Special Edition

Using

Microsoft®

Windows® 2000 Professional

Survival Guide

que®

Survival Guide: Installation

Always check the Microsoft Hardware Compatibility List to see if your hardware will run Windows 2000. (http://www.microsoft.com/hcl).

Installation is simple in the best circumstances. First, decide whether you're going to do an upgrade or a clean installation. Upgrades keep your current settings, and clean installs let you dual-boot with the previous operating system if there is one. Obviously, clean installs are the only way to go if the hard disk is fresh. Upgrades and dual-booting can be done from Windows 9x and Windows NT, but not from Windows 3.x. For Windows 3.x upgrades, upgrade to Windows 9x first. Dual-booting with Linux and triple- or quad-booting require other approaches (see Chapter 36, "Windows Script Host").

Insert the Windows 2000 CD into the CD-ROM and open read1st.txt, which is on the root directory of the disc. This file contains late-breaking installation information. If the computer has no operating system on it, you can boot from the CD. If the computer doesn't support booting from the CD (check the BIOS), you can make boot floppies (see "Making Replacement Startup Floppies" in Chapter 4, "Installing Windows 2000").

The CD should autostart the installation process. If you need to run it manually, run winnt.exe from DOS or winnt32.exe from Windows 9x or Windows NT. A wizard executes; follow its instructions. Use the Advanced options if you want to stipulate the directory and/or partition for the setup. You'll need to decide whether you want to convert your installation partition to NTFS if it's currently FAT (see Chapters 4 and 33).

Interface and Applications

The GUI of Windows 2000 is essentially the same as the GUI of Windows 98. However, there are a few changes, and things have been moved around. If you can't find a command, click Start, Help, and choose If You've Used Windows Before. The following are the major changes to the GUI:

- Any folder can have the directory tree showing or hidden.

- By default, the Start menus are personalized—they remember choices you've made. If you dislike this feature, click Start, Settings, Taskbar & Start Menu, and turn off Personalized Menus.

- Some Start menus, such as Control Panel, can be expanded off the Start button for easy access. Choose Start, Settings, Taskbar & Start Menu, and then click the Advanced tab.

- If you have Y2K concerns with programs using only two-digit years, check the Control Panel, Regional options, Date tab. You can control how two-digit years are entered, for a period of 100 years.

- Windows 2000 supports the single-click Web-like GUI option that Windows 9x does. Go to Control Panel, Mouse, Buttons to change this setting if you don't like the mode your system is in.

The following are other tips to keep in mind:

- If you have a dead application, press Ctrl+Alt+Delete, and then click Task Manager. Select the task and click End Task. Windows will keep running.

- To switch between apps quickly use Alt+Tab.

- To quickly launch programs, add program shortcuts to the quick-launch bar at the bottom of the screen by dragging them to the bar. You can reposition them by dragging left or right.

- To add programs, typically add them using the program's supplied setup utility on the CD or floppy. Otherwise, use Control Panel, Add/Remove programs. Usually, you'll use this applet to remove programs and associated settings.

System Maintenance

A collection of supplied troubleshooters will help with many types of hardware problems. Click Start, Help, Troubleshooting.

If your system won't boot, restart it a few times. If that doesn't help, reboot and press F8, and then check out the Safe mode options on the menu. In Safe mode, remove potentially problematic drivers and services. Use the emergency repair disk (ERD) if Safe mode doesn't work. Always have an emergency repair disk updated and handy (refer to Chapter 33).

If you suspect you're having hard disk media problems, run an error check. Right-click on the drive, choose Properties, Tools, Error Checking, Check Now (refer to Chapter 33).

Keep a gigabyte or so of hard disk space available on your system drive. You can use Disk Cleanup to help. Right-click on a drive and choose Disk Cleanup. Disk Cleanup also can compress NTFS drives.

Use Windows Update to keep your system up to date. Click Start, Windows Update.

If you want to convert FAT to NTFS, add new drives, create dynamic disks, or resize partitions, use the Disk Manager. Right-click My Computer and choose Manage, Storage, Disk Management (see Figure 1).

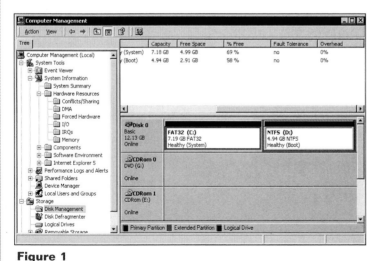

Figure 1

Connecting to the Internet

If you'll connect to the Internet with a dial-up connection, first install your modem. Windows automatically sets up Plug and Play modems. If you use an external or non–Plug and Play modem, install it, and then go to the Control Panel and select Phone and Modem Options. Select the Modems tab. If your modem isn't listed, click Add and use the Install New Modem Wizard to set it up.

To enter Internet service provider (ISP) information, whether you're using a dial-up or LAN connection, start up Connect to the Internet on the Windows desktop or click Start, Programs, Accessories, Communications, Internet Connection Wizard. The wizard can automatically help select an ISP for you, or you can enter information for your own existing ISP account.

If you're connecting to the Internet with a LAN, cable, or DSL connection, set up your network card first. Then view Settings, Network and Dial-Up Connections (see Figure 2). View the properties sheet of your local area connection. Select Internet Protocol and click Properties. Enter your assigned IP information and DNS numbers on this first page, and then click Advanced and select the DNS tab. Enter your business or ISP's domain under DNS Suffix for This Connection. Also, be sure to verify the proxy settings on the Connection page in the Internet Options control panel.

Advanced, Dial-up Preferences can
enable or disable automatic dialing
to your ISP

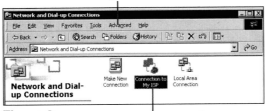

Figure 2   Make a new connection
for each ISP or city access
number you use

Setting Up a Workgroup LAN

Setting up a LAN with Windows 2000 is a snap. Your LAN administrator will handle all of this if you're part of a corporate network, but you can also "roll your own" network of two to ten computers at home or work (see Figures 3 and 4).

Install LAN adapters in each of your computers. Your best bet is to buy inexpensive PCI 10BASE-T network cards—you can get these for about $15 each. Just be sure to buy a card that's listed on the Windows 2000 Hardware Compatibility List. Add a 10BASE-T network hub and CAT-5 patch cables to run from each computer to the hub. Installing in-the-wall wiring adds complexity and expense, but it's worth the trouble if the computers are spread out in different rooms.

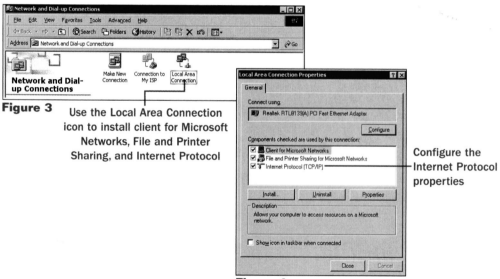

Figure 3   Use the Local Area Connection icon to install client for Microsoft Networks, File and Printer Sharing, and Internet Protocol

Configure the Internet Protocol properties

Figure 4

When your network is set up, My Network Places, Computers Near Me should show all your computers. To share folders or printers, just right-click a folder or printer, select Sharing, and enter a Share As name. Be sure to read up on security issues in Chapters 26 and 32. A LAN adds special risks if you have an Internet connection.

Using a Corporate LAN with Active Directory

In a corporate network environment, most network resources and settings are managed by the network manager. Microsoft's Active Directory lets network managers install software in your computer automatically, configure your network, and manage security. In fact, security can be controlled so well that many of the configuration and setup options listed in this book might not be available to you.

When you log on to Windows 2000 in a Windows 2000 domain-based network, add your company's domain name when you sign in. You can enter *username@domain* or enter your username and domain name separately in the login dialog. To manage your own computer, log in as Administrator@*machine*, where *machine* is the name of your computer.

The Active Directory lets you search your company's directory quite easily. Click Start, Search and choose For Printers or For People (see Figure 5). To look for people, set Look In to Active Directory.

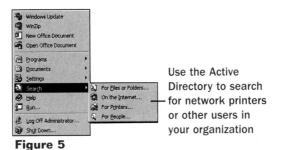

Use the Active Directory to search for network printers or other users in your organization

Figure 5

You can also search from My Network Places, Directory. Right-click a domain and select Find. This dialog lets you search for printers, users, published shared folders, or other information.

On an Active Directory network, if your domain user account is set up with a roaming profile, your My Documents folder and all your settings and preferences will appear at any computer you use anywhere in your organization.

Remote and Dial-Up Networking

Establish dial-up or VPN connections to remote LANs using the Make New Connection Wizard in Network and Dial-Up Connections. Choose Dial-Up to Private Network for modem access, or choose Connect to a Private Network Through the Internet for a VPN connection.

When you establish the dial-in connection, you'll need to provide a login name and password for the remote network. Here's a tip: It's best if you use the same login name on your own home or portable computer that you use on any accounts on networks at work.

If you're connecting to a Windows 2000 network, leave the security settings alone. For other network types, you might need to change the connection's security settings as specified by the other network's administrator.

Road warriors will appreciate Offline Folders, Web Folders, and Internet Printing Protocol Support (see Figures 6 and 7).

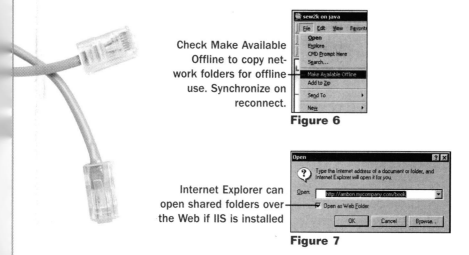

Check Make Available Offline to copy network folders for offline use. Synchronize on reconnect.

Figure 6

Internet Explorer can open shared folders over the Web if IIS is installed

Figure 7

If you've installed Internet Information Services in your computer, you even access your own shared folders and printers through the Internet this way, as long as your computer has a dedicated Internet connection. Support is provided automatically.

Special Edition

Using

Microsoft®
Windows® 2000
Professional

Robert Cowart

Brian Knittel

A Division of Macmillan USA
201 West 103rd Street
Indianapolis, Indiana 46290

Special Edition Using Microsoft® Windows® 2000 Professional

International Standard Book Number: 0-7897-2125-2

Library of Congress Catalog Card Number: 99-65440

Printed in the United States of America

First Printing: February, 2000

02   01   00   4   3   2

TRADEMARKS

WARNING AND DISCLAIMER

Associate Publisher
Jim Minatel

Acquisitions Editor
Jill Byus

Senior Development Editor
Rick Kughen

Managing Editor
Matt Purcell

Project Editor
Tonya Simpson

Copy Editor
Chuck Hutchinson

Indexer
Kevin Kent

Proofreader
Benjamin Berg

Technical Editors
Jim Cooper
Vince Averello
Kyle Bryant
Mark Reddin

Team Coordinator
Vicki Harding

Media Developer
Craig Atkins

Interior Designer
Ruth Harvey

Cover Designers
Dan Armstrong
Ruth Harvey

Copywriter
Eric Borgert

Editorial Assistant
Angela Boley

Production
Stacey DeRome
Dan Harris
Heather Hiatt-Miller
Ayanna Lacey
Tim Osborn
George Poole
Mark Walchle

CONTENTS AT A GLANCE

CONTENTS

ABOUT THE AUTHORS

Robert Cowart (lead author) has written more than 30 books on computer programming and applications, with more than a dozen on Windows. His titles include *Windows NT Unleashed, Mastering Windows 98, Windows NT Server Administrator's Bible*, and *Windows NT Server 4.0 No Experience Required*. Several of his books have been bestsellers in their category and have been translated into more than 20 languages. He has written on myriad computer-related topics for such magazines as *PC Week, PC World, PC Magazine, PC Tech Journal, Mac World*, and *Microsoft System's Journal*. In addition to working as a freelance consultant specializing in small businesses, he has taught programming classes at the University of California Extension in San Francisco. He has appeared as a special guest on the PBS TV series *Computer Chronicles*, CNN's *Headline News*, ZD-TV's *The Screen Savers*, and ABC's *Peter Jennings World News Tonight*. Robert resides in Berkeley, California.

In his spare time, he is involved in the music world, presenting chamber-music concerts and playing classical piano. He's also a teacher of the Transcendental Meditation technique and meditates regularly, in hopes of rewiring his inner computer.

Brian Knittel has been a software developer for more than 20 years. After doing graduate work in nuclear medicine and magnetic resonance imaging technologies, he began a career as an independent consultant. An eclectic mix of clients has led to long-term projects in medical documentation, workflow management, real-time industrial system control, and most importantly, 12 years of real-world experience with MS-DOS, Windows, and computer networking in the business world. He contributed to several of Robert Cowart's other Windows books prior to this one. Brian lives in Albany, California, between the tidal wave zone and the earthquake fault.

DEDICATION

To Elaine, for all her support, and to Results, the international grassroots lobby dedicated to ending world hunger, poverty, and illiteracy.

—Bob

To my parents, for letting me follow my curiosity down whichever paths it led, even when this required installing teletypes in the basement.

—Brian

ACKNOWLEDGMENTS

Just as with Windows 2000 itself, this book is the result of a team effort. We couldn't have produced it without the great team at Que, the assistance of contributing writers, and the patience and support of our friends, so we want to express our appreciation.

We would like to thank Ken Savich for general technical editing, writing portions of the hard disk and multiboot sections, and providing the detailed information on UNIX internetworking; Melvin Backus for his work on operating system multibooting; Dr. Steve Cummings for sharing what he knows about Data Sharing; Rebecca Tapley for showing how to use FrontPage Express and how to publish sites on the Internet; Jamie Bumsted for graciously showing how to manage users; Tyler Regas for his expertise in Macintosh internetworking; Martin O'Reilly for his work on the Windows Script Host section; and Tom Syroid for additional help with the hard disk management section. Thanks to Pete Cocke (*Il Professore*) for hours and hours of formatting and to Harry Summerfield for masterful writing and rewriting in the "Network Security" chapter.

The staff at Que did an amazing job. A series as well-known and consistently as professional as *Special Edition Using* cannot be maintained without a steady hand such as that provided by Associate Publisher Jim Minatel. Jim offered timely guidance, yet remained in the background to allow authors, acquisitions editors, and developmental editors to do their jobs. Thanks to Acquisitions Editor Jill Byus, who, with great patience, kept us on track with gentle prodding and copious exclamation points!!! Our almost daily interactions over the course of nine months were with Development Editor Rick Kughen, who developed this monster by himself. His humor, technical insights, and graciousness are deeply appreciated. We would especially like to acknowledge the technical editors and the editorial, indexing, layout, art, proofing, and other production staff at Que who labor away largely unseen and often unthanked. You all did a marvelous job.

Hats off to Jim Price for inviting us into the Que family of authors and agreeing to work on this title with us. It has been an honor.

No book could make it to market without the real-world personal relationships developed between booksellers on the one hand and the publisher's sales and marketing personnel on the other. We've had the opportunity to meet sales and marketing folks in the computer publishing world, and we know what a difficult job selling and keeping up with the thousands of computer titles can be. Thanks to all of you for your pivotal role in helping to pay our mortgages!

Finally, we want to acknowledge those who made it possible for us to get through the months of writing. Bob thanks first his agent, Chris Van Buren, for standing by him with encouragement on down days and sharing his excitement after his successes. Many thanks for fighting for better contracts, keeping things in perspective, and phoning in long distance (even from Brazil!) for conference calls. And, as always, thanks to friends and family who, even though accustomed to seeing him disappear for months on end, allow him back in the fold when the project is over. This goes for Elaine, in particular, whose daily support and patience made such a difference.

Brian wants to thank Chris Van Buren for representing him on this project. He also adds a special mention to the Baguette Quartette, for music through many long nights; Bryce Carter for guidance; Pete Cocke for his friendship (and tour planning); and Mike Holloway for housesitting while Brian spent four months in the office writing.

TELL US WHAT YOU THINK!

As the reader of this book, *you* are our most important critic and commentator. We value your opinion and want to know what we're doing right, what we could do better, what areas you'd like to see us publish in, and any other words of wisdom you're willing to pass our way.

As an associate publisher for Que, I welcome your comments. You can fax, email, or write me directly to let me know what you did or didn't like about this book—as well as what we can do to make our books stronger.

Please note that I cannot help you with technical problems related to the topic of this book, and that due to the high volume of mail I receive, I might not be able to reply to every message.

When you write, please be sure to include this book's title and author as well as your name and phone or fax number. I will carefully review your comments and share them with the author and editors who worked on the book.

Fax: 317-581-4666

Email: opsys@mcp.com

Mail: Associate Publisher
Que
201 West 103rd Street
Indianapolis, IN 46290 USA

INTRODUCTION

We would like to thank you for purchasing or considering the purchase of *Special Edition Using Microsoft Windows 2000 Professional*. It's amazing the changes that 15 years can bring to a computer product such as Windows. When we wrote our first Windows book back in the mid-eighties, our publisher didn't even think the book would sell well enough to print more than 5,000 copies. Microsoft stock wasn't even a blip on most investors' radar screens. Boy, were they wrong! Who could have imagined that a little over a decade later, anyone who hoped to get hired for even a temp job in a small office would need to know how to use Microsoft Windows, Office, and a PC? Twelve Windows books later, we're still finding new and exciting stuff to tell our readers.

Some people (including the U.S. judicial system) claim Microsoft's predominance on the PC operating system arena was won unethically through monopolistic practices. Whether or not this is true (we're going to stay out of the politics in this book), we believe that Windows has earned its position today through reasons other than having a stranglehold on the market. Consider that Windows NT 3.1 had 5 million lines of code. Windows 2000 weighs in with over 29 million. This is a lot of work, by anyone's accounting. Who could have imagined in 1985 that any decent operating system a decade and half later must have support for so many technologies that didn't even exist at the time: CD-ROM, DVD, CD-R and CD-RW, Internet and intranet, USB, APM, ACPI, USB, RAID, Web-TV, email and newsgroup clients, UPS, fault tolerance, disk encryption and compression…? The list goes on. And could we have imagined that a Microsoft Certified System Engineer certificate (MCSE) could prove as lucrative as a medical or law degree?

Although rarely on the bleeding edge of technology, and often taking the role of the dictator, Bill Gates has at least been benevolent from the users' point of view. In 1981, when we were building our first computers, the operating system (CP/M) had to be modified in assembly language, recompiled, and hardware parts soldered together to make almost any new addition (such as a video display terminal) work. Virtually nothing was standardized, with the end result being that computers remained out of reach for average citizens.

Together Microsoft and IBM changed all that. Today Joe and Jane Doe can purchase a computer, printer, scanner, Zip drive, keyboard, modem, monitor, and video card over the Internet, plug it in, install Windows, and they will probably work together. The creation and adoption (and sometimes forcing) of hardware and software standards that have made the PC a household appliance the world over can largely be credited to Microsoft, like it or not. The unifying glue of this PC revolution has been Windows.

Yes, we all love to hate Windows, but it's here to stay. Linux is on the rise, but for most businesses, at least for some time, Windows and Windows applications are "where it's at." And Windows 2000 ushers in truly significant changes to the landscape. That's why we were excited to write this book.

WHO IS THIS BOOK FOR?

We all know this book will make a hefty doorstop in a few years. (You probably have a few already. We've even written a few.) Yes, it is a large book. If you think it contains more information than you need, you can think of it as a reference that will be there as you grow into this product. We couldn't possibly cover all the features of the product, even with 1,400+ pages, so don't worry that we had to make up stuff! And we all know that computer technology changes so fast that it's sometimes easier just to blink and ignore a phase than to study up on it. Windows 2000 is definitely a significant upgrade in Windows technology—one you're going to need to understand. Because Windows 2000 is the next step in the NT line, rest assured it will be around for some time.

Is Windows 2000 so easy to use that books are unnecessary? Unfortunately, no. True, as with other releases of Windows, online help is available. As has been the case ever since Windows 95, however, no printed documentation is available (to save Microsoft the cost), and the Help files are written by the Microsoft cronies. You won't find criticisms, complaints, workarounds, or talk of third-party programs there.

By contrast, in this book's many pages, we focus not just on the gee-whiz side of the technology, but why you should care, what you can get from it, and what you can forget about. The lead author on this book has previously written 12 books about Windows, all in plain English (several bestsellers), designed for everyone from rank beginners to full-on system administrators deploying NT Server domains. The co-author has designed software and networks for more than 20 years. We work with and write about various versions of Windows year in and year out. We have a clear understanding of what confuses users and system administrators about installing, configuring, or using Windows, and (we hope) how to best convey the solutions to our readers.

We spent close to a year considering and reconsidering our table of contents, testing Windows 2000 betas through numerous builds, participating in the Microsoft beta newsgroups, documenting and working through bugs, and installing and reinstalling Windows 2000 on a variety of networks and computers. The result is what you hold in your hands.

While writing this book, we tried to stay vigilant of four cardinal rules:

- Keep it practical.
- Keep it accurate.
- Keep it concise.
- Keep it interesting, and even crack a joke or two.

We believe that you will find this to be the best book available on Windows 2000 Professional for the intermediate to advanced user. While writing it, we targeted an audience ranging from the power user in the small home office to the Workstation system administrator in a major corporation. Whether you provide PC support in your office or company or you need a user-level book for the folks you support, this book will cover it all.

We're also willing to tell you what we don't cover. No book can do it all. As the title implies, this book is about Windows 2000 *Professional*. We don't cover the Server versions of Windows 2000 (Server, Advanced Server, and Datacenter). However, we do tell you how to connect to and interact with other operating systems, including Windows NT Server, 2000 Server, Mac OS, Linux, and variants of Windows, over the LAN.

We worked hard not to assume too much knowledge on your part, yet we didn't want to assume you aren't already experienced with Windows. The working assumption here is that you are already conversant at least with some form of Windows, preferably 9x, and possibly with NT 4. However, we provide a primer on the Windows 2000 interface to cover the likelihood that many shops will be upgrading from Windows 3.x into 2000 and will be new to the Windows 9x-style interface.

How Our Book Is Organized

Although this book advances logically from beginning to end, it's written so that you can jump in at any location, get the information you need quickly, and get out. You don't have to read it from start to finish, nor do you need to work through complex tutorials.

This book is broken down into six major parts. Here's the skinny on each one in a nutshell:

Part I, "Introducing Windows 2000 Pro," introduces Windows 2000 and explains its features, new elements, and the design and architecture behind Windows 2000. It then explains how to read your hardware and software in preparation for installation and describes the installation process itself.

Part II, "Getting Your Work Done," is, well, about getting your work done. Perhaps the bulk of workstation users will want to study and keep on hand this part as a reference guide. Here, we cover using the interface, running programs, organizing documents, sharing data between applications, printing documents, and managing fonts.

Part III, "Windows 2000 and the Internet," introduces you to Windows 2000 networking, Internet style. We start with Internet connection options and then move into the Internet tools. We provide in-depth coverage of Outlook Express for mail and newsgroups, Internet Explorer for Web surfing, and NetMeeting for audio and videoconferencing; we also describe how to create your own Web sites with FrontPage Express and serve them with IIS. We also included sections on Internet diagnostic utilities such as Ping, Telnet, and ipconfig.

Part IV, "Networking," deals with networking on the LAN. Our development editor said this section "has more hands-on, get-dust-bunnies-in-your-hair advice than I've ever seen in any Windows book." Of course, he gets paid to say things like that, but it might well be true. In Part IV, we explain the fundamentals of networking and walk you through planning and installing a functional LAN. We cover the use of a Windows 2000 network, whether it's a worldwide corporate network or a small workgroup LAN; give you a chapter on dial-up, remote, and portable networking; and finish up with crucial security tips and troubleshooting advice that the Windows Help files don't cover.

Part V, "System Configuration and Customization," covers system configuration and maintenance. We tell you how to work with Control Panel applets, provide tips and tricks for customizing the graphical user interface for most efficiency, and describe a variety of ways to upgrade your hardware and system software (including third-party programs) for maximum performance.

Part VI, "System Administration and System Maintenance," dives even deeper into system administration and configuration, with coverage of supplied system administration tools such as the new Microsoft Management Console (MMC) and its plug-ins. We also provide techniques for managing users; information on policies and LAN administration; means for managing the hard disk, including multiple file formats such as NTFS5; and details on setting up multiboot machines with Windows 9x, DOS, Linux, and Windows 2000. We cap off this part with coverage of the Registry and with an introduction to automating Windows 2000 via the Windows Script Host.

The two appendixes in this book are on the accompanying CD-ROM.

Appendix A, "Command-Line Reference," contains a guide to Windows 2000's command-line interface, listing all commands by function and explaining the new command-line interpreter.

Appendix B, "Keyboard Shortcuts and Mouseless Survival Guide," consists of a collection of keyboard shortcuts you can use when or if you mouse dies, or you simply prefer to use the keyboard. It's an exhaustive list. We think you'll be surprised by some of the useful shortcuts.

CONVENTIONS USED IN THIS BOOK

Special conventions are used throughout this book to help you get the most from the book and from Windows 2000 Professional.

TEXT CONVENTIONS

Various typefaces in this book identify terms and other special objects. These special typefaces include the following:

Type	Meaning
Italic	New terms or phrases when initially defined.
Monospace	Information that appears in code or onscreen or information you type.
Initial Caps	Menus, dialog box names, dialog box elements, and commands.

Type	Meaning
Words separated by commas	All Windows book publishers struggle with how to represent command sequences when menus and dialog boxes are involved. In this book, we separate commands using a comma. Yeah, we know it's confusing, but this is traditionally how the *Special Edition Using* book series does it, and traditions die hard. So, for example, the instruction "Choose Edit, Cut" means that you should open the Edit menu and choose Cut. Another, more complex example would be "Click Start, Settings, Control Panel, System, Hardware, Device Manager."

Key combinations are represented with a plus sign. For example, if the text calls for you to press Ctrl+Alt+Delete, you would press the Ctrl, Alt, and Delete keys at the same time.

TIPS FROM THE WINDOWS PROS

Ever·wonder how the experts get their work done better and faster than anyone else? Ever wonder how they became experts in the first place? You'll find out in these special sections throughout the book. We've spent a lot of time under the Windows hood, so to speak, getting dirty and learning what makes Windows 2000 tick. So, with the information we provide in these sections, you can roll up your shirt sleeves and dig in.

SPECIAL ELEMENTS

Throughout this book, you'll find Notes, Cautions, Sidebars, Cross-References, and Troubleshooting Tips. Often, you'll find just the tidbit you need to get through a rough day at the office or the one whiz-bang trick that will make you the office hero. You'll also find little nuggets of wisdom, humor, and lingo that you can use to amaze your friends and family, not to mention making you cocktail-party literate.

BOB AND BRIAN'S "SIGNATURE" TIPS

Tip #0

We specially designed these tips to showcase the best of the best. Just because you get your work done doesn't mean you are doing it in the fastest, easiest way possible. We'll show you how to maximize your Windows experience. Don't miss these tips!

NOTES

Note

Notes point out items that you should be aware of, but you can skip them if you're in a hurry. Generally, we've added notes as a way to give you some extra information on a topic without weighing you down.

CAUTIONS

| Caution | Pay attention to cautions! They could save you precious hours in lost work. Don't say we didn't warn you. |

TROUBLESHOOTING NOTE

 We designed these elements to call attention to common pitfalls that you're likely to encounter. When you see a Troubleshooting note, you can flip to the end of the chapter to learn how to solve or avoid a problem.

CROSS-REFERENCES

Cross-references are designed to point you to other locations in this book (or other books in the Que family) that will provide supplemental or supporting information. Cross-references appear as follows:

→ To learn more information about how Windows 2000 already has a good head start at becoming a standard in the corporate network environment, **see** "Windows NT/2000 Evolution in a Nutshell," **p. 14**.

SIDEBARS

Sidebars
Sidebars are designed to provide information that is ancillary to the topic being discussed. Read this information if you want to learn more details about an application or task.

Introducing Windows 2000 Pro

1

INTRODUCING WINDOWS 2000 PROFESSIONAL

In this chapter

AN OVERVIEW OF WINDOWS 2000 PROFESSIONAL

When Microsoft decided to improve upon Windows NT 4, the development team was given the mandate of producing a mainstream operating system for PCs that integrated the best business-related features and strengths of Windows 98 into the already popular and successful Windows NT. We believe they have come close to that mark with Windows 2000 Professional.

In addition to the features that Windows NT 4 already boasted, such as increased security over Windows 98, an advanced file system (NTFS), support for multiple CPUs, remote administration, and support for complex hard disk arrangements (RAID), Windows 2000 Professional now features a simplified user interface, improved Plug and Play, even more sophisticated mass storage features, power management, and support for a broad range of hardware devices. Additional reliability, security, and administration flexibility round out the package owing to the new file encryption system and application management tools.

In writing Windows 2000, the Microsoft team claims it wanted to make Windows 2000 Professional the "easiest Windows yet." That's a tall order for an industrial-strength operating system for which administrators pay hundreds of thousands of dollars annually to attend training programs such as the Microsoft Certified Systems Engineer (MCSE) courses, something necessitated by the complexity of NT. But from our examination, it would be safe to say that Windows 2000 Professional makes bold moves in the direction of simplicity of management, despite the fact that this NT-based product is incredibly ambitious and in some ways extremely complex.

In lock step with naming conventions the applications group at Microsoft has been keen on (Office 97 and Office 2000), and in line with two previous operating systems, Microsoft decided to dub this operating system Windows 2000. This naming scheme is a bit confusing because up until now Windows NT versions were named 3.1, 3.51, and 4. Of course, the folks at Microsoft must certainly have understood they were taking the risk of confusing us all in the process.

Considering the potential public bewilderment and the fact that Microsoft operating systems are notoriously late, the reasoning behind the name Windows 2000 seemed sketchy at best to those of us in the press. It has lead us to ask obvious questions: Is Windows 2000 the next installment in the popular Windows 95 and 98 line, or is it the next version of Windows NT? And will there be no more Windows 9x releases? What should I install on my home or small-business machine? You will surely see a plethora of articles devoted to clearing up the naming-issue confusion.

At least Microsoft also said it will use the tag line "Built on Windows NT technology" with Windows 2000 to help the many customers who know and understand the value of the Windows NT architecture.

Note

Windows 2000 does not herald the end of the Windows 9x platform. Windows 98 Second Edition will be followed by another operating system officially announced by Microsoft. The next release of Microsoft Windows 98—code-named Millennium—will support new PC designs that do not include conflict-causing legacy hardware such as Super I/O. Low-cost PCs designed to run Millennium and meet an emerging "Easy PC" specification may give the Win9x code base a longer run than many of us expect, perhaps even into 2002.

On the plus side, there actually is some intelligent reasoning behind this naming maneuver on Microsoft's part, if you're interested. With millions of marketing-research bucks at its fingertips, Microsoft surely doesn't take lightly actions such as product name changes—especially not for its flagship products such as Windows or Office.

Despite the fact that Windows NT has a very healthy following in the corporate workplace, Microsoft has for years hoped to pull the two lines of Windows (the consumer line of Windows 95 and 98 and the more businesslike NT products) together. Even Microsoft acknowledges the inherent limitations and bugginess of Windows 9x, which is—despite what the Microsoft representatives might say in court—still just a graphical user interface shell on top of some version of MS-DOS. Portions of Windows 9x are still written in 16-bit code (Windows NT code is all 32-bit), and the operating system itself can be compromised by older or poorly written 16-bit programs that were really designed for a much simpler, pre-Windows operating system (DOS).

The following sections, "A Little Windows NT/2000 History" and "Windows NT/2000 Evolution in a Nutshell," primarily discuss the history and evolution of NT 4 because it lays the groundwork for what we know as Windows 2000 today.

A LITTLE WINDOWS NT/2000 HISTORY

As you surely know, Windows is a *graphical user interface (GUI)* and *operating system (OS)* that is the heart and soul of your computer. Without it, you can't run your favorite programs, copy a diskette, or even enter text from the keyboard. You could use another operating system such as MacOS, Linux, or OS/2, but the clear frontrunner in operating systems for personal computers these days is Windows from Microsoft Corporation. This said, let's step back in time for a moment to better put this Windows 2000 into its historical context so that when we cover the new features of Windows 2000 later in this chapter, you will have a little better perspective.

Many versions of Windows led up to the release of Windows 2000. Windows started out at version 1.0, though you don't hear much about that nowadays. Well, actually you didn't hear much about it then, either. It left a lot to the imagination.

Various versions of Windows have appeared since those days in the early-to-mid-1980s, including Windows 2, Windows 286, Windows 386, Windows 3.0, Windows 3.1, Windows 3.11, Windows for Workgroups, Windows 95, and Windows 98. It was not at all clear until well into the late '80s that Windows was going to dominate the PC market. The market battles included numerous software contenders such as Digital Research (with its *Gem* operating system interface), Quarterdesk Office Systems with DESQview, and IBM with its answer to Windows 2 called TopView. Challenging the foothold the IBM PC had in hardware were primarily Apple, Atari, and Commodore.

The times were rough and tumble, and the options for the consumer were many—as were the headaches. At one point, reading the daily computer news was like watching professional wrestling on TV. Back in 1988, Bill Gates recognized that Novell had made major inroads into corporate settings by reliably interconnecting PCs with its NetWare product. NetWare was *the* networking operating system of choice (often running on PCs designated as NetWare "server" computers), for connecting large numbers of PCs in corporate settings.

IBM and Microsoft, who had partnered on previous projects (notably the development and marketing of Microsoft-DOS, also known as PC-DOS when IBM sold it), agreed to combine forces against their common enemy to develop the next version of Windows, which would be called OS/2. Unfortunately, an intense and rather unsavory falling out between IBM and Microsoft developed in 1989 and 1990 over the project.

The two software giants had originally decided to work together on creating the next version of a robust multitasking operating system with a graphical user interface. But disagreements on several pivotal points about how the project would progress resulted in the emergence of two separate and competing products—OS/2 and Windows NT.

What had begun as a friendly collaboration between Microsoft and IBM devolved into charges, threats, and retaliation as Microsoft fought for the dominance of its Windows operating system over IBM's OS/2.

The result was an out-and-out war between separate, competitive project teams, each company vying for leadership in the industrial-strength PC operating system arena. And as is so often the case, Microsoft won. Oddly, both Microsoft and IBM sold OS/2. But that same year also saw sales of Windows reach 1 million, even though there was a shortage of Windows-based programs for people to use with it.

Still, Novell NetWare continued to dominate the corporate *local area network (LAN)* market. Not being one to sit back and watch any potential cash cow of the PC software industry wander out of the barn, and recognizing the limitations of Windows 3.11, Bill lead Microsoft into the corporate operating system battle by hiring a team of programmers to write a new OS from the ground up.

Dave Cutler was the man in charge, a fellow who had proved his abilities at DEC, where he developed a serious operating system called VMS. The whole idea was to write a bulletproof, industrial-strength system for microcomputers that took full advantage of the capabilities of Intel's new breed of 32-bit processors. A big part of the idea also was to leave behind all the 8- and 16-bit "legacy" code in MS-DOS, much of which was responsible for the crashability of Windows 3.x (Windows 95 hadn't been invented yet, obviously, because it was 1988). A key feature of Windows NT was that it was designed from the ground up as *the* future operating system for PCs, whether in the corporate setting, the *SOHO (small office/home office)*, or single-computer setting.

> **Note**
>
> *VMS*–Virtual Memory System–is a virtual memory operating system used with DEC VAX and Alpha minicomputers and workstations. VMS, which is both multiuser and multitasking, was introduced in 1979. The first VAX minicomputer was introduced at the same time. According to `Webopedia.com`, DEC (now owned by Compaq) now refers to VMS as *OpenVMS*.

In July 1993, the first versions of Windows NT were released under the names Windows NT 3.1 and Windows NT Advanced Server 3.1. It wasn't actually new technology per se; it was just new to PCs.

> **Note**
>
> Windows NT stands for New Technology (not New Testament as someone asked, looking over my shoulder in a coffee shop near a seminary, where I'm writing).

One of the essential qualities of Windows NT was that it was based on a client/server model in which the internals of the operating system are divided into two primary sections (client and server), much as mainframe systems are.

Also, NT incorporated dynamic disk caching, which meant it could span multiple hard drives when it ran out of RAM to use for storing data. (Windows 3.x and 9x use only a single hard disk for caching.)

NT also included serious *fault tolerance* (the capability to withstand power outages, disk crashes, and so on) and supported fancy hard disk setups (such as RAID and mirroring), which could increase hard disk storage speed, capacity, and data safety dramatically. And with the assistance of the Windows NT Advanced Server product, NT could effectively *internetwork (page 649)* literally thousands of PCs fairly effectively. Management tools for system administrators made management, even across the local area network, much easier than it had been for previous versions of Windows. Installing the operating system remotely, controlling users' rights and privileges, monitoring network traffic and fine-tuning, internetworking with Macs, and so on, were now possible on a fairly reliable platform. Major operating system functions, called *services*, could be started and stopped by an administrator without rebooting the machine—just like on a "real" operating system such as UNIX.

Despite detractions of Windows NT from people in the UNIX world, NT has its roots in UNIX to some degree, actually. Computer scientists at Carnegie Mellon working to develop new operating system models between the years 1985 and 1994 created the basis of a small and efficient operating system called the *Mach microkernel*. A microkernel is a sort of concentrated, scaled-down version of the internals of a major operating system such as UNIX. Dave Cutler and his team adapted concepts of the Mach microkernel (a kernel is the heart of an operating system) to run on an Intel-based PC with a Windows-like graphical user interface on top of it. Although it looks just like the consumer Windows product, under the hood a very different animal is at work.

Note

Work on the Mach operating system was started in 1985 at Carnegie Mellon University's School of Computer Science. Parts of the Mach operating system have been incorporated into several commercial operating systems, including Encore's Multimax, NeXT OS, MachTen for the Macintosh, Omron's Luna, and DEC's OSF/1 for the DEC Alpha.

Though not new, technically, Windows NT 3.1 was still exceptional in comparison to its progenitors. Both versions of Windows NT 3.1 boasted a preemptive multitasking scheduler; the fault-tolerant, journaling file system of Windows (NTFS); support for multiple CPUs; fully 32-bit Windows-based architecture; powerful domain-level security; and file and print services; to name but a few.

Note

Don't be thrown by the technical terms if you don't recognize them. You don't have to know what they mean to be able to use Windows 2000. There will not be a quiz. But these terms will be explained more fully in the next chapter, in case you want to better understand the internals of Windows NT and Windows 2000.

WINDOWS NT/2000 EVOLUTION IN A NUTSHELL

Not long after the release of 3.1, Windows NT 3.5 followed in September 1994. A fairly significant upgrade, it offered improved stability, better performance, and more competent system management tools. In June 1995, the next update appeared—Windows NT 3.51. Always running a little behind the consumer line of Windows in terms of user niceties, 3.51 at least attempted to include some of the hardware support that Windows 95 offered, such as wider application and support for PCMCIA cards (credit-card-sized devices—modems and NICs, for example—commonly used by portable computers). Whereas 3.1 had negligible acceptance, NT 3.5 and 3.51 marked the beginning of more rapid adoption.

At this juncture, it became clear to observers that Microsoft was seriously gunning for Novell. NT 3.5 included NetWare integration tools, culminating with *FPNW* (*File and Print Services for NetWare*) in 1996. FPNW provided regular NetWare file and print services on an NT Server machine. When installed on a Windows NT server, FPNW let regular NetWare client PCs access the NT server as though it were a NetWare server. It was clear that Microsoft was willing to go to great lengths to entice Information Systems (IS) managers to convert to NT by making the transition from NetWare to NT a smooth one.

The next big update arrived under the appellation *Windows NT 4.0*, which was released in July 1996. A serious face-lift to the look and feel, by adding the GUI of Windows 95, was its major attraction, along with support for much more hardware (limited hardware support has always plagued NT users). Also integrated was Internet Explorer (IE) 2.0, which marked the first time NT shipped with a Web browser included. In Microsoft's attempt to supplant the installed base of NetWare servers, NT 4 made it easy for system administrators to connect to existing NetWare servers. People began to use NT for "application serving," while continuing to use NetWare servers for printer and file serving due to its superior (real or perceived) security.

> **Note**
>
> NT 4 originally shipped with Internet Explorer 2.0 and Internet Information Server (IIS) 2.0. With service pack 3 (SP3), Internet Explorer 3.0 was included. It wasn't until SP4 in 1998 that Internet Explorer 4.0 and IIS 4.0 were included with NT.

> **Note**
>
> As of 1998, more than 60 percent of corporate PCs were estimated to still be running the aging Windows 3.1 operating system. Many of them were expected to jump directly to Windows 2000 Professional, passing up Windows 95 or 98 altogether. At that time, Microsoft estimates were that the LAN market was seriously underpenetrated, with only 40 percent of small businesses online and fewer than 50 percent networked, according to sources within Microsoft. Due to the delay in shipment of Windows 2000 and the increase in anxiety about Y2K compliance in the interim, many of those companies have taken the leap and upgraded from Windows 3.x to 95, 98, or NT 4.0 Workstation. It remains to be seen how seriously this intermediate upgrade will affect their willingness to upgrade to Windows 2000 Professional.

Windows NT 4.0 has gained significant market share in the several years before this writing, due in no small part to widespread support training for administrators and the plethora of ancillary support systems that Microsoft continues to spawn, such as SQL Server, Exchange Server, and Internet Information Server. The allure of a one-stop shop for professional systems installers and managers is a strong one, and Microsoft continues to offer integrated solutions and support for everything from word processing to Web-based transaction processing.

Windows NT was a sleeper at first, selling a mere 34,000 licenses in fiscal 1994. But some of us believed it would catch on when users realized how strong a product it really was (I among them, writing one of the first NT books in 1993). Microsoft has now sold more than 20 million licenses of Windows NT Workstation and more than 3 million licenses of Windows NT Server (and we expect to see a major increase in that number with the release of Windows 2000 for reasons you'll discover in this book).

The NT 4.0 platform hasn't been bumped up in version number (that is, a version 4.1 has not been released as of this writing), but it has several service packs of system upgrades, and something called an *option pack*. Features added to NT 4.0 included such esoteric goodies as the following:

- Transaction Server
- News Server
- SMTP Server
- Internet Information Server (IIS) 4.0
- Internet Explorer 4.0

- Integrated public key and certificate authority functionality
- Streaming-media support for displaying Web-based sound and video
- Support for Component Object Model (COM)
- Web browser improvements such as 128-bit encryption
- Additional server technologies
- SmartCard support
- Clustering
- Reliable synchronous and queued transaction support
- Better symmetric multiprocessor (SMP) scalability

That brings us to the next entry in the Windows evolution journal—Windows 2000 (which, incidentally, includes all the items in the preceding list).

THE BIRTH OF WINDOWS 2000

Realizing the inherent limitations of Windows 9x (namely, its DOS roots), the folks at Microsoft (and Windows users) have hoped for merging of the NT and Windows 9x operating systems. Most of the crashing problems we all experience with Windows 3.x and 9x are the result of non-client/server architecture and the nonprotected system kernel of those operating systems.

Yet Windows 9x has a more refined interface, broad hardware support, and better support for DOS programs and for games than does NT. If only the best of Windows 9x could be rolled into a new NT version, we'd be in fat city, right? We'll talk more about this issue from an architectural point of view in Chapter 2, "The Design and Architecture of Windows 2000 Professional," but suffice it to say Microsoft certainly understands this ideal scenario and hopes to stop selling Windows 9x as soon as it can, probably sometime in the year 2001. Eventually, all variants of Windows—whether running in a TV set, in a handheld organizer, or in a high-power corporate server—will be based on the NT kernel simply because of the elegance of the design.

Note

If you have any doubts that Microsoft originally intended Windows NT to become the only operating system it hoped to be selling in the near future, consider this: A little-known fact is that Windows CE (the operating system in those little handheld computers) is actually a subset of Windows NT and is made up of 32-bit code derived from the Windows NT product line.

Tip #1

Although many intermediate-level Windows users (such as yourself, most likely) will be installing and using Windows 2000 Professional, it's overkill for the computer in Junior's bedroom. It's really a replacement for NT Workstation rather than something to take the place of a Windows 95 or Windows 98 computer. The initial release of Windows 2000 fell somewhat short of Microsoft's hope to move away from the legacy of 16-bit code and other problems inherent in Windows 9x because time and resources were too slim to create and ship a "consumer" version of 2000 along with Professional and Server. A consumer edition will come in time, though, probably in 2001. This consumer edition of Windows 2000 is expected to take the place of Windows 9x.

Windows 2000, like NT 3.x and 4 before it, is a multithreaded, preemptive multitasking operating system with full 32-bit memory addressing. It runs programs written for DOS, Windows 3.x, Windows 9x, Win32 character and GUI, POSIX 1003.1, and character-based OS/2 (IBM Presentation Manager through 1.3). However, based on the extreme paucity of information on the Microsoft Windows 2000 site on the topic of OS/2 and POSIX, it seems evident to us that little emphasis is being put on developing or extending compatibility of non-Microsoft operating systems.

Note

During development of what is called Windows 2000, early versions of the operating system were called NT 5.0. Microsoft renamed NT 5.0 to Windows 2000.

As authors and beta testers, we worked with Windows 2000 for close to a year during its development, and we can say based on our testing that it's darned good stuff. Microsoft seems to have gotten it right this time—or at least *enough* right. The company was cautious and made clear from the start that, just like Robert Mondavi wines, it wouldn't release this operating system before its time—that is, before beta testers deemed it very stable.

WHAT'S NEW IN WINDOWS 2000?

At this point, you're probably wondering what is new in Windows 2000. As I'm writing these Windows books, people always ask me whether the new version of Windows is different enough to warrant upgrading. I can definitely say this is a major upgrade, on the order of the difference between Windows 3.11 and Windows 95. Windows 2000 is a huge accomplishment. Estimates are that by the time it was released, it contained about 29 million lines of code (see Table 1.1). In that code, you will find much to enjoy.

TABLE 1.1   LINES OF CODE COMPARISON

Operating System	Lines of Programming Code
NT 3.1	6.5 million
NT 3.5	10 million
NT 4	16.5 million
Windows 2000	>29 million
Windows 2000 Advanced Server	>33 million
Windows 2000 Datacenter	>40 million

Much of this significant size increase is due to enterprise-capable features such as a multi-domain directory, called *Active Directory (page 33)*, which was added in hopes of wooing Novell NetWare Directory Service (NDS) and UNIX-based corporations to move over to NT. (Oops, there I go again. We all better get used to saying Windows 2000.) The Active Directory architecture replaces the older master and multiple-master domain structures of NT, which date all the way back to LAN Manager days. The transaction-intensive and mission-critical nature of corporate computing demands a solid operating system with many features that typical Windows and PC users have no idea about, features long built into UNIX and other major systems.

Because so many improvements have been made to added features in Windows 2000, in this section we'll quickly run through what is new and what each new feature does. Table 1.2 highlights some of the key improvements found in Windows 2000 Professional and points you to the chapter in which they are covered.

TABLE 1.2 COVERAGE OF NEW AND IMPROVED WINDOWS 2000 FEATURES

Feature	Chapter in Which It Is Covered
Vastly improved setup	4
Improved interface: My Documents and Pictures, custom toolbars, intelligent menus, new help system, search function	5
Multimedia improvements: DVD, DirectX 7, image color management, scanner and digital camera support	6, 9, 28
Hardware support: Plug and Play, multiple monitors, FireWire	28
Active Directory	19, 22
IntelliMirror	33, 19
Enhanced Web browsing with IE 5	12
Better email and news reader with Outlook Express 5	13
Improved mobile support and power management	28
Microsoft Management Console (MMC)	29
Installer/Remover	28
Kerberos security	19
Modem sharing	24
OpenType font support	10

SETUP

Let's start our coverage with Setup because that is the place where most of us begin our love/hate relationship with Windows, unless Windows is preinstalled by an Information Systems (IS) manager, a vendor, or an original equipment manufacturer (OEM). Following in the footsteps of Windows 98, installation has become simpler. Of course, the easiest upgrade path is from a previous version of NT. A new Setup Manager also can be used to script unattended upgrades. So you can simply insert the installation CD, run your customized upgrade script, and take a coffee break. Assuming all goes as expected, your system will be running Windows 2000 when you get back, which should be in about 30 minutes.

→ For more details on how the improved Windows 2000 setup utility makes your life better, **see** Chapter 4, "Installing Windows 2000 Pro."

Tip #2	If you were using NTFS under NT 4, your file system is automatically upgraded to a new version of NTFS that might not be usable by NT 4. If you plan to dual-boot NT 4 and Windows 2000, make sure you have upgraded NT 4 to Service Pack 4.

If you're upgrading from another operating system such as Windows 9x, the road might be a little rougher, though not terribly so. As with the installation routine for Windows 98, far fewer interventions are required during setup, and they appear mostly at the beginning of the process. One great feature is that Windows 2000 Professional reads and writes to the FAT32 file system. This means you don't have to reformat large Windows 95 and 98 hard disks to NTFS before doing the installation. Assuming you don't want or need the added security and indexing capabilities of NTFS, you can stick with FAT32 and just cruise through the installation. If you're using disk compression under Windows 9x and want to upgrade from that, you must manually decompress the files before you upgrade.

Setup is generally much friendlier than it was in previous versions of NT. You will be issued warnings in the case of programs that might not upgrade successfully from Windows 9x, or hardware that the installer can't find drivers for, and so on—which are nice touches. If you want to keep Windows 9x on the machine and dual-boot it, you can just specify another directory (such as WINNT) and do a fresh install into that. Your Windows 9x directory and settings will be spared invasion and will remain as they were. When you boot up your machine, you'll be prompted to choose the operating system you want to use.

As with Win9x setup routines, a Smart Recovery mode kicks in if setup crashes during hardware detection or some other point of the process. In the worst-case scenario, such as when hardware looks incompatible or the system keeps crashing and then recovering, you'll have the option to gracefully bail out.

GENERAL SYSTEM IMPROVEMENTS

With the advent of the PC, information administrators in corporations began to lose control of corporate data. What afforded workers a certain amount of computing freedom ended up a double-edged sword. Data loss, corruption, and accidental duplication continue to be a headache for PC-enabled companies 20 years later. Ideally, we would be able to meld the portability and personal control of desktop-based computing with the reliability, security, and the administrative control associated with the terminal-mainframe model of computing.

Note

We think it's a little ironic that business computing has come almost full circle in the past 20 years. In the seventies and early eighties, workers had terminals on their desks, tying them to the company mainframe computers. Then PCs appeared and were standalone units fully disconnected from the corporate data source. Next, PC users wanted to share data with one another, so LAN arrangements became popular. In the last few years or so, a significant amount of new PC technology has been precipitated by the need for data security and centralized data storage. To some degree, then, what we're creating with advanced operating systems such as NT and millions of PCs is not all that dissimilar to the arrangement back in the seventies. The only difference is that the terminals are fully functional desktop computers powerful enough to do much of their own computing.

In any case, Windows NT was a move in the direction of helping centralize and secure data in the corporate enterprise, and has done that fairly well. Now Windows 2000 delivers even more power, controllability, and reliability for both the administrator and the average worker bee, who might not even be connected to a LAN. (In fact, I'm running Windows 2000 Professional on a standalone laptop.)

"Okay, so what's in it for me?," you ask. If you or your organization is considering a move to Windows 2000 Professional, you're probably asking this question. We think that anyone who uses it, assuming your computer is powerful enough, will enjoy the system's easier user interface and increased reliability.

→ To learn more about the hardware you'll need to successfully run Windows 2000 Pro, **see** "Hardware Requirements," **p. 98**.

Speaking generally, one of the best aspects of Windows 2000 Professional is that it just plain works. You can just install it and get to work. And it keeps on ticking. That's all most of us want, right? Even in beta testing, it proved very reliable and smooth. We expect that with Windows 2000 Professional and Server together, organizations can build an overall client/server infrastructure that stays up and running for long periods of time, helping to ensure higher levels of productivity across the enterprise. This reliability is becoming increasingly important as Web sites become more central to doing business and they must be up 24 hours a day. The explosion of Internet technologies, the rate of change, and the intensity of competition will be greater than anyone imagined a few years ago.

Second, we've noticed that Windows 2000 is fast. Even before optimization (that's typically the last step before a software product ships), Windows 2000 Professional ran very quickly on test machines; significantly faster than Windows 98 on the same machines with 64MB of RAM. After optimization, performance was notably better still.

Tip #3

If you want to go whole hog with Windows 2000 Pro, you can take advantage of its support for scalable memory and multiprocessors. So you can bump your RAM up as far as 4GB (if you can afford it and your machine can take it), and you could add up to two symmetric multiprocessors.

Because IE 5 is packaged with the release version of Windows 2000 Professional, you'll notice faster browsing, simply due to IE's improvements. But in addition, Windows 2000 Professional has faster hard disk indexing than NT 4 or Win9x, meaning you can locate the information you need quickly and easily, whether you're searching your computer's hard drive or the Web.

For companies, probably the most compelling reasons to make the switch to Windows 2000 are architectural, and many pertain to services provided by Active Directory, available on the three flavors of Windows 2000 Servers: Standard Server, Advanced Server, and Datacenter Server. Datacenter Server will be the "top dog" of 2000 Server and will support 32 CPUs, huge memory capacity, advanced clustering, load balancing, and fail-over technology. Even without the Server variants, Windows 2000 Professional offers mobile and roaming enhancements, reliability improvements, trouble-prevention and management tools, and services that reliably install, maintain, and remove applications. An NTFS update with encryption and Plug and Play device detection and configuration are attractive as well.

> **Note**
>
> Although we'll discuss Windows 2000 Server from time to time, you'll need to refer to another book for the detailed information you need to set up and run Windows 2000 Server. We suggest picking up a copy of *Special Edition Using Microsoft Windows 2000 Server*, published by Que.

INTERFACE IMPROVEMENTS

As one magazine article on Windows 2000 said, "When it comes to looks, NT 5.0 puts the Windows in Windows NT." Windows NT 4 was beginning to look a bit dated, and Windows 2000 Professional definitely sharpens the image, both on the surface level of icons and such and in interface features and intelligence.

STARTUP AND START MENU IMPROVEMENTS

From the get-go, Windows 2000 looks different. As you boot, pressing F8 brings up an option menu much like the one in Windows 95 and 98, letting you boot into alternative modes such as "safe mode" to do troubleshooting (see Figure 1.1). You see the usual little progress dots across the top of the screen as device drivers are loaded, just like in NT 4, but when the splash screen hits, it's more attractive and has a progress bar.

As in Windows 98, Windows 2000 includes a Windows Update option on the Start menu for simplifying connection to the Internet for system upgrades.

Next, the Start button menuing system has been made more intelligent. Instead of your having to look through all your application shortcuts on the Start menus, often in scrolling lists, Windows 2000 Professional just shows you the most recently used programs. This feature is called the Windows 2000 *adaptive user interface* and is brought to you from Office 2000— known in Office-speak as *personalized menus and toolbars*. It keeps tabs on which applications you use most often and promotes them by placing them farther up your Start menu. The built-in "intelligence" continually monitors your use of programs that you access from the Start menu, making it easy for you to keep your Start menu clean.

Figure 1.1
New startup options in Windows 2000 Professional offer various troubleshooting options if you simply press F8 at boot time.

```
Windows 2000 Advanced Options Menu
Please select an option:

Safe Mode
Safe Mode with networking
Safe Mode with Command Prompt

Enable Boot Logging
Enable VGA Mode
Last Known Good Configuration
Directory Services Restore Mode (Windows 2000 domain controllers only)
Debugging Mode


Use ↑ and ↓ to move the highlight to your choice.
Press Enter to choose.

Press ESCAPE to disable safeboot and boot normally
```

Note

As we'll discuss later, you can turn off this feature, thankfully, because it can be annoying, at least to some. Whether you choose to do so depends on your work style. See Figures 1.2 and 1.3 for examples of the classic Windows menu system and Windows 2000 Personalized menus.

Figure 1.2
Here, you see a mess of Start button short-cuts and scrolling lists.

Figure 1.3
With the adaptive user interface turned on, only the Most Recently Used (MRU) Start button shortcuts are shown.

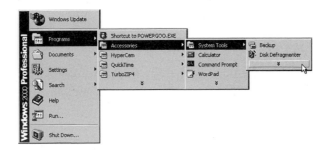

You might decide this feature is pretty spiffy, letting you access your frequently used applications a lot faster. You can still get to your lesser-used programs; they are just moved down a level on the menus. If you linger on a choice such as Programs for a few seconds or click on the little down arrows, the entire list will eventually appear, so you still can find that goofy game or recipe program you installed last year. But for most purposes, cutting out the distraction of those erratically used listings is a boon. You can turn off this feature if you decide you don't like it.

In general, the clutter has been cleaned up. For example, the Channel Bar, MSN, or Outlook Express shortcuts aren't just plunked down on your desktop without your asking.

The following is the rundown of a few other interface niceties:

- New wizards—Several new wizards have been added to simplify common tasks such as adding hardware.

- My Documents and Pictures—As in Windows 98, a My Documents folder is the default location for storing your work. A new My Pictures folder below My Documents is the prefect place for your digital photographs. It comes complete with a viewer. Drop any JPG, GIF, or TIF file into the My Pictures folder, and you can easily view it, zoom in, or zoom out. No editing or slideshow features have been added, though.

- Customizable toolbars—You can drag toolbars, such as the Web address toolbar, around on the desktop or add them to the taskbar at the bottom of the screen. Additional personalized Start menu and taskbar settings are available from the Taskbar Properties dialog box (see Figure 1.4).

- Radio toolbar—In all Explorer windows, you can add a Radio toolbar, from which you can easily choose radio stations to listen to while you work.

- Smarter Open dialog boxes—Many dialog boxes, such as the ones you use to open and save files, now remember the most recently entered filenames. Open dialog boxes also sport an iconic representation of the common locations in a new left pane, called the *Places Bar* (see Figure 1.5).

- Customizable Explorer toolbars—The toolbars are customizable, just like in IE or MS Office.

Figure 1.4
In this dialog box, you can choose new options for taskbar properties.

Figure 1.5
New Open dialog boxes include the Places Bar at the left.

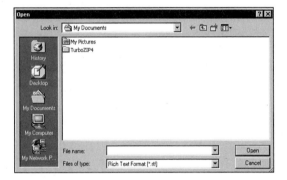

- Desktop button from Win9x—With this button, you can quickly minimize all working windows from the screen so that you can see the desktop. Click again on this button and all the windows reappear in their previous sizes and locations.

- Improved help system in enhanced HTML—This much improved, fully searchable HTML-based help system has links to the Web (if you're online). The Help viewer displays an integrated table of contents and index, including the search results at the same time you are viewing a Help topic (see Figure 1.6). It also includes the Favorites tab, which you can use to bookmark topics. This feature enables you to quickly display topics that you refer to often. The Favorites tab is available only in the main Windows Help file.

- New balloon help tips—Novice users will appreciate the new balloon help tips that pop up, such as when you let your mouse pointer hover over certain icons, or when network connections are made, reporting the connection speed (see Figure 1.7).

Figure 1.6
The new help engine is more friendly, has Web links, and includes a Favorites tab.

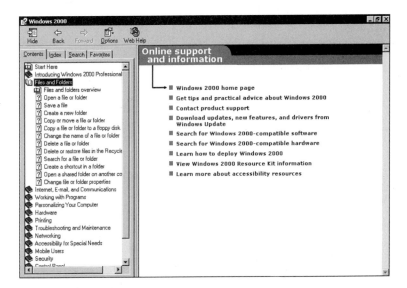

Figure 1.7
Little help balloons appear from time to time, such as when you hover the mouse pointer over certain items.

ENHANCED SEARCH FEATURE AND HISTORY

Although the new interface frills provide a bit of comfort and ease for the weary computer user, we all expect increased efficiency and functionality from a new operating system. Improved searchability and the ability to recall past activities will be welcome additions to any user's bag of tricks.

The Find option on the Start button menu was a real boon in Windows 9x. It has now migrated to Windows 2000 Professional and grown up. You can search from any and all Windows Explorer windows. When you search the Internet, the LAN, or your local hard disk, you use the same dialog box now. You can search for a file, folder, network computer, person, Web topic, or map. Note that if you're running on a Windows 2000 Active Directory network, files are indexed across the network by Active Directory (see later in this chapter) for faster searching. You can display a thumbnail view of search results to see what files or other items have been found. If the network you're on is using the new MS Index Server, the discovered items are also ranked according to closeness of match, just like search engines do.

Pressing the Windows key + F or choosing Search from the Start menu brings up the box you see in Figure 1.8. This integrated, easier-to-use search feature helps you find information on your computer, your network, or on the Web. Notice that the name of the feature was changed from Find to Search.

Figure 1.8
The new search tool is much more inclusive than the one in Windows 98. Local and Internet searching are supported from one unified box.

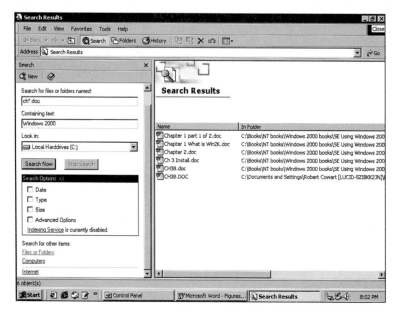

A History pane is also available in any and all Explorer boxes (from My Computer, Windows Explorer, or IE). It can be useful for retracing your steps over the past few weeks. Using this feature, much like the journaling feature in Outlook, you can easily review what you were doing, say, a week ago, or you can reopen a file you edited or even see which folders you had open. Figure 1.9 illustrates the History pane.

Figure 1.9
A History pane is now an option in Windows Explorer.

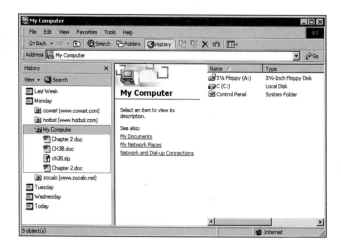

ACCESSIBILITY AND LANGUAGE SUPPORT HAVE BEEN EXPANDED

Using computers is hard enough for those of us who have full mobility and physical abilities, considering how cryptic and idiosyncratic Windows is. For many folks, just the physical act of using a computer poses an additional challenge. Windows 2000 Professional has risen to the level of Windows 98 in terms of support for people with such accessibility challenges. The "sticky keys" and "mouse keys" options for the motor impaired have been added, as have the screen magnifier for the visually impaired and display system and program sounds as visual cues for the hard of hearing. Windows 2000 also has a "narrator" function that reads the screen contents out loud.

Built-in support is now included for viewing and editing more than 60 language character sets, which means you can run programs such as email and text editing in different languages on a single version of Windows. If you want full language support (dialog boxes, help system, and other details in another language), you'll have to purchase a new version, the multilanguage edition of Windows 2000 Professional.

INTERNET CONNECTIONS AND SOFTWARE

Like the rest of us, Microsoft has taken to the Internet in a big way. Numerous tools have been added over the last several years to help get us all connected (and addicted) to the Internet. Just as in Win9x, you can now connect to the Internet through the Internet Connection Wizard. In addition to getting you connected through an Internet service provider, or ISP (even finding one in your local area, assuming you have a modem connected to the phone line), Windows 2000 can help you make your connection via your local area network or set up a connection based on a preexisting ISP account, should you already have one.

One of the most compelling reasons to upgrade either to Windows 98 Second Edition or to Windows 2000 is to benefit from a feature that was long outstanding from Windows products—modem sharing. Even though fax/modem sharing was built into Windows several years ago, the capability to share an Internet connection was not. Instead, each computer needed its own dial-up Internet connection, or the LAN used an external box called a *router* that, in turn, connected to the Internet. Windows 2000 Professional comes with Internet sharing built in, software that essentially performs the same task as a router. Whether you're running a small LAN in your home, with a few computers, or a larger collection of machines at work, you might find Internet Connection Sharing very useful.

Despite many folks' hopes that Microsoft wouldn't win the browser war and Netscape would stand a chance, Internet Explorer 5 has received rave reviews for speed and its overall feature set. It is fast and helps you be productive on the Web—and it is built into Windows 2000 Professional. Using what Microsoft calls IntelliSense technology, Internet Explorer 5 has nifty features such as the capability to remember what you type into forms (such as name and address); IE suggests that information the next time you hit the form, helping to complete it for you. IE also lets you save complete pages or sets of pages (with working graphics and links) to your hard disk for fast, offline browsing.

With the integrated search capability, you can search for and view information on the World Wide Web directly from your browser, without directly using a search engine such as Yahoo!. You can also select from and customize the list of available search services used with each search category and fine-tune other Internet searches.

Active Desktop has been an option since IE 4—not that it ever caught on as well as Microsoft would have liked. Regardless, it is included in Windows 2000. It appears to be less buggy in Windows 2000 than in Windows 9x, and because the multitasking in Windows 2000 is more elegant, you can expect it to take less of a toll on system speed.

The Windows 2000 platform integrates the most comprehensive set of Internet technologies across all facets of the client and server operating systems. Internet standards such as HTTP, DNS, TCP/IP, and LDAP are native protocols to both Windows 2000 Server and Windows 2000 Professional. The platform integrates the very latest in advanced Web application services such as Internet Explorer 5, Internet Information Services 5.0, Active Server Pages, and COM+ across the client and server, and more. This means that the Windows 2000 platform provides the fastest time-to-market for your Web solutions.

REMOTE ACCESS IMPROVEMENTS

With the increase in popularity of road warriordom and telecommuting, remote access has become an issue for many computer users. I'm pleased to report that Windows 2000 Professional not only runs fine on laptop computers, but the remote access tools built into it are somewhat in excess of the combination of both Windows 98's and NT 4's. As with *Remote Access Services (RAS)* in NT 4, you can connect to, view, and work with files back at the office with a secure login.

Thankfully, now you can create, monitor, connect to, and alter all the Internet and remote connections settings from one location rather than hop around between various dialog boxes and control panel applets. Most of these settings are driven by wizards, to make it easier for anyone not comfortable with making these kinds of settings.

HARDWARE IMPROVEMENTS

One of the continued gripes about NT 4 is the relative paucity of hardware support, at least when compared to the consumer versions of Windows. Microsoft is attempting to rectify this situation with Windows 2000—at least to some extent. Literally, thousands of printers, network devices, modems, scanners, and digital cameras are supported with drivers tested and approved by the QC labs at Microsoft—on average, not quite as many devices as Windows 98 supports, but far better than the case with NT, and Microsoft promises to bring Windows 2000 Professional on par with 98.

In the meantime, if you have rare, discontinued, or otherwise nonstandard hardware, be sure to check Microsoft's Hardware Compatibility List at www.microsoft.com/hwtest/hcl. If you're in a position to influence corporate deployment of Windows 2000 Professional, you might additionally want to look into compatibility information and any possible testing utilities before you buy additional Windows 2000 Professional upgrades. Check the Microsoft Windows 2000 Professional Web site and the Windows 2000 installation CD.

For high-end servers, Windows 98 can't compare to Windows 2000. Windows 2000 supports advanced features such as 4GB of RAM, multiple processors, and *clustering*. (Clustering allows several computers to share processing tasks and also distributes risk.)

→ To learn more about hardware support issues, **see** Chapter 3, "Getting Your Hardware and Software Ready for Windows 2000."

The following is the lowdown on the newly added hardware support, help, and troubleshooting:

- New Device Troubleshooters (online help) can be reached from Control Panel Device Properties boxes and from the Windows Help menus.

- Infrared support has been added, typically for printers, but other devices such as hand-held computers use IR, too.

- Gamers and multimedia types will be happy to know that Windows 2000 Professional has strong support for DirectX and OpenGL games (and Multimedia in general), which NT 4.0 doesn't have or sorely lacks. Using DirectX 7.0, you can run consumer and professional 3D titles; use videoconferencing; use new devices, such as USB audio and digitally connected joysticks; and hear richer, clearer sound.

- Native support of Zip drives for backup has been added.

- Windows 2000 provides full support for Digital Video Disc (DVD) playback. With DVD Player, you can play feature-length films and have instant access to advanced DVD features, including movie chapters, optional closed-caption support, and your choice of viewing formats.

- Windows 2000 Professional supports IEEE 1394 FireWire, a high-speed connection type that enables you to use even high-end digital video and audio devices.

- Using image color management helps calibrate the colors on your monitor so that the hue and saturation more closely match that of your color printer. This feature helps you get predictable output on your printer.

- As in Windows 98, Windows 2000 Professional lets you connect up to four monitors to your PC, each with different information or applications in them, if you want. This capability is particularly good for demanding applications such as editing video, following the stock market, and so on.

- Full support of the Advanced Configuration and Power Interface (ACPI) power-management standard enables the operating system to direct power management on a wide range of mobile, desktop, and server computers and peripherals. ACPI can better control battery consumption, hard disk and screen power down, and peripheral restart after entering standby mode than APM (Advanced Power Manager) could. I was pleased to see that Windows 2000 Professional can power down my Dell Inspiron 7000 laptop in "hibernate mode" quickly, remembering all the files and applications I had open, and then restore the identical work space days later without a hiccup.

Support for ACPI

ACPI gives the operating system greater control over ACPI-compliant hardware and lets the hardware provide the operating system with information about itself. For example, ACPI-ready systems with ACPI-compliant hardware add-ons can have Windows 2000 turn off individual peripherals to save power, depending on what the PC is doing at any given moment. These peripherals could be modems, video cards, hard disks, or even external devices such as scanners or monitors. Of course, Windows 2000 won't turn off a network PCMCIA card during a file transfer, but it could choose to save power by powering down your monitor and video card. And a new ACPI-compliant CD-ROM drive can lock itself if an unauthorized user tries to remove a disk.

Windows 98 also supported ACPI but was somewhat buggy. Effective use of ACPI relies on several factors, only one of which is the operating system. Because ACPI is relatively new, not all hardware complies with the standard. Even though 2000 has support for "legacy" systems that have older BIOS dates and ISA hardware, you won't see the same advantages as you will on brand-new machines with the latest cards and BIOSes. Your machine might be BIOS upgradable to support ACPI. If not, it's probably not a big deal. You are more than likely going to upgrade at some point to a new computer to run Windows 2000 Professional anyway. Make sure to check the ACPI specs on it and get one with the ATX (rather than AT) specification so that the power supply can also be powered down or put into a sleep state by the motherboard and operating system.

Note

With an eye toward the future, Microsoft has built in to all versions of Windows 2000 support for Intel's new Pentium III and Pentium III Xeon processors. These processors use the Intel Single Instruction Multiple Data (SIMD) set that allows a database to perform multiple parallel tasks. The Xeon sports Extended Server Memory Architecture (ESMA) and will allow workstation and server applications to access between 4GB and 64GB of dedicated memory. When applications are written to exploit these features, Xeon-powered boxes will meet or exceed the speed and efficiency of Dec's Alpha workstations.

PLUG AND PLAY AND OTHER GOODIES

Windows 2000 also adds support for *Plug and Play (PnP)*, meaning you can add new stuff to your computer, such as a printer, video card, USB port, and so on, and Windows will attempt to automatically assign it resources and add drivers. It does so, assuming the add-on hardware is Plug and Play compatible and the computer's BIOS is Plug and Play compliant. Windows 2000's Plug and Play is also enhanced by the Advanced Configuration and Power Interface (ACPI), as explained previously, and by a few other technologies brought over to Windows 2000 Professional from Windows 9x:

- Universal Serial Bus (USB)—With Universal Serial Bus, you can connect the latest generation of Plug and Play devices to a desktop or laptop computer without having to manually configure them. You can also chain together up to 127 peripheral USB devices, transmitting data between them at rates up to 12 million bits per second. USB may eventually replace all serial and parallel ports on PCs. USB is typically used for mouse devices, scanners, and cameras at this point.

- IEEE 1394 (FireWire or I-link or Lynx)—IEEE 1394 provides a higher-bandwidth connection for devices that require even faster data transfer, such as scanners and video cameras. It supports speeds up to 400 million bits per second. Up to 63 devices can be supported per 1394 controller, and controllers can be bridged to support multiples of 63. The 1394 interface is more expensive, but the throughput is higher. It will be used mostly for demanding duties such as video editing.

- AGP graphics and related—Windows 2000 supports new display devices such as Accelerated Graphics Port (AGP), multiple video cards and monitors, OpenGL 1.2, DirectX 7.0, and Video Port Extensions.

- Asynchronous Transfer Mode (ATM) technology—ATM can handle voice, data, and video simultaneously, enabling a new generation of business applications that support real-time voice and video streaming. It also integrates smoothly with other network technologies, including Frame Relay, Ethernet, and TCP/IP, whether they are deployed concurrently or incrementally.

- Comprehensive removable storage device support—This support enables you to take advantage of large storage media such as Digital Video Disc (DVD) and Device Bay. Device Bay is a specification developed by Intel, Compaq, and Microsoft. Device Bay is a bit like the PCMCIA specification because devices are a specific shape and size and have a standardized electrical connection to the computer. The difference is that Device Bay is for faster and larger items than PCMCIA. Device Bay will be useful for items such as modems and disk drives, and let users easily replace or upgrade these types of devices. The electrical interface will probably be a mix of USB and 1394 (FireWire).

- Support for more processors in an SMP (symmetric multiprocessing) configuration—Windows 2000 Professional does not have this feature, but Server does, supporting up to two processors.

- Support for VLM (very large memory) accessing—This technique allows applications to access large areas of memory without having to read or write to the hard disk. The VMS operating system (OpenVMS v. 7.1) uses this technique and is now available in Windows 2000 Professional.

FILE SYSTEM IMPROVEMENTS

Realizing the inherent security and efficiency limitations in the old DOS (FAT 16) file system, Microsoft has developed two improved file systems over the last several years—FAT32 and NTFS. NTFS was introduced with NT 3.1; FAT32 with Windows 98. Each has its strengths and weaknesses. FAT32's big advantage is that it's highly compatible with FAT16 yet supports larger disk drive partitions and divides the drive into smaller clusters than FAT16, thus economizing on disk space. However, it's not nearly as secure as NTFS.

Microsoft's updates and tweaks to NTFS in NT 4 service packs pushed NTFS's security even further, but now, Windows 2000 gives the file system a major shot in the arm, with the new NTFS 5.0 version. Now file caching for networked and shared drives is an option, and 128-bit file and folder encryption is built in. Caching speeds up access to the files as well and allows users to work with them offline.

To top it all off, two ambitious new technologies are most central to the file system updates: IntelliMirror and Active Directory.

INTELLIMIRROR AND ACTIVE DIRECTORY

Although it's sort of a confusing name (is it from Intel, or is it just intelligent?), *IntelliMirror* is really a collection of utilities that administrators will use to manage Windows 2000 Professional systems on a network.

Tip #4

> If you visit Microsoft's Web site or read its marketing materials, you'll see the word *IntelliMirror*. IntelliMirror is Microsoft's term for the net effect of several systems that let your preferred—and management-enforced—settings and applications appear on the desktop of any computer you use on your organization's Windows 2000 Server-based network. IntelliMirror is more of a concept than a specific feature of Windows. When you read *IntelliMirror*, you can mentally translate that term to the technologies that really do the work: Active Directory's Group Policies, Remote Installation Service, Roaming User Profiles, and Offline Folders. We'll address each of these topics separately throughout this book.

When combined with Windows 2000 Server and Windows 2000 Professional, IntelliMirror makes a new generation of management capabilities possible:

- Systemwide policies can be administered from a central location via Active Directory and Group Policy. You can use group policies to configure systems to meet the varying needs of particular groups of users. For example, you might want to set up a "policy" for the accounting group in your company, to ensure the staff has the latest software, data files, and rights to work with those files, whereas the sales force would have other programs and would not have access to accounting's file. Each team could have its own desktop arrangements and configurations and even be prevented from changing certain elements of its setup.

- The installation, maintenance, and removal applications can be better controlled. If files are missing when you or a user tries to start it up, you'll be notified, and the application will attempt to "heal" itself by finding the missing file. (See "Improved Application and File Management" later in this chapter for more details.)

- Users can roam around the network and have their documents, settings, and applications follow them. A user can simply log on to another computer using his or her ID and password and bring up his or her own settings. This means you can switch machines at any time and still have access to all your data.

- Remote installation and even replacement of computers on the network can be accomplished easily using what Microsoft calls "Remote Operating System Installation." A manager can just connect your computer to a server, and the system will magically install Windows 2000 Professional or a complete image of the operating system and your applications (probably not your data files, though, depending on where they are stored). Hook up your laptop, and you're ready to hit the road. Even better, if your computer dies, you can just drop a new PC in its slot, and you're working again.

ACTIVE DIRECTORY   *Active Directory* makes many of these whiz-bang features work. You might have heard a great deal of talk about it in the press, but the skinny on it is as follows. Active Directory is really a big database of stuff on the network: users, resources (such as printers), and network policies that can help coordinate the efforts of computer users on the LAN.

Who will use Active Directory? Finding Joe down the hall is no big shakes for a small company, so who cares if Windows 2000 Professional has an amazing tool that can find him, his printer, his computer, or whatever else he might have shared? But in a firm with hundreds or thousands of computers, printers, hard drives, data files, and other shared peripherals, efficiently finding and using those resources can be a challenge. If a user moves from one office to another, what happens then? Using Active Directory, the system manager can alter that user's network privileges, shared items, and links to applications and data files quickly and easily.

> **Note**
>
> As with NT, Active Directory isn't actually new technology. Exciting products such as Novell's NetWare Directory Service (NDS) perform pretty much the same functions (sometimes just called *directory services*). If you're using NDS, some means of synchronizing NDS and Active Directory services between Windows 2000 Server should be available by the time Windows 2000 Professional ships. If not, products from other vendors will do the job.

MORE STABILITY

Stability of performance is the calling card of NT, and also of Windows 2000 Professional— not that anything is perfect or that any operating system is crashproof. UNIX and Linux advocates will allege that NT is no paragon of stability, but it certainly is the most complete, best-supported (in terms of applications and trained support personnel) PC operating system that is relatively solid. The PC market is primarily application-driven and only secondarily driven by an operating system's features. Windows is here to stay as long as hundreds of applications are written and updated each year for it. Windows 2000's strength derives from how it runs applications and yet still protects the kernel of the operating system.

We'll talk more about how the internals of NT and Windows 2000 are organized and how they function in Chapter 2, but for now, consider this point: When Windows 2000 Professional runs a program, it automatically assigns that program to an exclusive area of your system's memory. No other programs can touch that area of memory. Nor can that program or other programs gain access to the area of memory in which the basics of the operating system are running. If this type of security breach were allowed, NT would exhibit the kind of crashing Win9x is known for, and is the primary reason why Windows NT was written. Some other well-designed operating systems have protected kernels and separate memory allocated for each application, too. Various flavors of UNIX are cases in point, as is the BeOS.

To further protect the operating system internals, Windows 2000 Professional implements two other strategies. The first is called *code signing*. Code signing requires a file to be officially "signed" before it is written into the system subdirectory. This strategy prevents bogus, untested, or virus-ridden files from being introduced into the operating system's directory and subsequently loaded at bootup. The second is called *pool tagging*. Pool tagging segregates device driver memory from system memory, allowing vendor-written device drivers that will not jeopardize system integrity to run in memory.

IMPROVED SYSTEM MANAGEMENT

Now let's look briefly at what Windows 2000 Professional has to offer you as a manager of either a single computer or hundreds of machines in a large office setting. Will your work life really be less complicated, and should your company's operating costs be lower? Most likely, because Windows 2000 provides you with centralized control over all the PCs in your organization. You'll also be able to use a new class of applications that are easier to deploy, more manageable, and more reliable. As a result, you will be able to provide better service with less hassle. Following are a few examples of Windows 2000 features that can improve an IT administrator's work life.

The most important new management tool in Windows 2000 Professional is called Microsoft Management Console (MMC), which is shown in Figure 1.10.

Figure 1.10
The Microsoft Management Console is a flexible control panel that accepts plug-in modules.

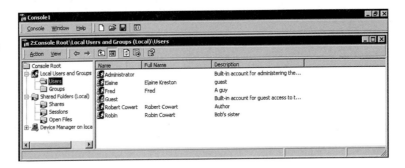

The Microsoft Management Console is a one-stop shop that you can use from your own desk to do the following and more:

- Check the status of remote machine
- Automatically install new applications
- Upgrade old applications
- Repair damaged applications
- Manage devices
- Manage security

In addition to MMC, an improvement to the Windows Management Architecture alerts administrators to possible impending hardware or software problems. Microsoft has implemented industry standards called WBEM (Web-based Enterprise Management) and WMI (Windows Management Instructions) that empower help-desk teams to diagnose problems using a variety of third-party management tools. These tools gather information about a workstation to aid in diagnosing problems.

Another big area of annoyance for administrators is keeping track of updates for deployment across a whole sea of users. This is version control management. Management tools have been added to Windows 2000 Professional to help in service-pack slipstreaming, so a company can keep one master image of the operating system on a network and deploy it to individual PCs as necessary.

Windows 2000 Professional has borrowed the Windows Update feature from Windows 98, enabling managers and users to keep their systems up-to-date via a simple connection to the Web. Just click Start and choose Windows Update. Now a hard disk defragmenting utility is also available, so no third-party defrag program (such as Norton Utilities) is required.

Tip #5	Consider the common headache of running out of disk space. It's a bummer, right? Some third-party programs can help out. Seagate has one called Remote Storage Service (RSS); it's a Hierarchical Storage Management (HSM) system that may come bundled with Windows 2000 Professional (check your release disks). Here's how it works: When your disk starts bogging down, RSS locates lesser-used files and transfers them to a tape or network drive or other backup medium. When needed, the files are called from the backup medium.

Another interesting and useful feature for keeping track of files is something borrowed from the Macintosh and from some graphics files (such as JPGs); it's called *native property sets*. To help you find and index files, users can add metadata, such as the revision number or some other descriptive title, to each file. By default, Windows 2000 Professional assigns every file a unique ID. This ID or metadata remains part of the file even if renamed or moved. If your network is using Microsoft Index Server, finding the file even among thousands of machines would be quick. You can add metadata to any file by using the Summary tab of the Properties dialog box (see Figure 1.11).

The following is a short list of other management tools and tricks incorporated into Windows 2000 Professional with the IT manager in mind:

- A System Prep tool is now available for cloning one system onto multiple machines.
- An improved Backup tool handles more kinds of media than in the past, including floppies, hard drives, tape, and CDs. An "automated system recover" option is included for backing up entire partitions (and the operating system itself) and restoring them in case of a hard disk crash.
- You can now boot off a network drive if your hardware supports such a drive.

- You can search for and manage network files based on username, and you can set quotas on disk usage and network resources based on user, group, or individual volume.

- Less rebooting is required. According to Microsoft sources, more than 75 scenarios that required a reboot in Windows NT Workstation 4.0—for example, adding a protocol or a new device required a reboot—have been reduced to 7 in Windows 2000. Windows 2000 Professional stops and restarts services to recognize new protocols or devices rather than requires a system restart.

- You now can find controls for settings more easily. The Control Panel now acts as the single configuration point for the OS, dial-up connections, scheduled tasks, administrative tools, and so on. Using the Control Panel is much easier than jumping from folder to folder looking for the applet you need.

Figure 1.11
Windows 2000 lets you add meta information to any file through native property sets for easy indexing.

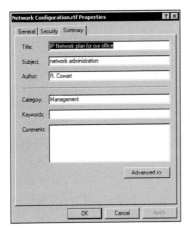

NEW WIZARDS

Several new wizards (well, new to NT; some have been in Win9x for a while) make system configuring easier and eliminate some of the guesswork that used to be involved in making all those settings in dialog boxes. The following are just a few examples:

- Hardware Wizard—You could consider this wizard a single stop for all your hardware settings (see Figure 1.12). You can use the Hardware Wizard to add, configure, remove, troubleshoot, or upgrade the peripherals. The wizard automatically configures any detected hardware and installs device drivers during setup or when you add or remove hardware. You can easily swap devices, such as floppy drives, CD-ROMs, DVDs, batteries, or PC cards.

- Network Connection Wizard—This wizard lets you start up network connections on-the-fly, whether in the office or at home (phoning into the Internet via your ISP), creating a Virtual Private Networking (VPN) connection to a LAN in another location, or whatever. The Network Connection Wizard is also used to set up direct connections to other computers, directly through infrared, parallel, or serial connections (see Figure 1.13). Note that infrared connections between computers are now supported for an ad hoc instant (slow-speed) cable-less LAN.

Figure 1.12
You can use the Hardware Wizard to add, remove, or troubleshoot a piece of hardware.

Figure 1.13
You can use the Network Connection Wizard to create several different types of connections.

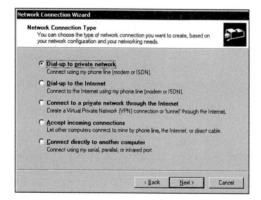

- Add Printer Wizard—This wizard makes it easy to set up and connect to local and network printers, even from an application, right from the Print dialog box (see Figure 1.14). No more fishing around for the Printers folder. The wizard automatically tries to determine the make and model of your printer without forcing you to scroll through a list of options.

IMPROVED APPLICATION AND FILE MANAGEMENT

Application management is a major chore, even in a single-user environment. Keeping programs up-to-date and running smoothly on a corporate LAN can be a Herculean effort. A seemingly simple job of moving data and applications from one computer to another can blow the better part of your day. As any veteran Windows user knows, one of the reasons for this is the plethora of dynamic link library (DLL) files that clutter your directories and on which your applications and operating system rely. These files can get lost, and version conflicts between them can lead to application and even system crashes.

Figure 1.14
You can choose or create a new printer without opening the Printers Control Panel.

If your network (workstations and server) is running Windows 2000 IntelliMirror then Active Directory and the Windows Installer Service work together to make light work of managing your applications. (Even on a standalone system, the Add/Remove Applications applet is smarter than in previous versions of Windows and can clean house more thoroughly when you remove an application.) In previous versions of Windows, a typical new application installed itself using an install program (for example, SETUP.EXE) that dumped files in specific locations on your system and hoped it all worked. Unless you have a third-party program such as Uninstaller sniffing around, you don't get much notice of what goes where either. Newer program setup routines are supposed to be written in such a way that they keep track of this information for later removal, but not all programs mind their manners.

By contrast, the Windows Installer Service uses MSI files (or Windows Installer Package, which basically is a simple relational database) to dictate where files should be placed on your system under a wide variety of situations. For example, if you're delivering the application to users from a LAN application server, you would have one setup, whereas a standalone system would have another. Rather than using absolute or assumed folder locations and names, MSI files rely on variables supplied by the operating system for such information as the location of the operating system itself (it's not always C:\WINNT, which can confuse older programs). Whereas older programs might place the new program's DLL file specifically in C:\WINNT\System32, the Windows Installer Service will manage the file placement itself and copy the file to the correct directory, even if it's something like C:\win2k\System32. In essence, the installer makes a system call to Windows and says, "Place our DLLs in the system directory." The upshot is that the operating system (via

Active Directory) keeps track of the whereabouts of all DLLs in use by applications or the operating system on a given computer.

Now, what's really cool is that the Active Directory database can be used to direct any number of activities related to applications management. Some of the key Active Directory features include

- Application pushing—Managers can "push" applications or upgrades to users. When the user logs on, the applications or upgrades will download across the network automagically. This means the IT manager doesn't have to configure each machine individually or even remotely. He or she can just set up rules that apply to the user or a set of users and then relax. There are some interesting push options, too, such as whether the application is *assigned* or *published*. If the application is assigned, the Windows Installer Service sets up a shortcut for the application in the Start menu. When the end user clicks the shortcut for the first time, the application is automatically downloaded, installed, and launched. If the application is published, any end user who has permission can install it using the Add/Remove Programs applet from Control Panel (see Figure 1.15). And finally, if a user double-clicks on a file but it won't open because no program is associated with it, the Windows Installer Service automatically searches for the published application that supports it. If the Windows Installer Service finds a match, the service automatically installs the application and launches it, without intervention from the user or an IS tech. Is this feature great or what?

Figure 1.15
Windows 2000 Professional users can install "published" applications from a centrally managed server.

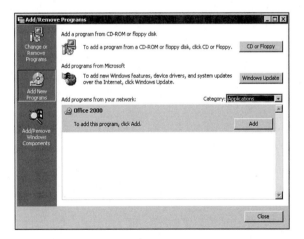

- Resiliency—Assigned programs are persistent. This means that even if a user deletes a program assigned to his or her workstation, the program is *advertised* again (a dialog box mentions its availability) the next time the user logs in to the computer. As a result, the assigned program is always available for the user.

- Automatic application healing—This phrase sounds pretty weird to be used in the context of computer programs, I know, but this feature is certainly something many

Windows users have wished for. Somehow the system seems to get messed up automatically, so why is it too much to expect that it might heal the same way? Here's how it
works: The maker of a software program can declare as part of its MIS file what files
are supposed to be installed and where. When you run a program, it looks around to
see whether all key files are present undamaged. If not, the program will repair itself by
attempting to find the needed files across the network server on a local CD-ROM, and
so on.

■ Automatic system healing—Much like the System File Checker in Windows 98,
Windows 2000 Professional can detect and repair corrupt system files, too. As we mentioned, new applications all too often overwrite critical files with their own versions,
sometimes causing previously installed software (including the operating system itself)
to break. Windows 2000 guards against system file corruption (unintentional or malicious) by maintaining a list of some 300 files that are automatically replaced by the
operating system when they are overwritten. This feature could cause conflicts with
software whose installers try to replace or update system files, but those are the breaks.
Software companies have to start dealing with Windows 2000 Professional's built-in
protection.

■ Manual healing—Optionally, a user can choose to do a more complete repair from the
Add/Remove Programs Control Panel, as described previously. If a program encounters
a problem during installation (for example, the hard disk contains insufficient space to
complete the installation), the installation fails. When the installation fails, this feature
will undo all the installation that has occurred up to that point, ensuring that a failed
installation leaves the computer in the same known good state the computer was in
before the installation began.

■ Resources sharing—The Windows Installer service also aids in cooperation between
programs that share files (components), ensuring more reliable interoperation among
them. For example, Microsoft Office components (Excel, Word, and PowerPoint) share
many files. The Installer service checks versions and keeps track of shared components,
which helps to ensure that applications work well with one another and work separately,
even when one of them is removed from the system.

■ Uninstalling applications—One of the reasons that hard disks jam up is that programs
you thought you uninstalled are not fully removed. In addition to helping set up and
configure programs, the Installer service also helps remove programs and their associated files completely and reliably. For example, the Installer service's refcount function
ensures that components that are shared between applications continue to work properly even when one of those applications is deleted from the computer.

IMPROVED NETWORK MANAGEMENT

As we have mentioned, Active Directory sits at the center of this new operating system, particularly when it comes to network management. Active Directory presents serious competition for Novell's NetWare Directory Services (NDS) by providing the extent of control that
IS managers need to deploy large-scale installations and manage large numbers of users,

groups, policies, and data using an integrated interface from a single location. Much of this technology comes from Microsoft's Exchange Server and even includes utilities to help in importing data from NDS or Exchange Server.

Like some other Microsoft products we have known and worked with, the relationship with the competition's product (in this case, NDS) is one way. Whereas Exchange and Active Directory can run concurrently and synchronize easily, NDS cannot. Only importing of NDS data is supported by Windows 2000 (Server, in this case, though we think the discussion is germane in this overview)—not exporting *to* NDS. Therefore, the two services cannot effectively synchronize. This limitation is obviously a ploy to encourage Novell shops to come on over to the Microsoft side of life, though third-party programs will appear to expedite this function, no doubt.

Network administration capabilities in Windows 2000 Server are extensive, to say the least:

- In addition to what we've already discussed, typical administrator chores, such as moving a user between groups, can be easily achieved in just a few minutes with a few mouse clicks.

- Windows 2000's Quality-of-Service (QoS) support guarantees bandwidth to users and groups for network-hungry activities such as videoconferencing.

- Disk quotas can be set for network resources based on users or groups of users or individual volume. For example, the sales department could be limited to using 250MB of disk space on the server.

- Windows 2000 lets an administrator hunt for and manage network files based on who is using them.

- Windows 2000 can now apply service packs to servers used for disgorging system files into remote installations (a.k.a. installation shares). Using this feature, an administrator can update one installation share with a service pack, and any user who installs from the updated version will automatically receive the upgraded OS. This means less user downtime and reduced IS costs.

EASIER CONNECTIONS

Making network connections work properly has never been easy. If some protocol isn't missing, then the workgroup setting is wrong, nothing is shared, or printer and file sharing isn't turned on. These examples are just a few of the possible bugaboos. Windows 2000 Professional makes things easier by putting all network- and dial-up network-related connection settings into a folder. It's now called the *Network and Dial-up Connections* folder. By right-clicking My Network Places (what used to be Network Neighborhood) and choosing Properties, you can get there fast (see Figure 1.16).

Instead of your having to tromp through separate locations for Dial-Up Networking and Ethernet adapters, all these settings are consolidated. By right-clicking an existing connection and choosing Properties, you get access to most of what you need for TCP/IP settings, workgroup ID, Virtual Private Network, Modem update, and so on (see Figure 1.17).

Figure 1.16
You can make network connections from one area of the operating system now.

Figure 1.17
Here, you can find properties for dial-up connections.

Notice the new help feature, the additional help links over on the left. Microsoft is attempting to take some of the confusion out of certain folders and some dialog boxes, such as the Network and Printers folders and the Delete Shortcut dialog box, by creating hotlinks that can lead the user to other settings, help, or related applications. We like this feature.

BETTER SECURITY

Sometimes you might wonder whether reliable security is really possible in a world where kids are hacking into the Pentagon's computers. Out of necessity, security technology is improving daily, and Microsoft has been in one of the leading positions in building encryption into PC products, to wit 128-encryption for IE, tracking down holes in JavaScript, and so on. Of course, someone can always sneak through a back door, but by and large the chances of someone stealing your credit card number over the Internet or hacking into your corporation are about as great as your getting into an airplane accident—or at least I suppose (don't sue me if I'm wrong).

Of course, if someone has a motive, that's another story. And people do have motives when it comes to big companies handling large amounts of money or sensitive records. You don't want to make it easy for national secrets to walk out the door on floppy disks, regardless of who the perpetrator is. Then you have to consider the person (like your two-year-old, for example) who has no motive at all but who can always seem to figure out how to format your hard disk or erase that report due tomorrow.

NT has always boasted C-2 level U.S. Government security, one reason it's been installed in venues such as the U.S. Social Security Administration. Permission could easily be set and granted to groups of users. Passwords could be assigned on a folder-to-folder basis, and fancy authentication and trust relationships between NT Server machines were supported. Windows 2000 Professional has all these features, but it goes well beyond, certainly exceeding Windows 98's security (what security?).

If you're a system administrator, IntelliMirror will likely be the primary reason for upgrading your systems, but enhanced security will be another serious attraction. For example, not only can you prevent end users from installing or removing software from a system, but you also can encrypt even individual files with a single click to thwart prying eyes. Kerberos-based security makes life easier, too, allowing you to access all password-protected accounts and resources (such as email and network drives) with a single login.

Note

> Researchers at MIT developed Kerberos to enable users on a public network (such as the Internet) to exchange information such as email, credit card information, or other data securely. It works by assigning a unique key, called a *ticket,* to each user as he or she logs on to the network. Every message created by a given user contains that user's ticket. Using a clever arrangement of encoding the tickets, Kerberos can unscramble the received messages without allowing prying eyes to read the messages during transit.

You'll also have SmartCard-based authentication (just insert your card in a reader to log on) and Public Key Infrastructure (PKI), which is encryption for disk volumes and network communications. PKI is still under development in the industry, and no accepted standard exists, but it's on the way. Suffice it to say, Microsoft is on the security bandwagon in a big way with Windows 2000.

The file system encryption encrypts each file with a randomly generated key. The encryption and decryption processes are transparent to you, the user. Likewise, Kerberos is really nonintrusive. You log in once, and as long as you don't log out, you have access to virtually any network environment, eliminating the need to request and regrant permission access every time a user logs on to a different resource on the network.

Windows 2000 Server/Professional's security systems can also do the following:

- Verify that email came from the claimed sender
- Prevent email from being viewed or edited by other users
- Ensure that applications and drivers come from known sources
- Protect software from tampering after it is installed
- Port credentials and other private information between computers at work, at home, or on the road

MOBILE COMPUTING SUPPORT

As Table 1.1 indicates, when it's finished, Windows 2000 Professional is likely to top out at more than 30 million lines of code. That's enough programming to run a mission to Mars, don't you think? Is this the ultimate in Bloatware? Well, yes on both counts. Windows 2000 Professional is a truly a huge operating system. Yet, despite the operating system's large size, Microsoft is making a serious play to woo notebook users into its corral. If you have a decently empowered Notebook, you can seriously consider making the upgrade. The following are some of the improvements aimed at road warriors:

- Offline folders—This option is one of the biggest advantages for mobile users. After you set up this option, Windows 2000 Professional prepares your laptop for use offline. You declare which files or folders you want to have access to when you're not connected, and the Synchronization Manager does the rest. Now you can easily take all your critical documents with you for work on the road or at home. When you're back online, the Synchronization Manager takes care of updating to the network server as necessary, assuring that everyone has the latest versions of documents available to work with.

  The feature is not unlike the Make Available Offline feature for synching Web pages in IE, but applied to network files and folders instead (see Figure 1.18). And it's a bit like the Windows 9x Briefcase, except it's on steroids. (Briefcase was typically used for synching between desktop and portable machines using floppies.) This feature works with any files shared over a Microsoft network that supports Server Message Block-based (SMB) File and Printer Sharing, including Windows 95, Windows 98, and Windows NT 4.0. Unfortunately, this list doesn't include Novell NetWare networks (surprise).

Figure 1.18
Windows 2000 enables you to make folders available offline.

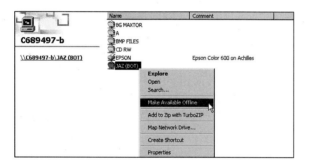

- Cutting-edge power management features—Windows 2000 offers a slew of new power management features. Like Windows 98, Windows 2000 supports Advanced Configuration and Power Interface (ACPI). This means that hardware makers can create systems and peripherals that work closely together to minimize power usage. Although this capability is useful on the desktop, it's critical on battery-powered laptops. It also means you can hot-dock your laptop, and Windows 2000 Professional will figure out what happened, adjust itself as necessary, load necessary drivers, activate peripherals, and so on. Older systems used Advanced Power Management, a BIOS-based power system. ACPI lets the operating system handle power management instead. Laptops and desktops running Windows 2000 Professional and Server now have both Standby and Hibernate functions available for pausing your work and resuming where you left off without having to boot up and open your applications again.

- Remote Access Services (RAS)—With this feature, you can take your laptop on the road and dial into a corporate or small business LAN using conventional phone lines. RAS in Windows 2000 Professional includes *RIP Listening*, a service that learns alternative routes to the network you're dialing into, obviating the need for the user or administrator to specify IP addresses to the route table. Windows 2000 Professional "listens" and updates the route table automatically as it discovers IP addresses that work. This capability can speed up throughput, cutting down on retires and lost packets.

- Virtual Private Networking (VPN)—This feature is sometimes termed *Point-to-Point Tunneling Protocol (PPTP)*. If you have an Internet connection while you're on the road, you can set up Windows 2000 Professional back at the office to "tunnel" into the corporate LAN through that connection and work as though you were in the office. If you have a national or international ISP, you can cut your long-distance phone bill significantly, making a local call rather than using RAS to dial long distance. VPN is easier and more secure under Windows 2000 than NT 4. By using Active Directory on Windows 2000 Server, an administrator can apply strict security measures for access, including password encryption and authentication. Group policies make it easy for the administrator to define a group profile such that all users who are assigned to that profile must comply with authentication rules set for the group before gaining entry. Extensible Authentication Protocol and 128-bit data encryption can also be applied. *L2TP*, a more secure version of PPTP, is now supported. And finally, an even more secure version of tunneling, *IP Security Protocol (IPSEC)*, allows virtually everything above the networking layer to be encrypted.

INTEGRATION WITH EXISTING ENVIRONMENTS

Realizing it has a tough row to hoe if its survival depends on moving every serious business off other operating systems, Microsoft seems to have decided to at least marginally play ball with UNIX and NetWare shops. Windows 2000 Server and Professional have been designed with interconnections to other kinds of servers in mind, emphasizing instead their advanced management and interface offerings as the carrot that will draw potential purchases and slowly woo users into the Microsoft camp. We agree that those realities are significant. If end users are relieved of worries over which server their applications and data are on, and if administrators can easily deploy and manage PC operating systems and groups of users, this translates into significant value and reduced cost of ownership.

Both Windows 2000 Professional and Windows 2000 Server are designed to work with your existing systems, networks, and applications. For example, the products will leverage investments in applications such as Microsoft Office 97 on the client and Microsoft Exchange 5.5 on the server, as well as most existing third-party applications. As mentioned earlier, Windows 2000's capability to synchronize with Novel NDS is somewhat limited, but at least they can coexist.

What about UNIX? Well, Microsoft actually provides an add-on component called Windows NT Services for UNIX. The add-on pack makes it easier than ever for technical-workstation users to move to a single desktop solution. Windows NT Services for UNIX includes the following components:

- An NFS client and server
- A Telnet client and server

- Scripting tools
- Password synchronization
- Virtual Private Networking

Of course, integration with and migration from Windows 9x and Windows NT 3 and 4 operating systems are fairly painless. Upgrading from Windows 3.11 requires a bit more sleight of hand. You must upgrade first to Win9x and then to Windows 2000 Professional. Still, it's possible, and assuming your computer is powerful enough, upgrading will be worth the hassle.

Short of upgrading to Windows 2000 Professional, any Win9x computer can still play on the network with Windows 2000; you'll just be missing some of the goodies, such as decent security. But this is nothing new—we're used to that from networking Win9x machines into NT 4. However, the Windows 2000 Servers and Professional workstations will not be compromised in any way by hanging Windows 9x stations on the network.

As far as we could determine at the time of this writing, OS/2 systems aren't supported on the Windows 2000 network at this time, though there are certainly going to be third-party efforts to make it so.

WHAT IS NOT IN WINDOWS 2000 PROFESSIONAL

Windows 2000 Professional is intended to be the direct replacement for Windows NT 4.0 Workstation and is designed for PCs that are either standalone or networked. The network can contain a wide mix of clients and optionally can have servers such as Windows 2000 Server. What are the limitations?

- Web serving is more limited than with Server. The number of simultaneous connections is 10.
- Two CPUs are supported in Windows 2000 Professional as opposed to four in Server, eight in Advanced Server, and thirty-two in Datacenter.
- Windows 2000 Professional does not include Internet Information Server 5.0 or the Active Directory controller.

You also should be aware that DOS applications that expect direct hardware access will not run (see Chapter 2), including many games written for the DOS platform. Such programs and games will stand a better chance of running on the Win9x platform than on Windows 2000 Professional.

Tip #6

To check whether your computer is ready for Windows 2000, you might want to visit Microsoft's Hardware Compatibility list at www.microsoft.com/hwtest/hcl. You might also want to try running the Windows 2000 compatibility program, which you can find on the Windows 2000 installation CD.

You can test for ACPI compatibility, too, to see whether you'll get the most out of Windows 2000's power management capabilities, by visiting http://www.microsoft.com/HWDEV/acpihct.htm#Public.

DIFFERENCES BETWEEN PROFESSIONAL AND WINDOWS 2000 SERVER

As mentioned earlier, Windows 2000 comes in several flavors—not including Windows 3.1, 95, and 98.

Our apologies for this rather extended discussion of the merits, features, and comparisons of the various versions of Windows and Windows 2000 Professional. The length of this chapter alone is testimony to the breadth of this product. Congratulations if you have read this discussion thoroughly. Even if you aren't ready for the pop quiz (especially if you aren't ready, perhaps), Table 1.3 will help consolidate a few of the concepts discussed herein. It might even shed some light on a few differences between the Microsoft operating systems that were not discussed here.

Most of the breakdown you'll hear in discussions around the water cooler will focus on Professional and Server, but there are two others as well. The Windows 2000 Server family consists of three editions:

- Windows 2000 Standard Server
- Windows 2000 Advanced Server
- Windows 2000 Datacenter

The Standard edition is aimed at small- to medium-sized businesses, whereas the Advanced and Datacenter editions are designed to meet the needs of mission-critical deployments in medium, large, and Internet service provider (ISP) organizations. Even though this book is designed and written for the Windows 2000 Professional user, knowing about the other products can be of some value either in planning an upgrade strategy for the future or for at least understanding the operating systems that your workstation is attached to and dependent on.

TABLE 1.3   VARIOUS CAPABILITIES OF WINDOWS 2000 PROFESSIONAL COMPARED TO EARLIER VERSIONS OF WINDOWS

Feature	Windows 3.1	Windows 3.11 (Windows for Workgroups)	Windows 9x	Windows NT 3.xx
Virtual memory management (paging file on hard disk)	Yes	Yes	Yes	Yes
Multitasking type	Cooperative	Cooperative	Preemptive	Preemptive
Multithreading	No	No	Yes	Yes
Number of CPUs (maximum)	1	1	1	2 native, 4 with OEM-modified HAL
Maximum RAM supported				
Access security	No	No	No	Yes
Kerberos security	No	No	No	No
Runs real-mode device drivers	Yes	Yes	Yes	No
Runs 16-bit Windows and DOS applications	Yes	Yes	Yes	Yes
Runs 32-bit Windows applications	No	No	Yes	Yes
Runs OS/2 applications	No	No	No	Yes
Runs POSIX applications	No	No	No	Yes
Supports DOS FAT16	Yes	Yes	Yes	Yes
Supports DOS FAT32	No	No	95 OSR2 and 98 only	No
Supports OS/2 HPFS	No	No	No	Yes
Supports NTFS	No	No	No	Yes
Supports Disk Compression	DiskSpace or third-party products	DiskSpace or third-party products	Yes	No
File encryption	No	No	No	No
RAID support/levels	No	No	No	Yes
Built-in networking	No	Yes	Yes	Yes
Built-in email	No	Yes	Yes	Yes
Minimum Intel CPU required	286	286	386	386
Supports RISC chips	No	No	No	Yes/MIPS R4000 Alpha
Supports Active Directory	No	No	Planned	No

Windows NT 4 Workstation	Windows NT 4 Server	Windows 2000 Professional	Windows 2000 Server	Windows 2000 Advanced Server	Windows 2000 Datacenter Server
Yes	Yes	Yes	Yes	Yes	Yes
Preemptive	Preemptive	Preemptive	Preemptive	Preemptive	Preemptive
Yes	Yes	No	Yes	Yes	Yes
2	4	2	4	8	32
		4GB	4GB	64GB	64GB
Yes	Yes	Yes	Yes	Yes	Yes
No	No	Yes	Yes	Yes	Yes
No	No	No	No	No	No
Yes	Yes	Yes	Yes	Yes	Yes
Yes	Yes	Yes	Yes	Yes	Yes
Yes	Yes	Yes	Yes	Yes	Yes
Yes	Yes	Yes	Yes	Yes	Yes
Yes	Yes	Yes	Yes	Yes	Yes
No	No	Yes	Yes	Yes	Yes
No	No	No	No	No	No
Yes	Yes	Yes	Yes	Yes	Yes
Yes	Yes	Yes	Yes	Yes	Yes
No	No	Yes	Yes	Yes	Yes
No	Yes	No	Yes	Yes	Yes
Yes	Yes	Yes	Yes	Yes	Yes
Yes	Yes	Yes	Yes	Yes	Yes
Pentium	Pentium	Pentium	Pentium	Pentium	Pentium
Yes/R4000 Alpha	Yes/R4000 Alpha	Yes/DEC Alpha	Yes/DEC Alpha	Yes/DEC Alpha	Yes/DEC Alpha
No	No	Yes	Yes	Yes	Yes

continues

TABLE 1.3 CONTINUED

Feature	Windows 3.1	Windows 3.11 (Windows for Workgroups)	Windows 9x	Windows NT 3.xx
Supports clustering	No	No	No	No
Supports load balancing	No	No	No	No
Supports Novell NDS	No	No	No	No
Includes Web server/maximum number of connections	No/unlim	No/unlim	Yes/10	No/umlim

The No/unlim entries mean no server was provided, and Microsoft did not restrict what you could do with other vendors' TCP/IP-based software on your computer. In the fall of 1996, Microsoft's licenses were reworded to restrict the number of connections allowed to be made to the computer, regardless of the means or software's vendor.

WINDOWS 2000 SERVER STANDARD EDITION

The center point of the three versions is Active Directory services, which we've already discussed. Active Directory runs on the servers to support management of users, groups, security services, and network resources. Next, the servers all have Internet and Web services built in, enabling your organization to utilize the latest and greatest Web technologies such as streaming video and audio, CGI, Java, and such. And for application services, just as in Windows NT Server 4.0, they all support COM+, transaction and message queuing, and XML support.

Now the differences begin. In response to the ever-increasing progress in microprocessor speeds and lowering costs, Windows 2000 Server also supports both uniprocessor systems and dual CPU (two-way symmetric multiprocessing, or SMP) systems. Up to 4GB of physical memory is possible. The bottom line: The standard Windows 2000 Server is the right match for small- to medium-sized businesses and Web servers, even if you have many workgroups. Support of remote offices is built in through various means, so branch offices can be part of your corporate landscape too and still be supported by the vanilla edition of Server.

Another interesting feature is Terminal Services, which essentially is a "thin client" service. Using really dumb PCs and only a single server, you can concoct a LAN. Code that is small enough to fit on a floppy disk runs on the terminal machines, with the desktop, data files, and applications all running on the Server machine. Most people running Windows 2000 Professional will not care about this feature because, by definition, they obviously have a pretty zippy computer. But if you're in the market for an easy way to have an administrator control users' environments, or if you have major budgeting constraints, check out Terminal Services.

Windows NT 4 Workstation	Windows NT 4 Server	Windows 2000 Professional	Windows 2000 Server	Windows 2000 Advanced Server	Windows 2000 Datacenter Server
No	Yes, only in Enterprise Edition				Yes
No	No	No	No	Yes	Yes
Yes	Yes	Yes	Yes	Yes	Yes
Yes/10	Yes/unlim	Yes/10	Yes/unlim	Yes/unlim	Yes/unlim

WINDOWS 2000 ADVANCED SERVER

Windows NT 3.x had an "Advanced Server," too. The Windows 2000 version is a fair bit more comprehensive though, so don't assume it simply has been renamed. Advanced Server now supports a comprehensive clustering infrastructure for high availability and scalability. It supports as much as 64GB of physical memory (if you can afford it). It can also do some serious data handling by up to eight CPUs running in tandem (SMP). The bottom line: Use this version of Server when, in addition to what is offered by the vanilla Server, you also need database capabilities (for example, inventory control, online transactions, and so on), high availability clustering, and network and component load balancing.

WINDOWS 2000 DATACENTER SERVER

When you're ready for serious rocking and rolling, check out the Windows 2000 Datacenter Server. It's the top-of-the-line Windows 2000 version, sporting all the goodies of the previous two, but imagine plugging in up to 32 CPUs along with that 64GB of RAM. If you intend to set up shop next door to Amazon.com and compete with them selling books, or if you're starting your own private space program, this is the Windows 2000 version for you. It can dish out and organize vast amounts of data, perform econometric and scientific or engineering analyses, and handle big-time online transaction processing. If you're consolidating several preexisting servers into Windows 2000, that might be another reason for looking into this product. Microsoft claims this version has the muscle to support upward of 10,000 simultaneous users in some workloads, while continuing to provide record-setting price performance in transaction processing.

CHAPTER 2

THE DESIGN AND ARCHITECTURE OF WINDOWS 2000 PROFESSIONAL

In this chapter

DEFINING WINDOWS 2000

As was made clear in Chapter 1, "Introducing Windows 2000 Professional," Windows 2000 is Microsoft's top-flight operating system, designed to meet the rigors of major corporations and power users, application developers, and Web servers. Though some, particularly UNIX enthusiasts, might take issue with claims about NT's capabilities, it continues to prove itself as a viable alternative to UNIX and its cousins. It's also the most obvious upgrade to the Win9x line of systems for the smaller, growing company looking for a more robust computing platform.

If you've kept up with NT during its evolution by reading magazines and Web pages, you might already know a bit, if not a lot, about how Windows NT and 2000 work, how its architecture differs from Win9x, and what its various modules do. If so, you can skip or skim this chapter. But if you find computer science interesting, read on. In this chapter, we'll talk about what makes Windows 2000 Professional tick, discuss the modules that make up Windows 2000 Professional, and describe what makes it different from other operating systems from Microsoft, notably Windows 3.x and Windows 9x.

> **Note**
>
> Most NT users (or those considering a switch to NT) are highly computer-literate, so we will dispense with detailed explanations of fundamental computer terminology.

Let's start with a capsule description: Windows 2000 is a *multithreaded, preemptive multitasking* operating system with full 32-bit memory addressing with protected memory space for all 32-bit applications. It supports DOS, Windows, Win32 GUI and character-based applications, and POSIX-compliant and character-based OS/2 1.x applications; it also includes integrated networking, security, and administration tools. It is based on a client/server model. It can run on single or multiple CPUs (up to 32 CPUs in a single box in the top-end Server version called Datacenter). It supports Intel processors as well as the Alpha RISC (reduced instruction set computer) chips from DEC. Extensive management tools, integrated emailing and Internet services, and compatibility with other Windows operating systems and services (such as Exchange Server) round out the Windows 2000 package.

→ Do you think *preemptive multitasking* is a ten-dollar word? You're not alone. To learn what it means, **see** "Preemptive Multitasking." **p. 55**.

By virtue of its internal design, you could say Windows 2000 is an operating system designed to run other operating systems—or at least to emulate them. This is possible only because its design is so modular. Think of the Windows 2000 kernel almost the way you think of your computer's CPU. A CPU is a general-purpose computing device that simply does what it is told, whether that's running spreadsheets, calculating pi to a million digits, cruising the Internet, or rendering video special effects. The CPU interacts with the world through ports; PCI, AGP, SCSI, EIDE, and ISA buses; and various other physical pathways.

So you could think of the CPU like a genie or a "black box." Instructions go in one side, and results come out the other. Like a CPU, Windows 2000's microkernel is a capable and flexible "black box," too. Instead of hanging hardware off it, however, Windows 2000 has services, file systems, and other modular subsystems glomming on to it. You could think of these modules sort of like plug-ins in the same way that PhotoShop or a Web browser has plug-ins. Because of the kernel's elegant design, it's easily *extensible* using this same kind of approach. Just by supplying plug-ins, the Windows 2000's kernel can provide a set of services generic and powerful enough to support a diverse range of operating system personalities. For example, it can concurrently support DOS, 16-bit Windows, 32-bit Windows, OS/2, and POSIX-compliant UNIX applications. It's so modular that it can conceivably support future operating systems and file systems, too.

This chameleon-like capability is partly owing to the fact that the system kernel is fully object-based. That is, it has a consistent interface or system "hook" for each of the many tasks that the central operating system performs. If you know anything about object-oriented programming, this concept is similar. All services provided by the kernel are represented by objects, and each has a consistent interface, naming system, and mechanisms of protection. This increases reliability and the ease with which programs and ancillary system services can interact with the kernel. In a word, this keeps the bug count down.

Each of these operating system environments runs in what is called a protected subsystem. Programs that run in protected subsystems (for example, POSIX applications) don't make direct calls to the kernel. Instead, they make requests of the appropriate subsystem. The subsystem then makes the requests of the kernel.

Tip #7	In addition to its likeness to the Mach microkernel, NT and Windows 2000 are similar in design to the Spring (especially how it uses objects) and to Plan 9 (mostly the way Plan 9 names objects and allows access to those objects) operating systems. Plan 9 is a new computer operating system and associated utilities. It has been built over the past several years by the Computing Science Research Center of Lucent Technologies Bell Laboratories, the same group that developed UNIX, C, and C++.

With a little bit of general discussion behind us, now let's get into some of the detail of the operating system's architecture and what some of the technical terms mean—client/server, preemptive multitasking, multithreading, and so on. Half of these adjectives probably sound like marketing hype, so the next sections contain the initial breakdown of this terminology. Further discussion is found later in this chapter.

PREEMPTIVE MULTITASKING

As undoubtedly you know (though you might be surprised how many Windows users do not take advantage of it), all versions of Windows make it possible to run multiple apps at one time, easily allowing the user to switch between them at will. Only one program is in the "foreground" where the user can interact with it, yet all the apps are technically running.

Note

In this book, we'll use the term *apps* to mean applications. We might occasionally use the term *programs* as well. All three of these terms are interchangeable and refer to programs you run on your computer, such as Microsoft Word. We've chosen to use the word *apps* because it uses less ink and it's being widely used in the press these days, so we figure you know what it means.

In the past, DOS utility programs such as Software Carousel worked this way, sort of; we called them *switchers*. But really they only suspended one application while resuming another. That's not what we're talking about these days. Today's modern PC operating systems can keep a profusion of apps running and computing all at the same time. The finer points of how Windows 2000 keeps them running have been the center of much discussion over the years since NT was introduced.

Suffice it to say, coordinating multiple simultaneously running apps is no small feat—and doing it smoothly is even tougher. One of the big attractions of Windows 2000 Professional is that it manages multiple apps more smoothly than its predecessors—especially Windows 3.x.

Consider an analogy. (If you've read Bob's other NT books, you'll be familiar with this one.) Think of a major intersection with a traffic cop standing in the middle and blowing a whistle. If everyone pays attention to the cop, and the cop is intelligent about things, traffic flows reasonably well and nobody crashes.

Now, suppose you have a spreadsheet recalculation in progress, a COM port receiving a fax, and you're typing a letter at the keyboard. As you know, all these activities can occur simultaneously under Windows 3.x or Win9x, although not always smoothly. Sometimes there are flies in the ointment.

Particularly in Windows 3.x, simultaneous application execution might or might not proceed as you would expect, with one program hogging the computer and not releasing it for use by the others. This result is based on the way their "traffic cop" (task scheduler) handles requests from the operating system for attention and processing by the CPU. At issue is just how CPU time is doled out so that one app doesn't appear to be dead in the water while another one runs. (Divvying up CPU time between apps or other processes is called *time slicing*.) Apps running under Windows 3.x were written to relinquish CPU time at regular (very short) intervals so that other apps (tasks) can be serviced. Not all applications work this way religiously, however, and Windows 3.x itself can't enforce adherence to the standard. A poorly written Windows 3.1 application can actually hog the CPU for enough time to effectively kill some time-dependent applications, such as data-acquisition programs. Try formatting a disk using File Manager (not in a DOS window) while trying to run a communications session (or anything else), and you'll see what we mean.

Windows 3.1's method of multitasking is called *cooperative multitasking*. By contrast, Windows 9x, Windows NT, and Windows 2000 utilize *preemptive multitasking*. Under this scheme, the task scheduler actually empowers the traffic cop to direct traffic as it sees fit. The apps do not control how much CPU time they receive, but rather the scheduler does, preempting one program in favor of another as it sees fit and democratically time slicing.

Note

Preemptive multitasking is not only used in NT but also in Win9x, UNIX, the Amiga operating system, and OS/2, among others. Cooperative multitasking is used in Windows 3.x and the Macintosh's MultiFinder OS.

Windows 9x programmers borrowed from the preemptive multitasking of NT technology and plugged that functionality into Windows 95 and 98. However, because those operating systems' architectures are generally less elegant than NT and 2000, the results are less impressive. Windows 9x suffer for several reasons, owing principally to the legacy from which they derive—DOS. The need to successfully run older DOS and 16-bit Windows programs requires real-mode execution capabilities. In real mode, the kernel is unprotected, exposed to the code of errant applications. This can crash the system. Also, Win9x is a combination of older 16-bit code from the Windows 3.x days, blended with some of NT's 32-bit code. Although capable of running a wide variety of programs, and with extensive support of new technologies (DVD, FireWire, USB, and so on), its design leaves the system vulnerable to crashing.

One result of preemptive multitasking is that the user no longer must consider the resources a certain task will consume, nor does the user have to allow the processing of one task to finish before starting another. Process mixes that previously might have caused problems in Windows 3.1 shouldn't cause even a hiccup in 2000. Background communications sessions, for example, shouldn't drop data while other CPU-intensive tasks are running.

Now consider another example. Any veteran Windows 3.x user almost instinctively allows one program to fully launch before trying to launch another. The hourglass cursor implies the user should wait. In Windows 2000, the hourglass cursor is often replaced by a *startglass* cursor, which is an hourglass with a pointer on it. The pointer is still functional, and as long as you keep double-clicking on icons, programs keep loading.

Tip #8

Actually, the number of programs that can load and execute in Windows 2000 Professional is limited by the amount of virtual memory available, as set by the paging file size (similar to the swap file in Windows 3.x and 9x). In Windows 2000, the recommended paging file's size is equivalent to 1.5 times the amount of RAM in your system. After you try to load more programs or documents into memory than the paging file can handle, performance will lag, or you will simply be prevented from opening more applications or files. If you decrease the size of either the minimum or maximum page file settings, you must restart your computer to see the effects of those changes. Increases normally do not require you to restart, however.

In Windows 2000 Professional, it's not only rare that any one task will be capable of hogging the CPU, but more pressing tasks can be given a higher priority than others. For example, keyboard input, mouse movement, or data coming in through a port could be given special attention by the Windows scheduler. This topic is explained in the next section.

HOW WINDOWS 2000 HANDLES TIME SLICING

In NT-based (including Windows 2000) and Windows 95/98 systems, processes have priorities that determine when and how often they are given time slices. The four categories of priority, from highest to lowest, are as follows:

- Real-time processes—These processes have the highest possible priority. The threads of a real-time priority class process preempt the threads of all other processes, including operating system processes performing important tasks.

- High-priority processes—These processes perform time-critical tasks that must be executed immediately for the operating system to run correctly. The threads of a high-priority class process preempt the threads of normal or idle priority class processes. An example is Windows Task List, which must respond quickly when called by the user, regardless of the load on the operating system.

- Normal priority—These processes have no special scheduling needs in terms of time.

- Idle priority—These processes are those whose threads run only when the system is idle and are preempted by the threads of any process running in a higher priority class. An example is a screen saver.

So, if a task in a higher group needs CPU time, it will get the time, and the processes under it won't compete for that time. The *idle* level is at the bottom of the totem pole, which means any normal app gets all the CPU time it wants, while idle processes are put on hold.

If two processes are in the same category—for example, if two "normal" apps both want to run (both have screen updates to do or keystrokes to process)—then they fight over the time they get.

Windows 2000 has some intelligence and can automatically assign or reassign processes to different priority levels. Windows tries to sense what a program is up to, and if the program is well-behaved, or if it's a highly human-interactive program, Windows tries to adjust priorities to make the user's experience better. For example, if Windows notices that a program is dealing mostly with mouse and keyboard events followed by inactivity (low CPU demand), it will consider this a very interactive app and can afford to boost its priority. An app that is getting little user interaction and is gobbling up lots of processor time in big chunks will probably get reduced a bit. The result is that the user will have the experience of the computer being snappier in overall response than with an operating system that doesn't monitor applications, such as Windows 3.x.

MULTITHREADING

You might have heard the term *multithreading* bandied about in discussions about NT and wondered whether it was a new interface for computer-controlled sewing machines. No, it has to do with *threads*, which are subprocesses within an application. This section delivers the scoop on multithreading and why it's an important part of NT technology and Windows 2000 Professional.

All tasks performed by Windows 2000 can be classified as processes. During any given period of time, Windows 2000 is executing a wide variety of processes. They might include checking a user's password, keeping track of the system's clock, accessing data from a disk, printing a word processing document, doing a memory fetch from RAM, or performing a mathematical calculation.

Going a step further, processes can often be broken down into separate threads. In fact, the scheduling of events by the process scheduler in Windows 2000 is actually based on the thread unit, not the process. Although most processes contain only a single thread, they can consist of multiple threads if the programmer dictates.

The important point is that programs devised to take advantage of Windows 2000's capability to service threads can be run very smoothly—more smoothly than under non-NT-based Windows versions.

Tip #9	In addition, as explained later in this chapter, the architecture of Windows 2000 allows threads in a single application to be offloaded to secondary CPUs in the case of multiprocessor systems, further smoothing thread execution.

THE CENTRALITY OF APPLICATION SOFTWARE

If the demand were only for a serious operating system with most or even all the features described previously, NT (and now Windows 2000) might not have stood a very good chance of becoming *the* corporate industrial-strength operating system of choice for the PC platform. Corporations heavily invested in PC-based information systems could have adopted some form of UNIX en masse by now—or for that matter, IBM's OS/2 Warp. But the success of an operating system, particularly in a business setting, has more to do with application availability than with any other variable.

Apple was aware of this basic OS truth when it dispersed its Apple evangelists to entice application developers into writing programs for its new brainchild, the Macintosh. Without application availability, the Macintosh never would have taken off. Its predecessor, the Lisa, went over like a lead balloon for just that reason. The demise of the NeXT "cube" is another good case in point. It was a terrific machine, but due to a scarcity of applications, loyal users of PCs and Macintoshes just wouldn't be wooed away. (Of course, its lofty price didn't help any either.)

The operating system market isn't only application-driven, however. Cost practicalities figure in, too. As the PC market has matured, users and IT managers have become less prone to overnight conversions from one type of machine, or even application, to another. The learning curve and data commitments involved in today's systems and applications are much greater than they were back in the days of the Apple II or CP/M, or even in the more recent days of Windows 3.x or Win9x. Purchasing, deployment, and training costs for local area networks (LANs), wide area networks (WANs), Internet commerce, and so on can be significant. This is true even for standalone systems. So it behooves MIS professionals to seriously consider the long-term investment cost of conversions to new applications, hardware, and training when they're shopping for operating systems. Over the last 10 years, compatibility and interoperability have become more and more of an issue when people are making critical hardware and software choices. This is why Microsoft has been so big lately about its Zero Administration of Windows (ZAW) program and emphasis on lowered TCO (Total Cost of Ownership) for Windows 2000.

WHERE DOES WINDOWS 2000'S ARCHITECTURE FIT INTO THE CORPORATE LANDSCAPE?

As you might be well aware, before the invention of the PC, corporations relied on mainframe and minicomputers to handle their workload. Office workers interacted with the mainframe computers through *dumb terminals* sitting on their desks, or at points of sale, inventory control in warehouses, and so on. In this scenario, MIS directors and IT personnel could fairly easily control the data people were working with because only one copy of it was available—in the mainframe. They could also manage users' access to that information through centrally located access controls, rules, passwords, and so on; they could also automate system backup. Upgrading the applications or operating system on the mainframe was relatively simple compared to today's scenarios, as well, because they had to deal with only one computer.

With the rise in popularity of the PC, however, MIS folks have had to deal with a whole new set of issues stemming mostly from duplicated data and application files, disparate and conflicting data file formats, and means of interconnecting users spread across the corporate enterprise. Initially, old-school IS managers protested the introduction of the PC into the workplace, fearing loss of control and rightly being concerned about the potential for chaos (and the extra work of untangling it). It took until the mid- to late-eighties or so before managers began to come to terms with the incontrovertible fact that individual workstation PCs were here to stay. And by this time, corporate workers became so addicted to the freedom of running their own print jobs or calculating a spreadsheet right at their desks without submitting a batch job to the IS person down the hall that they were loathe to give up their PCs anyway.

But, ironically (as mentioned in Chapter 1), the evolution of the corporate PC network has paralleled the proverbial reinvention of the wheel to some degree. Notwithstanding the liberation afforded us through the marvels of the PC powerhouses we now have on our desks, this democratization of CPU time in the workplace has lead to some very real issues concerning data integrity. In a sense, personal computing was great because it took a portion of the workload away from the MIS departments, but it left a gaping hole in the area of data integrity. In so-called mission-critical or line-of-business applications, large and often valuable corporate databases can't realistically be put in the hands of everyday users without jeopardizing the health of a company's data processing backbone.

These concerns have, of course, spawned whole new PC-related industries. I remember writing a series of *PC Magazine* articles in the mid-1980s that reviewed 13 local area networking systems available at the time. The idea that networking is built into Windows sounds crazy now, but networking PCs was a burgeoning industry rife with aspiring startups. Novell was the winner of much of the LAN battle, leading the industry in add-on networking products for DOS and Windows and spurring Microsoft on to add increasingly sophisticated networking internals to Windows. On the mini-computer side, the downward price spiral of workstations running UNIX or UNIX-like operating systems has brought multitasking, mainframe-like power to many smaller corporations.

Windows 2000 (like NT before it) inherits much from both of these growth patterns (PCs growing up and mainframes downsizing), integrates popular Windows-based programs, and rolls in the Internet's riches. Windows 2000 with Active Directory, IntelliMirror, and enhanced security and networking capabilities promises to fill any remaining holes that NT left gaping. NT has already made serious inroads into the Novell camp. Now with Windows 2000 and the likelihood that millions of Windows 3.1 users will upgrade, we expect to see a new era of high-end computing on the desktop. Following are some of the reasons why. Note that much of these reasons have to do with the Windows 2000 Professional architecture.

PART

I

CH

2

→ To learn more about how Windows 2000 already has a good head start at becoming a standard in the corporate network environment, **see** "Windows NT/2000 Evolution in a Nutshell," **p. 14**.

Here's a brief recap:

- Windows 2000 runs on popular Pentium 166 and higher PCs (albeit with some probable hardware upgrades). Thus, millions of popular desktop PCs in the business place can actually run Windows 2000.

- It runs most existing Windows applications, especially NT and Win9x programs. Therefore, thousands of apps were available for Windows 2000 the moment it was released.

- It offers security and robust kernel solidity—features that many corporations and governmental institutions require for their mission-critical applications.

→ To learn more about Windows 2000's capability to protect against crashing, **see** "More Stability," **p. 33.**

Consider these additional key features that make Windows 2000 an attractive operating system for the power user or corporate computing MIS professional:

- Windows 2000 is written from the ground up as an operating system. It's not just a GUI laid on top of DOS.

- It has the look and feel of Windows. Windows users don't have to be retrained to use Windows 2000 Professional. This point is especially true of Win9x users (less so for Windows 3.x users).

- It has scalable architecture. This means that Windows 2000 can run on different types of computers—from single CPUs (both Intel x86 and RISC chips) to multiple processor-based systems (sometimes called symmetric multiprocessor, or SMP, systems).

- It has high reliability. Unlike DOS and DOS/Windows, Windows 2000 incorporates a robust microkernel design that prevents a single misbehaving application from pulling down the whole system.

- It offers application compatibility. Windows 2000 can run a mix of any of these classes of applications: DOS, Windows 3.x, POSIX-compliant, MS OS/2 1.x character-based programs, and NT 3.x- and 4.x-compliant applications. A command prompt window similar to the DOS prompt supports execution of DOS, 16-bit Windows, POSIX, OS/2, and 32-bit NT applications from the command line.

- It offers complete support for COM+ and Windows Object Linking and Embedding (OLE) version 2.0. (OLE allows programs to share data in ways more sophisticated than simple cutting and pasting.) The Component Object Model (COM) lets one program call another one for a specific function, such as spell checking or creating a spreadsheet document. Windows handles all the details. Both OLE and ActiveX are based on COM.

- Windows 2000 also offers advanced file system support. It can work with four basic types of file systems: FAT, FAT32, and two types of NTFS. (NT 3.5 supported the OS/2 "HPFS" system, but that support was dropped in NT 4.) FAT (DOS's file scheme) is widely used. NTFS is the proprietary Windows NT file system. Because Windows 2000 supports an installable file system, future file systems are easy to add. Aside from being able to convert FAT16 and FAT32 partitions to NTFS, Windows 2000 Professional's file system offers advanced security features, supports long filenames (up to 256 characters), and provides automatic error correction if a bad sector is detected. A new, more advanced version of NTFS accompanies Windows 2000, adding encryption. Advanced features allow creation of "stripe sets" in which multiple disks are used simultaneously to speed disk I/O, and "mirrored disks" are used to increase data safety through storage redundancy.

→ For additional discussion of Windows 2000 Professional's file system support, **see** "File System Improvements," **p. 31**.

- Windows 2000 has a built-in networking solution. Like most modern operating systems, it doesn't need software add-ons to perform LAN, Internet, or WAN networking. Remote access is also supported in the native system. Windows 2000 Professional has peer-to-peer networking built in, so without a server, you can hook up a few workstations and be running a network. NT supports industry-standard network protocols, with built-in drivers for TCP/IP, NetBEUI, Novell IPX/SPX, and other transports. Windows 2000 is compatible with popular existing networks such as Novell NetWare, Banyan VINES, Macintosh, and Microsoft LAN Manager. Remote access for dial-up service is supported for Professional, with a two-caller limit for simultaneous access.

→ To read more about Windows 2000's improvements in the area of network manageability, **see** "Improved Network Management," **p. 40**.

- As covered in Chapter 1, Windows 2000 provides U.S. government C-2 rated security features. For most intents and purposes, NT has very good security that can prevent an unauthorized user from gaining access to the system or in other ways gaining access to files on the hard disk. The new file encryption increases the security level. Tools for assigning permission levels for various tasks are supplied, providing great flexibility in security arrangements.

→ For additional details on security improvements in Windows 2000, **see** "Better Security," **p. 42**.

■ Multiple users can have accounts on the same NT machine, and users can "float" from machine to machine using IntelliMirror. A user account on a machine includes a user-name and password and a series of user privileges assigned by the administrator. A user can hide directories or files from other users and set custom desktop, Start menu, and Control Panel settings. Logging on to the system automatically activates all saved set-tings from the user's previous sessions. If a user has been assigned high enough privi-leges, he or she can share or stop sharing system resources on the network, such as printers and files, or can alter the rights other network users have when accessing them.

■ Windows 2000 Professional fits into the complete Microsoft product line. Assuming you don't mind being held hostage, this is a good thing. Microsoft has been fairly good at designing products that mesh. Windows 2000 Professional fits not only with the Server of Windows 2000, but also with other Windows platforms, SQL Server, BackOffice, Exchange Server, IIS, and new products as they emerge. So, if you're using Windows 3.x, Windows for Workgroups, Win9x, or NT 3.x or 4, migration to Windows 2000 Professional should not be too difficult. Most applications will work fine (although 16-bit applications typically run slower) under NT.

PART

I

CH

2

WINDOWS 2000 VERSUS DOS, WINDOWS 3.X, AND WINDOWS 9X

Although some Windows 2000 Professional users will be making a lateral (detractors would say downward) move from UNIX or OS/2, most newcomers will be migrating upward from one DOS/Windows platform or another. When we say *DOS/Windows*, we mean typically DOS 5 or DOS 6 and Windows 3.1, but we could also mean Windows 9x. Even though you don't exit to DOS when you quit a Windows 9x session, it's still there.

The following sections compare Windows 2000 to DOS/Windows setups and briefly discuss the advantages and disadvantages of NT over its predecessors. Subsequently, we discuss other operating systems such as OS/2 and UNIX.

THAT OLD DOGGY DOS

Despite the enormous popularity of Windows 3.x and 9x (we're probably talking about more than 100 million users combined), these GUIs are really only shells placed on top of DOS. We all know that Windows 9x crashes more than we would like, even though it's a miracle that it can run at all, considering the number of combinations of hardware that it has to be compatible with. (But that's another story.)

The real fly in the ointment is DOS—not that DOS is any slouch, of course. After all, it has been estimated that more than a couple hundred million copies of DOS are in existence and that more than 10,000 applications are available for it. As a result, no responsible MIS pro-fessional or computer user would want to discount the importance of DOS compatibility when making an operating system choice. All too often, programs—whether major applica-tions or minor utilities—are available only in a DOS version.

As strong a workhorse as it is, DOS never was designed to be a multitasking operating system, much less to have a graphical user interface tacked on top of it. In other words, Windows has been a "kludge job"—something held together with spit and baling wire. As any veteran Windows user knows, strange and frustrating anomalies often crop up in Windows as a result of this funky union.

As you probably know from far too much experience, when one Windows program (or DOS program running under Windows) crashes, it's likely that your whole system will lock up. You'll have to reboot, and you'll probably lose some work (unless your apps have auto recovery features like Word does; in fact, necessity was the mother of invention there!). Due to internal redesigns, crashing was decreased in Win95 (believe it or not) and further decreased in 98. But we're still plagued by limitations in the architecture of DOS preventing the building of a crash-proof shell.

WINDOWS 2000 DOES DOS

How does Windows 2000's DOS work, and how does Windows 2000 run DOS programs without the inherent limitations of DOS? Easy. It just doesn't run on top of DOS. When Windows 2000 Professional boots, DOS does not, not even invisibly as it does in Windows 3.x and 9x. Of course, NT technology does have a kernel operating system, as we've discussed, one responsible for much of what old DOS does—for example, keyboard and screen I/O, managing loadable device drivers, and handling disk I/O requests. As explained earlier, NT can emulate distinct operating systems through plug-in modules called *environment subsystems*. DOS is one of them, essentially running as a program on top of NT. Very neat. The DOS environment subsystem provides all the system services that DOS normally does. However, these functions are integrated seamlessly into NT; they don't sit below it.

Not very many people are DOS lovers anymore, but if you are one, you needn't feel abandoned while using Windows 2000. Using nothing but the keyboard, many DOS diehards can achieve a greater throughput of work than they can using menus, dialog boxes, and the mouse. Don't worry, as with NT 4, Windows 2000 still supports this strategy by supplying backward compatibility between their operating systems. It has a "DOS box" (called the *command console*) similar to the one in Windows 3.x and 9x. It has a rich command set in the command interpreter (see Appendix A, "Command-Line Reference"), and the box is sizeable (not limited to 24 lines, thank goodness) and scrollable. When dir listings roll off the top of the window, as shown in Figure 2.1, you can get back to them.

The DOS box in Windows 2000 is not a DOS session per se, as it is in Windows 3.x and 9x. It is achieved through DOS emulation through a 32-bit application called CMD.EXE, which is a superset of MS-DOS that not only provides MS-DOS compatibility but also lets you run Windows, OS/2, and POSIX applications from the command line.

Figure 2.1
Note the scrollbar in this DOS box (command console) in Windows 2000 Professional.

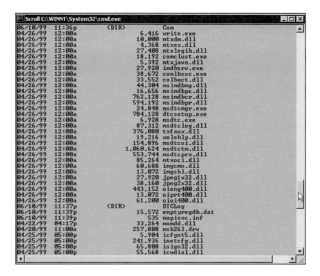

PART

I

CH

2

Tip #10	The DOS session that is created when you run a DOS application from the command window (CMD.EXE) is quite flexible in that it is configurable. Just as DOS that boots on a PC can be configured from AUTOEXEC.BAT and CONFIG.SYS, the DOS session that gets created within NT can be configured with loadable device drivers, TSRs, and so on.

→ To learn more about configuring a DOS session created by NT, **see** "Maintaining and Optimizing System Performance," Chapter 30.

When you launch a DOS program under Windows 2000 Professional, a *virtual DOS machine (VDM)* is created. The VDM tricks the DOS program into thinking it's running on its own PC. Windows 2000 sets up one VDM for each DOS application you run. Each VDM has all the services needed to handle both 16-bit and 32-bit DOS calls, in compliance with DOS 6. A full 16MB of standard DOS (segmented) application and data memory space is supplied to the VDM. In case they are needed, popular memory managers are supported. Figure 2.2 illustrates how virtual DOS machines run independently of one another on top of NT.

Figure 2.2
Several DOS sessions can run on top of NT in virtual DOS machines (VDMs).

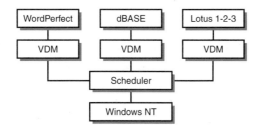

Limitations? Yeah. For security reasons and to protect the kernel, DOS apps must be kept isolated. To do so, the DOS environment subsystem intercepts all I/O processes, checks them out, and then routes the data to their destinations. This process is handled by I/O interceptors, which in turn hand data to the *NT Executive* for dispatching. (You'll find more details about the Executive later in this chapter.)

Any traditionally designed DOS programs that perform their I/O using standard DOS system calls will run under NT as expected. Those that write directly to hardware for which device drivers prevent direct access—for example, the hard disk drivers—will be thwarted by the security monitor, leading to an error message and termination of the nasty program. Typical programs that pull these kinds of hijinks are disk caching and communications applications. One of the unexpected advantages here is protection against DOS-based viruses because most viral programs attempt to write directly to the hard disk boot tracks or directories, which Windows 2000 won't permit.

DOS device drivers are another limitation under Windows 2000's DOS environment subsystem. If your DOS application requires a loadable device driver to operate (something that was formerly installed with a line in CONFIG.SYS), you might have trouble running it under Windows 2000 Professional because the driver won't be loaded. If you try to make it load (by including it in CONFIG.NT), it likely will not work. The NT architecture doesn't allow user-supplied device drivers to be loaded in the DOS subsystem because device drivers attempt to access hardware directly.

If your program tries to write to and read from COM and LPT ports, the screen, or the keyboard, Windows 2000 Professional will handle that task smoothly, but other direct memory, disk, or hardware control won't be permitted.

Most DOS programs that use the mouse driver will work because the mouse driver entry points are emulated. The same is true for the keyboard; the hardware is emulated because so many DOS programs used it. The point is that your program can't *be* a mouse driver, but it can *use* one.

Sample programs that could be problematic are old DOS TCP/IP programs using the "packet driver" interface.

WINDOWS ON WIN32 (WOW)

So how does Windows 2000 Professional run older 16-bit Windows programs? Is this really an issue? Sure, with 60 million people still running Windows 3.x, you can bet that a lot of folks want to continue running their pet rock simulator programs or, more importantly, expensive hand-coded applications for banks and such. Just as with DOS applications, 16-bit Windows programs run in a VDM created on-the-fly by Windows 2000.

Here's how it works: When you launch a 16-bit Windows application in Windows 2000 Professional, information in the header of the file informs NT that it's a 16-bit Windows program and creates a VDM, just as when you run a DOS program. The VDM includes DOS and an emulation of Windows called *Windows on Win32 (WOW)*. As with DOS emulation, the Windows emulation fakes all the standard system calls (called APIs in Windows, for application programming interface). When a program makes a call to a standard Windows 3.x API, WOW intercepts the call and routes it to the appropriate source— usually the NT Executive or a Win32 API call. Some APIs are mapped to internal code integrated into the WOW environment. The Windows NT 32-bit graphical display interface (GDI) manages the display of the application onscreen for image and text display, window locations, and so on.

But wait until you hear the interesting catch. Unlike virtual DOS sessions, each 16-bit Windows program does not get its own VDM. After the first application is run, launching additional 16-bit Windows apps doesn't create an additional VDM and WOW session for each one. Doing so is no more necessary than running multiple copies of normal Windows 3.x when you want to run Terminal and Notepad at the same time. This arrangement is necessary to allow maximum Windows 3.1 compatibility, as well as DDE and OLE communication between applications.

After a WOW VDM environment is launched the first time, additional Win 3.1 applications are just dumped into it as separate program threads, as shown in Figure 2.3.

PART

I

CH

2

Figure 2.3
Multiple 16-bit Windows applications run in the same VDM.

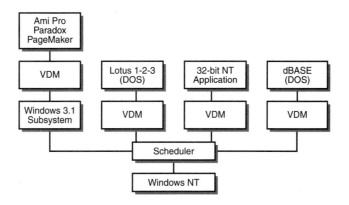

Another advantage of this arrangement is that Windows 2000 has less software overhead to manage, and because the NT thread manager is preemptive, no unruly application is allowed to hog the CPU's attention and slow down your other applications. This scenario, of course, differs from how an unruly application could behave when running under real Windows 3.x. The bad news is that because all 16-bit Windows applications are running in a single VDM, an errant application can pull down the whole VDM like a house of cards (see Figure 2.4). This one application won't crash Windows 2000, but conceivably it could crash any running 16-bit Windows applications.

Tip #11	Although the WOW VDM might crash all your open 16-bit apps due to a single misbehaving one, there's a silver lining. You don't actually have to restart NT to launch the WOW environment again. You can just run another 16-bit Windows application, and the WOW is reinitialized.

Figure 2.4
One crashed 16-bit
Windows program can
pull down the WOW
VDM but not the
whole system.

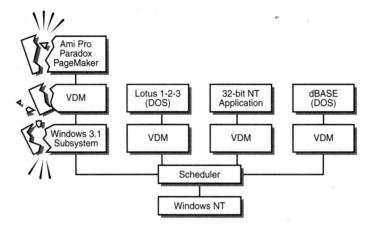

As you have probably surmised, the rules governing DOS apps apply here as well: Only well-behaved 16-bit Windows applications are likely to run successfully under Windows 2000 Professional. Some Windows 3.x programs write directly to the Windows GDI (usually to speed up display performance) instead of making calls to the API. In Windows 2000 Professional, the GDI isn't going to be located where the application expects it, so these unruly programs will bomb.

WINDOWS 9X IN LIGHT OF NT AND WINDOWS 2000

For many users, references to Windows 3.x and 16-bit programs seem a relic from the distant past. I'm among those folks, actually, but have to acknowledge the great panoply of programs still running about out there in the world. I probably unwittingly ran a 16-bit program in the last couple of days, whether a utility, photo editor, paint program, or something. Still, it's true that today's most viable programs have already been translated into 32-bit versions. Truth be told, before a program earns the Windows 9x seal of approval from Microsoft, it must be written in all 32-bit code and runnable under NT-based systems such as Windows 2000 Professional.

Well aware of the architectural limitations of the DOS/Windows 3.x marriage, Microsoft set out to create a bridge of sorts between the two worlds of NT technology and DOS-based systems. That bridge was Windows 95, later to become Windows 98. But it was only a temporary fix, intended to last only a few years while the cost of hardware dropped and while waiting for older, underpowered PCs to fade away.

To encourage developers to migrate their applications to 32 bits, Microsoft whetted the appetite of the public, making them hungry for features that the new platform offered: Plug and Play, long filenames, memory protection, preemptive multitasking, and faster program execution. Even other players in the industry, such as DEC and IBM, offer tools for porting VMS and OS/2 programs to the Win32 API.

Despite the technical advances built into Windows 9x, such as USB, Plug and Play, a 32-bit file system, and a flashy interface, Microsoft knows full well that Windows 9x isn't the kind of tool that serious businesses can rely on. One faulty 16-bit or 32-bit application can pull down the whole operating system, not just the 16-bit VDM, as is the case when running under an NT system. As mentioned earlier, this situation occurs because critical portions of Windows 9x are exposed in unprotected memory. Any renegade program can wreak havoc on it. This was by design, incidentally, to better provide backward compatibility with older programs. After a program crash, Windows 9x will run longer than Windows 3.x will, typically, because "house cleaning" is more expertly handled. As most Windows 9x users know, however, when you kill off a stuck program through the Task Manager error dialog box, the chances of the system becoming "unstable" are pretty good—another vote for Windows 2000 Professional, as we see it, unless you're a gamer. Users heavy into playing games on their computers will probably be sticking with Windows 9x (particularly 98) for some time at least. Fast games need access to the internals of the operating system and to hardware, and Windows 98 was engineered with this use in mind.

PART

I

CH

2

Tip #12	The Microsoft NT team isn't actually deaf to the needs of gamers—support for DirectX is built right into Windows 2000 Professional. DirectX gives game programmers the hooks to execute high-speed graphics without having to directly access the hardware. Windows does that for the program, but does it very quickly. As more and more games are converted to DirectX, folks will begin running them on the Windows 2000 platform.

How Does Windows 2000 Professional Compare to OS/2?

If you're a Windows maverick, you probably thought OS/2 bit the dust some time ago. Nope. It's still around. At the time of this writing, IBM was still selling Warp version 4 for the client, and Warp Server/Warp Server Advanced on the server side. True, IBM has killed the software division that created and maintained the OS/2 product line, so we'll probably see a sharp falloff of sales in the ensuing years.

As mentioned in Chapter 1, OS/2 and Windows 2000 hail from similar roots. They are both multithreaded, preemptive-multitasking operating systems. However, OS/2 doesn't run 32-bit Windows programs, only 16-bit 3.x applications. It also runs only on Intel processors (or compatible processors, such as those from AMD and Cyrix), not Alpha. And it runs Win 3.x apps by actually running a copy of Windows 3.x under OS/2 (supplied in the package). OS/2 supports up to 64 processors, and IBM seems to be pushing its Internet connectivity capabilities as its biggest strength. As with NT-based products, the kernel is protected, and it sports an advanced file system (HPFS), which is much like the earlier version of NTFS. Both systems are similar in design, supporting long filenames (though NTFS is limited to 254 characters instead of 256, but who's counting). However, with Windows 2000's encryption and active directory, Windows 2000 clearly has the upper hand at this point. Windows 2000 also provides additional access controls for files and support of various redundant array of inexpensive drives (RAID) technologies such as striping and disk mirroring, which are in excess of OS/2's capabilities.

OS/2 is good at multitasking, although it handles I/O queuing requests slightly differently than Windows 2000 does (some say less efficiently), which can cause performance penalties. However, OS/2 is supported by IBM and integrated into the total solutions planning, incorporating products ranging from laptops to mainframes. If you're running an IBM shop, with IBM and Windows 3.x apps, you might have ample reason to stick with OS/2, but otherwise, due to its inability to run 32-bit programs, it just doesn't compete with Windows 2000 Professional.

HOW DOES WINDOWS 2000 PROFESSIONAL COMPARE TO UNIX AND LINUX?

As mentioned in Chapter 1, Windows 2000 has its roots in UNIX. UNIX is a very popular multitasking operating system developed at Bell Labs in the early 1970s. It was designed by programmers for programmers. In fact, the language C was developed just to write UNIX. Even though UNIX has become a friendlier operating system with the addition of Windows-like interfaces such as MOTIF, it's still relatively user-unfriendly, requiring cryptic commands much like DOS.

Because it is written in C, UNIX can run on any computer that has a C compiler, making it quite portable. Early on, AT&T decided to give away its source code to universities around the world, who picked it up for their computer science departments. AT&T also licensed UNIX to several companies during that time, for a fee. In later years, the licensing price became miniscule as a result of an antitrust settlement against AT&T when Ma Bell was broken up by the Department of Justice. By the end of the 1970s, numerous institutions were running UNIX. The UNIX trademark is now owned by OpenGroup, though the source code is owned by the Santa Cruz Operation (SCO).

Unfortunately, to avoid even the licensing fees to AT&T, UNIX lookalikes sprung up over the years. Without the proper license, these versions could not call themselves UNIX, only UNIX-like. And as these clones proliferated, cross-compatibility became an issue. More than a handful of versions (dialects) of UNIX have appeared, the primary contenders being AT&T's own, known as *System V*, and another developed at the University of California at Berkeley, known as *BSD4.x*, *x* being a number from 1 to 3. Other popular brands of UNIX these days are HP-UX from HP, AIX from IBM, Solaris from Sun, and SCO's version, UnixWare.

In 1984, industry experts were brought together to create guidelines and standards for UNIX clones, in hopes of creating a more coherent market. The result was a single UNIX specification, which includes a requirement for POSIX (Portable Operating System Interface for UNIX) compliance. Accepted by the IEEE and ISO, POSIX is a standard that makes porting applications and other code between variants of UNIX as simple as recompiling the source code.

UNIX has been the predominant operating system for workstations connected to servers, mostly because of its multiuser capabilities and its rock-solid performance. NT has been making inroads due to the extensive number of development tools and applications for the Windows platform. However, a relatively new variant of UNIX has been making some inroads into the workstation market. The emergence of a new version called Linux is revitalizing UNIX across all platforms.

Linux

Linux is a UNIX look-alike, which is not a port of a preexisting operating system, but rather it was written from the ground up. It's the brainchild of Linus Torvalds, who wrote the kernel, and a handful of computer programmers. The idea was to create an operating system for PC (Intel boxes mostly) that was an alternative to Windows, was based on UNIX, and would be POSIX-compliant. Like all variants of UNIX, Linux has many of the features of NT and Windows 2000, such as true multitasking, virtual memory, shared libraries, intelligent memory management, and TCP/IP networking.

Linux is an open system, and programmers worldwide are invited to participate in its building and refinement. Unlike other flavors of UNIX that were based on licensed source code, Linux is based on Minix, which mimics in a way that does not infringe on the UNIX license. That's why it's practically free.

Actually, the term *Linux* pertains only to the kernel. What people have come to refer to as Linux is actually a collection of separate pieces of code, the majority of which are GNU. It was not until Linux came together with GNU that the full power of the Linux OS (what GNU enthusiasts would called GNU Linux) crystallized.

Tip #13	GNU stands for, oddly, *GNU is Not UNIX*. It's another UNIX-compatible software system envisioned as a completely free and nonproprietary system, available for anyone to download, share, and modify. The only rule is that no entity can limit the free redistribution of the products—sort of the opposite of capitalism. GNU was developed by the Free Software Foundation (FSF) and was started in 1983 by Richard Stallman at the Massachusetts Institute of Technology. Linux packages come with numerous GNU tools and utilities, and GNU itself has used the Linux kernel. However, no actual connection exists between the two other than redistribution bundling by Linux suppliers. The GNU people are actually working on their own kernel called HURD to replace the Linux kernel in GNU systems.

The several popularly distributed Linux versions are differentiated mostly by the selection of tools and utilities bundled with them. The most popular package at this point is Red Hat Linux. If you want to go it alone, you can acquire Linux for free, but buying some commercially bundled packages makes the job of installation and support easier because you get support. Technically, the distribution of the software must be free, in accordance with the GNU General Public License (GPL) agreement governing the distribution of Linux and the collected modules that accompany it.

The number of Linux systems in place and the number of users are difficult to calculate because many users don't bother with the commercial packages, and registration is not required. The Linux newsgroups are some of the most heavily read on the Net, so the number is likely in the hundreds of thousands, but firm numbers are hard to come by.

Although Linux currently runs primarily on Intel 386/486/586-based PCs, people are working on ports to other platforms, such as MIPS R4600, PowerPC, DEC Alpha, and the ARM family of processors. Others are in progress.

Tip #14	Another popular version of UNIX that runs on the PC platform is called FreeBSD. Briefly, FreeBSD 2.X is a UNIX-like operating system based on U.C. Berkeley's 4.4BSD-lite release for the Intel 386 platform. It is also based indirectly on William Jolitz's port of U.C. Berkeley's Net/2 to the Intel 386, known as 386BSD, though very little of the 386BSD code remains. You can find a fuller description of what FreeBSD is and how it can work for you at www.freebsd.com.

WINDOWS APPLICATION COMPATIBILITY WITH LINUX

IT professionals willing to get under the hood and poke around and learn Linux's ways are impressed with its solidity. Though Linux is not commonly used as a business productivity workstation, it is being embraced by some for back-end Web servers or transaction servers where reliability is a high priority.

But as with all operating systems, Linux success will depend on application availability, how rigidly it can be standardized, and the cost of maintenance and training. It's really only due to the large number of community-produced applications for Linux, including several graphical user interfaces, Web browsers and tools, and image and word processors that Linux is a viable operating system. The preponderance of software packaged in Linux distribution is GNU software. The GNU project was a way to produce UNIX-compatible operating systems that were free of licensing and cooperative restrictions. As with Linux itself, some applications are free and some are commercial.

An MS-DOS emulator can run DOS itself and some (but not all) DOS applications. We have heard that it can now run Windows 3.1 in enhanced mode. But generally speaking, you can't run Windows programs under Linux. A project called WINE is underway to build a Windows emulator for Linux, but no delivery date is set at this time. The only reliable way to run Windows programs on a Linux system is to dual-boot.

→ To learn more about dual-booting Linux, **see** "Windows 2000 and Linux," **p. 1316**.

Mainstream applications written for Linux are arriving, however, making Linux something to keep an eye on. For example, Corel has made a Linux version of WordPerfect available (it's free for the download, or you can pay $49 and get it on CD, with a T-shirt and some other goodies) and is prepared to soon release its entire productivity for this operating system.

Microsoft, of course, doesn't want to develop Linux versions of either its programming languages or applications such as Office, for obvious reasons.

Obviously, as a capitalistic enterprise, Linux doesn't cut it for the entrepreneur, unless he or she is willing to look at the world through a radically new set of glasses. Giving away your software doesn't net you much. Then again, people are giving away PCs to sell the advertising, so go figure. The world of computing might be changing more than we know. But because applications developers for the Linux environment are supposed to distribute their source code along with the applications, this is a daunting shift of worldview for a behemoth such as Microsoft, which works overtime to protect its intellectual property. The upshot is that you're out of luck if you want to run Word, Excel, or Access, Internet Explorer, or any other Microsoft programs on a Linux box.

Windows Versus Linux

When it comes to actual performance tests, some independent field testing has shown superior speed performance by Windows NT-based computers compared to Linux servers. In addition, Windows has the following specific advantages over Linux:

- Uptime guarantees by some original equipment manufacturers (OEMs) as high as 99 percent.
- Journaling file system for higher reliability and crash recovery.
- Compatibility testing and guarantees for operating system and applications.
- More than 8,000 NT-based applications versus only hundreds for Linux.
- Clustering and base-load balancing.
- Long-term roadmap of operating system deployment plans.
- Larger hard disks and maximum file sizes. Linux's maximum file size is 2 gigabytes; Windows 2000's limit is 18.4 quintillion bytes.
- "Synchronous I/O," which allows smoother running in Windows 2000 when multiple threads are being processed and waiting for input or output. It improves SMP scalability as well.
- Consistent GUI across all tools.
- International versions available.
- Dedicated support network, with close to one-half million Microsoft-certified trained professionals and engineers.

We believe that the entire Linux/Windows controversy comes down to this: Microsoft offers lots and lots of powerful stuff (which you can use to build very sophisticated software) from the C compiler, to the component-nature of Excel and other apps, to the ASP scripting language, COM, and so on. These tools let you leverage everything Microsoft offers to make very powerful applications. As people used to say in the sixties and seventies, nobody ever lost his job buying IBM. Now it's safe to say nobody ever lost his job buying Microsoft. True, you're locked into Windows because the stuff you build on Windows systems can't be ported to UNIX variants, but that's the price you pay for the tools, the user base, and the support and training. Although increasing support options are available for Linux (see www.linuxcare.com) enterprise-level support for the OS will still be spotty by the year 2000.

Linux might be a decent choice for the small-business owners or IS professionals who need to build low-cost servers for Web, email, or file sharing. This operating system is designed for those uses, and the popular Red Hat and Caldera Linux packages make installation relatively painless (not as easy as Windows 2000 Professional, though, mind you). If you're thinking of using Linux on your PC, beware—you might be biting off more than you can chew. The manuals that come with Linux—even the commercial versions—are dense. It is not always headache-free. But if you have a good understanding of computer technology and insist on switching from Windows to something more stable and more flexible, Linux might be the choice for you. If nothing else, using Linux will be a learning experience.

WINDOWS 2000 ARCHITECTURE CLOSE UP

As you probably surmised from the discussion thus far, Windows 2000 is a complex and capable operating system—certainly a far cry from its DOS/Windows 3.1 and Windows 9x predecessors, and even far exceeding NT 4. We've talked at some length about aspects such as *IntelliMirror (page 32)*, *Active Directory (page 32)*, and other high-end capabilities. Now we'll go a bit deeper into the inner workings of NT technology, discussing its architectural design and some specific differences between 16-bit Windows and Windows 2000.

AN OVERVIEW OF WINDOWS 2000 DESIGN

Now that we've looked at Windows 2000 in relation to other Microsoft operating systems, let's look at some of its inner workings. Obviously, writing 29 million lines of code wasn't undertaken lightly or handled by a small band of hack programmers. Such a project can't be undertaken lightly or without extensive forethought. Coding began only after a thorough architectural design and line of attack were agreed upon by the main programmers and system architects involved. Much of the design, coding, and thinking behind NT were the work of Dave Cutler, who, you might recall from Chapter 1, also developed an operating system for the DEC PDP-11 (called RSX-11M) and the VMS operating system that runs on the DEC VAX system.

> **Note**
>
> Although it began with about 10 members, the NT/2000 programming team is reported to have eventually grown to many hundreds, possibly as many as a thousand.

The NT design model included several primary higher-order goals separate from applications, tools, or utilities—that is, inner functionality mostly invisible to the user. Although the team had other considerations and features in excess of these, the main architectural premises were to make NT-based systems be

- Secure
- Compatible with existing code
- Easily extensible
- Scalable by adding CPU

■ Portable to other hardware platforms

■ Networkable, with distributed processing

The next sections briefly examine what each of these design goals means and how NT implements them. Then we'll look at the architectural model and the components of NT.

WHICH SYSTEM MODEL TO USE?

Over the years, operating systems engineers have developed many basic theories (and resulting models) that are employed when they design a new operating system. Before designers start coding, they first must decide which of the several overall architectural schemes they intend to built upon. Because operating systems are extremely complex, a basic blueprint is needed as a guide map, or programmers will easily get lost writing "spaghetti code"—code that is undisciplined, redundant, or worse, simply unfathomable by subsequent programmers who attempt to repair or extend it. Also, decisions at critical junctures are more difficult to make without the guidance of such a model.

Complex operating system code is written in numerous layers and generally falls into these groups:

■ Monolithic

■ Layered

■ Client/server

What's common among the three models is that they each break down tasks into one of two categories: *user tasks* and *kernel tasks*. This distinction between the nonprivileged user mode and privileged kernel mode is important in understanding how NT is designed.

From our earlier discussions, remember that the kernel must stay protected at all costs, to keep the operating system up and running. Only code with high-level permissions can run in kernel mode, typically code that will need access to system hardware or data. All external programs, such as the apps you run, even many device drivers, run in user mode. When it's time to save a file or access a hardware port, the kernel is asked to do so by the user mode code through an interaction across the user/kernel boundary. If the kernel honors the request, the data is passed to the destination. Note that this process is still handled by the kernel rather than the kernel just granting direct hardware access to the user mode program code.

Boot-track-altering virus programs are obvious examples of the kinds of code that is prevented from operating effectively by this "containment field" approach. Boot-track viruses attempt to mess up your system by writing directly to the boot track (typically track 0) of your hard disk, hoping the operating system won't notice until the next time you try to boot. Because all such requests must be passed to the kernel for authorization, Windows 2000 Professional can prevent such a breach, within limits. A very smart program that knows exactly what hardware is in your machine could conceivably go around the operating system.

THE THREE OPERATING SYSTEM MODELS

Getting back to the three types of models, we'll explain each one and where Windows 2000 Professional fits into the scene.

MONOLITHIC OPERATING SYSTEMS

Think chaos when you think *Monolithic*. In this kind of model, basically one mess of code acts as the operating system. You don't have much in the way of control over the messages that run around inside the monolith, as it were. Unlike the Monolith in *2001: A Space Odyssey*, which we assume was omnipotent, this kind of monolith ain't that smart.

Although numerous functions and/or procedures are built into the system, each one is permitted to call another one at will, without anyone running the switchboard (see Figure 2.5). The upside of this arrangement is that it's easier to build and requires less software overhead. The downside is, you guessed it, less security and more crash potential. Internal message collisions or just plain unfriendly programs can bring down the system. The other drawback is that this type of system lacks the modularity required to easily update the system or extend it to incorporate new technologies, environment subsystems, and such.

Figure 2.5
This flow diagram illustrates a monolithic operating system.

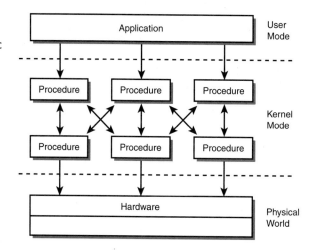

LAYERED OPERATING SYSTEMS

Systems using the layered operating system model incorporate various levels, much like the floors of a building. Imagine the elevator running up and down between floors, delivering messages. The boss works on the top floor, and guards prevent lower floors from directly accessing higher levels. But messages can be sent down to lower levels without intermediaries. If rules about the passage of messages between levels are instituted, the operating system stands a better chance of protection from renegade or poorly coded applications (see Figure 2.6). Because this type of system is more modular than the monolithic variety, it's more easily *extensible (page 55)* and updateable through the replacement of independent layers or modules.

Figure 2.6
This flow diagram
illustrates a layered
operating system.

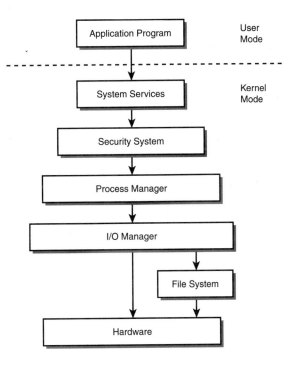

CLIENT/SERVER OPERATING SYSTEMS

Now we're ready for the model upon which Windows 2000 is based—the client/server model. It is the most sophisticated of the three, but don't confuse the terminology. Often when people bandy the term *client/server* about, they are referring to a networking arrangement, wherein independent client workstations are connected to a server box, which makes services such as applications or files available for the clients' use.

→ For more details about client/server networking and how it works with Windows 2000, **see** Part IV, "Networking."

In the operating system context, however, the client and server are on a more macro level, deep within the operating system, so the term refers to the supply and demand for services and resources. Typical clients would be applications, asking for services such as accepting keyboard presses, mouse movements, and the like. When requests like this are made, a portion of the operating system called the *NT Executive* registers them and puts them in line for servicing.

You could think of the Executive as a broker that decides which service should get the request. The nifty thing about Windows 2000 is that it not only supports local services (called *Local Procedure Calls*, or *LPCs*), but also something called *Remote Procedure Calls*, or *RPCs*. Using RPC, the NT Executive could pass on a request for a service that is actually supplied by another computer somewhere across the network. Using this approach, multiple computers attached across a network could act much like a parallel-processing super computer. Likewise, the Executive could send service requests to another processor in the same machine (see Figure 2.7).

Figure 2.7
This flow diagram illustrates a client/server operating system.

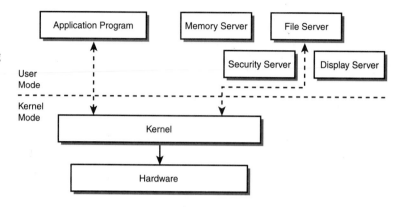

COMPATIBILITY

As discussed earlier, compatibility with existing software systems and applications was a primary design goal for the NT and Windows 2000 programming groups. So let's now take a gander at how the client/server model as applied to NT allows for it to achieve compatibility with existing file systems, applications, and other operating systems from both the Microsoft and non-Microsoft camps.

Recall that Windows 2000 Professional is compatible with the following hardware and software, through the use of plug-in environment subsystems and other software trickery:

- Applications—DOS, 16-bit and 32-bit Windows, OS/2 version 1.x character-based (except on MIPS and DEC Alpha, where OS/2 compatibility is not available at all), LAN Manager, and POSIX-compliant applications

- Disk file systems—FAT, FAT-32, NTFS

- Local area networks—NetWare, Banyan VINES, LAN Manager, Windows for Workgroups; connectivity for TCP/IP, SNMP, SNA, NetBEUI, and data link control (DLC); remote access services to support X.25 protocols

ENVIRONMENT SUBSYSTEMS PROVIDE COMPATIBILITY

Compatibility is a thorny issue, especially when it comes to running applications written for other operating systems. It could be termed a binary compatibility problem because the binary code of the applications in question was compiled for not only different operating systems but in some cases for different CPUs. For example, compatibility is a problem in the case of Windows 2000 Professional running on the DEC Alpha, when you want to run Word or some other app written for the Intel platform.

As discussed earlier, Windows 2000 Professional provides an elegant means of attaining compatibility by using *environment subsystems*. An environment subsystem's job is to intercept each binary code request of a CPU or operating system and translate it into appropriate instructions that Windows 2000 and the native CPU it is running on can faithfully execute.

Recall that an environment subsystem is a module that emulates a given operating system, enabling Windows 2000 to run programs written for the foreign operating system even though the machine is really running Windows 2000. How is this result achieved? Let's consider a POSIX program. When such a program runs in the POSIX subsystem, for example, Windows 2000 does the following:

1. The first job is to figure out what kind of program it is. Often the type can be determined by the header information in the application's executable file. If the program is not recognized, Windows 2000 will bag the execution of the application and issue an error message.

2. Assuming the type of executable is recognized, Windows 2000 summons the pertinent environment subsystem and runs it.

3. Windows 2000 then loads the application into the environment subsystem and starts running it.

PART

I

CH

2

While running in the environment subsystem, a foreign application assumes it's the only program running on the machine. For example, if you're running a DOS application, when the app asks to print to the printer port, write to the screen, read the keyboard, or read a sector from the hard disk, it "thinks" and acts like it's really interacting with DOS, even though it isn't. The DOS environment subsystem fakes out the program by emulating the DOS environment effectively, translating the DOS API to the NT API. These requests by the program are handed to the Executive, which doles them out to the respective destinations and then messages back to the DOS subsystem, which in turns interacts with the DOS application, which is never the wiser as to what is going on.

Of course, the environment subsystem must know all the APIs in the system it's emulating and include a translation map to the Windows 2000 API. This is just like doing simultaneous translation at the United Nations, but instead of the translation being from one word to another, it's more like from one task to another. Typical tasks would be saving a file to the disk, for example.

The following are some interesting and useful advantages of running a foreign program under emulation in Windows 2000:

■ Additional security—The operating system is protected from any badly written programs you have in your arsenal. For example, NT prevents programs of various types from "stepping on each other," which can cause system crashes. This result is achieved by virtue of the fact that each subsystem is given its own memory space that can't be touched by other subsystems or programs. For this reason, the environment subsystems are called protected subsystems.

■ Additional functionality—Because Windows 2000 supports multiple CPUs and superfast CPUs such as the Alpha, you could significantly increase the speed of execution of an application or task. Or, working through Windows 2000's executive and I/O functions, an application could write data on disk in several different formats for advantages such as encryption, data security through mirror sets and password protection, or faster access through stripe sets.

ENVIRONMENT SUBSYSTEM BREAKDOWN

So by now you get the idea of how environment subsystems work in general. How about a little more detail?

For starters, understand that five environment subsystems are in use: Win32, DOS, Windows 3.x, OS/2, and POSIX. And you know that Windows 2000 is based on the client/server model, where major areas of the operating system act as servers to applications (clients) that request them. The environment subsystems are treated by Windows 2000 as servers. Clients and servers in the Windows 2000 architecture can have a one-to-many relationship, so an environment subsystem can handle a bunch of applications at one time without replicating itself and using up a lot of memory. Thus, you could run, say, 10 DOS programs at once, all being handled by the same DOS environment subsystem. Or you could run several Windows 3.1 applications. Same idea.

If you have multiple programs running in the same environment subsystem, the subsystem's API server decides which one to service first. Another point is that each subsystem operates in user mode rather than in kernel mode. This mode helps to protect the kernel of the operating system from a subsystem or application that goes awry. (Recall that user mode is outside the kernel and can't mess with it directly.)

Now we're ready for a little scoop about each subsystem.

WIN32 SUBSYSTEM

The Win32 subsystem is the big daddy of the subsystems and is highly important to Windows 2000's overall functioning. It's important because the Win32 subsystem provides control for the basic Windows 2000 interface, including screen, keyboard, input, and mouse activities for whatever you're doing in NT. Even if another environment subsystem is providing services for a foreign application, it calls upon the Win32 environment subsystem for these services. Because it's also used to run 32-bit programs written for NT, this subsystem performs double duty. Figure 2.8 depicts the relationship between the other subsystems and the Win32 subsystem.

Figure 2.8
The relationship of the environment subsystems.

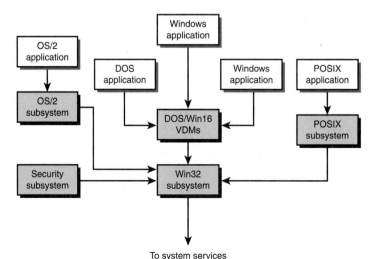

To system services

DOS SUBSYSTEM

The DOS environment subsystem is interesting because DOS was never intended to be a multitasking operating system, yet its subsystem allows for multiple DOS sessions to run simultaneously. When you try to run a DOS program, NT launches the DOS-environment protected subsystem, which in turn creates a virtual DOS machine (VDM). Recall that a VDM is an emulator that sets up a sort of virtual PC with its own 16MB of segmented memory space, required device drivers, support for most memory managers, and I/O system call support. In the case of DOS applications, each new DOS application you launch gets its own VDM and separate "DOS window," just as in Windows 3.x.

When an I/O request is trapped (detected) by the subsystem, it's passed on to the NT Executive (or, in some cases, the Win32 API) and processed accordingly. An application that attempts to write directly to hardware is terminated, and a message to that effect appears onscreen.

PART

I

CH

2

Tip #15	The DOS VDM window under NT is compatible with all the specifications of DOS 5.0, and it operates properly as long as the DOS application behaves itself—that is, as long as the application uses the DOS system calls for all input and output and doesn't try to access hardware directly.

16-BIT WINDOWS PROTECTIVE ENVIRONMENT

Consider now the 16-bit Windows protected environment subsystem. This one is interesting in its own right because it's dependent on the DOS emulator in a DOS VDM. When you launch the first 16-bit Windows application, NT creates a new VDM for it with 16MB of dedicated RAM. When the VDM loads, the Windows emulator (WOW, discussed earlier in this chapter) loads up and supplies a multitasking simulation of Windows 3.1. Just as with real Windows 3.1, it is a cooperative multitasking environment rather than preemptive as in Windows 2000. Although it provides all the APIs of 16-bit Windows, its internal structure is significantly different. System calls made by an application are mapped to Win32 calls and executed by the Win32 subsystem or the NT Executive.

As with DOS programs, any Windows application that attempts direct hardware access will fail; the call is trapped by NT and the application is terminated. However, unlike when multiple DOS applications are running, multiple Windows applications don't need additional VDMs. Each new 16-bit Windows application launched after the first one is set up as a separate thread within the same instance of WOW in the VDM.

The OS/2 environment subsystem supports only character-based programs, so this one isn't as complicated as you might think. It's not that much more complex than the DOS environment subsystem, and in some ways, it's simpler. OS/2 character-based applications are designed with 32-bit multiuser capabilities in mind, so the environment subsystem for this type of program has a little less mapping to do, and setting up a virtual DOS machine isn't necessary—only a subsystem that properly maps the OS/2 calls to the relevant NT services. As a side point, note that NT won't run OS/2 2.x applications, but only character-mode applications that will run under OS/2 version 1.x. For many folks, this means that Windows 2000 Professional doesn't really run OS/2 programs after all.

Before moving on to the POSIX subsystem, we need a little background information about what POSIX is. Although UNIX is very popular and ubiquitous, many different interface standards are in existence for UNIX applications and systems today. UNIX is "open source" code that's in the public domain, so many institutions have taken it upon themselves to modify it. The upshot is that a plethora of additions and modifications have been made to UNIX, but not much in the way of standards for graphical user interfaces, and applications portability between differing UNIX-based systems can be somewhat limited. It's sort of the opposite situation to the Windows camp, where Microsoft controls the code and interface standards and everyone must write code that complies with the standard or else the app won't work.

POSIX is an attempt to standardize UNIX application code so that it can be more easily ported to other systems. Windows 2000 Professional's POSIX subsystem supports only character-based applications, so once again, the subsystem is not as complex as it would be if a GUI such as Motif or the X Window System were being emulated. No VDM is created— just a protected space to run the application and a call interceptor that remaps calls to the Win32 environment subsystem and NT Executive.

EXTENSIBILITY

A friend of mine looked at the word *extensibility* last night and asked, "What is extensibility? Is that a word in the English Language?" Flexibility and extensibility were among the highest priorities for NT-based systems designers because they allow applications and operating system software to be upgraded quickly and in a cost-efficient manner. The upgrading typically extends the functionality of the software. Owing to the quickly changing face of computer hardware and application hardware requirements, extensibility of an operating system is key to its continued success.

Windows 2000's modularity of design renders extensibility fairly easy. NT was intentionally written in such a way that modifying it for future upgrades and porting it to other computer platforms are possible with relatively little hassle. The environment subsystems are a case in point. They can easily be removed or new ones added. They aren't even loaded into memory unless they're needed. Likewise, all the other major portions of NT are written and function as modules: the security subsystem, the hardware abstraction layer (HAL), and the NT Executive (kernel, I/O manager, object manager, security reference monitor, process manager, Local Procedure Call [LPC] facility, and virtual memory manager).

How does extensibility work? If you've experimented with the Windows Control Panel, Windows Explorer, or the Windows 3.x File Manager, you might know that they are all modular and extensible (though they're much simpler programs, of course, than Windows 2000 Professional). So are the Microsoft Office programs, using Visual Basic for Applications (VBA). They can easily be upgraded to supply new services to the user, thus requiring no changes to the core application. For example, simply adding .CPL files to the system directory (for Control Panel) is all you must do to get new applets to show up in Control Panel. A wonderful side effect of this modularity is that many system services in Windows 2000 can be started through Control Panel's Services applet, after NT is booted and running.

SCALABILITY AND SYMMETRIC MULTIPROCESSING

All versions of Windows 2000 can take advantage of multiple CPUs, from 2 (in Windows 2000 Professional) up to 32 (in Windows 2000 Datacenter). Windows 2000 uses the CPU strategy called symmetric multiprocessing (as opposed to asymmetric multiprocessing) as its model for *scalability*. Figure 2.9 helps illustrate the differences.

Figure 2.9
In symmetric multiprocessing, all processing, including the operating system and applications, is spread among available CPUs. In asymmetric multiprocessing, the operating system code is run by one CPU, and other CPUs run applications.

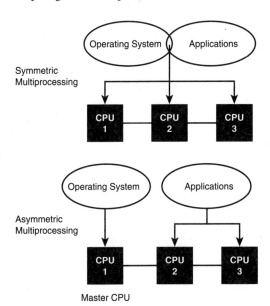

In the *symmetric* arrangement, the CPUs reside in one cabinet and share the same memory. As business increases, additional CPUs can be added to absorb the increased transaction volume. The end result of employing symmetric methodology is that the operating system is less likely to come to a standstill if the master CPUs cease functioning for some reason. Also, because operating system tasks can be shuffled off to other processors, the system runs more smoothly and (possibly) with greater throughput. On the downside, if one CPU fails, the entire SMP system can die. One way around this problem is to cluster two or more SMP systems together. Clustering can increase fault resilience because, if one SMP system fails, the others pick up where it left off.

SMP arrangements were first pioneered on the UNIX platform by Encore, Sequent, and Pyramid. Other large companies such as IBM, NCR, and Unisys and smaller systems such as OS/2 and NetWare from Novell employ SMP, too. With the price of CPUs dropping, systems designers have no reason not to utilize it, and you can expect to see more and more multi-CPU boxes showing up in discount computer lines.

Applications must be designed specifically to take advantage of SMP architecture. Even if a developer writes a program using the Win32 API, this doesn't mean that the program can use multiprocessors. The program must specifically utilize the multithreading hooks in the API.

Asymmetric operating systems are easier to design and build, whereas an efficient use of symmetric processing is more difficult and requires that the operating system itself be *threaded*—broken down into separate processes. The benefits, however, are great. For example, operating system subtasks can be routed to different processors, increasing system efficiency and making it less likely that CPUs are underutilized. I/O processing could be handled by one CPU while, for example, the security subsystem is handled by another.

MPP PROCESSING

In SMP, CPUs are assigned to the next available task or thread that can run concurrently. In another scheme, called *massively parallel processing (MPP)*, a single chore is broken up into separate pieces, which are processed simultaneously. MPP is similar to SMP, except that SMP CPUs share the same memory, whereas in MPP each CPU has its own memory. Although MPP complicates the process of the CPUs communicating with one another and increases the software overhead. But MPP systems don't suffer from slowdowns that can occur when SMP CPUs try to access the same memory simultaneously. Figure 2.10 illustrates how SMP and MPP handle memory.

Figure 2.10
An SMP arrangement of CPUs is shown on top, and an MPP arrangement of CPUs is shown on the bottom.

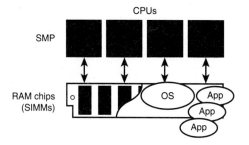

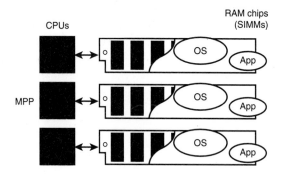

SCALABILITY

Scalability refers to an operating system's capability to take advantage of additional resources—particularly additional CPU resources that might be added to a computer's hardware arsenal. When installed on a uniprocessor machine, Windows 2000's thread manager sends all processes to the only CPU in the system. When only one processor is available, however, system performance can be slowed by bottlenecks in the single-thread queue.

Windows 2000 is intelligent in its detection of multiple CPUs and its assignments of tasks to them. Windows 2000 will automatically redirect threads and processes to available CPUs, increasing system operational throughput. Both RISC and CISC systems support easy installation of extra CPUs or CPU cards. In most cases, simply installing the CPU and rebooting Windows 2000 are all that's required to prod the thread dispatcher into divvying up the workload between processors.

PORTABILITY

A *portable* operating system is one that can run on numerous hardware platforms. Portability has been the strong suit of UNIX for years, with that operating system appearing on myriad platforms ranging from 8-bit Zilog Z-80s (running in tandem) to "big iron" mainframes. UNIX is still the workhorse behind the majority of powerful workstations the world over, ranging from DEC to Sun, IBM, Silicon Graphics, and Hewlett-Packard, to name but a few. Because UNIX is the prime target on Microsoft's seek-and-destroy map, it behooves Windows 2000 Professional to be portable as well.

Portability is nothing new to the world of the Wintel box, of course. Most of us have migrated upwardly several times in just the past five years. I've carried my data files and many programs over from Windows 3.0 up through the ranks of Windows 3.1, 3.11, 95, 98, NT, and now Windows 2000 Professional. The hardware has ranged from the 4.77MHz 8086 to 400MHz Pentiums and K6-2 machines. MS-DOS is a good example of a portable operating system, running on today's powerful Intel boxes just as well as the wimpy PCs of the eighties.

Owing largely to the vast numbers of PC clones in the workplace today, hardware prices have been forced down to rock-bottom levels, making powerful systems available even to students on shoestring budgets. This situation has probably led Microsoft to focus less on platform independence and more on hardware support, which is extensive in Windows 2000. That's probably why beginning with NT 4, Microsoft dropped support of the MIPS R4000 RISC chip and began supporting only Intel (and compatible) and DEC CPUs.

Still, Microsoft has designed Windows 2000 in such a way that dependence on Intel could become a thing of the past. With a recompilation of NT's modules (using software compilers), other future CPUs can be accommodated.

32-Bit Windows 2000 Application and the DEC Alpha Chip

Microsoft claims that 32-bit Windows 2000 and NT applications are fully portable to the DEC Alpha chip, requiring only a "simple recompile." Actually, this claim doesn't represent the whole picture. Applications still require troubleshooting, and software developers must decide whether they have the requisite support resources before jumping onto a new hardware platform. However, Compaq (which now owns DEC) is selling a DEC-developed product called DIGITAL *FX!32* that provides fast and transparent execution of 32-bit x86 applications on the Windows 2000 Alpha platform. What this product does is pretty amazing. For starters, consider that the Alpha chip is seriously faster than the Pentium at about the same price. That's great, but no application software is available for it, compared to Wintel boxes. So who wants to move over to an Alpha box for fear of software incompatibility? Hold on. FX!32 is an emulator (and more) that seems to effectively let Alpha/NT systems run most 32-bit Wintel applications at Pentium speeds. FX!32 now ships with every Alpha workstation and server that Digital (Compaq) sells and is also available for download from the Internet.

If it were only an emulator, that would be cool enough, assuming it could run your x86 programs quickly on the Alpha. But it's not only an emulator, it's also an intelligent translator. It gradually moves your applications over to the native Alpha instruction set. Here's how: At first, when you run your Windows 2000-based applications on the Alpha, they run about 30 percent slower than native Alpha NT code applications. But the Alpha is fast anyway, so it's no biggie. Then through a combination of binary translation and software emulation, and with absolutely no intervention on your part, FX!32 automatically starts performing a background translation process. Not only do you not need to act, you'll probably never realize any translation is afoot: FX!32 runs completely in the background.

The next time you run the non-Alpha app, FX!32 looks around for a "translation table," recording the work it has done thus far, and uses whatever translated, optimized code it finds. Each time you run the app, it gets a little faster because the translator has more native code to work with and will need to perform less emulation.

Although these features sound terrific, don't jump too fast, though, unless you really understand the Alpha product line. With the multi-CPU Intel-compatible boxes (check out inexpensive motherboards from the likes of SuperMicro), building your super server or workstation using more traditional parts might be easier than going with the Alpha boxes. Doing so could also ensure a higher compatibility with existing Windows-compatible software and hardware. For raw computing power, though, Compaq/DEC offers some seriously big-time, multi-CPU boxes. You might want to check them out on the Compaq Web site.

INTERNETWORKING WITH WINDOWS 2000

Another of the major architectural design mandates for the programming team was to ensure that NT technology had networking built in and that it could internetwork with the most popular protocols and clients. Of course, NT—like its lowly 9x and even 3.11 counterparts—does include networking. Windows 2000 Professional supports peer-to-peer networking but not client/server style. Just plug in your network, hook up your cards, name your workgroup, and you're pretty much up and running (oy, it used to be so much more challenging!).

If you already have an existing network, you can probably jack your Windows 2000 Professional workstation right into it because support for all the popular protocols such as TCP/IP and NetBEUI and clients such as the Microsoft network client and Novell NetWare are included. This type of plug-and-play functionality was well implemented in NT and even better organized and expanded in Windows 2000 Professional. Whether you're interested in giving up your existing investment in another network operating system is another question, but with the move afoot in the direction of the NT server, and with the significant advantages of IntelliMirror and Active Directory services available, not to mention the diminutive price tags on kick-butt computers, large enterprisewide networks should definitely be checking out the potentially rosy bottom line for conversion to the Windows 2000 line of workstations and servers.

Note

Of course, when you're pricing network server software (and even application software), licensing fees are an issue to factor in. Although the upfront cost of NT Advanced Server might be higher, the overall cost impact might be lower, depending on the software licensing and per-user charges. You should check with your vendor on those issues.

PART

I

CH

2

THE SECURITY SUBSYSTEM

We made a couple of references to the *security subsystem* in the context of extensibility earlier in the chapter. Like the environment subsystems, another class of systems called *integral* subsystems offers services to the NT kernel, and the security subsystem is one of them. Like the environment subsystems, the security subsystem runs in user mode, and its job is, as the name implies, to provide security for the operating system. All transactions within the operating system and with outside forces (typically people) that have been deemed by Windows 2000's programmers to be potentially "life" threatening to the system are observed or controlled in one way or another by the security subsystem.

An obvious job of the security subsystem would be to prevent unauthorized use of files or hard disk volumes without correct password (assuming passwords were required to access that resource). Any user who hasn't been granted the requisite rights will be bounced at the door.

Of course, all potential users have access codes, passwords, and eventually iris or fingerprint pattern matching, and so on. Whatever cost of entry is applicable to your computers and resources and has been assigned by the system administrator, the security subsystem's task is to ensure the rules are enforced.

Virtually all aspects (inner and outer) of NT are overseen by security management services that make NT quite secure. Windows NT meets U.S. Government requirements for what is called C2-level security. It isn't the highest level of security an operating system can achieve, but it's respectably high and good enough for the bulk of work run on computers. Windows 2000 Server has a domain-based security model, which makes it easy to scale to enterprise levels by adding additional controllers or by subdividing domains. With Windows 2000's newly incorporated advanced security technologies such as Kerberos authentication, Public Key cryptography, digital certificate support, and native encryption of files and SmartCard support, security has been bumped up a major notch.

Tip #16

Windows 2000 also meets E3-level security as defined by the U.K. government. Windows 2000 will be upgradable to B2-level security in future custom versions.

Note

To read about how the Gina system enhances security, see "Windows Wizardry: Protecting Against Viruses and Trojan Horses," at the end of this chapter.

THE NT EXECUTIVE

During the course of this discussion, we've referred several times to the NT Executive. Although you might have thought we were talking about *you*, we weren't. Nope. Next to the kernel (and we're not talking about KFC), the Executive is the heart of NT's architecture. It's the top cop, and it includes everything except the protected-mode subsystems and the actual hardware.

If you haven't been put to sleep already, it's time for a little review. As you might remember, the operating system code can run in two modes: user (unprivileged) mode and kernel (privileged) mode. Recall also that all the subsystems (such as the Win32, DOS, POSIX, and OS/2 environment subsystems and the security) run in user mode. By contrast, the NT Executive runs in kernel mode. Table 2.1 shows the breakdown.

TABLE 2.1   USER AND KERNEL MODES COMPARISON

Mode	User Mode	Kernel Mode
Major Elements	Environment Subsystems: POSIX, OS/2, DOS, Win-32	NT Executive: object manager, virtual memory manager, process manager, LPC facility, security reference monitor, I/O manager, HAL
	Security subsystem	

NT Executive has access to all the critical internal data structures and procedures of NT. Figure 2.11 shows where the Executive fits into the picture.

If you study the figure a bit, you'll notice that the Executive is made up of all the components below the dark line, except for Physical Hardware. Thus, the Executive provides all the native services that the environment and security subsystems can't—virtual memory management, I/O, thread scheduling, and so on. When a subsystem needs a service performed, it sends the call to the appropriate NT Executive manager. NT then runs in the restricted kernel mode momentarily, protecting itself from foreign intervention, and performs the action. When the task is completed, control returns to the originator of the request.

Necessary elements of the Executive are the primitives. The NT Executive primitives represent an important design concept because they allow for multiple subsystem compatibility. Without them, applications running in the different subsystems might clobber one another. For example, applications running in the Win16 and OS/2 modules ask for resources differently and could request the same service simultaneously. The primitives negotiate such contentions between the environment subsystems.

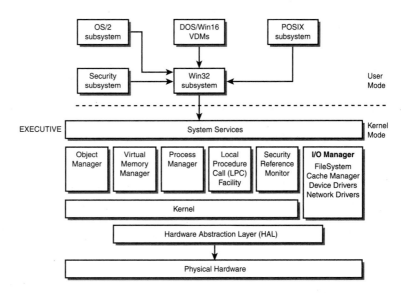

Figure 2.11
The NT Executive forms the heart of Windows NT and Windows 2000.

ABOUT THE SYSTEM SERVICES

Okay, one last major section and we're finished. In Figure 2.11, notice the section called System Services. Actually, when a subsystem asks to have a service performed (such as saving a file to the hard disk or sending a print job to the printer port), the request goes through the Win32 subsystem and is then passed to the System Services module to handle it. The System Services module then sends the message to the appropriate manager, such as the I/O manager. The same would be true of any other service, such as asking for the creation of a new thread by the process manager when a new program is launched.

As implied by Figure 2.11, the System Services module runs interference between the various managers and the environment subsystems. This is another example of modularization that Windows 2000 benefits from because updates to independent sections are more easily made. As security protocols, file systems, or memory management schemes evolve, they can be plugged into Windows NT technology products, for example, even as the System Services module stays the same. In a sense, it's reminiscent of how the cable TV companies are using their existing infrastructure to connect computers now, something they had never thought about five years ago.

THE EXECUTIVE MODULES

Now we're left with just a few remaining subportions of Windows 2000 Professional to analyze. Let's consider the remaining eight sections of the Executive:

- Object manager
- Virtual memory manager
- Process manager

- Local Procedure Call facility
- Security reference monitor
- I/O manager
- Kernel
- Hardware abstraction layer

This chapter isn't an operating systems Ph.D. design class, so we'll spare you all the details of these modules. Because you're either a power user or a professional who is managing an NT-based installation, we'll focus briefly on the tasks addressed by the various modules.

OBJECT MANAGER

Windows 2000 isn't actually an object-oriented operating system, but NT does use so-called "objects" as the basic operating element for interaction between user mode and kernel mode—for example, when a subsystem needs access to shared resources. What's an object? An *object* is something that represents a service that can be shared by more than a single process. For example, a physical device such as a hard disk could be shared by several applications. When hard disk access is requested, the source subsystem calls the service manager and asks for it, as you know. The service manager, in turn, calls the object manager, which creates a new object that represents the request. Even more subtle processes such as threads can be objects.

Why use objects and not just have the System Services directly make the request to the I/O services? Why have another middle man? By creating objects, Windows 2000 (and human programmers) can more easily keep track of system resources such as shared memory, ports, processes, and files. In a sense, creating objects democratizes important events and resources within a Windows 2000 session by giving them a handle. After being given a handle, all these types of objects—whether a physical resource, a process, or an event—can be dealt with uniformly by the object manager and other modules of Windows 2000. For example, the security reference monitor can examine an object for validation or prevent unauthorized use of it.

The object manager makes sure that objects aren't running amok. For example, objects could be created willy-nilly by an out-of-control program, or objects could be left over after a program crashes and has been terminated by either the system or manually by the user (using the Task Manager).

VIRTUAL MEMORY MANAGER

You might know what *virtual memory (VM)* is. If you're a seasoned Windows user, and you haven't thrown up your hands in frustration reading as theoretical a chapter as this one, then you no doubt do know. But just in case, let's go through a quick preamble.

Like the name implies, VM is simulated RAM created by sleight of hand with the help of your hard disk. When the system runs low on RAM because too many programs are loaded, data files are loaded, or operating system activity is using it up, Windows uses hard disk space to simulate what looks like RAM space to applications. This is done a little like the way you edit a long document on a computer screen. You can see only a little of the document at a time. The rest of it is stored offscreen.

Like that, the operating system can temporarily "swap" data in RAM to the hard disk to free up some RAM for the requested activity. The result is what looks and acts like a computer system with more RAM chips than are physically present. When needed, the data is read back into RAM without the application's being aware of it. Because hard disk space is so cheap, using it is more cost effective than buying a slew of RAM. The downside is that hard disks are a lot slower than real RAM, so swapping takes its toll on system performance. When RAM is really low, almost everything you do on your computer causes the hard disk to "thrash."

So, what does the *virtual memory manager* do? Just like in Windows 3.x and 9x, it manages the virtual memory for the system. But in Windows 2000 Professional and NT-based systems, it goes beyond that. The manager prevents processes from overwriting other virtual memory "pages" on disk. It can also be called upon to prevent swapping, forcing the use of real RAM to provide faster program performance for applications that might require it.

Process Manager

The *raison d'être* of the process manager is to help programs and internal processes execute. When you run an app, and the application requests that a process be run, the request is sent down through the environment subsystem to the Win32 subsystem, to the systems services, and then to the object manager. The object manager, in turn, creates an identity for it and passes it on to the process manager, which spawns a new thread and supplies it to the process in question. The object and the thread remain alive as long as needed. The process kills off the thread after its job has been fulfilled.

The importance of the process manager is hard to underestimate. Hundreds of processes can seem to be executing simultaneously because the process manager quietly plays traffic cop to the threads waiting to execute. The process manager can cause any application's threads to be executed, suspended, restarted, or terminated.

Local Procedure Call Facility

The job of the Local Procedure Call facility, also known as the LPC facility, is to help threads talk to each other. (Sounds like a cartoon or a joke, right? So these three threads walk into a bar…. Just kidding.) Remember that applications are composed of processes which are composed of threads and that Windows 2000 is a multithreading operating system, meaning it can run multiple threads simultaneously (well, virtually simultaneously, by switching back and forth between them quickly).

A typical thread arrangement can be found in an everyday office application, a spreadsheet program. Suppose you want your spreadsheet to do a calculation and then pass that calculation to a report that is being run at the same time. If these two processes of calculating and generating the report are written as separate threads, they must communicate with each other to internally do the data exchange. Normally, no easy avenue exists for this data passage because threads are executed by the CPU as separate entities.

In a case in which one thread must send data to another thread belonging to a separate process, the LPC facility steps in. Such message passing is achieved through requisition of a temporary memory pool from which the data is handed off to the second thread. After the handoff, the memory is freed up for other use.

SECURITY REFERENCE MONITOR

The purpose of the security reference monitor is to prevent unauthorized access to objects, after they are created by the object manager. Unauthorized access could happen intentionally or accidentally, but in either case, it should be prevented from happening for the sake of system security. Access to objects is given to users, processes, threads, and events. As mentioned previously, a security subsystem works in tandem with the reference monitor to keep security tight.

Consider this example. Let's say you're a user who wants to open a file in Photoshop. You run Photoshop, which begins a process. The process is tagged with your rights and permissions on the system (given to you by your system administrator). You try to open a file you've been working on. Because everything in Windows 2000 is treated as an object, the object manager checks to see what the access control specs on the file are. The object manager then supplies this information to the security reference monitor, which then compares your permissions to those of the file in question. If the two match up favorably, then you get access to the file. If not, you don't, and you'll see a warning dialog box, explaining that you're attempting something illegal.

Incidentally, Windows 2000's security reference monitor is intelligent in the way it does its security checks. It attempts to avoid redundant security checking. After a person or process is authorized to access an object the first time, subsequent accesses are permitted. This way, the system won't be strangled by doing repeated security access checking.

I/O MANAGER

Interfacing with the outside world often takes a little spit and baling wire. As a result, getting printers, modems, data-acquisition devices, video displays, SCSI devices, keyboards, mouse devices, and other such real-world objects to work correctly and efficiently is often a nightmare. It's a well-known fact that programmers often have to work around an operating system (DOS or the combination of DOS and Windows, for example) just to get an application or peripheral to work efficiently enough to keep users happy.

The I/O manager's job is to organize the drivers and other routines used to get data into and out of the computer. In Windows 3.x and 9x, you often must reboot the computer for new device drivers to take hold. Having to reboot is a bummer when all you want to do is activate a mouse or a network card. In Windows 2000, many I/O software drivers can be loaded on-the-fly, without restarting the system. This capability is of particular importance on large networks, where taking down the server just to load a new driver would be a nuisance. Also, NT's I/O system is designed so that removing and installing new drivers of any sort (including file system drivers such as those for FAT and NTFS) can be done as a module replacement.

PART

1

CH

2

Note

Unfortunately, not all NT-type drivers can be loaded and unloaded without a reboot. For example, loading a new video or tape backup driver requires a reboot.

The I/O manager's job, as you might expect, is simply to process the I/O requests of applications. The following describes how the I/O manager handles an I/O request: When an application asks for an I/O service, such as sending data to a printer, the message first goes through the environment subsystem running the application. It's then passed through System Services to the I/O manager. The I/O manager determines which driver should be used and sends the data to the proper driver in the form of an I/O request packet, or IRP. The driver then processes the data accordingly for the physical device. This procedure often entails some sort of translation—for example, into PostScript code for that type of printer or into HPCL code for an HP printer. After the data is successfully sent to the device (through the hardware abstraction layer explained later in this chapter), the driver returns the IRP to the I/O manager, which then deletes the packet. Figure 2.12 details this process.

Figure 2.12
This diagram shows the direction and order of flow of I/O processes.

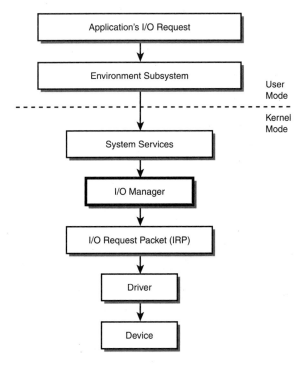

SYSTEM KERNEL

We've already devoted a fair amount of verbiage to the kernel. The important point of the kernel is that it's the most essential and central portion of the operating system, and after it loads into memory when you boot up, great care is taken by the rest of the operating system to keep it invulnerable to accidental attack. Almost everything that happens in

Windows 2000 passes through the kernel in one way or another. Even though the kernel is a scaled-down and somewhat anemic version of the kernel in mainframe systems, it still has quite a lot of responsibility, including the following:

- The kernel works primarily in the area of scheduling and dispatching threads and processes. Therefore, it continually queues up data, sends it to the CPU(s), and routes it after processing.

- The kernel also handles interrupts from various sources—the keyboard or other physical devices—and is responsible for managing *exceptions*, which are error conditions resulting from system violations such as divide-by-zero errors or attempts to write over protected memory areas.

- It synchronizes multiple CPUs (by carefully managing how data threads are divvied up between them).

- It prepares and restarts the system in case of a power failure.

HARDWARE ABSTRACTION LAYER (HAL)

"Open the Pod bay doors, HAL. HAL?" If only Windows 2000 Professional had been in control when Dave was trying to get in, it all might have ended differently. We might have ended up with Windows 2001, too. Who knows, we still have time for another one. Anyway, Kubrick's HAL probably had a hardware abstraction layer too, so let's talk about it.

Imagine you were building an operating system that was supposed to work on a jillion different brands of computers with that many combinations of hardware installed. The way to deal with that and ensure that new programs could find a printer or a modem somewhere when you choose File, Print is to "virtualize" the hardware. Well, that's how the hardware abstraction layer works. The interface between Windows 2000 and the hardware it's running on is all managed by the HAL. Porting Windows 2000 to another type of computer requires only replacing the hardware abstraction layer and some of the I/O drivers.

Based on its experience with installable device drivers in DOS, then with even greater system independence with Windows, Microsoft apparently has realized that keeping hardware as far out of the operating system as possible is the way to ensure success. After all, one of Windows' strongest selling points has been that software drivers for thousands of different screens, printers, mouse devices, SCSI devices, sound cards, video cards, and a panoply of hardware items can easily be written for it and plugged into it.

Windows 2000 takes this approach of hardware isolation a step further by using not only device drivers, but a whole replaceable layer of the operating system responsible for interacting with the hardware. The hardware abstraction layer, or HAL, is this layer. It's the final barrier between the system hardware (including the CPU, memory, I/O ports, keyboard, video, and so on) and the rest of NT. The only parts of NT that communicate directly with the HAL are the kernel and the I/O drivers. Applications, the other executive modules, and the environment subsystems don't know anything about what type of computer they're running on, what type or number of processors are involved, or whether the system is on a network.

The theory of the replaceable HAL ensuring relatively effortless porting of Windows 2000 to other hardware platforms is probably overly optimistic. Many other variables can contend with (such as caches and hardware memory managers) the ways in which disparate CPUs schedule and process data, and so on. It is often difficult for all these variables to be addressed by recoding just the HAL. It's more likely that some adjusting in the rest of the operating system may be necessary as well. Still, the idea is good, and some OEM systems on the market ship with their own HAL, for best taking advantage of hardware peculiarities of their boxes. Certainly the use of a HAL is a good move in the direction of hardware independence and portability for Windows 2000. By abstracting the hardware layer of a system as much as possible, rewrite time to adapt Windows 2000 to new hardware platforms will be minimized.

PART

I

CH

2

WINDOWS WIZARDRY: PROTECTING AGAINST VIRUSES AND TROJAN HORSES

Speaking of security, one way Windows 2000 Professional increases security is through an option that prevents trojan horse viruses from breaking into your computer. Trojan horses are programs that act like another program, fooling the user, and typically grabbing the information the user enters, later using it against the system. A good case in point is a program that pretends to be a network or workstation login dialog box. The user then types in a name and password, and the program steals it, later using it to gain entry to the system, even to the network. Data theft, erasure, or corruption can then occur.

To ensure that a sign-on box is legitimate, Windows NT always required that you press Ctrl+Alt+Delete to sign in. Counterintuitive to Windows 3.x users, this keypress didn't reboot the system. (In fact, you couldn't reboot the system this way, no matter how many times you pressed this key combination.) What it did was flush the portion of RAM where a trojan horse could be residing and bring up a true login dialog box.

In Windows 2000 Professional, trojan horse protection at sign-on is an option. We suggest you turn it on. To do so, follow these steps:

1. Choose Control Panel, Users and Passwords.
2. Select the Advanced tab.
3. Select Require Users to Press Ctrl+Alt+Delete Before Logging On.

In general, we also suggest you learn about viruses and how they are commonly spread. You can accidentally bring viruses into the network by loading a program from a source such as the Internet, online bulletin board, or even email attachments. Keep your eyes peeled for unusual or unexpected onscreen messages, missing files, or the inability to access your hard disk. If you do suspect something, install an antivirus program and run it as soon as possible. Use at least one well-trusted commercial antivirus program, and keep it up-to-date. And make a point of scanning floppies before putting them into your computer.

Even power users or administrators shouldn't regularly work logged in as Administrator. Doing so leaves the system more open to viruses, which can wreak serious damage if activated from an account with Administrator permissions. Users should log on as members of the Users group so they will have only the permissions necessary to perform ordinary, everyday tasks.

CHAPTER 3

GETTING YOUR HARDWARE AND SOFTWARE READY FOR WINDOWS 2000

In this chapter

HARDWARE REQUIREMENTS

So much for the hype about Windows 2000, all its new features, and some of the details of its design and architecture (assuming you survived the exciting computer-science theory in Chapter 2, "The Design and Architecture of Windows 2000 Professional"). So, the question at this point is, "Are you really going to install it?" If you are, you should go ahead and read this chapter and the next one. In this chapter, I'll coach you on preparing for the installation and checking your hardware and software requirements; then I'll discuss some compatibility issues that might affect your product-purchasing decisions. The next chapter covers more specific installation issues, such as choosing disk formats, upgrading versus installing fresh, and dual-booting. I'll also walk you through the setup procedure.

Of course, if Windows 2000 Professional is already installed on your PC, you can probably skim this chapter and skip to Chapter 4, "Installing Windows 2000." You should at least take a brief look at this one because it includes some discussion that might affect software and hardware installation decisions you might make when using Windows 2000 Professional in the future. Understanding what you can do and shouldn't expect from an operating system is always good background material when you use as complex a tool as a computer on a regular basis. Pay particular attention to the section about RAM and hard disk upgrades, how to access the online Hardware Compatibility List (HCL), and how to find the Windows 2000-approved applications list at Microsoft.com.

As you'll learn in the next chapter, the Windows 2000 Setup program automatically checks your hardware and software and reports any potential conflicts. Using it is one way to find out whether your system is ready for prime time. It can be annoying, however, to find out something is amiss at midnight when you're doing an installation, especially when you could have purchased RAM or some other installation prerequisite the previous day when you were out at the computer store. Likewise, you don't want to be technically capable of running Windows 2000 Professional only to experience disappointing performance. To help you prevent such calamity or surprise, the first part of this chapter will cover hardware compatibility issues.

Let's start with the basics. The principal (and minimal) hardware requirements for running Windows 2000 Professional and Server are as follows:

Windows 2000 Professional Minimum

Pentium 166 (or equivalent) or higher CPU (Pentium II or III recommended)

64MB RAM (128MB recommended)

1GB hard drive with at least 650MB of free disk space

Windows 2000 Server (All Flavors) Minimum

Pentium 166 (or equivalent) or higher CPU (Pentium II or III recommended)

64MB RAM (128MB recommended)

2GB hard drive with at least 850MB of free disk space

Notice that the only difference between Professional and Server is the 200MB of additional free space on the hard disk. Also note that these are Microsoft's suggested minimums, and not necessarily what will provide satisfactory or exceptional performance. Some users have reported that they have installed on lesser machines. Microsoft tries to quote minimum requirements that will provide performance the average user can live with.

Table 3.1 compares system requirements for popular operating systems.

TABLE 3.1   HARDWARE REQUIREMENTS BY OPERATING SYSTEM

OS	CPU (Minimum Required/ Recommended)	Memory (Minimum Required/ Recommended)	Disk space (Minimum Required/ Recommended)
Windows 98	P166 MMX/PII-300	16MB/64MB	300MB
Windows NT 4.0 Workstation	P166	48MB	300MB
Windows NT 4.0 Server	486DX/P166	32MB/64MB	No information available
Windows 2000 Professional	P166/PII-300	64MB/128MB	650MB/500MB
Windows 2000 Server	P166/PII-300	64MB/128MB	850MB/1GB
Novell NetWare 5	Intel 386	64MB/256MB	500MB/1GB
Red Hat Linux 5.2 Server	P166	16MB	1620MB

Surprised that you can run this operating system on a machine that's only a 166MHz Pentium? I guess everyone is getting spoiled and thinks that's a pokey old processor. But think back just a year or two, and you may recall that 166MHz was considered fast. I've actually heard of people running NT on 33MHz machines with decent performance, assuming the system had enough RAM. However, Windows has grown in complexity with each iteration. Recall that now Windows 2000 Professional has something in the range of 29 million lines of programming code in it as opposed to the 5 million in Windows NT 3.1. So, some additional horsepower is clearly a good idea.

Tip #17

With the plummeting prices of CPUs these days, there's no reason not to upgrade your CPU or just get a whole new system for Windows 2000 Professional. I have never been unhappy with a faster machine. In fact, I'm writing this book on a 300MHz Pentium II laptop with 128MB of RAM, in July 1999. I'm sure in a year, that will sound like yesterday's news. Of course, I paid a pretty penny for it–something on the order of $3,400–because of its DVD drive and brilliant, large 15-inch screen. In the seven months since I bought it,

continues

continued

> prices of desktop machines have crashed so hard that I just purchased, for testing Windows 2000, a 400MHz AMD K6-2-based system with 128MB of RAM, a 13GB hard disk, and 44X CD-ROM drive, all for $630! Thanks to the fact that RAM prices have finally plummeted as far as other hardware and that Intel was busted for monopolizing the CPU market, PC clones are becoming almost free.

Note

> Some ISPs and advertisers *are* giving away PCs for free, or next to nothing, if you purchase their services or look at their customers' ads. Just watch. In a few years, newborn babies will be issued PCs along with their lifetime cell phones and Social Security numbers.

Anyway, based on what you can get for a song these days, you shouldn't have any difficulty hustling up a machine that will run Windows 2000 Professional adequately. A few years ago when I was writing about Windows NT 3.1, the cost of admission was significantly higher; you had to be on the bleeding edge of computing to build a quality NT-style workstation.

As a consultant, I get more phone calls and emails asking what kind of computer to buy than on any other topic. Despite the rapid de-escalation in prices and apparent exponential increase in computing speed, putting together a machine to run Windows 2000 Professional successfully for your needs might not be as easy as you think. Whenever I build a new system, I'm surprised by twists I hadn't considered, new hardware standards I didn't know even existed, and so on. You probably know the story.

If you're a power-user type or hardware jock running the PCs at your company, you probably spend your coffee breaks poring over magazines like *Killer PC* or belong to the Captain Number Crunch fan club. You can find some blindingly fast stuff, such as accelerated 3D AGP video cards, ultra-wide SCSI2 drives on the 100MHz PC bus, and so on. As much fun as it is for speed freaks, a screamer PC that will take the computing Grand Prix doesn't necessarily a good NT box make. And as much as everyone is hoping that Windows 2000 Professional will broaden hardware and application compatibility over the annoying confines that NT 3 and 4 suffered, it's still a protected and somewhat picky system. Hardware that purrs away happily under Windows 9x might not necessarily cut it under Windows 2000 Professional. Before you go cutting purchase orders and checks for your personal PC or 20 for the office, think twice.

OPTION 1: USING WHAT YOU'VE GOT: ENSURING COMPATIBILITY VIA THE HCL

You can take three basic approaches to ensure hardware compatibility. The first is really simple. Microsoft has done most of the compatibility testing for you already and posted that information in its Hardware Compatibility List (HCL), which is available on the Internet. Items on the list have been tested by the staffers at Microsoft and are guaranteed to perform adequately with Windows 2000 Professional. Before you install, upgrade, or purchase new hardware (from the motherboard on up), consult the list at the following address:

```
http://www.microsoft.com/hwtest/hcl
```

For your edification when selecting new or affirming preexisting hardware, you can check out a special Windows 2000 hardware compatibility site on the Web. You can find it at the following address:

```
ftp://ftp.microsoft.com/services/whql/win2000hcl.txt
```

There, you'll also find a text-based list of hardware specific to Windows 2000. Also, to find general information about Windows 2000 Professional, including compatibility, check out the following:

```
http://www.microsoft.com/windows/professional/default.asp
```

The first site has an interactive list displaying hardware compatibility for all Microsoft operating systems. Figure 3.1 shows the result of my search for the Sound Blaster sound card. The interface is a little Spartan, and the first field you fill in is not explained. The upshot is that you can type a word to narrow the search, such as `Presario` or `SCSI`, and then choose the subcategory of hardware you want the site to search, such as `system/mobile uniprocessor` (that means *laptop computer* in layman's terms) or `Printer`. Then click Go. You might have to try several approaches to find the item you want. The list is quite large, so keep trying with a slightly different approach if your item doesn't come up the first time. Also, make sure to click The Icons Below Mean, and read that information. A check mark implies a lower compatibility rating than does the Windows icon. Note that the Windows logo indicating that the driver is available will take you to the download spot for the driver if you click it— very convenient.

 For a complete list of URLs related to upgrading to Windows 2000, see "Compatibility and Upgrade Help," in the "Troubleshooting" section at the end of this chapter.

PART

I

CH

3

Figure 3.1
Use the online Microsoft Hardware Compatibility List to check on your hardware either before you purchase or decide to upgrade to Windows 2000 Professional.

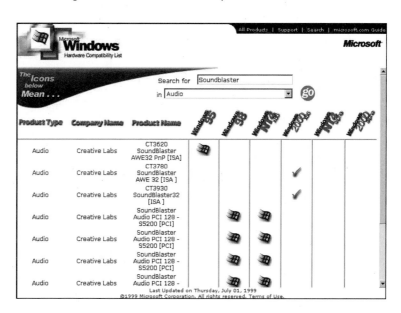

If you don't have online access, you can look at the list on the CD, though it may not be as up-to-date. You can view the Hardware Compatibility List by opening the Hcl.txt file in the Support folder on the Windows 2000 Professional CD. If your hardware isn't listed, Setup may not be successful.

Don't know what's in your system or not sure if you thought of everything that might conflict with Windows 2000 Professional? No problem. You can run the Windows 2000 Compatibility Tool (testing program) either from the Microsoft Web site or the CD. This program detects your hardware and verifies compatibility. You can find it in the Support\Ntct folder on the Windows 2000 Professional CD. Otherwise, you can download the tool from this site:

`http://www.microsoft.com/windows/common/ntcompto.htm`

When you run the program, a report is generated telling you whether your computer cuts the Windows 2000 Pro mustard.

> **Note**
>
> The Windows 2000 Professional Setup program also runs a compatibility test producing a similar listing. The Setup program is covered in Chapter 4.

What do you do if some component of your system (or your entire computer) doesn't rank high enough to appear and isn't listed in the compatibility list? Well, you can wing it and just install onto the computer in a separate directory (dual-boot); then see what happens. If this approach doesn't work, you can revert to using your old operating system. You should also approach the hardware manufacturer and ask whether a Windows 2000 driver is available for the component.

> **Tip #18**
>
> Some people say that you don't need to ensure availability of drivers for Plug and Play devices. Although the idea was that all officially sanctioned Plug and Play devices (bearing the PnP logo) are automatically supported by Windows, this isn't always true. Check carefully to see that any new PnP device you're considering comes with drivers for, or has been tested with, Windows 2000 Professional. If the box says "Designed for Microsoft Windows 2000" and bears the Windows 2000 logo, you're probably home free.

Make sure to take a hard look at peripheral compatibility before you upgrade. Windows 2000's new system architecture requires completely new drivers for most I/O-based peripherals and controller hardware. DOS device support and Windows 9x virtual device (VXD) support are a thing of the past.

OPTION 2: CHOOSING A WINDOWS 2000-READY PC

Sometimes, with new operating systems, it's easier to take the opportunity to start fresh, not just with your hard disk, but with a whole new computer. Every year or so, even subtle advances under the hoods of PCs are put in place. Typically, not a lot of hoopla surrounds these advances, but manufacturing consortia are busy at work coming up with new standards, such as APM, ACPI, CardBus, USB, IEEE 1394 (Firewire), and so on.

It isn't a bad idea to just bite the bullet and shell out for a new machine once every two years or so. I'm a holdout myself, even though I'm a techno-junkie. The bottom line is that I'm cheap, so I try to squeeze out every last CPU cycle from my computers and keep them running for a very long time. I'm still using an old 386 machine running DOS as a router to the Internet. Clearly, I don't like to participate in the throw-away society's idea of planned obsolescence. But every time I upgrade to a new computer, I notice a significant number of niceties across the board—quicker response, more inclusive power management, reduced energy consumption due to lower chip count, more CMOS setting options, faster CD-ROM, and so on.

If you have decided to start fresh and purchase new PCs for your personal or corporate arsenal, let me suggest an easier way to choose them than to check each piece against the HCL. Just as with the individual hardware item listings in the HCL, Microsoft's testing lab awards the "Windows-Ready PC" merit badge to computers that cut the 2000 mustard. You can find a shortcut to checking out brand new ready-to-roll Windows 2000 PCs at this address:

```
http://www.microsoft.com/Windows/2000ready/Partners.asp?site=ntw
```

You'll find mostly brand name boxes there, so don't expect to get a budget computer with a Windows 2000 logo on it just yet. It will take awhile for them to show up. My recent purchase was guaranteed to run NT 4, though, and that was enough for me. Sure enough, it installed and booted Windows 2000 just fine. Prior to the release of Windows 2000, the logoed PC came preinstalled with Windows NT Workstation 4.0.

WHAT YOU GET WITH A WINDOWS 2000-READY PC

When you purchase a Microsoft-sanctioned Windows 2000 computer, you get more than you asked for, but I guess that's capitalism and, besides, with bloatware being so prevalent these days, it's better to prepare for the coming need for bigger and faster everything.

As of this writing, all Windows 2000-ready PCs meet the requirements shown in Table 3.2.

TABLE 3.2 WINDOWS 2000-READY PC REQUIREMENTS[1]

Feature	Requirements
Operating system	Preinstalled with Windows NT Workstation 4.0 Service Pack 3 and the Windows NT 4.0 OPK supplement, which prepares computers for the proposed new European currency and includes bug fixes for Year 2000.
RAM	Include at least 64MB of RAM.
Logo rating	Meets "Designed for Windows" logo for Windows NT Workstation 4.0 and Windows 98 requirements (PC97 or higher).

continues

PART

I

CH

3

TABLE 3.2   CONTINUED

Feature	Requirements
Power Management	Supports Advanced Configuration and Power Interface (ACPI) for laptops to increase battery life, among other benefits.
CPU and CPU cache	Desktop machines come with at least a 300MHz Pentium II with 128KB L2 cache or equivalent performance; laptops include at least a 233MHz Pentium-class processor with 128KB L2 cache or equivalent performance.

[1]The requirements listed in Table 3.2 are preferred. They exceed the minimum requirements to run Windows 2000. See the beginning of this chapter for the minimum requirements.

Tip #19

I've noticed that all the computers linked to from the Microsoft site are Intel-based boxes. Big surprise. The Intel-Microsoft relationship goes back way before AMD or Cyrix hit the scene, and is still somewhat of an old-boy network. Suffice it to say, you can count on Pentium-compatible products to work as well. Keep your eyes peeled for reviews in the magazines, comparing performance of competing CPUs running various tasks under Windows 2000 if you really want the latest skinny as the CPUs evolve. Both my co-author and I are running Pentium IIs and AMD K6-2 processors with Windows 2000 Professional quite successfully.

OPTION 3: UPGRADING YOUR COMPUTER

Don't want to purchase a whole new computer, but your hardware isn't all on the HCL? Or you have some old, stodgy disk drive, SCSI controller, video adapter, motherboard, or some other piece of gear that you want to upgrade anyway? You're not alone. The PC upgrade business is booming, as evidenced by the pages and pages of ads in the backs of computer rags and the popularity of computer "swap meets," where precious little swapping is going on except that of hardware components for the hard-earned green stuff. If only my co-author and I had written Scott Mueller's book on PC upgrading, we would be very happy authors. It's perennially one of the best-selling computer books.

Buy It or Build It?

I have a word of caution about the "building your own" mindset. I started in PCs back before IBM got into the fray, and in those days, you had no choice but to build your own microcomputer. Lots of the building required using a soldering iron, too (and close proximity to the freezer to thrust burned fingers into).

The notion of a completely packaged PC ready to go was sort of disgusting to hobbyists, of course, at least at first. I've been through about 20 PCs so far. After my first few fully integrated (packaged) systems, it started to dawn on me that I didn't have to spend half my time under the hood, and I could really get some work done. I was pretty much hooked, even though I get stung by the upgrade bug once in a while, adding peripherals, hard drives, scanners, CD-RW drives, and backup devices.

Overall, though, my advice is this: If you think you're going to save a lot of time and money while building yourself a better mousetrap than you can get from some serious vendor or systems integration house, "fugget about it!" as Crazy Eddie says. Any company worth its salt has engineers and testers whose job is to iron out the software and hardware incompatibilities that you don't want to lose sleep over.

If you want to upgrade what you have, that's not necessarily terrible, but if you want to build a new system from the ground up, I advise against it. Save yourself some agony, and buy a computer from a reputable dealer, preferably someone who will guarantee it to work with the operating system you have in mind. Especially when you're dealing with local clone builders, you should get that guarantee in writing. Get as much in the box as you can, including video, audio, modem, network card, CD-ROM, hard disk, floppy drive, USB and serial and parallel ports. The basic system with keyboard, mouse, and drives should all work and boot. You can add the frilly stuff like CD-R, Jazz, Zip, and SCSI later if you want to.

The next few sections describe upgrading your PC for Windows 2000 Professional in case you want to take that route.

THE MOTHERBOARD AND CPU

So, you want to upgrade? Okay. Here's point number one: Don't bother upgrading just your CPU without upgrading the motherboard, too. I know lots of CPU upgrade kits are available, but you're not going to experience much in the way of improvement with them. Your money is better spent by upgrading the whole motherboard, possibly with a new generation of CPU along with it. Motherboard improvements roll down the pike every few months, and adding a new CPU to an old design isn't going to net you much. Motherboards are pretty cheap—typically under $100 even for a good one, such as an Intel, Supermicro, or ASUS (this number is sans CPU). Don't get a motherboard from a company that doesn't put its name on the board, doesn't have a good Web site for technical support, or doesn't have a phone number. It's not worth saving a few bucks. Also, check the Microsoft HCL, of course, to see whether it's been tested. You should get one with the memory cache and the latest system memory (as of this writing, it was 100MHz memory) and the chipset that was designed to make it work optimally with the CPU you selected. (See the next section to learn about the importance of chipsets.)

Tip #20	If Windows NT 4 SP4 is successfully running on your current computer, you should have no trouble using the same machine for Windows 2000 Professional. You should not require a hardware upgrade, even though you might enjoy the increased performance by doing it, or you want access to newer hardware standards such as OnNow, USB, Firewire, and so on that your current computer doesn't sport.

Ideally, you'll want a box with a modern motherboard with a fast CPU. So, get your hands on a real Plug and Play box or motherboard (check that it has an actual Plug and Play BIOS) that supports the ACPI power management scheme (not just APM) *and* a reasonably quick processor (in the 300 to 500MHz range), such as a Pentium Celeron, Pentium, Pentium Pro, Pentium II, Pentium III, AMD K6-2, or K6-3. It should have a 100MHz internal bus, support for AGP graphics, a flashable BIOS for later upgrading, and it should be designed around the processor you have in mind.

When you install Windows 2000 on an ACPI-based system, you might need to update the ACPI BIOS to get the full benefits of Plug and Play and power management. If you don't do the update, you might have any of the following problems:

- You can't install Windows 2000 because of an ACPI BIOS error.
- After you install Windows 2000, power management or Plug and Play functionality is not present.
- After you install Windows 2000, power management or Plug and Play functionality is present but doesn't work correctly.

If you do have any of these problems, you need a BIOS update. To obtain an update, contact your system manufacturer.

Tip #21	Many motherboard manufacturers' sites provide an easy way to download a BIOS upgrade and install it via their Web pages. On some motherboards, you have to enable BIOS upgrading by changing a jumper setting. I suggest that you disable the jumper when you're not upgrading to prevent viruses or some runaway program from messing with your BIOS settings.

If you're interested in running Windows 2000 on an existing machine, you can get relatively meager but workable performance with productivity applications such as word processors (assuming you use a slim word processor, not something huge such as the entire Microsoft Office suite) on a Pentium running at around the 166MHz level with 32MB of RAM minimum. Don't skimp on the memory on a slower-CPU machine (see more details about memory later in this chapter). Adding another 32MB increases the perceived speed appreciably because it decreases your disk swapping.

For more demanding application mixes, such as graphics, computer-aided design, heavy database use, or network printer or communications servers, bump up the CPU to a Pentium II-class processor in the 200 to 300 MHz range with 64MB of RAM minimum. And for a snappy system, don't hesitate to purchase a motherboard with a 400 to 700MHz PII or PIII class machine. Don't overpay on the latest, fastest processor, though. It's not worth being on the bleeding edge.

If you're going to be running applications that can actually benefit from multiple processors (check with the software vendor because not all applications do; it depends on how they are written), then you should consider going full bore with a dual-CPM motherboard. Note that you can use only one brand of processor on a dual-CPU motherboard: Intel. No exceptions. CPUs must conform to the MPS SMP standard to work, and others do not.

Suffice it to say that older 386- and 486-based machines are now out of the picture. I have heard of people installing Windows 2000 Professional on 486 machines, and you can try it if you don't value your time, but I don't recommend it. If you want to keep these machines in service, put less-demanding versions of Windows on them, and network them as clients into your Windows 2000 LAN.

Note

All versions of Windows 2000 support the new Single Instruction Multiple Data (SIMD) instruction set included in Intel's Pentium III and Pentium III Xeon processors. The SIMD set allows a database to perform multiple parallel tasks, and its support for multiple floating-point operations is expected to provide improved application stability. Another feature of the Xeon is called Extended Server Memory Architecture (ESMA). This feature lets workstation and server applications access greater amounts of RAM (4GB to 64GB). Intel claims that when applications are written to exploit these features, Xeon-based computers will rival the speed of Alpha workstations from DEC/Compaq. (NT 4 will also be able to exploit these features with Service Pack 5.) Because the Alpha platform was dropped from Windows 2000, it's not as though you have a choice anyway. It's just interesting to note how the performance of the Xeons will compare.

The Importance of the Chipset

Keep in mind that the CPU is only a very small part of the overall design of a motherboard and computer. Many people ask me about upgrading their computers by simply dropping in a (relatively) expensive CPU chip or going through all kinds of machinations to speed-double the chip, and so forth. Just like you don't become Arnold Schwarzenegger or Rambo by getting a brain transplant, you can't create a super computer just by upgrading the CPU. Efficiency of the CPU is interdependent with several variables, such as the support chipset and the internal system bus speed. In fact, contrary to popular belief, the efficiency of the computer is more affected by the chipset than by any other factor—not the CPU nor the video nor the hard disk.

The CPU can be changed. The memory can be upgraded. The hard disk can be swapped. But the motherboard has been designed around the capabilities of the chipset, and until you change the motherboard, your PC will function largely the same. You cannot upgrade the chipset on a motherboard; you have to replace the board. The following are some examples of what properties the chipset dictates:

- Memory type—FPM, EDO, BEDO, SDRAM, parity-checking, ECC
- Secondary cache—Burst, pipeline burst, synchronous, asynchronous
- CPU type—486, P-24T, P5, P54C/P55C, Pentium Pro, Pentium II
- Maximum memory bus speed—33, 40, 50, 60, 66, 75, 83, 100MHz
- PCI bus sync—Synchronous or asynchronous to memory bus speed
- PCI bus type—32-bit or 64-bit
- SMP capability—Single, dual, trio, or quad CPU support
- Support for other features—AGP, IrDA, USB, PS/2 mouse
- Support for built-in PCI EIDE controller and every possible EIDE feature you can imagine—DMA mode, PIO mode, ATA/33, and so on
- Built-in PS/2 mouse, keyboard controller and BIOS, and real-time clock circuitry

You can see that the chipset is at the very heart of much of what the computer does. Because it cannot be upgraded, though, there isn't much talk about it, and people tend to forget about its centrality. Equally important to the overall design of the chipset is how well the CPU and chipset engineers communicated during the design of the chipset. Doing your homework on the latest chipsets and their compatibility/performance with specific CPUs will serve you well.

SLOTS, RAM, AND HARD DRIVES

When you're scoping out a motherboard, think about how many slots you will need for plug-in boards. More and more hardware is built onto the main boards now because very large-scale integration chips make it possible (VSLI); therefore, you'll tend to have fewer needs for slots. Often network support, audio, and even AGP video are built into the motherboard. If you want to use your own sound card and special super-duper video adapter, you can save a few bucks by getting the bare-bones version of the same motherboard. However, if you want to avoid the hassle and keep slots open, buy the motherboard with this stuff integrated on it (such as on-board audio, which provides lower-cost—and lower-performance—audio capability that should suit your needs, unless you're a hard-core gamer or audiophile). For one thing, all the parts are guaranteed to work together. If you think you'll want to add your own boards for the motherboard-included functions, make sure you can turn them off (usually with jumpers or software settings in the BIOS).

As of this writing, most motherboards were strong in PCI slots and weak in the quickly aging ISA slots. Most have only one ISA slot. And most motherboards now have an AGP (accelerated graphics port) for plugging in a fast video card. AGP is based on the PCI bus but fine-tuned for the needs of high-performance 3D graphics. Because I like to be ready for most anything, I recently opted for five PCI slots, one AGP, and one ISA, which seem to be enough for my needs.

Finally, consider the size of the board and the type of case and power supply you now have. The newer boards are ATX-compliant. These motherboards don't fit in the older AT-style cases and don't work with the AT power supplies either. ATX power supplies allow the software to control the power states of the PC, including sleep, suspend, soft power down and up, and so on. I suggest getting a new box and power supply and opting for the ATX version of whatever motherboard you're considering. A new box and power supply shouldn't cost you more than about $60.

For the budget minded, the Socket 7 and Super 7 motherboards are terrific. These de facto industry-standard designs originated by Intel can be used for most any fifth-generation processor, such as the AMD K5 and K6; the Intel Pentium and Pentium MMX; the IDT C6; and the Cyrix/IBM 6x86, 6x86L, and 6x86MX processors. Good Socket 7 motherboards can be had for less than $100 without CPU.

Note

> Super 7 technology was designed by AMD to compete with Intel's expensive Slot 1 technology. Socket 7 processors and motherboards are significantly cheaper than their Slot 1 counterparts and offer similar performance. In 1999, Intel introduced the Socket 370 design, which abandons the slot architecture in favor of the cheaper socketed-processor design. Recently, AMD reversed the tables yet again and introduced the K-7 Athlon processor, which plugs into a new slot design called Slot A.

If you really want to delve into the research, check the Usenet newsgroups. Point your news reader to

```
alt.comp.periphs.mainboard
```

You can find many other motherboard groups as well, addressing specific brands, but this is the place to start. You'll have your reading cut out for you.

Tip #22

> Check the Web site www.motherboards.org for in-depth information about the latest motherboards, chipsets, types of RAM, and much more. You can even find information on building you're own computer. It's a pretty amazing site.

Tip #23

> Annoyed by the noise your computer makes? Me too! Why should that fan and hard disk have to make so much noise? They don't. Ambient noise generated by the cooling fans and the hard disk drive has been a critical hurdle plaguing the PC's capability to fully penetrate the home and become an appliance. TVs, telephones, and VCRs produce less then 26 decibels of noise, whereas PCs produce between 36 and 48 decibels when operating. A PC is considerably louder than the typical living room, and this noise is particularly a problem as you add more PCs to an office, especially a home office, which is otherwise quiet. It's one reason many folks opt for laptops. Hard drive noise adds to the noise of the PC power supply fan, and as hard drives become faster, with the 7200RPM and 10,000RPM spindle speeds, the noise level increases. There is a solution. Several companies are combating noise in PCs by offering noise suppression kits. When you're upgrading or buying a new PC, you might think about the noise factor. Check www.silentsystems.com for more details on this issue.

RAM

Like other versions of Windows NT, Windows 2000 Professional intelligently uses the memory it finds in the system. And it loves memory! The cheapest and easiest upgrade you can make to your PC is to add RAM. If your computer seems to "hit the hard disk" every time you click something or move the mouse around, Windows is doing way too much disk swapping. You should be able to quickly switch among 5 to 10 programs without a lot of wait or noise from your PC. Go get some new memory that matches the kind of board you have (read the motherboard or your PC's manual), and *carefully* install the memory. Unplug the computer. Open the case, and find the RAM slots. Touch the metal case with your other hand before inserting the RAM. (RAM chips are very susceptible to damage by static electricity.) Get the fastest kind of memory that your motherboard can take advantage of.

Modern motherboards automatically detect memory you install (no switch setting is necessary), and Windows 2000 Professional reads this setting and uses it as necessary. In general, the more memory you have installed, the better. Microsoft suggests 128MB for decent system performance. If you're running lots and lots of programs at once, I even suggest more on the order of 256MB, but I've found 128MB adequate for even running 10 or more programs, while many folder windows were open, along with a couple of browser windows.

I'm writing this chapter on a PII 300 with 128MB laptop, and it's plenty zippy. I typically have more than 10 programs and/or windows open, playing MP3 files, checking email in the background, and browsing the Web. Another machine of mine has only 64MB and does a fair bit more disk swapping. Although Microsoft says you can run with as little as 32MB, I'd put 64 as the minimum. At this point, memory is so inexpensive that there is no reason not to upgrade if you need to.

As you might know, there are several different RAM specs. If you have a choice between DRAM (Dynamic), EDO (Extended Data Out) RAM, and SDRAM (Synchronous Dynamic RAM), choose SDRAM. If not that then buy a motherboard or machine that supports EDO. The motherboard (and chipset) has to be designed to take advantage of EDO's or SDRAM's faster data transfer capability. If you buy SDRAM, you'll more likely be able to transfer it to future motherboards and systems. A new kind of RAM called RDRAM will likely replace SDRAM in the near future.

You should ensure that the motherboard has a decent amount of system cache on it. This issue is totally different from the system RAM. A hotly discussed topic in the computer magazines, cache RAM is very fast RAM used by the CPU to temporarily store data as it is sent to and from system RAM, speeding up memory fetches. RAM caching has been shown to increase system speed considerably. When you're shopping for a notebook or desktop computer, go for a 128KB cache minimum, and preferably 256KB or 512KB. If your computer is very old, it might not have a built-in cache or even an option to add one. Some CPUs have a cache built into them. The Pentium and Pentium Pro, for example, have 8KB internal cache. The Intel Pentium MMX and Pentium II have 16KB. The Pentium Overdrive has 32KB.

 If you can't seem to get your newly installed RAM to be detected, see "RAM Not Recognized" in the "Troubleshooting" section at the end of this chapter.

HARD DISK

You need approximately 650MB of free hard disk space to install Windows 2000 Professional. This amount is just a little indication of Windows 2000 Professional's storage hunger. With bloatware on the rise (programmers figure why bother making programs fast and tight with storage being so cheap, I guess), it behooves you to have lots of storage space online. Like upgrading RAM, upgrading the hard disk is easy these days—even on the pocketbook. Get down to Costco, or check www.buycomp.com for the latest prices on hard disks. They are continuing to plummet. For less than a couple hundred dollars, you can get a huge hard disk. The 650MB you need for the installation will look like nothing.

As with RAM, modern motherboards autodetect and configure hard disks when you insert them. Using EIDE, you can get a drive up and online pretty easily. Hard disks typically come preformatted, but you should read the instructions with the drive for details. The biggest nuisance with drive upgrades is figuring out whether to ditch the old one or keep it, which will be the boot drive, and how to back up and restore. The EIDE spec allows for four drives, one of which is probably your CD-ROM. That typically leaves room for three, unless you have a CD-RW or something in the box. There are too many options to cover here, but the easiest upgrade path is to make the new drive a slave on the primary IDE channel. Make sure to set jumpers on the drives' circuit as necessary, and ensure that you have the necessary cables to hook up the drives. Jumper your boot drive as *master* and the secondary drive as *slave*.

Unlike NT, Windows 2000 can be installed on large removable media. The Setup program doesn't look to determine whether the target volume is removable. The %SystemRoot% (WINNT) folder is typically on a fixed hard disk, but it could be on a removable disk, such as a Jaz drive. One application would be to install, say, Linux on one removable drive, Windows NT 4 on another, Windows 98 on a third, and so on.

→ To learn more details about multibooting schemes, **see** Chapter 34, "OS Mix and Match."

Chapter 4 describes in detail partitioning schemes and file systems for storing your operating system and data, so I won't go into those details here. Suffice it to say, you'll want a large and fast hard disk. So what else is new? Hard disks and video controllers are typically the major bottlenecks in PCs, so do pay attention to them if performance is an issue of concern for you. Though SCSI used to be the hands-down winner in the speed wars, the newer ultra-DMA (sometimes called Ultra-ATA) drives are cheaper and almost as fast (33MB/sec). ATA/66 has a transfer speed of 66MB/sec. High-performance systems such as big servers still use SCSI, but you shouldn't go out of your way to buy a SCSI controller card and drive unless you go for Ultra2/Wide SCSI and a high-spindle-speed (10KB) drive, which will get you 80MB/sec transfer rates. (Fast-Wide SCSI and Ultra-SCSI are only 20MB/sec.) You'll want a drive with a fast access time, too: less than 10ms (milliseconds) average access time. ("Average access time" is a specification that will likely be advertised along with the drive's price.)

PART

I

CH

3

Note

Although FDISK can handle all your drive partitioning and file system chores, you can resort to a much easier way.

PartitionMagic—one of the most popular PC utilities on the market today—allows you to easily partition drives without first backing up your data and then spending all day reloading your operating system, applications, and data. You can use PartitionMagic as a replacement for FDISK and/or use it to tweak your drive partitioning after completing your drive setup with FDISK.

continues

continued

> If you decide to change partitioning later, simply run PartitionMagic and reallocate your partitions. PartitionMagic also makes it easy to switch among FAT, FAT32, and NTFS file systems.

MONITOR/VIDEO CARD SUPPORT

Because a doggy, older video card can bring even a snappy system to a crawl when you scroll the screen or move a window around, you'll want to find yourself a fast AGP card. Microsoft has made the move to support video as nicely in Windows 2000 Professional as it did in the 9x platform, even more so in some ways. You have the option of connecting up to four monitors, for example, and using them together. You should check your video cards' specs and the HCL to see whether they will work in multimonitor arrangements before purchasing, though.

Of course a vanilla VGA card will work with Windows 2000 Professional, so you don't have to stress about getting the latest. But if you're thinking about upgrading here, get an AGP board that has the bells and whistles you want—TV support, video capture, fast 3D for games, whatever. Decide the resolution you want to use, and make sure the card supports the number of colors you'll need at that resolution. You'll want at least 64,000 colors for most work; 256 colors is too few even to make icons on the desktop look good anymore, much less to render digital photos in typical Web pages. If you have a 17-inch monitor, you'll want to be running in at least 800×600 resolution, more likely 1024×768. All modern video boards support these resolutions easily with even 4MB of video RAM on the board. Make sure the board can run at 72Hz refresh rate at the color depth and resolution you desire, too, so you won't see flicker on your screen. (P.S. Your monitor needs to be able to do it, too. Check the monitor specs. Some older monitors can't run at, say, 1024×768 while refreshing at 72Hz.)

If you're thinking of using a flat-screen monitor, I highly recommend it. Both my co-author and I have 15-inch LCDs and love 'em. Nothing comes close to their clarity, they make no noise, they use little power, and regaining some desk space is a plus. However, choosing an adapter for these newfangled screens gets a bit complicated. Because LCD panels are digital by nature (every pixel on the screen has a discrete address), they display the clearest image when driven by a digital video board, just like in a laptop computer. Some screens such as the Mag models are supplied with a digital adapter card for this reason. The monitor does not attach to a standard VGA analog video adapter, though. You can use it only with the supplied card. Other LCD monitor brands, such as the NEC, give you greater flexibility, plugging into any analog video card. You can hook it up to, say, an ATI All-In-Wonder card and watch TV on it, capture video, and so forth. But it isn't quite as clear as digital setup because the pixel control is less accurate. The analog signals from the card have to be converted into digital addressing for the pixels. Eventually, flat panels and video adapters will both have digital *and* analog connectors on them, so you won't have to choose before you buy. So far, though, I haven't seen them.

Tip #24	Laptop and other flat-panel screens look very good at only one resolution—the so-called "native resolution." Other resolutions can be displayed, but they tend to look blocky. Some LCDs look better than others in nonnative resolutions due to built-in antialiasing firmware. And, unlike standard CRT monitors, LCD monitors look best at low refresh rates. If you buy an LCD monitor, be sure to set the refresh rate to 60Hz. It will probably look clearer that way. You don't have to worry about flicker on an LCD monitor; it's not an issue, and any advertising about high refresh capabilities of an LCD monitor is bogus and misleading. The pixels are transistors and simply don't flicker because they don't have to be refreshed in order to stay on.

Windows 2000 Professional comes with a large complement of 32-bit driver support for many devices, including a wide variety of video cards. It's quite likely that your card is going to be recognized, but you should check with the HCL just to make sure.

PART I

CH 3

PLUG AND PLAY ITEMS

Plug and Play (or *PnP*, as it is commonly abbreviated) has brought a new level of sophistication to the PC. Much of the headache of PC upgrades stemmed from internal conflicts between plug-in boards and peripheral devices that were not easily detected by the operating system and too difficult for users to configure. Installing even a simple modem was often an exercise in failure for many users as they struggled to determine and set the board's jumpers, dipswitches or software settings to use an available IRQ (Interrupt Request). With PnP, you just plug in a board, screen, printer, scanner, or other peripheral, and reboot.

The PnP idea was introduced with the Apple NuBus on the Mac II and was later picked up by Microsoft and the PC industry. It appeared in an operating system when Windows 95 hit the streets. Since then, a plethora of PnP devices have shown up. PnP doesn't always work as advertised, but most of the time it does, and it's a big step in the right direction. With Windows 2000 Professional, the NT platform now supports PnP. The PnP portion of Windows is extensive, and bringing it over to the NT platform was one of the complications that delayed the release of NT 5 (Windows 2000).

Note	As you probably know, older legacy hardware that isn't Plug and Play compliant will work fine in a PnP-enabled computer. Windows 2000 Professional does a good job of detecting some older non-PnP hardware, although a lot of the old crusty stuff isn't going to make it onto the Windows 2000 Professional HCL. The real question is whether the manufacturer or Microsoft supplies an NT or Windows 2000 driver for it. All NT-based operating systems rely on what is called the Windows Driver Model (WDM)—32-bit drivers designed specifically for NT and Windows 98. Windows 98 also supported older 16-bit drivers, but NT and Windows 2000 Professional do not. WDM drivers are loaded and unloaded dynamically based on entries in the Registry, and the Plug and Play manager is called on to create, start, and stop devices that have been detected.

For PnP to work, the system BIOS, the operating system, and related hardware drivers all have to work together. All modern motherboards are PnP-enabled. Some older legacy computers from the 486 days are not. This point is not particularly germane unless you intend to try running Windows 2000 Professional on a 486.

The main point is that, in preparation for Windows 2000 Professional, you should buy only PnP designed for Windows 9x and Windows 2000. This point applies mostly to boards, but it is pretty spiffy to plug in a PnP printer, scanner, or mouse and have it detected and the correct driver installed.

If your computer contains ISA cards, they might be set in a manually configured mode in which the user has to declare the card's resources. Examples are sound cards, network cards, or modems. If your ISA cards have an ISA Plug and Play mode, you should set them that way. Check the manual that came with the hardware to see whether it has such a mode.

Tip #25	To be permitted to display the "Windows 2000-compatible" logo, hardware and software must be PnP-capable. Look for this logo or the Plug and Play moniker when buying.

PREPARING YOUR SOFTWARE FOR WINDOWS 2000 PROFESSIONAL

In preparation for upgrading or installing Windows 2000 Professional fresh, you need to consider software compatibility issues in addition to the hardware issues described previously. Chapter 1, "Introducing Windows 2000 Professional," and Chapter 2, "The Design and Architecture of Windows 2000 Professional," describe how Windows 2000 Professional is largely backward-compatible with DOS, Windows 3.x, and Windows 9x applications. However, you should be aware of some limitations. If you've been exclusively running NT, and your stable of software has tested acceptably on that platform, you're in pretty good shape for Windows 2000 Professional. There are some exceptions, of course, and software makers are busily upgrading their programs to comply with the requirements as the bugs are being worked out of Windows 2000 itself. In some ways, older software will run better under Windows 2000 Professional than it did under DOS, Windows 3.1, or Windows 9x environments.

Anyway, the good news is that Windows 2000 Professional will be highly compatible with many DOS and Windows 3.x applications, and certainly with 32-bit programs that were designed for Windows 9x and Windows NT. In addition, any old Windows 3.x software will benefit from having a face-lift—nicer borders, more options in the dialog boxes, smoother functioning, an increased capability to work with larger files, and so forth. The bad news is that Windows 2000 Professional *won't* be able to run some programs and utilities, at least not in their current incarnations. You'll either need updates to the software or have to bag such programs altogether. The payoff, as explained in Chapters 1 and 2, comes down primarily to increased reliability and security.

In general, if you have your arsenal of programs and utilities chugging away under Windows NT successfully, your applications will upgrade to Windows 2000 Professional with only minor incident. The Setup program will alert you about any needs or incompatibilities. If you want to better understand the vagaries and nuances of Windows 2000 Professional's application restrictions, read on.

CLASSES OF PROGRAMS

You are probably aware of a distinction to be made between types of programs. Most programs folks use on a daily basis are called *productivity applications* or simply *applications*. They include programs such as Microsoft Word, Microsoft Access, Adobe PhotoStyler, Dreamweaver and other Web page editors, CAD-CAM programs, video and sound editing programs—just to name a few of the thousands that are available. Typically, such programs help you produce documents in a certain line of work. These applications run at the highest level of the computer system, well on top of the operating system, and don't get down into the nitty-gritty of it.

By contrast, *utilities* are programs that try to get down deeper into the operating system and are used to manage the computer. Programs such as virus eradicators, hard disk partitioning and image backup tools, hard disk organizers, user interface tweakers, and power management tools fall into this class of programs. Norton Utilities, NT Disk Administrator, and McAfee Anti-virus are examples.

Even though people don't typically distinguish between utilities and applications and simply use the word *application* (or just *program*) to refer to any program, technically, they are different. As you'll see, it's more likely that plain old *applications* are going to work under Windows 2000 Professional than will utilities you want to bring over from less-empowered iterations of Windows.

<table>
<tr><td>Tip #26</td><td>If you have a program that uses 16-bit drivers, you need to get 32-bit drivers from the software vendor to ensure that the program functions properly after the upgrade to Windows 2000.</td></tr>
</table>

LEGIT APIS VERSUS HARDWARE TWIDDLING

As you may recall from Chapter 2, when applications need help from the operating system to, say, print or write a file to disk or accept keyboard input, the environment subsystem passes the request to the Executive. The NT Executive runs in protected mode so that the applications (or utilities) can't threaten the stability of the system. The requests that applications make are known as *API calls*. (API stands for *application programming interface*.) APIs are built into each environment subsystem and make up a set of tricks or canned functions the programmer can call upon.

The NT Executive, kernel, and hardware abstraction layer (HAL) take care of the rest of the work after the request is made. Recall also that the non-Win32 environment subsystems

PART
I

CH
3

turn their calls over to the Win32 subsystem, which then routes them to the Executive. Thus, the environment subsystems have to translate native Windows 3.x, OS/2, DOS, and POSIX calls into Win32 calls, which are then passed to the Executive using API calls the Executive understands. A lot of interpreting goes on, and lots of middle management.

For general applications, all this is just peachy because most applications just want traditional access to hardware: keyboard input, screen output, printing, and reading and writing data files on disk. APIs are a great help here, as is the Executive, because applications programmers don't have to handle the drudgery of system housekeeping on their own. The existence of an API makes writing Windows programs much easier.

As you might have suspected, any program or utility that wants to work directly with hardware, or makes calls that would otherwise be trapped because they don't exist in the Windows 2000 environment subsystems, will fail or will likely be crippled in some way. Typically, Windows 2000 shuts them down after generating an error log and displaying an error dialog onscreen. Exceptions are legitimate calls to COM and LPT (serial and parallel) ports made by DOS programs in the course of traditional procedures such as dialing a modem or printing a document. Many DOS communications programs expect to access the serial port UART (the chip that runs the serial port) directly, for example. NT virtualizes the PC serial and parallel ports in the 16-bit subsystem, intercepting the request and sending it through the Executive as legitimate. The port is emulated in software, basically, and the DOS program is none the wiser. DOS programs that try anything more sophisticated, such as writing to the hard disk tracks or doing fancy stuff with the ports, screen, or keyboard, will be trapped.

In Windows 3.x, API end runs often were neither perceived nor prevented, resulting in system breaches and crashes. This was particularly a problem with DOS programs because they assumed they had control of the entire computer (DOS isn't a multitasking operating system). Windows 3.x allowed this use, so games and utilities programmers took advantage of this "feature" to write some pretty audacious programs. DOS-based viruses are a good case in point. Viruses make a hobby of fiddling with the innards of your operating system (typically by altering data on the hard disk), with insidious effects. Windows 3.x couldn't prevent such security breaches because it had no way of knowing they were occurring. Windows 2000 is much better at preventing them. The BIOSs of modern PCs can also detect attempts to futz with the boot tracks of the hard disk, too, though the feature can be defeated through a setting in the BIOS Setup utility.

Windows 9x was somewhat better at protection than 3.x, though not by a great margin. Portions of the *kernel* were protected, and if a program acted improperly, you stood a better chance of being able to kill it without bringing down the whole operating system. The designers of Windows 9x achieved a higher degree of hardware isolation by virtualizing all the hardware, the same approach used in NT and 2000. Every physical piece of hardware in the computer is accessed only by *virtual device drivers* (called *VxDs* in Windows lingo). When an application wants the use of a device, it asks the operating system for it via the API call. Then the operating system validates the request and passes it along to the device driver, which in turn handles the actual communication with the device.

HARDWARE-BASED DEVICE-PROTECTION CAPABILITIES

The Intel CPUs have capabilities that come to the rescue, to some degree, in helping prevent hardware access breaches, yet still handle the request. The CPU works in concert with the operating system to achieve the desired result. When a DOS program running in Windows tries to access hardware, Windows maps the DOS API call to the Win32 API. This procedure is fine until a direct call to hardware is attempted. An intelligent feature built into Intel 386 and subsequent chips (486, Pentium, Pentium II, and Pentium III), called the *I/O permission bitmap*, comes to the rescue by noticing this request and putting up a red flag.

As mentioned in Chapter 2, when an application is run, Windows 2000 Professional detects what type of program it is—whether DOS, Windows 3.x, 32-bit Windows, POSIX, or OS/2. When the VDM (virtual DOS machine) for a DOS program is set up, it provides all the basic services of a PC, and it also creates an I/O permission bitmap for the application. The bitmap is essentially a table with entries for each of the computer's internal ports (there are many, used for different things, such as the system clock, network boards, and so on), and it shows which, if any, of the ports allow direct access. If the DOS program tries to access hardware outside this accepted list of virtualized hardware, the red flag goes up, Windows 2000 Professional notices it, and the program is terminated, typically accompanied by an entry in the system error logs.

WHY SHOULD YOU CARE?

Enough theory. What does this mean to you and to your application choices? As I mentioned earlier, not a lot of your personal or corporate software medley hails from the 32-bit Windows camp. Most of them will probably run fine after the upgrade. But if you're upgrading from Windows 3.x or 9x and you've been running 16-bit programs, especially hard disk utilities, you might have trouble running them. Unlike Windows 98's DOS mode, which lets you run particularly demanding DOS programs by temporarily exiting Windows, Windows 2000 Professional has no such mode. You should upgrade or jettison such programs.

Caution

Even though you might be able to run some of your older disk utilities by forcing the issue doesn't mean that it's advisable. Windows 3.x programs, for example, don't know about long filenames and can truncate long filenames or at least not display them or accept them in dialog boxes, which can be annoying. Running such programs is not recommended, and I suggest you put them in cryogenic suspension.

As you'll learn in the next chapter, when you perform an upgrade installation of Windows 2000 Professional, Setup examines the applications you have installed and attempts to warn you of incompatibilities. In some cases, you'll just be told to bag the program. In other cases, you'll be prompted to contact the maker for updates, called *upgrade packs*, or to insert the disks with upgrade packs on them at the appropriate time.

Also, as you know, because Windows 9x and NT have been out for a few years now, plenty of available 32-bit programs are Windows 2000 Professional-compatible. Windows 2000 Professional itself also comes packed with more utilities than you can beat with a stick. And you can find scads of 32-bit utility programs from third-party vendors written for Windows 9x to accomplish what your DOS or Windows 3.x did. You'll also find some workarounds in Windows 2000 for accommodating picky DOS programs. You can fine-tune each DOS program's environment with startup files (AUTOEXEC.BAT and CONFIG.SYS), and numerous DOS *properties settings* can assist as well. Still, even they don't allow an overzealous DOS program to access your hard disk because doing so could prove harmful.

WINDOWS 2000-APPROVED APPLICATIONS

So, which programs are really ready for Windows 2000? The logo requirements for Windows 2000-ready software are similar to those discussed previously for hardware. Just check the product's packaging or the Web page description of the product you're thinking of purchasing. If it's NT 4–compatible, chances are good that it will run under Windows 2000 Professional, but that's not guaranteed. I suggest you contact the maker or check a few sites on the Web first.

Microsoft hosts a site of Windows 2000 Professional-ready software at the following address:

```
http://www.microsoft.com/windows/professional/deploy/compatible/
```

You also can access a Directory of Windows 2000 Applications that lists products compatible with the Windows 2000 platform. You can search the directory by company or product name to find applications you're interested in. The product information in this catalog is provided by Independent Software Vendors (ISVs) and by Microsoft application teams. The list continues to expand as vendors test and add their products, so visit the following address from time to time to see what's new:

```
http://www.microsoft.com/windows2000/ready/
```

You can also search the Directory of Windows 2000 Applications to find applications that use more sophisticated Windows 2000 technologies, such as Active Directory, IntelliMirror, and Windows Installer. Because they're based on advances in Windows 2000 technology, these products deliver improved levels of reliability and manageability. The address is as follows:

```
http://www.microsoft.com/Windows/professional/deploy/compatible/CompatApps.asp
```

TROUBLESHOOTING

RAM NOT RECOGNIZED

I've added RAM to my computer, and it doesn't seem to show up.

You must check several things when adding RAM to ensure that it shows up correctly in Windows. If the BIOS detects the RAM, you can be assured that it will be detected in

Windows, so don't worry about any settings within Windows per se. Just do what is necessary for the computer to report the correct amount of total RAM when it is booting or from within the BIOS. Older machines used to require switch settings or BIOS setting adjustments when you added RAM, but virtually all new computers do not. Of course, you can and should always consult the manual supplied with your computer when performing a RAM upgrade. Follow this checklist:

- Make sure you purchased the correct type, form factors, and capacity of RAM.
- Make sure the RAM is the correct speed for the computer.
- Double-check that the RAM is inserted correctly and firmly seated in the computer. With the power off, try removing and reinserting it.
- Make sure you inserted the RAM in the correct slot. Most computers have a few slots for RAM. Many motherboards require that RAM slots be filled in a specific order, or autodetection of RAM will not work.
- If it's still a no-go, remove the RAM (turn off the power first, of course), carefully package the RAM in an antistatic bag, and return it to the dealer to be tested.

COMPATIBILITY AND UPGRADE HELP

Where can I learn more about compatibility and upgrade options for my Windows 2000 computer?

Microsoft maintains several resources for Windows 2000. You can check the following:

- The Microsoft Deployment Resources Web site includes operating system migration guides, pointers to training resources, and a strategic upgrade white paper. You can find this information at the following address:
  http://www.microsoft.com/windows/professional/deploy/deploying/deployguide.asp
- The Hardware Compatibility List provides quick access to compatibility information for a variety of equipment vendors, computer systems, and specific peripherals by name and type. It's located at this address:
  http://www.microsoft.com/hwtest/hcl
- An updated list of Windows 2000 device drivers is available at this address:
  http://www.microsoft.com/windows/compatible
- You can check Windows 2000 software compatibility at this site:
  http://www.microsoft.com/windows/professional/deploy/compatible/default.asp
- Microsoft's Windows 2000 Ready program can help you find workstations and servers that are 100 percent Windows 2000-compatible. Check with your PC vendor to see whether existing products can be retrofitted to comply with Microsoft's specifications. Go to the following address:
  http://www.microsoft.com/windows2000/ready)
- In its Windows 2000 upgrade paper, Microsoft includes a more detailed list of application compatibility tests that you can perform; it's available at the following address:
  http://www.microsoft.com/windows/professional/technical/default.asp

TIPS FROM THE WINDOWS PROS: SHOPPING FOR THE RIGHT HARDWARE AND SOFTWARE

Many people ask how I decide what hardware and software to purchase or discard when preparing for an operating system update such as Windows 2000 Professional. Here are some personal notes.

When I want to use one of my old utilities or applications for my Windows 2000 Professional machine, I first check to see whether what I want to do is already covered by some other program. A better mousetrap is always around. Consider zip utilities, for example. I used to use DOS-based zip programs; then I moved on to WinZip. Until Windows 2000 Professional, I used Windows 98 Plus! which includes native support for zip in the GUI, so I could zip and unzip right in the Explorer interface. Come Windows 2000 Professional, and I was wondering what to use. I popped onto the Web and did a search or two and came across Turbo Zip. I think the link said something about working with NT, so I gave it a shot. Now I'm using Turbo Zip. It works fine under NT and Windows 2000 Professional.

As for productivity applications, I'm game to try anything I was using under Windows 98: PhotoShop, Adaptec Easy CD Creator, CoolEdit 96, Excel 97, Word 97, Ulead Media Studio, Real Jukebox MP3 player, Front Page Express, Cute FTP, ThumbsPlus, even some 3.x applications such as Collage Image Capture (for capturing screen shots for this book). I trust that Windows 2000 will alert me if the application isn't safe to use.

If I hear that the 32-bit version of the application is available and will run faster (I usually assume it will at least have some nifty new features, such as better Save As and Open dialog boxes, support for more file formats, or something), I'll spring for it if the price isn't too outrageous or if an upgrade option is available.

I used to hang with Netscape Navigator, but frankly I like Internet Explorer better mostly because I love the F11 feature that increases the browser size to the full screen so that I can see the maximum amount of text at one time. Also, because I use Outlook Express for my mail, and they are integrated pretty nicely, I go for the package deal. However, Internet Explorer relies heavily on ActiveX, which is known for its security holes and is nonportable to other operating systems.

Whom Can You Trust?

Web browsers were originally supposed to be totally portable, so in reality, Microsoft is working against that vision of the Web. Instead, it is attempting to trap us into a Microsoft world. For a more fully compatible browser that is faster and smaller, I suggest Opera. It is based on the Sun Microsystems Java interpreter, so it's maximally compatible with Java because Sun wrote Java. Of course, neither Netscape nor Opera (nor other brands of browsers) will run ActiveX technologies from Microsoft. Therefore, on some sites—particularly on the Microsoft sites—you will lack some functionality. But that's the price you pay for additional security.

It's true that ActiveX objects are digitally signed, so their origin can be traced, which prevents them from being easily distributed by malicious people. When a Web page wants to use an object that isn't already installed on your system, a screen appears, and you get to decide whether to trust the vendor. However—and this is the big problem—you're trusting them more than you might think. You're not only trusting that the object will do what it says it does, but that it can't be used to do things the author didn't intend. Malicious people can exploit ActiveX objects to wreak havoc on your system. Microsoft's own ActiveX objects, supplied with Windows, have been a notorious source of security risks. Nearly every week I read about one that lets any user read any arbitrary file on your computer. This is the basis of the problem with ActiveX. Java has security boundaries. ActiveX doesn't.

A few years ago, after first starting to use Windows 95, it took me several months to get used to using the desktop and the taskbar. But soon I was converted. Anyone upgrading from Windows 3.x will probably go through the same confusion at first. Whereas my home base had been the 3.x Program Manager and File Manager, I quickly became addicted to dropping folders and documents right on the desktop, dragging files to a floppy drive on the desktop, and so forth. With the Windows 9x interface on NT since NT 4 and now more fully integrated into Windows 2000 Professional, the conversion evolves. It's getting easier and easier to copy files around, drop them in email, or view images using thumbnails in an Explorer window. The need for many of the shell add-ons that I once used in Windows 3.x has vaporized.

When it comes to hardware, although I'm an experimenter and always want to try out the latest gizmos, I'm hard-core practical. Got that from my parents, I guess. Trying out new hardware and returning it aren't nearly as easy as deciding not to purchase software after trying the demo for free. It's also not as easy as learning from other's failures. As the saying goes, "Learn from other people's mistakes because you won't live long enough to make them all yourself." Too bad you can't try hardware for free; shipping charges, restocking fees, and hassles with sales people are too much for me to worry about. I don't buy new hardware unless it's on the Microsoft HCL for the operating system that I'll be using with the system. It's that easy. I have too much weird off-brand hardware sitting in closets around my office or that I've donated to local community groups just because it didn't work with my operating system. Before I purchase, I also look around to see what the most popular item in a niche is. I bought a PalmPilot even though the CE devices have broader functionality, for example. Buying mainstream means I'll have more add-on products, supplies, cables, media, drivers, and online support from users. That support is worth the extra few dollars or loss of bleeding-edge features any day.

And finally, I usually go for version 2.0. If a product catches on and has industry-wide support, I'll go for it, but not until then. I never bought a Sony Beta VHS, a nine-track tape player, or an Atari or Timex-Sinclair computer. My new computer is a Socket 7-based AMD K-6 uniprocessor on an ASUS motherboard. I checked the newsgroups and various Web sites before getting it and didn't push it to beyond 400MHz. I didn't go with multiprocessors or Ultra SCSI II. Internal timing with super-fast computers can be problematic, so why push it? When the PVII 1000MHz job comes out, I'll upgrade. I just wanted reasonable processing power and mostly reliability.

CHAPTER 4

INSTALLING WINDOWS 2000

In this chapter

CHOOSING AN UPGRADE PATH

This chapter describes the variety of installation options available for Windows 2000 Professional. Even if your system is already installed, you might be interested in reading through this chapter for some helpful information about dual-booting various operating systems, considering whether you should install Windows 2000 Server, and working with multiple formats of disk partitions (FAT, FAT32, and NTFS).

Due to improvements and standardization in user interfaces and to Microsoft-imposed installation procedures for Windows programs, setup of application programs nowadays is typically a piece of cake and self-explanatory. Likewise, installation of all newer Windows versions has grown increasingly automated since the 3.x days. Windows 98 Setup is typically a breeze, for example; you just answer a few questions up front and then have a cup of coffee while the rest of Setup's machination progresses automatically. Because Windows 98 is more of a consumer-oriented product, a simple installation experience for the user is a necessity, and makes good business sense for Microsoft. However, partly owing to upgrade path complexities and partly to the expanded feature set, things aren't quite so simple with the Windows 2000 Professional installation.

This chapter covers the installation issues you will need to ponder under differing scenarios. I won't go deeply into the blow-by-blow because the Setup windows offer enough basic explanation, and you've no doubt been through enough installations of Windows by now to know the score. Instead, I'll describe the basic decision tree you'll have to mull over before committing to Windows 2000 Professional and the path you'll follow to get Windows 2000 Professional up and running. Along the way, I'll discuss why you might make one choice over another and what to do when the process goes awry.

You can choose from a hefty handful of potential upgrade and installation scenarios:

- Clean installation on a new drive
- Upgrade a 95 or 98 system
- Upgrade an NT 3.x system
- Upgrade an NT 4 system

Note

> You cannot upgrade a Windows 3.x system directly. It would have been nice if Microsoft had included a direct means for upgrading from Windows 3.x, but it was probably felt that the bulk of machines still running Windows 3.x wouldn't have the CPU, RAM, or hard drive required for the upgrade anyway. If this is not the case for your machine, you can upgrade by migrating through Windows 9x. See "Upgrading a Windows 3.x Machine" later in the chapter.

In each category of upgrade, you have two important subchoices:

- Whether to create a dual-boot system or upgrade your existing operating system
- Whether to keep your existing FAT file system or upgrade to NTFS

I'll break down descriptions by preexisting operating systems and tell you what you can expect when upgrading. Look for the section that applies to you. Also, check the general discussions about dual-booting and upgrading your file system because they apply in all cases. You can find a more in-depth discussion of multibooting in Chapter 34, "OS Mix and Match."

Note

In addition to this chapter, you should also read the file Read1st.txt, which you can find on the root directory of the Windows 2000 Professional CD. This file contains last-minute installation information Microsoft didn't publish until it released the final version of Windows 2000 Professional.

As mentioned in Chapter 1, "Introducing Windows 2000 Professional," Windows 2000 also supports installation capabilities attractive to the IS professional, such as *push* installations and automated installations that require no user intervention.

For more information about these kinds of sophisticated deployment processes and automated installation tools, you should seek the aid of Microsoft's Windows 2000 Professional Resource Kit. There, you can find instructions for creating automated installation scripts. I'll cover the basics of automated installations at the end of this chapter.

PART

I

CH

4

CHOOSING BETWEEN WINDOWS PROFESSIONAL OR SERVER

For purposes of this chapter, I'll assume that based on information in Chapter 1, you've decided to install Windows 2000 Professional rather than Server. That's a big assumption on my part, so let's talk about it a bit here. Installation of an operating system isn't something to take lightly because changing your mind midstream isn't always easy or achieved without repercussion. It will behoove you at this juncture to consider whether you want to install one of the Server flavors rather than Professional.

The basic rule of thumb is this: You should install Server if you need centralized services for a group of workstations. Server gives you everything that Windows 2000 Professional does, but in addition, you garner all the advantages of centralized control. For example, user authentication information is stored on one central machine, so managing a network is *much* simpler using Server than Professional (where user information is stored on each individual computer). You get Active Directory (which is good for locating resources such as printers and files), far easier control over those resources, higher-level networking services (such as RAS Server, DHCP, DNS, and WINS), and more powerful management tools. Of course, these features require training and sophistication to use, so you have to take into consideration your level of expertise and the amount of time you have to bone up on Server topics.

Forget Professional and install Server when you have these needs:

- You want tools for easily managing IP addresses. Unless you have a router to automatically assign IP numbers to new workstations as you add them, doing so manually can be a nuisance. Server includes Dynamic Host Configuration Protocol (DHCP) support, meaning that it assigns an IP address to new computers as they are plugged into the LAN. If you plan to run TCP/IP as your primary network protocol, and you want to integrate the LAN with the Internet, you'll end up wanting DHCP.

- You want your network's manager to be able to configure and manage all network settings from one computer. You want to be able to add a new computer and assign passwords, privileges, and access to printers and other resources without running around the office. You should be able to configure once and then manage anywhere.

- You want to be capable of supporting more than 10 simultaneous connections, such as a Web server or database server. Windows 2000 Professional has the same connection limit as Windows NT 4 Workstation. It denies incoming connections to the Web server or database file (for example) when the eleventh simultaneous connection is attempted.

Tip #27

Managing a network with Windows Professional is like trying to hold ping-pong balls underwater. When you get up to about 10 balls, two hands just aren't enough. You need central management tools at that point. That's when it's time to add in at least one Windows Server to the network.

- You want your users to have their *profiles* follow them from machine to machine, complete with security settings, privileges, applications, and so forth.

- You need full support for telecommuters. With Windows 2000 Professional, you can call into your remote computer, but Remote Access Services (RAS) to the entire office network are limited. You do not have as extensive security to prevent a hacker dialing in and using a guest account, for example. With Server, you have full access to the network you're dialing into, including enhanced security.

- If you have 10 users or more, you should consider setting up one Server. Even with fewer users, it's common that you'll have a temp in the office, or Joe might want to surf the Web with Lisa's computer while she's out at lunch. This kind of movement of personnel between computers is most efficiently managed from a central location and suggests the need for heightened security, which is what Server is all about.

Note

Of course, you should consult a book that specializes in Server, such as *Special Edition Using Microsoft Windows 2000 Server* by Roger Jennings (also published by Que) for the nitty-gritty on Windows 2000 Server.

Note

If you're the proud owner of a DEC/Compaq Alpha computer, you probably are already aware of Microsoft's decision not to offer Alpha support for Windows 2000. This is a sad development because the Alpha is a fast and relatively inexpensive machine. This might also result in the Linux platform taking over the Alpha platform and giving Microsoft more of a run for its money. Alpha users who want to run some version of NT have to stick with NT 4.

CLEAN INSTALLATION VERSUS UPGRADE

Assuming you've ruled out the Server version (which is likely, because why else would you have bought this book?), let's begin to talk about installing Professional. The next major question you must ask is whether to upgrade from an existing operating system or install fresh. Windows 2000 Professional supports upgrading from the following operating systems:

- Windows 95 (all releases)
- Windows 98 (all releases)
- Windows NT 3.51 Workstation
- Windows NT 4.0 Workstation (including service packs)

Most Windows veterans know by now that doing a fresh installation is usually the most beneficial approach in the long run, even though it means more work up front installing applications and reentering personal settings, Dial-Up Networking details, and so forth. You probably have some seat-of-the-pants experiences with Windows operating systems becoming polluted over time by wacko applications that mysteriously trash the Registry or *.DLL files that have been erased or overwritten.

With a clean installation, such worries can be forgotten. It's like selling off that lemon of a car you've been wrestling with for the last five years. And yes, you'll lose lots of settings that are annoying to input again, such as dial-up and TCP/IP settings, email accounts, address books, and so forth. As you learned in Chapter 1, Windows 2000 Professional is somewhat self-healing. Because system files and DLLs are protected against trampling, you're going to have a more sturdy system in the long run anyway, and some programs will let you import settings, such as address books and mail, from the folders in which these things are stored. If your system is acting a little wonky already anyway (unexpected crashes, for example), a clean installation just might iron out some wrinkles.

When you choose to upgrade over an existing operating system, you also run the possibility that some applications won't work properly afterward because they aren't compatible with Windows 2000 Professional. In this case, the sensible route is to upgrade to Windows 2000-compatible versions of the programs as soon as you can.

Table 4.1 compares performing a clean installation versus upgrading your existing Windows installation.

PART

I

CH

4

TABLE 4.1   CLEAN INSTALLATION VERSUS UPGRADING

Perform a new installation when you can answer "yes" to any of the following:	Consider upgrading when you can answer "yes" to all the following:
You've just purchased a new hard disk or reformatted it.	Your current operating system supports upgrading.
The operating system you have on your computer isn't among those on the upgrade list.	You want to fully replace your previous Windows operating system with Windows 2000.
Your computer has an operating system already, but you're ready to kill it and start fresh with Windows 2000 Professional.	You want to keep your existing files and preferences.
You want to create a dual-boot configuration with Windows 2000 and your current system. (Note that Microsoft recommends using two partitions to do so.)	You're ready to chance that in some rare cases, applications or hardware won't immediately work as they did under the old operating system.

DUAL-BOOTING VERSUS SINGLE BOOTING

In addition to the upgrade/fresh installation issue, you also must consider the single/dual or multiboot issue. Dual-booting is a scheme that lets you keep your old operating system and install Windows 2000 Professional as a fresh installation. When you boot up, you are given a choice of operating system to start, as you can see in Figure 4.1.

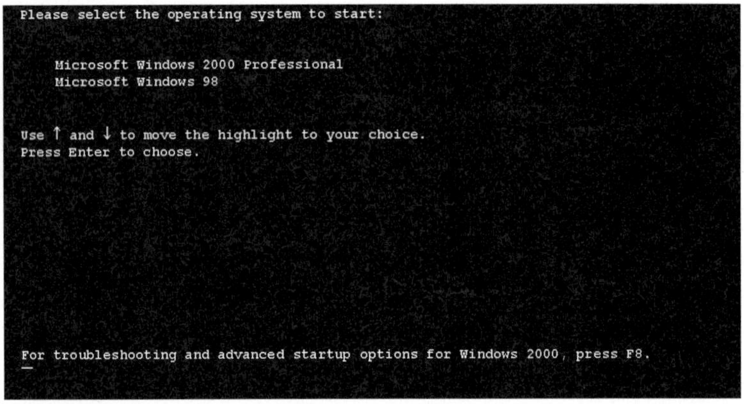

Figure 4.1
When a system is set up for dual-booting, a menu like this appears at boot time.

```
Please select the operating system to start:

    Microsoft Windows 2000 Professional
    Microsoft Windows 98

Use ↑ and ↓ to move the highlight to your choice.
Press Enter to choose.




For troubleshooting and advanced startup options for Windows 2000, press F8.
```

Windows 2000 officially supports dual-booting with the following operating systems:

- Windows NT 3.51, Windows NT 4.0
- Windows 95, Windows 98
- Windows 3.1, Windows for Workgroups 3.11

- MS-DOS
- OS/2

> **Note**
>
> Surprised that Linux isn't listed? Microsoft isn't going out of its way to help you run Linux in case you haven't guessed. But if you turn to Chapter 34, you can read more details about how to use Linux. You also learn how to dual-boot more than two operating systems.
>
> If you really want to learn all the ins and outs of dual-booting operating systems, pick up a copy of *The Multi-Boot Configuration Handbook* published by Que.

PROS OF DUAL-BOOTING

I can think of a couple of good reasons for dual-booting. The following are some of the more common reasons:

- I dual-boot on a couple of my machines because I run lots of Windows 9x tools, hardware-specific programs such as video editing programs, CD-writers or rewriters, and so on. Also, I'm always testing new programs. No matter how much I would prefer to run just a single operating system, sometimes I need to run Windows 9x to get a driver or some application to work. So, it makes sense for me to dual-boot.

- If you're a gamer, chances are you prefer the Windows 9x platform. Lots of attention went into making Windows 9x the preferred gamer's platform. Support for *DirectX*, direct access to hardware, DOS compatibility, broad hardware compatibility, and multiple monitor support are a few of the reasons. Windows 2000 does incorporate DirectX and other game-specific optimizations such as various kinds of video and audio hardware acceleration. However, a greater number of games are likely to run on the Windows 9x platform successfully than on Windows 2000. For the full scoop on compatibility with your favorite games, check with some gaming magazines or the makers of the games in question. Configuring game controllers is covered in Chapter 29, "Customizing via Control Panel Applets."

- If you're regularly testing or running lots of different kinds of software and own an abundance of hardware, or you're a new hardware junkie like me, being stuck with just a single operating system is like being in jail. Choose to dual-boot, even though this choice can cause some headaches, as described in the following section.

- If you have doubts about compatibility with your hardware or software and don't want to blow away your existing operating system, use dual-boot for awhile and then do an upgrade installation over your existing operating system when you are more confident it will work and you like Windows 2000 Professional.

CONS OF DUAL-BOOTING

The cons of dual-booting are not insignificant, but you should be aware of them before deciding to dual-boot your machine:

PART

I

CH

4

- You must reinstall many applications, particularly ones that make Registry entries, such as Office, or ones that put portions of themselves (for example, DLL files) in the operating system directory. You must run the Setup routines for each such program once for each operating system. Your applications still work in both environments, and contrary to what you might think, you don't have to duplicate all the files on disk; they install into the same directories under each operating system. Still, you must go through the process of installation again.

- Some applications that run in both environments just don't behave properly or cooperate as you would hope. This is especially true of ones that share the same data files or futz with the Registry. An example is Outlook Express (OE). I tried to set up OE5 to work under either operating system so that I could send and receive email regardless of how I booted. I tried by relocating my mail message store to a new directory and pointing OE to it, under each operating system. I did the same to the Windows Address Book (WAB) file that OE uses (it requires editing the Registry under each operating system). This trick should have worked perfectly, but it didn't. Even though Outlook Express running under each operating system knew where to look for my address and mail files (I stipulated an independent directory right off the root directory not under Windows/profiles), some data got weirded out when I switched between operating systems. The moral is that if a program itself tweaks the Registry or alerts your data files to what operating system has been working with it, and then you reboot in the other operating system (each operating system has its own Registry files, remember), unexpected incompatibilities can crop up.

Note

Some programs are, obviously, less picky because they are not as integrated into the operating system. Netscape seems to live quite peaceably in a multiboot arrangement, mail and all.

- Any application that relies on the operating systems' rights settings, user identities, or multiple profiles will likely not interrelate properly between the operating systems. As you probably know, both Windows 9x and Windows 2000 can be set up with multiple-user settings stored on the same machine. Applications that take advantage of these settings often store individual settings in the Registry and in folders such as Windows\profiles or C:\windows\application data or, in the case of Windows 2000, C:\documents and settings. In any case, because applications sometimes look to the operating system for information about a user's individual settings, whether it's gleaned from the Registry or user-specific folders such as the Desktop folder, things can go mighty awry if you're hoping to run certain applications under either operating system, and you're not a bit crafty. One way to live with this situation is to focus on using one operating system and use the other only when some application or hardware refuses to run in it.

- Upgrading to Windows 2000 pulls in all your preexisting settings, such as email accounts, LAN settings and dial-up connections, machine user accounts, and so on. If you dual-boot, you have to create them from scratch for the new operating system.

■ Security is a biggie. Is security an issue for you? Do you need to keep prying eyes at bay? Unless you're going to set up a separate partition or drive with NTFS and encryption on it, you're increasing the chances of security breaches by dual-booting. Drive, volume, partition, and file security are minimal under Windows 9x because FAT16 and FAT32 partitions can be altered by anyone who can boot the system in DOS or a DOS-based operating system. If you want to dual-boot and still have some decent security, then you should install Windows 2000 Professional on a second drive, formatted in NTFS; alternatively, you can create an NTFS partition on your main drive and install into it. Use the NTFS partition for your Windows 2000 files and encrypt sensitive data files. When installing, you are given the option of converting to NTFS. (Encryption can be performed after Windows 2000 is installed.)

→ To learn more details about file and folder encryption, **see** "Encryption: How It Works, How to Use It," **p. 1254**.

■ The only Microsoft operating systems that can read NTFS partitions are NT and Windows 2000. If you want to dual-boot and gain the advantages of NTFS, remember that you can't access any data files on the NTFS partitions when you're running DOS, Windows 3.x, or Windows 9x. (Linux, however, can read and write to NTFS partitions.)

Tip #28	Installing into a new directory leaves your existing operating system intact and lets you stipulate the target directory (such as c:\win2k). Note that you must choose the "advanced" options during Setup if you want to install this way.

PART

I

CH

4

PRECAUTIONS WHEN DUAL-BOOTING

If, after reading the pros and cons, you think you want to set up a dual-boot system, consider the following precautions in addition to those listed previously. This part is going to take a little studying, so put on your thinking cap.

■ Each operating system should be installed on a separate drive or disk partition.

■ Microsoft doesn't suggest mixing file systems in dual-boot arrangements because it complicates matters. To quote the documentation, "…such a configuration introduces additional complexity into the choice of file systems." My experience while writing this book was that mixing Windows 9x on FAT and Windows 2000 Professional on NTFS seemed to work acceptably well. Both NT 3.x and 4.0 coexisted fine with NTFS and FAT partitions/drives in the same computer in the past, even in dual-boot situations. Microsoft's warning is probably just an admonition against burdening the operating system and your applications with multiple file systems *and* multiple operating systems on the same machine. Admittedly, mixing them does complicate things. If you want to play it safe, go with the lowest common denominator of file systems for the operating systems you're installing. Typically, it is FAT or FAT32. (See the discussion on file systems later in this chapter.)

- Installation order is important in some cases. To set up a dual-boot configuration between MS-DOS/Windows 3.x or Windows 95 with Windows 2000, you should install Windows 2000 last. Otherwise, important files needed to start Windows 2000 could be overwritten by the other operating systems. For dual-booting between Windows 98 and Windows 2000, installation order is irrelevant.

- To set up a dual-boot configuration between MS-DOS/Windows 3.x or Windows 95 with Windows 2000, the primary partition (that is, the one you boot from) must be formatted as FAT. If you're dual-booting Windows 95 OSR2 or Windows 98 with Windows 2000, the primary partition must be FAT or FAT32, not NTFS. These two rules make sense because, without third-party drivers, Windows 9x can't read or exist with NTFS, and Windows 95 can't read FAT32.

- As I mentioned in the cons list earlier, non-NT operating systems (except Linux) can't access NTFS partitions. But this situation is worse than that, actually, because NTFS has been upgraded in Windows 2000. NT 4 with Service Pack 4 can access a new NTFS partition but can't read files created by Windows 2000 Professional. So, this effectively prevents dual-booting NT 3 or 4 with Windows 2000, unless you stick exclusively to the FAT file system for both operating systems.

→ To learn more details about the complications involved with dual-booting NT and Windows 2000, **see** "Precautions When Dual-Booting Windows NT and Windows 2000," **p. 133**.

- You can install Windows 2000 on a compressed drive if that drive was compressed using the NTFS disk compression utility, but not if made with DoubleSpace or DriveSpace or some other disk compressor such as Stacker. If you're going to dual-boot with Windows 9x, remember that the compressed DoubleSpace and DriveSpace partitions won't be seen by Windows 2000 Professional, and any NTFS partitions, compressed or not, will be invisible to Windows 9x without third-party drivers.

- In the slim chance that you're currently dual-booting OS/2 and DOS, and then you install Windows 2000, the Setup program reduces this to a dual-boot situation instead of a triple-boot system. Not very nice, actually. You end up with a dual-boot system with boot choices between Windows 2000 Professional and the last operating system you booted prior to installing Windows 2000 Professional. If you want to keep all three, check out the program called BootMagic from PowerQuest or System Commander. For a no-added-expense approach, you can use the OS/2 Boot Manager in its own 2MB partition. Windows 2000 switches the active partition, but you can boot with a DOS floppy and use FDISK to change it back to the boot manager partition.

- Sometimes an operating system reconfigures your hardware through soft settings. Suppose you install some new hardware and run Windows 98. That operating system will detect it and might do some software setting on the hardware that works with Windows 98 but which conflicts with Windows 2000. This problem should be rare because most hardware these days is Plug and Play-compatible and should be configurable on-the-fly as the operating system boots up. But be aware of the possibility. A good example is that two operating systems might have different video display drivers for the same video adapter, causing you to have to manually adjust the screen size and orientation when you switch between them.

PRECAUTIONS WHEN DUAL-BOOTING WINDOWS NT AND WINDOWS 2000

You must follow some weird rules when dual-booting Windows NT (3 or 4) and Windows 2000 Professional. Mostly, they have bearing on which file systems you can use. For folks testing Windows 2000 while keeping the tried and true NT 4 around, they can pose a bit of an annoyance. Here's the list:

- You should upgrade to at least NT 4.0 Service Pack 4 if you want to dual-boot with Windows 2000 Professional sharing NTFS partitions. Upgrade first and then install Windows 2000 Professional; or your NT 4 system will not boot.

- If your hard disk is formatted with only NTFS partitions, Microsoft recommends against dual-booting Windows 2000 and Windows NT. It makes this recommendation because NT and Windows 2000 Professional use slightly different versions of the NTFS specification, and they will bump into one another. Either use FAT32 or, when you're installing Windows 2000, opt *not* to upgrade to NTFS 5.

- Computers dual-booting Windows NT and Windows 2000 must have different computer names under each boot configuration if the computers are connected to an NT domain. Otherwise, the domain controller is given conflicting information about the workstation, and it deals with these two types of workstations in slightly different ways (for example, security tokens).

Note	For more detailed information about configuring your computer to dual-boot, see Chapter 34, which is devoted to this topic.

| Tip #29 | To install more than two operating systems, check the program called BootMagic from PowerQuest (www.powerquest.com). This program is included with PartitionMagic version 4 and above, or can be purchased separately. It allows you to set up multiple booting systems, including Windows 9x, Windows NT, Windows 2000, Windows 3.x, MS-DOS 5 or later, PC-DOS 6 or later, Open DOS, OS/2 3.0 or later, Linux, and BeOS.

Another program called System Commander from Vcomsystems is similar to BootMagic. It boots many different operating systems and has a lot of features. |
| --- | --- |

WHICH FILE SYSTEM: FAT, FAT32, OR NTFS?

The next major consideration on the preinstallation agenda is determining what type of file system you intend to use. The rules and regulations discussed in the preceding section might have narrowed down this choice for you. Still, you'll likely want to read about the pros and cons of the various file-keeping schemes in use on Windows 2000 machines and consider a few details on how they influence your installation.

Note

Windows 2000 doesn't know about compressed drives such as those created with DriveSpace or DoubleSpace. You have to decompress them before installing to Windows 2000. Decompressing can be a real pain if your disk space is totally packed. You might have to decompress in stages, moving data off the hard disk to backup media or another drive.

As mentioned in the previous sections on dual-booting Windows 2000 and a second operating system, it's a good idea to think about what file system you're going to use, preferably before installing Windows 2000 Professional. Although you can use utilities in Windows 2000 Professional and external utilities such as PartitionMagic to convert partitions between file systems after the fact, forethought and advance partition preparation are the better path. Let's do a little review of file systems you can use and advantages of each.

A file system is a scheme by which data files and directories (folders) are stored and retrieved on a random access disk, whether a floppy disk or hard disk. Tape and other media have file systems as well, but here I'm talking only about hard disks. Windows 2000 supports several file systems: the NT File System (NTFS) or one of the file allocation table file systems (FAT or FAT32).

In the beginning, there was FAT, and it was good. FAT is the system that DOS uses; it's been around for a long time, since the early eighties. A file allocation table is basically a table of contents of the disk that the operating system uses to look up the location of a file, even if the file is broken up in pieces (sectors) scattered across the disk's surface. The FAT scheme brought relatively simple, reliable, and efficient floppy and small hard disk storage to the PC. It's also the scheme that, unlike the Macintosh file system, brought the confining 8.3 file-naming convention that many of us learned to live with and hate.

When NT 3.x appeared, it included NTFS as an acknowledgment of the shortcomings of the FAT system. NTFS provided long filenames, more security and fault tolerance, better disk compression, support for hard disks up to 2 terabytes (that's big), and support for advanced multiple-disk arrangements such as striping and mirroring (RAID schemes). Also, as drives become larger, efficiency of disk storage doesn't fall off under NTFS as it does with FAT.

Windows 95 brought long filenames to FAT through some sleight of hand, but still the system was not good at dealing with the newer large drives and wasted a bunch of space on them when it stored tiny files. So, to both provide good backward compatibility with FAT disks and still offer support for large drives, Windows 95 OSR2 and Windows 98 both included a *third* file system called FAT32. Essentially a beefed up FAT file system, FAT32 isn't as robust as NTFS, and it's not compatible with NTFS. The FAT32 system eliminated the 2GB upper limit on partition size support (it also can run as high as 2TB) and increased effective storage capacity by lowering the cluster size on large drives. NT 4 can't read or work with FAT32, nor can DOS and Windows 3.x. However, now Windows 2000 Professional can.

The bottom line? As with NT 3 and 4, NTFS is the recommended file system for use with Windows 2000. NTFS has all the basic capabilities of FAT as well as all the advantages of

FAT32 file systems. The weird thing is that now you have to think about three different file systems when considering dual-booting. When you consider that you have at least six Microsoft operating systems to choose from and three file systems, the combinations get complex. Therefore, understanding the limitations of each is important.

Tip #30	You can convert an existing partition to NTFS during Setup, but if you want to wait, you can convert it later by using a command-line utility called convert.exe (covered later in this book). Another approach is to use PartitionMagic, which is discussed later in this chapter and in Chapter 33, "Managing the Hard Disk."

One of the prime points to remember is that if you're dual-booting, only NT systems can read NTFS partitions. If you don't care about accessing the NTFS partition from, say, Windows 98, this is not a big deal. It simply does not appear in Windows 98's Explorer and is not available from Windows 98 applications. This is the main reason Microsoft doesn't want you to mix file systems; it simply confuses people.

When you're running partitions larger than 32GB, you should really format them as NTFS. If you choose to use FAT, anything over 2GB should be formatted FAT32.

Note	File systems are terribly complex and a subject far beyond what we can cover in a Windows book. For the most part, you don't need to know more than what is presented here, unless you are naturally inclined to learn everything you can about complex topics. In that case, I recommend that you pick up a copy of *Upgrading and Repairing PCs, Eleventh Edition*, by Scott Mueller (also published by Que). Chapter 27 of this book, "Troubleshooting Your Network," takes a long look under the hood of your hard drive and explains how each of the file systems—FAT16, FAT32, and NTFS—manages your data.

PART

I

CH

4

DISK PARTITIONING TIPS

In case you don't know, disk partitioning is a scheme by which you can have a single hard disk look like multiple hard disks to the operating system. If you partition a disk into, say, two partitions, the operating system displays disks C and D rather than just C. You split up the space on the drive between the partitions based on your needs.

One of the most notable needs for disk partitioning was to accommodate operating systems that imposed limitations on the size of partitions. As hard disks grew in size, partitioning was required in order to use the entire disk. Because FAT had a limitation of 2GB, users relied on partitioning or other software driver schemes to get around this imposed top end. Another common reason for partitioning is for running dissimilar operating systems, ones that cannot read from or write to a common file system. Because each partition can have its own disk format, this could often circumambulate such requirements. One partition could be FAT, another NTFS, and another HPFS (for OS/2), and so on. Any hard disk can contain up to four partitions.

Some people use partitions for dividing up their data rather than for accommodating different file systems. You might want a partition to organize information—for example, one for backup data, one for documents and data files, one for applications only, or for the operating system only. Then you can more easily design your backup strategy.

Note

> Some people even create a separate partition to store the Windows paging (swap) file. This is discussed in Chapter 30, under the heading "Optimizing Virtual Memory (Paging) File and Registry Sizes."

Note

> When you do a new installation of Windows 2000 Professional, the Setup program looks around and automatically selects an appropriate disk partition as the destination based on size and format. You can override the choice by clicking the Advanced Options button during Setup, though.

If you're going to dual-boot, you should install on a separate partition. Either create one or use one that is already present. The reason for using a separate partition for each operating system is to prevent Setup from overwriting important files belonging to the other operating system. If you have unpartitioned (different from unused) space on your disk, Setup can create a partition during installation.

If you intend to dual-boot Windows 9x and Windows 2000, Windows 9x should be on the first partition.

→ If you're considering creating a system that is bootable in more than one operating system, **see** "Dual-Booting Versus Single Booting," **p. 128**.

The exact options you have during Setup change depending on your existing hard disk configuration. You might have as many as four options when partitioning your hard disk:

- If you have adequate unpartitioned space, you can create a new Windows 2000 partition in that space and install Windows 2000 Professional in it.

- If the hard disk is unpartitioned (no partitions at all—freshly formatted) you can create and size the Windows 2000 partition.

- If the disk does have an existing partition, but you don't care what's in it, Setup lets you delete the partition and create a new one of your chosen format for installing Windows 2000 Professional. Beware, though; deleting an existing partition creams *every file* on the partition.

- If the existing partition is large enough, you can put Windows 2000 on it. Contrary to what the Microsoft documentation says, installing on an existing partition doesn't overwrite all data on that partition. If you choose a separate directory from an existing operating system (for example, the default C:\winnt), Setup leaves any existing C:\windows directory alone. You can dual-boot, but you have to reinstall your applications. But, the better approach is to play it safe and create a new partition to install into.

Tip #31

Don't install Windows 2000 on a partition that is less than 1GB. Although Windows requires only 650MB (only!), you'll want the additional free space later for future additions and modifications to the operating system.

FILE SYSTEM CONVERSION LIMITATIONS

This section lists a few ridiculous warnings and limitations—ridiculous because these steps are not required if you use PartitionMagic. Due to limitations of Setup and Microsoft's supplied disk tools (FDISK, for example), you should be aware. First, most conversions between file systems are multistep processes involving backing up and then restoring the partitions after reformatting.

For example, although converting to NTFS during installation is easy, if you change your mind and want to revert to FAT, you have to back up all your files on the NTFS partition, reformat the partition as FAT (which erases all the files), and then restore the files from backup. The same is true of converting a FAT partition to FAT32. One workaround is to use the FAT32 converter in Windows 98 or 95 OSR2. Each of these operating systems has a tool that converts FAT16 to FAT32 quite easily and nondestructively.

Second, you can't restore an NTFS 4 (file system from NT 4) partition after you convert it to NTFS 5 (file system from Windows 2000). No easy way out on that score. There should be support soon for NTFS 5 file formats via tools like PartitionMagic to do this, though.

PART

I

CH

4

GETTING YOUR NETWORK INFORMATION TOGETHER

As part of the installation procedure, you are asked details about your network connection (assuming you're going to run the computer in question on a local area network; if not, just skip over this part).

You must supply the following information:

- Is the computer going to join a domain or a workgroup? You can answer Workgroup if you don't know and later change to a domain. Ask someone who knows. If you select the Domain option, you'll have to ask your network administrator to create a new *computer account* to allow you to join that domain or to edit your existing account to reflect the new computer name.

→ To learn more information about networking settings, **see** "Setting Your Computer Identification", **p. 729** and "Configuring Protocols," **p. 726**.

Note

A computer account is a specific type of account that an NT Server administrator makes to allow a given computer to join the domain. In an NT Server domain, both computers and users have accounts on the server.

- Are you already part of a network? If so, collect the following information, scribble it down on a piece of paper, and keep the paper handy:

  Name of your computer

  Name of the workgroup or domain

  TCP/IP address (if your network doesn't have a DHCP server)

→ If you need help configuring network settings, **see** "Answering the Networking Questions," **p. 142**.

IT'S BACKUP TIME!

Okay, so you're ready to do the installation. Need I say it? If you're upgrading from a previous version, Setup is supposed to let you back out and restore your system to its previous state if you panic in the middle. I've actually backed out of Setup a few times successfully and a few times unsuccessfully. Setup does lots of stuff to your operating system and hard disk files, and particularly if it bombs halfway through the process, things could get sticky. So ask yourself, "Do I have important data on my computer?" If so, back it up. Can you afford the downtime incurred should you need to reinstall your applications and operating system? If not, back them up, too.

Backing Up to a Disk Image

One technique I like for doing serious backups is to make a disk image of my main hard drive. With a disk image, if the drive dies or I have some other catastrophe, such as a new operating system installation goes south, I can just restore the drive to its previous state—boot tracks, operating system, data, and applications—all in one fell swoop. I use a program called DriveImage from PowerQuest for this task, though some people swear by a competing product called Norton Ghost. Either one is a powerful tool for making backups and recovering from a dead operating system. These programs work by copying your hard disk sector by sector and storing the whole image in a huge, single file on another drive. The large file they create contains all the necessary information to replace the data in the original tracks and sectors.

If you have a CD-writer, you can use a CD-R as the backup medium and tell the drive image program to break the image file into 650MB chunks. If you have a CD-RW drive, it can provide a very cost efficient (though slow) means of backing up and restoring. It also works with a second hard disk in the computer, a second partition on a hard disk, and removable media such as or Zip or Jaz drives. Another approach is to store an image on a hard disk across the LAN on another workstation, though recovering from the remote station is a little more complex than from a local drive.

If you must back up data only and don't care about reinstalling your applications or operating system (this backup approach is easier, of course), you can use some backup program or simply copy the files onto other drives using Windows Explorer or some other utility. How you back up your files depends on your current operating system. If you're running Windows 9x, one obvious approach is to employ the Windows Backup program (by choosing Start, Programs, Accessories, System Tools, Backup). You might have to install it if it's not there. To do so, open the Control Panel, choose Add/Remove Programs, and then select Windows Setup. If you're using Windows NT 3.51 or Windows NT 4.0, Windows Backup is installed by default. Remember, in Windows NT, you need a tape drive installed for the Backup tool to work. If you're in doubt about the use of the Backup program in Windows NT, check the Windows Help system.

→ To learn more details about backup strategies, **see** "Backup Tools and Strategies," **p. 1261**.

Okay, enough for the safety speech. I just remembered I was captain of the Safety Patrol in grade school. Guess I can't help myself.

FRESH INSTALLATION PROCEDURE

The three basic types of fresh installation procedures are as follows:

- Install on a brand new disk or computer system
- Wipe the disk, format it, and install
- Install into a new directory for dual-booting (see the multiboot discussion earlier in this chapter)

If you intend to use either of the first two methods, make sure you are equipped to boot your computer from the CD-ROM. Most of today's breeds of computers support booting from the CD-ROM drive. Doing so might require changing the drive boot order in the BIOS, but try it first without. With no floppy disk inserted and a clean hard disk, the CD-ROM drive should be scanned next. The Windows 2000 Professional CD-ROM is bootable and should run the Setup program automatically.

On an older computer, you might have to ensure you can boot into DOS from a floppy and have CD-ROM access. People preparing to set up Windows on older computers often overlook this point. They wipe the hard disk and then boot up with a floppy only to find the CD-ROM drive isn't recognized, so they can't run the Setup program on the CD. If you have the boot floppy for Windows 2000 Professional, your CD-ROM drive will mostly likely be recognized upon booting, assuming your CD-ROM drive is among those supported.

 If you can't get DOS to recognize your CD-ROM drive, see "DOS Won't Recognize the CD-ROM Drive" in the "Troubleshooting" section at the end of this chapter.

> **Note**
> Remember to check Chapter 3, "Getting Your Hardware and Software Ready for Windows 2000," to ensure your hardware components meet the minimum requirements to run Windows 2000.

Installation takes about 30 minutes or so on a speedy machine. Refer to the following sections if you have questions about the steps of the process. The process is fairly similar for each category of installation, with the addition of the software compatibility report when you're upgrading from an older operating system.

PART

I

CH

4

TYPICAL FRESH SETUP PROCEDURE

If you're installing into a fresh directory, and you can boot an operating system that is supported for the purpose of Setup (Windows 9x or NT), just boot up, insert the CD, and choose Install Windows 2000 from the resulting dialog box.

If Windows doesn't automatically detect the CD when you insert it, you must run the Setup program, winnt32.exe, manually like this:

1. In Windows 9x or NT 4, choose Start, Run. Or in Windows NT 3.51 or Windows 3.1, switch to the Program Manager, and choose File, Run.

2. In the resulting Run box, enter this command, replacing d with your CR-ROM drive's letter:

    d:\i386\winnt32.exe (if you're running NT 4 or Windows 9x)

    d:\i386\winnt.exe (if you're running DOS or Windows 3.1)

3. Press Enter.

4. Follow the instructions that appear.

If your computer has a blank hard disk, or your current operating system isn't supported, the process is different. You have to start the installation either by using the supplied Setup startup disks or by booting from the Windows 2000 Professional CD (this approach works only if your computer is newer, and the CD-ROM drive can be booted from). Setup automatically runs if you boot from the CD-ROM.

Follow these steps to start the Setup process from the floppies:

1. Turn off the computer.

2. Insert the Windows 2000 Setup startup Disk 1 into your A: drive.

3. Start your computer. After the computer boots and Setup runs, follow the instructions that appear.

4. On the splash screen displayed when Setup starts, choose Install Windows 2000 Professional. Notice the Advanced Options button in one of the first dialog boxes that appears after you run Setup. Clicking it brings up the options displayed in Figure 4.2.

Copying all the Setup files to the hard disk has two advantages. First, you can save yourself some time because the file copying and decompressing process is faster from the hard disk than from a CD-ROM drive. Second, the next time Windows 2000 Professional needs access to Setup files (when you add new hardware, for example), you won't have to insert the CD-ROM. Just browse to the correct directory. Copying the approximately 4,000 files (yes, that's *thousand*, amounting to

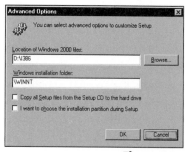

Figure 4.2

about 200MB) from the CD takes about 10 minutes on a reasonably fast system (400MHz K6-2 with an EIDE hard drive, for example).

If you have multiple partitions on your hard disk, you might want to choose the target partition in addition to the target folder. Which one you choose depends on where you want to have the operating system files stored. If you want to stipulate the partition, check the last box. You are prompted to choose the partition at the appropriate time. Microsoft recommends installing into a separate partition from your normal boot partition (typically C:) if you plan to dual-boot, incidentally. See the discussion about differing file system formats and the section about disk partitions later in this chapter, as well as Chapter 34.

Tip #32	If you want to install Windows 2000 Professional into a separate partition, make sure the partition is preexisting or that you have some unpartitioned space on your hard drive. Sorry to state the obvious, but Setup doesn't let you change the *size* of existing partitions on-the-fly, even though it does convert from FAT to NTFS and does create NTFS partitions from an unpartitioned space.
	If you have a large hard disk all in one partition (typical with today's cheap drives as they come from the factory) and want to split it, use a utility program such as FDISK, NT's Disk Administrator tool, or PartitionMagic (I highly recommend PartitionMagic). If you want to install into an NTFS partition, remember that FDISK can't create NTFS partitions. As a workaround, you either have to convert the target partition to NTFS during or after Setup or use a utility such as PartitionMagic that can make or convert FAT partitions to NTFS. Note that the NTFS partition does not have to be formatted in advance of your running Setup; as long as it exists as a partition, Setup will offer to format it as NTFS for you.
	The main advantage of having multiple partitions on a hard disk these days is to support different file system formats. You can use FAT or FAT32 on one partition to run DOS or Windows 9x, for example and use an NTFS partition for Windows 2000.

After you answer the initial questions, Setup reboots in character mode, and you have the option of repairing a Windows 2000 installation or setting up a new one. Choose the latter (but remember the Repair option if and when a system of yours dies; it reinstalls the system files for you nondestructively or lets you poke around on the drive and examine log files and such).

→ To learn more details about recovering a trashed installation of Windows 2000, **see** "The Recovery Console," **p. 1285**.

After the temp files are copied onto the hard disk (and your target partition is created and/or formatted, if necessary), the Setup Wizard runs and performs the following tasks:

- Performs hardware detection (about 10 minutes).
- Requests that the user input regional settings.
- Requests that the user input name and organization, computer name, and administrator password.
- Requests that the user input date and time settings.

PART

I

CH

4

- Installs network components (about 5 minutes) and asks for some settings. You can go with Typical settings and adjust them later because this option will service most needs. Setup also requests that you enter a workgroup or domain name. See the next section for more details.

- Installs Windows 2000 components (about 5 minutes).

- Registers components (about 10 minutes). Hang on. This part seems to take forever.

- Saves settings (less than 1 minute).

- Removes temp files (less than 1 minute).

Just follow the onscreen instructions. Check the next section about network settings if your machine is connected to a network.

 If the Windows installer crashes during the installation, see "Windows Crashes During Installation" in the "Troubleshooting" section at the end of this chapter.

 If Windows refuses to boot after the installation is complete, see "Windows 2000 Fails to Boot After Installation" in the "Troubleshooting" section at the end of this chapter.

ANSWERING THE NETWORKING QUESTIONS

As I mentioned previously, during Setup, you are asked some details about your network, and you must make a few choices. Here's some commentary on those choices:

- Computer name—Choose a computer name that is unique. It must differ from any other computer, workgroup, or domain names on the network. You'll probably want to enter your name or a name of your own choosing, though Setup supplies some cryptic name for you. You might want to coordinate naming your computer with your LAN administrator, if you have one.

- Administrator password—An Administrator account is set up automatically during each installation, just as in NT. The Administrator account is assigned full rights, allowing the administrator to create user passwords, set up new accounts, and mess with all the computer's settings as a manager. When you specify a password for the administrator, enter it, write it down somewhere safe, and remember it!

Caution

You should definitely assign a password. If you leave this field blank, anyone can get into the system settings by just entering Administrator as the username and pressing Enter with no password.

Also, after setting up this account, you should change the Administrator's username. Hackers typically try to hack this account first because they know that people often do not change the Administrator username. By knowing that the username is Administrator, they are one step closer to hacking into the system. See Chapter 26 for more information about network security.

- Networking settings—Select the Custom settings option if you want to manually configure network clients, services, and protocols. But do so only if you're an expert in these matters and know that the typical settings won't cut it. You'll probably be fine with the default settings, and you can change them later if not.

- Workgroup or computer domain—During Setup, you must join either a workgroup or a domain.

A *workgroup* is a more casual collection of connected computers than is a domain. Any computer can join a workgroup. To join a workgroup on the LAN, you just supply the workgroup name. All computers set for the same workgroup name can share files, printers, and other resources. The Setup program suggests a name, but if you already have a workgroup in your office, use that name.

A *domain* is a collection of computers that an administrator creates. Domains offer more security and control than workgroups do. Ask your system administrator if you don't know the domain settings. He or she has to create a computer account for you before you can join the domain. If you're upgrading from Windows NT, your existing computer account is used to identify you. If you have the right privileges already, you can create the account during the Setup process, but you have to enter the username and password that matches the entry in the domain controller (server) for the preexisting account. A wizard for Network Identification will walk you through joining a domain. If you run into trouble joining a domain (the network server doesn't allow it), join a workgroup first, and join the domain later.

UPGRADING OVER AN EXISTING OPERATING SYSTEM

If you're upgrading rather than performing a clean installation, the process is a bit different. Setup checks on the advisability of upgrading and asks a few more questions. This section provides a few points concerning the upgrade or dual-boot with preexisting operating systems. The steps and screens you see here are for upgrading over Windows 98. Similar screens apply to the other operating systems.

Caution

Let me add an additional note about network connections when you're upgrading. If you're upgrading a Windows 95 or Windows 98 computer that's a member of a Windows NT or Windows 2000 domain, you must check a few things in advance, or you'll end up wasting some time. Ideally, you should make sure the Windows 9x machine is connected to the domain and working properly because the user profile for the upgraded workstation needs to be stored on the domain controller.

If the domain isn't available during Setup, the user's preferences are placed in a local user account on the workstation computer, and you have to copy the profile to the domain profile after joining the domain. So, to avoid that situation, follow these steps:

1. Ensure that the computer's workgroup is set to the domain you participate in by choosing Start, Settings, Control Panel, Network. Then select the Identification tab, and verify the workgroup.

PART

I

CH

4

continues

continued

> 2. Create a computer account on the domain server if it doesn't exist already. The computer must have access to the domain during Setup.
>
> 3. Upgrade the Windows 9x machine to Windows 2000 Professional.
>
> If you don't follow these steps, you'll have to copy the profile to the domain later. To do so, choose Control Panel, System, User Profiles, Copy.

To begin the upgrade process, follow these steps:

1. Start the Setup program as explained in the "Typical Fresh Setup Procedure" section. The Setup Wizard starts, and the dialog box shown in Figure 4.3 appears.

Figure 4.3
The initial question about upgrading.

2. Assuming you want to upgrade your existing Windows installation, click Yes in the Microsoft Windows 2000 CD dialog box.

3. Clicking Yes leads to two choices. You can upgrade or do a clean installation into a new directory. Choose Upgrade. It's the recommended choice anyway, so don't fret. The following sections provide some guidance through the remainder of the upgrade process.

LICENSE AGREEMENT

When you get to the license agreement, read it and prepare to give away your first-born child. Then click I Agree.

> **Note**
>
> Corporate attorneys know that people don't read these software agreements. I've even heard reports of software in which the agreements make you promise not to write a review of the software without alerting the manufacturer first. I'm sure some interesting, precedent-setting cases will occur in the upcoming years.

COMPUTER EXAMINATION

The computer examination part of the process includes a search for incompatible hardware, software, or settings and creation of an *upgrade report* that you can print or save. Along the way, you are asked whether you have any *upgrade packs* for programs that need them in order to work properly with Windows 2000 Professional. If you have any (typically from the makers of your applications), you can report them at this point (see Figure 4.4). Packs apply only when you're upgrading from Windows 95 or 98, and you are prompted to insert the packs during the installation process.

Figure 4.4
Adding upgrade packs for applications. Click Add to create the list of upgrades you have on disk.

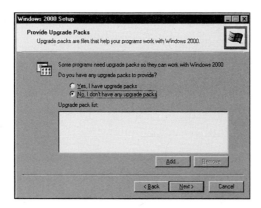

UPGRADING THE FILE SYSTEM

Now comes a biggie: Should you upgrade to NTFS?

If you intend to use other operating systems such as Linux, DOS, Windows 3.x, or Windows 9x on the same drive, you can't upgrade to NTFS. Well, that's not exactly true. You can, but it's a hassle to return the drive to its earlier FAT16 or FAT32 state. Microsoft doesn't provide the utilities to do so, but you can use a third-party utility program such as PartitionMagic from PowerQuest. (It's a great tool, by the way. I recommend that everyone have a copy for making, removing, and resizing partitions nondestructively on-the-fly.) If you want to play the middle ground between FAT and NTFS, choose not to upgrade to NTFS. After installation of the operating system, you can create an NTFS partition on your drive for storing sensitive data you want to better protect. You could also convert the whole drive to NTFS later after you get used to Windows 2000 Professional and migrate out of your FAT dependence.

→ If you want to know more information about deciding whether you should change file systems, **see** "Which File System: FAT, FAT32, or NTFS?" **p. 133**. Also, Chapters 33 and 34 contain additional information about file systems and formats.

UPGRADE REPORT

Next, Setup creates an upgrade report summarizing everything that might not work with Windows 2000 Professional and giving you a chance to point to files the makers of your hardware or software might have available (check their Web sites) for the update. (See Figure 4.5.)

PART
I
CH
4

Tip #33	If you don't have upgrade files, you might skate by anyway. In Figure 4.5, for example, notice the two potential compatibility problems on one of my machines, but they didn't cripple the installation.

Figure 4.5
Possible conflicts with the new operating system are reported before the installation begins in earnest.

The upgrade report is actually a pretty spiffy HTML-based dialog box detailing what might not work anymore if you go ahead and do the installation. It has a link to the Windows 2000 Hardware Compatibility List (HCL) for easily checking to see whether the Brand X video board you just bought really won't work or if the compatibility test was just out of date. Do check the list, assuming your computer is on the Internet.

Although your list might be long, it might not be catastrophic news. Most of the stuff my systems showed turned out not to cause problems. For example, I know that the video card I have is supported, as is the Epson printer. Both were listed as potentially problematic. Most of the other things such as shares, Recycle Bin, backup files, and DOS startup file issues were no big deal. The new operating system takes care of most of these issues, mostly due to Plug and Play and good hardware detection during Setup. Plus, I probably did have some old junk in my AUTOEXEC.BAT and CONFIG.SYS files that's no longer valuable. The DOS exceptions were Sound Blaster drivers that DOS-based games used—the kinds of things that most Windows 2000 Professional users are not going to worry about.

If you see anything listed about your video card, disk controller, sound card, or tape backup, you might want to check on those items a little more closely and download a driver update pack from the manufacturer before you update. Basically, you should take seriously anything that might suggest incompatibility that will prevent basic operation or bootability of the system, and you can acknowledge but not sweat the rest.

Tip #34

> If you just want to run the upgrade report and not execute the complete Setup program, insert the installation CD in the CD-ROM drive, or connect over the LAN to the CD. Then issue the following command:
>
> `winnt32 /checkupgradeonly`
>
> This command generates just the report.

As with the fresh installation instructions, you can just follow the rest of the instructions as they come up on the screen. Your computer might have to restart several times in the process. If the computer seems to be stuck, wait several minutes to ensure it's really hung.

Then reboot it. Windows 2000 Professional uses an "intelligent" Setup feature that should restart where it left off. Eventually, after much spinning of your CD and blinking of hard disks lights, the system will boot up in Windows 2000. You can then turn to Chapter 5, "Using the Windows 2000 Interface," to set up an account and begin using it.

UPGRADING A WINDOWS 3.X MACHINE

To upgrade a Windows 3.x machine, think carefully. Check Chapter 3 for hardware requirements for Windows 2000 Professional. Assuming the machine can cut the mustard, you can do the following:

1. Upgrade to Windows 95 or 98.

2. Try to get everything working correctly before moving ahead, but if you can't get a piece of hardware to work, don't fret. The upgrade to Windows 2000 Professional might solve the problem.

3. After you have successfully upgraded to 9x, do the upgrade to Windows 2000 Professional.

4. Use the system troubleshooters in Windows 2000 Professional to solve driver and hardware problems if devices are not working properly after the installation.

Can you dual-boot a Windows 3.x machine? Sure. Just install into a second partition or directory (preferably a partition). Setup then creates BOOT.INI (the multiboot instructions, stored on the root of the primary disk drive), leaving DOS/Windows 3.x as one of the boot options, with Windows 2000 Professional being the other option.

→ If you are considering having your machine dual-boot Windows 3.x and Windows 2000, **see** "Dual-Booting Versus Single Booting," **p. 128**, and **see** Chapter 33, which discusses setting up multiboot machines in great detail.

PART

I

CH

4

MAKING REPLACEMENT STARTUP FLOPPIES

You don't need the startup floppies unless you can't boot up the machine from the hard disk or can't initiate Setup from your CD-ROM, hard disk, or across the network for some reason. If you do need them, and you've lost the ones that come with the CD or yours are damaged, you can make a fresh set.

Note

Although Setup startup disks contain different information than the Emergency Repair Disk, you can use an Emergency Repair Disk from Windows 95 OSR 2 or Windows 98 to boot up a system to gain CD-ROM support.

Follow these steps to create new startup floppies:

1. Collect four blank, 1.44MB formatted 3.5-inch disks. Label them Setup Disk 1, Setup Disk 2, and so forth.

2. Insert the first disk into the floppy disk drive, and insert the Windows 2000 Professional CD into a machine with a workable CD-ROM drive.

3. Choose Start, Run, and type the following:

   ```
   d:\bootdisk\makeboot.exe a:
   ```

   (Replace d with the letter of your CD-ROM drive and a with the letter of your floppy drive.)

4. Follow the onscreen directions.

TROUBLESHOOTING

WINDOWS CRASHES DURING INSTALLATION

I tried to install Windows 2000, but it crashes while installing.

The trick with any Windows Setup is to get it to complete without crashing or freaking out about some setting you try to make during the process. Hold off doing anything fancy—stuff like network settings, screen savers, video display settings, and so on—until well after you have finished the installation. Just get through the installation as simply as possible, and then poke around and tweak your settings later.

Windows Setup is intelligent. It keeps tabs on where in the process things stalled. Simply restarting Setup should result in its picking up where it left off. This, at least, is some consolation. Next time around, keep it simple, and get by with as few settings as possible. Just make the necessary ones. Sometimes a machine will hang when you're playing with the Regional settings, language, or something you can easily change later. Also, avoid the Advanced settings if you don't need them.

At a certain stage, Setup switches from character-based screens to graphical screens (GUI mode). If, at this point, Setup crashes, your video display card might not be compatible with Windows 2000. Make sure you checked your system's innards against the Hardware Compatibility List, as discussed earlier in this chapter. Also, ensure that you meet the minimum requirements in terms of RAM and hard disk space. If you get a blue screen of death and a Stop error, Windows generally will give you some arcane troubleshooting advice, such as a message reading Video Display Driver Cannot Be Loaded. Maybe your video card isn't supported. Check the hardware compatibility list again.

DOS WON'T RECOGNIZE THE CD-ROM DRIVE

I can't get DOS to recognize my CD-ROM drive, so I can't install Windows 2000.

The following are a few other workarounds for those weird occasions when you just can't get DOS to recognize your CD-ROM drive:

- The preferred method is to create the boot floppies from the Windows 2000 Professional CD. See the section "Making Replacement Startup Floppies," earlier in this chapter.

- Create an Emergency Startup Disk (ESD) from Windows 98. As of Windows 98, popular CD-ROM drivers are dumped on the ESDs when you create them by choosing Control Panel, Add/Remove Programs, Startup Disk.

- Use an old DOS startup disk with installable device drivers for the CD-ROM drive on it as stipulated in the AUTOEXEC.BAT and CONFIG.SYS files on the floppy. Creating such a disk typically takes a little knowledge of MSCDEX command-line arguments, and you need the driver supplied with the CD-ROM drive.

- Using your existing operating system or a floppy disk with network client software on it, connect to the network and run Setup from a remote CD-ROM drive. This process can take some work if you have to boot in DOS, however. You must know lots of network settings and use the command line to get them going. Your network administrator might have to tell you the exact path of the setup command. You're looking for the file winnt32.exe on the CD-ROM when you are told or you discover the correct path to the drive. When you find that file, either double-click it from a folder window, or use the Run command, type in the full pathname of the file (for example, computername\\D:winnt32.exe), and press Enter.

- Another solution is to copy all the appropriate CD-ROM files to your hard disk one way or another (even using LapLink or Microsoft's direct-cable connection between two computers are two approaches I've used successfully). You need all the files in the root directory of the CD and everything in the I386 folder (assuming you're installing into a Wintel box.) When files are on the hard disk, switch to the folder you stored the file in, and run winnt32.exe.

WINDOWS 2000 FAILS TO BOOT AFTER INSTALLATION

I got through the installation, but Windows 2000 won't boot now.

You can take several steps when an installation doesn't seem to have worked out. As I mentioned in the first troubleshooting tip, you can try to determine when Setup failed. If, by observation, you can determine the point at which it failed, you might be able to avoid whatever it was you did the first time around. Restart Setup, and see whether reinstalling will help.

While you're installing again, note that Setup asks whether you want to load any SCSI drivers at a certain point. At about this point, you can opt not to install support for power management. Try opting out of the power management. You can install it later by choosing Control Panel, Add New Hardware. Sometimes power management can cause problems on a machine that doesn't support it correctly, or not at all.

The Recovery Console built into Windows 2000 allows attempted repairs to what could be a damaged Windows 2000 installation. Refer to Chapter 33 for coverage of the Recovery Console.

Finally, you can contact Microsoft. They might have you make copies of the setup logs (there are several of them): setuplog.txt, setupapi.log, and setupact.log.

These files are modified as setup progresses and are time stamped in the left margin of the log file. Look to see whether there are any long delays in the setuplog.txt file. Registering DLL files can take awhile on some systems. When Setup appears to be hung, press Shift+F10 to open a DOS window, and then open the log in a text editor and examine it. Recheck the log file a few minutes later to see if anything has changed, noting the time stamps. You just might have to wait longer before bailing out.

TIPS FROM THE WINDOWS PROS: RUNNING SETUP IN UNATTENDED MODE

If you intend to install Windows 2000 on a bevy of computers, answering all these questions repeatedly can prove an exercise in inefficiency. Instead, you can create a special script to automate the process. A Setup Manager Wizard will help you design the script, or you can base yours on the example supplied on the Windows 2000 CD.

The script you create is called an *answer file*, and it is used to install Windows 2000 Professional in so-called *unattended mode*. In this mode, nobody needs to interact with the computer during installation. The script simply supplies the answers that you would normally have to enter from the keyboard, such as acceptance of the license agreement, workgroup and computer name, network details, and so on. The script can fully automate or only partially automate the Setup process. For example, you might want to supply defaults for the user but let him or her change them. A script can additionally stipulate the creation of special folders, execution of programs upon completion of Setup, location of Setup files, and more.

Of course, creating answer files makes sense only when you're installing Windows 2000 Professional on multiple computers with a hardware complement that you know will install Windows 2000 properly; otherwise, you can waste more time trying to troubleshoot what happened in your absence. As you know, sometimes unexpected developments occur during Setup that might require intervention. The Setup routine is fairly successful at detecting hardware when doing installations, so it's worth a try if you're deploying a large number of machines.

The best way to check out all the deployment support tools is as follows:

1. Go to the I386\support\tools folder on the CD.

2. Open the deploy.cab file (if you have WinZip installed, it opens and displays the items), or you can right-click the .cab file and choose Explore. Figure 4.6 shows the contents.

3. Create a folder on your hard disk, and extract the contents there. (You can't run the Setup Manager Wizard—setupmgr.exe—from the CD.)

Note

You should pay special attention to Deptool.chm and Unattend.doc. Start your reading there to learn about creating answer files.

4. You can run the Setup Manager Wizard by double-clicking setupmgr.exe. The program runs and displays the dialog shown in Figure 4.7.

Figure 4.6
The contents of the deploy.cab file. Note in particular the Help file and the unattend.doc file.

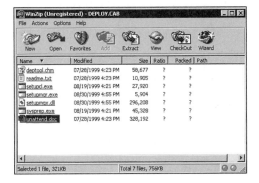

Figure 4.7
The Setup Manager Wizard creates answer files for you to use in automating Windows 2000 Professional (or Server) installations.

For detailed information about creating an answer file, see the Microsoft Windows 2000 Unattended Setup Parameters Guide on your Microsoft Windows 2000 CD under \support\toolsdeploy.cab\unattend.doc. This file provides the complete list of unattended Setup parameters to use in Windows 2000 unattended answer files. Included in this documentation are the necessary section headings, parameter values, definitions of the parameter functions, and examples.

You also might want to look at the file named unattend.txt, located in the I386 folder on the Windows 2000 CD. You might want to use it as a template. Typically, you should at least modify variables such as computer name, username, company name, passwords, and workgroup. However, there are many more possibilities.

When you have your answer file together, you can start Setup this way:

```
Winnt32.exe /unattend[num]:[answer_file]
```

or

```
Winnt32.exe /unattend parameter
```

Tip #35

The Setup program, winnt32.exe, is very flexible and has a number of options, most of which apply to bulk and network installations. If you're interested in reading about them, run the program from a command line, using the ? argument; just type the following:

```
D:winnt32 /?
```

This command produces a window listing all the command-line variations.

GETTING YOUR WORK DONE

CHAPTER 5

USING THE WINDOWS 2000 INTERFACE

In this chapter

WHO SHOULD READ THIS CHAPTER?

Before going on in this book, make sure you've read the introduction and installed Windows correctly on your computer (installation is explained in Chapter 4, "Installing Windows 2000"). When those hurdles are completed, you can return here to learn about the user interface. You may wonder why an advanced book such as this would include coverage of something as basic as the user interface. This is a decision that was primarily driven by the knowledge that many users of Windows 2000 Professional will be upgrading from Windows 3.x or NT 3.x machines that have seen their day. For those users, savvy as they may be with Windows concepts, the Windows 9x, NT 4, and 2000 interfaces are different enough to warrant full coverage. Even if you're a veteran user of the newer-style interface of Windows 9x and NT 4, you may be unaware of some features have been woven into Windows 2000 Professional; therefore, you should at least skim through this chapter.

As you read along, feel free to experiment because that's how you'll learn the most quickly. Experience is the best teacher, especially with computers, and you probably won't blow up your computer by trying stuff. When we think of a suggestion to keep the fire department (or more likely the tech support professional at $100 an hour) away from your house, we'll let you know.

Of course, you can take a break from your experimenting at any time by closing this tome of deathless prose (bookmark the page, first) and turn off or log off your computer. If you don't know how, just jump to the end of this chapter and read the section titled "Exiting Windows Gracefully." Also, if at any time you don't understand how to use a Windows command or perform some procedure, read the section in the next chapter that covers the built-in Windows Help service.

STARTING WINDOWS 2000

At this point, you should have Windows 2000 Professional installed and working. If you ran into trouble, you have our sympathies at the very least, if not our help in person. You can always write us by visiting our Web site at www.helpwin2k.com. You can send an email from there as well as find useful information and links about various versions of Windows. We try to keep it up-to-date and add new insights into the functionality of Windows as we discover new features.

After rebooting several times at the end of installation, the Setup Wizard finally does a real, normal boot. This takes a little time, and you may see a blank screen, the little dots (or progress bar) appear across the top or bottom of the screen, slowly, one at a time. (Each dot represents a device driver loading into memory.)

During this first boot, you can create a new user account as well as register your copy of Windows 2000 with Microsoft. When you're fully in, it's time to make initial adjustments to the operating system, check your network settings, screen and desktop schemes, and so on, and poke around in your new operating system.

Note

Be sure to remove any floppy disk you might have in the A: drive, and the Windows 2000 CD from the CD-ROM drive. Otherwise, the computer might not boot up Windows 2000 properly. It may try to boot from the A: drive or from the bootable Windows 2000 Professional CD.

LOGGING IN TO WINDOWS 2000

Logging in the first time for new accounts is different than if you upgraded from a previous operating system. If you upgraded, Setup transfers your user profile from the previous operating system and uses it to create a new user account in Windows 2000 Professional. In that case, simply log in using your old username and password (see Figure 5.1).

Figure 5.1
Signing in using an old user account name and password.

If you didn't have a user account under the previous operating system, you'll have to create a new one. Only a user with administrative privileges can create new accounts, so this means you have to log in as Administrator. If you didn't have a preexisting identity from the previous operating system, you wouldn't have been able to log in by now anyway, unless you used the Administrator name and password you created during setup.

In any case, assuming you now see the logon box, do the following to log on as Administrator and set up a new account for yourself:

1. Press Ctrl+Alt+Delete if prompted to do so. Note that this does not cause the computer to reboot in NT and Windows 2000 Professional. It's a security measure that clears out "Trojan horse" viruses that can reside in memory.

PART

II

CH

5

Trojan Horses

You might recall from your past readings, or perhaps high school history class, that the term *Trojan horse* derives from a portion of Homer's *Iliad*, in which the Greeks offer a huge wooden horse to the Trojans, their enemy, supposedly as a peace offering. Only after the Trojans drag the horse inside their city walls do they realize they've been invaded. In the dead of night, Greek soldiers disgorged from the horse's hollow belly, threw open the city gates, and allowed their Greek soldiers to pour in and capture Troy.

In computers, a Trojan horse is not dissimilar. It provides an enemy's clever entry into your computer, masquerading as something that it isn't. Once in your computer, Trojan Horses act like viruses (however, they don't replicate and are complete, standalone applications), waiting to do their damage. For example, they may cleverly present a dialog box that looks like the logon box, waiting for an unsuspecting user to type in a name and password, only to share it with the hacker for a later break-in. Others can alter or destroy data on your

continues

continued

hard disk or can tunnel past your *firewall (page 831)* and into your company's servers. Some Trojan horses could even attack another computer system outside of your office, while making you appear to be the perpetrator of the crime. One of the most insidious types of Trojan horses is a program that claims to rid your computer of viruses but instead introduces viruses onto your computer.

The Ctrl+Alt+Delete key combination forces Windows 2000 to clear memory and any potential Trojan horses residing there. This only works if this feature is enabled. (See "Exiting Windows Gracefully," later in this chapter.)

2. Type the Administrator password that you created during setup. (You wrote it down, didn't you?)

3. Press Enter.

Windows 2000 Professional starts, and the Welcome screen appears. At this point you can now take the tour of Windows 2000 Professional to learn about new features, or you can install a new Internet connection if you're not yet connected. The tour requires the CD to be inserted and takes about 10 minutes to read. There isn't much, if anything, in the tour that isn't covered in Chapter 1, "Introducing Windows 2000 Professional," however.

When you're finished taking the tour or using the Connection Wizard, you should move ahead and create a user account (or multiple user accounts, if you're planning to be the system administrator for this computer). The next section explains how to create new accounts.

CREATING A NEW USER ACCOUNT

Although anyone who wants to use a computer could simply log in using the Administrator account, it doesn't make much sense to give everyone in your home or office the ability to completely trash the system. Therefore, you'll want to safeguard the Administrator password, sign in as Administrator, and create user accounts for each user. The Guest account can be used for visitors, ascribing to them minimal rights, but even that account has its dangers. It's safest to set up personal accounts for each user. This system of accounts empowers an administrator to closely keep track of user activities, and it can be fine-tuned to prevent or permit access to programs, folders, printers, and other resources on a person-by-person basis.

→ To learn more about managing user accounts, **see** "Guest and Administrator Accounts," **p. 1195**.

User profiles are stored in the computer in a user database, in which each account is identified by a user name and a password, both of which the user types when logging on to the computer. There are two types of user accounts in Windows 2000: domain and local. During setup, you were asked whether the computer is a member of a domain. If you answered yes, you'll be creating a domain-based user. If not, you'll be creating user accounts for the individual computer, and if you're networked, you'll be part of a peer workgroup rather than a server-based domain. Part IV, "Networking," discusses the differences between domains and workgroups in detail. If you're currently in doubt about which you're connected to, skip to that part of the book and do some reading, or you can ask someone who knows the topology of your network.

> **Caution**
>
> You should create user accounts on the workstation machine only if your computer isn't part of a domain. If it is part of a domain, the administrator running the domain must create an account for your computer before you install Windows 2000 as well as create an account for you as a user. Contact your network administrator before you install Windows 2000 Professional onto a fresh computer with no previous account on the domain. This will save you time and trouble later on.

To create a new user account, follow these steps:

1. Click the Start button, point to Settings, and then click Control Panel.
2. Double-click Users and Passwords.
3. Click Add. The Add New User Wizard appears.
4. Follow the instructions that appear. Figure 5.2 shows an example of a new user. Enter the user name and password and then choose the level of access you want to give the user.

Figure 5.2
Adding a new user account on a computer that's not in a domain.

After you've added your user account, you're ready to log off as Administrator and log on using your new account. Here's how:

1. Click Start, Shut Down.
2. From the drop-down list, choose Log off Administrator and click OK.
3. Log in using the new name and password.

REGISTERING YOUR COPY OF WINDOWS 2000

After you're installed and signed in, you can register from the Welcome dialog box, which should be in the middle of your screen. This means of registration is for those who have a modem or are online. If you can scare up the registration card in the Windows 2000 Professional box, fill it out and mail it in.

PART

II

CH

5

Why register? If you call or contact Microsoft tech support for help, they'll want to look you up in their database to see whether you're a registered user. They probably won't hassle you if you're not, but you never know. It depends on who you get on the phone. Registering also gives you access to Windows Update, the online extension of Windows 2000 on the World Wide Web.

According to Microsoft, "registration ensures that you receive product support, product update information, and other benefits. The process takes only a few minutes." You can decide. You can register from this box now, or you can close the box and open it later by following these steps:

1. Clicking Start, Run.
2. Enter Welcome and press Enter.
3. The Welcome box appears. Click Register Now.

Another way to run the Registration Wizard is to enter regwiz /r in the Run box.

If you want to register now, just click through the steps and follow the directions onscreen. When asked whether you want to send information about the system inventory, you can choose Yes. It's not like Microsoft is going to steal your Visa card number. Just knowing what kind of hardware is in the computer helps Microsoft be more accurate in supporting typical system configurations in the future.

USING WINDOWS 2000–INTERFACE UPDATE

Now that you're logged in and running, you can start using Windows 2000 to get familiar with it and maybe even get some work done. If you're an experienced Windows user, especially if you've used Windows 9x before, you can skim this chapter to get the gist of the new features of Windows 2000. The interface is essentially the Win9x GUI, with only a few twists, such as smart Start menus. If, on the other hand, you're new to Windows, make sure you read this chapter with some attention to detail because it covers Windows 2000 interface concepts and skills that you'll need to have no matter what your line of work is or what you intend to do with your computer. A solid grasp of these concepts will also help you understand and make the best use of the rest of this book.

WINDOWS IN BRIEF

Just as you can have different files on your desk that you switch between during the day, you can switch between windows easily, just by pointing to one and clicking the left mouse button on it or by using some shortcuts that we'll cover later. On a decent computer, you can easily have 10 to 20 documents open at once. Most of what you'll do onscreen to run and work with your program is achieved using the mouse pointer or the menu commands.

A *window* is simply the frame or box that an application or document is displayed in on your monitor (see Figure 5.3).

Figure 5.3
Windows are frames that hold information of some sort on the screen.

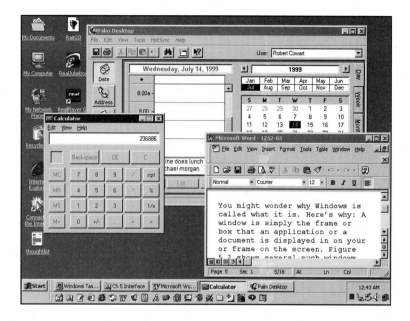

To expedite the sharing of information between documents, Windows includes an internal facility called the Clipboard. If you've used any version of Windows in the last 10 years, you know what this is about already. Using the cut and paste method, you can share data, pictures, video, sounds, and text among similar, or even dissimilar, document types. For example, you can copy a section of a photograph from a PhotoShop window into a company report or a Web page–design window you're working in. You can also take some spreadsheet numbers and dump them into an email you're writing about how quickly your Internet stocks are growing! Essentially, Windows is the glue that lets dissimilar programs work together. Due to the common interface between all Windows programs, once you learn to use one Windows program, learning subsequent ones is fairly easy. This is because similar techniques (menus, buttons, icons, and so on) are used to control most all Windows applications.

However, Windows is more than just an operating system and graphical user interface. Like other versions of Windows, Windows 2000 Professional includes a broad collection of useful programs, from a simple arithmetic calculator to fancy system and network management tools. This list also includes a word-processing program called WordPad, a drawing program called Paint, Internet Explorer for cruising the Web, Outlook Express for email, NetMeeting for video and telephone conferencing over the Internet, utilities for keeping your hard disk in good working order, and a data-backup program—just to name a few.

PARTS OF THE WINDOWS 2000 SCREEN

At this point, you should be booted and signed in. Now the Windows 2000 starting screen (called the *Desktop*) appears, as shown in Figure 5.4. Take a look at your screen and compare

PART

II

CH

5

it to the figure. If you're used to the Windows 3.x desktop, this is quite different. You don't have the Program Manager (or File Manager) to run your programs from but instead have an interface that emulates a physical desktop and office a bit more.

Your screen might look a bit different from the one shown in the figure, but the general landscape will be the same. You may see a Welcome to Windows 2000 box, accompanied by music and an optional tour of Windows, or get some help about Windows. Just click the close button (the X in the upper-right corner) to close the Welcome box. We'll discuss the Help system and the Windows tour later. When you close the Welcome box, it will ask you whether you want to see it every time you boot up and log on. That's up to you. Click Yes or No. If you find it a nuisance, click No, but you might want to click Yes so that it runs the next time you start up your computer. You can always turn it off later.

Figure 5.4
The Windows 2000 desktop. This is where you can organize your work and interact with your computer.

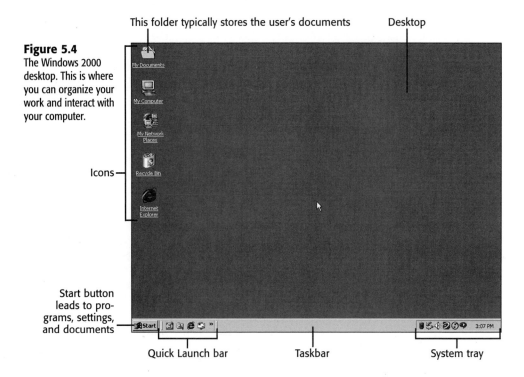

This folder typically stores the user's documents   Desktop

Icons—

Start button leads to programs, settings, and documents

Quick Launch bar   Taskbar   System tray

Note

If you or someone else has used your Windows 2000 setup already, it's possible that some open windows will come up on the screen automatically when Windows boots (starts up). It's also possible that you'll see more icons on the Desktop than what's shown in Figure 5.4, depending on the options chosen when Windows 2000 was installed and whether other applications were loaded before upgrading.

There are three primary areas of the screen to explore: the Desktop, icons, and the taskbar (and, optionally, the channel bar). All you really must know to use Windows 2000's interface are these essential building blocks and then how to manipulate a window and its commands. If you've been using Windows 3.x, you already know the latter. You just need to be brought up to speed on the advanced 9x interface specifics. As mentioned in the introduction, for the purposes of this book, we assume that you have basic Windows proficiency and have either been using Windows 3.x or 9x. Therefore, we skip subjects such as how to click the mouse, what double-clicking is, and how to scroll a window. (We're as relieved as you are.)

THE DESKTOP

Let's start with the Desktop. This is your home base while doing your work in Windows. Unlike the Program Manager in 3.x, it's always on the screen as the backdrop, and you can put files and folders right on it for storage. It's analogous to a real desktop in this way. It also serves as a handy temporary holding area for files you might be copying from, say, a floppy disk to a hard disk folder. Like the Mac, the Windows 2000 Professional Desktop has a trash can (called *Recycle Bin*) that holds deleted work objects such as files and folders until you empty it. It also has often needed items such as a path to network computers (now called *My Network Places* instead of *Network Neighborhood* in Windows 9x) and My Computer. Just as in Windows 3.x, you'll do all your work in Windows 2000 Professional using graphical representations of your work projects (called *icons*).

The Desktop analogy is a bit corny, but once you get used to the Desktop, you'll wonder how you ever got along without it, especially if you're a veteran Windows 3.x user. It's a very easy medium for organizing your various activities. For example, you can put your most-used folders and documents right on the Desktop so that you don't have to fish around in your hard disk directories to get to them. Every time you boot up, they're waiting for you on the Desktop.

ICONS

As you probably know, the small graphical representations of your programs and files are called *icons*. Windows 2000 uses icons to represent folders, documents, programs, and groups of settings (such as dial-up connections). For example, Recycle Bin and My Computer are icons. Graphically, icons got a facelift in Windows 2000 Professional, compared to Windows 3.x. They were also given additional functionality. They can now directly represent items in your computer, or they can be shortcuts to those items. *Shortcuts* provide easy means of getting to programs and documents from multiple locations without duplicating the files themselves. You simply duplicate the icons, which don't take up much disk space. Shortcuts are discussed later.

Icons that look like little folders are just that—folders. In Windows 9x and Windows 2000, directories were renamed *folders*. This is a term taken from the Mac OS. You use folders to keep related files together, and they can be nested, just like directories in DOS or Windows 3.x. Folders have replaced Program Manager groups, too. The functionality is the same; only the terms have changed.

Another kind of icon is called a *taskbar button*. These buttons appear on the taskbar at the bottom of the screen when you minimize the program or window to get it off the screen for

PART

II

CH

5

the moment. Technically, it's called a *minimized window*. We'll cover this kind of icon later, when we discuss the taskbar and running your programs.

> **Note**
>
> Just as in Windows 9x and NT, when minimized, a program is still running and a document is still open. They're just removed from display on the screen. For example, a program can be rendering a video effect, fetching your email, or calculating a spreadsheet while minimized.

MINIMIZE, MAXIMIZE, AND CLOSE BUTTONS

In Windows 3.x there were only two buttons in the upper-right corner of any window, and they had small up and down arrows in them. These were the *minimize* and *maximize* buttons, for making a window as large or as small as possible. In Windows 9x and 2000, there are three buttons, and they look a bit different. Minimize and maximize are still there, but a single-click close button has been added. This new button eliminates the need for double-clicking the control box or choosing File, Close to close an application (these techniques varied too much between applications, thus confusing users).

Using these new buttons, you can close any application (including a DOS box) with a single click on the "X" button.

Assuming that you're looking at a maximized window, the button with the small horizontal line in it is the minimize button. The one to its right is the maximize button, and the third one is the close button. These are little control buttons with which you quickly change the size of a window, as you'll learn in a moment.

There are essentially three sizes a window can be

- Minimized—The window becomes an icon at the bottom of the Desktop (or of the application's window if it's a child window), where it's ready to be opened again and takes up a minimum of screen space.

- Normal—The window is open and takes up a portion of the Desktop, the amount of which is determined by how you manually size the window, as explained in the next section. This is also called the *restored* size.

- Maximized—The window takes up the whole Desktop. When you maximize a document window, it expands to take up the entire application window. This might not be the entire screen, depending on whether the application's window is maximized. After a window has been maximized, the maximize button changes to the *restore* button (an icon of two overlapping windows). Restored size is neither full screen nor minimized. It's anything in between.

The usual mouse techniques for resizing a window apply. Just grab the edge of a window (the cursor turns to a double-headed arrow when you're positioned appropriately) and drag it. Release when it reaches the size you want. Some windows in the new interface have a serrated tab in the lower-right corner, thus making it a little easier to grab them for resizing.

With Windows 2000 Professional's "full window drag" effect, you'll see the contents of the window resize as you drag the window edge, or when you drag the whole window. To drag the whole window, grab its title bar (it must be sized smaller than the screen).

Note

A much overlooked trick is one that toggles a window from full screen to restored size. Just double-click the title bar of the window.

DIALOG BOX CHANGES

As you might know, when Windows or a Windows application wants input from the user or issues an alert, it presents a *dialog box* onscreen. For example, a dialog box will always appear when you select a command with an ellipsis (…) after it. Dialog boxes have evolved over the years, especially in the Windows 9x interface, and they continue to evolve in Windows 2000. Two primary changes to dialog boxes are described in the following subsections.

TABS NOW ADDED TO DIALOG BOXES

Dialog boxes are sometimes confusing and overwhelm the user with too many input choices. The newer 9x interface helps organize overzealous dialog boxes by using *tabs* (see Figure 5.5). Related settings are stored on each tab. Just click a tab to bring up its settings.

Figure 5.5
Newer-style dialog boxes have tabbed pages to help organize settings.

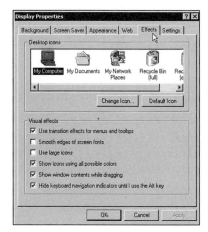

PART

II

CH

5

THE NEW FILE OPEN AND SAVE AS BOXES

The 9x interface also updated the look of File dialog boxes (sometimes called simply *File boxes* or *Browse boxes*). These are the boxes you use when opening and saving documents. Choosing File, Open from almost any Windows program will bring one up on your screen, asking which document file you want to open and where it is on your computer or network. File boxes went through a major redesign after it was finally figured out that novices were thoroughly confused by them.

Now the new design function is more intuitive and very similar to the file boxes used on the Mac. Some older programs, when run under Windows 2000 Professional, will still use the old-fashioned 3.x-style File boxes and might not even allow long file names to be displayed or entered. You'll just have to live with it. Check out the new Open dialog box in Figure 5.6. The list of items down the side (My Computer, My Documents, and so on) is new in Windows 2000 Professional, although the rest of it is much the same as in Windows 9x. The new iconic bar is known as the *Places bar* and was first introduced in Office 2000.

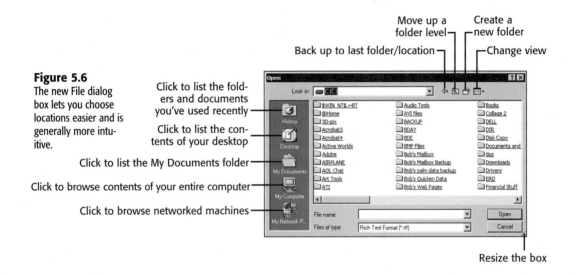

Figure 5.6
The new File dialog box lets you choose locations easier and is generally more intuitive.

Move up a folder level
Create a new folder
Back up to last folder/location
Change view

Click to list the folders and documents you've used recently
Click to list the contents of your desktop
Click to list the My Documents folder
Click to browse contents of your entire computer
Click to browse networked machines

Resize the box

Note

If you're new to Windows, mark this section with a paper clip and refer to it when you must save or open a file for the first time. File boxes can be confusing.

The redesigned File dialog boxes in the 9x interface were a welcome relief from the confusion caused by the older boxes. Saving and finding files is still confusing to lots of folks, but that's the nature of computers, and especially files, to the masses. The new File box at least helps cut down the work. One click on My Documents will get you to your document files, assuming you store them there. (More about My Documents in a bit.)

USING THE NEWER-STYLE FILE BOX   Here's a blow-by-blow account on using the new-style File box when you're opening or saving files:

1. Notice the Look In section at the top of the box. This tells you which folder's contents is being displayed in the window below. You can click this drop-down list to choose the drive or folder you want to look in, if the buttons on the left don't offer the options you want. (Again, some programs won't offer these buttons.) The drop-down list includes My Documents, My Computer, all your drives, and the network. Basically you're just trying to drill down from the top level (My Computer) to find the folder where you want to store or retrieve a file (see Figure 5.7).

Figure 5.7
You can quickly get to areas of storage via the Look In list or the buttons on the left.

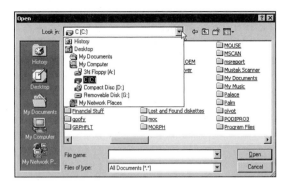

2. If the file is on your desktop or in a folder on the desktop, click the Desktop button. That will instantly display the contents of the desktop (ditto for My Documents). Saving files in My Documents is not a bad idea actually. (I've finally gotten more hooked on storing mine there, because many programs default to this location, and it's a hassle to poke around and find alternative folders.)

3. You can create a new folder using the Create New Folder button in the dialog box's toolbar if you want to save something in a folder that doesn't already exist. This can help you organize your files. The new folder will be created as a subfolder to the folder shown in the Look In area. (After creating the new folder, you'll have to name it by typing in a new name just to the right of the folder.) After creating the folder, double-click it to switch to it.

4. The object is to display the target folder in the window and then double-click on it. Therefore, if the folder you want is somewhere on your hard disk (typically drive C:), one way to display it is to click My Computer and then double-click the entry for the C: drive. All the folders on your C: drive appear in the window. (Don't forget, you can resize or scroll the box's contents to see more files and folders.)

5. In the large window, double-click the folder you want to look in. If you don't see the folder you're aiming for, you may have to move down or back up the tree of folders a level or two. Just back up a level by clicking on the Up One Level button. You can move down a level by double-clicking a folder and looking for its subfolders to then appear in the window. You can then double-click a subfolder to open it, and so on.

6. Click the file you want to open. If you're saving a file for the first time, you'll have to type in the name of the file.

7. If you want to see only certain types of files, open the Files of Type box to select the type of files you want to see (you can select a certain kind of document or all files). If the options offered don't suit your needs, you can type in DOS-like wildcards in the File Name area and then press Enter to modify the file list accordingly. For example, to show only Lotus 1-2-3 worksheet files, you'd enter *.WK? in the File Name area and press Enter.

PART
II

CH
5

When the file you want is visible in the File box at the left, double-click it or highlight it and click OK.

Tip #36

> Here's a trick: To quickly jump to a file in a long list, click once on a folder or file in the box (any one will do) and then type the first letter of the item you're looking for. That will jump the highlight to the first item that starts with the letter and probably bring your target into view. Successive key presses will move through each item that starts with that letter.

MY COMPUTER AND WINDOWS EXPLORER, NOT FILE MANAGER

In Windows NT 3.x, you work with your hard disk and files using the File Manager. In the Windows 9x and 2000 interfaces, File Manager is replaced by Windows Explorer and My Computer. In Chapter 6, "Organizing Your Work," we'll talk much more about how these tools work and how to organize your documents and applications using them. However, it's important to know for the following discussion that you find and manage your files and folders are using My Computer and the Windows Explorer. If you've used a Macintosh, this system is much like the Finder.

A File Manager program was actually supplied with Windows 95 and 98, as was a version of Program Manager, as a help for folks migrating from Windows 3.x. However, Windows 2000 Professional doesn't include File Manager.

Tip #37

> Surprisingly, Windows 2000 does include a Program Manager. Just type `Progman.exe` in the Run box.

File Manager wasn't included because, for starters, it doesn't work with long filenames. Second, it doesn't exploit the advancements in the interface, such as links to the Web, and lacks the flexibility in cutting, copying, and pasting objects between locations, including networked workstations.

USING THE NEW WEB VIEW

We've all been amazed at the meteoric rise in popularity of the Web. Who could have imagined just a few years ago that TV ads, radio ads, and even billboards would include Web sites as part of a corporation's identity? Any professional who doesn't have a Web site is yesterday's news.

Note

> Hey, we even have a Web site for this book and our other books (go to www.helpwin2k.com).

Because so many people have become accustomed to using the Web, it made sense for Microsoft to consider not only integrating a Web browser closely with the operating system and applications such as Office but also to change the view of the Desktop and folder windows so they more closely emulated the look and feel of the Web. The idea was to provide an interface that could smoothly mesh what's stored inside your computer with all the stuff out there on the Internet. A few adjustments to the Windows interface helps make the transitions a bit more seamless.

For example, one of the most basic differences between the Windows way of doing things and the Web's way is the number of times you click to open something. On Web pages, you click once on a link to go to a new Web page. In Windows, you double-click. This is one of the options that can easily be changed in Windows 2000 Professional, thus making the whole workstation begin to act more "Web like." If you use the Web a lot, you might want to be operating in this alternative Web view. We actually prefer it and find it cuts down on clicking (and the resultant finger wear over the course of a day's work). You also don't have to remember whether you're on a Web page or looking at folders and files on the hard disk.

Web view was introduced with Internet Explorer 4 on the Windows 9x platform. It was technically IE 4 that provided the new functionality. In Windows 2000 Professional, this functionality appears to be built into the operating system and is not dependent on IE. The upshot is that the Windows Explorer (the internal part of the operating system by which you look can examine the contents of your disk drives) acts much like a Web browser.

Note

> If you're coming from Windows 3.x, you can think of the Windows Explorer as being much like the File Manager, but on steroids. More about using Windows Explorer can be found later in this chapter.

Note

> In the chapters on using the Internet (Chapters 11–18), we'll cover the ins and outs of getting connected; browsing the Web; using search engines; creating and serving Web pages; and using email, newsgroups, and so forth. However, what's relevant here is how the Windows 2000 Web view affects how you work with files and folders.

PART

II

CH

5

Here are the key Web view effects integrated into Windows 2000 Professional (see Figure 5.8 for a sample window):

- Opening a file or folder can be done with one click instead of a double-click. Such items are underlined just like links on Web pages.

- Your desktop can be made active, displaying Web page information (such as your home page) or streaming data gathered from the Internet, such as news, weather reports, traffic reports, stock tickers, and so on.

- My Computer and Windows Explorer have Back, Forward, Search, and History buttons, just like a Web browser.

- The toolbars in Folder and Explorer windows are customizable and have address lines, just like a browser. You can type in a Web address, hit Enter (or click Go), and the window will adjust appropriately to display the content. If you enter a Web address, that page will display. If you enter a drive letter (C:, for example), its contents will be displayed.

- Every folder on your system can be customized with a background color, picture, hot links, instructions, and so forth. Basic customizations can be made without knowledge of HTML coding, through a wizard.

- Many of the Windows preset folders already have hot links to relevant sites, help files, and troubleshooting tools.

There are many more features and options in the interface, but we'll get to those in the sections on customizing with the Control Panel as well as in the Windows Explorer and My Computer coverage.

Figure 5.8
A typical Explorer window reached through My Computer. Notice the browser-like features, especially in the toolbar.

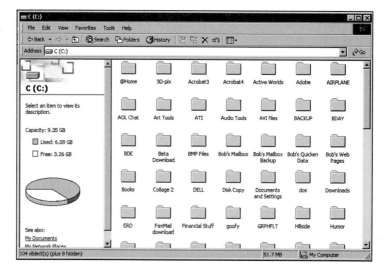

TURNING THE SINGLE-CLICK WEB VIEW ON AND OFF

Although many people like the single-click option in the Windows 9x interface, it's not turned on by default in Windows 2000. However, because we like it, you might find screen shots in this book that show it, and you may want to try it yourself. Don't confuse your friends by changing their settings, though. They'll suddenly be opening two copies of the same document when they double-click it. To turn on single-clicking, follow these steps:

1. Choose Start, Settings, Control Panel.

2. Double-click Folder Options. The Folder Options dialog box appears, as shown in Figure 5.9.

3. Click the Enable Web Content in Folders button to enable the option. This is probably already turned on by default. This option enables links and a Web-like view of folders contents.

4. Select Single-click to Open an Item (Point to Select) to turn on that option.

Figure 5.9
Turning on single-clicking and Web view.

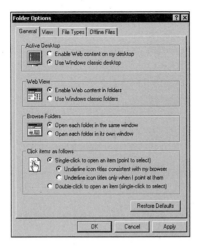

5. Click OK.

Now your Desktop should have changed its look, as you see in Figure 5.10.

Figure 5.10
Files, folders, and other documents have a line under them like Web links after Web view is turned on. Now a single-click acts as a double-click.

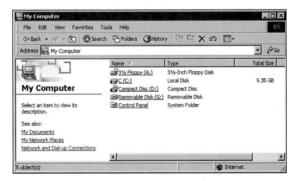

An important skill with Web view is *pointing*. Normally you select an object by clicking it. However, with the single-click option on, you select an object by just pointing to it. You don't click; instead, you just hover the mouse pointer over the item. At first, the pointer takes the shape of a pointing hand.

Caution

If you turn on single-clicking, be careful not to click on things unless you're ready to execute some action. You'll have to retrain yourself a bit if you're really used to double-clicking. You select by hovering, and you run a program or open a document with one click. Clicking a folder makes it open. Click a file and it opens. Click a program and it runs. To select a range of items in a list, hover the pointer over the first one to select it; then hold down the Shift key and then hover the pointer over the last item in the range.

If you're the controlling type, you might want to fine-tune other aspects of your folders' behavior. Click Start, Settings, Control Panel, Folder Options; then click the View tab. You'll see a bevy of options that affect how folders and their contents are displayed (see Figure 5.11).

Figure 5.11
Additional folder display options.

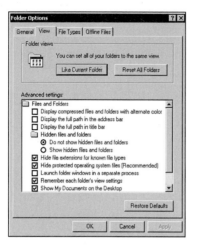

Change any settings you like. (Some of these are pretty technical, though. If you don't understand a setting, don't touch it.) These settings will be explained in the relevant sections of this book. See Chapter 6, "Organizing Your Work," for more details about many of these settings.

PROPERTIES AND THE RIGHT-CLICK

Ever since Windows 95, a common theme that unites items within Windows is the aspect called *properties*. Properties are pervasive through Windows 9x, Windows NT 4, and Windows 2000; they provide a means for making changes to the behavior, appearance, security level, ownership, and other aspects of objects through the operating system. Object properties apply to everything from individual files, to folders, printers, peripherals, screen appearance, even to the computer, itself, or a network or workgroup. All these items have property sheets that allow you to easily change various settings that apply to these objects. For example, you might want to alter whether a printer is the default printer or whether a folder on your hard disk is shared for use by co-workers on the LAN.

You can see a typical set of properties in Figure 5.12, which displays the properties for the C: drive (hard disk) on a computer. Notice that there are several tab pages on this sheet. Some property sheets only have a single page, whereas others may have many.

Property sheets are very useful and often serve as shortcuts for modifying settings that otherwise would take you into the Control Panel or through some other circuitous route. With some document files (for example, Word files), you can examine many settings that apply to the file, such as the creation date, author, editing history, and so forth. A typical printer's property sheet contains security, color management, location, name, and share status information.

Figure 5.12
A typical property sheet for a hard disk.

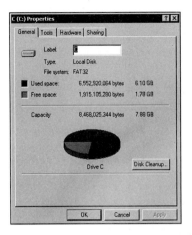

Although everyday users might not have need for property sheets, power users certainly will. As you use property sheets, you'll also become familiar with and accustomed to another aspect of the Windows 2000 Professional interface: the right-click. Until Windows 9x, the left (primary) mouse button was the one you did all your work with unless you were using a program that specifically utilized the other buttons, such as some art programs. However, Windows 9x instituted the use of the right-click to bring up various "context-sensitive" menus in programs and throughout the interface. These have been incorporated into Windows 2000 Professional. (Right-clicking simply means pointing to something and clicking the rightmost mouse button.) Microsoft Office has been using right-clicking for some time to bring up shortcut menus for such things as Cut, Copy, and Paste operations and formatting options.

PART
II

CH
5

Here are some typical uses of right-click context menus:

- Sharing a folder on the network
- Changing the name of your hard disk and checking its free space
- Changing a program's icon
- Setting the Desktop's colors, background, screen saver, and so on
- Adjusting the date and time of the clock quickly
- Closing an application by right-clicking on its icon in the taskbar and choosing Close
- Displaying a font's technical details

As an example of the right-click, simply get to an empty place on the Desktop and right-click on it. Right by the cursor, you'll see a menu that looks like the one shown in Figure 5.13. Notice that you can slide up and down the menu to make choices. Choose Properties down at the bottom of the list. You'll see the Properties settings for the your Desktop (as well as general video display, screen saver, and other related items).

Figure 5.13
Setting your screen and video properties is as easy as right-clicking on the Desktop and choosing Properties.

Here are some other examples of what right-clicking can do for you:

- Right-clicking on any window's title bar produces a menu containing the Restore, Move, Size, Minimize, and Maximize commands.

- Right-clicking on and dragging an icon from the Explorer or a Folder onto the Desktop creates a shortcut icon and places it on the Desktop in one move. (The Desktop and shortcuts will be explained later.)

- In many applications, selecting text and then right-clicking produces an edit menu at the cursor location that lets you choose Cut, Copy, or Paste.

- Right-clicking an empty area of the taskbar gives you a menu that lets you manage the display of all the windows you have open. For example, you can tile all open windows or set the properties of the taskbar. (The taskbar is discussed in more detail later in this chapter.)

- In the Explorer, right-clicking on a file lets you work with it in various ways, depending on the file type. You can open the document, send it to an email recipient, run a program, install or set up a utility such as a screen saver, play a sound file, and so forth.

If you want to use Windows most efficiently, make a habit of right-clicking on objects to see what pops up. You may be surprised to see how much time you can save with the resulting shortcuts.

RUNNING YOUR APPLICATIONS

If you're just upgrading from Windows 9x, you already know how to run applications, how to switch between them, and how to manage them. If you're upgrading from Windows 3.x, however, the procedures for launching programs are a bit different from what you're used to, and you'll need a quick primer to get up to speed. Even though your programs, themselves, may work very much the same way under Windows 2000 Professional as they do with Windows 3.x, how you get them going differs. This is because the Program Manager, although available, isn't at the heart of Windows 2000 the way it was in Windows 3.x and NT 3.x.

Note

To run Program Manager, click Start, Run, and enter `progman.exe`. You'll have to manually add program groups, programs, and documents to your program groups. They're not migrated into Program Manager as you install programs. This is discussed in more detail in the section "Running a Program from the Program Manager."

Note

Starting with this chapter, we're going to assume that you understand the choice between single-click mode and double-click mode (see descriptions earlier in this chapter). Some of the figures in the book might have icons, files, or other object names underlined, whereas other may not, based on what mode the computer was set in when the screen shots were grabbed. Don't let it throw you. Also, when we say "double-click something," we mean run it or open it by whatever technique is applicable based on your click setting. Also, when we say "click on it," that means select it. Remember that if you have single-clicking turned on, that means just hovering the pointer over (that is, pointing to) the item.

HOW TO LAUNCH YOUR APPS

You can launch your applications under Windows 2000 Professional in a number of different ways, as is the case with many other things in Windows. You'll probably end up employing the technique that best fits the occasion. Regardless of which one you use, you'll soon come to think of the old Program Manager as clunky by comparison, and you'll be a convert to the Windows 9x/2000 interface.

To run an application, you can perform the following tasks (ranked in order of ease of use):

- Use the Start button to find the desired application from the resulting menus.
- Add an application shortcut to the quick launch bar at the bottom of the screen and click it to run.
- Open My Computer, browse through your folders to find the application's icon, and double-click it.
- Use Windows Explorer to find the application's icon, and double-click it.
- Run the old-style Windows 3.x Program Manager, open the group that contains the application's icon, and double-click it.
- Find the application with the Start, Search command and double-click it.
- Enter command names from the command prompt. DOS, OS/2, POSIX, and Windows programs can be launched this way. You must know the exact name and most likely the folder in which it's stored.
- Press Ctrl+Alt+Del and choose Task Manager. Click on New Task and then type in the executable filename for the program (for example, `word.exe`).

PART

II

CH

5

You can use an alternative approach, opening a document that's associated with a given app, as a trick to open the application:

- Locate a document that was created with the application in question and double-click it. This will run the application and load the document into it. With some applications, you can then close the document and open a new one if you need to.

- Right-click on the Desktop or in a folder and choose New. Then choose a document type from the resulting menu. This creates a new document of the type you desire, which, when double-clicked, will run the application.

Here's how to open an existing document in an application (ranked in order of ease of use):

- Click Start, Documents and look among the most recently edited documents. Clicking one will open the document in the appropriate application.

- Use the Start, Search command to locate the document.

- Run the application that created the document and check the document's MRU (most recently used) list on the File menu. It may be there. If so, click it.

In the name of expediency, we're not going to cover all these options. Once you get the hang of the most common approaches, you'll understand how to use the others. Notice that some of the approaches are *application-centric*, whereas others are *document-centric*. An application-centric person thinks, "I'll run Word so I can write up that trip expense report." A document-centric person thinks, "I have to work on that company manual. I'll look for it and double-click it."

RUNNING PROGRAMS FROM THE START BUTTON

The most popular way to run your applications is with the Start button, which is located down in the lower-left corner of your screen. When you install a new program, the program's name is usually added somewhere to the Start button's Program menu lists. Sometimes you'll have to drill down a level or two to find a certain program, because software makers sometimes like to store their applications under their company names (for example, Real Networks creates a group called Real, which you have to open to run the Real Player or Real Jukebox). Then you just find your way to the program's name, choose it, and the program runs. Suppose you want to run the calculator. Here are the steps to follow:

1. Click the Start button.

2. Point to Programs.

3. Point to Accessories. If you don't see Calculator in the resulting list, this means that personalized menus are enabled (see Chapter 1). Just hover the pointer over Accessories and then choose Calculator.

Tip #38

The personalized menu is a feature that came over from MS Office, and some people find it helpful and time saving. We find it a pain and confusing. If you do too, turn this feature off. Click Start, Settings, Taskbar, Start Menu and uncheck Use Personalized Menus.

Note that all selections with an arrow pointing to the right of the name have submenus—meaning that they'll open when you click them or hover the pointer over them. These groupings are essentially the same as Program Groups in Windows 3.x's Program Manager. There may be several levels of submenus. For example, to see the Fax Queue submenu, you have to go through Programs, Accessories, Communications, Fax menu.

By default, Windows 2000 Professional uses personalized (smart) menus. This keeps the program listing cleaner by showing you only the programs you've most recently used. If you don't see the one you want, it may still be in the Start menu, but just not displayed. If you see a double arrow, just hover the pointer over it, and all the hidden programs will appear in a few seconds. Sometimes because of the length of a list, the list might need to scroll off the screen. In this case, you'll see arrows at the top or bottom of the list, as shown in Figure 5.14.

Figure 5.14
A scroll arrow appears if there are too many programs to fit on the screen at once.

Just click the arrow to scroll the list, release the mouse button when you see the one you want, and then click it.

PART

II

CH

5

Tip #39

Sometimes, spotting a program in a list is a visual hassle. Press the first letter of the program you're looking for and the cursor will jump to it. If there are multiple items starting with that letter, each key press will advance one item in the list. Also, pressing the right-arrow key will open a submenu. The Enter key will execute the highlighted program. Items in the lists are ordered alphabetically, although folders appear first, in order, with programs after that.

Often you'll accidentally open a list that you don't want to look at (say, Documents). Just move the pointer to the one you want and wait a second. You can also press the Esc key for the same effect. Each press of Esc closes one level of any open lists. To close down all open lists, just click anywhere else on the screen, such as on the Desktop or another window. All open Start button lists will go away.

 If a shortcut on your Start menus doesn't work, see "Shortcut Doesn't Work" in the "Troubleshooting" section at the end of this chapter.

Running a Program from My Computer

If you're a power user, chances are good you'll be sleuthing around on your hard disk using either the My Computer approach or the Windows Explorer (more about that in the next chapter). I certainly have programs floating around on my hard disk that do not appear in my Start button program menus, and I have to execute them directly.

In general, the rule for running programs without the Start menu is this: If you can find and display the program's icon, just double-click it. It should run. The My Computer icon lets you do just this. My Computer is usually situated in the upper-left corner of your Desktop. Opening it provides a very Mac-like way of moving through the stuff in your computer, such as drives, files, the Control Panel, and network and dial-up connections.

Tip #40	Right-clicking My Computer and choosing Manage launches a powerful computer manager program called *Microsoft Management Console* (MMC). This is covered in Chapter 31, "System Management and Configuration Tools."

In Windows 9x, a Printers folder is included here as well, but that's eliminated in Windows 2000 Professional, thus requiring a visit to the Control Panel instead.

Getting to a program you want can be a little convoluted, but if you understand the DOS directory tree structure or you've used a Mac, you'll be able to grasp this fairly easily. Click a drive to open it, and then click a directory to open it. Then double-click the program you want to run. Figure 5.15 shows a typical directory listing reached through My Computer. It also shows the HotSync program for my Palm Pilot being launched.

Here are some notes to remember:

- You can get to the Desktop quickly by clicking the Show Desktop icon just to the right of the Start Button.

- Folders are listed first, followed by files. Double-clicking a folder will reveal its contents.

- If you want to see more files or folders on the screen at once to help in your search, you have several options. The Large Icon view can be annoying because it doesn't let you see very many objects at once. Check out the View menu and choose Small Icons, or you can use the View tool on the toolbar to change the view.

- The Details view will show the sizes of files and other information about the files and folders, such as the dates they were created. This is useful when you're looking for applications because the Type column will indicate whether the file is an application program.
- If you want to see the folder tree, click the Folders button on the toolbar. This is covered more in Chapter 6.

Figure 5.15
A typical directory as shown through My Computer, and a program being double-clicked.

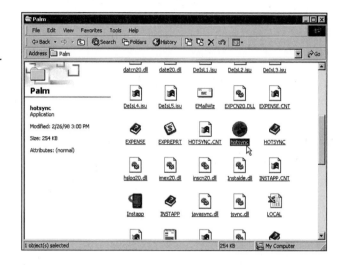

Tip #41

In Windows 9x, you can click repeatedly on the View button to cycle through the available views. This doesn't work in Windows 2000 Professional, unfortunately. You have to open the list and choose a view.

PART
II
CH
5

Tip #42

Pressing Backspace while in any folder window will move you up one level in the directory tree. Also, the Back and Forward buttons work just like they do in a Web browser—they'll move you forward and back through folders you're already visited.

Of course, many of the files you'll find in your folders are *not* programs. They're documents or support files. To easily find the applications, choose the Details view and then click the column head for Type. This sorts the listing by type, putting applications at the top of the list.

Note

Applications, registered file types, and certain system files will not have their file extensions (the last three letters after the period) displayed. Hidden system files and directories will be invisible, too. This choice was made to prevent cluttering the display with files that perform

continues

continued

duties for the operating system but not directly for users. It also prevents meddling with files that could cripple applications and documents, or even the system at large. Personally, I like seeing as many details about files as possible, so when I first install a system, I open My Computer (or any folder window), choose Tools, Folder Options, View, and turn off Hide File Extensions. In Chapter 6, "Organizing Your Work," we'll cover all the options you can use when displaying folder windows.

RUNNING A PROGRAM FROM THE WINDOWS EXPLORER

If you're the kind of person who prefers a bird's-eye view of your computer, you probably used the File Manager in Windows 3.x. As explained in more detail in later chapters, the Windows Explorer is like File Manager on steroids. It uses a "tree" approach (a hierarchical display) to your PC and is well suited to organizing your folders and files, as well as running programs.

Just as with the My Computer approach, you'll need to know where your applications are stored to execute them. Nowadays, most programs are stored in C:\Program Files\. This means finding them shouldn't be that difficult. Here's how:

1. Click Start, Programs, Accessories, Windows Explorer.

2. Click the plus sign (+) next to My Computer to see the local storage on it.

3. Click the drive in question and then click the folder you're headed for. In Figure 5.16, you can see a search for the RealJukebox program.

Figure 5.16
Windows Explorer lets you easily poke around your computer, Desktop, network, or the Internet.

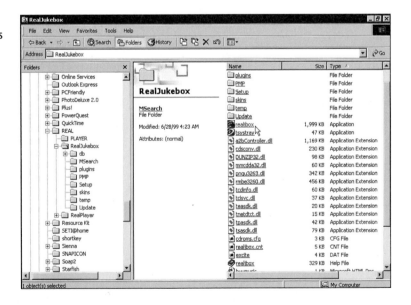

Note

Windows 9x includes the Windows 3.x File Manager, which you can run by entering `winfile` into the Run box. However, File Manager isn't included in Windows 2000 Professional.

Obviously the items on the left side are folders. Scroll down to the folder that contains the program you're looking for (folders are listed in alphabetical order). If a folder has a plus sign next to it, it has subfolders. Clicking the plus sign displays the names of any subfolders.

If you prefer to see small icons or details in the right-hand pane, you can change the view the same as when you're using the My Computer folders (see "Running a Program from My Computer," earlier in the chapter).

In Windows 2000, the distinction between My Computer and the Windows Explorer is very subtle. In fact, by clicking the Folders button on the toolbar, you can toggle back and forth between these two views into your computer's contents.

RUNNING A PROGRAM FROM THE PROGRAM MANAGER

Although it's a bit odd, you can organize your programs in Windows 2000 Professional in such a way that they're runnable from a Windows 3.x-style Program Manager. An administrator could use this approach to ease the move to the Windows 2000 GUI for his or her users. The Program Manager is hidden away, though. Many Windows 2000 Professional users will never know it's included in the package.

As mentioned previously, existing program groups (Start button groups) are not pulled into Program Manager during an upgrade or when you're installing new programs into a Windows 2000 Professional system. However, it doesn't really matter. If you haven't done so already, you can make new groups and program icons to launch them. Here's how:

1. Click Start, Run.
2. Enter progman and press Enter.
3. From the resulting box, choose File, New.
4. Enter a name for a new program group, assuming you want to create one.
5. At this point you can manually set up program items for the group by choosing File, New, Program Item. Alternatively, as a shortcut, you can drag and drop documents and applications from any folder (for example, My Computer, Windows Explorer, and Find).

PART
II

CH
5

Tip #43

Program Manager groups are imported from Windows 3.x into Windows 9x Start button groups during the Windows 9x setup process. If you then upgrade to Windows 2000 Professional, your Program Manager items can be imported to Windows 2000 Professional's Start button groups.

RUNNING APPLICATIONS WITH THE SEARCH COMMAND

The Search command is covered in detail in Chapter 6, "Organizing Your Work." However, this section will briefly cover how to use this indispensable tool to run your programs. Windows 2000 Professional (just like Windows 9x) has a Search command that will hunt through your hard disks (or the network or Internet for that matter) for files, folders, and other such objects. In Windows 9x, this feature is called *Find*, whereas in Windows 2000, it's spiffed up significantly in its capabilities and called *Search*. Of course, just as with My Computer and Windows Explorer, it helps if you know the filename of the program you're looking for, but at least Search cuts you some slack if you don't know the whole name, because you can enter just part of the file's name.

Search will slog through a specified disk or the whole computer (including multiple disk drives) in an attempt to locate the folders or files that meet your criteria. Once they're found, you can work with these objects however you like. If a found object is a program, you can run it.

Using the Start, Run command for launching a program is easier than searching for it, but only if you know the exact name of the program, and if the program is in the search path. If it's not, the program won't run and you'll just get an error message saying the program can't be found.

Here's an example of how I use Search to run a program. I have the program called Remapkey somewhere on my computer. This is a small utility program I downloaded off of the Net, and it doesn't have its own setup program, so it was never added it my Start menus. I could add this program to the Start menu, as you'll learn how to do in Chapter 6, "Organizing Your Work," but I don't use it that often. I just want to run it occasionally. Therefore, I use the Search command. Here are the steps I follow:

1. I click Start, Search, For Files and Folders.
2. In the resulting Search box, I enter the name of the program or a portion thereof (see Figure 5.17).
3. I double-click the program name and the program runs. Note that I've set the Look In section to My Computer.

As a default, it will search your C: drive, which is usually fine unless you have multiple hard disks on your computer and want Search to comb through them all.

USING THE MRU DOCUMENTS LIST

A feature introduced with Windows 9x is a Start menu that remembers the last 15 documents you've worked on. Find it by clicking Start, Documents. It's possible that by revisiting a project you've been working on, you can run the program you want. This list is maintained by Windows 2000 between sessions and is part of a user's profile. Logging in to the workstation will bring up the list. Only the last 15 documents are remembered, though, and some of these won't be items you'd think of as documents. Some of them might actually be programs or folders.

Figure 5.17
Choosing Search from the Start menu lets you search the computer for a program or folders. You only have to enter a portion of the name, if you don't mind possibly finding a broad range of files.

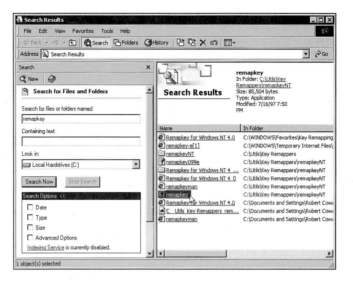

Notice the My Documents choice at the top of the list. This is a shortcut to the My Documents folder, which has become the default storage location for many Windows applications.

Lots of Windows programs nowadays have a feature that lists the files you were most recently working on (typically in their File menus). The contents of the Documents menu is sometimes pretty bogus, because it lists items such as the last 15 photos you looked at—not very helpful if you're looking for the letter you wrote last week.

Tip #44	You can clean up the Documents list if you want to start fresh (or don't want someone to know what you've been working on). Click the Start, Settings, Taskbar & Start Menu, Start Menu options and then click the Clear button.

Note	You can place program shortcuts on the top of the first Start menu, on the desktop, or in any folder. This is a real timesaver, and it takes up only a small amount of disk space. Shortcuts are covered in Chapter 6, "Organizing Your Work."

SWITCHING BETWEEN APPLICATIONS

As you know, one of the attractions of Windows is that it lets you run multiple programs at a time. You can also have a bunch of folders or Web pages running simultaneously. When you boot up, any Web pages or folders that were open when you shut down will reopen with their current content displayed.

Despite this capability, many users still work on one project or in one window at a time. Pretty silly, and not very efficient. In Windows 3.x, you switched between running programs

PART
II

CH
5

with Alt+Tab. Microsoft realized that people weren't taking advantage of task switching because that key combo wasn't easily discoverable. Therefore, it added the taskbar at the bottom of the screen. Alt+Tab still works, and I use it all the time because I'm keyboard oriented. However, if you're a mousy type, you'll like the taskbar.

Tip #45

> If you like using the Alt+Tab method but find you often bypass the task you're heading for by Alt+Tabbing too quickly, here's a little tip: Press Shift+Alt+Tab to move backward through running tasks. (You're just adding the Shift key to the usual Alt+Tab key combo.) You can simply back up a task or two, then release.

It's simple. When you run each new program or open a folder, another button is added to the taskbar. Simply clicking a button switches you to that program, window, or folder. Depending on the resolution of your screen, once you have about 10 or so programs up, the names on the buttons get truncated to just a few letters. To better read them, you can create another line or two of buttons on the taskbar. Grab the upper edge of the taskbar (position the cursor so that it turns into a double-headed arrow) and then drag it upwards a half inch or so and release. Of course, you lose some screen real estate when you do this. In that case you can set the Taskbar properties so it hides unless you move the cursor to the bottom of the screen, at which point it pops up for a minute so you can use it. To do this, right-click an empty area of the taskbar, choose Properties, and turn on Auto Hide.

Note

> You can reposition the taskbar on the right, left, or top of the screen. Just click any part of the taskbar other than a button and drag it to the edge of your choice.

Tip #46

> In Windows 3.x, pressing Ctrl+Esc brought up the Task List. It no longer does: It opens the Start menu as though you clicked the Start button. To see a list of running tasks, switch to one. To shut one down if it has crashed, press Ctrl+Alt+Del; then click Task Manager.

USING THE HELP SYSTEM

"Earl Gray tea, hot," says Picard. And that's what he gets. Despite all the advances in PCs and PC software, until we have one that's as smart as the computer on the USS Enterprise in *Star Trek*, we're going to need help.

By now, we've all tried to use Help systems in Windows and in Windows programs. Do they work? Well, sort of. With a little digging you can often come up with something useful or interesting, or at least something that might send you looking in the right direction. In the worst of programs, help consists of repeating the obvious: "The File menu is used for opening and saving files." Great.

The Windows Help system has evolved over the past 10 years or so from something very funky to the slick, new HTML-based utility packaged with Windows 2000. The Windows Help engine itself has been a pain for us as writers to document. Each version of Help has had its own interface, quirks, and capabilities, just enough to confuse many users and mandate a bunch of rewrites. Often, the help that pops up from within an application when you press F1 has some proprietary interface.

As much as online help files help, Brian and I still think there's a lot to be said for books. (Of course, we *would* say that!) There's just something people like about books: For example, books don't require batteries. You can take them with you; you have a sense of how many pages there are, how long a section or a chapter is, just by thumbing through it. There's the familiar table of contents and the index. They don't break if you drop them. Using them doesn't really take much know-how (except the ability to read—a skill that shouldn't be underestimated), and you can skim through a book very easily in hopes of searching for a given topic. We think books are going to be around for quite some time, despite the rise of e-books and Web-based instruction.

Despite our obviously self-serving opinion about the superiority of books in print, it's no small feat for publishers to keep up with the latest version of a program, and so there we have it—online help files. Besides, you don't always have a book on hand when you're having trouble with a program or Windows, so there's another rationale for electronic help.

For help with individual applications, press F1 or click File, Help and hope the writers of the Help file did their homework. Once in a while you'll be delightfully surprised. More and more companies are posting help files and FAQs (frequently asked questions) online, so check the company's Web site before giving up hope. As for the Windows 2000 Help file, I'm pleased to say it's impressive. Even if it's not packed with personality or seat-of-the-pants insight, it is chock full of information. You could easily spend a week, on and off, reading through it. As mentioned in Chapter 1, there are built-in troubleshooters, cross-references, links to Web resources, and the ability to search using Boolean rules (AND, OR, NOT, and NEAR) and phrase searches, just like in Web-based search engines.

The Help system uses a sensible layout similar to the Windows 9x Help system. It has four tabs: Contents, Index, Search, and Favorites. The last tab is new, letting you save specific pages that you refer to frequently, for easy lookup.

Because you've undoubtedly used Help engines before, I won't belabor the techniques for using them. Suffice to say that for weekend reading you might start with the Contents tab. However, when you have a specific need or question, start with the Index tab. Type in a keyword and then scroll through the results to find something relevant, select it, and click Display. When worse comes to worst, your last resort is to search the whole Help file for an occurrence of a word or phrase. For that, click the Search tab. It pores over the entire Windows Help file and, with a little luck, will dish up some helpful info. Don't overlook the Web links built into the Help pages if you're online.

The newest version of the Help system uses CHM files (compiled HTML), some of which even use animation. Also of note are two items on the first page of the Help system:

- There is a text link called If You've Used Windows Before. Clicking this link will help you learn Windows 2000 equivalents to features you've used in Windows 98 or NT.
- The Find It Fast link explains the syntax you can use while searching, much like in a Web-based search engine. This is an animated page with audio instructions.

EXITING WINDOWS GRACEFULLY

When you've finished a Windows 2000 session, you should properly shut down or log off to ensure that your work is saved and that no damage is done to the operating system. Shall we reiterate? Shutting down properly is very important. You can lose your work or otherwise foul up Windows settings if you don't shut down before turning off your computer. If multiple people share the computer, you should at least log off when you're finished so that others can log on. Logging off protects your work and settings from prying eyes. When you shut down, Windows does some housekeeping, closes all open files, prompts you to save any unsaved work files, and alerts the network that you and your shared resources are no longer available for consultation. The doctor is out.

There are several ways to shut down the computer, all or only some of which might apply to your machine. Newer machines will have more shutdown features because they're likely to have advanced power management built into them via ACPI.

Here are the steps for correctly exiting Windows:

1. Close any programs that you have running. (This can almost always be done from each program's File, Exit menu or by clicking the program's close button.) If you forget to close programs before issuing the Shut Down command, Windows will attempt to close them for you. If you haven't saved your work, you'll typically be prompted to do so. Some programs, such as DOS programs, you'll have to manually close. Windows will alert you if it can't automatically close an open program. Quit the DOS program and type exit at the DOS prompt, if necessary.

2. Click Start, Shutdown. You'll see the dialog box shown in Figure 5.18.

Figure 5.18
How do you want to shut down? Choose the desired option from the drop-down list and click OK.

3. Choose the desired option and click OK.

Here are some points to consider:

- If your computer has Advanced Power Manager (APM) or *ACPI* built in, you should have a Standby option in the Shutdown list. This will certainly be the case with PCs fitted with ATX motherboards (as opposed to the older AT-style PC) and power supplies. The ATX motherboards have standby capability that Windows 2000 Professional should recognize and utilize. If your system isn't APM or ACPI enabled, you'll probably just have Log Off, Shut Down, and Restart options.

- Logging off clears personal settings from memory and puts the computer in a neutral state, waiting for a user to enter a user name and password to log on. However, it doesn't bring the system to its knees. Logging off will not stop running services, which can include some applications, such as Web services, file sharing, print sharing, UPS support, and scheduled tasks, to name a few.

Tip #47	In NT, logging on always requires pressing Ctrl+Alt+Delete first. This key combination flushed potential Trojan horse viruses from memory as a security measure (see the earlier sidebar that describes Trojan horses). In Windows 2000 Professional, this is not the default. If you want this "three-finger salute" security measure implemented in your system, go to Control Panel, Users and Passwords, click the Advanced tab, and click Require Users to Press Ctrl+Alt+Delete Before Logging On.

Standby puts the computer in a suspended state, letting you quickly come right back to where you were working before you suspended the PC. This means you don't have to exit all your applications before turning off your computer. You only have to choose Standby. This also saves energy, because the hard drives, CPU, CPU fan, some internal electronics, and possibly the power supply and fan will go into a low-power state. Your monitor, if Energy Star compliant, should also go into a frugal state of energy consumption. When you want to start up again, a quick press of the power switch (on some computers a key press on the keyboard will do) should start up the system right where you left off. Make sure to press the power button for just a second or so. Anything over four seconds on most modern computers in a standby state will cause the computer to completely power down.

Be aware that Standby will hold your system state only so long as the computer has power. If the power fails, everything stored in the computer's RAM will be lost. You'll end up doing a cold boot when the power is restored or you hook up to your AC adapter to your laptop again. The moral is to be cautious when using Standby. You should save your work before going into standby mode, if not close important documents.

One of the most welcome features of Windows 2000 Professional in my opinion is *hibernation*. Like standby mode, hibernation lets you pause your work, and resume later, without laboriously shutting down and reopening all your applications and files. But unlike Standby,

PART

II

CH

5

Hibernate isn't volatile. If the AC power fails or batteries run flat, it doesn't matter because Hibernate stores the system state on a portion of the hard disk rather than keeping the system RAM alive in a low-power state. After storing the system state to the hard disk, the computer fully shuts down. When restarted, a little internal flag tells the boot loader that the system has been stored on disk, and it's reloaded into memory.

Hibernation requires as much free hard disk space as you have RAM in your PC. If you have 128MB of RAM, you'll need 128MB of free disk space for hibernation to work. If Hibernate is not an option on your shutdown menu, you can turn on the feature from the Power Options in Control Panel (see Figure 5.19.) The dialog box will report the amount of disk space needed for your system in case you're unaware of the amount of RAM in your system.

Figure 5.19
Turning on the hibernation feature.

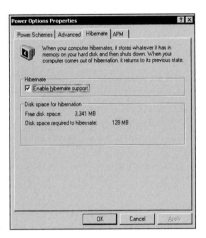

When you choose Hibernate from the shutdown menu, Windows 2000 Professional has to create a fairly large file on disk. In my case, for example, it's 128MB in size. On a 300MHz Intel Pentium 300, the entire process takes about 35 seconds. Restarting takes about the same amount of time. Remember, if you're going to put the machine to sleep for more than a few hours, use Hibernate or just do a complete shutdown, closing your applications and documents.

DEALING WITH A CRASHED APPLICATION OR OPERATING SYSTEM

Even though Windows 2000 Professional is fairly immune to crashing, the applications that run on it are not necessarily so robust. Not to be cynical, but many IS professionals don't consider any version of Windows worth their trouble until version 2 or a couple of service packs hit the streets, because they know bugs tend to be prevalent in first-release software. With an operating system as complex as Windows 2000, you can bet there are a few gotchas lurking.

If your system is really still stuck but you can get the Task Manager up, see "Forcing Your Computer to Shut Down" in the "Troubleshooting" section at the end of this chapter.

 If your laptop computer won't shut down no matter what you do, see "Ctrl+Alt+Delete Doesn't Work" in the "Troubleshooting" section at the end of this chapter.

My point here is that you're going to bump into some unstable behavior from time to time. If you notice that a program's not responding, you may have a crash on your hands. To gracefully survive a crash, possibly even without losing any of your data, you can try the following steps:

1. Try pressing Esc. Some programs get stuck in the middle of a process and Esc can sometimes get it back on track. For example, if you accidentally pressed Alt, this activates the menus. A press of Esc will get you out of that loop. If you've opened a menu, two presses of Esc or a click within the application's window may be required to return to normal operation.

2. Can you switch to the app to bring its window up front? First try clicking any portion of the window. If that doesn't work, click its button in the taskbar. Still no? Try using successive presses of Alt+Tab. If you get the window open and responding, try to save any unfinished work in the app and then try to close it by clicking the close button or selecting the File, Exit.

3. If that doesn't work, try right-clicking the program's button in the taskbar and choosing Close from the pop-up menu.

4. If that doesn't work, press Ctrl+Alt+Delete and choose Task Manager. Notice the list of running applications. Does the one in question say "Not responding" next to it? If so, click it and then click End Task (see Figure 5.20).

Figure 5.20
Killing a crashed, dead application.

TROUBLESHOOTING

SHORTCUT DOESN'T WORK

I click a shortcut somewhere in my Start menus and nothing happens or I get an error message.

Windows isn't smart enough, or, to put another way, it would be too much software overhead for the OS to keep track of all the shortcuts and update them, as necessary, when the files they point to are moved or deleted. A system that's been in use for some time will certainly have "dead" shortcuts, just as Web pages have broken links floating around. When you click a shortcut icon anywhere in the system—be it the Start menus, the Desktop, or in a folder—and you get an error message about the program file, click OK and let Windows take a stab at solving the problem by searching for the application. If it's found, the shortcut will be "healed" by Windows 2000. It will work again next time you use it.

If that doesn't work, try to search using Start, Search. See whether you can track down the runaway application. If you're successful, you'll probably be best off erasing the bad shortcut and creating a new one that points to the correct location. You can create a new shortcut by right-clicking the app's icon and choosing Create Shortcut. Then drag, copy, or move the shortcut to wherever you want, such as onto the Start button.

Also, a good trick to help you sort out a bad shortcut or to follow where its trail is leading is to right-click the icon and choose Properties, Find Target.

Tip #48	Remember, moving folders containing applications (for example, Office might be in `C:\Program Files\MSOffice`) is a bad idea. Once installed, many programs want to stay where they were put. Chapter 6, "Organizing Your Work," talks more about this.

FORCING YOUR COMPUTER TO SHUT DOWN

The system is acting sluggish, nonresponsive, or otherwise weird.

If your system is really acting erratically or stuck in some serious way and you've already killed any unresponsive programs, press Ctrl+Alt+Delete. This should bring up the Windows Security dialog box. Click Shut Down. If you get this far, there's hope for a graceful exit. You might have to wait a minute or so for the shutdown command to take effect. If you're prompted to shut some programs or save documents, do so. Hope for a speedy shutdown. Then reboot.

CTRL+ALT+DELETE DOESN'T WORK

Even Ctrl+Alt+Delete doesn't do anything.

If Shut Down doesn't work from the Windows Security dialog box (Ctrl+Alt+Delete), it's time to power-cycle the computer. Press the power switch to turn off the machine. On a machine with APM or ACPI support (one that can perform a soft power down), this can require holding the power button in for more than four seconds. You could lose some work, but what else are you going to do? Sometimes it happens. This is one good reason for saving your work regularly, and looking for options in your programs that perform autosaving. As writers, we set our AutoSave function in MS Word to save every five minutes.

Incidentally, I've known laptops to not even respond to any form of command or power button when the operating system was fully hung. I've even had to remove any AC connection, fully remove the main battery, wait a few seconds, and then reinsert the battery and reboot. Removal of the battery is important; otherwise, the battery keeps the computer in the same stuck state, thinking it's just in standby mode.

TIPS FROM THE WINDOWS PROS: WORKING EFFICIENTLY

The interface is your portal into the operating system and therefore into your computer. You're likely to be using it every day, so it behooves you to work the system as effectively and efficiently as possible. As writers and programmers on deadlines, we're using our computers at breakneck speed most of the time. Cutting corners on how you control the system interface can save you literally hundreds of miles of mousing around on your desktop over the course of a few years. Here are our top timesaving and motion-saving tips for using Windows 2000 Professional:

- To get to the Desktop, press the Windows key and M at the same time. To reverse the effect, press Shift+Windows+M. This is a real timesaver. If you prefer the mouse, use the Desktop button on the left side of the taskbar. It does the same thing.

- Change between apps with Alt+Tab. Aiming for an application's little button on the taskbar is a hassle. You'll get tendonitis doing that all day.

- Buy an ergonomic keyboard, split in the middle. Try not to rest your wrists on a hard surface. Cut a mouse pad in half and use Velcro, tape, or glue to affix it to the palm rest in front of the keys, if you're a leaner.

- Double-click a window's title bar to make it go full screen. Editing in little windows on the screen is a hassle and requires unnecessary scrolling.

- To close a program or window, press Alt+F4. It's that easy. Alternatively, right-click its button on the taskbar and choose Close. Aiming for that little X in the upper-right corner takes too much mouse movement.

- Put all your favorite applications, dialup connections, folders, and documents on the Quick Launch bar. Forget about the Start button. You can put about 20 things down there on the Quick Launch bar, for easy, one-click access. Use it. When an item falls out of use, erase it. They're only shortcuts, so it doesn't matter if you erase them.

- Use Standby and Hibernate! Don't boot up every time you turn on your computer. It's a waste of valuable time. Keep your favorite programs open: email, word processor, picture viewer, Web browser, spreadsheet, whatever. Yes, do save your work, maybe even close your document, but leave the apps open and keep the machine in standby or hibernate mode.

- If you use a laptop in the office, get a good external keyboard to work with it. Your hands will probably be happier, and you'll type faster. Also, get a pointing device that works best for you. Those "pointing stick" mice are *slow* to work with. You might like yours, but they're not nearly as quick or nature to use as a mouse or trackpad because they map pressure to motion, which is unnatural, and it's really easy to overshoot your target. Try a few different pointing devices and come up with one that works best for you.

- Discover and use right-click shortcuts whenever possible. For example, in Outlook Express, you can easily copy the name and email address of someone from the Address Book and paste them into an email. People are always asking me for email addresses of mutual friends or colleagues. I click on a person's entry in the Address Book and press Ctrl+C (for copy); then I switch back to the email I'm writing and press Ctrl+V (paste). Then Ctrl+Enter, and the email is sent.

- Also in Outlook Express, you can reply to an email with Ctrl+R. Forward one with Ctrl+F.

- In Internet Explorer, use the F11 toggle to go full screen. This gets all the other junk off the screen. Also, use the Search panel in the left column to do your Web searches. You can easily check search results without having to use the Back button. And speaking of the Back button, don't bother moving the mouse up there to click Back. Just press Alt+left arrow. The left- and right-arrow buttons with Alt are the same as the Back and Forward buttons.

- In most Microsoft applications, including Outlook Express and Internet Explorer, F5 is the refresh key. In OE, for example, pressing F5 sends and receives all your mail, so long as the Inbox is highlighted. In IE, it refreshes the page. In Windows Explorer, it updates the listing in a window (to reflect the results of a file move, for example). Remember F5!

- In Word, Excel, and many other apps, Ctrl+F6 is the key that switches between open windows within the same app. No need to click on the Window menu in the app and choose the document in question. Just cycle through them with Ctrl+F6.

- In whatever apps you use most, look for shortcut keys or macros you can use or create to avoid unnecessary repetitious work. Most of us type the same words again and again. (See, there I go.) As writers, for example, we have macros programmed in MS Word for common words such as *Windows 2000 Professional, Control Panel, Desktop, Folders,* and so on. Bob has created a slew of editing macros that perform tasks such as "delete to the end of line" (Ctrl+P), "delete line" (Ctrl+Y), and so on. In Word, press Alt+T+A and check out the AutoCorrect and AutoText features.

→ **See** Chapter 28, "Tweaking the GUI," to add more timesaving tricks to your arsenal.

CHAPTER 6

ORGANIZING YOUR WORK

In this chapter

AND YOU THOUGHT YOU LEFT THE HOUSEKEEPING CHORES AT HOME

As I was writing this, a U.S. Federal Court judge was making his decision regarding alleged unfair business practices by Microsoft. Bill Gates might have a difficult challenge convincing the court that Windows has increased national productivity. Even I wonder about that one, and I'm an advocate of personal computing!

You have to admit that a heck of a lot of folks' primary computing activities are playing Solitaire and sending email. It makes me think that perhaps if we shut them all off, the GNP decline and the negative U.S. trade deficit would both turn around.

If not engaged in apparently frivolous activities, you certainly can lower your daily workplace productivity by chores as silly as organizing your programs, folders, documents, shortcuts, and so forth. Sometimes it seems like there's no end to the organization capabilities of computers—and the need to organize the items we make with them.

Which brings us to this chapter about organization. Whether or not you end up assimilating the bulk of this book's more advanced technical coverage, you're likely among the millions of users who actually do use their computers to get work done, creating documents in programs as diverse as Adobe Premiere, Microsoft Access, C++, CyberStudio, Lotus Notes, and Excel. The complexity of today's computer-based workplace requires organization and understanding of basic housekeeping chores like never before. Unlike a real desktop, we users can hide our devilish habits, our "Bad Housekeeping Seal of Approval," by sweeping our poor file mismanagement under a pretty desktop background. Who would know? However, carelessly strewing files around the hard disk comes back to haunt you when you can't find the program or the document you desperately need to run or open.

This chapter covers some of these basics, many of which will be known to the veteran Windows buff, but all of which are absolute requirements for survival in your Windows workplace. We'll explore the best ways to organize your own work within Windows 2000, how to install apps and add them to the Start menu and Quick Launch bar, how to efficiently use the folder system, and how to crank up the Windows Explorer.

> **Note**
>
> If you're an advanced user of Windows, feel free to skim this chapter en route to the more advanced topics in subsequent chapters. (You still might find some good tricks in here, though.) If you've recently upgraded to Windows 2000 from Windows 3.1 then more rapt attention here would be in order, however, because many of the procedures will be new to you.

START BUTTON AND QUICK LAUNCH BAR MANAGEMENT

Something every Windows adept wants to do is cut down on clicks and unnecessary mousing about. Clicks are annoying. Why should you have to maneuver through all those menus just to find the programs you run every day? There are three easy shortcuts you should know about for running your oft-used programs: the Start button, the Desktop, and the Quick Launch bar. I'll take them in order.

When you install new programs, their setup utilities will typically create a shortcut icon on the Desktop so you can easily launch the program by clicking it. However, this is a bummer for a couple of reasons. For starters, it clutters the Desktop. Secondly, it's a hassle to get back to the Desktop because it can be obscured by whatever windows you might have open. This was the whole reason for the Start menu in the first place—it's always visible. Even if it's set on AutoHide, simply moving the pointer to the bottom of the screen causes it to reappear.

Tip #49	Better yet, if you have a keyboard with the Windows key on it (check to the left and right of the spacebar), you can press that to open the Start menu. This is especially useful if you have the taskbar hidden.

Going back as far as Windows 95, you could drag and drop items onto the Start button and Windows adds them to the first-level menu. With a single click of the mouse, no matter what you're doing in Windows 2000, you'll be able to quickly access programs if you put them here on your Start menu. As is the case with many Windows procedures, there are a number of ways to add items to the Start menu. What's more, this isn't limited to programs. You can also add often-used folders or individual documents here. The easiest way is to simply drag the application, folder, or document's icon onto the Start button and release it. Windows will then create a *shortcut* and place that shortcut on the Start button's opening menu.

Note	In Chapter 5, "Using the Windows 2000 Interface," we mentioned that shortcuts are aliases or pointers to an item, not the item itself. Creating a shortcut this way doesn't duplicate the document, folder, or application. It just points to that object.

Even since Windows 98, the Start button has gained additional functionality whereby you can reposition items on all its pop-up menus by dragging them around. Prior to that you had to use either Explorer or the taskbar properties sheet to rearrange menus. We'll get to that in a bit. The easier trick is simply to drop an object on the Start button using these steps:

1. Find a likely victim to put on the Start menu: an icon on a file, folder, or application. It can be a shortcut icon or the original icon. You can find such an icon in a folder via My Computer and Windows Explorer, on the Desktop, in the Find box, or displayed in any other window that supports drag-and-drop techniques.

2. When you've located the object you want to add, just drag it to the Start button and drop it. Notice that as you do this, the icon of the object gains a little arrow below it. This means the Windows GUI is creating a shortcut for it, a small (approximately 1KB)

PART

II

CH

6

file with an .LNK extension that contains nothing but pointers to the file, folder, document, or other source object.

The next time you click the Start menu, your shortcut will appear at the top of the list, above Windows Update.

There are certain limitations to the items you can create shortcuts for. If shortcuts for an object can't be created, either nothing will happen when you drag and drop it or Windows will issue an error message or suggestion. For example, Windows won't let you drag an applet out of the Control Panel. If you try to put one on the Start menu, you'll be asked if you want to create a shortcut on the Start menu (or anyplace else for that matter) instead. Because you wanted to create a shortcut anyway, just answer yes.

If you want to rename or remove items from the Start menu, you can open the menu, right-click the item, and choose Rename or Delete. Figure 6.1 shows an example.

Figure 6.1
You can remove or rename a shortcut icon, or even re-sort the listing of a menu, by right-clicking it and choosing the appropriate action.

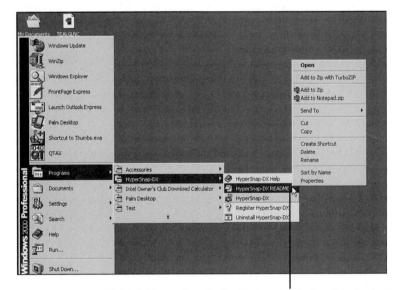

Right-clicking an item in the Start menu displays this shortcut menu, enabling you to delete and rename the item, among other things

QUICK LAUNCH SHORTCUTS

As of IE4, the Quick Launch toolbar was added to the taskbar options, and this very useful feature has migrated upward into Windows 2000 Professional. We mentioned this toolbar a bit last chapter as a way to organize your applications. Actually, Quick Launch is just one of the several toolbars you can add to the bottom of your screen (or sides or top—you can drag it to the edge of your choice). However, more about the other ones in a minute. As the name implies, Quick Launch, like the Start menu, makes it super easy to run your applications or open specific folders or documents without hunting for them. If you're not already using the Quick Launch bar, you'll want to start taking advantage of it.

It's simple to use. The Quick Launch toolbar is turned on by default when Windows 2000 is installed, with only a few items on it. However, you can add icons to it using the same drag-and-drop techniques described earlier for the Start button. Just drag items from most any source in the Windows interface, such as Windows Explorer, the Search box, the Desktop, and the Control Panel, and drop them on the Quick Launch bar. (The Control Panel is covered in Chapter 28, "Tweaking the GUI"). You can add folders, local or network drives, and even a local or network printer, just to name a few. Then, to open an item on the toolbar, you just click it once.

Tip #50	If the Quick Launch bar has been removed, you can add it again easily. Right-click an empty spot in the taskbar, and from the pop-up menu, choose Toolbars. Look to see that Quick Launch has a checkmark beside it. If it doesn't, choose Quick Launch. This will turn on that toolbar.
	If the checkmark is there already, you've got the Quick Launch bar hidden or "torn off" and floating around somewhere, as explained in a few pages. One you find the bar, drag it back to the taskbar and drop it there. It will reunite.

When dropping an object on the bar, you can choose the position it will fall into, between existing ones. Just move the cursor left and right. You'll see a black insertion point (I-beam cursor) indicating the target.

As shipped, the bar has a few useful items on it (depending on your point of view). The first of them is the Show Desktop button. As mentioned in the last chapter, clicking this button alternately minimizes and restores all windows in your current workspace—very useful. Then there are the Outlook Express and Internet Explorer icons. Once you have more than a few items on the bar, you can drag the icons left and right to rearrange them if you want to. After you've added more than a few icons, they won't all be in view at once unless you adjust the size of the taskbar to make room for them. If you don't, you'll have to scroll the Quick Launch bar, which makes it less quick! In Figure 6.2, you see a sample collection of Quick Launch items. Notice that there's a folder on it as well as a printer. Opening the printer brings up the printer's print queue for observation or management (see Chapter 9, "Printing, and Faxing with Windows 2000," for coverage of printer installation and management).

PART

II

CH

6

Tip #51	Placing a folder on the Quick Launch bar is an easy way to get to documents quickly that you might have buried deep within the hard disk directory structure and otherwise would require many mouse clicks to reach. Simply drag any folder you like to the Quick Launch bar and release.

If you decide you want to remove an item from the bar or rename the item, right-click it and choose Delete or Rename.

Figure 6.2
The Quick Launch bar
can contain shortcuts
(links) to your favorite
places and programs.

Folder shortcuts can be added, too

OTHER TOOLBARS

The Windows 2000 Professional taskbar is quite flexible, much like the toolbars in Office.
Check it out. There are several preexisting toolbars you can turn on, or you can create your
own if you have special needs. Here's how:

1. Right-click an empty portion of the taskbar and select the Toolbars menu. There are
   five options to choose from.

2. Choose the type of bar you want by clicking it. The checkmark indicates it's turned on.

Here's what each of the additional toolbars does:

- Address—Adds an address text line, where you can enter a URL, drive letter, network
  resource address, folder name, or even an executable name such as CMD, which will bring
  up a command prompt box. Entering a URL will take you to the Web page, FTP
  address, and so on. This works just like the address bar in IE or in the Address line of a
  folder window or the Windows Explorer window. An appropriate window will appear
  when you enter a resource name and press Enter.

- Links—This toolbar is a repeat of your quick links from Internet Explorer. Without
  running Internet Explorer, you can connect to your favorite Web sites.

- Desktop—Dumps copies of all your Desktop items into a new bar. Now you don't have
  to redisplay the whole Desktop just to click My Computer or the Recycle Bin. On the
  other hand, if you have tons of stuff on your Desktop, all those icons aren't going to fit
  into a skinny little toolbar either. Toolbars will scroll if overly full, so there's nothing to
  worry about. It's just a hassle to scroll them.

- New Toolbar—Leads you to a Browse box from which you can choose an object such as
  a folder or drive or an item such as My Network Places, My Documents, or Control
  Panel.

As you turn on toolbars, they're added to the taskbar, making a mess, basically. Each portion
will have a little sizing handle on it, just like in Internet Explorer. However, rather than sizing them, you'll want to increase the vertical size of the taskbar so that each toolbar has a
line of its own. Just grab the top line and pull up.

Toolbars can be torn off the collection, incidentally, causing them to float, if you so desire.
(This is a feature borrowed from the Mac OS, by the way.) Follow these steps:

1. Display the Desktop.

2. Grab any toolbar just to the right of its handle (not on it). A four-headed arrow must
   appear for this to work. When it does, you're grabbing the right spot.

3. Drag the toolbar away from the edge of the screen, out onto the Desktop, and release. Now you can move it to any position you like, as well as resize it, by dragging its border.

You can use this same dragging technique to rearrange the toolbars relative to one another. It takes a little trial and error to arrange them, just as it does in Internet Explorer, but it's possible.

MANAGING YOUR START BUTTON MENUS

As you install more and more programs, your Start menus can start to get messy. The items on them can fall out of alphabetical order, for one thing, or after a while you may decide you'd like to reorganize your items into more logical groupings. This section explains how to manage your Start menus.

Tip #52	To simply rename, re-sort, or delete items in a Start menu, just click Start and navigate to the item. Highlight it and right-click. Then choose from the list.

MANAGING START MENUS WITH DRAG AND DROP

Most of us just accept the Start button arrangements that various app setup programs impose on us, however disorderly or cryptic. When we're installing programs, we choose the "express setup" defaults for expediency, and then we have to live with the results, such as program groups that are a company's name (for example, Real or Symantec) instead of the program we want to run (for example, Jukebox or Norton Utilities).

However, you're not a captive here. Just rename and/or reorganize your groups and group items. For everyday rearrangement tasks, you can use the drag-and-drop approach right from the Start menus. The Windows 2000 GUI allows you to drag and drop items to and from the various Start, Programs menus. This means you can easily rearrange, rename, or delete them without using Explorer windows, as was required in Windows 95. Dragging items around in your program groups takes a little bit of practice. For example, suppose you want to move an item from one group to another. Here are the steps you would take:

1. Open the source group and click the item.

2. Drag it over to the destination group. Hover over the destination group name and in a few seconds, the group will open, and you can position the object among the other entries in the group. Figure 6.3 shows a move in progress.

Figure 6.3

| Tip #53 | To cancel a drag-and-drop move in the middle of the process, don't drop the item. Just press Esc. It will then remain unchanged in its original location. |

| Tip #54 | You can drag items from the Start, Program menus to the Quick Launch bar to quickly add an icon there. It will not be removed from the Start menus when you do this. The Windows GUI creates a shortcut on the Quick Launch bar, leaving the original shortcut in place. |

 If your Start menu is becoming really cluttered, see "Cluttered Start Menu" in the "Troubleshooting" section at the end of the chapter.

MANAGING START MENUS WITH PROPERTIES

New in Windows 2000 Professional is a set of Start menu properties that simplifies management tasks as well as lets you choose popular additions to the Start menus easily. For example, how many times have you wanted to open up a particular Control Panel applet such as Device Manager without actually loading the whole Control Panel window and visually scanning for the correct icon to double-click?

Check out the new features here by choosing Start, Settings, Taskbar and Start Menu. Then click the Start Menu Options tab. Figure 6.4 illustrates this dialog box.

Figure 6.4
You can do some cool Start menu management from this dialog box.

Most of the option boxes are self-explanatory and control whether subitems are displayed for direct access. For example, Expand Control Panel means that Control Panel will have a submenu of its applets to choose from, without you opening the Control Panel. The last two options in the box are a tad more cryptic:

- Scroll the Programs Menu—If this is on and you have an overgrown collection of program choices, they'll scroll up and down on the screen in a single column. Turn it off, and you'll get multiple columns of programs (Windows 95 style).

- Use Personalized Menus—If this is on, Windows maintains the MRU (most recently used) list of programs, hiding others from view. The idea is to clean up the screen and make it easier to find the programs, commands, settings, and documents that you use most often. This is a feature that grew out of Office. Internally, Windows watches your actions and applies a mathematical formula (algorithm) to calculate which items to display. Unless you linger too long on a menu or click on the little double arrows at the bottom of the programs menu, only your most-recently used items will show. You can always double-click a command to expand the list fully. Turn it off if the personalized menus bug you. Many users, particularly new users, find personalized menus confusing, for a number of reasons. In particular, menus between different machines don't look the same. This throws off users moving from computer to computer or those users trying to help one another. Advanced users find them annoying simply because Microsoft is fiddling with the GUI to the point of being obtrusive.

MORE SERIOUS START MENU MANAGEMENT

You might want more control when managing or customizing your Start menu. For example, occasionally an uninstall program doesn't remove all the entries, or you want to delete a bunch of them at once or just graphically rearrange items using an interface more like Windows Explorer. You have a couple choices:

- Use the buttons in the Taskbar Properties dialog box previously shown in Figure 6.4.
- Right-click the Start menu and choose Explore.

Using the Add button in the Taskbar Properties dialog box runs a wizard that walks you through creating a new menu or item. Nothing terribly difficult there. You use a Browse box to pinpoint the item and then choose where on the menu structure you want it added.

You can click the Remove button to bring up a Browse box to pinpoint the item to kill off. However, you already know that you can delete an item without going into this box. Just right-click the item on the Start menu and choose Delete.

The Advanced tab *is* useful, however, and leads to the same location as right-clicking the Start button and choosing Explore. The result is that you'll be running Windows Explorer with the user's Start Menu folder selected. Figure 6.5 shows a sample directory.

→ To learn more about Windows Explorer, **see** "Using the Folders Bar (a.k.a. Windows Explorer)," **p. 226**.

Check out the directory tree in the figure and notice that the path is

`C:\Documents and Settings\Robert Cowart [LUCID-5ZIBKK2JN]\Start Menu`

You'll also see that there's a branch for each user, the administrator, and the default user. (There are duplicates here—for example, two Robert Cowarts—because Windows 98 coexisted on the computer and has it own collection of menu settings.) Unless you have administrative rights, you won't be allowed to alter the settings of other users.

PART
II
CH
6

Figure 6.5
Exploring the Start menu for the current user provides the advanced user with a powerful tool for customization.

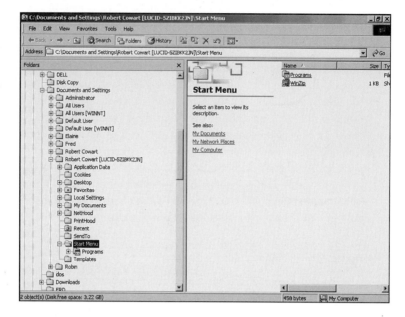

Significance of the All Users and Default Users folders will be covered in Chapter 32, which covers user management.

Clicking the plus sign (+) next to Programs opens up its contents. Figure 6.6 illustrates this. You can see that the folders under Start Menu, Programs are treated specially by the operating system. These folders have special icons, and anything put in these folders will appear on the Start menus. You can now drag and drop items as well as cut, copy, paste, rename, and delete them.

Caution

Although you can drag and drop items into your menus using this interface, use caution. You don't want to actually copy executables into these folders. The contents of all Start menu folders should be limited to shortcuts (icons with the small curved arrow beneath them). The interface will allow you to copy or move any kind of files (including EXE files) into the folders, but this isn't a good idea because moving programs from their own folders can cause them not to work. If you must use this interface for creating new objects, leave the source object where it is and create a shortcut in the Start menu folder. Do this by right-click-dragging the item into the desired folder. Upon release, a pop-up menu will ask whether you want to use the Copy, Move, or Create Shortcut option in the destination. Choose Create Shortcut.

What if instead of adding a program or document to a Start menu you want to add a folder? Doing this can give you a shortcut to that folder as one of the options on your Start menu. The only catch is that you can't do it from the Browse box. If the Browse box is open, close it by clicking Cancel. Then enter the full path name of the folder.

Figure 6.6
Folders under
Programs contain pro-
gram groups with
shortcuts to programs
and files in the
groups.

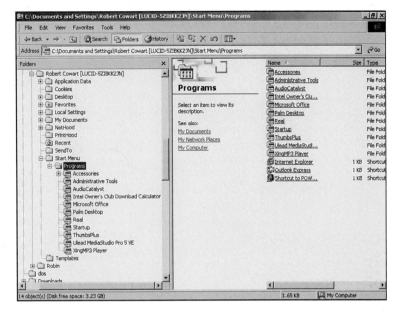

Just as with Program Manager icons in Windows 3.x, removing a shortcut from the Start
button menus does not remove the actual item from your hard disk. For example, if you
remove a shortcut to Word for Windows, the program is still on your computer. It's just the
shortcut to it that's been removed. You can always put the shortcut back on the menus again
using the Add button.

Here are some tips for working on your Start menus in the Windows Explorer view:

- Click the topmost folder (Start Menu) to adjust the contents of the Start button's first-
  level menu. All items in the right pane will appear at the top list that appears when you
  click the Start button.

- An easy way to change an item's name is by highlighting it (either click once or point,
  depending on your interface settings) and then press F2. Alternatively, you can right-
  click the name and choose Rename from the right-click menu. Type in the new name
  and press Enter.

- You can drag items in the right pane to destination menus in the left pane. Just drag and
  drop.

- Creating a new program group is a two-step process. First, click in the left pane on the
  menu you want to add to the group below. For a top-level group, click Programs. Now
  right-click in the right pane and choose New, Folder. Name the folder. Then open that
  folder and add items however you like.

USING THE SEARCH WINDOW

One of the first rules of organization is to know where things are, and how to keep them in their rightful places. The Search command from the Start menu is a tool often used in this mission. It can be invaluable for those of us who are too lazy to *get* organized—you can just do a search for that file you know you stored *somewhere* but couldn't remember to save your life. Yes, indeed, it's a wonderful tool for the absent-minded. However, this chapter is dedicated to organization, and in that spirit, let's look on the bright side. If you're interested in organizing your stuff (the lexicon's term *du jour* for anything in your computer), you must find it first. The Search command can offer a major assist in the sleuth.

As we mentioned in Chapter 1, "Introducing Windows 2000 Professional," Windows 2000's Search feature is new and wholly superior to anything in any version of Windows to date. It can find a needle in a haystack, and it doesn't much matter where the haystack is or what else is in it. The Search window will find people, computers, Web pages, files, folders, and programs. It will look on the Web, on the local machine, or across the intranet (LAN). In the context of this chapter, let's focus on organizing your programs, files, and folders, however. In the chapters covering network issues (Part IV) and the Internet section (Part III), we'll cover searching for other kinds of information.

In Windows 9x and NT 4, Search was called *Find*. The name has changed, as has the functionality of the look of the window. Just click Start and choose Search (or as a shortcut I use all the time, press Windows+F). This will bring up the Search window, as shown in Figure 6.7. I've maximized the window and set it up to perform a search of all files starting with the letters *ch* that are Word files (or that have an extension of .DOC, at least). Notice that I've also narrowed the search to include only files that have the word *Clipboard* in them, because I wanted to quickly find what I had said about the Clipboard in other chapters.

Figure 6.7
The new Search box is multitalented. Use it to seek out documents, folders, computers, and other stuff.

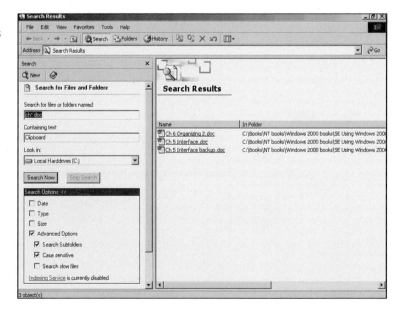

You can use standard DOS-style wildcards in your searches for files. For example, in Figure 6.7, notice that I've used the * character, which substitutes for a character string of any length (* replaces any number of characters, whereas ? replaces one character).

Just as with the Find box in Windows 9x and NT, you have to be a bit crafty when filtering the search. If you enter a long filename with spaces between the words, the search will likely end up becoming too broad. For example, if you entered

`Annual Report 2`

in the Search For area, the result would be any file with the word *Annual*, *Report*, or *2* in any part of its name. This is annoying. Also, using quotes around the string, as when conducting a Web search, doesn't help either, unfortunately. I was trying to find a folder called `Ch 3` and the only way to exactly find it was to enter `Ch*3` as the criterion. So keep in mind that you should use DOS-style wildcards when searching for items that contains spaces in their names.

When you click the Date, Size, Type, or Advanced option, the Search Options area of the window expands for you to enter the relevant search criteria. Experiment with other aspects of the Search box, such as searching the Internet or turning on the Indexing Service.

The Indexing Service is new to Windows 2000 Professional. This tool scans files and folders on your hard disk and builds a database of the words it finds in those documents. This database helps speed up file and directory searches when you're looking for words within files or keywords in file descriptions. The database also helps the Internet Information Services Web server perform Web site searches.

→ To learn more about the new Windows Indexing Service, **see** "Indexing," **p. 1255**.

The Indexing Service can index the following types of documents in several languages:

- Text
- HTML
- Microsoft Office 95 and later
- Internet mail and news
- Any other document for which a document filter is available

PART

II

CH

6

The Indexing Service is designed to run continuously and requires little maintenance. After it's set up, all operations are automatic, including index creation, index updating, and crash recovery if there's a power failure. For information about administering the Indexing Service, see Chapter 18, "Using Internet Information Services to Host a Web Site."

ORGANIZING YOUR FILES AND FOLDERS

This section discusses tricks of the trade for organizing your documents and files on the local machine. I'll discuss the folder system and then point out the differences and advantages of the Windows Explorer as a means for maintaining your file system. If you're already adept in using these tools, you may want to skim this discussion just to pick up some tips that might be new to you.

If you're like most people, you're already a card-carrying member of the My Computer users clan or you're addicted to the Windows Explorer. Or, if you're really a geek, like Brian, you use a DOS box to do all your file management. Personally, I can't see doing that for most chores, because the GUI makes such light work of hard disk housekeeping. I'll admit, though, that there are some times when the old `c:>` prompt comes in handy for such things as batch-renaming of files. I was a File Manager convert early on with Windows 3.0, and now I use Windows Explorer to do most of my work in Windows 9x and Windows 2000.

For example, you can rename a whole directory full of files using the DOS `rename` command much more quickly than via the GUI. Say, for example, you have a bunch of files named `report01.doc`, `report02.doc`, `report03.doc`, and so on. Your company has been purchased by the Acme Roadrunner Supply Co. and now you want to rename the files `Acme01.doc`, `Acme02.doc`, and so on. With the DOS-style `rename` command, you can type `rename report*.doc acmeco*.doc`.

MAKING NEW FOLDERS

Hard disks have a way of collecting data files at an exponential rate, and soon you'll find yourself overwhelmed by a staggering number of files, many of which you don't remembering creating. Hard disk management tools such as Defragmenter, Backup, and Disk Cleanup are covered in Chapter 7, "Using the Simple Supplied Applications," so I won't go those that here. Suffice it to say that knowing how to view the contents of local or network computer mass storage devices and even floppy drives is a central part of everyday computer management.

As with a real-world filing system, folders are the building blocks of data organization. The Windows operating system, itself, has evolved over the years to utilize folders as it grew more and more complex.

Tip #55

If you poke around through My Computer or Windows Explorer, you'll discover a complex tree of folders under both WINNT and Program Files. These typically are branches of your hard disk that you'll not want to make modifications to. In fact, you'll be warned against it when you view your WINNT folder (or wherever you chose to install the Windows 2000 Professional files).

Moving files around in the WINNT folder can cripple the operating system. Likewise, your applications can suffer potential incapacitation if you're not careful while poking around in the Program Files tree. It's not advised unless you know what you're doing. Moving system files and program files should be left primarily to the Windows Setup program and specific application setup programs.

Note

More advanced issues, such as Ffile and folder encryption, will be covered in Chapter 33, "Managing the Hard Disk." File and folder sharing for use by others on the LAN is covered in Chapter 22, "Using a Windows 2000 Network."

Many users take the approach of dumping all their files on their Desktop for easy access, or alternatively into their My Documents folder. Some older programs default to their own directories for storage, which really makes for trouble. There are plenty of reasons to organize your files: You'll know where things are, you'll be more likely to make backups, and you'll be less likely to accidentally erase your doctoral dissertation that was in the WordPerfect directory that you deleted so you could install a new word-processing program. Whoops.

In Windows 9x, storing important documents on the Desktop is potentially disastrous because that folder actually exists *under* the Windows directory. Therefore, during a complete reinstallation of Windows, forgetting to backup the C:\Windows\Desktop directory could lead to a sudden disappearance of anything on the Desktop. Microsoft seems to have wised up, and in Windows 2000, the Desktop is now under C:\Documents and Settings.

Saving all your files in one directory without sorting them into folders makes creating backups and clearing off defunct projects that much more confusing. It's difficult enough to remember which files are involved in a given project without having to sort them out from one another. Although the Save As dialog boxes for most programs (see the last chapter) have a button for creating new folders, even this doesn't mean you're going to remember where things are or that you won't want to create new folders later to rearrange your work.

 If you're worried about losing your data files during the reinstallation, see "Preventing Data Loss When Reinstalling Your OS" in the "Troubleshooting" section at the end of the chapter.

With that preamble in mind, just think folders, folders, folders. When in doubt, over-organize. The low cost of hard disk space these days provides us all the opportunity we need to be efficient organizers, thus easing the process of data backup and recovery.

To create new folders, do the following (then we'll quickly cover how to move items between the folders):

1. Get to the Desktop. If you want to create a folder, skip to step 4.

2. Open My Computer and click the drive where you want to store the new folder.

3. Open the folder under which the new directory will go.

4. Right-click on a *blank* area in the window (or on the Desktop) and choose New. Make sure you're not clicking an existing file or folder! Wait a second or two for the shortcut menu to pop up and then choose Folder (see Figure 6.8).

PART

II

CH

6

Figure 6.8

5. A new folder appears called New Folder. Its name is highlighted and ready for editing. Whatever you type will replace the current name. Press Enter to complete the naming process.

If you're coming from Windows 3.x, remember, long names are acceptable, even with spaces between words. Therefore, a folder could be named *My Brain Surgery Home-Exam Essay Questions.*

Tip #56	A name can contain up to 255 characters, including spaces. However, it's not recommended that you create folder names that long because most programs can't interpret extremely long filenames. Very long names will be truncated (shortened) at times for display onscreen, so something a little more modest is a good idea. I like to keep filenames down to about 20 characters or so for easy display in folders, on the Desktop, and in Windows Explorer. Certain characters are not acceptable as folder (or file) names. Filenames mustn't contain the following characters:
	`\ / : * ? " < > ¦ .`
	However, remember that if remote users will be looking at your files, they may need shorter names. This will be true of anyone connected via an operating system that doesn't understand long names, such as Windows 3.x machines.

Obviously, after you have folders created, you'll have the option of saving your work in those folders or moving items to them when you get into a hard disk housekeeping frenzy.

MOVING AND COPYING ITEMS BETWEEN FOLDERS

Moving files and folders from place to place is simple once the destination is created. As usual, there are multiple ways to do this:

- Drag and drop
- Cut, copy, and paste using menus
- Cut, copy, and paste using standard shortcut keys (Ctrl+X, Ctrl+C, and Ctrl+V)

Tip #57	Pressing Backspace while in a folder window moves you up a level in the directory structure. Also, pressing Home takes you to the first item and pressing End takes you to the last. Pressing Enter opens the selected item.

For drag and drop, first position the source and destination windows on the screen at the same time so you can drag from one to the other. You can drag document icons, shortcut icons, or folder icons—the procedure is the same for all of these. When you drop an item, be sure to drop it on an empty space in the destination folder, not on top of another icon—otherwise, you put the source item *inside* the item under it. If you accidentally do this, just open the target and drag the object out again, or, if the incorrect destination was a folder, open any folder and choose Edit, Undo Move or right-click in any folder choose Undo

Move from the pop-up menu. (Do this immediately after making the mistake, though. In other words, don't do any other copying or moving in between.) Also, if you press Esc *before* you drop an object, the process of dragging is canceled.

Figure 6.9 illustrates the process of dragging and dropping an item from the Desktop into a folder.

Figure 6.9
Working with folder windows and objects is as simple as dragging from the source to the destination and then dropping.

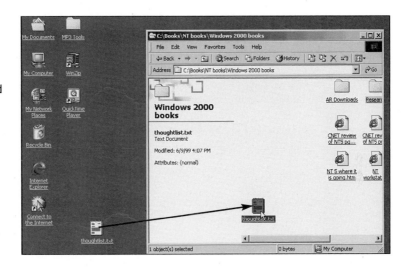

 If you get lost while dragging and dropping files, see "Drag and Drop Confusion" in the "Troubleshooting" section at the end of the chapter.

 If you accidentally dropped a file in the wrong folder and now can't find it, see "Dragged and Lost" in the "Troubleshooting" section at the end of the chapter.

SELECTING SEVERAL ITEMS

You can select a bunch of items at once to save time. The normal rules of selection apply:

- Draw a box around them starting in the upper-left corner and dragging to the lower right.
- Press the Ctrl key and select each additional object you want to work with (remember, if in single-click mode, this just means pointing and waiting a second—no clicking). Use this technique to select a bunch of noncontiguous items.
- Select the first of the items, hold down the Shift key, and click the last item. This selects the entire *range* of objects between the starting and ending points.

After several items are selected (they will be highlighted), right-clicking any one of the objects will bring up the Cut, Copy, Paste menu. The option you choose will apply to *all* the selected items. Also, clicking anywhere outside of the selected items will deselect them all, and Ctrl-clicking (or pointing) to one selected object will deselect it.

PART

II

CH

6

Tip #58	Take a look at the Edit menu in any folder window. There are two commands at the bottom of the menu: Select All and Invert Selection. These can also be useful when you want to select a group of files. Suppose you want to select all but two files; select the two you don't want and then choose Edit, Invert Selection. Ctrl+A is a handy shortcut for selecting all files or folders in the active window.

Tip #59	Drag-and-drop support is implemented uniformly across the Windows 2000 Professional interface. You can drag and drop most objects in Windows 2000 using this same approach. In general, if you want something placed somewhere else, you can drag it from the source to the destination. For example, you can drag items from the Search box into a folder or onto the Desktop, or you can add a picture attachment to an email you're composing by dragging the picture file into the new email's window. Also, the destination folder does not have to be open in a window. You can drop items into a closed folder icon for the same effect.

Arranging your screen so you can see source and destination is graphically lovely and intuitively reassuring, because you can see the results of the process. However, it's not always the easiest to set up. Once you get familiar with the interface, you'll want to try the Cut, Copy, and Paste methods of moving files and folders. In the Windows NT and 3.x interfaces, Cut, Copy, and Paste are reserved for data within applications, such as text and graphics. In the 9x and 2000 interfaces, they also apply to files, folders, and other interface objects.

Without making the source and destination windows or folders visible at the same time, you can copy or cut an item (or group of items) and copy or paste it into the new folder location, using the familiar Edit menu choices or shortcut keys. The right-click menu works, too. Here are the steps:

1. Select the item or items to be moved.

2. Choose Edit, Cut.

3. At this point, failing to paste the file into a destination or pressing Esc will abort the cutting and copying process. Nothing will be lost. The file will remain in its original location. However, if you open the destination folder and either right-click in it and choose Paste or open its Edit menu and choose Paste, it will magically show up in the new location. If, when you go to paste, the Paste command is grayed out, it means you didn't properly cut or copy the object. Try again. Remember, you must use the Cut or Copy command on a file or other object immediately before using the Paste command.

Note that if you want to make a copy of the file rather than move the original, you'd choose Copy rather than Cut from the menu. Then, when you use the paste command, a copy of the file appears in the destination location.

Finally, to delete items, don't use Cut. Cutting is reserved for moving (before subsequent pasting). If you cut a folder or file and then don't paste it, the GUI will assume you changed your mind—it won't be altered. Therefore, you might be surprised to find that it's still right where you last saw it. This is not standard Windows behavior, because in a program such as a text editor, cutting deletes the selection even if you don't bother to paste it elsewhere. If you want to delete a folder, file, or other object, highlight it and choose File, Delete, press Del, or click the X in the toolbar. The icon should fully disappear and not leave a ghost behind, as is the case when cutting.

As an alternative to this method, you can delete almost anything in Windows by dragging it into the Recycle Bin. You'll always be asked to confirm the deletion. There's no easy way to turn off this sometimes-annoying confirmation query. If you throw something away, you can get it back until you empty the trash, as explained in the section "Managing the Recycle Bin," later in this chapter.

Caution

Deleting a folder deletes all its contents, too. That content could include additional subfolders. Use the Delete command with forethought when nixing folders.

Caution

Don't try moving program files unless you know they have not registered themselves with the operating system and they can harmlessly be moved around between folders. If you must move applications, use a tool specifically designed for this, such as MagicMover from PowerQuest, a program bundled with PartitionMagic (see www.powerquest.com).

MOVING VERSUS COPYING

The Windows 2000 GUI will usually assume you are *moving* an object rather than making a copy of it during a drag-and-drop procedure. When you're moving items between folders, and folders between drives, this is the logical assumption. However, it's not always what you want. The general rule about moving versus copying is simple. When you *move* something by dragging, the mouse pointer keeps the shape of the moved object (see Figure 6.10).

Figure 6.10
The cursor looks like the object when you're moving it.

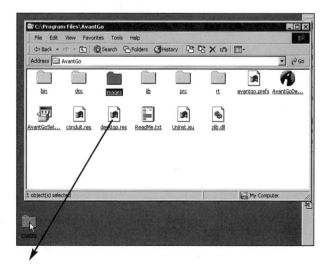

However, when you *copy*, the cursor takes on a plus sign (see Figure 6.11).

Figure 6.11
The icon is given a plus sign when you're copying it.

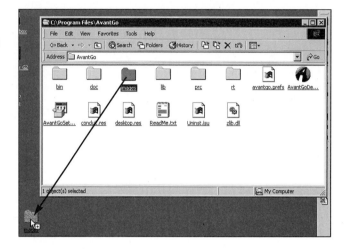

When using drag-and-drop methods, you can easily switch between copying and moving by pressing the Ctrl key as you drag. In general, holding down the Ctrl key causes a copy. The plus sign will show up in the icon so that you know you're making a copy. Pressing Shift as you drag ensures that the object is moved, not copied.

This trick isn't always reliable, however. Therefore, when I'm in doubt about whether the GUI is going to copy or move an item, and it's a critical item, I ensure the correct operation. Here's the trick: The easiest way to fully control what's going to happen when you drag an item around is to *right-click and drag*. Place the pointer on the object you want to move, copy, or make a shortcut for and then press the right mouse button (or left button if you're left handed and have reversed the buttons) and drag the item to the destination. When you drop the object, you'll be asked what you want to do with it, as shown in Figure 6.12.

Figure 6.12
This menu pops up when you right-click-drag an item to a new location.

Choose your desired option. Being able to create a shortcut this way is pretty nifty, too. Often, rather than dragging a document file (and certainly a program) out of its home folder just to put it on the Desktop for convenience, you'll want to make a shortcut out of it. Clicking the shortcut will then run the app, open the document, or do whatever the real McCoy does when you click it.

Tip #60

> It's not uncommon that, due to a slip of the wrist (or a finger on a touchpad), you'll realize you've accidentally dragged an item, such as an entire folder, from one location to another. Sometimes you won't even know what you've done—a folder just suddenly disappears. All you can assume is that it has been dragged and dropped into a destination folder somewhere. Instead of going hunting, you should just check the Edit menu to see whether there's an option at the top of the menu called Undo Move. If there is, choose it to reverse the action.

ORGANIZING DOCUMENT FILES

All the preceding discussion about copying and folders applies to the files that are in those folders, too. Moving and copying documents works just like moving and copying folders—you just drag and drop or use Cut, Copy, and Paste. When you want to copy files using the drag-and-drop technique, you press the Ctrl key while dragging. If you want to create a shortcut, you right-click-drag and choose Shortcut from the resulting menu.

Notice, however, that right-click menus for documents have a few more choices on them than they do for folders—Open, Open With, and Print. In Windows 9x, there's also Quick View, a feature that lets you display the most popular file formats quickly and easily from the file's right-click menu or folder window. However, Quick View isn't included in Windows 2000. Here's what these extra menu options do:

- Open—Use this option to open the document with the associated program, assuming there is one. File types become associated with an app typically during installation of the program. *Associations (page 1046)* can be made manually later when necessary. (See "Managing File Associations," later in this chapter.)

- Open With—Enables you to open the file with a program other than the one it's associated with. You'll be presented with the Open dialog similar to the one shown in Figure 6.16, listing the installed programs that Windows knows about. Choose the program from there. If the program you want to use isn't listed, click Other and browse around until you find it.

- Print—This option secretly opens the associated application and prints the documents to the default printer. You don't get to choose the printer. (See Chapter 9 for more about printing.)

RENAMING FILES

When renaming a file, be careful not to change the extension—unless, of course, you intend to, for purposes such as having the file open in a different application than the one originally intended. This won't be an issue if the extension of the file isn't showing because then you're prevented from altering the extension. However, if you have elected to display extensions of registered file types (see the discussion in Chapter 5, "Using the Windows 2000 Interface," and the discussion later in this chapter about folder options) and you change a registered file's extension, you'll see an error message when you finalize the name change.

PART

II

CH

6

The message will alert you that the file might not open correctly when clicked. Just click No to the message and rename the file again, making sure to give it the same extension that it had before.

PUTTING ITEMS ON THE DESKTOP

As mentioned several times in passing, the Desktop is a convenient location for either permanent or temporary storage of items. Many folks use the Desktop as a home for often-used documents and program shortcuts. I'm quite fond of using the Desktop as an intermediary holding tank when moving items between drives, computers, or to and from floppy disks. It's particularly good for pulling found items out of a Search window or other folder while awaiting final relocation elsewhere.

Here are some quick notes about use of the Desktop that you should know about. For starters, you can send a shortcut of an object to the Desktop very easily by right-clicking it and choosing Send To, Desktop (thus creating shortcut).

Second, remember that the Desktop is nothing magical. Actually, it's just another folder with a few additional properties, prime among them is that you can have active Internet-based information in it, such as stock tickers, weather, and the like (see Chapter 12, "World Wide Web," for more details). Also, each user on the machine can have his/her own Desktop setup, with icons, background colors, screen saver, and such.

The major feature of the Desktop is that whatever you put on it is always available by minimizing or closing open windows or more easily by clicking the Show Desktop button on the Quick Launch bar. Keep in mind that some items cannot be moved onto the Desktop—only their shortcuts can. For example, if you try dragging a Control Panel applet to the Desktop, you'll see a message stating that you cannot copy or move the item to this location.

If you must be able to access a Control Panel applet from the Desktop, just create a shortcut to the applet and place it on the Desktop. However, in other cases when you're copying and moving items around, particularly when using the right-click method, you'll be presented with the options of copying, moving, or creating a shortcut to the item. What's the best choice?

Here are a few reminders about shortcuts. Remember that they work just as well as the objects they point to (for example, the program or document file), yet take up much less space on the hard disk. For this reason, they're generally a good idea. What's more, you can have as many shortcuts scattered about for a given object as you want. Therefore, for a program or folder you use a lot, put its shortcuts wherever you need them—put one on the Desktop, one on the Quick Launch bar, one on the Start menu, and another in a folder of your favorite programs on the Desktop.

Tip #61	Shortcuts take up the minimum amount of disk space that your file system and hard disk allows. This minimum unit is called an *allocation unit*. Typically, this is less than 1KB of space on a FAT32 partition, or about 512 bytes on NTFS.

Make up shortcuts for other objects you use a lot, such as folders, disk drives, network drives and printers, and Web links. From Internet Explorer, for example, drag the little blue E icon that precedes a URL in the address bar out to the Desktop to save it as a shortcut. Clicking it will bring up the Web page.

Caution

> Remember that shortcuts are not the item they point to. They're aliases only. Therefore, copying a document's shortcut to a floppy or a network drive or adding it as an attachment to an email doesn't copy the document itself. If you want to send a document to some colleagues, don't make the mistake of sending them the shortcut unless it's something they'll have access to over the LAN or Web. If it's a shortcut to, say, a word-processing document or folder, they'll have nothing to open. Remember, if the icon has a little curved arrow on it, it's a shortcut, not the real thing.

In Windows 9x, the link between shortcuts and the objects they point to can be broken. This happens typically when the true object is erased or moved. Clicking the shortcut results in an error message. In Windows 2000, this problem was addressed in an ingenious way. Shortcuts are adjusted when linked objects are moved. The operating system keeps track of all shortcuts and attempts to prevent breakage. Shortcut healing is built into Windows 9x, but it's more clunky and happens only when you try to use the shortcut, thus resulting in delays while the operating system hunts the entire hard disk for a possible match. (Often the suggested match doesn't come close.)

If you're in doubt about the nature of a given shortcut, try looking at its properties. You may find it telling, or at least interesting. Right-click the shortcut and choose Properties. Figure 6.13 shows an example.

Figure 6.13
A shortcut's properties.

Clicking on Find Target will locate the object the shortcut links to and will display it in a folder window.

Tip #62	To quickly bring up the Properties dialog box for most objects in the Windows GUI, you can highlight the object and press Alt+Enter.

SAVING FILES ON THE DESKTOP FROM A PROGRAM

Because the Desktop is a convenient place to plop files and folders, modern applications' Save As boxes list Desktop as a major option. Figure 6.14 shows a Save As box from WordPad.

Figure 6.14
Saving to the Desktop is easy in modern applications.

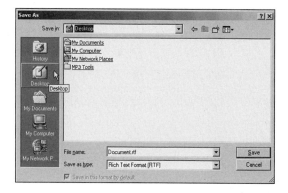

Even if the app's dialog box doesn't have the Desktop icon in the left pane, the drop-down list at the top of the box will have it. Windows 3.x programs don't know about the Desktop, so things get a little trickier. Saving a file to (or opening one from) the Desktop from a Windows 3.x program takes a little more doing. Still, you can do it. Here's how:

1. Open the Save, Save As, or Open dialog box from the File menu as usual.

2. In the dialog box, select the drive that contains Windows. This is probably your C: drive.

3. Switch to the `Documents and Settings` directory. Then look for your `Desktop` subdirectory. As mentioned earlier, it's going to be on a path similar to this, for most machines:

        C:\Documents and Settings\Robert Cowart\Desktop

It can be a pain to locate the Desktop in a Windows 3.x program's Save As box, because long filenames will be truncated to 8.3-style names and have ~ marks imposed on them. Here's how that works: For 16-bit programs, Windows removes spaces, shortens long names to six characters, and inserts a ~ character and then a number. If two files have the same first six characters (for example, `Bob's resume` and `Bob's resume revised`), the number is incremented for the second file. Therefore, those files appear as `bobres~1` and `bobres~2`.

Figure 6.15 shows an example of locating Bob's Desktop from a Windows 3.x–style dialog box.

Figure 6.15
Saving a file to the Desktop from a Windows 3.x–style dialog box.

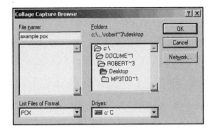

Note

The location of the Desktop folder for a user will not be on the local machine if *IntelliMirror (page xxx)* is being used on a network using Windows 2000 Server in such a way that the user's Desktop will follow him or her from workstation to workstation. In this case, the Desktop will be in a folder on the server and will be more difficult to locate from an old-style Save As dialog box. Just use another folder to save the file and then move it to the Desktop using My Computer or Windows Explorer.

WORKING WITH FLOPPY DISKS

Despite the huge storage capacities of today's hard disks, wimpy little floppies are going to be with us for awhile. They're great for quick-and-dirty backups, posting files in the mail, and "sneaker-netting" some work down the hall. Even if you have a Zip drive or higher-capacity type of floppy disk in your machine, the way you work with them remains the same. This section explains formatting, moving, and copying files to and from floppies.

You can work with floppies through multiple avenues, just as you can the hard disk or network drives:

- My Computer–style folder window
- The Send To option
- Windows Explorer
- The command prompt

I'll cover the first two items here. Windows Explorer is covered later in this chapter. For DOS-type commands, refer to the command reference in the back of this book or open a command prompt window and type copy /? to read some help information about the copy command.

COPYING TO AND FROM A FLOPPY WITH MY COMPUTER

You know from earlier parts of this chapter how to copy and move files between folders. Moving files to the floppy disk isn't much different. You can open a window to display the contents of your floppy disk by opening My Computer and clicking the floppy disk icon (typically called *Floppy A*) or switching to any open folder window, clicking the Address drop-down list, and choosing 3 ½" Floppy (A:). Figure 6.16 shows an example of floppy contents displayed this way.

Figure 6.16
Display the contents of a floppy drive by choosing the appropriate floppy from the Address list.

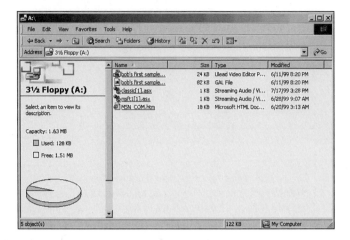

Note

If you don't have a floppy disk in the drive, you'll see an error message when you try to access it.

Most programs' Save As boxes will have a similar choice for saving files directly to the floppy disk.

When the floppy drive's contents are displayed, you can easily work with it just as you do with other folders. Drag items to and from the window to other folders or to the Desktop. Note that when you replace one floppy disk with another, the computer doesn't know about it automatically. After you change the disk, the contents of an open floppy disk window will still be the same, even though the disk holds a completely different set of files. You'll have to update the contents of the floppy disk's window by pressing press the F5 key or choosing View, Refresh.

Tip #63

The F5 key works to refresh the display fairly universally across the Windows GUI and in some other programs as well. For example, in Internet Explorer, F5 refreshes the Web page, and in Outlook Express, F5 updates the Inbox by checking for new mail.

Sometimes when using a floppy disk you'll see an error message alerting you that the disk has not yet been formatted, that the disk can't be read, or something else, such as the disk is write protected.

Why Do Good Floppies Sometimes Report as Bad Under Windows 2000?
Sometimes, when you access a floppy disk from your Windows 2000 computer (this can happen in Windows NT, too) the following error message appears:

`STOP: The disk media is not recognized, it may not be formatted.`

This is annoying, especially when the same disks on the same computer work correctly with MS-DOS or Windows 9x. The disks work correctly after you format them with Windows 2000 or Windows NT. This seems to happen on disks that are preformatted or that were manufactured without the media descriptor byte written to the disk. MS-DOS and Windows 9x don't require the media descriptor byte on a floppy to be set, so they don't protest when looking at the floppy's contents. The media descriptor field specifies a value that identifies the type of media. Some device drivers use the media descriptor to determine quickly whether the removable media in the drive has changed.

The upshot for you is that you'll sometimes have to format a floppy using Windows 2000 before you can use it, even if it has been formatted on another supposedly compatible operating system. Formatting is discussed later in this chapter.

On 3 ½-inch disks, there's a little tab on the back of the disk that must be in the closed position for the disk to be written to. You'll have to remove the disk and change the position of the tab; then reinsert the disk and try again. Note that if you recycle disks used for software distribution, sometimes they don't have write enable/protect tabs on them. If there isn't a little sliding tab on the disk, try another one or firmly affix a piece of tape over the hole that looks like it should have a tab (it's the larger of the two holes). Use tape with some good stick to it, because you don't want this tape to fall off inside the drive.

COPYING FILES TO A FLOPPY WITH SEND TO

By far the easiest way to copy files and folders to a floppy disk is via the Send To option on the right-click menu. In other chapters, we'll talk more about the Send To feature and how to customize it. Microsoft has provided this shortcut, and it's terrific if you use floppies a lot. Here's how to use it:

1. Right-click any file or folder icon.

2. Choose the Send To option. Depending on your computer's setup, you'll have differing choices in the Send To list (see Figure 6.17). You'll at least have one floppy disk option.

Figure 6.17

PART

II

CH

6

Tip #64

The Send To option is very handy. You can customize the Send To list for other purposes, such as sending a file to a viewer program, to the Desktop, to a compression program such as WinZip (if installed), a network destination, and so on. Just add the destination shortcuts to the `C:\Documents and Settings\`*username*`\SendTo` directory and they'll show up in the Send To list. (Replace *username* with the user's name.)

COPYING FILES TO A FLOPPY'S SHORTCUT

A shortcut to a floppy works as a drag-and-drop destination. Therefore, a convenient setup for copying items to a floppy is to create a shortcut of the floppy drive and place it on the Desktop. When you want to copy items to the floppy drive, insert a disk in the drive, adjust your windows as necessary and drag and drop objects on the shortcut.

FORMATTING A FLOPPY DISK

If the disk isn't formatted, you'll also get an error message, and you'll have to format it before it can be written to. The easiest way to format a disk is to find the floppy's icon (such as in My Computer) and right-click it. Then choose Format. You'll be presented with a Format dialog box. Choose Quick Format to simply erase all the files on the disk. For a full format, checking the validity of the disk media and ensuring that there are no remains of any traceable data on the disk, do not check Quick Format.

You cannot choose a format other than FAT for a floppy disk. Nor can you alter the allocation unit size. You can change the disk label if you want to label the disk, although this is optional.

Unlike under Windows 9x, you cannot format a floppy to boot the operating system. If you want to create an emergency boot disk to attempt to restore a trashed operating system or boot for some other reason, that's done from the Backup application in the administrator's tools. Refer to Chapter 33 for details about this program and system-recovery operations.

If you want the floppy disk to be able to boot up the computer, you have to create an emergency repair disk (ERD). Click Start, Programs, Accessories, System Tools, Backup. On the Tools menu, click Create an Emergency Repair Disk. Follow the instructions that appear on your screen

---

Tip #65

To see how much room is left on a floppy, look in the left pane of the floppy window (refer to Figure 6.16). Alternatively, you can right-click a floppy's icon and choose Properties.

FOLDER DISPLAY OPTIONS

Chapter 5, "Using the Windows 2000 Interface," briefly introduced some of the folder view settings when we talked about the Web view and single-click versus double-click settings. In this section, we'll briefly cover the various settings that affect your view of files, folders, and drives.

In its attempt to create a unified user interface, Microsoft has added numerous standard buttons to all Explorer windows. Some of these tools derive from Web browsers, and some worked their way up from Windows 3.x's File Manager. We now have toolbars with Back, Forward, Search, and History buttons from Internet Explorer, as well as Cut, Copy, Paste, Undo, and View buttons, which classically pertain more to file management on the local computer. For the novice, this is a pretty strange mix of bedfellows. Then again, you can type a URL into any folder's address line and it will bring up a Web page. We'll all just have to get used to this kind of seamless integration.

The default settings for folder viewing will probably be fine for most of your daily rummaging around in the file system. As mentioned in Chapter 5, the most frequent changes people make is whether they want single-click or double-click view as well as the style of listing (large icons, list, details). However, there are lots of additional goodies you can alter, some of which are super useful, some nice for a change of scene, and some downright superfluous.

Take a look at the View menu from any folder window or Windows Explorer window.

Between this menu and the Tools, File Options dialog box, you can control the following items:

- Which toolbars appear on all Explorer windows
- Whether the Explorer bar is displayed and what goes in it
- Whether folders look vaguely like Web pages and whether they're customized with backgrounds and color or custom HTML code
- The size and order (sort) of items being listed, including thumbnail-views of images
- Whether file extensions (the last three letters after the period) will be displayed
- Whether system and hidden files are displayed or are invisible
- Which programs are associated with given file extensions
- Whether clicking a folder opens a separate window or uses the current one
- Which of a zillion column headings should be in the details display
- And much more

The list of options is fairly staggering, so we're not going to bore you with them all here. Many of the options are self-explanatory. I'll cover the most salient ones and point you in the direction of the rest.

SORTING AND TIDYING UP THE LISTING

Regardless of the size and resolution of your screen, you can never see enough of a folder listing. It serves to tidy up the listing and arrange icons because it lets you see more stuff at one time. Here are a few of the basic tidying tricks.

First, when your Desktop (or a folder's) contents are displaying as large icons, they can get jumbled up. Quickly organize them by right-clicking any free space on the Desktop or in the folder and choosing Arrange Icons and then the appropriate command:

Command	Description
By Name	Sorts the display of objects alphabetically based on the name. Folders always appear first in the listing.
By Type	Sorts the display of objects according to type. (The type is only visible when you list the objects' details.) Folders always appear first in the listing.
By Size	Sorts the display of objects in increasing order of size. Folders always appear first in the listing.

continues

continued

Command	Description
By Date	Sorts the display of objects chronologically, based on the date the object was last modified.
Auto Arrange	Keeps the objects lined up nicely at all times. It doesn't ensure that they'll be in any particular order, however. This is a toggle: Choose it once to turn it on and again to turn it off.

The Arrange menus for some specialized windows offer additional options, such as in the case of My Computer. The Recycle Bin window will have its own settings as well.

Of course, if you have the display set to show details (View, Details), you'll have column heads to click for quickly sorting the table of files. Simply click the column heading control above the desired column. For example, to sort by size (something that is often useful when sleuthing out those files that are consuming all your disk space), click the Size heading. The first click sorts in ascending order; the second reverses the order.

Unless you specify that all folders should look like the one you're modifying, most of the basic view settings you make to a folder do not affect other folders. When you close a folder, its settings are stored on disk and will apply the next time you open it. The size, position, listing type and order, and auto-arrange settings are stored with the folder itself and are not global. More global settings such as Web view, single-click versus double-click, and the advanced settings detailed later will affect *all* folder windows, including the Desktop.

VIEWING THUMBNAILS AND PICTURES

As mentioned in Chapter 1, Windows 2000 Professional adds a couple useful features when it comes to viewing images and HTML pages. I tend to prefer standalone programs such as ThumbsPlus for viewing images. However, the rise in popularity of digital photography and Web page design has encouraged Microsoft to add some functionality to the folder system for limited viewing of pictures in several formats, as well as HTML pages.

Windows 98 started the trend with the Thumbnail view in folder windows and Windows Explorer, but it was slow and buggy. Switching to Thumbnail view often crashed Explorer or didn't go into effect until you backed off the folder and then reloaded it. Windows 2000 Professional speeds things up and adds a specialized folder, My Pictures, that even includes a rudimentary image viewer (with a few stupid limitations, I might add). My Pictures is the default location for storing digital photographs and scanned images.

Organizationally speaking, how you store photos depends on the number of them you have. Bob has hundreds of them, being into digital photography. He has a master photo folder with many subfolders, broken down into subjects. Figure 6.18 shows this.

Come up with a system that works for you, adding subfolders when one folder becomes overwhelmed with pictures or you realize it's too general. Once you have your photos organized, making backups of them is a good idea. Bob uses CD-RW discs to store photo files and keep the hard disk on the computer freed up. An extensive photo library can eat up even large disks quickly.

Figure 6.18
This is one way to store photos on your hard disk.

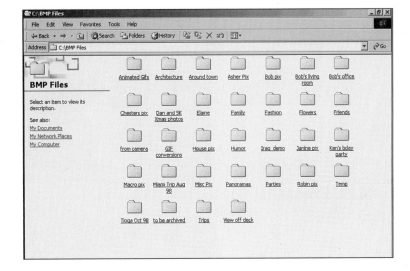

Whether or not you splurge on a good cataloging and viewing program for your photos, you can still use the Thumbnail view to look at your images for easier sorting. Here's how:

1. Copy or move all your photos into folders using your own logical design.
2. Using My Computer or Windows Explorer, browse to that folder.
3. Choose View, Thumbnail. Your photos take a few seconds to render as thumbnails. Figure 6.19 shows a display of a typical collection of photos.

Tip #66

The first time you display thumbnails for a directory, Windows 2000 creates a database of thumbnail images called thumbs.db, which is stored as a hidden file in the same folder as the pictures. To speed up display of thumbnails, only the thumbnails actually showing in a folder window are rendered. When you scroll the window to see others, they'll render while you wait. Beware: The thumbnail files are not small. An exact ratio is difficult to determine, but as an experiment I enabled Thumbnail view for a directory with 7MB worth of JPEG files (39 files) of various typical sizes that a digital camera would produce. Windows created a 1.3MB thumbs.db file. Thumbs.db files won't show up in your folder, even if you enable hidden files to be viewed (see next the section), probably because they're considered system files. If you do a search for thumbs.db, though, it will show up and you can delete such files should you want to.

PART

II

CH

6

Thumbnail view works with the same image file types that Internet Explorer does: BMP, GIF, JPG, and HTML. Unless you've installed a program that changes the file associations (most picture-editing programs such as PhotoShop will, by the way), opening one of these pictures or HTML files by double-clicking will run Internet Explorer and load the file into its window.

Figure 6.19
Displaying thumbnails of JPEG photos stored in a folder.

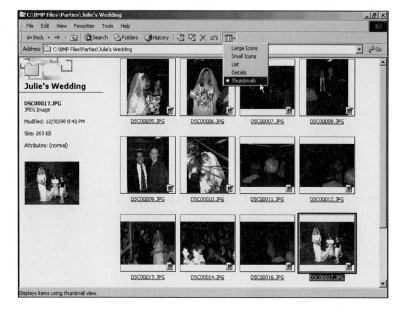

Two other points: Files types other than those listed will be displayed as icons only, so don't bother with thumbnail view for folders that don't primarily contain pictures or Web pages. Even if you don't turn on Thumbnail view, you can see a thumbnail of a picture file. Just select the file and it will be rendered in the left side of the folder window, as shown in Figure 6.20.

Figure 6.20
Selecting a picture file or Web page file will display it if you have Web view turned on in Explorer.

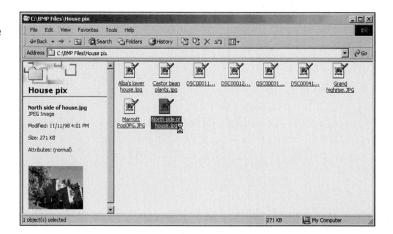

PICTURE VIEWER

If you're working with only a small number of files and don't need to break them up between folders, the My Pictures folder is the place to put them. As mentioned in Chapter 1, this folder has a picture viewer with a zoom function that makes looking at your pictures fairly painless (assuming you have a decent eye). It has some limitations, such as being able to view only the images in that folder. You'd think that subfolders to the My Pictures folder might also have the viewer function, but no go. (However, you can customize any folder to have the features of the My Pictures folder using the Customize This Folder option, covered in Chapter 28.)

My Pictures is a subfolder to My Documents. Therefore, click My Documents and then My Pictures. Figure 6.21 shows the folder with a few pictures in it.

Figure 6.21
The My Pictures folder has an image viewer in it.

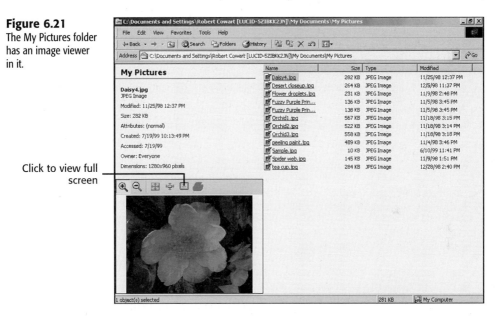

When you click the Full Screen button, the window for the picture will expand to full screen size. The percentage of the screen now filled with the picture depends on the size and resolution of the image.

Experiment with the view buttons on both the small and the larger viewers to see what they do. To make the zoom buttons work, click the tool; then click the picture. Each click zooms either in or out, depending on which zoom tool you've activated.

EXPLORER BAR OPTIONS

New to Windows 2000 Professional are the Explorer bar options, which extend the functionality of both My Computer and Windows Explorer. If you've used the Windows

PART

II

CH

6

Explorer before, you might wonder why we covered the folder system so thoroughly in this book without showing the Windows Explorer. Well, it's because the folder system forms the basis for the Windows Explorer, and unlike the Windows 9x and NT 4 interfaces, you don't actually have to run Windows Explorer to get its functionality. As with other aspects of Windows, these two modes of looking at your computer's data are merging. This will become clear as we show you a few pictures and discuss the Explorer bar settings.

The Explorer bar options are found in Internet Explorer as well as Windows Explorer, and you may be familiar with the concept from Internet Explorer already. In Internet Explorer you can view History, Favorites, Search, or Folders in a pane on the left side of the window. This feature has been added to any and all folders now. If you choose Folders as the left pane, you have what we used to call the *Windows Explorer*. If you like, you can still run Windows Explorer from Start, Programs, Accessories, but the result is the same as adding the Explorer bar to a folder window.

Tip #67	Like listening to the radio? Have a full-time Internet connection? Just add on the Radio toolbar and you've got a zillion-channel radio attached to a folder, Windows Explorer, or Internet Explorer window. Just choose Toolbars, Radio. Once you have the radio bar up, click the Radio Stations button and choose Radio Station Guide. The rest is self-explanatory.

To turn on one of the Explorer bars, click Search, Folders, or the History button on a folder's toolbar or choose View, Explorer Bar and then choose the bar you desire. Only one can be on at a time. The purpose and brief description of each Explorer bar option follows:

- Search bar—Adds the same functionality as the Search window (reachable from the Start button on the taskbar). Use it to search for files, folders, network computers, people, and Web pages.

- Favorites bar—Lists all your Internet Explorer (Web) bookmarks, displayed in a format that's similar to hard disk folders. Use this to revisit your bookmarked Web pages easily while viewing folders. When you click a link, assuming you're online, the right pane switches from local folders and displays the Web page. The toolbar changes to display Internet Explorer tools such as the Home and Refresh buttons.

- History bar—Displays the last several week's worth of Web pages visited. Click a week or a day to open the list of sites visited. Clicking a site will revisit it (assuming you're online), displaying the results in the right pane.

- Folders bar—Displays the contents of the local machine's hard disk, floppy disks, network connections, Control Panel, Recycle Bin, Desktop, and so on. This creates the same view as if you ran the Windows Explorer program from the Accessories group.

USING THE FOLDERS BAR (A.K.A. WINDOWS EXPLORER)

The Search window has already been covered in previous sections, and History and Favorites will be covered in Chapter 12, because they pertain to Internet Explorer and the World Wide Web. Therefore, let's focus on the Folders bar.

For a bird's-eye view of your computer, turning on the Folders bar is the way to go. It makes copying, moving, and examining all the contents of your computer easier than navigating up and down the directory tree through folders. If you're doing housekeeping, copying and moving items around from one folder to another or across the network, or hopping back and forth between viewing Web pages and your local hard disk, mastering this view will serve you well.

Turning on the Folders bar turns any folder window into the Windows Explorer. Introduced with Windows 95, the Windows Explorer is a very capable tool, and the one that both authors and most power users prefer over the folder system. (I covered the folder system in this chapter first, because most of its settings and procedures apply to the Windows Explorer, too, and because many people delve into their PCs' innards via My Computer simply because it's on the Desktop.)

Some have said that Windows Explorer is like the Windows 3.x File Manager on steroids. Unlike the Windows 3.x File Manager, Windows Explorer doesn't let you open multiple windows, however. On the other hand, Explorer is more flexible in design and allows you to copy files, folders, or other objects from anywhere to anywhere, without needing multiple windows. Also, Windows Explorer is a portal into more aspects of your computer than is File Manager. Whether you want to examine the Control Panel, the local area network, the Internet, your hard disk, or the Recycle Bin, it can all be done with a minimum of effort from the Explorer.

Let's take a quick look at the Windows Explorer and what's new or different about it, relative to the folder system.

As mentioned previously, there are two ways to bring up the Windows Explorer view of your computer (see Figure 6.22):

- Open My Computer (or any folder) and choose View, Explorer Bar, Folders.
- Click Start, Programs, Accessories, Windows Explorer.

Figure 6.22
The basic Windows Explorer screen, showing the computer's major components on the left and the contents on the right.

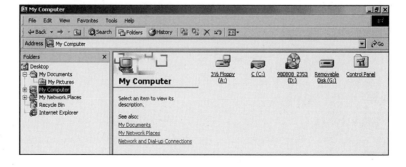

Tip #68

As an easy way into Windows Explorer, I always keep a shortcut to it on the Quick Launch bar, immediately to the right of the Show Desktop button.

DISPLAYING THE CONTENTS OF YOUR COMPUTER

When you run Windows Explorer, all the objects constituting your computer appear in the list on the left. Some of those objects may have a plus sign (+) next to them, which means the object is collapsed; it contains subitems that aren't currently showing. For example, the hard disk drive shown in Figure 6.23 is collapsed. So is My Network Places (which you won't see unless you have network options installed) and the floppy drive (drive A).

Click an item in the left pane to see its contents in the right pane. If the item has a plus sign, click it to open up the sublevels in the left pane, showing you the relationship of the folders and other items in a tree arrangement. In Figure 6.23 you can see that several items (Control Panel, CD-ROM, the network, and so on) have been opened in this way. Notice that the + is replaced with a minus (-) sign, indicating that the object's display has been expanded. Clicking the minus sign causes that branch to collapse. This interface should be nothing new, because it's well integrated into many Web pages and programs nowadays.

Figure 6.23
Click the plus sign to open sublevels of an object.

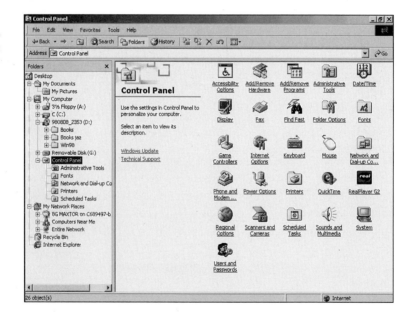

Click the Desktop icon at the top of the tree. Notice that all the objects on your Desktop appear in the right pane.

If you open a local disk drive or disk across the network, you can quickly get a graphical representation of the disk's folder layout. Then click a folder to see its contents. By right-clicking on disks, folders, or files, you can examine and set properties for them. The straight lines connecting folders indicate how they're related. If you have more folders than can be seen at one time, the window will have a scrollbar that you can use to scroll the tree up and down.

Notice that there are two scrollbars—one for the left pane and one for the right. These scroll independently of one another—a feature that can be very useful when you're copying items from one folder or drive to another.

You can customize the toolbars, just as you can in most of the interface. The Toolbars, Customize option lets you fine-tune the button arrangement on the Explorer window.

WORKING WITH FILES AND FOLDERS IN EXPLORER

Working with folders and files in this view is simple. As explained previously, you just click an item in the left pane, and its contents appear in the right pane. Choose the view (Large Icons, Small Icons, List, or Details) for the right pane using either the toolbar's View button or the View menu. In Details view, you can sort the items by clicking the column headings, just as explained earlier in this chapter.

Now here's the good part: Once you select the source item in the left pane and its contents are displayed in the right pane, you can manipulate them. You can drag items to other destinations, such a local hard disk, a floppy drive, or a networked drive. You can drag and drop files, run programs, open documents that have an association, and use right-click menu options for various objects. For example, you can right-click files or folders and choose Send To, 3 ½ Floppy to copy items to a floppy disk.

With a typical hard disk containing many files, once its folders are all listed in the left pane, some will be offscreen. Because the two panes have independent scrollbars, dragging items between distant folders is not a problem. Here's the game plan:

1. Make sure the source and destination folders are open and visible in the left pane, even if you have to scroll the pane up and down. For example, a network drive should be expanded, with its folders showing (using and mapping network drives are covered in Chapter 22).
2. Click the source folder in the left pane. Now its contents appear to the right.
3. Scroll the left pane up or down to expose the destination folder. (Only click the scrollbar, not a folder in the left pane; if you do, it will change the displayed items on the right side.)
4. In the right pane, locate and drag the items over to the left, landing on the destination folder. The folder must be highlighted; otherwise, you've aimed wrong.

This technique will suffice most of the time. Sometimes it's too much of a nuisance to align everything for dragging. In that case, use the cut/copy-and-paste technique discussed earlier in the chapter. Remember, you can copy and paste across the LAN as well as between your local drives.

Here are a few tips when selecting folders:

- Only one folder can be selected at a time in the left pane. If you want to select multiple folders, click the parent folder (such as the drive icon) and select the folders in the right pane. Use the same techniques described earlier for making multiple selections.

- When a folder is selected in the left pane, its icon changes from a closed folder to an open one. This is a reminder of which folder's contents are showing in the right pane.

- You can open a folder by clicking it, typing a letter on the keyboard, or moving the highlight to it with the arrow keys. When selected, the folder icon and name become highlighted.

- You can jump quickly to a folder's name by typing its first letter on the keyboard. If there's more than one folder with the same first letter, each press of the key will advance to the next choice.

- The fastest way to collapse all the branches of a given drive is to click that drive's plus sign.

- You can quickly rearrange a drive's folder structure in the left pane by dragging folders around. You can't drag disk drives, however, although you can create shortcuts for them (for example, a network drive) by dragging them to, say, the Desktop.

- If a folder has subfolders, those will appear in the right pane as folder icons. Clicking one of those will open it as though you had clicked that subfolder in the left pane.

- When dragging items to collapsed folders (ones with a plus sign), hovering the pointer over the folder for a seconds will cause it to open.

- You can use the right-click-drag technique when dragging items if you want the option of clearly choosing Copy, Move or Create Shortcut when you drop the item on the target.

- You create a new folder the same way as in a My Computer window. In the left pane, click the folder you want to create the new folder *under*. Right-click in the right pane and choose New, Folder.

- Delete a folder by clicking it in either pane and then clicking the X in the toolbar, choosing File, Delete, or pressing the Del key. You can also use the right-click menu.

Caution

Although powerful, the folder view is also dangerous. It makes accidental rearrangement of your hard disk's folders extremely easy. When selecting folders, be careful not to accidentally drag them! The icons are small, and this is easy to do accidentally, especially over in the left pane. A little flick of the wrist and a click of the mouse, and you've dragged one folder on top of another folder. This makes it a subfolder of the target. Remember, the left pane is "live" too. Rearranging the directory tree could cause programs and files to be hard to find and even some programs to not work. If you think you've accidentally dragged a folder (its subfolders will go, too) into the wrong place, open the Edit menu. The first choice will probably read *Undo Move*. Choose it, and the folders or files you dragged will be returned to their previous locations.

FOLDER OPTIONS FROM THE TOOLS MENU

Although the factory-installed options for viewing and working with the disk and folders system are acceptable for most work, you may want to fine-tune them to your preferences.

We've already covered a few of the settings, such as the Web view and single-clicking versus double-clicking, in previous chapters. However, there a plethora of additional options that affect the display of files and folders throughout your system.

WHAT THE FOLDER SETTINGS DO

Folder settings can be reached from any folder or in the Windows Explorer. Just choose Tools, Folder Options and click the General or View tab. You'll see the options displayed in Figure 6.24 (the General and View tabs are shown). The settings are somewhat like some options boxes available in Internet Explorer that really let you get into the nitty-gritty of the Explorer's display settings.

Figure 6.24
Two groups of settings for folder display and behavior.

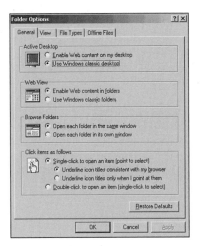 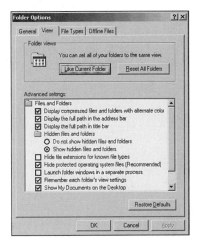

The various settings are described in Table 6.1.

TABLE 6.1 FOLDER DISPLAY SETTINGS

Setting Name	Notes	Does It Affect All Folders or Only the Current One?
Browse Folders. Applies only when the Folders bar is turned off (that is, you're running in a My Computer folder rather than a Windows Explorer–style window).	**Open each folder in the same window:** With this setting, if you open a folder from within another folder (as an example, open My Computer and then open the C: drive), the window stays put. Only the content changes. **Open each folder in a new window:** With this setting, each time you open a folder from within an existing folder, a new window appears. This can create clutter on your screen but lets you drag and drop items between folder windows.	Global

continues

TABLE 6.1   CONTINUED

Setting Name	Notes	Does It Affect All Folders or Only the Current One?
Display compressed files and folders with alternate color	When on, files and/or folders that you've set to be compressed will show up in a different color so you can spot them easily. Only NTFS partitions support compression.	Global
Display the full path in the Address bar	When this is on, the entire path name of an open folder will be displayed in the Address bar of the folder's window. Normally, only the name of the folder itself is shown. For example, a full path name might be C:\Fred's work\Budgets\2001, whereas the folder name alone would display as 2001.	Global
Display the full path in the title bar	Same as previous, but it applies to the display in the title bar of the window (the very top line of the window).	Global
Hidden files and folders	**Do not show hidden files or folders**: When this is on, files marked Hidden or System won't be displayed. (To check or alter the Hidden setting for a file or folder, right-click it and choose Properties.) **Show hidden files and folders:** When set to on, Hidden or System files appear in listings. They appear as "ghost" images, grayer than normal items.	Global
Hide file extensions for known file types	When this is on, files with recognized extensions won't have their last three letters (and the period) showing. Unrecognized (unregistered) file types will still show their extensions. Turn this off to see all extensions, even if they *are* registered in Windows 2000. The reasoning behind hiding file extensions when possible is that it reduces distraction on the screen. It also is an attempt on Microsoft's part to move away from the legacy of DOS and to reduce confusion for users. Once the extension is set and then hidden, you can more easily rename document files without fear of accidentally changing the extension, which would prevent the file from opening in the correct program.	Global
Hide protected operating system files	When set to on, this protects important system files by not displaying them. Be cautious when turning this setting off. There's an extra level of protection provided by the file folder system as well, incidentally. Click the WINNT folder on the boot drive and you'll see a message warning you about even viewing the contents of the folder. This setting does not affect that warning.	Global

Setting Name	Notes	Does It Affect All Folders or Only the Current One?
Launch folder windows in a separate process	This is different from the browsing option at the top of this table. This option, if on, determines that each folder is opened in a separate part of memory (that is, as a separate program). When you open each folder in a separate part of memory, the stability of Windows 2000 is increased. Normally if Explorer (the underlying program that displays folders and files) crashes, all folders will. By setting this option on, the computer's resources will be taxed more when opening multiple folder windows, but because they will be running independently, they'll be less likely to pull one another down in the event of a crash.	Global
Remember each folder's view settings	The Windows documentation states that when this is on, settings for each folder, such as location on the screen, window size, toolbar settings, listing type (Large Icon, Small Icon, List, or Details), will be retained when you close the folder window. When you next open the folder, they'll go into effect.	Global
Show My Documents on the Desktop	If this is off, the My Desktop Documents folder doesn't show on the Desktop. Because some people don't use My Documents as a location for their work, turning it off cleans up the Desktop a bit. It's also a way of hiding your documents from view. This folder will still be available from a folder window or Windows Explorer, though.	N/A

Tip #69

> Of all these settings, the only ones I really prefer to turn on are full pathname, file extensions, and hidden files. Being an old DOS guy, I like to see all the files on the drive and also see the file extensions. Be aware, though, that turning on the display of all files can be a little dangerous because anyone using the computer could browse to your Windows directory and see all your system files, possibly deleting some of them accidentally. System files do not contain personal information, but they contain data and programming that are responsible for making Windows work correctly.

PART

II

CH

6

The View, Customize This Folder command runs a wizard that makes it easy to choose a background image, background color, or even a more elaborate display in a given folder's window. Whenever you or someone else opens this folder, the custom display will appear. Try running the wizard. It will walk you through the steps of customization for a folder.

After you get a folder looking the way you like, you can opt to have all other folders use the same display arrangement. Just click the Like Current Folder button. Click the Restore

Defaults button if you decide you have been mucking around too much and want to return your system to its default state.

MANAGING THE RECYCLE BIN

As you know, when you delete a file or folder, it heads directly to the Recycle Bin. The Recycle Bin temporarily holds such objects until it fills up or you empty it. Because items are not actually *erased* from your computer when you delete them with the Delete command, you can get them back in case you've made a mistake. This is a terrific feature. How many times have you accidentally erased a file or directory and realized you goofed? For most people, even a single accidental erasure is enough. With the Recycle Bin, all you have to do is open its folder, find the item you accidentally deleted, and click the Restore button to return the item to its original location.

Tip #70	This doesn't happen when you delete a file or folder from a command prompt window, incidentally. In that case, it's erased permanently, and you don't have the option of retrieving it.

The Recycle Bin is actually a special folder on your hard disk, as you might imagine. This folder or directory is called `Recycled` or `Recycler`, typically on your C: drive. Also, it's a hidden file. You won't normally be able to see the folder in Explorer or a folder window unless you turn on hidden folders, as explained in the preceding section. CD-ROM drives, even though given a logical drive letter, do not have `Recycled` directories for the obvious reason that you can't delete their files or folders. The Recycle Bin is a weird entity. It's actually a shared resource that the system treats in mysterious ways. For example, each logical drive has its own Recycle Bin in it, but the contents will show up identically in each of them.

As mentioned, the Recycle Bin will hang onto your deleted items only until you empty the bin, or until they fall off the list of contents because the bin became too full. After that, they're gone. At that point, your only hope is to try one of the "undelete" programs, such as one from PC Tools or Norton, the one supplied with DOS 5 or 6—if your hard disk is formatted with FAT or FAT32—or a program such as Undelete for NT from PowerQuest.

Tip #71	Because files aren't actually erased until you empty the Recycle Bin, you won't increase your available disk space until you do just that. If you're running low on hard disk space, check what's in the Recycle Bin. You may want to empty it.

RESTORING SOMETHING YOU ACCIDENTALLY TRASHED

The one major goodie to know about the Recycle Bin is how to get back something you accidentally trashed. (This page alone may make this book worth your investment!) Here's how:

1. Find the Recycle Bin one way or another, such as by going to the Desktop or via a folder window.

2. Click the Recycle Bin icon. The folder will list all the items you trashed since the last time the Recycle Bin was emptied. When viewing the contents of the Recycle Bin, switch to Details view because you can see a lot about when the items were deleted, their original location, their type, and their size. You can also sort on those criteria.

3. Poke around to find the item you accidentally trashed. When you find it, highlight it by clicking it. (You can select multiple items using the techniques described earlier in this chapter.) Some information about the item shows up in the left panel if you have Web viewing activated (see the preceding section), or you can right-click it and choose Properties to see some info about it.

Tip #72	You can quickly restore an item from the Recycle Bin or Windows Explorer by right-clicking it and choosing Restore.

4. Right-click the item (or choose File, Restore). This will move all selected items back to their original locations. Figure 6.25 shows an example in which I'm restoring several screen captures for this chapter (good thing I found them).

Figure 6.25
My Recycle Bin before emptying it.

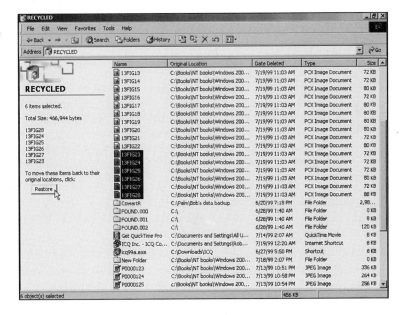

EMPTYING THE RECYCLE BIN

Make a regular habit of visiting the Recycle Bin and emptying it. Otherwise, it just clogs up space on your hard disk. It's always a good idea to have plenty of free disk space for Windows and your programs to work with, so regularly emptying the trash, just like at home, is a good practice.

The easiest way to empty the Recycle Bin is to right-click it from the Desktop and choose Empty Recycle Bin.

ADVANCED RECYCLE BIN PROPERTIES

The advanced Recycle Bin settings are worth considering. They affect how your Recycle Bin works. Recall that when you delete files, they aren't actually erased. They get moved to the Recycle Bin, which is actually a directory on your hard disk. If your hard disk is modest in size or getting crammed, decreasing the size of the Recycle Bin might be in order. In some cases, you might even want to *increase* its size. The options in the Recycle Bin's properties sheet are therefore worth a gander.

To get to the setting, right-click the Recycle Bin icon, either on the Desktop or in Explorer. Then choose Properties.

There are several settings here to contemplate. First, notice that each of your local hard disks or partitions will have a tab. If you choose the Configure Drives Independently option, you'll use those pages to make individual drive settings. Otherwise, you'll just use the global page.

If you don't want to be able to reclaim deleted files, check the Do Not Move Files option. This will speed up deletion. It will also free up disk space immediately upon deletion of files. If you share the computer with other users and security is a high priority, turning this option on may be worth considering. You lose the ability to restore deleted files, but at least your deleted files will not be reclaimable by others.

Tip #73

> On the other hand, deleted files retain the security properties they had when in their original locations. Therefore, if you set a file's security permissions such that only you can access it (via its property sheet's Security tab) and then you delete the file, it will not be available to any prying eyes that may examine the Recycle Bin. You can still reclaim the file if you need to, and your security remains intact. For more about volume, folder, and file security settings, see "Securing Your Files and Folders," in Chapter 32, "Managing Users."

As a default, 10 percent of each drive is used for the Recycle Bin. When you delete a file on drive C, it goes to drive C's Recycle Bin until you empty the bin. When you delete from drive D, (if you have a second hard drive or partition), it goes into that drive's Recycle Bin. As the Recycle Bin fills up, older files will be erased to make room for newer ones, once the 10 percent amount it reached. Practically speaking, the Maximum Size setting determines the number of files or amount of file space allocated for recycling before files begin to be permanently erased. It also determines the maximum file size that will be recoverable. If a file you're deleting is larger than the percentage allocated, Windows will tell you that it can't be put in the Recycle Bin—it will have to be instantly deleted.

If you work with very large files or have a particularly small hard disk, you may want to increase this percentage to, say, 20 percent. That way, you can still restore such a file after accidental deletion.

The final check box about confirmation is normally turned on, requiring you to confirm before Windows 2000 will empty the bin. If you find this annoying, uncheck this box.

Tip #74	If you want to leave confirmation on, but sometimes want to irreversibly delete files without being asked about it, you can. The technique is to highlight the files and Shift-drag them to the Recycle Bin. You won't be able to restore the files, because they're instantly deleted from the hard disk.

When you empty the Recycle Bin, all Recycle Bins are cleared out, regardless of the drive or partition. The Recycle Bin is a systemwide aggregated storage space that can span several drives. You can't purge individual Recycle Bins. However, you *can* permanently delete individual items that are in the Recycle Bin. Just open the Recycle Bin, right-click an item and choose Delete (or click the X in the toolbar). Answer Yes to the confirmation question and the selected item is erased.

Note	In Windows 95, when you delete a folder, the folder doesn't move to the Recycle Bin. Only the files in the folder do. They're removed from their folder. In Windows 2000 (as with Windows 98), deleting a folder causes the entire folder to appear the Recycle Bin and be removed from the source location. If you restore one file that used to reside in the deleted folder, Windows 2000 re-creates that folder in its original location and restores the file into it. You can't open a folder that's in the Recycle Bin in hopes of restoring one file in it. You must restore the whole folder, and then delete what you don't want.

MANAGING FILE ASSOCIATIONS

Contrary to the ways documents and their source apps are organized on the Mac, PC-based operating systems have a flaky way of linking the two. They use the file extension to, in essence, link documents and the programs that create, edit, or run them. On the Mac, every document file is embedded with a "creator" signature that cannot be easily changed or mucked with by something as simple as changing the file extension. On the PC, the file extension is the basis for the association between document and creator application, and the connection is fragile.

The file extension scheme is a throwback to DOS days, and Microsoft has tried to get around it by hiding extensions of known document types by default. This way, it's less likely the user will accidentally modify the file extension and thereby prevent the file from launching the correct app when clicked.

As you probably know, file associations are contained in an internal database maintained by Windows. The database is not much more than a fancy list of file extensions and matching applications (and their locations) used to open, edit, or print each type of document and stored in the Registry.

When you install an application, the setup program for the app makes the necessary changes to the Registry to include itself as one of the apps in the system, and it declares its related file extension(s). Sometimes there are conflicts, however, because extensions are only three letters long (some are four, but three is standard), and some programs fight over who gets what documents.

For example, HTM (Web pages), MID (MIDI), and MP3 files are regularly fought over by makers of competing software. Netscape and Microsoft both want to woo you to their browsers for viewing HTM files. Real Networks and Microsoft fight over the media playing software (Real Player versus Windows Media Player). And there are zillions of photo-editing programs for retouching GIF and JPEG files. Install a new program, and it takes over the associations.

All this is very annoying to the user, because we're repeatedly hassled by dialog boxes alerting us to the fact that all our "whatever" files are not currently set to be played or viewed by "whatever" program. There's a war going on within our own computers being fought by companies that likely don't care about us; they just want to be king of the hill. What's worse is that sometimes the file associations are changed beyond repair. While writing this book, both of us authors developed system problems that prevented playing certain types of streaming video and sound files. This was apparently the result of installing some products from Real Networks. However, this is a petty rant compared to the next issue.

The biggest problem with the association scheme was that once an extension was registered, it was difficult to open that type of document with another app. There were ways around this, such as opening the app, finding the document via Explorer, and dragging the document into the app's window. Or by using the File, Open command on the app and browsing to the document you wanted to open.

Another approach I've used was to change the extension on the fly. I used to do this a lot, say, with TXT files that I wanted to open in Word. You just highlight the filename, press F2, edit the extension to .doc, and press Enter to save the new name. Then Enter again (or double-click) to open the file. This is too much work, though.

As mentioned earlier in this chapter, Microsoft has thoughtfully added the Open With command to the context menu in Windows Explorer. This lets you try to open a document with the application of your choice, or forever change an association. Brilliant improvement! See Figure 6.26.

Figure 6.26
Opening a document with an app that's not its associated app is now easily possible with the Open With command, which opens this dialog box.

For a one-shot opening, this is the way to go. For example, suppose you want to open a JPEG image in Adobe Photo Deluxe just to fix up some red-eye problems but later want to use Thumbs Plus or Fireworks to resize it or change its resolution for posting on the Web. If the program you're shooting for isn't listed (and it might not be, because not all apps, especially utilities, register themselves with the OS), click the Other button and go searching for the app (EXE) file you want to work with.

→ To learn another technique for quickly choosing the target application, **see** "Tweaking the Send To Folder," **p. 1017**.

Notice the check box at the bottom of the dialog box called Always Use This Program to Open These Files. This option is great. It makes it very easy to change the default association for an extension. In the past, changing the association meant wandering through more boxes and futzing with some rather cryptic settings.

THE CRYPTIC SETTINGS

If you want to get into more of the nitty-gritty of file associations, you can. Short of editing the Registry (which we don't recommend), there's another way in. From any Windows Explorer folder, choose Tools, Folder Options, File Types tab (see Figure 6.27).

Figure 6.27
Changing more detailed file association settings can be done from this box.

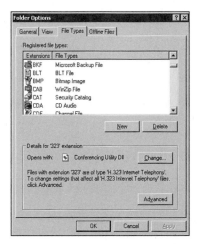

As mentioned, don't bother with this approach unless you must specify details about how parameters are passed to the application when you double-click a document or must use separate applications for, say, printing and editing the same document.

The Change button takes you to the dialog box shown in Figure 6.26. The Advanced button is the one you'll want to play with for detail adjustments (see Figure 6.28).

PART
II

CH
6

Figure 6.28
Setting deeper details of file association.

First, choose the activity you want to alter (for example, Open, Edit, Print); then click Edit to change the properties there. Note that you're going to be getting into some hairy relationships between this file type and the OS, such as how DDE messages are sent (see Figure 6.29). For example, you'll see lines such as the following:

```
[REM _DDE_Direct][FileOpen("%1")]
```

Figure 6.29
Details for DOC files' open action.

Our advice is to tread lightly in the DDE section. Only play around with the Application Used to Perform Action section, unless you understand DDE communication pathways within Windows.

Tip #75

Before getting too far into trying to change associations from the OS side, try looking through your app for an option that allows it to make the necessary changes to the OS. This is often a more effective approach.

TROUBLESHOOTING

PREVENTING DATA LOSS WHEN REINSTALLING YOUR OS

When I reinstalled Windows, my data files were erased, too.

As explained in Chapter 33, some folks preach a strict separation of OS, data, and applications. This segregation provides an increase in fault tolerance. When or if your OS partition dies, you can reformat it, reinstall the OS, and your data is still in tack. If your apps are on yet another partition, you have one level more of the same type of protection. You might want to read Chapter 33 for more about this and similar arrangements.

CLUTTERED START MENU

My Start menu is such a mess. What can I do to clean it up from time to time?

Things will fall out of order on your Start menu, particularly on the Programs submenu. Click Start, Programs and then right-click anywhere on the resulting menu and choose Sort by Name.

DRAG AND DROP CONFUSION

While dragging items around, I got lost or distracted by another window. How do I back out of the process?

This is a good one. If the destination is obscured from view, or even if you change your mind in the middle of a drag-based move or copy, no big deal. Just hit the Esc key. It cancels the process. This is true of the right-click Cut and Copy commands as well, not just when dragging. When you cut a file, its icon changes to gray, waiting to be pasted somewhere. Just hit Esc, and the process is terminated. The file's icon becomes full color again.

DRAGGED AND LOST

While dragging items around, I got lost or distracted and dropped something in the wrong place. I've lost a whole file or folder.

Not a problem. Just go to any folder or the Windows Explorer window and choose Edit, Undo. Check that the Undo action (Undo Move, Undo Copy, and so on) matches what you thought you did, first. The last action that Windows Explorer did will be reversed. It might be something you did yesterday. Therefore, make sure the object you think you lost is actually missing, first. Then make sure the Undo action looks like the action you think you accidentally took. For example, if you think accidentally moved something, make sure you see Undo Move on the menu before you choose the Undo command.

IDENTIFYING QUICK LAUNCH ITEMS

I want to change the pop-up note on the Quick Launch bar items so I can tell what they are.

If you have a bunch of items that look the same, this is a good idea. Folders all look the same, for example. By default, all Quick Launch items are given names. However, you can change them by going into the Quick Launch button's properties and selecting the General tab.

TIPS FROM THE WINDOWS PROS: ORGANIZING YOUR FILES

Telling other people how to organize their computers is about as invasive and ineffective as telling them how to arrange their pantries or closets. Everyone's style is different, and it evolves over time. If you have a long history with PCs, you likely have had numerous strategies that evolve to follow the technology. One year you're keeping all your important data on floppies. The next year, it's on Zip disks. This year it's across the LAN or in Web folders, offsite. With the drop in hard drive prices and increase in capacities, it's now very practical to sport multiple drives and partitions on a single machine, so your storage options are myriad.

Then, there are all the approaches for arranging your Desktop, folders, Start menus, Quick Launch items, and so forth. Here are some tips for keeping your work straight and your apps flying as well as increasing your overall computing efficiency in Windows 2000 Professional:

- Start with your hardware. Have enough RAM in your machine and a speedy-enough processor to make switching between folders, apps, and documents really fast. As I write this, I have 25 icons in my taskbar, on a 300MHz Pentium II with 128MB RAM, and it's plenty fast. If you're hearing even 5 seconds of disk grinding waiting for apps or windows to change when you press Alt+Tab or click taskbar buttons (apps that are already running, mind you, I'm not talking about launching closed apps), your computer probably needs help. (See Chapters 3, "Getting Your Hardware and Software Ready for Windows 2000," and 30, "Maintaining and Optimizing System Performance," for information about upgrading your hardware).

- Keep your Desktop relatively clear. Putting stuff on the Desktop can lead to a visual mess if you do much work at all. It's difficult to see everything at once because you're stuck with Large Icon view, which doesn't lend itself to a top-down approach. It's preferable to use My Documents. My Documents will follow you while roaming on the LAN (if IntelliMirror is set up to support it via Windows 2000 Server), for one thing. Of course, a few shortcuts or folders you're working with for the duration of a project are okay on the Desktop. However, when you're finished with the project, clean up.

- Turn off personalized menus. They're confusing.

- Keep several instances of Windows Explorer open at all times. Rather than hopping around in one copy of Windows Explorer between folders, just to open files and such, have one for each drive, partition, folder, LAN drive, and so on that you work with. Then you can just press Alt+Tab to get to the one you want, quickly.

- Rather than dragging files between folders when you're organizing things, get used to cutting/copying and pasting. That way, you don't need to do all that adjusting of the source and destination windows just to move a silly file. Cut or copy it, Alt-Tab to the destination folder, right-click the exact destination, and choose Paste.

- Can't find a file? Don't waste more than a minute looking for it manually! Press Windows+F to start a search. Type in all or part of the filename and let Windows find it for you. In the meantime, go back to work on something useful. Check the Search window when the hard disk stops grinding.

- Set your programs to autosave your work and/or make backup copies when you open document. For example, I have Word set to autosave every five minutes and make a backup copy whenever I open a document. (See Chapter 33 for much more about file safety.)

PART

II

CH

6

CHAPTER 7

USING THE SIMPLE SUPPLIED APPLICATIONS

In this chapter

WHAT IS ALL THIS?

Although you no doubt have collected your own arsenal of workhorse programs to assist you in your daily chores, Windows 2000 Professional, like past versions, comes replete with numerous freebie utility programs to handle common, everyday tasks. These utility programs range from the bizarre to the useful—from pinball and solitaire to streaming video, CD and DVD players, word processing programs, and a calculator, to name but a few. Whether they are intended for entertainment or as daily helpmates for such tasks as jotting down simple notes or making quick calculations, none of these programs require a degree in rocket science to figure out. They are fairly self-explanatory, and it's also likely you've used them before in their previous versions. Therefore, this chapter covers them only briefly, suggests a few tips, and leaves the rest to you and the Windows Help file. This chapter is offered as reference material (listing updates to the utilities in Windows 2000 Professional when applicable) and as a brief introduction to beginners.

Tip #76	To see a complete listing of programs supplied with Windows 2000, open the Help file, click the Search tab, and search for DVD. Then click Programs That Ship with Windows 2000.

NOTEPAD

Notepad has been around since Windows 3.0. It's a simple, no-frills editor that does no fancy formatting (though it does enable you to change the display font) and is popular for composing "clean" ASCII files. I use Notepad for jotting down quick notes or for editing program code, batch files, and the like. You could say Notepad is a *text editor*, whereas WordPad (see the section later in this chapter) is a *word processor*. Unlike WordPad, Notepad cannot view or edit Word (.DOC) or Rich Text Format (.RTF) files. It's also much leaner, requiring much less memory, and it starts up faster. It's a perfect tool to call up whenever you need to view a simple README.TXT file or fine-tune some HTML code.

Tip #77	You can right-click on the desktop or in a folder; choose New, Text document; and create a Notepad file on the spot. Using it this way is a good technique for taking down a quick memo, making notes about a phone call, or keeping a to-do list on your desktop.

Text-only files contain text characters and nothing else—no character formatting such as italics, bold, underlining, or paragraph formatting information such as line spacing. Sometimes such files are called ASCII files, plain ASCII files, or simply *text files*. As of Notepad 5, the Save As dialog box now allows you to save in several "text only" file formats: ANSI, Unicode, UTF-8, and big-endian Unicode. These formats provide you greater flexibility when you're working with documents that use different character sets. The default is ANSI, and unless you are inserting non-U.S. characters, you should use this format when you save files.

Though visually boring and lackluster, text files do have some important advantages over formatted text documents. Most importantly, they are the lowest common denominator for exchanging text between different programs and even between different types of computers. Literally, any kind of word processor and many other types of programs, from email tools to databases, can share textual information using simple text files, regardless of computer type or operating system.

ASCII, ANSI, and Unicode—Alphabet Soup Anyone?

ASCII stands for American Standard Code for Information Interchange. Standard ASCII is a 7-bit character-encoding scheme used to represent 128 characters (upper- and lowercase letters, the numbers 0 through 9, punctuation marks, and special control characters) used in U.S. English. Most current Intel-based systems support the use of extended (or "high") ASCII, which is an 8-bit system. The 8th bit allows an additional 128 special symbol characters, foreign-language letters, and graphic symbols to be represented. Even with 8 bits, ASCII is not capable of representing all the combinations of letters and diacritical marks that are used in the Roman alphabet. DOS uses a superset of ASCII called *extended ASCII* or *high ASCII*. A more universal standard is the ISO Latin-1 set of characters, which is used by many operating systems, as well as Web browsers.

ANSI stands for the American National Standards Institute. Windows uses the ANSI character set, which is very similar to ASCII. Windows 3.x and Windows 95 support the ANSI character set, which includes 256 characters, numbered 0 to 255. Values 0 to 127 are the same as in the ASCII character set. Values 128 to 255 are similar to the ISO Latin-1 character set but naturally have extensions and incompatibilities.

Unicode, which uses 16 bits, goes beyond ASCII and ANSI. Developed by the Unicode Consortium between 1988 and 1991, Unicode enables almost all the written languages of the world to be represented using a single character set. Using Unicode, 65,536 possible characters can be represented, approximately 39,000 of which have now been assigned, 21,000 of them being used for Chinese ideographs.

Because ASCII files are clean, ASCII is the preferred medium for sending text-based English communications over the Internet and via other information services such as BBSs. However, HTML email is gaining a quick foothold because of its use on the Web, and with the high popularity of Microsoft Word, .DOC files are running a close second. You can be fairly sure that a .DOC file attachment can be read by remote email recipients, especially if they are running Windows. But don't count on it. To be sure your recipients can read an email message or a text file on a disk, stick with the simple text files such as ones Notepad creates.

Source code used to generate computer programs is often stored as text files, too. Because files are clean, without extraneous codes for formatting, program *compilers* (software that converts the source code into a working program) are not confused. Good examples of simple ASCII program code or configuration file code are WIN.INI, SYS.INI, PROTOCOL.INI, BOOT.INI, CONFIG.SYS, and AUTOEXEC.BAT in many Windows computers that control various aspects of Windows, all of which can be edited with Notepad. HTML code for Web pages is another example. You can safely edit Web-page HTML in Notepad.

Windows recognizes any file with a .TXT extension as a text file and opens it in Notepad if you click it. For this reason, README files supplied with programs—even some supplied with Windows—are stored as .TXT files. Take a look around on the Windows 2000

Professional CD, and you'll find some pithy files about setup, networking, and so on. After you open them in Notepad, turn on the word wrap feature (by choosing Format, Word Wrap) to view the document correctly.

NOTEPAD'S LIMITATIONS

As I mentioned previously, Notepad does no formatting. In fact, it does so little that it doesn't even wrap lines of text to fill the window unless you tell it to. Notepad can't properly render or print formatted documents created with WordPad, Microsoft Word for Windows, WordPerfect, or any other fancy word processor. You can open them, but they look like gibberish. Also, it doesn't have any fancy pagination options, though it does print with headers and footers via the Page Setup dialog box. Although you can change the font in Notepad 5, font information isn't stored in the file. Font choice is a personal preference for viewing and printing, and applies to all files you open in Notepad.

Tip #78	Be careful about opening formatted text files with Notepad. If you accidentally save the file, the formatting is stripped out of it, and the file can become useless. If you want to examine executable files or initialization or control files used by programs, I suggest a file viewer intended for this purpose, such as FVIEW. Many utility programs for this purpose are available on the Web. One such program is called QuickView Plus. It's a full version of the quick viewers supplied with Windows 9x.

Notepad files used to be limited in size to about 50KB. That's no longer the case. Even very large files can be loaded into Notepad 5.

RUNNING NOTEPAD

To run Notepad, click Start, Programs, Accessories, Notepad. Notepad then appears on your screen (see Figure 7.1). When it does, you can just type away.

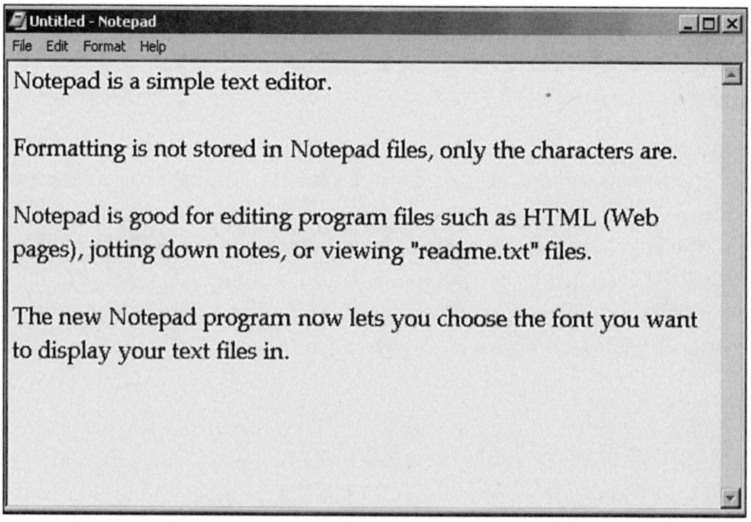

Figure 7.1
You can use Notepad to edit simple text.

Untitled - Notepad

File   Edit   Format   Help

Notepad is a simple text editor.

Formatting is not stored in Notepad files, only the characters are.

Notepad is good for editing program files such as HTML (Web pages), jotting down notes, or viewing "readme.txt" files.

The new Notepad program now lets you choose the font you want to display your text files in.

Of course, you can choose File, New to start a new file at any time. If you've made changes in the previous file, Notepad gives you the expected opportunity to save it before creating the new file. You use the standard File, Open and File, Save As commands.

You should turn on word wrap when you're entering text unless you're entering program code that is line oriented. When you do, the text wraps within the constraints of the window. If you resize the window, the text rewraps to fit the available space. Note that the word wrap setting doesn't affect the text file itself. That is, Notepad does not insert line feeds or carriage returns at the points where the lines wrap.

As with most Windows text programs, the keys shown in Table 7.1 have the effects shown here.

TABLE 7.1 KEYS IN NOTEPAD

Key	Moves Insertion Point To
Home	Start of the line
End	End of the line
PgUp	Up one window
PgDn	Down one window
Ctrl+Left Arrow	Start of previous word
Ctrl+Right Arrow	Start of next word
Ctrl+Home	Start of the file
Ctrl+End	End of the file
F5 (particular to Notepad)	Inserts the time and date
Ctrl+Backspace	Deletes a word to the left
Del	Kills letter right
Backspace	Kills letter left

 If you can't see all the text in a Notepad window, see "My Text Is Chopped Off" in the "Troubleshooting" section at the end of this chapter.

SETTING MARGINS AND ADDING HEADERS AND FOOTERS

Despite the paucity of formatting options for onscreen display, you can format printed output to some degree. Use the File, Page Setup command for establishing headers and footers. Enter your desired footing and heading text. Margin changes and header and footer settings aren't visible on the screen but do print. You can also include the special codes shown in Table 7.2 in the header and footer fields. You can enter these codes alone or within a text string.

PART

II

CH

7

Code	Effect
&d	Includes the current date
&p	Includes the page number
&f	Includes the filename
&l	Forces subsequent text to left-align at the margin
&r	Forces subsequent text to right-align at the margin
&c	Centers the subsequent text
&t	Includes the time of the printing

TABLE 7.2   FORMATTING CODES FOR NOTEPAD

When you print a document, Notepad 5 now lets you choose the page range, the number of copies, and the printer to which the job will be sent. See Chapter 9, "Printing and Faxing with Windows 2000," for more details.

WORDPAD

For more capable word processing than Notepad can accomplish, you can use WordPad. Though it's not Word or WordPerfect, it works fine for most everyday writing chores. It includes most of the formatting tools people need for typical writing projects, and the price is right. You can edit documents of virtually any length, it supports drag-and-drop editing, and it can accept graphics pasted to it from the Clipboard. WordPad supports the following:

- Standard character formatting with font, style, and size
- Standard paragraph formatting with changing line spacing, indents and margins, bullets, justification, and right and left alignment
- Adjustable tab stops
- Search and replace
- Headers and footers
- Pagination control
- Insert and edit graphics
- Undo
- Print preview

It doesn't do tables, columns, indexes, master documents, outline view, legal line numbering, or anything really groovy, though. Go get Word, WordPerfect, Ami Pro, or something else if you have that level of needs.

SAVE AND OPEN OPTIONS

WordPad can save and open files in several formats:

- Rich Text Format—This choice is the default. The Rich Text Format is used more and more as a common format for exchanging documents between word processors, though few, if any, use it as their primary format (it's sort of like an Esperanto for word processors). The Rich Text Format preserves the appearance as well as the content of your document. Graphics and other objects are saved in the file along with the text but may be lost when you open the file with another application.

- Word for Windows 6.0—This choice stores the document in the same format used by Microsoft Word for Windows, version 6.0. If you open the document with Word, all the text, character and paragraph formatting, graphics, and other objects are preserved. If you have Word installed, incidentally, double-clicking a DOC file you created and saved in WordPad opens it in Word, not WordPad. (Later versions of Word, such as Word 2000, should be able to display, edit, and print the file, assuming you installed the Word 6 converter with Word. If not, check Office Setup.)

- Text Files—See the discussion of text files earlier in the chapter.

- Unicode—See the discussion of Unicode earlier in the chapter.

WordPad correctly opens even incorrectly named (wrong extension) RTF and Word 6 files if you select the All Documents option in the Files of Type area in the Open dialog box or type the document's full name. If a file's format isn't detected by WordPad, it is opened as a text-only file. Note that if a document has formatting information in it created by another application, it will likely appear as garbage characters mixed with the document's normal text.

RUNNING AND EDITING IN WORDPAD

To Run WordPad, choose Start, Programs, Accessories, WordPad. The WordPad window then comes up. Figure 7.2 shows an example of a Notepad file.

Figure 7.2
WordPad includes moderately sophisticated word processing features.

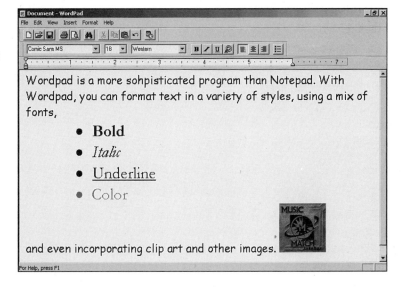

As with most Windows programs these days, you don't have to memorize what each button on the toolbar does. Just position the mouse pointer over the button, and wait for a few seconds. A pop-up description will appear. In addition, the status bar at the bottom of the screen displays a longer help message. Try working with them now to get an idea of what all the buttons do.

When you're doing lots of editing and formatting in WordPad, check the View menu. You can turn on as many of the toolbars as you need to quickly change formatting, tab locations, and so on. A check mark next to a bar's name means it's on. They are toggle settings.

You can drag and drop or "tear off" the various toolbars. Just position the mouse pointer over the far left edge of any bar (don't click a button); then drag the bar where you want it. If you drag the bar to the bottom of the WordPad window, the bar merges with the lower portion of the window. You can also drag the toolbar to the right side of the window so that it becomes a horizontal strip fused with the right window edge. (This trick doesn't work with the Format Bar because the list boxes for typeface and size are too wide to fit in the narrow strip.)

Editing is simple in this program and complies with Windows standards and then adds a few rules of its own. I'll outline them very quickly. Just enter your text as usual. Line wraps happen automatically and are readjusted if you resize the window, change the margins, or change the font size. You can move the cursor around with a click of the mouse or by using the control codes listed for Notepad in Table 7.2.

You can double-click a word to select the whole word. To select the entire document quickly (select all), move the cursor to the left edge of the document until the arrow changes direction, and then Ctrl+click. To select an arbitrary area, click and drag the pointer over the text. Release when the text is highlighted. You can also select areas of text by pressing Shift and using the arrow keys. The spot where you first click (beginning of the selection) is called the *anchor point*. You can triple-click to select a paragraph. After text is selected, you can format it with the toolbars and format menu commands.

To move blocks of text, either select and use Cut, Copy, and Paste from the Edit menu, or drag it with the mouse to the new location and drop it.

Tip #79	To insert characters that aren't available on your keyboard, such as ™, ®, or ©, use the Character Map accessory, covered later in this chapter.

WordPad handles each paragraph as a separate entity, each with its own formatting information, such as tab stops. To apply changes to multiple paragraphs, select them first.

To undo the last command, choose Edit, Undo; click the Undo button (the curving arrow) on the toolbar; or press Ctrl+Z.

Undo can undo the following errors: block deletions, anything removed by pressing Del or Backspace (as a unit), blocks replaced by typing, new text typed (back to the last time you issued a command), and character and paragraph formatting changes (if you select the Undo command immediately after making the change).

ADDING GRAPHICS TO A WORDPAD DOCUMENT

You can insert a graphic—and other *OLE* objects—into a WordPad document in one of two ways: by creating the object from scratch as you insert it or by inserting an existing object stored in a disk file. The basic steps required are similar for either method, but they vary slightly in detail.

- Select Edit, Paste to insert a graphic you've put on the system Clipboard.

- Select Insert, New Object to create a new graphic using another program or an existing file. In the Insert Object dialog box, choose the type of graphic object you want from the list, and click OK. At the insertion point, an area opens for the graphic. You create the graphic in the second program and then exit the graphics program using the appropriate command (typically Exit and Return) and return to WordPad.

- Click the graphic, and then drag the picture's handles (the small black squares along the edges) to resize the image.

After you've pasted the graphic, you have only crude control over positioning it where you want it in the document. You can't move a graphic around with the mouse, and no menu command is available for this purpose. Instead, you must "push" the picture around in your document with ordinary typing, the Backspace key, or the Tab key, or you can cut and paste it into a new location.

Tip #80

When you insert an existing object from a file, the Insert Object dialog box offers a Link check box. If you check this box, any changes to the source file will be reflected in the WordPad file. For more details about sharing data among applications, the Clipboard, OLE, and COM, see Chapter 8, "Sharing Data Between Applications."

DISPLAY OPTIONS

A few WordPad preferences affect viewing of files. You can check the View, Options dialog to see them. All the tab pages except General Options in the Options dialog box pertain to the various types of documents that WordPad can open: Text Only, Rich Text Format (RTF), Word for Windows, Windows Write, and Embedded. Each of these pages offers identical choices. These settings affect display only; none of these choices affect the way your document prints.

Tip #81

If you are upgrading from Windows 3.x or NT 3.x, you've probably used Windows Write, the predecessor to WordPad. Although WordPad beats Write in the looks department, Write actually had greater functionality in some respects. If your word processing needs are so great that they warrant purchasing a high-end program such as Microsoft Word, and you don't mind the clunky look of Write (and older Save As dialog boxes), you might want to keep it around. (Copying WRITE.EXE from the Window 3.x computer to your Windows 2000 computer should do the trick.)

PART
II
CH
7

The following features are missing in WordPad but present in Write:

- Printed headers and footers.
- Full paragraph justification (so that text is flush on both the left and right sides of a paragraph). WordPad has only left, center, and right alignment.
- Double-spacing and 1 1/2-spacing for paragraphs. WordPad permits only single-spaced paragraphs.
- Decimal tabs, allowing you to line up columns of decimal numbers.
- Superscript and subscript character formats.
- A "Regular" character format command, allowing you to remove all styles (bold, italic, underlining, superscripts, and subscripts) from selected text with a single command.
- Capability to insert a hard page break (useful for creating documents with sections).
- The capability to search for nonprinting characters such as paragraph marks, tabs, and page breaks with the Find command.

 If you have trouble inserting tab stops where you want them, see "Adding and Modifying Tab Stops" in the "Troubleshooting" section at the end of this chapter.

Tip #82

Although WordPad can open Write documents, items that WordPad doesn't recognize are converted or discarded. For example, WordPad converts decimal tabs to ordinary tabs, and it simply discards headers or footers.

PAINT

Paint is a simple drawing program that creates and edits bitmapped images (BMP files). Using free-form drawing tools, text, and special effects, you can create projects such as invitations, maps, signs, wallpaper for your desktop, and you can edit images linked into documents created by other programs (see Chapter 8 for more details about linking and embedding).

Let me explain why Paint is called a bitmapped image editor. Your computer's screen is divided into very small dots (*pixels* or *pels*) that are controlled by the smallest division of computer information—bits. A *bitmap* is a collection of bits of information that creates an image when assigned (*mapped*) to dots on the screen. This bitmap is similar to one of those giant electronic billboards in Times Square, New York, that can display the score, a message, or even a picture by turning on and off specific light bulbs in the grid.

Being a bitmapped drawing program, rather than an object-oriented drawing program, Paint has some significant limitations to keep in mind—also some advantages. After you paint a shape, you can't move it independently. You can use the computer to remove an area of the painting and place it somewhere else—as if you were cutting out a piece of the canvas and pasting it elsewhere. But all the dots in the area get moved, not just the ones in the shape you're interested in. Because a given bitmapped image has a fixed number of dots, its resolution is also fixed. It doesn't look any better or sharper by printing it on a higher-resolution printer.

By contrast, object-oriented graphics programs such as CorelDRAW, Adobe Illustrator, or Micrografx Designer treat each shape as a separate entity that can be manipulated and moved independent of other items. In addition, object-oriented graphics always appear and print at the maximum possible resolution of the device you're using. Windows 2000 Professional doesn't come with an object-oriented graphics program. Simple object-oriented graphics modules are included in some word processors and spreadsheets.

Windows 3.x had a bitmapped drawing program called Paintbrush, but Windows 2000's Paint has more features. Generally, the two programs are very similar in functionality, though. In Paint, the right mouse button actually does stuff (like you can paint with it). You get two new tools: the eyedropper and the pencil. Manipulating selections is much easier now that they have resize handles, and you can rotate them or even use them as a brush shape. Print Preview lets you check your work before you print, saving paper and time. It's easier to work with text by virtue of the Text toolbar (for setting fonts, sizes, and styles). And you can undo three previous commands, not just one. Some features were dropped, such as the Color Eraser tool. Also, you can't save files in the PCX (PC Paintbrush) format, and shadow or outline text styles are history.

An addition to Paint that appeared in the Windows 98 version and carries over is the capability to save files in JPG and GIF formats in addition to the usual bitmapped (BMP) formats. But you can do so only if the appropriate Office 97 (or later) Graphics Import Filters are installed. If you have installed Office with those options, the Open and Save As dialog boxes in Paint will include GIF and JPG extensions. Otherwise, only BMP files are supported. If what you want to do is edit photo images (typically JPG, TIF, or GIF) created with a digital camera or scanner, you should use another program such as Adobe PhotoShop or PhotoDeluxe, Microsoft PhotoDraw, Paint Shop Pro, Kai Photo Soap, or another of the many popular programs designed specifically for photos.

STARTING A NEW DOCUMENT

To bring up Paint, choose Start, Programs, Accessories, Paint. When the Paint window appears, maximize it. Figure 7.3 shows the Paint window and its component parts. I've loaded a BMP-file photograph into the program by double-clicking on a BMP file I found using the Search tool.

WORK AREA, TOOLBOX, TOOL OPTIONS, COLOR PALETTE

You create the drawing in the central area (or *work area*). Down the left side, the *Toolbox* holds a set of tool buttons for painting, drawing, coloring, and selecting. You choose colors from the *Color Box* at the bottom of the window. The status bar offers help messages on menu choices and displays the coordinates of the mouse pointer.

The object is to choose a tool and start fiddling around. You'll soon learn which tool does what. Hovering your mouse pointer over a tool displays some pop-up text with the tool's name. Some of the tools are a little difficult to figure out, but if you open Help and look up the tool, you can find descriptions there for each of them.

Figure 7.3
The Paint window.

When you're starting a new picture, you must attend to a few details; then you can get on with painting.

1. If a picture is open, choose File, New to erase the previous image.

2. Choose Image, Attributes to set the picture size and whether it's color or black and white.

You can alter the size of the overall canvas when you're painting, so don't lose any sleep over adjusting the size. However, after you convert to black and white, you can't revert to color because the color information is literally discarded.

Remember that an image prints smaller on paper than it appears onscreen because the printer's resolution is much higher (each dot is smaller). Also, if you increase the resolution of your screen, the picture will look smaller because each component dot is smaller.

To estimate the printed size, determine the *DPI* of your printer and do the math. For example, say you want a printout of 3×5 inches on the printed page, and your printer's resolution is 300 dots per inch. In this case, you would want an image that was 900 pixels wide and 1,500 pixels high (or vice versa). Remember, too, that if your picture is wider than it is tall, and if its printed width is more than about 8 inches, you need to change the page orientation for printing from Portrait to Landscape. To do so, just choose File, Page Setup, and select the appropriate button.

Maximum picture size is limited by available memory and color setting. Black-and-white pictures use far less memory than color pictures do, so they can be much larger. Paint lets you know if you set a picture size that's too large to fit in memory. A black-and-white image is not the same as a grayscale image, in which you can paint with 16 or more separate shades of gray. Black and white have only two colors—black and white. Duh. To create a grayscale image, you must place the desired shades of gray on the palette.

Tip #83

You can resize a picture with the mouse by dragging the handles on the edges of the white workspace; however, the direct entry method in the dialog box is more accurate.

WORKING WITH THE PAINTING TOOLS

Before beginning to use a tool, you set the color to paint with. You need to set two colors: background and foreground. One of the most fundamental techniques to learn is selecting a color to paint with. In Paint, you control both foreground and background colors independently.

The foreground or drawing color is the main color you paint with. For example, when you add strokes with Paint's paintbrush, draw lines or shapes, or even when you type text, these items appear in the currently selected foreground color. The term *background color* is somewhat different. Many of the tools (such as the Brush, Pencil, and the Shape tools) let you paint with the so-called background color just as you would with the foreground color. All you have to do is hold down the right mouse button instead of the left one as you paint. The background color also determines the fill color for circles, squares, and other enclosed shapes; the fill color inside text frames; and the color with which you erase existing parts of the picture. If you select a section of the picture and drag it to another location, the resulting "hole" is filled with the background color. You can change the background color as many times as you like.

An alternative technique for selecting colors is using the Eyedropper tool, which lets you "suck up" a color that already appears in the picture. That color becomes the new foreground or background color for use with any of the painting tools.

Tip #84

You can start a new picture with a certain color as the "canvas." Before you paint anything on the picture, choose the desired background color, and click anywhere over the work area with the Paint Can tool.

After you have the colors selected, you can use the tools to draw like this:

1. Click the tool you want to use to select it.
2. Position the pointer in the work area where you want to start painting, selecting, or erasing, and then click and hold the mouse button.
3. Drag to paint, select, or erase. Release the mouse button when you are through.

Some tools (for example, the polygon tool) require multiple clicks. When some of the tools are selected, the area below the grid of buttons provides options for the selected tool. The options are different for each tool.

UNDOING MISTAKES

Every addition you make to an image eventually melds into the picture and can't be undone. However, the program does keep track of the three most recent additions, allowing you

PART

II

CH

7

some small degree of rethinking. Each time you make a new change, Paint "forgets" the fourth most recent change, and it becomes permanent.

To undo a change, press the fairly universal Undo command key, Ctrl+Z, or choose Edit, Undo. You can undo an undo by choosing Edit, Repeat.

OPENING AN EXISTING PICTURE

You might often use Paint simply as a viewer of BMP files. Web browsers do not open BMP files for display, so when you double-click a BMP, it runs Paint (unless the system association for BMP files has been set to another program) and opens the file.

To see the maximum image amount at once, choose View, View Bitmap. The picture fills the entire Paint window; all the other screen elements, including the title bar, menu bar, and scrollbars, disappear. Clicking anywhere on the screen or pressing any key returns you to the working screen.

 If you have opened a photographic picture for work in Paint, and it looks splotchy and uneven, see "Photos Look Terrible in Paint" in the "Troubleshooting" section at the end of this chapter.

ZOOMING IN FOR DETAIL WORK

One of the best features of Paint is pixel editing. You can zoom in closely to edit a picture, dot by dot, and can choose from five magnification levels: normal, 2×, 4×, 6×, and 8×(800). Figure 7.4 shows a picture at highest magnification, 8×(800). In Paint, you can use any of the standard painting tools at any magnification level. Use the Pencil tool to best change the color of one dot at a time.

Figure 7.4
An image magnified for pixel editing.

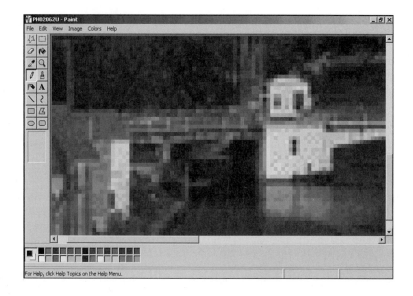

SAVING YOUR WORK

You can choose from several different BMP formats for saving Paint files, the variations pertaining to the number of colors stored in the file. Normally, you can just let Paint choose the correct format for you, but sometimes knowing which format to use comes in handy.

The following are the available formats and their descriptions:

- Monochrome bitmap—Use when you have only two colors (black and white) in your picture.
- 16-color bitmap—Use when you have 16 colors or fewer in your picture.
- 256-color bitmap—Use when you have more than 16 and fewer than 257 colors in your picture.
- 24-bit bitmap—Use when you have more than 256 colors in the picture.

Use the lowest possible setting, based on how many colors you have been painting with. The more colors you save, the larger the file. However, saving a picture with a format that has fewer colors may ruin it, losing the detail.

Tip #85	When a picture is displayed in the Paint window, you can set it to be the wallpaper on the computer's desktop. Just choose one of the File, Set as Wallpaper options.

IMAGING

In stark contrast to Paint, Imaging (made by Kodak) isn't intended for drawing as much as for viewing images, scanning text or graphics, and making annotations on them. It can optionally fax scanned or otherwise acquired images. You could think of Imaging as a combination of something like Visioneer's PaperPort (for scanning documents), a graphics image viewer such as ThumbsPlus or LView Pro, and Delrina's WinFax Pro (for some faxing capabilities).

VIEWING IMAGES

If you don't have another image-viewing program of choice, the most likely use of Imaging would be to view documents and images onscreen. It can successfully open TIF, GIF, JPG, BMP, PCX, DCX, WIF, XIF, or AWB files.

Note	AWB is the extension Windows 98 uses for its fax file format.

Images are compressed and converted to 200×200dpi grayscale images for efficient disk storage and faxing when you store them in this format. You can view images in normal size, as thumbnails, or an arbitrary size you set. You also can annotate, email, and print them.

To run the program, choose Start, Programs, Accessories, Imaging. Figure 7.5 shows an open JPG file (a picture I took of an orchid) for viewing. Imaging has two modes: Preview and Edit. Figure 7.5 shows Edit mode.

Figure 7.5
A JPG file open in Imaging.

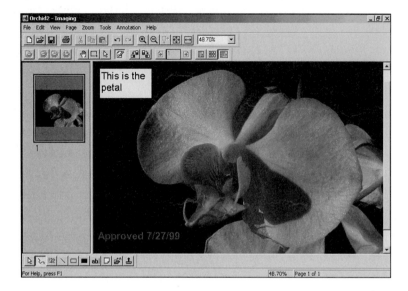

Hover your mouse pointer over a tool on the toolbars to see a short pop-up description of what the button is for. Check particularly the Rotate and Zoom buttons, which are especially useful when you're viewing images and scanned text. Each click on the + or - buttons increases or decreases the zoom. The Zoom menu has additional zoom options. If you want to rotate all the pages in a multipage document, choose Page, Rotate all Pages. Choosing View, Full Screen (Ctrl+F) is particularly useful for getting as much of an image onscreen as possible.

EDITING AN IMAGE

To edit an image, you switch to Editing mode. You can click the Edit button, or choose File, Open File for Editing. When you're in the Editing screen, you can alter the view in additional ways. Just click each of the three buttons on the bottom right of the toolbar, or open the View menu to see them:

- Page view—Shows only the image
- Thumbnail view—Shows only a small thumbnail of the image, which is useful when you're viewing a document with a number of pages, such as a multipage scanned image
- Page and Thumbnail views—Show images and thumbnails

When an image is open, you can make some modifications, such as adding annotations, adding rubber stamp marks (for example, "Draft"), and so on.

Tip #86

> In previous versions, Imaging let you edit only TIF, AWB, or BMP files. Even though you could view GIF and JPG files in their native formats, you needed to save them as either TIF or BMP files before you could annotate or otherwise edit them. This was annoying. In Windows 2000 Professional, you can now annotate JPG files, too. However, when you save the file, the annotations become permanent. If you save as a TIF file, you can reopen the file and move or delete the annotations.

SCANNING IMAGES

You can scan pictures and text right into Imaging if your scanner has a TWAIN device that works with Windows 2000 Professional. Using this type of device is easier than using a big program such as PhotoShop. If you're intending to do a lot of document scanning, I recommend a program such as Visioneer's PaperPort and a page scanner such as the PaperPort Strobe because it lets you feed in sheets very quickly and organize them in a folder system much like the Windows Explorer.

Note

> TWAIN is an acronym for *Technology (or Toolkit) Without An Interesting Name.* Somebody has a sense of humor out there. It's a standard driver interface allowing scanners and digital cameras to deposit data into Windows-based graphics editing programs. All modern scanners and many cameras are now shipped with TWAIN drivers.

To scan, follow these steps:

1. Turn on your scanner, and insert the page, photo, or whatever.
2. Choose Tools, Scan Options, and choose the format for the scan.
3. If you have multiple TWAIN devices, choose the one you want first via File, Select Device.
4. Click the appropriate scan button from the four available. Alternatively, choose File, Acquire Image, and select from there. (If these buttons and the menu choice are grayed out, you don't have a TWAIN driver installed.)

ANNOTATING IMAGES

When you have one of the editable file types open in the edit screen, you can annotate it in various ways, such as by highlighting, rubber stamping it with prefab words such as "Draft," or writing your own text on it. Figure 7.5 shows a sticky note (which appears yellow onscreen), a straight line pointing to the petal, and a rubber stamp that included the date automatically.

Unlike Paint images in which alterations meld into the image, the annotations and marks you make in this program can stay independent. You can move, edit, or remove them, at least for a time. After you make the annotations permanent, though, they are set. As I mentioned previously, JPG file annotations are made permanent after you save the file to disk.

PART

II

CH

7

If the status title bar of the Imaging window says (Read Only) after the document name, you cannot annotate. This means you're viewing a file format that Imaging can only display, not edit or save. Save the file first as a JPG, TIF, BMP, or AWS document; then reopen it and try annotating it again.

At the bottom of the window is an Annotation toolbar (see Figure 7.6). If it's not there, choose View, Toolbars, and turn on Annotation.

Figure 7.6
The Annotation toolbar.

Check out the Annotation toolbar functions for such tasks as selecting objects; drawing freehand lines; drawing a highlighted rectangular area; drawing straight lines; drawing a hollow box, filled boxes, or boxes with text inside; adding sticky yellow notes; adding a box with text stored in a TXT file on disk; and adding rubber stamps. You can use a canned stamp or create your own text stamp or an image stamp. (Click Annotation, Rubber Stamps to create a new stamp.)

Tip #87

The characters %x in a stamp's text print the current date as part of a stamp. Examine the Received stamp's settings, and you'll see that it's Received %x, which prints in the form Received 10/10/98 on the image.

To change the properties of an annotation, right-click it, and choose Properties. In the Properties dialog, you can change font size, color, and so on. Each kind of annotation has its own properties. For example, lines defining boxes have line width and color, and text has font properties.

Tip #88

You can set the properties for the whole picture or scanned page, too. Just right-click the picture or page; then fill in the boxes.

NAILING DOWN ANNOTATIONS

Until you save a BMP or JPG file, or choose Annotations, Make Annotations Permanent, you can move, edit, and reset their properties. With TIF files, you can move the annotations next time you load the file. If this command is grayed out, check to see that annotations are not hidden from view. To do so, choose Annotations, Show Annotations.

It's good practice to make annotations permanent before exporting a document to another application because it more than likely won't recognize annotations. If you don't, the annotations might be lost.

FAXING IMAGE DOCUMENTS

You can prepare fax image files from Imaging, but you should prepare the image correctly, or else the appearance of the resulting fax might be less than the recipient had hoped.

Remember that an image can have different horizontal and vertical resolutions. For example, images received from fax transmissions typically have resolutions of 200×100 pixels per inch. Also, a color document will fax more successfully if you first change it to grayscale. Don't forget that you should not fax an image that is larger than the target fax machine's paper size.

To make necessary setting modifications to an image prior to faxing, follow these steps:

1. Choose Page, Properties.
2. On the Color, Compression, Resolution, and Size tabs of the Properties dialog, click the settings you want.
3. After you make the changes on all tabs, click OK.
4. Choose File, Print, and then choose Fax.

→ To learn more about setting up and using the Windows 2000 fax services, **see** Chapter 9, "Printing and Faxing with Windows 2000."

CALCULATOR

The Calculator is a quick and dirty onscreen version of two traditional pocket calculators: a standard no-brainer calculator and a more complex scientific calculator for use by statisticians, engineers, computer programmers, and business professionals. They are good for adding up your lunch bill, a list of inventory items, or the mortgage payment on your office building. But neither calculator sports a running tape that you can use to backtrack through your calculations.

To run the Calculator, choose Start, Programs, Accessories, Calculator. A reasonable facsimile of a hand-held calculator then appears on your screen, as shown in Figure 7.7. You can switch between modes by choosing View, Standard or View, Scientific. The program always remembers which type was used last and comes up in that mode.

Figure 7.7
The Scientific Calculator.

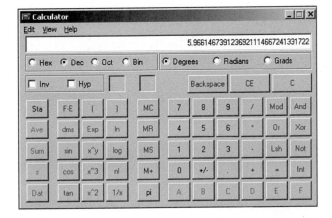

Tip #89	To quickly see a little help about any Calculator button, right-click the button, and choose What's This?

Tip #90	To add a series of numbers or to find their mean, use the statistical functions on the Scientific Calculator. This way, you can see all the numbers in a list before you perform the calculation instead of having to enter them one at a time. And don't let the idea of statistics make you nervous; the technique is very simple.

Most of the operations on the Standard Calculator are self-explanatory, but a couple of them—square roots and percentages—are just a bit tricky. Check the Help file for more information. Table 7.3 provides a quick reference chart of keyboard shortcuts.

TABLE 7.3   KEYBOARD SHORTCUTS FOR THE CALCULATOR

Button	Key	Button	Key
%	%	(	(
)	)	*	*
+	+	+/-	F9
-	-	.	. or ,
/	/	0 to 9	0 to 9
1/x	r	=	= or Enter
A to F	A to F	And	&
Ave	Ctrl+A	Bin	F8
Byte	F4	Back	Backspace
C	Esc	CE	Del
cos	o	Dat	Ins
Dec	F6	Deg	F2
dms	m	Dword	F2
Qword	F12	Exp	x
F-E	v	Grad	F4
Hex	F5	Hypo	h
Int	;	Inv	I
ln	n	log	l
LSH	<	M+	Ctrl+P
MC	Ctrl+L	Mod	%
MR	Ctrl+R	MS	Ctrl+M

Button	Key	Button	Key
n!	!	Not	~
Oct	F7	Or	|
PI	p	Rad	F3
s	Ctrl+D	sin	s
SQRT	@	Sta	Ctrl+S
Sum	Ctrl+T	tan	t
Word	F3	Xor	^
x^2	@	x^3	#
x^y	y		

COPYING YOUR RESULTS TO OTHER DOCUMENTS

Tip #91　　　　You can copy information to and from the Calculator using the Windows Clipboard. Just use the standard Windows Copy and Paste commands.

You can prepare a complex equation in a text editor such as Notepad and then copy it to the Calculator for execution. For example, you can enter the following:

((2+8) +16) /14=

or

(2+(8+16)) /14=

Mind your parentheses, and make sure to include the equal sign, or click = on the calculator; otherwise, the result will not appear. You can omit the parentheses if you use extra equal signs, like this:

2+8=+16=/14=

Some special characters can be included in your equations to activate various Calculator functions:

:e　　　　If the Calculator is set to the decimal system, this sequence indicates that the following digits are the exponent of a number expressed in scientific notation; for example, 1.01:e100 appears in the Calculator as 1.01e+100.

:p　　　　Adds the number currently displayed to the number in memory.

:c　　　　Clears the Calculator's memory.

\　　　　Places the number currently displayed into the Statistics box, which must already be open.

:m　　　　Stores the number currently displayed in the Calculator's memory.

:q　　　　Clears the Calculator.

:r　　　　Displays the number stored in the Calculator's memory.

PART

II

CH

7

CHARACTER MAP

Character Map is a utility program that lets you examine every character in a given font and choose and easily insert into your documents special characters, such as trademark (™ and ®) and copyright symbols (©), foreign currency symbols and accented letters (such as ¥) and nonalphabetic symbols (such as fractions, ¾), DOS line-drawing characters (+), items from specialized fonts such as Symbol and Wingdings, or the common arrow symbols (↑, ↓, ←, and →). Some fonts include characters not mapped to the keyboard. Character Map lets you choose them, too, from its graphical display. The Program Map displays Unicode, DOS, and Windows fonts' characters.

Character Map for Windows 2000 Professional is larger and updated from the one in Windows 98. Now you can choose the character set, rearrange the items in a font (such as grouping all currency types together) to eliminate hunting, and search for a given character.

Character Map works through the Windows Clipboard. You simply choose a character you want to use, click Copy, and it moves onto the Clipboard. Switch to your destination application (typically a word processing file), position the cursor, and choose Paste.

USING CHARACTER MAP

To run Character Map, follow these steps:

1. Choose Start, Programs, Accessories, System Tools, Character Map. When the window appears, check the Advanced View box to see more. The window then appears as shown in Figure 7.8. All the characters included in the font currently selected are displayed.

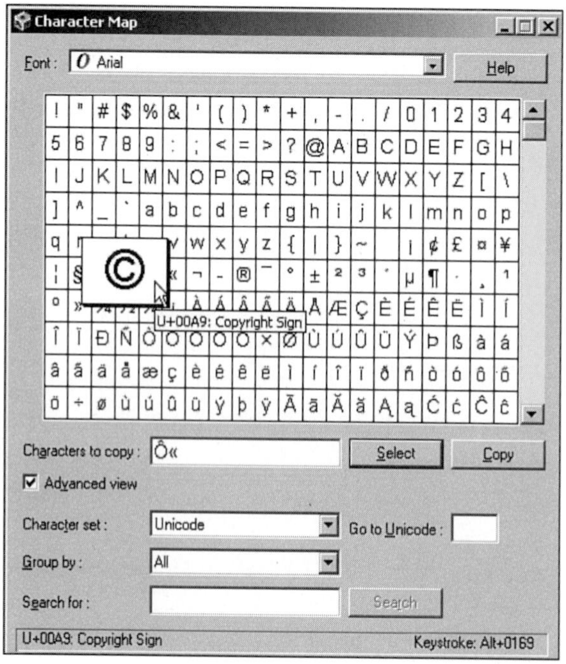

Figure 7.8
Character Map with advanced options showing. You can double-click a character to put it in the copy list.

2. Choose the font you want to work with from the Font list.

3. By default, the Character Set is Unicode. This means all the characters necessary for most of the world's languages are displayed. To narrow down the selection, choose a language from the drop-down list.

4. To examine an individual character, click a character box, and hold down the mouse button to magnify it. You can accomplish the same thing with the keyboard by moving to the character using the arrow keys.

5. Double-click a character to select it, transferring it to the Characters to Copy box. Alternatively, after you've highlighted a character, you can click the Select button or press Alt+S to place it in the Characters to Copy box. You can keep adding characters to the copy box if you want to paste several into your document at once.

6. Click the Copy button to place everything from the Characters to Copy box onto the Windows Clipboard.

7. Switch to your destination application, and use the Paste command (typically on the application's Edit menu) to insert the characters into your document. In some cases, you may then have to select the inserted characters and format them in the correct font, or the characters won't appear as you expected. You can, of course, change the size and style as you like.

Tip #92	If you know the Unicode number of the item you want to jump to, type it into the Go to Unicode field. The display scrolls as necessary, and the desired character is then highlighted, ready for copying.

Choosing from a Unicode Subrange

A useful new feature in the latest version of Character Map lets you choose a subrange from the Unicode. Unicode was designed intelligently with characters grouped in sets. You can choose a subset of a font's characters to help you locate a specific symbol. To check out this feature, open the Group By list, and choose Unicode Subrange. When you choose this option, a box like the one in Figure 7.9 pops up.

Click the subgroup that you think will contain the character you're looking for. Good examples are currency or arrows. Make sure to open the Group By list again, and choose All when you want to see all the characters again.

Entering Alternative Characters from the Keyboard

At the bottom right side of the Character Map dialog box is a line that reads

`Keystroke:`

PART

II

CH

7

Figure 7.9
Choosing a subset of a
font to select from.

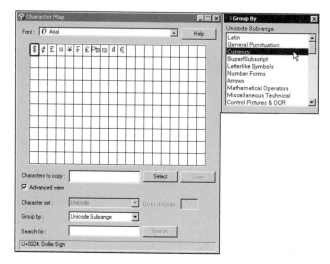

For nonkeyboard keys (typically in English, anything past the ~ character), clicking a character reveals a code on this line—for example, Alt+1060. This line tells you the code you can enter from the keyboard to quickly pop this character into a document. Of course, you must be using the font in question. For example, say you want to enter the registered trademark symbol (®) into a Windows application document. Note that with a standard text font such as Arial or Times New Roman selected in Character Map, the program lists the keystrokes for this symbol as Alt+0174. Here's how to enter the character from the keyboard:

1. Press Num Lock to turn on the numeric keypad on your keyboard (the Num Lock light should be on).

2. Press and hold Alt, and then press 0+1+7+4 (that is, type the 0, 1, 7, and 4 keys individually, in succession) on the number pad. (You must use the number pad keys, not the standard number keys. On a laptop, you must activate the number pad using whatever special function key arrangement your computer uses.) When you release the Alt key, the registered trademark symbol should appear in the document.

Tip #93

> Not all programs accept input this way. If this approach doesn't work with a program, you'll have to resort to the standard means of putting characters into the Clipboard explained previously.

SOUND RECORDER

Sound Recorder is a no-frills utility for creating and playing WAV files. If you want to use it, your system obviously needs a sound card recognized by Windows 2000 Professional, as well as an input source such as a CD player, microphone, and so on. The program lets you capture sound, edit it, do some rudimentary manipulation and effects, and save it for later playback. In the last couple of years, Microsoft has started to include Media Player with Windows, and automatically associating WAV files are now associated with that player instead. So, unless you specifically open a WAV file in Sound Recorder, it won't play there when double-clicked in an Explorer window.

Although Sound Recorder is not a full-featured Windows-based sound recording program such as SoundForge or CoolEdit, the simple sound files you create with it can be put to a variety of uses. For example, you can assign them to system events or attach them to email to a friend who can play WAV files on his or her computer.

Tip #94	If you want elaborate recording and editing control for semi-professionally preparing WAV files for cutting CDs and the like, definitely download a copy of CoolEdit 96 off the Web. (It's shareware.) I use this program for my classical music home-recording business. It's an amazing program, especially for the price. If you want to go full bore, get SoundForge, or for top end, check Sonic Solutions.

Editing is basic: You can remove portions of a file (though only from one point to the end or to the beginning of the file). You can also add an echo effect to a sample, play it backward, change the playback speed (and resulting pitch), and alter the playback volume.

PLAYING A SOUND FILE

To play an existing WAV file, follow these steps:

1. Make sure that your sound system is working properly. If you can hear the startup sound when you boot up Windows, you're probably in business. If it doesn't work, refer to the section in Chapter 29, "Configuring via Control Panel Applets," on installing new hardware and using the system troubleshooters.

2. Run Sound Recorder by choosing Start, Programs, Accessories, Entertainment, Sound Recorder. The Sound Recorder window then appears.

3. Either drag and drop a file on the Sound Recorder window or choose File, Open and browse to the file. Notice that the length of the sound appears at the right of the window, and the current position of the playback is indicated by a slider, as shown in Figure 7.10.

4. To start playback, click the Play button, or press the spacebar. (Hover your mouse pointer over each button if you're in doubt about what each one does.) Pause by pressing the spacebar again. As a sound plays, the wave box displays a representation of the sound a bit like an oscilloscope would, and the playback slider moves to the right.

Figure 7.10

You can click the rewind and fast-forward buttons to move to the start and end of the sample, or press the PgUp and PgDn keys to jump forward or backward in increments. You can also drag the slider around and then click Play to start playing a sound. You also can drag the slider back and forth to see how the wave box displays a facsimile of the frequency and amplitude of the sample over time.

RECORDING A NEW SOUND

Tip #95

A simple way to create a new sound file is to right-click on the Desktop or in a folder and choose New, Wave Sound. Name the file, and then double-click it. Finally, click the Record button.

Recording a new sound is easy. Just get your input source ready, as follows:

1. Choose File, New.

2. Check the recording format before you begin. Sound Recorder can record in numerous file formats, mostly pertaining to sampling rate. Choose File, Properties, and click Convert Now. A dialog box then appears, showing some details about the recording format, as shown in Figure 7.11.

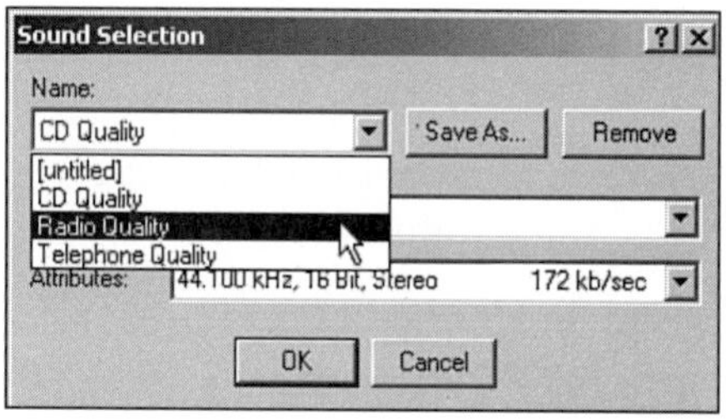

3. Choose a preexisting format scheme here. Choose a combination of data-recording format and "attributes" or sampling rate. Together, they make up a format scheme. The default setting is PCM, 8KB, 8-bit mono, which will consume 7KB of disk space per second. For best results, use one of the sound schemes provided. If you're just recording voice, stick with the default. For higher qualities, click the drop-down Name list, and choose Telephone, Radio, or CD Quality.

Figure 7.11

Notice that the Attributes section in the dialog box reports the amount of disk space consumed per second of recording. Be certain to consider space requirements when making new files. The higher quality recording formats such as CD-Quality stereo can use around 150 to 200KB per second.

Tip #96

If you accidentally record at a higher quality level than you wanted to, don't worry. You can convert to a lower quality and regain some hard disk space by choosing File, Properties, Convert Now.

4. To proceed with the recording, click the Record button. The Position time starts clicking away, and incoming sounds should wiggle in the graphical display area. If you don't see any activity there, you should check the validity of your input and use the Volume Control accessory (covered later) to assure that the input devices are enabled and that the relative volumes (you can have more than one input active at a time) are appropriate.

Tip #97

A major limitation of this program is the maximum recording time. The maximum time varies depending on your recording format, but it's pretty lame. At the default setting (PCM, 22.050-KHz 8-bit mono), you can record for only up to 65 seconds.

5. Click Stop when you're finished recording.

6. Play back the file to see whether you like it.

7. Save the file by choosing File, Save As. Enter a name (you don't have to enter the WAV extension; the program does that for you).

EDITING SOUNDS

Sound files can be edited in a number of interesting, useful, and fun ways, within limits. For example, you can do the following:

- Increase or decrease the volume
- Increase or decrease the speed and pitch
- Remove unwanted parts of a sound
- Add echo to a sound
- Reverse the sound
- Mix two samples together
- Convert a sound to another format for use by a particular program

Tip #98

Even though samples are limited in time while you're originally recording, you can fake out the program during the editing process to allow you to make longer files. To do so, you can insert a second file into an existing one or start recording at a spot within an existing file. Use care, though, as you may run out of memory if your file becomes very long because of inserting files into one another. The amount of free physical memory (not virtual memory) determines the maximum size of any sound file.

The following are some general tips for editing sound files:

- You can play with a file before you save it, or you can choose File, Open to open a sound file you want to edit. If you want to add echo, reverse the sound, increase or decrease volume, or increase or decrease speed, open the Effects menu and choose appropriately. Most of the effects can be "undone" by choosing their opposite effect.

- To clean up files, you can cut out data from a point where you position the slider to either the beginning or the end. For example, you might want to cut out the beginning of a sound when you were clearing your throat. To do so, adjust the slider to just before the point where the good sound starts (play it several times to make sure you have the right spot), and choose Edit, Delete Before Current Position. You can do the same for the end of the sample by choosing Edit, Delete After Current Position.

PART

II

CH

7

- You can mix two existing sound files together for some very interesting overlap effects that are much richer than single sounds. Open the first file; position the cursor where you want to begin the mix; choose Edit, Mix with File; and then choose the second file-name.

- To insert an existing sound file into a preordained spot, move to the spot using the slider; choose Edit, Insert File; and then choose the filename. The file is then added at the spot. Anything after the insertion point in the original file is trashed.

Tip #99	You can put a sound into the Clipboard for pasting into another Windows program by just choosing Edit, Copy.

- If you think you've messed up a file and want to revert to the last version you saved so that you can start tinkering again, choose File, Revert.

Tip #100	Some programs require a particular sound file format to use sounds. Typically, programs that require proprietary sound formats supply their own conversion or import tools for pre-existing wave files. You're usually better off using those tools when they are available than a dinky accessory such as Sound Recorder.

It's fun and often instructive to include vocal instructions or sound effects to text-based documents such as Word or WordPad files. You can add a sound file link in another document like this:

1. Open the sound file in Sound Recorder.

2. Choose Edit, Copy.

3. Using a word processing program such as WordPad, open the document in which you want to link the sound, and then click where you want to insert the sound.

4. Choose Edit, Paste Special. Click Paste Link; then click OK. A link now appears in the destination document. Clicking it should play the sound file.

Read more about object linking and embedding in Chapter 8.

 If you're having trouble with distortion creeping into files you're doing special effects on, see "Distorted Sounds" in the "Troubleshooting" section at the end of this chapter.

VOLUME CONTROL

The Volume Control accessory is a no-brainer, pretty much. It provides a pop-up volume control sporting balance, mute, and other controls for your audio subsystem. Whether you're playing radio stations from the Web, CDs from your CD player, listening to TV if you have a TV tuner card, doing online conferencing with NetMeeting, or recording sound files, you need access to these controls from time to time. Of course, if you don't have a working sound card installed, this accessory isn't available, or at least it won't do anything.

A little known fact for many people is that this accessory has two sets of controls—one for recording and one for playback.

1. To open the volume controls, choose Start, Programs, Accessories, Entertainment, Volume Control. A shortcut is to double-click the little speaker icon in the taskbar.

   Your sound system's capabilities and possible changes that past users have made to the application's settings will determine the format of the volume controls you'll see. On one of the computers on my LAN, the controls look like what you see in Figure 7.12.

Figure 7.12
The basic volume controls for setting playback volume. Another set is available for record levels.

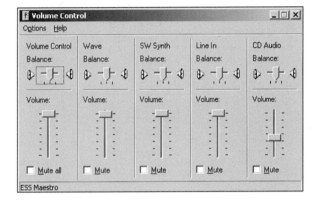

2. Obviously, you alter any volume control's setting by dragging the volume up or down. Change the balance between right and left channels by dragging the Balance sliders left or right. Mute any source input by checking the Mute box in its column.

3. Controls for some input sources are probably not showing. Check out the Options, Properties command. It offers options for turning on various volume controls and possibly special features. Figure 7.13 shows an example. Because audio controls operate differently for different sound cards, check out any Help files that might be available from your audio controls.

Figure 7.13
The Properties dialog box for typical volume controls.

PART

II

CH

7

If you are doing any sound recording, be sure to see the recording controls, too. Open the Properties dialog box, and choose Recording. Sometimes you'll want to see the playback and the recording controls at one time. Here's a tip: Run the Volume Control application twice. Set one for playback and the other one to record. Then adjust them onscreen so that you can see each side-by-side.

> **Note**
>
> Some sliders in one module are linked to sliders in other modules. Adjusting the Volume setting on one affects Volume settings on the other mixers, for example.

To quickly adjust or mute the sound output from your system, or to adjust the master volume level (useful when the phone rings), click the little speaker icon in the system tray, near the clock, as shown in Figure 7.14.

Figure 7.14
Quickly setting the master output volume.

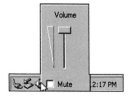

If your system suddenly doesn't have any sound at all, see "No Sound" in the "Troubleshooting" section at the end of this chapter.

CD PLAYER

The CD Player accessory has been given a facelift in Windows 2000 Professional. It's the same Deluxe CD Player you got with Windows 98 Plus! This time, though, it's supplied with the stock Windows product, so you don't need an add-in program to get the goodies. This CD Player application looks hip and has Internet functionality built in. It not only plays your CDs like most Windows-based CD players do, but it also can hit the Web to download all the artist, disc, and track information about a CD, storing it in a database in the computer. Next time you insert the CD, the player identifies the CD and can display the database listing for that CD, even if you're offline.

You can also create playlists of your favorite tunes. Playlists act like those intelligent CD players that remember which songs on a CD you hate. You can block them out so that, when you insert a CD, only your favorite tunes play in the order you want to hear them.

Assuming your computer has a CD-ROM drive and sound card, the program can play standard audio CDs with all the controls you would expect on a "real" CD player, and more. For example, a few clicks, and you can put your CD up for "trade," scan the Web for bios and discographies of artists, or get suggestions for music-related Web sites about CDs with similar music that you might like. They're really making it easy for us to spend our money.

Of course, for decent sound, you need a good pair of speakers, maybe even with a subwoofer attached. You can find plenty of good sound systems designed for computers these days; however, you can just use your existing stereo system, fed by a wire from the "line out" of your sound card, going to an "aux" input on your receiver or amp.

To run the player, choose Start, Programs, Accessories, Entertainment, CD Player. The CD Player looks like the one shown in Figure 7.15.

Figure 7.15
The spiffy new CD Player.

Tip #101

Have you installed another CD player program such as Real Jukebox and now find that inserting a CD brings up a program other than the Windows CD Player? Do you want to revert to using Windows CD Player instead of the other program? Reclaiming your CD Player from another program that has registered itself as the CD Player of choice can be done. Here's how: Open any Explorer window, and choose Tools, Folder Options. Then select the File Types tab. Scroll down to Audio CD in the File Types column. Click Advanced, click Play, and then click the Edit button. Choose a new program using the Browse button. You're looking for %SystemRoot%\system32\cdplayer.exe. Another way to reassign CD playing is from some CD players' options or preferences menus.

If you have a data CD or no disc loaded, you are alerted with one of the following messages:

```
Data disk loaded
No disc loaded
```

Just insert an audio CD, and you're in business. You don't have to be on the Internet to use the Player; you just get more features if you are.

BASIC PLAYING CONTROLS

The CD Player window looks much like the front panel of a typical CD player in a sound system. It has Play, Stop, Pause, Eject, Track Advance, Track Back, and Forward Fast/Rewind buttons. The Track and Disc buttons let you choose a track by name or drive (if you have more than one CD-ROM drive on your computer).

To control the volume, click the volume knob, and move the mouse around. You'll see how it works. The blue neon display is a faux LED readout telling you which track is currently playing, and the time count up or count down for the track or the whole CD.

SETTING PREFERENCES

To set preferences in CD Player, choose Options and then choose Preferences. The Preferences dialog box shown in Figure 7.16 appears.

Figure 7.16
Setting some preferences makes the CD Player more fun.

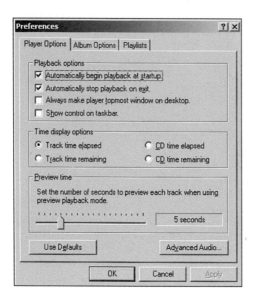

Tip #102

Notice the Tiny View command on the Options menu in the CD Player. It makes the player really small for placement on the screen when you're doing other work. Choose Options, Full View to return to normal view.

The options are self-explanatory. Notice the option for controlling the amount of preview time. You can insert a CD and have the program play a bit of each track for you. The button below the Eject button on the Player lets you choose the mode: Standard, Random, Repeat Track, Repeat All, or Preview. Just choose Preview to hear a few seconds of each track. When you hear a track you like, click the Play button to play the entire track.

You can also control the display of time information in the main readout of the CD Player window. The standard setting shows elapsed time for the track currently playing. If you prefer, you can instead see the time remaining for the current track or for the entire disc. You set this option in the Options, Preferences dialog box.

Tip #103

To get help with CD Player, press F1.

OTHER PLAY OPTIONS

CD Player also offers a bunch of other play options, mostly having to do with using the Internet and creating playlists.

Downloading CD information is the most important of the Internet connectivity features. (The others are mostly commercial.) The basic gist of using the feature follows: Choose Options, and then select the Album Options tab. If you're on the Internet full-time, check the Enable Internet option. The Player automatically looks for album information when a CD is inserted, and if the album is found on the CD database service, the information is sucked into the database stored on your computer. When you bump into a CD that isn't detected, you can try another info provider (change the Primary Provider from the drop-down list) and click Download Now.

To see the names that have been pulled into your database, click the Playlists tab. This tab provides the list of tracks currently in your CD drive, as well as in your database as a whole. To create a personal playlist of a CD (to avoid tracks you don't like), expand Albums in Database, click a CD, and click the Edit Playlist button. In the Playlist area of the resulting dialog box, add or remove the tracks as desired.

CD Player always selects the tracks it plays from the playlist. Before you make any modifications, the playlist contains all the tracks on the disc, and you'll hear every track when you play the disc. After you've created your own playlist, though, CD Player plays only the tracks on the list. If you select Random Order play, the program randomly selects tracks from the playlist, not from all the tracks on the disc.

You can edit an individual track or CD name by clicking it once, or highlighting it and pressing F2 on the Playlists tab from the Options dialog box. Then edit the name, and press Enter. If you have corrected an album's information and want to upload it to the Internet CD info provider, you can click the Internet Upload button on the Edit Playlist tab.

Cataloging a Disc

When you load a disc that hasn't been cataloged, you get a message that the CD isn't found on the Web. You can proceed as follows:

1. Click OK. A new album called No Album Information Available is added to the Playlists tab.

2. Double-click this album, and a new dialog box comes up, as you can see in Figure 7.17.

3. Enter the artist and title names.

4. Select each track from the Available Tracks drop-down list, and type the names. You can type in the first track name and then press Enter. The next track name comes up ready to be edited. You don't have to use the mouse.

5. Click OK to close the dialog box.

You can change any of this information at any time. When you're satisfied with your entries, go on to create a playlist as described here, or click OK to return to CD Player. The disc information then appears in the appropriate areas of the window.

PART

II

CH

7

Figure 7.17
Inputting details of a CD that isn't recognized.

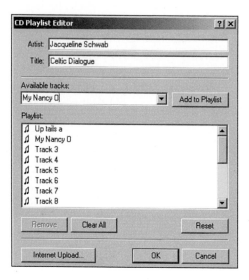

WINDOWS MEDIA PLAYER

Media Player is a little application whose popularity and capabilities have both been growing. Media Player's evolution has been spurred by the infiltration of streaming audio and video across the Web, as well as by the new MP3 craze as a distribution medium for CD-quality music distribution. Think of Media Player as the major competitor to Real Network's multiformat player, but with the capability to wear a few more hats.

The types of media files that can be played by Microsoft Windows Media Player are shown in Table 7.4. When you open a stored file that has one of the extensions listed in the following table, either by double-clicking a file icon or a link in a Web page, Media Player starts up and begins playing it.

TABLE 7.4 MEDIA FILES THAT WINDOWS MEDIA PLAYER CAN PLAY

Type of Product or Program	Filename Extensions
Native Microsoft formats	.AVI, .ASF, .ASX, ., WAV, .WMA, .WM, .WAX
RealNetworks RealAudio and RealVideo (version 4.0 or lower)	.RA, .RAM, .RM, .RMM
Moving Pictures Experts Group (MPEG)	.MPG, .MPEG, .M1V, .MP2, .MPA, .MPE
Musical Instrument Digital Interface	.MID (MIDI), .RMI
Apple QuickTime, Macintosh AIFF Resource	.QT, .AIF, .AIFC, .AIFF, .MOV
UNIX formats	.AU, .SND

Media Player can also send control information to multimedia devices such as audio CD players or video disc players, determining which tracks to play, when to pause, when to activate slow motion, and so on.

Media Player uses a simple interface that's consistent across these various media types, which makes it easy to use. I hate to be a sell-out, but I have to say that the audio codecs (compressors/decompressors) that Microsoft has developed for streaming audio in its Windows Media products are superior to those of Real Networks, in most regards. I listened to a chamber music concert over the Web, "aired" by the Australian Broadcasting Company. Both formats were offered from the site, and the Windows Media (Microsoft) audio frequency response was superior, save for some time-distortion artifacts. Real Audio's transmission didn't have the timing problems but didn't sound as good.

In any case, you're certain to see a quickly evolving arena of media players and format types on the market, boasting more and more high-tech capabilities, especially as DSL, cable, and other high-bandwidth connections to the Internet fall into place. Originally just a player for .WAV, .MIDI (MIDI), and CD-ROM–based video (competing with Apple's QuickTime), Media Player is becoming well integrated into the Internet.

For the most part, you don't have to worry about how or when to run Media Player. When you bump into one of the above file types, either by clicking on a filename on your local computer or a link on a Web page, it should pop up on the screen—that is, unless you have installed a competing product such as a QuickTime player or Real Network's player and allowed those players to change your system associations for any of the file types. During installation, some of the nicer programs ask whether you want the setup program to alter your file associations. Others do not. You might have to restore the file associations listed from time to time if you play around with installing and deinstalling various players from other companies.

Although I'm impressed with Media Player's capabilities, I am hopeful that Microsoft won't squash the competition and that the streaming media and multimedia arena stays healthily competitive.

RUNNING MEDIA PLAYER

You can run Media Player manually by choosing Start, Programs, Accessories, Entertainment, Windows Media Player. Or, as I said previously, it will run when you double-click a file associated with it or a Web link that tries to download or stream a file associated with it. At that point, the Media Player pops up and starts doing its thing. Figure 7.18 shows an example of a video/audio program being played.

You can open the View menu and choose the size of the picture you want. Alternatively, press Alt+Enter to toggle between full-screen and windowed mode, though the video tends to get pixilated (blocky) when running full screen with Web-based formats.

PART

II

CH

7

Figure 7.18
Media Player playing a
video stream from the
Internet.

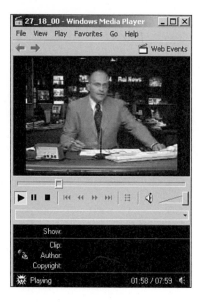

Tip #104

Click the speaker icon to mute the audio when you get a phone call. Remember, it's not a TV; it's more like a VCR. Unless the program you are watching is live, you can click Pause and resume the playing when your phone call's over.

Media Player is intelligent enough to scale appropriately, both in size and in network speed. When it detects a slowdown in data delivery, it tries to negotiate with the server to receive a data format that will keep the show going, though at a lesser quality of video and/or audio. Depending on the server and the stream type, this might or might not be successful. For example, an .ASF file created by the Windows Media tools and served by a Windows Media server will autoscale. The same file served by a traditional Web server will not.

Looking for content? It's busting out all over. Open the Favorites menu and check out all the potential programming you can enjoy (or wade through). If that is not enough, click the Web Events button in the upper-right corner of the screen to see a Web page with a zillion links to streaming or downloadable audio and video.

To listen to the radio, check Chapter 12's coverage of the radio toolbar with Internet Explorer, or open any folder window and turn on the Radio toolbar from the View menu. Then click the Radio Stations button.

Tip #105

You can view closed captions if the program or device you're playing supports it. Just choose View, Captions. Not all media files provide closed captioning, however. When captioning is turned on, the player window increases in size, vertically, to accommodate the captioning text. The video portion of the window might shrink to make room.

PROBLEMS WITH STREAMING

The most common problem you'll experience with Media Player and the Web (as opposed to playing local files, which should be problem-free) is interrupted video and audio performance. It can be annoying and is typically caused by the following:

- High volume of traffic on the Internet or local area network
- Transient problems on a network or server
- A connection speed too low to support the media file you're trying to play
- A buffering time that is too short
- A media file that uses the wrong bandwidth setting
- The wrong bandwidth setting in Media Player

When you first start a streaming session, you are often asked how fat your "pipe" is (how fast your Internet connection is). Try the link again at a slower speed. Your ISP or LAN connection might not be as fast as you think. Also, check for lost packets by choosing View, Statistics to see some interesting numbers on throughput. If the number of lost packets is high, you may have a poor connection. If network slowdowns are frequent, increasing the buffer size might help prevent the rendering from stopping unexpectedly. (Make the change on the Advanced Playback settings tab.)

Choose View, Options, Advanced, Change. Then check the various settings there. Also, check the Help file for the troubleshooter. You might find some tips there.

EVER EVOLVING MEDIA PLAYER

Because Media Player is ever evolving and often easily upgraded via Web download, I'll not try to document it in depth here. You are better off reading the menu options and Help file for the latest version. The trick with this class of program (just as with many aspects of the Web) is simply to experiment.

Tip #106	For the latest updates and news about Media Player, open the Go menu and click Windows Media Player Home Page. Or choose Help, Check for Upgrades.

TROUBLESHOOTING

MY TEXT IS CHOPPED OFF

I can't see all the text in a Notepad window. Where did it go?

You must manually turn on word wrap to get the text in a file to wrap around within the window. By default, word wrap is turned off, which can be annoying. The good news is that word wrap is now a persistent setting. After you turn it on and then close Notepad, it should be on the next time you run it. If you need to edit program code, make sure to turn it off, or your program lines will wrap, making editing and analysis of code more confusing.

If you still can't see enough text, remember that Notepad 5 now supports font changing for display. Change the display font from the Format menu. Choosing a monospaced font (for example, Courier) may help you line up columns. Choosing a smaller font and/or a proportional font (for example, Times) will cram more text into the window.

ADDING AND MODIFYING TAB STOPS

Inserting and adjusting tab stops in WordPad is a pain. Is there an easy way?

You can easily insert and adjust tabs in WordPad by clicking in the ruler area. Choose View, Ruler to turn on the ruler. Then click in the ruler area where you want to insert a tab stop. You can drag the cursor left and right to see a vertical rule to align the stop. To kill a tab stop, drag it out of the ruler area into the document.

PHOTOS LOOK TERRIBLE IN PAINT

I've opened a photo in Paint, and it looks terrible. Why?

You probably have your display set to too few colors. When too few colors are available to the video display, it "bands" the colors, making photos look like a topographic map. Each sharp delineation between similar colors in the picture is called a *band*, for obvious reasons. Normally, the colors would blend together evenly. But if the video display's driver is set to 16, or even 256, colors, this is too few to render most photographic images properly.

Typically, they have well over 256 colors. You need thousands of colors to display an attractive photograph. As I said earlier, to edit photos in any professional manner, you should use a program designed for photographic retouching. Still, you can cut and paste, do some pixel editing, add text and so forth, with Paint. First, however, check your display settings by right-clicking the desktop, choosing Properties, and then Settings. Make sure you have your system set to run in 16-bit color or higher.

DISTORTED SOUNDS

I've been using the speed increase/speed decrease controls, and robot-like distortion has entered my sound file. What gives?

The speed increase/speed decrease commands are not quite the same as redo/undo commands in some other programs such as a word processor. After you use the speed increase command once, the file is altered in such a way that decreasing the speed adds distortion. To check this out, record a short wave, and increase the speed 10 or 100 percent. Then decrease it the same amount. You'll notice weird overtones in the sound file. They are s imply an artifact of this less-than-perfect sound editor. You should save a file in pristine condition before playing around with the effects. That way, you can revert to the saved version if you don't like the artifacts that can creep in as you apply effects. Better yet, get a full-featured sound editor if you're serious about making sound files.

No Sound

I'm adjusting the volume control from the system tray icon, but I just don't get any sound.

Total loss of sound can be caused by myriad goofs, settings, hardware conflicts, or program malfunctions. Troubleshooting your sound system isn't always easy as a result. You should consult other chapters in this book that deal with the Control Panel and the Device Manager for serious problems. One tip is in order here: If you're using a laptop computer, ask yourself whether the sound stopped working after you hibernated or suspended the system. I've noticed this problem on several laptops, and this bug might not have been worked out of Windows 2000 Professional for your soundchip set. Try rebooting the computer, and see whether the sound comes back to life.

TIPS FROM THE WINDOWS PROS: CREATING PROFESSIONAL RECORDINGS

So, you want to make real recordings with the Sound Recorder program? Forget about it. If you want to make professional-sounding CDs with your PC, you can do it, but some tricks are involved.

I sponsor a classical music concert series and wanted to record the concerts. Eventually, people started asking for CDs of the concerts. Here's the inside scoop on how I create the CDs.

Because I love new technology, and tape annoys me (with the hassle of getting to a specific spot on the tape and editing the tape), I have to admit that the first thing I ruled out was using a DAT for the initial recording. For the best recordings, you'll probably want to use a DAT recorder (even a DAT Walkman from Sony will do a credible job) or record directly into a high-quality recording sound board in the PC. A good example is the GadgetLabs Wave (8 lines in, 24 out), www.gadgetlabs.com. You'll also want a very fancy program such as SoundForge, or for multi-tracking, Cubase. Hard drive speed matters. Any UltraDMA IDE disk should handle at least 12 simultaneous tracks. Faster ones can do 24 and more.

But, hey, DATs, fancy sound cards, and programs can cost a lot of money. I was interested in seeing what I could get out of my system using the basic 16-bit sound card that came with the computer and my Sony minidisc sound recorder. Turns out you can do a pretty decent CD this way. You just need the following:

- Stereo or mono recording device of some sort. Even a Walkman Pro cassette recorder will do.
- Computer with a line-in jack on the sound card.
- Optionally, a stereo digital reverb unit to add some "room" sound.
- CoolEdit, a shareware program available over the Net.
- CD-R or CD-RW recorder installed and working properly in your computer. They are really cheap these days.
- CD-R or CD-RW program, such as Adaptec Easy-CD or Easy-CD Pro.

Here's what you do:

1. Record the music you want to put on the CD. Use a good-quality microphone. Also, spend a couple hundred dollars on a good mic. It's probably the best place to put your money. I use an AKG uni-point stereo condenser mic. For the machine, I prefer using a mini-disk recorder because I can then remove the stuff I don't want to put on the CD very easily. (I just mark the beginning and the end of the sections I don't want and then delete them with a press of a button. Voila! This way, I can eliminate applause, people tuning up, and so forth.) I can also number the tracks just the way I want. But you can use whatever source you want.

2. After you have your material ready, connect the player's line out to the PC sound card's line in. (Optionally, run it through your digital reverb unit to add some nice reverb, but not too much! You can easily overdo reverb.)

3. Run CoolEdit in the PC, check the input levels, and set as necessary. Begin your recording. You can record each track individually, or you can run all of them together and later cut and paste individual sections into tracks and save them as separate WAV files to put on the CD. Figure 7.19 shows an example of a WAV file being recorded and edited.

Figure 7.19
CoolEdit in action.

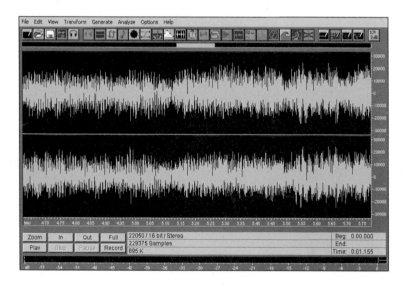

4. Edit the individual WAV files using the amplitude envelope adjustment in CoolEdit to fade in at the beginning of the track and fade out at the end of the track, if you care. You can use presets called "fade in" and "fade out" in the program, which are used just for this purpose. Fading makes the transitions between tracks sound smoother because the background noise doesn't suddenly disappear.

5. Insert a blank CD in your recorder. Then run Adaptec Easy CD or Easy CD Pro. (I paid the extra $99 for Pro because it makes nice CD jewel-case inserts.) Line up the WAV files in the order you want to record them, insert the blank CD, and start cutting.

6. Make up a nice cover for your CD using the Adaptec program, PhotoShop, or whatever.

Tip #107

If you use Adaptec's program, you can use this trick to put a photo on your CD cover: You must open the JPG or other photo picture in a program such as PhotoShop and then select the portion of the photo you want to use. Then switch to Adaptec CD Pro and paste the image from the Clipboard. You'll go nuts trying to do this by opening an image from the Adaptec program. It doesn't allow you to paste the image.

7. Use a program such as CD Stomper Pro (check `http://www.octave.com/accessories/cdlabels.html`) to create your CD's label.

8. Print the label, and place it on the CD. Print the cover art on glossy paper using one of the many available inexpensive inkjet printers such as one from Epson. Then cut, fold, and insert the cover art/liner notes into the CD jewel case. You're finished.

Figure 7.20 shows a completed CD cover in the jewel case.

Figure 7.20
A finished, self-produced CD cover and labeled CD.

Tip #108

CoolEdit offers a noise reduction option that you can use to get rid of pesky tape noise and noise introduced by the cheesy electronics you might have used to create your recordings. Check it out. It can use the brains of your computer to dramatically reduce the noise level and make up for the fact that you made your professional-looking CD with a sound studio that cost you a tiny fraction of what the pros dish out.

PART

II

CH

7

CHAPTER 8

SHARING DATA BETWEEN APPLICATIONS

In this chapter

WORKING WITH THE WINDOWS CLIPBOARD

You could say information is infectious—it seems driven to hop from one document to another. Because transferring data is such a common task, this chapter offers considerable detail on the techniques you can use to facilitate the process.

The most basic sort of information sharing relies on the Windows Clipboard. As you're probably well aware, you can cut, copy, and paste information from one application to another with relative abandon—assuming both applications allow you to work with the kind of information you're transferring (text, graphics, or musical notes, for example).

Note

Although the Clipboard is a necessity for *ad hoc* data transfers, it's still a crude tool that requires lots of fussing on your part. You can make it much more effective by supplementing it with a utility such as ClipBook Viewer, discussed later in this chapter. Windows 2000 also offers a different sort of vehicle for live data exchange: object linking and embedding (OLE). With OLE, a single document can contain information taken from multiple applications–information that remains editable using the application from which it originated.

Almost all Windows applications use the Clipboard for everyday, on-the-fly data-transfer operations. The Clipboard lets you move text, graphics, spreadsheet cells, portions of multi-media files, and OLE objects from one location to another. It supports both 16-bit and 32-bit Windows programs and can even move text to and from non-Windows programs, within the constraints I explain later in this chapter.

Information cut or copied to the Clipboard goes into system memory (RAM and virtual memory), waiting there until you paste it to a new location elsewhere in the same document or in another document. Even then the data remains on the Clipboard until it's replaced by new cut or copied information or until you exit Windows. The upshot of this arrangement is that you can paste the same information as many times as needed, into as many different locations in your documents as necessary.

Want to know what information currently resides on the Clipboard? Run the ClipBook Viewer utility that comes with Windows to view the Clipboard contents as well as to store Clipboard information on disk (in CLP files or ClipBooks) for later retrieval.

Note

Some Windows applications maintain their own independent Clipboard-like storage areas for cut or copied data. These proprietary clipboards overcome some of the weaknesses of the main Windows Clipboard. For example, whereas the Windows Clipboard can hold only one chunk of cut or copied data at a time, Microsoft Office 2000 has its own clipboard that stores up to 12 chunks. In Office 2000 apps, a special toolbar pops up as the Office clipboard fills up. The toolbar displays each chunk of data with an icon identifying the data's source application, and you can paste the chunks in any order you need them into your Office 2000 documents.

→ To learn more about ClipBooks, **see** "Using ClipBook Viewer," **p. 295**.

COPYING, CUTTING, AND PASTING IN WINDOWS APPLICATIONS

Windows 2000 maintains time-honored Windows standards (most of them date all the way back to Windows 2.0) for selecting, cutting, copying, and pasting information. This section offers a brief review of the techniques you need. In summary, four steps are required to transfer data from one place to another via the Clipboard:

1. Select the data. The techniques required to select data depend on the type of information in question and the application you're using. If you're working with text, you can drag across the characters to be selected, or, if you prefer a keyboard approach, hold down the Shift key while you use arrow keys and other cursor movement keys to expand or reduce the selection. Many programs let you select entire lines or paragraphs using techniques such as clicking or double-clicking in the left margin. Selected text appears in reverse colors.

   With graphics and other nontext information, selection techniques vary, but you typically just click on the item you want to select, Shift+click to select a series of adjacent items, or drag over adjacent items to select them together. In many applications you can also Ctrl+click to select nonadjacent items. You can usually tell that an item has been selected by the appearance of an outline or small rectangles on its perimeter.

2. Cut or copy that data to place it on the Clipboard. Choose Edit, Copy to place the selected data on the Clipboard without disturbing the original. You can also choose Edit, Cut to put the information on the Clipboard and remove it from the source document. Many applications let you right-click over the selection and choose Copy or Cut from the shortcut menu that pops up. With the keyboard, the standard shortcuts are Ctrl+X for Cut and Ctrl+C for Copy; however, some applications don't abide by these conventions.

3. Identify the destination for the information by selecting the destination document and, if appropriate, navigating to a specific location in that document.

4. Paste the data into the destination document. With the mouse, choose Edit, Paste or choose Paste from the shortcut menu. Using the keyboard, pressing Ctrl+V does the trick, except in the odd, nonstandard application. With any of these techniques, the contents of the Clipboard will appear in the new location.

If the Paste command fails to paste the data into the destination document, see "Paste Command Doesn't Work" in the troubleshooting section at the end of this chapter.

If the pasted data doesn't look like you expected, see "Pasted Data Doesn't Look Right" in the troubleshooting section at the end of the chapter.

> **Note**
>
> Almost all Windows applications have Cut, Copy, and Paste commands on their Edit menus, but that doesn't mean these commands are always available. If you haven't selected anything to be cut or copied, for example, the Cut and Copy commands will be inactive—they appear grayed out on the Edit menu and you can't choose them. For its part, the Paste command can be grayed out even if data is currently on the Clipboard. This happens when the application doesn't recognize the data format in which the Clipboard data is stored.

> **Note**
>
> Many Windows applications place cut or copied information onto the Clipboard in multiple formats. For example, suppose you copy some text from Microsoft Word. When the copy operation is complete, the Clipboard will contain at least four representations of that same text: a plain text (nonformatted) version, a version in the Rich Text format, a version in HTML, and a picture (an image of the text stored as a line, or *vector*, graphic). When you paste, the destination application communicates with the Clipboard to decide which format to use. In some cases, the application also has a command that lets you take manual control and decide the right format for yourself. At any rate, the availability of all these formats means that you have a better chance of successfully pasting the data into the destination document.

USING THE CLIPBOARD WITH NON-WINDOWS APPLICATIONS

DOS applications are fair game for copy and paste operations, even though they weren't originally designed to work with the Windows Clipboard. You also can copy and paste items from POSIX and character-based OS/2 applications. The only trick is that the non-Windows program must be running in a window, not in full-screen mode. Note, too, that you can only *copy* data from a non-Windows program to the Clipboard, not cut it.

COPYING INFORMATION TO THE CLIPBOARD FROM NON-WINDOWS APPLICATIONS

Copying data from a non-Windows application is a little trickier than from Windows applications, but not much. Before I detail the steps, you should know that in the case of DOS programs, both text and graphics can be copied to the Clipboard. Windows 2000 can detect when an application is running in character mode or graphics mode. If the selected data is text, it's transferred to the Clipboard as text characters. Graphics data is moved to the Clipboard in bitmapped format. Either way, you can then paste the data into any Windows program that will accept that type of data (again, Clipboard text can also be pasted into most character-based non-Windows applications).

> **Tip #109**
>
> Certain DOS programs look like they're running in character mode when in fact they're using graphics mode to display letters, numerals, and punctuation. Copying "text" from such a program places graphics data on the Clipboard. You may be able to paste the image into a Windows word processor—because most of them do accept graphics—but you won't be able to edit the text itself. Note that most DOS programs that can display text as graphics let you switch into a true text mode—do so if you want to copy text rather than graphics to the Clipboard.

With that detail out of the way, follow these steps to copy information from a DOS program running in a window:

1. Make sure the DOS program is running in a window, not in full-screen mode. To toggle a DOS program between full-screen and a window, just press Alt+Enter. (Note, however, that a few DOS applications run only in full-screen mode.)

2. Open the source document—the one you're going to be copying from—in the DOS application.

3. To activate the special mode used to select information for Clipboard copies, open the DOS window's control box (click the icon at the left side of the title bar) and choose Edit, Mark.

4. Drag the mouse pointer over the desired text or graphics region, beginning in the upper-left corner and dragging to the lower-right corner. As shown in Figure 8.1, the selected material is highlighted as you drag. Release the mouse button to complete the selection.

Figure 8.1
Selecting text in a DOS application.

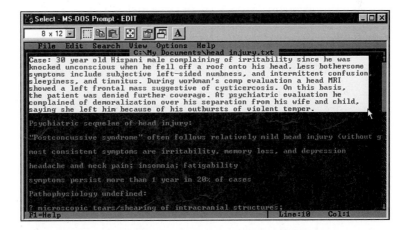

> **Note**
>
> When you're in select mode in a DOS window, you can only select—you can't use the program normally until you exit select mode. Copying the selected information to the Clipboard automatically turns select mode off, but you can also do so by pressing Esc or right-clicking on the window. Note that the word Select appears in the window's title bar when you're in select mode.

5. To copy the selection to the Clipboard, open the Control menu again and choose Edit, Copy.

If the data you copied from a non-Windows application seemingly can't be copied, see "Cannot Copy Non-Windows Data to the Clipboard" in the troubleshooting section at the end of this chapter.

PASTING INFORMATION INTO NON-WINDOWS APPLICATIONS

Within some significant limits, you can paste data from the Clipboard into non-Windows applications as well as copy information from them. The main caveat to remember is that you can only paste plain-text characters—any formatting the text may have contained is lost. Graphics simply can't be pasted into a non-Windows program.

Tip #110

> To transfer graphics from the Clipboard into a non-Windows program, you first must paste the image into a program such as Paint or CorelDRAW and then save the image in a file that can be read by the destination DOS graphics program.

Follow these steps to paste unformatted text into a non-Windows application:

1. See to it that the application is running in a window. If it's currently in full-screen mode, press Alt+Enter to window it.

2. In the destination application, place the cursor at the location where the pasted text should be deposited.

3. With the destination application's window still active, be sure the window isn't in select mode. If select mode is active, press Esc.

4. Open the Control menu of the destination application's window. There, choose Edit, Paste.

When you paste into a non-Windows application, Windows transfers the text characters by feeding them into the system's keyboard buffer. In human terms, the process works by tricking the destination application into thinking you're typing the text at the keyboard. Be forewarned that some programs can choke when fed keyboard characters more quickly than a person could type them. Figure 8.2 shows an example of text pasted into Edit, a Windows-supplied text editor.

Figure 8.2
When pasting text into a non-Windows application, the formatting can leave something to be desired.

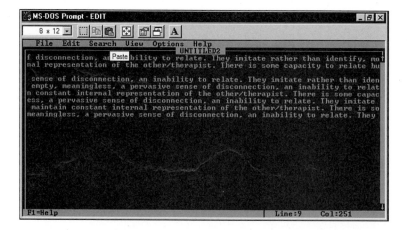

CAPTURING SCREENS AND WINDOWS

Windows lets you capture whatever you're currently viewing on the screen, placing the captured image on the Clipboard. You can use the images to illustrate Help files, Web pages, or printed documentation explaining how to use, say, a custom spreadsheet or database solution you've designed—or any software, for that matter.

You can capture screen information from both Windows and non-Windows applications. The Clipboard records the capture as a bitmap image that you can paste into a graphics program such as PhotoShop or Windows Paint. There, you can save it in any format available in the destination application.

Tip #111

> Rather than paste a captured screen image immediately into another application, you might want to simply store it on disk for later use. In that case, you can use ClipBook Viewer to store the image in a CLP file on disk or to transfer it to a ClipBook. For details, see "Saving the Clipboard's Contents in Disk Files," later in this chapter.

Tip #112

> The Windows built-in screen capture feature works fine as far as it goes, but it's rudimentary. Many commercial and shareware programs give you much finer control over the process. Strong contenders in this market include Collage, FullShot, HyperSnap, and Corel Capture, which comes with the CorelDRAW suite.

CAPTURING THE ENTIRE SCREEN

Here's how to capture a duplicate of the entire screen onto the Clipboard:

1. Set up the screen as you want it to look in the captured image, with as many windows open as you like in any suitable arrangement.
2. Press the Print Screen key, which may be labeled Prt Scr. The screen image is transferred to the Clipboard immediately.

Note

> If you don't get the expected results from the Print Screen key, try Shift+Print Screen or Alt+Print Screen, which work on some keyboards.

CAPTURING THE ACTIVE WINDOW

To place a copy of a single window on the Clipboard, follow these steps:

1. Activate the window you want to capture. You can capture an individual dialog box by displaying it and making sure that it's active (the clue is the title bar color).
2. Position and size the window to taste.
3. Press Alt+Print Screen (or on some keyboards, Shift+Print Screen) to place a image of the active window on the Clipboard.

COPYING FILES USING THE CLIPBOARD

The Clipboard has special powers when you use it with entire files via Windows Explorer or My Computer. When you copy or cut and then paste a file from one folder on your hard disk to another, or to a destination on the network, the Clipboard serves as a way station for the file. You can verify this by copying a file from Windows Explorer (select the file and choose File, Copy) and then examining the Clipboard contents in ClipBook Viewer—you should see the filename. Behind the scenes, the Clipboard recognizes that it now contains not just text but a reference to the file itself. That way, when you perform a Paste operation, Windows knows to paste the entire file (not just its name) to the new location on disk.

You can also use Windows Explorer to embed or link existing disk files into open documents using the Clipboard. After cutting or copying the file, switch to the destination document, and then identify the location for the pasted material (if the program allows you to do so). When you then perform the Paste operation, Windows creates an OLE object representing the file in the document.

→ To learn more about OLE, **see** "Object Linking and Embedding in Windows 2000," **p. 302**.

CREATING A SHORTCUT TO A SPECIFIC DOCUMENT LOCATION

Did you know you can create a shortcut to a portion of a document? It may sound weird, but you can. Try this:

1. Select a portion of an Excel spreadsheet, a line of text in a Word document, or some data in Access.
2. Use Edit, Copy to copy the data to the Clipboard.
3. Get to the Desktop and right-click on an empty portion and then choose Paste Shortcut (if this option is grayed out, you did something wrong or the source app doesn't support this feature).
4. Either leave the source document and app open or close them. It doesn't matter. (If asked to save the document, you should, because this new shortcut has to be recorded in the source document in order for the next step to work.)
5. Open the shortcut you just created. It should run the app, open the document, and take you to the *exact* location of the selection. Very spiffy.

Why would you want to do this? Here's one idea: You could in essence leave a message on your desktop to remind yourself to check a formula in a cell or a paragraph of a document in progress, without typing lots of instructions into the document itself or even having to remember where the document is located.

USING CLIPBOOK VIEWER

Like earlier versions of Windows, Windows 2000 comes with the ClipBook Viewer utility to help you manage the contents of the Clipboard. ClipBook Viewer lets you perform the following tasks:

- See what's currently on the Clipboard
- Save the Clipboard's current contents to a file and open previously saved Clipboard files
- Store related Clipboard items in the ClipBook for later use.

RUNNING CLIPBOOK VIEWER

Depending on how your system was set up, the shortcut for the ClipBook Viewer utility may be located in one of several likely hiding places. Look for it in the Start, Programs, Accessories submenu or in the System Tools submenu of Accessories.

If you don't find the shortcut in any of these places, the ClipBook Viewer program, itself, is stored in the Windows\System32 folder. The program file is called CLIPBRD.EXE. Use the standard techniques for running the program via Windows Explorer or the Run command on the Start menu.

As shown in Figure 8.3, the ClipBook Viewer has two separate windows, labeled Clipboard and Local ClipBook. If both windows aren't visible when you start the program, use the View menu to restore the missing one.

Figure 8.3
Here's the ClipBook Viewer in action.

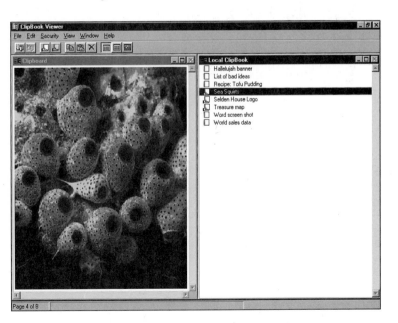

EXAMINING THE CLIPBOARD'S CONTENTS

The Clipboard window of ClipBook Viewer shows you the current contents of the Clipboard. In other words, what you see here is what will appear in the destination document when you do a paste. Viewing the Clipboard contents can be especially useful when you're not sure whether you've managed to transfer the correct chunk of information to the Clipboard—selecting just the right information can sometimes be difficult, especially with graphics. By checking the Viewer, you can see instantly if you succeeded.

SELECTING A FORMAT FOR CLIPBOARD DATA

The ClipBook Viewer's View menu lets you choose the format in which to display the information stored on the Clipboard. Recall that the Clipboard often receives several versions of the cut or copied data, each version representing the data in a different format. For example, a picture cut or copied from Paint can be viewed in the Picture, Bitmap, Device Independent Bitmap, and Enhanced Metafile formats.

A given format may be ideal for pasting into one application but wrong for another, so multiple formats increase the chances that you'll be able to successfully paste the data. At any rate, the available formats are listed in black on the View menu, and you can switch between them at will. Choose the Default menu item to switch back to the format that was originally used to display the data.

SAVING THE CLIPBOARD'S CONTENTS IN DISK FILES

When you cut or copy new information to the Clipboard and then log off of Windows or shut down your system, poof go the contents of the Clipboard. However, there's a way to store those contents for later use, even spanning logoffs and shutdowns—by saving them in a CLP file using ClipBook Viewer. When you later want to paste that information into a document, you just open the CLP file to bring its contents back onto the Clipboard.

Another reason to save Clipboard contents in a file is to share them with other users. Your Clipboard isn't available to other users, but you can make the data it contains accessible in the form of a CLP file.

Note

> The CLP format is unique to the Clipboard and isn't readable by most other programs. To use CLP files, you must open them in ClipBook Viewer and then perform a Paste operation—you generally can't open them directly in the destination application.

With all that in mind, here's how to save the Clipboard contents in a CLP file:

1. Start ClipBook Viewer.
2. Choose File, Save As to display the Save As dialog box.
3. Type in a filename.
4. Click OK to save the file.

LOADING A STORED CLIPBOARD FILE

Of course, saving a CLP file is only useful if you plan to reuse it in the future. To load a stored CLP file back into the Clipboard using ClipBook Viewer, follow these steps:

1. In ClipBook Viewer, activate the Clipboard by clicking the Clipboard icon.
2. Choose File, Open to display the Open dialog box.
3. Select the file you want to open.
4. If the Clipboard already contains information—which is usually the case—you get a message informing you that the existing data will be replaced by the file you're opening. Be aware that when you open a CLP file, the information that was on the Clipboard is deleted permanently—you can't retrieve it. Click OK to proceed.

When the CLP file is open and its contents are on the Clipboard, the information acts just like you cut or copied it there directly. In other words, you can paste it repeatedly into any document you like.

CLEARING THE CLIPBOARD

Turn-of-the-millennium PCs might have gobs of RAM and capacious hard disks, but system resources are still at a premium. Of course, a short snippet of text placed on the Clipboard has no appreciable impact on system performance. However, because the Clipboard can store entire database tables and multimegabyte multimedia files, and because the Clipboard often stores several copies of the same information in different formats, the Clipboard can become an important drain on the memory available to your applications.

For this reason, don't leave a large amount of information just sitting idle on the Clipboard. As soon as you've pasted the data the last time, replace it by copying a brief snippet of text (a single character or word will do). Voilà, for all intents and purposes, you've just emptied the Clipboard and released the memory used by the previous contents.

> **Note**
>
> The Performance Monitor utility can show you the amount of free memory currently available. Check it before and after clearing the Clipboard to see how much memory you've freed. Performance Monitor is covered in Chapter 31, "System Management and Configuration Tools."

If ClipBook Viewer is running, you can completely clear the Clipboard as follows:

1. In ClipBook Viewer, select the Clipboard window by clicking its window or choosing Clipboard from the Window menu.
2. Choose Edit, Delete, click the delete button on the toolbar, or press Delete.
3. When a message appears asking whether it's all right to deep-six the Clipboard contents, click OK. They're history.

USING CLIPBOOKS

As useful as it is, the Clipboard is a rudimentary tool with several important deficiencies. These include the following:

- You can only have one item at a time on the Clipboard. Copying or cutting a new item deletes the existing Clipboard information. Copying a new item erases the previous one.
- The Clipboard isn't network aware—you can't share its contents with other users.
- You can't control what information makes it to the Clipboard or the format it arrives in.

Stored CLP files offer partial relief from the first two problems. However, storing and retrieving Clipboard files individually is a pain. It's a time-consuming process, and it can be hard to come up with a meaningful, memorable name for each file—a vital step, because you can't see what's in the files before you reload them.

The ClipBook feature eases the pain. Note ClipBook's benefits:

- The ClipBook stores up to 127 separate Clipboard content items as pages.
- You can label each ClipBook page to make it easier to find the one you're looking for.
- You can display the pages in miniature thumbnails (another aid for tracking down the right item).
- You can share pages individually on your network.
- ClipBook enhances the process of linking items over the network to documents on other computers.

WORKING WITH THE CLIPBOOK VIEWER

The ClipBook Viewer's toolbar, previously shown in Figure 8.3, gives you immediate access to 10 useful functions. Table 8.1 lists the buttons and what they're for.

TABLE 8.1   VIEWER TOOLBAR BUTTONS

Button	Function
Connect	Opens a ClipBook on a network computer
Disconnect	Closes a ClipBook you've been accessing via the network
Share	Shares the current ClipBook page on the network so other users can access it
Stop Sharing	Turns off sharing on the current page
Copy	Pastes the contents of the current ClipBook page to the Clipboard
Paste	Pastes the information on the Clipboard to the ClipBook
Delete	Erases the contents of the current ClipBook page (clears the Clipboard itself if its window is active)

Button	Function
Table of Contents	Lists the ClipBook pages by name
Snapshots	Displays thumbnails (tiny images) of the ClipBook's pages
Full Page	Displays the contents of each ClipBook page at full size, one page at a time

WORKING WITH CLIPBOOKS

The ClipBook feature is an enhancement for the main Windows Clipboard, not a replacement. Information you cut or copy from a document still gets transferred to the Clipboard and must be pasted from it to the destination. ClipBook's job is to store Clipboard items for ready reuse, making it easy to find and transfer the items back to the Clipboard when you need them. You can share ClipBook pages with others who have ClipBook Viewer installed on their computers, and they can share their ClipBook pages with you. Figure 8.4 shows how this works.

Figure 8.4
Items are added to the ClipBook when you paste them from the Clipboard.

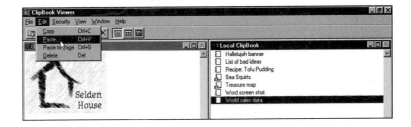

To add an item to a ClipBook, follow these steps:

1. Cut or copy the information to the Clipboard from the source application.

2. Open or switch to ClipBook Viewer.

3. Click the Paste button or choose Edit, Paste to create a new page for the information. Type a name for the page in the resulting Paste dialog box, as shown in Figure 8.5. (You must supply a name for each new ClipBook page.) If you want other network users to be able to access the item, check the Share Item Now box.

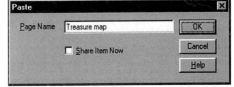

Figure 8.5

PASTING FROM CLIPBOOK

To paste an item from a ClipBook into a document, start by transferring the information back to the main Clipboard. You can then paste it using any standard paste technique. Here are the steps:

1. Open or switch to ClipBook Viewer.

2. Locate and activate the page that has the information you want to paste.

3. Click the Copy toolbar button or choose Edit, Copy. A copy of the item is placed on the Clipboard.

4. Switch to the destination application and do the paste.

SHARING CLIPBOOK PAGES ON THE NETWORK

To share a ClipBook page so that others on the network can copy its contents into their documents (or link to it via OLE), follow these steps:

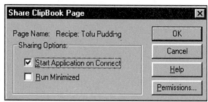

1. Select the page in ClipBook Viewer.

2. Click the Share button or choose File, Share. The dialog box shown in Figure 8.6 appears.

3. If you're sharing an item that's to be linked or embedded via OLE, check the box labeled Start Application on Connect.

Figure 8.6

Tip #113

With the Start Application on Connect check box checked, the application from which the ClipBook data was taken runs whenever a remote user accesses a document into which that data has been pasted. Check the Run Minimized box so that you don't have to see the application's window on *your* screen.

Note

By default, other users on the network can paste from shared ClipBook pages or link the data they contain into other documents. However, network users can't change the data.

To stop sharing a local ClipBook page:

1. In the local ClipBook window, click the ClipBook page you want to stop sharing.

2. On the File menu, click Stop Sharing.

SPECIFYING PERMISSIONS FOR SHARED CLIPBOOK PAGES

You can control the permissions that regulate how much access network users have to ClipBook data on a page-by-page basis (of course, you must, yourself, have permission sufficient to allow you to change the permission level).

By default, all network users can read a shared ClipBook page (that is, users can copy the information on the page to their own Clipboards) and can link the information to their own documents. If you like, however, you can restrict such access to specific users or groups of users. You can even increase permission levels for some pages (or some users), thus permitting the ClipBook data to be altered or deleted.

To change the permissions for a particular page, follow these steps:

1. Activate the desired ClipBook page.

2. Choose Security, Permissions. You'll see the dialog box shown in Figure 8.7.

Figure 8.7
Use this dialog box to change permissions for a ClipBook page.

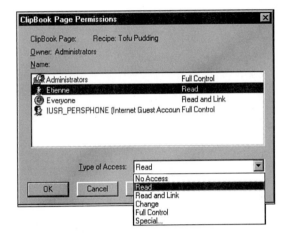

3. Select the user or group whose permission level you want to alter.

4. Choose the desired permission level in the Type of Access field.

Tip #114

To prevent a user or group from accessing a given page at all, select the user or group and then click Remove.

You can also add new users to the permissions list in the Permissions dialog box. Here's how:

1. Choose Security, Permissions.

2. Click the Add button to display the Add Users and Groups dialog box (see Figure 8.8).

3. If you don't see the user's name, use the List Names From field to select a different domain or computer. Then click the Show Users button to display the individual users who belong to that domain or computer.

4. Once the user or group you're looking for is visible, select that entry and then click Add.

5. Specify the permission level in the Type of Access box.

6. Click OK.

Figure 8.8
As shown here, you can add more users to the list of those who have access to a Clipboard page.

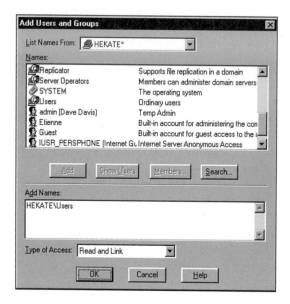

OBJECT LINKING AND EMBEDDING IN WINDOWS 2000

The Clipboard works fine when you want to take information from one document as is and place it into another, breaking the connection between the data and the source document. However, there are many situations when this isn't the ideal system for information transfer. These fall into three main categories:

- The destination document doesn't understand, and won't accept, the information you want to paste into it.

- You expect the information in the source document to change and you want the destination document to reflect those changes whenever they occur.

- You want to be able to edit the transferred information directly in the destination document. In other words, you don't want to have to reopen the original document, make your changes, and then recopy and repaste the data into the destination document.

To accommodate all these scenarios, Windows offers an information-sharing technology called *object linking and embedding* (OLE). OLE passes information from one program to another in the form of *objects* that retain their connection with the source application. That connection enables you to edit the contents of the object using the source application, even though the object appears to be part of the destination document.

> **Note**
>
> An OLE object can encompass one spreadsheet cell or an entire spreadsheet; a single database field from one record or the full database table from which that field is drawn; an individual graphic element such as a line or box or a fully realized work of computer art.

UNDERSTANDING OLE'S BENEFITS

Consider a typical use of OLE in constructing your basic business document, such as a financial report. You would use a Windows word processor such as Word, WordPerfect, or Word Pro to create the text, but you'll surely be including financial analysis calculated in a spreadsheet application such as Excel, Quattro Pro, or Lotus 1-2-3. Cutting and pasting the data would be one way to move the figures into the final report, but the calculations are always changing.

Instead of trying to keep up with these changes by repeatedly copying and pasting, you can use OLE to *link* the desired cells in the spreadsheet directly to the report document. When the calculations change in the spreadsheet, the new figures appear automatically in your report. Figure 8.9 shows a Microsoft Word document containing linked Excel data.

Figure 8.9
The figures in this Word document represent cells in a linked Excel worksheet.

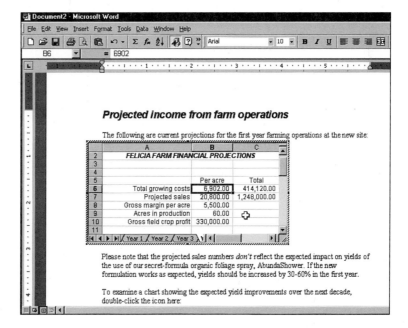

Linking has an added benefit: It allows you to edit the source information from within the document into which it has been linked. Using the same example, suppose you're working on the report text in Word when the latest sales results arrive. All you need do is double-click the linked cells in the report to open the spreadsheet from which they come. The source application (in this case Excel) appears on your screen, allowing you to make whatever changes are appropriate in the original data. When you finish editing and close Excel, you're returned to Word and your report, where you can see the new calculations.

This same technique lets you link charts, graphics, word processing documents (or portions thereof), and multimedia files to other documents. A linked chart, for instance, will be automatically redrawn whenever it's changed in the application that created it.

REMEMBERING DDE

OLE is based on a more primitive data-sharing technology called *Dynamic Data Exchange* (DDE). Although most applications released since the early '90s use OLE for user-initiated data sharing, you may still run across programs that rely on DDE. DDE-based data links are typically complicated to set up because DDE's standards are loose and have been interpreted differently by different software developers. It's vital to read the manual and consult whatever other resources the software publisher provides.

UNDERSTANDING LINKING VERSUS EMBEDDING

As it's full name implies, OLE supports two types of data sharing: linking and embedding. Here's how they work:

- When you embed an object in a document, the information can only be accessed in the destination document—it isn't stored in a separate file you can open independently in the source application. However, embedding does create a connection to the source application, thus allowing you to edit the embedded object with that application's tools. Embedding is the default type for most OLE connections in Office.

- A linked object represents all or part of a source document, stored in its own disk file. You can open the linked object from within the destination document, but you can also open the source document on its own in the source application.

The bottom line is this: Use a linked object when you want to be able to edit the information separately with the source application, even when the destination document isn't open. If you simply want to be able to edit the information using the source application, embed the object instead.

Note

Because a linked object is based on a separate file, the same object can be linked to different documents as many times as you like.

Also, you should know that *compound document* is the term for a document that contains one or more OLE objects.

Note

Be aware that DDE and OLE put a significant drain on system resources. These days, the typical new PC finally has enough speed and memory to make good use of OLE. However, if you have performance problems, consider upgrading your system.

WORKING WITH OLE SERVERS AND CLIENTS

OLE-aware applications can play two distinct roles in the information-sharing process:

- An *OLE server* is a program that can serve as a source application. In other words, it can create an object to be embedded or linked. As previously shown in Figure 8.9, Excel is the server.

- An *OLE client* is a program capable of accepting a linked or embedded object. Word is acting as the client in Figure 8.9.

The typical mainstream business application can act as both an OLE server and an OLE client. A spreadsheet program such as Excel can furnish chart and worksheet objects to a word processor or a desktop publishing program, and it can also accept objects from a word processor or a graphics program. However, many applications can function in only one of these roles. Sound Recorder and Paint, for example, act only as OLE servers—they can't accept linked or embedded documents.

WORKING WITH OBJECT PACKAGES

Objects containing static visual content ordinarily appear in the destination document more or less as they would be displayed by the source application. When placed into a spreadsheet, for example, a word processing document object shows the same text with the same formatting as it does in the word processor.

However, you can also display objects as icons representing the underlying content. Such iconized objects are called *packages* (see Figure 8.10). Packages are required for multimedia objects such as video and sound clips because their content can't be displayed. You can also choose to package objects that do contain static visual content. That way, they don't occupy much space onscreen, but their content is available to interested users. Of course, packages aren't practical for visual content you intend to print out.

Figure 8.10
The icon in the middle of the window represents a packaged object.

the use of our secret-formula organic foliage spray, AbundaShower. If the new formulation works as expected, yields should be increased by 30-60% in the first year.

To examine a chart showing the expected yield improvements over the next decade, double-click the icon here:

Chart: standard vs enhanced yields

Research crops

The farm plans to undertake an ongoing research program designed to identify crops that will perform well in our climate and that offer superior nutritional benefit. Possible candidates for inclusion in this program include:

- Chandra chinensis

- Lococutus bryoninia

- Fortunia fortunii

Packages have one advantage over nonpackaged OLE objects: They allow you to incorporate documents from OLE-unaware applications into your destination document. This is a handy way to provide the user with quick access to supplemental material that isn't reachable via OLE. Again, this technique is only useful for documents that are to be viewed onscreen rather than printed out.

Tip #115	You can even place executable files such as EXE, PIF, BAT, and CMD files into packages. By embedding a set of such packages into your document, you can readily build a simple customized command center for software tasks you or another user commonly perform.

EMBEDDING AND LINKING OBJECTS: PRACTICAL TECHNIQUES

For most people, the hardest part about OLE is remembering the difference between embedding and linking. By contrast, the procedures for placing embedded or linked objects in your documents are actually quite straightforward. Just be aware that the specific steps required vary somewhat from application to application.

EMBEDDING AND LINKING OBJECTS THROUGH THE CLIPBOARD

One way to embed or link objects is via the Clipboard. The technique is much the same as the one used to paste ordinary Clipboard data. Follow these steps to embed or link an object into another document:

1. Run the source application and open the document containing the information you want to embed. Remember, the source application must be able to function as an OLE server.

2. In the source document, select the information you want to transfer. If you're creating a link, be sure to save the source document before going on.

3. Choose Edit, Copy or press Ctrl+C to copy the information to the Clipboard. So far, these are the same steps you would use to place ordinary (non-OLE) information on the Clipboard.

4. Switch to the destination document and, if appropriate, specify the location in the document that's to receive the object.

5. Here's where the procedure might part company with a standard Paste operation:

   - In some applications, activating the standard Paste command (Edit, Paste or Ctrl+V) creates an embedded object automatically, assuming the source app is an OLE server and the destination doc is an OLE client.

   - When you embed in other programs, and whenever you link, you must use an alternative pasting command. In Word, for example, you should choose Edit, Paste Special and then choose an object format for the pasted information. If you're creating a link, select the Paste Link radio button before clicking OK. Some programs have an Edit, Paste Link menu command.

EMBEDDING AND LINKING OBJECTS THE DRAG-AND-DROP WAY

Depending on the applications involved, you should be able to create objects in your destination document through simple drag-and-drop techniques. Here are some examples of what you can do:

- Drag a file created by an OLE server application from Windows Explorer or My Computer to the destination document. If the destination document isn't visible, drag to its icon on the taskbar and hold it there until the destination document appears; then drag to the correct location.

- Drag a selection from a document open in an OLE server application to the destination document. Use the technique covered in the previous paragraph to drag to a document window that isn't currently visible.

Note

Holding down Ctrl+Shift while you drag is supposed to create a linked object rather than an embedded object. However, I haven't been able to get this technique to work when dragging objects into Microsoft Office documents.

INSERTING EMBEDDED OR LINKED OBJECTS

Many OLE applications let you insert objects into the document you're currently working with, without having to start the source application separately. Microsoft Office applications, for example, have an Insert, Object command (Figure 8.11 shows the resulting dialog box in Microsoft Word).

Figure 8.11
Use this dialog box to insert an OLE object in a Microsoft Word document without manually starting the source application.

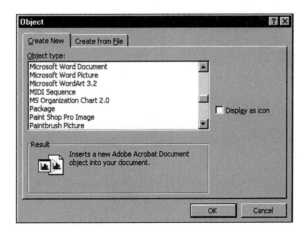

Using such a command, you can insert objects with either of two techniques:

- You can create a brand-new object and embed it into the document (linking isn't possible with this method).

- You can embed or link an existing disk file into the document.

EMBEDDING NEW OBJECTS

In an Office application, follow these steps to insert a new embedded object that you create from scratch:

1. Position the insertion point where you want the object to appear in your document (or use a comparable technique as appropriate to your application).

2. Choose Insert, Object.

3. In the Object dialog box that appears, select the Create New tab (refer back to Figure 8.11).

4. Locate and click the type of object you want to create from those listed in the Object Type area. All OLE servers registered on your system are listed there.

5. If you want to insert the object as a package, check the box labeled Display As Icon.

6. Click OK. At this point, the object is inserted into your document and the application associated with the object type you chose starts. If the source and destination applications are of reasonably recent vintage, your document remains active, but the source application's toolbars and menus appear there. With older applications, the source application appears in a separate window.

7. When you're through creating the object, click elsewhere in the document to restore the application's standard menus and toolbars (if you had to create the object in a separate window, you must choose File, Exit to return to the original document).

CREATING OBJECTS FROM DISK FILES

Here are the steps for inserting an existing disk file into a document as an embedded or linked object in Microsoft Office applications:

1. Position the insertion point where you want the object to appear in your document (or use a comparable technique as appropriate to your application).

2. Choose Insert, Object.

3. In the Object dialog box that appears, select the Create from File tab (refer to Figure 8.11).

4. Click Browse to locate the file you want to insert using a standard Office File dialog box. When you find the right file, click it and then click OK to open it. You're returned to the Object dialog box.

5. If you want to link the object into your document, check the box labeled Link to File. To embed the object, leave this box cleared.

6. If you want to insert the object as a package, check the box labeled Display As Icon.

7. Click OK to insert the object.

CREATING PACKAGES

I've already covered one method for creating packaged objects—the Insert, Object command—in the section "Inserting Embedded or Linked Objects." The only other dependable method for creating packages is using the Object Packager utility supplied with Windows. You can use Windows Explorer to create packages. However, although this technique is quicker, it doesn't always work.

PACKAGING DOCUMENTS AND FILES WITH OBJECT PACKAGER

The Object Packager program comes with Windows 2000, but you might not find it in the Accessories submenu. If not, you'll find the PACKAGER.EXE file in the WINNT\System32 directory. You'll also find the PACKAGER.CHM file (the Help file for the application).

Object Packager allows you to package any sort of file, be it a document from an OLE-aware application—in which case the package can contain a linked or embedded object—a non-OLE document, or any application or other executable file. (To run the executable file represented by a package, you just double-click the package icon.)

→ You can also use the Object Packager to package commands for the command line. **See** "Packaging a Command for the Command Prompt," **p. 310**.

Here's how to create a package containing a complete file using Object Packager:

1. Run Object Packager. Again, if it's not on one of the Program menu's submenus, search for the PACKAGER.EXE file. The window of this modest-looking program sports two panes: Content and Appearance (see Figure 8.12).

Figure 8.12
Create packages with the Object Packager utility.

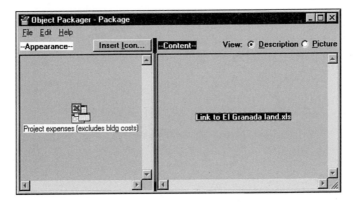

2. Click the Content window to select it.
3. Choose File, Import to bring up the Import dialog box.
4. Locate and select the file you want to package.
5. Click OK. The icon and filename of the chosen file appear in the Appearance and Content windows, respectively.

6. To change the icon associated with the package, click the Insert Icon button. To change the text that appears beneath the icon, choose Edit, Label.

7. Choose Edit, Copy Package to place the package onto the Clipboard.

8. Switch to the destination document and position the insertion point where the package is to reside.

9. Use the Paste command to place the package into the destination document. It appears as it did in Object Packager's Appearance pane.

Note

> This technique works with any type of file, be it a document or executable program. It can only package embedded objects, however. To package an entire document as a linked object, use Windows Explorer to locate the document file, click the file icon to select it, and choose Edit, Copy. Switch to Object Packager. There, select the Content pane (this is a must) and choose Edit, Paste Link. Then choose Edit, Copy Package (not Edit, Copy) to create the package.

PACKAGING PART OF A DOCUMENT

You can package a selected part of a document, rather than the document as a whole, as long as the source application is an OLE server. If this test is met, follow these steps:

1. Create or open the source document. As always, save the document before proceeding if you want to create a linked object.

2. Select the information you want to place in the package.

3. Choose Edit, Copy.

4. Switch to Object Packager and—this is important—select the Content pane.

5. From Packager's menu, choose Edit, Paste to create an embedded object or Edit, Paste Link for a linked one.

6. If you like, change the icon shown in the Appearance pane by clicking Insert Icon or change the label beneath the icon by choosing Edit, Label.

7. Choose Edit, Copy Package. (Important: Don't choose Edit, Copy or you'll wind up with an ordinary object, not a packaged one.)

You can now switch to the destination document and paste in the finished package.

PACKAGING A COMMAND FOR THE COMMAND PROMPT

Object Packager lets you quickly create packages containing single commands to be executed at the command prompt. Because Windows 2000 can execute Windows 2000, DOS, OS/2, and POSIX commands at the command prompt, you can accomplish lots of work with this technique. Here's how to proceed:

1. Start Object Packager.

2. Choose Edit, Command Line.

3. Type in a valid command in the resulting dialog box.

4. Click OK. The Content pane displays the command you entered.

5. Click the Insert Icon button to assign an icon to the command. Choose Edit, Label to change the text beneath the icon.

6. Choose Edit, Copy Package.

7. Switch to the destination document and paste in the package.

Tip #116	To create a package that executes a series of commands, use a text editor to compose a batch file with the desired commands and then package the batch file using the standard technique outlined earlier. You might also want to read Chapter 36, "Windows Script Host," to learn about the power of the Windows Scripting Host for automating native Windows 2000 functions.

WORKING WITH LINKED AND EMBEDDED OBJECTS IN YOUR DOCUMENTS

After you've successfully placed an OLE object in a document, it appears there in one of two forms:

- If the object comprises static visual content (such as text, spreadsheet cells, a chart, or graphics), it appears in the document in that form. You can look at the information, but to edit it you must double-click the object, as discussed in the next section.

- Packaged objects, including executable files and multimedia objects such as video or sound clips, appear as icons. To play or run the object, just double-click it. If the packaged object is an ordinary document, double-clicking opens it in the source application.

Tip #117	Right-clicking an object should bring up a shortcut menu containing all the commands available for working with that object.

EDITING LINKED AND EMBEDDED OBJECTS

The procedure for editing the contents of a linked or embedded object varies somewhat, depending on the type of object:

- If the object displays static visual content, double-click the object to edit it.

- If the object represents a multimedia clip or other content that can be played, double-clicking won't work. Instead, click once to select the object and choose Edit, *Objecttype* Object, Edit. You can also right-click the object and choose Edit, *Objecttype* Object, Edit from the shortcut menu.

What happens next depends on the capabilities of the source and destination applications, and on whether the object is linked or embedded. Here's the breakdown:

- If you're editing an embedded object and if you're working with up-to-date OLE applications, you can edit the object *in place*. In other words, the object remains visible in context in your document, but the editing tools of the source application appear. When you finish editing, just click elsewhere in the document to restore the destination application's menus and toolbars.

- If you're editing an embedded object and you're using older OLE applications, the object opens in the source application. After completing your edits, choose File, Close to close the source application and return to the document (answer Yes to any dialog boxes you see).

- Linked objects are always open for editing in the source application. When you finish making changes, choose File, Save and switch back to your document, where the changes will also appear.

Note

Changes made to a linked object will appear in all documents to which the object has been linked.

TENDING TO LINKED OBJECTS

The whole point of linking objects via OLE is to take the hassle out of keeping your data current. Ordinarily, you can sit back and let Windows worry about updating the content shown in your document whenever the source document for a linked object changes. Once in a while, however, you need to step in to set things right.

UPDATING A LINK MANUALLY

You might want Windows *not* to update a linked object automatically. Perhaps the source document is going through substantial revision. Rather than distracting yourself with a series of inaccurate, intermediate versions, you may prefer not to update the object until those revisions are complete.

Follow these steps to specify that a link should be updated manually—that is, only when you say so:

1. Select the linked object in the destination document (clicking it should do the trick).

2. Choose Edit, Links to display the Links dialog box (see Figure 8.13). It lists all the linked objects in the document by the source document's filename. Note that the target object is already selected, assuming you followed step 1.

Figure 8.13
Change link settings in
this dialog box.

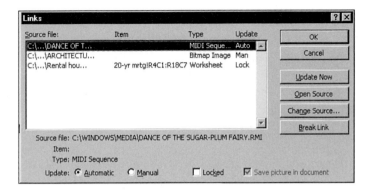

3. Click the Manual button. When you click OK, the procedure is complete.

Tip #118

To update a link after you've set it to manual updating, open the Links dialog box again, select the link, and click the Update Now button.

To switch back to automatic updating, repeat steps 1 and 2 and then click the Automatic button when you get to step 3.

FIXING BROKEN LINKS

If someone renames a linked object's source document or moves it to a new location on disk, the link is broken and you won't see the correct data in your document. Use the Links dialog box (previously shown in Figure 8.13) to fix such problems. Follow these steps:

1. Select the object and choose Edit, Links to display the Links dialog box.

2. Click the Change Source button. In the resulting dialog box, browse for the file containing the source object.

3. Click OK to return to the Links dialog box where the new path of the source document is displayed.

4. Click OK in the Links dialog box. If the link is set for automatic updating, the current contents of the source object appears in your document.

 If a link suddenly disappears, see "Linked OLE Objects Disappear" in the "Troubleshooting" section at the end of this chapter.

BREAKING LINKS

Sometimes it makes sense to break the link between an object in a document and its source document. You would want to do so to preserve the contents of the object in their current state, thus protecting them from ever being updated. Once you break a link, Windows substitutes a static copy of the information contained in the object.

To break a link, select the object, choose Edit, Links to open the Links dialog box, and click Break Link.

> **Note**
>
> Breaking a link makes sense only if the destination application can display the object's data in static form. If you break a multimedia object's link, you're left with an icon that doesn't do anything. A better approach would be to delete the linked object altogether and create an embedded object from the source document. That way, your destination document will still contain active information, but the information won't change unless you edit the object.

MANAGING OBJECTS ON THE NETWORK

Windows 2000 permits you to enhance your documents with linked and embedded objects derived from source documents located anywhere on your network. All the linking and embedding techniques described earlier in this chapter work equally well with network documents as they do with those stored on your own PC. The only caveat is that you must have permission to open the source document you want to work with.

DEALING WITH INACCESSIBLE DOCUMENTS

When a document contains linked objects based on source documents stored elsewhere on the network, an error occurs if the source document is unavailable over the network. If the directory containing the document hasn't been shared, if the network computer has been shut down, or if the network itself has crashed, you and your application won't be able to get at the source document to display the object.

Whatever the cause, here are the choices to ponder when you see a message such as one telling you that the server is unavailable:

- Wait longer and hope the problem rights itself. The server may respond to your computer's request after it finishes a big job.
- Click the Cancel button in the error message. Then call your friendly Help Desk staffer to alert him or her to the problem. Because a response may take hours to weeks, change your priorities.

UNDERSTANDING OLE SECURITY AND PERMISSIONS

As you know, each Windows 2000 user has a specific set of privileges when it comes to which disks and directories he or she can access and which documents he or she can view or edit. When you use OLE to build compound documents over a network, the complexities of the Windows security system can become an issue. The text in a document could come from a file the user has read/write (full) access to, whereas an embedded portion of a spreadsheet is supplied by a workstation or a directory to which the user has only read privileges.

One way to reduce the security hassle is to stick with embedded objects whenever possible. An embedded object is a full-fledged part of your document. Once you've created an embedded object in the first place, you can count on having access to it from then on.

Linked objects, by contrast, are references to completely separate source documents, each of which maintain a distinct set of permissions. If someone changes the permissions for the source document of a linked object, the document may become inaccessible to you, and you may no longer be able to access or edit the linked object's content.

TROUBLESHOOTING

PASTE COMMAND DOESN'T WORK

I'm sure I placed information on the Clipboard but the Paste command won't work.

The problem is that the destination document doesn't recognize the format of your Clipboard data. You may be able to work around this obstacle by first pasting the data into another application that does accept the information and then copying and pasting from this way station app into the intended destination document. Alternatively, try saving the selected information to disk in a file format that the destination app can import.

PASTED DATA DOESN'T LOOK RIGHT

My pasted data sometimes looks quite different in the destination document than it did in the original.

You might be able to get better results by pasting the data in another format, if the destination application allows this. Look for a command in the destination app such as Edit, Paste Special that lets you select from all the Clipboard formats the application recognizes. Try each format in turn to see which gives the best results.

If you still don't get the desired results, try inserting the foreign data as an OLE object into the destination document. The information will appear exactly as it did in the original application. The take-home message: OLE is a good solution for preserving the appearance of transferred data, even if you don't need OLE's live connection to the original application.

CANNOT COPY NON-WINDOWS DATA TO THE CLIPBOARD

Nothing seems to happen when I try to copy information from a non-Windows program to the Clipboard.

Remember that you must first enter the special mark mode before selecting information with the mouse. First, be sure that you're running the program in a window, not in full-screen mode. Then open the window's control box and select Edit, Mark. Then press Enter or choose Copy from the control box's Edit menu.

LINKED OLE OBJECTS DISAPPEAR

A linked OLE object disappeared from my document.

This happens because the disk file in which the object appears has been moved from its original location or is inaccessible over the network. If you're dealing with a moved file, move it back where it was or relink the file from its new location. If someone has deleted the file, you're out of luck unless you have a backup copy.

Tip #119

This talk of backups brings me to make this suggestion: When you back up documents containing linked OLE objects, always back up the files for those objects as well. When you're planning the backup procedure, remember that each OLE object file carries the filename extension used by its source application, which is usually not the application used to create the main document. Remember, too, that a linked OLE file may be stored in a completely different location than the main document file.

TIPS FROM THE WINDOWS PROS: SUPERCHARGING THE CLIPBOARD AND WORKING WITH SCRAPS

I'm not a shill for software vendors, but believe me, one of the single most important steps you can take to be more productive in Windows is to install a Clipboard extender utility. Clipboard extenders are designed to fix the myriad shortcomings of the Windows Clipboard. They succeed far better than the ClipBook Viewer described earlier in this chapter.

The basic mission of a Clipboard extender is to automatically store every cut or copied item. That way, you can then paste any item at any time thereafter, even when it long ago vanished from the Clipboard itself—or even if you've shut down your system since you originally cut or copied the item. Choosing the item you want to paste is very convenient—one keystroke pops up a window listing the available items over your current application, and you can paste directly from there. You can organize the stored items into groups, edit the content of text items, and combine multiple items collected at different times into one for convenient one-step pasting.

The two best Clipboard extenders are Clipmate and SmartBoard 2000. Add one of these inexpensive gems to your Startup folder, and it will quickly become indispensable.

After you've installed a Clipboard extender utility, you also should become familiar with using Windows scraps. A little known fact about the Windows GUI is that you can easily drag a portion of a document on the desktop for use in another application. This creates what's called a *scrap*, somewhat like double parking your car while running into a store to grab a quart of milk.

Here's how to use it: In your document, select the text or graphic that you want to copy. Drag it to the desktop. Once on the desktop, the text or graphic becomes a scrap, which you can drag to other documents or programs. Figure 8.14 shows an example of such a scrap. Notice that Windows figured out to create a new document of the same type as the source document (in this case, Word).

The scrap document created can be opened again later just by clicking it. Technically, opening is achieved via the *shell scrap object handler*.

Unfortunately, not all applications will do this. Only the ones that support OLE drag-and-drop functions will. For example, Notepad won't.

Figure 8.14
Creating a scrap for later use by dragging a selection onto the desktop.

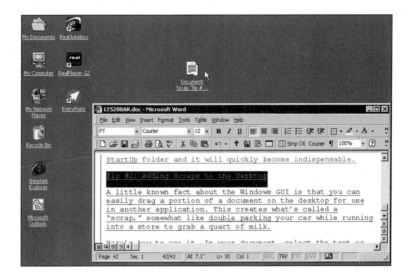

CHAPTER 9

PRINTING AND FAXING WITH WINDOWS 2000

In this chapter

WINDOWS 2000 PRINTING PRIMER

As with other versions of Windows, before you can print from Windows 2000 Professional, you need to install a printer and the requisite printer driver on your computer. During Windows setup, a printer might have been detected and installed automatically, eliminating the need for you to install a printer manually. In this case, a default printer is already installed, and printing should be fairly effortless from your Windows applications. You can just print without worrying about anything more than turning on the printer, checking that it has paper, and choosing the File, Print command from whatever programs you use.

If you didn't have your printer on or connected during setup, or it isn't a Plug and Play printer, this process might not have happened with success, however. Sometimes, simply plugging in a new printer or having Windows 2000 Professional do a scan for new hardware is enough to get things rolling. I'll talk about installation procedures later, but regardless of your current state of printer connectedness, as a user of Windows 2000 Professional, you should know how to control your print jobs, print to network-based printers, and share your printer for others to use. This chapter covers these topics.

> **Note**
>
> You might want to take advantage of HTML-based printing over the Internet to Windows 2000 Server-attached remote machines—a new and very cool feature in Windows 2000. That topic is covered in Chapter 22, "Using a Windows 2000 Network."

When you print from an application, the application passes the data stream off to Windows, which in turn *spools* the data to a specified printer. Spooling is the process of temporarily stuffing onto the hard disk the data to be transmitted to the printer and eventually printed at the relatively slow pace that printer can receive it. Spooling lets you get back to work with your program sooner. Additional documents can be added to a printer's queue, either from the same computer or from users across the LAN.

Windows 3.x and Windows NT 3.x included a standalone program called Print Manager, the interface for adding printers, doing the spooling, and managing the print jobs. Since Windows 9x and NT 4, the term *Print Manager* has been dropped, even though the same functionality is provided by the Printers folder.

In essence, the Print Manager was internalized. Windows 2000 is no exception. At least to the casual user, print management works much as it does in Windows 9x and NT 4: You add printers, check the status of the queue, and manage print jobs from Start, Settings, Printers, or via the Control Panel's Printers folder (both approaches open the Printers folder). (Note that you cannot reach the folder from My Computer anymore.) After you open the folder, you can check or manage the queue and set properties for a particular printer by double-clicking a printer's icon. This action opens a window and displays the print queue for that printer, along with menus for management tasks.

> **Note**
>
> As you learned in Chapter 2, "The Design and Architecture of Windows 2000 Professional," Windows 2000 prevents any application from writing directly to the printer port. Some older programs, especially DOS programs, might try to write this way. In Windows 2000, however, any such attempt by an application to directly write to hardware is trapped by the security manager and either is rerouted to the Windows 2000 printer driver or simply fails. Because Windows 2000 emulates hardware ports in software, most DOS programs should be able to print successfully.

Using the printer spooler, Windows takes control of all printing jobs, whether from OS/2, POSIX, Win32, Win16, or DOS applications. The spooler receives the jobs, queues them up, routes them through the correct printer driver, and passes them on to the desired printer. When there's trouble (for example, ink or paper outage or paper jams), it also issues error or other appropriate messages to print job originators.

> **Note**
>
> I'll refer to the spooling and other printer management capabilities of Windows 2000 Professional's GUI, taken as a whole, as *Print Manager*.

The Print Manager in Windows 2000 Professional has the following features:

- It lets you easily add, modify, and remove printers right from the Printers folder by using the Add Printer Wizard. Browsing for LAN-based printers to connect to has been made very simple. With Web printers (Internet Printing Protocol, or IPP) installed, printers can be shared securely over the Internet, without using *Virtual Private Networking (VPN)*, but rather via the HTML protocol.

→ To learn more about IPP, **see** "Using Printers over the Internet with IPP," **p. 768**.

- The intuitive user interface uses simple icons to represent printers that are installed (available to print to) on the workstation. You don't need to worry about the relationship of printer drivers, connections, and physical printers. You can simply add a printer and set its properties. After it is added, it appears as a named printer in the Printers folder.

- You can easily share a printer over the LAN by modifying a few settings on the printer's Properties sheet. Your printer then acts as a printer server, even though it's running Windows 2000 Professional (not Server). Shared printers can be given a meaningful name and comment, such as *LaserJet in Ted's Office*, which identifies it to LAN-based users surfing for a printer.

- Groups of users (administrators, guests, power users, and so forth) can be assigned rights for ownership, sharing, and queue management.

- Thanks to Windows 2000's multithreading and preemptive multitasking, 32-bit programs tend to print quite smoothly. Most applications let you start printing and immediately go back to work, while spooling and printing occurs in the background. (This isn't true for 16-bit programs, which tie up the given application until output to the spooler is completed.)

- The priority level of a print job can be increased or decreased.

- Multiple applications can send print jobs to the same printer, whether local or across the LAN. Additional documents are simply added to the queue and are printed in turn.

- Default settings for such options as number of copies, paper tray, page orientation, and so forth are automatically used during print jobs, so you don't have to manually set them each time.

- You can easily view the document name, status, owner, page count, size, time of submission, paper source and orientation, number of copies, and destination port of jobs. You can also pause, resume, restart, and cancel jobs; plus, you can rearrange the order of the print queue. In addition, you can temporarily pause or resume printing without causing printer time-out problems.

- You can choose whether printing begins as soon as the first page is spooled to the hard disk or after the last page of a document is spooled.

- You can set color profiles for color printers, assuring accuracy of output color. Associating the correct color profile with all your publishing tools helps to ensure consistent color application throughout the publishing process.

- You can set printer properties, such as times of day when a network printer is available for use.

- You can choose from a multitude of form drivers—canned form sizes such as stationery, business letter, legal, and envelope sizes—to include as part of the printer driver.

- You can specify a pool of printers as the default printer for a machine. When you print a document, the first available printer is used, and a notification is sent to you when the job is finished.

- The system can audit the use of network print servers locally or remotely for later review by an administrator.

Tip #120

By default, all users can pause, resume, restart, and cancel printing of their own documents. However, to manage documents printed by other users, you must have the Manage Documents permission as set by the system administrator.

→ To learn more details about managing print jobs as a system administrator, **see** "Tracking Printer Users," **p. 786**.

ABOUT PRINTER DRIVERS

Printer drivers in Windows 2000 consist of three types of files:

- Configuration (printer interface) file—This file is responsible for displaying the Properties and Preferences dialog boxes and their settings when you configure the printer. The file has a .DLL extension.

- Graphics driver file—This file is the heart of the driver because it effectively translates device driver interface (DDI) commands from the printing application and operating system into commands that the target printer can understand and print from. Each driver translates a different printer language. For example, the file Pscript5.dll translates the PostScript printer language. All graphics driver files have the .DLL extension.

- Data file—This file stores information about the capabilities of particular printers, such as whether they can print double-sided, which paper sizes are acceptable, whether color and grayscale capabilities are offered, and so on. This file can have a .DLL, .PCD, .GPD, or .PPD extension.

PART

II

CH

9

You can find driver files in the \system32\spool\drivers... directory. Sometimes accompanied by a help file, these files form a cohesive unit, working cooperatively to successfully print. When you're installing a new printer, the configuration file queries the data file and displays the available printer options. Later, when you print, the graphics driver file queries the configuration file about the current state of the options settings so that it can generate the appropriate printer commands.

INSTALLING AND CONFIGURING A PRINTER

If your printer is already installed and operational at this point, you can skip this section and skim ahead for others that might be of interest. However, if you need to install a new printer, modify or customize your current installation, or add additional printers to your setup, read on.

The following sections cover how to do the following:

- Set up or install a new printer on your system
- Select the printer port and make other connection settings
- Set preferences for a printer
- Install a printer driver that's not listed
- Set the default printer
- Select a printer when more than one is installed
- Remove a printer from your setup

Tip #121	As discussed in Chapter 3, "Getting Your Hardware and Software Ready for Windows 2000," and Chapter 4, "Installing Windows 2000," before you install a new piece of hardware, it's always a good idea to check the Microsoft Hardware Compatibility List (HCL) either on the Web or on the Windows 2000 Professional CD. You should at least check with the manufacturer or check the printer's manual to ensure it's compatible with Windows 2000 Professional. Also, you should check for the possibility of another file, PRINTER.WRI, for additional help information about installing and using printers.

The basic game plan for installing and configuring a printer is as follows:

- Plug it in. The newer USB printers are detected when you simply plug them into the USB port. Your printer might be found and then configure itself fairly automatically. If the printer is not recognized, scan for new hardware.

- If the printer doesn't configure itself, you can run the Add New Printer Wizard (or setup program if one is supplied with your printer).

- Select the printer's port and relevant port settings, if necessary, via the wizard.

At this point, you should have a functioning printer. You might want to make alterations and customizations to the printer setup, though. For example, you can do the following:

- Choose the default printer if you have more than one printer installed.

- Set the default priority level of jobs you send to the printer from this workstation.

- Set job defaults pertaining to paper tray, two-sided printing, scaling, type of paper feed, halftone imaging, the time file header information (such as a PostScript "preamble") is sent to the printer, and paper orientation.

- Check and possibly alter device-specific settings such as DPI (dots per inch), memory settings, and font substitution.

- Share the printer, and specify its sharename so that other network users can use your printer from afar.

- Declare a separator file, usually one page long, that prints between each print job. Using such a file is good for networking printing so that jobs have a cover sheet with the user's name on it.

- Arrange security for the printer by setting permissions (if you have Administrator privileges).

Note

Printer security issues such as setting permissions, conducting printer access auditing, and setting ownership are covered in Chapter 22.

ADDING THE PRINTER

In earlier versions of Windows, adding a printer was called *creating* a printer. This language was somewhat bizarre in my estimation. This process is now called *adding* a printer—a somewhat more sensible phrase. What it really means is hooking up the printer, installing a printer driver, setting some preferences, and, if the printer is networked, sharing the printer for common use and giving the printer a network name.

You might want to add a printer in a few different instances, not all of which are obvious:

- You're connecting a new physical printer directly to your computer (obvious).

- You're connecting a new physical printer to the network (obvious).

- You want to print to formatted disk files that can later be sent to a particular type of printer (not so obvious).

- You want to set up multiple printer configurations (preferences) for a single physical printer so that you can switch among them without having to change your printer setup before each print job (timesaving idea).

Tip #122

Each time you add a printer, Windows creates an icon for it in the Printers folder. Although each is called a printer, it is actually a virtual printer, alias, or named virtual device much the way a shortcut represents a document or application in the GUI. Each physical printer can have multiple aliases, each with different settings. For example, one could print in landscape orientation on legal-size paper, whereas another printer would default to portrait orientation with letter-size paper and a lower priority for network print jobs so that your local print jobs would always be processed first. If you simply select the desired "printer" at print time, those settings go into effect.

PART

II

CH

9

As I'm sure you know, but I'll mention just for the record, you can't make a Windows printer do anything useful without a *printer driver*. A driver is a file whose job is to translate the data you want to print so that your printer knows how to print it. Windows 2000 Professional comes stocked with drivers for more than 3,500 brands and models of printers, and because many printers are functionally equivalent, a driver for a popular brand and model of printer (for example, an Epson or a Hewlett-Packard) can perform perfectly well for other types. If Windows didn't come with a printer driver for your printer, don't despair. Just contact the printer manufacturer, or comb its Web site for a Windows 2000 driver. Because Windows 2000 drivers might not be available for all devices, in a pinch, you can try a Windows NT driver (Windows 9x VxD-based drivers do not work).

→ To learn more about installing a manufacturer-supplied printer driver, **see** "What to Do If Your Printer Isn't Listed," **p. 332**.

A basic printer driver can at least get your text and graphics printed in some pedestrian manner, even from a sophisticated printer. A full-featured printer driver goes further, taking advantage of all your printer's capabilities, such as its built-in fonts, high-resolution graphics features, fancy paper handling, and utilities for cleaning the nozzles or printing test pages, and so on.

INSTALLING A NETWORK PRINTER

You must be logged on to a machine either as a Power User or Administrator to add a new printer. If you're logged on to your machine without these user rights, you must rectify the situation first. After you jump that hurdle, you can start the Add Printer Wizard.

Read this section to learn how to add a network-based printer to your setup. If you want to add a local printer, skip down to the next section, "Installing a Local Printer."

When you install a network printer, if the printer driver isn't on your computer, don't worry; Windows copies the driver from the remote computer sharing the printer. You can get started like this:

1. Open the Printers folder, either by choosing Start, Settings, or by going through the Control Panel. The Printers folder opens, listing installed printers (if any exist) and the Add Printer icon. Double-click the Add Printer icon to launch the Add Printer Wizard if it doesn't start automatically.

2. Click Next. You then are asked whether the printer is local or network. Because I'm describing how to install a network printer in this section, choose Network, and then click Next.

3. Tell the wizard where the printer is, as shown in Figure 9.1.

Figure 9.1
When you choose a network printer, you can browse for the printer or enter the printer's path manually. For a Web-shared printer, you must enter the URL.

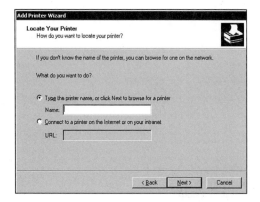

Unless you're a glutton for punishment or the LAN is not currently up, don't bother typing a complicated printer pathname. Just leave the Name field blank and click Next. Up comes a browse list of the printers on the network. For example, Figure 9.2 shows the network printer Epson Color 600 on Achilles.

4. You might have to double-click Entire Network or click the + (plus) sign next to a computer icon to display the printer attached to it. Either way, just highlight the printer you want to connect to, and click Next. You can also connect to a printer by dragging the printer icon from the print server's Printers folder and dropping it into your Printers folder, or by simply right-clicking the icon and then clicking Connect.

If you really must specify the name of the printer, use the form *printserver_name**share_name* (standard UNC path).

If the printer is shared over the Web, you can enter its URL, as in this example: `http://www.company.com/corp-printer`

If you're on a network running Active Directory, you can search for it by clicking Find a Printer in the Directory. If you're not working on an Active Directory network, this option is grayed out.

Figure 9.2
You can choose a network printer to install from the list. Double-click a + (plus) sign next to a network server or workstation to display its shared printers.

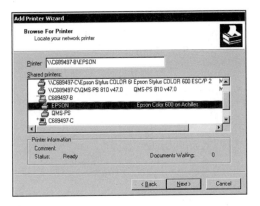

Tip #123

For a remote printer to be available for connection, it must have been added to the host computer's setup (the computer the printer is directly attached to) using the steps in "Installing a Local Printer," later in the chapter. It must also be shared for use on the network.

→ To learn more details about networking printers, and about using and sharing printers over the Internet, **see** "Sharing Printers," **p. 783**.

5. Answer any additional questions in the wizard dialog boxes. For example, you'll be asked whether you want the printer to be your default printer. The default is the printer that will be chosen by applications unless you specify otherwise. If your workstation can't determine what brand or model of printer you're connecting to, the wizard might ask you to choose this information from a list. You might also be asked to supply the printer driver if it's not found on the printer server's machine or on yours. You should be asked only if you are connecting to a printer running on a non-Windows 2000 machine.

The printer should now be connected and listed in your Printers folder, as shown in Figure 9.3. You can now use it just as though it were attached to your own computer. There might be some limitations to the amount of control you have over the printing, depending on the network security assigned to you and to the printer.

INSTALLING A LOCAL PRINTER

Installing a local printer is a bit more complex than connecting to an existing network printer. For starters, unless Windows finds the printer automatically (via Plug and Play), you must specify the location where the printer is physically connected, specify what you want to name it, and specify a few other pieces of information.

Figure 9.3
Added network print-
ers appear in the
Printers folder. Notice
that network printers
have special icons. A
check mark appears
above the default
printer.

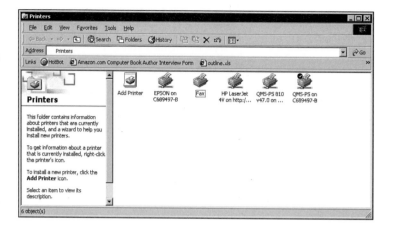

The procedures vary, depending on how the printer is connected to your computer:

- Parallel printer port
- USB/Firewire (IEEE 1394)
- Infrared

Tip #124

You must be logged on as a member of the administrator's group to add a local printer to a computer.

Here's the basic game plan, which works with most printers:

1. Connect the printer to the appropriate port on your computer according to the printer manufacturer's instructions.

2. Windows 2000 automatically installs most printers. However, for older printers, you might be required to provide additional information, such as make and model, to complete the installation.

3. Read the description that applies to the kind of connection your printer uses and proceed as directed:

   Parallel Port   Connect the printer to your computer (typically you don't have to shut down the computer to attach parallel devices, though doing so might be a good idea). Then open the Printers folder, and double-click Add Printer to start the wizard. Now click Next. Click Local Printer and turn on Automatically Detect My Printer. Then click Next again to start the Found New Hardware Wizard. Follow the instructions on the screen to finish installing the printer. The printer icon is then added to your Printers folder.

USB or Firewire

Just install a USB-based or IEEE-based printer. Windows 2000 will detect it and automatically start the Found New Hardware Wizard. Because USB and Firewire are hot-pluggable, you don't need to shut down or restart your computer. Simply follow the instructions on the screen to finish installing the printer. The printer icon is then added to your Printers folder.

Infrared

Make sure your printer is turned on and within range of your computer's infrared eye. Also, make sure your infrared service is installed properly. You can check its setup via the System applet in the Control Panel if you have doubts.

Windows might detect the printer automatically and create an icon for it. If not, open the Printers folder, and double-click Add Printer to start the Add Printer Wizard. Click Next. Choose Local Printer, and check Automatically Detect My Printer. Then click Next again to start the Found New Hardware Wizard. Follow the instructions on the screen to finish installing the printer. The printer icon is then added to your Printers folder.

IF THE PRINTER ISN'T FOUND OR IS ON A SERIAL (COM) PORT

If your printer isn't found using the options in the preceding section, or if the printer is connected via a COM port, you must fake out Plug and Play and go the manual route. To do so, just follow these steps:

1. Open the Printers folder, and run the Add Printer Wizard again.
2. Click Next.
3. Click Local Printer, make sure that Automatically Detect My Printer is not checked, and then click Next.
4. Select the port the printer is connected to in the resulting dialog. Figure 9.4 shows the port dialog box; the options and what they mean are as follows:

Options	Notes
LPT1:, LPT2:, LPT3:	The most common setting is LPT1 because most PC-type printers hook up to the LPT1 parallel port.
COM1:, COM2:, COM3:, COM4:	If you know your printer is of the serial variety, it's probably connected to the COM1 port. If COM1 is tied up for use with some other device, such as a modem, use COM2. If you choose a COM port, click Settings to check the communications settings in the resulting dialog box. Set the baud rate, data bits, parity, start and stop bits, and flow control to match those of the printer being attached. Refer to the printer's manual to determine what the settings should be.

continues

continued

Options	Notes
File	This is for printing to a disk file instead of to the printer. Later, the file can be sent directly to the printer or sent to someone on floppy disk or over a modem. When you print to this printer name, you are prompted to enter a filename. (See the section "Printing to Disk Option.")
Network Printer	See Chapter 22 for a discussion of this setting.
Create a New Port	Create a New Port is used to make connections to printers that are directly connected to your LAN and are to be controlled by your computer. Its use is covered elsewhere in this book as part of the procedure to install network-connected printers.

Figure 9.4
Choosing the port for a printer. Ninety-nine percent of the time it is LPT1.

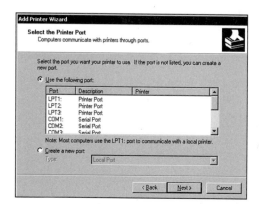

5. Select the manufacturer and model of your printer in the next dialog, as shown in Figure 9.5. You can quickly jump to a manufacturer's name by pressing the first letter of the name, such as E for Epson. Then use the up- and down-arrow keys to hone in on the correct one.

   If the wizard finds an existing driver on your machine that will work with the printer, you can elect to keep it or replace it. It's up to you. If you think the replacement will be newer, go for it. By contrast, if no driver is listed on the machine, you might be prompted to install it or insert a disk, such as the Windows 2000 Professional setup disk.

6. Name the printer. The name then appears in LAN-based users' browse boxes if you decide to share this printer. As the dialog box states, some other servers might have trouble with filenames longer than 31 characters if you share the printer.

7. Set whether you want this printer to be your default printer.

Figure 9.5
Choose the make and model of your printer here. If you can't find the exact model, try a variation on the model number or a printer that your printer is supposedly compatible with (check the printer's manual).

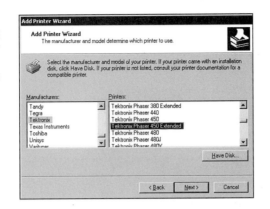

8. Click Next. Choose whether you want to share the printer on the LAN. If not, skip to step 10. If so, click Share As and name the share. If you're connected to any DOS and 16-bit Windows users, you might want to limit this name to 12 characters because that's the maximum length those users can see. This share name is different from the printer's name, which you entered in step 6.

9. Click Next. Now you can fill in additional information about the printer that people can see when browsing for a printer over the LAN, such as where it is and anything else, like a cute joke or something goofy. Something like `Joe's Laser Printer in Room 23` would be useful. Although these fields are optional, by filling in the location, you at least let users know where to pick up their documents.

10. Click Next. You then are asked whether you want to print a test page. Doing so is a good idea. Choose Yes or No, and click Next. You then see a display of all the printer details, as shown in Figure 9.6.

Figure 9.6
You can check the details of your printer before finalizing it. Click Back if you need to alter anything.

11. Assuming that everything looks cool, remember whether you chose to print a test page. If so, make sure your printer is turned on and ready to print. Then click Finish. Some files are copied between directories. You might be asked to insert disks again. The test

page is then sent to the printer; it should print out in a few minutes. Then you are asked whether it printed okay. If it didn't print correctly, click Troubleshoot, and the Help system pops up with the Print Troubleshooter running. The troubleshooter can walk you through a logic tree of troubleshooting. If the page printed okay, click Yes, and you're finished.

When you're finished, the icon for the printer appears in your Printers folder.

Tip #125	If you're going to share the printer with LAN users running Windows 95 and 98, Windows NT, or Windows 3.x on Intel, MIPS, Alpha, or PowerPC platforms, they need different printer drivers than Windows 2000 machines do. You must install the drivers appropriate to their operating systems so they don't have to hunt around for driver files or they're not prompted to insert disks into their machines when they try to connect to your printer. You can do so by opening the Properties sheet for the printer, clicking the Sharing tab, and then clicking Additional Drivers.

→ For more details about sharing printers for use by workstations running other operating systems, **see** "Installing Extra Printer Drivers," **p. 784**.

WHAT TO DO IF YOUR PRINTER ISN'T LISTED

If your printer isn't detected with Plug and Play and isn't listed in the selection list, don't worry; there's still hope. Many off-brand printers or models are designed to be compatible with one of the popular printer types, such as the Apple LaserWriters, Hewlett-Packard LaserJets, or one of the Epson series. Also, many printer models are very similar and can use the same driver.

Make your first stop Microsoft's online Hardware Compatibility List to see whether the printer in question has been tested with Windows 2000 Professional. If it has, check the Microsoft drivers site, call the manufacturer, or check the manufacturer's Web site for the latest driver and download it. If the printer isn't on the HCL, determine whether the printer has a compatibility mode in which it can emulate a particular brand and model of printer that is. For example, some offbeat printers have an HP LaserJet compatibility mode.

You can find the Microsoft site for drivers at

http://www.microsoft.com/NTServer/nts/exec/vendors/freeshare/Other.asp#drivers

Next, you can search for drivers on the Web. You can find a list at this Windows 2000 support site:

www.helpwin2k.com

Assuming that you have obtained a printer driver, follow these instructions to install it:

1. Open the Printers folder, and run the Add Printer Wizard.
2. Click Next, choose Local Printer, and then turn off the check box for autodetect.
3. Choose the correct port, and click Next.
4. Click Have Disk.

Tip #126	If you're online, you can click the Windows Update button to query the Microsoft site for additions to the list of printers that are supported. If your printer isn't already on the standard list, connect to the Internet and try this approach. Your printer driver might be newly available over the Net from Microsoft.

5. Instead of selecting one of the printers in the Driver list (it isn't in the list, of course), click the Have Disk button. You're now prompted to insert a disk in drive A:. Insert the disk, or click Browse to get to a disk or network volume that contains the driver. The wizard is looking for a file with an .INF extension, which is the standard file extension for manufacturer-supplied driver files.

6. Click OK. You might have to choose a driver from a list if multiple options exist.

7. Continue through the wizard dialog boxes as explained previously.

PART

II

CH

9

Tip #127	If none of the drivers you can lay your hands on work with your printer, try choosing the Generic/Text Only driver. This driver prints only text—no fancy formatting and no graphics. However, it does work in a pinch with many printers. Make sure the printer is capable of or is set to an ASCII or ANSI text-only mode; otherwise, your printout might be a mess. PostScript printers typically don't have a text-only mode. The text-only driver (sometimes called a *null printer driver*) that came with Windows NT actually cheated a bit because it added carriage returns and escape codes to control the placement of text. The Generic/Text Only printer driver included in Windows 2000 is cleaner and doesn't impose carriage returns, spaces, or escape codes to your print job.

CHANGING A PRINTER'S PROPERTIES

Each printer driver has a Properties sheet of associated settings (typically enough to choke a horse). The basic settings are covered in this chapter, whereas those relating to network printer sharing you'll find in Chapter 22.

As I explained earlier in this chapter, a driver consists of several files that dictate, among other things, the options available on its Properties sheet. Because of the variations possible, the following sections describe the gist of these options without necessarily going into detail about each printer type.

The settings pertaining to a printer are called properties. When you add a printer, the wizard dumps the icon for it in the Printers folder, and it's ready to roll. At that point, you can alter its properties or accept the default properties. If you are logged on with Administrator privileges, or if the administrator has given you the correct privilege, you can then alter the properties as follows:

1. Open the Printers folder.

2. Right-click the printer whose properties you want to examine or alter. The printer's Properties dialog box then appears, as shown in Figure 9.7.

Figure 9.7
A typical printer's
Properties dialog box.
The settings available
vary between printers.
Some have fewer
tabs.

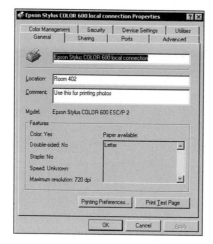

3. Change any of the text boxes as you see fit. (Their significance was explained earlier in this chapter.)

Tip #128	You can also press Alt+Enter to open a highlighted printer's Properties dialog box. This shortcut works with many Windows 2000 Professional objects.

Tip #129	If all you want to see is a printer's location, queue status, number of pending jobs, comments, or waiting time, you can highlight that information in the Printers folder. That information shows up on the left side of the window. You should bother with the Properties sheet only to actually alter aspects of the printer, such as the driver and default print settings.

Any printer's Properties sheet can have as many as eight tabs: General, Sharing, Ports, Advanced, Color Management, Security, Device Settings, and Utilities. Table 9.1 shows the general breakdown. Keep in mind that the tabs can vary depending on the capabilities of your printer.

TABLE 9.1   PROPERTIES SHEET TABS

Tab	What It Controls
General	This tab lists the name, location, model number, and features of the printer. From this tab, you can print a test page. You also can set default printing preferences, including the paper size, page orientation, paper source, pages per sheet (for brochure printing), affecting all print jobs. (You should rely on your application's Print Setup commands to control an individual print job's choice of paper orientation, paper source, and so on, which will override these settings.) Some color printers might have settings for paper quality, color control, and other utilities on this tab.

Tab	What It Controls
Sharing (see Chapter 22 for more)	On this tab, you can alter whether the printer is shared and what the share name is. You also can set drivers for other operating systems by using the Additional Drivers button.
Ports	On this tab, you can add and delete ports; set time-out for LPT ports; and set baud rate, data bits, parity, stop bits, and flow control for serial ports.
Advanced	This tab controls time availability, printer priority, driver file changes, spooling options, and advanced printing features such as booklet printing and page ordering. The first two settings are pertinent to larger networks and should be handled by a server administrator. The Advanced settings vary from printer to printer, depending on its capabilities. Booklet printing is worth looking into if you do lots of desktop publishing. Using this option, you can print pages laid out for stapling together small pamphlets.
Color Management	On this tab, you can set optional color profiles on color printers, if this capability is supported. (See "Color Management" later in this chapter.)
Security (See Chapter 32 for more)	Here, you can set who has access to print, manage printers, or manage documents from this printer.
Device Settings	The settings on this tab vary greatly between printers. For example, you can set paper size in each tray, set the amount of RAM in the printer, and substitute fonts.
Utilities	This tab contains options for nozzle cleaning, head cleaning, head alignment, and so on, depending on printer driver and printer type.

PART

II

CH

9

Tip #130

To assign a printer to an infrared port, open the Printers folder, right-click the printer, and choose Properties. Then click the Ports tab. Make sure the port selected under Print to the Following Port(s) is the infrared (IR) port. Setup and use of the infrared port are covered in Chapter 23, "Windows Unplugged: Remote and Mobile Networking."

Considering the rich collection of options here, I could fill a book describing them and their combinations. The use of many of them will be self-evident. The following sections group some of the basic options, with some notes about each.

→ For more details about printer sharing, printer pooling, port creation and deletion, and other server-related printing issues, **see** Chapter 22. (Check Table 9.1 for specifics.)

COMMENTS ABOUT VARIOUS SETTINGS

Table 9.2 describes the most common settings from the Properties dialog box for both PostScript and HP-compatible printers.

TABLE 9.2   THE OPTIONS IN THE BASIC SETUP DIALOG BOX

Option	Description
2 Sides	This option enables or disables double-sided printing for printers that support this feature.
Available From/To	This option specifies times when the printer is available for use. At other times the printer can still be printed to, but physical printing is attempted only during available hours. As a way of managing printing priorities when the number of physical printers is limited, you can create multiple printer setups based on the same physical printer. For example, you can set one of the printers to off-hour availability (during the night or over lunch hour). Then you can instruct users to send their low-priority print jobs to that printer.
Configure Port, LPT Port Timeout	This option specifies the amount of time that will elapse before you are notified that the printer or plotter is not responding. The setting affects the printer you've selected and any other local printers that use the same printer driver. If you print to a pen plotter, you might need to increase the port timeout setting to allow more time for the plotter to clear its buffer. The default setting is 90 seconds, which is long enough for most purposes. If printing from your application regularly results in an error message about transmission problems, and retrying seems to work, you should increase the setting. The maximum is 999,999 seconds.
Configure Port, Serial Port Settings	Settings here pertain to the serial port's communications settings, such as baud rate and parity. The serial port's baud rate, data bits, parity, stop bits, and flow control must match that of the printer's, or you're in for some garbage printouts. If you have trouble, check the printer's DIP switch or software settings and the printer manual to ensure that the settings agree.
Default Datatype	This setting usually doesn't need changing. The default is RAW. A very specialized application might ask you to create a printer with another datatype setting for use when printing its documents.
Enable Advanced Printing Features	When this option is checked, metafile spooling is turned on, and options such as Page Order, Booklet Printing, and Pages Per Sheet might be available, depending on your printer. For normal printing, you should leave the advanced printing feature set to the default (Enabled). If compatibility problems occur, you can disable the feature. When the option is disabled, metafile spooling is turned off, and the printing options might be unavailable.
Enable Bidirectional Support	This option lets the computer query the printer for settings and status information.
Enable Printer Pooling	You can use this option to set up a printer pool. This means that several printers are connected to the same server but to several different ports on that server. Everyone on the network can send print jobs to the same virtual printer, but the server doles out the jobs to the first available printer. Documents sent to the server are automatically routed to the first available printer. All printers must work with the same printer driver (typically but not necessarily the same make and model of printer). Choose the ports the printers are on, and check Enable Printer Pooling. (See Chapter 22 for more details on pooling.)
Font Cartridges	For this option, you choose the names of the cartridges that are physically installed in the printer. You can select only two.

Option	Description
Font Substitution	TrueType Font Substitution Table: Used for PostScript printers to declare when internal fonts should be used in place of downloading TrueType fonts to speed up printing. See Chapter 10, "Font Management," for more details on font substitution.
Form-to-Tray Assignment	For this option, you click a source, such as a lower tray, and then choose a form name to match with the source. When you choose a form name (such as A4 Small) at print time, the printer driver tells the printer which tray to switch to. You don't have to think about it. You can repeat the process for each form name you want to set up.
Hold Mismatched Documents	This option directs the spooler to check the printer setup and match it to the document setup before sending the document to the print device. If the information does not match, the document is held in the queue. A mismatched document in the queue does not prevent correctly matched documents from printing.
Keep Printed Documents	This option specifies that the spooler should not delete documents after they are printed. This way, a document can be resubmitted to the printer from the printer queue instead of from the program, which is faster.
New Driver	You use this button to install an updated driver for the printer. It runs the Add Printer Driver Wizard.
Orientation	This option sets the page orientation. Normal orientation is Portrait, which, like a portrait of the Mona Lisa, is taller than it is wide. Landscape, like a landscape painting, is the opposite. Rotated Landscape means a 90-degree counterclockwise rotation of the printout.
Page Order	This option determines the order in which documents are printed. Front to Back prints the document so that page 1 is on top of the stack. Back to Front prints the document so that page 1 is on the bottom of the stack.
Page Protect	If turned on, this option prevents the printer from printing until an entire page is imaged inside the printer. It's available only on printers with enough memory to store an entire graphics page in internal RAM.
Print Directly to the Printer	This option prevents documents sent to the printer from being spooled. Thus, printing doesn't happen in the background; instead, the computer is tied up until the print job is completed. There's virtually no practical reason for tying up your computer this way, unless your printer and Windows are having difficulty communicating or you find that printing performance (page per minute throughput) increases significantly when this option is enabled. When a printer is shared over the network, this option isn't available.
Print Processor	You usually don't need to change this setting. The default is WinPrint. A very specialized application, however, might ask you to create a printer with another print processor for use when printing its documents.
Print Spooled Documents First	This option specifies that the spooler should favor documents that have completed spooling when deciding which document to print next, even if the completed documents are a lower priority than documents that are still spooling. If no documents have completed spooling, the spooler favors larger spooling documents over smaller ones. You should use this option if you want to maximize printer efficiency. When this option is disabled, the spooler picks documents based only on priority.

continues

TABLE 9.2   CONTINUED

Option	Description
Printer Memory	This option specifies how much memory the printer has installed.
Printing Defaults	You click this option to view or change the default document properties for all users of the selected printer. If you share your local printer, these settings are the default document properties for other users.
Priority	Printers can have a priority setting from 1 to 99. The default setting is 1. Print jobs sent to a printer that has a priority level of 2 always print before a job sent to a printer with a level 1 setting if both setups use the same physical printer.
Resolution	Some printers can render graphics in more than one resolution. The higher the resolution, the longer printing takes, so you can save time by choosing a lower resolution. For finished, high-quality work, you should choose the highest resolution. (On some printers, this choice is limited by the amount of memory in the printer.)
Separator File	A preassigned file can be printed between jobs, usually just to place an identification page listing the user, job ID, date, time, number of pages, and so forth. Files also can be used to switch a printer between PostScript and PCL (HP) mode for printers that can run in both modes. You just type the name DEFAULT.SEP for a basic page before each PCL print job. You also can choose other separator files by clicking the Browse button and switching to the SYSTEM32 directory. PSLANMAN.SEP prints a basic ID page on a PostScript printer, PCL.SEP switches the printer to PCL mode, and PSCRIPT.SEP switches to PostScript mode.
Use Printer Halftoning	Halftoning is a process that converts shades of gray or colors to a pattern of black and white dots. A newspaper photo is an example of halftoning. When the arrangement of dots (pixels) on the page is varied, a photographic image can be simulated with only black and white dots. Because virtually no black-and-white printers and typesetters can print shades of gray, halftoning is the closest you get to realistic photographic effects. Normally, Windows 2000 Professional processes the halftoning of graphics printouts. Only printers that can do halftoning offer halftone options.

Note

If you can't figure out what an option does, you can always click the Help button in the upper-right corner of the Properties dialog box and then click an option. A description of the option should appear.

Tip #131

You can access the Printing Defaults tab through two paths: one by choosing Printing Defaults from the Advanced tab and the other by choosing Printing Preferences from the General tab. What's the difference? On the Advanced tab, you choose Printing Defaults when you're setting the default settings for the printer, period. Subsequent users inherit these settings as the "recommended" set of settings, as it were. Then, from the General tab, you can make your own preferred settings by choosing Printing Preferences. These settings are user-specific.

Tip #132

Another set of properties is available for shared printers. To locate them, right-click an empty spot within the Printers folder, and choose Server Properties. The Server properties list ports and show the collective list of all installed drivers in use. Here, you can define forms and set events and notifications. The last tab is covered in Chapter 22 because it's a network topic.

REMOVING A PRINTER FROM THE PRINTERS FOLDER

You might want to remove a printer setup for several reasons:

- The physical printer has been removed from service.
- You don't want to use a particular network printer anymore.
- You had several definitions of a physical printer using different default settings, and you want to remove one of them.
- You have a nonfunctioning or improperly functioning printer setup and want to remove it and start over by running the Add Printer Wizard.

In any of these cases, the approach is the same:

1. Make sure you are logged on with Administrator privileges.
2. Open the Printers folder.
3. Make sure nothing is in the print queue. You must clear the queue for the printer before deleting it. If you don't, Windows 2000 will try to delete all jobs in the queue for you, but it unfortunately isn't always successful.
4. Select the printer icon you want to kill, and choose File, Delete (or press the Del key).
5. Depending on whether the printer is local or remote, you see two different dialog boxes. One asks whether you want to delete the printer; the other asks whether you want to delete the connection to the printer. In either case, click Yes. The printer icon or window disappears from the Printers folder.

Tip #133

The removal process removes only the virtual printer setup from the Registry for the currently logged-in user. The related driver file and font files are not deleted from the disk, however. Therefore, if you want to re-create the printer, you don't have to insert disks or respond to prompts for the location of driver files. This is convenient, but be aware that if you're tight on disk space, any printer fonts and related screen fonts could possibly take up considerable room. If you're tight on space, use the Fonts applet from the Control Panel to remove them, as described in Chapter 10.

PRINTING FROM WINDOWS APPLICATIONS

When you print from 16-bit or 32-bit Windows applications, the internal Print Manager kicks in and spools the print job for you, adding it to the queue for the selected printer. The spooler then spools the file to the assigned printers, coordinating the flow of data and keeping you informed of the progress. Jobs are queued up and listed in the given printer's window, from which their status can be observed; they can be rearranged, deleted, and so forth. All the rights and privileges assigned to you, as the user, are applicable, potentially allowing you to alter the queue (as discussed later), rearranging, deleting, pausing, or restarting print jobs.

If the application doesn't provide for a specific printer (typically through a Print Setup dialog box), the default printer is used. You set the default printer from the Printers folder by right-clicking a printer and choosing Set as Default Printer.

When an application prints to the default printer, all settings previously made to the printer's Properties sheet go into effect, controlling the print job. The exact appearance of your printed documents might vary from program to program, depending on the degree to which your Windows application can take advantage of the printer-driver setup. Some programs, such as Write, enable you to change fonts, for example, whereas other rudimentary ones don't.

Printing from DOS Applications

Printing from DOS is an especially thorny proposition these days. Many DOS applications are out there still, and newer operating systems have to be clever to print acceptably despite all the new operating system and printer features.

In fact, if you choose a default printer that your DOS application can't support, your printouts might be garbled. For example, if you're running WordPerfect 5.1 for DOS and have it installed for an Apple LaserWriter, but the default Windows printer is set to an Epson inkjet, your printouts will be nothing but a listing of PostScript commands. Make sure your non-Windows applications and your default printer are in accord before you try to print.

In other words, a DOS application will print to LPT1 if specified, not the default printer as specified in Windows. To print to a network printer, you would have to capture a port and have the DOS application print to that port.

Like the NetWare `capture` command, the `net use` command enables MS-DOS and Windows applications to print to a specific port. For example, you type `net use lpt1: \\server\share`.

PRE-PRINTING CHECKLIST

To print from Windows applications, follow these steps:

1. Check to see that the printer and page settings are correct and the right printer is chosen for your output. Some applications provide a Printer Setup or other option on their File menu for this task. Recall that settings you make from such a box override the Job Default settings made from the printer's Properties sheet. If the application has a Print, Preview command, use it to check that the formatting of the document is acceptable.

2. Select File, Print from the application's window, and fill in whatever information is asked of you. Figure 9.8 shows the Print dialog for WordPad for Windows 2000. (Print dialogs for older applications differ.) Notice that you can just click a printer's icon to choose it. When you do, its printer driver kicks in, changing the options on the tabs. You can also find a printer on the LAN or print to a file, using their respective buttons. Two other tabs, Layout and Paper/Quality, could be useful. For advanced options such as halftoning and color matching, select the Layout tab and click Advanced.

PART

II

CH

9

Figure 9.8
Preparing to print a typical file.

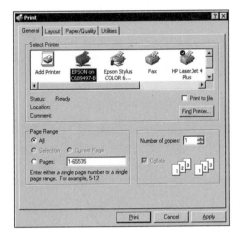

3. Click OK (or otherwise confirm printing). The data is sent to the spooler, which writes it in a file and then begins printing it. If an error occurs—a port conflict, the printer is out of paper, or whatever—you see a message such as the one shown in Figure 9.9.

Figure 9.9
A typical error message resulting from a printer problem.

You can attempt to fix the problem by checking the cable connection, the paper supply, and so forth. Then click Retry. If you run into more serious trouble, you can run the Troubleshooting Wizard from Help.

For most users, following these steps is all you'll ever need to do to print. The remainder of this chapter deals mostly with how to work with the printer queues of your own workstation printer or of network printers, and how to alter, pause, delete, or restart print jobs.

 If you receive printer errors when attempting to print a document, see "Printer Errors" in the "Troubleshooting" section at the end of this chapter.

 If nothing happens when you send a print job to the printer, see "Nothing Happens" in the "Troubleshooting" section at the end of this chapter.

PRINTING BY DRAGGING FILES INTO THE PRINT MANAGER

As a shortcut to printing a document, you can simply drag the icon of the document you want to print either onto an icon of a printer or into the printer's open window (from the Printers folder). You can drag the file from Explorer right onto the chosen printer's icon or open window to see it added to the print queue for that printer.

When you drop the document, Windows realizes you want to print it, and the file is loaded into the source application, the Print command is automatically executed, and the file is spooled to the Print Manager. Figure 9.10 shows an example of dropping a Word document on a PostScript printer.

Tip #134	Documents must have associations; otherwise, printing by dragging them to Print Manager doesn't work. Also, you obviously don't have the option of setting printing options when you print this way. All the defaults are used.

Figure 9.10
You can print a document or several documents by dragging them onto a destination printer in the Printers folder. The files must have application associations.

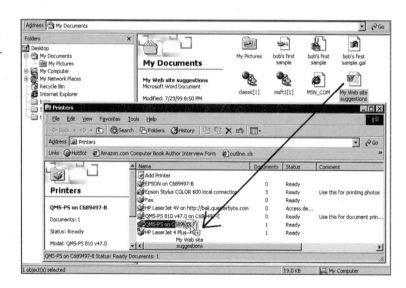

 If you're having trouble printing, you're getting "garbage" printouts, or you're getting only partial pages, see "Printer Produces Garbled Text" in the "Troubleshooting" section at the end of this chapter.

 If only half of the page prints correctly before the printer starts printing garbage text, see "Only Half of the Page Prints Correctly" in the "Troubleshooting" section at the end of this chapter.

WORKING WITH THE PRINTER QUEUE

After you or other users on the network have sent print jobs to a given printer, anyone with rights to manage the queue can work with it. If nothing else, it's often useful to observe the queue to check its progress. This way, you can better choose which printer to print to or decide whether some intervention is necessary, such as adding more paper. By simply opening the Printers folder, you can see the basic state of each printer's queue, assuming you display the window contents in Details view (see Figure 9.10 as an example).

For each printer, the window displays the status of the printer (in the title bar) and the documents that are queued up, including their sizes, status, owner, pages, date submitted, and so on.

Figure 9.11 shows a sample printer's folder with a print queue and related information.

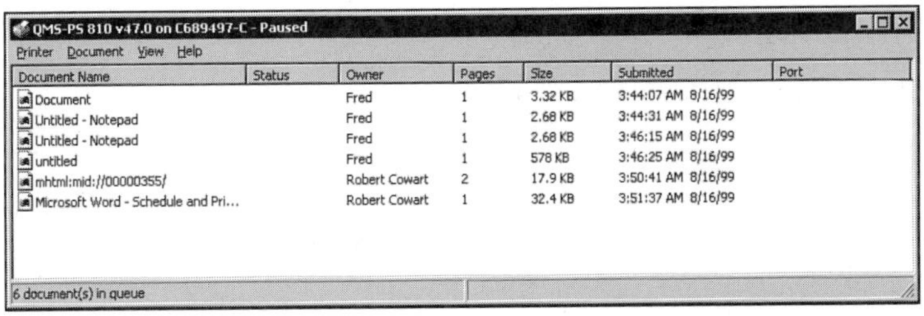

Figure 9.11
A printer's folder showing several print jobs pending.

Document Name	Status	Owner	Pages	Size	Submitted	Port
Document		Fred	1	3.32 KB	3:44:07 AM 8/16/99	
Untitled - Notepad		Fred	1	2.68 KB	3:44:31 AM 8/16/99	
Untitled - Notepad		Fred	1	2.68 KB	3:46:15 AM 8/16/99	
untitled		Fred	1	578 KB	3:46:25 AM 8/16/99	
mhtml:mid://00000355/		Robert Cowart	2	17.9 KB	3:50:41 AM 8/16/99	
Microsoft Word - Schedule and Pri...		Robert Cowart	1	32.4 KB	3:51:37 AM 8/16/99	

QMS-PS 810 v47.0 on C689497-C - Paused

Printer   Document   View   Help

6 document(s) in queue

Tip #135

When print jobs are pending for a workstation, an icon appears in the system tray, near the clock. You can hover the mouse pointer over it to see the number of documents waiting to print. Right-click it to choose a printer's queue to examine in a window.

To keep network traffic down to a dull roar, Windows doesn't poll the network constantly to check the state of the queue. If you are printing to a network printer and want to check the current state of affairs on the network printer, choose View, Refresh or press F5 to immediately update the queue information.

DELETING A FILE FROM THE QUEUE

After sending a file to the queue, you might reconsider printing it, or you might want to re-edit the file and print it later. If so, you can simply remove the file from the queue. To do so, right-click the document and choose Cancel, or choose Document, Cancel from the menu. The document is then removed from the printer's window.

If you're trying to delete the job that's printing, you might have some trouble. At the very least, the system might take some time to respond. Sometimes canceling a laser printer's job while it's printing in graphics mode necessitates resetting the printer to clear its buffer. To reset, either turn the printer off and then on, or use the Reset option (if it's available).

Note

Because print jobs are spooled to the hard disk, they can survive powering down Windows 2000. Any documents in the queue when the system goes down, whether due to an intentional shutdown or a power outage, reappear in the queue when you power up.

PAUSING, RESUMING, AND RESTARTING THE PRINTING PROCESS

If you need to, you can pause the printing process for a particular printer or even just a single document print job. This capability can be useful in case you have second thoughts about a print job, want to give other jobs a chance to print first, or you just want to adjust or quiet the printer for some reason.

To pause a print job, right-click it and choose Pause. Pretty simple. The word Paused then appears on the document's line. The printing might not stop immediately because your printer might have a buffer that holds data in preparation for printing. The printing stops when the buffer is empty. When you're ready to resume printing, just right-click the job in question, and choose Resume.

Tip #136	Pausing a document lets other documents continue to print, essentially moving them ahead in line. You can achieve the same effect by rearranging the queue, as explained in the section titled "Rearranging the Queue Order."

In some situations, you might need to pause all the jobs on your printer, such as to add paper to it, to alter the printer settings, or just to shut up the printer for a bit while you take a phone call. To pause all jobs, open the Printer's window and choose Printer, Pause Printing. Obviously, you can just choose the command again to resume printing, and the check mark on the menu goes away.

Should you need to (due to a paper jam or other botch), you can restart a printing document from the beginning. Just right-click the document, and choose Restart.

REARRANGING THE QUEUE ORDER

When you have several items on the queue, you might want to rearrange the order in which they're slated for printing. Perhaps a print job's priority has increased because you need it for an urgent meeting, or you must get a letter to the post office. Whatever the reason, you can easily rearrange the print queue like this:

1. Click the file you want to move, and keep the mouse button pressed.
2. Drag the file up or down to its new location. A solid line moves to indicate where the document will be inserted when you release the mouse button.
3. When you release the mouse button, your file is inserted in the queue, pushing the other files down a notch.

VIEWING AND ALTERING DOCUMENT PROPERTIES

Like everything in Windows, each document in the printer queue has its own properties. For a more detailed view of information pertaining to each document, you can open the

Properties sheet for it by right-clicking it and choosing Properties. You can change only two settings from the resulting dialog box (see Figure 9.12):

- The print priority
- The time of day when the document can be printed

Figure 9.12
Altering the properties for a print job on the queue.

> **Note**
>
> As a shortcut, you can open a document's properties by just double-clicking it.

Setting	Description
Priority	All documents normally have the same priority, 1. You can increase this number to as high as 99 to push the print job through. The job with the highest priority is printed before all other jobs on that printer. Remember, however, that when you create a printer, it can have a priority setting, too. That setting overrides the document setting you make here. Therefore, even if you increase the priority of a print job to 99, it won't print before a job with a priority of 1 that's been sent to the same physical printer via a setup with a higher priority.
Only From	You can specify that a job be printed only between certain hours, such as night (when the network printing load is low) or during lunch hour. Make sure the hours are compatible with the hours the printer is set for, as described earlier in this chapter.

CANCELING ALL PENDING PRINT JOBS ON A GIVEN PRINTER

Assuming you have been given the privilege, you can cancel all the print jobs (purge the queue) on a printer. In the Printers folder, right-click the printer, and choose Cancel All Documents, as shown in Figure 9.13. A confirmation dialog then appears.

Figure 9.13
Canceling all print jobs on a given printer.

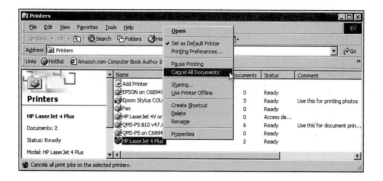

PRINTING TO DISK OPTION

Sometimes, printing to a disk file rather than to a printer can be useful. What does printing to a disk file mean? It means that the same data that normally would be sent to the printer is shunted to a disk file, either locally or on the network. The file usually isn't just a copy of the file you were printing; it contains all the special formatting codes that control your printer. Codes that change fonts, print graphics, set margins, break pages, and add attributes such as underline, bold, and so on are all included in this type of file. Print files destined for PostScript printers typically include their PostScript preamble, too.

Printing to a file gives you several options not available when you print directly to the printer. Sometimes print files are used by applications for specific purposes. For example, you might want to print part of a database to a file that will later be pulled into a company report. Or you might want to print an encapsulated PostScript graphics file that will be imported into a desktop publishing document.

Another advantage is that you can print the file later. Maybe your printer isn't hooked up, or there's so much stuff on the queue that you don't want to wait, or you don't want to slow down your computer or the network by printing now. In any case, you can print to a file, which is significantly faster than printing on paper. Later, you can use the DOS COPY command or a batch file with a command such as COPY *.PRN LPT1 /B to copy all files to the desired port. This way, you can queue up as many files as you want, prepare the printer, and then print them without having to be around.

Tip #137	Be sure to use the /B switch. Because the print files are binary files, the first control-Z code the computer encounters will terminate the print job.

Another big advantage is that you can send the file to another person, either on floppy disk or as email. That person can then print the file directly to a printer (if it's compatible) with Windows or a utility such as the DOS COPY command. The recipient doesn't need the application program that created the file, and he or she doesn't have to worry about any of the printing details—formatting, setting up margins, and so forth. All the information is in the file.

In some applications, this choice is available in the Print dialog box. If it isn't, you should modify the printer's configuration to print to a file rather than to a port. Then, whenever you use that printer, it will use all the usual settings for the driver but send the data to a file of your choice instead of to the printer port. Just follow these steps:

1. In the Printers folder, right-click the printer's icon, and choose Properties.

2. Click Ports.

3. Set the port to File, and close the dialog box.

The next time you or another local or network user prints to that printer, you'll be prompted to enter a filename, as you can see in Figure 9.14. The file is stored on the machine where the print job originated. Predicting where it will end up is difficult unless you stipulate the path in the filename. It's up to the application you're printing from. If you don't stipulate the full pathname, do that first, and then use the Start, Search command to look for the file.

Figure 9.14

Tip #138

If you want to print the file as ASCII text only, with no special control codes, you should install the Generic/Text Only printer driver. Then select it as the destination printer.

Tip #139

If you want to print to an encapsulated PostScript file (.EPS), you can print to a printer that uses a PostScript driver (the Apple LaserWriter or the QMS PS-810, for example) or set up a phony printer that uses such a driver. No physical printer is needed. Then you can modify the properties of the printer via the Properties, Details, Job Defaults, Options dialog box to set an encapsulated PostScript filename.

COLOR MANAGEMENT

Color management is the process of producing accurate, consistent color among a variety of input and output devices. In Windows, the color management system (CMS) maps colors between devices such as scanners, monitors, and printers; transforms colors from one color space to another (for example, RGB to CMYK); and provides accurate onscreen or print previews.

Because each printer, monitor, and scanner has slightly different color characteristics (such as hue, tint, saturation, and brightness), how is this issue handled? Normally, it's not. Most people out there in the computing world simply plug in their equipment and go. When you print an image on your inkjet printer, you take what you get. Or you adjust the image in some application such as Photoshop, knowing that your printer requires bumping up the blue range or the red range. Some printers come with color adjustment software of their own, as do some monitors and/or video display cards. One of my cards from ATI (the All in

Wonder Pro) has very nice color adjustment software. All I must do is print an image, hold it up to the screen, and adjust the screen color to match. Now I know that what I see is what I'll get.

For a more elegant solution, you can use color management. Windows 2000 incorporates a color system called LinoColorCMM, which was developed by Heidelberger Druckmachinen AG. By adding a color profile for each piece of color-related hardware in your computer, you can ensure consistent color output and display.

Just like a printer needs a printer driver or a scanner needs a TWAIN driver, each piece of hardware needs its own color *profile*. A profile is a file made by the hardware manufacturer (or Microsoft) specifically for the device, and it contains information about the color characteristics of the hardware. You simply associate the profile with the device via the device's Properties sheet, and the color system does the rest. Only if a device supports color management does its Properties sheet have a Color tab on it, however.

Windows 2000 Professional comes with about 20 color profiles, which you can find in the *systemroot*\System32\Spool\Drivers\Color folder (where *systemroot* is the folder that contains your Windows 2000 files, typically WINNT). Even though some profiles are included with Windows 2000, you might need to obtain a profile for your particular hardware. Check with the manufacturer. You can use the following procedure to add a color profile to a printer:

1. Open the Printers folder.

2. Right-click the printer that you want to associate with a color profile, click Properties, and then click the Color Management tab. Notice that the tab has two settings: Automatic and Manual. Normally, Windows uses the Automatic setting, in which case it assigns a color profile to the printer from those it has on hand. If you want to override the default, click Manual (see Figure 9.15).

Figure 9.15
You can set or check the color profile for a printer from the Color Management tab of the printer's Properties sheet.

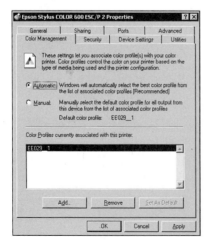

3. Click Add to open the Add Profile Association dialog box.

4. Locate the new color profile you want to associate with the printer. You can right-click a profile and choose Properties to read more about the profile. Because the filenames are cryptic, this is the only way to figure out what device a color profile is for.

5. Click the new profile, and then click Add. Keep in mind that you can associate any number of profiles with a given piece of gear. Obviously, only one can be active at a time, however. After you open the profile list, click the one you want to activate. For sophisticated setups, you might have reason for multiple profiles on, say, a printer, but it's not likely that many users who are not designers or artists will bother.

You can use the same approach to add profiles for other hardware pieces, such as displays and scanners. Just bring up the Color Management tab of each item through its Properties sheet.

PART
II

CH
9

> **Note**
>
> For a video display, open the Settings tab, click Advanced, and then click the Color Management tab.

FAXING

Faxing is a function that Microsoft has dropped in and out of Windows (almost literally) for years now. Windows 95 had faxing capability built into Microsoft Exchange. When Exchange became Windows Messaging, this capability disappeared. Outlook Express didn't fax, and even though Kodak Imaging (which was supplied with Windows 98) had some fax-related features, Windows 98 didn't have native faxing capabilities, so it was meaningless. Well, finally, Windows 2000 has faxing capability built in and ready to roll.

You install and use Windows 2000's faxing feature just like most of the third-party fax programs have taught in the past—as a printer, which is called a *fax printer*. After the fax printer is set up, to send a fax, you simply choose to print your document to the fax printer. Choosing this option runs a wizard that prompts you to enter some information about the recipient (such as phone number), and the rasterizer optimizes the output for a fax machine rather than a printer, dials the phone, and then sends the fax image to the remote fax machine. That's all there is to it. You can even use a cover page editor and a fax management tool to view and edit your faxes, set preferences, and review logs of fax events. The good news is that you don't need a degree in Sanskrit to figure out faxing anymore. (Windows Messaging and Microsoft Exchange in the Windows 9x products were too complex, not to mention buggy.) In Windows 2000, faxing is easy.

The Windows 2000 faxing feature supports scanned graphic images and automatically converts graphics to a .TIF file format before you fax them. Also, it supports classes 1, 2, and 2.0.

> **Note**
>
> Some mail programs can send email and fax messages simultaneously. For more details about that, look for the related sidebar later in this chapter.

Windows 2000 faxing can't be shared among several users on the LAN the same way you can share regular printers. This feature is different from Microsoft Exchange, which did allow network faxing. If you need to do shared faxing, you should look for another product. See the following note for some links. You can, however, send and receive faxes using more than one fax device (for example, fax modems, should you have more than one), but this scenario is rather unlikely. You're more likely to need to set up multiple copies of the same fax printer with different settings. You could, for example, have two fax printers with different settings for time to send, paper size, and paper orientation. You can also define customized printing preferences such as billing codes, which can be tracked in the fax event log.

You set up multiple fax printers in pretty much the same way you create regular printers: You just use the Add a Fax Printer button on the Control Panel's Fax applet and set up the properties for that fax printer. When it's time to send a fax, you then choose which one you want to send through, putting its properties into effect.

 If you can't seem to add a fax printer, see "Fax Printer Can't Be Added" in the "Troubleshooting" section at the end of this chapter.

> **Note**
>
> For a collection of links about faxing and NT, check out the following sites:
>
> `http://www.ntfaxfaq.com/`
>
> `http://www.faximum.com/faqs/fax`

All you need to get started faxing is a fax device, such as a fax modem; it cannot be just a plain data modem. Simply put, the problem is that the modulation methods (tones) used to communicate data are different from those used to communicate faxes. Typically, the modulation schemes used for fax are synchronous half-duplex, whereas those used for data (at least by most UNIX and PC people) are asynchronous and full-duplex.

Because most modems these days are fax modems, chances are good that your computer already has the Windows 2000 fax services installed and ready to roll. If not, you must install a fax device or fax modem.

In this day of Plug and Play, attaching a fax device will probably prompt Windows 2000 into installing the fax service and a fax printer. If, for some reason, Windows doesn't sense that you've attached a fax modem even when you reboot, you can use the Add/Remove Hardware Wizard. (See Chapter 29, "Customizing via Control Panel Applets," for coverage of the Add/Remove Hardware applet and the Modem applet, both in the Control Panel.)

> **Note**
>
> For more information on modem compatibility with faxes, see the Microsoft Windows Hardware Compatibility List at the Microsoft Web site (`http://www.microsoft.com/hcl`).

Several options are available in the Fax program group (you can reach it by choosing Start, Programs, Accessories, Communications, Fax) that you can use for management of faxes and of the fax service. Table 9.3 lists these commands and their purposes.

TABLE 9.3   FAX-RELATED COMMANDS

Command	Action
Fax Queue	Allows you to view, cancel, resume, or pause a sent fax.
Fax Service Management	Allows you to set up your fax device to receive faxes; to set security permissions; to set the number of rings before the fax is answered and the number of retries attempted before the fax send is discontinued.
My Faxes	Allows you to view, print, or delete sent and received faxes. This folder also stores all cover pages. You can create and edit the cover pages.
Send Cover Page Fax	Allows you to fax a cover page only. This option accesses the Send Fax Wizard.

GETTING SET UP

After you install your fax gear, you can get started by entering your fax-related settings like this:

1. Choose Control Panel, Fax. You then see the dialog shown in Figure 9.16.

Figure 9.16
You can enter your fax properties into this dialog.

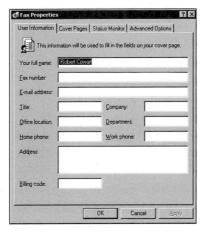

2. Enter the relevant information into the User Information tab. You can skip the stuff that is not relevant. This data will be printed on your cover pages.

3. Click the Cover Pages tab, and notice that probably nothing is listed there. You can skip this tab for the time being. Modifying an existing page is easier than making a new one. Alternatively, you can browse to the location of the several cover pages supplied with Windows 2000. The two types of cover pages are Common and Personal.

Personal pages are the ones you create and save. Common ones are for all users on the machine to use. Common cover pages are stored in

C:\Documents and Settings\All Users.WINNT\Documents\My Faxes\ Common Coverpages

Personal cover pages will be stored (after you make them) in

C:\Documents and Settings*User Name*\My Documents\Fax\Personal Coverpages

(Be sure to change the drive letter based on the partition that Windows 2000 is installed on, of course.)

When you're ready to send a fax, you have the option of adding a cover page to it.

4. Click the Status Monitor tab, and check the boxes that meet your needs. If you're using the same phone line for voice and fax, turn on the last check box, Enable Manual Answer. This option lets you screen a call to hear whether it's a voice or fax call, without the fax modem picking up automatically.

5. Click Advanced, and then click Add a Fax Printer. After some hard disk grinding, you are notified that a fax printer was "created successfully."

6. Click OK, and you should be ready to roll.

 If you can't get your fax printer installed, see "Fax Printer Can't Be Added" in the "Troubleshooting" section at the end of this chapter.

SENDING A FAX

The Fax service should now be running and your fax printer installed. You should now be ready to send a fax. To do so, just follow these steps:

1. Open the document you want to send.

2. Choose File, Print. From the standard Print dialog box, choose Fax as the printer. Set up the particulars as necessary (page range and so on), and click OK.

3. The Fax Wizard then begins and walks you through the process of preparing the fax. If this is the first time you've used the wizard, it asks whether you want to edit your personal information. If you already entered it following the instructions from the preceding section, you don't need to do that, though you can check it for correctness if you want.

4. Fill in the recipient and dialing information as prompted. You can add multiple names to the list. If you have fax numbers in your address book, you can use it as a source for your list. Note that unless you have Dialing Rules checked, you can't enter area codes in the (area code) text box. You can still enter the whole number manually, over in the right text box, however. Don't forget the 1 ahead of the area code if you use this technique. Click the Add button to add the first recipient, and repeat the process for each additional recipient. (This way, you can do a bulk faxing if you need to. This feature is one of the true advantages of faxing with a computer rather than a hardware fax machine.) See Figure 9.17 for an example of a fax headed for two recipients.

Figure 9.17
Adding recipients to
the fax transmission
list

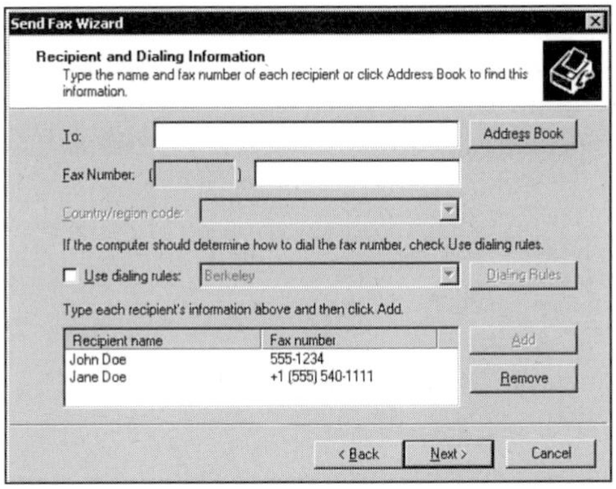

→ You can apply dialing rules to the transmission if you are on the road or in a location that has specific requirements for phoning, such as outside-line access numbers and the like. To learn more dialing rules, **see** "Dialing Rules," **p. 1056**.

5. Click Next, and choose a cover page if you want to. Use the Cover Page Template drop-down list. Then enter the subject and any notes you want to appear on the cover page.

6. Click Next. On the next wizard page, enter the timing for fax transmission. Typically, it is Now, but the When Discount Rates Apply option is interesting. (See the description of Fax Service Management in the following section to see how to set the timing.) Alternatively, you can specify a time in the next 24 hours. Enter an optional billing code. The billing code appears in the fax event log for outbound faxes. You can use it to assign costs of faxing documents to a specific account.

Tip #140	The billing code setting applies only to the selected printer. If you want to provide different billing codes for different purposes (such as faxes sent by different departments), you can create a different printer for each billing code.

7. Click Next. You then see a summary page reporting the full details of your soon-to-be-faxed document. If you approve, click Finish. If not, walk back through the wizard and make corrections.

8. When the Fax Monitor appears on your screen, as shown in Figure 9.18, you can check the status of the call from it. Close the monitor if you want.

FAX MANAGEMENT UTILITIES

You should not be surprised when I tell you that Windows 2000 Professional has a fax management application much like the Computer Management snap-ins. It's called Fax Service Management. The interface is similar, and you can set many options. You use this application to do the following:

- Set up your fax devices to receive a fax

- Change security permissions for users set up to use the fax devices

- Declare how many rings occur before a fax device answers a fax

- Determine how many retries are allowed before the fax device aborts the fax send

- Set up where to store the sent or received faxes

- Set priority in sending faxes

- Set the amount of detail for the event log

- Suppress personal cover pages, enforcing the company fax-cover page design

Figure 9.18
When you finish the fax, the Fax Monitor reports its progress.

You run Fax Management by choosing Start, Programs, Accessories, Communications, Fax, Fax Service Management. You then see the window shown in Figure 9.19.

Figure 9.19
You can manage faxes from this application.

Poke around in this application to familiarize yourself with it. As you can see, two primary branches appear in the left pane: Devices and Logging. Click Devices, and then right-click a specific device (a fax modem) to make settings and view or change properties. To enable the fax device to receive a fax, for example, you just right-click and set the Receive check box on (that is, Receive if the check box is off). The Send option should already be turned on, by default.

Make sure the phone line is connected to your fax modem. Your system should now be in standby mode, waiting for a fax. A fax icon is added to the system tray, too.

When a fax comes in, the Fax Monitor pops up, apprising you of the progress of the fax, as shown in Figure 9.20.

Figure 9.20
The Fax Monitor reports progress of the incoming fax.

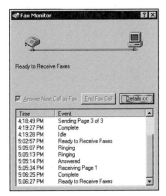

When reception of a fax is complete, the little fax icon wiggles down in the system tray. Clicking it brings up the My Faxes folder. If you open the Received Faxes folder, you see icons for each received fax. Double-click the fax icon, and it opens in an Imaging (Kodak Imaging) window. You can then size, scale, rotate, print, and edit it in various ways.

A shortcut to the My Faxes folder is to right-click the fax icon and choose My Faxes. Note also the options for Fax Queue and Fax Monitor Properties on the same menu. The Queue is just like a printer queue, as discussed earlier in this chapter, and the same commands apply here.

Each fax is converted to a TIF file when it arrives. Because TIF is a nonproprietary format, you can view or edit it with almost any graphics image program. However, using the supplied Kodak viewer and editor is easy enough.

 If your system refuses to receive incoming faxes, see "Cannot Receive a Fax" in the "Troubleshooting" section at the end of this chapter.

→ To learn more details about the supplied Imaging program, **see** "Imaging," **p. 259**.

Tip #141	As long as the fax service is running and you have enabled your fax modem to receive faxes, the fax icon appears in the system tray. Double-clicking it brings up the Fax Monitor.

INCOMING FAX STORAGE

By default, incoming faxes are converted to TIF files and are dumped into the Received Faxes folder (which you open by choosing Start, Programs, Accessories, Communications, Fax, My Faxes). But you can configure a fax setup to actually print your documents on paper as they come in. To shunt all incoming faxes to a physical printer for automatic printing, follow these steps:

1. Run Fax Service Management.

2. Click Devices in the left pane, and then click the Fax device in the right pane.

3. Open its Properties sheet.

4. Click the Received Faxes tab. Check the Print On box, and choose the destination printer.

For more details, open Fax Service Management and choose Action, Help. If you're an administrator, you might want to set some of the defaults, determine the level of detail in fax logging, and set permissions.

Fax Resolutions

With all the talk about digital cameras, scanners, and cameras these days (and their respective resolutions), you might be wondering about fax resolution. Here's the skinny on that: The standard resolution for faxes is 3.85 scan lines/mm (approximately 98dpi vertically) with 1728 pixels across a standard scan line of 215mm (approximately 204dpi horizontally).

An additional, popular setting on many fax machines is called "fine" resolution. This setting scans 7.7 lines per millimeter (approximately 196dpi vertically) with the same resolution horizontally as with the normal setting.

Can some fax machines go higher? Yes. Many so-called Group III fax machines use nonstandard frames to negotiate higher resolutions. Some go as high as 300×300dpi (similar to older laser printers) and even 400×400dpi, but have to be talking with other fax machines made by the same manufacturer for this scheme to work. Manufacturers are working to set standards to support this level of resolution between machines of dissimilar manufacture.

The resolution you get on your printouts or as viewed on your computer screen depends on many factors. First, the screen resolution depends on the resolution of the source fax machine or computer. Second, it depends on the group of fax your system is employing and, finally, on the resolution of your display or printer. If what you intend to send someone is a high-resolution picture, you should always try to acquire a good color or grayscale scan of the image. Then you can attach it to an email as a GIF, TIF, or JPEG file. Generally speaking, it will look better than sending it as a fax.

Sending Faxes Over the Internet

The problem with sending faxes is that you don't always have a phone line available (as when you are in an office connected to the Internet via a LAN), or you don't want to pay for long-distance phone calls or high per-page charges to use a hotel fax machine. The problem with receiving faxes is that you aren't always there to receive the fax when it comes in. Isn't there a way to send faxes over the Internet?

Internet faxing is in development as of this writing, and there are various ways of both sending and receiving faxes using the Internet. If you're using an email program capable of faxing (such as newer versions of Microsoft Outlook), you can configure it to send and receive faxes. Several services (commercial as well as free) offer to accept email messages and fax them to the specified phone number. Some even let you fax from portable, wireless devices such as PalmPilots.

The following are some links to information about email-based faxing services:

http://www.jfax.com

http://www.interfax.ca/

http://www.efax.com/

You can read a FAQ about this topic, courtesy of savetz@rahul.net (Kevin M. Savetz) at this address:

ftp://rtfm.mit.edu/pub/usenet/news.answers/internet-services/fax-faq

TROUBLESHOOTING

PRINTER ERRORS

I receive error messages when I try to print. What's wrong?

When an error occurs during a print job, Windows tries to determine the cause. If the printer is out of paper, you might see a Paper Out message in the status area. At other times, the message is ambiguous, and the word Error might appear in the status area. Add paper; make sure that the printer is turned on, online, and correctly connected; and make sure that the settings (particularly the driver) are correct for that printer.

NOTHING HAPPENS

I try to print, but nothing happens. How do I proceed?

If your print jobs never make it out the other end of the printer, work through this checklist:

- First, ask yourself whether you printed to the correct printer. Check to see whether your default printer is the one you are expecting output. If you're on a LAN, you can easily switch default printers and then forget that you made the switch.

- Check the settings in the Print dialog box carefully before you print. Is there something to print? Do you have to select some portion of your document first?

- Next, check to see whether the printer you've chosen is actually powered up, online, and ready to roll.

- If you're using a network printer, is the station serving the printer powered up and ready to serve print jobs?

- Check the cabling. Is it tight?

- Does the printer need ink, toner, or paper? Are any error lights or other indicators on the printer itself flashing or otherwise indicating an error, such as a paper jam?

PRINTER PRODUCES GARBLED TEXT

When I print, the printout contains a lot of garbled text.

If you're getting garbage characters in your printouts, check the following:

- You might have the wrong driver installed. Run the test print page and see whether it works. Open the Printers folder (by choosing Start, Settings, Printers), open the

Properties sheet, and print a test page. If that works then you're halfway home. If it doesn't, try removing the printer and reinstalling it. Right-click the printer icon in the Printers folder, and choose Delete. Then add the printer again and try printing.

- If the printer uses plug-in font cartridges, you might also have the wrong font cartridge installed in the printer, or your text is formatted with the wrong font.

- Some printers have emulation modes that might conflict with one another. Check with the manual. You might think you're printing to a PostScript printer, but the printer could be in an HP emulation mode; in this case, your driver is sending PostScript, and the printer is expecting PCL.

ONLY HALF OF THE PAGE PRINTS CORRECTLY

My printer prints about half of a page, and then it starts printing garbage.

This problem is a rare occurrence nowadays, but it's still possible if you're running a printer off a serial port. Serial printers use more complicated "handshaking" than parallel ones do, and the result can be something called *buffer overruns*. The computer is supposed to receive a message from the printer when its internal buffer is filled with data and waiting for the print head to catch up. If the computer doesn't get this message, it continues to send data to the printer. At that point, the data becomes scrambled or is possibly dropped altogether. Try several documents. If your printer regularly prints about the same amount of text or graphics and then flips out, suspect a buffer-related problem. On serial printers, buffer problems can often be traced to cables that do not have all the serial-port conductors (wires), or they're not in the correct order. Make sure the cable is the correct kind for the printer. USB printers are also serial in nature; they just are running on a bus that is faster than the old COM-type serial ports. Overruns are less likely, however, because the USB protocols for printers are more standardized.

Also, remember that because the print spooler requires some free hard disk space, you might also want to check on it. Always be sure to have at least a few megabytes of space available on your system partition.

FAX PRINTER CAN'T BE ADDED

I can't add a fax printer.

If you're are unable to add a fax printer, you might not have sufficient user rights. See your system or fax server administrator.

CANNOT RECEIVE A FAX

My system can't receive a fax. What's wrong with it?

Here's a quick checklist of common stumbling blocks:

- Have you plugged in the phone line properly?
- Is your modem installed and working properly?

- Is it a true fax modem, not just a data modem?

- Did you enable fax reception via the Fax Service Management application (the default setting is off)?

- Is another device (for example, an answering machine) picking up the phone before your fax modem is? Check the ring settings for the fax modem and/or answering machines. Consider using the option that lets you screen for a fax first and then activate it manually (see the faxing section earlier in the chapter).

- If your computer goes into standby mode and doesn't wake up to receive incoming faxes, you might need to turn on an option in the computer's BIOS to "wake on ring." This option wakes up the computer any time it senses the ringer voltage on the phone line. If a fax is coming in, it takes the call. If it's not fax, the computer goes back to sleep.

TIPS FROM THE WINDOWS PROS: CHOOSING A PRINTER NAME

Windows 2000 supports the use of long printer names. With this capability, you can create printer names that contain spaces and special characters. However, if you share a printer over a network, some clients do not recognize or correctly handle the long names, and users might experience problems printing. Also, some programs cannot print to printers with names longer than 32 characters.

For printers that are shared, the entire qualified name (including the server name, \\PRINTER2\PSCRIPT, for example) must be fewer than 32 characters.

- If you share a printer with a variety of clients on a network, use 31 or fewer characters for printer names, and do not include spaces or special characters in these names.

- If you share a printer with MS-DOS computers, do not use more than eight characters for the printer's share name. You can lengthen the name by adding a period followed by no more than three characters, but you cannot use spaces in the name.

CHAPTER 10

FONT MANAGEMENT

In this chapter

A LITTLE WINDOWS FONT HISTORY

Since the days of Windows 3.0, one of the big attractions to Windows was that it included a unified system for displaying and printing text across all Windows applications and printers. Prior to Windows, font management on the PC was a nightmare. Switching between typefaces and typestyles (italics, bold, and so on) in DOS-based applications was definitely *not* a WYSIWYG (What You See Is What You Get) experience. For example, in WordPerfect or Word for DOS, you often had to resort to Control-key codes for input and view color-coded characters onscreen at best. You had to remember that blue text meant bold, for example. If you had a monochrome monitor (as most were), you were limited to monocolor cues. Font size changes weren't displayed onscreen, and finer points such as kerning and justification and special effects such as outline, shadow, and so forth were out of the ballpark.

When print time came, not only were there typically no spoolers (you couldn't get back to work until the print job was done), but the line and page breaks you could expect to see on paper rarely paralleled what you saw onscreen. The whole process was more like WYSIMWYG (What You See Is Maybe What You'll Get) or WYSIWYW (What You See Is What You Want).

Printers such as the HP LaserJet came with their own plug-in font cartridges that gave you maybe a few typestyles and sizes and an accompanying font-management program you had to install on the PC. Worse yet, each program solved font dilemmas in its own way, not sharing its wealth of fonts or font-management utilities with other MS-DOS programs. A friend of mine who later opened his own computer book publishing company (Peachpit Press) started his fortune writing books about this arcane area of PC existence.

Eventually, DOS word processors evolved to run in "Graphics mode," yet they were still nothing much to write home about. Screens were still black or blue with white text on them; fonts and typestyles weren't displayed with much definition, nor were they easily selectable.

The Macintosh had it all over the PC in the desktop publishing arena, and had the PC not caught up with offerings such as Ventura Publisher (which ran on the GEM operating system, not Windows, incidentally, and pretty darned fast even on a 286-based AT), I should think Apple would be the frontrunner in personal computers today. With Adobe on its side producing PostScript printers and fonts (albeit at a much higher price and copy protected at that), *DTP* (desktop publishing) quickly became a buzzword as celebrated 10 years ago as *WWW* or "dot com" are today.

Everyone's cousin-once-removed was pulling all-nighters converting gas stations into desktop publishing shops (including yours truly, who typeset computer books for a living). Fonts were a spin-off business, and everyone with a Macintosh started getting font happy. The side effect of font mania was the plethora of posters, brochures, and newsletters riddled with visually incompatible typefaces. It was enough to make professional type designers, typesetters, and graphic artists livid, not to mention leaving them hungry for clients who now thought they could do a cheaper (if not better) job back at the office.

Not to be outdone of course, Gates and his team caught on fast enough, developing their own font system and building it into the then quickly evolving Windows. This new system helped to plow under Digital Research's GEM, and even Adobe to a great degree. With Windows 3.1 came TrueType fonts, and things began to work just about as well as on the Macintosh. A user with only a single printer driver and one pool of fonts could effectively lay out and print complex documents across a broad spectrum of applications such as on Lotus 1-2-3 for Windows, Ami Pro, Paradox, Microsoft Access, PowerPoint, and so on. Economy CD-ROM packages appeared down at the local Kompu-Mart blistered with fonts you would never really want to use—except to let Junior make his Keep Out sign for the bedroom door. But it was fun anyway.

Each new version of Windows has improved on the font situation. Installing, removing, and managing fonts threw many a Windows 3.x user for a loop because the system tools were scanty. With time, it became common knowledge that after you installed a zillion fonts, your system could take a performance hit, especially notable in slow booting. This hit occurred because all the fonts, font names, and font directories had to be checked out and loaded at boot time. As a result, third-party font-management programs popped up in the market-place, improving on the rudimentary Font utility supplied in the Windows 3.x Control Panel. For example, they displayed all your fonts, let you print sample pages of your fonts, and loaded and unloaded fonts in groups to circumvent the slowdown problem. Some of these packages also had built-in font-conversion capabilities, producing TrueType fonts from other types such as Adobe Type 1 or bitmapped fonts, and could create novel display type by applying groovy effects to fonts you already had installed.

Windows 95 came with a set of new stock fonts, such as Courier New, Times New Roman, and Arial, in place of Courier, Times, and Helvetica (holdovers from the PostScript days). Windows 95 also added a spiffier font-management folder (built into the system with special attributes). This font management folder was further tuned up in Windows 98.

Windows 2000 benefits, of course, from all these developments, not the least of which is that the unstoppable march of printer technology has brought the price of full-color print-ing in the 1200dpi range down to below $100. This price boggles my mind, considering I'm sitting here next to my trusty 300dpi QMS PS-810 laser printer for which I was soaked $4700 10 years ago. (Then again, it still works, and it's printed 38,689 pages. Let's see where the little photo printers are in 10 years!)

As with all previous Windows versions, upon a fresh installation, you are left with but a tawdry selection of fonts for your document design excursions. You might be among the many who will remain happy with a limited selection and possibly never feel the need to add to the collection. More likely, though, you'll at some point want to augment your rudimen-tary workhorse fonts with a few more cheery or colorful ones to spruce up your documents. So, in this chapter, I'll explain a bit about font technology, how to add and remove fonts from your system, how to choose and use fonts wisely, how to procure new fonts, how to create fonts of your own, and how fonts interact with Internet Explorer.

FONT OVERVIEW IN WINDOWS 2000

Microsoft continues the move toward improved font management in Windows 2000. As in Windows 9x, when you open the Control Panel and choose Fonts, a Fonts folder opens. (In reality, it's the folder X:\winnt\fonts; just replace X with your startup drive letter.) It is one of those specially treated system folders that, when displayed under Windows Explorer or in a folder window, magically has its own unique menu and right-click commands with options to let you do the following:

- Add and remove fonts
- View fonts in various ways
- List fonts by similarity of looks
- List only the basic font family name and hide variations such as bold and italic to make selection easier

Tip #142	Relative to Windows 98, Microsoft decided to reduce the number of paths to the Fonts folder. You can now reach it only from Control Panel or by drilling down through the folder system to \winnt\fonts.

A LITTLE FONT PRIMER

Anyone interested in fonts should first become acquainted with basic typographic nomenclature. Let's start at the top.

The word *font*, as used in Windows, really refers to a typeface. Those people in typesetting circles believe the term is misused in PC jargon, and you should really be calling, say, Arial a typeface. But, oh well. There goes the language (again). Technically, a font is a specific set of characters, each of which shares the same basic characteristics. So, Arial Italic is a font, whereas Arial is a typeface (made up of a collection of the fonts Arial Roman, Arial Bold, Arial Bold Italic, and Arial Italic). In any case, in Windows-talk, you call a family such as Arial a font, and that's that.

Fonts are specified by size as well as by name. The size of a font is measured in *points*. A point is 1/72 of an inch.

Figure 10.1 shows several popular font styles.

Windows 2000 Professional comes with a basic stock of fonts (about 30). The exact number of fonts depends on the printer or printers you have installed and the screen fonts you have chosen to install.

→ To learn more about installing printers, **see** "Printing and Faxing with Windows 2000," Chapter 9.

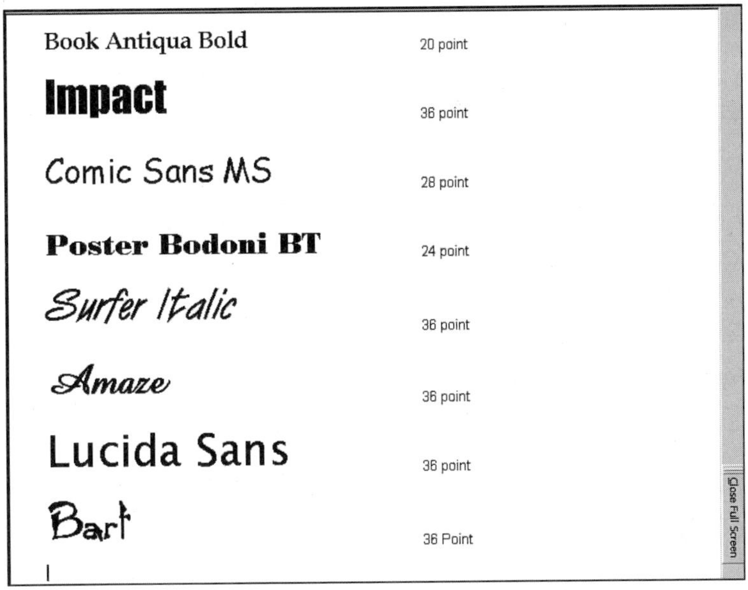

Figure 10.1
Fonts are used to more effectively reach an audience.

Book Antiqua Bold	20 point
Impact	36 point
Comic Sans MS	28 point
Poster Bodoni BT	24 point
Surfer Italic	36 point
Amaze	36 point
Lucida Sans	36 point
Bart	36 Point

Close Full Screen

> **Note**
>
> *Screen fonts* control how text looks on your screen. They come in predefined sizes, such as 10 points, 12 points, and so on.
>
> *Printer fonts* are fonts stored in your printer (in its ROM), stored on plug-in cartridges, or downloaded to your printer by Windows when you print. Downloaded fonts are called *soft fonts*.

⚡ *If your screen fonts (such as text under icons on the desktop) seem too large or too small, see "Icon Fonts Too Large or Small" in the "Troubleshooting" section at the end of this chapter.*

Let's start with the basic classifications of font types. Three essential classes of fonts are used in Windows, and an understanding of them will help you manage your font collection. Windows 2000 provides three basic font technologies: *outline*, *vector*, and *raster*.

OUTLINE FONTS

In the past, if you used a printer like the LaserJet II, you might have been limited to the two fonts that come standard with that printer (Courier and Line Printer). If you wanted to print any other fonts, you had to buy a cartridge containing a few additional fonts, or you had to buy soft fonts. These fonts had to be individually rendered by the vendor in each size that might be required. These fonts were often costly and required a tremendous amount of hard disk space. If you wanted to display the fonts onscreen, you had to create yet another set of screen fonts that matched the printer fonts.

Although folks such as Hewlett-Packard sold presized (bitmapped) fonts, Adobe Systems first popularized scalable fonts, which it called Type 1 fonts (cute name, eh?). This technology was part of the PostScript page-description language and allowed users to choose a wide range of font sizes and styles all from relatively small font description files. It was a major breakthrough in PC-based fonts. The files were, in essence, mathematical descriptions of the curves in each character in a font. Rather than load a bitmap (picture) of each possible letter into the printer or on the screen, the printer or computer could twiddle the numbers in the formula and resize the characters on-the-fly.

These fonts were called PostScript fonts back then (a trade name), but specifically they were Adobe Type 1 fonts, and generically they fall into a class called *outline fonts*. They have this name because the font file contains information about how to draw the outline of each character, using its formulas and "hinting" algorithms to help smooth lines and curves regardless of font size and also improve the look of specific letter pairs when adjacent to one another.

Although PostScript fonts looked great and could print on any PostScript-equipped printer or even high-resolution typesetting machine, the downside of using PostScript fonts is that a PostScript printer or typesetting machine has to interpret all the instructions in the outline font itself. It essentially needs a powerful computer inside to calculate the PostScript formulas and render the fonts and PostScript graphics on the paper. So, PostScript printers have both a PostScript interpreter and a rasterizer inside the box, which makes PostScript printers very expensive.

TrueType provides the same advantages as Adobe's Type 1 fonts, namely that with a single font file, you can make the type appear in whatever size you want, either onscreen or printed. But the big advantage is that the computing and rasterizing are done in the computer, not in the printer. TrueType-compatible Windows printers now sell for less than one-tenth what PostScript printers cost, largely because they can be very stupid. Your PC and Windows 2000 Professional can do all the cogitating and then pass simple commands to the printer.

The tug of war between Adobe and Microsoft (Type 1 versus TrueType fonts) has finally come to an end, as both companies have agreed to create a superset of their respective technologies, dubbed *OpenType*. (See "A Little TrueType History" later in this chapter.) OpenType, which is built into Windows 2000 Professional, converts your older Type 1 and TrueType fonts to the new format. It also provides some additional features that fix limitations in the other formats, such as providing ligatures (special font pairs to improve readability), providing alternative characters within the same font, and helping in embedding of compressed font information into documents such as Word files and Web pages.

→ To learn more about font embedding, **see** "Embedding Fonts in Documents," **p. 375**.

You must consider a few other advantages of OpenType and TrueType. For starters, printed output looks the same (perhaps with some differences in smoothness or resolution), regardless of the type of printer. Also, because of the careful design of the screen and printer display of each font, TrueType and OpenType provide much better WYSIWYG capabilities than previous fonts.

Tip #143
> Windows 2000 ships with a CD-ROM collection of Far East OpenType fonts, which you can install to view or print Far East documents and Web pages.

OpenType and TrueType also allow users of different computer systems to maintain compatibility across platforms. For example, because TrueType is also integrated into System 7, the Macintosh operating system, a document formatted on a Macintosh using TrueType fonts will look exactly the same on any Windows PC (after Windows 3.1 and later).

Finally, because OpenType is an integrated component of Windows, any Windows program can use OpenType fonts. These fonts can be easily scaled (increased or decreased in size), rotated, or otherwise altered from any program that calls upon the Font Registry in the Windows system.

A LITTLE TRUETYPE HISTORY

Originally designed by Sampo Kaasila and a team of about 10 others, TrueType was a project that Apple Computer started around 1987. It later became a joint venture between Microsoft and Apple, which intended to avoid the licensing costs involved in using Adobe's PostScript fonts.

Actually, Adobe's PostScript fonts worked wonderfully for printing, and the cost was not exorbitant (even though the printers were). However, a screen display methodology was needed so that printer output matched the screen more closely. Adobe developed such a technology called *Display PostScript (DPS)*, which, together with print PostScript, met this need and formed a complete font solution for PCs and Macintoshes. But both Apple and Microsoft were loathe to hand over control of key parts of their operating systems—not to mention millions of royalty dollars—to Adobe. (DPS was too slow for the target machines anyway, ending up primarily on Steve Jobs's NeXT computer, which is now history.) To make matters worse, Apple was annoyed that Adobe was undercutting the sales of its PostScript printer (the LaserWriter) by licensing PostScript to other printer makers, such as QMS. The upshot was that Apple and Microsoft teamed up against the burgeoning Adobe to create their own font-display and font-printing solution. Microsoft was to create the printing portion of TrueType, while Apple would do the system display portion.

The system needed attractive typefaces (fonts) to work with, and the first TrueType fonts— Times Roman, Helvetica, and Courier—became well known when they were released with the Macintosh's System 6.0. Microsoft introduced TrueType into Windows with version 3.1, in April 1991, and included similar fonts created with the aid of the Monotype company. Windows 3.1 shipped with TrueType versions of Times New Roman, Arial, and Courier.

Soon afterward, Microsoft began rewriting the TrueType rasterizer to improve its efficiency and performance and remove some bugs (while maintaining compatibility with the earlier version). The new TrueType rasterizer, version 1.5, first shipped in Windows NT 3.1. There have since been some minor revisions, in Windows 95, NT 3.x, Windows 98, and Windows NT 4. New capabilities include enhanced features such as font smoothing (or

PART

II

CH

10

more technically, grayscale rasterization). The TrueType engine became fully 32-bit, much more reliable, and the grayscale rasterization enhanced onscreen text substantially.

Adobe counter-attacked in two phases. The first part was to release its very inexpensive Type Manager that could plug into Windows 3.1 and MacOS. This release was an attempt to continue the life of Type 1 fonts. The second was to release the formulas for Type 1 fonts so that other type foundries could produce fonts. But this effort was too little too late. Apple's and Microsoft's partnership had produced an efficient and solid technology that worked and that gave them both the control over their respective operating systems, without any licensing fees to Adobe.

The next major event was that an agreement was struck between Adobe and Microsoft to end the font wars and collaborate on OpenType, which incorporates both TrueType and Type 1 fonts. The benefit of this collaboration to Adobe is that it is back in a player's position in font technology. To the end users, it simply means that all their fonts work, with no headaches. No more Adobe Type Manager if you want to use Type 1 fonts. OpenType handles all fonts with a unified Registry, which means that both Type 1 and TrueType fonts will be seen reliably across all platforms supporting OpenType. Also, Adobe is working on converting existing Type 1 fonts to the new OpenType format.

So, Windows 2000 Professional includes full support for OpenType for this reason.

VECTOR FONTS

The second type of font in this three-ring circus is the *vector font*. Vector fonts use straight line segments and formulas to draw letters. They can be easily scaled to different sizes. These fonts are primarily used on printing devices that only draw lines, such as plotters. Plotters need to use vector fonts because they don't know about *rasterizing*.

Tip #144	Rasterizing is a method of creating images, much the way a TV does. For example, a TV fills the picture tube with an image from the top down, drawn with successive lines composed of dots. Rasterizing printers work more or less the same way. This is why the print head of a typical dot-matrix or inkjet printer moves from side to side, drawing one line (or band of lines) with each pass, as the paper is pulled through the printer.

Vector fonts are more suitable for devices such as plotters that can't use bitmapped characters because they draw with lines rather than dots. Vector fonts are a series of mathematical formulas that describe a series of lines and curves (arcs). They can be scaled to any size, but because of the process involved in computing the shape and direction of the curves, generating these fonts can be quite time-consuming.

Actually, PostScript, TrueType, and OpenType fonts are technically vector fonts, but because the printers and screen themselves can calculate and draw quickly, the performance is pretty good. Vector fonts are supported in Windows 2000 Professional only because many programs, such as those in the CAD/CAM arena, still depend on them. Windows 2000 supports three vector fonts: Modern, Roman, and Script.

Raster Fonts (Bitmapped Fonts)

Raster fonts, sometimes called bitmapped fonts, are essentially little predrawn pictures (bitmaps). A font consists of a collection of these pictures, one for each character, in a given size. Typically, today's Windows bitmap font files contain a handful of sizes to choose from, but the selection is fairly limited.

Five bitmapped fonts come in Windows 2000 Professional: Courier, MS Serif, MS Sans Serif, Small, and Symbol. Based on the resolution of your video adapter, Windows chooses the font files that take best advantage of your particular display. Figure 10.2 shows a character map of a bitmapped font.

→ To learn more about the Character Map, **see** "Character Map," **p. 266**.

Figure 10.2
Typical bitmapped font displayed in Character Map.

Part II CH 10

Bitmapped fonts are used for special purposes, such as in Command Prompt boxes, dialog boxes, and in other programs that don't know about TrueType and OpenType fonts. Notepad used to be a good example, but now Notepad 5 can display text in the OpenType font of your choice. In general, you should limit yourself to displaying bitmapped fonts in the sizes provided or in something close to multiples of their original sizes if you want the fonts to look decent. Of course, when you start playing with the scaling, bitmapped fonts just don't look as good as TrueType or OpenType fonts at the same size.

 If dialog boxes are displayed in unreadable fonts or with type that is too large or too small, see "Dialog Box Fonts Are Unreadable" in the "Troubleshooting" section at the end of this chapter.

Font Substitutions

Fonts are readily available on the Internet these days, so finding fonts you might need is no biggie. You just download them and drop them into the Fonts folder (see the section later on adding fonts). Also, OpenType makes it easier to compress and incorporate fonts into your documents so that, when you share them with others, they are displayed correctly even if the recipient doesn't have the fonts installed in his or her system.

But what if you have older documents that were formatted with fonts not in your system and that you can't acquire? Some word processors, such as Word, have an option to substitute missing fonts with present fonts. In Word, choose Tools, Options, Compatibility, Font Substitutions. If all the fonts you need to print the document are installed in the system, you are told that everything is hunky dory. If not, you can make changes. Check the help file for the word processing program for details.

Another kind of font substitution pertains only to PostScript printers. Because PostScript printers have internal fonts, printing is faster using them than forcing Windows to download a similar font file into the PostScript rasterizer and then commence printing. For example, the Windows Arial font and the PostScript Helvetica font are virtually identical. So, you can tell your PostScript printer driver to just use the Helvetica font in the printer whenever you print a document formatted with Arial. Likewise, Times can be substituted for Windows's Times New Roman.

A font substitution table is responsible for setting the relationship of the screen and printer fonts. In Win9x, this table is stored in the WIN.INI file under [FontSubstitutes]. In NT 4 and Windows 2000 Professional, you can find it in the slick dialog box that's attached to the printer's icon in the Printers folder. Here's how to edit the font substitution table:

1. Choose Start, Settings, and then click Printers.
2. Right-click the printer you want, and choose Properties.
3. Click the Device Settings tab.
4. Click the + to the left of Font Substitution Table. You then see a list like the one in Figure 10.3.

Figure 10.3
The font substitution table for a PostScript printer controls what fonts in the printer will be used in lieu of TrueType fonts in the Windows 2000 operating system.

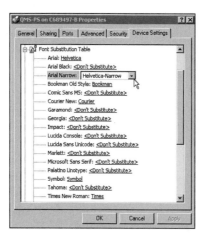

5. Click a link next to a to select the TrueType font from the font substitution table.
6. Click to select the substitution font, or click Download as Soft Font from the Change Setting list.
7. Click OK.

Microsoft's Special LCD Font Technology: ClearType

Remember the eight-track tape player? (Oops, there I go dating myself again.) Okay, how about an LP record? Well, add to the list of soon-to-be-landfill items those fat, heavy, heat-producing old CRT (Cathode Ray Tube) monitors. Yup, soon you're going to have more room on your desk for paper-clip organizers and pen holders. In a year or two, having a CRT will stigmatize you as a relic of the past. You won't want any part of it. And the likes of NEC, Mag, Sony, and the rest will see to it, gently "encouraging" us all to shell out fairly big time for the privilege of reading LCD (liquid crystal displays) instead of glowing phosphor ones.

But technology marches on. We're being quickly converted to LCDs regardless of what's on our desktops. Wrist watches and calculators have used LCDs for years. Now PalmPilots, cash registers, ATMs, pay phones, and even gas pumps are using them. And, of course, all laptop computer displays are LCD in one form or another. Soon to proliferate the market will be *ebooks*—electronic gadgets you can read plug-in or downloadable books on, complete with text, graphics, hot links, and more.

Realizing the increasing popularity of the LCD for text display, the folks at Microsoft who were working on TrueType and OpenType got to thinking about improving that technology. Because the pixels on an LCD are square rather than round, and because their focus is perfect (there is no bleeding between dots, which tends to smooth out the look a tad), low-to-medium resolution LCDs tend to display text with a choppy look. To worsen the matter, many pixels in LCDs are typically on or off—there are no shades of gray to soften the edges. Microsoft came up with ClearType, which it claims will make words on your LCD screens look as smooth as the words on a piece of paper.

It does so by improving on this "on/off" pixel addressing, instead addressing the area beyond the traditional pixel boundary. The result will be letters on the computer screen that appear smooth, not jagged. Essentially, ClearType is not dissimilar from the font smoothing in TrueType screen fonts. It's just tailored to LCD technology, using shades of gray (or color) to fill in the tiny gaps between and around the pixels that construct onscreen characters.

Although ClearType font technology works with existing systems such as CRT monitors or LCD panels being driven by analog video display boards, you're going to see noticeable improvements only on color LCDs driven by digital control boards, such as those found in laptops and high-quality flat panel desktop displays.

The advantages gleaned from ClearType are less obvious as the resolution of the LCD panel increases. Low-resolution LCDs form blockier characters because they have fewer pixels to work with. On high-resolution LCDs, pixels are smaller, so pixelation is less obvious to the eye.

ClearType was originally going to be included in Windows 2000. It was pulled, close to release time. Look for it in a service pack or as an after-market product.

How Do TrueType and OpenType Work?

Now let me share a little scoop on how the TrueType/OpenType system works.

Note

From this point onward, I'll use the terms *OpenType* and *TrueType* interchangeably because they are so closely related.

OpenType fonts have certain interesting similarities to bitmapped and vector fonts. Here's how: An OpenType font contains a description of the series of lines and curves for the typeface—just like a vector font does. When you enter a character into a document, the application asks Windows to generate the bitmap of that character in the desired size and font and dump it on the screen because a screen is a raster display device, just like most printers (the image consists of dots). It's the task of the Windows Graphical Device Interface (GDI) to create the best possible representation of the character on your screen, based on the resolution and other factors.

But wait, there's more. As I mentioned earlier in passing, good OpenType fonts include "hints," some of which help the GDI render the font in smaller point sizes. Hints, along with grayscale rasterization (screen font-smoothing), help make OpenType fonts look better onscreen. Because the resolution of a typical monitor is considerably less than even a 300dpi printer, many fonts simply don't look right onscreen. They just don't have enough pixels to accurately reproduce the font at smaller point sizes.

So, to display a character at a tiny point size (say, 5 or 6), it relies on the hinting instructions located in a TrueType font. The result is that the characters look smoother. Hinting is also important for printing (hey, I'm a poet). If you check the printout of some small text on a decent high-resolution printer (for example, a 300dpi laser), you'll likely see certain mis-shapen characters. An *O* might not be perfectly round; the slant of a *W* might not be truly straight, but it still looks good. Hinting ensures you get high-quality fonts output, despite the resolution limits of today's printers.

Onscreen font smoothing is another factor that can affect how well fonts look onscreen. Smoothing has no effect on printing but does affect onscreen display, especially of small fonts on screens running in lower resolutions, such as 640×480 and even 800×600. Font smoothing (grayscale rasterization) uses shades of gray to smooth out the otherwise rough edges of small fonts displayed onscreen. Basically, this technique fools the eye into thinking the "jaggies" are gone, when actually they are filled in with pixels that, if black, would look just as jagged or even worse. If you make them lighter in color, the letters simply seem to look less irritating, even though the edges can look a little fuzzy at times.

Tip #145

When you select a different font or a new point size, Windows 2000 Professional creates bitmaps for the entire character set in the new size or style. This process happens only once during a Windows session. After first generating the bitmaps, Windows places them into a memory cache, where they can be quickly accessed the next time they are required. In earlier versions of Windows, this process used to cause a slight delay that was detectable by the user. Now it all happens very smoothly.

OPENTYPE FONT FAMILIES

On the grossest level, OpenType fonts are organized into font families. As with humans and other animals, a *family* is a group of items (in this case, typefaces) with similar characteristics. A family is more distantly related, however, than the members of a given font; there is more variation among them. Windows 2000 Professional recognizes five basic font families: Decorative, Modern, Roman, Script, and Swiss.

Swiss and Roman are the most common of these families, with the Roman family containing the majority of serif fonts. Sans-serif fonts such as Arial are generally members of the Swiss family (not Robinson). Check out Figure 10.4, which compares the Roman and Swiss families. (Serifs are discussed later in "Classes of Fonts.")

Figure 10.4
Here, you see two fonts, Times New Roman (a Roman font) and Arial (a Swiss font).

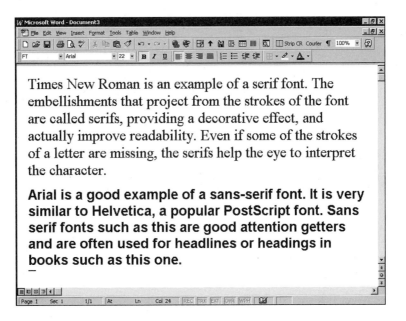

Times New Roman is an example of a serif font. The embellishments that project from the strokes of the font are called serifs, providing a decorative effect, and actually improve readability. Even if some of the strokes of a letter are missing, the serifs help the eye to interpret the character.

Arial is a good example of a sans-serif font. It is very similar to Helvetica, a popular PostScript font. Sans serif fonts such as this are good attention getters and are often used for headlines or headings in books such as this one.

SPECIAL CHARACTERS

All OpenType fonts contain special characters, such as foreign-language accents (è), trademark (™), copyright (©), currency such as this yen mark (¥), and special punctuation such as the em dash (—), and so on. Windows 2000 Professional complies with Unicode specifications, which means that a large number of the world's languages can be represented by these newer fonts.

 If foreign-language fonts don't appear properly, see "Foreign-Language Fonts Don't Appear" in the "Troubleshooting" section at the end of this chapter.

Most better word processors let you insert odd characters such as these using a symbol lookup tool, but if not, you can use the Character Map or keyboard commands, as discussed in Chapter 7, "Using the Simple Supplied Applications."

When it comes to inserting offbeat symbols that are not represented by your keyboard, you should also be aware of two other fonts: WingDings and Symbol.

- WingDings is very versatile. This font contains a bizarre collection of symbols and characters that can be used to add special impact to documents, a bit like clip art. You'll find items such as religious icons, a book, envelopes, zodiac signs, and even the official Windows logo.

■ Symbol contains the complete Greek alphabet along with numerous mathematical symbols.

Figure 10.5 displays all the characters of these two fonts.

Figure 10.5
WingDings and Symbol fonts are supplied with Windows 2000 Professional for special purposes. Use the Character Map or your word processor's Insert Symbol command to view, choose, and insert these symbols into documents.

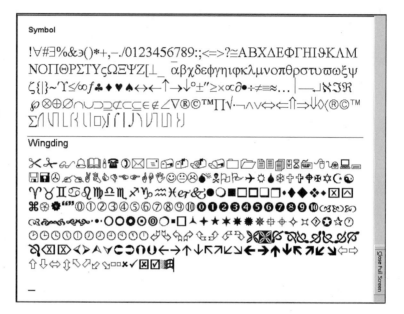

 Tip #146

If all you want to do is examine all the characters in a given font, you can do that from the Fonts applet in the Control Panel, as explained later in this chapter.

⚠ *If dialog boxes are displayed in the wrong language, see "Dialog Box Fonts Are Unreadable" in the "Troubleshooting" section at the end of this chapter.*

HOW WINDOWS USES YOUR FONTS

Ideally, only fonts that work properly with your printer should show up in the fonts list in your applications. But what happens if you have multiple printers installed on a computer? In that case, all the fonts on the computer can show up in the fonts list, which leaves you to determine appropriate fonts, based on your printer of choice. In the case of multiple installed printers, the fonts list can change based on which printer is set as the default printer, so be aware of this fact when you're formatting documents for printing. Set the default printer first, and make sure the fonts you want to use can actually print properly on your chosen output device.

As an example, check Figure 10.6. There, you'll see the fonts list for my QMS PS-810 PostScript laser printer. Notice the icons next to the fonts. Some are TrueType fonts, whereas others have the little printer icon next to them. The printer icon means they are printer fonts—that is, fonts that are resident inside my printer. The printer driver for the laser printer knows which fonts are resident in the printer, and it informs the operating system, which in turn informs Word. Thus, changing the default printer from the Printers folder immediately changes the available fonts list in applications.

→ To learn more about installing printers and setting the default printer," **see** "Installing and Configuring a Printer" **p. 323**.

Figure 10.6
A typical drop-down fonts list within an application. This one is from Word 97. Notice the icons to the left of the fonts. The TT means TrueType. The little printers indicate fonts internal to a printer.

PART

II

CH

10

The way Windows displays your chosen font on the screen depends on what kind of font it is. For an OpenType font, the operating system uses its internal font scaling system to generate a screen font that very closely matches what it will send to the printer, as explained earlier.

If the font is a nonscaling font, though, the plot thickens: Windows then looks around for a screen font that corresponds to the one you've chosen to print with. If it finds a match, it uses that font. If no exact match exists, then Windows substitutes the closest thing it can find. In the worst of cases, the screen font might look completely different from the printed font in style. Still, the line and page breaks should be accurate. When you print the document, Windows checks your printer driver file and the system, looking for the fonts you specified. If the fonts exist, Windows knows whether they're already resident in the printer or must be scaled or downloaded from the hard disk. If a font is missing, Windows again makes an effort to substitute a similar one.

 If someone sent you a document in which font layout looks obviously way off, see "Document from Another User Is Displayed Improperly" in the "Troubleshooting" section at the end of this chapter.

EMBEDDING FONTS IN DOCUMENTS

As I mentioned earlier in this chapter, an extension of the OpenType specification provides an *application programming interface (API)* for applications to embed fonts in documents. If an OpenType font is embedded in the document, you can open and view the document correctly on a system that doesn't have the document's fonts resident. Not all applications can embed fonts this way, but more and more can display them at least.

TrueType's greatest advantage is that it ensures that the fonts you see onscreen are the fonts you get on paper. Embedded TrueType takes this one step further by ensuring that the fonts used to create a document are the ones used to view, edit, and print it.

Note

Embedding can even use a compression technique to reduce the size of the font as much as possible, by limiting the characters to only those actually in the document. This capability is particularly useful when you're embedding fonts into Web pages.

Three options for font embedding are controlled by the font vendor. These options affect how you can use the font after you open a document containing them. The options are read-only embedding, read-write embedding, or no embedding at all.

Read-only is the most common type, allowing the person loading the document only to display or print the file, not to edit it. This option protects the font from being copied without the font manufacturer being paid for the product.

Obviously, with common fonts supplied by Microsoft with Windows 2000 Professional, copying fonts is not a problem, nor even a consideration. You wouldn't bother embedding TrueType fonts that any Windows 3.x, 9x, NT, or Windows 2000 users likely have in their systems. Those popular fonts are read-write fonts anyway and can be printed, viewed, and edited regardless of whether the fonts themselves are installed on the system.

Read-write fonts also allow you to save the fonts to disk for installation into the system and later use with future documents. For obvious reasons, this approach isn't really popular with folks who professionally develop fonts. But many freeware fonts are available online, most of which are read-write enabled.

In contrast, some font makers choose to prevent embedding of their fonts. If you try to save a document that contains such a font, your application creates a file with no font information in it other than the font name.

Tip #147

Obviously, to be sure a recipient will be able to display and edit a document, you should format your documents using only the popular fonts everyone has or has substitutions for. You can't go wrong with Times, Times New Roman, Courier, Courier New, Arial, Helvetica, Symbol, and the latest addition, Verdana.

EMBEDDED WEB FONTS

Microsoft and other vendors have created a means of embedding OpenType and TrueType fonts into Web pages for the same reasons listed earlier for normal documents. Web designers have felt hog-tied in their use of fonts, being restricted to basically two classes of fonts—serif and sans-serif—and a few styles such as bold, italic, underline, blinking (yuck), bullets, and colors.

A tool from Microsoft called *Web Embedding Fonts Tool*, or *WEFT*, lets Web authors create font objects that are linked to their Web pages. When an Internet Explorer user views the pages, he or she sees them displayed in the font style contained within the font object. Of course, the catch is that the user must be using Internet Explorer to view the page. (Surprised?)

A competing product from Bitstream (a premier maker of fonts) is called WebFont Maker. With this product, you can add fonts to your pages, knowing that both Netscape Communicator and Microsoft Internet Explorer will display your pages with the font formatting intact—a slightly more egalitarian approach.

Figure 10.7 shows an example of a Web page containing an embedded font. The page links to several font objects that are downloaded, cached, temporarily and privately installed, and then used to render the text on the page.

Figure 10.7
A screen capture of a Web page viewed in Internet Explorer.

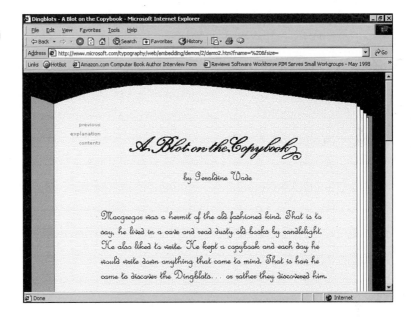

PART

II

CH

10

In the case of WEFT, if the viewer of the page doesn't have Internet Explorer, the results depend on which browser he or she is using and which fonts are installed in his or her system. The user either sees the text displayed in the second choice font as specified by the particular Web page or in his or her default font.

Due to the need for small files to keep page loading quick even over slow Internet connections, font embedding for the Web has to be efficient. Font objects created by WEFT differ from traditional font files; they are compressed and are usually subsetted (they contain only the characters used by a particular site or page). The embedded font file is therefore much smaller than ordinary TrueType fonts.

Tip #148

For more information about embedding fonts into Web pages, check the Web. A good site I've used is `http://shift.merriweb.com.au/fonts.html`. A Web search will also lead you to some controversial articles posted by font designers, decrying the industry's decision to allow font embedding, claiming it will dry up their sources of revenue due to font copying, just as some feel that MP3 files will threaten the sales of audio CDs.

Tip #149

> Another effective way to share documents with people who might not have the same fonts you have in your possession is to use .PDF formatted files. PDF, or PostScript Display Format, files are created by the Adobe Acrobat program. You've probably come across Acrobat-formatted files on the Web or as part of online documentation on CDs. PDF files can contain detailed formatting information, graphics, fonts, indexing, tables of contents, hot links, and other controls for creating customized, easily sharable documents with others. As long as the recipient of the document file (the PDF file) has the Acrobat Reader, he or she can view your document. The Acrobat Reader is easily and freely downloadable from the Internet. You have to use the full-blown version of Acrobat to create the files, however. If protection of files is an issue for you, you can also encode PDF files to prevent copying your text and/or graphics from the document, ensuring against copyright infringement.

BUILDING A FONT COLLECTION

Windows 2000 comes with a set of trustworthy TrueType fonts that will meet your needs for many occasions. Most folks get by just fine with Times New Roman, Courier New, and Arial, with maybe an occasional character from Symbol or WingDings. What else could you need? Why should you purchase or download freeware or shareware fonts? And how do you install them and choose which fonts to use in your documents? Let's look at these topics in order.

The prime reason to expand your collection of fonts is simply to make your documents look spiffier, express your message with more alacrity, or convey a specific mood such as formal, festive, or casual. Professional typographers know that readers, even unconsciously, are influenced by the fonts they spy on a page of text—whether a brochure, a business card, or even in an online document such as a technical document or Web page. The more fonts you have at your disposal, the greater likelihood you'll have one that fits the situation and conveys the message and mood you intend. In addition, looking beyond the stock Windows fonts helps you create an identifiable corporate style for your printed documents, as the typefaces you choose can become associated with you or your business in the minds of those who read your documents regularly.

After you've settled on the font format you're going to use, your next task is to decide how to acquire the fonts. Will you pay for them or download freebies over the Net? The number of typeface designs available for Windows totals in the thousands and is still growing. With that much variety, selecting a set of fonts that's right for you can be a daunting proposition.

CLASSES OF FONTS

Having a basic understanding of font classifications is a good idea before you start purchasing fonts and designing your own documents. (See Figure 10.8 for some examples that will help clarify the following discussion.)

The two primary categories of fonts are *serif* and *sans-serif* designs. As a look at Figure 10.8 will show you, serifs are the little embellishments that extend from the main strokes of the character. Serifs often are added to improve readability. As the name implies, sans-serif fonts lack these embellishments, making for a cleaner look. Sans-serif fonts tend to work well for headlines (most newspapers use them), whereas serif fonts are traditionally used for body text (this book is a good example). Combining one serif and one sans-serif font in this way will look good together, but two sans-serif or two serif fonts will clash.

Figure 10.8
Serif fonts are easily identified by the platforms or "feet" that rest on the baseline. Proportional fonts are generally better suited for professional documents.

The next major classification of fonts has to do with the spacing between characters. In *monospaced* fonts, every character occupies the same amount of horizontal line space. For example, *l* and *W* get the same amount of linear space. By contrast, *proportionally spaced* fonts give differing amounts of line space, depending on the character. A *W* gets more space than an *l* or an *i*. The body text in this book uses proportionally spaced fonts, making it easier to read. The advantage of using monospaced fonts is that they allow you to easily align columns of text or numbers when you're using a simple word processor such as Notepad or sending email. You can use the spacebar to align the items in the columns, as you would on a typewriter.

Tip #150

For easier alignment, numerals in most proportionally spaced fonts are monospaced. But in proportionally spaced fonts, you still have the problem with the spacebar. A press of the spacebar in a monospaced font advances the cursor one full block, just as any character does. In a proportional font, the spacebar moves the cursor only a small increment. So, it's still difficult to align rows of characters using the spacebar. If your word processing program has tab stops, setting them and then using the Tab key can help overcome this problem. Using tabs can be problematic when you're reading a document in a program other than the one it was created in, however, because not all programs translate tabs identically. Aligning columns in email, for example, is a dicey proposition at best because email programs use different fonts and often give users the option of choosing the display font on their own. It might or might not be a monospaced font. Using HTML-based (rich-text) email is one solution to this problem, though not all email client programs can handle it properly. See Chapter 13, "Email," for more details about HTML mail.

If you can't get columns of text or numbers to align in a document someone has sent you, see "Text Columns Out of Alignment" in the "Troubleshooting" section at the end of this chapter.

Two other categories of fonts (after headline and body text) are ornamental and nonalphabetic symbols. *Ornamental* (sometimes called *display)* fonts have limited application. They are often fun in the short term, or for a one-shot deal such as a poster or a gag. They often attract attention but are too highly stylized to be suitable for body text, and they can distract the readers' attention from your message. Windows doesn't come stocked with any decorative fonts. One that was popular a few years ago (and overused!) was Zapf Chancery. You should use ornamental fonts sparingly and only when you want to set a special mood.

Symbol or pi fonts contain special symbols such as musical notes, map symbols, or decorations instead of letters, numbers, and punctuation marks. Good examples are Symbol and WingDings.

→ To learn more about symbol and other nonkeyboard characters, **see** "Character Map," **p. 266.**

PROCURING FONTS

Due to increased interest in typography generated years ago by desktop publishing technology and now with the Web, the number of font designers and vendors has exploded. Fonts are included as part of even cheesy applications packages, as well as in the better word processing programs. And the Web is riddled with sites pushing everything from high-class fonts from respected foundries down to $2 fonts.

Many leading font vendors, including Bitstream, Monotype, SWFTE (now owned by Expert Software), SoftKey, and others, are producing TrueType font collections. Although you can find these collections in most software stores, Web downloads are easier. Quite charitably, Microsoft has a site that lists all the type foundries known to it, with descriptions and links. Check out this very helpful site:

`http://www.microsoft.com/typography/links/links.asp?type=foundries&part=1`

If that link dies for some reason, check back at the primary Microsoft fonts site and click around the following:

`http://www.microsoft.com/typography/default.asp`

Other sites you might find of interest are as follows:

- Agfa/Monotype's site:
  `http://www.monotype.com/`
- Bitstream:
  `http://www.bitstream.com`
- Adobe Systems:
  `www.adobe.com`
- And for some cheapie (and free) fonts, check the following:
  `www.buyfonts.com`
  `www.fontcafe.com/showcase/`

I've also seen numerous cheapie CD-ROMs that pack hundreds of TrueType fonts on them in several computer stores. For example, Walnut Creek CD-ROM offers 2000 TrueType fonts for $39.95. To locate it, check the following:

www.cdrom.com

> **Note**
>
> Although shareware and freeware TrueType fonts are plentiful, be aware that not all TrueType fonts have sophisticated hinting built in. Therefore, they might not look as good as fonts from the more respectable font foundries. Some reports from users indicate that funky font files can make your system freak out a bit. In general, though, even the free TrueType (OpenType) fonts will look very good, and you'll be hard pressed to notice the difference.

Expert Font Sets

Many of the cheapie fonts you'll come across will work okay for general letter writing, garage-sale posters, and greeting cards. When you want hardcore professional typesetting, though, you'll want a professional typeface that contains the following key elements:

- Small caps—These smaller than normal capital letters are a complete set of uppercase letters that look better for corporate names and the like. An example would be QUE BOOKS.

- Ligatures—In some letter combinations beginning with the letter *f*, the *f* touches the subsequent letters (for example, *fi*). Ligatures are replacements for these unsightly combinations.

- Old-fashioned numerals—Number characters in most fonts look kind of funky. They are designed to perform nicely in tables, spreadsheets, and so forth, but they don't have a polished look that conveys professionalism. Numbers in nifty typefaces actually have descenders just like lowercase letters such as *y* and *g* do. They are also proportionally spaced rather than monospaced.

A FEW FONT USAGE TIPS

Choosing the correct fonts for a particular job is something that can take a great deal of experimentation. Numerous tomes are devoted to the subject of typography and graphic design, so I'll leave at least the esoterica to the experts and give you only a few pointers.

If you have an eye for design, use it and trust it. Time-tested combinations of fonts tend to work well together and form the backbone of most typographic designs. If you analyze several technical computer books, for example, you'll find pretty much the same kinds of fonts being used. One solution is to purchase a set of fonts from a well-respected font company such as Adobe Systems and Monotype. Font sets from respected vendors often come with several fonts chosen for a specific type of document, along with design tips for using the fonts appropriately.

Regardless of how you acquire your fonts or even use the ones supplied with Windows 2000 Professional, you should use some care when designing your documents. "Less is more," as the old saying goes. Attractive fonts by themselves aren't enough to win the day because the primary purpose of a font is to convey the meaning in your text.

Whitespace on a page is important to not overwhelm the reader. One important area of whitespace is the space between lines, which is called *leading* (as in the element lead, which the letters in a letter press were made of in olden days). With body text, the leading between two lines of text should be about 20 percent greater than the size of the font. With headlines, the leading should be about the same as the font size.

Another area of whitespace is margins. You should make your margins generous. Don't crowd text closely to the edge of the paper, and allow plenty of space between columns as well.

Don't give in to font mania. You might have a snazzy collection of fonts, but don't mix too many fonts in the same document. Use one font for the main body of your text and a larger, bold version of the same font for headlines. You can get away with using a third font for sidebar text, but you'll run the risk of clashing font designs.

If you use two or more font sizes, be sure they contrast adequately. If your main text is in 12-point Times New Roman, use at least 14-point type for the subheadings.

Avoid using underlining and capitalization on large areas of text. Underlining is now confused with Web links, for one thing, and uppercase looks like you're SHOUTING and is difficult to read. Use italics with discretion, typically for single words only. It, too, is hard to read in long passages.

MANAGING A SYSTEM'S FONT COLLECTION

Windows 2000's font management works the same way as Windows 9x's and NT4's does. In short, you can perform several simple techniques from the Control Panel's Fonts applet (or the \Windows\Fonts directory in Explorer) that let you do the following:

- Add new fonts to the system
- Remove unnecessary fonts, freeing disk space
- View fonts onscreen or print out samples of each font you have
- Display groups of fonts that are similar in style

ADDING FONTS

Some font sets come with an installer. In that case, you can just run it as instructed. The fonts are dumped into the fonts directory, and the system adds them to the Font Registry, whereupon they can be used from your applications. If no installation program came with your fonts, or if you want to add some fonts to your system that you downloaded from the Internet or otherwise acquired, just follow these steps:

1. Open the Control Panel, and run the Fonts control applet. The resulting folder window appears, looking

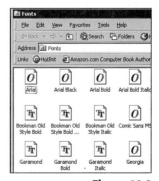

Figure 10.9

much like any other folder. Figure 10.9 shows an example. All fonts currently installed in the system appear in this folder, with each font style being a separate file. The TrueType fonts have the TT icon, OpenType fonts have an O icon, and bitmapped or vector fonts have an A icon. Using the buttons on the toolbar or the View menu, you can alter the form of the display.

Tip #151	Some printer-font installation programs copy font files to another folder, yet those fonts still appear in the font picklist in your applications. In that case, the fonts aren't displayed in the Fonts folder, though they still work.

If you elect to turn on Details view in this folder, you can see that bitmapped and vector fonts are stored on disk in files with the extension .FON; TrueType and OpenType font files have the extension .TTF.

2. Choose File, Install New Font. The Add Fonts dialog then appears. Browse to the location of the font files you want to install. Use the Network button if the files are across the LAN. It runs the Map Network Drive Wizard. After you target the source folder, all the fonts in that location are listed in the dialog box.

3. Select the fonts you want to install. Note that if you want an entire font family, you have to select all similarly named files. In Figure 10.10, I'm installing all the Book Antiqua fonts. If you try to install a font that's already in your system, the installer won't let you, so don't worry about accidentally loading one you already have.

Figure 10.10
Choosing the font files to install.

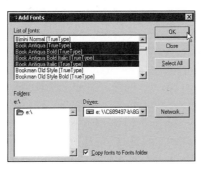

Tip #152	Just as in Explorer, you Shift+click to select a range or Ctrl+click to select individual non-contiguous fonts.

4. Choose whether you want the font files copied into the Fonts folder as part of the installation process. They work either way. Copying into the Fonts folder keeps things tidier, though it does make a copy of the file, using up more disk space. I like to copy them into the Fonts folder so that I know where all my fonts are. If you use this approach, you can later erase any duplicate source files to save disk space. (Fonts range from about 80 to 400KB each, averaging about 200KB.) If you choose not to copy the files, shortcut icons appear in your Fonts folder instead of normal font icons.

PART

II

CH

10

Tip #153

Don't turn off the Copy check box unless you know that the source files will be available when you want to use the font. If the source files are on a CD-ROM, a floppy, or a workstation on the LAN, you'll probably be better off if you copy them onto the local hard disk.

5. Click OK to finalize the operation. After the installation process is complete, all newly added fonts are added to your font list and are visible in Windows applications that offer font selection.

Tip #154

You can copy fonts into the system by dragging the font files into the Fonts folder. This one-step process is quick and dirty. You don't have options doing it this way, though; by default, fonts are copied into the Fonts folder.

DISPLAYING AND PRINTING FONT EXAMPLES

You can easily acquire a large selection of fonts, thus easily forgetting what you have on hand. Several utility programs are available to help you keep track of fonts or show a little example of them in font selection lists within applications and such. Check the Web for such programs. (Try www.download.com and choose Utilities and then Fonts. You'll be amazed at the number of font utilities. Most NT-compatible ones will work on Windows 2000 Professional.)

The Fonts folder has a few tricks of its own to make font management a bit easier. For starters, you can view and/or print the characters in any font easily by following these steps:

1. Open the Fonts folder.
2. Double-click any icon in the folder. The font then opens in the font viewer. In Figure 10.11, I've displayed a font called Jokerman and maximized the window.
3. If you need printouts, just right-click a font and choose Print, or open the font as per above and click the Print button. To print multiple fonts in one fell swoop, select them first, and then choose File, Print. You get a one-page printout for each font.

Tip #155

The font viewer displays a font's character set regardless of the location of the font. So, if you want to check out the font's look before installing it, just open the floppy disk or other folder containing the font, and double-click it.

FONT VIEWING OPTIONS

As I mentioned earlier, each font style (normal, bold, italic, and bold italic) is stored in its own file. All these files can clutter the display when you're just poking around the Fonts folder to see what you have installed. You can choose a viewing option to cut down on the clutter by showing only one icon per font family instead of four. Just choose View, Hide Variations.

Figure 10.11
Double-clicking a font in the Fonts folder displays its characters in a window. Numbers in the left margin indicate point size for each line of the display. Notice the copyright information.

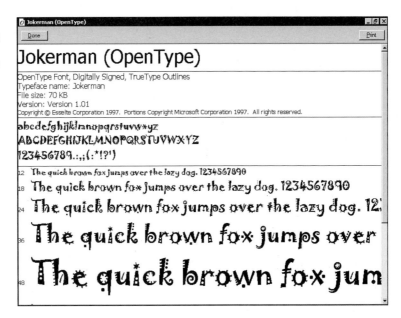

To return the view to showing all font files listed separately, choose the command again to toggle the check mark off in the menu.

VIEWING FONTS BY SIMILARITIES

TrueType and OpenType fonts often contain within them *Panose* information, which helps the operating system determine how to substitute fonts for one another when needed. Included in a font's Panose information are tidbits such as whether it is a serif or sans-serif font. The font listing can be sorted according to Panose information, relative to a given font. For example, you could list the fonts that are similar in look to, say, Times, in case you're looking for an interesting serif font that everyone hasn't seen already.

To use this feature, just choose View, List Fonts by Similarity, or click the related toolbar button. Then, from the drop-down list, choose the font you want to compare to. The font must be one endowed with Panose information; otherwise, Windows 2000 Professional won't have a reference point. Figure 10.12, for example, shows a listing comparing Arial Italic to my other fonts.

All bitmapped and vector fonts, some older TrueType fonts, and pi fonts such as WingDings and Symbol don't have Panose information stored in them. The Fonts folder simply displays No Panose information available next to the font in this case.

Figure 10.12
Font listing by similarity to Arial Italic. Notice the three categories of similarity: Very similar, Fairly similar, and Not similar.

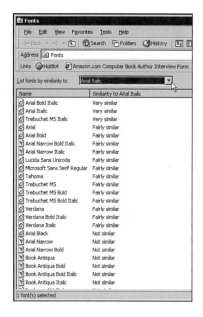

HIDDEN SYSTEM FONTS

Some fonts are normally hidden because they are required by the system. If a user accidentally deleted them, the system wouldn't work. For example, dialog boxes wouldn't have text in them. Unless you turn on viewing of hidden files via the Folder options in an Explorer window, you won't see these fonts. If you do turn on viewing of hidden files and then view the Fonts folder in Details view, you'll see an H in the Attributes column. Figure 10.13 shows an example of hidden files in the Fonts display. Make sure not to delete or move these files.

→ File viewing options are covered in "Folder Display Options," **p. 220**.

Tip #156

Programs that are multilingual-aware automatically use a font that contains multiple character sets. If you are using a program that is not multilingual-aware, such as Notepad, the font might appear as black boxes or lines. To make the text appear correctly, you might need to manually select a font that contains multiple character sets. Both Tahoma and Microsoft Sans Serif font support multiple character sets.

REMOVING FONTS

Fonts consume space on your hard disk. A typical TrueType font consumes between 50 and 200KB of disk space. If you're a font monger, you could easily chew up a gigabyte or two with fonts you end up never using. You can keep them online on CDs if you're a pro and need them. In that case, install them with the Copy to Fonts Folder option cleared; then insert the CD when the fonts are needed. Or spread fonts across the network, and rely on network drives for the fonts. Just make sure the network font server is available and mapped properly to the computer doing the document creation and/or printing.

Figure 10.13
If hidden files can be viewed via your system settings, you'll see the system files that should be protected. They are all bitmapped fonts used primarily for screen display.

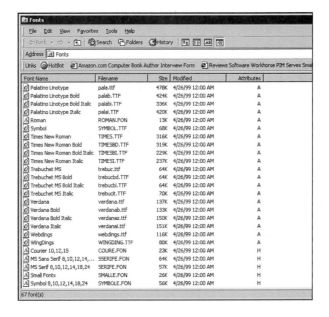

PART

II

CH

10

Tip #157 | A little-known fact is that even if an italic or bold font has been removed, Windows can still emulate it on-the-fly. It won't look as good as the real thing, but it will work.

If you get on a spring-cleaning jag and decide to remove some fonts, follow these steps:

1. Open the Fonts folder.
2. To remove an entire font family (normal, Bold, Italic, and Bold Italic), turn on the View, Hide Variations setting. If you want to remove individual styles, turn off this setting so you can see them.
3. Select the font or fonts you want to remove.
4. Press the Del key; choose File, Delete; or right-click one of the selected fonts and choose Delete.
5. When a dialog box asks you to confirm the removal, choose the Yes button. The font is then moved to the Recycle Bin.

Tip #158 | You can also drag a font file to another folder, but the default is for that operation to create a copy of the font and not remove it from your arsenal of system fonts. If your aim is to organize your seldom-used fonts into folders, the easiest way would be to right-click and drag them into the new folders, and then choose Move from the resulting context menu. Finally, you can install them as necessary, with the Copy to Fonts Folder option cleared.

TROUBLESHOOTING

FOREIGN-LANGUAGE FONTS DON'T APPEAR

When I'm running a specific program, I can't see the correct foreign-language fonts in dialog boxes, display menus, and within my documents.

You might have this problem if the program you are using doesn't understand how to use Unicode fonts. Recall that Unicode fonts are extended fonts that have support for multiple languages built into them. To work around this problem, you can try the following procedure:

1. Open Control Panel, Regional Options
2. On the General tab, click Set Default.
3. Under Select the Appropriate Locale, select the language version of non-Unicode programs that you want to use.

Note that only non-Unicode programs are affected by alterations to the system locale, and you might be prevented from altering the locale setting if you don't have administrative privileges or if the network policy settings conflict.

TEXT COLUMNS OUT OF ALIGNMENT

Sometimes when I read email or another document that contains columns of text or numbers, they are out of alignment.

You can have this problem if the document was formatted with a monospaced font and you're viewing it in a proportionally spaced font. Select the text in question, and change the font to Courier, Courier New, or some other monospaced font. If your program doesn't allow altering the font of selected text, it might allow you to change the font of all displayed text. Email programs often fall into this category. Look for the relevant option setting within the application. For example, in Outlook Express, you choose Tools, Options, Read, Fonts.

DOCUMENT FROM ANOTHER USER IS DISPLAYED IMPROPERLY

I received a complex document that doesn't look right at all. I suspect something is wrong. The text is readable, but I suspect either the author of the document must have had too many drinks or some technical glitch must have happened.

This problem is yet another symptom of the document's font or fonts not being installed in the system that's displaying it. The document probably looks just fine on the computer that its author was using. If you're not going to be printing it or proofing it for layout but care only about the textual content, don't worry about it. If you need to print the document or proof it for line breaks, layout, page arrangement, and so forth, it's imperative that you have the document's font or fonts on your computer. Have the author send you the fonts, or purchase them if they are not free. Then install them as explained in this chapter. Finally, reopen the document.

Note that even if the correct fonts are not available in the system, most layout programs indicate what they are *supposed* to be. To find out, click any text in question, and look at the program's toolbar. For example, Microsoft Word indicates in the Standard toolbar the name of the font in which the text is formatted. That's the font you're going to need to have in your system to see the text displayed properly.

Dialog Box Fonts Are Unreadable

Fonts in all my dialog boxes look very weird or unreadable.

You can have this problem for a couple of reasons. First, ensure that the regional settings are correct for your area (see "Document from Another User Is Displayed Improperly"). Next, choose Control Panel, Display, Appearance and click Message Text. Look to see what font size you have chosen for dialog box messages, and change it if necessary.

Dialog boxes that programs display can also get weird if you have removed necessary system fonts such as MS Sans Serif and MS Serif. Check the Fonts folder to see that they are available. Replace them from another system if necessary.

Icon Fonts Too Large or Small

My icon fonts are too small (or too large).

If your screen fonts (such as text under icons on the desktop or in Explorer windows) are the wrong size, you can change the system fonts to another size. Choose Control Panel, Display Properties, Settings, General, and look for the fonts setting. Then choose another size. You might have to reboot.

Tips from the Windows Pros: Using the Private Character Editor

Tired of the same old letters, numbers, and symbols? Want to create your own language? Or more seriously, do you have a need to design your own font modifications? Professional design tools are available for doing so, of course, and you can pay some bucks for them if you're a professional font designer. Fontographer is a reasonably good example of such a commercially available tool (do a Web search if you're really interested). But for many users who might need special characters or company logos, or lexicographers or translators who might need to create their own fonts, the Private Character Editor (PCE) that comes with Windows 2000 does the basics.

Using Private Character Editor, you can create up to 6,400 unique characters (such as special letters and logos) for use in your font library. PCE contains basic tools for creating and editing characters, along with more advanced options. After you have created your own characters, anyone using the computer they are installed on can insert the characters into most documents just as easily as inserting special symbols such as the © symbol.

Using a drawing program much like Paint, you can create your own characters and store them in the "private" character area of any Unicode font. As discussed earlier, Unicode fonts have private areas in them, which are essentially empty key codes for storing personalized characters.

To open Private Character Editor, choose Start, Run, and then type eudcedit. The program appears, as shown in Figure 10.14.

Figure 10.14
Use Private Character Editor to create and save your own characters.

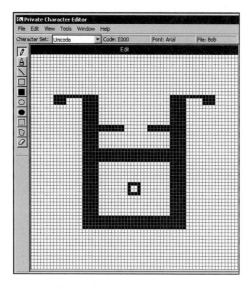

You can draw each character yourself from scratch, or you can start by copying a character from another font. In either case, after you have a few characters drawn up, you then can link them either to all the Unicode fonts in your system or to a specific one. Then the private areas of those fonts are altered, and now contain your personal font character outlines. You can insert them by using the Character Map application described earlier in this chapter.

See the Help information in the Private Character Editor for more information on the details of usage.

WINDOWS 2000 AND THE INTERNET

CHAPTER **11**

INTERNET AND TCP/IP CONNECTION OPTIONS

In this chapter

GOING WORLD WIDE

You're itching to start selling all that stuff in your attic on eBay, aren't you? (If you don't know what eBay is, where have you *been* for the past few years?) Well, first things first…you must make your connection with the Internet before you can connect your debris with all those collectors out there.

In this chapter, you will find information about choosing an Internet service provider (ISP), making the connection through a modem or other link, and installing and configuring your system.

This chapter tells how to connect a single computer to the Internet. You can take one of several routes:

- If your computer is part of an existing local area network (LAN) with Internet access, you can skip this chapter entirely because Internet access will come along as part of your Windows 2000 installation. In fact, if you are part of a corporate LAN, it is probably a violation of your company's security policy to establish your own independent connection. (If it's not, it should be!)

- If you are setting up a LAN for a workgroup, you might want to provide Internet access to the entire LAN through one connection. You should skip ahead to Chapter 24, "Connecting Your LAN to the Internet," and decide whether you want to connect your LAN. You can use the instructions in this chapter to set up the one connection; Chapter 24 will tell you how to share it with the rest of your workgroup.

- If want to use your existing ISP account and connection technology, you can skip the introductory sections and go right down to "Installing a Modem in Windows 2000."

- If you need to make a clean start with the Internet, read on!

WHAT IS THE INTERNET, ANYWAY?

If you have, perhaps, been stranded on a desert island for the last five years or so: The Internet is the global network of computers, an amazing worldwide phenomenon. To appreciate what the Internet has become, you might appreciate a bit of historical background.

In the 1960s, the United States Department of Defense Advanced Research Project Agency commissioned the development of a network technology that could endure missing links, lost data, and bad connections yet still function. This network, called the ARPAnet, was installed between a few major defense contractors, universities, and government agencies. The ARPAnet used special-purpose network routing computers and cross-country leased data lines, and was the origin of the *Transmission Control Protocol/Internet Protocol (TCP/IP)* used on the Internet today.

Academic and corporate researchers worked together, in a largely communal effort, to develop software to take advantage of this network. Email came first, followed in the mid 1970s with file transfer and remote terminal access, as the network was used to share access to the world's few supercomputers. Next came discussion forums called *newsgroups*. In 1981, 213 computers were connected by this network.

As the usefulness of email became apparent, more and more universities and companies clamored to join the growing network. The TCP/IP protocol was implemented on the newly affordable Ethernet network technology, to connect computers at a fraction of the former cost. The UNIX operating system was given to universities free of charge by AT&T Bell Laboratories, and tens of thousands of graduate students worldwide, across countless disciplines, began using this powerful operating system with the emerging Internet to develop communication systems barely imaginable only a few years before. For example, a particle accelerator in Switzerland could be controlled by physicists in Berkeley; astronomers in Egypt could see through a telescope in Hawaii. By 1989, the network had grown to 80,000 computers.

In 1990, the military gave the network to the National Science Foundation (NSF), and it was renamed the Internet. It was commonly accepted then that 1200 bits per second (bps) was plenty fast for a telephone data connection by modem, and 9600 bps was the theoretical limit.

Meanwhile, Tim Berners-Lee, a member of a high-energy physics research group in Switzerland, developed a computer publishing system that let authors include references from one document to another, forming a sort of "web" of information. This concept had been around for more than 25 years (if you're interested, search the Web for references to Theodor Nelson and the Xanadu project), but this technology really worked, and more importantly, it was public, free, and ran over the Internet. Berners-Lee called his document communication technology the *Hypertext Transfer Protocol (HTTP)*, but it soon became known as the *World Wide Web*.

As the tools for network connectivity matured, interest in the Internet grew. By January 1992, nearly a million computers were on the Internet. Modem speeds reached 9600, 12,000, even 14,400 bits per second by the mid-nineties. Networking over the telephone became practical.

In 1993, 60 "Web servers" were in use worldwide. The system was functional, but it was entirely text-based and not really interesting. Then something completely unforeseen happened; graduate students at the University of Illinois added a graphical user interface to the original Web-navigating software and called their program Mosaic. The result was breathtaking. Mosaic tied computers, networks, information, and typography together in a way that wasn't new, but it was usable in a way computers had never been. The rest you probably know: Heads snapped. Companies flocked to the new technology. Stock prices rose! And somehow within a year or two, Internet service providers had sprung up nearly everywhere, selling access to the Internet by modem for just dollars a month.

By 1994, counting Internet-connected computers was no longer possible, but about 7 million people used the Internet. In 1996, that number rose to 31 million. Microsoft, late to recognize the importance of the Internet, jumped on the bandwagon and began to incorporate Mosaic's features into its operating systems.

PART

III

CH

11

By the year 2000, approximately 300 million people worldwide will have access to the Internet. For about the cost of a movie per week, nearly any computer in any home or office can be connected to the rest of the world at speeds of 56,000 to 10 million bits per second. Libraries, cafés, airports, and bookstores now sport Internet terminals as required equipment. There's even an Internet café in Katmandu, Nepal. Sipping tea there right now, someone is probably buying this book online.

What does it all mean? It means that the "analog age"—which brought the record player, the telephone, the radio, and television—is over, and the digital age has truly arrived. This global digital network will soon be the single conduit for all our communication and entertainment needs.

WHAT KIND OF CONNECTION?

Not long ago, you had one choice to make for your Internet connection: which brand of modem to buy. Now, options abound, and you can choose among several technologies, speeds, and types of Internet service providers. Your choice of a way to connect your computer to the Internet involves a trade-off between performance and cost; more money gets you a faster link. However, the balance points are changing rapidly.

CONNECTION TECHNOLOGIES

A huge technology shift is taking place, as high-speed digital connection services are being deployed worldwide. The telephone system as you know it will undergo a dramatic change in the next decade. It's likely that per-minute and distance-rated telephone charges will disappear entirely, and you'll pay a flat rate for data connectivity over which you can talk, send email, shop, or browse the Web.

Digital is in, analog is out, and all the players in the telecommunications industry are fighting to be first to get a multimegabit data connection into your home. They hope you'll stay with them as things change in the coming years.

These changes are occurring now, but gradually and only in certain locations. So, you'll have to check availability in your area for both the new and old technologies, as well as evaluate your needs for speed, portability, and quality of customer service. Telephone modems will eventually become obsolete, but this process will take awhile.

Let's take a look at the basic Internet connection technologies appropriate for an individual user.

ANALOG MODEM

Standard, tried-and-true dial-up modem service requires only a telephone line and a modem in your computer. The connection is made when your computer dials a local access number provided by your ISP. ISPs typically have local numbers for every community they serve, whether they're regional or nationwide providers. Costs vary between $15 and $25 per month, so it pays to shop around. Dial-up service is available just about everywhere in the world.

Modems transmit data at a top speed of 33Kbps and can receive data at up to 56Kbps from a suitably equipped Internet service provider. In real life, you will usually obtain download speeds of 40 to 50Kbps. This speed is adequate for general Web surfing—that is, reading text and viewing pictures. You will find it woefully inadequate for viewing video or for voice communication, however, despite any software vendor's claims to the contrary (that is, unless you consider repeatedly shouting "Hello? Hello? Did you hear that?" to be communication).

56K—More or Less

Everyone thought analog modem speeds had topped out at 33.6Kbps. You see, all telephone signals are turned into digital signals—streams of numbers—for transmission between telephone company switching centers. Because the signals are sampled at a fixed rate, the frequencies the telephone system can transmit are limited: Signals varying too quickly simply aren't sampled often enough to notice the changes, so very high-frequency signals are simply lost. The need to carefully sample the signal sent by your modem limits the rate at which you can send data. To get a good representation, they need at least two or three samples per cycle of an incoming signal. That's the basic reason for the limit in modem transfer speeds. It turns out that they can't clearly track signal changes representing much more than 33 thousand bits per second.

Now, most ISPs connect to the telephone company through digital telephone lines, and their modems work directly with the stream of numbers sent by the telephone switch. They send a stream of numbers back to the telephone company, and only at your telephone central office does an analog signal get reconstituted and sent to your modem.

This system of delivery gave some modem engineers a very clever idea. They realized that in the reverse direction, from the ISP to you, no sampling operation takes place. Whatever stream of numbers they send back is simply converted into an analog signal and sent to your modem. Because they didn't have to worry about sending a signal that varies slowly enough that it could be sampled two or three times per waveform, they could send a faster-varying signal to you than you can send to them, and thus more bits per second—56,000, to be precise. The concept worked, and it upped download speeds by almost 70 percent. When various manufacturers' competing technical specifications were straightened out, the 56K modem became the standard for ISP connections.

The story doesn't end there, however. Just to show that technology is no match for bureaucracy, the Federal Communications Commission set limits on the amount of "signal energy" that a telephone line can legally carry. A wildly varying 56Kbps signal crosses their line, so for purely legal reasons, "56K" modems are actually limited to 53.3Kbps.

These 56K modems must test the conditions of the telephone line every time they connect and determine the maximum speed that the connection will support. (If you have one, you're familiar with the boingy "sonar" sound it makes when connecting; that's the sound of the modem testing the current line conditions.) In real life, 56K modems rarely connect at even 50Kbps, so the FCC's limit isn't all that baneful.

One other thing I should point out: Remember that these modems are really 33.6Kbps modems, and the higher speed applies only to receiving data from a special-purpose digitally connected modem, the expensive sort that ISPs buy. If you dial up another, regular 56K modem, 33.6K is the limit in both directions.

You'll see the acronym *PPP* associated with Dial-Up Internet service. The *Point-to-Point Protocol* is a standardized way for computers and ISP network equipment to communicate the details of a temporary connection. The PPP system handles the details of communicating your username and password to the ISP, agreeing on a temporary Internet Protocol address for your computer, and other such management details.

ISDN

Integrated Services Digital Network (ISDN) was supposed to have completely replaced the analog telephone network by now. ISDN service can carry two independent conversations over one standard telephone wire pair and can carry voice or data on either or both connections. ISDN service is actually a different type of telephony; you can't plug ordinary telephones into an ISDN line. Despite many interesting features, ISDN voice service hasn't caught on well in the United States because it's more expensive than standard telephone service, and the telephones cost up to $300 each. ISDN modems for computers cost in the neighborhood of $200 to $300 and can carry data at 64 or 128Kbps, depending on whether you use one or two of its channels to connect to your ISP. Until recently, that was pretty impressive. ISDN had the well-deserved reputation of being difficult to order, install, make work, and use. It's now just about effortless, thanks to improved Windows software, better hardware, and more concern on the part of telephone companies (just in time for it to become obsolete).

ISDN service is available in much of North America and Europe (it's quite popular in England and Germany), but coverage is limited in rural areas because ISDN signals can travel only a limited distance from the telephone company switching office.

DSL

Digital Subscriber Loop (DSL) service is a new technology that sends a high-speed digital data signal over the same wires used by your standard telephone line, while that line is simultaneously used for standard telephone service. This means that you can get DSL service installed without adding an extra telephone line. DSL service can also be set up so that the data rates are different coming from and going to the Internet. This setup saves you money, and because most Web surfing involves sending out a very small request and receiving a relatively large amount of data back, it's fine if the upload speed is lower than the download speed. This type of service is called *asymmetric*, and what is amazing is that its pricing is comparable to standard analog modem service, with data rates up to 30 times faster!

Depending on the mix of speeds, DSL gets various names—Symmetric, Asymmetric, High-Speed, and ISDN—so you'll see the acronyms *SDSL*, *ADSL*, *HDSL*, and *IDSL* or the collective *xDSL*. As far as I'm concerned these distinctions are unimportant, so I just call it DSL.

The telcos (that's short for telephone companies) have a strong interest in DSL for two reasons: One, they're about to enter a to-the-death battle with cable TV companies to compete for your local telephone service; and two, hours-long modem calls tie up their equipment, which was designed and provisioned for short-term voice calls. On the other hand, they are terrified that DSL will eat into their extremely lucrative high-speed, dedicated data services like frame relay, and it will. They've realized that there's no way out, though, so the best thing is to do the damage themselves.

DSL service is available in many major metropolitan areas but will be deployed nationwide soon. DSL is even more restricted than ISDN by distance from the telephone company office, and the maximum available speed falls sharply when the distance is more than half a mile. This restriction may prohibit DSL from ever making it into rural areas.

CABLE MODEM

Cable modem Internet service is provided by your local television cable service, which sends high-speed data signals out through the same distribution system it uses to carry high-quality TV signals. Cable Internet service comes in two flavors: bidirectional and unidirectional. With *bidirectional* service, data travels to and from your computer via the TV cable. In *unidirectional* service, the cable system can only carry data signals *to* you, so you must establish a standard dial-up modem connection to carry data from you to the Internet. This service is awkward, but it does give you a much higher download speed (Internet to you) than the dial-up connection could provide alone.

Cable modem service has none of the distance limitations of ISDN or DSL. The service is spreading slowly because it costs companies quite a bit to make their existing cable systems capable of carrying the digital signal. Still, they want to use their wires to provide standard telephone service as well, and eventually advanced services such as movies-on-demand, so they have a big incentive to get cable Internet service online and get you hooked on it so that you're more inclined to purchase future services.

One criticism of cable service is that data speeds tend to drop during high-use times such as the early evening. It's the fault of the technology. High-speed optical fiber connects a "hub" in each neighborhood, where the data is piped into the cable wires. Each neighborhood shares one fixed amount of bandwidth, typically 10Mbps. If you're the only one downloading at a given moment, you might see speeds up to the full 10Mbps (assuming you're downloading from a server with that fast a connection). But if many people are downloading simultaneously, the data rate each individual sees can drop well below DSL speeds. This situation has generated quite a bit of distress, and some customers have even sued their cable service providers, but I expect this situation to improve as profits are plowed back into improving the technology. (They will plow their profits back into the technology, won't they?)

Note You can find a quirky and fascinating Web site devoted to high-speed Internet access, especially via cable, at http://www.teleport.com/~samc/cable1.html.

SATELLITE SERVICE (DIRECPC)

Satellite service is similar to unidirectional cable modem service, in that the link from you to the Internet is made by a standard dial-up connection. But the similarity ends there: The download connection, from the Internet to you, comes via satellite, through a small dish and receiver you bolt to your roof or the side of your house. Satellite service was quite expensive until recently, when competition from cable and DSL forced prices down. Satellite's big advantage is that it's available anywhere in the continental U.S. with a view of the sky. The disadvantage is that installation requires both a rocket scientist and a carpenter, the service plans all are based on limited hourly usage, and the system suffers from the same slowdowns that affect cable service. Check out www.direcpc.com.

WIRELESS

In some major metropolitan areas, wireless Internet service is available through a small radio transmitter/receiver. They're small enough to attach to the lid of a laptop computer with velcro. Data transfer rates are typically in the 33Kbps range but improving. Service is limited to a few cities. If you live in a covered area, and surfing the Net while sitting in the park under a tree appeals to you, you should investigate wireless connectivity. Visit www.ricochet.net for an example.

Right now, it's an emerging technology, but by 2005, I wouldn't be surprised if it moves to the top of my list of choices. The cellular telephone companies are going to push it in a big way.

Tip #159	If you're considering satellite or wireless service, be sure the providers offer support for Windows 2000. This service might take a long while to become available.

CHOOSING A TECHNOLOGY

The following are some points to consider in making a choice:

- How many hours per month will you spend online? Some ISPs offer unlimited usage, whereas others have a limited number of hours per month included in the base price. These providers might offer several plans with different monthly allowances.

- What will the telephone charges be, if any, for that time? Even if your ISP is local, in some regions even local telephone calls carry a per-minute charge, and this rate can differ between residential and business service.

- Do you travel and need national access to your Internet account? Some ISPs provide local numbers nationwide, others provide toll-free access for an additional charge, and still others have no wide-area access, so you would have to pay for a long-distance call. Your travel patterns will dictate which approach makes the most sense.

- How much speed do you need or want? (If you're sharing your Internet connection, see Chapter 21, "Instant Networking," for more discussion of this topic.) Do you routinely transfer large files over the Net, or do you want to attempt to use voice- or videoconferencing? In either case, you'll want the fastest connection possible. If you just want to browse the Web, an analog modem might be fine.

- Do you want to host a Web site on your own computer rather than an ISP's? Hosting a Web site requires a dedicated, always-on connection.

- What technologies are available in your area, and which will be deployed in the near future?

- How much are you willing to spend to buy new equipment—for example, an ISDN or xDSL modem? These modems typically cost three or four times what an analog modem costs, so you might not want to buy one just to replace it a few months later with a different type.

→ For more information on ISDN, xDSL, and cable modem service, **see** Chapter 24, "Connecting Your LAN to the Internet." That chapter describes these technologies with a focus on using them to connect a LAN to the Internet, but you still might find the information helpful.

- Finally, if have Internet access on your LAN at work, see whether your company can provide you with dial-up or dedicated Internet access at home. If you want to telecommute, it's in their best interest to give you a good, fast, secure connection.

Keep these questions in mind as you evaluate your connection options.

You will eventually have to make a decision somehow, and price is going to be one big factor. I hate to show even approximate dollar amounts here because competition between the technologies is having a big effect on rates and options. For example, where DSL or cable modem service are available, some telephone companies are slashing prices for ISDN service. But here goes anyway, just to give you a general idea of what you have to choose from. Table 11.1 summarizes the costs and speeds for different ways for a single computer user to access the Internet. These prices show typical prices after applying discounts and special offers.

PART
III

CH
11

TABLE 11.1 INTERNET CONNECTION OPTIONS FOR THE INDIVIDUAL USER

Method	Approximate Cost, $ per month	Approximate Setup and Equipment Cost	Time Limits in hours	Availability	Download Speed
Analog Modem	$15 to 25	$150	10 to unlimited	Worldwide	33 to 56Kbps
ISDN	40 plus ISDN toll charges	300	10 to unlimited	Limited, unlikely to expand	64 to 128Kbps
DSL	50 and up	100	Unlimited	Limited but growing	312Kbps to 6Mbps
Cable Modem	40	50	Unlimited	Limited but growing	1 to 10Mbps
Satellite	30 and up	350	25 and up	48 states	400Kbps

(To give you a relative feeling of what the numbers mean in the Download Speed column, I might just as well have written: Modem: "Yawn." ISDN: "Hmmm." DSL, cable, and satellite: "WOW!")

When you factor in telephone costs, ISP fees, and the value of your own time waiting for dialing and downloads, you might find some surprising results. In California, for example, businesses pay nearly $18 per month per telephone line plus one cent per minute even for local calls. With telephone charges factored in, DSL service at $50 per month ends up costing the same as 20 hours of basic analog dial-up service, and it's about 30 times faster.

Finally, remember that you have three costs to factor in:

- The cost of hardware required to make the connection
- The cost of installation and setup
- The monthly cost for telecommunications and Internet service

Try to estimate how long you'll keep the service, and amortize the startup and equipment costs over that time frame when comparing technologies.

OTHER CONSIDERATIONS

That's the overview of the technologies. Now, besides cost, you need to consider some other factors before making a decision.

For Internet access at home or work:

- Is DSL or bidirectional cable service available in your area? Get one of them if you can. You won't regret it. You can call your cable TV company, telephone company, and local ISPs to find out whether these services are available. You can also check www.covad.com, www.northpoint.net, and www.athome.net.

Tip #160

These services are particularly well suited for connecting a group of computers, either directly or via Internet connection sharing. You'll learn about this topic in Chapter 24.

- If DSL and cable aren't available, and you still crave serious speed, consider satellite or ISDN service.
- There's nothing wrong with using a modem. (And when I was your age, I had to walk three miles through the snow to get to school.)

FACTORING IN TRAVEL

You must remember that ISDN, DSL, and cable service are wired into place when you install them, so they don't provide for access when you travel or roam about town. However, some DSL, cable, and ISDN providers include a standard modem dial-up account at no extra charge just to compensate for this factor.

If you want Internet connectivity when you travel, you have three basic choices:

- For occasional or personal travel, you can forgo national access. Just find an Internet cafe or get Internet access at your hotel.

- If you want to use your own computer for occasional travel, you can always place a long-distance call to your own ISP. Subtract the cost from the money you might save using a less expensive local ISP versus the higher prices of a national ISP to see which solution would be best.

- If you travel frequently, choose a national ISP with local access numbers in the places you visit frequently or toll-free access with an acceptable surcharge.

Choosing an Internet Service Provider

Several different kinds of businesses offer Internet connections, including large companies with access points in many cities, smaller local or regional Internet service providers, and online information services that provide TCP/IP connections to the Internet along with their own proprietary information sources (I'm talking about AOL here, of course).

ISPs are a lot like long-distance telephone companies. First of all, almost all of them are simply selling access to a fast connection they bought from some other ISP. Very few so-called "Tier 1" providers are out there—that is, ISPs that actually have high-speed data networks across the country and to the rest of the world. Then, each has its own set of rate plans to choose from, so different from each other that there's no simple way to compare them.

Local ISPs are typically less expensive than national providers because they don't have these big networks to maintain. They can also get away with selling more bandwidth than they actually have, on the assumption that not everyone will try to download at the same time. They can buy one 30Mbps connection and sell 100 1Mbps connections to their subscribers, as an example. This actually isn't a problem as long as the company pays attention to its aggregate data transfer rates and buys more capacity as it grows. And this problem affects all ISPs: the small, the large, and AOL.

| Tip #161 | In my opinion, getting good customer service is more important than saving a few dollars a month. As you narrow down your list of potential ISPs, call their customer support telephone number and see how long it takes to get to talk to a human being. This experience can be very illuminating. |

Points to Consider

The following are a few points to consider in choosing an ISP:

- Can you have multiple email accounts (for family members or employees)? If so, how many?

Part

III

Ch

11

■ Does the ISP offer 56Kbps support? If so, which standard? It should be V.90, not the older X2 or K56Flex standards.

Note

If you have an X2 or K56Flex modem, check the manufacturer's Web site to see whether it can be flash upgraded to V.90. Many of these modems can be upgraded by software you can download for free or for a small fee.

■ Will the ISP let you create your own domain name? For example, Sue Jones might want the email address sue@jones.com rather than something like sejones343@ix.bighost.com. Sometimes creating your own domain name costs extra, but it has a certain prestige and gives your correspondents an easier address to remember. You can decide whether having one is worthwhile.

■ Does the ISP provide you with a newsreader account so you can interact with Internet newsgroups? It should, and it shouldn't restrict which newsgroups you'll have access to unless you are trying to prevent your kids or spouse from seeing "dirty" messages or pictures.

■ Do you want your own Web page available to other people surfing the Net? If so, does the ISP provide online storage room for it? Does it support Microsoft FrontPage extensions? How many "hits" per day can it handle, in case your page becomes popular? How much storage do you get in the deal? (It usually doesn't take more than a few megabytes.) Do you want the ISP to create a Web page for you?

■ What is the charge for connect time? Some ISPs offer unlimited usage per day. Others charge by the hour or have a limit on continuous connect time.

■ Does the ISP have local (that is, free) phone numbers in the areas you live, work, and visit? If not, calculate the tolls. Using an ISP that charges more per month but has local access might be cheaper.

■ Does the ISP have many points of presence or an 800 number you can use to call into when you are on the road?

■ Does the ISP have too much user traffic to really provide reasonable service? Ask others who use the service before signing up. This is a major problem with some ISPs, even biggies such as AOL. Smaller providers often supply faster connections. Remember that even if you can connect without a busy signal, the weakest link in the system will determine the speed at which you'll get data from the Net. Often that link is the ISP's internal LAN, which connects its in-house computers. It's hard to know how efficient the ISP really is. Best to ask someone who's using that provider.

 If you have access to the Web, try checking the page www.thelist.com. You'll learn a lot about comparative pricing and features offered by ISPs, along with links to their pages for opening an account. Another good site is www.boardwatch.com.

| Tip #162 | No matter which service you choose, wait a month or two before you print your email address on business cards and letterhead. If the first ISP you try doesn't give you the service you expect, take your business someplace else. |

| Tip #163 | If you want to set up a Web site or a domain like your friend Sue Jones, remember that you don't have to get that service from your ISP. You can have a Web site and domain set up anywhere, and have mail forwarded to your ISP's mailbox. Some companies offer small-volume Web sites and a domain name for $5 to 10 a month. You can decide which is the least expensive approach. |

The following sections describe the major categories of ISPs you have to choose from.

National ISPs

The greatest advantage of using a national or international ISP is that you can probably find a local dial-in telephone number in most major cities. If you want to send and receive email or use other Internet services while you travel, finding a local number can be extremely important.

These name brand services carry a small premium in price, but in exchange you get nation-wide local access, 24-hour customer support, and Big Corporate indifference to your special needs. (Alas, there's always a trade-off.)

The ISP industry is both expanding and consolidating quickly, so I hesitate to say I can give you anything like a complete list. Half of these companies might have eaten the other half before you see this, but here goes. You might investigate the following:

AtHome	www.home.com (Cable only)
ATT WorldNet	www.att.net
CompuServe	www.compuserve.com
Concentric Networks	www.concentric.net
Covad	www.covad.com (DSL only)
EarthLink	www.earthlink.net
IBM Internet Services	www.ibm.net
MCI Worldcom	www.mci.com
MindSpring	www.mindspring.com
Microsoft Network	www.msn.com
Northpoint	www.northpoint.net (DSL only)
PSINet	www.psinet.com
Verio	www.verio.com

LOCAL ISPs

The big national and regional services aren't your only choices. In most metropolitan areas, and in many cities and countries, smaller local service providers also offer access to the Internet.

If you can find a good local ISP, it might be your best choice. Check local computer magazines, advertisements in the business section of your newspaper, or best of all, ask friends and colleagues for recommendations. A local company might be more responsive to your particular needs and more willing to help you get through the inevitable configuration problems than a larger national operation. Equally important, reaching the tech support center is more likely to be a local telephone call.

Unfortunately, though, the Internet access business has attracted a tremendous number of entrepreneurs who are in it for the quick dollar; some local ISPs are really terrible. I've heard stories of frequent busy signals, slow downloads, dropped lines, and unexpected downtime rather than consistently reliable service (not to mention the ISP that attempted to finance its failing business by posting extra charges to customers' credit cards, including mine). If a deal seems too good to be true, there's probably a good reason.

To learn about the reputations of local ISPs, ask friends and colleagues who have been using the Internet for a while.

ONLINE SERVICES

Online services are more than ISPs. They sell dial-up access to their own private computers and provide special, valuable content such as stock quotes, email, discussion lists, instant messages, and chat rooms. Wait a minute! Isn't that exactly what you get on the Internet now? Yes, it is, and that's why most of the online services such as CompuServe, Prodigy, and GEnie either are gone or have collapsed, becoming little more than ISPs now.

AOL is the exception, having grown up right in the middle of the Internet boom as a full-fledged online service, with proprietary software, exclusive content, and hefty fees. AOL survives because it provides Internet access as well as its proprietary, value-added content. It's easy to use, and apparently people find some comfort in their love/hate relationship with it because AOL has more than 18 million subscribers. (I've never used it, but I do have a nice set of coasters made from all the CDs I've received from them in the mail over the years.)

A few of the older online services still survive as ISPs with special paid-members-only content pages, but it's harder to call them true online services now because they rely entirely on standard TCP/IP Internet technology.

So, an online service such as AOL can offer you an advantage in providing both Internet access and exclusive content for you and your family. Just beware that this type of service is not primarily an ISP. Its vested interest is in having you view its own sites, not the Internet's. And if software conflicts occur between its software and your favorite hot new Web browser, you probably won't find that service too helpful.

MAKING A DEAL

Regardless of which ISP you choose, be sure to ask whether you can get a special deal. It's a competitive business, so asking for favors doesn't hurt.

- Can you get a discount by signing up for a year or longer term contract?
- Will the ISP waive the setup or installation fee?
- In the case of DSL or cable service, in addition, will it provide a free network adapter, a free modem, and free inside wiring when it installs the service?

The DSL market is so competitive now that, with careful shopping, you might get all three of these deal-sweeteners. All in all, it can save you up to $500. (The prices in Table 11.1 reflect prices after the typical discounts are applied.)

RELYING ON THE INTERNET CONNECTION WIZARD

One of the welcome additions to later versions of Windows 95 has continued into Windows 2000. It's the inclusion of easy signup software for the major information services and selected ISPs in the U.S. Evidently, this was done in reaction to complaints that Microsoft Corporation was gaining unfair advantage by bundling software for its own service, The Microsoft Network. Any one of these services will get you connected to the Internet, using a "name brand" so to speak. The Internet Connection Wizard will connect via modem to a toll-free line operated by Microsoft, offer you a choice of ISPs, and sign you up for service, without your having to lift, well, much more than a finger.

Before you let the wizard narrow the range of choices for you, you'll probably want to do some research on your own. Then you can use the wizard to see if it recommends your ultimate choice. If it does, you can let it help you set up the account.

CHOOSING EQUIPMENT

You need to purchase equipment compatible with the particular type of Internet service you'll be using. The six types of service I described earlier all use different types of equipment:

Standard Dial-up	Requires an analog modem
ISDN	Requires an ISDN modem or adapter
DSL	Requires a DSL router or modem and an Ethernet adapter
Cable	Requires a cable modem and an Ethernet adapter
Satellite	Requires a dish, transceiver, satellite modem, and analog modem
Wireless	Requires a wireless modem

In all but the first two cases, you will probably have to accept the hardware chosen by your ISP, so there's little to discuss until I get into installation later.

SELECTING A MODEM

All modems sold now are capable of 33.3Kbps transmission toward the Internet (upstream) and up to 56Kbps reception from the Internet (downstream). Many have fax capability, and some can record and play back voice, so they can serve as the basis of a voicemail system. If you don't already have a modem, these tips can help you choose a model:

- Above all, get a modem that appears on the Windows 2000 Hardware Compatibility List. Check `http://www.microsoft.com/hcl` before you buy. An unlisted modem probably won't work.

- Choose a modem that is compatible with the fastest service level provided by your ISP. It should be V.90 for 56Kbps service. If your ISP still uses X2 or K6Flex modems, ask when this problem will be fixed.

- Get a modem with fax capability so that you can send and receive faxes directly from your computer. Almost all modems have this capability now.

- If it appeals to you, check into voice capability. If the modem comes with Windows 2000-compatible software, you might be able to use your computer as a voicemail system.

- Avoid anything called a "winmodem." This type of modem has no on-board processing power and relies on your computer's processor to do the work of encoding and decoding the data the modem transmits and receives. You have an incredibly powerful computer. Why make it do the dirty work? More importantly, many "winmodems" don't come with Windows 2000 drivers.

If you have a desktop computer, you will have to choose between an internal and an external modem. If you have a portable computer, you will have to choose between an external modem and a credit-card size PCMCIA (or PC Card) modem.

The three forms have their own pros and cons:

- An internal modem has fast access to data because it's plugged right into the computer data bus. But it has no indicator lights to tell you when data is successfully transmitted or received, and it takes up a precious expansion slot inside your computer.

- An external modem has lots of nice flashing indicator lights but requires a separate power plug for its power supply and requires you to plug it into an available high-quality, high-speed serial COM port. Also, if the external modem gets turned off or unplugged, it loses its configuration settings and must be reinitialized by shutting down and restarting whatever communication software you are using.

- A PC Card modem has no lights, but it is small. It fits right into the built-in slots in a portable computer, which is great for traveling. PC Card modems can be plugged into some cell phones for true road-warrior action. (The cell phone must be set to "analog" mode for this type of modem to work.) You can even find PC Cards containing both a modem and a network adapter built into the same card for the ultimate in space efficiency!

SELECTING A DSL MODEM OR ROUTER

You will probably have no choice in the equipment used for DSL service. Most DSL providers supply a chosen brand of DSL modem, and they usually throw in one network adapter as well. If you plan to connect more than one computer now or in the future, you should see if you can get a DSL router rather than a simple DSL modem. A router has additional software inside that permits multiple connections and provides important firewall protection. Many models provide a built-in Ethernet hub for up to eight computers. I've used the Flowpoint and Farallon Netopia models, and they're both great.

Tip #164	Configuring a DSL router, especially for firewall protection, requires considerable expertise, so you might want to ask your ISP to configure it for you. Ask the ISP to block Microsoft Networking, RPC, and SNMP traffic at the very least, as discussed in Chapter 26, "Network Security."

You'll also need an Ethernet network card to connect your computer to the DSL modem. In many cases, the ISP will provide this card free of charge. (The providers want things to work and the installation to be easy, so it's less expensive for them to give you a card they know works than to figure out the various cards they would run into otherwise.)

If you need to purchase a card yourself, you can choose from many models. It probably doesn't matter which you choose, as long as you follow these suggestions:

- Buy a card that is listed on the Windows 2000 Hardware Compatibility List at www.microsoft.com/hcl. Don't touch one that isn't!
- Be sure to get a Plug and Play adapter.
- Get a 10/100BASE-T PCI model if your computer has a free PCI bus slot. You can get a 16-bit ISA card if not, and you can get a plain 10BASE-T card if it's considerably cheaper. The faster card will not work faster here but might be more valuable to you in the future.

Network cards are so inexpensive now that I base the decision on "How far do I have to drive to get it?" rather than "How much does it cost?"

SELECTING AN ISDN MODEM

If you want to use an ISDN service, you will need an ISDN modem. Internal and external ISDN modems are really two different animals. Internal ISDN modems are treated by Windows as network adapters, and external ISDN modems are, well, modems. The difference is this: Windows sees an external ISDN modem through a serial COM port and communicates with it using standard modem commands. An internal ISDN modem can be configured directly by the computer hardware, and Windows has more control over it. As a result, you can get extended features such as telephony, voice interfaces, and so on.

Which is best? It's hard to say. External modems are simpler to configure and manage, and you get the blinking lights to tell you things are working. But, to get full use of their high speed (128Kbps and possibly much more, if data compression is enabled), you'll need to be sure to use a high-quality, high-speed COM port, which might require adding a plug-in card to replace the low-quality COM ports on most motherboards.

Internal modems are a bit more difficult to install and configure, but there's no problem with the high data rate because they're plugged right into the computer's bus on the motherboard. For that reason, they're a less troublesome choice.

Whichever you decide to use, I suggest that you shop around and, of course, be absolutely sure that whichever modem you select is certified for use with Windows 2000. Old ISDN cards that you might have used with Windows 9x or Windows NT might not be supported by Windows 2000.

ISDN equipment is designed for either of two ISDN wiring interfaces: "U" or "S/T." Unless you have more than one ISDN device or telephone plugged into your ISDN line, you should order a modem that is advertised as having a "U interface with a built-in NT-1."

SELECTING HARDWARE FOR CABLE, WIRELESS, OR SATELLITE

For wireless, satellite, or cable modem service, most likely you will have to use the equipment provided by your ISP. You will also need an Ethernet network card, which I discussed previously.

ORDERING THE SERVICE

Ordering standard dial-up modem Internet service is really quite simple. Just call the ISP, talk to the sales department, and ask the sales representative to mail or fax you instructions for configuring Windows 2000. At the very least, you'll need this information:

- Access telephone number(s) in your area, for your modem type
- Does the service provide DHCP for automatic configuration?
- If not: the DNS addresses (these numbers indicate the Internet address of servers that look up the names like www.que.com and turn them into network addresses)
- Type of post office server: POP3 or IMAP
- Names of SMTP mail server, post office server, and NEWS server
- Account name and password

Ordering ISDN service is quite a different matter. The most difficult part is getting the ISDN telephone line ordered and installed correctly because ISDN service has a bewildering number of options, all specified in telephone-companyese. What you want is standard "2B+D, two data and voice" service with no extra-cost features.

Tip #165   Your best bet is to have your ISP order the telephone line for you. Most ISPs will make these arrangements for you. If they won't, some ISDN modem manufacturers–for example, 3COM–will order your ISDN service for you.

In addition to the ISP information I listed previously, you'll need this information from your telephone company:

- Switch type—for example, 5ESS, DMS, or Custom
- SPIDs
- Directory numbers

→ You'll find a longer discussion about ordering ISDN service in Chapter 24, "Connecting Your LAN to the Internet."

Ordering cable, DSL, or satellite service is also quite easy because the ISP will take care of all the details for you. The provider first checks to see whether your neighborhood qualifies for the service. It calls you back with the news, and then schedules an installation appointment.

Even if someone else installs and configures your service, be sure to get a paper record of the setup information:

- Does the service provide DHCP support?
- If not: your IP address, subnet mask, and gateway IP address, and the IP addresses of their *DNS* servers
- Type of post office server: POP3 or IMAP?
- Names of SMTP mail server, post office server, and NEWS server
- Account name and password

After the service is installed, you're ready to configure your Windows 2000 computer.

Installing a Modem in Windows 2000

In Windows 2000, communications control functions are located in a central application programming interface (API), which moves data between your modem and individual communications programs. One of the benefits of this design is that you can configure Windows 2000 to work with your modem just once, rather than repeating the process for each application program that uses a modem.

The procedures described here apply to analog modems as well as external ISDN modems.

Install your modem according to the manufacturer's instructions. Insert an internal modem into a free slot inside the computer. Install an external modem by cabling it to a free COM port plug or a PC card modem by simply plugging it into your portable. If you have an external modem, connect its power supply, and turn it on.

PART

III

CH

11

Tip #166

If you're installing a non–Plug and Play internal modem, be especially careful not to have it conflict with any internal COM ports built into your motherboard. Check the manufacturer's

continues

continued

instructions. The easiest approach is usually to configure the modem as COM2 and to disable the motherboard's built-in COM2 port using the BIOS setup program that is accessible when you first power up the computer.

If your internal modem is Plug and Play (PnP) compatible, Windows 2000 should automatically detect it when you turn on your computer and log in as Administrator. If you have PCMCIA (credit-card style) modem, simply inserting the card while the computer is on should result in Windows detecting it and loading the appropriate software driver.

If you're using an external modem or an older internal modem ("older" means anything made before late 1995 that isn't PnP aware), you might need to add it to the configuration manually by following these steps:

1. Choose Start, Settings, Control Panel.

2. Open the Phone and Modem Options applet. Then select the Modems tab, as shown in Figure 11.1.

Figure 11.1
The Modems tab identifies the modems currently installed in your system.

3. If Windows 2000 has already detected your modem, its name appears in the Modems tab. If the correct modem is already listed, you can close the dialog box now and skip to step 7.

   If no modem is listed, or if the name on the list does not match the modem you want to use, click the Add button to run the Install New Modem Wizard.

4. The wizard can try to detect your modem's make and model automatically, or you can choose to tell it the model yourself. If you simply click Next, Windows attempts to locate the COM port and determine the type of modem

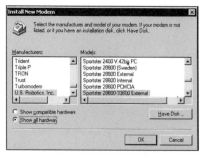

Figure 11.2

you have. You can try this procedure and see whether Windows is successful. If it is, click Next. Otherwise, click Change, and select Show All Hardware in the Install New Modem dialog box, as shown in Figure 11.2.

5. Locate the manufacturer and model of your modem in the dialog box. If you find the correct make and model, select them and click OK. If your modem came with a driver diskette for Windows 2000, click Have Disk, and locate the installation file for the modem.

Otherwise, you didn't follow my advice and used a modem that isn't on the Hardware Compatibility List. Select a similar model by the same manufacturer if you can. I should warn you that this procedure might not work because Windows 2000 is more sensitive to modem model variations than you might have been used to with Windows 3.1 or 9x. Later you might be able to download the proper driver from Microsoft's www.windowsupdate.com site or from the modem manufacturer.

6. After you select the modem type, click OK and then Next.

7. Click Finish to complete the installation. The modem then appears in the list of installed modems in the Phone and Modem Options dialog box.

8. Select the Dialing Rules tab.

9. Select My Location, and click Edit.

10. Enter the General tab information for your current location, as shown in Figure 11.3.

Figure 11.3
In the Edit Location dialog box, you can record the dialing instructions for your current location. The important settings are Country, Area Code Access for an outside line, and Disable Call Waiting.

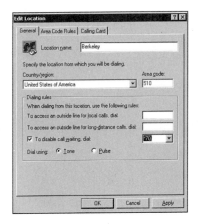

11. Enter the name of your location—for example, home, Berkeley, or another name that will distinguish the current telephone dialing properties. Set the country, area code, and dialing rules information.

If your telephone system, for example, requires you to dial a 9 to make an outside local call, enter 9 in box labeled To Access An Outside Line For Local Calls, Dial. Make a corresponding entry for long-distance access.

If your telephone line has call waiting, check To Disable Call Waiting, and choose the appropriate disable code.

I'm going to assume that your ISP access number will be a local call in the same area code. If this is not the case, you might want to fill in the Area Code Rules table for the ISP access number. (If you don't know the number yet, don't worry; you can come back and fix it later.)

12. Click OK.

INSTALLING MULTIPLE MODEMS

Windows 2000 supports *modem aggregation* (also called *Multilink* or *Multilink PPP*), making several simultaneous connections to your ISP to increase the total speed of your transfers. This process is a little tricky; it requires multiple modems and an ISP that supports synchronization of multiple modems, or a compatible setup on your corporate LAN.

You'll see this possibility mentioned in many Windows books, but to be honest, it's an obnoxious technology and one you can ignore if you can wait for DSL or cable service. It requires two telephone lines, two modems, and manual management on your part. It works, but it's a little bit like riding two skateboards at once. Go buy a bike.

ISDN modems, on the other hand, can make multiple channel connections and do not require the addition of a second line or modem. The two channels are built into one modem, and you can take advantage of this to get extra speed, as long as you're willing to pay the extra charges imposed by your ISP and telephone company.

INSTALLING INTERNAL ISDN ADAPTERS

Internal ISDN modems or adapters are treated by Windows as network adapters, not modems. Plug and Play adapters should be set up the first time you log in after installing the adapter. Log in as Administrator to be sure that you have sufficient privileges to install hardware drivers.

For older non–Plug and Play adapters, you must get up-to-date Windows 2000 drivers from the manufacturer's Web site, along with installation instructions.

INSTALLING A NETWORK ADAPTER

DSL and cable service providers usually provide and install an Ethernet network adapter for use by their services. If you're lucky, this will be the case. You won't have to lift a finger, in fact, as long as the installer is familiar with Windows 2000. You will just need to log in using the Administrator account, and supervise while the installer does his or her stuff. Take notes of what he or she does.

If you want to purchase or install the network adapter yourself, install it according to the manufacturer's instructions. This process should involve no more than inserting the card into your computer, powering up, and logging in as Administrator. The Plug and Play system should take care of the rest for you.

After installation, confirm that the network adapter is installed and functioning by following these steps:

1. Right-click My Computer, and then select Manage.
2. Open the Device Manager in the left pane.

   The list in the right pane should show only "first-level" items. Under Network Adapters, you should see no items listed with an exclamation mark icon superimposed.

If the network adapter appears and is marked with a yellow exclamation point, follow the network card troubleshooting instructions in Chapter 27, "Troubleshooting Your Windows 2000 Network."

The service installer will connect your telephone line to a device called a *splitter*, which separates the radio-frequency DSL carrier signal from the normal telephone signal, and will install a wire to bring the DSL carrier signal to a jack near your computer. The jack connects to the DSL modem, the DSL modem plugs into your network adapter, and you're ready to configure your connection.

INSTALLING A SATELLITE OR WIRELESS CONNECTION

Installing satellite or wireless modems is not terribly tricky, but the procedure is very specific to the type of hardware you're using. Unfortunately, I have to leave you at the mercy of the manufacturer's instruction manual.

One bit of advice I can give: Installing a satellite dish is difficult, and it's best to hire a professional dish installer for this task. The job involves mounting the dish on your roof or to the side of your house, aiming it precisely at an invisible target in the sky, running a cable into the house (being careful to weatherproof the holes you have to make), and routing the cable through the attic or the walls. (Our editor Rick Kughen didn't have the benefit of this sage advice when he installed his, and he offers this observation: "About halfway through the ordeal, I decided that I really wished I had paid the $199 installation fee.")

CONFIGURING YOUR INTERNET CONNECTION

If you're like me and can't resist poking around, you've already tried running Outlook Express or Internet Explorer and have already seen the Internet Connection Wizard, which tried to call, well, who knows where to get you signed up with an Internet account.

Now that your modem is installed and ready to go, it's time to head off to see the wizard.

Tip #167	Have your Windows 2000 Setup CD handy. The wizard might need to install some Windows 2000 files to set up your Internet connection.

Choose Start, Programs, Accessories, Communications, Internet Connection Wizard. You then see the wizard shown in Figure 11.4.

PART

III

CH

11

Figure 11.4
The Internet
Connection Wizard
has three starting
paths, depending on
whether you want
Microsoft to suggest
an ISP.

Now, your path from here depends on whether you

- Want Microsoft to give you a list of suggested ISPs
- Have an existing ISP account
- Want to enter all your ISP's information manually

The first two choices are for analog modem or ISDN access only. If you take this route, go on to "Using a Referral ISP."

Otherwise, skip to "Making and Ending a Dial-Up Connection," or "Configuring a High-Speed Connection" later in this chapter.

USING A REFERRAL ISP

If you want the wizard to help you choose an ISP, select I Want To Sign Up For A New Internet Account, and click Next. Windows then makes a toll-free call to Microsoft's ISP referral server and downloads a list of ISPs in your area.

Internet Explorer then displays a list of available ISPs in your area. You can follow the onscreen instructions to establish an account with one of them, if you choose. If you choose not to, or if none are available, you are given the chance to manually configure an ISP account.

TRANSFERRING AN EXISTING ACCOUNT TO THIS COMPUTER

If you have an existing dial-up account with an Internet service provider, choose the wizard's I Want To Transfer... option, and click Next.

Windows then dials the Microsoft Referral service to see whether your current ISP is known. If you are currently using one of the listed ISPs, simply follow the instructions shown to retrieve the account settings for your Windows 2000 computer. Otherwise, indicate that you want to perform a manual Internet account setup, and click Next.

MANUALLY CONFIGURING AN ISP ACCOUNT

If you want to enter your own ISP account information, make the third choice in the wizard's first screen, and click Next. You then need to complete three dialog boxes using the information provided by your ISP.

The first (shown in Figure 11.5) asks for the local access telephone number for your ISP.

Figure 11.5

In the manual Internet account connection information dialog, enter the local access number for your ISP.

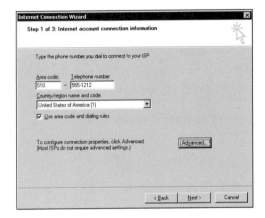

Caution

Be sure to use a local number. Your ISP will not help pay your phone bill if you choose a toll number by mistake!

Proceed as follows:

1. Enter the local access number for your ISP, including area code and telephone number. You should also be sure to check Use Area Code and Dialing Rules.

   If your ISP has provided you with a list of DNS server addresses and has indicated that they will *not* be sent to your computer automatically, click the Advanced button. Otherwise, click Next and go on to step 2.

   You'll see two tabs for Advanced connection properties (see Figure 11.6). On the Addresses tab, you manually enter the DNS server addresses.

   The Connection tab will almost certainly not be required. (In the early days of dial-up Internet service, the options listed here were rarely used, and today they should not be required at all. If they are, you need a new ISP!)

   If your ISP indicates that you need to do so, select Always Use The Following, enter the IP addresses provided by your ISP, and click OK. Then click Next to proceed.

2. Enter the username and password provided by your ISP in the Internet Account Logon Information dialog box (see Figure 11.7). Click Next.

Figure 11.6
In the Advanced Connection Properties dialog, you can enter your ISP's DNS addresses, if necessary.

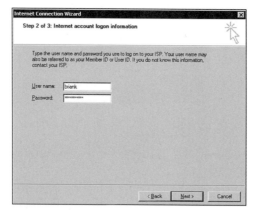

Figure 11.7
The Internet Account Logon Information dialog box requests only the login ID and password provided by your ISP.

3. Give the connection a sensible name. The Configuring Your Computer dialog box (see Figure 11.8) asks only that you give a name to the connection information being saved. This name is displayed as part of the sentence Dialing xxxxx, so I like to use the name of the ISP rather than the default name Connection to 555-1212 provided by Windows. You can change it as you see fit and then click Next.

4. Aha! It turns out that there are more than three steps after all. The next dialog asks whether you want to set up an Internet email account. Any information you provide here will be used by Outlook Express to receive and send email via this account. You can configure this information now or later when you first fire up Outlook Express.

These steps are explained in Chapter 13, "Email," so for now you can just choose No and then Next. If you want to, though, you can plow through the Mail account setup dialog boxes now to get this job over with.

You'll need the following information:

- Your email address
- The name of the POP or IMAP server at your ISP (and which type is used)
- The name of the SMTP server at your ISP

Figure 11.8
Here, you can name the Internet dial-up connection.

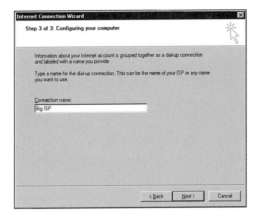

5. The wizard will want to immediately dial your ISP. Uncheck the box if you do not want to dial immediately. Click Next to finish the configuration wizard.

That's it. Your connection is ready to use. If you have no other LAN or dial-up connections, you can simply fire up Internet Explorer to automatically dial. You can choose Start, Settings, Network and Dial-up Connections to use or modify your dial-up configuration at any time.

PART
III

CH
11

ADJUSTING DIAL-UP CONNECTION PROPERTIES

As configured by the wizard, your dial-up connection is properly set up for most Internet service providers. It's unlikely that you would need to change any of these settings, but just in case, and because I know you're curious, I will walk you through the various settings and properties that are part of a dial-up connection. I'll explain dial-up connection properties in detail in Chapter 23, "Windows Unplugged: Remote and Mobile Networking."

You can view the connection properties by selecting Start, Settings, Network and Dial-up Connections. Right-click the icon for your dial-up connection (see Figure 11.9), and select Properties. You'll see five tabs, which I will run through in order. Few settings need to be changed for an ISP connection. I'll list a few here that you might want to check if you encounter problems dialing into your ISP.

Figure 11.9
Select a dial-up connection to modify in the Network and Dial-Up Connections window.

- The General tab contains modem properties and the ISP telephone number. If you have multiple modems, you can choose which of one or more of these modems will be used for this particular connection.

- Using the Configure button for the modem, you can set the maximum speed used to communicate from the computer to the modem. As for external modems—if you don't have a special-purpose high-speed serial port—you might want to reduce this speed from the default 115200 to 57600.

- Using the Alternates button for the telephone number, you can add multiple telephone numbers for your ISP, which can be automatically tried, in turn, if the first doesn't answer.

- On the Options tab, you can change the time between redial attempts if the connection fails.
  - You can check Redial If Line Is Dropped to maintain a permanent or *nailed-up* dial-up connection.
  - You can select a time to wait before hanging up the line when no activity occurs. By doing so, you can help cut costs if you pay an hourly rate to your ISP.

- The Security tab controls whether your password can be sent in unencrypted form. It's okay to send your ISP password unsecured. It's *not* okay to check Automatically Use My Windows Login Name and Password if you also select Allow Unsecured Password. You send your Windows name and password when you're dialing into a Windows remote access service rather than a commercial ISP.

- The Networking tab determines which network components are accessible to the Internet connection. If you're dialing a standard ISP, you should uncheck everything except Internet Protocol. You'll learn more about that in Chapter 26.

- On the Internet Connection Sharing tab, you can share this dial-up connection automatically with other users on a LAN. You'll learn more details on that in Chapter 24.

SETTING UP SLIP AND/OR LOGIN SCRIPTS

As I mentioned earlier, today's ISP equipment directly connects your incoming modem calls to a call-processing service that uses the Point-to-Point Protocol (PPP) to work out the details of your connection.

In the early years of the Internet boom, though, it wasn't unheard of to find ISPs using the archaic Serial Line Internet Protocol (SLIP) and text-based login systems. Text-based login systems required an incoming caller to read messages and type responses to a login screen and then activate the PPP or SLIP software. The SLIP protocol is used by some older UNIX-based Internet hosts, but again, it is quite rare today.

If your ISP really requires SLIP or a manual login, you might find it easier to find a new ISP than to configure this type of login process. If you're stuck with it, however, Windows 2000 has the capability to handle these types of Internet connections.

If you need to connect to a SLIP connection server, bring up the dial-up connection's properties page, and select the Networking tab. Under Type of Dial-Up Server I Am Calling, select SLIP: UNIX Connection. SLIP has no provision for automatic configuration, meaning you must also select Internet Protocol in the Components list, select Properties, and then enter the IP address and DNS server addresses assigned to you by the ISP or remote network's manager. On the Advanced tab, you can set the SLIP frame size if you're instructed to do so.

To set up an interactive or scripted login, bring up the Security tab. You can manually perform the login each time you dial by selecting Show Terminal Window.

You can edit or select a *login script* by checking Run Script. If you check this box and click Edit while the script name is still set to its default value (none), Windows displays the contents of the default script file SWITCH.INF. This file contains detailed instructions on writing login scripts. You should print its contents before undertaking this unpleasant task.

If you have a preconfigured login script from a previous version of Windows 9x or NT, you can place it in \WINDOWS\SYSTEM32\RAS and select it using the Browse button next to the Run Script check box. Windows 2000's dial-up manager supports both the Windows NT SWITCH.INF script language and the Windows 95 scripting language.

CONFIGURING A HIGH-SPEED CONNECTION

If you're using an Ethernet network adapter to connect your Windows 2000 computer to a DSL or cable Internet service, the installer will probably set up your computer for you. If this doesn't happen, here's approximately what you will need to do. More specific instructions will have to come from your ISP.

1. In the Internet Connection Wizard, select I Connect Through a Local Area Network (LAN), and click Next.
2. Uncheck Automatic Discovery of a Proxy Server, and click Next.
3. You can choose to set up your Internet mail account information at this time. Proceed through the wizard either way, until you select Finish.

Now you might need to configure the Ethernet card using information specified by your ISP. Your ISP will tell you whether your network card must be manually configured or if the DHCP protocol is available through its service.

If your ISP uses the DHCP protocol to configure client network adapters, your connection should begin working immediately and automatically. You're ready to go. If you need to manually configure IP addresses and network information, follow these steps:

1. Choose Start, Settings, Network and Dial-up Connections.
2. Right-click the Local Area Connection icon, and select Properties.

3. Uncheck all items *except* Internet Protocol in the Components Checked Are Used by This Connection list. Unchecking these items, as shown in Figure 11.10, helps minimize your computer's exposure to hacking via the Internet.

Figure 11.10
If you have a LAN card used to connect to a cable or DSL modem, uncheck all network components except Internet Protocol.

4. Be sure that Internet Protocol is checked. Then select it, and click the Properties button.

5. Select Use the Following IP Address, and enter the IP address, Subnet mask, and Default gateway information provided by your ISP, as shown in Figure 11.11.

Figure 11.11
Here, you can add the network address, subnet mask, and DNS information supplied by your ISP.

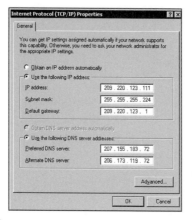

Tip #168

When you're entering TCP/IP dotted-decimal numbers like 1.2.3.4, the spacebar advances the cursor across the periods. This technique is much easier than using the mouse to change fields.

6. Select Use the Following DNS Server Addresses, and enter the two DNS addresses provided by your ISP.

7. Click the Advanced button, and select the WINS tab in the resulting dialog box, as shown in Figure 11.12.

8. Select Disable NetBIOS Over TCP/IP as an additional security measure. Selecting this option will also prevent hostile Microsoft Networking activity via your Internet connection.

9. Click OK and then OK again.

When setup is complete, you will have a Dial-Up Networking connection profile for your ISP.

If you have several ISP accounts, ISP access numbers for different cities, or both personal and business dial-up connections, you can add additional connections following the same procedure.

Figure 11.12
Here, you can disable NetBIOS over TCP/IP to further help prevent hostile attacks on your computer via the Internet.

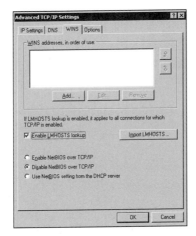

PART

III

CH

11

MAKING AND ENDING A DIAL-UP CONNECTION

If you use a dial-up connection with an analog modem or ISDN line, after you've set up an icon for your ISP, making the connection is a snap:

1. Select the connection icon in Network and Dial-Up Connections.

2. When Windows displays a connection dialog box (see Figure 11.13), enter the login name and password assigned by your ISP. Check Save Password so that you won't need to retype it every time you dial.

Note

If you have not chosen to have Windows prompt you for the phone number, the dialog will appear differently than what is shown in Figure 11.13. If you select Prompt for Phone Number in the properties sheet for your connection, the lower half of the dialog showing Dial, Dial From, and Dialing Rules will not appear.

Figure 11.13
When you want to initiate a dial-up connection, enter your user ID and password, and check Save Password to simplify connecting in the future.

3. Check that the phone number is correct, including area code and any required prefix numbers. You might need to correct your current location (Dialing From) and/or the Dialing Rules if the prefix or area code isn't correct.

4. Select Dial to make the connection.

Windows then dials your ISP and establishes the connection; if it works, a connection icon will appear in the tasktray with a temporary note indicating the connection (see Figure 11.14).

Figure 11.14

If the connection fails, Windows displays a (usually) sensible message explaining why: There was no dial tone because your modem in unplugged, there was no answer at the ISP or the line is busy, or you user ID and password failed. In the latter case, you'll get three tries to enter the correct information before Windows hangs up the phone.

(Of course, if you use a dedicated, always-on Internet connection, you won't have to fool with dialing and hanging up connections at all. To be honest, I don't know which I like more about my DSL connection—its lickety-split speed or the fact that I don't have to wait for a modem connection to be made.)

CHECKING THE CONNECTION STATUS

The tasktray connection icon shows two tiny computer screens, which are normally black. They flicker when data activity occurs on the dial-up connection, momentarily turning green to show that the modem is active. The two indicators represent data you're sending and data returned from your ISP, respectively. This icon is actually a decent troubleshooting tool because you can immediately see whether modem activity is taking place.

If you let your mouse cursor hover over the connection icon, a small pop-up window shows the number of bytes transmitted and received over the current connection.

If you right-click the connection icon, a pop-up menu appears. This menu contains the following options:

- Disconnect—Hang up the connection
- Status—View the Connection Status dialog
- Open Network and Dial-Up Connections—Bring up the whole dial-up networking control panel

Choosing Status from this menu opens the Status dialog box, as shown in Figure 11.15. The dialog displays the number of bytes transmitted and received during the connection and the number of transmission errors detected; it also has buttons to let you disconnect or adjust the connection properties.

Figure 11.15
In this dialog box, you can see connections statistics, such as the length of time you've been connected and the number of bytes sent and received.

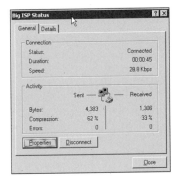

PART

III

CH

11

For what it's worth, in practice, I've found that I've never once needed to use this status dialog.

HANGING UP A DIAL-UP CONNECTION

After you finish with your Internet connection, simply right-click the connection icon in your tasktray, and select Disconnect. Windows will hang up the dial-up connection and remove the icon from the tasktray in a few seconds.

CHANGING THE DEFAULT CONNECTION

If you don't establish a connection manually before using an Internet program such as Internet Explorer, Windows will go ahead and dial your ISP automatically when you start these programs. If you don't want Windows to dial automatically, or if you have defined multiple dial-up connections, you can tell Windows which, if any, of the connections you want it to dial automatically.

To change the default settings, follow these steps:

1. Open the Control Panel, and run the Internet Options applet. Alternatively, within Internet Explorer, you can choose Tools, Internet Options.

2. Select the Connections tab, and highlight the dial-up connection you want to use for Internet browsing (see Figure 11.16).

Figure 11.16
In the Internet Properties dialog, you can specify which dial-up connection to use automatically when an Internet application is started.

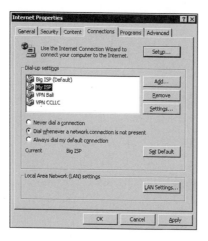

3. If you use a standalone computer or a portable computer that sometimes has Internet access via a LAN, select Dial Whenever a Network Connection Is Not Present.

    If you want to use the modem connection even while you're connected to a LAN, you can select Always Dial My Default Connection.

    Finally, if you don't want Windows to dial automatically at all but prefer to make your connection manually, you can choose Never Dial a Connection.

4. If you have actually changed the default dial-up connection, click Set Default.

5. Click OK.

MANAGING MULTIPLE INTERNET CONNECTIONS

Life would be so simple if computers and people just stayed put, but that's not the way the world works anymore. Portable computers now account for more than half of the computers sold in the United States. Managing Internet connections from multiple locations can be a little tricky.

I'll talk a bit more about the ins and outs of traveling with your computer in Chapter 23, where the topic is remote networking.

The issue comes up with plain Internet connectivity as well, so let me share some tips:

■ If you use a LAN Internet connection in the office and a modem connection elsewhere, bring up the Connections tab of the Internet Properties dialog box, and choose Dial Whenever a Network Connection Is Not Present, as I discussed in "Changing the Default Connection."

- If you use different LAN connections in different locations, see "Multiple LAN Connections" in Chapter 23.

- If you use a dial-up Internet service provider with different local access numbers in different locations, life is a bit more difficult. It would be great if Windows let you associate a distinct dial-up number for each dialing location, but it doesn't. The best solution is to make separate connection icons for each location. After you set up and test one connection, right-click its icon and select Create Copy. Rename the icon using the alternate city in the name; for example, I might name my icons "My ISP Berkeley," "My ISP Reno," and so on. Finally, open the Properties page for the new icon, and set the appropriate local access number and dialing location.

  In this case, it's best to tell Windows never to automatically dial a connection (as shown in "Changing the Default Connection") because it will not know which of several connections is the right one to use; it might dial a long-distance number without you noticing.

TROUBLESHOOTING A NEW INTERNET CONNECTION

The first time you establish a dial-up connection is the most difficult because everything is new: new hardware, new software components, new procedures, and new usernames and passwords. If the connection doesn't work, you'll have to be very thorough in determining exactly what went wrong.

In troubleshooting hardware and software over the last 15 years or so, I've always found that the phrase "It doesn't work" isn't terribly useful. I always ask, "What *does* happen?"

Let's start in the middle: When you attempted to make a connection (in the Internet Connection Wizard or from Internet Explorer), did you hear the modem dial your ISP?

- If you didn't, then you know that you have a hardware problem to resolve before you can worry about anything else.

- If you did, you know that the modem and telephone line are working, so you can concentrate on connection configuration details such as protocols, username, and password.

TROUBLESHOOTING MODEM HARDWARE PROBLEMS

Before delving in to the more difficult problems, try to eliminate the easy ones first:

1. Be sure that your modem is connected to a functioning telephone line jack (check it with a regular telephone) and that the telephone cable is plugged into the correct jack on the modem. Modems generally have two jacks, one for the wall and one for an extension telephone. Some modems don't care which jack you use for which, but some do. If you have an external modem, be sure it is connected to the correct COM port on your computer and is powered on.

2. With analog modems (not ISDN), listen in with an extension telephone (use a two-jack extension coupler if necessary) to be *sure* that no dialing is taking place. You'll feel pretty silly if the only problem was that the modem wasn't making any sounds you could hear. Some external modems have volume controls. Make sure yours is set in the middle of its range.

   If dialing is actually taking place, run the Phone and Modem Options from the Control Panel. Select the Modems tab, select Properties, and then turn up the speaker volume.

3. If you have a voicemail system that uses a stutter dial tone to indicate that you have messages waiting, your modem may not dial when the stutter is active. In this same Control Panel dialog, you can disable Wait for Dial Tone Before Dialing.

4. Check the Device Manager for COM port conflicts. Right-click My Computer, select Manage, and open the Device Manager. Open the Modems and Ports items in the right-hand pane. No entries should be marked with a yellow Exclamation Point icon. If some are, you can use the Windows Troubleshooter to help diagnose the problem. Right-click the device, and select Properties. Then click the Troubleshooter button.

5. If you have an external analog or ISDN modem, be sure that it's plugged in and turned on. When you attempt to make a connection, watch for flickering in the Send Data LEDs. If you don't see flickering, your modem cable might not be installed correctly. If you do, but no dialing is taking place, you also might want to turn down the data connection speed between the modem and the computer as I mentioned in "Adjusting Dial-Up Connection Properties" earlier in this chapter.

6. If you have an analog or ISDN modem, and dialing is taking place but no connection is made, in the Device Manager or Control Panel Phone and Modem Properties, view the modem's Properties dialog. Select the Diagnostics tab, and check Append to Log. Close the dialog, and try to make the connection again. Go back to the Properties dialog, and select View Log. This log may indicate what is happening with the modem. Be sure to uncheck Append to Log when you're finished.

7. If the connection to the ISP fails because Windows is dialing 1 and an area code even though it's a local call, or is dialing an incorrect area code, check control panel Phone and Modem Properties to be sure that your current location information, including area code, is correct. If correcting this information doesn't fix the problem, go to the Connection properties, and uncheck Use Area Code and Dialing Rules to prevent Windows from adding a 1 and area code.

Note

If you'd like to learn more about troubleshooting hardware conflicts, I recommend that you pick up a copy of *Upgrading and Repairing PCs*, published by Que.

TROUBLESHOOTING CONNECTION CONFIGURATION PROBLEMS

If your modem is making contact with your ISP, but the connection fails to function properly, one of two things may be happening:

- You are being disconnected because of an incorrect username, password, or protocol selection.
- You are connected, but you can't access the Internet anyway.

You can determine which is happening by viewing the connection log, as instructed in step 6 in the preceding section. The log tells you why the modem is disconnecting. You can contact your ISP with this information to help determine the cause of the problem.

If the connection is established, but you still can't use the Internet, see Chapter 16, "Internet Diagnosis Tools," for more troubleshooting tips.

Tips from the Windows Pros: Staying Connected While Traveling Abroad

As I said earlier, you can choose an ISP with regional local access numbers to let you connect without toll charges wheresoever you roam in your home country. But what about when you travel overseas?

Actually, you usually don't have to go far to find an Internet terminal. You can rent PCs with Internet connections for roughly $1 to $10 per hour almost anywhere. Listings of Internet cafés and computer parlors are now a required element in guide books (for example, the fantastic *Rough Guide* series), and Tourism Information centers in most towns can direct you to the nearest rental centers.

If you want to connect your own computer, however, connecting is a bit more difficult. The following are some tips I've picked up in travels through Mexico, Australia, and Europe:

- Do your research before you leave. Search the Internet to find at least one Internet location and/or ISP in each area you'll be visiting. Print these pages and bring them along, being sure to get the local address and telephone number. You might find a more convenient location or better service after you arrive, but this way you have a place to start.
- Most Internet cafés won't let you hook up your own computer. Some will. You can find Kinko's Copy centers, for example, in many large cities in North America, Europe, and Asia; they're outfitted with fast computers, fast connections, and at least one bay with an Ethernet cable that you can use to connect your own laptop. Bring a PCMCIA Ethernet card, and you're set. (You will have to configure it using the Local Area Connection icon in Network and Dial-Up Connections, as you'll learn in Chapter 21, using the setting provided by the rental center.)
- Bring some formatted floppy disks with you. If you need to transfer files and can't hook up your own computer, you can at least use the floppy disks.
- If you normally receive email through a POP mail server at your ISP, use one of the free email services such as Hotmail or Yahoo! Mail to view your home email via the Web while you're traveling. Use a different password, not your regular password, for

the free account. Set up the free service to fetch mail from your ISP, using what is called *external* or POP mail. Set the mail service to "leave mail on the server" so you can filter through your mail the normal way when you get home. Delete the free account, or change its password when you return home.

These steps will (a) let you read your mail from virtually any Internet terminal in the world and (b) protect your real mail password from unscrupulous types who might be monitoring the network traffic in the places you visit.

- If you're staying a reasonable length of time in one country, you can sign up for a month of Internet service. For example, in Australia, I used ozemail.com, which gave me local access numbers all over the Australian continent. A month's service cost only $17, with no setup fee. After I found an adapter for Australia's curious telephone jacks, I was all set.

- If you do use a foreign ISP, configure your email software to use the foreign ISP's outgoing mail (SMTP) server, but keep your incoming POP server pointed to your home ISP. (This step is important because most ISPs' mail servers won't accept mail from dial-up users outside their own networks.)

- Get power plug adapters and telephone plug adapters from a travel store, telephone accessory store, or international appliance store before you leave, if you can.

CHAPTER **12**

WORLD WIDE WEB

In this chapter

ORIGINS AND DEVELOPMENT OF THE WORLD WIDE WEB

The World Wide Web (also called WWW or the Web) has worked its way into virtually every aspect of modern life, an astounding fact considering that just a short decade ago it was nothing more than an idea living inside a computer scientist's head. That scientist was Tim Berners-Lee, who, while working at the European Laboratory for Particle Physics (CERN), needed to devise a way in which scientific data could easily be shared simultaneously with physicists around the world. Along with Robert Cailliau, he designed the first Web browser in 1990 to allow scientists to access information remotely without the need to reformat the data.

This new communications technology developed by Berners-Lee and Cailliau transmitted data to viewers via the Internet, which by the early 1990s already existed as a global network linking numerous educational and government institutions worldwide. The Internet served for decades as a means for exchanging electronic mail (email), transferring files, and holding virtual conversations in newsgroups, although data shared online was typically static and text only. The new idea provided data in hypertext format, which made it easier for far-removed scientists to view the electronic library at CERN's information server. The hypertext data could even incorporate graphics and other file formats, a practice virtually unknown to Internet users of the time.

Despite a relatively small initial audience, the hypertext concept quickly caught on and by 1993 more than 50 hypertext information servers were available on the Internet. That year also saw the development of Mosaic, the first modern and truly user-friendly hypertext browser. Mosaic was produced by the National Center for Supercomputing Applications (NCSA) at the University of Illinois with versions for the X Window System, PC, and Macintosh. Mosaic served as the basis for a number of browsers produced by commercial software developers, with Netscape Navigator and Microsoft Internet Explorer eventually becoming Mosaic's best known offspring.

The world was eager when undergarment maker Joe Boxer published the first commercial Web site (www.joeboxer.com) in 1994. President Bill Clinton and Vice President Al Gore had already popularized the idea of an "information superhighway" during their 1992 political campaign, and by the next year it seemed that everyone wanted to get online and see what this new World Wide Web of information had to offer. A high level of media coverage meant that by 1995 most of the general public knew what the World Wide Web was, and they wanted to be part of it.

The rest, as they say, is history. In its current form, the Web exists on hundreds of thousands of servers around the world. The system of naming and addressing Web sites is implemented by a number of private registrars contracted by the United States Government. Today you can go shopping, play games, conduct research, download tax forms, check the status of a shipment, find directions to a new restaurant, get advice, or just plain goof off on the World Wide Web.

The hypertext concept has grown as well, even outside the confines of the Internet. To make interfacing with the Web more seamless, Microsoft has structured much of the Windows 2000 interface (as well as Windows 98) in a Hypertext Markup Language (HTML) format. Thus, you can use the same program—in this case, Internet Explorer 5—to browse the World Wide Web, your company's intranet, the contents of your own computer, and other network resources.

WHAT'S NEW IN INTERNET EXPLORER 5?

Internet Explorer 5 (IE5) comes delivered as an integral part of Windows 2000. Whereas with Windows NT 4, a Web browser was simply another program you added in, Windows 2000 uses the basic code behind IE5 to control Windows Explorer, My Computer, My Network Places, and many other aspects of the user interface.

If you have used Internet Explorer 4, IE5 will look and act in a familiar way. But it does offer a few new features that make IE5 significantly easier to use:

- Simpler "pushed" content—The previously convoluted subscriptions feature has been simplified to a single check box in the Favorites dialog, and the Active Desktop Channels have been eliminated.

- Integrated Web searching with the Search Assistant—The Search Assistant pools the resources of several popular search engines into a tool that works as a customizable part of the browser (see Figure 12.1).

Figure 12.1
Using the Internet Explorer 5 Search Assistant, you can easily search for different kids of information online.

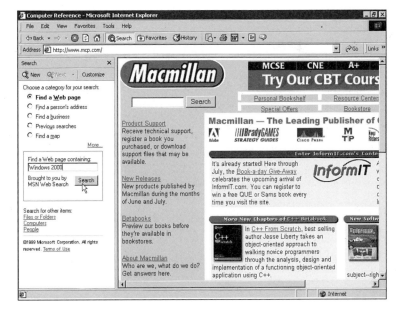

PART

III

CH

12

- AutoComplete when entering Web Uniform Resource Locators (URLs)—IE5 uses your browsing history to make it easier to revisit places you have already been.
- Integration with Microsoft Office 2000 products—If you have Office 2000 components such as Word 2000 or FrontPage 2000, you can easily use them to edit a Web page you are currently viewing with IE5.

INTERNET EXPLORER 5 QUICK TOUR

Web browsers have become so ubiquitous that we'll assume here that you are already familiar with the basics of Web browsing. And because many Windows 2000 elements such as Windows Explorer, the Control Panel, and My Network Places use the background code of IE5, you are probably already familiar with the location of common toolbar buttons, menus, and other screen elements.

Still, IE5 does have some new features, so an overview of how to use some of them is provided here. This overview will be especially useful if you are switching from an earlier version of Internet Explorer or another Web browser such as Netscape Navigator.

→ You must have a connection to the Internet configured on your computer before you can connect to the Web. **See** "Configuring your Internet Connection," **p. 415**.

You can begin browsing the Internet by launching Internet Explorer using the IE5 button on the Quick Launch toolbar, the IE5 desktop icon, or by choosing Start, Programs, Internet Explorer.

Tip #169	You can "transform" virtually any Explorer-based window in Windows 2000 into an Internet Explorer window by typing a Web URL in the Address bar and pressing Enter.

If you connect to the Internet via a dial-up connection, you may be prompted to connect. When the connection is established, Internet Explorer probably opens to the MSN (The Microsoft Network) home page, as shown in Figure 12.2. Some PC manufacturers—such as Compaq—customize IE5 before delivery so that you see their home page instead.

 Did a Web page freeze your browser? See "Internet Explorer Crashes on Certain Web Pages" in the "Troubleshooting" section at the end of the chapter.

As you probably know, Web pages change frequently, so the page you see will almost certainly look different from Figure 12.2. The general layout of the IE5 window might also be somewhat different from what is shown here, although if you have performed a standard installation of Windows 2000 and have not done any customizations, it should look like this.

Tip #170	Want even more space to view Web pages? Press F11 to change the view to get rid of some screen elements and make more room for Web documents. If you don't like what you see, press F11 again to toggle back.

Address bar

Toolbar

Links bar

Figure 12.2
Internet Explorer opens with MSN, the default home page, displayed.

Status bar

If you visit a few Web pages frequently, consider creating buttons for them on the Links bar. But first click and drag the Links bar to a more visible portion of the screen. It should look something like Figure 12.3. If you want to customize the Links bar, keep these tips in mind:

- The Customize Links button is not very useful. It merely takes you to a Microsoft-hosted Web page that provides instructions on how to do what is already described here.

Figure 12.3
The Links bar is a handy place to store your most frequently visited Web sites.

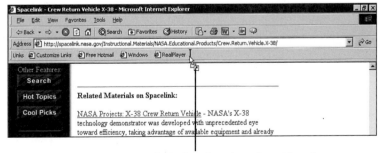

Drag and drop a Web site icon here from the Address bar

PART
III

CH
12

- You can remove unwanted buttons by right-clicking them and choosing Delete from the menu that appears.

- The easiest way to add a Web page to the Links bar is to drag the icon for the page from the Address bar and drop it on the Links bar. Figure 12.3 demonstrates this technique.

- To save room, consider placing the Links bar on the same "line" as the Address bar. If you are using 800×600 or greater screen resolution, you should have enough space onscreen for them to fit beside each other.

As you probably know, you can navigate around the Internet by typing Web addresses into the Address bar or by clicking hyperlinks on a page. The mouse pointer turns into a hand whenever it is over a link. Among the most useful features of the IE5 interface are the Back and Forward buttons. When you click the Back button, you return to the previously visited page, and clicking Forward moves you ahead once again.

 Are you frustrated because Internet Explorer tells you that a site you visit often is unavailable? See "What Happened to the Web Site?" in the "Troubleshooting" section at the end of this chapter.

Notice that next to both the Back and Forward buttons are downward-pointing arrows. If you have been browsing for a few minutes, click the down arrow next to the Back button. A menu similar to that shown in Figure 12.4 should appear showing a backward progression of the Web pages you have visited. Click a listing to move back several pages simultaneously rather than one at a time.

Figure 12.4

→ If you want something else to be your home page, **see** "Customizing the Browser and Setting Internet Options," **p. 450**.

ENTERING URLs

Every Web document you view in IE5 is identified by a unique address called a *Uniform Resource Locator (URL)*. When you visit a Web page, for example, the URL for that page appears in the Address bar of Internet Explorer. URLs for links also appear in the status bar when you hover the mouse pointer over a hyperlink.

URLs are broken down into three main components. To illustrate, consider these URLs:

```
http://www.mcp.com/
```

```
http://www.irs.treas.gov/prod/forms_pubs/forms.html
```

```
http://www.proaxis.com/~kcunderdahl/garage.htm
```

Each of the listed addresses conforms to this scheme:

```
protocol://domain/path
```

The protocol for all World Wide Web documents is http, short for *hypertext transfer protocol*. The protocol is followed by a colon and two forward slashes and then the domain name. The domain often—but not always—starts with www. Following the domain is the path to a specific document file. You may notice that the first URL listed here does not actually show a path; this is usually okay because Internet Explorer automatically looks for a file called default.htm, index.htm, home.html, or something along those lines in the root directory of the domain.

Tip #171	If you get an error message when trying to visit a URL, remove the path from the address and try again.

When you type a URL into the Address bar in IE5, a built-in feature automatically reviews your browsing history and presents a number of possible matches. A list appears directly under the Address bar and shrinks as you type more characters, thus narrowing the search. If you see a desired URL appear in the list, click it to go directly to that page. This feature is called AutoComplete and is part of a technology package that Microsoft calls IntelliSense.

AutoComplete can save keystrokes, but it can also be incriminating if others use your computer and user profile. AutoComplete works with Web form data as well, which means that others could see your user IDs, passwords, and other sensitive data for various sites. If you are concerned about others viewing your data, disable the feature by doing the following:

1. Choose Tools, Internet Options.
2. Click the Content tab to bring it to the front, and then click AutoComplete.
3. Remove check marks next to the items you do not want affected by AutoComplete.
4. You can further safeguard existing information by clicking either of the two Clear buttons in the AutoComplete Settings dialog. Click OK when you are finished.
5. To prevent existing Web URLs from being compromised, select the General tab in the Internet Options dialog, and click Clear History. Click OK to close the Internet Options dialog when you're finished.

PART

III

CH

12

Note	If no one else has access to your Windows 2000 user profile, AutoComplete doesn't present a security problem. In this case, you should be able to safely leave the feature enabled.

VIEWING YOUR COMPUTER'S CONTENTS FROM A BROWSER WINDOW

IE5 is a fully integrated part of the Windows 2000 operating system. The graphical user interface presents system resources in HTML format, so browsing the contents of your computer is no more complicated than browsing the World Wide Web.

Open Internet Explorer 5 if it isn't already open. Now follow these steps:

1. In the Address bar, type c:\ (where c: is the hard drive on which Windows 2000 is installed), and press Enter.

2. The contents of your hard drive should be displayed, similar to Figure 12.5. Your view settings determine the exact layout of the window. Notice that the window is virtually identical to what would be displayed in My Computer if you had opened that instead.

Figure 12.5
The contents of the computer's hard disk are displayed in Internet Explorer. The drive letter may be different on your PC.

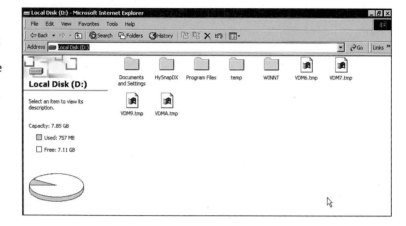

3. Double-click the icon for the WINNT folder. Some folders do not automatically show their contents. Look for a blue hyperlink on the left side of the window to reveal the contents.

Just as with My Computer or Windows Explorer, you can manage system resources in the IE5 window. You can use the Back and Forward buttons to move through your system resources just as you can with Web pages. If you want to browse the Web again, just enter another URL in the Address bar to replace the address of your local resources.

BROWSING OFFLINE

If you have a permanent Internet connection that is never interrupted or shut off, consider yourself fortunate. A permanent connection—such as what you might have through your company's network—allows you a great deal of flexibility in terms of what and when you download from the World Wide Web.

Alas, not all users have this sort of flexibility in their daily computing. Internet Explorer offers you the ability to download Web pages into cache for offline viewing. This feature can be useful in a variety of situations. For example, you can set up IE5 to download specific Web sites in the background every time you go online. You can also download Web sites onto your portable computer so that you can view them later while you're on the plane. In IE4, this capability was called Subscriptions, but setting up a page for offline viewing involved a complex and challenging process.

Note

Internet Explorer works just fine whether or not an Internet connection is available. However, if no connection is available, it can view only files stored on the local computer or other available network resources. The IE5 status bar displays this icon when you are working in offline mode.

The process of downloading a Web site for offline browsing is fairly simple. Your first step, obviously, is to browse to the Web site you want to make available offline. For best results, open the main or index page of the Web site first. Now try the following:

1. Choose Favorites, Add to Favorites.

2. In the Add Favorite dialog, click the Make Available Offline option to place a check mark next to it, as shown in Figure 12.6. You can also change the name if you like; the name entered here is what will be shown in your Favorites list.

Figure 12.6
In this dialog, you can check the Make Available Offline option and click Customize.

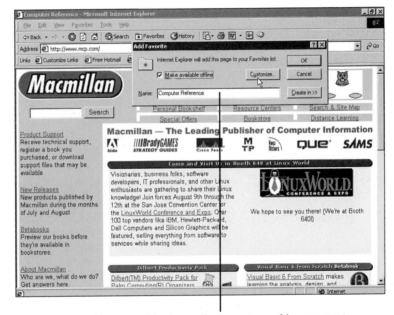

You can safely change the name to anything you want

PART

III

CH

12

3. The Offline Favorite Wizard guides you through the process of setting up offline browsing. Click Next in the introductory dialog to open the window shown in Figure 12.7. Depending on the layout of the site, this screen could contain the most important options that you will set.

Figure 12.7
Here, you can choose how many link levels you want to make available offline.

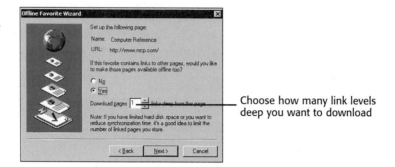

Choose how many link levels deep you want to download

4. Usually, you will probably want to choose Yes when asked whether you want to down-load pages that are linked to the one you are making available offline. For example, if the main page is a list of news stories, the next level of links probably contains the actu-al stories. Viewing a list of stories won't do you much good without also being able to read the stories!

5. If you chose Yes in the preceding step, select the number of levels you want to down-load. The exact number will depend on the layout of the site.

Tip #172

If you aren't sure how many levels to download, cancel this process, and browse the Web site to get a feel for it. Too many levels could result in a lot of unwanted content, and not enough will leave you trying to click links that are unavailable.

6. Click Next after you have decided if and how many link levels you want to download. In the next window, you must choose between downloading the pages manually or auto-matically. If you will browse offline only occasionally—say, on a laptop—choose the first option and skip to step 8. Otherwise, select the second option, and click Next to create a schedule for downloads.

7. Select a schedule to synchronize the download process. In Figure 12.8, a schedule has been set to download the pages when the computer is least likely to be in use. You can also choose to have the computer automatically connect to the Internet for you if a con-nection does not already exist when the synchronization time comes.

Figure 12.8
In this wizard window, you can set a schedule for downloading pages to read offline.

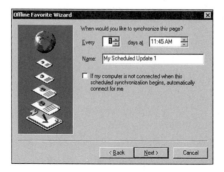

8. Click Next when you are finished setting your schedule. If the Web site requires a username and password, you must enter it in the last window of the wizard. Click Finish when you're finished. If the Add Favorite dialog is still open, click OK to close it.

VIEWING PAGES OFFLINE

Now that you've set up a schedule and have downloaded some pages for offline viewing, you are ready to actually read them offline. To do so, just follow these steps:

1. Open Internet Explorer. If you are prompted to establish an Internet connection, click the Work Offline button. Internet Explorer will probably load a copy of your home page from cache, so it will appear as if you are online when, in reality, you aren't.

2. To view a synchronized offline page you have set up and downloaded, click Favorites and choose the page's listing from the Favorites menu. You can view the page and click links that have been downloaded.

 3. Notice that if you move the mouse pointer over a link that has not been downloaded, the pointer hand has a not available symbol next to it.

If you click a link that isn't available, you are asked whether you want to connect or remain in offline mode. If you do not or cannot connect, you cannot open the link.

DEALING WITH MULTIMEDIA BROWSING AND DOWNLOADING

When the World Wide Web first debuted as a method for sharing scientific data among physicists, the hypertext format of the data was specifically chosen to lend itself to sharing information in many different formats. For early Internet users, the ability to download pictures and other graphics in conjunction with Web pages was both exciting and profound.

Today, Web pages with pictures in them are commonplace. Web developers continue to push the multimedia horizon further out, with many sites now featuring audio tracks and moving video. You can even listen to radio stations and other broadcasts live over the Web.

In addition to multimedia-rich Web sites, you'll also find that the Web is a good place to download new software. You can find many places to download freeware, shareware, software updates, and even purchase full versions of some programs.

IMAGES

Believe it or not, graphics-rich Web sites used to be controversial. Some people believed that graphics would put too much of a strain on the bandwidth capacity of the Internet, but those gloom-and-doom predictions have not come to pass. Backbone improvements have helped the Net keep pace with the ever-growing appetite for multimedia on the Web, and images are now not only commonplace but in many cases expected.

Internet Explorer supports two basic graphics formats used in Web pages:

- JPEG—Short for Joint Photographic Experts Group, this format allows pictures to be compressed significantly, reducing download time and bandwidth. Photographs on Web pages are often in the JPEG format.

- GIF—Short for Graphical Interchange Format, this format is often used for buttons and other simple icons used on Web pages.

The exact format used for each image is not apparent when you view the page. Usually, the specific format used is not important unless you plan to copy the graphics and use them for some other purpose. For Web use, the formats are essentially interchangeable.

By default, IE5 displays graphics used in Web pages. If you have a very slow Internet connection—say, 14,400 bps or slower—you might want to change this option. With graphics disabled, only the text of Web pages will be downloaded to your computer, with placeholders indicating where graphics should be. You can open graphics individually by right-clicking the placeholder and choosing Show Picture.

 What if some graphics on a page open, but others don't? See "Some Graphics Don't Appear" in the "Troubleshooting" section at the end of the chapter.

Tip #173

Although the idea of speedier downloads might seem appealing, many Web pages now rely so heavily on graphics that they do not include text links. This means you cannot navigate the site without the images. Don't disable this feature unless you deem it absolutely necessary.

To disable automatic downloading of graphics, follow these steps:

1. Open Internet Explorer and choose Tools, Internet Options.

2. Click the Advanced tab to bring it to the front, and scroll down the list of settings until you see the list of Multimedia options, as shown in Figure 12.9.

Figure 12.9
In this dialog, you can choose which multimedia elements you want to open automatically when you view Web pages.

3. Remove the check mark next to Show Pictures to disable automatic downloading of graphics. Click OK when you're finished.

Besides choosing whether you want to download pictures, you can do other things with online graphics:

- You can save graphics on your hard drive for future use. To do so, just right-click a picture you want to save, and choose Save Picture As from the shortcut menu. You can then select a location to save the graphic.

- Set a graphic as your Windows desktop wallpaper by right-clicking the image and choosing Set as Wallpaper.

Caution

Before you use any graphics you find on the Web, check the Web site for a copyright statement or other information about terms of use. You should obtain permission before you use any copyrighted material.

AUDIO AND VIDEO

A growing number of Web sites offer audio or video content in addition to standard text and graphics. The terms *audio* and *video* when used in conjunction with Web content can mean a few different things:

- Basic audio files—such as MIDI music files—that play in the background while you view a Web page.

- Video files on Web sites that download and then play automatically, or when you click a Play button.

- Video media that plays using the Windows Media Player.

- Animated GIFs that give the appearance of a video signal but with a significantly reduced bandwidth requirement. They display a series of GIF frames that simulate video and are often used in logos.

- Streaming audio or video that you choose to open and listen to or watch.

You might have noticed that, when you visit some Web sites, a song starts to play while you read the page. Audio isn't nearly as common as graphics in Web pages because some people find it annoying. If you come across a Web page that contains a song you would rather not hear, the most obvious solution is to simply turn your speaker volume down or mute the Windows volume control.

Likewise, some Web sites contain video files and animations set to download and play automatically. MPEG and AVI video files are usually very large, and if you have restricted

PART

III

CH

12

bandwidth capacity, you might want to consider disabling them. Animations usually aren't as large as video files, but if your connection is very slow, you can disable them as well. Follow the instructions in the preceding section regarding images to disable other types of multimedia downloads.

Before you get too excited about Web-based video, it is important to remember that in spite of the great "gee-whiz" technological appeal, audio and video quality will pale in comparison to what is produced by a plain old television set. Whereas a broadcast TV signal may deliver 30 or more frames per second (fps), typical Web-based streaming videos provide just 10 to 15fps (or even fewer). MPEG and AVI videos are better but still generally limited to fewer than 25fps.

MPEG AND AVI VIDEOS

By default, MPEG and AVI files are played using Windows Media Player 6.0. When you click a link for an MPEG or AVI film, it must first download, and depending on your connection speed, downloading may take awhile. These files are, by nature, very large; the 29-second MPEG clip shown in Figure 12.10 is 1.3MB.

You might notice that Media Player opens as soon as you click the link. It remains blank, however, until the entire file is downloaded. When the download is complete, the Media Player window automatically resizes to fit the file's resolution and begins playing, as shown in Figure 12.10.

Figure 12.10
An MPEG video plays in the Windows Media Player.

Notice that the Media Player contains standard Play, Pause, Stop, Skip, Rewind, and Fast Forward buttons similar to a CD player. You might want to customize certain elements of the Media Player:

- To view the video in full-screen mode, click View, Full Screen, or press Alt+Enter. It reverts to the normal view when the video is complete. Depending on your display hardware and the format of the video file, playback quality may be diminished in full-screen mode.

- You can choose to have the video continuously repeat playback by opening the Options dialog (by choosing View, Options). On the Playback tab, select the Repeat Forever option.

- On the Player tab of the Options dialog, you might find it handy to select the Open a New Player for Each Media File Played option if you want to keep several video files available at the same time.

- MSN maintains a schedule of online "media" events. You can click the Web Events button in Media Player to jump instantly to their schedule.

Before you close the Media Player window, consider whether you want to save the video you downloaded. Downloaded files are normally saved to cache, so they won't necessarily be accessible later. If you want to save the video, choose File, Save As and save it to a safe location.

STREAMING BROADCASTS

Another type of sound or video you might play over the Internet is *streaming audio* or *streaming video*. Streaming audio/video is a format in which a signal "plays" over your Internet connection in real-time, as opposed to playing from a file that was first downloaded to your hard drive.

When you first access a streaming signal, a portion of the signal is buffered in *RAM* on your computer. This buffer helps provide a steady feed if connection quality wavers. If the signal is received faster than it can be played, the additional data is buffered. However, if your connection deteriorates significantly, the signal may break up and not play smoothly. Streaming broadcasts are not written to a disk cache file, so retrieving the signal later from your own PC will be impossible.

Most streaming audio signals require a minimum 14.4Kbps connection speed, but even that low speed provides a relatively low-quality broadcast. Streaming video signals generally require at least a 28.8Kbps connection. For most streaming broadcasts, a 56Kbps or greater connection is most desirable.

Streaming audio signals are often used to play various types of audio signals over the Web. For example, CDNow (www.cdnow.com)—an online music retailer—offers you the ability to listen to sample audio tracks from many of the CDs it sells. Also, you can listen to many radio stations and programs—such as the Art Bell Show (www.artbell.com)—over your Internet connection instead of a radio.

Streaming video is used by a number of information providers to send newscasts and other broadcasts across the Web. Many *Star Wars* fans, for example, utilized streaming video in early 1999 as a means for viewing new movie previews over the Web. MSN (windowsmedia.msn.com) provides links to a number of online video resources, streaming and otherwise.

To access streaming audio or video signals, you need to have an appropriate plug-in program for IE5, such as the RealPlayer G2 from Real Broadcast Network (www.real.com), QuickTime from Apple (www.apple.com/quicktime/), or Windows Media Player 6.0, included with Windows 2000. After you have downloaded and installed the appropriate streaming player (following the installation instructions provided by the player's publisher), you can access the streaming signals over the Web.

Although the Windows Media Player can handle many formats, most broadcasts require a specific player. Check the Web site that hosts the streaming media you want to play for specific requirements. RealPlayer is by far the most common application used for streaming audio, and QuickTime is used by many streaming video providers. Some Web sites may offer a choice of player formats; the NASA Web site (www.nasa.gov) lets you choose either Media Player or RealVideo format for most of its streaming broadcasts.

→ To learn about downloading programs from the Web, **see** "Downloading Programs," **p. 448**.

To use a streaming media player, follow these steps:

1. Locate a link to an audio clip or video signal you want to access, and click it.

2. Your streaming media player should open automatically, as shown in Figure 12.11. As you can see here, the RealPlayer G2 includes standard Play, Pause, and Stop buttons. The Windows Media Player and Apple QuickTime work in a similar manner.

Figure 12.11
A streaming audio clip of a song plays using the RealPlayer G2.

3. When you are finished listening to the streaming signal, click the Close (x) button for the player.

When you access a streaming signal from the Web, pay special attention to the bandwidth requirements. Many signal providers provide scaling of signals from as low as 14.4Kbps up to 56Kbps. Choosing a signal that is scaled higher will provide a higher quality broadcast, but only if your connection can handle it. If you choose a larger signal than you have bandwidth for, the signal will arrive too fragmented to use. For example, suppose you use a dial-up connection that typically runs at 24Kbps to 26Kbps, and the broadcaster offers signals in either 14.4 or 28.8 flavors. Although you might be tempted to opt for the 28.8Kbps signal because your connection is *almost* up to it, you will probably find that the 14.4Kbps broadcast provides a more usable signal.

MP3 AUDIO

MP3 is an audio file format that is quickly growing in popularity. MP3 is the file extension for files using MPEG Audio Layer 3, a coding scheme for audio tracks. MP3 files are small, on average about one-twelfth the size of CD audio tracks, while at the same time they maintain a high sound quality. One minute of CD-quality MP3 music requires approximately 1MB of storage space.

Controversy has surrounded MP3 since its introduction. The small size of MP3 files makes it relatively easy to pirate music and illegally distribute it over the Internet, thus circumventing copyright laws. Nevertheless, MP3 has become extremely popular, even among people who never break the law.

Tip #174

The bottom line is this: Distributing or downloading MP3 files from any artist without permission is theft. Although many artists, particularly new artists, willingly provide audio tracks for free download as a means for building a fan base, many MP3 sites contain audio files that have been pirated. If you have questions about the legality of MP3 files you find on the Internet, the best (and most moral) thing for you to do is not to download them.

If you would like to learn more about the MP3 format and how to determine whether the MP3 files you find on the Web are legal for download, see www.mp3.com.

MP3 files can be played by many different applications, including Windows Media Player 6.0, RealPlayer G2, and QuickTime 4. A number of consumer electronics companies are also now producing devices that allow you to play MP3 files away from your computer. Diamond Multimedia's (www.diamondmm.com) pocket-sized Rio player works like a portable CD or tape player, allowing you to take MP3 music anywhere. You can transfer MP3 files to the player's storage via a Universal Serial Bus (USB), parallel, or serial port connection.

MSN provides links to some free MP3 downloads at windowsmedia.microsoft.com/music/. Another good resource is MP3.com (www.mp3.com). After you have downloaded an MP3 file, you can play it using the Windows Media Player, RealPlayer, QuickTime, or any other MP3-compatible player.

PART

III

CH

12

Tip #175

Sound quality is affected not only by your hardware, but also by the player application. Experiment with several different programs to see which one you prefer.

When you click a Web page link for an MP3 file, your default MP3 application will probably open. It may or may not be the application you want to use. Also, the MP3 file will be inconveniently saved in IE5's cache. You can exercise a bit more control over the whole process by following these steps:

1. When you see a link for an MP3 file, right-click the link and choose Save Target As.

2. Select a safe location in which to save the file download.

3. When the download is complete, open the desired player application manually, and choose File, Open to open and listen to the file. If you click Open in the File Download dialog, your default MP3 player will open.

DOWNLOADING PROGRAMS

Although the World Wide Web is most often thought of as a source of information and entertainment, it is also an excellent place to obtain new software or updates for existing programs.

You can find numerous excellent resources for downloading free or trial versions of software. One great source is TUCOWS (www.tucows.com). Most Web sites that offer software downloads provide instructions, and you need to follow specific instructions for installation provided by the software publisher. But when you're downloading, these general rules apply:

- Some Web sites require you to choose a mirror site for your download. Normally, you are asked to select a location that is geographically close to you, although you are usually free to choose any site you want.

- Select a location for saving the download files that you will remember. If you can download the files to a removable disk, it will be safest.

- Check with your network administrator before installing any new software to find out what your company policies are.

- Scan all downloads with virus-scanning software before you install them.

- Many downloads come in a compressed .ZIP format. If you download such a file, you need an appropriate compression program such as WinZip (www.winzip.com) to decompress it.

Tip #176
Downloads are quickest when Internet traffic is low, such as late at night. If you are given a choice of mirror sites for a download, keep in mind the local time for each site; servers located where current traffic is lower usually are faster.

During the download process, a window similar to Figure 12.12 showing the download progress appears. Notice that it also shows an estimation of the time remaining in the download.

Figure 12.12
Download progress is shown in this dialog. If you can't wait that long, click Cancel.

In addition to downloading new software, you can also frequently download updates to software you already have. Check the manufacturer's Web site from time to time to see whether new updates, patches, or bug fixes are available. Another great source of information on software updates is the Versions! Web site (www.versions.com).

Tip #177	Create a Software folder in your Favorites list, and add the manufacturer Web sites for software you own to the folder. Doing so will make it easier to periodically check for updates later.

Trouble with PDF documents on the Web? See "PDF Files on the Web" in the "Troubleshooting" section at the end of the chapter.

CUSTOMIZING THE BROWSER AND SETTING INTERNET OPTIONS

One of the most important features of Internet Explorer 5 is the capability to tailor it to your own specific needs. Every user sets up IE5 differently based on programs used, favorite Web sites, bandwidth capability, security needs, and so on.

You can make most customizations in the Internet Options dialog, which you can access either through the Windows Control Panel or by choosing Tools, Internet Options in IE5. The dialog contains six tabs, each holding a number of unique preference settings. Figure 12.13 shows the General tab.

Check each tab in the dialog to customize your own IE5 settings. Table 12.1 describes some of the key preference settings you can change.

PART

III

CH

12

Figure 12.13
On the General tab, you can set general preferences for your home page, temporary cache files, history, and browser view options.

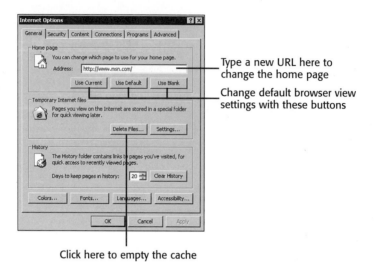

Type a new URL here to change the home page

Change default browser view settings with these buttons

Click here to empty the cache

TABLE 12.1   IMPORTANT INTERNET OPTIONS

Tab	Option	Description
General	Home Page	The home page is the first page that appears when you open Internet Explorer. It is probably set to MSN or has been customized by your PC's manufacturer. Consider changing this page to your company's home page or something else you find more valuable.
	Temporary Internet Files	When you view a Web page, the files for the page are saved on your hard drive as *Temporary Internet Files* (also called *cache*). You can clear all files from the cache or change the amount of disk space they are allowed to consume.
	History	A record of the Web sites you have visited is maintained by IE5. You can change the length of time these records are kept or clear the history altogether.
	Colors, Fonts, and so on	You can customize default colors, fonts, languages, and set accessibility options here.
Security	Zones and Levels	You can set security options for IE5. See "Setting Security Preferences" later in this chapter.
Content	Content Advisor	You can control the capability to view objectionable content on your computer. See "Controlling Objectionable Content" later in this chapter.

Tab	Option	Description
	Certificates	When a Web page tries to run a script or install a piece of software on your computer, you can accept certificates from the publisher to authenticate their identity and trustworthiness. See "Setting Security Preferences" later in this chapter.
	AutoComplete	You can enable or disable AutoComplete when typing Web URLs, email addresses, or form data.
	Wallet	You can store personal information such as credit card numbers, your address, and other data that may be required for online shopping transactions.
	My Profile	You can create a profile for yourself in the Microsoft Address Book.
Connections		You can set up preferences for your Internet connection, whether it be through a dial-up or network connection.
Programs		You can select default programs for various actions. See "Setting Default Mail, News, and HTML Editor Programs" next.
Advanced		You can set various (but obscure) options for browsing, multimedia, Java scripts, security, and searching.

SETTING DEFAULT MAIL, NEWS, AND HTML EDITOR PROGRAMS

Using the Programs tab of the Internet Options dialog, you can decide some default programs for a variety of Internet-related tasks. If you have not installed any other Internet software packages, you probably won't have too many choices here, but if you use different programs, these options can be useful. Figure 12.14 shows the default program settings you can make on the Programs tab, and Table 12.2 describes the various options you can set.

PART

III

CH

12

Figure 12.14
On the Programs tab, you can choose the default programs for the various Internet tasks you perform.

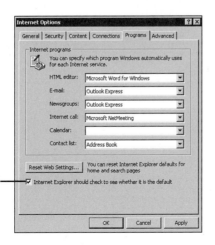

Remove this check mark if you want another installed Web browser (such as Netscape Navigator) to remain the default

TABLE 12.2   DEFAULT INTERNET PROGRAMS

Program	Description
HTML Editor	If you are a Web developer, make sure the correct editor is listed here. This will simplify editing during your testing process. The list might include Word 2000, Notepad, FrontPage 2000, or another installed editor.
E-mail	This program will open when you click the Mail button on the IE5 toolbar or when you click an email link on a Web page.
Newsgroups	If you link to or open a newsgroup URL, the reader listed here will open.
Internet Call	Microsoft NetMeeting is the default Internet Call client, but if you have another call program, you can select it here.
Calendar	If you have a calendar program such as Outlook, you can set it here.
Contact List	The default list is the Microsoft Address Book. You should set this to the Address Book used by your favorite email and calendar program.

⚠ *Email links in Web pages can cause many frustrations. See "Email Link Troubles" in the "Troubleshooting" section at the end of the chapter.*

SETTING SECURITY PREFERENCES

In many ways, the World Wide Web is a safer place than the "real" world, but it does present its own unique dangers as well. The greatest hazards involve sensitive and private information about you or your company being compromised, or in having your computer infected with a software virus. IE5 incorporates a number of security features to protect you from these hazards, and those features can be customized to suit your own needs, browsing habits, and company policies.

Begin by opening the Internet Options dialog from the IE5 Tools menu if it isn't already open, and click the Security tab to bring it to the front (see Figure 12.15).

Figure 12.15
On the Security tab, you can customize security settings for various Web zones.

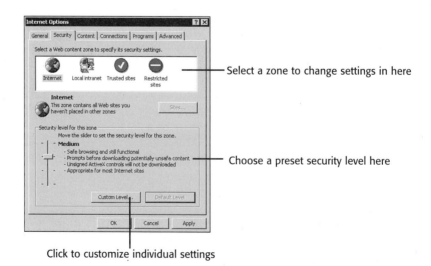

Select a zone to change settings in here

Choose a preset security level here

Click to customize individual settings

You first need to select a zone for which you want to customize settings. The four zones are shown in Figure 12.15.

Internet	This zone applies to all resources outside your LAN or intranet.
Local Intranet	This zone applies to pages available on your company's intranet. They are usually more trustworthy and can justify less restrictive settings.
Trusted Sites	You manually designate these sites as trusted. To designate a trusted site, browse to the site, open this dialog, select the Trusted Sites zone, and click Sites. Here, you can add the site to your Trusted Sites zone list. Trusted sites usually allow lighter security.
Restricted Sites	Designated in the same manner as Trusted Sites, Web sites listed here are ones you specifically find untrustworthy. They should have the strictest security settings.

Caution

Before you designate a Web page as trusted, try to remember that even the most diligently maintained sites can be compromised. Recent "hacker" attacks at Web sites of the FBI, U.S. Army, and others make the practice of designating any Web site as "trustworthy" questionable.

Each zone has its own security preferences, which you set. The easiest way to set preferences is to choose one of the four basic levels offered in the dialog. The default level is Medium, and for most Web users, this setting works best because it provides a good balance of security and usability. The High setting offers the greatest possible security, but you might find that the level is so restrictive that it's difficult to browse your favorite Web sites.

Likewise, the Low and Medium-Low levels make browsing much easier because you aren't presented with dialogs and warnings every time a potentially hazardous activity begins. Because these two levels leave too many doors open to virus infection and other dangers, they are not advisable in most situations.

Besides setting a basic security level, you can customize individual settings. First, choose a basic level (such as Medium), and then try these steps:

1. Click Custom Level to open the Security Settings dialog, as shown in Figure 12.16.
2. Browse through the list of options, and apply custom settings as you see fit.
3. Click OK when you're finished. A warning dialog appears, asking whether you really want to apply the changes. Choose Yes.

The items in the Security Settings dialog that most deserve your attention are those pertaining to ActiveX controls and Java applets. Review these settings carefully, especially those for

PART
III

CH
12

ActiveX controls, because of the unique hazards they can present. The ActiveX standard contains loopholes, so unsigned controls can run virtually any OLE-compliant operation on your system. Java, on the other hand, is relatively—but not entirely—secure.

Figure 12.16
You can scroll through this list to make custom security setting changes.

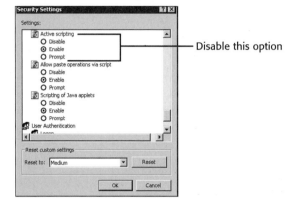

Disable this option

You should also consider what level of cookie security you are willing to live with. A *cookie* is a small text file that some Web sites can leave on your computer in cache. Because cookies are text only, they cannot contain a virus or other harmful content. However, they can contain personal information such as a record of Web pages you have visited, how long you spent at a page, how many times you have visited, personal preferences for a Web page, and even user IDs and passwords. It is for these reasons that cookies are regarded by many people as an invasion of privacy.

You can disable cookies, or you can choose to have IE5 prompt you every time a site attempts to leave a cookie in your cache. However, keep in mind that some Web sites make such heavy use of cookies that you could find it difficult—if not impossible—to browse the Web normally.

Tip #178

A major security hole in IE5 involves the option Allow Paste Operations via Script, which is enabled in all security levels but High. It allows any Web site to see the contents of your Windows Clipboard via a scripted Paste operation. If you have been working with sensitive information in another program and used a Copy or Cut command, that information could be compromised by unscrupulous Webmasters. To be on the safe side, change this setting to Disable or Prompt no matter which security level you use.

USING ENCRYPTION

The Advanced tab of the Internet Options dialog has a number of other security settings that deserve your attention. In particular, most of the security settings here deal with *certificates*. Certificates can be saved on your computer and serve to authenticate your identity or the identity of the server you are connected to. They also provide for secure encrypted communication over secure Web connections.

IE5 supports *Secure Socket Layer (SSL) encryption* technology developed by Netscape. It supports 128-bit encrypted SSL sessions, the highest level of data encryption available in the online world. SSL encryption works using a pair of encryption keys, one public and one private. One key is needed to decrypt the other. Certificates facilitate this use by including the following information:

- The issuing authority, such as VeriSign
- The identity of the person or organization for whom the certificate is issued
- The public key
- Time stamps

Thus, the certificate provides and authenticates the basis for an encrypted session. The identity is re-verified, the private key is shared, and encryption is enabled.

Another encryption protocol supported by IE5 is *Private Communication Technology (PCT)*, developed by Microsoft. PCT is similar to SSL encryption, except that it uses a separate key for identity authentication and data encryption. Thus, in theory, PCT should provide slightly enhanced security versus SSL.

Again, encryption protocols can be enabled or disabled on the Advanced tab of the Internet Options dialog. If you disable a protocol, any page you try to access on a secure server that uses that protocol will not open in IE5.

→ Learn how to obtain a digital certificate for yourself in "Handling Digital IDs," **p. 481**.

CONTROLLING OBJECTIONABLE CONTENT

The World Wide Web holds the most diverse range of information and content of any library in the world. That diverse range includes a great deal of material that you might deem objectionable, and there is no perfect way of protecting yourself from it short of never going online. However, IE5 incorporates a feature called the Content Advisor, a tool to help you screen out much of the things you or the other people using your computer would rather not see.

The Content Advisor evaluates Web content based on a rating system. The included rating system is developed by RSACi (Recreational Software Advisory Council on the Internet), but you can add others if you want.

You must enable the Content Advisor manually, but after it is set up, the Advisor can be password-protected so that only you can adjust the settings. To enable the Content Advisor, open the Internet Options dialog, and perform the following:

1. Click the Content tab to bring it to the front, and click Enable to open the Content Advisor dialog.

2. The Content Advisor dialog contains four tabs, as shown in Figure 12.17. On the Ratings tab, you can move the slider back and forth to set a rating level in each of the four categories presented.

Figure 12.17
On the Ratings tab, you can move the slider back and forth to change the rating level.

Move this slider to change the rating level

Select a rating category here

Click here to learn more about the ratings system

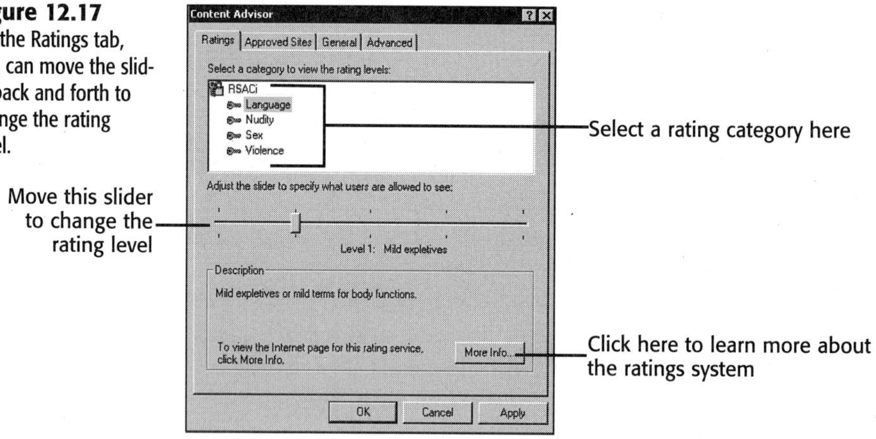

3. Click the Approved Sites tab to bring it to the front. List specific Web sites here to control access to them. Click Always to make it easily acceptable, or click Never to restrict access.

4. On the General tab, choose whether unrated sites can be viewed. Keep in mind that many objectionable sites will not be rated. You can also set a password to let people in unrated or restricted sites on a case-by-case basis, or you can add another rating system here.

5. Click the Advanced tab. If you plan to use a ratings bureau or PICSRules file you obtain from the Internet, your ISP, or another source, add it here. Click OK when you're finished.

RSACi and other organizations provide content rating systems based on the PICS (Platform for Internet Content Selection) system developed by the World Wide Web Consortium, or W3C (www.w3.org/PICS/). They work using meta tags in the code of a Web page. The tags are usually generated by the rating organization after a site developer follows a brief rating procedure. Developers can then place the PICS meta tag in the header of their HTML code, where it is identified by IE5's Content Advisor when you try to open the page. The tag identifies the types and levels of content contained in the site, and the Content Advisor allows or disallows the site based on the content settings you have chosen. If you want to screen Web sites using a system other than RSACi's, you must install an appropriate PICSRules file provided by the rating organization.

Of course, rating is voluntary. Developers set the rating levels in the meta tags based on their own evaluation of the site content, so you never really get a surefire guarantee that the tag accurately represents the site. RSACi periodically audits rated sites, and Web developers generally *try* to rate their sites as accurately as possible. It is a voluntary system, after all, and providing inaccurate ratings defeats the purpose of voluntary rating in the first place.

OTHER INTERNET SETTINGS

A number of other settings deserve your attention. On the Content tab of the Internet Options dialog, check the AutoComplete and Wallet option groups to make sure they do not contain information that you are concerned about being compromised. AutoComplete makes it easier to fill in data fields on forms and URLs in the Address bar, but if other people use your user identity, they could end up seeing your personal information because of these settings. Likewise, the Wallet is designed to store deeply personal information such as credit card numbers, so protect this information if others have access to your PC and identity.

You should also scroll through the Advanced tab settings again. If you are a Web developer, you might want to disable the Enable Page Hit Counting option to ensure that your own visits to the site don't skew the data collected by your counter.

One setting you probably should *not* enable is the Print Background Colors and Images option. If a Web page uses anything but a plain white background, a printed copy of it will waste a considerable amount of printer ink and probably be harder to read.

Review the Search settings on the Advanced tab. In previous versions of Internet Explorer, if you wanted to visit a Web site with a fairly simple URL such as www.mcp.com, all you had to type was mcp and press Enter. Internet Explorer would assume the missing www. and .com and fill it in for you. But now, if you type only mcp in the Address bar, IE5 opens a Search window in the Explorer bar. In theory, this is supposed to make searching easier, but if you've been using IE for a while, you might find it annoying.

You cannot completely restore the previous function of "assuming" the missing bits of the URL, but you can modify the way in which this feature works. The different search options will have the following results:

- Display results and go to the most likely site—The default setting, it opens the Explorer bar search window. In some cases, the "most likely" site will also appear in the main window, but it may or may not be what you were hoping for.

- Do not search from the Address bar—No search is made of any kind. Typing a single word in the Address bar will generally result in a Page not available error.

- Just display the results in the main window—No attempt is made to find a close match, nor is the Explorer bar opened. A search engine will open in the main window.

- Just go to the most likely site—In theory, this setting should work as in previous IE versions, but in practice it does not. It first looks for a match within the Microsoft Web domain and then tries to find a match at large. Select this option, and then type mcp in the Address bar to see what we mean.

Under Security, check Empty Temporary Internet Files Folder When Browser Is Closed to discard cache files you don't want others to see. This setting can also be useful if disk space is limited, but you shouldn't use it if you want to be able to view pages in offline mode later.

EFFECTIVELY SEARCHING THE WEB

You've probably heard that you can find virtually anything on the Web, and if you've spent much time online, you're probably left wondering where it all is. Finding information on the World Wide Web is a fine art, but Internet Explorer 5 makes the process much simpler than it used to be.

The new Search Assistant is one of the most significant new features of IE5. You can click the Search button on the IE5 toolbar to open the Search Assistant in a separate window (called the Explorer bar) on the left side of Internet Explorer, as shown in Figure 12.18.

Figure 12.18
The Search Assistant opens and allows you to search for several different kinds of information.

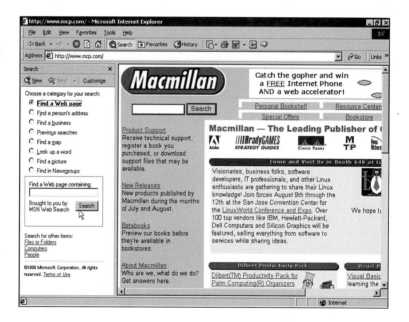

As you can see, you can choose to search for Web pages, people, businesses, maps, words, pictures, newsgroups, or even revisit a previous search. If you do not see all the categories shown in Figure 12.18, click More in the Assistant window. Notice that some links at the bottom allow you to search for files and other resources on the local computer or network as well.

The Search Assistant pools the resources of several major Internet search engines to help you conduct your search. If you have a favorite search engine, you can specify that it be used first by following these steps:

1. Click Customize in the Search Assistant window.

2. The Customize Search Settings dialog opens, as shown in Figure 12.19. Here, you can add or remove search engines from each category, and you can even remove categories that you never use. Add or remove check marks as you see fit.

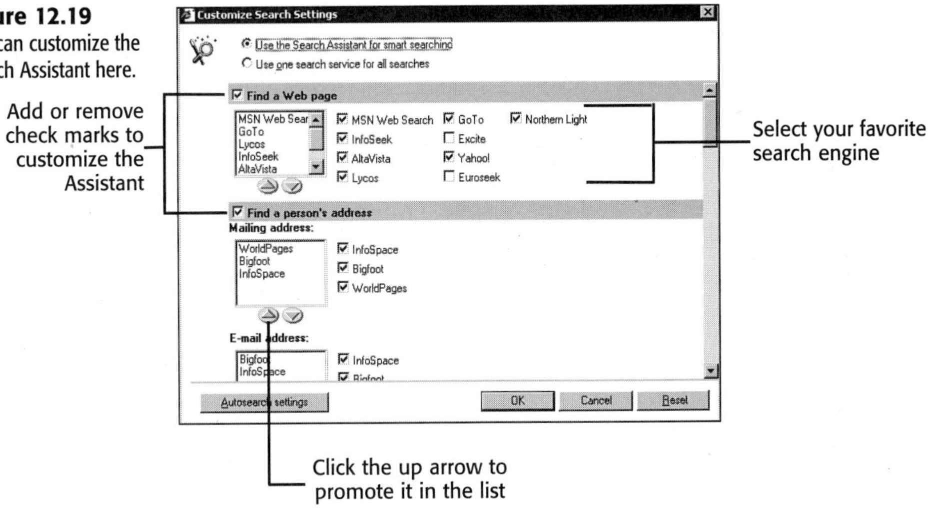

Figure 12.19
You can customize the Search Assistant here.

Add or remove check marks to customize the Assistant

Select your favorite search engine

Click the up arrow to promote it in the list

3. Notice the list box in each category. These boxes list the search engines that will be used in the order in which they will be used. To move a listing up or down in the list, select it and click the up and down arrows under the list box to promote or demote it.

4. Click OK when you're finished.

When you're finished customizing your Search Assistant preferences, you are ready to begin searching. You can type a word or phrase in the search text box, and click Search. If you type a single word—such as antiques—the search will probably yield a list of results too big to be useful, so you should use more words to be more specific. You will probably get better results by searching for antique furniture instead.

Search results are displayed in the Assistant window, 10 at a time. You can click directly on a search result to link to that site, or you can click Next to see the next 10 results. If you're still not happy with the results, click Use Advanced Search to display more options, as shown in Figure 12.20.

PART
III

CH
12

Figure 12.20
The Advanced Search options help you perform a more directed search.

The options you choose depend on the search you are conducting. Consider for a moment a search for antique furniture. This search yields every page that contains these two words, even if they are not in the same paragraph. To remedy this situation, click the drop-down arrow next to Find, and change "all words" to "the exact phrase." Look through the other options to see what else you might want to try.

If you don't like waiting for each page of 10 search results to download, consider changing the number of results displayed per page to something higher. Click the drop-down arrow next to Results/Page, and select a larger number such as 20 or 50. Keep in mind that increasing the number of results will slow down the actual search process a bit, but you might find that you more than make up that time in saved download time.

When you're finished searching, close the Search Assistant to get it out of the way. You can revisit a previous search at any time by choosing that search category in the first Search Assistant window (refer to Figure 12.18).

TROUBLESHOOTING

WEB PAGE ERRORS

An error occurs when I try to visit a specific Web page.

Try clicking the Refresh button to reload the page. If you still don't have any luck, remove the path information (that would be everything after the domain name) from the URL in the Address bar, and press Enter.

EMAIL LINK TROUBLES

When I click an email link, Outlook Express opens, but I prefer a different email program.

Open the Internet Properties dialog, and change the default mail program on the Programs tab. You should be able to select any installed email client (such as Outlook, Outlook Express, Eudora, Netscape Mail, and so on) here.

SOME GRAPHICS DON'T APPEAR

Some pictures on a page don't open.

If the Web page contains many pictures—say, a dozen or more—the graphics at the bottom of the page often do not open. Right-click the placeholder boxes for the images that didn't download, and choose Show Picture from the menu that appears.

INTERNET EXPLORER CRASHES ON CERTAIN WEB PAGES

A Web page freezes Internet Explorer.

Some Web pages contain poorly developed scripts or ones that needlessly strain your Internet connection. Scripts that try to detect the brand and version of browser you are using frequently cause this problem. Click the Stop button on the IE5 toolbar, and close and reopen the program if necessary. You can try disabling most scripting operations in the Security settings dialog, but doing so might cause the offending Web page not to display properly.

PDF FILES ON THE WEB

When I try to view a PDF document on a Web site, a `Bad Parameter` *error occurs.*

PDF documents are frequently used to distribute tax forms, government documents, technical manuals, and other materials over the Web. They must be read using a program called Adobe Acrobat Reader, which can be downloaded (`www.adobe.com`) and installed for free. The program is designed to work as a plug-in for your Web browser, but versions 3.0 and 3.1 of the Reader had some compatibility problems with Internet Explorer. This incompatibility results in an error when you try to view a document directly over the Web. The solution is either to obtain a more current version of the Reader or to download the PDF file to a local disk and read it from there. To do so, right-click the link that leads to the PDF file, and choose Save Target As from the shortcut menu that appears. Save the document to disk, and then read it offline.

WHAT HAPPENED TO THE WEB SITE?

I get a lot of `Page not available` *errors, even on major commercial sites.*

The most obvious suggestion is to check your Internet connection. Your server may also be having a temporary problem, or high Internet traffic is preventing your access. But another thing you should consider is whether the page you are trying to visit is on a secure Web server. Choose Tools, Internet Options, and click the Advanced tab to bring it to the front. Scroll down to the group of security settings, and see whether any of the encryption protocols supported by IE5 are disabled. If, for example, you are trying to visit a page that uses PCT encryption but Use PCT 1.0 is disabled, that page will not open.

TIPS FROM THE WINDOWS PROS: FINDING AND USING PDF DOCUMENTS ON THE WORLD WIDE WEB

Perhaps you saw the photograph on the cover of *Time Magazine* a few years ago of Bill Gates in a forest, sitting atop a tree-sized stack of papers while holding a single compact disk in his hand, suggesting that digital information storage could save trees. It can, but it isn't easy.

The problem with digital documents is that, even with the best available technology, they are still not as easy to read as a paper book. Computer monitors put considerably more strain on your eyes, and the PCs themselves are too bulky and/or clumsy to carry with you to a comfortable reading location. Furthermore, current digital storage technologies have a shorter shelf-life than paper. Most CDs begin to deteriorate and lose their data after 10 to 20 years, but properly stored paper can last for centuries.

Still, digital documents have many advantages. First and foremost is cost: A single compact disc can contain hundreds of books yet cost less than $1 to manufacture. Printing the same amount of data on paper would cost hundreds, if not thousands, of dollars. Electronic books can be searched quickly, efficiently, and more thoroughly than printed ones. And, of course, digital documents are much easier to distribute.

 One of the most popular methods for producing and distributing electronic books online is via PDF (Portable Document Format) files. PDF documents can be read using the Adobe Acrobat Reader, a free program offered by Adobe Systems, Inc. (www.adobe.com). PDF books can have the appearance and properties of a paper book but without the paper. They also have the advantage of being compatible across many platforms, with versions of the Reader software available for Windows, Macintosh, OS/2, and various incarnations of UNIX. A PDF document link on a Web page is usually identified by the PDF icon.

PDF is used for a wide range of documents:

- It is used for government documents such as tax forms and educational materials.
- Technology companies such as Intel distribute technical documents and white papers in PDF.
- Private and commercial publishers produce and distribute electronic libraries of PDF books both on CD and the Web.
- News agencies produce PDF weather maps and other news material.

You can obtain the Acrobat Reader from many sources. If you own any other Adobe software—such as Photoshop or PhotoDeluxe—the reader is probably already installed on your computer. Look for a program group called Adobe or Adobe Acrobat in your Start menu. You can also download it for free from the Adobe Web site.

The Acrobat Reader version 3.01 (or later) integrates nicely with Internet Explorer to read PDF documents directly over the Web. The Reader is generally distributed in one of two versions: one with Search and one without. Actually, the only difference between the versions is that Acrobat Reader with Search has an extra plug-in called ASRCH32.API. This search plug-in works only with PDF documents that have been indexed by the publisher. This is normally done if a series of PDF books is produced and the publisher wants to enable the reader to search all the books at once. If this is the case, an index file with a .PDX extension accompanies the PDF files. PDF Search indexes are rare, so for most Web-related uses, you don't need to worry about it.

Acrobat Reader works as a plug-in for Internet Explorer. When you click a link for a PDF document, it opens Acrobat Reader within IE5, as shown in Figure 12.21.

Figure 12.21
A PDF document has been opened using the Acrobat Reader as a plug-in to Internet Explorer.

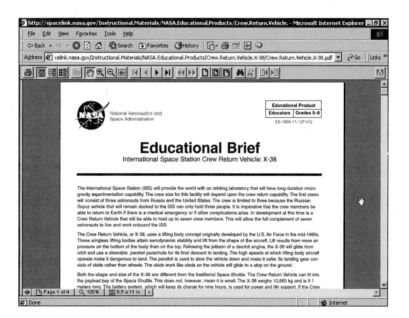

PART
III

CH
12

Sadly, having problems with this whole procedure is not uncommon. Reading PDF documents over the Web can be problematic, but most of those problems can be solved if you first save the PDF document to your hard drive. Rather than click the PDF link to open the file in IE5, right-click it and choose Save Target As from the shortcut menu that appears. Save the document to a safe location, and then open it manually using the Acrobat Reader outside the IE5 session. Saving the PDF document in this manner has the added advantage of making the document available to you for future reference, without having to relocate it again on the Web.

CHAPTER 13

EMAIL

In this chapter

CHOOSING AN EMAIL CLIENT

From the start, the Internet has been touted as a means for enhancing human communications, and among the many communication tools available in the online world, few have had the impact of electronic mail (email).

Email began innocently enough in the early 1970s when engineer Ray Tomlinson developed a way for users on remote machines connected via ARPAnet (the predecessor to the Internet) to leave messages for each other. Tomlinson began with an existing messaging program called SNDMSG that only allowed users to leave messages on a local machine. He developed a transfer protocol to allow SNDMSG files to be sent over a network and chose the @ (at) sign to distinguish the server location from the sender and recipient.

To fully understand the nature of email, you should keep in mind that, at its most basic level, it is simply a way for users to send messages to each other over a network. This network could be a local area network (LAN) run by your company using MS Exchange Server software. In this situation, the network server manages all message traffic. The server can also act as a gateway to other servers, allowing you to send mail beyond the local network. If you have an email account with an Internet service provider (ISP) or other Internet-based service, the provider's server acts as your gateway to other mail servers across the Internet.

Email messages traveling through Internet gateways utilize the mailto: Internet addressing protocol. Individual mail packets travel the same Internet backbone and pathways as other online traffic, meaning that outgoing messages can reach their destination gateway in a matter of minutes or even seconds.

Email has been criticized by some as diminishing the art of written communication by making letter writing into a less formal exchange. You may or may not agree, but the fact is, if your daily work requires you to use a computer, chances are you are also expected to use email for much of your business communication.

Given that email is a must, you must decide which email client you plan to use for reading, composing, and sending messages. You have a number of options available to you, and which one you ultimately choose will depend not only on your personal preferences but also professional needs.

Windows 2000 includes an excellent email client called Outlook Express 5 (OE5), which is actually a companion program to Internet Explorer 5. It is a multifeatured program designed to appeal to a variety of email users, but it isn't for everyone. OE5 can also function as a newsgroup client, making it a "one-stop" program if you routinely communicate via email and use newsgroups.

→ To learn more about using Outlook Express to read newsgroups, **see p. 497**.

Outlook Express is relatively compact as Windows applications go. If you want an efficient program that can handle your email needs without a lot of extra fluff, OE5 is a pretty good choice. However, it does lack a few features that you might want or need, so read the next couple of sections to find out if you should be using a different client.

Note

This discussion assumes you have a choice in email clients. Check with your company's Information Systems (IS) manager to find out whether you must use one specific client.

WHAT IF YOU LIKE OUTLOOK 97, 98, OR 2000?

If you use Microsoft's Office suite, you're probably familiar with Outlook. Outlook is the primary communications tool included in the Office package, and many professional PC users like it. However, don't be misled by the name similarity between Outlook and Outlook Express. OE5 is not a "lite" version of Outlook; these two applications are actually quite different. Aside from the name and a few basic interface similarities, the only thing they have in common is the capability to handle email.

Outlook includes many features that Outlook Express does not, such as the following:

- A personal calendar
- An electronic journal
- Fax capability
- Compatibility with Microsoft Exchange Server

In addition, Outlook's system of managing personal contacts is far more advanced than that of Outlook Express. If the ability to integrate a heavy email load with your personal scheduler on a daily basis is important to you, Outlook is the clear choice.

One thing that Outlook cannot do that OE5 does is communicate using newsgroups. Outlook is also bigger, requiring more disk space, more RAM, and slightly more patience on the part of the user.

If you are already using Outlook and like the Calendar and Journal, stick with it. Furthermore, if your company's network or workgroup uses Exchange Server for mail services, Outlook is the only fully compatible upgrade to that system. Outlook is also Messaging Application Programming Interface (MAPI) capable, which means it can share mail with other MAPI-capable programs on your system. Outlook Express is not MAPI-capable.

Outlook is clearly the heavier duty application, but if you adhere to the KISS (Keep It Simple, Stupid) principle, find that you prefer to keep a schedule on your good old paper desk calendar, and don't use Outlook for anything but email, you might be better served by Outlook Express. And if you also access newsgroups on a regular basis, you might find it easier to consolidate your online communications into one program instead of two.

PART
III

CH
13

Tip #179

One more solution is to use both Outlook *and* Outlook Express. If you have a hard time keeping your personal and business communications apart, try using Outlook for your work email and Outlook Express for your personal ISP mail account.

OTHER EMAIL CLIENTS

Microsoft isn't the only company producing high-quality email clients. One of the most popular alternatives is Eudora Pro from Qualcomm (www.eudora.com). Eudora offers an excellent package of mail management and filtering features, as well as compatibility with the latest Internet mail standards. Like Outlook Express, it is considerably more compact than Outlook, but it does not incorporate a newsgroup reader. Some unique Eudora features include the following:

- Voice messaging capability
- Integrated McAfee VirusScan protection for viruses propagated in mail attachments
- Built-in compression agent to shorten download times on slow dial-up connections

A free version of Eudora called Eudora Light is available, but it lacks so many of the features available in the identically priced Outlook Express that, at this point, it isn't worth your consideration.

Another popular email client is Netscape Messenger, which comes as part of the Netscape Communicator package. Messenger is comparable to Outlook Express in terms of mail management and newsgroup capability, and its interface is clean and uncluttered. One drawback is that Messenger does not allow you to configure multiple email accounts or identities, a must for most professional users today.

Numerous other email clients exist, but the ones mentioned here are best suited to the business email user. You can find a more complete list of email clients online in the Yahoo! directory. To find it, surf to

```
http://dir.yahoo.com/Computers_and_Internet/Software/Internet/Electronic_Mail/
```

OUTLOOK EXPRESS QUICK TOUR

You can choose from many different email clients. Covering them all would be beyond the scope of this book, so for now, we will assume that you have chosen Outlook Express 5. It comes free with Windows 2000 and will meet many of your electronic mail needs.

The greatest strength of OE5 is its simplicity, but you would not know that from looking at the opening screen shown in Figure 13.1. This view can serve as a gateway to the rest of OE5's features, but otherwise it is almost useless.

Tip #180

You'll probably find that you spend more time in the Inbox than in any other place in Outlook Express. For that reason, place a check mark next to When Outlook Express Starts, Go Directly to My Inbox.

Folder Bar

Figure 13.1
The opening view of
Outlook Express is
not very useful. You
can configure the
program to open
directly to the Inbox
instead.

Folder list

Your personal
contacts

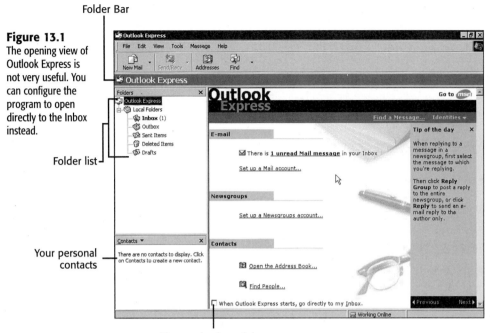

Place a check mark here

Outlook Express is installed during a normal installation of Windows 2000, so it should be ready to open. You can launch it either by clicking the Outlook Express button on the Quick Launch toolbar, or by choosing Start, Programs, Outlook Express. When you do, you should see a window similar to Figure 13.1. If you already have an email account set up, OE5 automatically checks for new mail when you open the program.

→ If you haven't set up an account yet, **see** "Setting Up an Email Account," **p 470**.

If this is the first time you've opened OE5, notice that you have one unread mail message. Click the link to go to your Inbox and read the message, which is actually just a welcome letter from Microsoft.

When the Inbox opens, as shown in Figure 13.2, you'll see that the right side of the window is divided. The upper half is a list of messages in your Inbox, with unread messages shown in boldface. The lower half is the Preview Pane, which shows a preview of whichever message is selected above. You can use the scrollbar to read more of the message.

The Preview Pane is useful, but some people don't like it. To open a message in a separate window, double-click it.

PART

III

CH

13

Figure 13.2
The Inbox includes a list of new messages and a Preview Pane that you can use to read them.

Click once to select a message

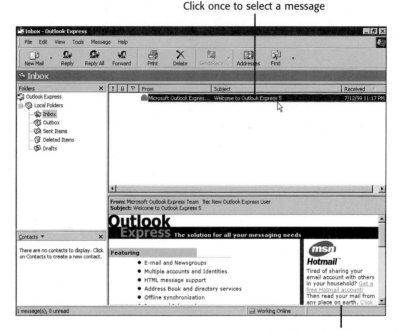

Read the selected message here

If you always prefer to read mail in this manner, you can hide the Preview Pane to make more room for Inbox messages. To hide that pane or make a variety of other adjustments to the Outlook Express interface, try these steps:

1. Choose View, Layout.

2. In the Window Layout Properties dialog (see Figure 13.3), select or deselect the screen elements you want to show or hide. We suggest you deselect the Folder Bar, as well as the Preview Pane if you don't plan to use it.

3. Experiment with the settings, and click OK when you have OE5 looking the way you want it.

Take a look at the other screen elements. The Folder list shown in Figure 13.4 is handy because you can use it to quickly jump to any part of Outlook Express, including news-groups if you have an account set up.

 Does Outlook Express always seem to check for new mail at the wrong time? See "Making OE5 Less Automated" in the "Troubleshooting" section at the end of the chapter.

SETTING UP AN EMAIL ACCOUNT

Before you can send or receive electronic mail, you need to have an email account. There is a good possibility that your account has already been configured by your company's IS department or that some software from your ISP took care of it for you. Otherwise, you'll have to set it up yourself.

Figure 13.3
You can customize the Outlook Express interface here.

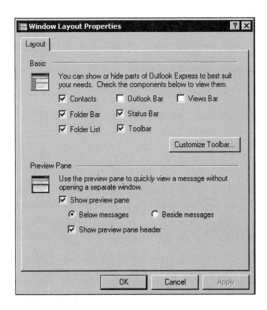

Figure 13.4
The Folder list can serve as a directory to virtually all Outlook Express resources.

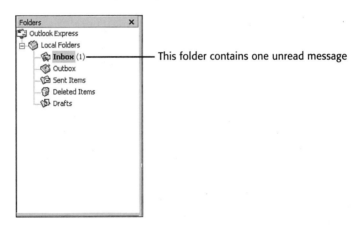

This folder contains one unread message

PART

III

CH

13

You can set up an account directly from Outlook Express by following the instructions listed here. These steps also work for setting up a second or third account or mail identity on the same machine. If you are setting up an email account at the same time you are configuring your Internet connection, begin with step 4.

1. In Outlook Express, choose Tools, Accounts.

2. In the Internet Accounts dialog (see Figure 13.5), click the Mail tab to bring it to the front.

Figure 13.5
You can review your email accounts here or add a new one.

Click the Mail tab

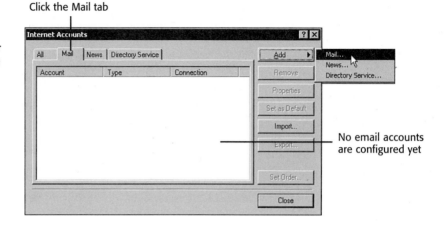

No email accounts are configured yet

3. Click Add, Mail.

4. The Internet Connection Wizard opens to a dialog asking for your display name. This is the name that other people will see when you send them mail, so choose carefully. Click Next after you've entered a name.

5. The next wizard box asks for your email account address, which should have been provided by your company or ISP. You can also choose to sign up for a free HTTP mail account from Hotmail at this time. Click Next after you've entered the address.

6. You must enter the types and names of your email servers in the next dialog, which is shown in Figure 13.6. Again, this information is provided by your company or ISP. See the next section for an explanation of the different server types.

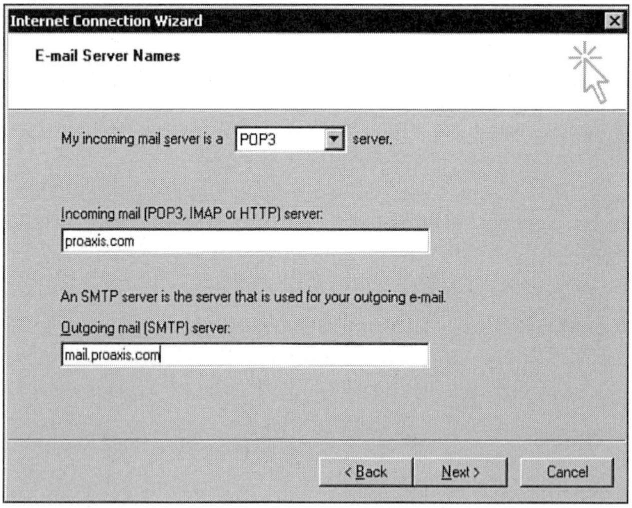

Figure 13.6
You can enter the types and names of your email servers here.

7. The next dialog asks for your login name and password. Do not check the option Remember Password if other people have access to your computer. Check the SPA (Secure Password Authentication) option if required by your email provider; then click Next. Click Finish in the final dialog. Your new account should now be listed in the Internet Accounts dialog, as shown in Figure 13.7.

Figure 13.7
The new mail account is now shown in the Internet Accounts dialog.

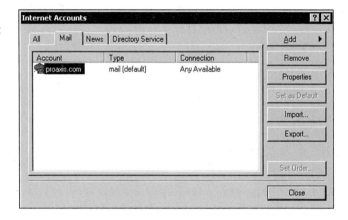

The only other piece of information that Outlook Express needs is which network or dial-up connection it should use when sending and receiving mail. You probably don't need to select this connection because OE5 automatically assigns your default connection to all mail accounts. However, if you need to change the connection used for a given account, open the Internet Accounts dialog and follow these steps:

1. Click the Mail tab to bring it to the front, and select the account you want to change. Click the Properties button on the right side of the dialog.

2. Click the Connection tab. If you need to use a specific connection, place a check mark next to Always Connect to This Account Using, and select a connection from the drop-down menu.

3. Click OK and Close to exit all the open dialogs.

 If you routinely encounter server errors when sending or receiving mail, see "Missing Mail Servers" in the "Troubleshooting" section at the end of the chapter.

WHAT ARE POP, IMAP, SMTP, AND HTTP?

You've probably noticed the veritable alphabet soup of acronyms that exist for the many different kinds of email servers. Unlike so many other cryptic terms thrown around in the PC world, these acronyms are actually worth remembering.

First, a basic understanding of how email flows across networks (including the Internet) is important. Usually, when you send a message, Outlook Express transfers it to a *Simple Mail Transfer Protocol (SMTP)* server. An SMTP server is controlled by the sender, meaning that

PART
III

CH

13

it waits for you to push mail through it. After you send the message to your SMTP server using OE5's Send command, no other interaction is required to deliver the message to its final destination.

To receive mail, you probably use either a *Post Office Protocol (POP)* or *Internet Message Access Protocol (IMAP)* server. POP and IMAP servers differ from SMTP servers because they wait for the recipient's signal before forwarding the mail. In other words, messages stay on the server until you tell it that you want your mail. You do so by using OE5's Receive command.

POP and IMAP differ in that POP servers forward all messages directly to your local machine, whereas IMAP servers maintain the messages on the server until you delete them. When you check for mail on an IMAP server, a list of message headers is downloaded, but the actual message bodies stay on the server (like newsgroup messages). An IMAP server comes in handy if you travel a lot and want to be able to check messages on the road with your laptop or PDA, but don't want to remove them from the server until you can download the mail to a more permanent location on your home desktop.

Another type of email server is a *Hypertext Transfer Protocol (HTTP)* server, such as the one offered by Hotmail. An HTTP mail account is even more useful for frequent travelers because it doesn't even require you to take a computer or any software with you. You can access your HTTP account using a Web browser on any computer with access to the Internet, and generally the only information you will have to provide is your login name and password. Outlook Express can be used to read and send mail using an HTTP account.

SETTING UP AN HTTP MAIL ACCOUNT WITH HOTMAIL

Microsoft has made it easy to configure an email account with Hotmail in Outlook Express. The account is free, and because it is an HTTP mail account, you might appreciate being able to use it on the road from any computer with Internet access. The Hotmail account limits you to 2MB of server space, so don't use your Hotmail email address for receiving large quantities of mail or file attachments. When your mailbox fills up, messages will be bounced back to the sender.

The easiest way to configure a Hotmail account in OE5 is to choose Tools, New Account Signup, Hotmail. Choosing these commands opens a wizard that takes you step-by-step through the setup process. Be prepared to provide information such as your name and geographic location. You will also be asked for your age, but testing has shown that you can pretty much enter anything you want into that field.

When it is configured, the OE5 Folder list displays a folder group called Hotmail. The Hotmail account has its own Inbox, Sent Items, and Deleted Items folders. In terms of downloading and deleting messages, HTTP mail accounts work in a similar manner to IMAP accounts.

If you are configuring an HTTP mail account from another provider, such as Yahoo! Mail, simply follow the instructions for setting up any other type of email account. You enter the HTTP server address in the same location where you would otherwise enter the POP or IMAP server address.

Tip #181

You can always check your Hotmail account from another computer by visiting www.hotmail.com in a Web browser and entering your username and password at the Hotmail Web site. If you are checking mail away from home, you can leave the messages you receive on the server so that they will still be available for download later using OE5.

One point to keep in mind about Hotmail is that although the free Hotmail account can be helpful when you're traveling, you must use it periodically to keep your account active. For example, you need to log on to your Hotmail account at least once during the first 30 days of membership and once every 90 days beyond that.

READING AND PROCESSING INCOMING MESSAGES

After you have an account set up, you are ready to begin downloading and reading mail. To get started, open Outlook Express if it isn't already, and go to the Inbox. Outlook Express automatically checks for new mail when it first opens. Otherwise, click the Send/Recv button on the toolbar. New messages appear as shown in Figure 13.8.

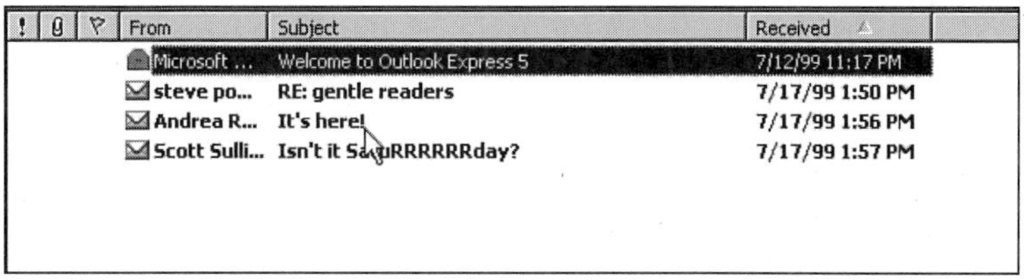

Figure 13.8
The Inbox shows three new messages.

!	0	∇	From	Subject	Received △	
			Microsoft ...	Welcome to Outlook Express 5	7/12/99 11:17 PM	
			steve po...	RE: gentle readers	7/17/99 1:50 PM	
			Andrea R...	It's here!	7/17/99 1:56 PM	
			Scott Sulli...	Isn't it SatuRRRRRRday?	7/17/99 1:57 PM	

Tip #182

If you receive a message from someone you plan to communicate with regularly, open the message, right-click his or her name in the message header, and choose Add to Address Book. By doing so, you add the person to your contacts list so that sending him or her mail in the future will be easier.

When you reply to a message, you need to be wary of a few things. First, when you click the Reply or Reply All button, make sure the correct person or persons are listed in the To: and Cc: fields. Anyone listed in those two fields will receive a copy of the message, so make sure you aren't airing your dirty laundry any more publicly than you intended. The section "Creating and Sending New Mail" discusses addressing messages more thoroughly.

When you reply to a message, Outlook Express automatically places the text of the original message in the reply, and an angle bracket (>) is inserted at the beginning of each line. This method of replying to plain text messages is fairly standard, and so many email users are accustomed to this feature that you might want to just leave it alone. However, you can change it if you want by following these steps:

1. Choose Tools, Options in Outlook Express.
2. Click the Send tab to bring it to the front, and then click the Plain Text Settings button.

3. In the Plain Text Settings dialog (see Figure 13.9), click the drop-down arrow, choose a different character to place at the beginning of each quoted line, and click OK when you're finished.

Figure 13.9
You can modify default settings for plain text messages here.

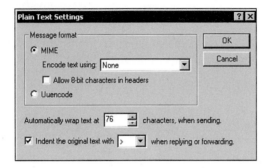

The rest of the reply process is fairly straightforward. You just type in your own text and click Send on the toolbar when you are ready to deliver the message. When you're composing your reply, you should keep in mind these important points:

- Consider editing the quoted text in the reply down to the text you actually intend to respond to. Most people don't appreciate reading four pages of quoted text followed at long last by "Me too."

- Include enough of the original text to help the recipient understand exactly what you are replying to. If the recipient doesn't read your reply for several days, he or she might not remember what his or her original statements were.

- Breaking up quoted text with your own inserted comments is usually acceptable, but make sure it is obvious which words are yours. Figure 13.10 illustrates this reply technique.

 Having trouble with a stubborn account password dialog? See "Password Trouble" in the "Troubleshooting" section at the end of the chapter.

DELETING MESSAGES

How and when messages are deleted depends on what kind of mail server you use. If you receive mail from a POP server, deleted messages remain in the OE5 Deleted Items folder indefinitely, similar to "deleted" files in the Windows Recycle Bin.

You can permanently delete them by right-clicking the Deleted Items folder and choosing Empty 'Deleted Items' Folder from the shortcut menu that appears. If you have an IMAP mail server, the Deleted Items folder is emptied automatically when you log off the mail server.

You can change the way Outlook Express handles items in the Deleted Items folder. To do so, choose Tools, Options, and select the Maintenance tab to customize when and how mail messages are deleted.

Figure 13.10
Quoted text and reply text are interspersed throughout the message, but there is little doubt as to who wrote what.

CREATING AND SENDING NEW MAIL

The process of creating and sending new mail is almost as easy as receiving it. You can use either of two good methods for opening a New Message composition window:

- Click the New Mail button on the OE5 toolbar.
- Double-click a name in your Contacts list. A New Message window opens with that person's name listed in the To: field.

Addressing messages properly is extremely important. A single misplaced character in an email address can send the message to the wrong person or to no one at all. A typical email address looks like this:

bob@mcp.com

The addressing scheme follows this format:

mailto:*account@domain*

You do not need to type mailto: at the beginning of an email address; the protocol is assumed by all modern email clients.

PART

III

CH

13

Tip #183

Some mail servers are case sensitive. If you're not sure, just type the whole address in lowercase letters.

Notice that OE5 has two address fields, To: and Cc: (short for Carbon copy). The To: field is the only required field when sending email; all the others, including the subject and even the message body, can be blank. The To: field usually contains the email address of the primary recipient, although it can contain more than one address, as shown in Figure 13.11. You separate multiple addresses with a semicolon (;).

Two people are listed in the To: field

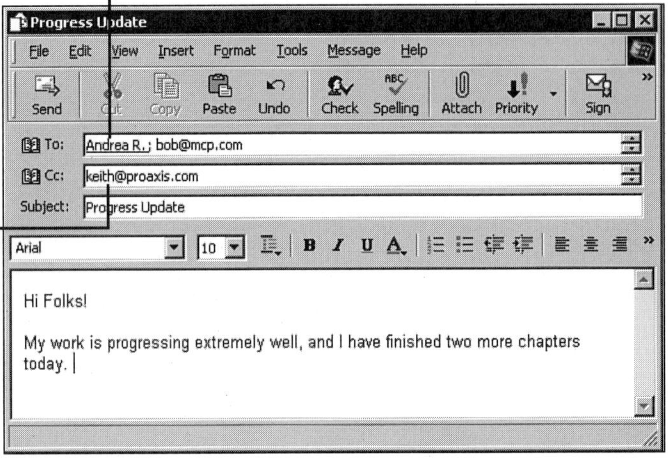

Figure 13.11
A new message has been addressed to several people.

One person will receive a carbon copy

When you are finished composing the message, just click Send on the toolbar. If you do not want your message sent right away, choose File, Send Later. The message is then sent to the Outbox folder and will be sent to your mail server the next time the Send command is given.

If you don't like the name that is being assigned to your outgoing mail, see "Identity Crisis" in the "Troubleshooting" section at the end of the chapter.

SENDING AND RECEIVING ATTACHMENTS

Of the many features that make email a versatile method for communication, perhaps the most useful is the capability to send files along with an email message. You can attach any electronic file stored on disk to an email message in Outlook Express and then send it to someone else.

Note

Some email accounts, particularly HTTP accounts, do not allow you to send or receive file attachments with messages. Check with your account provider to find out whether you have this capability. Also, make sure that the recipient has the capability to receive attachments.

Attaching a file to an outgoing message is easy. In the message composition window, click the Attach button on the toolbar, and locate the file you want to send in the Insert

Attachment dialog. After you have selected the file, click Attach. The file attachment should appear in the header information, as shown in Figure 13.12.

Figure 13.12
A file has been attached and will be sent along with the message.

Attached file —

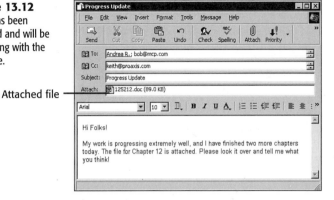

Before you send any attached files, consider the bandwidth it will require. Even if you have a very fast network or Internet connection, if the recipient connects to the Internet via a modem, downloading the attachment could take a long time. In general, you should avoid sending any attachments that are larger than one or two megabytes unless you are sure the recipient can handle them.

One more thing: If you or the recipient uses a 56Kbps or slower Internet connection, it is usually a good idea to compress large attachments with a program such as WinZip (www.winzip.com) before you send them.

In addition to sending file attachments, you can also receive them. They show up in the header information of messages you receive. Right-click the attachment, and choose Save As to save it to disk. If the attachment is a picture file, it often appears in the body of the message.

Caution

Computer viruses often propagate themselves via email attachments. Simply downloading an infected attachment does not harm your computer, but opening the attached file could have dire consequences. If possible, save the file attachment on a separate disk, and then scan it with antivirus software. Be especially wary of any attachment you weren't expecting (even from people you know), executable attachments, or anything that comes from a source you are unfamiliar with.

SETTING UP A SIGNATURE

If you use email for much of your personal and business communication, you probably like to "sign" outgoing messages with an electronic signature file. These signatures frequently include additional information about you, such as an email address, title, phone number, company name, Web URL, or a witty quote. Outlook Express makes it easy to set up a standard signature that will be included in every message you compose. You can configure your own signature by following these steps:

1. Choose Tools, Options. Click the Signatures tab to bring it to the front.

2. Click New to begin typing a new signature. Type your signature information as shown in Figure 13.13.

Figure 13.13
You can create a standard signature for your outgoing messages here.

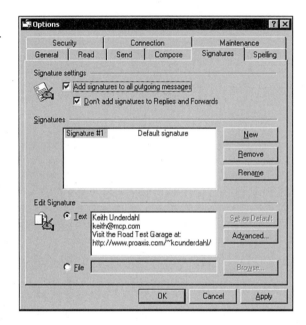

3. If you have multiple email accounts, click Advanced and select the account or accounts you want this signature to be used with.

4. Place a check mark next to Add Signatures to All Outgoing Messages to enable this feature. Notice that, by default, your signatures will not be added to replies and forwards. Click OK when you're finished.

Tip #184

Consider creating several signatures, with varying levels of personal information. You can then choose a signature in the message window by selecting Insert, Signature.

CREATING FANCIER MAIL

Electronic mail has been around for several decades, and until a few years ago, all email was formatted as simple text. That meant no special characters or fancy formatting. These early emails utilized a message format called *uuencode*, short for UNIX-to-UNIX encode. You don't need to be running UNIX to read uuencoded messages, though; virtually any email client you are likely to encounter—including OE5—can read and send messages in this format.

To address the shortcomings of ASCII-based uuencode email, the *Multipurpose Internet Mail Extensions (MIME)* specification was developed. MIME, which is supported by most modern email clients, allows the use of graphics, file attachments, and some special non-ASCII characters in email messages.

A third, newer way to enrich email is to apply message formatting using HTML code, the same type of code used to construct Web pages. HTML is the default format for new messages you create in OE5, although replies are typically formatted in whatever manner they were originally sent to you.

Applying special formatting to HTML messages is easy. Outlook Express provides a formatting toolbar similar to what you would see in a word processing program, where you can choose such formatting options as bold, italic, and so on. You also can give HTML messages graphic backgrounds by choosing one of the stationaries provided by OE5.

The only problem with HTML messages is that not all modern email clients can view them properly. Messages formatted in this manner may appear with a huge quantity of gibberish at the end of the message if the recipient doesn't have an HTML-compatible client. Likewise, mailing lists usually cannot handle HTML formatting in messages that are sent to them. If you send HTML messages to the list, your odds of getting "flamed" are high.

On the other hand, most mailing lists and users in general can handle MIME messages. To change the default sending formats for outgoing messages, open the Options dialog in OE5. On the Send tab, choose HTML or Plain Text. If you choose Plain Text, your default message format will actually be MIME. If you want to change to uuencode, click the Plain Text Settings button, and choose the appropriate options in the dialog that appears.

Tip #185	If you happen to know that your recipient is using some truly ancient technology to download and read email, such as Telnet and a text reader, send messages to that person uuencoded.

 Is the formatting of your outgoing messages creating discontent among your recipients? See "Recipients Don't Like My Mail Formatting" in the "Troubleshooting" section at the end of the chapter.

PART

III

CH

13

HANDLING DIGITAL IDs

Electronic mail is a reasonably secure method of communication, but for some uses, it might not be secure enough. One significant problem involves identifying the people you are communicating with. Hiding or falsifying your identity on the Internet is relatively easy, meaning that some unscrupulous person could be masquerading as one of your associates.

To combat this problem, several companies offer digital IDs that help verify your identity. Secure email messages can be signed using a digital ID, authenticating the identity of the sender. Using these IDs is extremely useful if you must share sensitive information via email.

You can obtain a digital ID for yourself by following these steps:

1. Choose Tools, Accounts in OE5, and then select the Mail tab. Select your mail account and click Properties.

2. On the Security tab, click Get Digital ID. Choosing this option will launch your browser and automatically go to the Web site of VeriSign, a *certificate* issuing authority for Digital IDs.

3. Follow the instructions provided by the Web site to obtain and install a Digital ID. As of this writing, a free 60-day trial ID is available from VeriSign.

After you have installed a Digital ID for yourself in Outlook Express, you can digitally sign any outgoing message by clicking the Sign button on the message window toolbar.

Other individuals can also send digitally signed email to you. Signed messages have a red flag attached to them in the Inbox, as shown in Figure 13.14. The message header also displays a special flag, and Outlook Express shows you an explanatory message about digital signatures before displaying the message.

Figure 13.14
A digitally signed message has been received, verifying the identity of the sender.

This flag indicates a signed message

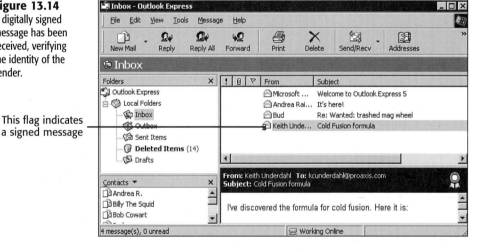

> **Caution**
>
> Digital signatures only authenticate the identity of the sender; they do not provide any additional security measures—such as *encryption*—for the email contents.

USING THE ADDRESS BOOK

You don't have to communicate via email for very long before you mistype someone's address. Email addresses are often cryptic, and some are even case sensitive. It is for this reason that the Address Book is such an important feature of Outlook Express. The

Address Book is a safe place to store contact information—including email addresses—for the people you communicate with.

Before going through the inner workings of the Address Book, keep in mind that this single feature goes by two different names within OE5. Sometimes it is called the Address Book, and other times it is called the Contacts list.

You can open the Address Book in its own window by choosing Tools, Address Book. It appears as shown in Figure 13.15.

Figure 13.15
You can open the Address Book in its own window to easily manage your contacts. Use the View menu to turn off the display of folders and groups.

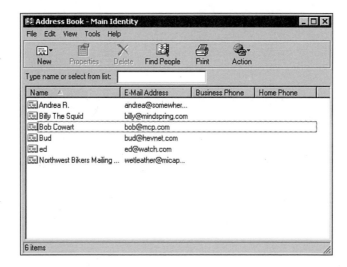

If you have too many unwanted entries in your Address Book, see "Thinning Your Contacts List" in the "Troubleshooting" section at the end of the chapter.

ADDING, EDITING, AND REMOVING ENTRIES

The Address Book is useful only if you have some names listed in it. Aside from that, the easiest way to add someone to your Address Book is by doing the following:

1. Open a message sent to you by someone you want to add to the Address Book.

2. Right-click the individual's name or email address in the message header, and choose Add to Address Book.

3. A Properties sheet opens for the entry, but don't close it yet. Click the Name tab to bring it to the front, as shown in Figure 13.16. If the person uses a nickname, you might need to edit the name entries on this tab so that they are displayed correctly in your Contacts list. Pay special attention to the Display field.

4. Review all the other tabs in the Properties sheet, and enter any other information about this person you feel appropriate. Click OK when you're finished.

PART

III

CH

13

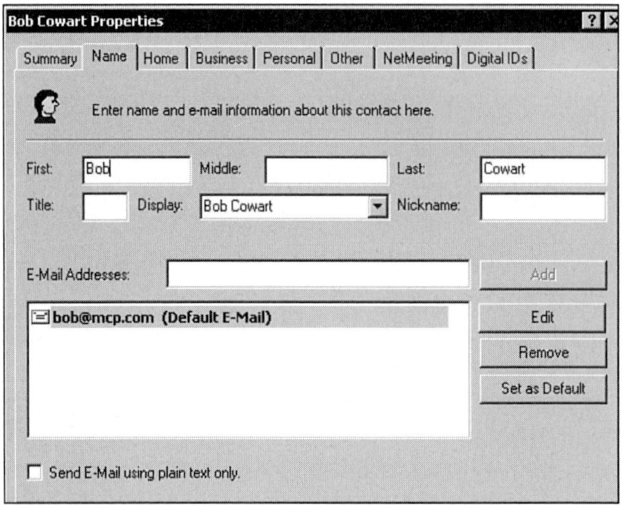

Figure 13.16
Go through all the tabs on the Properties sheet, and enter any information about this contact you feel appropriate.

Tip #186

By default, people's names are automatically added to your Address Book when you reply to one of their messages. To avoid an excess of unwanted entries, you can disable this feature on the Send tab of the Options dialog.

Creating Distribution Lists

Sending a single email message to several people is not unusual. As you learned earlier, you can enter multiple email addresses in the To: and Cc: fields of a new message window, separating each one with a semicolon. However, even using the Address Book to enter these multiple addresses can get tiresome, especially if you frequently send messages to the same group of people.

To simplify this task, you can create *distribution lists* in the OE5 Address Book. You can group many people into a single list, and when you want to send a message to all of them, you simply choose the distribution listing from your Address Book. Distribution lists can be created for co-workers, customers, friends and family, or any other group you communicate with. To create a list, just follow these steps:

1. Open the Address Book if it isn't already.
2. Click New, and select Group from the menu that appears.
3. On the Group tab of the Properties dialog that opens, type a descriptive name. For example, if you are making a list of people you work directly with, consider using the name of your department.
4. Click Select Members. In the Select Group Members dialog, select a name from your Address Book, and click Select. Repeat until you have selected all the names you want in the distribution list.

5. Click OK when you are finished selecting names from the Address Book. As you can see in Figure 13.17, each member is listed under Group Members. Check the Group Details tab to see whether you should enter any information there, and click OK when you're finished.

Figure 13.17
A distribution list has been created for sending mass emails.

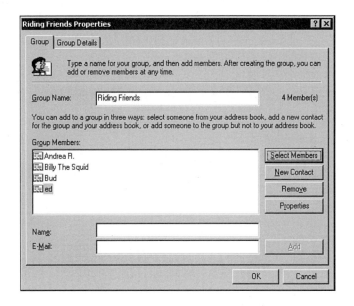

A listing for the group then appears in your Address Book. When you are composing email for the group, simply select the group name from your Address Book to automatically send the message to all group members.

FINDING PEOPLE WHO AREN'T IN YOUR ADDRESS BOOK

A number of people-search directories exist on the Internet to help you locate individuals. Outlook Express does a good job of integrating these search engines into the program, making it easy for you to search for people and add them to your Contacts list.

Tip #187

No matter how obscure a name may seem, you would be amazed at how many other people in the world share it. When you locate someone in an online directory, first send that person an email inquiry to confirm that he or she is indeed the person you are seeking *before* you share any sensitive information with him or her.

To find people who aren't in your Address Book, follow these steps:

1. Open the Address Book if it isn't already. Click Find People on the Address Book toolbar.

2. In the Find People dialog, click the drop-down arrow next to Look in, and select a directory service. No single directory is ideal, so you might need to try searching through several directories before you find the person you are looking for.

3. Click Find Now. A search of the directory service you selected in step 2 is conducted, and results are displayed, as shown in Figure 13.18. If the person is not found, a dialog tells you so. Try another directory or a different spelling for the name.

4. After you have located the person you are looking for, select his or her listing, and click Add to Address Book. Click Close when you are finished searching.

Figure 13.18
A listing has been found in the VeriSign directory service.

PRINTING YOUR ADDRESS BOOK

Outlook Express enables you to print your Address Book. This capability comes in handy, especially if you use the OE5 Address Book as your main source of contact information. As wonderful as the electronic Address Book may be, sometimes a printed copy of it still is easier to use day to day.

You have several options for printing Address Book information. To begin, choose File, Print to open the Print dialog. Under Print Range, select whether you want the current selection (make sure you selected the correct name or names) or the entire list. You must then choose a Print Style as described here:

Memo   This mode prints all available information for each entry. It requires the most paper but also provides the most information.

| Business Card | Business Card mode is similar to Memo, but the print is smaller and less information is provided. Information is generally limited to name, email address, phone numbers, and company name. |
| Phone List | As the name implies, this mode prints only phone numbers for each listing. |

Set any other printer options—such as the number of copies you want—and click Print to print the list.

HANDLING UNIQUE MAIL SITUATIONS

Most email-related tasks are straightforward, whether they are reading and composing mail, addressing and sending messages, or using the Address Book. However, each person uses this communication medium in a different way, and Outlook Express 5 has enough features to deal with many contingencies.

HANDLING MULTIPLE EMAIL ACCOUNTS FOR THE SAME USER

A growing trend in electronic mail communications is users having more than one email account. These accounts may be on the same server or on different servers altogether. Outlook Express can be configured to handle multiple email accounts, even if they are on separate servers.

Each mail account needs to be configured in Outlook Express. Follow the steps listed in "Setting Up an Email Account" earlier in this chapter to learn how to configure a new email account. After you've set up the account, select it in the Internet Accounts dialog and click Properties. If you need to use a specific connection for the account, visit the Connection tab, and choose the correct one there. Close the dialog when complete.

Normally, OE5 checks all accounts when looking for new mail, even if they use different server accounts. However, if you have specified that an account use a specific connection, you will see the dialog shown in Figure 13.19 when you try to use that account on another connection.

Figure 13.19
Here, you must decide whether you want to switch connections or try to locate the server on the current connection.

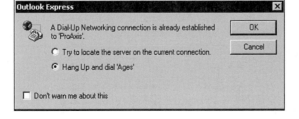

PART

III

CH

13

You can set up an unlimited number of email accounts in OE5. You can even set up multiple accounts using the same email address and server information. Each account can serve a separate identity for you.

When you compose a new mail message, it is automatically addressed for your default mail account. The default account can be set in the Internet Accounts dialog. You can change the account used for an individual message manually, as follows:

1. Click New Mail in Outlook Express to begin composing a new message.

2. In the New Message window, select an identity from the drop-down menu next to From: in the header, as shown in Figure 13.20. The identity used here identifies you to the recipient and also determines the Reply to: address used if the recipient replies. Figure 13.21 shows the same message window with a new identity applied.

Figure 13.20
You can choose an identity for your new message here.

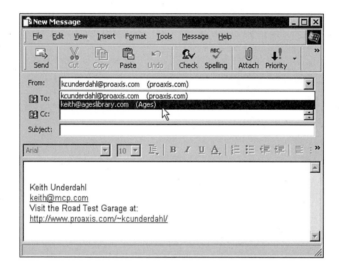

Figure 13.21
A new identity has been chosen.

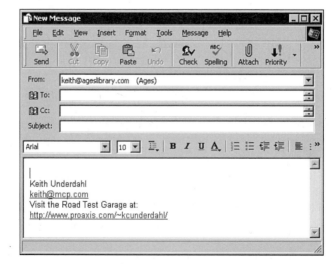

⚠ *Does Outlook Express check for new mail in some of your accounts but not in others? See "Checking Mail in Multiple Accounts" in the "Troubleshooting" section at the end of the chapter.*

ORGANIZING YOUR MAIL

You don't have to receive very much mail to realize that your Inbox can get pretty cluttered in a hurry. You probably find that you need to save many of the messages you receive, but you can't leave them all in the same place. The best way to save important mail and stay organized is to organize your mail into folders, just like files are organized on your hard drive.

The process of creating folders and storing messages in them is quite simple:

1. Right-click the Inbox in the OE5 Folder list, and choose New Folder from the menu that appears. The Create Folder dialog opens, as shown in Figure 13.22.

Figure 13.22
You name your new folder in this dialog and click OK to create it.

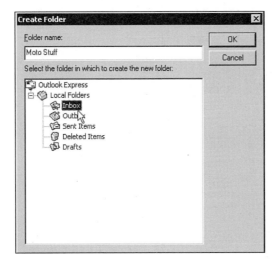

2. Type a descriptive name for your folder under Folder Name. Check the folder list in the lower half of the dialog to make sure that the correct folder is selected to create your new folder in.
3. Click OK to create the folder.

The new folder appears in the OE5 Folder list, under the folder you created it in. You can simply drag and drop messages from the message list to the folder you want to store them in.

FILTERING YOUR MAIL

Some people receive a lot of mail. Many email users—especially those who subscribe to mailing lists—receive dozens or even hundreds of messages per day. Wading through all this mail for the really important stuff can be challenging (to say the least), so OE5 includes

PART
III

CH

13

a mail filtering feature similar to Outlook's Inbox Rules that helps you direct certain kinds of mail to specific locations. For example, you might want to direct all mail from a list you are subscribed to into a special folder where it can be read later.

You can even use mail filters to delete mail you don't want to see at all. Mail can be filtered by content, subject, or sender information. If you are frequently being bothered by someone, you can simply set up OE5 to send all messages from that person to the Deleted Items folder.

To set up a filter, perform the following:

1. In Outlook Express, choose Tools and select Message Rules, Mail. If the Message Rules dialog opens, click New.

2. Select a condition from box 1 of the New Mail Rule dialog. Place a check mark next to the condition or conditions you want to apply.

3. Select an action in box 2. This action will happen if the condition specified in box 1 is met.

4. Follow the instructions in box 3. They will be specific to the conditions and actions you set in boxes 1 and 2. As you can see in Figure 13.23, we have set up a rule that automatically sends a reply to every incoming message. The reply states that we are away from the office until a certain date.

Figure 13.23
You can create mail rules to filter your mail and automate certain tasks.

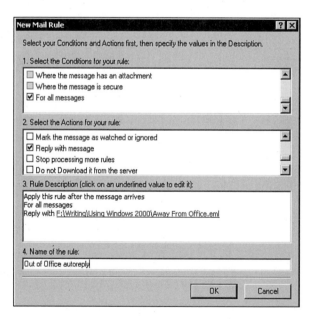

5. Check the description in box 3 to make sure the correct action will take place. Name the rule in box 4, and click OK when you are finished.

The rule then appears in the Message Rules dialog with a check mark next to it. You can open this dialog at any time to edit, disable, or remove any rules.

Tip #188

> Although an "out of office" auto reply rule as demonstrated here can be useful, do not enable such a rule if you are subscribed to any mailing lists. Every incoming message from the list triggers a response from Outlook Express. Those responses go back to the mailing list, generating more list traffic that will be sent to your account, resulting in more auto replies, and so on. See where this loop is going?

To block mail from a specific sender, you can use the Blocked Senders tab of the Message Rules dialog. You can open this tab directly by choosing Tools, Message Rules, Blocked Senders List in Outlook Express. Click Add in the dialog, and type the person's email address in the Add Sender dialog. After you add the address, that person's name appears in your Blocked Senders list, as shown in Figure 13.24. Notice that you can opt to block newsgroup messages from that person as well.

Figure 13.24
Messages from people in this list are automatically sent to the Deleted Items folder.

Tip #189

> If you are traveling away from home, consider setting up a message rule in Outlook Express to forward all incoming messages to your Hotmail account. That way, you can read all your mail on the road, no matter which of your addresses the messages are sent to.

PART

III

CH

13

BACKING UP MESSAGES

One of the unique aspects of electronic mail is that it can serve as a permanent record of your communications. Mail that seems insignificant now may be invaluable in the future, and many people back up all their correspondence on a regular basis to ensure that a record is kept for all time.

You can save copies of individual messages by choosing Save As from the File menu in the message window. Choosing this option opens a standard Windows Save dialog, where you can choose a location and name for the file. It is saved with the .EML extension.

Backing up an entire folder is a bit trickier. OE5 folders are saved on the hard drive with the .DBX extension, but by default they are hidden files living in hidden folders. After you display them, do the following:

1. Click Start and choose Search, For Files and Folders. In the first search box, type DBX and click Search Now. A file for each folder appears with the search results in the right side of the window, as shown in Figure 13.25.

2. Locate the file for the folder you want to back up, and save a copy of it on a disk or other safe location.

Figure 13.25
Using the search box, you can search for .DBX files and save them in a safe place.

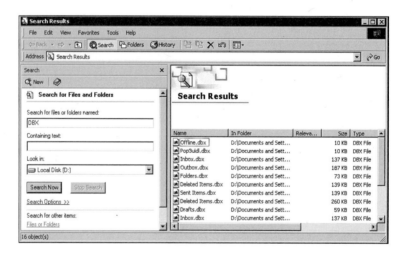

If other people use this computer, make sure you are backing up folders for yourself. Your username should appear in the folder path listed under In Folder.

DEALING WITH SPAM

A hot topic in email circles today is the subject of commercial advertisements mass-delivered via electronic mail. This type of unsolicited mail is generally referred to as *spam*, a name attributed in Internet lore to a Monty Python musical skit pertaining to the pink meat product of the same name. This type of mail is so offensive to some people that a few states have even enacted laws against it.

Some groups are also working with the U.S. Federal Government to ban unsolicited electronic mail and place identification requirements on people and organizations who send advertisements via email. Countless anti-spam organizations exist, with one of the foremost being CAUCE, the Coalition Against Unsolicited Commercial Email (www.cauce.org).

The real problem with spam is that scam operations are rampant and difficult to detect. Spam also has an impact on Internet traffic, requiring a considerable amount of bandwidth that many people feel would be better used for other purposes.

If you have been online for very long, you've almost certainly received some spam yourself. You can protect yourself from receiving a lot of spam by taking some basic precautionary measures:

- Avoid giving out your email address whenever possible. Some Web sites funnel you through pointless registration procedures that do little else than collect email addresses.
- If you post to newsgroups periodically, alter your Reply to: email address for your news account in such a way that "spam bots" searching newsgroups for email addresses will not be able to send you mail correctly. Many people put "Nospam" in front of their address, a modification that will be easy for humans to correct when sending you a valid reply.
- Don't register with too many online directories. Some directories can be used as email address archives for spammers. The trade-off is that someone looking for you will have a harder time.

Alas, no matter how careful you are, some spam will get through. Many spams contain instructions for getting yourself removed from their list. Follow through whenever possible, because removing yourself from existing lists could prevent your address from being sold to other spammers.

You can also check with your local, state, or federal laws from time to time to find out whether there are regulations against spam that apply to your account. If so, you may have legal recourse against spammers. The CAUCE organization mentioned earlier is a good starting point to search online for information about laws in your area.

TROUBLESHOOTING

PASSWORD TROUBLE

The server will not accept my password.

Many email servers are case sensitive. If the Caps Lock key on your keyboard is on, it could cause the password to be entered in the wrong case. This is true even if you have configured Outlook Express to remember your email address so that you don't have to type it in every time you check mail.

PART

III

CH

13

IDENTITY CRISIS

I don't like the name Outlook Express is using to identify me in outgoing messages.

The name Outlook Express uses could be indicative of several things. First, if you have multiple accounts or identities configured in Outlook Express, make sure that you are selecting the desired one in the From: field when you send the messages. You can also open the Internet Accounts dialog and check the Properties sheet for your email address(es). The Name field under User Information on the General tab is the name used to identify you on outgoing mail.

CHECKING MAIL IN MULTIPLE ACCOUNTS

I have several mail accounts, but OE5 doesn't check all of them when I click Send/Recv.

Open the Properties sheet for each of your mail accounts in the Internet Accounts dialog. On the General tab is an option labeled Include This Account When Receiving Mail or Synchronizing. Make sure a check mark appears next to this option for each of your mail accounts.

THINNING YOUR CONTACTS LIST

Several people in my Contacts List shouldn't be there, including spammers.

By default, OE5 adds an entry to the Address Book for every source you reply to. You can disable this feature by opening the Options dialog in the Tools menu. On the Send tab, disable the option labeled Automatically Put People I Reply to in My Address Book.

RECIPIENTS DON'T LIKE MY MAIL FORMATTING

People on my mailing list are sending me hate mail because of machine characters or strange attachments that accompany each of my posts.

HTML messages are not compatible with most electronic mailing lists. Change your default mail sending format to Plain Text on the Send tab of the OE5 Options dialog.

MISSING MAIL SERVERS

When I try to go online and check mail, an error occurs stating that the server could not be found.

Assuming that the server information for your account is correct, you probably have a problem with your connection. OE5 should automatically dial a connection if one is not present, but if it doesn't, open the Internet Properties icon in the Windows Control Panel. On the Connection tab, select the option Dial Whenever a Network Connection Is Not Present, and click OK to close the dialog.

MAKING OE5 LESS AUTOMATED

I want/don't want Outlook Express to automatically check for mail periodically.

Go to the General tab of the Options dialog. If the option Check for New Messages Every XX Minutes is checked, OE5 automatically checks for new mail at the specified interval. Just below that option, you can also specify whether you want OE5 to automatically dial a connection at this time.

TIPS FROM THE WINDOWS PROS: FED UP WITH USENET? TRY A MAILING LIST

Email predates virtually all modern uses for the Internet. It is an outstanding medium for communication, although its primary limitation has traditionally been that it was designed with person-to-person communication in mind. To address this limitation, Usenet was developed in the late 1970s to allow more widespread dissemination of certain kinds of information.

If you've used Usenet newsgroups at all, you know about the benefits they can provide. They serve as message boards and open communications forums, where anyone can read or post messages. Newsgroups can be used to give or get technical advice for a certain product, discuss issues and interests with other like-minded persons, share software and other files, and more.

Alas, like anything else, newsgroups have their shortcomings. Foremost among them is the very openness that makes Usenet what it is; privacy and security are almost nonexistent because access is unlimited. People who post to newsgroups can also be the subject of victimization or can become the targets of spam simply because their email addresses appear in all their posts. And controlling the posting of inappropriate material to a given group is difficult.

To address some of these problems, many online users have come full circle back to email as a means for communicating in a forum. Some mailing lists perform essentially the same functions as newsgroups, but the distribution is much more limited. Members must subscribe to a mailing list to read it, and usually members are the only ones allowed to make posts.

Mailing lists are simple; you send a message to the list address, and it is then forwarded to every other list member. Every time another member posts a message to the list, you receive a copy. The list is managed by a list administrator who often, but not always, works directly with the mail server hosting the list. Often the administrator can be reached via the email address `listproc` or `majordomo` followed by @ and the name of the host server.

Lists exist for virtually any topic imaginable. If you want to try to find a mailing list to join, a good place to start would be Vivian Neou's mailing list search directory, available online at `www.catalog.com/vivian/`.

Lists vary widely in terms of message volume, ranging anywhere from only a few messages per month up to hundreds of posts each day. Many lists let you opt to receive one or two daily list compilations rather than a string of individual posts. These compilations are called *digests* and are especially useful with high-volume lists.

Before you join and start to participate in mailing lists, you need to keep two main issues in mind: Security and Netiquette. Security is largely determined by the list administrator, so you should check list policies for concerns before you join. You should also exercise caution when posting sensitive information to a list because, generally speaking, you won't know who is actually subscribed.

Netiquette is a little trickier. You've probably already read volumes on such topics as flame wars and the public airing of private laundry, but you should be aware of some issues unique to mailing lists:

- Don't post attachments. Most mailing lists, especially those offering a Digest mode, forbid file attachments, and for good reason. If you want to send a file to someone, do it off list.

- Send posts in plain text format. HTML formatting can wreak havoc on recipients' systems. Check with the list administrator to find out whether MIME or uuencode plain text formatting is best.

- Read and save the FAQ. Every list has a different procedure for subscribing, unsubscribing, switching to digest mode, or changing various other options. This information is usually contained in a list FAQ, which should also include guidance regarding list content and rules.

- Be conscious of the reply procedures for your list. Some mailing lists are configured so that a Reply action goes only to the original sender, and you must click Reply All to post a reply to the list. But with other lists, clicking Reply sends your response directly to the list. Again, double-check your list's FAQ to find out the correct procedure.

- Do not use an "Out of Office" auto-reply rule for your Inbox. Automatic replies to incoming messages can cause destructive feedback loops in lists that you are subscribed to. If you feel that you must use such a rule, unsubscribe or suspend your mailing lists before enabling it.

CHAPTER 14

Newsgroups

In this chapter

NEWSGROUPS AND THE INTERNET

With the overwhelming and still growing popularity of the World Wide Web since its inception in the early 1990s, you might easily forget that the Internet was around for more than two decades before the first Web page saw the light of a cathode ray tube. Before the inception of the Web, people used the Internet to access newsgroups. Newsgroups began in 1979 as a forum in which UNIX users could communicate with each other, and the concept grew steadily from there into what is now a global assemblage of people sharing information on virtually every topic imaginable.

Originally, news servers exchanged articles using UNIX-to-UNIX Copy Protocol (UUCP), which involves direct modem dial-up over long-distance phone lines. In 1986, the Network News Transport Protocol (NNTP) was released, allowing news to be transported via TCP/IP connection over the Internet. Most modern newsgroups use the NNTP protocol, and it is the only news protocol supported by Outlook Express.

Newsgroups are scattered on servers around the world, and the rough network used to carry newsgroup bandwidth is generally referred to as *Usenet*. We're not implying, however, that some authority provides oversight of Usenet. "Usenet is not a democracy" is one of the first statements you will read in virtually any primer or Frequently Asked Questions list (FAQ) on the subject, alluding to the virtual anarchy in which this medium exists. Usenet has become so large and diverse that a simple definition cannot possibly do justice.

What we can do, however, is roughly describe the types of newsgroups and news servers that you can access using Outlook Express 5 (OE5). Basically, the administrator of your news server determines which news feeds you will have access to. Feeds are passed along to the server from adjacent servers, providing a decidedly decentralized structure to Usenet. Each server maintains a list of message IDs to ensure that new articles are received at a given server only once. An individual server can control which feeds it propagates, although the interconnectivity of Usenet servers ensures that a lone server has little or no control of the overall distribution. Thus, the authority of a news server is generally limited to what clients (that would be you) can access and what kind of material those clients can post. Likewise, the decentralization of servers means that an article you post may take hours—or even days—to circulate among all other news servers.

> **Note**
>
> The terms *newsgroup* and *Usenet* are used almost interchangeably in today's online world, but it is useful to know that *newsgroup* refers to individual groups, whereas *Usenet* refers to the entire network of groups as a whole.

WHAT ABOUT MAILING LISTS?

Many users now take advantage of a popular alternative to newsgroups: electronic mailing lists. When a message is sent to a mailing list, everyone subscribed to the list gets a copy of the message via email. Some lists compile many messages into a single *digest* message that is mailed to members periodically, reducing the number of individual messages received by each person.

Many people prefer mailing lists because of their less-public nature. Mailing list posts are less public because the only people who can read them are other list members, and lists are generally less susceptible to spam and objectionable material. Furthermore, mailing list traffic comes in with regular email, making lists easier to deal with for some people.

Of course, mailing lists have drawbacks as well. The most significant is that mailing lists can dump dozens—or even hundreds—of posts into your email account daily. The sheer volume of mail can make it difficult to figure out what is important and what isn't.

→ Spam is a fact of life in both mailing lists and newsgroups. Learn more about spam in "Avoiding Spam," **p. 509**.

SETTING UP A NEWSGROUP ACCOUNT IN OUTLOOK EXPRESS

Outlook Express 5 (OE5) is included free with Windows 2000 and serves quite well as a news reader. If you already use OE5 for email services, you're probably already familiar with the basics of using this program. If not, you may benefit from a quick review of Chapter 13, "Email," which will help you master the fundamentals of using OE5.

You first must set up a news account in OE5. You might do so at the same time you set up an email account, but if not, you can configure it any time. Before you can configure your news account, you need to obtain a news server address, which should look something like this:

news.domainname.com

Your company might also have a news server account with a commercial provider. You can configure multiple server accounts in OE5, just as you can set up multiple email accounts.

As mentioned earlier, a news server provides you with news feeds from other news servers. Which feeds are available to you depends on decisions made by your server's administrator. For example, some news servers restrict feeds for all alt. (alternative) newsgroups because some of them contain highly objectionable material.

→ If you do not have a news server you can access, **see** "Locating News Servers," **p. 500**.

To set up your account in Outlook Express, follow these steps:

1. Open Outlook Express, and choose Tools, Accounts to open the Internet Accounts dialog. Click the News tab to bring it to the front, and then select Add, News.

2. Follow the instructions in the Internet Connection Wizard.

3. Type the name of your news (NNTP) server, as shown in Figure 14.1.

PART

III

CH

14

Figure 14.1
You enter the name of your news server here. If you use multiple news servers, you must set up an individual account for each one.

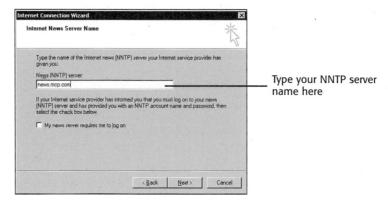

Type your NNTP server name here

4. Click Next, and then click Finish.

LOCATING NEWS SERVERS

Many ISPs and companies provide news server accounts to their Internet users, but you still might find yourself looking for a server on your own. This may be the case even if you have a news account available to you; some service providers censor the news content that is available, and if you want uncensored news, you must rely on a different source.

Censorship, Big Brother, and NNTP Servers

News feeds are censored for a variety of reasons. For example, your company's server may restrict feeds from `alt.`, `rec.`, and `talk.` groups to reduce the number of work hours lost to employee abuse or simply to reduce bandwidth. Many other servers restrict feeds that contain pornographic content for both legal and moral reasons.

Even if your news server provides a relatively unrestricted news feed, you should exercise care when deciding which articles you download from the server. Virtually all servers maintain logs of the activities of each login account. This means that your service provider can track which articles you download, and in most cases these logs can be subpoenaed and used against you in court.

In other words, Big Brother might be watching you download porn, bomb making instructions, and bootleg copies of *The Phantom Menace*. Be especially paranoid if you access a company news server; hours spent receiving otherwise legal content such as fruit cake recipes, Bill Gates jokes, and the like could still land you in hot water if the boss is logging your online activities.

Many news servers are available through virtually any Internet connection, but you'll pay for that connection. Typically, monthly charges for a personal news server account range from $10 to $20 per month and get higher for corporate or higher bandwidth accounts. If you plan to use newsgroups frequently, you might want to factor in this cost when you're shopping for an ISP. You can find a good list of commercial news servers in the Yahoo! directory at

```
http://dir.yahoo.com/Business_and_Economy/Companies/Internet_Services/
➥Usenet_Servers/Commercial/
```

SETTING UP A NEWSGROUP ACCOUNT IN OUTLOOK EXPRESS | 501

 If Outlook Express has trouble locating your news server, see "No News Server Connection" in the "Troubleshooting" section at the end of this chapter.

Deja.com (www.deja.com) offers a free alternative to commercial news servers by offering a Web-based news service. It does not charge for the service, although registration is required. Deja.com is also home to an online community area focusing on Usenet.

 If you cannot locate a particular newsgroup on your news server, see "Newsgroup Isn't Available on News Server" in the "Troubleshooting" section at the end of this chapter.

DOWNLOADING THE NEWSGROUP LIST

After you have configured Outlook Express for your news server, your next step is to download a list of newsgroups from the server. Depending on how many groups the server allows access to, this list could contain more than 75,000 newsgroups. In reality, most servers list less than half that number.

Why aren't they all listed? As you've already seen, some content might be censored by the server's administrator. In many cases, though, it is a much more practical matter: New groups are created so frequently that your server simply might not be aware of them. If you become aware of a newsgroup you would like to join, but it is not currently available on your server, try dropping an email message to the administrator and ask for the group to be added. Assuming the group falls within the administrator's guidelines for acceptable content, adding the group will take only a few seconds.

To begin downloading your server's list, follow these steps:

1. Click the listing for your news account in the OE5 Folders list, as shown in Figure 14.2.

2. A message appears stating that you are not currently subscribed to any newsgroups and asking whether you would like to view the list. Click Yes.

3. If this is the first time you have viewed the list, a dialog appears, as shown in Figure 14.2. Depending on the size of the list, downloading will take several minutes. You probably have time to go get another cup of coffee. When the process is finished, the list is downloaded, and you are ready to locate and subscribe to newsgroups.

Figure 14.2
The list of newsgroups downloads from your news server.

Click the news account listing to begin

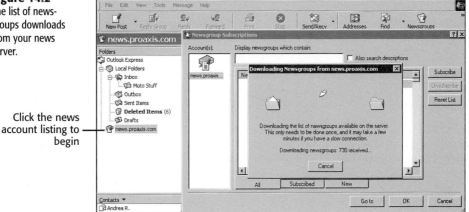

PART
III

CH
14

Tip #190

Although new newsgroups are created daily, the list that has been downloaded to your computer is static and doesn't show new groups. To make sure you have a current list, click Reset List in the Newsgroup Subscriptions dialog periodically.

FINDING AND READING NEWSGROUPS

Usually, when you read a newsgroup, you first subscribe to it. A subscription simply means you've placed a bookmark of sorts in Outlook Express for that group, making it easy to return to and follow conversations whenever you are using OE5.

Before you can subscribe to a newsgroup, you need to find one that piques your interest. Searching for a group in your downloaded list is fairly simple in OE5 (see Figure 14.3). If the list isn't already open, you can open it by clicking your news account in the Folders list. If the list doesn't open automatically, you can click the Newsgroups button on the toolbar.

Figure 14.3
You can begin typing a word to search the newsgroup list. The list automatically gets smaller as you type, showing only those groups with names that match what you typed.

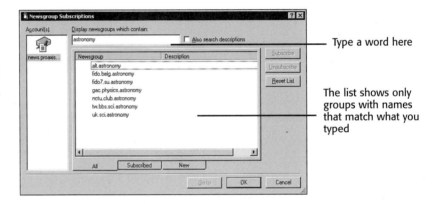

Type a word here

The list shows only groups with names that match what you typed

As you can see in Figure 14.3, as you type a word in the Display Newsgroups Which Contain field, the list of newsgroups shrinks. You can experiment by typing a keyword you are interested in, pausing after each keystroke.

Newsgroups are usually—but not always—named descriptively. In Figure 14.3, you can see the option to search newsgroup descriptions as well as their names, but very few groups actually have descriptions listed in this window.

Tip #191

If you don't find a newsgroup that interests you, try a search at Deja.com or another Web source to see whether other groups not currently available on your news server exist. There is no such thing as a "complete" list of newsgroups, so a search of several different resources will yield the best results.

SUBSCRIBING TO NEWSGROUPS

OE5 does not require you to subscribe to a group to view its contents. You can simply select a group from the list and click Go To to see messages posted to the group, but you might find it easier to manage the process by simply subscribing anyway. Subscribing to a newsgroup does not require any great level of commitment on your part because you can always unsubscribe with just two mouse clicks.

When you find a newsgroup you want to subscribe to, do the following:

1. Click once on the newsgroup name to select it, and then click the Subscribe button. An icon should appear next to the group name, as shown in Figure 14.4.

Figure 14.4
You can select a newsgroup and subscribe to it here. When you click Go To, this window automatically closes.

This icon indicates that you have subscribed

2. Click Go To at the bottom of the Newsgroup Subscriptions window. The window closes, and the 300 most recent posts are downloaded to your computer.

Actually, only the message headers are downloaded, and they appear listed in the OE5 window. The message contents are not downloaded until you choose to view a specific message.

MANAGING YOUR SUBSCRIPTIONS

Newsgroups you are subscribed to are listed in the OE5 Folders list, under the news account listing, as shown in Figure 14.5. If you have multiple news server accounts, individual subscriptions are listed as subfolders under the server you used to subscribe to them.

When you click a newsgroup's listing in the Folders list, the 300 most recent headers are downloaded.

→ If you want to change the number of headers shown, **see** "Customizing Outlook Express for Newsgroups," **p. 511**.

If you decide that you don't want to remain subscribed to a group, unsubscribing is easy. Just right-click the group's listing in the Folders list, and choose Unsubscribe from the shortcut menu that appears.

PART
III

CH
14

Figure 14.5
Subscribed news-groups are shown in the Folders list.

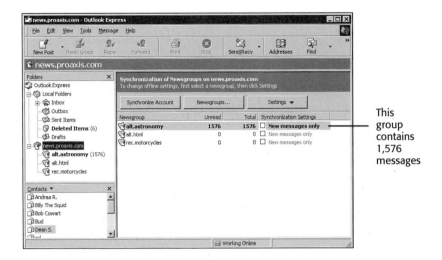

This group contains 1,576 messages

READING A NEWSGROUP

As you learned previously, when you first access a newsgroup using OE5, only the first 300 message headers are downloaded. You can download additional headers by clicking Tools, Get Next 300 Headers.

If you want to read a message, you need to manually open it. If you are using the Preview Pane, all you have to do is click once on the message header to cause it to download. If you are not using the Preview Pane, you can double-click a message to open it in a separate message window.

→ To learn how to show or hide the Preview Pane, **see** "Outlook Express Quick Tour," **p. 468**.

As you peruse the list of messages in the group, you need to understand the concept of *discussion threads*. A thread occurs when someone responds to a message. Others respond to the response, and this conversation becomes its own discussion thread. Messages that are part of a thread have a plus (+) sign next to them, and you can click this icon to expand a list of other messages in the thread. Figure 14.6 shows several expanded threads.

Figure 14.6
These messages are part of a thread.

POSTING MESSAGES TO A NEWSGROUP

Posting messages to a newsgroup is quite simple. Perhaps the easiest way to post is to reply to an existing message. This process works much the same as replying to regular email, except that you must take extra care to ensure that your reply is going to the right place. Notice that the toolbar has a new button—the Reply Group button—as shown in Figure 14.7.

Figure 14.7
You must choose your reply mode carefully.

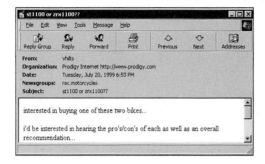

Each reply button serves a unique purpose:

Reply Group	Sends a reply back to the group
Reply	Sends a reply only to the original sender
Forward	Forwards the message to a third party

One aspect to watch carefully is that messages you post to a newsgroup are relevant. If the newsgroup is moderated, someone reviews all posts and removes those posts that are deemed inappropriate. Look for a newsgroup FAQ (Frequently Asked Questions) for more information on etiquette and rules as they apply to the groups you are subscribed to.

Caution

Information posted in newsgroups can be viewed by anyone, and we do mean *anyone!* Never post personal or sensitive information in a newsgroup.

Note

The default news message format is plain text. You should maintain this setting to ensure that your message can be read by other news readers.

MANAGING MESSAGES

By default, OE5 deletes messages from your computer five days after you download them, but you can change this option easily. Likewise, you can also set up Outlook Express to delete read messages every time you leave the group. You can review these settings by choosing Tools, Options. In the Options dialog, click the Maintenance tab to bring it to the front, as shown in Figure 14.8.

Figure 14.8
You can review your
message management
settings here.

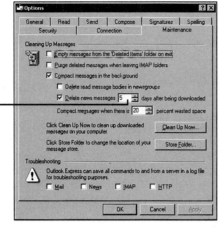

Adjust the length
of time read
messages are
saved

 If a message you read earlier becomes unavailable, see "Message No Longer Available" in the "Troubleshooting" section at the end of this chapter.

 If you're not sure which messages have been read and which haven't, see "Which Ones Are New?" in the "Troubleshooting" section at the end of the chapter.

If you want to maintain a record of the messages in your newsgroup, remove the check marks next to each Delete option shown in Figure 14.8. Messages remain in OE5 indefinitely if you deselect both of these options, and if the group has high traffic, these messages could eventually eat up a lot of disk space.

The better option is to save individual messages that you want to maintain. To do so, create a new folder for storing news messages under Local Folders in the OE5 Folders list, and then drag messages to the folder. You can also drag and drop newsgroup messages to any of your email folders, but you might find it easier to keep newsgroup and email correspondence separate.

READING NEWS OFFLINE

In Chapter 12, "World Wide Web," you learned that you can download Web pages for offline viewing. You can do the same with newsgroup messages, a capability that makes especially good sense if you must limit your Internet connection time or will be traveling with your laptop. OE5 calls this feature *synchronizing*.

> **Caution**
>
> Before you synchronize a newsgroup for offline viewing, check the size of the messages you will download. Some people post pictures and other large files into newsgroups, and they can add significantly to download time.

To begin downloading a newsgroup for offline viewing, click your news server account in the Folders list. A list of the groups you are subscribed to then appears, as shown in Figure 14.9. Now follow these steps:

1. Select the newsgroup you want to synchronize, and review the synchronization settings. By default, only new messages will be synchronized, but you can change this setting by clicking the Settings button and choosing another option.

2. Place a check mark in the box under Synchronization settings, as shown in Figure 14.9.

3. Click Synchronize Account. Messages are downloaded based on the synchronization settings you choose. Keep in mind that if you choose to synchronize all messages, the download could take awhile.

Figure 14.9
You synchronize messages for offline viewing by choosing the options shown here.

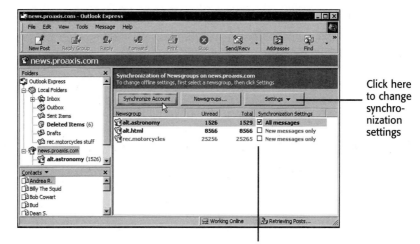

Click here to change synchronization settings

Place a check mark here

When the download is complete, you can get offline to read the downloaded messages. If you try to open a message that isn't available offline, a warning advises you of this fact.

 If, after you synchronize a newsgroup, some messages are not available, see "Some Messages Are Unavailable After Synchronizing" in the "Troubleshooting" section at the end of this chapter.

You can also select individual messages for offline reading. Choosing particular messages may be a better course of action, especially if the newsgroup has thousands of messages and you want to download only the first few. To do so, select the message headers in the newsgroup by Ctrl+clicking or Shift+clicking, right-click the selection, and then choose Download Message Later from the menu that appears. Then, when you choose Synchronize Account from the server account window shown in Figure 14.9, only the selected messages are downloaded.

NEWSGROUP SAFETY

It is no secret that many potential hazards exist in the online world, and nowhere is this more evident than in Usenet. Objectionable Web pages get all the media attention, but nowhere is objectionable—and often illegal—content more readily available than in

PART

III

CH

14

newsgroups. You can avoid most objectionable content simply by staying away from certain newsgroups, but you might still find the need to filter some of the content you receive.

Besides objectionable content, you must also consider that you become more vulnerable to victimization (or, for that matter, prosecution) when you participate in newsgroups unless you take some basic precautions. Remember, anyone in the world who has access to an Internet connection can see what you post in a newsgroup.

FILTERING UNWANTED MESSAGES

OE5 allows you to set up some message rules to filter certain messages. You can set up this feature, which is similar to mail message rules, as follows:

1. In Outlook Express, choose Tools, Message Rules, News.

2. In the New News Rule dialog, choose conditions for your rule in box 1. As you can see in Figure 14.10, you can select more than one condition. In this case, we're looking for messages in the `alt.astronomy` newsgroup that contain the word *Hubble* in the subject line.

3. In box 2, choose what you want to happen to messages that meet your conditions. In this case, matching messages will be highlighted in yellow. If the condition were looking for objectionable material, we would probably choose to delete it instead.

4. In box 3, review the rule description and enter any required information. For example, you will probably have to specify words or other pieces of information pertaining to the conditions you set.

Figure 14.10
You can create rules for filtering your news messages here. Be sure to check each box for relevant information.

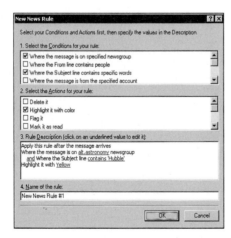

5. Click OK when you're finished, and click OK in the Message Rules dialog to close it.

You can modify or disable a rule at any time by using the Tools, Message Rules, News command.

→ You can also filter news by restricting senders. To learn how, **see** "Filtering Your Mail," **p. 489**.

PROTECTING YOUR IDENTITY

Besides objectionable content, the other great hazard involved with using newsgroups is the threat to your identity and personal information. You can avoid having personal information compromised on Usenet by simply not posting it. Don't post your home address or phone number, age (especially if you are young), or financial information (such as a credit card number).

You can also hide your identity if you do not want to reveal it. Outlook Express identifies you in all outgoing posts by whatever username you entered when you configured the account. If you are concerned about protecting your identity in newsgroups, consider changing the username for your news account to a nickname that your friends or associates will recognize but strangers won't. Figure 14.11 shows such a nickname in use.

Of course, there are limits to how much anonymity can be provided by simply changing the username and email address for your news account in OE5. Any message you post to a newsgroup can be easily traced back to your server, and your server maintains transaction logs that allow your real identity to be ascertained.

A more secure solution would be to use a *pseudonymous remailer*. A pseudonymous remailer is a server that assigns you an ID based on a proprietary scheme, and you send and receive anonymous posts through the server. Some remailers require you to use a specific news application, and it's never OE5. You can find a good list of pseudonymous remailers online at the following site:

```
http://www.stack.nl/~galactus/remailers/index-anon.html
```

AVOIDING SPAM

One of the most pervasive threats to your identity that exists in Usenet is spam (see "Dealing with Spam" in Chapter 13 for a definition).

Programs called *Spambots* do nothing but scan Usenet message headers for email addresses. These addresses are compiled and sold to companies that send out unsolicited advertisements via email. If you post frequently to newsgroups, your email address could get "vacuumed" in this manner, resulting in a greater volume of spam in your Inbox.

Fortunately, Spambots aren't intelligent, so defeating them is relatively simple. The most common tactic is to add a word to your email address that actual human beings will recognize as an anti-spam measure. It would look something like this:

```
bob@nospam_mcp.com
```

A person who wants to respond to you can easily remove the "nospam_" from your email address, but Spambots won't be able to recognize it, and the spam that was meant for you will end up bouncing back to the sender. You can change your reply address by clicking Tools, Accounts to open the Internet Accounts dialog. Then click the News tab, select your news account, and click Properties. Type the modified email address in the Reply Address text box, as shown in Figure 14.11, and click OK to close the dialog.

Figure 14.11
You can type a modified identity and reply address in this dialog to avoid spam and protect your identity in Usenet.

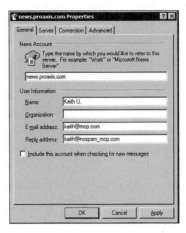

Modified email address

Responding to Anonymous Posters

You're not the only person trying to remain anonymous in Usenet. Trying to respond to a message you read can cause you a few problems, especially if you are trying to respond directly to the poster.

Obviously, there are different levels of anonymity. If the person is simply using a nickname, you should be able to respond to him or her normally. But if that person is also trying to conceal his or her email address, responding can get trickier. If an error message is returned to you when you try to send someone email (often called a *bounce*), check that person's email address to see whether he or she is using an anti-spam scheme as shown here:

```
bob@nospam_mcp.com
```

People who use this naming scheme usually have something in their signature files that says "To reply, remove 'nospam_' from the domain" or something to that effect.

If the email address is obviously not valid, and no clues to the individual's real address exist, your last resort may be to post to the newsgroup. But don't use this situation as an excuse to share a private response in a public forum. A typical response would look something like this:

```
Attn: bob@nospam_mcp.com
I wish to send you a response. Please contact me directly at rick@mcp.com.
```

This message should get the individual's attention. If not, there's not much else you can do.

CUSTOMIZING OUTLOOK EXPRESS FOR NEWSGROUPS

Outlook Express 5 comes with a fairly good package of preset options for reading and participating in newsgroups. Still, what works for the "average" user might not suit you. You can customize virtually every aspect of news reading in this program by reviewing the various settings available to you. To do so, follow these steps:

1. In OE5, choose Tools, Options.

2. Click the General tab to bring it to the front, and then remove the check mark next to Notify Me If There Are Any New Newsgroups if you plan to reset your group list periodically.

3. Click the Read tab, as shown in Figure 14.12. OE5 automatically downloads the first 300 headers at a time, but you can change that number here. You also might want to check the option Mark All Messages as Read When Exiting a Newsgroup. If you routinely ignore some posts in the group, selecting this option will help you determine which messages are actually new the next time you open the group.

Figure 14.12
You can set the number of message headers that will be downloaded when you open a group here.

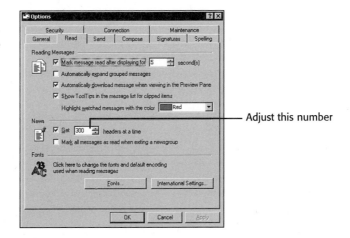

Adjust this number

4. Switch to the Send tab to make your default news-sending format HTML if you like, but doing so is not recommended.

5. Click the Signatures tab to bring it to the front, and create a new signature to be used exclusively with newsgroups. Your news signature could include instructions for removing anti-spam measures from your email address. After you have created the new signature, click the Advanced button to open the dialog shown in Figure 14.13. Here, you can select your news account to "assign" the signature to it. After you have assigned a signature, it will be used only with that account.

6. On the Maintenance tab, check the two news-related Delete options if you want to save disk space.

→ To learn more about setting the Delete options, **see** "Managing Messages," **p. 505**.

7. Click OK to close the dialog and save your settings changes.

PART

III

CH

14

Figure 14.13
You can assign your
new signature to your
news account here.

Place a check mark
here to assign the
signature

TROUBLESHOOTING

NEWSGROUP ISN'T AVAILABLE ON NEWS SERVER

A newsgroup I want to access isn't available on my server.

Click Reset List in the Newsgroup Subscriptions window. The newsgroup may be new and simply not shown in your current list. If the group still isn't there, try contacting the ISP or other service that hosts the list and ask that service to add it. Often new groups simply go unnoticed because so many of them are out there. Many news servers are willing to respond to such a request, unless they have a rule restricting or censoring the particular group.

SOME MESSAGES ARE UNAVAILABLE AFTER SYNCHRONIZING

I tried to synchronize the group, but some messages I click aren't available.

Obviously, you should first check that the settings for the group are correct. If the group isn't set to All Messages, and the Synchronize check box isn't checked, this could easily explain the missing message bodies. Another possibility is that the message was removed from the host server sometime after the header list was distributed. It can take up to 72 hours after a message is physically removed before it disappears from the header list.

MESSAGE NO LONGER AVAILABLE

A message I read earlier is no longer available.

The default settings in Outlook Express delete read messages five days after you have downloaded them. You can change this option on the Maintenance tab of the OE Options dialog.

WHICH ONES ARE NEW?

I can't tell which messages are new.

Open the Options dialog by choosing Tools, Options. On the Read tab, place a check mark next to Mark All Messages as Read When Exiting a Newsgroup.

NO NEWS SERVER CONNECTION

Outlook Express cannot locate my news server.

Do you need to use a separate Internet connection to access the news server? If so, choose Tools, Accounts, and then click the News tab in the Internet Accounts dialog. Look at what is listed under Connection next to your news account listing. If it says `Any Available`, click Properties and select the Connection tab. Place a check mark next to Always Connect to This Account Using:, and select the appropriate connection from the drop-down list.

TIPS FROM THE WINDOWS PROS: NEWSGROUPS AIN'T JUST FOR NEWS ANYMORE

Newsgroups began innocently enough as forums for UNIX users to find and offer support, but it didn't take long for them to explode as a means of online recreation. Today, no matter how obscure you think your hobby or personal interest may be, a newsgroup is probably already dedicated to it. And one of the great advantages of newsgroups is the fact that files can be easily attached to posts. Attachments can be in the form of pictures, sound files, movies, text documents, programs, or anything else imaginable. In this respect, newsgroups really shine when compared to mailing lists; most mailing lists strictly forbid attachments, but in Usenet they are welcome.

Newsgroups with the word *binaries* in their address are good places to find attachments. Naturally, you need to exercise some care before you download any messages with large attachments. First, ask yourself whether you have enough bandwidth to download the message. The OE5 message list doesn't always show the paper clip icon next to message headers like it should, but it does tell you the size of each individual message, as shown in Figure 14.14.

Figure 14.14
This newsgroup contains many messages with large attachments.

Note the message size here

Where's the paper clip icon?

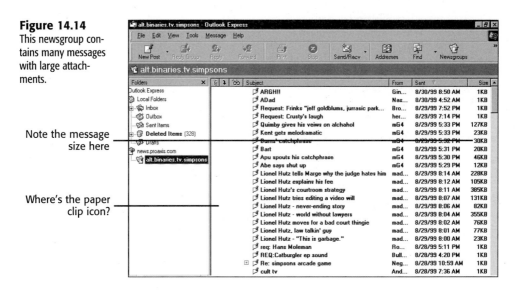

After you have determined that you can handle the message download, you should also keep virus safety in mind. If the attachment is a standard multimedia format, such as JPEG, WAV, GIF, MP3, or AVI, it should be safe. But if the attachment is an unknown format or is an executable (EXE) program, you should follow your standard antivirus protocols.

Some news attachments come as multipart files, meaning that a larger file is broken up over several consecutive postings. You can usually identify these types of posts by the Subject field, which identifies the message as part of a series. For example, you might see something like, "xfiles.avi (1/3), xfiles.avi (2/3), etc."

Multipart attachments must be opened together. Your first step is to identify each part of the series; if you miss even one portion of the series, it will not download or open properly. You Ctrl+click and Shift+click to select each member of the series. After you've selected all of them, right-click the series, and choose Combine and Decode from the shortcut menu, as shown in Figure 14.15.

Figure 14.15
You must make sure you select each member of a multipart attachment series before attempting the download.

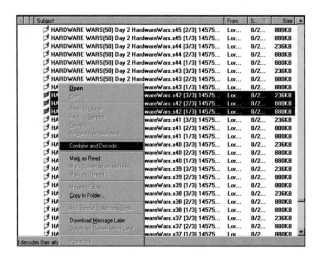

You are next presented with a dialog asking you to put the series members in order. They should be in numeric order, starting with part one at the top of the list. Use the Move Up and Move Down buttons to place them in the correct order. Depending on the size of the multipart attachment, the download may take awhile. When it is complete, a single message window opens with the attachment listed.

Multimedia attachments in Usenet can be a lot of fun. For example, the group alt.binaries.tv.simpsons usually contains WAV files of popular sound bites and catch-phrases from the television series *The Simpsons*. If you save downloaded WAV files in the \WINNT\Media folder of your hard drive, you can later assign those sounds to various Windows events. Wouldn't Windows 2000 be more enjoyable if each critical stop were accompanied by Bart Simpson's "Ay Caramba" rather than the monotonous Chord.wav?

Another gem to be on the lookout for in Usenet is MP3 music. MP3 files offer CD-quality music, but because they use about one-twelfth the storage space, they can be transported reasonably over the Internet. Look for any newsgroup with *mp3* in the address, but watch out for those bootlegs!

CHAPTER **15**

USING NETMEETING

In this chapter

THE EVOLUTION OF NETMEETING

The confluence of high-bandwidth Internet access and the unstoppable push toward corporate downsizing has had many repercussions on the nature of the workplace in the nineties. One of the effects has been the meteoric rise in the popularity of telecommuting. Computer-based tools to assist in telecommuting are on the rise as a result. Because so much of the work that telecommuting entails (computer programming, technical writing, interactivity with the corporate database) involves computers, tools such as Remote Access Services (RAS), Telnet, and Internet telephony have evolved to fill a growing need.

Although it was behind initially, Microsoft decided to jump into the Internet fray a few years ago, fearing it would be left in the electronic dust otherwise. Along with the development of email software, browsers, and other Net-related goodies, a special team at Microsoft worked quietly to integrate the latest in voice and videoconferencing tools into a single, inexpensive product. It's called NetMeeting, and in fact, it's so inexpensive that it's free. As part of the effort, Microsoft, in its usual fashion, hoped to pull in users who were, at the time, paying for products such as VocalTech's InternetPhone by giving away the Microsoft product for free.

Now in its third incarnation, NetMeeting 3.x has been going through growing pains once again. Version 2.x saw the inclusion of several features such as support for standards-based video, Web page integration of NetMeeting address links, and standards-based directory services.

Now in version 3.01, Microsoft has realized the interface for NetMeeting was too intense and confusing. Essentially copying (dare I say?) the AOL Instant Messenger/ICQ interface, NetMeeting is now much more intuitively arranged. The window is smaller, the buttons make more sense, and you don't have a mass of information on the screen to confuse you. Also, the functionality is broader. NetMeeting 3.01 was released June 18, 1999. Windows 98 Second Edition included a slightly less-inclusive version of NetMeeting 3.0 than comes with Windows 2000.

> **Note**
>
> NetMeeting was also bundled into Office 2000 and was integrated into Word, Access, Excel, and PowerPoint as a means for online collaboration. However, the version shipped with Office 2000 was 2.11.

THE DETAILS

NetMeeting is an Internet-based video and audio conferencing program based on common standards of Internet telephony. In addition to video and audio transmission (that can be used for traditional video teleconferencing or placing Internet telephone calls), it also contains a "whiteboard," keyboard chat mode (like AOL Instant Messenger or ICQ), and a few other goodies such as file transfer and Desktop Sharing. The whiteboard is great for sharing a drawing, map, picture, or other graphic and letting multiple folks in the conference edit it, point to objects, and so on. The chat window is the lowest common denominator for communications when both parties are not video or audio enabled.

Each feature is optional, so you can run chat only, for example, or audio without video. In fact, because the program is sometimes plagued by little gremlins (Internet traffic and incomplete connections?), resorting to one or another of the lower-level modes of communication is sometimes necessary anyway.

Other notable features include the following:

- You can set up meetings with up to eight other people. These people can be communicating in text chat, sharing a whiteboard, or working as a group on an application.

- A file transfer command lets you easily send files of any type between as many as eight other people at one time.

- Internet Telephony support lets you make audio phone calls with one other person. As with other Internet-based telephone products, this means you can talk to people anywhere on the Internet for just the price of the Internet connection (well, in addition to the computer). Your computer must have an audio system and microphone.

- Your Internet-based phone calls can optionally include video for videoconferencing. Again, this feature is limited to one-to-one calls, not group meetings. Of course, you need a video capture card and camera or some way to get video images into your computer, though.

- The application-sharing aspect of the program lets multiple people collaborate over, say, a word processing document, each being able to grab the cursor and make edits. It's pretty slick. You shouldn't confuse *application sharing* under NetMeeting, however, with the way the term is used in the context of LANs. In the world of LANs, the term only means letting people use the same program without having to have it on their local machine, by making it available on a server computer that they can all access. In the context of NetMeeting, application sharing takes on the additional meaning of people actually editing the same documents on those applications—while being able to see each other's changes in real-time. Even if the application isn't a true multiuser program, NetMeeting lets multiple people run the program and work on the same documents simultaneously.

- Using Desktop Sharing, you can log in to your computer from a remote computer running NetMeeting and completely control it as though it were local. Security is maintained by both encryption and optionally by certificate authentication so that not just anyone can connect in, nor could you accidentally log in to the wrong computer and have it snarf your password when you enter it. This feature is much like the programs Remote Control or PC Anywhere.

Tip #192

It's actually possible to have more than eight people in a meeting, but doing so takes a bit of trickery. By daisy-chaining groups together, you could theoretically have any number of participants. For example, the first group has 8 members in it, but one of them becomes a member of a second group that also has 8 members. The result is a 16-member group. But in reality, the number of participants is limited by bandwidth and processor speed.

You can create your own NetMeeting server for your own company if you want to host private (and more reliable) meetings. Doing so requires setting up your own *Internet Locator Server*, or *ILS*.

Of course, the video isn't TV quality, and the voice quality isn't as good as a typical telephone, especially if you're connected to the Net through a narrow pipe. But, hey, it's free. At the risk of sounding like a Microsoft ad, I'll say that NetMeeting could actually transform the way telecommuters do their everyday work, the way clubs hold meetings, or the way schools present instructional material.

Tip #193

Owing to the growing use of NetMeeting, numerous companies now sell add-on products such as cameras, microphones, headsets, video cards, and software additions. You can check them out via links from www.microsoft.com/netmeeting. You'll find a ton of information and links from there for good stuff about NetMeeting. Another good source is www.netmeet.net.

Another use of NetMeeting that comes to mind is distance learning, allowing presentations to be made or information to be disseminated to numerous people at the same time over the Internet or intranets. Also, it could be a boon for deaf or hard-of-hearing individuals who could use it to communicate more effectively in real-time with others in the workplace, the classroom, and the home. These features give NetMeeting substantial benefits over using traditional TTY devices.

In addition to using NetMeeting straight out of the box to share applications and to conference with other NetMeeting users, you can modify or incorporate NetMeeting into other media in various ways. Download the free *NetMeeting SDK* (the NetMeeting Software Developers Kit), and you can add conferencing support to your own Web pages, to Visual Basic applications, and to other ActiveX-enabled documents and applications.

The bottom line on this product? My experience with NetMeeting over the years and now with the new version 3 is that it's an exciting product that might change the way people communicate over the Net or the LAN. It points the way to the long-promised video phone (I'll date myself by saying I remember seeing one at the 1960 World's Fair in New York). Being able to talk to someone anywhere on the Internet for free, see each other's image at a fairly fast frame rate (I've seen about 15 frames/sec on a good day), and collaborate on a document all at once is pretty remarkable.

Note

In case you're unwashed in the nomenclature of frame rate, standard Hollywood-type movies run at a rate of 24 frames per second. (The screen image is updated every 1/24th of a second.) This speed is fast enough to fool the human eye and brain into filling the gaps between the frames. Even at this rate, however, you can still notice the flicker down at the movie theater, especially if you end up relegated to the front row of a sold-out box-office hit. Television was designed to operate at approximately 24 frames/sec so that movies and film (TV was invented well before videotape, remember) could be effectively transmitted over that medium. My point here is that 15 frames per second is going to look somewhat choppy to the uninitiated, but it ain't bad. If you've been watching any video clips on Web pages, you know how jerky Internet-based video can be. Fifteen frames looks way better than much of what you'll see over the Web, which often struggles in at even as little as 1 frame per second.

The technology just isn't ready for prime time, though. Unless you're willing to tinker a lot, using NetMeeting is still a bit like running a ham radio rig. Within the enterprise, with the right IS manager and strict hardware control (and possibly using a private corporate server), this tool could be very effective for communications. However, on the open Internet with the broad range of computers, transmission speeds, video and audio combinations, it can be frustrating. Performance is often unreliable, with spurious performance glitches (such as disappearing video or distorted audio) blemishing what will some day likely be a reliable, robust, and feature-rich product.

NEW STUFF IN NETMEETING VERSION 3.X

With the disclaimers out of the way, let's discuss NetMeeting 3, what it offers, and how to make it work as best you can. Let's start with new features over version 2.x. (If you've been using NetMeeting 2.x, this list will make some sense. If you haven't, don't sweat these details unless you're among the geekily interested.)

- The user interface is new. It's much more compact, with the video screen, dial interface, and participant list the focus of the window. (See Figure 15.1.)

- A Picture-In-Picture (PIP) display option displays both incoming and outgoing pictures in the main NetMeeting window.

- Audio and video work better in version 3.0, especially in low-bandwidth environments.

- Setting up NetMeeting and your hardware devices is easier than ever (and Microsoft seems to have gotten rid of many of the bugs that kept people from using some of its hardware).

- Call initiation has improved. ILS directory searching is now HTTP based, making it easier to find someone (yet more difficult to see a complete list of people who are available for cold calling). NetMeeting now supports H.323 and supports gateways and proxies better (though this capability will be of minimal use to most folks outside the enterprise). IP address issues that caused a caller's incorrect IP address to be registered in the ILS directory have been fixed.

Figure 15.1
The new interface is
more compact and
simpler.

- Individuals can more easily set up and host meetings. You can now set up encryption use for data-only meetings and require certificate-based authentication of individuals who want to join a meeting.

- You have the option to use DirectSound, which can decrease delay time in audio transmission. This option is off by default and can be controlled from within NetMeeting.

- Application sharing is much improved and available in full color. It's also faster and offers expanded control of viewing by the receiver. A participant can now share his or her "desktop" within a session, meaning that the remote user can take control of the computer. This capability makes NetMeeting a powerful tool for Internet-based Help personnel to walk stumped users through procedures or investigate settings on a computer themselves.

- The Software Development Kit (SDK) has been improved, with expanded documentation. However, I have some complaints: The SDK assumes you are a Visual C++ programmer. If you program in Visual Basic or JavaScript, no luck. Fine programmatic control is not included in the SDK.

The primary features that were removed in version 3.0 are

- Shared Clipboard
- Confusing interface

Noted limitations of version 3.0 are as follows:

- NetMeeting still cannot handle multiparty audio and video. If you need this functionality, you should check out White Pine's CUSeeMe Pro.

- The processes of adding and deleting ILS servers are still difficult for beginners, and the listing is still limited to 15 servers, even though more than 200 servers are available now. ILS servers are the remote machines that help facilitate meetings by providing a directory that users sign in to when they are online. After they are signed in, other users can scan the directory to find a potential call partner, either for a cold call or for a preplanned meeting.

- The interface, although an improvement, isn't consistent with Office 2000's. The interface isn't customizable either. It's really more like AOL's Instant Messenger or ICQ than Office. You can't resize the window or snap various windows, such as the whiteboard and chat window, together with the main window.

- Echoing can still be a problem when you're using audio.

- You can't broadcast audio and video in a one-to-many arrangement. You have to use Windows Media tools or third-party programs to do that.

VIDEO FEATURES

The following are some features of NetMeeting 3.x video support:

- Support for H.323 makes NetMeeting multipoint-enabled to support audio and video with multiple people, through the use of a multipoint conferencing bridge service.

- It complies with the ITU H.323 industry standard, which means it's interoperable with other popular audio and videoconferencing products such as CUSeeMe, even on other platforms such as Macintosh.

- Even if you do not have a video capture card or camera, you can receive video.

- Any video capture card or camera compliant with Video for Windows will work with it.

COMPATIBLE STANDARDS AND LANGUAGE VERSIONS

NetMeeting 3 complies with the following standards. Note that these industry standards have been ratified or proposed through the International Telecommunications Union (ITU) or the Internet Engineering Task Force (IETF):

- RTP/RTCP—Real-time protocol (RTP) and real-time control protocol (RTCP), both from IETF. RTP/RTCP is a packet format for sending real-time information, such as audio or video, across the Internet.

- T.120—Set of ITU protocols for transport-independent, multipoint data conferencing. It is the basis of the NetMeeting protocols that allow a group of people to interact via data (exclusive of video and audio).

- H.320—Set of ITU protocols for audio, video, and data conferencing over ISDN. It integrates with T.120. This set of protocols adds the advantages of the higher speed of ISDN lines.

- H.323—Set of ITU protocols for audio, video, and data conferencing over TCP/IP networks. It includes RTP/RTCP and integrates with T.120. The H.323 standard provides a foundation for audio, video, and data communications across IP-based networks, including the Internet. By complying to H.323, multimedia products and applications from multiple vendors can interoperate. H.323 is part of a larger series of communications standards that enable videoconferencing across a range of networks. Known as H.32X, this series includes H.320 and H.324, which address ISDN and PSTN communications, respectively.

- H.324—A suite of standards approved by the ITU that allows NetMeeting (and other brands of video and audio) conferencing to run effectively over plain old telephone service (POTS) rather than on a LAN. One of the main components of H.324 is the V.80 protocol that specifies how modems should handle streaming audio and video data.

- The capability to integrate with T.120—It is the predominant standard that you want your video and audio conferencing software to be compatible with, even if you decide to go with something other than NetMeeting, such as VDOPhone from VDOnet.

NetMeeting supports more than 20 language versions, including Brazilian Portuguese, Chinese (simplified), Chinese (traditional), Czech, Danish, Dutch, Finnish, French, German, Greek, Hungarian, Italian, Japanese, Korean, Norwegian, Polish, Portuguese, Russian, Slovenian, Spanish, Swedish, and Turkish.

SYSTEMS REQUIREMENTS AND PLATFORM COMPATIBILITY

To use the data, audio, and video features of NetMeeting, your computer must meet the following minimum hardware requirements:

- For Windows 2000, you need a Pentium 90MHz processor with 24MB of RAM (a Pentium 133MHz processor or better with at least 32MB of RAM is recommended).

- You need 4MB of free hard disk space (an additional 10MB is needed during installation only to accommodate the initial setup files).

- You need a 56,000bps or faster modem, ISDN, DSL, cable, or LAN connection.

- You need a sound card with microphone and speakers (a sound card is required for both audio and video support).

- You need a video capture card or camera that provides a Video for Windows capture driver (required for video support).

- Because, as usual, Microsoft has integrated NetMeeting into other aspects of the operating system and browser, it's preferable to have Internet 4 or higher on your machine. (You'll have at least IE 5 with Windows 2000, so don't worry, but you might want to know this requirement for any Windows 9x machines you use.) NetMeeting-enabled sites are beginning to show up, and they'll work best with IE. Not surprisingly, therefore, NetMeeting is included with Microsoft Internet Explorer through many different distribution mechanisms.

- The Macintosh, Linux, and UNIX platforms are still not supported although NetMeeting does allow you to interact with people using these platforms as long as they have compatible audio/video conferencing software and hardware.

Note

Windows 98 and Windows 98 Second Edition come bundled with NetMeeting (version 2.0 and 3.0, respectively), so you don't have to worry about those users not having it, though you must deal with some restrictions when interfacing with version 2.0 users. It's best to have all parties connect using the latest version, for the best feature set.

Before you decide to use it, consider whether you intend to use NetMeeting for data only (for example, chat, whiteboard, or file transfer) or for data plus voice and/or video. You can actually get away with a 14,400bps modem for data-only connections. Real-time voice and video are designed for TCP/IP networks only (no direct modem hookups) and eat bandwidth for breakfast, as mentioned earlier.

Tip #194

You should upgrade your hardware and drivers before you run NetMeeting, if possible. Getting it to recognize newly installed hardware isn't always effortless.

INSTALLING NETMEETING

By default, NetMeeting should be installed in your Windows 2000 Professional machine along with IE5. If it's not, open the Control Panel, and then choose Add/Remove Programs, Add/Remove Windows Components to install it.

If you're in doubt about having the latest version, just go to www.microsoft.com/netmeeting and download the latest version. Then install it following instructions on the site.

RUNNING NETMEETING FOR THE FIRST TIME

After you obtain the program, follow these steps to install it:

1. Choose Start, Programs, Accessories, Communications, NetMeeting. Then follow the instructions you see there.

2. Sign in with your name, address, and so on (see Figure 15.2).

3. Use the default server unless your administrator tells you to do otherwise.

Figure 15.2
Entering your personal user information for NetMeeting. This information might be displayed to the public, so enter only what you want to broadcast.

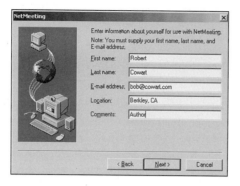

4. Fill in the connection speed you have for your workstation: 1440; 28800; cable, xDSL, or ISDN; or Local Area Network. (If you're connected to the Net through your local area network—a typical scenario in an office setting where you don't have a modem on your computer dialing out—choose Local Area Network.)

5. Do the audio tuning for settings. Make sure your microphone is set up; then click the Record button, and start reading the text in the box. Presumably, you successfully recorded some sound, and the sound level was set automatically. If it didn't take, you'll be told about it and advised what to do. You can return to the previous dialog box by clicking Back. Then you can try again after you plug in your mic, fix your sound card, or whatever.

6. Follow the instructions to finish the setup, typically just clicking OK and the Finish button.

If you have some conflicting hardware or software in your computer, you might see a message like the one in Figure 15.3. With any luck, it will be a sensible error message that you can do something about.

Figure 15.3
If a conflict occurs with existing settings or use of hardware, you'll see a message such as this during installation or when you run NetMeeting.

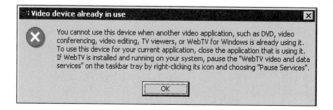

Tip #195

Some sound cards are capable of *full-duplex sound*, letting you talk and listen at the same time, like on a normal telephone (as opposed to half-duplex, which switches back and forth from transmitting and receiving like a CB radio). NetMeeting has more difficulty negotiating communications with half-duplex cards because only one person can talk at a time, and people get cut off. If you use NetMeeting a lot for voice communication, you should look into upgrading to a full-duplex sound system. Most current computers have full-duplex sound cards.

After you have NetMeeting properly installed, you'll see the basic NetMeeting screen in unconnected mode (the title bar reads `Not in a Call`, as previously shown in Figure 15.1).

If you're not connected to the Net, you'll see an error message saying the directory server could not be found, or you might see the Dial-up Connection box that normally comes up when you try to access the Internet from any application when you are not online. In any case, connect one way or another. Then move to the next section.

MAKING A NETMEETING CALL

The best way to learn how to use NetMeeting is to be in a call (a meeting) and play around with it. So, arrange to call up a friend (make a date via telephone or some other means such as AIM [America Online Instant Messenger], ICQ, or Microsoft Messenger). As an alternative, you can cold call someone who shows up in the listing server (ILS).

The way you use the directory has changed in version 3, so if you're used to seeing a large list that takes forever to appear or scroll, listing all kinds of sexually explicit thrill-seekers, forget about it. Microsoft has tried to clean up the look and feel of NetMeeting by relegating the ILS directory lists to a secondary window and including an HTML-based search window for looking up a person in the ILS directory (see the caution later in this section for more details about the ILS directory.)

You have several means for initiating calls:

- Cruise the ILS servers (hundreds are now available, but start with the Microsoft ones). Then choose File, Directory. You'll see a directory listing like the one in Figure 15.4. (Type the name of a different directory if you want to use another ILS.) From the list, double-click a likely victim, and that person will be hailed. (A little dialog box pops up on the recipient's screen asking whether he or she wants to accept the call.)

Figure 15.4
Using an ILS to find someone to talk to. You can find someone in the listing by entering a name in the Type Name field. Click the column heads to sort.

- In the top of the NetMeeting window, enter the IP address or DNS hostname of the party you want to call. (That person must be running NetMeeting at the time.) Then click the Call button.

- Open the Directory list, and choose another source, as shown in Figure 15.5. If you choose the Microsoft Internet Directory (MID), you'll get a search form to fill in. You can fill in just one line of the form or more. For example, just type `France` in the

Country line, and you'll see everyone on the currently logged ILS directory who lives in France. (Click the Help button on the Search page if you need to see examples.) The History list shows the names of people who have called you in the past.

Figure 15.5
You can locate people in ways other than via a long ILS listing, though they might not be online.

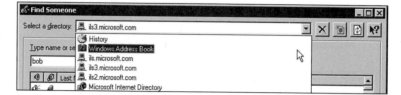

A speaker in the left column of a directory listing means the person has audio capability in his or her system. A little TV camera means that person has video. All the other poor fools have neither and are stuck groveling for attention because they are multimedia challenged.

Caution

If you are a parent or are offended by frank language or pornographic images, you should be aware that public NetMeeting servers are pretty heavily populated by people soliciting and/or offering such material. This is good reason to monitor NetMeeting use by minors.

Of course, NetMeeting is a safe and powerful collaboration tool when used professionally and responsibly. Generally, you can avoid unwanted material by initiating NetMeeting calls with friends and colleagues. When you're initiating calls to strangers, be sure to note the users' email addresses, locations, and comments in the ILS directory. Generally, you can determine the nature of what you'll see based on these clues. When in doubt, don't initiate a call.

A little blue computer screen with a red star next to it means the person is already in a meeting.

You might see lots of weird characters (letters, not people!) in the listing due to foreign language usage by some of the international users or tricks people play to be listed first (sort of like naming your company AAAA Rent-A-Car in the yellow pages).

ARRANGING TO RECEIVE A CALL

If you want to be available to be called, you have two choices:

- Log on to an ILS.
- Let people know your IP address so they can call you directly.

As you probably know, many people are connected to the Internet via a modem dial-up connection. When a connection is made, the user is assigned a temporary Internet address, just for the duration of the connection; the user gets a different address each time. But getting different addresses is problematic for some applications such as NetMeeting. Imagine if the phone company gave you a new number every day? How could anyone call you?

The Directory (formerly called the User Location Service, or ULS, and now also called the ILS for Internet Locator Service) enables you to find people to talk to on the Internet. The ILS servers provide a database so that people can find you and ring you up, even if your IP address changes. By using your other information, such as email address and name, the Directory does a lookup of your current IP address when you log on and then lets people find you that way.

If you have a static IP address, doing a lookup isn't an issue because your number never changes. Just tell people your IP address, like you would a phone number. They can enter it in their phone books or in NetMeeting's Speed Dial list for later use. Of course, you have to be running NetMeeting to receive their calls.

The upshot is that people can reach you by looking to see whether you're logged on to an ILS server, or, if you have a static IP address, they can ring you by calling you directly. If you don't have a static IP address, well, people can still call you directly, but you'll have to tell them your IP address at the time of the call.

A typical scenario goes like this:

1. Phone or ICQ a colleague, and say you want to initiate a NetMeeting at time x.

2. Give him or her your IP address, or ask for his or her number. Or say you're going to be logged in to `ils.microsoft.com` (or some other directory) at 10 a.m., and he or she should look for you.

If you go with the second approach, you need to make sure you're logged in to an ILS server. The default option is for NetMeeting to log you on automatically when you run the program. You can set this option by choosing Tools, Options. The easy way to check whether you're logged on to a server is to look for the little two-computer icon in the lower-right corner of the NetMeeting window. If it's grayed out, then you're not logged on anywhere. Click Call, Log On to connect to a server. An hourglass replaces the grayed-out computers until you are successfully logged on. Sometimes this process can seem like it takes an eternity. If it fails, click the Refresh button. Still no go? Try logging on to another server by choosing Tools, Options, General and changing the Directory setting.

Tip #196	To determine what your IP address is, connect to the Internet, and then run NetMeeting. Click Help, About Windows NetMeeting. Your IP address is displayed at the bottom of the window. To see what directory you're logged in to, hover the mouse pointer over the connection icon in the lower-right corner of the NetMeeting window. (The window has to be active for this trick to work.)

Microsoft has added a new directory service called Microsoft Internet Directory (MID). It is a Web site provided and maintained by Microsoft. When you do a search from the Find Someone window, this service is used to look up people. If you want people to be able to find you regardless of ILS server, just log on to the MID instead of any ILS at all.

Tip #197

If you're a Webmaster using Microsoft's Internet Information Service (IIS), you can set up your own User Location Service as a means of providing a way for people who are visiting your site to find each other.

GENERAL POINTS ABOUT CONNECTING

In version 2 of NetMeeting, you could filter the directory listing to show only certain categories of people, such as Adult or Personal. That feature is history.

When you call a person, a box appears onscreen indicating that the callee is being paged. That person's computer will ring or beep or display a message alerting him or that you are trying to reach him or her for a conference. If the callee doesn't want to answer your call or for some reason simply doesn't respond (he or she is eating lunch or something and forgot to log out) you'll see a dialog telling you that the person you are calling did not respond.

Click OK, and try again later. If you want, you can send an email if that person's email address is listed. If he or she does answer, your name will appear in the list, as shown in Figure 15.6.

If video is being used, you'll see that too, and you can play with the PIP setting. In Figure 15.6, I have PIP turned on. You can also open a new window with your outgoing video in it by choosing View, My Video.

Figure 15.6
Typical audio/video connection in action, accompanied by the whiteboard and chat window.

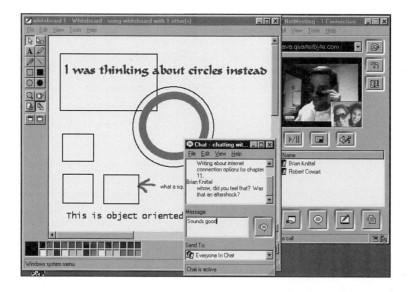

NetMeeting isn't the only conferencing system in use these days that is H.323 compatible. Other folks on the ILS directories might be using other setups. Or they might be using older versions of NetMeeting. If this is the case, when you try to call someone, you'll see a dialog box explaining that the person can't communicate with you over NetMeeting, or the connection might have some limitations.

When a meeting is underway, new incoming calls can be accepted, and your conference then includes multiple personalities. However, you can have video and audio between only two people.

TERMINATING A CONFERENCE

After you've finished with your call, just click the Hangup button. Of course, it's nice to say goodbye first rather than just disappear. You also might want to save the contents of your chat window and whiteboard if you want to refer to it or use the contents later.

AUDIO AND VIDEO ADJUSTMENTS

Whereas the pure data communications (chat and whiteboard) are pretty trusty, video and audio can use a little tweaking to get working correctly. See the "Troubleshooting" section at the end of this chapter for more dirt on this topic, but right here I'll tell you about some of the basic adjustments you can futz with.

SOUND ADJUSTMENTS

Let's start with the basics. You need good hardware, if possible. You'll get the best sound with a headset. Headsets keep the sound of the speakers from feeding back into the microphone. If you use speakers, keep the speakers turned down to prevent feedback, which can lead to echo problems. NetMeeting is fairly good about this, and Microsoft has been working to solve this problem, but it can happen.

Turning down the bass and increasing the treble (assuming you have tone controls on your computer speakers) can improve intelligibility. Your system might behave differently, however.

If you're having trouble with your sound, you can adjust the sound system in these three essential ways:

- You can run the Audio Tuning Wizard. Using this wizard is the best way to start making adjustments. Just choose Tools, Audio Tuning Wizard, and follow the instructions.
- Next, you can play with the two sliders on the bottom of the NetMeeting window. You first have to click the Audio button just under the video area to turn on the sliders. (This button is a toggle, incidentally.) You'll see check boxes to turn on the mic and speaker and sliders for each. The Audio Tuning Wizard adjusts them for optimum performance, but you might need to adjust them if people report that your sound is too quiet or too distorted. Test your settings with a few people to get their reactions before you finalize a setting. It could be the other person's system that needs help.

- Also, check the Microphone muting option. You adjust it from the Volume Control applet, available from the Control Panel, or easier yet, from the taskbar. Double-click the little speaker in the tray, down by the system clock to bring up the volume control. The microphone Muting should be turned on. Muting prevents the mic from playing through your speakers and producing feedback.

Caution

Be careful not to turn off the mic muting button while the speakers are turned on! The feedback can be deafening, not to mention damaging to your speakers and particularly irritating for your pets.

Finally, check the audio options by choosing Tools, Options and then selecting the Audio tab, as shown in Figure 15.7. You might want to play with a few settings here. Normally, though, you can leave them alone. For example, you should turn off full-duplex audio if you have a half-duplex sound system. Some people have reported that turning off DirectSound can help reduce the echo problem. If your mic is not cutting off so that the other person can speak, increase the silence detection manually (although automatic detection of silence is suggested).

Figure 15.7
Optional audio settings that might improve your connection.

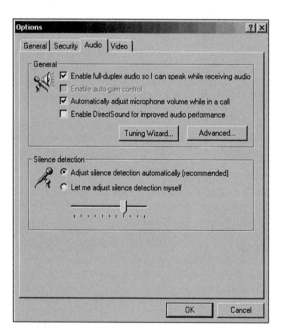

A couple of other settings on the Audio tab are interesting. The following are some notes about them:

- The Automatically Adjust Microphone Volume options should normally be left on. This way, you prevent your voice from dropping out when you speak quietly.

- Turn on the full-duplex option only if you know you have a card that supports it.

- Use care with the Advanced settings. You're changing the codecs (compressor/decompressor) software from here. Lots of choices are available, and they're for the brave only. Make sure you know what you're doing before messing with them. The list controls the order in which NetMeeting will attempt to use popular compression/decompression algorithms when sending and receiving sounds.

 If you still can't get your sound to work properly, see "Audio Problems" in the "Troubleshooting" section at the end of this chapter.

VIDEO ADJUSTMENTS

Most cameras and video capture equipment come with their own drivers and software to help you tune your video capturing. Check the manuals that came with your gear. But let me describe a few adjustments of note for the video portion of your show:

- Get your lighting and focus correct from the get-go. Most blurry or gray-looking bad images I've seen are the result of poor lighting. Put the camera in a good spot so you're not showing off your double chin. Oh, and use a decent camera.

 If you are having trouble with video, see "Video Problems" in the "Troubleshooting" section at the end of this chapter.

- You can pause the sending of video to comb your hair or yawn or whatever. Just click the Pause button under the video window. Click again to resume sending live video. Pausing video transmission can improve on sound if the voices are starting to break up. They break up because the video consumes large amounts of data bandwidth, often causing the audio to be delayed or lost.

- Right-click either video window, and you'll see several settings, including Properties, which brings up a bunch of settings to play with. Changing the Send Image Size controls how big your picture will look on the other guy's screen.

- The smaller the display size, and the fuzzier the image you send (faster video), the less data has to be transmitted per frame of video. So, if things are getting bogged down, try the small image size.

THE OTHER TOOLS

As I mentioned previously, you can use several other tools while in a conference:

- Chat window
- Whiteboard
- Application sharing

Then there is computer sharing, but I'll discuss that after the other three.

CHAT

Chat offers a simple window for writing back and forth to the person or people on the other end of the connection. Chat is very reliable, so if other modes of communication break down, you can always resort to the chat window. You can use chat by itself, or you can use it to whisper to one participant in the group while others continue using other modes. Up to eight people can use chat at once.

To use chat, simply click the Chat button at the bottom of the NetMeeting window. Type a message into the bottom section of the resulting window, and then click the large button to the right of the text entry area. Then your message is sent. Look back at Figure 15.6 to see a chat window in action.

If more than two people are in the chat, you can choose who sees your message. Just open the drop-down list at the bottom of the chat window, and choose the recipient before you click the Send button.

WHITEBOARD

Sometimes a scribble, a graphic, or a photo can be of help in a conversation. The white-board gives participants a canvas for drawing, writing text, and copying in portions of what's on the screen from another application. Users in the conference draw on the whiteboard at the same time. Using the basic drawing tools, you can sketch flow diagrams, org charts, and the like. The whiteboard is object-oriented (versus pixel-oriented), so you can move and manipulate the contents by clicking and dragging with the mouse. A cute little remote pointer (in the shape of a pointing finger) and a highlighting tool can be used to point out specific contents or sections of shared pages. You also can create and optionally save multiple pages of whiteboard contents.

To use it, click the Whiteboard icon in the toolbar, or choose Tools, Whiteboard. The whiteboard appears on everyone's screens. By default, "synchronization" is on, meaning that any changes anyone makes to the whiteboard can be seen by everyone. The highlighter and the pointing finger are particularly useful when you want to draw your audience's attention to something on the board. If you want to work on the page for a minute by yourself, turn off synchronization, do your adjusting, and then turn it back on (by choosing View, Synchronize).

You can easily copy stuff on your screen into the whiteboard. This capability can be useful for quickly transmitting a photo, scanned document, or portion of a document you're work-ing on. Just choose Tools, Select Area (or click the Select Area button in the toolbar; it's the bottom-left tool on the Whiteboard tool palette). Then switch to the program displaying the stuff you want to display on the whiteboard, and select it with the crosshair cursor. Your selection gets dumped onto the whiteboard for everyone to see.

If the whiteboard gets full of information that you don't want to part with, just create a new page by clicking the + (plus) tool in the lower-right corner of the whiteboard. If you don't care about what's on a page and are running out of room, just clear the page by choosing Edit, Clear Page.

Tip #198	When you optionally save the contents of the whiteboard, it gets an .NMW (NetMeeting Whiteboard) extension and gets dumped into the My Documents folder of the currently logged-in user.

SHARING DOCUMENTS AND APPLICATIONS

A truly valuable capability of NetMeeting is that it lets you collaborate on documents in real-time. Sure, telecommuters can send files back and forth to work for review by other folks, but some collaborative projects are best done in real-time.

Any Windows-based program can be shared among up to eight users, all of whom can witness what is going on. Only one person need have the program that is being shared because what's really being shared is the interface to the program, not the program itself.

To use this feature, you just run the program to be shared (on your local computer). Next, you share it by clicking the Share button (see Figure 15.8). Other folks in the conference can be allowed in on the action if you, as the sharer, allow control to be passed. You do so by clicking the Allow Control button in the Sharing dialog.

Figure 15.8
Sharing an application for observation and collaboration with others.

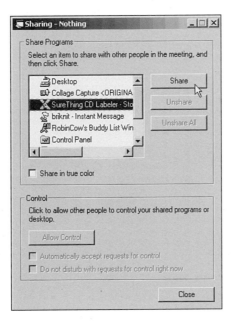

Remote participants will see a window with the shared application in it onscreen. When they want to take control of the mouse cursor and be allowed input from their keyboard, they must choose Control, Request Control. As the sharer, you are then asked to accept or deny the request. If you accept the request, the pointer now changes to include the controller's initials, and the remote participant can then interact with the program, edit a document, or even save it on disk locally or across the network. If you, as the sharer, want to regain control, just double-click your mouse over the application's window.

DOING FILE TRANSFERS ON-THE-FLY

If you press Ctrl+F; choose Tools, File Transfer; or click the File Transfer button, you can quickly send a file to anyone or everyone in a conference you're participating in. Intended recipients can accept or deny incoming files.

Caution	Of course, recipients should perform a virus check on every file they accept via NetMeeting before running it.

To send a file, follow these steps:

1. In the File Transfer window, choose File, Add Files. Then browse to the file or files you want to transfer. You can add any number of files to the file transfer queue. Alternatively, you can drag the files from any Explorer window into the File Transfer window.

2. In the File Transfer window, choose the recipient from the drop-down list. Then choose File, Send All or Send a File, or right-click a file in the list and choose from the menu shown in Figure 15.9.

Figure 15.9
You can send any number of files quickly and efficiently to any number of users in your meeting. Just drag them into this window, choose the recipient or recipients, and click Send.

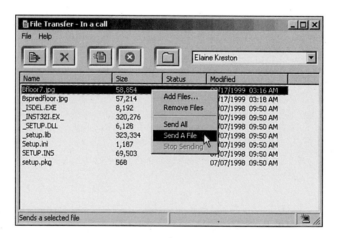

Tip #199	To change the folder where files are saved during transfers, click File, Change Folder. You'll find this menu in the File Transfer dialog box.

USING SPEED DIAL, VIEWING DIAL HISTORY, AND SENDING EMAIL

When you successfully connect to another party, that person's address is added to the Speed Dial list. To view the list, click the drop-down list at the top of the NetMeeting window, or open the Directory window and select Speed Dial from the Select a Directory drop-down. Using the Speed Dial list, you can easily reconnect with a party by double-clicking his or her name or IP address.

By contrast, the History list (which you can view from the Directory window if you choose History from the drop-down list) displays the names of everyone who called you and the times of the calls. Even if you don't answer the call, or you just ignore it (by clicking Ignore), it's added to the History list. Just double-click the caller's entry list to attempt to reconnect.

> **Note**
>
> You must have an address for the entry or the ILS reconnection to work. Notice that a couple of the entries in Figure 15.10 don't have addresses. You get an address-less entry when a direct call comes in from someone who knows your IP address and doesn't use the ILS directory.

Figure 15.10
Past incoming calls are added to the History list. You can double-click an entry to attempt a return call.

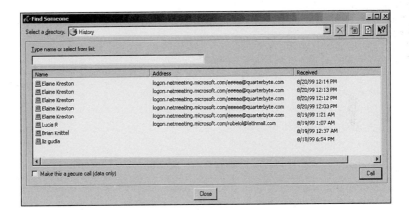

Often, the people you are trying to connect to are not online and running NetMeeting on their end. You have a couple of options at this point. As mentioned earlier, the best way of ensuring a successful meeting is to make an appointment in advance. But if the person is online, and you still can't connect, just send email. Assuming the other party has filled in his or her real email name in the Personal Properties box, you can right-click the entry in the History, Speed Dial, or directory lists and then choose Properties. You'll see that person's email address and can use it to send him or her email.

DESKTOP SHARING

One of the neatest new features in NetMeeting 3 is the capability to control one computer from another. The user of a remote computer can take over another computer just as though he or she were in front of it. This is something that cannot even be accomplished using virtual private networking or other remote access services because, even though those features allow for a great amount of security and convenience, they don't let you operate the remote machine using that machine's GUI.

Using Desktop Sharing is much like using Norton's pcAnywhere32 for NT or RemotelyPossible32 from Avalan Technology, although those programs have more features. Once again, the price is right for NetMeeting, though you should note that only machines running NetMeeting 3 (or later) can participate.

Taking over a computer using a remote control program is an excellent choice for when you're out of the office and need to look up something, even edit a document from afar.

Note

I suspect Desktop Sharing will be an incredible boon to Microsoft's support department (and other companies' as well) because, without requiring additional software, a tech support person can commandeer the user's computer and see what is going on (assuming the computer can boot, of course).

Of course, performance will be slower in a remote setting than if you were sitting in front of the computer you're controlling. This performance is the result of bandwidth limitations and the amount of graphical information that has to be transmitted. NetMeeting is fairly intelligent about how it controls the remote user's screen, however, so the performance is quite acceptable for typical tasks, such as editing a spreadsheet, writing a document, transferring files, and such. Don't expect to run a video game or watch a CD-ROM or DVD-ROM movie, though.

You can share a computer for remote control in two ways. One does not require or even offer the option of security, so you best be careful. Recall the previous section about application sharing. When you bring up the dialog from which to choose the application you want to share, just choose Desktop, as shown in Figure 15.11.

Follow these steps to share your desktop with a remote user:

1. Choose Tools, Sharing.

2. Unshare any other programs that you are currently sharing. You can't share the desktop and other programs at the same time.

3. Highlight Desktop and click Share. Now your desktop immediately shows up on the other participants screens. However, they can't manipulate anything on it until you click Allow Control. If you just want to demonstrate something on your desktop (for example, some kind of user training) without opening yourself up to a hostile takeover, don't click Allow Control.

Figure 15.11
You can give control of your desktop to another participant in a meeting by sharing the desktop.

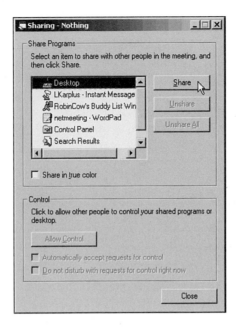

4. After you click Allow Control, a user can take over by clicking his or her image of your desktop. You will see a dialog box asking to give control to the requesting party. Click Accept, and the deal is done. The same rules for application sharing (see above) apply at this point; however, the remote user can now open folders, run new applications, and so on.

5. To regain control of the local computer, double-click your desktop, or press a key on your keyboard.

Tip #200

What's really going on here is that all your open applications are now shared, as is the desktop itself (actually Explorer.exe).

Caution

Here's a weird one. Two people in a meeting can share their desktops with each other, effectively reversing their machine locations. I can't think of why you would want to do so, and besides, you get a very strange side effect in the form of "desktop feedback," for want of a better term. Because each person's desktop is shown in the other's, they start to cascade, creating an endless number of windows within windows. Someone had better terminate, or you'll end up in one of those time warp *Star Trek* episodes that gives Captain Janeway an Excedrin headache.

SINGLE-USER IP-BASED DESKTOP SHARING

Almost as a standalone feature or program, NetMeeting lets you set up your computer in advance to receive calls from afar (not dial-up, only over the Internet using your IP address), allowing remote control. This capability is perfect for dialing in to your PC when you're on the road and need to check on something in your computer back home or run an application that isn't on your remote computer. As long as NetMeeting is running on both machines, and you leave the computer back home turned on, you're in business.

→ If all you need to do is copy files and folders to and from your remote machine, **see** the discussion about remote Web-based folder sharing in Chapter 24, "Connecting Your LAN to the Internet," **p. 847**.

Here's how you do it:

1. Install and set up NetMeeting on both computers.

2. On the computer you'll be dialing in to (I'll call it the "home" computer), click Tools, Remote Desktop Sharing.

3. In the resulting dialog box, turn on Enable Remote Desktop Sharing on this computer.

4. For security purposes, remote sharing should require a login and password when the connection is initiated. To read about it and to set up a password-enabled screen saver so that a local user near the home computer can't take over while you're in a session, click the Wizard button and follow the instructions. When the Screen Saver dialog box (display properties) comes up, choose the screen saver you want to activate and turn on the Password Protected check box. You should also choose Tools, Options; select the Security tab; and check the box for secure incoming calls.

5. Finish working through the wizard, and click OK to close the Remote Desktop Sharing Settings dialog box. You'll then see a new NetMeeting icon in the system tray (you probably have two there now).

6. You might want to write down your home station's IP address first, so choose Help, About NetMeeting, and look for the IP address at the bottom of the dialog box. Write it down on a piece of paper, and take it with you.

7. Remote sharing doesn't work with NetMeeting running, so close it.

8. Right-click the remaining NetMeeting icon in the system tray, and choose Activate Remote Desktop Sharing. (This step is very important!)

9. Make sure to leave the "home" computer turned on and with a live connection to the Internet. You can turn off the screen, of course, if you want to. If you don't want anyone messing with the computer, put a sign on it with a message such as "Don't Touch!" You might want to put the keyboard up on end next to the screen, under the desk, and so on.

10. Go on your vacation or road trip or to another computer in the office or at home, and connect to the Internet.

11. Run NetMeeting on your remote machine, and then initiate a call to the home computer by entering its IP address (or name) and clicking the Call button. If you receive an error message reading: The person you are calling only accepts secure NetMeeting calls, then choose Tools, Options, Security, and turn on security for outgoing calls. Then try again.

12. When you see a Remote Desktop Sharing Password dialog asking for user, password, and domain, enter the same username and password you normally do on your Windows 2000 Professional machine. If you're not on a domain, don't enter anything in that field. If you are, enter the domain name. Click OK, and you should see an image of your desktop on the remote machine. Figure 15.12 shows an example in which a Windows 98 machine is connected to a Windows 2000 Professional machine. The home computer's screen, mouse, and keyboard will lock up until the connection is broken.

Figure 15.12
You can see Remote Desktop Sharing of a computer across the Internet in action here. Because the home computer's screen resolution is 800×600, it fits easily in a window on the remote computer's (1024×768).

13. Complete the needed work on your home computer from the remote computer.

Tip #201

If a portion of the home computer's desktop blanks out, you can often get the window to "repaint" by dragging around another window on the home machine's desktop. For example, run Calculator on the home machine, and drag it around a bit. When the screen repaints, it should be filled in. Then minimize the Calculator. If you need to send a "three-finger salute" (Ctrl+Alt+Del) sequence to shut down or kill a process on the home computer, open the Control menu on the Desktop window, and choose Send Ctrl+Alt+Del.

14. When you're ready to disconnect, switch to the NetMeeting window and click the Hangup button, or choose Call, Hangup. Control of the keyboard and mouse then return to the home computer.

15. If you want to prevent someone from dialing in to the home computer, have someone right-click the NetMeeting icon in the system tray, and turn off Remote Desktop Sharing. Note that even if you don't turn it off this way, the next time you run NetMeeting from the home computer, it will turn off Remote Desktop Sharing.

Tip #202

When you're sharing desktops (either in this scenario or in a regular meeting among multiple people), it really helps if everyone in the meeting is running the same screen resolution. Otherwise, too much scrolling can be required on the various computers. This is true of application sharing as well. People can literally not be on the same page when editing a document, for example.

You can actually change the screen resolution of the home PC via its display properties, if you're having to scroll too much in your remote view window. Try knocking it down one notch below what your remote computer's screen resolution is. Be careful to select the correct machine's desktop to adjust, though! Right-click the home computer's desktop, or use its Control Panel to make the adjustment. Things can get confusing because you now have two desktops, Control Panels, My Computers, Networks, and so on.

Note

Note that you cannot drag and drop objects between the home computer's desktop and your Explorer because the image of the home computer's screen is only virtual. It's not a network; it's only a means to perform remote manipulation of a machine. (More advanced products such as pcAnywhere32 do include this feature, incidentally.) If you need to transfer files to and from a remote computer, use connection sharing or shared Web folders, as discussed in Chapter 22.

TROUBLESHOOTING

AUDIO PROBLEMS

I don't hear any sound when I run NetMeeting.

The following are some suggestions for dealing with audio problems. Take them in this order:

■ Check the mic, mixer, and speaker suggestions listed earlier in this chapter. Make sure to set the mixer so that the microphone is muted on the playback volume control set and selected on the record volume control set. For good measure, it might be sensible to use only the Wave device on playback and only the Microphone on record. You can add back others as you need them and determine that they don't cause problems in the mix.

- Run the Audio Tuning Wizard.

- Turn down your speaker volume so that it's not feeding into the microphone, or move the speakers away from the mic a bit. This trick can help prevent echo.

- Get yourself a decent headset. It's a cheap investment and is the most cost-effective improvement you can make to your NetMeeting system.

- If your audio gets choppy occasionally and/or freezes, this problem can be caused by having background processes running on your computer that take up considerable CPU slices. Typical programs that run without your knowing it are indexing programs such as Find Fast (a file indexing program in Microsoft Office that makes finding files faster), email programs that check mail every few minutes (turn down the check rate or turn off mail during your meeting), and even NetMeeting (when it updates or relogs you in to an ILS). Especially if you're logged in to a very popular ILS, you should log off it using the Call, Logoff command.

- Try lowering your throughput settings. Make sure you are considering traffic congestion on your pipe when making the choice of throughput speed. NetMeeting decides which codecs to use based on your claimed throughput. Often a cable modem, LAN, or even DSL service can be slower than you think. You and the other participants in your meeting might want to lower your bandwidth settings one notch and see what happens (by choosing Tool, Options, General, Bandwidth Settings). You have to change the settings and restart NetMeeting for them to take effect.

- If the problem isn't improving, uninstall NetMeeting. Next, clean out the program files\netmeeting directory if it's still there. Then reinstall the sound and video capture drivers for your computer and reboot. Download and reinstall the latest version of Internet Explorer for Windows 2000 from the Microsoft site. It often comes with NetMeeting bundled in. If not, then download and install NetMeeting from the Microsoft site, too (www.Microsoft.com/netmeeting).

VIDEO PROBLEMS

I'm having trouble with my video when running NetMeeting.

- Try changing the Video quality slider (by choosing Tools, Options, and then selecting the Video tab).

- Make sure your video capture software and hardware works with other applications, such as those supplied with the capture equipment. The problem might not be in NetMeeting, so rule that out first.

- Choose Tools, Options, and then select the Video tab. Check the settings there. If no capture device is listed, the video capture device is missing or not seen by Windows. In this case, choose Control Panel, System, Hardware, Device Manager. Next, open Sounds, Video and Game Controllers. Look for a video capture entry to see whether it's working. (Double-click it, and read the resulting dialog box. Is it working? Even if Windows reports that it's working, it might not be.) Try uninstalling it by right-clicking it and choosing Uninstall; then reboot. It should be detected and reinstalled. If not, click Computer (at the top of the list), and then choose Action, Scan for Hardware Changes.

- If you're sharing applications, drawing on the whiteboard, or sharing the desktop, everyone in your conference should be using the same screen size if possible. Otherwise, things can get confused, especially if one person maximizes or adjusts the size of a window beyond the capabilities of the other participants' monitors. People using smaller monitors or lower resolution can end up with windows that they can't see all of.

GETTING HELP

For additional troubleshooting tips, check the following sites:

`http://www.meetingbywire.com`

`http://www.netmeet.net/`

For Microsoft general information on NetMeeting, including the Resource Kit for system administrators and programmers, try this Web site:

`http://www.microsoft.com/netmeeting/`

For information about the international standards used in NetMeeting, check out some of the organizations in the industry responsible for defining, approving, and communicating standards. The following are some of the key organizations:

- *International Telecommunications Union.* The ITU, headquartered in Geneva, Switzerland, is an international organization through which governments and the private sector coordinate global telecom networks and services. ITU activities include the coordination, development, regulation, and standardization of telecommunications, and organization of regional and world telecom events. Check out its Web site at `http://www.itu.ch/`.

- *Internet Engineering Task Force.* The IETF is the protocol engineering and development arm of the Internet. The IETF is a large, open, international community of network designers, operators, vendors, and researchers concerned with the evolution of the Internet's architecture and the smooth operation of the Internet. For information, go to `http://www.ietf.org/`.

- *International Multimedia Telecommunications Consortium, Inc.* The IMTC is a nonprofit corporation founded to promote the creation and adoption of international standards for multipoint document and video teleconferencing. The IMTC and its members promote a Standards First initiative to guarantee compatibility between aspects of multimedia teleconferencing. For more information, check out `http://www.imtc.org/imtc/`.

TIPS FROM THE WINDOWS PROS: AVOIDING NETMEETING LURKERS

As you might have noticed, the ILS servers not only are hard to get logged on to, but once you do, they are a bit unfriendly. Most of the folks there seem to be lurking, waiting for some fresh meat. I even had trouble taking a screen shot of an ILS listing for this chapter without annoying the censors. What's more, when you log on to an ILS server, you see scores of folks whom you're not interested in talking to, and they can see you and can hassle you by calling you for a chat.

The solution is to use one of a growing breed of small messaging servers that alert people when their friends are connected to the Net and let them send short messages to each other in real-time. Essentially the same as the Chat box in NetMeeting, these programs are stand-alone applets that keep track of when people log in and off them, keeping a database much like the ILSs do. However, they are more private, so folks you don't know can't see you or bug you.

The first of such programs to become popular was ICQ from Mirabilis. Then AOL came out with its program, called Instant Messenger. Now Microsoft has launched its own, called MSN Instant Messenger.

All these programs let you keep track of your friends, co-workers, and other "buddies." They show you when your buddies are online and let you collaborate with your buddies in a lot of ways without even getting NetMeeting involved.

All three of them let you send simple text messages to one another. ICQ and MSN Messenger additionally let you invite a friend to initiate a NetMeeting session. ICQ also lets you transfer a file, send a greeting card, or get a friend's IP address. Figure 5.13 shows the interfaces of each of these three programs.

Figure 15.13
You can use a small Internet messenger service to alert your friends that you are online. ICQ and MSN Messenger can even be used to invite a friend to a NetMeeting visit.

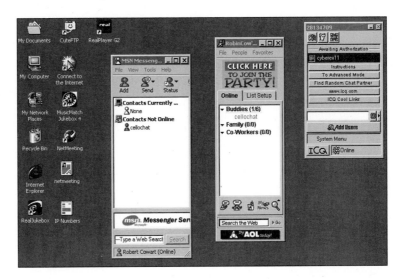

You should coordinate with your friends and colleagues on a messenger system to use because, at this point, a war is going on between them (especially AOL and MSN) over standards and equal access. So, settle on one, and set it to start up at boot time.

Note

To read about or download AOL Instant Messenger, go to `www.aol.com`.

To read about or download ICQ, go to `www.icq.com`.

To read about or download MSN Messenger, go to `http://messenger.msn.com`.

CHAPTER 16

INTERNET DIAGNOSIS TOOLS

In this chapter

IT'S GREAT WHEN IT WORKS, BUT...

Browsing the Internet is great fun—and very useful, too. In fact, watch as I instantly transfer millions of dollars from my secret Swiss bank account to.... Wait a minute, what's a 404 Server Not Found Error? What's going on? Did the modem disconnect? Is the IRS closing in on me? Help! *Where's my money?!*

If you've used the Internet for any length of time, this scene may seem all too familiar—except for the bit about the Swiss bank account (a guy can dream, can't he?). Connecting to the Internet and using the Web is an amazingly user-friendly experience, yet we can't escape the basic fact that it's a staggeringly complex system. If something goes wrong at any step along the way between your fingertips and a server somewhere off in cyberspace, the whole system comes to a crashing halt. Where do you begin to find and fix the problem?

Despite the amazing progress made simplifying the use of Internet hardware and software, diagnosing and fixing connectivity problems is still a dark and dirty job. Someone has do it, and guess what—most of the time that someone is you! In this chapter, I'll tell you what tools are available to help you and then show you the basic strategies to use when tracking down Internet problems.

WINDOWS TCP/IP UTILITIES

Windows 2000 comes with a set of command-line programs you can use to trace TCP/IP problems. Most of these programs are the Windows versions of standard utilities supplied with UNIX, the operating system on which virtually all TCP/IP software was originally developed. (Despite the claims of their respective PR agents, neither Microsoft nor Al Gore invented the Internet.)

Because most of these diagnostic tools are command-line utilities, you run them from the command prompt (Start, Programs, Accessories, Command Prompt). Most of them are actually sophisticated 32-bit Windows programs on the inside—they just don't have that nice graphical user interface.

In Appendix A, "Command-Line Reference," on the CD-ROM that accompanies this book, I give an introduction to the use of command-line utilities as well as command-line switches and arguments. If you're not familiar with these programs, you might take a look at Appendix A. You can also get online help from Windows for each of these programs. Look up "Command Line Reference" in Windows Help and pick the desired command from the alphabetical listing.

Note

Experiment with the utilities when your network and Internet connection are operating correctly to learn how the programs work and what output you should expect. I know from experience that when I'm using an unfamiliar program to diagnose an unknown problem, if the output looks wrong, it's hard to tell whether I'm using the utility incorrectly or I've really identified a problem.

Now, let's go through the Windows 2000 TCP/IP diagnostic and command-line utilities. I'll list them alphabetically. There's a lot to chew on here, so I'll go into detail only on the most important ones: ping, tracert, ipconfig, and nslookup. (Pathping is an up-and-comer, too.)

If you're a UNIX devotee, you'll find these utilities very familiar, if not identical, to their UNIX counterparts. If you're new to TCP/IP networking or debugging, you might find these utilities a little unfriendly. (Welcome to the world of networking!)

ADDRESS RESOLUTION PROTOCOL (ARP)

ARP sounds like the sound a hungry seal makes, but actually, it's the sound a computer makes when it's trying to find another computer on the same LAN. The Address Resolution Protocol is used to find out which computer on the LAN corresponds to a given IP address.

ARP

When LAN data is transmitted on an Ethernet or Token Ring LAN, it has to be directed from one computer to another using the physical address—or Media Access Control (MAC) layer address—built into each network adapter card. It's a little bit like sending a letter: When you want to address a letter to a friend, you start with her name, but you must look up her physical street address. In the same vein, the ARP protocol is used to resolve IP addresses, which are conceptual, into physical network card addresses, which are physically used to transmit the data.

When your computer needs to send data to another computer on your LAN, it broadcasts (sends to everyone at once) a request: "Will the computer that has IP address x.y.z.q please respond to me?" If that IP address is really assigned to a computer on your LAN, it will respond along the lines of "Here I am!" Also, its physical network card address will be in the response. This little conversation takes place using the conventions of the ARP protocol. From that point on, your computer can send data directly to the other computer, by addressing data packets to its physical address.

When data needs to go to a computer that isn't on your LAN but is out on the Internet somewhere, the gateway address comes into play. A *gateway* is a router or other computer that takes responsibility for passing on any TCP/IP data bound for places beyond your own LAN. When data is bound for some other network, your computer uses the ARP protocol, as described, to find the physical address of the gateway, and it sends the data there. The gateway then sends the data on its way.

As your computer communicates with others on the LAN, it gradually builds up a list of IP addresses of computers it has talked with and their physical addresses. Entries in this list are kept for a few minutes, in case they're needed again. Therefore, this list of addresses is dynamic, and it's sometimes called the *ARP cache*.

Now, how does this apply to TCP/IP debugging? The ARP table shows you which other computers your computer has successfully communicated with. The ARP function is a very low-level part of the networking system, and it can diagnose whether a problem is with hardware and basic TCP/IP network settings or with higher-level network protocols such as the File Sharing for Microsoft Networks services.

Usually, you diagnose network communication problems with the ping command first. Ping attempts to send a simple message to another computer that's supposed to be returned back (like that sonar "ping" sound that submarines make). If a ping test works between computers on LAN, well, you know that your network hardware and TCP/IP settings are correct. However, if it doesn't, the ARP table will show you at least whether the first part of network communication is working by determining the physical addresses of neighboring computers.

The arp command is used with the -a switch to print all known addresses. For example, typing

```
C:\>arp -a
```

on my computer produces this result:

```
Interface: 202.201.200.164 on Interface 0x1000003
  Internet Address      Physical Address      Type
  202.201.200.162       00-f3-14-a1-57-56     dynamic
  202.201.200.163       00-23-e3-a3-6b-71     dynamic
  202.201.200.172       00-83-35-4e-ac-8e     dynamic
  202.201.200.190       00-43-72-1f-00-9b     dynamic
```

The first line of the report

```
Interface: 202.201.200.164 on Interface 0x1000003
```

tells us that the IP address assigned to my computer is 202.201.200.164.

The rest of the report indicates that Windows has managed to contact four other computers on the LAN. The listing also shows the physical (MAC layer) addresses of their network cards and indicates that the addresses were discovered automatically (rather than having been entered by hand).

This listing tells us that these four computers are correctly cabled and can send data to and from my computer; we know this because they successfully exchanged ARP information.

IPCONFIG

Ipconfig is one of the most useful command-line utilities because it displays the current IP address information for each of your computer's network adapters and active dial-up connections. Because many networks assign addresses automatically, ipconfig provides the only way to find out what your computer's IP address is.

By itself, the ipconfig command prints out just IP addresses for your adapter and dial-up connections. For a computer with a network adapter, typing

```
C:\>ipconfig
```

returns the following (of course the IP, subnet, and gateway information will be different for your computer):

```
Windows 2000 IP Configuration
Ethernet adapter Local Area Connection:

        Connection-specific DNS Suffix  . : mycompany.com
        IP Address. . . . . . . . . . . . : 202.201.200.166
        Subnet Mask . . . . . . . . . . . : 255.255.255.224
        Default Gateway . . . . . . . . . : 202.201.200.190
```

Tip #203

ipconfig is the first command to use when diagnosing any TCP/IP networking problem. It tells you whether your network card or dial-up connection has been assigned an IP address and gives you the network gateway address. See the section titled "ping," later in the chapter, to learn about the second command you would use.

With the /all option, ipconfig adds domain name and DNS server information. For example, typing

```
C:\>ipconfig/all
```

returns the following:

```
Windows 2000 IP Configuration
        Host Name . . . . . . . . . . . . : AMBON
        Primary DNS Suffix  . . . . . . . : mycompany.com
        Node Type . . . . . . . . . . . . : Broadcast
        IP Routing Enabled. . . . . . . . : Yes
        WINS Proxy Enabled. . . . . . . . : No
        DNS Suffix Search List. . . . . . : mycompany.com

Ethernet adapter Local Area Connection:
        Connection-specific DNS Suffix  . : mycompany.com
        Description . . . . . . . . . . . : Realtek RTL8139(A)
                 PCI Fast Ethernet Adapter
        Physical Address. . . . . . . . . : 00-C0-CA-14-09-7F
        DHCP Enabled. . . . . . . . . . . : No
        IP Address. . . . . . . . . . . . : 202.201.200.166
        Subnet Mask . . . . . . . . . . . : 255.255.255.224
        Default Gateway . . . . . . . . . : 202.201.200.190
        DNS Servers . . . . . . . . . . . : 201.202.203.72
                                            201.202.213.72

PPP adapter My ISP:
        Connection-specific DNS Suffix  . :
        Description . . . . . . . . . . . : WAN (PPP/SLIP) Interface
        Physical Address. . . . . . . . . : 00-53-45-00-00-00
        DHCP Enabled. . . . . . . . . . . : No
        IP Address. . . . . . . . . . . . : 100.102.103.154
        Subnet Mask . . . . . . . . . . . : 255.255.255.255
        Default Gateway . . . . . . . . . : 100.102.103.001
        DNS Servers . . . . . . . . . . . : 201.202.203.72
                                            201.202.213.72
```

Note that I've shown both a local area connection and an active dial-up connection here. This display is a bit richer than the original. Here's what typing C:\>ipconfig /all shows:

Host name	The name you gave your computer.
Primary DNS suffix	The Internet domain to which your computer primarily belongs. (You might temporarily belong to others as well while using a dial-up connection.)

Node type	The method that Windows uses to locate other computers on your LAN when you use Windows Networking. This should be Hybrid if you have a Windows 2000 Server machine or a WINS server on your LAN; otherwise, the node type should be set to Broadcast.
IP routing enabled	Indicates whether Windows will pass packets from one LAN adapter or dial-up connection to another (if this computer has been designated an Internet gateway).
WINS proxy enabled	Not applicable for Windows 2000 Professional.
DNS suffix search list	Alternative domain names used if you type just part of a host name and the default domain does not provide a match.
Connection-specific DNS suffix	The domain name for this particular connection. This is most applicable to dial-up connections.
Description	The manufacturer's name for the LAN adapter or type of dial-up connection.
Physical address	The MAC layer or physical network address.
DHCP enabled	If set to Yes, this adapter is set to receive its IP address automatically. If set to No, the address was set manually.
IP address	IP address for this adapter.
Subnet mask	Identifies the part of the IP address that determines which addresses are part of the local LAN and which belong to outside networks.
Default gateway	Address to which to send packets destined to outside networks.
DNS servers	IP addresses of domain name servers.

Ipconfig displays most of the information in the Network and Dial-Up Connection Properties dialog box, but it shows their real-world values. This makes it an invaluable "first stop" when troubleshooting any network problem. If you determine that an Internet connection problem lies in your equipment somewhere (because you cannot access *any* Internet destinations), typing ipconfig /all will tell you whether your network setup is correct. I'll describe this process in detail in the section "Identifying Software Configuration Problems", later in the chapter.

NETMON

Although it's not a part of Windows 2000 Professional, I want to point out that Windows 2000 Server comes with a very powerful network traffic–analysis program called *netmon*. Netmon captures all the network traffic passing through a LAN, even packets sent between other computers. Netmon can analyze the data sent between computers to identify problems such as protocol errors, lost data, bad passwords, incorrect domain names, and more.

Netmon is a hard-core utility, and it's only available with Windows 2000 Server. However, I wanted you to see it so that you know what's available (if your LAN grows larger than 10 computers, you'll probably want to use Windows 2000 Server anyway). In Figure 16.1, netmon has captured a few seconds of data from my network. I can see each data packet, view its source and destination addresses, and see the data inside.

Figure 16.1
Network Monitor in Windows 2000 Server is a full-featured network protocol monitor, for *big* problems.

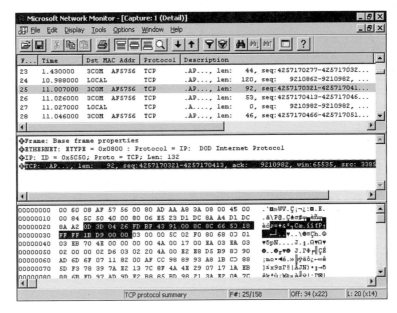

If you run into serious network problems, netmon (and a highly paid consultant) can usually solve them.

NETSTAT

Netstat displays information about current TCP/IP network connections and statistics. It's an interesting tool because it tells you which other computers are communicating with yours.

Netstat has several monitoring modes, which are discussed in the following subsections.

DISPLAYING ALL CURRENT TCP CONNECTIONS

You can display all current Transmission Control Protocol (TCP) connections with the following command:

```
C:\>netstat
```

The `netstat` command, by itself, displays all current TCP connections between your computer and others. TCP provides established data paths between two computers and is responsible for ensuring that data lost in transit is re-sent and that data packets received out of order get rearranged properly. In general, it also handles a sustained transfer of data between two computers. TCP is used for most network services that must transfer large amounts of data: Microsoft Networking over TCP, the World Wide Web, FTP, NetMeeting, Instant Messaging, Telnet, and so on.

Typing

```
C:\>netstat
```

returns the following:

```
Active Connections
   Proto  Local Address        Foreign Address           State
   TCP    java:nbsession       bali.mycompany.com:4497   ESTABLISHED
   TCP    java:2104            bali.mycompany.com:3389   ESTABLISHED
   TCP    java:2396            h-207-200-73-6.netscape.com:443  CLOSE_WAIT
   TCP    java:2405            207.211.106.90:http       CLOSE_WAIT
   TCP    java:2407            207.211.106.90:http       ESTABLISHED
   TCP    java:2408            207.211.106.90:http       CLOSE_WAIT
   TCP    java:2410            pop.myisp.com:pop3        TIME_WAIT
```

This listing shows the protocol in use (usually TCP), the host name and port number for this end of each connection, the host name and port of the remote or foreign end of each connection, and the state of the TCP connection.

TCP States

Like a phone call, which goes through several stages (dialing, ringing, talking, and hanging up), a TCP connection has many stages (or *states*), and you'll see a few of them in listings by netstat:

- LISTENING—Your computer has a service to provide and is waiting for some other computer to make a connection to it.
- SYN_SENT—Your computer has sent a "dialing" packet to the remote computer but nothing has come back yet.
- ESTABLISHED—The connection is established, and the two computers may send data back and forth.
- CLOSE_WAIT—Your computer has told the other side it's ready to hang up and hasn't heard back from the other side yet.
- TIME_WAIT—The connection has been closed, but the connection is remembered for a few more minutes. These entries may be ignored.

The SYN_SENT state is useful in debugging because it shows that your computer is trying to establish a connection. If the connection never proceeds past this state, you can tell that no response is coming back from the other computer. If ping can communicate with the remote machine, the problem is solely with the remote server program.

Connections in the ESTABLISHED state are exactly what they appear to be—current, active connections between your computer and the remote host shown.

TCP Ports Demystified

Port numbers, the items shown after the colons, are like the extension numbers in a large company's office: The main telephone number (IP address) gets you to the building, and the extension number (port number) connects you to the right department.

The port numbers tell you which service is involved on each connection. You'll find a file named `C:\Windows\System32\Drivers\Etc\Services` that lists most of the port numbers and services for standard TCP/IP utilities and Microsoft software. Note that if you upgraded from Windows NT to Windows 2000 (meaning you did not perform a clean install), the file path will be `C:\WinNT\System32\Drivers\ETC\Services`.

Here are a just few of the ports and their associated services:

Port Number	Protocol	Description
20, 21	FTP	File Transfer Protocol
25	SMTP	Simple Mail Transfer Protocol
80	HTTPS	World Wide Web
110	POP3	Post Office Protocol
139	NetBT Session	File/Printer Sharing
555	Doom	A computer game

You can think of it this way: When a computer runs the World Wide Web service, the WWW server program sits by extension number 80 waiting for the phone to ring. In TCP/IP language, we say that the service *listens* on port 80.

When a client computer connects to a service on one of these standard ports, the port on the client's side is a random number, usually greater than 1000. That's the secret to help unlock what's going on in a netstat printout: The side of the connection with the "known" port number is providing a service, and the side with the random port number is the client side. Netstat will print the name of the known port if it finds it in that `C:\Windows\...\Services` file; otherwise, it prints the number. Not all services are listed though. You can add names to your services file if you find that you use netstat and frequently must look up the services associated with the ports you see listed.

The first two lines of the listing tell us that computer bali is using a shared folder on my computer named java:

```
TCP     java:nbsession      bali.mycompany.com:4497   ESTABLISHED
TCP     java:2104           bali.mycompany.com:3389   ESTABLISHED
```

Notice the connection with an unrecognized number on bali, and the nbsession port on my end. This means bali has connected the nbsession (or file-sharing service) on my computer.

Here, my computer has just finished downloading a secure Web page from Netscape, using the secure Web page HTTPS protocol, port 443:

```
TCP     java:2396           h-207-200-73-6.netscape.com:443   CLOSE_WAIT
```

Note

How did I know that HTTPS was used? I peeked at the listing of port numbers at the end of Chapter 26, "Network Security." Port 443 is the server end of a secure Web page connection.

Next, here are connections from my computer to a different Web server:

```
TCP    java:2405          207.211.106.90:http      CLOSE_WAIT
TCP    java:2407          207.211.106.90:http      ESTABLISHED
TCP    java:2408          207.211.106.90:http      CLOSE_WAIT
```

It's not unusual for a Web browser to have several open connections at once, and here the browser is closing two of them.

Finally, from the following line you can tell that I had just checked my mail, and the connection to my ISP's POP3 mail server was gone but not forgotten:

```
TCP    java:2410          pop.myisp.com:pop3       TIME_WAIT
```

TIME_WAIT entries disappear after a few minutes.

DISPLAYING ALL CURRENT AND LISTENING TCP CONNECTIONS

If you add the -a option (meaning *all*) to the netstat command, netstat lists established connections as well as services on your computer that are waiting for other computers to make connections. This quickly shows you which network services your computer is offering to the LAN as well as to the world. For example, typing

```
C:\>netstat -a
```

returns the following:

```
Active Connections
  Proto  Local Address          Foreign Address          State
  TCP    AMBON:ftp              AMBON.mycompany.com:0    LISTENING
  TCP    AMBON:smtp             AMBON.mycompany.com:0    LISTENING
  TCP    AMBON:http             AMBON.mycompany.com:0    LISTENING
  TCP    AMBON:epmap            AMBON.mycompany.com:0    LISTENING
  TCP    AMBON:https            AMBON.mycompany.com:0    LISTENING
  ...
  TCP    AMBON:netbios-ssn      AMBON.mycompany.com:0    LISTENING
  UDP    AMBON:epmap            *:*
  UDP    AMBON:snmp             *:*
  UDP    AMBON:microsoft-ds     *:*
  ...
  UDP    AMBON:netbios-ns       *:*
  UDP    AMBON:netbios-dgm      *:*
  UDP    AMBON:isakmp           *:*
```

Note

> Note that I removed the active connections, which we saw earlier, as well as many of the listening connection ports.

This listing shows that Windows has many services waiting for connections using the both TCP and UDP protocols.

Unlike the TCP protocol, the User Datagram Protocol (UDP) is used to send brief messages back and forth between computers, and by network services that choose to take care of retransmitting lost data themselves. The Domain Name Service (DNS), the Windows network browser, and RealAudio are examples of services that use UDP data transmission.

In the listing, you can see that I have Internet Information Services installed on my computer, which provide FTP, email, and Web services. My computer also has Microsoft File Sharing (netbios-ns, netbios-dgm, and netbios-ssn) and the network-monitoring protocol SNMP.

Beyond the FTP, Web, and email servers, Windows seems to listen on 30 different ports, many of which are not listed as standard protocols; these are probably related to remote administration.

SAVING TIME WITH THE -n SWITCH

Note that when netstat lists remote computers and ports, it lists the name of the computers involved in each type of connection. This can be very time consuming when Windows has to query the Internet Domain Name Service to find the name of each computer connected to yours. If no name has been entered for a particular computer, netstat is forced to wait several seconds before it gives up and prints only the remote IP address.

Adding -n to the netstat command line skips this lookup business and prints only IP addresses. This can save you a lot of time if your computer is the target of many connections.

DISPLAYING PROTOCOL STATISTICS WITH THE -s SWITCH

Another, very different use of netstat is to view statistics for the number of packets sent and received in each protocol. Here are just some of the statistics printed by the command netstat -s:

```
IP Statistics           (comments)  Packets Received    = 4209
                                    ➥(total packets
                                    ➥received via TCP/IP)

    Received Header Errors          = 0     (bad packets received)
    Datagrams Forwarded             = 8     (packets routed to
                                            ➥other computers)

    Output Requests                 = 3373     (packets you sent)
    Reassembly Required             = 12    (packets too large for their
                                            ➥underlying network)


ICMP Statistics

                            Received    Sent
    Destination Unreachable    29        0       (replies from remote
                                                 ➥routers, saying
                                                 ➥"no go!"

    Echos                      11        111     (pings handled by
                                                 ➥this computer)

    Echo Replies               92        11

TCP Statistics
```

```
Active Opens             = 99   (connections established outbound)
Passive Opens            = 18   (connections made to this computer)
Segments Retransmitted   = 11   (packets resent due to errors)
```

Most of the statistics aren't really helpful in debugging connectivity problems. The Echos Received number, though, is useful when another computer can't ping yours. The statistics will show you whether the ping packets are at least making it to your computer.

NSLOOKUP

Nslookup queries the Domain Name System. Besides helping uncover name lookup problems, nslookup can give you a wealth of behind-the-scenes information on Web sites, *spam* (*page 492*) mailers, and anyone else who reveals themselves to you with an IP address.

> **Note**
>
> Nslookup is quite a complex program—in fact, an entire book could be written about it and the Domain Name System. I can't get into a lot of detail here, unfortunately. However, if you're interested in the topic, you should read *Concise Guide to Windows 2000 Dynamic DNS*, published by Que (ISBN: 0-7897-2335-2), and *DNS and Bind*, published by O'Reilly & Associates.

The Internet Domain Name System is really a sophisticated, distributed database. Its information is managed by thousands of computers worldwide, each responsible for a small piece of the whole puzzle. When you want to visit a Web site (say, www.mcp.com), what your Web browser really needs is the Web server's IP address. Windows communicates with DNS servers to get this information for most Internet applications.

Nslookup lets you bypass Windows and communicate with DNS servers directly, to get additional information. The most interesting DNS information comes in three forms:

- A (or *Address*) records, which record the IP address for each named network computer.
- PTR records, which serve the opposite purpose: They record the host name of a given IP address.
- SOA records, which list the email address of the person responsible for a domain's management.

If you just type the command nslookup, nslookup will start its own command prompt. You can type in any of its set of lookup commands, or you can type exit or press Ctrl+C to quit. You can also issue a single nslookup command right from the Windows command line, sticking it after nslookup.

Rather than describe the many nslookup commands, I'll just give you cookbook recipes for looking up three types of useful information, as discussed in the following subsections.

Tip #204	You can substitute any other IP addresses or names when you try these commands. You might explore nslookup's other commands by typing `help` at its command prompt, although I should warn you that they won't make much sense without detailed knowledge about DNS.

FINDING AN IP ADDRESS GIVEN A NAME

Finding an IP address is the simplest task: Just type the command `nslookup` *hostname*. For example, typing

```
C:\>nslookup www.bigcompany.com
```

returns the following:

```
Server:  ns1.bigisp.com
Address:  222.211.200.72

Non-authoritative answer:Name:    www.bigcompany.com
Address:  193.71.146.70
```

nslookup started by telling us which DNS server it asked and then tells us that the IP address we wanted is 193.71.146.70. What's this about a "non-authoritative answer"? It means that my ISP's DNS server already knew the answer to my query, because someone asked for it earlier in the day. This message just means it knows the answer; it didn't get it from the authoritative source this time. DNS servers remember (or *cache*) information for several hours to save time answering repetitive questions.

FINDING A NAME GIVEN AN IP ADDRESS

Looking up names in reverse is a little trickier. The information to find IP addresses given names is the bread and butter of domain name servers, but not everyone supplies them with the extra information needed to look up host names given an IP address. Although you might not get the information you want, when you've received spam mail or had a suspected break-in, you're willing to give it a shot.

First, see whether the reverse name information is available by typing this:

```
C:\>nslookup 193.71.146.70
```

If you're lucky, the output will look just like that shown in the previous example, and it has the following answer:

```
Name:    www.bigcompany.comAddress:  193.71.146.70
```

If this fails to work, you might be able to find out who owns the block of IP addresses to which this IP address belongs. Here's the recipe, using 193.71.146.70 as an example. Typing

```
C:\>nslookup> set type=SOA> 146.71.193.in-addr.arpa
```

PART
III

CH
16

returns the following:

```
primary name server = ns1.bigisp.net
        responsible mail addr = robert.bigisp.net
serial  = 1999061611        refresh = 3600 (1 hour)
        retry   = 3600 (1 hour)
        expire  = 604800 (7 days)
        default TTL = 21600 (6 hours)
> exit
```

SOA stands for Start of Authority, and TYPE=SOA is a request to learn something about the organization responsible for a set of DNS information. Next, I entered a peculiar address, entering just the first three numbers in the IP address, in reverse order, followed by in-addr.arpa. The response indicates the name of the DNS server responsible for knowing the names of the block of IP addresses 193.71.146.1 through 255 (ns1.bigisp.net) and the DNS manager's email address (robert@bigisp.net). This usually is the name of the ISP that serves the IP address we're interested in. If the first lookup had failed, I could have typed

```
> 71.193.in-addr.arpa
```

as well, which would tell who is responsible for the IP addresses 193.71.0.0 through 193.71.255.255. However, that covers a lot of ground and isn't very useful.

When you have the name of the primary name server or the responsible email address, your next stop is usually the World Wide Web. In this case, we could look up www.bigisp.net.

Also, see the section titled "Whois Database," later in this chapter.

FINDING THE OWNER OF AN IP ADDRESS

The SOA information you just saw can also be used to find out about a host name or IP address. Just cut off the host and enter the domain only. For example, typing

```
C:\>nslookup> set type=SOA> bigcompany.com
```

returns the following:

```
primary name server = ns1.bigisp.net
        responsible mail addr = admin@bigcompany.com
serial  = 1999061611        refresh = 3600 (1 hour)
        retry   = 3600 (1 hour)
        expire  = 604800 (7 days)
        default TTL = 21600 (6 hours)
> exit
```

This tells us that the DNS servers for bigcompany.com are really managed by the company's ISP, but we've also found an email address of a network administrator within the company.

PATHPING

Pathping is new to Windows's toolkit. It provides the function of tracert and adds a more intensive network traffic test. (If you're not familiar with tracert, you might want to skip ahead and read about it first. See the section titled "tracert.")

Pathping performs the route-tracing function faster than tracert because it sends only one packet per hop, compared tracert's three.

After determining the route, pathping does a punishing test of network traffic at each router by sending 100 ping packets to each router in the path between you and the host you're testing. It measures the number of lost packets and the average round trip time for each hop, and it displays the results in a table:

```
Computing statistics for 350 seconds...
                   Source to Here   This Node/Link
Hop  RTT    Lost/Sent = Pct  Lost/Sent = Pct  Address
  0                                            AMBON.mycompany.com
                                             ➥[202.201.200.166]
                                 0/ 100 =  0%   |
  1   2ms    0/ 100 =  0%     0/ 100 =  0%  190.mycompany.com
                                             ➥[202.201.200.190]
                                 0/ 100 =  0%   |
  2   2ms    0/ 100 =  0%     0/ 100 =  0%  129.mycompany.com
                                             ➥[202.201.200.129]
                                 0/ 100 =  0%   |
  3  25ms    0/ 100 =  0%     0/ 100 =  0%  w001.z216112073.
                                             ➥sjc-ca.dsl.cnc.net
                                             ➥[216.112.73.1]

 12  26ms    0/ 100 =  0%     0/ 100 =  0%  295.ATM8-0-0.GW2.
                                             ➥SCL1.ALTER.NET
                                             ➥[152.63.48.113]
                                 0/ 100 =  0%   |
 13  31ms    0/ 100 =  0%     0/ 100 =  0%  2250-gw.customer.
                                             ➥ALTER.NET [157.130.193.14]
                                 0/ 100 =  0%   |
 14  29ms    0/ 100 =  0%     0/ 100 =  0%  www.metricom.com
                                             ➥[204.179.107.3]
Trace complete.
```

The Source to Here column indicates the cumulative percentage of packet loss, going further along the path. The column This Node/Link indicates packet loss between and in each router along the way.

The results tell you which routers along the way are experiencing congestion, because they will not be able to return every echo packet they're sent, and they may take some time to do it. You can't quite trust these results, however, because many routers assign very low priority to these diagnostic packets. Pathping's results may be biased because its probe packets are less likely to be delivered and may take longer to return than normal data packets.

No Speed Demon

Performing the pathping test can take quite a while. By default, pathping sends packets 250 msec (one-quarter second) apart, so 100 probes at one-quarter second each for, say, 12 routers adds up to five minutes of testing. If some packets are lost, the time can be much greater because pathping waits up to three seconds for an echo to return.

You can cancel the test by pressing Ctrl+C, or you can perform a shorter test using those wonderful command-line switches. Pathping can be sped up with any one of several options:

Switch	What It Tells pathping
-n	Don't look up the names of the intermediate routers; just print the IP addresses.
-p *nnn*	Send test pings every *nnn* msec instead of the default 250 msec. Don't go lower than 100 msec if a modem Internet connection is used.
-q *nnn*	Send *nnn* queries per router rather than the default 100.
-w *nnn*	Wait at most *nnn* msec for an echo to return, instead of the default 3000, before considering it lost.

Here's a faster pathping test of the route to www.richochet.net:

```
C:\>pathping -n -p 100 -q 5 www.ricochet.net
```

This test takes only seven seconds instead of the nearly six minutes that the default settings would require. Of course, the results will be less statistically significant.

PING

If you try to browse the Internet or share files with other computers on your LAN and get no response, it could be because the other computer isn't getting your data or isn't responding in more sophisticated layers. After ipconfig, ping is the most useful tool to determine where your TCP/IP network stops working.

Tip #205

You can type ping *x.x.x.x*, replacing *x.x.x.x* with the gateway address or the address of any other operational computer on your network, and in an instant know whether your computer, network hardware, and cabling are operating properly. If echoes come back, the physical part of your network is functioning properly. If they don't, you can use tracert and other tools to see why.

See the section titled "ipconfig," earlier in the chapter, for another related command. Use these commands together for a quick one-two check to see whether an Internet connection is working.

Here's how it works: The ping command sends a few packets of data to any computer you specify using a special echo protocol. The other computer knows to send these packets right back where they came from. Ping lets you know whether the packets come back. Therefore, ping tests the low-level communication between two computers. If ping works, you know that your network wiring, TCP/IP software, and any routers in between you and the other computer are working. Ping takes several options, and three variations are especially useful. Here are the first two variations:

```
C:\>ping hostname
```

and

```
C:\>ping nnn.nnn.nnn.nnn
```

These variations transmit four packets to the host or IP address you specify and tell you whether they return. This command returns the following information:

```
C:\>ping www.mycompany.com
Pinging sumatra.mycompany.com [202.222.132.163] with 32 bytes of data:
Reply from 202.222.132.163: bytes=32 time<10ms TTL=32
Reply from 202.222.132.163: bytes=32 time<10ms TTL=32
Reply from 202.222.132.163: bytes=32 time<10ms TTL=32
Reply from 202.222.132.163: bytes=32 time<10ms TTL=32
```

The fact that the packets returned tells us that the computer can communicate with www.mycompany.com. It also tells us that everything in between is working as well.

Note

By the way, it's not uncommon for one packet of the four to be lost; when the Internet gets congested, sometimes ping packets are discarded as unimportant. If *any* come back, the intervening networks are working.

Another useful variation is to add the -t option. This makes ping run endlessly, once per second, until you type Ctrl+C. This is especially helpful if you're looking at indicator lights on your network hub, changing cables, and so n. The endless testing lets you just watch the screen to see whether any changes you make cause a difference.

Ping is a great quick test of connectivity to any location. If the ping test fails, use tracert or pathping to tell you where the problem is.

ROUTE

Most of us have at most one modem or one LAN adapter through which we make our Internet and other network connections, but Windows Networking components are sophisticated enough to handle multiple LAN and dial-up adapters in one computer. When multiple connections are made, Windows has to know which connections to use to speak with another remote computer. For the TCP/IP or Internet Protocol (IP) data, this information comes from the *routing table*. This table stores lists of IP addresses and subnets (blocks of IP addresses) as well as indicates which adapter (or *interface*) Windows used to reach each of them. You probably don't have to worry about routing unless one of the following scenarios is true:

- You use a dial-up connection *and* a LAN adapter simultaneously.
- You use multiple LAN adapters.
- You use Virtual Private Networking connections.

If you have trouble reaching an Internet destination and fall into any of these three categories, type route at the command line. You'll be shown a table that looks something like this:

```
===========================================================================
Interface List
0x1 ......................... MS TCP Loopback interface
0x2 ...0e c3 24 1f 09 3f ...... NDIS 5.0 driver
===========================================================================
===========================================================================
Active Routes:
Network Destination        Netmask          Gateway        Interface  Metric
        0.0.0.0          0.0.0.0   202.201.200.190  202.201.200.166      1
      127.0.0.0        255.0.0.0       127.0.0.1       127.0.0.1         1
 202.201.200.160  255.255.255.224  202.201.200.166  202.201.200.166      1
 202.201.200.166  255.255.255.255       127.0.0.1       127.0.0.1         1
 202.201.200.255  255.255.255.255  202.201.200.166  202.201.200.166      1
      224.0.0.0        224.0.0.0  202.201.200.166  202.201.200.166      1
 255.255.255.255  255.255.255.255  202.201.200.166  202.201.200.166      1
Default Gateway:    202.201.200.190
===========================================================================
Persistent Routes:
  None
```

There's a lot of information here, but for our purposes, we can boil it down to this: The entry for network destination 0.0.0.0 is the effective gateway address for general Internet destinations. This *can* be different from your LAN's specified default gateway, especially while a dial-up or VPN connection is active. That, in turn, may mean that you can't get to the Internet. If you have multiple LAN adapters, the issues are more complicated. Contact your network administrator for assistance.

→ If the gateway address is incorrect after you've made a dial-up connection, **see** "Routing Issues," **p. 833**.

TRACERT

Tracert is similar to ping: It sends packets to a remote host and sees whether packets return. However, tracert adds a wrinkle. In the first few packets it sends, it marks the packets, saying that they can't travel past one network router. Therefore, when they get to the first router between you and the host you're testing, the router returns them as undeliverable. The "undeliverable" message contains the IP address of the router that turned the packet back, so tracert has located the first step in the path between you and the final host. This first address is your LAN gateway (if you connect to the Internet via a LAN) or the modem-answering equipment at your ISP's office (if you're using a dial-up connection).

Tracert repeats the process, marking the packets as "can't pass more than two routers." When these packets are returned, tracert learns the IP address of the second step toward the desired host.

The number is stepped up one at a time, until the packets are returned by the target host. In this way, tracert maps out the path through the Internet between you and any other computer on the Net.

This makes tracert an extremely useful utility: When you can't reach a Web site or other network resource, tracert can quickly tell you how far data can get. By showing you the routers that do work, tracert tells you whether the problem is on your network and where you must fix it or whether the problem is out in the Internet, where you have no control. This alone makes tracert worth its proverbial weight in gold.

Here's an example that tests the route between my network and the Web server www.ricochet.com. Typing

```
C:\>tracert www.ricochet.net
```

returns the following:

```
Tracing route to www.metricom.com [204.179.107.3]
over a maximum of 30 hops:

 1   <10 ms   <10 ms   <10 ms   190.mycompany.com [202.201.200.190]
 2   <10 ms   <10 ms    10 ms   129.mycompany.com [202.201.200.129]
 3    20 ms    20 ms    20 ms   w001.z216112073.sjc-ca.dsl.cnc.net
                                ➥[216.112.73.1]
 4    10 ms    10 ms    10 ms   206.83.66.153
 5    10 ms    10 ms    10 ms   rt001f0801.sjc-ca.concentric.net
                                ➥[206.83.90.161]
 6    10 ms    20 ms    20 ms   us-ca-sjc-core2-f5-0.rtr.
                                ➥concentric.net [205.158.11.133]
 7    10 ms    20 ms    10 ms   us-ca-sjc-core1-g4-0-0.rtr.
                                ➥concentric.net [205.158.10.2]
 8    10 ms    20 ms    20 ms   us-ca-pa-core1-a9-0d1.rtr.
                                ➥concentric.net [205.158.11.14]
 9    10 ms    20 ms    20 ms   ATM2-0-0.br2.pao1.
                                ➥ALTER.NET [137.39.23.189]
10    10 ms    20 ms    20 ms   125.ATM3-0.XR1.PAO1.
                                ➥ALTER.NET [152.63.49.170]
11    10 ms    10 ms    20 ms   289.at-1-0-0.XR3.SCL1.
                                ➥ALTER.NET [152.63.49.98]
12    20 ms    20 ms    20 ms   295.ATM8-0-0.GW2.SCL1.
                                ➥ALTER.NET [152.63.48.113]
13    20 ms    20 ms    20 ms   2250-gw.customer.
                                ➥ALTER.NET [157.130.193.14]
14    41 ms    30 ms    20 ms   www.metricom.com
                                ➥[204.179.107.3]

Trace complete.
```

Between my computer and this Web server, data passes through 13 intermediate routers, owned by two ISPs.

PART

III

CH

16

Tip #206   When your Internet connection is working, run tracert to trace the path between your computer and a few Internet hosts. Print and save the listings. Someday when you're having Internet problems, you can use these listings as a baseline reference. When your Internet connection isn't working well, the tracert listing might not show DNS names for each of the stops, and you can refer to your printout. It's very helpful to know whether packets are stopping in your LAN, in your ISP's network, or beyond when you pick up the phone to yell about it.

Each line shows the time in milliseconds that the probe packets took to make the roundtrip between my computer and the router. If your Web connection seems unusually slow, you can find out where the bottleneck is from these numbers. Perform a `tracert` to the Web site you were visiting. If the roundtrip time takes a big jump at one of the routers listed, say 150 ms more than the previous router, the Internet is experiencing traffic congestion at that point. If none of the routers show large roundtrip times, the slowdown is at the Web server itself.

Tip #207

To be honest, the numbers shown in the listing are unusually low, relative to what I usually see. I usually expect times up to 150ms for a DSL *(page xxx)* connection, and up to 500ms with a modem connection. Roundtrip times also depend on the distance to the remote Web site. International sites are often more than 500 ms away, even with a DSL connection.

The times shown aren't all that reliable, in any case. Many ISP and Internet backbone routers assign a lower priority to tracert packets than to normal data. A busy router with lots of data waiting to go through a slow network channel might even discard tracert and ping packets. Therefore, a large jump in roundtrip times at a given router might not indicate that data is being held up there, but only your test packets.

I should point out a couple of tracert's oddities. First, notice in the example that I typed `www.ricochet.net`, but tracert printed `www.metricom.com`. That's not unusual. Web servers sometimes have many different names. Tracert starts with a reverse name lookup to find the canonical (or *primary*) name for a given IP address.

There's another glitch you might run into. Many organizations block tracert packets at the firewall between their LAN and the Internet, so tracert will never reach its intended destination. Instead, you'll see an endless list that looks like this:

```
14      *       *       *     Request timed out.
15      *       *       *     Request timed out.
16      *       *       *     Request timed out.
```

This continues up to tracert's limit of 30 probes. Just press Ctrl+C to cancel the test if this happens. If tracert was able to reach routers outside your own LAN or PC, your equipment's fine and that's all you can hope for.

Tracert also gives you a way to speed up the tracing process by eliminating the lookup of each intermediate router's name. Just to make things interesting, I guess, the option is `-d` instead of the usual `-n`. It's a faster way to use tracert, but when the listing doesn't have the router and host names, it's a little hard to interpret without the list that I suggested you make in advance.

WEB-BASED UTILITIES

There are some interesting Web-based Internet utilities, provided mostly by major networking companies, computer manufactures, and universities with network engineering research programs. I'll point you to two I've found very handy.

SPEED CHECK

Ever wondered how to find the real-world transfer rate of your Internet connection? Intel Corporation has a nifty Web-based program to measure transfer speeds using a Java applet. Check out `www.intel.com/home/club/dcalc.htm`. Figure 16.2 shows the calculator in action.

Figure 16.2
The Intel Download calculator measure the real-world speed of your Internet connection and lets you compare download times for different connection technologies.

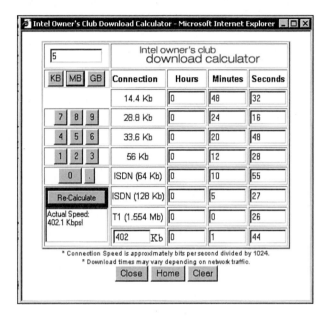

WHOIS DATABASE

Anyone registering an Internet domain name is required to file contact information with his or her Internet registry. This is public information, and you can use it to find out how to contact the owners of a domain whose customers have sent spam mail or with whom you have other concerns.

The .com, .edu, and .org domains all register with the U.S. InterNIC, which is managed by Network Solutions, Inc. You can look up domain contact information online using the whois service. Whois is a registered network protocol like finger. Although there are whois lookup programs out there, the simplest way to get at the InterNIC registry is through the following Web page:

`www.networksolutions.com/cgi-bin/whois/whois`

Links on that page lead you to similar lookup pages for the U.S. government and military domains (.gov and .mil) and for European and Asia/Pacific IP address registries.

THIRD-PARTY UTILITIES

If you want to be really well equipped to handle Internet and general networking problems, you can buy third-party utilities that are really much easier to use than the standard ones built into Windows. I really like WS_Ping ProPack from Ipswitch Software (www.ipswitch.com). This one utility packs almost all the TCP/IP tools into one graphical interface and adds other features such as whois for domain registration lookups, SNMP probing, and network scanning (see Figure 16.3). The registration fee is $37.50 U.S. for a single-user license. I rarely use or like add-ons like this, but I use this program every few days for one reason or another, and it quickly made my "must have" list.

Figure 16.3
WS_Ping ProPack is a great shareware utility, with many of TCP/IP debugging tools wrapped up in a graphical user interface.

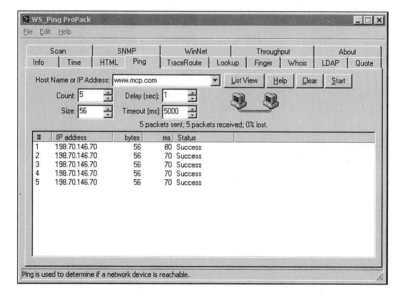

BEFORE YOU RUN INTO TROUBLE

As mentioned previously, the best tool to have on hand when you're diagnosing Internet problems is information about what you should expect when your connection is *working*.

It's very helpful to collect correct output of the TCP/IP diagnostic programs discussed, print it, and store the copies in a notebook for reference purposes. You can use the PrntScrn key to take a snapshot of the Command Prompt window and then paste the picture into a WordPad document as a super-fast way of recording this stuff. You can also redirect the output of the utilities into a file and print or import the files into a comprehensive document.

Here are some things to record:

■ The output of tracert to a sample Web site

■ The output of ipconfig/all on each of your computers

- The network hardware and protocol configuration dialog boxes in Network and Dial-Up Connections, as pictures snapped with PrntScrn
- The configuration of any routers or network connection equipment
- The settings for any dial-up connections used
- Diagrams showing network cabling, hubs, routers, and computers

In a business setting, documentation of your LAN configuration is a "due diligence" issue—it's not optional. Keep it up-to-date, and if you use an outside contractor for network installation or management, be sure that you're owed good documentation by contract.

This way, you'll be armed with supportive information when a problem does occur.

TROUBLESHOOTING

If you're having trouble using a Web site (say, www.hugebank.com), think of all the software and hardware between you and your money tucked away in Huge Bank's vault:

- Your network software
- Your modem or network card
- The physical connection to your ISP
- Your account at the ISP
- Equipment at the ISP's office
- Connections between ISPs around the world
- The Internet's connection to Huge Bank
- The Web server at Huge Bank
- Your account at Huge Bank

All these things must work with each other. They're like the links of a chain: If any one link fails, the chain is broken.

If you can't connect to an Internet site, you may know right away what the problem is. For example, if you're using a dial-up connection, you might get an error message stating "Your credentials have failed remote network authentication." This one is pretty self-explanatory, if not a bit stuffy, and you won't have trouble figuring out that you must check the user name and password you've entered (perhaps the Caps Lock key is on). However, if the cause or location of the problem isn't clear, what do you do?

Figures 16.4 and 16.5 show flowcharts to help direct you to the problem. The first chart is for dial-up connections to an ISP, and the second is for LAN connections. If you're having Internet connection trouble, follow the appropriate flowchart. The endpoints in each flowchart suggest places to look for trouble. I'll discuss these in the sections that follow.

Figure 16.4
Flowchart for diagnos-
ing dial-up Internet
connection problems.

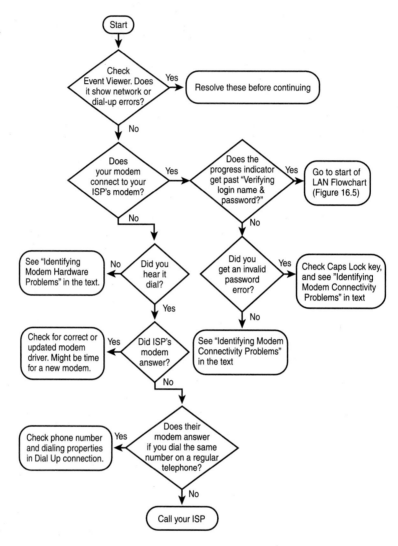

IDENTIFYING SOFTWARE CONFIGURATION PROBLEMS

Software configuration problems can easily be the cause of Internet connection problems,
and it's fairly easy to determine that this is the problem—you can't make any Internet connection whatsoever, although the Device Manager says your network card or modem seems
to be working correctly. The potential problems depend on the type of Internet connection
you use.

Figure 16.5
Flowchart for diagnosing wired or LAN connection problems.

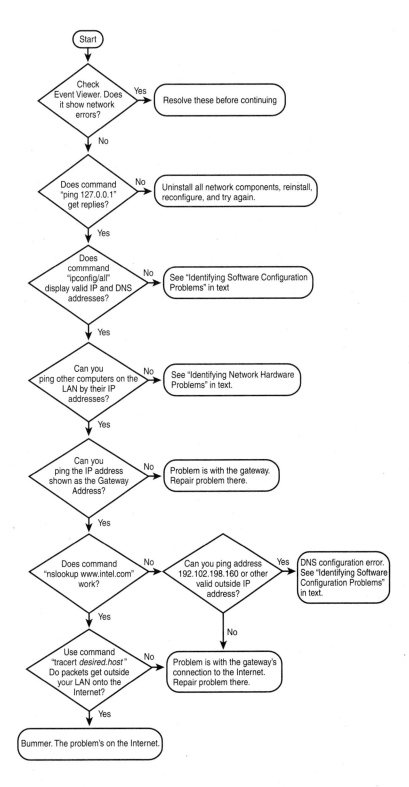

IF YOU CONNECT THROUGH A DIAL-UP CONNECTION

If you can connect to your ISP but, even though connected, still can't access any Web pages or Internet services, here are some steps you can take:

1. In Internet Explorer, select Tools, Internet Options. Select the Connections tab. Be sure you have selected the correct dial-up connection. Click LAN Options and be sure that Use a Proxy Server is not checked.

2. In Network and Dial-Up Connections, select your Dial-Up connection, right-click Properties, and select the Networking tab. The type of dial-up server should be PPP, and under Components Used By This Connection, only Internet Protocol should be checked (if you're calling an ISP). Additional protocols may be selected if you're connecting to your own office to use its network.

3. On the Network and Dial-Up Connections Security tab, be sure that Validate My Identity is set to Allow Unsecured Password for an ISP or Require Secured Password if you're connecting to your office LAN.

4. In a command prompt window, type `ipconfig /all` to be sure that you have a valid IP address and DNS server settings. Be sure you can ping the listed gateway IP address. If you can't ping the listed gateway IP, call the contact person at your ISP and tell him or her what IP address and netmask your computer is using. This person can tell you whether these numbers are okay or if they indicate a configuration problem.

5. Type `nslookup www.microsoft.com` to be sure that your DNS settings are correct. If the name lookup fails, verify that you're using the correct DNS values. See whether you can ping your DNS servers by their IP addresses. Your ISP's DNS servers may be offline. This happens from time to time.

IF YOU CONNECT DIRECTLY VIA A CABLE OR DSL MODEM

If your computer connects to a cable or DSL modem, you may have one or two network cards installed in your computer, depending on whether you're sharing the high-speed connection on your LAN.

Here's how to check for the proper settings:

1. In a command prompt window, type `ipconfig /all`. Be sure that your IP address and DNS information for the network card that connects to your high-speed modem is accurate.

2. If you're sharing a high-speed connection to a LAN using two network cards in your computer, be sure that you've enabled sharing on the correct connection! The connection to check as shared is the one that connects to your high-speed DSL or cable modem. The LAN connection is not the shared connection and should have an IP address of `192.168.0.1`.

IF YOU CONNECT THROUGH YOUR LAN

If you connect to the Internet via a connection on your LAN, the first question is, can you communicate with other computers on your LAN? Use the `ping` command to see whether you get responses from other computers on the LAN.

If you can communicate with other computers on the LAN but not the Internet, can anyone else on your LAN access the Internet? If no one can, the problem is in your LAN's connection to the Net. If your LAN uses Internet connection sharing, go to the sharing computer and start diagnosing the problem there. Otherwise, follow these steps:

1. Open a command prompt window and type `ipconfig /all` to view your TCP/IP settings. Check the following:
   - The DNS suffix search list and/or the connection-specific DNS suffix should be set correctly for your company's domain name or your ISP's domain name (if you don't have a company domain).
   - The IP address should be appropriate for your LAN. If you're using Internet Connection Sharing with Windows 2000, the number will be `192.168.0.xxx`.
   - If your IP address appears to be `169.254.0.xxx`, the sharing computer was not running the connection-sharing service when you booted up your computer. Get it started and then skip to step 2.
   - The default gateway address should be the IP address of your router or `192.168.0.1` (if you're using a shared Internet connection).
   - The default gateway address and your IP address should be identical in the first few sets of numbers, corresponding to those parts of the subnet mask that are set to 255.
   - The DNS server numbers should be those provided by your ISP or network administrator.
   - If your computer gets its IP address information automatically, DHCP Enabled should be set to Yes. If your computer has its IP address information entered manually, DHCP Enabled should be set to No.

     If your computer gets its settings automatically or uses a shared connection, continue with the next two steps.

2. Be sure the master router or computer is running. In Network and Dial-Up Connections, right-click your Local Area Connection icon and select Disable. Then select Enable to reset your network connection.

3. Repeat the `ipconfig` command and see whether the correct information appears now. If it does, you're all set. If not, the master computer or the router is not supplying the necessary information, and it needs to be set correctly before you can proceed.

These steps should take care of any software configuration problems, and there isn't much more that could be causing a problem, as long as your network hardware is functioning correctly. If none of these steps indicates or solves the problem, check that your network or modem hardware is functioning correctly.

IDENTIFYING NETWORK HARDWARE PROBLEMS

If you suspect hardware as the source of your Internet connection problems, check the following:

- Right-click My Computer, select Manage, and select Device Manager. Look for any yellow exclamation point (!) icons in the device list; if your network adapter is marked with this trouble indicator, you'll have to solve the hardware problem before continuing. See Chapter 30, "Maintaining and Optimizing System Performance," for hardware troubleshooting tips.

- Check the Event Viewer for informative error message that may indicate a hardware problem.

- If your LAN has indicator lights on the network cards and/or hubs, open a command prompt window and type ping -t *x.x.x.x*, where *x.x.x.x* is your network's gateway address. This forces your computer to transmit data once per second. Confirm that the indicator lights blink on your LAN adapter and the hub, if you have one. This test may point out a cabling problem.

- If your hub or LAN card's indicator doesn't flash, you may have a bad LAN adapter, the wrong driver may be installed, or you may have configured the card for the wrong media type. If you have a so-called combo network card, check the LAN adapter's Advanced properties in Network and Dial-Up Connections to see whether you can force it to use the correct 10BaseT or ThinNet medium and network speed.

IDENTIFYING MODEM HARDWARE PROBLEMS

Modems can have a greater variety of problems than network adapters. Here are a few steps you can take to determine what the problem might be:

1. Before getting too frustrated, check the obvious one more time: Is a functioning telephone line connected to the right socket on the modem? Unless you're using an ISDN modem, it also doesn't hurt to plug in an extension phone and listen for dialing and an answer. You must somehow put the extension on the "line" side of the modem, though, because most modems disable the "telephone" jack when dialing.

2. Check the Event Viewer for informative error messages that may indicate a hardware problem.

3. Right-click My Computer, select Manage, and select Device Manager. Look for any yellow exclamation point (!) icons in the device list; if a modem or port is marked with this trouble indicator, you'll have to solve the hardware problem before continuing. See Chapter 30 for hardware troubleshooting tips.

4. Create a log file of modem activity as described in Chapter 11, under "Troubleshooting Modem Hardware Problems," step 6. Attempt another connection. Go back to the Modem Diagnostics page and click View Log File. See whether the log file reports any useful error messages. Be sure to turn off the Append to Log setting when you've finished diagnosing problems.

5. Try reducing the Maximum Port Speed (computer-to-modem connection speed) setting in Modem Properties to 19200. If this solves your problem, you need a new modem, or, if you have an external modem, a higher-quality serial port card.

→ For more modem troubleshooting tips, **see** "Troubleshooting Modem Hardware Problems," **p. 427**.

IDENTIFYING MODEM CONNECTIVITY PROBLEMS

If your modem is attempting to dial but you don't get a good connection to your ISP, check for proper dialing and modem settings:

- In the Dial-Up Connection Properties Option tab, check Prompt for Phone Number and try to make the connection. This will show you the actual number being dialed. Verify that the call waiting code, outside line access codes, and area code are correct. These are set on the connection's General tab and in the Phone and Modem Options control panel.

- If the ISP's modem answers but you don't establish a connection, your modem may be incompatible; call your ISP for assistance.

- Create and view a log file of modem activity and look for error messages indicating a protocol negotiation error. Your ISP can assist with this as well.

- If your modem makes screeching sounds for about 15 seconds and hangs up, your modem is probably incompatible with the equipment used at your ISP, and one of you needs to get an updated modem. Before you buy a new one, note that some modems can be updated via software. Check the manufacturer's Web site for information.

- If your connection works but the modem disconnects after a certain amount of time, there are two possible causes. If your connection was sitting idle, you may have run into the Windows inactivity timer. View the connection's properties in Network and Dial-Up Connections and select the Options tab. Check the entry Idle Time Before Hanging Up; you may have left the connection idle too long. Increase the time (or stay busy). You might enable the modem log and see whether it provides an explanation if this recurs.

- If you don't think that idle time was the cause, your connection may have been interrupted by call waiting. On the connection's General tab, check Use Dialing Rules and select Rules and Edit. Verify that you've chosen to disable call waiting and have selected the proper call waiting turn off setting (for example, *70).

- If none of these are the cause, you may simply have a scratchy telephone line or a flagging older modem. This is an annoying problem and difficult to diagnose. Try changing modems.

TIPS FROM THE WINDOWS PROS: PINGING WITH LARGER PACKETS

While I was finishing this chapter, it appeared that my LAN's Internet connection had just stopped working. After a closer look, I saw that only downstream communication was affected, meaning my browser could contact Web sites, but information from the Web wasn't reaching my computer.

Therefore, I first tried pinging my ISP at the gateway address of my DSL modem. It worked just fine. In fact, I could ping any site in the entire Internet but could not view a single Web page. Data travels both ways. I called my Internet service provider and found out that pings from its network into my LAN work, too. The guy I spoke to suggested that I must have a software problem. However, that didn't make sense, especially because everything was working earlier that same day. Then I had a hunch. Ping, by default, sends very small packets: 32 bytes each, plus a few bytes of IP packet packaging. Requests for Web pages are very small, too (maybe 100 bytes). However, responses from Web servers are big and come in the largest packets possible—about 1500 bytes each. This meant the problem might not be the direction the data was taking. Instead, it could be the size of the data that was causing the problem.

I vaguely remembered that ping has a bunch of command-line options, so I looked up "ping" in Windows Help and saw that I could increase the size of its packets with the `-l` option. Typing

```
ping -l 300 www.anyplace.com
```

tells ping to send 300-byte packets. Aha! I found that only about 50 percent of these packets made the roundtrip. When I sent 500-byte packets, the success rate dropped to 10 percent. The tech support guy at my ISP tried this, too, and found the same thing from his end.

The diagnosis: a problem with the DSL equipment at the phone company central office (CO) or with the wiring between the CO and my building. The result: trouble ticket #6470 filed. Problem resolved.

The moral of this story is to be familiar with your friendly neighborhood command-line utilities.

CHAPTER **17**

GOING PUBLIC: CREATING WEB PAGES

In this chapter

ORIGINS OF THE WEB

The humble beginnings of the World Wide Web (or just the Web, as it is commonly known today) are a definite surprise when you consider just how widely known and used the Web has become today. The truth is, less than 10 years ago, a small band of scientists in Switzerland decided to create a network so they could share information with other scientists far away. The first, very early incarnation of the Web was used for journal articles, research, and proposals—highly specialized information that really applied to only a small group of people. Then the U.S. government took an interest, and the first recognizable form of the Web took shape.

Along with this type of progress came a difficult realization: Hypertext Markup Language (HTML), the computer language designed to create Web pages, was not really Web friendly. Designers and Web page readers wanted color and multimedia, not to mention true control over where text and graphics would appear. So, to make such changes possible, HTML was stretched a little to accommodate wider use of color, more graphics, sound, and video and to harmonize with *plug-ins*—small add-on utilities that could run animation and neat visual tricks inside a Web page without depending on HTML.

The good news today is that Web page technology is finally starting to truly reflect the needs and wants of the Web audience. Recent creations covered in this chapter, such as cascading style sheets and Extensible Markup Language (XML), are finally enabling Web page designers to get the freedom they want to provide Web site users with the results they love.

Who Owns the Internet?

It's important to understand that no one person, organization, or business "owns" the Internet. The Internet, by definition, is one humongous network that is kept alive and working by each of the millions of individual, international computers and servers connected to it. The Web also is just one small part of the Internet at large; the Internet is also made up of email, FTP sites, newsgroups, chat groups, and many other smaller parts.

The only two entities that possess any sort of control over the Internet are Network Solutions (formerly known as InterNIC, the Internet Network Information Center), which keeps track of domain or Web site names, and the W3C (World Wide Web Consortium), which develops and maintains standards for using HTML. To read more about domain names, or to see whether the domain name you want to use is still available, go to http://www.networksolutions.com, and to read more about HTML standards, visit http://www.w3.org.

Note

If you are a beginner, FrontPage Express is a good place to start. If you are a seasoned Web designer, however, you should stick to more advanced tools, such as DreamWeaver and FrontPage 2000.

For more information, see *Using Macromedia DreamWeaver* and *Special Edition Using Microsoft FrontPage 2000*, both published by Que.

KEY POINTS TO CONSIDER

No matter what kind of Web site you want to build—whether it's a personal Web site for you and your family, or a large corporate Web site to advertise your business and your product line—you must consider a few general questions about your new Web site:

- Who is the audience for this site?
- What information will this site contain?
- When do I want to launch the Web site?
- Where will the Web site be seen?
- Why do I need a Web site at all?

WHO IS THE AUDIENCE?

There are two dimensions to the first question: Who is the audience? On the one hand, you do want to think like a marketing person and ask yourself what kinds of people you want to attract to your Web site. If you represent a business, do you want to attract new clients or buyers for your merchandise? Do you want prospective employees or your competitors to get a certain message? If you're an individual, too, do you want to attract other people with your interests or hobbies, other people with children the same age as yours, or people who have the same breed of cat you have? These are all content questions, and you should consider them very carefully as soon as possible.

On the other hand—and this point is just as important—you want to ask yourself about the technological proficiency of the visitors you want to attract. Only a small segment of the Web-using population is extremely cutting edge in terms of their knowledge and their interests when it comes to advanced Web page design or technologies. So, do you need to have all the latest bells and whistles in trendy Web page creation if you're trying to appeal to, say, antique dealers? You *can* create a Web site that is simple technologically but that still maintains an elegant presentation. In fact, you might strongly consider keeping your Web site simple if you want to keep the focus of the users on the content of the Web page rather than how the Web site itself actually works. The more time you spend focusing attention on who will be looking at your Web site, the better off you'll be in the long run.

WHAT INFORMATION SHOULD THE SITE CONTAIN?

The second question is, by contrast, very straightforward: What information will your Web site contain? Business sites typically advertise the business itself, sometimes including advertising of their products or services, and sometimes including a way to purchase said products or services. They can also feature the company's mission statement, quarterly earnings and other stockholder/investor facts, employee profiles, driving and traveling directions, marketing and promotional information, and more. You can safely pick and choose among these contents for your own Web site if it does or does not sell something.

Personal sites are a free-for-all, with as much or as little personal information as you can imagine. You can find Web sites featuring live camera images broadcast from a person's residence 24 hours a day to Web sites tightly secured with passwords that give nothing away. In between, however, is the norm: biographical information, hobbies and extracurricular interests, lists of favorite links, and such. It is generally not a good idea to post your picture, your street address, your phone number, or other such personal information to your Web page (although if you're the type to broadcast from your living room all the time, perhaps privacy isn't such an issue). However, it is certainly always appropriate to give your email address, if only to get compliments on how great your Web site looks.

Tip #208	Functionally, there is no difference between the way an intranet and a public Web site works. You use the same kinds of software to create them, you can include all the same features and advanced technologies, and the users will not be able to tell an intranet from a public Web site at a glance. With this point in mind, all the examples in this book will be public Web sites found on the Web at large (because they offer the most variety and because intranets by nature are not easily accessible to review).

 If you're designing an intranet, see "Special Considerations for Designing an Intranet" in the "Troubleshooting" section at the end of the chapter.

WHEN SHOULD THE SITE BE LAUNCHED?

The third question—when do you want to launch the Web site?—is largely a business-oriented concern. If you've created or re-created a business Web site, and you really want to draw attention to it, you can coincide your site launch with the debut of a new product, a move to a new location, the hiring of a new CEO, or some other marketing-driven event. The most important point to consider, though, is which event is more important: Is it more important to launch the site by a certain date, or is it more important to give the site design process whatever time it needs for the sake of the site itself? Many businesses and corporations make the mistake of deciding a certain date is more important, and then the Web site isn't finished, needs to be scaled back, or makes a poor impression for some other reason. In this case, the site gets several visits at first, but none later, and the company wonders what went wrong.

WHERE WILL THE SITE BE SEEN?

The fourth question—where will the Web site be seen?—is also a business-only query. These days, Web sites fall into two categories: public Web sites that are openly accessible to anyone on the Internet at large and *intranets*, or closed sites, that are viewed by and networked among a private, limited number of people. Large companies, for example, like to make intranets for their employees so that the company handbook, logos, holiday schedules, and other such information are easily circulated. So, the type of Web site you are creating is also a consideration when you sit down to do your initial planning.

WHY IS A WEB SITE NEEDED?

The fifth and final question—why do you need a Web site at all?—is not a rhetorical one. All the current hype and discussion about the Web might make you feel as though you must have a Web site "just because" or you're going to be hopelessly behind the times. The truth is, a poorly planned, unfocused, or hastily developed Web site is worse than having no Web site at all—even for businesses. So, take some time to think about the reason you're creating a Web site, and make it a good one.

WEB SITE PLANNING STRATEGIES

After you've answered all the questions from the preceding sections, and taken a good long time about it, you can begin to plan the actual layout of your Web site. This section provides a few general recommendations about good site planning strategy.

Your site should be built to serve as many visitors as possible. Think quantity and quality with regards to this issue. If you're building a Web site with online ordering capability for a very popular product, invest in the hardware and the people power for support. Independent contractors and part-time staff cannot adequately support a highly active, customer service-oriented Web site. Also, realize that one-quarter to one-third of the users on the Web are using older versions of Netscape Navigator or Microsoft Internet Explorer, the two leading Web browsers. Why does this point matter? People who use certain older versions of Navigator and Explorer cannot view a Web page that uses certain common technologies, such as frames or JavaScripts. Unless you know your audience is likely to have the latest browser software, you should think twice about using technologies such as style sheets, Java applets, streaming video, or even certain types of graphics, too.

Depending on your budget, your feelings, and your time frame, consider creating two versions of your site: one for low-end users and one for high-end users. You can also be up front with the type of Web site you have by posting a disclaimer of sorts (see Figure 17.1). The objective here is to be as courteous to low-end users as possible without compromising your vision for your Web site.

Your site should provide an entryway or splash page. An entryway or splash page is the ideal place to direct traffic or warn low-end visitors in the manner just covered and/or to recommend a particular browser or browser version that works best for your site design.

 If you're concerned about the differences in the way Netscape Navigator and Microsoft Internet Explorer will display the same Web page, see "Browser Display Differences" in the "Troubleshooting" section at the end of this chapter.

PART

III

CH

17

Tip #209

> An entryway or splash page also makes a quick visual statement about the look and feel of your Web site, giving a nod to the thousands of casual surfers who like to decide whether to spend time on a Web site in the first three to five seconds they see it.

Figure 17.1
Protect low-end users by providing a warning, an alternative site, or both.

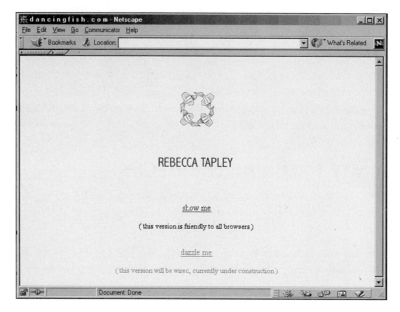

Your site should be easy to read and to navigate. Three factors are involved in following this basic principle of good design. First, visitors to your Web site should always know what page they are on and how to get to another place; a list of links or some kind of navigational element should be clearly visible and cleanly designed. Also, the links or buttons on the navigational element should be short and precise. If your Web site sells jeans, for example, the navigation bar should have buttons labeled something like Sizes rather than Sizing Chart and Checkout rather than Shopping Cart. Also, always have a button or link that returns the visitors to the front, or home, page. Give them the option to start over in case they get lost (and someone, somewhere, always gets lost no matter what you do).

Second, if you want visitors to read a large amount of text—which in Web-speak really means more than five or six lines—the sentences should be short and the paragraphs brief. The Web has become, first and foremost, a visual medium. E-zines, encyclopedias, newsgroups, and archives require visitors to spend a lot of time reading large portions of text, but these sites are the exception rather than the rule. Also, consider creating a print-only version of your Web site pages if your Web site contains anything people might want to print and keep, and/or the background of your site is dark or patterned. For example, if you provide warranty information, it's more likely to be printed than bookmarked, and if you have a dark background with white text or a patterned background that obscures text, the printed version of your site should be easy on the ink and the eyes.

Third, on the main page of your site and arguably on all the secondary pages leading off from it, the visitors to your Web site should not have to scroll down to see everything on the page. In design lingo, this is called asking a viewer to read "below the fold," which many casual visitors to a Web site will not do. A Web site, therefore, is not a printed brochure; it is not a magazine article; it is not a newspaper. Your readers are more than likely not going to turn the page to keep reading, even if the content is interesting. Instead, a Web site is mostly like, but not exactly like, a good television ad: It's concise, it's eye-catching, and it uses its limitations to their best advantage.

WHEN TO HIRE A PROFESSIONAL

Sometimes hiring a professional Web page designer is definitely better than attempting to design or plan a Web site yourself. You should probably hire a professional if the following points are true:

- Your goal is professional or business-oriented.
- Your time is limited.
- Your Web site will contain online ordering.
- Your audience is highly Web-savvy.
- Your site will be large (more than five or six individual Web pages).

The plain fact of the matter is, making a *good* Web site is not easy. It's also very true that your Web audience is getting smarter and more sophisticated all the time, so expectations are moving continually upward. Consequently, if your Web site has to sell something—a product, a company, an idea, or even yourself—paying someone experienced and talented to create the site for you is worthwhile.

Another axiom of professional Web page design is that it is time-consuming. Learning HTML and/or Web page design software takes a lot of time; then designing, testing, and launching a Web site takes a lot of time. But what about Web site maintenance? If you're creating a Web site about your business or company that has to grow with your business or company, you should try to think long term from the very start. You should also realize that somebody needs to keep tabs on your Web site all the time in case something goes wrong. Just because you can design a Web page yourself doesn't necessarily mean you have the expertise or (again) the hours to devote lots of attention to it. So here is another reason that hiring a professional is a good idea—or a better reason to hire a professional from the very beginning.

CHOOSING DESIGN TOOLS

If you're determined to design your Web site yourself, you can choose from a myriad of Web page design software tools. You might find FrontPage Express frustrating if you have some (or a lot of) Web page design experience. So let's talk about the different kinds of Web page design software based on proficiency, platform, and what you hope to achieve.

The simplest type of Web page design software to use is the WYSIWYG (what-you-see-is-what-you-get) family. "Wizzy-wigs" are designed for people who have little or no knowledge of HTML so they can use a group of tools and features to create Web pages instead. In a WYSIWYG tool, for example, you can drag an image into a blank Web page and resize it with the mouse before clicking and dragging it into position. The software writes the HTML instructions as you work depending on what you do. So, if you are a beginner, or the Web site you want to construct is a very simple one, you might choose to use a WYSI-WYG editor. The best ones are FrontPage or FrontPage Express and Adobe PageMill; they are available for both the Windows and Macintosh platforms.

The intermediate group of Web page design software is the largest and most versatile, if you are willing to spend a little bit of time learning the ropes. Adobe GoLive, Macromedia DreamWeaver, and netobjects Fusion are all excellent software products for Web page design (and they are available for both the PC and the Macintosh), but they are best for people who have a rudimentary knowledge of HTML. GoLive, for example, has its own easy-to-use tools to help you create QuickTime movies, JavaScript-enabled Web pages, and DHTML (Dynamic HTML), including style sheets—but these types of Web page components sometimes need a little tweaking to work at optimum. All these software products also write the HTML code "behind the scenes" as you use their tools and features, but code is much more complicated given the equally more complicated things you can do. Consider the software packages in this group a second tier of choices, which will perhaps be best for you if you start with something simpler and really get hooked.

The advanced group of Web page design software is the type of software that does little, if any, of the HTML writing for you. Allaire's HomeSite and Bare Bones Software's BBEdit are Web page design programs that forgo the colorful graphical interfaces, tools, and features and simply help you write cleaner code. In other words, you can use different tools to bring in and position an image; however, you cannot resize it with the mouse, and you must manually adjust the margins and other increments to position the image on the Web page. Experienced Web page designers sometimes prefer this kind of Web page design software because nothing gets between the designer and the Web page. This is not the type of software to begin with, however; it is rather the type to end up with, if and when you become very knowledgeable and experienced in writing HTML.

Tip #210

In Office 2000, Web publishing capabilities are available in every major software program, such as Word, Excel, and PowerPoint. It's definitely handy and appealing to think you can type out a proposal, report, or presentation using one of these software packages and then click a few options to publish on the Web. In truth, though, you cannot make the type of Web page or Web site you're accustomed to without actual Web page design software. So, you should use Office 2000 software for its primary function—to create and manage your business documents—and use Web page design software to build your Web site. The only exception to this rule is if your version of Office 2000 includes FrontPage. If FrontPage is included in the mix, you can design Web pages right from the Office environment without the aid of another WYSIWYG application.

You should have one more type of Web page design software at your fingertips, no matter what your proficiency: You should have browsers. Specifically, you should have as many versions of Netscape Navigator and Microsoft Internet Explorer as you can get your hands on and safely install on your computer. Why is having browsers important? Remember what I said earlier about the 25 to 30 percent of users who surf the Web with early browser versions. The only way for you to see what your Web site will look like to this segment of your audience is to see your site through their eyes—or, more specifically, through their browsers. And it also pays to see your site through the eyes of users on both the PC and the Macintosh, if at all possible. Unfortunately, this is easier said than done.

Keeping several versions of Navigator and Explorer on your computer is also easier said than done. Keeping two or three different versions of Netscape Navigator on the same machine is no trouble, but having several versions of Explorer is (unfortunately) next to impossible. Microsoft designed Explorer to install over older versions of itself, all but erasing the old version to make room for the new, and the solutions to this problem are simply too complex for the average nonprofessional Web page designer to contend with. If you work in an office where you can keep versions 3, 4, and 5 of Explorer on three separate machines, then that is the type of solution to this problem that I recommend. Otherwise, there's just not much you can do.

FRONTPAGE EXPRESS

FrontPage Express is not included along with Windows 2000 but is perfectly fine for most fledgling Web page designers. It's one of the WYSIWYG editors described in the preceding section, which means it has tools and features that help you create Web sites without requiring you to know any HTML at all.

If you upgraded to Windows 2000 from Windows 98 or a system on which Internet Explorer 4.0 was already installed, FrontPage Express will be available to you.

However, if you install a clean copy of Windows 2000 or purchase a computer with Windows 2000 preinstalled, you will have to locate and download FrontPage Express from the Microsoft Web site or copy it from another computer. The best approach is to go to www.microsoft.com/ie and poke around. As of this writing, FrontPage Express was available using the following steps:

1. First try the simple approach. Choose Start, Windows Update. From time to time, FrontPage Express is added to the Windows Update site. This will be the easier approach (if you find it there). If you don't find it, follow these directions.
2. Download Internet Explorer 5. An installation wizard starts.
3. Choose Install Minimal or Customize Your Browser.
4. Scroll down until you see FrontPage Express, and check that box.
5. Proceed with the remainder of the Internet Explorer installation and any other components you want to install. If you have existing bookmarks and cookies, the installer should maintain them.

If all else fails, do a search on the Microsoft site for FrontPage Express. You might find it that way as well.

Note

If you have Office 2000 Premium Edition, chances are that you already installed FrontPage 2000. If this is the case, don't fret about FrontPage Express because the FrontPage 2000 features are far more robust. In general, most of the Web design advice provided here will apply to FrontPage 2000 or most any other WYSIWYG Web site creation tool.

THE INTERFACE

To start FrontPage Express, simply choose Start, Programs, Internet Explorer, FrontPage Express. The FrontPage Express window then opens.

Take a good look at FrontPage's Standard toolbar. You'll be reassured to see that most of the tools are quite familiar. If you know other Microsoft Office software such as Word or PowerPoint, you'll already know at a glance what these tools do. If you're not sure what a certain button does, hover the mouse cursor over it, and a pop-up description will appear. Get to know the unfamiliar, Web-specific tools this way first. You can find a button here for everything from forms and tables to text boxes, buttons, lists, and indents.

Note also that you can change the font and font size, color, and style with other tools on the toolbars. These tools specifically resemble the same tools in Microsoft Word; Bold, Italic, and Underline look the same and are located in approximately the same places. You can increase or decrease the size of selected words by using the Increase Size and/or Decrease Size buttons, choose a color with the Text Color button, and select a different font from the Font drop-down menu.

Now start opening the drop-down menus. You'll also see many familiar tools in familiar places on these menus, and the ones you don't recognize are still organized logically. The Insert drop-down menu is particularly useful because it lets you drop in everything from images to video to scripts just by using your mouse.

BUILDING A BASIC WEB PAGE

In this section, I'll show you how to quickly start a new page that contains text, images, and links. To get started, you can use one of FrontPage's several wizards to help you create Web pages. To launch a wizard, follow these steps:

1. Choose File, New.
2. When the New Page dialog box appears, click one of the wizards listed in the box of choices. Then click OK to launch it. In this example, I'll use the Personal Home Page Wizard.
3. Choose the different types of information you want to publish about yourself. Click Next when you're finished.
4. Use the rest of the wizard's options and choices to round out the content of your Web pages, to name your Web site, and to make other customizations. Click Finish after you've finished; the wizard then renders your new bare-bones Web site.

Tip #211

> You can easily experiment with the various tools and menu options in FrontPage. If you want to add a line of text and bold it, for example, click at the place on the Web page where you want the text to appear. Then type it, highlight it with the mouse, and click the Bold button on the Standard toolbar. FrontPage is designed to work as much like Word 2000 as possible to lower the learning curve and to give you confidence.

ADDING IMAGES

To add an image to your page, do the following:

1. Click at the place in the Web page where you want the image to appear.
2. Click the Insert Image button on the Standard toolbar. The Insert Image dialog box then appears; this dialog box has two tabs.
3. If you have an image stored somewhere on your hard drive or desktop, select the Other Location tab. You can browse for the image by choosing the From File option, or write out the path to it with From Location. If you're inserting clip art, click the Clip Art tab. Either way, after you've found the image to insert, click OK. The image then appears in your Web page just where you want it to be.

To resize an image, click it once, and then reduce or enlarge it by dragging one of the black boxes that appear around the border. To specify more settings such as alignment, spacing, and alternative text, choose Edit, Image Properties.

ADDING HYPERLINKS

You might want two kinds of links in your Web pages: links to other pages in your site or links to other Web sites out there on the Web.

To add either kind of link, follow these steps:

1. Highlight the text (or image) that will serve as the link.
2. Click the Create or Edit Hyperlink button on the Standard toolbar. The Edit Hyperlink dialog box then opens.
3. If you want to link the Web page you're working on to another Web page in your site, click the New Page tab. Enter a name for this new page, and click OK to create an internal link.
4. If you want to link the Web page to another site on the Web, click the World Wide Web tab. Choose http: from the Hyperlink Type drop-down menu, and type the URL of the Web site to which you want to link.
5. Click OK, and FrontPage adds the link to your Web page in progress.

PART
III

CH
17

Note

One of the most attractive ways to arrange navigational links on a Web page (the ones that help the visitors move among different pages within your Web site) is to create an imagemap. An imagemap is a grid of "hot spots" or clickable hyperlinks arranged invisibly underneath an image. Creating an imagemap is a fairly intermediate Web page design task, so you can start out with plain links and graduate to imagemaps later.

Now that you've created a basic, no-frills Web page, it's time to take a look at some other options. Do you want to use tables, perhaps, or frames? How about animation or multimedia or DHTML? You must keep in mind some special considerations while making these decisions, so I'll cover them all in the following sections.

ADVANCED WEB PAGE DESIGN TECHNIQUES

Now let's cover some of the most interesting Web page design techniques using FrontPage Express and some real-life examples from the Web itself.

Note

As mentioned earlier in the chapter, FrontPage Express is a slimmed-down version of FrontPage 2000, which is a much more fully featured, robust Web page design product. If you find FrontPage Express is inadequate for your needs, visit Microsoft's site at http://www.microsoft.com to find more information on FrontPage 2000. FrontPage 2000 also is part of the Office 2000 Premium Edition. Though FrontPage Express is not included with Windows 2000 Professional, it is free from Microsoft.

TABLES

Tables are not an advanced technology, per se; rather, tables provide an option to organize and determine the overall look of your Web site. Tables are very widely used for aligning text, images, and other content on the Web because they enable a Web page designer to position elements quite precisely (see Figure 17.2). They are supported by every version of both browsers on both platforms, so they are very dependable. You can easily print out a Web page that uses tables, and you can always reload or use the Back button to return to a Web page that uses tables and see the Web page again without any display problems. So, tables have become a standard part of every Web designer's toolbox and a very important component of most Web sites.

To add a table to a Web page with FrontPage Express, do the following:

1. Open the Web page you want to edit, and put the cursor in the location where you want the table to appear.

2. Click the Insert Table button on the Standard toolbar. A small grid appears, enabling you to choose how many rows, columns, and cells you want in the new table. (Getting the hang of using this grid takes a little practice; count on making a couple of tries before you get what you want.)

Figure 17.2
A nicely composed Web page using tables to position and align contents. This site uses tables to align the company logo, links, and check boxes into separate parts of the page so that everything aligns properly.

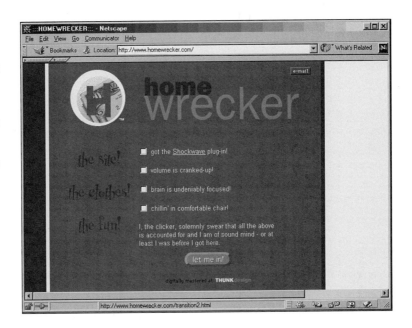

3. Use the arrow keys to put the cursor in the cell, or small box, you want to edit. Type some text, insert an image, or create a link as you like.

4. To edit the appearance, size, or alignment of the table, open the Table drop-down menu, and use the tools listed there. They are fairly self-explanatory and easy to figure out with a little noodling around, but Cell Properties and Table Properties are most useful.

5. Save your changes to protect your work.

Caution

FrontPage Express must not be used to edit Web pages containing Dynamic HTML or Script tags because it will strip this "enhanced" HTML right out of the file. As a general rule, it's best to edit a Web page file with the same editing tool used to create it. That way, the capabilities of the editor won't be outmatched by the contents of the HTML file it's editing.

Tip #212

A good shortcut for adjusting table and cell contents is to right-click in a cell and use the context menu. Be sure to check the vertical and horizontal alignment settings because they can be the solution when text doesn't line up properly. There is interaction between the alignment tabs for the text (in the toolbar) and the settings in the cells and table properties.

FRAMES

If you were to use a table to divide the contents of a Web page into three sections, you would be, in fact, dividing one Web page into three actual parts. This is not so with frames: If you look at a Web page that uses three frames to divide what you see into three parts, you are really looking at three separate Web pages (see Figure 17.3). The premise behind frame technology is a simple one: It's a way to keep important elements in place, such as a navigation bar or a banner ad, while the user of a Web site clicks various links and sees the results load up in one main viewing frame only.

Figure 17.3
Using frames for quick and easy navigation. This site is actually three separate Web pages. HotBot is a registered service mark of Wired Ventures, Inc., a subsidiary of Lycos, Inc. All rights reserved.

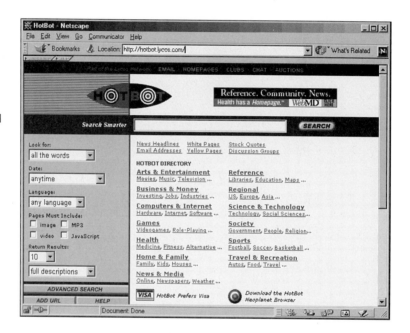

The catch—and it's a big one—is that frame technology is troublesome. Users with some earlier version browsers cannot view a Web page that uses frames at all. A frames-based Web page cannot be printed because it's not actually one page, and several other technologies cannot be combined with frames (certain JavaScripts, for example) without messing up the Web page layout if the users return to or reload it. For these reasons, both designers and users dislike using frames if any alternative is available. If your Web site plan is dependent upon frames, however, you do have a few options for making your Web site much more user-friendly. You can create a splash page that warns users about the frames in your Web page, and/or you can create a nonframes-based alternative page. These solutions are the most common workarounds for the problems created by frames.

If frames are not displayed properly in a browser, or if only part of a framed Web site is printed when you click the Print button, see "Printing Issues with Framed Web Sites" in the "Troubleshooting" section at the end of the chapter.

ANIMATED CONTENT

Largely two kinds of animated content are used for Web pages these days: the trusty GIF animation and the more advanced type of animation created with a utility such as Macromedia Flash. If you've ever seen a banner ad then you've seen a GIF animation; it is a series of individual GIF images played in a certain order with a certain time delay set between frames. This type of animation is most dependable and easy to use because a browser recognizes it as a GIF file, the original image file format that's been built into HTML ever since the beginning. Figure 17.4 shows a sample GIF-based banner ad.

Figure 17.4
Most banner ads are GIF animations.

Banner ads —

By using simple shareware products such GIF Builder, along with a series of individual GIFs you create and provide, you can easily create a GIF animation. If you're interested in a more sophisticated look that takes a little more expertise, a product such as Flash can make beautiful larger animations with great impact (see Figure 17.5).

The catch with Flash animations is that they require the Flash plug-in to run properly. As you learned earlier, a *plug-in* is a small software utility that gives your browser a helping hand with animations and multimedia, for example, that can't run on HTML alone. Typically, users download or install a whole variety of plug-ins when they add new browsers to their computers, but this has been the case only with the past two or three versions of the popular browsers (versions 3, 4, and 5 of Navigator and Explorer). So, it's still a good idea to treat plug-ins like I recommend you treat frames: Put a short description of technologies used in your Web site on the splash page, and/or provide a low-tech alternative to folks who don't want to download a plug-in.

Figure 17.5
Flash animations are bigger, bolder, and better than GIF animations.

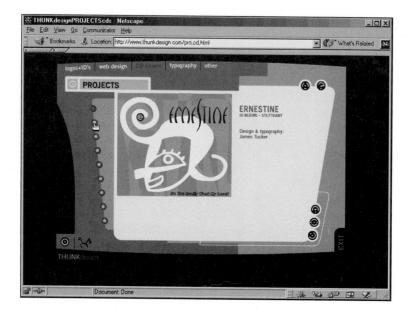

Using animations is still the fastest and most user-friendly way to add motion and interest to your Web pages because most Web page surfers use a regular modem. However, there are plenty of reasons to include sound or video in your Web pages, and some in-between technologies such as QuickTime provide you with the capability to create animations, sound files, and video clips with the same tools. So let's take a look at those tools next.

SOUND AND VIDEO

You'll encounter these three challenges with adding sound and video to a Web site:

- Knowing that your viewership will have fast enough Web access to avoid annoying them with the relatively choppy or slow downloads
- Gathering the right tools for the job
- Creating interesting content

Although it's true that the speed at which the average Web surfer is using to connect to the Internet is fairly slow, that problem will soon be a thing of the past. Although compression technology for sound and video files is ever improving, more tools for streaming Web-based audio and video files are hitting the streets every day.

If you intend to post standard video (for example, AVI and MPG) files on your site, think carefully. These files are large, and you will lose viewers unless they are very motivated and really want your video clip. The same is true of audio, although these files are smaller. The now popular MP3 standard for Web-based music dissemination has clearly demonstrated that Web surfers are willing to download files of this size for later listening. But building them into your page is another story. Whatever you do, make sure the page doesn't sit dead in the water until a large file loads into it because users on the Web are unwilling to wait 10 or 15 minutes (optimistically) for a Web page to come into view.

One way to ensure that your page doesn't just sit there is to use *streaming* media rather than static media. Streaming media loads the beginning of the file into the browser quickly and starts playing it. Static media requires the entire sound or video clip to download before playing commences. If you've used the Real Media player to watch or hear news over the Web, you've been on the receiving end of streaming media.

Recent technology from Microsoft called Windows Media and rival products from Real Networks and others are now making it possible to weave together interactive sites consisting of streaming video, audio, Flash animations, and other additions such as PowerPoint presentations into a single, coherent Web page. Microsoft is so bullish on this idea that it is giving away a whole suite of production tools for free. If you're looking for a way to disseminate your presentations over the Web, this is it.

PART
III

CH
17

I've seen sites using Windows Media, and the results are quite impressive. In a few years, when a significant portion of the computer populace has shifted to high-bandwidth Internet connections, streaming media will be taken for granted, and sites with only cartoon-like Flash or animated GIF will look as old as static text-based pages do today. If you want to deliver sound or video clips, using streaming media is the way to go. You'll need to ensure that your server supports it, and realize that your viewers may have to download a viewer such as Real Player or QuickTime viewer to see or hear your clip. If they are running Windows 9x or Windows 2000, your viewers will already have the Windows Media Player, which can play several popular streaming formats, including those created with the Microsoft tools, so you needn't worry there.

Right now, if a Web site has sound or video files on it, most likely they are links for downloading the files themselves. But more and more sites now integrate streaming media. Check out the Radio toolbar in Internet Explorer, for example, and click around on a few of the pages that present live streaming radio programs. It is possible to create an elegant, useful site with this strategy. If you want to create a biography of a movie star or famous entertainer, as in Figure 17.6, using a series of links to audio and video files can be a very good idea.

Static audio files present much the same problem as video, though less so. It's a nice idea to have a background soundtrack or sound effects to bring your Web pages to life, but the size of even a two- or three-second sound file can be prohibitive, especially if you don't use a streaming media format. Plan on using sound files judiciously, and don't depend on sound to make or break the overall impact of your Web page site design.

Figure 17.6
Video clips used to
their best advantage.

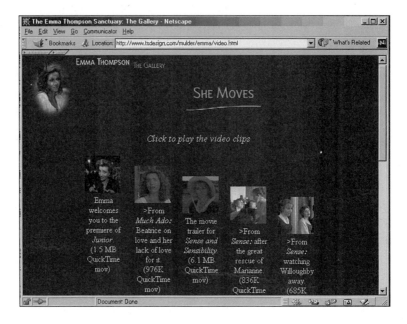

Tip #213

If you must have sound associated with your page, you can use MIDI files, which load more quickly. Check the Page properties settings, and set your "background sound" to a MIDI file. MIDI files are small and load quickly into a receiver's browser. You can't control the quality of the sounds as much because MIDI files essentially "play" the synthesizer built into the recipient's computer. On most computers, MIDI files sound pretty cheesy. You can set a MIDI file to play once or (annoyingly) loop forever. If you do include a MIDI file with your page, give the viewer a button for turning it off.

SCRIPTS

A script, generally speaking, is a bit of code inserted into HTML that allows the browser to display something HTML alone would not let it do. The most popular type of scripting in Web pages these days is JavaScript (which has no relationship to Java), and JavaScript is truly a godsend to Web page designers.

The sample Web page in Figure 17.7 illustrates a *rollover*, which is a JavaScript that transforms an area in a Web page when the mouse cursor rolls over it. *Mouseovers*, as they are popularly called, can trigger or pause a short animation; they also can substitute one graphic for another, thereby creating a color change or drop shadow; and they can perform many other interesting tricks. The two primary drawbacks to using scripted elements in a Web page are browser support and difficulty of execution.

Figure 17.7
JavaScript rollovers, among other cool effects. In this example, the image shading changes to blue when the mouse cursor is placed over it.

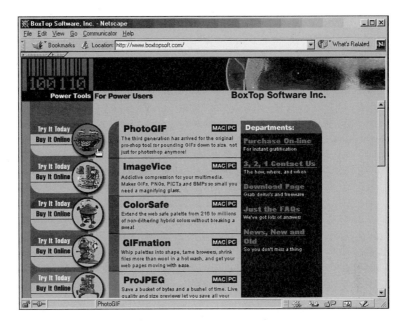

JavaScript is not supported by some earlier version browsers, so you're still leaving that 25 to 30 percent of your Web audience in the dust if you include scripted elements in your Web site. Also, JavaScript is not as simple to learn or edit as HTML; it is most like a true programming computer language and therefore very frustrating to learn. A software program such as FrontPage doesn't really allow you to modify or edit scripts, either; it can only drop them in after you've already finished your editing. So, if you want to do something in your Web page design that requires scripting, you should definitely hire a professional Web site designer to, at minimum, create the scripts for you.

THE CUTTING EDGE

Now let's take a look at the real cutting-edge stuff that has just arrived or is just around the corner: style sheets, embedded fonts, and the tantalizing prospects of XML and SGL. I'll show you real-world examples when and where I can, but sometimes it isn't possible. Some of these technologies are not quite supported yet (XML and SGL), and some are supported unreliably (cascading style sheets). What groups these technologies all together here is their usefulness; I'll explain the pros and cons as I go.

CASCADING STYLE SHEETS

Way back when the Web was created, the founders who were creating HTML didn't much care about the appearance of the information they were trying to send as long as it was readable. So (just as an example) they essentially wrote browser instructions that declared, "All text on a Web page will be this size in this font, all margins will be this wide, and that's that, end of story." Nowadays, some 10 years later, Web page designers have been tearing out their hair trying to get around these instructions so that they can have a little more choice and control.

Enter the idea of style sheets, which provide a way to override HTML's basic instructions about how elements will appear on a Web page without your having to write lots of HTML code. You can use style sheets to quickly and easily determine what every type of text on your Web page will look like, from headers to lists to plain text. You can use style sheets to turn off the underlining beneath your hyperlinks or make a link change color when you roll the mouse cursor over it. Also—and perhaps most important—you can position each image, link, and bit of text as freely as elements in a collage, making anything you like transparent or layered or even overlapped. In essence, style sheets give you complete control over the appearance and layout of your Web page.

What's the catch? Style sheets are not quite fully supported by the newest version 5 browsers of Navigator and Explorer, they're only marginally supported by version 4 browsers, and they are not at all supported by version 3 browsers or earlier. When they work, they work beautifully; but when they don't, your Web pages look terrible. So, most Web page designers do not rely on style sheets for anything essential; they try to create two sets of instructions in the same HTML document that they hope do not conflict. This is difficult, time-consuming, and too much of a headache for inexperienced Web page designers to work with—yet.

For more information on style sheets, check out the following links:

`http://www.webmonkey.com` for tutorials on style sheets

`http://www.w3c.com` for the official specifications

EMBEDDED FONTS

Suppose you've created a beautiful Web site design that depends on a specific font such as Desdemona. You can name Desdemona as the font that the browser is supposed to use, but the browser can use Desdemona only if the person visiting your Web page has that font installed on his or her computer. What happens if he or she doesn't? The browser will make a substitution, and that will ruin the look of your Web site.

Up until very recently, you had only two choices. One, you could create large GIFs containing all your text in Desdemona, which would make your Web page very large and long to download. Or two, you could bite the bullet and design around Navigator's and Explorer's default fonts. But now that embedded fonts are available, you can, in theory, create a "recipe" for your browser to follow, including the fonts themselves, which a browser will download and use for reference when displaying your Web page.

The theory part of this great new technology is that Navigator and Explorer use two different methods to embed fonts. They both depend on the style sheets method for writing instructions, but they work so differently it's just about impossible to make them work together in the same Web page. Microsoft's embedded fonts tool, WEFT (which it created in partnership with Adobe Systems), is in beta at this writing, so it doesn't quite have all the kinks worked out of it yet. Netscape, by contrast, has teamed up with Bitstream Technology, but Netscape has decided not to develop the technology itself. So again, Web designers are waiting for third-party software developers to make Bitstream's embedded font technology into something useful. In the end, however, you will still have two ways to use embedded fonts that will inevitably result in problems.

→ To learn more details about fonts and about embedded fonts in other kinds of documents, **see** "Embedding Fonts in Documents," **p. 375**.

For more information on embedded fonts in Web pages, check out the following links:

`http://www.webmonkey.com` for tutorials on style sheets and embedded fonts technology

`http://www.webreview.com` for more details on embedded fonts

`http://www.bitstream.com` for the official specifications on the Netscape side

`http://www.microsoft.com/typography/web/embedding/weft` for the official specs on the Explorer side

PART

III

CH

17

XML AND SVG

Now imagine that you are creating a Web site, and it contains an extensive catalog of hardware products. To make all the product pages in the catalog look the same, you must type (or cut and paste) the same formatting instructions over and over again. Wouldn't it be easier if you could somehow create your own customized tags, such as `<ITEM>` or `<PRICE>`, instead? Well, now you can, with Extensible Markup Language (XML). XML enables you to create all-new, completely customized tags that you can specify to do whatever you want them to do. You can make `<ITEM>` render every single hardware product on your Web site in a specific size, color, font, and style, and all you have to do is repeat the tag—not all the individual instructions. XML can also make the contents of your Web page more easily recognizable to search engines. Right now, Web designers and search engine bots largely depend on the `<META>` tag for specifying keywords. XML will make that type of hit-and-miss identification obsolete; it will greatly expand the accessibility of your Web page content, and it will improve the searching capability of search engines. So, your Web page will be easier to find, and it will be easier for you yourself to find what you're looking for when using a search engine.

Now imagine that you want to include drawings of all your hardware products in this online catalog. With current Web page technology, you would have to draw or scan in photos of every single item and upload them as GIFs or JPGs. But with Scalable Vector Graphics (SVG), you can make the browser do the drawing for you. SVG is like a whole new set of instructions that can render an image according to the specific guidelines you establish, just as HTML can render, color, and size plain text. These drawings can be as complex and intricate as anything Adobe Illustrator or any other vector-based graphics program can create, too. Additionally, though, SVG can render drop shadows and other gradients, simple animations, and filter effects—the kinds of effects you must use certain plug-ins and GIF animations to produce right now. So the main benefits here are functionality and download time. Imagine never having to wait for an image file to download because the drawing itself is efficiently embedded in the page code. The main drawback, however, is that SVG is part of XML, so you probably know where this discussion is leading.

Unfortunately, I'm covering XML and SVG at the end of this section because they are the least supported and furthest off of all the advanced Web page technologies I've included. There's a great deal of talk surrounding these two subjects (XML in particular) and a great deal to read about if you want a glimpse of that particular part of the future. But as of this writing, only Explorer 5 offers partial support for XML; Navigator 5 will not, and none of the earlier versions of these browsers offer any type of support. So, I'm talking about the future of Web page design, albeit not the far-off future.

For more information on embedded fonts, check out the following links:

`http://www.webmonkey.com` for tutorials on XML and SVG

`http://www.w3c.org` for the official specs on XML

`http://www.xml.com` for high-end development-oriented information on XML

Now let's cover a different kind of Web page content: elements in a Web page that sells products online.

SELLING ONLINE

A commerce site is one of the most ambitious and complex types of Web sites you can create. In addition to using Web pages that may or may not contain all the features and technologies already covered, a commerce site also includes a database, forms, and authorizations (for credit cards and passwords at least). In short, creating this type of Web site is not for the faint of heart, the newcomer, or even the person or company with a brief window of time. The following sections describe the basics of each area I've mentioned.

DATABASES

The idea of a commerce site sounds dazzlingly simple up front: It's like combining the best of television ads and catalogs into one single place to purchase. And this is absolutely true. On a commerce site, you can offer options and features to your customers that you can't give them in a 30-second television spot or on a printed catalog page. Figure 17.8 shows a sample commerce site.

Now just sit back a moment and think about what's required here. You'll want your Web site to keep up-to-the-minute records on what's available. You'll need it to know every size, color, variety, and type of product that's ready to ship, including returns, overstocks, discontinued items, or even sale items. You'll need it to calculate costs, tax, and shipping and handling charges for people all over the planet. And most of all, you'll need it to be easy to use.

A *database* is what you must keep track of what you have and what you don't have. A commerce site database is fundamentally no different than a regular database you might create in Access. However, an online database must calculate changes every minute, adding and deducting items and money all the time, 24 hours a day. Therefore, it must be active all the time, so you must make plans to keep your database on its own server that's outfitted to do exactly what the database needs it to do.

Figure 17.8
Mix and match products, read all the details, order with a credit card: the optimal commerce site experience.

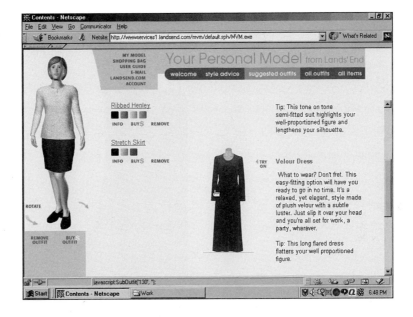

How does a database juggle all the data it must send and receive? It uses forms, so let's take a closer look at forms.

FORMS

A *form* is actually a type of element on a Web page; it's not simply a text field or list of radio button options to choose from. It is, first of all, whatever type of form field you see on the Web page; I just described two of the most popular ones, a text field and a list of buttons. But it is also a script that collects and relays whatever information is put into the form field. So, when you use forms, you must design and organize not just how all the form fields look on your Web page, but you also must write the code that translates form field information into something useful for you, such as an online purchase order, email, or a database entry. This task can be, in a nutshell, quite tricky.

FrontPage and other WYSIWYG editors make it easy to pick the type of form field you want and to position it on the Web page. However, it is not possible in any type of Web page design software to do much resizing or editing of forms. You can determine the length of a text box or the dimensions of a text box, but you cannot change the background or text color of what appears in that box, for example. WYSIWYG editors also do not help you create the scripts that process form information, and learning this skill quickly is really not possible. So, if you're building a commerce site with a shopping cart or ordering page, you should be able to create the page itself but might consider hiring a professional to write the scripts you need.

One alternative is to look around the Web for premade scripts that perform basic, oft-needed operations. Often they are written in Perl or CGI and are available for the taking. For example, I just put together a site that takes online registrations for an annual conference I sponsor. Potential registrants fill out about 20 fields such as name and address. To translate the fields into a piece of email sent to a registration company that handles the details of housing and conference fees, I used a free, canned script found on the Web. When a person fills in the form and clicks the Submit button, an email is generated with all the supplied information and is sent out to three email addresses I prespecified.

You might want to check out this well-known site, where you can find such premade scripts:

`http://www.worldwidemart.com/scripts/`

The third component of a commerce site is ordering, so let's look at authorizations.

AUTHORIZATIONS: PAYMENTS AND PASSWORDS

If you're taking the time to build a Web site to sell your products then you obviously want to make it easy for people to use your Web site. At this writing, it is easiest for people to use credit cards to pay for their purchases, to receive order confirmations, and to have some sort of identification on the site the next time they return to order again. All three of these functionalities are some form of authorization, or recognition of unique and private information that the users give to you by way of your Web site. To facilitate authorizations, you still need a database, forms, and scripting, but you also need security.

A database that is set up to process authorizations can store and recognize user IDs and passwords, accept and process several varieties of credit cards, produce and remember order confirmations, and work with different ways to safeguard online transactions. You can set up your Web site to work with *cookies*, which are small bits of important, distinct identifying information kept on a user's computer until your Web site requests it. Cookies can also be used to remember a users' track records at your site: what they purchased (and perhaps therefore what they will purchase again), how much they spent, which credit cards they used, and the previous Web sites they visited.

Tip #214

As discussed in Chapter 12, "World Wide Web," cookies can be turned off by users who feel that they are an invasion of privacy, so they cannot be entirely reliable as a means of tracking your site's users.

Developing this type of database and Web site is far outside the realm of part-time or spare-time site design, as is the job of keeping such a site current and functional. So, you definitely should hire a professional to create and maintain a commerce site that makes use of authorizations. I keep repeating myself because this bit of advice is so important. In the long run, you really want to spend your time doing your own job, or you want your colleagues or employees to do their jobs rather than feel consumed and overwhelmed by problems with a Web site.

Now that you've read about the important areas of Web site development, let's look at ways to publish and then to market your Web site.

MARKETING AND PUBLISHING YOUR WEB SITE

After you've created your wonderful Web site, you want to upload it to the Web to see it in action, and you want to spread the word that it's available. So, first I'll cover how to choose a service provider, then I'll help you explore FrontPage Express's publishing tools, and finally I'll talk a little bit more about how you can market and advertise your Web site.

CHOOSING A SERVICE PROVIDER

If you're creating a personal Web page, you'll have to find your own service provider unless you're a student at a university (colleges and universities typically offer services to students and faculty) or you work for a company with server space you can borrow. If you're creating a corporate or commerce Web site, you'll definitely need to find a service provider, and you'll have some special concerns to inquire about. So let's look at the basic factors you should keep in mind while you do your search.

COST AND SERVICES PROVIDED

You definitely want to know how much a service provider charges by the month and how much installation costs. You also must ask whether you must buy your own modem (though most newer computers come with internal modems already installed) or other hardware, especially if you want a super-fast connection, such as DSL or cable modem.

It's imperative that you know what you're paying for, so you might ask the provider these questions:

- How much space do I get for my Web site on the server? (I recommend a minimum of 10MB for personal sites and 20MB for corporate or commerce sites with a provider who can give you room to grow.)

- Do you have local access numbers or a toll-free access number? If I have to dial up using long distance, do I have to pay any additional charge?

- Is technical support or customer service available, and when?

- Do you supply a Web-based "control panel" for making changes to my account, such as script handling, changing the type of server (UNIX or NT), adding new domains, adding transaction capability, or adding streaming media?

- Do I also get email, or is email additional? (At a minimum, having email support can be a good idea so users have an address to write to if problems occur with the Web site; you need not necessarily use the service provider's account for your personal or business mail.)

You should also ask whether restrictions or different rates apply for corporate or commerce sites because traffic to such sites is typically much heavier. Some service providers pull the plug on your site if you use it to sell products and don't tell them. Other service providers are picky about the type of content you put on your Web site; be sure to read all the fine print in your user agreement with regards to censorship issues in case you have potentially sensitive content to upload.

TECHNICAL CONSIDERATIONS

At this writing, there's no reason why your service provider should not have fast connections to the Internet, backup servers in case of network failure, and full support for scripts. You should also have no trouble finding a service provider that can give you full security. You should ask for one of the more common security protocols, such as Secure Socket Layer (SSL) or Pretty Good Protection (PGP), though you'll have to pay more. Investigating Web site development and hosting through CyberCash or CheckFree might be worthwhile if you're going to rely on heavy credit card use. But don't be put off by the increased monthly charge for these services. Public anxiety about using credit cards on the Internet is a very real concern, and a significant number of potential customers will not buy something from your site if it's not secure.

Note

It is possible to build a database that will remember a customer's credit or debit card numbers as part of a user ID or customer account. However, if you want to add this functionality, you should make it optional. Many consumers want total control over their credit and debit cards, so give them their choice.

DOMAIN HOSTING

If you're creating a corporate or commerce site, or if you're creating a personal Web site to serve as a sort of resume for yourself, you might want your own domain name. If you spring for your own domain name, you'll pay a registration fee with InterNIC (though its monopoly on this service is coming to an end), the company that keeps track of domain names, but you'll never have to change URLs or even email addresses if you move from server to server. So, ask service providers whether they support domain hosting, and see what their terms and conditions are.

Caution

Be very careful when considering offers or deals from domain name registration services other than Network Solutions (formerly known as InterNIC). For the majority of the life of the Web, InterNIC had the monopoly on this kind of service, so other similar businesses are working hard to attract customers. Make sure their customer service and reliability are what you expect before you make your final decision.

For more information on all these hosting/service provider topics, check out the following links:

> `http://www.verisign.com` for general information about secure transactions and server hosting
>
> `http://www.cybercash.com` for information on taking credit card numbers on the Web
>
> `http://www.checkfree.com` for information on online payments
>
> `http://www.networksolutions.com` for domain name verification and hosting
>
> `http://www.pgp.com` and `http://www.ssl.com` for online security

PUBLISHING WITH FRONTPAGE

Publishing your Web site with FrontPage Express is easy if you already have an account with a service provider. To use the Web Publishing Wizard, follow these steps:

1. Select the file or folder you want to publish on the Web. (It's best to keep all your Web site pages, images, and other files in the same folder if you want to keep things simple; though, for complex sites, you should break them down into separate directories to help you better organize.)

2. Right-click the file or folder, and choose Send To, Web Publishing Wizard.

3. When the Web Publishing Wizard opens, read the introductory stuff, and click Next to get started.

4. Give the name of the Web server you're connecting to. This name is for your own benefit when you upload new or updated pages in the future, so it can be whatever you like. Click Next.

5. Type the URL of your Web site in the top box and the path to the folder or file you're uploading in the lower box. Click Next.

6. Type the URL again, and click Next.

7. Select the type of connection you're using: A LAN is any sort of networked connection such as a T1, DSL, or ISDN line or cable modem, whereas a dial-up connection is any type of regular modem that requires you to dial a number before you can connect to the Internet. Click Next.

   The computer then verifies that you have the proper FrontPage publishing extension, that the files are located where you said they were, and that a connection to your provider can be established.

8. Click Finish to publish your Web pages.

Tip #215

> You will no doubt have the experience of links on your pages failing to work properly, even when they point to your own pages, pictures, or whatever. Learning to debug your own page's links and understand where your files are on a server's site takes some time and experience. Don't give up. At first, it's confusing because the page may look fine in FrontPage Express yet not work from the Web server when opened in Internet Explorer. Or it might work fine in your copy of Internet Explorer, but on someone else's computer, it doesn't. Often the problem is that the images are in your computer on the hard disk, so FrontPage or Internet Explorer finds them there and loads them. You think your page is all finished until your clients can't see a thing except text. For starters, remember this one basic rule: Hover the mouse cursor over or click on a link on your published page. Look in the status line of the browser window or in the address line of the browser to see where the link is pointing. If it is pointing to anything on your hard disk (for example, C:\my Web page\picture.jpg) then you goofed. You didn't specify the correct *Web-based address* in the link; instead, you gave it the local address. The URL should be (in a simple site where everything is in one direction on the server) simply picture.jpg. Then it will load from the same directory in which the main Web page (typically called Index.html) is stored on the Web server.

MARKETING YOUR WEB SITE

If you pay attention to television and radio ads, to billboards, even to magazine and newspaper articles, you'll see URLs advertised everywhere. If you're debuting a commerce or corporate Web site, it's obviously good marketing to plaster your URL all over your usual marketing and promotional materials. But how do you advertise on the Web? Here's a short list of ideas:

- Consider joining a Web ring. If your Web site is personal or extracurricular, look into becoming part of a Web ring, or a group of Web sites all hyperlinked together. Doing so is a great way to associate yourself with other sites containing similar or complementary content to what's on your Web site. Instructions and conditions for joining vary depending on the category your site falls into.

- Create and distribute banner ads. If your Web site is corporate or commerce-oriented, you can advertise yourself on news or magazine sites, on search engines, or on any sort of other commercial site you can think of. Look into regional or local Web sites, such as those of your city's newspaper or magazine, or take it all the way to CNNOnline.

- List your site on search engines. Pay absolutely no attention to those services that promise to list your site in 1,000 places for $49.95; making your Web site search-engine friendly is a simple matter of inserting the <META> tag. If you look at the source or HTML code for your Web page, insert the <META> tag inside the <HEAD> tag and provide a list of keywords. These keywords should mirror whatever someone would type into a search engine to look for Web sites like yours. So, for example, if you sell pet supplies, some of your <META> tag keywords might be cats, dogs, birds, and even pet food (phrases are acceptable), all separated with commas. Then register your site with the top five search engines and indexes: Lycos, HotBot, AltaVista, Yahoo! and Excite. You'll reach the largest audience this way for the smallest amount of effort.

For more information, check out these Web sites:

`http://www.webring.com` for more information on Web rings

`http://www.lycos.com` for information on registering your site with Lycos

`http://www.hotbot.com` for information on registering your site with HotBot

`http://www.altavista.com` for information on registering your site with AltaVista

`http://www.yahoo.com` for information on registering your site with Yahoo!

`http://www.excite.com` for information on registering your site with Excite

Tip #216

Remember that there's a fundamental difference between a search engine (such as Lycos) and an index (such as Yahoo!). Someone who looks for a Web site using a search engine is searching, in theory, the entire Web, whereas someone using an index is searching only the limited list of Web sites that the index contains. This difference should definitely affect the way that Web surfers find your site; you should monitor the location of your Web site in an index to make sure it's listed in the proper category, and you should run test keyword searches on a search engine to make sure your Web site comes up.

You should be aware that the big search engines penalize sites that submit their pages too many times. Also, if people claim to know the tricks of given search engines, they have their work cut out for them. The better search engines change their rules all the time, to prevent Web site programmers and advertisers from faking them out, or "jamming" the engine. Keeping current with the major search engines is a job that can take some time and expertise.

TROUBLESHOOTING

SPECIAL CONSIDERATIONS FOR DESIGNING AN INTRANET

What kinds of things should I consider when building an intranet as opposed to an Internet Web site?

If you're designing an intranet—that is, you know your audience is going to be a finite number of people who are all likely using the same platform, system software, and browser—you must pay attention to the particular difficulties or challenges that come with designing for that specific audience. Although it's true that you will dramatically reduce the number of errors that crop up in Web page design because of platform, browser, and browser version differences, no one combination of these influences is trouble free. If you are using advanced Web page technologies such as style sheets and DHTML, particularly, you are going to run into support issues in which certain options work only on the Macintosh *or* the PC, or in Navigator *or* Explorer. So, be sure to build plenty of testing and redevelopment time into your intranet design schedule. You'll have fewer headaches to contend with than if you were designing a public site, but you'll still have a few.

BROWSER DISPLAY DIFFERENCES

I'm looking at the same Web page on Navigator and on Explorer. Why do they look different?

The very same Web page will look drastically different in Navigator versus the way it appears in Explorer for two main reasons. Neither of them is the result of error in your design, nor can they be "fixed" with HTML or other related code. You can only learn to design and otherwise work around them as already mentioned earlier in the chapter.

The first big difference in Web page display has to do with fundamental sizing. To put it briefly, everything on a Web page appears one-third larger than it does on the Macintosh: text, links, margins, padding, borders, table cells, everything. Only images remain the exact size you specify; everything else around them will look dramatically different. You can get around this difference only by designing for the middle of the road—by choosing font sizes, margins, and everything else after lots and lots of testing on both platforms—or by designing two completely different versions of your Web site. This solution is just as difficult and time-consuming as it sounds, too, which is yet another compelling reason to hire a professional and let someone else deal with the problem.

The second primary difference has to do with the way a page is viewed in Netscape Navigator versus the way it appears in Microsoft Internet Explorer: the left margin offset. In IE, a series of thumbtab navigational elements runs down the left side of the browser window, so IE scoots the entire Web site over to the right to compensate. You should always test the width of "readable" space on your Web page to make sure nothing runs off the right edge. Also, test pages with vertical designs or colored fields because the space behind the tabs might not contain this design or color, and your whole visual presentation might look funny.

The good news is that the third primary difference—color—is very nearly no longer an issue. Back in the early days of the Web, most Web users had 256-color monitors, so Web sites and Web site designs were restricted to a limited palette of 216 "safe" colors. That is, Windows and MacOS shared 216 colors in common in relationship with the monitor display. Nowadays, though, fewer than 10 percent of people on the Web are viewing Web pages with this kind of monitor, and all the new monitors on the shelves for new users display in the now-common millions of colors.

PRINTING ISSUES WITH FRAMED WEB SITES

When users try to print from a Web site with frames, only part of the site actually prints.

Web sites that use frames actually are made up of separate HTML documents—one for each frame in the site. To print a framed site, users must position the mouse pointer in the frame containing the information they want to print, click to activate it, and then issue a print command. Most sites have one frame dedicated to the content of the site, so clicking that area is a prerequisite to printing the content. As long as you don't mind that users can't easily print all the frames at once (which can be okay because, most likely, a secondary frame contains link buttons, ads, banners, and so forth) along with the site content, you'll be okay.

Remember, however, that not all browsers can display frames, and frames do confuse people because the Back and Forward buttons on browsers don't work consistently with framed pages, often requiring the use of the right-click context menu to navigate. For widest compatibility with browsers, I suggest you design your pages without using frames. You can still create a framed look that contains a left margin with buttons and a menu bar across the top, without actually using frames. You can find plenty of examples on the Web to look at, if you do a little cruising.

If you must use frames, be sure that the essential meat of each page is contained in a single window so that viewers can print out the important material.

TIPS FROM THE WINDOWS PROS: RUNNING MULTIPLE VERSIONS OF INTERNET EXPLORER ON ONE COMPUTER

All Web page designers—and the companies they design for—should be testing Web sites on as many possible versions of Netscape Navigator and Microsoft Internet Explorer as possible. It's easy to facilitate this kind of testing with Navigator; you can easily install and use all the different versions of Navigator on one computer. However, you cannot do this with all the different versions of Internet Explorer. Explorer is designed to install over the previous version and update certain Registry information so that if you attempt to keep two versions of IE on one machine—even if you store different versions on different zip disks or other large-storage media—you can still use only the more recent version. This is an increasingly difficult and urgent problem to resolve as IE steadily edges out Navigator as the public's browser of choice. So what do you do? Do you buy four different PCs to house the last four versions of IE?

An alternative solution is easy to utilize if you're handy with hardware. You can add a *disk tray* (also sometimes called a *disk cage*) to your PC that will enable you to have several versions of Explorer on one computer. A disk tray enables you to use numerous and removable hard drives. The tray itself is an open slot on the front of your PC, and the tray cartridges each hold one hard drive. You then insert, remove, and interchange the tray cartridges just as you insert, remove, and interchange floppy or zip disks. There is no interference with the Registry, so you can put one version of Explorer on each cartridge safely and reliably. Best of all, the tray/cage and hard drive casings each cost much less than $100, so the hard drives themselves are the most expensive part of this solution.

The other advantage to using disk trays is being able to comfortably use beta-version browsers without risking the welfare of your other software. You can designate one hard drive as your "beta" drive and use it only for beta or prerelease software. The rest of your software and your files can safely live on an entirely separate hard drive, and you need not worry.

CHAPTER 18

USING INTERNET INFORMATION SERVICES TO HOST A WEB SITE

In this chapter

OVERVIEW OF INTERNET INFORMATION SERVICES

Internet Information Services (IIS) is a collection of programs that make up Microsoft's industrial-strength IIS Web server platform. It's included for free as part of Windows 2000. Besides the basic Web (HTTP) server, add-ons include a File Transfer Protocol (FTP) server, an Indexing Service for site content searching, FrontPage and Visual InterDev publishing extensions, the ASP script processor, support for sophisticated multitier online transaction services, and a Simple Mail Transfer Protocol (SMTP) mail delivery server. In short, IIS is the Mother of All Web Servers.

Caution

If you are part of a corporate network, before you go any further, check with your network administrators because policies may prohibit you from setting up a Web site on your own. Many legitimate security concerns are involved, and in some companies, you could be fired for violating established security policies. Check first if you're not sure what's permitted.

WHAT DOES A WEB SERVER DO?

You're probably familiar by now with using a Web browser to view documents over the World Wide Web (WWW or Web), but you might not have seen what happens on the other side, from the server's point of view. We'll take you on a brief tour here. (If you already are familiar with the function of Web servers, you can skip on down to "Reviewing Components of IIS.")

In the most basic sense, a Web server works like a call desk librarian: When you request a book by name, the librarian looks up the book's location, fetches the desired tome, passes it across the counter, and goes on to the next patron as quickly as possible. If the desired book is not in the shelves, the librarian will say so and again go on to the next client. The interactions are brief and involve no interpretation of the content—that is, the content of the book—passing back and forth.

The roles of a Web server and Web browser are very similar. A Web browser sends a short request message to a Web server. The request is a text string, mostly just the Uniform Resource Locator (URL), which you type in or click. The server turns this virtual name into a real or physical filename and passes the appropriate HTML, image, or other type of file back across the Internet. When the URL refers to an executable program or a script file, instead of returning the file itself, a Web server runs the program and passes back whatever the program generates as its response.

Let's follow one of these request-and-response interactions through from beginning to end. It's simple, but each step can have variations, which will give us plenty to talk about later.

If you bring up your Web browser and type the URL http://www.mcp.com/index.html, the following sequence of events takes place:

1. Your Web browser looks up the computer name www.mcp.com, which turns out to have the IP address 198.70.146.70.

2. The browser sends a request to this IP address, consisting of a short string like this:
   GET /index.html HTTP/1.0

   This string says that the browser wants to get or read the file named /index.html, using the standard Web protocol, version 1.0.

   The Web server running at Macmillan Computer Publishing translates the *virtual* filename /index.html into a *physical* filename, which might be something like c:\inetpub\wwwroot\index.html. This is the file that the server will send back.

3. The Web server sends back a response, which has two parts: a descriptive header, followed by content. It might look something like what is shown in Figure 18.1.

Figure 18.1
A typical request and server response might look something like this.

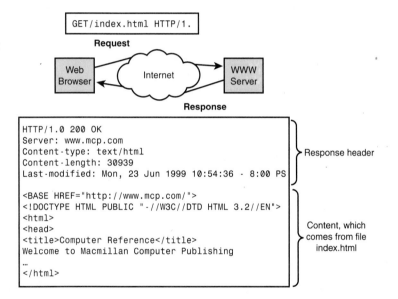

The response header tells the browser what to expect of the following content. The Content-type entry tells what format it's in so that it can be displayed appropriately: Is it plain text? an HTML file? a GIF image? a sound clip? Other fields tell the browser how and when it can keep a *cached* copy of the content so that at a future visit to the same Web site it can decide whether it needs to download the same information again.

In this case, your Web browser interprets and displays the HTML text it received and repeats the process to retrieve any image files listed in this HTML document.

This process is really pretty simple, but a few tricky variations can come into play.

A FOLDER BY ANY OTHER NAME IS...A VIRTUAL FOLDER

The translation of the URL filename into a physical filename is generally straightforward. When you set up your Web site, you specify which directory contains the documents that you want to publish. The Web site has a *home directory*, which is the starting point for the translation of URL names into filenames. For example, if the home directory is c:\inetpub\wwwroot, then the URL filename

```
/index.html
```

returns file

```
c:\inetpub\wwwroot\index.html
```

Any file or folder inside this home directory is available to Web browsers, as shown in Figure 18.2.

Figure 18.2
URLs refer to files and folders within the Web server's home directory. Virtual directories let other folders appear to be a part of this structure.

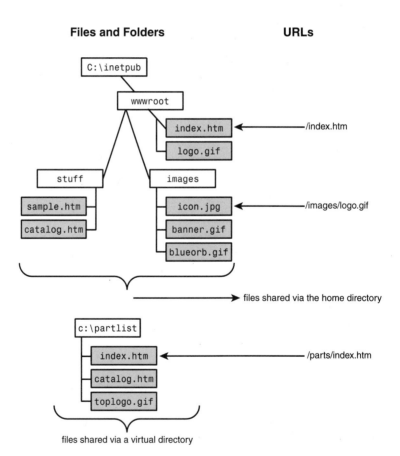

For example, the URL for the file

```
c:\inetpub\wwwroot\sales\catalog.html
```

would be

```
/sales/catalog.html
```

You can also add other folders from your computer to this mapping, even if they aren't inside the one home directory. They are called *virtual directories* because they appear to be part of and inside the home directory, but they aren't physically. You could instruct IIS to share folder c:\partlist with the virtual URL name of /parts, so that the URL

```
/parts/index.html
```

would return file

```
c:\partlist\bullet.gif
```

When IIS is installed, adding a folder to your Web site is a piece of cake: This process is integrated right into Explorer and is just a right-click away.

DEFAULT DOCUMENTS—WHEN "NOTHING" JUST ISN'T ENOUGH

A *home page* is a URL with no filename. So what does an empty or home page URL map to? For example, what file does www.mcp.com refer to? You might guess that it corresponds to just the name of the home directory:

```
c:\inetpub\wwwroot
```

Indeed, it does, and in this case a Web server looks for a *default document*. When a URL names only a folder and not a full filename, IIS looks first for a script file named default.asp. Failing that, default.html or default.htm will do.

If no default document can be found, IIS simply returns a listing of all the files in the folder, if "directory browsing" is permitted for the folder. The "default document" list is something that you can configure. (Different Web servers start with different lists. In the preceding example, a little experimentation shows that www.mcp.com and www.mcp.com/index.html return the same thing, so the Web server at Macmillan Computer Publishing must search for index.html.)

Tip #217

Default documents, in a way, provide some security to your Web site. Directory browsing is useful for sharing files, but it also lets visitors probe around your Web site's folders. Placing a default document in a folder prevents remote users from seeing what files are in the folder. Unless you explicitly link to files, these users won't see them.

MIMEs MAKE IT HAPPEN

Web browsers must be told how to interpret the content returned by the server. They don't know in advance whether they're going to get HTML text, a Microsoft Word document, an image, or something else. Whereas Windows Explorer determines a file's type from the end of its filename—for example, .doc or .html—Web browsers get this information from the Content-type field returned in the response header. This information is called a file's *MIME type*.

> **Note**
>
> You might have already guessed that we're not talking about the Marcel Marceau type of mime. MIME stands for Multipurpose Internet Mail Extensions. Prior to MIME, there was no standardized way to encode or name message content other than plain ASCII text. And in case you are still wondering, Marcel Marceau is a world famous mime–the undisputed master of the art.

MIME type names are agreed-upon Internet standards, and it's the Web server's job to know how to label each of the files it shares. IIS uses the Windows File Types Registry to map file types like .doc and .html into MIME types, and you can add to the list any special types of files you share.

 If people browsing your Web site see a screen full of random letters and numbers instead of your Web pages, see "Hyperlinks Return Gibberish" in the "Troubleshooting" section at the end of this chapter.

TO RUN OR NOT TO RUN

Remember the DOS command line? Recall the old DIR program and the listing of files that it created. The former is a little program file named DIR.COM, and the latter is the output of that program. You could copy either one—the program or its output—to a floppy disk.

Well, when a URL refers to a program file, a Web server either can return it to you as a file, which you can save or run on *your* computer, or the Web server can run the program on *its* side and return the program's output to you. This is the *crucial* feature that made the World Wide Web cause such a sensation and made the Internet explode into a global phenomenon. Programs on the server's side can do virtually anything: Search libraries, access your bank account, buy airline tickets, or move robots on the moon, and then return the results to you as a Web page.

These programs are generically called Common Gateway Interface (CGI) programs, or *server-side scripts*, when written in a language such as ASP, Perl, JavaScript, VBScript, or another interpreted language supported by the Web server. Useful CGI programs and scripts can be created with programming know-how, or can be purchased or downloaded from the Net. Because CGI programs and scripts run on the computer that hosts the Web site, they let you return information to remote visitors without giving them direct access to your computer's files.

For IIS, the distinction between "send it as a file" and "run it and return the output" is made by giving a Web-shared folder the read, script, or execute attributes. Folders with the read attribute treat scripts and executable programs as data to be returned directly. With the script or execute attribute, scripts and programs, respectively, are run on the server.

Let us just reassure you: You don't need to take advantage of all this complexity if you just want to publish some simple Web pages and make files available to Web visitors. IIS can publish Web pages out-of-the box with no programming.

REVIEWING COMPONENTS OF IIS

IIS version 5 is included with Windows 2000 Professional as well as Windows 2000 Server. The Professional version has the same capabilities as the Server version, except for two things.

First, the license agreement for Windows 2000 Professional restricts the use of your computer and any services it hosts to a maximum of 10 concurrent connections.

Second, the software does not support multiple Web sites hosted by one computer (that is, it does not support multiple *virtual domains*).

The bottom line is that it's legal to use Professional only for a low-volume site. Practically speaking, unless you're selling Viagra online or you get listed on Yahoo!'s Cool Site of the Day, you probably don't have to worry about this point.

Do You *Really* Want to Do This?

Before going any further, we should say: If you can get the hosting services you need from your Internet service provider (ISP), your corporate IS department, or just about anyone else, you might not want to bother with setting up your own Web server! There's no glory in hosting your own Web site, just hard work. Web servers at an ISP will have faster connections to the Internet, are probably backed up every night, *and* some poor soul with a pager tied around his neck is probably on call 24×7 in case something goes wrong with the server. With low-volume Web sites to be had for as little as U.S. $5 a month, including domain name service (DNS), mailboxes, FTP, and FrontPage support, taking this project on yourself hardly seems worthwhile.

Hosting a public World Wide Web site requires domain name service, which Windows 2000 Professional alone doesn't provide. Therefore, if you want your site to be accessible as www.mysite.com, you still need someone else or an add-on product to provide DNS support. This support alone can cost nearly as much as a full-service Web site package.

On the other hand, you might want to install IIS if you

- Want to host in-house communication within your company or workgroup.
- Want to share files or your printer over the Internet using Web Sharing.
- Develop custom Web programs or scripts, or use CGI programs that an ISP can't or won't provide.

- Want to write and preview Web pages and applications before deploying them to an online site.

- Think that a chance to participate in this global Internet thing is just too cool to pass by. (I have to admit that this was the reason *I* set up a Web server.)

Whatever your reason, IIS installed in all its glory will give you plenty to chew on. It provides a full range of services:

- World Wide Web (HTTP) Service—The WWW service is the basic component that lets your computer host Web pages. The WWW server supports server-side Java, JavaScript, and ASP scripting. It's the full-blown IIS 5 package except for the limit of 10 connections; also, this version doesn't let you host multiple Web sites—for example, for different domain names—as the Server version does.

  The WWW service gives you Internet Printing capability. The Internet Printing Protocol (IPP) lets you manage and print to your Windows printer from anywhere on the Internet. IPP can be used from Windows 95, 98, and Windows 2000 computers.

- File Transfer Protocol (FTP) Server—FTP lets remote users send and/or retrieve files from specified directories on your computer. FTP is a good interplatform file transfer system but poses some security risks, which we'll discuss in the next section.

- FrontPage 2000 Server Extensions—The FrontPage Extensions allow you to post Web pages and graphics to your server directly from the FrontPage design program. This capability greatly simplifies the process of copying a set of related files (a web) to the server's "online" directories. The Extensions also add searching and form-posting services to the WWW service, which you can include in your FrontPage-produced pages. FrontPage 2000 obeys Windows file security, so you can control who has permission to update files on various parts of your Web site.

  The Extensions also enable Web Sharing, which lets you share files with your printer via the Internet with a high degree of security. Web Sharing lets Internet Explorer 5 treat Web folders like regular Windows shared folders. You can view, copy, rename, and delete files over the Internet just as if you were using a local area network (LAN).

  If your computer is permanently accessible via the Internet, these two features alone are a good enough reason to install IIS.

- Internet Information Services Snap-in—This management tool permits you to configure and manage IIS from Administrative Tools on the Start menu, or from the Microsoft Management Console (MMC).

- Personal Web Manager—This simplified Web administration console is used for the simplest changes like the addition of a published folder. It also displays site traffic statistics such as requests per hour or visitors per day. This feature is borrowed from Windows 98's Personal Web Server.

→ If you're starting to get confused by Microsoft's seeming multiple personality disorder, **see** "What's This Personal Web Business Anyway?" **p. 615**.

- Indexing Service—The Microsoft Indexing Service automatically builds a database of your Web site's content and gives visitors a way to search for documents by keywords and phrases. It understands Microsoft file formats such as RTF and Word Document format, so searches can locate text in these documents as well as plain text and HTML files. It also respects Windows file and folder security and doesn't list files a remote visitor doesn't have permission to view. The Indexing Service also assists when you choose Search for Files and Folders.

- Visual InterDev RAD Remote Deployment Support—Visual InterDev is Microsoft's software development system for sophisticated Web-based services that access corporate database and multitier transactional systems. The Remote Deployment Support service lets VID developers install and test software on-the-fly.

- SMTP Service—SMTP (Simple Mail Transfer Protocol) is the foundation for virtually all email exchange on the Internet. The SMTP Service provided with Windows 2000 is designed to permit IIS and Windows Scripting Host applications to send mail, and it also works with Microsoft Exchange Server, which must be purchased separately. It is, however, only a delivery system and doesn't provide mailboxes or a Post Office Protocol (POP) service, so it's only half of what you need to host your own email system. On a Windows 2000 Server, it can also be used to transfer Active Directory data between distant installations.

Extensive online documentation is also available—4.6MB worth. It's helpful, but if you're going to get serious about Web site development using IIS, you might want to pick up copies of the following books:

- *Active Server Pages 3.0 by Example*, published by Que
- *Active Server Pages 3.0 from Scratch*, published by Que
- *Internet Information Server Administration*, published by New Riders
- *MCSE Training Guide: Internet Information Server 4, Second Edition*, published by New Riders

PART

III

CH

18

WHAT'S THIS "PERSONAL WEB" BUSINESS ANYWAY?

Seeing both Internet Services Manager and Personal Web Manager in your Administrative Tools menu might be a bit confusing. Both management tools can set up virtual directories and control basic features. You can use either one, depending on which is most familiar and comfortable to you. Either way, you're using the same powerful Web server.

But why two utilities to do the same thing?

Well, you might remember a program called Personal Web Server, or PWS, which was included with Windows 95. It was a simplified Web and FTP server with a nifty and very simple graphical interface called the Personal Web Manager. It wasn't as sophisticated as IIS, but it was not bad for simple Web publishing.

Windows NT came with Internet Information Server, a more sophisticated Web server that includes ASP, VBScript, and JavaScript for CGI programming, which makes it an extremely powerful tool. It was available with both NT Server and Workstation, and the only difference was that the Workstation version was restricted to 10 connections, just like PWS.

Microsoft probably didn't want to have to maintain two separate Web server platforms. So, in Windows 98, it slipped in the full IIS Web server, though the feature was still called Personal Web Server. The FTP service was removed, and the Personal Web Manager was updated to include a wizard that could set up a simple Web site, including a guestbook for visitors.

With Windows 2000, Microsoft has dropped the "Personal" title, and the FTP server is back—perhaps to make former Windows NT users more comfortable. Microsoft also threw in the Personal Web Manager to give something familiar to former Windows 9x users. It's the same old Personal Web Manager, less the wizard (which was overextended as it was; the poor old guy had to assist with everything from chart making in Excel to establishing Internet connections in Windows).

I hope you're not as confused now as I was when I tried to sort out the magically appearing and disappearing features. If you are, Table 18.1 might help make some sense of this information.

TABLE 18.1—FEATURES OF THE WEB SERVERS SUPPLIED WITH WINDOWS

Operating System	Web Server	FTP Server	Number of Connections	Number of Domains
Windows 95	PWS	Yes	10	1
Windows 98	IIS 3	No	10	1
Windows NT 4 Workstation	IIS 2	Yes	10	1
Windows NT 4 Server	IIS 2	Yes	unlimited	unlimited
Windows 2000 Professional	IIS 5	Yes	10	1
Windows 2000 Server	IIS 5	Yes	unlimited	unlimited

DETERMINING WHICH IIS SERVICES YOU NEED

IIS is a bulky and sophisticated suite of programs. Although they're not more difficult than they need to be, considering what they do, they're also not "entry-level" programs. They require forethought and oversight to make them useful and to manage the security risk that comes with global accessibility. Two familiar laws of nature come into play here:

As the number of components in a system increases, the number of ways it can fail grows exponentially.

Anything that can go wrong will.

Applied to IIS, these laws mean that you should not install what you don't need. Enough lecturing, now: What do you need?

BEFORE YOU GET STARTED

All IIS services require you to have a network using the TCP/IP protocol. These days, it would be very surprising if you did *not* because the Internet is everywhere, and you probably wouldn't be reading this book if you weren't either getting connected or already connected to it.

If you want to make Web pages available to others in your company, your computer needs to be connected to a local area network. If you want to publish Web pages on the Internet at large—that is, be part of the World Wide Web—you need a full-time Internet connection as well. If your site is available only a few hours a day while you're dialed in to your ISP, then few people will ever be able to see it. This kind of dedicated service is much less expensive today than it was only a few years ago, and can be had in some areas of the U.S. for under $50 a month. (You can read about Internet connectivity in Chapter 11, "Internet and TCP/IP Connection Options," and Chapter 24, "Connecting Your LAN to the Internet.")

Tip #218

IIS requires *lots* of memory. Don't even think of installing it in your system unless you have 128MB of memory or more. (We advise having 128MB anyway; you and Windows 2000 will both be much happier.)

Finally, you should install IIS on an NTFS-formatted disk so that it can take advantage of the Windows user-level security.

Tip #219

If you plan to install a LAN or IIS, you should share files only on a drive that is formatted with NTFS. NTFS lets you control access to files and folders based on Windows usernames and group membership, which the FAT formats can't. If you share data from a FAT-formatted drive, anyone can read or write over your files.

→ If you want to learn more details about choosing the best file system (NTFS, FAT32, or FAT) for your Windows 2000 Professional installation, **see** "Which File System: FAT, FAT32, OR NTFS?," **p. 133**.

NAMING SERVICE

If you plan to use IIS just to develop and test Web pages, or if you want to share pages on an office or corporate network, you don't have to worry about your computer being visible to the Internet at large. But if you want to host a public Web site with Windows 2000 Professional, you need the following:

■ A static, or permanent, IP address and Internet connection, as opposed to the dynamic, or temporary, number you get when using a dial-up connection to an ISP

- An entry in the Internet's domain name service so that people can find your site using a standard name like www.myfamouswebsite.com

Without both of these elements, you're a moving target, and nobody will be able to find or use your Web site on a consistent basis. Getting them set up is beyond the scope of this book, but here are a few hints:

- If you are part of a company network already connected to the Internet, your computer's network name may already be registered on the Internet.

- If you use a permanent Internet connection such as a cable modem, DSL service, frame-relay, or other dedicated link, you probably will get a permanent IP address from your Internet provider, or you can ask for one. With this information, the entire world can reach you if they know your IP address. For example, if your IP address·is 207.33.3.2, visitors can reach your Web site by using http://207.33.3.2

- Your ISP may provide you with domain name service, or you might be able to buy this type of service from a commercial Web site service for about U.S. $5 a month. You also have to register your domain name with a national Internet registry service, such as www.networksolutions.com, at around $70 for the first two years. Your ISP will probably take care of the paperwork, but you'll still be billed separately for the service and for the registration.

- If your network has Windows 2000 or Windows NT Server, your network administrator can set up domain name service for you because a DNS server is included with Windows 2000 and NT Server.

WORLD WIDE WEB

The World Wide Web service delivers static and dynamic Web pages and also offers file and document pickup (via Web pages or directory listings), database interactivity, and just about any other sort of information sharing. This is the core of IIS. If you can't or don't want to use a commercial or other hosting service for your pages, or if you want to host Web pages, develop Web applications, or share folders using the Web model, you should install the WWW service.

FRONTPAGE 2000 EXTENSIONS

You should install the FrontPage 2000 Extensions if you want to do any of the following:

- Use FrontPage (any version) or Office 2000 to develop Web pages
- Use your WWW service to use FrontPage's searching or form extensions
- Copy files to and from your computer via the Internet, using Internet Explorer 5 and Web Sharing
- Manage and use your printer via the Internet

The Extensions provide a way for Web-enabled applications to *publish*, or deliver, the composed HTML file and graphics to the Web server's online folders. Thus, the author doesn't have to manually drag files into the WWW folders or use the evil FTP service to copy them there. FrontPage Extensions also provide HTML Form processing services, in the form of some special CGI (Common Gateway Interface, or Web server extension) programs that can record or email form responses, and index or searching services that let Web site viewers search your Web site for keywords or phrases. They also include as standard equipment a CGI-based Web page system to manage your printers.

Note

If you want to learn more information about using the FrontPage 2000 Extensions, we recommend that you pick up a copy of *Special Edition Using Microsoft FrontPage 2000*, published by Que.

Tip #220

If you use Microsoft Office 2000, you might want to use the Office Server Extensions instead of the FrontPage Extensions. The Office Server Extensions provide additional services for Office users, and you can get them with the *Microsoft Office 2000 Premium Edition*. You can learn all about Office 2000 and the Server Extensions in *Special Edition Using Microsoft Office 2000*, published by Que.

PART

III

CH

18

FTP

FTP allows remote users to retrieve or deliver files to your computer. FTP, which is one of the original Internet applications, is available on virtually every Internet-connected system, from mainframe to Macintosh to PC, so it's really handy for file transfers between Windows and non-Windows computers. But the decision to install FTP should not be made lightly because FTP can create some severe security risks.

FTP permits two types of access: *anonymous* and *authenticated*. Anonymous access doesn't require a password and should be used to share folders for file-pickup only; you should *never* allow users from the Internet at large to write files to your computer (lest you find one day that someone has made your computer one of the Internet's prime repositories and distributors of pornography).

You can allow remote users to deliver files to your computer using *authenticated* access, but FTP doesn't encrypt passwords sent over the Internet, so this method is a security risk. The login name and password used are exposed while they are in transit over the Internet.

In most cases, if you only want to distribute files to the general public, you don't need to install FTP. The World Wide Web service can do the job nicely. The only two reasons to install FTP are as follows:

■ You need to let remote users pick up files from your computer, and their computers might not have Web browser software.

- You need to let remote users deliver files to your computer, and their computers aren't running Windows.

If you decide to install FTP, you must understand the security consequences and take great care configuring the service and the folders it makes public. We'll discuss the risks and configuration issues in excruciating detail later. You might want to read that discussion before you make your decision.

SMTP MAIL

The SMTP Mail service provided with IIS is required to send email from Web pages, ASP scripts, and FrontPage or Office 2000 Server Extensions. If you want to send mail from your Web server, you should install SMTP.

As a mail system, though, the SMTP service unfortunately doesn't provide you with mailboxes or any of the other user-side services that an email system needs. If you want to host your own email system, you need to purchase an add-on email server such as Microsoft Exchange Server or download a free or shareware mail server system.

Tip #221

I really like the EMWAC email system distributed by the European Microsoft Windows Academic Center and use it for my own company. Its development stopped in 1998, but it works, it's free, and it's great for a small workgroup. It includes a POP server, too. It uses the Windows account database as its user/password source. You use it for in-house and outside email. It also has great HTML-based help and setup files. You can download it from the following site:

`http://www.emwac.ed.ac.uk/html/internet_toolchest/ims/ims.htm`

If this information helps reassure you at all, Microsoft distributed an earlier version of the EMWAC server with its Windows NT 3.5 Resource Kit, before it developed the IIS Mail server.

From `http://www1.sica.com/ims/`, you can download an anti-spam and anti-relaying add-on for the EMWAC mail server. The installation instructions are a headache to decipher. It's free, though, so that's what you have to put up with.

OTHER COMPONENTS

The other components of IIS—online documentation, Management snap-in, and Personal Web Manager—are all handy to have. As Martha Stewart would say, "They are *good* things." We recommend installing them, so we'll go over their use later.

INSTALLING IIS

After you've decided which IIS services to install, follow these steps:

1. Choose Settings, Control Panel, Add/Remove Programs. Select Add/Remove Windows Components from the left pane.

2. Check Internet Information Services to install all the IIS services. Select Details, and deselect any components you have chosen not to install. The following list provides some recommendations for installing IIS:

Component	Should You Install?
Common Files	required
IIS World Wide Web Server	required
Internet Information Services Snap-In	yes
Personal Web Manager	yes
Documentation	yes
File Transfer Protocol (FTP) Server	probably not
FrontPage 2000 Server Extensions.	optional
Visual InterDev RAD Remote Deployment	optional
SMTP Service	optional

If you change your mind about using any of these services, you can always select Add/Remove Windows Components again later to add or remove components. We recommend letting IIS use the standard location for its home directory, c:\inetpub\wwwroot.

Note

If you had FrontPage Extensions installed under an earlier version of Windows that you upgraded to Windows 2000, you must still manually install the FrontPage Extensions here. They are not automatically upgraded and configured for Windows 2000.

PART

III

CH

18

When the installation is complete, Windows starts the services you installed, *except* the Indexing Service. If you want to search the IIS online documentation or want to use site-searching for your own content, start the Indexing Service now, as follows:

1. Right-click My Computer, and select Manage.

2. Open Services and Applications.

3. Right-click Indexing Service.

4. Select Start.

5. A dialog appears asking whether you want the Indexing Service to start whenever the computer is started. Select Yes or No.

The Indexing Service builds an index of its default content directories, which include the IIS online documentation and your Web site's home and virtual directories. (It also indexes your own Documents and Settings folder but doesn't make this information available to Internet visitors.) The indexing process will take a minute or two, during which you can tour the major components of IIS.

TAKING A QUICK TOUR

After you've installed IIS, you can take a quick tour of the major components that have been put into place. To do so, first start Internet Explorer, and enter the URL //localhost. Localhost is shorthand for "the IP address of this machine" and will display Internet Explorer's default installation Web page. You will see the default page shown in Figure 18.3. Internet Explorer will also fire up the online documentation for IIS in a separate browser window.

Figure 18.3
IIS serves you a welcome page when first installed. A remote browser, using your real IP address rather than localhost, would see a plain "Under construction" page.

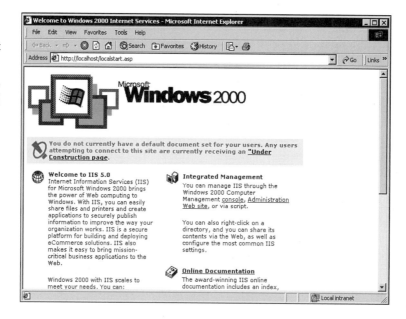

Congratulations! You have a Web site. Let's take a look at the built-in pages. If you find them as handy as we did, you might want to add them to your Favorites folder. (You learned how to use Internet Explorer's Favorites folder in Chapter 12, "World Wide Web.")

ONLINE DOCUMENTATION

Typing http://localhost/iishelp in the Address bar displays the IIS Online documentation, which has a built-in search and indexing feature. Check this documentation for the latest IIS news, release notes, and detailed instructions. (This documentation is a good place to spend a couple of hours.)

You can find the current IIS release notes at

//localhost/iishelp/iis/misc/default.asp

PRINTER MANAGER

Built into IIS for Windows 2000 is a nifty Web-based printer management console. When you type `http://localhost/Printers` in the Address bar, note that your installed printer(s) and any pending print jobs are listed on the page. You can view the printers on any machine in a Windows 2000 network by using the URL `http://machine/Printers`, replacing *machine* with the actual network identification name of another computer, its domain name, or its DNS name—for example, `judy.mycompany.com`. Because this page uses Windows user-level security, you can view but not manage the printer if you don't have a user account and adequate permissions on the other machines. It works only with Internet Explorer for the same reason. What you're viewing, of course, is generated by a CGI program that lets IIS return information from the Windows printer manager. It is installed, by default, with IIS.

If you are viewing this page from a different Windows 2000 computer or from a Windows 9x or NT 4 computer with the IPP (Internet Printing Protocol) add-on available from `www.windowsupdate.com`, you can also select Connect and install this printer as a remote printer. You'll learn about Web printing in Chapter 22, "Using a Windows 2000 Network."

SETTING UP A SIMPLE WEB SITE

PART
III
CH
18

Right out of the box, IIS is ready to serve up static Web pages and images. If you have files from an existing Web site, or if you can create and edit HTML files yourself, you can simply copy them into the home directory c:\inetpub\wwwroot and any subfolders you want to create. The default page name is initially default.htm, so give the file with your entry or home page this name.

With no further administration or fuss, other users on your network and/or on the Internet can view your Web site, using your computer's Internet domain name or, on a Windows LAN, by viewing `http://machinename`, where *machinename* is the Windows name of your computer. (You can find that name by right-clicking My Computer, selecting Properties, and viewing the Network Identification tab.)

You can also use Notepad, FrontPage, FrontPage Express, Word 2000, or another editor to create Web pages. Chapter 17, "Going Public: Creating Intranet and Internet Web Sites," describes how to download and use FrontPage Express.

If you're the impatient type, as I am, you probably skipped right past Chapter 17 and into the gritty details of configuring IIS. Now you have a Web server running and want to see it work. Okay, just follow these steps to build a *really* quick and dirty home page, just to prove to yourself that you really do have a Web server up and running:

1. Select Start, Programs, Accessories, Notepad.
2. Type the following text:

```
<HTML>
<HEAD>
<TITLE>This is My Home Page</TITLE>
</HEAD>
<BODY>
```

```
<P>Welcome to my completely spiffy new website, hosted by Windows 2000!
</BODY>
</HTML>
```

Be especially careful to get the angle brackets (< and >) right and to use the forward slash (/), not the backslash (\).

3. Select File, Save As, and enter `c:\inetpub\wwwroot\default.htm` as the filename. Click OK.

4. View `http:\\localhost` in Internet Explorer.

Now you have your very own home page. It's not much to look at, but now you can say you've coded Web pages by hand. This will impress people.

At the end of this chapter, we'll show you a quick way to have a Web page send email, too. It's *way* cool! (Web page programmers talk like that.) To add a link to a feedback page we'll show you at the end of the chapter, you can add the following line just before the `</BODY>` line at the bottom of the sample home page you just made:

```
<P><A HREF='\scripts\feedback.asp'>Send us your thoughts!</A>
```

When you're finished, you can create or copy other HTML documents and images into the wwwroot folder.

You'll also quickly find that IIS can deliver more than static Web pages.

Scripts and CGI programs let your Web server return information determined at the moment a page is viewed. These scripts and programs can perform tasks as simple as inserting the current date and time in the viewed page or accessing databases, creating complex images, retrieving images from cameras, or even turning on coffee pots and moving robots on command. At the simplest level, you can use scripting to embed information in a Web page on-the-fly. For example, you can use Notepad to create a file named time.asp in c:\inetpub\scripts, with this inside:

```
<HTML>
<HEAD>
<TITLE>What time is it?</TITLE>
</HEAD>
<BODY>
You viewed this web page at <% response.write time() %>,
<% response.write date() %>.
</BODY>
</HTML>
```

Then you can view `http://localhost/scripts/time.asp` in Internet Explorer. IIS copies most of the file literally. Stuff in between <% and %> is treated as *script* code, which are commands written in Visual Basic or JavaScript. There's just about no end to the complexity you can get into here. ASP scripts can be programmed to "remember" information about a Web visitor—for example, to remember a visitor's name entered on your home page as he or she visits other pages in your site.

If you are new to Web page building and want to learn how to populate the Web site you just created, skip back to Chapter 17 for the basics. If you've already built a site and are now interested in publishing it to the Web, stay here.

Note

The Web site-creating skills taught in this book are enough to help point you in the right direction if you are a beginner. You'll also find just enough information here to knock the rust off if you're a semiretired Web developer, and you want to get back up to speed quickly. If, however, you are a Web development professional or want to become one, you'll quickly outgrow the Web development skills we can teach within a Windows 2000 book. In that case, we recommend the following books as great starting places for learning more:

- *Special Edition Using Microsoft FrontPage 2000,* published by Que
- *Special Edition Using HTML 4.0,* also published by Que

Tip #222

Don't put anything into your Web folders that you don't want to be seen all over the world. Just because *your* pages don't link to a given file doesn't mean that someone *else* won't publish a Web page linking to it. One morning you might wake up and find that, through someone else, the world's search engines have indexed your "private" document and are leading people (and your mother-in-law) to it.

PART

III

CH

18

PUBLISHING TO YOUR WEB SITE WITH FRONTPAGE

If you have installed the FrontPage Extensions, you can use a purchased copy of Microsoft FrontPage, or you can download a free copy of FrontPage Express from Windows Update to write extension-enhanced Web pages.

You can locate a management tool for the FrontPage Server Extensions by right-clicking My Computer, selecting Administrative Tools, and then selecting Server Extensions Administrator. You should not need to use it unless you're undertaking more sophisticated projects than we can cover here. For most of your Web publishing work, you should be able to get by without meeting the Server Extensions Administrator.

If, while you're modifying pages on your Web site, your browser continues to load the old page and not the new one you just placed in the Web folder, see "Browser Doesn't Show Modified Web Page" in the "Troubleshooting" section at the end of this chapter.

MANAGING YOUR IIS SERVER WITH PERSONAL WEB MANAGER

Windows 2000 Professional includes a simple Web site management console called Personal Web Manager (see Figure 18.4). To bring up Personal Web Manager, right-click My Computer, select Manage, and then select the Personal Web Manager icon in the Administrative Tools window.

Figure 18.4
Personal Web Manager was borrowed from Windows 98's Personal Web Server. With a minimum of troublesome details, it lets you set up virtual directories and view statistics on the number of daily hits on your Web site.

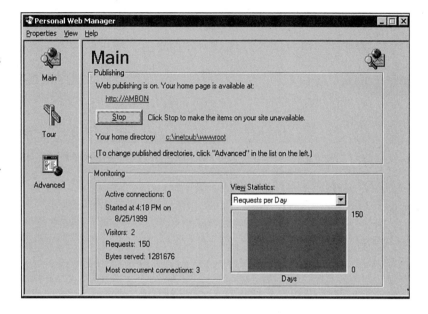

Personal Web Manager's left pane has three selections: Main, which displays simple statistics on the number of visitors to your Web site; Tour, which starts a charming but useless marketing slide show describing IIS; and Advanced, which lets you add and remove virtual directories from your Web site.

On the Main page, you can quickly view your own home page via a hypertext link, start and stop the World Wide Web service, and view statistics of activity on your Web site. You can view visitors or requests per hour or day. A *request* is a single interaction with the Web server to fetch a file or image. A *visitor* is counted when the server detects a series of one or more requests from the same IP address in a reasonable timeframe.

On the Advanced Options page (see Figure 18.5), you might want to verify or change the following options after you install IIS:

- Check Enable Default Document to permit IIS to search for a file with one of the listed names when a URL names just a folder. Your "home page" file should have one of the names in this list.

- Default Documents is the list of names to search for, in order, separated by commas, when you're searching for a default document.

Tip #223

We recommend adding default.html, index.htm, and welcome.html to the Default Documents list as well to maintain compatibility with other Web servers that use these names for the default document.

Figure 18.5
The Advanced Options page includes settings for the Web server as a whole; on this page, you can add and modify virtual directories on the Web server.

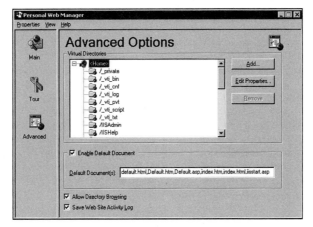

- Check Allow Directory Browsing to allow IIS to return a listing of all files in a folder when a default document can't be found. Unchecked, it hides the contents of folders without default documents.

Tip #224

We recommend leaving the Allow Directory Browsing option unchecked and enabling directory browsing only in selected folders using the management console. It's best not to invite snooping when you don't need to.

PART
III
CH
18

- Check Save Web Site Activity Log to record the times, dates, IP addresses, and requests of visitors to your Web site. (Analysis programs in the public domain can help you construct interesting charts describing the visits to your Web site.)

If you have installed FrontPage Extensions, several virtual directories are preinstalled for you; they are named private, _vti_bin_, and so on. You don't need to make any modifications to them.

You can add or alter the list of virtual directories by clicking Add or by selecting an existing directory and clicking Edit Properties. Figure 18.6 shows the properties for the Home directory itself.

The Access Permissions are as follows:

- Read—Allows a remote user to read, download, or view the contents of this folder.
- Write—Allows a remote user to write to or modify the contents of this folder. (Don't check this permission unless you know that it is required.)
- Script Source Access—Permits script files to be read as files rather than always executed on the server.

Figure 18.6
The virtual directory properties for the Home directory. Proper permission settings are crucial for maintaining security control over your Web server. You should never allow write access along with script or execute access.

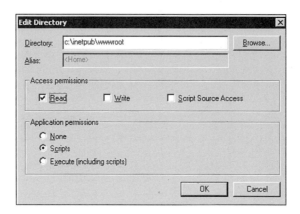

These permissions work in concert with the file permissions on the folders in an NTFS disk partition. Remote users get no more access than the most restrictive of the rights granted by either IIS or the file system itself. That is, if either prohibits reading files, a user will not able to read files.

The Application Permissions control what IIS does with .EXE and script files such as .ASP files:

- None—Means that applications are treated as plain files to be copied.
- Scripts—Means that script files are run as programs, but .EXE executable files are not run. The .EXE files will be copied to the user as data.
- Execute (Including Scripts)—Means that both EXE programs and scripts are run as CGI programs, when referenced by a remote browser.

Caution

Maintaining proper control over your Web server is crucial if it is connected to the Internet. Improper settings could allow a remote user to copy a malicious program to your computer and have IIS run it. *Never* give write access to a folder along with either script or execute access. This type of access would let a malicious user copy arbitrary files to your computer and run them there. Your Web folders should also be on an NTFS partition so that Windows can provide user-level access security.

If this topic seems too complex, well, we have two observations. One: It is. Managing IIS is the topic of an entire book this size. And two, to be honest, it's our experience that you will never need or want to modify any of these settings, other than the default document list and directory browsing check boxes. So, don't worry about it now.

If you want to add a virtual directory, adding it from Windows Explorer is easier than adding it from Personal Web Manager.

SHARING FOLDERS THROUGH EXPLORER

If you want to add to your Web site a folder that is not inside c:\inetpub\wwwroot, you can add it as a virtual folder by using Windows Explorer. To do so, right-click the folder in the Explorer display, and select Properties. Then click the new Web Sharing tab, and select Share This Folder. The virtual directory or Edit Directory dialog appears, as shown in Figure 18.7.

Figure 18.7
Here, you can set alias properties for a new virtual directory. The Alias name is the URL name this folder will have.

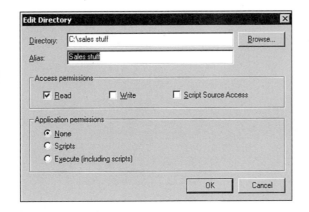

Enter the URL name you want to use for this folder, and change the Access and Application Permissions check boxes if necessary. For a folder that will hold Web pages and images, check Read. If this folder will also contain scripts and/or CGI programs that you want to have run by the server, check Scripts or Execute (Including Scripts). If you want to let remote users see the contents of the directory in the absence of a default document, check Allow Directory Browsing.

Tip #225

The best practice is *not* to enable the Scripts or Execute permissions unless you know you require them.

Tip #226

To minimize the number of folders requiring Scripts and Execute permissions, use the pre-installed Scripts folder for your scripts and CGI programs.

Remember that Windows file permissions will be in force as well as the permissions you set for Web sharing. If you want anyone in the world to be able to view these pages, be sure to set the file and folder permissions for these Web-shared folders to Read by Everyone, as you'll see in Chapter 22, "Using a Windows 2000 Network." Otherwise, viewers of the Web site will be asked for a Windows username and password.

PART

III

CH

18

If you do want to maintain control over who has the privilege to read Web pages in some or all of your Web folders, see the following section for an important warning about Windows security.

MANAGING YOUR SITE WITH THE COMPUTER MANAGEMENT CONSOLE

If you want more detailed control over access rights in your Web folders, or you have installed the FTP or SMTP services, you should take a look at the Internet Information Services management plug-in. To use it, right-click My Computer, select Manage, select Computer Management, and then open the Internet Information Services node, as shown in Figure 18.8.

Figure 18.8
The Computer Management console contains management tools for the Indexing Service, FTP server, Web server, and SMTP server.

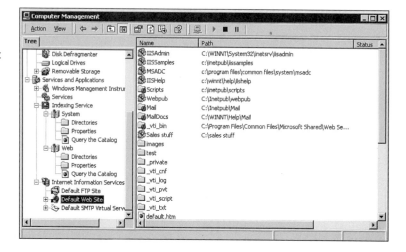

In this Explorer-like view of the folders shared by the Web and FTP services, you can take complete control of IIS's behavior, down to its treatment of individual files. It's very unlikely, though, that you'll need to manage your Web server at this level.

Besides seeing it once just to be familiar with its possibilities, you should use it, as shown here, to make a few small configuration changes after you've installed the World Wide Web Service:

1. Right-click the Default Web Site item, and select Properties. You then are presented with a complex dialog with nine tabs (see Figure 18.9).

2. Select the Performance tab to bring it to the front, and click the left side of the slider because you anticipate "Fewer than 10,000 hits per day."

3. If you plan to use FrontPage Extensions, select the Server Extensions page to bring it to the front, and under Performance, select the approximate number of pages you expect to have on your Web site: fewer than 100, 100 to 1,000, or more than 1,000.

Figure 18.9
On the Default Web Site Properties dialog, you can set properties for the Web server itself.

4. If you plan to use form and email processing with ASP scripts, FrontPage Extensions, and/or Mailing List services with the Office Server Extensions, select Specify How Mail Should Be Sent Settings, and make the following entries:

   Web server's mail address: Enter the email address of your Web server administrator.

   Contact address: Enter an alternative administrator's email address or other administrator contact information such as call 555-555-1212

   SMTP Mail Server: Enter the name of your network's or your ISP's SMTP mail receiver, often something like smtp.myisp.com.

5. Click OK to close the dialog.

You can use a security tool called the Permissions Wizard after you've been working with your Web site awhile. Using the Permissions Wizard is a quick-and-dirty way of setting Web access and NTFS file permissions on Web folders to make sure that the general public doesn't unexpectedly have write access to your Web pages. The wizard sets NTFS file permissions to permit read access by Everyone and write access only to Administrators. Then it sets Web permissions to either permit or deny public (anonymous) access, depending on whether you're setting up a public or private Web site.

The wizard grants write (that is, authoring) access only to Administrators, so you have to go back and manually add write, delete, and change permissions for other users or groups to the Web folder's NTFS permissions. However, the wizard does seem to take into account Web properties such as Directory Browsing, and grant or remove the NTFS List Folder Contents as appropriate.

PART
III

CH

18

You can follow these steps to use the wizard to enforce responsible access rights to your Web pages:

1. In the IIS Management console, right-click any Web-shared folder—for example, Default Web Site or Webpub. Select All Tasks, Permissions Wizard. Then click Next.

2. For a top-level Web folder, choose Select New Security Settings from a Template. Otherwise, for a subfolder in a Web folder, choose Inherit All Security Settings. Click Next.

3. If you chose to select new security settings, choose either Public Web Site or Secure Web Site. Secure disables anonymous access by visitors who don't have an account on your computer or domain. Click Next.

4. Choose Replace All Directory and File Permissions, and click Next.

If you want to grant authorship access to others, go back in Explorer and select the physical folder corresponding to the virtual folder you wizard-ized. (For Default Web Site, remember that the Web page files are really in c:\inetpub\wwwroot.) Right-click Properties, and then view its Security page. You then can add other *trusted* users or groups, giving them all rights except Full Control.

In case you are curious about what else you can do with the Management plug-in, the following are a few of the possibilities enabled by the other management tabs:

■ Under the Home Directory or Documents tabs, you can specify that a given document or folder is to be obtained from a different URL on a different Web server, using a process called *redirection*. Complex CGI programs called *ASP applications* are configured here as well.

■ On the Directory Security tab, you can restrict visitors to those at certain IP addresses. This tab also allows you to control whether anonymous access is allowed at all and whether clear-text passwords and/or encrypted passwords are required when a document is protected by user security. See the "Security Issues for Internet Services" section for more details.

■ On the HTPP Headers tab, you can limit the length of time that Web proxy servers and browsers can cache the content of your Web site. This tab also lets you provide content ratings (for example, violence, sex, nudity, or language) and the MIME-type associations mentioned earlier in the chapter. If you are publishing unusual file types and want your Web server to deliver the correct MIME type with them, check this section.

■ On the Custom Errors tab, you can design special Web pages or scripts to be used when a remote user specifies an incorrect URL. Web servers always return some sort of content. Even when a browser sends an invalid request, the server sends back a reply. This tab lets you select your own content files to be returned for each type of URL error.

Managing the FTP Server

If you have installed the FTP service, from the Computer Management console, right-click Default FTP Site to view its properties dialog.

To establish a secure server, make the following settings:

- On the FTP Site tab, be sure to check Enable Logging (see the "Log Files" section).
- On the Security Accounts tab, check Allow Anonymous Connections and Allow Only Anonymous Connections.
- On the Messages tab, under Welcome, enter a greeting followed by a warning of this sort:

```
All access to this server is logged. Access to this server is
allowed by permission only and unauthorized use will be prosecuted.
```

These settings establish a read-only FTP server, which can be used only to retrieve files from your computer.

> **Note**
> You should not enable writing to an FTP server without great consideration. Because FTP cannot encrypt passwords, if you permit nonanonymous access, the FTP server will permit remote users to enter their passwords and have them sent across the Internet without encryption. We'll discuss this issue later in more detail.

You can view and remove FTP site visitors from the FTP Site tab of the Default FTP Properties dialog by clicking Current Sessions. You can use Disconnect to remove any of them if, for some reason, you need to terminate their activity on your computer.

Log Files

By default, IIS services create log files in the Windows directory, usually in \Winnt\System32\LogFiles. The Web service log files are in subfolder W3SVC1 and are named ex*yymmdd*.log, where *yymmdd* are digits indicating the current date. A new log file is created on any day on which Web server activity occurs.

The FTP service follows a similar format, storing its log files in \Winnt\System32\MSFTPSVC1.

You can change the period for changing log files from daily to hourly, weekly, or monthly, or you can base this change on the log file growing to a certain size. To do so, you use the Default Web or FTP Site Properties dialogs. Just locate the Enable Logging check box, and click the Properties button next to it.

The log files are plain ASCII text files that contain a line for each file or page retrieved from the Web server. Each line contains the time, the browser's IP address, the HTTP method used (usually GET), and the URL requested.

If you are interested in analyzing the use of your Web site, several free or shareware analysis tools are available. Of course, you also can hire hugely expensive consultants for intense analysis of your Web server activity logs for marketing research, but this in-depth analysis is probably more than you want.

ENABLING SITE SEARCHING USING THE INDEXING SERVICE

If you want to let remote browsers search your Web site for documents of interest, you can install and configure the Indexing Service. This service periodically scours selected Web-shared folders and documents and maintains a list of all the words it finds in them. It actually maintains two separate indexes: one of your whole hard disk, for your use alone, and another of the Web folders for Internet searching. It's also sophisticated enough not to show results for documents Web visitors don't have permission to download. To install this service, follow these steps:

1. From the Computer Management console, open the Indexing Service section.
2. Right-click Web, and select Properties.
3. Select the Generation tab to bring it to the front (see Figure 18.10), and make the following choices:
    - Check Index Files with Unknown Extensions to include more than the expected .html and .txt files in the index. If you check this option, the Indexing Service will attempt to make sense of every file it finds in your Web folders.
    - Check Generate Abstracts. This option increases the size of the index in a large Web site but lets the search results return not only a filename but a paragraph or so of text from the beginning of each matching file. You can set the maximum size of this abstract if you want or leave the default setting of 320 characters.
4. Click OK. The Indexing Service updates the index automatically.

By default, the Indexing Service includes the IIS documentation in its index. You might find this information useful, but visitors to your Web site probably won't. You can open the Directories pane and remove the IIS documentation by selecting all the folders except \inetpub\wwwroot and any virtual folders you have added, double-clicking them in the right-hand pane, and checking No for Include in Index? (see Figure 18.11).

When you specify a folder, all its subfolders are included as well. You can prevent them from being included by specifying a subfolder and marking No under Include in Index.

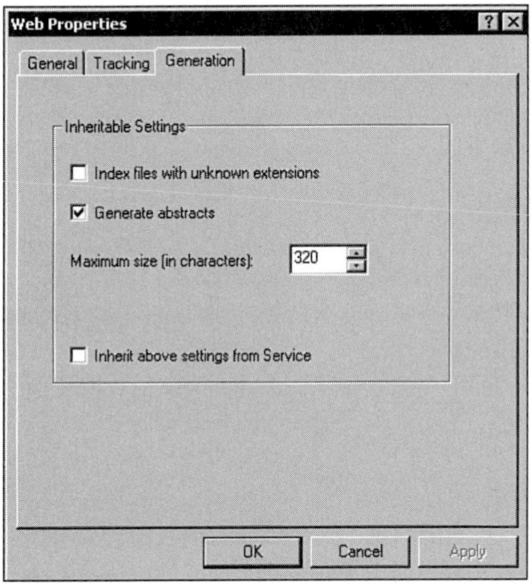

Figure 18.10
You can index generation properties for the Web index. Here, you can select the level of detail you want to include in the index.

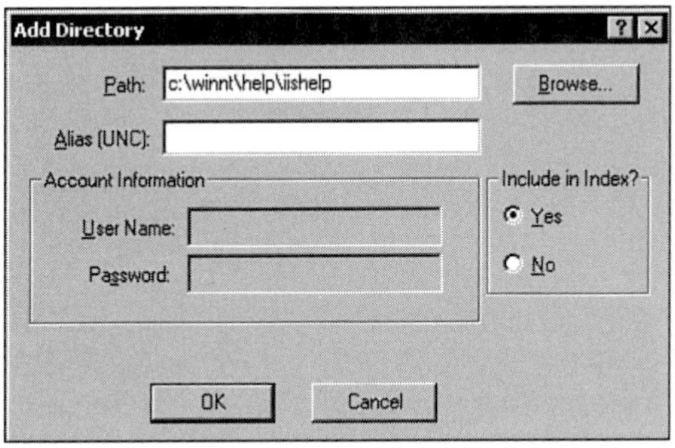

Figure 18.11
You can exclude documentation directories from your Web site index by using the Computer Management/ Indexing Services plug-in.

Also, when you specify folders, you can use wildcards in the names. We'll combine these two features in an example. In this example, you can index the entire hard drive, except the Temporary Internet Files folder, which is stored in each user's profile directory, and the Windows and Program Files directories:

```
c:\                                            yes
c:\Documents and Settings\*\Local Settings\Temporary Internet Files     no
c:\winnt                                       no
c:\program files                                 no
```

You can test the search engine by clicking Query the Catalog. The Management plug-in then displays a search query page in the right-hand page; you can use it to make sample searches.

To enable searching on your Web site, refer to Chapter 17, where you learned how to use the FrontPage Extensions.

SECURITY ISSUES FOR INTERNET SERVICES

Simply stated, if your computer is connected to the Internet, it's exposed to millions of people who can reach it in milliseconds from anywhere in the world, and many of whom have nothing better to do than to try to break into and damage your computer. Consider your connection to the Internet like the door to your house, and it's in a rough neighborhood: Don't leave the door unlocked.

Dealing with security is a little bit scary, but you can take a few steps to ensure your safety.

→ For a more detailed discussion of keeping your network safe from prying eyes, **see** "Network Security," **p. 931**.

FILE SECURITY

Your server's file system contributes to the security of data on it. You can do the following:

- Use NTFS for any drives containing folders you share using IIS.

→ For information on converting your file system from FAT to NTFS, **see** "File System Conversion Limitations," **p. 137**.

- Review directory permissions. By default, Windows assigns new folders Full Control permissions to the Everyone group. Examine folders you create under the \inetpub folder to be sure that only authorized users can write files there.

→ For information on setting folder permissions, **see** "Using a Windows 2000 Network," **p. 737**.

- Store executable and scripts files in a separate folder from Web pages so that they can be executed but not read.

AUTHENTICATION

If you use user restrictions to limit access to files or folders in your Web site, the Directory Security tab in the IIS Computer Management plug-in (which you open by right-clicking Default Web Site and choosing Properties) lets you permit or prevent Basic Authentication from being used to view protected Web pages.

Basic Authentication transmits unencrypted usernames and passwords across the Internet. This is a bad thing.

But you get a significant trade-off here. If you don't allow Basic Authentication, no Web browser other than Internet Explorer can view the protected pages. If you do allow Basic Authentication, usernames and passwords are transmitted across the Internet without encryption, which is a significant security risk.

These passwords aren't just for a Web page, remember; they're your Windows 2000 usernames and passwords, the keys to your computer and network domain.

Tip #227

> If you need to restrict access to Web pages but need to make them available to non-Internet Explorer users, we suggest that you create special single-purpose accounts to be used to access these folders.

USER ACCOUNTS

You can take several steps with user accounts to ensure tighter security:

- IIS services use a special user account named IUSR_*computername* when anonymous users access files through the Web or FTP. Control the rights of this account to limit what an anonymous visitor can see.

- Review user accounts often; check for accounts that were not created by an authorized administrator. Check to see that no unexpected users are listed as members of the Administrators group. Check permissions on the IUSR_*computername* account to see that they have not been increased.

→ For information on managing user accounts, **see** "Managing Users," **p. 1193**.

- Enable auditing of security policy modifications and access failures. Check the Security event log frequently for attempted privilege violations or unauthorized modifications.

- Choose difficult passwords. In particular, Power User and Administrator passwords should be more than seven characters long and contain numbers, upper- and lowercase letters, *and* punctuation characters.

- Limit account permissions and membership to the Administrators group to the minimum required. You'll hear right away if users need privileges they don't have, but you won't know users have privileges they don't need until it's too late.

→ For information on security management, **see** Chapter 26, "Network Security."

- Don't use the Administrator account for day-to-day use. Use a Users or Power Users account.

SERVICES

Our computer management philosophy is "keep it simple." The fewer services you run, the less likely that one will be configured incorrectly and become a security liability. Use care in configuring and managing your server. Here are some tips:

- Run only the services you actually need and use.

- Enable auditing of access failures and privilege violations.

→ For instructions on auditing access failures, **see** "Tightening Local Security Policy," **p. 965**.

- Use an encrypted connection if you are administering your computer remotely (over the Internet using the Management snap-in or using administration tools such as regedit).

- Back up your system frequently. Include the Registry in your backups, for example, by checking System State in the Backup System Tool or the equivalent in another program.

- Run virus checks regularly.

- Keep track of the services that should be running on your computer, and watch out for unknown services that may have been installed by rogue software or unauthorized users.

Web Permissions

Restrict access to files and folders to prevent unauthorized users from modifying your Web site by doing the following:

- To lock down access to your Web folders, synchronize Web and NTFS file permissions using the Permissions Wizard, as discussed earlier.

- Use the most restrictive access permissions possible. For example, the IUSR_*computer-name* account should have only read access to Web page directories and write access only to directories that require it.

- Never enable both execute and write permissions in the same folder. These permissions would permit an outside user to copy an arbitrary script or program to your computer and execute it.

Physical Security

Restrict physical access to your computer so that an unauthorized person doesn't take advantage of finding your computer logged in to a privileged account. Keep these points in mind:

- Keep your computer in a safe place.

- Log out when you are not present, and use the lock option on your screen saver.

Personnel Security

Most computer break-ins and thefts are inside jobs! Of course, you trust your fellow employees, but taking unnecessary chances doesn't make sense. Follow these guidelines:

- If you authorize more than one Administrator-level user, give each a different name and password to track changes.

- Disable accounts that are no longer needed, especially when employees are terminated.

- Require periodic password changes.

- Develop an official security policy, and educate users on important issues: no sharing of passwords, no use of unauthorized software, the importance of protecting against application macro viruses, and so on.

→ For information on establishing good security policies in your organization, **see** Chapter 26, "Network Security."

SPECIAL SECURITY ISSUES WITH FTP

As mentioned previously, FTP requires a user to log on for access and permits two types of connections: *anonymous* or *authenticated*. Authenticated connections require a Windows login name and password, and as you might guess, anonymous connections don't use passwords (well, technically, they do; they use the login name anonymous and accept anything entered as a password). The Microsoft FTP service can be configured to permit authenticated, anonymous, or both types of access.

On an Internet-connected system, using anonymous access is a great way to distribute files that you want anyone in the world to be able to download—for example, your company's product catalog. But you can use a Web page or a Web-shared folder with directory listing enabled to accomplish this task just as well.

For folders that are to *receive* files from the outside world or for sensitive files that you don't want everyone in the world to see, you certainly must make FTP require a username and password. This is the problem. FTP uses the Windows username and password system but does *not* encrypt passwords when they are transmitted across the Internet. They could be read by a hacker who has broken into an ISP's computers. So, FTP with anything but anonymous-only access is a severe security compromise.

The insult is especially severe to Windows 2000, which has so many enhanced security and encryption features. By just *permitting* authenticated access, FTP *invites* users to expose their passwords to snoops anywhere in the world. Imagine that you are on vacation overseas and want to add vacation snapshots to your personal Web site. If you use FTP to send the files, you will expose your login name and password to anyone with a network analyzer between your vacation spot and your office. This could mean handing governments, corporations, and individuals of unknown integrity the key to your computer. Is it worth the risk?

This is the FTP dilemma. If all you want is to publish files, you can configure FTP for anonymous-only access. This type of access is low risk, but you could just as easily use a Web page. If you want to allow remote delivery of files, FTP is great but is a security risk. People can deliver files to your computer in more secure ways: Email attachments, FrontPage publishing, Web folder sharing, network sharing, and Virtual Private Network (VPN) connectivity are just a few.

Still, you might decide that you want to use FTP to let others transmit files to your computer. We recommend the following to minimize the security risk.

Create separate virtual folders for incoming and outgoing files. (Create virtual folders in the Computer Management utility by right-clicking Default FTP Site, and selecting New, Virtual Directory).

- For folders with nonsensitive files, disable Write on the Virtual Directory properties sheet.
- For folders with sensitive files, create a Group for remote FTP access users.

In Explorer, you can assign permissions to this folder so that the remote user Group has read and write permissions, as do you.

Create special Users as members of this group, and remove the Log In Over Network and Interactive permissions from these accounts.

You can give these special accounts to remote users or clients to use as a *somewhat* secure file pickup and drop-off area. It's effective and, if the files being shared are not terribly sensitive, not terribly risky.

If you want to receive files from anonymous users, you must take even more extreme precautions. We really recommend against receiving these files because it makes your site vulnerable to abuse by people trading in illicit material—especially pornography and pirated software. If you absolutely need to be able to receive files from the general public, we suggest that you do the following:

- Create and format a separate partition on your hard disk for this folder so that someone can't fill your entire hard disk.
- Enable logging of anonymous access.
- Remove read and list permissions on this folder from user IUSR_*computername*. This way, people can send files to you but not see what else is already there.

TROUBLESHOOTING

CHECK TO SEE WHETHER IIS IS WORKING

I cannot access my IIS server from another computer.

Go to the computer running IIS, start Internet Explorer, and view the address `http://localhost`. If you see a Web page, then IIS is functioning. If you don't, try restarting it following the instructions in the next troubleshooting tip.

SERVER DOESN'T RESPOND TO REQUESTS

A Web browser locates my computer, but the status stays at `Contacting Server` *or* `Waiting for Response`. *No Web page is returned.*

Use the Internet Services Management tool to stop and restart the IIS Server. Open the Management tool, or locate Internet Information Services in Computer Management. Right-click Restart IIS. Then select Restart Internet Services on *machinename* and click OK.

HYPERLINKS RETURN GIBBERISH

When I click on my links, my browser shows a screen full of random letters and numbers.

Check the file-type to MIME-type mappings on the server and the MIME-type to application viewer on the browser. You can choose File, Save As to save the seemingly senseless information to a file with the appropriate name (for example, XXXX.GIF if you think you have downloaded a GIF file) and try to view it by double-clicking the file in Explorer. If it displays correctly there, then the only problem is the MIME-type mapping.

Browser Doesn't Show Modified Web Page

I have modified a file on my Web site, but the browser still gets the old version.

Click Refresh on the browser. If that trick doesn't work, shut down the browser, restart it, and try again. It's usually the browser's fault. If you still get the wrong version, confirm that you are viewing the correct virtual directory.

Tips from the Windows Pros

The addition of the ASP scripting language to IIS is probably the most powerful feature that Microsoft has added to the Web server market. ASP scripts can take full advantage of COM and ActiveX objects. These objects provide a way for scripts to perform very complex functions using simple Visual Basic scripts.

CGI programming was notoriously complex until ASP came along. Consider the example of adding a feedback form to a Web site. Marketing researchers say that a fill-in form is over *five times* more likely to be used than an email link. I tried it, and it's true. Just think: Adding a form will give you five times as many responses to your Web page.

Sending email with form data used to require an EXE program, which you probably had to pay extra for, and it was hard to configure. Not so with ASP. You can just use the mail-sending objects already built in! This fairly simple Web page lets viewers fill in information, and the text will be sent to you via email.

The following example is simplified, but it shows what ASP can do, and I hope it encourages you to use it.

The file feedback.asp is shown here. Put it into \inetpub\scripts. (First, though, you need to edit this file to add your own email address.) Then view //localhost/scripts/feedback.asp with Internet Explorer.

```
<HTML>
<HEAD>
<TITLE>Feedback Form</TITLE>
</HEAD>
<BODY BGCOLOR=White>

<% @ LANGUAGE="VBSCRIPT" %>
<%
    M_SendTo    = "brian@company.com"
    M_Subject   = "Feedback from web page"

    If request.ServerVariables("REQUEST_METHOD") = "POST" Then
        process_form        ' POST means form is being submitted
    else
        display_form        ' otherwise: GET means form is to be displayed
    End If
```

```
sub display_form     ' send HTML codes to display the form

    response.write "<H1>Feedback</H1>"
    response.write "<P>We'd like to hear from you! Please fill in
                       our feedback form."
    response.write "<FORM NAME=FEEDBACK METHOD=POST ACTION='feedback.asp'>"
    response.write "<P>Your email address: <INPUT NAME=EMAIL
                                             TYPE=TEXT SIZE=60>"
    response.write "<P>Your name: <INPUT NAME=NAME TYPE=TEXT SIZE=40>"
    response.write "<P>Comments: <TEXTAREA NAME=REMARKS ROWS=6
                              COLS=60></TEXTAREA>"
    response.write "<P><INPUT TYPE=SUBMIT VALUE='Send!'>"
    response.write "</FORM>"
end sub

sub process_form      ' get data from Request.Form object,
                        mail with a CDONT object

    if request.Form("EMAIL") <> " then
M_MailFrom = request.Form("EMAIL")
else
M_MailFrom = M_MailTo)
    end if

    Set objSendMail = CreateObject("CDONTS.NewMail")
    objSendMail.From    = M_MailFrom
    objSendMail.To      = M_MailTo
    objSendMail.Subject = M_Subject
    objSendMail.Body    = request.Form("NAME") + " said: " +
                            request.Form("REMARKS")
    objSendMail.Send
    Set objSendMail = Nothing

    response.write "<H1>Thank You!</H1>"
    response.write "<P>We appreciate your comments."
    response.write "<P><A HREF='/'>Click here to return to our home page</A>"
end sub

%>
</BODY>
</HTML>
```

When you post a remark, a file should appear in c:\inetpub\mailroot\Pickup before the SMTP service sends it on its way.

PART IV

NETWORKING

CHAPTER **19**

OVERVIEW OF WINDOWS 2000 NETWORKING

In this chapter

NETWORK CONCEPTS

A revolution is going on now, and it compares to the one Johannes Gutenberg started in 1456 when he pioneered the use of movable type. The ability to print in quantity made it possible for the first time for the common man to gain knowledge by himself. This new revolution is based on global connectivity, and its impact is on our ability to *disseminate* information by ourselves. We now take it for granted that we can share information, preach, publish, talk, and touch the rest of the world through our computers. Networks have radically changed the way the world communicates.

Networks aren't limited to just the work environment anymore. Most homes with a computer quickly end up with two or more, and it's not long before it seems sensible to tie them together with a network. So, whether you have one now, a network is probably in your future. In this chapter, you'll learn how networking works and how Windows 2000 provides the tools to help you become part of the connected world.

> **Note**
>
> This chapter is designed to provide some basic networking concepts. If you have been networking computers for some time, feel free to skip ahead. If you are new to networking, stick around. This chapter will help get you pointed in the right direction.

WHY YOU REALLY NEED A NETWORK

I probably don't have to convince you of the value of tying your computers together with a network, even if you have only two. With a network, you can do the following:

- Use any printer attached to any computer.
- Share files, that is, get at files stored on one computer from another. At home, having this capability might mean you can finish that letter you were writing yesterday using your kids' computer because they're now using yours to manage their stock portfolio. In the office, a network lets workers share information quickly and facilitates the creation of a centralized documentation system.
- Share CD-ROMs.
- Back up networked computers with one common backup system—for example, a tape drive.
- Use network-enabled application software, such as databases, workgroup scheduling and calendar programs, and email. Network-enabled software is designed to give multiple, simultaneous users access to information that is updated in real-time.
- Share a single Internet connection among several computers, saving on telephone lines and connection costs.

A network can justify its cost with printer sharing alone because providing each workstation with a network connection costs less than providing each with a printer. But how hard is it to put together?

No Longer a Dark Art

It doesn't seem possible that it was only 10 years ago that I installed my first network in a client's office. Installing it was nerve-wracking because it had cost my client thousands of dollars in hardware and software above the cost of the computers alone, and although he didn't know, I had never installed networking software or a file server before. Networking was reputed to be a costly, mystical, and dark art, and I soon found that this reputation was well-deserved. The network eventually worked. For several thousand dollars, my client got 10 computers that could read and write the same database file.

Now a network card can cost less than a movie (with popcorn), you can buy network cables at the corner hardware store, and first-class networking software is, well, nearly free...it's free if you would have bought Windows anyway. And for the price of a dinner, you can be connected for a month to *tens of millions* of other computers and people all over the world, sharing everything from your political views, your family tree, your deepest secrets, and your cookie recipes. And you probably take it for granted that you should just be able to plug and play.

In the next few chapters, you'll learn how to use Windows networking to connect to the computer in your basement, to the rest of your office workgroup, or to a worldwide corporate enterprise. You may still need to learn an incantation or two, but fear not, they're no longer in Latin.

One other point: I'll be using the word *resource* frequently in this chapter. By *resource*, I mean a shared folder or printer on someone else's computer, which you can access through the LAN.

Network Neighborhoods

Windows 2000 has, right out of the box, all the software you need to communicate and share information with other computers. Windows 2000 Professional can fill several roles, depending on the way it's connected to other computers. It can be any of the following:

- A standalone computer working in complete isolation. An example might be the simple home computer.

- A standalone computer connected to others via a modem. An example is a laptop computer with a modem used to connect to an office or to the Internet. This computer works in isolation some of the time but can socialize when needed. You can think of this type as a *remote workstation*.

- A member of a small workgroup of computers with no central "server." An example might be a computer in a small office, one of 5 or 10. The computers share resources with each other but are essentially independent. This computer is a *peer* in what is called a *peer-to-peer* network; no one computer has an intrinsically special role in making the network work. All the participants are on equal footing; they are peers. Not all the computers need to use Windows 2000 either; Windows 2000 can peer with Windows NT, 95, 98, and even 3.1.

- A member of a group of computers working under the stewardship of a central server. This computer is probably one of a group of a dozen or more. The designated master computer or server contains, at least, centralized username and password information, which it passes out as a service to the other computers on the network. This computer is the *client* in a *client/server* network. Windows 2000 Professional can be the client of a Windows 2000 Server, or a Novell NetWare or Banyan VINES server.

- A member of a client/server network that is in turn connected to other networks. An example is a computer in a branch office of a large company. This computer is participating in an *enterprise* network, where special consideration has to be made to management, security, and the allocation of resources of many, many computers and people spread out over a wide geographical area.

Windows 2000 has all the stuff to participate in any of these network environments. The one thing it can't do is take the central, or server, role of a client/server or enterprise network. For that, you need at least one computer running Windows 2000 Server or one of its more upscale versions: Advanced Server or DataCenter.

In the next few chapters, you'll learn how to configure and tune up Windows 2000 Professional in each of these environments. If you already understand how networks work, you can skip ahead to "The Many Faces of Windows 2000" later in this chapter. If not, check out the following sections for an introduction to the concepts and terms you should know.

NETWORK FORM AND FUNCTION

What makes a network tick? Let's start by looking at Figure 19.1, the first sort of network you probably built.

Figure 19.1
Did your first network look like this?

Don't laugh! A tin can telephone has many of the attributes of a computer network. The basis of a network is a *physical transport*: a means of carrying raw information (for example, words) over a physical medium (string) between hardware interfaces (cans). When you first used a tin can phone, you found out right away that you couldn't speak at the same time as the person on the other end, so you had to work out a *protocol* to trade off: You probably said "over" after you spoke. Finally, you found that there's a limit to how long the string could be for the phone to work. If the string was too long, you couldn't hear.

Computer networks have these components and limitations, too. The raw information in a network is digital data (bits), carried over a physical medium (usually wires or optical fibers) between hardware interfaces (network cards plugged into your computer), according to a mutually agreeable protocol. Although a tin can network probably isn't too particular about the type of can you use, a computer network is because the endpoints have to use the same sort of electrical or optical signals.

SIZE MATTERS

A computer network is often called a *local area network*, or *LAN*. A LAN is a group of computers connected by a physical medium that supports a relatively high rate of data transmission, say one million bits per second (Mbps) or more, in relatively close proximity, say within one building, all able to communicate directly with each other. Imagine 10 cans on strings, all tied together in the center.

The electrical nature of LAN communication limits the physical distance allowed between computers. LANs can be extended using optical fiber cables, carrying data as pulses of light, to connect groups of computers sharing a more traditional (and inexpensive) electrical connection. You might hear this arrangement called a *campus network* or *metropolitan area network*.

A *wide area network*, or *WAN*, is a group of two or more LANs tied together over longer distances. Historically, these connections were much slower, between 56 thousand bits per second (Kbps) and 1Mbps because long-distance connections were extremely expensive. A 56Kbps connection between San Francisco and Chicago (with a guaranteed throughput of only 16Kbps) cost about $2,500 per month in 1996.

In addition to your data, LANs carry quite a bit of "chatter" between the member computers. This overhead communication occurs as computers broadcast questions, asking for the location of needed resources, and as servers broadcast announcements of the services they provide. A slow WAN connection cannot tolerate carrying this chatter, so special devices called *routers* examine and make decisions about the data to be sent back and forth between the disparate geographical areas.

Long-distance data connections are much faster and less expensive now than in the past. Using the Internet, a 400Kbps connection between any two points in the U.S. can be made for as little as $200 per month. So, as high-speed, long-distance connections become more commonly available, the distinction between LANs and WANs will fade.

PART

IV

CH

19

Grab the Net!

Seems like every computer buzzword these days has "net" in it somewhere. *Internet*, intranet, extranet, internetwork...the whole situation is getting pretty confusing! Let me clear up what these terms mean:

To *internetwork* is to connect two or more LANs somehow, by any means, over any distance. They can be LANs on two different floors of the same building or LANs in two different countries. The point is that the LANs are somehow connected via a router, a long-distance leased-line connection, a satellite link, and so on.

continues

continued

An *internet* (note the lowercase *i*) is the result of two or more distinct, separate networks that have been connected together through some intermediate means. If data from one network can reach the other, it's an internet.

But when I say *the Internet*, I mean the global, public worldwide Internet, which grew out of the U.S. Department of Defense ARPAnet Research network. This is the Internet that ISPs sell access to. (If you made money in the stock market in the late 1990s, thank the Internet.)

Intra means *within* or *inside*. An *intranet*, then, is that part of an organization's network which is inside the organization, out of the reach of the public. Your LAN is an intranet if it has no Internet connection or if it has a firewall in place. This word has also taken on a less precise meaning: Some people use *intranet* to refer to the shared resources on a private network, usually based on standard Web and Internet Protocol technology. For example, a Web server on a company's LAN, which is accessible within the company's network but not from the outside world, might be called an *intranet site*.

Another popular term is *extranet*. It is a marketing concept rather than a technical term. It refers to a public Internet Web site that is controlled by usernames and passwords, so it's "members only." For example, a business might give valued customers access to usually private resources such as an order-entry system or pricing and inventory records. So, an extranet is like an intranet in that it provides privileged resources, but it has outside ("extra") access.

Now, just to help confuse the issue, some Internet companies have started selling *intranet* services to businesses. These companies host Web sites solely for the use of the employees of subscribing companies. They're publicly available via the Internet, and access is controlled by a password. They are really just portal services like My Yahoo. If I were feeling really generous, I might call them *outsourced extranets*. But *intranets*? Nope.

MAKING THE CONNECTION

As you know, a LAN consists of a group of computers connected together using some sort of electrical medium. You can choose from several different electrical media. They differ in the way they format and electrically represent the data sent between computers. You may have heard of some of them already. The others are waning in popularity and you won't be hearing of them again, so don't feel any need to memorize.

- *ARCnet*, *AppleTalk*, and *StarLan* were early network technologies but are hardly used now because they are so much slower than modern technologies. (I personally have very fond memories of my first ARCnet.) AppleTalk is still occasionally used. AppleTalk LANs today typically run only from a Macintosh to its printer and end there.

- *Token ring* was developed by IBM and is still used in businesses that are "blue" to the core, but nobody else in his right mind would install it now because it's slower and much more expensive than Ethernet.

- *Ethernet*, the first hugely successful computer networking technology, was developed by Xerox, Intel, and Digital Equipment Corporation. Ethernet has grown so popular and common that you hardly need to use the word anymore: Most networks are Ethernet networks. Ethernet comes in 10Mbps (million bits per second) and 100Mbps varieties. A connection at 100Mbps is fast enough to transmit the contents of this book in a second or two. Gigabit Ethernet is also available, though it's a new technology and not well standardized between manufacturers.

- *ATM-24* is a very high-speed LAN technology that had some promise to be the next high-speed desktop networking technology, but it has not found wide acceptance. It's based on *Asynchronous Transfer Mode, or ATM*, networking and is widely used in the telecommunications and Internet industries for very high-speed backbone networks. A *backbone* is a term for an ultra-fast connection between the separate parts or sites of a large network. For example, it might refer to the set of links between major network sites of a corporation, the national network of a telephone carrier, or the high-speed Internet links between major ISPs.

No, These Aren't Bank ATMs

ATM uses very small data packets called *cells*, which have none of the addressing and physical addressing overhead of Ethernet, instead relying on a "permanent virtual circuit" technology. Paths between remote computers are established by trading location and IP address information just once. Each connection is assigned an identifier called a *permanent virtual circuit number*, a four-byte number, which is all that the data packets have to carry to be transported through ATM routers.

Therefore, every router in the path between any two computers has to keep track of each established connection by its identification numbers to know where to send incoming ATM cells. This type of routing is a sharp contrast to TCP/IP routing, in which routers examine and route packets independently from each other. ATM routers can handle extreme data rates because they have so much less work to do per packet, at the expense of needing to manage connection information for possibly millions of connected computers.

Most ATM traffic is carried over fiber-optic cables, and to get back to the LAN discussion, it has not found wide acceptance as a basic office LAN technology.

The signals transmitted across a LAN are generated and interpreted by electronics in each computer. Some computers have built-in network interfaces; otherwise, each computer in a LAN needs a *network interface card*, or *NIC*. I may also refer to them as *network cards*.

The electrical signals have to be carried by some sort of wiring system. Network interface cards are designed to use one of the standardized varieties of network cabling, which are described in the following sections.

PART
IV

CH
19

THICK ETHERNET

The original design for Ethernet used a *very* expensive, 1/2-inch thick cable that could carry the 10Mbps Ethernet signal up to 500 meters. It was named 10BASE5 for this reason (this name makes sense to an engineer). The high cost was acceptable when only a few computers in a building were connected, but it was largely superceded by Thin Ethernet.

THIN ETHERNET, OR THINNET

Thin Ethernet uses coaxial cable similar to television cable. It is also called 10BASE2 Ethernet, which indicates that the network runs at 10Mbps and has a maximum wiring length of 200 meters or 660 feet. Thin Ethernet cables end in distinctive twist-on connectors called bayonet connectors, or BNC.

The wiring for thick or thin Ethernet runs from computer to computer in a daisy-chain fashion called a *bus* network, as shown in Figure 19.2.

Figure 19.2
Thin Ethernet network cabling runs from computer to computer in a single unbroken line called a bus.

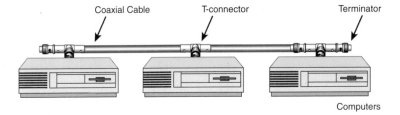

Coaxial Cable   T-connector   Terminator

Computers

UNSHIELDED TWISTED-PAIR (UTP)

Unshielded Twisted-Pair, or UTP, has become the most common network carrier, and is so called because like-colored pairs of wires in the cable are gently twisted together for better immunity to electrical interference from fluorescent lights, radio signals, and so on. This inexpensive type of cable is also used for telephone connections, although the network variety is of a higher quality and is certified for its capability to carry high data rates. UTP cables are terminated with eight-wire RJ45 connectors, which are wider versions of the ubiquitous modular telephone connectors.

UTP cabling can carry token ring signals but is most commonly used for Ethernet networking. You can buy two varieties of UTP-based Ethernet hardware; I'll explain the 10BASE-T variety first.

If you've been paying attention, you might guess that the *10BASE* part means 10Mbps, but *T*? The *T* stands for twisted pair, and you just have to *know* that the maximum permitted cable length is 100 meters, or 330 feet.

Unlike ThinNet's all-in-a-row bus wiring pattern, 10BASE-T devices are connected to a central device called a *hub* in what is called a *star* network, as shown in Figure 19.3. If any cable in a bus network breaks, the whole network fails. If a cable in a star network fails, only the computer connected by that cable goes offline.

The maximum cable distance from hub to computer of only 100 meters or 330 feet limits 10BASE-T's usefulness in a large building or campus LAN. Hubs can solve this problem by serving to several close-by computers and then connecting to each either other with ThinNet or fiber-optic cable, which forms a "backbone" connecting groups of computers, as shown in Figure 19.4.

10BASE-T and ThinNet Ethernet cards now cost about the same (typically $10 to $75 each), and some NICs have both types of connectors. Hubs have fallen in price to as little as $5 per port, so there is now no economic argument in favor of ThinNet; as a result, I expect it to virtually disappear (although existing networks using ThinNet could be in existence for years to come).

Figure 19.3
Unshielded twisted-pair network with a hub, forming a star pattern.

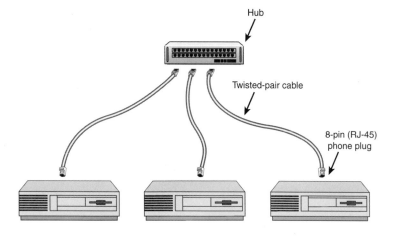

Figure 19.4
In larger LANs, 10BASE-T hubs are connected together to span larger distances. Hubs can be connected using 10BASE-T, ThinNet, or fiber-optic cabling.

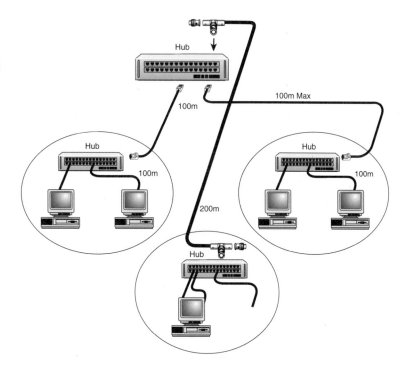

Tip #228	Because thin Ethernet cable has only one wire, like our tin can network, only one device at a time can "speak." In networking parlance, this is called a *half-duplex* network. 10BASE-T is usually half-duplex, too. 10BASE-T cards from some manufacturers can operate in full-duplex mode—two network cards can "speak" to each other simultaneously—if all the cards and hubs in the network are so capable.

continues

continued

Operating this way can help boost communication rates somewhat, but it does not double them. Most computer-to-computer conversations are just like the ones you dread being trapped in at parties: One person does most of the talking, while you just nod and say "uh huh" every so often. In a full-duplex network, the "uh huhs" don't have to interrupt the nonstop talker, so the conversation goes a little bit faster—but not much. Full-duplex network cards are labeled 10BASE-Tx or 100BASE-Tx by their manufacturers. Paying extra for this feature is generally not worthwhile for the average office network, but it's nice if it comes standard with the network hardware you end up buying.

FAST ETHERNET

Fast Ethernet is a 100Mbps version of Ethernet over UTP cable. It is also called 100BASE-T or 100BASE-Tx. (The x stands for full-duplex, which is standard with 100BASE-T networking hardware.) The hardware is 10 times faster but not too much more expensive than 10BASE-T hardware. Everything I said previously about 10BASE-T applies to Fast Ethernet as well. However, the cable required to carry this high-speed signal is a bit more expensive and requires more care in its installation. Hubs and network cards cost a bit more, too.

OPTICAL FIBER

Optical fiber is capable of gigabit (1000MBps) speeds and can also carry data over runs of several miles, quite a bit farther than standard Ethernet. Optical fiber is not generally run directly to individual computers, but between hubs and routers between buildings, to form the "backbone" of a campus network, as shown in Figure 19.5. Optical fiber cables can carry 10 or 100Mbps Ethernet data, as well as more advanced, even higher-speed data formats called *Fiber Distributed Date Interface (FDDI)* and *Asynchronous Transfer Mode (ATM)*.

Figure 19.5
Optical fiber cable linking two 100BASE-T hubs via a fiber "uplink" port. Cables contain pairs of fibers because each fiber can carry information in only one direction.

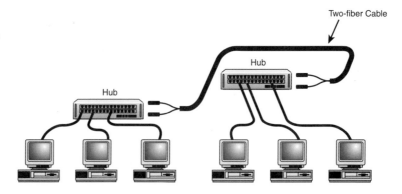

Two-fiber Cable

Hub

Hub

GIGABIT ETHERNET

Gigabit Ethernet is a new technology whose standards are not yet stabilized. It's expensive (now), but a hundredfold increase in speed is nothing to sneeze at if you're involved in high-speed videoconferencing or other such intensive communication work. It's also used for the backbones of large networks and for fast server-to-server connections.

WIRELESS ETHERNET

Wireless Ethernet is becoming reasonably priced now. Using wireless network adapters, you can connect computers in a small area (for example, an office setting) via radio, as illustrated in Figure 19.6. The data rate is only a few million bits per second, but it's great for networking laptops. It has always seemed silly to me to have a portable computer tied down by network and power wires. Starting in the year 2000, wireless network products will achieve 10Mbps speeds or more and will become more economical. For business use, they may achieve parity with wired networks, when the cost of wiring and maintenance are factored in. For convenience, wireless probably can't be beat.

Figure 19.6
Wireless hub connecting computers to a standard twisted-pair network.

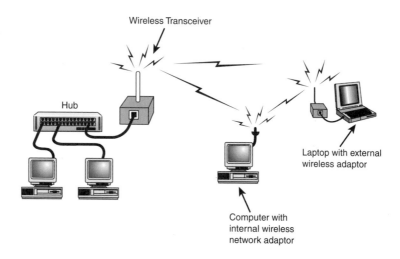

Wireless Transceiver

Hub

Laptop with external wireless adaptor

Computer with internal wireless network adaptor

PART

IV

CH

19

THE OSI MODEL

If you've read about networks in any other computer book, you've probably seen a diagram similar to the one in Figure 19.7, the OSI Standard Network Model. The International Organization for Standardization (ISO) and Institute of Electrical and Electronic Engineers (IEEE) developed this model—I think to help computer book authors fill lots of pages trying to explain it. It's in every computer book I've ever seen.

I will spare you the usual long explanation of this diagram because I don't think it's very helpful as an introduction to networking. But I do think it helps illustrate that networks are composed of modular components, *conceptually* stacked one on top of the other, each performing a job for the component above it, using the components below. The parts are interchangeable in that you may often choose between several components to do a given job. As long as the job is done correctly, the layers above don't really care how it's done.

Figure 19.7
The OSI Standard Model for Computer Networks–a required figure in almost every computer book. Networks are built from components, each of which performs a job for a higher-level component in the "stack."

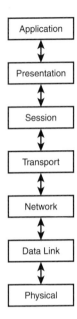

The components in this stack communicate with their corresponding components in the other computers on the network. As you go down in these stacks, the layers are less concerned with *interpreting* the data they handle and more with simply *moving* it somewhere. The higher level components interpret and communicate with each other to reassure each other that the data they have sent was correctly received, and they rely on the lower levels to actually transport that data from one computer to another.

That's the OSI network model in two paragraphs.

In the real world—at least in the Windows world—the stack of components that make up Windows networking really does exist. Figure 19.8 shows the Windows network model. When you want to access a remote network resource somewhere inside the operating system, the following actions occur:

- A *network client* composes data messages to communicate these desires to the remote computer, using an agreed-upon file sharing protocol.

- These messages are packaged according to a *transport protocol*, which specifies how messages are to be broken into manageable pieces, how the pieces are to be addressed to member computers, and how to re-request missing or garbled pieces as they are received.

- The packaged message pieces are called *packets* and are physically carried by a *data link or framing protocol* that determines how to arrange the bits of information in each packet for transmission.

- The bits are converted into electrical pulses or flashes of light and carried from one computer to another through a *physical medium* that carries the pulses or flashes to another computer.

- The pulses or flashes work their way up the network components on the other side and are finally delivered to a *server* component that satisfies the request by sending data back through the same system to the client.

Figure 19.8
A practical Windows network model, with actual Windows network components.

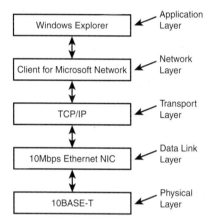

The Data Link level is handled entirely by the hardware in a *network interface card* (NIC), When you buy a network card, you're buying a data link protocol and the attachment to the physical medium. Because the card is what you'll actually see and have to describe to Windows, from this point on, I'll talk about adapters rather than data link protocols.

NETWORK CLIENTS

Microsoft provides two network clients with Windows 2000: the Client for Microsoft Networks and a Client for Novell NetWare networks. Novell supplies its own version of the NetWare client, so you actually have a choice of three.

These components, at the top of their network stacks, communicate with their corresponding top-level components in other computers to read and write files, queue printer data, read the contents of folders for display in Explorer, and so on. The Client for Microsoft Networks uses the *Server Message Block (SMB)* and *NetBIOS* protocols to speak to other Windows computers, Windows 2000 Servers, and IBM OS/2 LAN Manager Servers. You won't ever encounter SMB or NetBIOS directly in your dealings with Windows Networking; they're part of the Client and Server software.

The Novell client can communicate with Novell NetWare-based file servers using the built-in *NetWare Core Protocol (NCP)*, or with a Windows 2000 Server network service called File Services for Novell Networks. File Services for Novell and File Services for Macintosh are available only with Windows 2000 Server and its more advanced versions.

PART

IV

CH

19

These services allow a Windows 2000 Server to share files and printers with Novell workstations and Apple Macintosh computers.

PROTOCOLS

As you learned previously, transport protocols define how data is arranged and sent in a coordinated fashion between computers.

Transport Control Protocol/Internet Protocol, or TCP/IP, is one such transport protocol which forms the basis of the Internet. TCP/IP is actually a set of many protocols that are used to provide the services that higher-level network components need: resolving computer names into network card and IP addresses, guaranteed transmission, and Internetwork routing. The *TCP* part, or *Transmission Control Protocol*, is the method an IP-based network uses to guarantee that data is sent end-to-end without errors. I'll go into more detail about TCP/IP in a little bit.

Internetwork Packet Exchange/Sequenced Packet Exchange, or *IPX/SPX*, was developed by Novell for its NetWare network software. Like TCP/IP, IPX/SPX is really a set of protocols that provide many services, including name resolution, guaranteed transport, and Internetwork routing.

NetBEUI was developed by IBM for its original IBM PC Network; it provides similar services to TCP/IP and IPX/SPX, except that it doesn't have a mechanism to route data to remote networks. NetBEUI can transport data between computers only on the same physical LAN. With the increasing popularity of the Internet and WANs, NetBEUI is not fully up to the task and is losing favor.

The Client for Microsoft Networks can use any of these three protocols to send its messages to a file server; all that's required is that both the client computer and server computer have at least one of the same protocols installed. In contrast, the NetWare client requires the IPX/SPX protocol. Windows 2000 Professional supports a few other transport protocols that aren't used by the file service clients:

- *AppleTalk* and its Ethernet-based counterpart *LocalTalk* are used in Apple Macintosh networking. Windows Professional cannot share files directly with Macintosh computers, although Windows 2000 Server can. Windows Pro provides support for AppleTalk in order to use Apple printers connected directly to the LAN.

- *DLC* is an IBM networking protocol, but you won't run into it directly unless you're working on a corporate network with IBM mainframes. In that case, if it's used, your company's network management staff will want to take care of this task for you. It is also used by some network-connected printers.

- *Point-to-Point Protocol*, or *PPP*, is used to carry Internet Protocol data packets across a modem connection. This protocol is used to establish most all modem connections to Internet service providers.

■ *Point-to-Point Tunneling Protocol*, or *PPTP*, is used to create *Virtual Private Networks*, or *VPNs*. PPTP takes data destined for a private, hidden network, repackages the data for transmission across the Internet, and at the other end unpackages the data to be released into the private, protected network. I'll go into greater detail explaining VPNs in Chapter 23, "Windows Unplugged: Remote and Mobile Networking." For the purposes of this chapter, I'll point out that you don't need to install or configure it directly in Windows 2000 because you might have done so with Windows NT or 9x.

Tip #229

You might be interested to note that PPTP is not, strictly speaking, a transport protocol. It actually straddles several network layers. It acts like a network adapter on its top side, taking packets from any transport protocol (see Figure 19.9). It encrypts and repackages the data into TCP/IP packets and then acts like a transport protocol itself to send them through a network adapter or dial-up connection across a network (usually the Internet) for unpackaging on the other side.

Figure 19.9
PPTP acts like an network adapter on its "top" side and like a transport protocol on its "bottom." It delivers data destined to a remote network by repackaging it for transmission over the Internet.

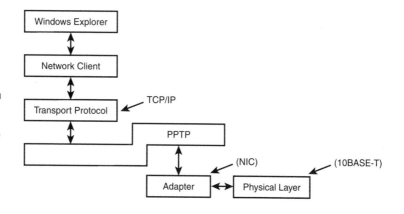

PART

IV

CH

19

NETWORK ADAPTERS

Earlier in the chapter, I described the popular physical media and data link protocols used in LANs when I described UTP and coaxial cable media, and mentioned the Ethernet and token ring data link protocols. As I said, they are usually lumped together for convenience.

Tip #230

Now you know that when I say "10BASE-T Ethernet," I'm really describing two different things: 10Mbps Ethernet framing over UTP cable. The next time you meet someone at a cocktail party and can't think of a good opening line, you can share this fascinating fact as an icebreaker.

At the physical level, network cards send packets of data through their physical medium from one to another. Network cards have two ways of sending data: directly, from one card to another; and broadcasting, which sends the same data packet to *every* card on the network. Each network card has an address (like a phone number) that is actually built right into the hardware of the network card. It is called the *physical network address* or *media access control (MAC)* address. When a data packet is addressed directly to a MAC address, only the one intended computer receives and examines the data. When a broadcast is made, every computer receives and must examine the data to see whether it needs to pay attention to that data.

RESOLVING A BIG PROBLEM

The preceding sections pretty much cover the technology for sending data from computer to computer. Next, let's look at how networks find computers by name.

My computer's physical network address is 00-C0-CA-14-09-2F, but I certainly don't want to know that. I want to view files on the computer named Java. It's up to the network software to *resolve* the name Java into its MAC address 00-C0-CA-14-09-2F. How this is accomplished depends on the transport protocol in use: NetBEUI or TCP/IP. The difference between the two is significant.

BURNING BRIDGES WITH NETBEUI

I'm sure you've tried to find a friend in a crowded airport lobby. The quickest way to find him or her is to stand up on a chair and shout out his or her name. Works like a charm, even though it momentarily interrupts everyone around you. NetBEUI resolves names this way. It broadcasts a request to every computer on the network: "Will the computer named Java please send me a message with your MAC address!"

This approach is fine when the desired computer is on the same physical LAN wire; in fact, it's great as it works without any configuration at all. But when two LANs are separated by a WAN link, NetBEUI's technique would require that the broadcast message be sent across the WAN. The WAN link would *have* to transmit every broadcast on every connected LAN to every other connected LAN to be sure that every computer could be found. This type of network-to-network connection is called *bridging*. It's the term for sending data between two networks based entirely on MAC-level addressing.

Bridging equipment can learn by listening that two MAC addresses are on the same side of the WAN and not transmit them, but broadcasts must always be sent across. Remember that WAN links are historically slow, on the order of 64Kbps, and with a few hundred computers sending a broadcast every minute or so, the WAN link would be fully occupied, carrying only broadcast messages and no useful data.

So, NetBEUI is considered a bad choice for networks with wide area links because it requires that remote networks be bridged. Today's faster networks help, but there's a better way.

THE IP ROUTE

An *Internet Protocol*, or *IP*, based network takes a more sophisticated approach to finding computers by name. Each computer in an IP network is given an *IP address*, which I'm sure you've seen before; it's a number like 198.70.146.70. Every IP data packet carries this IP address along with it, so IP packets have *two* addresses: their IP address, contained in the data packet, and their MAC layer address.

On an IP network, a *name service* is run on a designated computer to do the job of turning names into IP addresses. This is a huge advantage because the job of looking up names is separated from the job of routing data from one computer or LAN from another. First, let's look at how an IP network sends data to local or remote LANs.

When data is sent using IP, the sending computer determines whether the destination computer is on the same physical LAN. If the destination computer is on the same physical LAN, the sending computer uses the stand-up-and-shout approach: It broadcasts a request for computer number 198.70.146.70 to please identify itself (in IP lingo, it *ARPs*), and with that information can deliver the packet to its destination.

When the IP address is *not* a local address, the sending computer forwards the packet to a *router*, which forwards the packet out across the WAN or the Internet, which is just a *very large* IP WAN. Routers along the way relay the packet from one router to the next by examining the IP address. The backbone routers of an IP WAN or the Internet know exactly where to send every IP packet based on its IP address. Eventually, the packet finds its way to a router on the destination LAN, where the router ARPs and sends the packet to its intended computer.

How does a router or computer tell whether an IP address is local? The answer is in the *subnet mask*, that mysterious 255.255.255.something number that you've probably entered into at least one home computer to connect to the Internet.

An IP address is a series of four numbers between 0 and 255. It can be written in binary as a 32-bit number, as in this example:

`11000110 01000110 10010010 01000110`

A network mask can also be written in binary; for example, 255.255.255.240 is

`11111111 11111111 11111111 11110000`

The part of an IP address next to the ones in its subnet mask is called the *subnet number*, and the remainder is the *node number* or node address.

IP address	11000110 01000110 10010010 01000110
subnet mask	11111111 11111111 11111111 11110000
subnet number	11000110 01000110 10010010 01000
node number	110

Every computer on an IP LAN must have the same subnet number. If the subnet number of a destination IP address matches the sender's subnet number, the address is local: shout, get the MAC address, send directly. If the subnet number differs, the computer simply punts: It sends the packet to a designated *gateway*, a router whose job it is to ultimately deliver the packet.

Tip #231	You probably suspect that this description is an oversimplification. It's not, actually, for the simple case I've described. What I've left out are details about how routers decide which of several possible directions to send a given packet and how they communicate new routes and traffic reports to each other. For a detailed look at the IP protocol and network technology, you might check out the following books:
	Practical Cisco Routers, ISBN: 0-7897-2103-1, Que
	Upgrading and Repairing Networks, Second Edition, ISBN: 0-7897-2034-5, Que

Note	If you're interested in the nitty-gritty details of Microsoft's implementation of network protocols, including TCP/IP timing, tuning, and Registry entry details, check out `http://www.microsoft.com/windows2000/library/default.asp`.

BINARY/DECIMAL CONVERSION

The four numbers of the IP address really correspond to a 32-bit binary number. For convenience, IP addresses and network masks are written in what's called *dotted decimal notation*. To get the binary version, you convert the four decimal numbers from decimal to binary and string them together. To get the dotted decimal number from the binary, you divide the 32-bit string of bits into four sets of eight and convert them each to decimal.

I hate to open a can of worms by going into binary-to-decimal conversion—this description could take half of a chapter by itself if I explain carefully. It's not really necessary for this discussion, but in brief, the process goes like this:

To convert an IP address's decimal number to binary, get a list of the powers of two, like this:

```
1, 2, 4, 8, 16, 32, 64, 128
```

Starting with the *largest* number in the list, go through each of these powers of two in turn. If you can subtract it from the number to be converted without going negative, do so, and write down a 1. Otherwise, write down a 0. With the result of your subtraction, repeat the process with each smaller power of two. Converting 240 to binary looks like this:

240 – 128	= 112, so you write:	1
112 – 64	= 48, so you write:	1
48 – 32	= 16, so you write:	1

16 – 16	= 0, so you write:	1
0 – 8	would be negative, so you write:	0
0 – 4	ditto	0
0 – 2	ditto	0
0 – 1	ditto	0

The result is read top down: 11110000. Try it yourself. Converting 10, you should get 00001010. With 255, you should get 11111111.

For a full IP address or network mask, you convert each of the four decimal numbers separately and string the four resulting binary numbers together. For example, 255.255.255.240 gives 11111111 11111111 11111111 11110000.

Converting binary to decimal is a little easier. First, you take the same list of the powers of two:

1, 2, 4, 8, 16, 32, 64, 128

Starting at the *right* side of the binary number and working toward the left, you add any powers of two that correspond to 1 in the binary number. Let's convert 10100010 as an example. Starting at the right, the 1 bits correspond to 2, 32, and 128. So, the result is 2 + 32 + 128 = 162. Spread out, the process looks like this:

0 is rightmost,	corresponds to: 1	Equals
1	2	2
0	4	
0	8	
0	16	
1	32	32
0	64	
1	128	+ 128
		162

Try the whole procedure with the network mask you saw earlier: 11111111111111111111111111110000. Divide it into four parts of eight bits each: 11111111 11111111 11111111 11110000. Convert each of these parts to decimal independently. The first three parts are 11111111, which has all bits set to 1: 1 + 2 + 4 + 8 + 16 + 32 + 64 + 128 = 255.

The last part is 11110000, or 16 + 32 +64 + 128 = 240.

So, the dotted decimal version is 255.255.255.240.

WINDOWS NETWORKING AND TCP/IP

To return the discussion to name resolution, let me describe how a TCP/IP network turns names into addresses. Two name resolution systems are involved: WINS and DNS.

WINS

The *Windows Internet Naming System*, or *WINS*, was introduced with Windows NT, which was the first Microsoft operating system that allowed Microsoft File Sharing to operate over the TCP/IP protocol. Windows users are used to using one-word names to identify computers, and networks can contain computers using NetBIOS and IPX/SPX as well as the TCP/IP protocol. Microsoft developed WINS as an integrated address resolution system. It learns the names of all the computers connected to each network connected to any server running WINS and makes these names available to TCP/IP-based computers on those networks. When a new computer appears on the network, the computer registers itself with the WINS server so that other computers can find it by name.

More importantly, WINS servers trade information across a WAN or the Internet, making name service available out of the reach of NetBEUI-based computers. The addition of WINS and TCP/IP to Microsoft networking made file sharing across a WAN a much more efficient operation, as it removed the requirement for bridging NetBEUI packets across a WAN link.

It works like this: A WINS server responds to broadcasts ("Will a WINS server please tell me the address of the computer named Java?"), but on a large network, you can tell Windows to direct its request to a specific WINS server at a particular IP address. This way, a TCP/IP-based client can find computers across a WAN link, through TCP/IP's capability to efficiently route directly addressed packets from network to network, without the need to send broadcast packets across the link as well.

Tip #232	Windows 2000 supports WINS, but it's no longer really necessary. When you use Windows 2000 Server to manage the network, Windows 2000 can use the standard Internet-style DNS system to locate network resources.

DNS

Domain name service, or *DNS*, is the name resolution system used by all Internet-based software. The domain name service is a sort of distributed database system that looks up names such as www.mcp.com and returns IP addresses such as 198.70.146.70. It also provides *Inverse DNS* information, which tells you that IP address 198.70.146.70 is www.mcp.com.

You can use DNS-based naming with Microsoft Networking, too; that is, you can tell Windows Explorer to view \\server.mycompany.com. Windows tries WINS first, if it's set up, and then attempts to resolve the name using DNS. If DNS succeeds, Windows then goes ahead and uses Microsoft File Sharing to connect to the computer using the TCP/IP protocol.

Caution

I will warn you many times that you must somehow put up a barrier between the Internet access and Microsoft Networking on your computer, even if you only use a modem to connect to the Internet. When you're connected, your shared files are vulnerable to attack by hackers if you're not adequately prepared.

On Windows 2000 Server-based networks, in fact, Microsoft is encouraging the use of DNS even within a company, rather than the old-fashioned single-word computer names. Microsoft is making this use easier by tying Windows 2000 Server's DNS service into the *Active Directory*, which identifies all Windows 2000 computers, networks, users, and resources.

DNS was designed for the original 1970s Internet with its fairly static database; entering new computers and domains was time-consuming. The DNS server provided with Windows 2000 Server, however, interacts with the Microsoft networking system on a dynamic basis to learn the names of computers as they plug into and leave the network.

THE MANY FACES OF WINDOWS 2000

Now you know what makes a network work. I've described how a network is composed of layers of software and hardware whose purpose is to let high-level client and server software provide useful services to you and the operating system. Security is a major concern in networks: We can't have the mailroom staff looking up the executives' salaries.

The Windows approach to network security varies, depending on the type of network community to which it's connected. The following sections describe what these different network types are and how Windows 2000 changes with each one.

THE WINDOWS PEER-TO-PEER NETWORK

On a peer-to-peer network, Windows 2000 Professional is a terrific member workstation, and you can set up shared folders with just the click of a mouse. Professional is also quite friendly with Windows 95, 98, and Windows for Workgroups, and treats them as peers, too. It can attach to Novell NetWare and Banyan VINES servers as well, if they're part of your network.

The downside of the peer-to-peer network is that each Windows workstation manages its own separate username/password database. Because there's no centralized control over user privileges, obtaining access to shared folders and printers on your LAN can be hit or miss. If you haven't been added as a user of the computer whose shared resources you want to use, you're out of luck. Users might then be tempted to make their shared folders accessible to "Everyone", and that's *very risky* from a security standpoint, especially if you're connected to the Internet by modem. Everyone means *everyone*; even some high school hacker in Hamburg can get at your files.

→ To learn more about shared folder security, **see** "Specific Configuration Steps For Windows 2000," **p. 963**.

To locate resources on a peer-to-peer network, you might have to hunt around a bit. Either you must know the name of the computer whose resources you want to use, or you have to poke around My Network Places (called Network Neighborhood in earlier versions of Windows). Poking around is fine on small networks but can be cumbersome on large networks with more than a few dozen computers.

Administration of the computers on a peer-to-peer network is handled on an individual basis also. Each computer has its own privileged "Administrator" account, so anyone with his or her computer's Administrator password can have at the Windows setup and configuration. Restricting the damage that individual users can inflict on the computers is rather difficult, though possible, but this type of control would itself have to be administered to each computer individually.

THE WINDOWS 2000 SERVER NETWORK

When a Windows 2000 Professional computer is part of a domain managed by Windows 2000 Server, something different happens: Windows Pro relinquishes the job of identifying users and their passwords to Server. This is a *good* thing. As part of a domain, when you log in on any member computer, your identity is actually verified by the Server, and you are automatically recognized by every Windows 2000 and NT computer on the whole network. Permission to view files, of course, can be granted or taken away by the owner of each computer; I'll explain how to manage permissions in Chapter 26. The point is that with a common user database, you can easily maintain good security practices because you can easily control access to resources properly.

When you're part of a domain (or group of domains), locating shared resources is no easier than it is on a peer-to-peer network. Either you need to know the name of the workstation or server you want to use, or you have to burrow through the domains and computers displayed in domain-sized groups on My Network Places.

Finally, as part of a Server-based network, the domain administrator—that is, the administrator of the Server computer—can exercise some serious control over what users of each computer can see and do, thanks to the Windows profile and policy systems. These features have two effects:

- They provide a way to deliver the same desktop, Control Panel, and software settings to a user no matter which computer he or she uses.

- They let the domain administrator individually remove or "lock down" Windows features and Control Panel options that change network, display, hardware, and network settings for individuals or groups of users. Management costs are reduced by removing the users' ability to customize (equivalently, mess up) their own computers.

Quite a personality change, isn't it? Of course, exercising this kind of control is completely up to the Domain administrator.

THE ACTIVE DIRECTORY NETWORK

Finally, when Windows 2000 Professional is a member of a Server network with Active Directory, an even more comprehensive management structure comes into play. With Active Directory, the network administrators can do everything I mentioned in the preceding sections *plus* delegate management responsibilities to lower levels in the chain of command, at just about any level of detail they desire.

For example, a large company with many small branch offices could let branch managers assign users at their branches to departmental groups but not change their passwords. The network administrator could let the San Francisco network manager change network settings but not the Winnemucka manager, and so on. The level of what Microsoft calls *granularity* in control and delegation is nearly unlimited.

This capability could mean one of two things to you, the Windows 2000 Professional user:

- Nothing at all because you're not part of an Active-Directory based network
- Nothing at all because you are locked out of all this fun stuff by your network manager

I'm only partly kidding. If you're a Windows Professional user on an Active Directory network, these management features affect you only when they prevent you from doing something. The only new thing you have to learn is the telephone number of the network manager who's responsible for your computer. (This manager, on the other hand, has so much new to learn that he or she is probably in a class somewhere right now, on the verge of tears).

Active Directory services also let network managers assign application software to users or groups, so your desktop automatically picks up icons for software you haven't even installed but your organization thinks you need. When you go to use it, boom, it installs itself. (It works this way in theory anyway, and I'm sure as Windows 2000 matures through several Service Packs, this feature will actually be used in the real world.)

Active Directory also lets you search for network resources and organizational information in a very useful, unified way. The Active Directory is designed to contain all kinds of information about the resources on a network, the network's users, and the structure of the organization itself. We're all used to the searching power on the World Wide Web, and now Windows 2000 brings us the same power to search on a company's worldwide network. Want to find the email address of your pal Sal in the Sonoma Sales Center? No problem, Active Directory can find it in a flash. Need to find a printer in your building that can print on both sides in color? One click, and you'll have it.

PART
IV

CH
19

THE WINDOWS OFFLINE/REMOTE NETWORK

Windows 2000 Professional can also exhibit Multiple Personality Disorder: Meet the remote workstation. Windows can behave like a standalone computer when you're working at home or toting your laptop around the field, and then it can act like a domain member when connected to a Server-based network by modem or docking port.

An additional feature Windows offers to the remote user is the "offline" file. Windows lets you mark files or folders for offline use and copies them from the network to your hard drive. When you're disconnected from the network, you have access to this copy, even though it still appears to be in a folder on another networked computer. When you reconnect, by modem or by plugging into the office network, Windows automatically synchronizes the "offline" files, copying anything you changed back to the network and retrieving any updated files from the network to your hard disk.

| Tip #233 | Offline files are similar to the My Briefcase function offered by Windows 9x. The advantage to offline files, however, is that they appear to stay in their original locations. Windows invisibly keeps track of the offline copies, so you don't have to worry about dragging files to and from the briefcase folder. |
| | I have to admit I never understood My Briefcase anyway, and I suspect few people did. |

WINDOWS 2000'S NETWORK SERVICES

Besides file and printer sharing, Windows 2000 provides many other network services. You may never interact with some of these services directly, but their presence makes Windows the amazing application platform it is.

Let's take a tour of Windows network services. I'll describe what each service is, why it's useful, and perhaps a bit about how it works, and I'll tell you where to find out how to install, configure, or use it, if appropriate.

FILE AND PRINTER SHARING

Networking software was developed to share and transfer files between computers (America Online Buddy Chat came later, if you can believe that!). Windows 2000 comes with the following features:

- Client for Microsoft Networks, which gives access to files and printers shared by Windows for Workgroups; Windows 95, NT, and 98; as well as OS/2 LAN Manager.

- File and Printer Sharing for Microsoft Networks, which lets Windows Professional share files and printers with users of those same operating systems. Windows Pro is limited to 10 simultaneous connections from other computers, which makes it less wonderful than Windows 2000 Server on larger LANs.

- Web Sharing, which is a new technology that provides secure file copying to and from shared folders over the Internet, using the Web's Hypertext Transfer Protocol. The new part is that it uses full Windows security and the Windows Explorer user interface, while the underlying technology is based on the World Wide Web and Microsoft's Internet Information Server.

- Client for Novell Networks, which gives access to files and printers shared by Novell NetWare file servers.

- UNIX Print Services, which lets you use and share printers with computers using the UNIX operating system's LPR protocol.

Unlike Windows 2000 Server, however, Pro has no tools to share files with Apple Macintosh computers or to use Macintosh shared folders.

→ For information about installing, configuring, and using Microsoft network software, **see** Chapters 20 through 23.

→ For information about interacting with Novell and UNIX servers, **see** Chapter 25, "Networking Mix and Match."

ROAMING USER PROFILES

When Windows Professional is connected to a Windows Server Domain, besides simply validating usernames and passwords, Server can supply Pro computers with a *profile* for each user as he or she logs in.

A profile contains information that helps Windows Professional make its desktop and folders look the same no matter which physical computer you use. User profiles contain the following:

- Desktop icons and shortcuts
- The contents of your My Files and Documents folder
- Your configuration and preference settings for all the software you use, from your Word preferences to your choice of screen savers
- Management settings that control, for example, whether you are allowed to change Control Panel entries

Roaming user profiles are covered in more depth in Chapter 32, "Managing Users."

PART

IV

CH

19

DISTRIBUTED APPLICATIONS

Windows 2000 provides network protocols which let software application developers write programs that interact across a network. You will probably never have to install, configure, or even know such protocols exist; you'll just use the programs that use them and happily go about your business. But someone may mention them, so you should be familiar with their names: RPC and COM+.

RPC

Microsoft's remote procedure call (RPC) network protocol allows software to be split into pieces that run on different computers and interact across a network. The RPC mechanism is used, for instance, when a user on one Windows computer pauses print spooling on another. It's the basis of most of Windows's remote management capabilities; these are more sophisticated things than the authors of the basic file sharing protocols made allowances for.

COM+ (FORMERLY COM AND DCOM)

The former Component Object Model (COM) and Distributed COM (DCOM) services have been combined in Windows 2000 to the upgraded COM+ service. COM provides software developers tools to build highly modular software in a variety of languages. You should be happy it exists and happier if you never hear about it again.

To learn more about COM and DCOM, pick up a copy of *COM/DCOM Unleashed*, published by Sams Publishing.

VIRTUAL PRIVATE NETWORKING

Windows 2000 Professional can connect to remote LANs through the Internet using Virtual Private Networking (VPN). This very secure technology makes it safe to use Microsoft networking over the Internet.

→ If you're interested in learning more about Virtual Private Networking, **see** "Virtual Private Networking," **p. 830**.

REMOTE ACCESS

If you travel with a laptop or often work from a location outside your physical LAN, you can still use RAS (Remote Access Service) to interact with people and files on your network.

→ RAS is covered briefly in this chapter; for more detailed coverage, **see** "Dial-Up Networking," **p. 798**.

CONNECTION BY MODEM

Windows Professional allows you to configure a modem for incoming connections as well as outgoing. You can provide access to your LAN via modem, for example, to retrieve files from your office while you are at home or in the field. At most, two incoming connections are permitted with Pro.

→ To configure Remote Access, **see** "Enabling Dial-In Access to Your Computer," **p. 813**.

INCOMING VPN

Windows Professional also allows you to connect to your LAN via the Point-to-Point Tunneling Protocol (PPTP); that is, it lets you create a Virtual Private Network. If your LAN has a full-time Internet connection, it will (or it should) have a firewall installed, thus preventing you from using file sharing directly from the outside world. A VPN connection lets you safely penetrate the firewall to gain access to your LAN over the Internet.

WINDOWS TERMINAL SERVICES

Windows 2000 Server provides a sort of remote-control system called Windows Terminal Services. Terminal Services let you use a Server computer remotely. Your applications run on the Server while you use your computer's display, keyboard, and mouse. The Service itself runs only on Windows Server, but the Client, or terminal side, is available for Windows Professional, NT, 95, 98, and 3.1.

Terminal Services was designed with two distinct purposes in mind. The first was to let inexpensive, slow computers run applications on a fast, beefy server. Think of the checkout lines in a store: Here, several terminals all run the same single application. Using a bunch of cheap "terminals" might make sense, providing just screens and keyboards for a program running on one computer in a back office. The second use of Terminal Services is to let administrators take control of a Windows Server computer from afar, for maintenance purposes, from a computer running any Microsoft platform. Both the server software and the client-side software come only with Windows 2000 Server. When you have it, you can distribute the client-side software wherever necessary.

CONNECTION SHARING

Windows 2000 Professional has a new feature that appeared in the Windows 98 Second Edition as well: Connection Sharing. This feature lets one Windows Pro computer with a modem or high-speed Internet connection provide Internet access to all users of a LAN. This access is somewhat limited, however. It requires that the LAN use the Windows built-in automatic IP address configuration system, so it's incompatible with WAN configurations. It also requires that the computer with the modem or high-speed connection be left turned on all the time.

Connection sharing is described in more detail in Chapter 24, "Connecting Your LAN to the Internet."

ACTIVE DIRECTORY

As discussed earlier in this chapter, Windows 2000 introduces a new service called the *Active Directory* (AD). Active Directory combines a name/address directory, management and security services, and wide-area replicated database technologies to provide a foundation for all of Windows 2000's networking functions. If your network is managed by a Windows 2000 Server with AD installed, this service is automatically and transparently made available to you. AD is entirely based on TCP/IP technology, and for this reason, all Windows 2000 computers should use TCP/IP as their primary, if not only, network protocol.

→ To learn how to use Active Directory services, **see** "Searching the Network," **p. 753**.

Active Directory is a true *distributed database*. "Distributed" means that information about separate parts of a geographically dispersed network are automatically copied from region to region, from server to server, so that the same information is available at all locations. Any of the information can be managed from any location, and the changes made automatically propagate throughout the network. This might not matter or make sense to the user of an eight-person network, but to the manager of a corporate network that spans several continents, the ability to manage a given computer just as easily from Canada as from Canberra is *very* appealing indeed.

Active Directory is a true database: It can store any sort of information. Out of the box, it's used to store usernames, passwords, group membership, privileges, and other security information, as well as the names of computers and network printers. But it can also be used by software developers to store arbitrary information about software applications, such as the location and names of the nearest database servers—anything that would be useful to have spread throughout an organization's network.

The most significant part of AD is that it's hierarchical: It arranges information in user-defined groups called *containers*, which can be nested to any depth. The purpose of this hierarchy is to let AD represent the real structure of an organization. AD lets a network manager define groups by geographical region, department, workgroup, function, or whatever categories make sense to the organization. Each grouping can contain other groups, until finally actual users and/or their computers, printers, and other resources are entered.

The purpose of this feature is to enable network managers to assign usage and management privileges to these "containers" at appropriate levels rather than to individuals. Network privileges, like the right to access certain files or the right to manage user accounts, can be associated with these containers. A network manager therefore can grant access to users based on the organization's own structure rather than on a user-by-user basis or through "flat" enterprise-wide groups.

For example, let's say a company has East Coast and West Coast divisions and an accounting department in each (see Figure 19.10).

Figure 19.10
Active Directory lets network managers define groups based on actual organizational structure. These groupings model the organization's chains of command. The resulting structure can then be used to sensibly control access privileges and to delegate management rights.

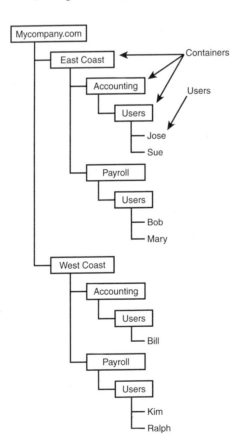

If the network manager grants read and write privileges to a shared network folder to the East Coast container, then all users anywhere in the East Coast structure (Jose, Sue, Bob, and Mary) get access rights to the folder. If Jose is granted "manager" rights to the East Coast Accounting group then he can control the user accounts for Sue and himself.

Management of all East Coast printers could be granted to a network manager by granting him management rights to the East Coast container. He then would get the right to manage any printers within the entire container, across all its subdivisions.

Active Directory can be integrated into the domain name system for a company's network so that, for example, a computer in the East Coast accounting division could be named `bigbox.accounting.eastcost.mycompany.com`.

Active Directory is used internally by Windows tools such as Explorer, My Network Places, and the Printer Manager. User-written programs can get access to the directory's contents through a programming interface called Active Directory Services Interface (ADSI) or more generally through an Internet protocol called Lightweight Directory Access Protocol (LDAP), which is an industry standard for directory queries and responses. Email programs, for example, can be designed to use LDAP to search for email addresses, regardless of the underlying network system, whether it's Windows 2000 networks, Novell NetWare, or others.

INTRANET/INTERNET SERVICES AND TOOLS

Finally, Windows 2000 comes with a full complement of applications and tools that Internet and UNIX users expect on a TCP/IP-based computer. They're not part of Windows Networking, technically speaking, because they don't use the Networking Clients. They communicate with other computers using TCP/IP directly. These tools include the following:

Internet Explorer (Web browser)

SNMP Agents

Telnet

Ping

FTP

NetMeeting

nslookup

pathping

tracert

Outlook Express (SMTP/POP mail client)

Internet Information Server (Web server)

PART

IV

CH

19

SECURITY

Finally, Windows 2000 Professional, when it's part of a Windows 2000 Server-based network, supports the use of two very sophisticated network security systems to encrypt network traffic and to communicate passwords and information about user rights between computers.

Windows 2000 Professional supports the IPSec TCP/IP data encryption standard. IPSec provides a means for each of the data packets sent across a network to be encrypted (scrambled) so that an eavesdropper with a wiretapping device can't glean passwords or other sensitive information from your data while it flows through the wires of your building, through airwaves in a wireless network, or across the Internet.

Windows 2000 also supports the Kerberos network authentication protocol, which was developed at Carnegie-Mellon University and is now widely used in secure distributed network operating systems. Kerberos manages the identification of computer users on a network to eliminate many network security risks, such as the recording and playback of passwords.

Tip #234

Both IPSec TCP/IP data encryption and Kerberos network authentication protocol are activated under the control of the administrator of Windows 2000 Server and are invisible to you as a Windows 2000 Professional user.

Note

If you're really into security—and I mean really into security—I recommend that you grab a copy of *Microsoft Windows 2000 Security Handbook*, published by Que (ISBN: 0-7897-1999-1). Better hang on to your hat, though....

TIPS FROM THE WINDOWS PROS: BECOMING A NETWORKING PROFESSIONAL

I've found that modern network software works perfectly the first time about 99 percent of the time. When things go wrong, however, you quickly find that the diagnostic tools are nowhere near as sophisticated, automated, or helpful as the installation tools. You often need a more complete understanding of network technology and structure to diagnose a broken network than you do to install one, and more to the point, a more complete understanding than I can give you in a general-purpose book like this.

So, the big tip for this chapter is this: If you're planning to set up a network for more than a few computers, or you're setting up a network in a business situation, you should have some pretty solid expertise at hand for the times when problems arise. You might have a consultant install and maintain your network, or you might at least establish a relationship with a consultant or technician whom you can call if you run into trouble.

If you want to become a networking professional yourself, I recommend the following books as places to continue your training:

Upgrading and Repairing Networks, Second Edition, ISBN: 0-7897-2034-5, Que

Practical Network Cabling, ISBN: 0-7897-2247-X, Que

Practical Windows Peer Networking, ISBN: 0-7897-2233-X, Que

CHAPTER **20**

PLANNING YOUR WINDOWS 2000 PRO NETWORK

In this chapter

CREATING A USEFUL NETWORK

How often do you think about scissors, and how often do you use them? I'd be willing to bet that you use scissors at least once or twice a day but never actually give the scissors themselves a thought—unless they're ill-fitting, squeaky, or dull. When you use good scissors, you're thinking about what you want to cut, not the tool itself.

I see computers exactly this way: They're nothing more than big, overgrown scissors. When they're doing their job properly, you shouldn't notice them. You should be able to look right through the glass on your screen at what you're working on. When a local area network (LAN) is involved, it shouldn't be any different. When I design and install LANs for my clients, my goal is to make the LAN reliable and functional but not noticeable—in other words (and I make no apologies for this), boring.

As you learned in Chapter 19, "Overview of Windows 2000 Networking," Windows 2000 networks are quite different when Windows 2000 Server is involved. You get a whole raft of services that Windows Professional doesn't provide; plus, you get centralized management. If your Windows Pro computer is part of a Windows 2000 Server network, all the planning will necessarily be done when Server is set up. In that case, you can skim this chapter or skip it entirely. If you're joining a Server network, you need only add a network card and connect by using the steps in Chapter 21, "Instant Networking."

In this chapter, you'll learn what you need to do to design a kind of stable, functional (and boring) LAN for your home or for a small workgroup by using Windows 2000 Professional. This network can include Windows 95 and 98 computers and even Windows 3.1 machines if you like. In Chapter 21, you'll learn the nitty-gritty details of installation and setup.

But the first step is to do your homework.

UNDERSTAND YOUR REQUIREMENTS

You must plan your network around your own needs. What do you expect from a network? The following are some tasks you might want it to perform:

- Share printers
- Share CD-ROMs
- Share files
- Share applications
- Share an Internet connection
- Send faxes from one modem, directly from Windows applications
- Receive faxes directly in one computer and print or route them to individuals
- Provide access to a wide area network (WAN) or other remote site
- Provide access via modem or the Internet from home or other places
- Host a Web site

- Back up multiple computers with a single tape drive
- Provide connectivity for voice and/or videoconferencing

You should make a list of your goals for installing a network. You have to provide adequate capacity to meet these and future needs, but you also don't need to overbuild.

If your only purpose is to share a printer and occasionally copy a file between two or three computers, you can spend as little as $25 per computer. On the other hand, if you need access to large databases, fast Internet connectivity, and centralized backup of all workstations, you need to plan and invest more carefully.

LEARN HOW PEOPLE WORK

When planning your network, you have to decide what kind of equipment to get, where to place it, and how many shared devices, such as printers, you'll need.

Consider how the people who will use it actually work. What tasks do people perform every 10 minutes? Every hour? Once a day? Every six months? Put your attention (and money) into making the things done frequently easy. For things done infrequently, it's enough that they're just possible.

My theory is that you *should* have to get up and move around at work. Being able to get up breaks up the day and provides time for stretching, exercising, socializing, and just finding a change of scenery. All these factors increase productivity, if done enough but not too often. I recommend these rough rules of thumb:

- Something you use several times an hour should be in your reach.
- Something you use a few times a day should be within 20 feet.
- Something you use once a day should be 100 feet away.
- Something you use once a week can be a 15-minute walk away.

For example, if you send many faxes every day from documents you create right on your computer, you should get a fax modem and use the Windows built-in Fax service, or even get a shared fax hardware or software system for your network. If you send a fax only once every couple of months, just go to a local copy center, and pay someone else a couple of dollars. Why bother setting up software you'll have forgotten how to use each time you need it? Get out of the office, and buy someone an unexpected gift while you're at it.

For the receptionist who addresses 30 or 40 envelopes every day, put one of those instant label printers right on his desk. For the artist who renders images all day every day, attach a high-speed color printer directly to her computer. But it doesn't hurt the accounting staff to have to walk across the building to use the postage meter once a day.

Your next step is to consider how you want to organize information on the computers on your network. Do your users

- Need to share information quickly?

PART

IV

CH

20

- Collaborate on projects?
- Contribute to and use a common repository of information of use to the group as a whole, such as office procedures or product literature?

If so, I encourage you to choose one computer to be used as a "main machine," the computer where most shared files and folders are stored. I call it a main machine because, whether or not you're using Windows 2000 Server, the idea is the same: If all common information is stored in once place, the following points are true:

- It can all be backed up in one operation.
- Finding files is easier.
- You can get at your own files, should you need to use someone else's computer.

You can organize shared folders on this main machine in such a way that individual users have private, secure storage space, as well as common, group folders for shared information. You can even tell Windows to store your desktop, settings, and My Documents folder on this main machine. Doing so is possible with Windows 2000 Professional, and easy with Windows 2000 Server.

On the other hand, if your work habits are very much independent or, for instance, in a home network, this sort of centralized organization isn't very important.

ARE YOU BEING SERVED?

Now you'll have to make the Big Decision. You learned about the differences between Windows Professional and Windows Server in Chapter 1, "Introducing Windows 2000 Professional," and again in Chapter 19, "Overview of Windows 2000 Networking." Windows 2000 Server provides a raft of networking services that Professional doesn't have, but you must learn how to configure and support them.

Here, I'll force the issue and say that you have to decide whether to include Windows 2000 Server in your network. If you want it, you'll get its extra network goodies, but at the cost of more training, more sophisticated management requirements, and a little more cost.

The primary trade-offs between Professional and Server boil down to those shown in Table 20.1.

TABLE 20.1 PRIMARY DIFFERENCES BETWEEN WINDOWS PRO AND SERVER

Network with Windows 2000 Professional Only	Network with Windows 2000 Server
This network provides at most 10 connections to other computers.	Connections to the server are unlimited.
The cost is low.	This network costs a few hundred dollars more, plus additional fees for Client Access Licenses.

Network with Windows 2000 Professional Only	Network with Windows 2000 Server
Configuration is simple (relatively, anyway!).	This network is complex to configure and administer.
Each machine must be administered independently.	Administration is centralized.
Provides rudimentary remote access, connection sharing, and WAN support.	The features are sophisticated.
Managing file security is difficult when you have more than one user per computer.	Centralized user management eases the task of managing security.
This network works with Windows peers only but can use Novell servers.	Internetworks with Windows, Macintosh, and Novell clients.

For me, the 10-connection limit with Windows 2000 Professional is the main dividing line. You can work around the limit by connecting your workstations to other computers only as needed and by not having a main machine that all users look to for shared files. But this is exactly what you'll find you need as your network grows to this size or larger! So, if you have a network of more than 10 computers, I encourage using at least one copy of Windows 2000 Server.

You can certainly use Server with smaller networks, too. What other reasons would you have for using Server?

- You want to connect your LAN through a WAN or through the Internet to another LAN at another location; that is, you want to join a Server domain somewhere else.
- You want to support multiple, simultaneous remote dial-in or Virtual Private Network (VPN) users.
- You want to exercise strict security controls, restrict your users' ability to change system settings, or use automatic application installation.
- You want to share files and printers with Apple Macintosh computers on your LAN.

If you decide you need or want Windows 2000 Server, you should get a copy of *Special Edition Using Microsoft Windows 2000 Server* (published by Que) and a box of Alka Seltzer before you go any further.

WHEN TO HIRE A PROFESSIONAL

You've probably heard this old adage: "If you want something done right, do it yourself!" It is true to a point. At some point, though, the benefit of hiring someone else outweighs the pleasure of doing it yourself.

PART

IV

CH

20

For a home network, you should definitely try setting it up yourself. Call it a learning experience, get friends to help, and if things still don't work, treat yourself to a truly humbling experience and watch a high-school-aged neighbor get it all working in 15 minutes. As long as you don't have to run wires through the wall or construct your own cables, you should be able to manage this job even with no prior networking experience. When something is called "Plug and Play" now, it really is.

For a business, however, the balance tips the other way. If you depend on your computers to get your work done, getting them set up should be your first concern, but keeping them working should be your second, third, and fourth. If you have solid experience in network installation, installing Windows 2000 will be a snap. But your business is hanging in the balance, and you should consider the cost of computer failure when you're deciding whether it's worth spending money on setup and installation. Hiring a good consultant and/or contractor will give you the following:

- An established relationship. If something goes wrong, you'll already know whom to call, and that person will already know the details of your system.
- A professional installation job.
- The benefit of full-time experience in network and system design without your paying a full-time salary.
- Time to spend doing something more productive than installing a network.

You can choose a full-service consultant who will handle wiring and hardware and software setup; you can farm these jobs out to different contractors, or you can do some of the work yourself. Just be sure that all the parties involved clearly understand their responsibilities and coordinate their schedules to mesh together effectively.

If you do want to hire someone, it's important to choose your consultant or contractor very carefully. The following are some tips:

- Ask friends and business associates for referrals before you go to the yellow pages.
- Ask a consultant or contractor for references, and check them out.
- Interview a few consultants before committing. Pay attention to the kinds of questions they ask. Does it seem like they're trying to gain an understanding of *your* business and your particular needs? Do they ask you the questions I posed in the preceding sections? Do they explain your options in understandable language? Do they make you feel comfortable and taken care of, or do you feel that you're being herded like a sheep?
- Look for experience and reliability. Also, look for someone who seeks balance and appropriateness in the solutions he or she suggests to you.
- Ask for billing details up front. Does this person charge by the hour or at a fixed rate? Does he or she sell equipment, or does he or she shop for you? Does the contractor get commissions or kickbacks on equipment purchased on your behalf?
- Find out what the contractor's guaranteed response time is, should problems or failures occur in the future.

- If you get a written contract (and you probably should), be sure to run it by your lawyer before signing. Be sure that the contract contains provisions to protect you as well as the contractor.

- Be sure that documentation is one of the contractor's "deliverables." You should get written documentation describing your system's installation, setup, and configuration, as well as written procedures for routine maintenance, such as making backups, adding users, and so on.

Even if you do hire someone else to build your network, you should stay involved in the process and understand the choices and decisions that are made.

PLANNING FOR ADEQUATE CAPACITY

After you've looked at your requirements and work habits, make a diagram of your office or home, showing computer locations, and indicate where you want to place special shared resources, such as modems, printers, a main machine, and the like. Remember that shared resources and the computers they're attached to need to be *turned on* to be used. So, for example, your office's main printer should probably be connected to a computer that will be on and accessible all the time.

WORKSTATIONS

You clearly need at least one workstation for each worker (or family member) who needs simultaneous access to a computer. Consider having an extra computer or two for the following:

- Guest workers
- Visiting salespeople, now that the Internet is widely used for sales and ordering information
- Shared use of special one-of-a-kind hardware, such as CD recorders, multimedia, video-conferencing, and so on
- A "warm spare" to have on hand in case a computer fails

You can use your designated main machine as an ordinary workstation as long as it's going to be on all the time. It should be one of your fastest computers with lots of memory—at least 128MB of RAM for Windows Professional. If your main machine is also to run Internet Information Server (IIS) for your intranet or is to receive incoming calls by modem from remote users, you might want to leave it alone to do just that job. Having it do only one job isn't necessary, though. Windows does a remarkable job of serving many masters well. Just don't match up your "main machine" with a user who's constantly rebooting, playing with strange and unreliable hardware or software, surfing the Net, or otherwise engaging in practices that may "take out" your office's most important computer.

PART

IV

CH

20

⚠ *If you anticipate that people will bring their own assorted computers to your network, see "LAN Must Support Visitors with Unknown Hardware" in the "Troubleshooting" section at the end of this chapter.*

PRINTERS

Printer sharing works *very* well with Windows, and Windows Professional can share printers with Windows 9x as well. You definitely won't need a printer for every user on your LAN. You can spend the money you save getting a faster, more durable shared printer or on different printer types, such as color, laser, or duplex (two sided).

Remember that you can purchase printers that connect directly to your network so that they can be located away from your workstations. You'll pay several hundred dollars extra for this capability, but you'll get added flexibility and printing speed. However, they still need to use a Windows 2000 computer as a print spooler, so you'll still need to leave their controlling computer on all the time. On the other hand, one Windows 2000 computer can manage quite a few networked printers.

For each printer, you should estimate the workload you're going to subject it to. For each printer, estimate the monthly duty cycle using this equation:

Number of users using printer

$\times$

Number of pages printed by each user per day

$\times$

22 workdays per month

Purchase printers that were designed to print at least this many pages per month. If you overwork a laser printer, you'll find that it will soon start to squeak, smell of ozone, and jam frequently. For example, a printer shared by 10 people each printing 40 pages per day will print 8,800 pages per month, so it should be a model designed to print 10,000 pages per month or more.

Higher duty-cycle printers are typically a bit more expensive but are much more reliable and faster than standard consumer-rated printers.

STORAGE CAPACITY

The first computer I used had an amazing 2MB of hard disk space. I have since filled up 10MB, 40MB, 80MB, 200MB, 600MB, and 2GB drives in succession. Initially, each of them seemed enormous, unlimited, ending forever the fear of running out of disk space. Alas, I have learned that software is like a gas: It expands to fill all available space.

Curiously, network disk drives shared by many users usually do *not* fill up much faster than disks used by an individual. They don't fill up any faster because most shared folders contain documents, and word processing documents are very small relative to today's operating systems. If your users save lots of large, high-resolution images or video clips, though, it could be another story.

You should estimate the amount of shared storage required by the main machine on your network as follows:

- Divide your users according to the type of information they'll store: mostly documents, mostly images, and so on.

- Estimate the amount of storage each type of user will need. If possible, survey existing computers, subtracting the disk space used by applications and operating systems from total disk space used. For example, the average storage needed for a documents-only user could be 100MB; for a user who stores images, it could be 500MB or more.

- Multiply the number of users in each group by their estimated storage requirement.

- Add in space required by any shared database files, common applications, shared image banks, or documents.

- Add the space required by Windows 2000 and the *virtual memory pagefile*, approximately 600MB.

Estimating the storage space will at least let you eliminate the risk of getting a disk drive smaller than you need. You can and should get a larger drive. Disk capacity is much less expensive than files lost because of full hard drives and less expensive than lost time and effort. Eight to 20GB disk drives are almost ridiculously inexpensive, so this isn't a place to scrimp and save.

Tip #235	You can easily add a second hard drive later and use Windows 2000's *Spanned Volume* feature to extend the apparent size of your original disk, without having to move files or reorganize your file system.

Windows 2000 Professional doesn't offer Server's disk RAID (mirroring, duplex, or striping) protection features, so you don't have to consider them.

BACKUP SYSTEM

You must include at least one tape backup system on your network if it's for business use. Your tape backup system should ideally be large enough to back up the entire hard drive of your main machine on one tape. I recommend getting a Travan tape storage system and a better backup software package than the Microsoft Backup utility included with Windows Professional. The Windows Backup utility is almost adequate, but for business purposes, you should have something that is convenient, that lets you save different backup configurations, and that lends itself to automatic scheduling.

Some backup software can be configured to back up not only the machine with the tape drive, but also other machines, via your network. This type of backup works only when the computers are left turned on, but it can be a real boon in a business environment. A system that performs automatic daily backups of every computer in the office is a valuable insurance policy. I've used Network Associates's Arcserve for this purpose; it's rather difficult to install and set up, but it's really a first-class system. Backup Exec is another good bet.

→ To learn more about network backups, **see** "Install and Configure Backup Software," **p. 731**.

NETWORK BANDWIDTH

Most network hardware you will encounter moves data at either 10Mbps or 100Mbps. To be honest, with a network of 10 or fewer computers, you probably would never notice the difference between the two.

A 10Mbps network works just fine if you have 10 or fewer computers. If you install applications on a server or main machine and execute them directly over the network, you might notice an improvement in startup time with a 100Mbps network. But if you install all your applications on each of your computers, you probably would never notice the difference.

There is a small incentive to use a 10Mbps network, in fact. If you want a high-speed Internet connection and choose Digital Subscriber Line (DSL), a Cable modem service, or a routed *frame relay* connection, you will find that most of the equipment provided comes with a 10Mbps Ethernet connection. Also, network connection cards for laptops are also typically 10Mbps.

You can certainly choose to use 100Mbps networking for all or most of your equipment and, if necessary, add a second 10Mbps network card to one Windows 2000 Professional computer to route TCP/IP and SPX/IPX data traffic between the two different speed networks; this configuration, however, can be more difficult.

In any case, if you choose to use unshielded twisted-pair network cabling, you should use Category 5 (CAT-5) cable, connectors, patch cables, and other components throughout. That way, if you ever decide to upgrade to a faster network platform, you will not need to re-cable your office. The extra investment now will be very small compared to redoing everything later.

> **Note**
>
> I'll discuss network types and cabling in more detail later in this chapter and go into installation in Chapter 21.

POWER SURPRISE

One of the last things people think about when planning a network is the fact that every computer and external device has to be powered. You might be surprised how often people plan a network and get all their hardware together, only to realize that they have no power outlet near their file server or have placed 10 devices next to one outlet. The result can be a tangle of extension cords and a reprimand from the fire marshal.

Furthermore, your file server(s) or main machine(s) should be protected with an *Uninterruptible Power Supply*, or *UPS*. These devices contain rechargeable batteries and instantly step in if the AC power to your building should fail. When a power failure occurs during the exact instant that your computer is writing data to its hard disk, you're almost guaranteed some sort of data corruption: lost data, missing files, corrupted database index files, or worse.

⚠ *If the AC power supply in your area is intermittent or unreliable, see "AC Power Is Unreliable" in the "Troubleshooting" section at the end of this chapter.*

BACKUP POWER

The three types of risk from power failures are as follows:

- Loss of productivity—If any computer or any component on your LAN loses power, it's pretty clear that any work that depends on it will stop. If computer downtime means your business stops cold, then you should consider trying to keep your computers and entire network functioning during brief power outages.

- Loss of data—If any component of a network fails, then any file that was being saved or modified at that exact moment will be corrupted or lost. You must consider the cost of losing a file change or of having to repair database files versus the cost of providing backup power to every computer and file server, as well as every network device.

- Damage to file systems—If power fails during the exact instant that a computer is writing data to its hard disk, the disk itself can become corrupted, resulting in lost files, damaged directories, or, in the worst case, an unbootable system.

The only two levels of protection worth considering are as follows:

- Full Protection, with backup power for every computer and every component of your network, to protect against all three types of risk

- Basic Disaster Insurance, with backup power for your most important computers, to avoid just file system damage

In the "Full Protection" scenario, your entire network and all computers will keep functioning as if nothing had happened when the power goes out. You can continue working for a short time but should shut down before the batteries run out of juice—5 to 90 minutes, depending on your budget. This option costs about $150 to $400 per computer and/or localized group of network equipment. Only laser printers would be left on standard power because they're *really* power hungry, and providing adequate battery power for them is prohibitively expensive.

In the "Basic Insurance" scenario, your only concern is to avoid catastrophic damage to your file servers and/or peer-to-peer computers with important shared folders and valuable data. If the power fails, work on unprotected workstations will cease immediately. You can then shut down the protected computers manually, let the UPSs automatically shut them down, or just let the backup power fail. Even if you can't save in-progress files and close applications, at least by the time your UPS fails, your computer will be idle and won't be writing to its hard disk. It's not great protection, but it avoids catastrophe.

There really aren't any sensible approaches in between these two. So, you should decide what level of protection to shoot for. Engineers use a pretty cold-hearted formula for

PART

IV

CH

20

making decisions like this. It's called "computing the expected cost," and here's how you do it. Calculate these two numbers:

Expected annual cost of providing backup power =

(Cost of equipment)

÷

(the estimated lifetime of the equipment in years)

and

Expected annual cost of not providing backup power =

(estimated cost of losing data because of a failure)

×

(the probability in percent of a failure in any given year)

÷100

> **Note**
>
> If you can think of several different failure scenarios with different costs and probabilities, you should work out the expected cost for them as well and add them together.

For example, on a network with one main file server and eight workstations, you might spend ($400 + 8 × $150) = $1,600 for backup power equipment that might last three years. Estimated cost: about $530/year.

The cost of suffering a major failure might be six hours of a consultant's time at $120 per hour, plus $1,000 in lost income for a day; with a 50 percent probability of this sort of loss in a given year. The expected cost is (6 × $120 + $1,000) × 50 / 100 = $860 per year, which is more than the cost of providing full backup power.

The Full Protection plan appears to be worthwhile in this case. For a home system, where loss of income is not an issue, or if computer experts are in abundant supply, you might come to a different conclusion.

Whatever your decision, you can use these tips for planning backup power:

- Don't plug laser printers into a UPS.
- Calculate the total power consumption required at each equipment location. The following are some rough estimates for power consumption:

Ordinary computer	200 watts (also called VA)
Loaded-up file server	400 watts
CRT monitor	100 watts

You'll need a UPS capable of providing the combined power requirement of the equipment at each location.

- If your UPS is larger than you need, you'll get more running time when the power goes off. But if it's too small, it will not be able to run your equipment at all.

- Try to get UPS devices with a cable and/or software that will signal Windows when the AC power has failed and when the batteries are about to run out. This way, Windows can shut itself down gracefully when necessary.

For full protection, follow these guidelines:

- Buy name-brand backup power supplies from a reputable vendor—for example, American Power Conversion, Tripp-Lite, or Best. You definitely get what you pay for here. Avoid nameless clones like the plague.

- Don't forget hubs, routers, DSL or cable modems, or modem-sharing devices; they'll need backup power, too.

- Remember, oversized UPSs mean more time, but this is helpful only if *all* your equipment is running. Most UPS manufacturers publish a chart showing running time *versus* power load. You should use these charts to buy appropriately sized backups to give every UPS about the same running time.

PLUGGING IN

Plan ahead for power. Count the number of cords and external "block" power supplies you'll need at each installation location in your network. The following are some rough estimates for power consumption:

Ordinary computer	1 amp
Loaded-up file server	3 amps
CRT monitor	1 amp
Laser printer	10 amps

You should check your own laser printers, if you have any, for their rated power consumption. Other devices such as inkjet printers and modems don't draw enough power to worry about.

Check your circuit breakers or fuse box to ensure that you don't attempt to draw more than the rated amount of power for a given circuit, noting that several outlets may share one circuit.

Don't plug laser printers to power strips at all; these high-power devices should be plugged directly into their own wall outlet.

If you set up a network with hubs, external modems, wireless bridges, DSL or cable modems, printers, and other various peripherals, you'll quickly find out that each manufacturer has given you an external block power supply that takes up two or three positions on a power strip. You might need several power strips to accommodate these devices on a larger network installation. You should avoid daisy-chaining power strips; plug each into its own wall outlet.

Tip #236	I find it helpful to plug a power strip into a UPS when connecting several low-consumption devices such as modem or hub power supplies. I write "UPS" all over these power strips with a red marker so that nobody uses them for laser printers or other devices I don't want on the UPS.

Finally, in an office situation, if you clump your Server or "central" computer, laser printers, office copiers, and fax machine together as many people do, *please* call in an electrician to ensure that you have adequate power circuits to run all these energy-sucking devices.

CHOOSING A NETWORK AND CABLING SYSTEM

If it's a network you want, you're going to have to connect these darned things together somehow. In the following sections, I'll describe the possibilities in excruciating detail; then I'll give you a checklist to help you make a decision.

→ For details on these cabling systems, **see** "Making the Connection," **p. 650**.

If your network is small and/or temporary, you can run network cables along walls and desks. Otherwise, you probably should keep them out of the way and protect them from accidental damage by installing them in the walls of your home or office. As you site and plan your network, consider how the network cabling is to be routed.

 If you can't or aren't allowed to drill through your building's walls, see "Can't Drill Through Walls or Ceilings" in the "Troubleshooting" section at the end of this chapter.

10BASE2 ETHERNET

10BASE2, or ThinNet, Ethernet is a 10Mbps Ethernet system. It's about as inexpensive as is possible; you can connect two computers for $25 if you're careful shopper.

CABLING

10BASE2 Ethernet uses RG-58 coaxial cable, which looks similar to television cable. It's typically black, about a quarter of an inch in diameter, and inexpensive.

You can buy premade cables in lengths of up to 50 feet and can use *barrel connectors* to join them to produce longer cables. You can also buy bulk cable and attach connectors with a crimping tool, but if you don't already know how to use this tool, I suggest that you don't bother learning now. 10BASE2 cabling is disappearing rapidly now that the cost of 10BASE-T network cards and hubs is so low.

10BASE2 cabling must be run in a single line from one computer to the next to the next, with a twist-on terminator plug at each end of the chain.

CONNECTORS

10BASE2 connectors are smart-looking twist-on jobbies called *BNC* connectors. The network card end is cylindrical with two small "Frankenstein neck" pins on the sides. The cable plug fits over it and twists on to lock in place.

TRADE-OFFS

BNC connectors are quite reliable, and the components are all very cheap, but the cables themselves are easily damaged by pulling or kinking. The problem with ThinNet is that damage to any cable, or any loose connector or terminator, takes down the entire network. Trying to diagnose a failed ThinNet network is no fun.

10BASE-T ETHERNET

10BASE-T Ethernet networks use *unshielded twisted-pair cabling*, commonly called *UTP*, *twisted-pair*, or *phone wire*. This last name is a little dangerous because I'm not talking about the thin, flat, ribbon-like cable used to connect a phone to a wall jack, nor is it likely that phone wire installed in an old home in the 1930s will work either.

10BASE-T NICs are available for as little as $5, as either ISA or PCI cards, and are made by network equipment manufacturers you've heard of. Name brands include Intel, 3COM, and Farallon. Middle-tier brands include Kingston, D-Link, Edimax, Boca, and Cnet. You also can use the (almost) nameless clones from the corner computer store. Actually, almost any of them will work equally well in your LAN. Many cards are designed to be software compatible with the NE2000, one of the earliest 16-bit Ethernet cards, manufactured for or by Novell Corporation. The most important point is to buy only cards that appear on the Windows Hardware Compatibility List. Surprisingly, many of the clone manufacturers are listed.

Some 10BASE-T NICs are available in a "combo" format that has a BNC connector for connection to a 10BASE2 network and an RJ45 jack for connection to a 10BASE-T network.

Tip #237	Many combo cards automatically sense which type of network they're on, but some older versions don't and require you to run a configuration program under DOS (and I do mean DOS) to set the card to one mode or the other. I suggest avoiding this kind of card because you might find that you can't configure it from a Command Prompt window in Windows 2000.

CABLING

10BASE-T networking requires a cable with certain physical and electrical properties, certified to properly carry the 10 million bit per second electrical signal. UTP cable is rated according to the maximum data rate it can carry:

Rating	Highest Data Rate	Used For
CAT-1	Less than 1Mbps	Telephone (voice)
CAT-2	4Mbps	IBM Token Ring
CAT-3	16Mbps	10BASE-T Ethernet
CAT-4	20Mbps	16Mbps Token Ring
CAT-5	100Mbps	100BASE-Tx Ethernet, TPDDI, ATM

10BASE-T requires at least CAT-3 certified cable. You *can* use cable with a higher rating, though.

> **Note**
>
> Sources vary on the transmission speeds of UTP. CAT-3 is often rated up to 10Mbps under certain conditions. CAT-4 is usually rated up to 16Mbps only, though some sources rate it at 20Mbps. The moral of the story is that speed can vary.

> **Tip #238**
>
> I recommend installing CAT-5 cable and connectors for all new wiring. That way, you'll be able to upgrade later to 100BASE-T just by adding new network cards and a hub. They will cost less to upgrade than the wiring.

If you want to use existing in-wall wiring for your network, you should be sure it's at least CAT-3 certified. If the cable has eight or more wires with color-matched pairs twisted together, it's *probably* CAT-3 compliant.

CONNECTORS

10BASE-T networks use modular telephone connectors with eight pins, dubbed RJ45 for reasons known only to the telephone industry. These connectors are the wider cousins of the standard RJ11 connectors used for telephone extension cords. They're reliable, very inexpensive, and a pain to attach. Buy premade cables, or hire someone to install the cabling for you, if you possibly can.

HUBS AND SWITCHES

10BASE-T networks of more than two computers require a central hub, a device to which every device on the LAN must connect. Hubs recondition the electrical signal received by any "sending" computer and transmit data back out to each of the others. Hubs are connected to the twisted-pair cable from each device on the network via an RJ45 jack, called a *port*. Hubs are available with anywhere from 4 to 32 ports each and, if necessary, can be connected together for larger networks.

Hubs were once very costly but are now available for about $5 per port; that is, a four-port hub for a four-computer network can cost as little as $20. Hubs can also be used to join a 10BASE2 network to a 10BASE-T network, letting you use both types of cabling at once. I'll show you how to join them in Chapter 21.

Hubs are an extra expense, but they provide two very important features:

- First, they separate the computers electrically so that failure of any one cable doesn't bring down the entire network.
- Second, they have flashing lights for each port, which indicate that the connection is sound and that data is moving. They're great diagnostic tools (and very satisfying to watch).

Switches are hubs on steroids. Whereas a hub is a simple repeater that forwards received data to every device on the LAN, a switch is very selective about forwarding. It monitors network traffic and learns, when data is addressed directly from one computer to another, that it need only send it out the particular port leading to the destination computer, as shown in Figure 20.1

Figure 20.1
An Ethernet switch can route several separate network conversations at once.

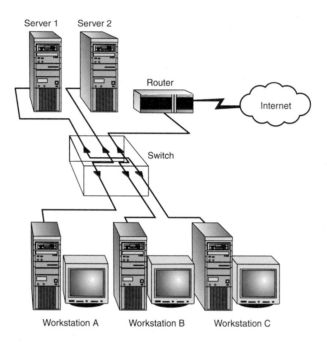

Switches can let a LAN carry on many simultaneous conversations because data can come in fully half of the ports and go out the other half. They multiply the data-carrying capacity of a LAN manyfold.

Do you need a switch? No, not for the type of LAN I'm talking about. Switches really help when network traffic is directed at many servers and other distinct LAN segments. If you have only one main machine, most network traffic will be between that one machine and the others on your LAN. You probably won't benefit enough to justify the additional cost of a switching hub.

Probably the only reason to use a switching hub is if you are installing 100BASE-Tx Ethernet.

TRADE-OFFS

10BASE-T networking requires the purchase of a hub if you have more than two computers. You also have to string wire from each computer to a hub, so you need to do more wiring. On the other hand, 10BASE-T is easy to install, inexpensive, and easier to troubleshoot than 10BASE2.

100BASE-Tx Ethernet

100BASE-Tx is a supercharged twisted-pair Ethernet network, and although it's 10 times faster than its 10BASE-T predecessor, it's perhaps only twice as expensive. The *x* stands for Extended; not only does 100BASE-Tx talk 10 times faster than 10BASE-T Ethernet, data can be simultaneously sent and received between a pair of computers. This type of communication is called full-duplex, and it's standard with 100Mbps Ethernet.

Many 100Mbps network cards will also operate at 10Mbps if they find themselves connected to other 10Mbps network cards; they are labeled *10/100 cards*. The entire network must be 100Mbps capable, or else the cards will degrade themselves to the lowest common denominator.

Cabling

100BASE-Tx networks send data 10 times as fast and are much pickier about the quality of the wiring they use. This isn't surprising; think of the difference between a normal street and a racetrack. Bumps and turns that your car takes in stride could cause a high-speed racer to spin out of control and crash. The same is true with network wiring: High-speed networks need high-quality wiring. CAT-5 certified cable must be used throughout. At no point on the network is more than one-half inch of any pair of wires to be left untwisted. It's that picky.

Connectors

100BASE-Tx networks require the same CAT-5 quality components for jacks, connectors, terminal blocks, patch cables, and so on. CAT-5 wall-mounted jacks are particularly expensive, but if you look inside, you'll see why. They don't have any loose wires; the jack and connector terminals are soldered to a printed circuit board to control the electrical properties of the connections inside the box. It's that picky.

Hubs and Switches

100BASE-Tx hubs are more expensive than 10BASE-T, but the costs have fallen to the neighborhood of $20 per port, instead of the $300 of a few years ago. Switching hubs are also available, as I mentioned previously, because it's sometimes sensible to connect a server at 100Mbps to workstations at 10Mbps.

Mixed Networking

If you are updating an existing network or are connecting two separate networks, you must consider several things.

Dual-Speed Hubs

If you have some 10Mbps devices and want to add new 100Mbps devices without upgrading the old, you can buy a dual-speed hub, which connects to each computer at the maximum speed it permits.

You should be wary of some *Autosensing 10/100Mbps Hubs*, which purport to let you connect both 10 and 100Mbps devices. Some of these hubs force the entire network to run at 10Mbps if any one device runs this lower speed. Read the specifications carefully if you mix fast and slow devices on one network. You want a device with *N-way autosensing* switches or ports.

MEDIA CONVERTERS

You can also purchase a small device called a *media converter* to connect a 10Mbps network to a 100Mbps network. These devices are available in any pairing of 10BASE2, 10BASE-T, and 100BASE-Tx; they're really just two-port hubs.

SWITCHING HUBS

If you have several users who place high demands on a single server, a device called a *10/100Mbps switching hub* might help. This hub has one 100Mbps Ethernet port and multiple 10Mbps ports. The hub sorts things out so that the high-speed port can communicate with each of the slower ports simultaneously, at full-bore speeds.

Tip #239

Do you have an existing 10BASE-T network you would like to speed up? Instead of replacing all the wiring and network cards in all your computers, you can put a 100Mbps Ethernet card in your file servers and use a switching hub to connect the server to the workstations. Using this card effectively gives every computer its own full 10Mbps channel to the file server at a minimal cost.

If you try this approach, be very sure of what you're buying, however. Some switching hubs permit only one computer to be attached to each port. Others let you connect a 10BASE-T hub to a port, allowing several workstations to share one 10Mbps connection. The switch must be capable of noting multiple network or MAC addresses for each port.

WIRELESS NETWORKING

One way to build a network without hubs, cables, connectors, drills, swearing, tools, or outside contractors is to go wireless. They *call* it Ethernet. Why not really transmit data right through the proverbial Ether? Radio frequencies in the 900MHz and 2.4GHz band are reserved for close-range data communications, and several new products are making radio-based networking both affordable and easy. Prices are falling to the point that wireless connectivity is now competitive with even the most inexpensive 10BASE-T hardware, when installation cost savings are factored in. This technology is coming of age, so I'll go into a little extra detail here.

You'll find a big range of capabilities and prices in these products, however. Wireless networking products seem to be oriented either to the consumer or business market. Consumer device characteristics

- Typically deliver under 1Mbps advertised speed, 400Kbps real-world throughput,
- Cost $80 to $120 per adapter

- Use proprietary protocols and do not interoperate with products from other vendors
- Are peer-to-peer devices with no way to connect directly to a wired Ethernet LAN
- Use a fixed frequency, typically in the 900MHz band
- And most importantly, are unlikely to ever have Windows 2000 drivers or support

These products include Zoom Telephonics's HomeLAN (www.zoom.com), Diamond Multimedia's HomeFree (www.diamondmm.com), and Intelogis's Passport (www.intelogis.com).

In the coming years, I expect that the consumer class devices will boast improved speeds at the same cost, but if you look at them, be *very* careful to check for Windows 2000 compatibility. Some of the manufacturers I spoke with indicated that they had no plans to develop Windows 2000 drivers.

Business-oriented devices, on the other hand, typically

- Offer 2Mbps rated speed, with about 1Mbps actual throughput
- Cost $150 to $350 per adapter
- Are standards based, capable of interoperation with other vendors' products
- Are peer-to-peer devices that can communicate directly with each other
- Can be bridged to a wired LAN through an optional device called an *Access Point*, bridge, or base unit, costing typically $400 to $1,000
- Use the 2.4GHz frequency band
- Use either the Spread-Spectrum Direct Sequence or Frequency Hopping technique for security

These products include Webgear's Aviator Pro (www.webgear.com) and Proxim's Symphony (www.proxim.com).

Both business and consumer products typically come with modem connection-sharing software that may also be called *proxy software*. This software lets all the computers on a wireless LAN share an Internet connection made through just one of the computers (which would have to be left on all the time, running the proxy software, for this to work). You might also be able to use Windows connection sharing to accomplish this type of connection.

Tip #240

Wireless technology is fairly new, and manufacturers are having a difficult time meeting standards and achieving interoperability. Before you invest in any wireless gear, search for product reviews on computer magazine Web sites. Don't touch any product that doesn't advertise itself as Windows 2000 compatible, and ask for a guarantee from your vendor. Be sure that any product you buy is software-upgradable.

If you use a dedicated Internet connection service such as DSL, cable modem, or frame relay, check individual product specifications to see whether they can share your dedicated connection. Chapter 24, "Connecting Your LAN to the Internet," offers more details.

You'll also find what I would call "top-end products" that have

- 10Mbps throughput
- Prices in excess of $500 per computer
- Access Point or Bridge devices in the $3,000 range

These products include Nortel Networks's Baystack 600 (www.nortelnetworks.com), Lucent Technology's WaveLAN (www.lucent.com), and BreezeCOM's BreezeNET (www.breezecom.com).

I don't recommend these products for home use or for the average business right now. By the year 2001, wireless products capable of 10Mbps speeds should be in the $200 range and will be seriously worth considering.

How to Choose a Wireless Connectivity Product

The consumer and business product lines are fairly well matched to their intended markets. The following questions will help you make a decision:

- Do you need high-speed connectivity to all your computers for heavy-duty file sharing, database access, video- or voice conferencing?

  If so, forget wireless for now, unless you're willing to pay a total of nearly $1,000 per computer. Alternatively, use a wired network for most of your computers, and add an Access Point and 2Mbps or faster wireless network cards for computers that can suffer along with 1Mbps throughput.

- Do you already have or need to install a fixed-wire network?
- Do you routinely transfer files of several hundred thousand bytes or more?
- Do you use network applications such as databases, Lotus Notes, Access, and so on, using files shared on the network?
- Do you have dedicated high-speed Internet service of 700Kbps or more?

  If so, you need a business-type wireless network with a real-life transfer speed at least as fast as your Internet connection.

You might not need an Access Point if you

- Do not use the NetBEUI protocol
- Have a Windows 2000 or NT computer you can leave turned on all the time
- Put both a wired NIC and a wireless NIC in this computer, to let it act as a router
- Understand TCP/IP networking sufficiently well to create a separate subnet for the wireless segment of the LAN
- Use a fixed or DHCP-based IP address scheme with either a DHCP server on both the wired and wireless segments of the network, or with Windows 2000 or NT Server acting as the routing computer

In this case, Windows 2000 acts as a router to transfer data between the wired LAN and the wireless computers. The tricky part is getting IP addresses assigned correctly to both parts of the network. (Unfortunately, if you want to use Internet Connection Sharing in this setup, you'll have to get Windows 2000 Server because the sharing software included with Windows 2000 Professional doesn't support a two-subnet LAN.)

Otherwise, you should get a hardware Ethernet-to-Wireless Access Point. This device acts as a bridge, so it supports the NetBEUI protocol and does not require setting up a separate IP subnet for the wireless segment of the LAN.

- Can you tolerate modem Internet connection speeds and pokey, but functional, peer-to-peer networking file transfers?

    If so, you can get away with a consumer wireless network product if it's Windows 2000 compatible.

I recommend researching the current state of the art before you make your decision because these products are evolving quickly. Check current computer magazines and Web sites for product reviews.

Tip #241

Search the Internet for vendors selling these products, and search for reviews of products. Online stores and reviews may help you discover products and manufacturers you hadn't heard of before.

Finally, you will have to choose between the two different wireless technologies described next.

WIRED WIRELESS CONNECTIVITY

You can use your home's or office's existing power or telephone wiring to carry data. Wait a minute! This is wireless networking? Well, it is if you're in the marketing department of the companies selling this type of "wireless" network adapter. These devices require no new wiring—that's true—because they transmit their radio signals over your existing AC or telephone wiring, using a transmitter/receiver device that plugs into a wall socket or telephone jack (see Figure 20.2). These devices don't interfere at all with the normal operation of your power outlets or telephones; the extra signal just hitchhikes along the wires. The advantage of using them is that you can plug into any socket in your house. However, these devices don't let you work completely unplugged; you can't sit under a tree in your back yard and surf the Net with them.

These products currently include the slow consumer-class devices, but I expect that faster 10Mbps devices will appear soon enough. These products are relatively inexpensive—about $70 per computer. However, they have several disadvantages:

- The data rate is low, about 500Kbps.
- Some devices connect to your computer through the printer port, and they are not supported by Windows 2000.

- No Access Point bridge devices are available.

- Some product reviewers have reported that connections are not reliable; some electrical outlets don't provide a good connection.

- The telephone wire products must all be plugged into the same telephone line.

- Several vendors have indicated they are unlikely to ever provide Windows 2000 support for their low data-rate products.

Figure 20.2
Wired-wireless networking uses existing household power or telephone wiring to carry a radio frequency signal between networked computers.

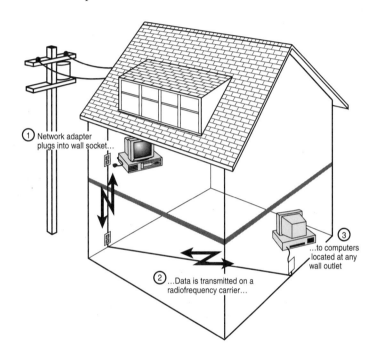

① Network adapter plugs into wall socket...

② ...Data is transmitted on a radiofrequency carrier...

③ ...to computers located at any wall outlet

TRULY WIRELESS NETWORKING

Real wireless products use a network card (internal ISA or PCI card for desktop computers or PC Card for laptops) with a small protruding antenna. Figure 20.3 shows a typical family of wireless products: a twisted-pair to wireless access point, a wireless modem for shared dial-up Internet connectivity, an internal wireless network card, and a PC network card for laptops.

These devices use radio signals sent through the air instead of through building wiring, so they are truly wireless. Two frequency bands are used: 900MHz and 2.4GHz. These frequency bands are reserved for data networking, so you don't have to worry about interference from cell phones or cordless telephones. The 900MHz products provide lower data rates and seem to have more problems with coverage; you might find that some parts of your office or house get a poor signal and low data rates. The coverage of these devices is typically 150 feet indoors and 300 feet outdoors.

Access Points cost $300 to $1,000 depending on the manufacturer, and if you suspect that cost and quality go hand in hand here, you're probably right.

PART
IV

CH

20

Figure 20.3
Typical wireless network equipment. Clockwise from the upper left: Access Point, modem, ISA adapter, PC card adapter. (Photo used by permission of Proxim.)

PRINTING AND FAXING

Shared printers simply need to be connected to host Windows 2000 computers with a standard parallel printer cable. If the printer needs to be farther than 10 feet away from a computer, you have three choices:

1. Get a really long cable, and take your chances. The electrical signal for parallel printers is not supposed to be stretched more then 10 feet, but I've gotten away with 25 feet in the past. Buy a high-quality shielded cable. You may get data errors (bad printed characters) with this approach.

2. Use a network-capable printer. You can buy special network printer modules for some printers, or you can buy special third-party "print server" modules, which connect to the printer port and to a network cable. Network supply catalogs list a myriad of these devices.

3. Use a printer-extender device. These devices turn the high-speed parallel data signal into a serial data connection somewhat as a modem does, and I recommend against using them because they result in very slow printing.

If your network includes Windows 95, 98, NT 3 or 4, or Windows 3.1 computers, collect the CDs or floppy disks containing the printer drivers for these operating systems for each of your printers. Windows 2000 lets you load in the printer drivers for the older operating systems and lets these computers automatically download the proper printer driver when they use the shared printer. This feature is *very* slick!

PROVIDING INTERNET CONNECTIVITY

Of course, you'll want to have Internet access on your LAN, and it's far better to have one connection to the Net for the entire LAN than to let each user fend for himself or herself.

Windows 2000 has a built-in connection-sharing feature, and you can also use external devices to make the connection. This topic is important enough that it gets its own chapter. I recommend that you read Chapter 24, "Connecting Your LAN to the Internet," now as you plan your network.

You also must be sure to study Chapter 26, "Network Security," to build in proper safeguards against hacking and abuse.

For now, you should start by researching the availability of DSL, cable, and other high-speed Internet connection options that are being deployed nationwide.

PROVIDING REMOTE ACCESS

You can also provide connectivity *in* to your network from the outside world, either through the Internet or via modem. This connectivity lets you get at your LAN resources from home or out in the field, with full assurance that your network is safe from outside attacks. Chapter 23, "Windows Unplugged: Remote and Mobile Networking," covers remote access.

For now, if you aren't planning to have a permanent direct Internet connection, you might want to plan for the installation of a telephone line near one of your Windows 2000 computers so that you can set up a dedicated modem connection for incoming remote access.

TROUBLESHOOTING

CAN'T DRILL THROUGH WALLS OR CEILINGS

My lease and the physical limitations of my building prevent me from drilling through walls or the ceiling to install network cabling.

In this case, you can install wires along baseboards, around doors, and so on. It's not as pretty, but because network wiring is low voltage, it's not risky to do so as it is with power wiring. (My office has a cable shamefully strung through a skylight, across the ceiling, and into a closet.) You also can use products called *wiring channels* to conceal the wires run along baseboards and rubber guards to protect them where they might be trod upon. You can find these products in the hardware store or in business product catalogs.

AC POWER IS UNRELIABLE

The AC power in my area is unreliable, failing frequently for significant periods of time.

In many areas of the world, the power grid is unreliable or unavailable. In these areas, UPSs aren't just for the occasional glitch but frequently serve as the main power source for normal operation, bridging the gaps in standard power service.

Because the required runtimes will be longer, the cost of UPSs to back up standard computer hardware can be prohibitive. In this case, consider building your network entirely with portable computers (laptops). Laptops use very little power and have built-in batteries that can often run long enough to work through power outages. I've even seen laptops used as file servers for large networks in this situation. You'll still need UPSs for routers, hubs, and so on, and possibly even the laptops.

LAN MUST SUPPORT VISITORS WITH UNKNOWN HARDWARE

My office frequently gets visitors who need to use my LAN or Internet connection and who come with various types of computer hardware.

You can set aside a workspace for random visitors by providing two types of network connection: 10BASE2 and 10BASE-T. (Almost all portable 100BASE-T cards automatically adjust to 10BASE-T speeds, so just the 10MHz connections should cover all the bases.) A small, inexpensive 10BASE-T hub *with a coax connector*, costing about $30, will make this easy. Provide a live coax T-connector and a live 10BASE-T patch cable, and your visitors will be able to connect to your LAN.

TIPS FROM THE WINDOWS PROS: SHOPPING FOR A NETWORK

This chapter covered a lot of territory and presented many options. After you've made all your decisions, shopping is not as daunting as it might seem. To show you what you need when all the planning is done, I've drawn up a shopping list for a typical small network.

In this network, I'm planning for the following:

- Seven Windows 2000 and/or Windows 9x workstations
- One Windows 2000 workstation designated as the "master" station, on which I'll set up communal shared folders
- A 10BASE-T network
- Full power protection for all workstations

The following is my shopping list for the network hardware and accessories:

- Seven network (PCI or PC Card) 10BASE-T cards
- One PCI network card as a spare, or to be used to connect a computer to a DSL or cable Internet service provider

- One 8-port 10BASE-T hub (or three 4-port hubs if groups of computers are widely separated).
- One 8GB (internal) Travan tape drive and eight tapes
- One backup software package, single-server version
- Six 200-watt UPSs, for the six ordinary workstations
- One 400-watt UPS, for the main machine and the hub
- Three surge-protected power strips
- Cable clips or staples

and either

- Eight CAT-5 patch cables, lengths as needed to reach from hub to computers (one is a spare)

or

- Bag of 20 (or so) RJ45 crimp-on connectors
- RJ45 crimping tool, diagonal cutters, and cable stripper
- Spool of CAT-5 cable, enough for the job plus some spare

In the next chapter, we'll continue with network installation and setup.

CHAPTER 21

INSTANT NETWORKING

In this chapter

CREATING YOUR OWN LAN

Do you remember the days when you could fix your own car, but local area networks (LANs) were the domain of technical wizards with expensive and mysterious tools? It seems like the situation is the other way around now. When I open the hood of my car, I can't make heads or tails of the jumble of black boxes, wires, hoses and…*things*, and I don't even know whether a carburetor is in there somewhere. LANs, on the other hand, have become so simple that just about anyone can install one in his or her home or office in an afternoon.

This chapter is directed toward a small group of users, at home or at work, who want to set up a LAN for themselves. This type of LAN is called a *peer-to-peer network* because no one computer has a central role in managing the network. This type of network doesn't take full advantage of all of Windows 2000 Professional's networking capabilities, but unless you have dozens of computers to network, you probably don't *need* all those capabilities. For you, a peer-to-peer network may be just the thing to let you share files and printers with your co-workers or housemates.

If you want to create or join a network managed by Windows 2000 Server, you probably won't have to do any of this work on your own. Your network administrator or support staff should manage all this work for you. If you have to do the job yourself, you can follow the instructions here; just be on the lookout for notes addressed specifically to you. This chapter doesn't cover the configuration of Windows 2000 Server, however.

> **Note**
>
> If you are adding your Windows 2000 Professional computer to an existing LAN, you should first check with your network manager (or children) for advice, instructions, and configuration information before performing this task on your own.
>
> If you are part of a Windows 2000 Domain network, or if your company uses Windows 2000's Remote Installation Services and Management features, you might not need to, or even be able to, view or change any of the network settings or control panels described in this chapter.
>
> If you want to learn how to configure your own Windows 2000 Server, I suggest that you pick up a copy of *Special Edition Using Microsoft Windows 2000 Server*, published by Que. Because the Workstation and Server flavors of Windows are entirely different beasts, two full-length books (tomes, if you will) are required to cover them.

Chapter 20, "Planning Your Windows 2000 Pro Network," describes the components, options, and trade-offs in setting up your own LAN. If you haven't chosen a network cabling system and designed your network, read Chapter 20 now. Otherwise, I'll assume you have done your homework, have finished your shopping, and are ready to put it all together! Creating a LAN is going to be easier than changing the spark plugs in my car (I think—if my car has spark plugs, that is).

INSTALLING NETWORK ADAPTERS

I've made this point before, but it's worth repeating: Before you purchase a network card, be sure to check the Windows 2000 Hardware Compatibility List (HCL). You should purchase cards that appear on the HCL or that are marked by the manufacturer certifying their compatibility with Windows 2000. You can find the HCL at http://www.microsoft.com/hcl.

If your adapter was already installed when you set up Windows 2000, it may already be ready to go, in which case you can skip this section and jump down to "Wiring a Computer to an Existing LAN." Follow these steps to see whether the adapter is already set up:

1. Right-click My Computer and select Manage.

2. Select Device Manager in the left pane, and open the Network Adapters list in the right pane.

3. Look for an entry for your network card. If it appears and does not have a yellow exclamation point (!) icon to the left of its name, the card is installed and correctly configured. In this case, you can skip ahead to "Installing Network Wiring."

   If an entry appears but has an exclamation point icon by its name (see the example in Figure 21.1), the card is not correctly configured.

Note

If you see an exclamation point icon in the Network Adapters list, skip ahead to Chapter 27, "Troubleshooting Your Windows 2000 Network," for tips on getting the card to work before proceeding.

Figure 21.1
The Device Manager indicates trouble with a network adapter by displaying an exclamation point icon next to its name.

4. If no entry exists for the card, follow the instructions for non-Plug and Play (PnP) adapters later in this chapter.

If you're installing a new card, follow the card's instructions for installing with Windows 2000. If it does not have specific Windows 2000 instructions, try one of the procedures listed in the following sections, depending on the type of card you have purchased.

INSTALLING A PLUG AND PLAY NETWORK ADAPTER

If you have purchased a PCMCIA (PC Card) adapter, external USB network adapter, or a standard internal *Plug and Play* card, the installation should be a snap. Just follow these steps:

1. If you have an internal Plug and Play card, shut down Windows, shut off the computer, open the case, install the card in an empty slot, close the case, and restart Windows. Log in as Administrator or other Power User. Windows displays the New Hardware Detected dialog when you log in.

Tip #242

If you've never worked inside your computer, you can check out one of the many hardware upgrade books available to help you get started. Working inside is not as hard as you might think. You should be sure to guard against static electricity damage (known by gearheads as ESD, or electrostatic discharge) to the internal components by using an inexpensive ESD kit available at any computer or electronics store. If you need assistance beyond the instructions that came with your NIC, I recommend *Upgrading and Repairing PCs, Eleventh Edition*, published by Que.

If you have a PCMCIA or USB adapter, just plug it in while Windows is running.

2. The New Hardware Detected dialog might instruct you to insert the Windows 2000 CD-ROM. If Windows cannot find a suitable driver for your network card, it may ask you to insert the floppy disk that came with the network card.

   If you are asked, insert the floppy disk and click OK. If Windows says that it cannot locate an appropriate device driver, try again, and this time click the Browse button. Locate a folder named Windows2000 (or some reasonable approximation), W2K, or NT5 on the floppy, and click OK.

Note

The exact name of the folder containing your device driver varies from vendor to vendor. You might have to poke around a little on the disk to find it.

→ For more detailed instructions about installing hardware and drivers, **see** Chapter 30, "Maintaining and Optimizing System Performance."

3. After Windows has installed the card's driver software, it automatically configures and uses the card. Check the Device Manager to see whether the card is installed and functioning. Then you can proceed to "Installing Network Wiring" later in this chapter.

INSTALLING A NON-PLUG AND PLAY NETWORK CARD

If you have an older network card, one that predates Plug and Play technology, you either can buy a new one or see whether the card is listed on the Windows Hardware Compatibility

List. If it is not listed, kiss it goodbye and get a new network card. If it is listed, you still might decide it's easier to just go get a new card. Compare the preceding instructions for a Plug and Play card to the 14 steps that follow. If seeing all these extra steps isn't enough motivation to get a new card, I don't know what is! A new card can cost less than a movie and popcorn, and who needs all those fat calories anyway?

Note

Microsoft recommends that you not use old 8-bit network cards with Windows 2000, even if they are listed on the Hardware Compatibility List. These cards include the Novell NE-1000, the 3COM 3C509, and others.

If I haven't convinced you to buy a new card, follow these instructions:

1. If you are using a computer that had a LAN card installed before you upgraded to Windows 2000, you might be able to use the card as is. See what its current configuration settings are, and if you can tell, skip ahead to step 7.

2. Before you install the card, you must determine what configuration settings are required for the card and which settings to use. The following typical settings must be made:

   - IRQ (Interrupt Request) Level
   - I/O Port
   - Memory address
   - EPROM or BOOT ROM Enable
   - EPROM or BOOT ROM Memory Address

   Your card might not have all these options; check your network card's manual to see which are required. The documentation should also list all the possible values for each setting, alone or in suggested combinations. (You need to know what the acceptable values are, even if you don't use one of the suggested combinations.)

   To determine which values you can use in your computer, right-click My Computer and select Manage. In the left pane, open System Information and then Hardware Resources.

3. Select the IRQs list, which displays the IRQ values already in use. For example, #1 will be used by Keyboard, and #4 probably will be used by Communications Port COM1 (see Figure 21.2). You can't use these numbers for your network card. Also, whether or not they're listed, you can't use 1, 2, 6, 8, or 13.

4. Check the list of IRQ numbers allowed by your network card, and choose one that is not already in use. Write down this number.

PART

IV

CH

21

Tip #243

Lower numbers are better, if you have a choice, because they give the network card greater priority over other devices when competing for the processor's attention.

Figure 21.2
Here, you can see IRQ
values already in use.
If your network card
allows any IRQ value
from 1 to 15, I suggest
that you choose 11.

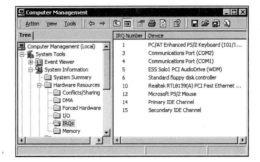

5. Repeat this process for the I/O port value (usually shown as a range of numbers—for example, 300-30F), checking the documentation's list of allowed values against the I/O display in Hardware Resources, which lists I/O ports already in use. Choose a setting that doesn't overlap any port value in use. (No one setting is better than any other here.)

6. If your card is one of the few that require a memory address setting, compare the list of allowed values against the Hardware Resources list of memory addresses already in use, and choose an unused value. Write down this value as well.

Tip #244

You do not need to select a Boot ROM or EPROM address. These addresses are used only for computers without hard disks that need to boot up using files stored on a network server. You need to disable only the Boot ROM option.

7. If the network card uses jumpers and pins to record these settings, follow the card's instructions to set the IRQ and I/O address and to disable the Boot ROM option. If the card has no pins, but it's not Plug and Play, you have to boot your computer with an MS-DOS startup disk and use the card's software setup utility.

8. Shut down the computer, power it off, and install the card.

9. Restart the computer, and log in as Administrator or other Power User. Choose Start, Settings, Control Panel, and then choose Add New Hardware. The Add New Hardware wizard opens.

10. Click Next. Click Add/Troubleshoot a Device and click Next. Windows checks for new Plug and Play hardware, which it does not find. Windows then displays the Choose a Hardware Device dialog (see Figure 21.3). Select Add a New Device, and click Next.

11. Windows asks whether you will let it try to guess what the new hardware device is. If you're feeling lucky, you can let Windows search for the new hardware itself, so just click OK. This approach works only if your network card is listed on the Windows 2000 Hardware Compatibility List.

Otherwise, or if Windows fails to determine the correct adapter type, select the No, I Want to Select the Hardware from a List option. Click Next, choose Network Adapters, and click Next again.

Figure 21.3
The Choose a Hardware Device dialog appears when Windows does not detect new Plug and Play hardware. Select Add A New Device to install the driver for a new network card.

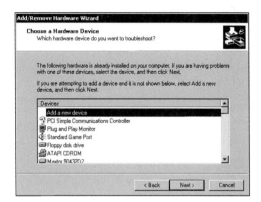

12. Locate the card's manufacturer and model, as shown in Figure 21.4. If you find it, click Next. If you can't find it and you have a floppy disk from the manufacturer with a Windows 2000 compatible driver, select Have Disk. The Install from Disk dialog then appears. Click Browse, and locate the Windows 2000 driver INF file. Finally, choose Open and click OK.

Figure 21.4
In this dialog, you can choose the device's manufacturer and model number.

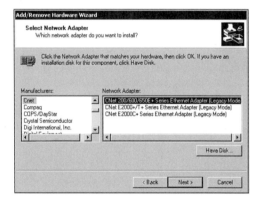

Tip #245

If you can't find the manufacturer and model and don't have a Windows 2000 driver diskette, you cannot use this network card.

I've found manufacturers' names and Web sites for some anonymous network cards by searching the Net for any model or part numbers I can find on the cards. This approach works sometimes, and I've been able to download up-to-date drivers. Try www.hotbot.com or www.altavista.com.

Or just get a new card.

PART
IV
CH
21

13. Windows should tell you that you have to enter the device's hardware settings manually. Select the first resource type, and click Change Settings. In the resulting dialog,

scroll up and down the Value setting until you find the value you chose earlier in Steps 3–6. Windows should display No Devices Are Conflicting under Conflict Information (see Figure 21.5). Click OK, and repeat this step for each resource type in turn.

14. Click OK when you're finished. Then click Next to proceed with the installation. Finally, the wizard indicates that the installation is complete. At this point, select Finish and allow Windows to restart your computer.

Figure 21.5

That wasn't so bad, was it? Now you need to connect your computer to the others.

INSTALLING NETWORKING WIRING

Installing the wiring is the most difficult task of setting up a network. If it involves climbing around in the attic or under a building, drilling through walls, or working in an office telephone closet, calling in a professional is probably best. Personally, I find it a frustrating task and one I would rather watch while sipping coffee and eating pastries. Hiring someone to do the job might cost $30 to $75 per computer, but you'll get a professional job, and if you consider that the price of network cards has gone down at least this much in the last few years, you can pretend that you're getting the wiring thrown in for free.

Tip #246

Look in the yellow pages under Telephone Wiring, and ask the contractors you call whether they have experience with network wiring. The following are some points to check out when you shop for a wiring contractor:

- Ask for references, and check them out.
- Ask for billing details up front: Do they charge by the hour or at a fixed rate? Do they sell equipment themselves, or do you have to supply cables, connectors, and so on?
- Ask for prices for parts and labor separately so that you know whether you're getting a good deal and can comparison-shop.
- Find out what their guaranteed response time is, should problems or failures occur in the future.
- Ask what their warranty terms are. How long are parts and labor covered?

GENERAL CABLING TIPS

You can determine how much cable you need by measuring the distance between computers if you're using coaxial cable or between your computers and your hub locations if you're using twisted-pair cable.

Remember to account for vertical distances, too, where cables run from the floor up to a desktop, or go up and over a partition or wall.

If you have to run cables through the ceiling space of an office building, you should check with your building management to see whether the ceiling is listed as a *plenum* or air-conditioning air return. You may be required by law to use certified *plenum cable* and follow all applicable electrical codes. Plenum cable is specially formulated not to emit toxic smoke in a fire.

When you're installing cables, be gentle. Don't pull, kink, or stretch them. Don't bend them sharply around corners; you should allow at least a one-inch radius for bends. And don't staple or crimp them. To attach them to a wall or baseboard, use rigid cable clips that don't squeeze the cable, as shown in Figure 21.6. Your local electronics store can sell you the right kind of clips.

Figure 21.6
Use rigid cable clips or staples that don't squeeze the cable when you nail it to a wall or baseboard.

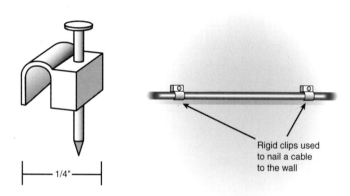

1/4"

Rigid clips used to nail a cable to the wall

Try not to run network cables near AC power cables. If you can't avoid it, be sure a network cable crosses a power cable at a right angle and doesn't run parallel to it to minimize the transfer of electrical interference from the power cable to the network cable.

Avoiding Electrical Interference

Electrical interference from fluorescent lighting, radio stations, and other electronic devices is a networker's nemesis. UTP cabling is inexpensive because it forgoes *shielding*, the metal sheath that protects coaxial and shielded twisted-pair cables from interference. Shielding reduces interference, but it adds a lot to the cost of cabling.

To compensate for this lack of protection, when you use UTP cable, you need to use good network wiring practices:

- Use only cable that is certified for the type of network you're installing (for example, CAT-3 or CAT-5).
- Keep network cables away from AC power wiring and away from electrically noisy devices such as arc welders, fluorescent lights, diathermy machines, and the like.
- Use high-quality jacks, plugs, patch cables, and other components.
- Don't solder, splice, or unwrap the twisted-pair wire.

PART

IV

CH

21

You can run network cables through the habitable area of your home or office by routing them behind furniture, around partitions, and so on. Just don't put cables where they'll be crushed, walked on, or run over by desk chair wheels.

If your cables don't need to pass through walls, you can either purchase premade cables or build them from crimp-on connectors and bulk cable stock. Making your own cables requires about $75 worth of tools (a cable stripper, diagonal cutters, and connector crimper) and more detailed instructions than I can give here. Making just a few cables certainly doesn't make buying the tools worthwhile. Factory-assembled cables are also more reliable than homemade ones because the connectors are attached by machine. They're worth the extra few dollars.

Tip #247

If you do make your own cables, be sure to buy spare connectors in case you make a mistake or two. I always end up cutting off at least one goof-up.

Note

If you really want to get into the nuts and bolts, so to speak, of pulling your own cable, you have a lot to learn. The good news is that you *can* learn it; it's not as tough as you might think. The bad news, of course, is that it takes time and patience. A good starting point is Que's *Practical Network Cabling*, which will help you roll up your shirtsleeves and get dirty (literally, if you have to crawl around through your attic or wrestle with dust bunnies under too many desks at the office).

WIRING WITH COAXIAL CABLE

For Thinnet (10BASE-2 Ethernet), you must use RG-58 cable. Ordinary television cable or existing ARCnet cable does not work.

Tip #248

I recommend using cable with a stranded center conductor rather than a solid wire because this type of cable is more flexible and less likely to kink or break.

If you're running cable through walls, you need to drill pretty big holes if you use cable with the connectors already attached. If you can use bulk cable, pull the cable through first, and attach the connectors afterward.

If you attach the connectors yourself, be sure to ask for the correct crimp-on connectors for the cable you buy. The size of the hole in the center pin used for stranded versus solid conductor cable is different.

Tip #249

T-connectors are supplied with coax-only network cards, but "combo" network adapters (which accept either coax or twisted-pair cable) usually do *not* include the T-connector. Don't forget to check the box when you buy your network card to see whether you need to buy T-connectors as well, lest you have to make two trips to the store. Figure 21.8 (later in the chapter) shows a detailed illustration of a standard T-connector.

WIRING WITH UTP CABLE

Chapter 20 described the requirements for UTP cabling and the differences between CAT-3 and CAT-5 cable. I'll repeat the main points here.

Keep in mind these points for 10BASE-T networking:

- Old household telephone wire probably won't work. If the wires are red, green, black, and yellow: no way. The cable must have color-matched pairs of wires, each with one wire in a solid color and the other white with colored stripes.

- If you want to use existing wiring for a 10BASE-T network, you should be sure that the wiring is at least CAT-3 certified. If the cable has three or more pairs of color-matched wires twisted together, it's probably CAT-3 compliant.

- I suggest that you use CAT-5 components for any new cabling and components you buy.

For 100BASE-Tx networking, you must use at least CAT-5 quality wiring and components throughout: cables, jacks, plugs, connectors, terminal blocks, patch cables, and so on.

WIRING WITH PATCH CABLES

If your computers are close together and you can simply run prefabricated cables between your computers and hub, you've got it made! Just plug (click!), and you're finished.

IN-WALL UTP WIRING

When you use longer, more complex in-wall wiring systems, you should carefully examine your wiring system plan to be sure that each pin of the jack at one end is connected to the same pin at the jack at the other end. If a pair of wires gets switched or connected to the wrong pins, the computer served by that wire simply cannot access the network.

If you have to put RJ-45 connectors directly on the ends of cables, be very careful to match up the proper wire pairs to the proper pins in the jack. Look at Figure 21.7 carefully, and note that one of the wire pairs is split up, between pins 3 and 6. Splitting the pairs is required!

In standard Ethernet UTP wiring, the choice of color-to-pin correspondence is not as important as consistency from end-to-end so that pins 1, 2, 3, and 6 of your Ethernet card end up connected to pins 1, 2, 3, and 6 at your hub. The best practice is to wire all eight wires through end to end. This wiring pattern is used for patch cables and all card-to-hub connections.

PART

IV

CH

21

Figure 21.7
Standard Ethernet UTP wiring.

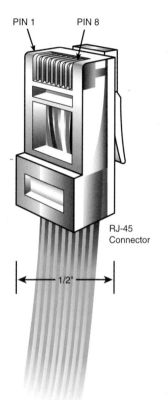

TIA/EIA 568A Standard

PIN	DATA	WIRE COLOR
1	TX+	White/Green
2	TX–	Green
3	RX+	White/Orange
4	–	Blue
5	–	White/Blue
6	RX–	Orange
7	–	White/Brown
8	–	Brown

RJ-45
Connector

1/2"

PIN 1   PIN 8

Tip #250

If you're starting to think making your own cables might be somewhat of a hassle, you're right. If you're not feeling experimental, or you are currently enrolled in anger-management courses, consider hiring a pro.

Otherwise, when you're trying to get the wires into the connector in just the right order and find that they tend to shift sideways and switch places as you shove them into the connector for crimping, think of the bearclaw and cup of steaming black coffee I'd be having right about then.

OUT OF THE (PHONE) CLOSET

If you're wiring an office, running all your network wiring alongside the office's phone system wiring to a central location may be most sensible. For 10BASE-T, you might even find that your phone wiring is already CAT-3 certified, and you can use spare pairs on the phone system wiring for at least some of your network connections.

But in this case, you might have to face the Phone Closet for the first time. In most office buildings, telephone and data wiring are run to a central location on each floor or in each office suite. Connector blocks called *punchdown blocks* are bolted to the wall, where your individual telephone extension wires are joined to thick distribution cables maintained by the phone company or the building management.

These commercial wiring systems are a little bit daunting, and if you aren't familiar with them, it's best to hire a wiring contractor to install your network wiring.

USING MORE THAN ONE TYPE OF WIRING

If you're building a 10BASE-T network, you don't have to stick with just one type of wiring. You can purchase a hub with twisted-pair connectors and a BNC connector so that you can mix and match cabling types. The only constraints are that you can't design a network in which more than three hubs separate any two computers, and cable can't exceed the maximum length for the type of wire: 100 meters (330 feet) for 10BASE-T or 200 meters (660 feet) for 10BASE-2.

CONNECTING TWO COMPUTERS

If you are connecting just two computers, yours is the easiest possible network installation: You can simply run a cable from one computer to the other, and you're finished. You can run the cable across a desk, a room, or—if necessary—through the walls. Just be sure not to exceed the distance limit: 200 meters (660 feet) for 10BASE-2 coaxial cable or 100 meters (330 feet) for 10BASE-T twisted-pair cable.

CONNECTING TWO COMPUTERS WITH COAXIAL CABLE

If you are using coaxial cable (10BASE-2) wiring, you need one length of RG-58 coaxial cable with BNC connectors at each end, two T-connectors, and two 50-ohm BNC terminators, as shown in Figure 21.8.

CONNECTING TWO COMPUTERS WITH UTP CABLE

For 10BASE-T and 100BASE-Tx networks, you have to use a *crossover cable* to directly connect two network cards. This cable is different from the patch cable described previously; it reverses the signals between its two ends so that the send and receive signals from one computer connect to the receive and send signals, respectively, on the other. You can purchase a crossover cable at a computer store or make one using connections, as shown in Figure 21.9. Be sure to use a CAT-5 cable if you're using 100BASE-Tx network cards.

If you must run your wire through walls, you can use the jack-and-patch-cable system shown in Figure 21.10, using a crossover cable as *one* of the two patch cables.

I recommend making the crossover in one of the patch cables because you can simply discard this cable if you ever add more computers and have to add a hub to your network. The long cable between computers should use the normal wiring pattern so that it doesn't cause confusion later.

→ With that, you're finished! You can skip ahead to "Configuring the Network" on page **724**.

Figure 21.8
When you're connecting two computers using coaxial cable, first connect the T-connectors to the network cards in the computers, and then connect the cable and terminators to the T-connectors.

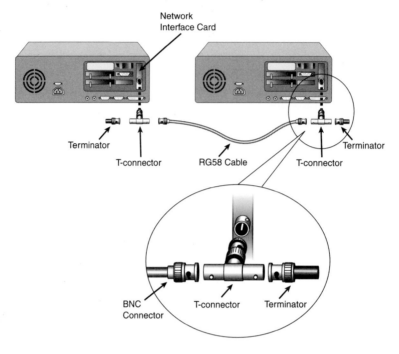

Figure 21.9
A crossover cable for 10BASE-T or 100BASE-Tx wiring reverses the send and receive wires so that two network cards can be directly connected.

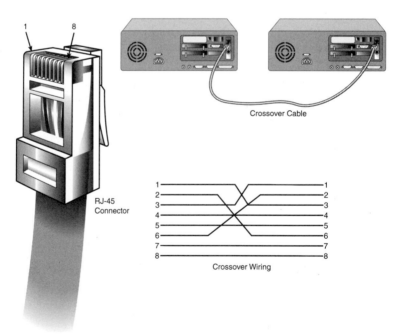

Figure 21.10
When you're connecting two computers using patch cables with a longer run of wire between two jacks, you can use a crossover cable as one of the two patch cables.

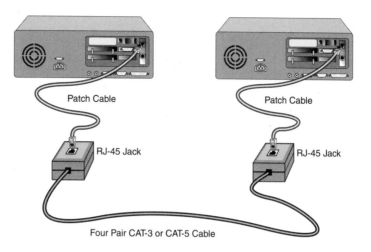

Patch Cable

Patch Cable

RJ-45 Jack

RJ-45 Jack

Four Pair CAT-3 or CAT-5 Cable

CONNECTING THREE OR MORE COMPUTERS

Installing three or more computers is only a little more complex—and then only if you're using twisted-pair cabling. In the following sections, we'll go through the connection types.

CONNECTING THREE OR MORE COMPUTERS WITH COAXIAL CABLE

Connecting multiple computers' 10BASE-2 wiring with coaxial cable is as easy as connecting two: You just have to remember that the computers must be connected so that the cable runs in a single line from one computer to the next and then to the next with no branches (see Figure 21.11).

Figure 21.11
Coaxial cable must chain the computers together in a single-file fashion, with no "branches." Terminators go on each end of the chain.

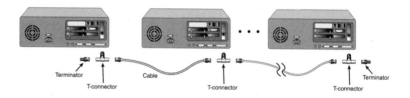

Terminator

Cable

Terminator

T-connector

T-connector

T-connector

If you need to join two lengths of coaxial cable to gain a greater length, you *cannot* solder or splice them. You can use BNC connectors on both of the ends to be joined and connect them with a special BNC-to-BNC connector called a *barrel adapter*. You also can use these adapters when adding a new computer to an existing network, as shown in Figure 21.12.

CONNECTING THREE OR MORE COMPUTERS WITH UTP CABLE

If you have chosen a 10BASE-T or 100BASE-Tx network, your first job is to choose a location for the center of your network: the hub. Because each computer must connect to a hub,

PART

IV

CH

21

you should put one or more hubs in places where running cables out to individual computers is convenient.

If you are installing longer runs of UTP cable through walls, ceilings, and so on, I recommend that you run the cables to wall-mounted jacks at each computer and use a 5- to 10-foot patch cable to connect the computer to the jack, as shown for the computers in Figure 21.13.

Figure 21.12
You can add a computer to a 10BASE-2 network like this. A barrel adapter is used to join BNC cables. You can use the barrel adapter to add a new computer to the middle of an existing network with minimum disruption to the existing wiring.

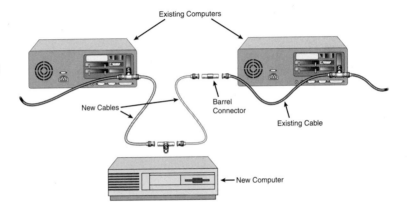

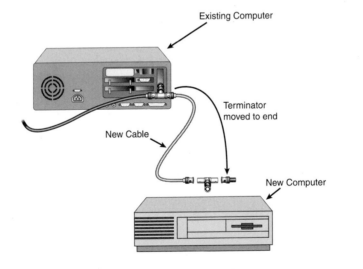

Tip #251

Even if you're using 10BASE-T network cards and hubs, you should use CAT-5 wire, jacks, and connectors. CAT-5 components are required for higher speed network systems such as 100BASE-Tx. Using them will cost a little more now, but you'll be glad you did it if and when you decide to upgrade your network in the future. Completely replacing the wiring will cost you a lot more.

Figure 21.13
This UTP wiring scheme uses jacks for each computer and a patch panel near the hub. All components must be rated CAT-5 for 100BASE-Tx networks and at least CAT-3 for 10BASE-T.

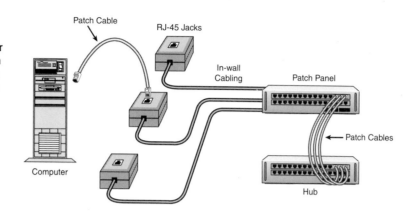

Patch Cable

RJ-45 Jacks

In-wall Cabling

Patch Panel

Patch Cables

Computer

Hub

Tip #252

Be sure to get at least one spare patch cable that is longer than the others you buy. One computer always ends up being farther from the jack than you thought.

For in-wall wiring, twisted-pair cable comes with varying numbers of wires in the jacket; the most common types are four- and eight-pair. An Ethernet connection requires only two pairs of wire, but the best practice is to connect all eight wires (four pairs) from end-to-end through your cabling system. So, you can connect one jack to a four-pair cable or two jacks to an eight-pair cable.

When you're installing the jacks, be sure not to untwist more than half an inch of any pair of wires.

CONNECTING THREE OR MORE COMPUTERS AT THE HUB END

At the hub end, you can put connectors directly on the incoming wires, you can use the wall jack and patch cord system you used at the computer end, or you can wire the incoming cables to a *patch panel* that contains between 8 and 32 RJ-45 jacks, as shown for the hub in Figure 21.13. Be sure to follow the color-coded labels on the patch panel so that the wires in each cable end up connected to the correct pins in the jacks. You can then run short patch cables between the patch panel and your hub.

I like the direct-cable method best when using four-pair cable (which carries one connection) and the terminal block method when using eight-pair cable (which carries two connections). The problem with eight-pair cable is that you can't crimp two connectors onto it. You have to connect it to a jack of some sort, and if you're doing that, you might as well use the terminal block to take up the least amount of room.

PART

IV

CH

21

Wire Color Coding
Telephone professionals deal with cables carrying tens or even hundreds of wire pairs all day, every day, all over the world. So, standardized numbering and color-coding schemes were developed so that workers could approach an unfamiliar telephone system and make some sense of the wiring they faced.

The standards cover UTP network wiring as well. Using standardized parts, wiring technicians can connect cables to jacks, punchdown blocks, and patch panels following the designated color scheme and trust that the wires will end up routed properly. For example, pin 1 at one end will wind up connected to pin 1 at the other.

The two different standards for terminal blocks and RJ-45 wall jacks are designated T-568A and T-568B. The only difference is in which wire colors are assigned to each pin of the jack. It doesn't matter which you use, as long as you get components that all use the same flavor. If you have a choice, use T-568A because it is the one preferred by the international standards organizations.

CONNECTING THE HUBS

Hubs usually come with those annoying plug-in power supplies that take up the space of two or three plugs on your power strips or electrical outlets. (With all the progress made in networking technology in the past decade, no one has figured out a way around this problem.) Wherever you put your hubs, you'll have to find a way to get AC power to them.

Tip #253	When putting hubs in office telephone closets, I usually either build a small shelf or bolt them directly to the plywood wall sheathing in the closet. You can also screw power strips to the wall where they'll be out of the way and close to your hubs.

Chapter 20 described mixing 10BASE-T and 100BASE-Tx. Be sure to read the discussion of mixed-speed hubs, switching, and media converters in that chapter if you have a mixture of 10Mbps and 100Mbps network cards or devices.

ADDING NETWORK-CAPABLE PRINTERS

If you have a printer that directly attaches to LANs, by all means, plug it into your network. If you are using coaxial cable and your printer has only a 10BASE-T connector or vice versa, or if you use 100BASE-Tx networking and your printer is capable only of 10BASE-T connections, you have to use a media converter to connect the printer, as shown in Figure 21.14.

Figure 21.14
You can add a network-capable printer to the LAN by using a direct connection, a media converter, or a hub.

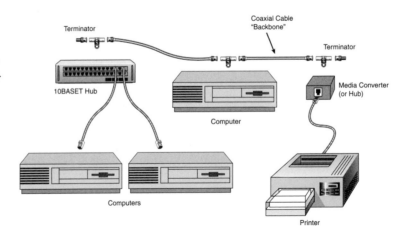

Using a four-port hub with a BNC connector is probably the cheapest way to connect a BNC device to a UTP network or vice versa. You must remember to use T-connectors and terminators at each end of the coaxial cable run, even if only the hub and a printer are connected to it, as shown in Figure 21.14.

WIRING A COMPUTER TO AN EXISTING LAN

If you are adding a new computer to an existing LAN, you should try to get a network card that matches the existing network type and speed. You may have some flexibility with the wiring type, as you'll learn here.

WIRING A COMPUTER TO AN EXISTING THINNET NETWORK

If your existing LAN uses 10BASE-2 coaxial cable, you have a choice. You can stick with coax and get a 10BASE-2 network card, or you can start the move to 10BASE-T by adding a 10BASE-T network card and a network hub with both coax and UTP connectors. These hubs can cost under $40.

You can add your new computer or hub to the middle of the network chain or at the end, as previously shown in Figure 21.12. Remember that 10BASE-2 is a *bus* network, and any breaks or problems with the cabling stop the whole network. Be careful and quick when changing the cabling.

> **Caution**
>
> When you unplug any cables or terminators to add your new computer, the entire network stops working. You should warn any other LAN users in advance of changing cable connections. Have other users save their work before you start. Your new cable arrangement might not work, disrupting their network connections, and then you'd have dozens of angry people chasing you around the office.
>
> After you've made the changes and have tested the network to be sure it works, go back and tell all the other users they can start working again. You might be surprised how often people forget this step.
>
> And you would be right if you guessed that I learned both of these things by experience.

If you have added a hub, plug your computer's 10BASE-T network card into the hub using a patch cable.

WIRING A COMPUTER TO AN EXISTING 10BASE-T NETWORK

If you can reach a cable from your computer to the nearest hub, and it has an unused connector, you can simply plug in using patch cable.

If the nearest hub is more than 20 feet away, you can add a new RJ-45 jack near your computer and run in-wall wiring to the hub.

If your hub has no unused connectors, you need to expand your network with an additional hub. Consider how many new connections you expect to make, and purchase a hub with enough room for growth; you can get hubs with 4 to 32 ports.

You must unplug one cable from the original hub to open a connection port. Connect this cable and your new computer to the new hub. Finally, connect the new hub's *cascade port* to the original hub's free port, as shown in Figure 21.15.

> **Note**
>
> A cascade port is a hub connector designed to be connected to another hub. Some hubs have a separate connector for this purpose, whereas others make one of the hub's regular ports do double-duty by providing a switch that turns the last hub port into a cascade port. Refer to your hub's manual to see what to do with your particular hardware.

Figure 21.15
You can expand your 10BASE-T network by cascading hubs. The instructions included with your hub describe how to con-nect two hubs using a patch cable. Some hubs have a special cascade port, whereas others have a switch that turns a regular port into a cascade port.

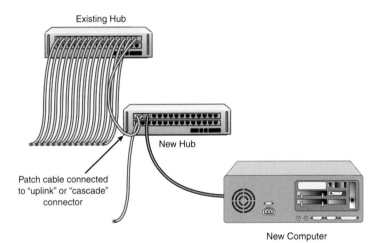

Existing Hub

New Hub

Patch cable connected to "uplink" or "cascade" connector

New Computer

CONFIGURING THE NETWORK

When your wiring is in, you're ready to configure Windows 2000. With today's Plug and Play network cards and with all the needed software built in Windows 2000, configuring should be a snap.

If you're using a UTP network, as you install network cards and plug them into the cables running to your hub, you should see a green light come on at the hub for each computer you power up and connect. There might be an indicator on the back of the network card as well. These lights indicate that the network wiring is correct.

 If you don't get green lights, stop immediately and get the wiring fixed. Check out "Hub Lights Do Not Come On" in the "Troubleshooting" section at the end of this chapter.

CONFIGURING NETWORK ADAPTERS

You should have configured your network adapters as you installed them, as described at the beginning of this chapter. To check whether your network adapters are installed and functioning, right-click My Computer, select Manage, open the Device Manager, and then open the Network Adapters list (refer to Figure 21.1). If your adapters are listed and have no yellow exclamation point (!) icons, you're all set. If not, follow the instructions for configuring network adapters earlier in this chapter.

ADDING CLIENTS

When your network card and its drivers are installed, Windows knows the card is there but doesn't have any networking software attached to it. Follow these steps to attach the networking protocols and services you chose in Chapter 20:

1. Choose Start, Settings, Network and Dial-Up Connections. Select Local Area Connection, and click Properties. You should see a Properties dialog with your network card named at the top under Connect Using. The list below Components Checked Are Used By This Connection will be blank.

2. Click Install, and from the list in the resulting Select Network Component Type dialog (see Figure 21.16), choose Client, and then choose Add.

Figure 21.16

3. From the list of Network Clients, choose Client For Microsoft Networks, and click OK. Windows may direct you to insert your Windows 2000 Installation CD to obtain needed files.

Tip #254

> If Windows asks whether it can restart, select Yes. For previous versions of Windows, I would have suggested selecting No because you would face further restarts as you added other network components. With Windows 2000, you aren't asked to restart more than once, so you might as well get it over with right away.

4. If you have Novell NetWare servers on your network, you can install the Client Service for NetWare, which is described in Chapter 25, "Networking Mix and Match."

ADDING SERVICES

If you want to share files, folders, or printers on your computer with others on your network, click Install, select Service, and click Add. Select File and Printer Sharing for Microsoft Networks, and click OK. Finally, make sure a check mark appears next to File and Printer Sharing.

ADDING PROTOCOLS

You learned about networking protocols in Chapter 20. If you don't know which protocols you should install, read Chapter 20 now. The following is an executive summary:

Internet Protocol (TCP/IP)   Add it.

NWLink IPX/SPX/NetBIOS	If you added the Novell client, NWLink is already installed.
NWLink NetBIOS	Probably not.
NetBEUI	If you have Windows for Workgroups computers that use folders you share with this computer, add it. If you have Windows 9x computers without TCP/IP, add it. Otherwise, no.
AppleTalk	Add it only if you want to directly access an AppleTalk-based printer attached to your network.
DLC	Add it only if you have DLC-based network-connected printers from IBM or Hewlett-Packard.

> **Caution**
>
> This summary is provided with the caution that you're not excused from reading Chapter 20!

For each protocol you need to use, click Install, select Protocol, and click Add. Select the protocol that you want to use, and click OK, as shown in Figure 21.17. Repeat this process for any additional protocols you want to use. The list in Figure 21.17 shows only protocols that have not yet been installed, so yours will probably differ from the one in this figure.

Figure 21.17
To add a protocol, choose a desired protocol from the list and click OK.

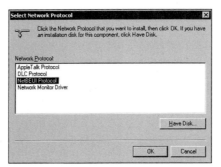

If Windows asked you whether it could restart, and you didn't believe me and selected No, restart it now by choosing Start, Shutdown, and selecting Shut Down and Restart.

CONFIGURING PROTOCOLS

You need to make configuration settings for only two protocols: NWLink and TCP/IP.

NOVELL (NWLINK)

In the very unlikely event that you have an old Novell NetWare version 2 server on your network, see Chapter 25 for notes on configuring the NWLink IPX/SPX/NetBIOS Compatible Transport Protocol.

TCP/IP

Normally, the TCP/IP protocol requires you to assign several parameters or values:

- IP Address
- Subnet Mask
- Default Gateway
- DNS Domain Name
- Preferred DNS Servers

If all the Windows 2000, Windows NT, and Windows 9x computers on your network are left to configure themselves automatically, they will, and you can leave the TCP/IP protocol settings alone. (If you're really interested, check out how this works in the following sidebar.)

Automatic Configuration Without DHCP

Dynamic Host Configuration Protocol, or DHCP, is a network service that lets computers receive their TCP/IP configuration automatically over the network. It's great because a network administrator can make all the settings once in a DHCP server configuration program and not have to deal with managing individual setups for tens, hundreds, or even thousands of computers. DHCP service can be provided by Windows 2000 and NT Server, UNIX servers, and even many network routers.

If a computer is set for automatic configuration, it broadcasts a message on the LAN when it boots, basically saying "Help! Who am I?" The LAN's DHCP server responds, assigns an IP address to the computer, and sends other information such as DNS server addresses, the domain name, and so on.

What's interesting is that a Windows TCP/IP network will still work even without a DHCP server.

Here's what happens: When each computer on the LAN is booted up, during its startup, it cries "Help!" as usual. But this time, there's no answer. The computer repeats the request a couple of times, to no avail. So, it picks an IP address at random from the range 169.254.0.1 through 169.254.0.254. (These addresses were reserved by Microsoft for this purpose and will never conflict with other computers on the Internet.) The computer sends a broadcast to the LAN asking whether any other computer is using this address. If none answers, then the computer continues on its merry way. If the address is already in use, the computer tries others until it finds one that is unclaimed.

This system will let each computer obtain an IP address, but it doesn't provide it with other network information such as gateway addresses, domain names, and DNS server information. Because this system is only for the simplest of LANs with no server and no permanent outside connections, that's fine. The other information comes if and when these computers dial out to the Internet independently.

Finally, just to be on the safe side, each computer bleats its "Help!" request every five minutes in the hope that there really was a DHCP server that had just been temporarily indisposed. If a DHCP server actually does come online later (perhaps the server computer had been turned off while the others booted up) then the Windows computers discard their made-up IP configuration for the real thing.

When Internet Connection Sharing is in use, the picture is a little different. The sharing computer actually acts as a DHCP server because it has to give the others its own IP address as the gateway and DNS server address for the LAN. This topic is covered in Chapter 24, "Connecting Your LAN to the Internet."

If you are setting up a LAN connection to the Internet, see Chapter 24 for a discussion of TCP/IP configuration.

If you have to join your computer to an existing TCP/IP network, you might have to do a little more work. Contact the network manager to obtain instructions for assigning the TCP/IP parameters. If your network has a DHCP server, you can leave the TCP/IP settings on Automatic, and your computer will obtain all its network settings from the DHCP server. (This is *so* slick!)

Otherwise, your network manager will give you the required settings for the five parameters listed above.

To configure settings for the TCP/IP protocol, follow these steps:

1. In Local Area Connection Properties, select the Internet Protocol (TCP/IP), and click Properties to open the dialog shown in Figure 21.18.

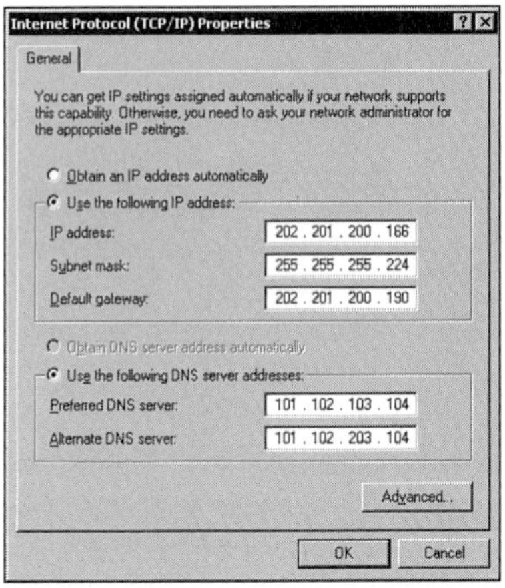

Figure 21.18

To configure TCP/IP parameters, select Internet Protocol and click Properties, or choose File, Properties.

2. Select Use the Following IP Address, and enter the required IP address, subnet mask, and default gateway address, as shown in Figure 21.18. Of course, you need to enter *your* IP address information.

3. Enter one or two DNS server addresses.

4. If your LAN is not connected to the Internet, you're finished, so just click OK. Otherwise, if your LAN has access to the Internet via a direct connection or Connection Sharing, click the Advanced button, and select the DNS tab, as shown in Figure 21.19.

5. Make sure that Append Primary and Connection Specific DNS Suffixes is selected and that Append Parent Suffixes of the Primary DNS Suffix is *not* checked.

6. Under DNS Suffix for This Connection, enter your company's registered domain name, or use your Internet provider's domain. This setting is used only if you use a computer name without a domain name in your Web browser, so it's not terribly important. But this setting is helpful, for instance, if you want to refer to your own Web server as "www."

Figure 21.19
You can enter your LAN's registered Internet domain name here, if you have a permanent connection on your LAN.

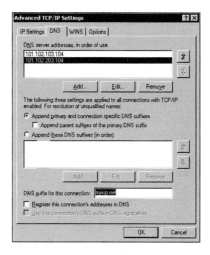

SETTING YOUR COMPUTER IDENTIFICATION

After you've configured your network, the next step is to make sure that each of the Windows 9x and 2000 computers on your network are members of the same domain or workgroup.

If you are part of a Windows 2000 network domain, your system administrator will give you the information you need to set your computer identification.

> **Note**
>
> Your domain administrator must know about your new computer in advance and must create a *computer account* for it before you try to add your computer to the domain. As you have a username and password, so does your computer. Refer to Chapter 4, "Installing Windows 2000 Pro," for more details.

If you are setting up your own network of Windows computers without Windows 2000 Server, right-click My Computer and select Properties. On the Properties dialog, click the Network Identification tab. Check each of the Windows 2000 Pro computers on your network. Do they each have a different full computer name and the same workgroup name? If so, you're all set. If not, click the Network ID button, and prepare to answer the wizard's questions.

Click Next on the wizard's first screen, and you are asked to select the option that best describes your computer:

- This computer is part of a business network, and I use it to connect to other computers at work.

- This computer is for home use and is not part of a business network.

The answers make a significant difference. If you choose the "business" route, Windows configures your computer for a higher standard of security than it will for home use. This

PART
IV

CH
21

choice is described in Chapter 4. If you're setting up a network now, I suggest that you select the "business" option at this point.

The wizard's next asks you to choose from one of the following responses:

- My company uses a network with a domain.
- My company uses a network without a domain.

If you are joining an existing network with a Windows 2000 Server, check With a Domain, but you should consult your network manager first.

Otherwise, if you are building your own network as described in this chapter, select "Without a Domain" and click Next.

The last question asks for a name for the network workgroup. Enter a name for your network (using only letters and numbers), such as ACCOUNTING or MYNETWORK, or leave the default setting WORKGROUP in place.

Click Next and then click Finish to complete the setup. You need to let Windows restart your computer if you changed the Workgroup setting.

Caution

You must make sure that every computer on your network uses the same workgroup name if you want them to be able to share files and printers.

NETWORK SECURITY

Now that you have a LAN—even if it's just a simple peer-to-peer LAN—you should be worried about network security and hackers. Why? Because you'll certainly be connecting to the Internet, at least intermittently, and when you do, you risk exposing your network to the entire world. These risks are not as far-fetched as you might think.

Refer to Chapter 26, "Network Security," to find out what risks you'll be exposed to and what you can do to protect your LAN.

At the very least, you should take this one precaution to be sure you have minimal protection. For each of the computers on your LAN that connect to the Internet via modem, do the following:

1. Right-click your Internet Dial-up connection icon in Network and Dial-Up Connections.
2. Select the Networking tab.
3. See whether File and Printer Sharing for Microsoft Networks is checked; if it is, uncheck it.
4. Click OK.

These steps *unbind*, or disconnect, the File Sharing service from your dial-up connection and prevent people on the Internet from attempting to view your shared files and folders while you're dialed in to your ISP.

CHECKING OUT THE NEIGHBORHOOD

Your network is finally ready to go. After you have configured, connected, and restarted each of your computers, double-click My Network Places on your desktop. If you are *not* part of a Windows 2000 Domain, select Computers Near Me. If your network is up and running, you should see one icon for every computer you've connected.

 If you don't see other computers in the Network Neighborhood, see "Network Neighborhood Shows No Other Computers" in the "Troubleshooting" section at the end of this chapter, and read Chapter 27, "Troubleshooting Your Windows 2000 Network."

If you are part of a Windows 2000 Domain, select Entire Network, Entire Contents, Microsoft Windows Network, and click your own domain's icon to see the list of connected computers.

Congratulations: Your network is up and running! But before you continue on to Chapter 22, "Using a Windows 2000 Network," there's one unpleasant task left: backups. I really suggest doing this now.

INSTALL AND CONFIGURE BACKUP SOFTWARE

Install a tape backup unit and, preferably, a good commercial backup software package on at least one main computer on your network. Follow the instructions on the software to configure it to perform automatic backups.

The Windows backup utility is almost adequate for business use, but for business purposes, you should have something that is convenient, that lets you save different backup configurations, and that lends itself to automatic scheduling.

Backups should ideally be made automatically every day. Typically, I suggest using a schedule that looks something like this:

- Friday: Full backup—entire hard drive, reset archive flag. Use two different Friday tapes for alternate weeks.
- Monday through Thursday: Differential backups, backing up every file that is new or changed since the last full backup. Use a different tape for each day of the week. A Saturday backup is optional.

The time of day for backups is up to you. I prefer backups to run automatically in the early morning hours, around 2 AM or so, so that nobody is using files when the backup occurs; when files are in use, typically they are not backed up properly. This means that you should change tapes every morning and insert the next day's tape. For example, on Thursday morning, remove Thursday's tape and insert Friday's. Friday's backup occurs at 2 AM Friday. On Friday, remove Friday's tape and insert a Monday (or Saturday tape, if you use a Saturday backup).

Notice that this means your full backup will contain Thursday's work but not Friday's. This is a tradeoff. Your goal is to have each week's full backup protect the week's work. If the full backup is to contain Friday's work, you'll have to do backups in the late afternoon, which is a bad idea—who's going to hang around until 6 PM on Friday to change a tape? The alternative is to leave Friday's tape in the computer all weekend. This exposes it to theft, damage, fire, or loss due to being overwritten. That's why I prefer the schedule I recommended and its "Thursday compromise."

This scheme is quick and requires at most two tapes to fully restore your system after a crash: the most recent Friday full backup and the most recent incremental backup.

Keep a supply of spare tapes on hand. Replace these daily and weekly tapes once a year. You might also consider setting aside a full Friday backup tape once every few months as a permanent archival copy.

Keep your Friday backup tapes off-site. If you forget to bring in a used tape on Friday, use a new tape.

Configure the backup software to exclude certain files, if you can:

~*.*	Any file or folder starting with a tilde
*.tmp	Any file with extension .tmp
*.bak	Any backup file
.ff	Fast-find index files
.ci	IIS Index Server index files
pagefile.sys	Virtual Memory paging file

I'm getting a little ahead of myself here, but here's an idea to plant in your head: Be sure to test your backup system at least once a month by viewing a tape directory or by restoring a single file from the tape. This will not only ensure that your backup system is functioning properly, but will maintain your skill in operating the backup-and-restore software.

TROUBLESHOOTING

HUB LIGHTS DO NOT COME ON

One or more UTP hub link lights do not come on when the associated computers are connected.

First, be sure that the computer is powered up. If that's not it, the problem lies in one of the cables between the computer and the hub. Which one is it? To find out, do the following:

1. Move the computer right next to the hub. You can leave the keyboard, mouse, and monitor behind. Just plug in the computer, turn it on, and use a commercially manufactured or known-to-be-working patch cable to connect the computer to the hub. If the

light doesn't come on regardless of which hub connection socket you use, you probably have a bad network card.

2. If you were using any patch cables when you first tried to get the computer connected, test them using the same computer and hub socket. This trick may identify a bad cable.

3. If the LAN card, hub, and patch cables are all working, then the problem is in whatever is left, which would be your in-wall wiring. Check the connectors for proper crimping, and check that the wire pairs are correctly wired end-to-end. You have to use a cable analyzer if you can't spot the problem by eye. These devices cost about $75. You connect a "transmitter" box to one end of your cabling, and a "receiver" at the other. The receiver has four LEDs that blink in a 1-2-3-4 sequence if your wiring is correct.

NETWORK NEIGHBORHOOD SHOWS NO OTHER COMPUTERS

The Network Neighborhood doesn't show any other computers when I boot up.

If you've eliminated the network card and any UTP wiring as the source of the problem, you can use Windows own built-in diagnostic tools to help. Here's how:

1. The first thing to check is whether all computers on the network are using the same workgroup name. On each computer, right-click My Computer, select Properties, and view the Network Identification tab. Be sure that the Workgroup name is the same on every computer, If it's not, use the Network ID button to correct it.

2. Next, be sure the LAN hardware itself is working. Check the Device Manager to be sure that your network card is operating properly. If not, see whether you have configuration conflicts. Repeat the process I gave previously to choose acceptable configuration values for your network card. Be sure you're using an approved network card and have up-to-date drivers for it. If the Device Manager gives you a message that reads The Card Is Not Functioning, you almost certainly have the wrong drivers. Check with the vendor to see whether up-to-date Windows 2000 drivers are available for you to download over the Internet.

3. If you have a UTP LAN, make sure all the expected indicators on your hub are lit.

4. On each computer, start a command prompt. Then type the command `ipconfig`.

5. When you see IP addresses listed, be sure each computer has a different IP address. They should all be similar but different. For example, they might look like 209.203.104.x, where the x is different for each computer. If not, check the Internet Protocol properties on each computer to be sure each was correctly configured.

6. Type `ping x.x.x.x`, where `x.x.x.x` is the computer's own IP address. It should have four "replies," which look like this:

   `Reply from x.x.x.x: bytes=32 time<10msec TTL=128`

   If not, remove, reinstall, and reconfigure the TCP/IP protocol.

7. Type `ping x.x.x.y`, where `x.x.x.y` is one of the IP addresses of the other computers on your LAN. If the replies don't come back, your network hardware is at fault. Check the wiring as follows:

On a ThinNet LAN, be sure that the cable is run from computer to computer, with a terminator at each end. You can disconnect a computer from the middle of the network and terminate the chain of computers there. Test communications between computers on this halved network. You can keep shrinking the network to isolate the problem by lopping off computers and moving the terminator up to close off the end of the smaller chain of computers, until you get down to just two. At some point, the pings will probably start working, and you will have found the bad segment of cable: It's in the part of the network you just removed.

On a 10BASE-T or 100BASE-T LAN, see whether an "activity" LED flashes on your network card when you type a ping command. If it doesn't, the problem is your network card. If it does, you might have to get a cable testing device to find out what's wrong with the wiring. (A professional installer will have one…it's time to call for help!)

Another possibility with combination 10/100BASE-T network cards is that the cards might not have decided to use the correct speed. You can force them to use one speed or the other in the Device Manager by viewing the network card's Properties page and selecting the Advanced tab. This tab usually has a Link Speed/Duplex Mode property. Set all the cards to the appropriate value for the type of hub you are using.

8. If the ping commands work between computers, be sure that each computer's Network Identification has the same workgroup name. This information is on My Computer's Properties page.

9. If none of these steps help, see whether the Event Log has any helpful error messages. To do so, right-click My Computer, select Manage, and view the three logs under the System Tool Event Viewer.

10. Finally, you can use a diagnostic program called NETDIAG.EXE, which might be on your Windows 2000 Installation CD. Use the Search for Files command to see whether it is. If you can find this program, run it on one of your connected computers to see whether it has any helpful suggestions.

TIPS FROM THE WINDOWS PROS: GRASSROOTS NETWORKING

Despite their becoming so inexpensive and simple to install, networks are extremely complex systems under the hood. It's hard enough to solve the problems that creep up from time to time in an existing, functional LAN, but new LANs are worse because *everything* is untested, and a little problem in any one part can mess up the whole thing. Where do you start looking for the problem?

The answer is an exercise in delayed gratification! It's exciting to see all the new equipment, parts, and cables all over the building, but as much as I'd like to hook it all up and see what happens when I turn on the switch for the first time, I've found that it's best to start small.

Whenever I build a new network, I put two computers side-by-side on one desk. They can be two regular computers for a peer-to-peer network, or a Windows 2000 Server and a regular workstation for a Server-based network. I wire them together in the simplest possible way, usually with two short patch cables and a hub.

This technique gives me the smallest possible, least complex system to start with. It's much easier to solve a networking problem when you can see both computers' screens at the same time.

When I have these two computers completely configured and tested, I start adding components one at a time: a network printer, an Internet connection, a tape backup system, an uninterruptible power supply, and so on.

When something goes wrong during this technique, I know it must have something to do with the last component I added, and I'm not searching for a needle in a haystack.

Finally, when I have all the parts working, I take the two computers to their final locations and see whether they still work with the real-world wiring. Then I add workstations to the network one at a time. Attaching them this way is not as much fun as assembling the whole thing at once, but I've found that staying up all night diagnosing problems on a new network is even less fun.

CHAPTER 22

USING A WINDOWS 2000 NETWORK

In this chapter

Windows 2000 Was Made to Network

Aside from finally finding a use for the right button on the mouse, almost all the advancements in the Windows platform over the last 10 years have been made in the area of networking. Back in Windows version 3.1, network software was an expensive add-on product—an afterthought—cumbersome to install and manage. Not so anymore! Networking is built right into the heart of Windows 2000, such that Windows isn't even happy without a network attached.

Okay, I'm exaggerating. But the truth is, Windows 2000's personality does change for the better when it is connected to a network, and the change depends on the type of network to which it's attached. In this chapter, I'll show you how to use Windows 2000 networking and share tips for making the most of whatever type of network you have.

First, though, here's an important point that should come as very good news: In Windows 2000, using files and printers on the network is exactly the same as using files and printers on your own hard drive. The look and feel are identical. The only new tasks you have to learn are how to find resources shared by others and how to make your own computer's resources available to others on the network.

The Many Faces of Windows 2000 Networking

Notice that I use the word *resource* frequently in this chapter. When I say *resource*, I mean a shared folder or printer on someone else's computer, which you can access through the LAN or the Internet. *The American Heritage Dictionary* defines a resource as "an available supply that can be drawn upon when needed." That's actually a perfect description of a network resource: It's there for you to use—provided you can find it, and provided you have permission.

The ways of finding resources and managing permissions change depending on the type of network you have. I talked about these network models in detail in Chapter 19, "Overview of Windows 2000 Networking," but here's a quick review:

- Workgroup Network (Peer to Peer)—A workgroup network, also called a peer-to-peer network, does not have a Windows 2000 Server computer. On this network, each computer manages its own user list and security system.

- Domain Network—A domain-based network uses Windows 2000 Server to provide a centralized user security base. All computers on the network look to a *domain controller*, or primary server, for usernames, group memberships, and passwords. File and folder security on member computers (including Windows 2000 Professional) can still be locally managed.

- Active Directory Network—Active Directory (AD) adds a distributed, global user directory to a domain network. It not only provides a user and password database, but it also provides a way for management permissions to be delegated and controlled; this capability is very important in large, spread-out organizations.

- Remote Network—Windows 2000 Professional functions very well on a standalone computer, but it also lets you connect and disconnect to networks or get remote access by modem, WAN (wide area network), or the Internet. Windows provides special services to help you deal with this on again/off again network relationship.

Most network functions are identical regardless of your network type. The following are four notable differences:

- Domain membership gives you the capability to control who uses your computer's resources, using a list of users and groups of users that includes every user in the domain.

- On a domain network, the administrator can also set up roaming profiles so that your settings, preferences, My Documents folder, and so on are centrally stored on the network and are available to you on any computer on your LAN or even at other network sites.

- Active Directory gives you added search functions to find users and printers on your network. These search functions appear as added icons and menu choices that non-AD network computers don't have.

- In a domain or Active Directory network, the network administrator can use policy functions to restrict the network management features you can use. For example, you might not have the option to map network drives or add network protocols in such a strictly controlled LAN. Rather than rouse up a protest for computer freedom, though, be thankful that you'll have less maintenance and futzing to do yourself.

Note

I'm already tired of typing *Active Directory* over and over, so as I go along, I'll sometimes abbreviate it as *AD*—thought I should warn you!

Members of a Windows network with AD have some options—menu choices and buttons in dialog boxes, for example—that workgroup network users don't have. If you are using a workgroup network, don't feel left out. Because a workgroup typically has fewer than 10 computers, the searching and corporate-style management functions provided by AD simply aren't necessary.

In this chapter I'll try to point out the differences you might encounter depending on your network type. However, it's difficult to generalize about AD networks because AD's policy-based restrictions are so comprehensive that an AD network user might have even less control over his or her computer's network settings than a workgroup user. If you are on a domain or Active Directory network and can't find an option I show you, call your network manager to see whether its use has been restricted.

WORKGROUP VERSUS DOMAIN NETWORKING

On a Windows domain-based network, user accounts are set up on the domain servers. Domain users are known by every computer on the network. When you're establishing who can and can't have access to folders and printers you share on the network, this is a good thing because you'll be able to choose users and groups from the entire list of all users in your organization. You can grant access to specific individuals, departments, sites, or other groupings even though those users might be scattered around the globe.

In a workgroup network, however, it's a different story. Each computer in the workgroup has its own list of usernames with passwords. If you have only, say, an Administrator and a Bob account in your computer, and someone down the hall has an Administrator and a Mary account in her computer, you can't designate "Mary" as someone with permission to use a certain shared folder you've set up. And, the Administrator account on one computer might have a different password than the Administrator account on another, making management a nightmare and over-the-network administration impossible.

→ To learn more details about user management on Windows 2000, **see** "Users on a Workgroup LAN," **p. 1202**.

HOW NETWORK SECURITY WORKS

The domain system works so well because each user is assigned a unique identification number called a *Security Identifier (SID)* that every computer in the domain recognizes.

> **Note**
>
> "Oh no," I can hear you say, "this is going to get technical and messy." You're right; it is. So, I'm going to give you an out. You don't have to read this section now. If your computer is part of a domain network, you probably will never care how this part of your network works. If you are part of a workgroup network, you'll eventually run into the problems I'm about to discuss. When you do, come back and read this section—it might make more sense then.

Say your friend Bob logs on to his computer. It looks up his SID in the domain's directory, and that number becomes part of his *access token*, a numeric ID badge that is flashed to remote computers when he tries to access network resources.

Because all domain computers use the same user database, if Mary grants Bob rights to a particular folder on her computer, Bob's SID is listed in her computer with the notation "can read this folder." When Bob tries to access the folder from across the network, his access token is sent along with the request. Mary's computer compares his SID to its list and finds a match. It therefore decides Bob is a trustworthy guy and passes back data from the folder.

Mary can designate which users get access to her files, and she can specify any user or group by name from the entire domain.

In a workgroup network, however, there is no global correspondence between usernames and SIDs. Mary can't grant Bob rights to her folder because Bob's SID is stored only in Bob's computer.

Suppose Mary thinks of a solution: She creates a Bob account on her computer and gives that Bob access to her shared folder. But her computer generates its own random number to use as Bob's SID. When the real Bob tries to read the file, his access token will have a different SID than Mary's computer expects. The two accounts might have the same username, but because they were set up from different computers, they're really different accounts.

> **Note**
>
> For this reason, Windows displays the computer or domain name with accounts: COMPUTER1\Bob and COMPUTER2\Bob are distinctly different accounts, as different as COMPUTER1\Bob and COMPUTER1\Cuthbert.
>
> On the other hand, a domain login such as MYCOMPANY\Bob is recognized by every computer on the MYCOMPANY domain.

So, does Mary's computer reject Bob's request? Not yet! A very important backup mechanism comes into play. Mary's computer recognizes that the SID Bob gave her comes from a different computer. Her computer asks Bob's computer for his username and password (encrypted, of course). It then checks to see whether there is a Bob account on her computer and checks to see whether the password that Bob sent matches the password set for her Bob account. If it does, then her computer assumes that the two Bobs are equivalent from a security standpoint—not identical but close enough to treat in the same way. Our Bob would get access to the shared folder.

What would have happened if there were no Bob account on Mary's computer, or if the password didn't match? Mary's computer would see whether its Guest account was enabled, and if it was, it would have assumed that the Bob making the request was equivalent to Guest, and granted access accordingly.

JUST THE FACTS

Does this process sound complicated? Well, it should—it is, somewhat. But I can distill it down into three practical realities for workgroup network users:

1. You can assign user or group access rights to files on your computer if—and only if—you set up accounts for each visiting user on your computer. I suggest choosing one central computer for this purpose, to simplify your life. Alternatively, you can set up all users on all computers.

2. Each user needs to physically go around and set the same password on each computer on which he or she has an account.

3. Don't enable the Guest account. It might be tempting to avoid steps 1 and 2 by enabling Guest, but Guest access also applies to hackers trying to break in through your Internet connection, even through a temporary dial-up connection. And, by default, Guest is a member of the group Everyone, and Everyone has full rights to all files. This all adds up to a potential disaster.

Because your workgroup LAN probably has 10 or fewer computers, this really shouldn't be a big burden. Chapter 32, "Managing Users," goes into all the details, so if you have a workgroup LAN, read Chapter 32 and work out a safe, manageable plan for establishing user and group security on your LAN.

TRADITIONAL AND WEB SHARING

In Windows 2000, you can actually get to shared folders and printers in two ways: through traditional LAN methods and via the World Wide Web. This last method shouldn't come as much of a surprise these days; I think even my washing machine has a Web interface now.

The traditional methods are based on the Microsoft Networking protocol (NetBT, also called SMB), which has been around for a very long time. It actually dates back to the days when IBM ruled the PC world and Microsoft was an obscure but up-and-coming company. (Have things changed or what?!)

The new Internet technologies are called WebDAV (Web Distributed Authoring and Versioning) or Web Sharing, for file sharing, and Internet Printing Protocol (IPP), for printer sharing. They're both based on the Hypertext Transfer Protocol (HTTP), which means that file and print operations can be carried out safely across the Internet, even through corporate firewalls. They require Web server software on the computer that is sharing the files or printers—but that's fine because Windows 2000 comes with it.

With Web sharing, you can work with files and folders shared by a remote computer just as you would with files found in My Computer, Explorer, or traditional network shared folders. Using IPP Printing, you can connect to a shared printer over the Internet and use it exactly as you would a local or LAN-based printer.

Although the look and feel are virtually identical to traditional LAN sharing, the Internet-based methods are not as speedy as ordinary LAN sharing, so they're meant only for remote users who need to get at shared files and printers back home.

WHAT'S IN A NAME?

Virtually the only difference you'll notice between local and networked files is their names. If you've found the use of the backslash character to be an annoying and peculiar convention, you'd better hang on to your hat because slashes of all persuasions are in your future in a big way.

Let's look at the names of shared network folders and files. Each computer on your network (or on an intranet or the Internet) has a name, and every folder or printer that is offered up for shared use on the network must be given a share name as well. For example, if I want to give officemates the use of my business documents, I might share my hard disk's folder c:\documents and give that folder the share name docs.

Figure 22.1 shows the relationship between my computer named Ambon, its hard disk, and the shared folder, from the point of view of another computer named Bali.

THE UNC NAMING CONVENTION

I can specify the location of a file on my hard drive with a drive and path name, like this:

```
c:\documents\quotations\roofing bids.xls
```

Figure 22.1
Sharing makes a folder, or even a whole hard drive, accessible to the LAN. Ambon shares folder \documents as docs, and Bali can use this folder by its network name \\ambon\docs.

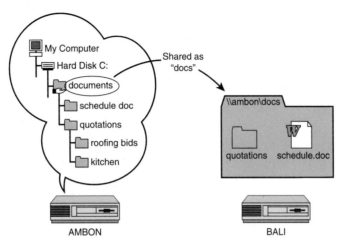

A folder shared from one computer...   ...can be viewed on another

Another user can refer to the same file from a different computer using a syntax called the *Universal Naming Convention*, or UNC:

```
\\ambon\docs\roofing bids.xls
```

The double backslash indicates that the name ambon is the name of a computer on the LAN rather than the name of a folder in the top directory of the local hard disk. Docs is the share name of the folder, and everything else specifies the path and file relative to that shared folder.

If the computer whose files you want to use is on a LAN using Active Directory or is part of a distant company network, you may also specify the remote computer name more completely, as in the following:

```
\\ambon.mycompany.com\docs\roofing bids.xls
```

Or, if you know only the remote computer's IP network address, you can even use a notation like this:

```
\\192.168.0.10\docs\roofing bids.xls
```

No matter which way you specify the remote computer, Windows finds it and locates its shared folder docs.

Shared printers are also given share names and specified by their UNC path. For example, if I share my HP LaserJet 4V printer, I might give it the share name *HPLaser*, and it will be known on the network as \\ambon\HPLaser. Here, it's not a folder but rather a printer, and Windows keeps track of the type of resource. You can use Explorer to view either type of name, and Windows will either present a list of files or a list of pending printouts.

NAMING FOR WEB-BASED SHARING

The new Internet-compatible technologies are based on the World Wide Web's Hypertext Transfer Protocol (HTTP) and use the Web's traditional forward slash rather than the back-slash.

A Web folder name looks just like a standard Web URL:

```
http://ambon/docs
```

or

```
http://ambon.mycompany.com/docs
```

The difference is that when you open a Web folder, instead of just displaying a listing of files, as it might if you visited a regular Web page, Windows displays the files in a standard Explorer folder view. You can do anything to the files that you would do in a normal folder: delete, rename, drag files in and out, and open and save files with applications.

IPP printers shared by Windows 2000 use a similar naming scheme, but I'll wait until the section "Using Other IPP Printers," later in this chapter, to get into the messy details about that. If you're connecting to a Windows 2000 computer from across the Internet, it's enough to view the printers page by typing

```
http://ambon.mycompany.com/printers
```

This allows the built-in Web pages to take care of all the work for you.

MY NETWORK PLACES

How do you find the folders and printers floating around out there somewhere in the Network Twilight Zone? If you've been using Windows 9x or Windows 2000 for any length of time, you might have guessed by now that you can do the job in several ways.

 My Network Places appears as a desktop icon after you install any network components in Windows 2000; it's the starting place for finding network resources.

My Network Places gives you a way to browse, search, and bookmark network resources, including shared folders, Web pages, FTP sites, and so on. You can view My Network Places in two ways:

- Open the My Network Places icon on your desktop.
- If you have Web Content enabled for folder views, open My Computer, and select the My Network Places entry.

When you select My Network Places from the My Computer window, you get the Folder view of My Network Places, as shown in Figure 22.2.

My Network Places is meant to be a place to collect shortcuts to commonly used remote network resources like shared folders, Web pages, and the like. When you first install

Windows, My Network Places doesn't have any of your shortcuts, of course; it starts with the following:

- Add Network Place—Opens a wizard to create network or Internet shortcuts.
- Entire Network—Lets you browse through your LAN as you would through folders of a hard disk, and appears if you are or ever were on a Workgroup LAN.
- Computers Near Me—Provides a quick way to view the computers in your workgroup. (This icon appears only if your computer is part of a workgroup network. Domain network users don't get it.)

Figure 22.2
My Network Places is the starting point for searching and opening network resources. This is the Folder view. You can switch to the Explorer view by choosing View, Explorer Bar, Folders.

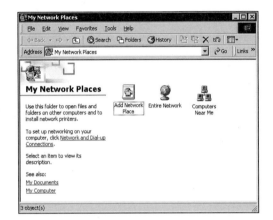

Where Are Computers Near Me?

If you belong to a workgroup network, the Computers Near Me icon displays all the computers in your workgroup. That makes sense because workgroup networks usually are all in one building or office.

On a domain network, determining which "Computers Are Near Me" is not easy because a network can span the globe. With a domain network, Microsoft felt that the word *near* could be misleading, so Windows doesn't display the Computers Near Me icon for domain network users. Besides, on a domain network, Microsoft wants you to use Active Directory to search for computers near you based on location or other criteria, rather than poke through a folder to find them. You can get to the list of computers, if you drill down at least four layers through Entire Network, but it's not very convenient to do so.

I suggest that you open Entire Network on your computer and browse through it to see the computers and resources available on your network.

USING SHARED FOLDERS

LANs were developed to exchange files between computers. Older methods of exchanging information, like dispatching couriers with papyrus scrolls or carrying floppy disks from room to room, just can't match the immediacy of a LAN. File sharing comes down to this: You can tell Windows that other users on the network can use the files in one or more folders on your hard disk, or even on the whole hard disk. Let's say I want to share a folder named C:\bookwin2000. For its share name on the network, I give the folder the name book, as shown in Figure 22.3.

Figure 22.3
Sharing a folder on my computer.

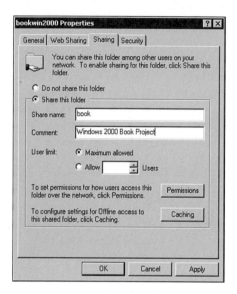

Other network users can see that book is a shared folder attached to my computer when they browse through My Network Places. It looks like any folder on their own computers.

If they open it, they'll see the same folders and file listings I see in c:\bookwin2000, illustrated in Figure 22.4. The information about filenames, dates, and contents is sent over the network. If they drag a file into the folder, all users can see it there (providing they refresh their view of the folder). If I edit a file in the shared folder, the next time users open the file, they'll get the changed version. That's network file sharing in a nutshell; the rest is just a matter of details.

There are two ways to treat file sharing on a LAN. One is to let people exchange information in a serial fashion. You work on a file and save it. I work on it, then it sits around awhile, and then someone else takes it. Email transfers, floppy disks, and papyrus scrolls work the same way but are slower. Most programs are designed to use *exclusive access* when using a network file. This prevents two users from attempting to make changes at the same time. If you attempt to use a shared file at the same time as another user (whom you probably can't even see), you get an error message stating that someone else is using the file.

Some applications, though, are designed for *concurrent file access*. A LAN can let many people read and write from the same file at the same time. Floppy disks and scrolls can't do this. Of course, only some application software is designed to manage this kind of work; when several people are saving information at the same time, some file locking mechanism has to be used to keep one person's work from overwriting another. This is the bread-and-butter of database and other shared-data applications such as Access, Visual FoxPro, Paradox, and others.

Figure 22.4
A network user examining the shared folder (above) sees the same files the owner of the shared folder sees (below).

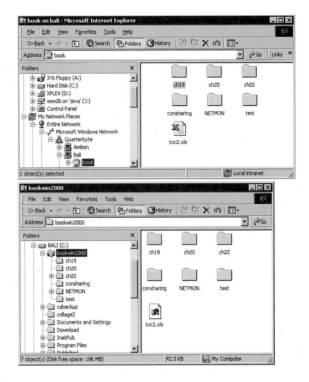

It's very important to note that Microsoft File Sharing and Novell NetWare networking support concurrent file access, but the Internet-based Web Sharing protocol does not. WebDAV or Web Sharing permits only one person to modify a given file at a time. This is fine when all you want to do is copy files into or out of a shared folder, but it doesn't support database access.

MAPPING DRIVE LETTERS

If you frequently use the same shared network folder, you can make it a permanent houseguest of your computer by *mapping* the network shared folder to an unused drive letter on your computer—one of the letters after your hard drive's C: and the CD-ROM drive's D: (assuming you have not already changed your drive mappings). You can give the shared folder \\server\shared the drive letter J:, for example, so that it appears that your computer has a new disk drive J:, whose contents are those of the shared folder.

Mapping gives you several benefits:

■ The mapped drive appears along with your computer's other real, physical drives in My Computer for quick browsing, opening, and saving of files.

- Access to the shared folder will be faster because Windows opens and maintains a connection to the sharing computer.

- MS-DOS applications can use the shared folder through its assigned letter. Most legacy DOS applications can't accept UNC-formatted names like \\server\shared\subfolder\file, but they can use j:\subfolder\file.

- If you need to, you can map a shared folder using an alternative username and password to gain access rights you might not have with your current Windows login name.

If you've used Novell or older Windows networks in the past, this might be the only way you've ever used a network! Good news: You still can.

To map a drive, select Tools, Map Network Drive in any Explorer window (such as My Computer or Windows Explorer). Or you can right-click My Network Places and select Map Network Drive.

Next, select an unused drive letter from the drop-down list, as shown in Figure 22.5. If possible, pick a drive letter that has some association for you with the resource you'll be using: E for Editorial, S for Sales—whatever makes sense to you.

Figure 22.5
You can select an unused drive letter to use for the drive mapping.

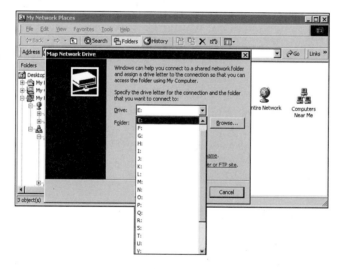

Then select the name of the shared folder you want to assign to the drive letter. You can type the UNC-formatted name if you know it already—for example, \\servername\ sharename—or you can click Browse to poke through your network's resources and select the shared folder. Find the desired shared folder in the expandable list of workgroups, computers, and share names, as shown in Figure 22.6, and click OK.

On an Active Directory network, the browse listing includes an additional icon called Directory that you can expand to view shared resources grouped according to your network's organizational structure. You still have to pick through the organizational tree to find the desired computer and its shared folders, however.

Figure 22.6
Browsing for a shared
folder. You can open
the list view to see
network types, work-
groups, computers,
and shared folders.

Tip #255

On an AD network, if you want to search for a computer by name, you must search using
the Directory tool in My Network Places. When you find the computer, explore it or one of
its shared folders, and then drag its location from the Address bar into My Network Places.

After you select the shared folder, the folder name appears in the dialog, and you have two
options:

- If you want this mapping to reappear every time you log
  in, check Reconnect at login. If you don't check this box,
  the mapping disappears when you log off.

- If your current Windows username and password don't
  give you sufficient permission to use the shared
  resource, or if your username won't be recognized at the
  other computer because your account name is different
  there, select Connect Using a Different User Name. Choosing this option displays a
  Connect As dialog, as shown in Figure 22.7. Here, you can enter the alternative username and password, and click OK. (On an AD network, you can select Browse to view
  valid usernames by location if you need help.)

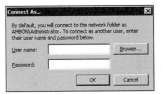

Figure 22.7

Note

Some Save As dialog boxes (particularly older 16-bit applications) show a Network button.
Clicking it brings up the Map Network Drive Wizard, so you can make a last-minute drive
mapping at the time when you're most likely to want to do it.

After you map a drive letter, the drive appears in your My Computer list along with your
local disk drives. You might notice a couple of funny things about these drives:

- If you haven't used the network drive for a while—20 minutes or so—it might turn
  gray, indicating that the network connection to the remote computer has been disconnected. When you use the drive again, it will reconnect and turn black.

- If the remote computer (or you) really go offline, a red diagonal line appears through
  the drive. You can still explore the drive if you've marked any of its folders to be available while you're offline.

If you enjoy the more esoteric aspects of networking, there are a couple of nifty features for you—mapping a drive to a subfolder and mapping shared folders with no drive letter.

MAPPING A DRIVE TO A SUBFOLDER

When you're setting up a mapped drive and you browse to find a shared folder, notice that Windows lets you delve into the shared folders themselves. If you drill down into a subfolder and select it as the location to use in mapping a drive letter, you'll find that the mapped drive starts at the subfolder. The subfolder becomes the drive's root directory, and you can't explore upward into the shared folder that contains it.

NetWare users call this the *map root* function. See Figure 22.8, in which I've selected the subfolder ch22\images from the shared folder \\bali\book. If I map drive E: to that folder, drive E: will contain the contents of folder \\bali\book\ch22\images, and it can't be made to see up into \\bali\book\ch22. The root, or top-level, directory of E: will be the images folder.

Tip #256	This feature is most useful to administrators, to set up scripts to map drives based on a user's login name. For example, mail might be stored in subfolders of \\server\mail according to username. Mapping drive M: to folder \\server\mail\%username% lets users get to their mail (directly) via drive M: and discourages users from poking around in other peoples' mail folders.
	This way, users can configure their mail programs to get mail from drive M:, and the same configuration will work for everyone.

Figure 22.8
By delving into a shared folder, you can map the root directory of a drive letter to a deeper point in the share.

Mapping a subfolder can be a good thing because it makes any program that uses the mapped drive letter see just that subfolder as the drive's root directory.

MAPPING A SHARED FOLDER WITHOUT A DRIVE LETTER

You can make an established connection to a shared folder, keeping it readily available for quick response without assigning it a drive letter. Follow the procedure shown earlier in this chapter for mapping a drive letter. When you select the letter to map, go all the way to the bottom of the Drive letter drop-down list, and select (None), the last choice. Continue through the rest of the process as described.

Mapping a shared folder to None doesn't add the mapped folder to your My Computer list, but it does make for speedier response from the server when you're accessing that folder.

EXPLORING AND SEARCHING THE NETWORK

Of course, before you can use a network resource, you have to know where to find it. You can look through your network for shared folders and printers by exploring in the following areas:

- Computers Near Me—If you have a workgroup LAN, using Computers Near Me is a quick way to display a folder containing all the known computers in your workgroup.
- Entire Network—Entire Network lets you peruse all the workgroups, domains, and network types that make up your network. It's a bit like exploring My Computer and viewing the contents of your hard drives and CD-ROM drives.

When you first try to view Entire Network, Windows throws up a little smokescreen: It displays a page suggesting that you might want to use its searching tools before plowing into the entire contents of the network. This makes good sense if you know what you're looking for, but not if you are just poking around.

You can select any available search tools:

Search for printers (if you have AD)

Search for computers

Search for people (if you have AD)

Search for files or folders

Or you can select View the Entire Contents to get past the smokescreen page and see all the members of the network.

Whichever windows or views you choose to browse, you will find that the contents are arranged hierarchically:

Entire Network

    Microsoft Windows Network

        Domain or Workgroup

            Computers

                Shared folders

                    Contents of shared folders

Tip #257

If you'll be using shared folders, Web sites, FTP sites, or Web folders repeatedly, add them to My Network Places for a quick return later. You can use the Add Network Place Wizard to do so, or you can just drag a network folder icon or Web page location into My Network Places, as shown in Figure 22.9. Dragging the icon creates a shortcut in My Network Places that you can use later.

UNDERSTANDING SHARED RESOURCES

If you do a bit of poking around, you might find that some computers share folders that might not make much sense. Windows 2000 Domain Server computers, in particular, offer many network resources to member Windows 2000 computers that are used by automatic services or for maintenance. Table 22.1 shows some of the shared resources you might see and what they do.

Figure 22.9
You can drag the folder icon from Explorer's Address bar to My Network Places, to the desktop, or to another folder to make an instant shortcut to the shared folder.

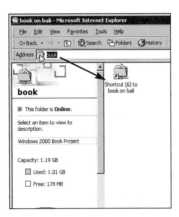

TABLE 22.1 TYPICAL ADMINISTRATIVE FOLDERS SHARED ON A WINDOWS 2000 SERVER

Folder	Description
CertEnroll	Contains data used to provide Security Certificates to member computers if your network has its own Certificate Authority. This share is used only by the Certificate Wizard.
NETLOGON	Used only by the domain login system.
Published	Contains installation packages for published and assigned application software, which might be available to or forced into your computer. When using the Add/Remove Software Control Panel via the network, files are automatically retrieved from the Published folder.
SYSVOL	Used only by the domain login system.
Printers	Mirrors the computer's Printers folder; can be used by an administrator to install or control printers across the LAN.
Scheduled Tasks	Mirrors the computer's Scheduled Task list; can be used by an administrator for remote maintenance.

Of these folders, only Printers and Scheduled Tasks are of interest, and then only to administrators. The others are used by the operating system and should not be modified.

Any other shared resources were put there by the computer's owner or administrator for LAN users.

SEARCHING THE NETWORK

You can locate shared folders or printers by exploring My Network Places, or you can use the search links found in Entire Network. Users with Active Directory at their disposal have more searching choices than those without Active Directory.

SEARCHING FOR PRINTERS

Active Directory networks provide a very powerful printer search tool. In a large corporate network, hundreds or thousands of network printers might be scattered over a large area. Search for Printers lets an AD network user find just the right type of printer using a powerful query form, which I'll show you in "Finding a Printer in the Active Directory" later in this chapter.

SEARCHING FOR COMPUTERS

If you want to quickly locate shared resources on a computer whose name you already know, with or without AD, select Search for Computers. You can enter either the full computer name or a fragment of its name. Windows lists the matching computers, as in Figure 22.10.

Figure 22.10
When you're searching for computers by their network names, you can enter full or partial names. Select one of the matching computer icons to explore its shared contents.

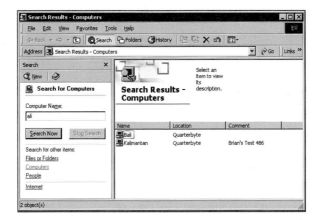

You can explore any of the listed computers to view its shared folders or printers; if you delve into the shared folders, you can open or copy the available files as you find them.

SEARCHING FOR PEOPLE

On an Active Directory network, My Network Places and the Start button's Search menu both offer a nifty search tool called Find People, shown in Figure 22.11.

You can search by name or email address in the Active Directory or in any of several Internet directories, such as Yahoo People Search, Infospace Business Directory, and WhoWhere Internet Directory, by selecting the directory under Look In.

Using the Advanced tab of Find People (shown in Figure 22.12), you can perform a more specific search.

Figure 22.11
Using Find People, you can search by name or email address in the Active Directory or in any of several Internet Directory services.

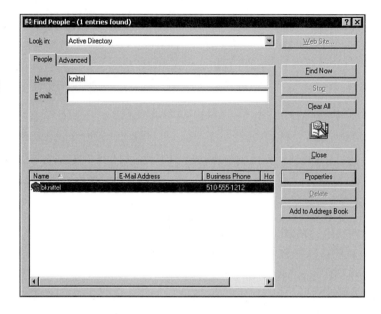

Figure 22.12
Advanced searching properties let you specify multiple searching criteria.

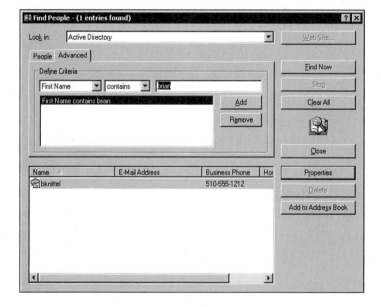

To perform an advanced search from the Start menu, follow these steps:

1. Choose Start, Search, For People, and select the Advanced tab.

2. Select the first drop-down list (Name is the default value), and choose a criterion from the list. The searchable attributes include First Name, Last Name, Email, and Organization.

3. Under the second drop-down list (contains is the default value), select a comparison type. The choices are Contains, Is, Starts With, Ends With, or Sounds Like.

4. In the third box, which is empty by default, enter the name or address, or a fragment.

5. Choose Add to add a condition; highlight a condition and click Remove to delete a condition.

6. Enter more filtering items if you want, or select Find Now to begin the search.

The two search tabs on the Find People dialog operate independently of one another, so selections on one tab do not influence searches made with the other.

You can open any entries returned by the search to view comprehensive information about the user, as shown in Figure 22.13. The information is spread out over five tabs:

- General contains name, address, and telephone number.

- Address contains complete postal address information.

- Business shows job title, department, the person's manager, and any managed employees.

- NetMeeting indicates direct connection information for NetMeeting chat/voice/video-conferencing, and includes a Call Now button.

- Digital IDs lists any digital email-signing certificates on store for the user; they contain public keys that can be used to encrypt or validate email messages.

Figure 22.13
Find People returns
information about the
user.

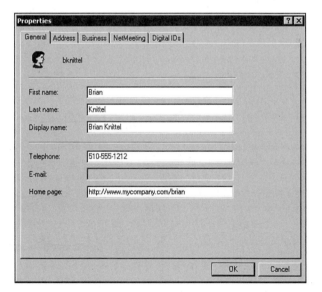

> **Note**
>
> You can change and update any of the information for your own account made available for user-level editing by the domain administrator. You also might be able to edit the information for employees you manage, if this is permitted on your network.

SEARCHING FOR FILES OR FOLDERS

The button labeled Search For Files and Folders is available on Entire Network as well. When you select Search for Files and Folders here, the In setting is initially set to Entire Network. You can't actually search the entire network this way; you have to select a computer and shared folder for the search.

On an Active Directory network, the domain administrator may choose to list, or *publish*, some shared folders in the directory; they might contain important resources that the company wanted to make widely accessible and easy to find. See "Advanced Active Directory Searching" later in the chapter for more information.

If you are trying to find a particular shared folder and it has not been explicitly published in the directory, you're out of luck; there's no other way to find it besides browsing.

Tip #258	If you have Administrative privileges on a network computer (that is, you are logged in as Administrator or an equivalent account and your administrator credentials are valid on the remote computer), you can have Explorer view the special shared folder C$. C$ displays the entire contents of the computer's hard drive. Windows automatically shares a network computer's entire hard disk for use by administrators.

ADVANCED ACTIVE DIRECTORY SEARCHING

I've already shown you how to find users and computers on an Active Directory network and have promised to talk about finding printers shortly.

I'd like to point out that the Active Directory contains information on many more objects than just users, computers, and printers. It includes shared folders, organizational units, certificate templates, containers (business groupings), foreign security principals, remote storage services, RPC services (used for advanced client/server software applications), and trusted domains. It can also contain information for other objects defined by your own organization. Most of this information is used only by domain administrators to configure Windows networks over vast distances; however, you can search for anything and can specify your qualifications based on more than 100 different criteria.

To make an advanced search, open My Computer, select Entire Network, and select View the Entire Contents of the Network to display the directory's top organizational level.

Tip #259	If you find getting to the Active Directory as cumbersome as I do, drag the Directory icon to your desktop and let Windows create a shortcut to it. Leave the shortcut on your desktop or drag it down to your Quick Launch toolbar.

Right-click an organizational unit and select Find, or choose menu File, Find to display the full-scale directory search tool (see Figure 22.14).

Figure 22.14
Using the advanced
Active Directory search
tool, you can use a
simplified form for any
of several categories
of directory objects, or
use the Advanced tab
to construct queries
using any of the
object's fields.

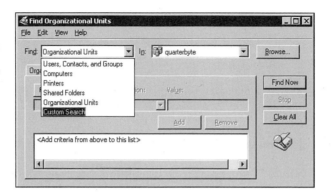

Using the advanced search tool, you can use a quick form-based search for any of the most
useful objects, similar to the forms you saw when you searched for users. You can also use
the Advanced tab to build specific queries such as "Last Name Starts with xxx." But this is
the full-blown search system, and here you'll have 53 fields to choose from when searching
for users; everything from Assistant to zip code: A to Z, if you need. For example, Figure
22.15 shows what to do if you need to know who belongs to a particular international ISDN
telephone number.

Figure 22.15
Advanced searches let
you dig into the most
arcane information
imaginable, but where
else would you find
information like this?

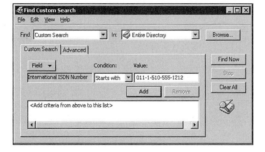

If you choose Custom Search, you have the whole gamut of fields to choose from, and in
the Advanced tab, you can enter LDAP (Lightweight Directory Access Protocol) queries
directly for submission to the AD service, as shown in Figure 22.16. This is the native query
syntax for Active Directory, and it's available here mostly for system debugging. (Strangely,
in Custom Search, any qualifiers set in the form-based search are applied along with a manually entered LDAP query; you should be sure to clear out the form if you are not likely to
need LDAP directly.)

ADDING NETWORK PLACES

By using the Add Network Place icon, you can add shortcuts in My Network Places to various network resources, for a quick return when you need them in the future. I find
Windows a bit hyper-helpful with its Favorites, Histories, Shortcuts, and now Network

Places. However, this aid is actually useful because entries in My Network Places appear in the list of choices in every application's Save As dialog, as shown in Figure 22.17.

Figure 22.16
Querying the Active Directory Server directly with its native LDAP query syntax.

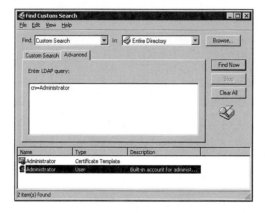

Figure 22.17
My Network Places is handy because you can select network folders when you're saving files in any application.

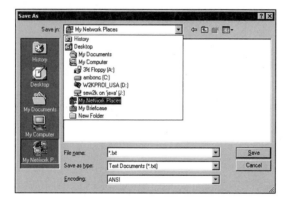

Tip #260

If you find you frequently use a certain shared network folder, put a shortcut to the folder in My Network Places so that you can quickly select it when using the Save As option in an application.

You can also put a network folder shortcut on your desktop for convenient access. Simply copy the shortcut from My Network Places to your desktop.

To add a new network place, do the following:

1. Select the Add Network Place icon. The Add Network Place Wizard asks for the name of the network resource, as shown in Figure 22.18.
2. Enter one of the three types of network resources you can call a Network Place:
   - A UNC name for a shared folder, such as \\server\share

- A URL for a Web folder, such as `http://host/share`
- The name of an FTP site, such as `ftp://host` or `ftp://host/subfolder`

You can also choose Browse to search through an Explorer-like view of the Entire Network, as in Figure 22.19.

PART

IV

CH

22

Figure 22.18
The Add Network Place wizard lets you enter a UNC name, a URL for Web folders, or an FTP site.

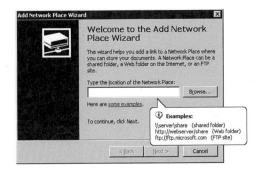

Figure 22.19
Using Browse, you can select a workgroup or domain, computer, and shared folder using an Explorer-like view. On an AD network, the Directory item lists the same computers, but they're organized by business units and locations.

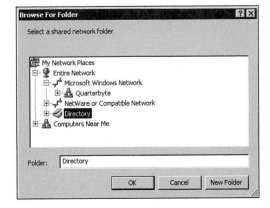

3. Click Next, and enter a name for your Network Place Shortcut. Then select Finish. A shortcut icon appears in My Network Places, and Windows pops up an Explorer window showing the contents of the remote shared folder or site.

Tip #261

When you're browsing through your network or browsing the Internet using Internet Explorer, you can drag network folders or Web page addresses to My Network Places to instantly make a Network Place shortcut, bypassing the Add Network Place Wizard entirely.

Likewise, you can drag the address from the Explorer window's Address bar to your desktop or to a folder to make an instant network shortcut.

USING WEB FOLDERS

Windows 2000 computers running Internet Information Services (IIS) can share folders using another file sharing system called WebDAV (Web Distributed Authoring and Versioning), or Web Sharing. Because it's based on the standard HTTP protocol, you can access Web folders on your office PC from home or from another LAN halfway around the world.

You can access folders that have been shared with the Web Folder sharing features of Office 2000, FrontPage 2000, and Internet Explorer version 5 or higher. To use these shared folders, you don't even have to be using Windows 2000; you can access these three applications from Windows 9x and Windows NT 4 as well.

Web folders let you view, use, and manage files and folders over the Internet just as if you were using them on your PC or on your LAN. You get exactly the same look and feel.

To use a folder that has been shared using Web Sharing, you need to know the folder's URL. It is set by the manager of the Web server you're using. In Internet Explorer 5, you can't use a link in a Web page to pop open a Web folder. You have to use the following procedure instead:

1. Select File, Open.
2. Enter the Web folder's URL, being sure to start with `http:`, and mark the Open as Web Folder check box, as shown in Figure 22.20.
3. Click OK.

Figure 22.20

An ordinary folder view appears, as in Figure 22.21. You can treat it in the usual way: Drag files in and out, create new folders, and rename and delete files. These operations take much longer than with LAN file sharing, however. And you might be prompted to enter your login name and password. It's safe to do so, even over the Internet.

Figure 22.21
The Web Folder view looks just like an ordinary Explorer folder view.

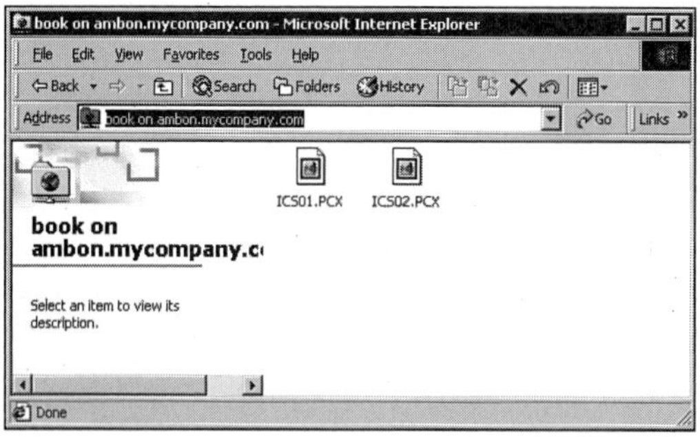

You can also view a Web file using the Add Network Place Wizard in My Network Places. When you're asked for the location of the network place, enter the Web folder URL starting with `http:`.

> **Note**
>
> After you open a Web folder, you might be tempted to create a shortcut to it by dragging the address from the Address bar in the Explorer window. This approach doesn't work if you opened the Web folder by choosing File, Open; you get a Web page shortcut instead.
>
> If you opened the Web folder by using the Add Network Places Wizard, however, or by opening an existing Web folder icon, you get a working folder shortcut. Strange!

> **Note**
>
> When Internet Explorer has switched to an ordinary Windows Explorer view, the File, Open command is no longer available. It's inconvenient because you must open another Internet Explorer window to view a different Web folder. You can't just type a new address because you need to mark the Open as Web Folder check box in the Open dialog box.

If you see an empty folder, or if you see a plain listing of filenames and dates without icons, see "Web Folder Appears to Be Empty" or "Directory Listing Appears Instead of Web Folder" in the "Troubleshooting" section at the end of the chapter.

Using Printers on the Network

Whether you're part of a large corporation or a small workgroup, or even if you're a home user with just two computers, network printing is a great time and money saver. Why connect a printer to each computer, when it will spend most of its time idle? Why not let several people share one printer and keep it busy? By not having to buy a printer for each user, you can spend the money you save more constructively on faster, higher-quality, and more interesting printers. You might add a color photo-quality printer or a transparency maker to give your network users more output choices.

Windows 2000 really excels at network printing. Here are some of the neat features of Windows 2000 network printing:

- Windows can print to any of hundreds of printer models, whether they're attached to a computer or connected directly to the LAN.

- It can send printer output to other operating systems. Novell, OS/2, and UNIX printer support is built into Windows 2000 Professional, and users of Novell, Macintosh, and UNIX networks can print to Windows shared printers if the printer's network uses Windows 2000 Server.

- Users of Windows NT versions 3 and 4 and Windows 9x can attach to a Windows 2000 network printer, and the correct printer driver for their operating system can be delivered to their computers automatically.

- You can print to and monitor a Windows 2000 printer over the Internet with new Internet Printer Protocol (IPP) support.

→ To learn more details about monitoring a printer via an Internet connection, **see** "Using Printers over the Internet with IPP," **p. 768**.

- Printer data is sent to a spooler on the computer that shares the printer. The printer data is stored on the hard disk while the printer catches up, making printing seem faster to user applications. More than one person at a time can send output to the same shared printer; their print requests simply queue up and come out in first-come, first-served order.

Because the software to do all this comes with Windows 2000 Professional, and you can hook computers together for as little as $25 each, printer sharing alone is a good reason to install a network.

The best part is that from the user's standpoint, using a network printer is no different than using a local printer. Everything you learned about printing in Chapter 9 applies to network printers; the only difference is in the one-time step of adding the printer to Windows. Later in the chapter, I'll describe how to share a printer attached to your computer; right now, let's look at using a printer that has already been shared elsewhere on the network.

USING SHARED PRINTERS

Windows can directly attach to printers shared via Microsoft Networking services, whether from Windows 2000, NT, 95, 98, Windows for Workgroups, OS/2, or even the Samba service from UNIX, and also to printers managed by Novell NetWare.

→ To learn how to use Windows with a Novell NetWare network, **see** Chapter 25, "Networking Mix Match."

To use any networked printer, you have to set up the printer in your Printers window by using the Add Printer Wizard, just as you would have to do with a locally attached printer. Using a networked printer is even easier, though, because you don't have to physically touch the printer.

The first step is to find the shared printer you want you use. Windows provides a nifty find-a-printer feature for users of an Active Directory network; it lets you find shared printers based on features such as location and capabilities. If you don't have an Active Directory network, you don't have this feature, nor is it likely that you would benefit from it because your network is probably all in the same building and not spread over a continent. In this case, you can skip to the section "Locating a Suitable Printer" later in this chapter.

FINDING A PRINTER IN THE ACTIVE DIRECTORY

If you do have Active Directory, notice that For Printers appears as an option on the Start button's Search menu.

This feature will come in handy if you're a business traveler using the network in an unfamiliar office, or if you're in such a large office setting that you aren't familiar with all the printing resources on your network. Personally, I don't have this problem; my company's printer is in the next room. But if one day you need to find a printer that can print 600dpi color on a Japanese Chou #3 Envelope (rotated), Active Directory will let you know whether your company has one.

Using the Active Directory printer search tool, you can search for printers three ways: by name and location, as shown in Figure 22.22; by printer capabilities; or by more advanced attributes.

Figure 22.22
Using the Printers tab in the Active Directory printer search tool, you can search for printers by printer name, location, and model.

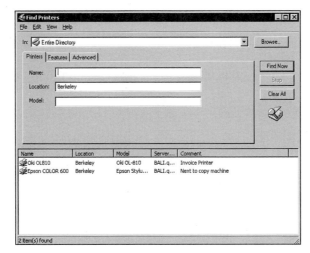

You can choose a major organizational unit to begin the search from the In drop-down list; you can search the entire directory, choose a major organizational unit, or select Browse to select a more regional subunit. See what choices In has on your network to see whether restricting the search makes sense for your company; otherwise, let the search use the Entire Directory.

Searching by the printer share name, location, or printer model is straightforward; just type a name or part of a name, and select Find Now. What works best when searching by Location depends on how your organization has set up the Active Directory. Yours might use cities, addresses, floors and room numbers, or another system. At any time, you can change your selection criteria and select Find Now again to update the search listing and refine or expand your search.

You can find all the printers in the directory by entering no information in the Find Printers dialog box: Just click Find Now.

Tip #262

View the entire directory the first time you use Find Printers. This will give you an idea of how location and printer names are organized in your company. If too many names are listed, you can click Clear All to clear the search listing and then restrict your search using a location name that makes sense for your network. For example, if your company has put floor and room numbers like 10-123 in the Location column, you might restrict your search to printers on the 10th floor by searching for 10- in Location.

To search for printers based on capabilities you need, select the Features tab, as shown in Figure 22.23. Here, you can limit the directory display to just printers with required color and finishing capabilities, speed, resolution, and available paper sizes.

Figure 22.23
Using the Features tab, you can select printers based on printing capabilities such as speed, resolution, and color capability.

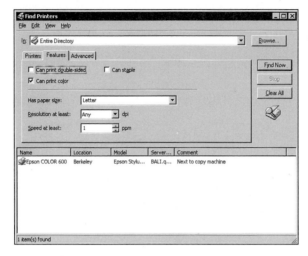

> **Note**
>
> The name and location attributes you select on the Printers tab, the capabilities you select on the Features tab, and any advanced search restrictions on the Advanced tab all operate together to limit the final result, even though you can see only one of the tabs at a time.

If these selections aren't specific enough for you, you can really nail down what you want on the Advanced tab, as shown in Figure 22.24.

Figure 22.24
Using the Advanced tab, you can select printers based on the full range of information stored in the Active Directory.

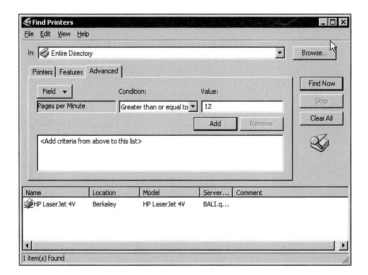

This tab lets you list your requirements in no uncertain terms. To perform an advanced search, follow these steps:

1. Select Field, and choose a criterion from the list. The searchable attributes include Asset Number, Input Trays, Installed Memory, and Printer Language; you can choose from 27 different attributes.

2. Under Condition, select a comparison type.

   - For numeric fields, the choices are Greater Than or Equal To, Less Than, and so on.

   - For text fields, the choices are Starts With, Ends With, Is (Exactly), or Is Not.

   - For capabilities such as Can Staple, you can choose True or False. You can also choose Present and Not Present to test whether a field is blank.

3. Under Value, enter the desired asset number, number of trays, megabytes of memory, printer language, and so on. Then click Add.

4. Enter more filtering items, or select Find Now to begin the search.

Remember, anything you entered on the Printers or Features tabs factors into this search as well.

 If your Windows displays `No Printers Match the Current Search`, *see "Can't Find Any Printers in Active Directory" in the "Troubleshooting" section at the end of this chapter.*

You can adjust the search results by double-clicking any of the filtering items you entered; just change the settings and select Add or Remove, and then click Find Now.

Using these three tabs, you should be able to quickly narrow down the possibilities enough to choose a suitable printer.

Installing a Printer You've Found in the Directory

After you've found a printer, what do you do with it? You have two options available by right-clicking a printer in the search results list: You can connect to it or open it. Connecting installs the printer on your computer; in other words, it adds the printer to the list of those your computer can use. Open displays the printer's current print jobs. If you try to open a printer that you haven't yet installed, installation takes place automatically.

You can also connect by double-clicking the chosen printer. The steps involved in installation from the Find Printers tool are similar to those described in the following section, which is written for those unfortunate souls without Active Directory. Because you've already identified the printer you want to use, skip down to "Selecting a Printer Driver" later in the chapter.

Installing a Network Printer Without Active Directory

To use a shared printer, you have to install the printer in your Printers folder, just as you would with any printer, as I described in Chapter 9, "Printing and Faxing with Windows 2000."

Display the Printers windows from Settings on your Start menu. Select the Add Printer icon, and click Next. This time, though, select Network Printer rather than Local Printer, and choose Next.

Next, you have to identify the shared printer. If you know its network name already, you can type it into the Name box in UNC format—for example, \\bali\laserjet—as shown in Figure 22.25. Click Next to finish installing the printer.

Figure 22.25
You can enter a UNC shared printer name if know it, or you can leave the Name field blank and choose Next to browse the network for a shared printer.

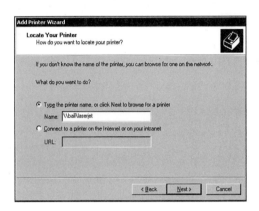

The following sections help you locate and install proper drivers for printers on a non-Active Directory network.

LOCATING A SUITABLE PRINTER

If you don't know the name of the printer you want to use, you can browse through the network. You went through something like this already when you were mapping shared folders to drives, but this time there's no Browse button. Just leave the Name field blank, and choose Next.

On a workgroup network, the network display appears, as shown in Figure 22.26, to let you probe into domains or workgroups, computers, and their shared printers. Select the printer you want, and click Next to finish the installation.

Figure 22.26
You can browse your workgroup network for shared printers by opening the list view of networks, domains, workgroups, and computers. Shared printers are found listed under each computer. It helps that the list includes only computers with shared printers.

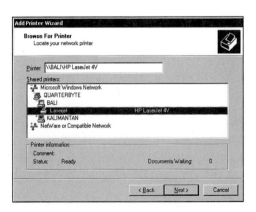

SELECTING A PRINTER DRIVER

When you've chosen a printer, Windows automatically looks to the computer sharing that printer for the correct software driver for Windows 2000. If it finds the driver, that driver is instantly downloaded to your PC, and the installation completes without your having to look up the printer's model number, hunt for the right driver disks, or otherwise lift a finger.

You might hit a snag, though, if the sharing computer doesn't have the correct Windows 2000 printer driver for you. You might have this problem if the remote computer isn't running Windows 2000. In this case, Windows pops up a message saying "The server on which the printer resides does not have the correct printer driver installed. If you want to install the driver on your local computer, click OK."

If you want to use the printer, well, now you have to lift a finger. Click OK, and Windows displays the Add Printer Wizard with its list of known printer manufacturers and models, as shown in Figure 22.27. Choose the correct make and model from the list, and then click OK.

Figure 22.27
The driver selection dialog appears if Windows requires you to select the proper printer driver for a network printer.

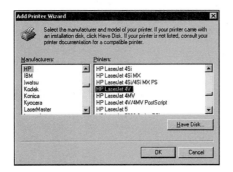

→ If you can't locate the correct printer model in this list and need more detailed instructions on installing printer drivers, **see** "About Printer Drivers," **p. 322**.

FINISHING THE INSTALLATION

If you are adding a second or subsequent printer, Windows asks whether you want this newly installed printer to be set as your default printer. You can choose Yes or No, as you like; then select Next. You can always change your choice of default printer later, as I'll show you in the next section.

When you click Finish, the wizard adds the printer to your list of printer choices, and you're finished. The network printer is ready to use in any application. The whole process takes about 15 seconds from start to finish.

SETTING A DEFAULT PRINTER

If you've installed more than one printer, you can choose one to be the default printer in your Windows applications like this:

1. Right-click your preferred printer.
2. Choose Set Default Printer.

You might select the printer closest to you as your default printer and select alternative printers only when you need one for its special features or when your usual printer is backlogged.

TESTING THE NETWORK PRINTER

When the new printer appears in your printer window, you might want to verify that you can actually use the printer and that its output is correct. To do so, right-click the printer icon, and select Properties. Select Print a Test Page to ensure that the network printer is working correctly.

USING THE NETWORK PRINTER

When the network printer is set up, you can use it in exactly the same way as you use a locally attached printer, so all the printer management discussion in Chapter 9 applies to network printers, too. The only difference is that the remote computer's administrator might not have given you management privileges for the printer, so you might not be able to change the printer's properties.

It's probably best that you don't have that capability anyway because changing the hardware setup of someone else's printer without permission is considered bad form. If you view the printer's Properties page and have access to all the usual printer configuration tabs—Sharing, Ports, Advanced, Security and Device Settings—don't make any changes without the permission of the printer's owner. Changing the port, for example, certainly makes the printer stop working, and the remote user probably won't figure out why for quite some time.

You can view and manage the printer's list of pending documents, as shown in Figure 22.28. All the printer management instructions in Chapter 9 apply to network printers as well: You can pause the printer, change document parameters, and cancel print jobs. The only difference is that, without printer management rights on the remote computer, you can't cancel or alter the properties of anyone's print jobs but your own.

Figure 22.28
Double-clicking a networked printer's icon displays pending jobs for the printer. You can cancel or change the properties of pending documents, provided you have printer management rights on the remote printer.

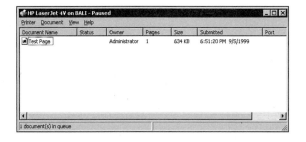

USING PRINTERS OVER THE INTERNET WITH IPP

A new feature in Windows 2000 is the capability to install and print to a shared printer through the Internet as easily as you can through a LAN. The Internet Printing Protocol (IPP) was developed by a group of network and printer technology companies at the initiative of Novell Corporation and Xerox Corporation. They saw the need for a standardized way to provide reliable, secure, and full-featured print spooling functions over the Internet.

The vision was that business travelers should be able to send reports back to their home offices via the Internet and use the same technology to print reports or presentations in a hotel's business center or a commercial copy service center. A consortium of network and printer vendors started the process, Microsoft and Hewlett-Packard joined in, and the result is IPP.

IPP is based on the Hypertext Transfer Protocol (HTTP), which runs the World Wide Web, so it's simple and can pass safely through network firewalls. In Windows, IPP uses Windows' own safely encrypted username and password security, so your printers are protected from abuse by anonymous outsiders.

As with all the shared resources I'm discussing, using and providing these services are really separate things. You can use IPP to reach a printer without providing the service yourself, and vice versa. In this section, I'll talk about using the service.

The magic of IPP is that after you've installed the printer icon, you can use the remote printer in exactly the same way as you use any Windows printer. The printer queue, management tools, and other operations are all exactly the same, as long as you're connected to the Internet or the appropriate intranet LAN.

SELECTING AN IPP PRINTER BY ITS URL

You can connect to a remote printer via IPP in two ways.

If you know the URL of the IPP-connected printer, you can use the Add Printer Wizard, as I discussed earlier in this chapter. The URL is supplied by your network administrator, if the printer is on your company's intranet, or by a hotel or service bureau after they've gotten your credit card number.

1. Follow the instructions I gave earlier for adding a network printer.

2. When you are asked to enter the printer name, choose Connect to a Printer on the Internet or On Your Intranet instead of browsing the network, as shown in Figure 22.29.

Figure 22.29
Adding an Internet-connected printer using IPP. This URL is fictitious, but the hope is that soon you will be able to send output to a printer at a copy center or service bureau as easily as to a printer in your own home or office.

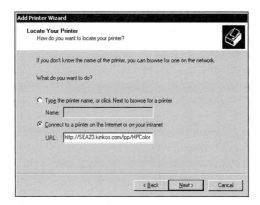

3. Enter the URL provided by your administrator or the service you are using, and select Next.

4. You might be prompted for a username and password. If so, enter the name and password supplied by the vendor or, if you are using an intranet, your network username and password.

5. Continue with the installation procedure described above; you might need to select a print driver if the remote print server doesn't provide it automatically.

When the new printer icon is installed, you have a fully functional Windows printer. You can view the pending jobs and set your print and page preferences as usual as long as you're connected to the Internet (or the LAN, in a service establishment).

Tip #263	If you use a printing service, remember to delete the printer from your Printers folder when you leave town; you don't want to accidentally print reports in Katmandu after you've returned home.

SELECTING AN IPP PRINTER VIA THE WEB

If you can reach the Web site of a Windows 2000 computer that sports both Internet Information Services (IIS) and a shared printer, Internet printing is a snap. When you install IIS on Windows 2000, it automatically enables IPP and provides a Web page interface with which to monitor and connect to any printers you share.

The Web pages aren't a feature of IPP, by the way. They're a set of Web pages installed with Internet Information Services that let you view and manage shared printers over the Web. If you want to print to the printer, then IPP comes into play.

If you view the URL http://*computername*/printers, replacing *computername* with the actual hostname of the remote computer, you get a display like the one shown in Figure 22.30.

Figure 22.30
Windows 2000's Web Interface for printer management. The home page gives a quick overview of all shared printers. You can select a printer to view or manage for more detail.

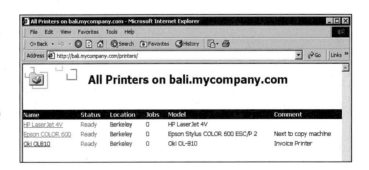

Selecting one of the printers brings up a detailed printer status page, as shown in Figure 22.31. The printer status page lists queued print jobs and current printer status. If you're using Internet Explorer as your Web browser and have IPP printing software installed in

Windows, clicking Connect sets this printer up as a network printer on your computer, drivers and all. You can select the printer and use it immediately, right over the Internet.

Figure 22.31
The printer status page shows current print jobs; using it, you can manage the printer and queued documents. The Connect hyperlink installs the printer on your computer.

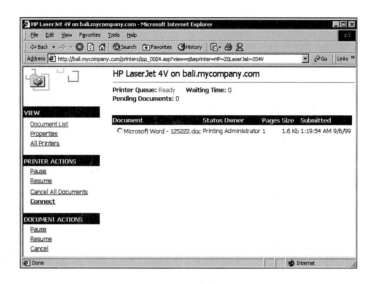

You can get IPP software for Windows 95, 98, and NT 4 computers from http:// windowsupdate.microsoft.com. These operating systems can connect to IPP printers as well and, if they use Internet Explorer version 5, can use the Web interface to make the connection.

If you view a Windows 2000 computers/printers Web page and can select printers but don't have the Connect option, see "No Connect Option for Web Printing" in the "Troubleshooting" section at the end of this chapter.

USING OTHER IPP PRINTERS

You can buy an IPP-capable printer and plug it directly into your LAN. An IPP-capable printer will probably provide Web-based management and status, which is a great way to monitor its health from across the country (or across the room).

→ To learn more about installing network-ready printers, **see** "Adding Network-Capable Printers," **p. 722**.

In a workgroup, it might not get a registered hostname, so you might need to refer to it by its assigned IP address, as in http://192.168.0.24/hplaser4. The installation instructions for the printer tell you what URL to use.

When you know the URL for the intranet- or Internet-accessible printer, follow the instructions in the section "Installing a Network Printer Without Active Directory" earlier in this chapter. You don't have to search for the printer, though. When you get to the screen shown in Figure 22.25, choose Connect to a Printer on the Internet or on Your Intranet. Enter the URL, and then go on installing the printer as instructed earlier.

When it is set up, you can use the printer as if it were directly connected to your PC.

Tip #264

Connect to the printer this way with just *one* of your Windows 2000 computers. Share the printer from that computer with the rest of your LAN. This way, you can make installation easier for everyone else.

USING UNIX AND LPR PRINTERS

In the UNIX world, most shared printers use a protocol called LPR/LPD, which was developed at the University of California at Berkeley during the early years of UNIX and the TCP/IP protocol.

Note

If you have a UNIX background, you might be happy to know that the familiar UNIX `lpr` and `lpq` utilities are available as command-line programs in Windows 2000.

→ For more information about UNIX printing, **see** "Internetworking with UNIX," **p. 900**.

Manufacturers such as Hewlett-Packard make direct network-connected printers that accept the LPR protocol as well. You can connect one of these printers to your LAN, configure its TCP/IP settings to match your LAN, and immediately print without running a cable from a computer to the printer. This way, you can place a printer in a more convenient place than could be reached by a 10-foot printer cable.

You can install a Windows printer that directs its output to an LPR print queue as easily as you can install a directly connected printer (as long as Print Services for UNIX is installed). Follow these steps:

1. Choose Start, Settings, Printers, and then select Add Printer.
2. Select Local Printer. (You choose Local because Network connects only to Windows and IPP shared printers.) Uncheck Automatically Detect and Install My Plug and Play Printer, and click Next.
3. Select the Create a New Port option, and choose LPR Port in the Type box, as shown in Figure 22.32.
4. In the Add LPR Compatible Printer dialog, enter the IP address or hostname of the UNIX or printer server and the name of the print queue on that server, as shown in Figure 22.33.
5. Select the manufacturer and printer model as usual, and proceed with the rest of the printer installation.

If you find that you entered the wrong IP address, hostname, or print queue name, Windows might not let you change this information. Bring up the printer's Properties page, highlight the LPR port, and select Properties. If Windows doesn't display a dialog to change the IP information, uncheck the LPR port. Delete the port, and add a new LPR port with the correct information. Then check the port to connect your Windows printer to the LPR server.

Figure 22.32
You can add an LPR port to connect to a UNIX print queue.

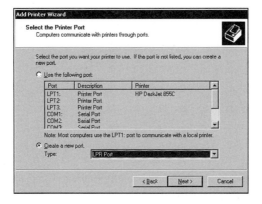

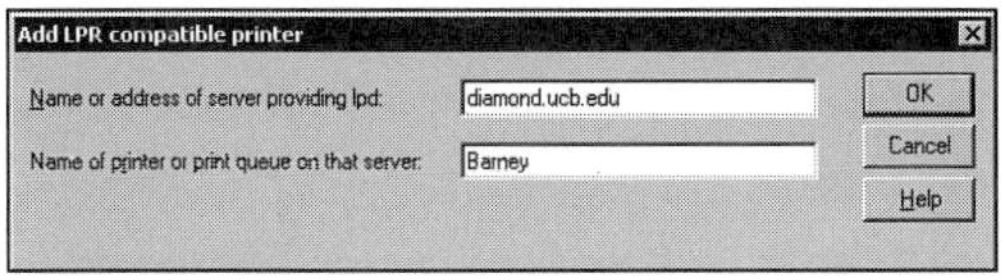

Figure 22.33
In this dialog, you enter the IP address or hostname of the print server and the queue or printer name.

USING APPLETALK PRINTERS

If your network has AppleTalk printers attached, you probably have Macintosh users on your LAN. If you want to share files with Macintosh users, you need to have Windows 2000 Server on your network because it includes File and Printer Services for Macintosh Networks. These services let Macintosh and Windows users access shared printers and folders on each others' networks as if they were their own.

→ To learn more details about internetworking with Macintosh computers, **see** "Internetworking with Macintosh," **p. 915**.

Windows 2000 Professional doesn't provide such services, so without Server you can't share files and printers with Macintosh users. You can print to AppleTalk-based printers that are directly attached to your LAN, however. You can then share access to the AppleTalk printer with other Windows users.

To use an AppleTalk printer on your computer, you first need to install the AppleTalk Protocol capability, as follows:

1. Right-click your LAN connection in Network and Dial-Up Connections, and select Properties.

2. Select Install. In the Select Network Component Type dialog, highlight Protocol and click Add.

3. In the Select Network Protocol dialog that appears, as shown in Figure 22.34, highlight AppleTalk Protocol and click OK.

Figure 22.34
In this dialog, you can add the AppleTalk Protocol to your Local Area Connection.

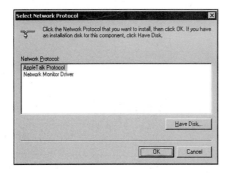

4. When Windows has finished, highlight AppleTalk Protocol and select Properties.

5. Check to see whether AppleTalk zones have been defined on your network; if they have, they appear in a list in the Properties dialog. If they're there, select the zone to which the printer is assigned from the drop-down list, and click OK. Otherwise, just close the properties page.

6. Close the Local Area Connection Properties dialog by clicking OK.

   Now you can install the printer.

7. Choose Start, Settings, Printers, and then select Add Printer.

8. Select Local Printer (because Network connects only to Windows and IPP printers). Uncheck Automatically Detect and Install My Plug and Play Printer, and click Next.

9. Select the Create a New Port option, and choose AppleTalk Printing Devices in the Type box, as shown in Figure 22.35.

Figure 22.35
In this dialog, you can add a local printer and select AppleTalk Printing Devices as a New Port.

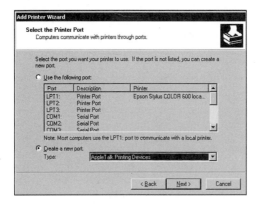

10. Windows scans for AppleTalk printers and displays any zones and printers it finds. Choose the desired printer, as shown in Figure 22.36, and click OK.

11. Windows displays a dialog box asking "Do you want to capture this AppleTalk printing device?" *Capturing* means that your Windows computer will get exclusive use of the

printer, and no other computers on the LAN will be able to directly access it. If you have Macintosh computers on your LAN, capturing the printer will not be appreciated. In this case, select No. However, if you have no Macintoshes on your network, you can select Yes. Share this printer so that other Windows users can use it through Windows printer sharing from your computer. Capturing the printer forces others to use the shared connection, and that ensures proper queuing, rather than the free-for-all that normally ensues with AppleTalk printers.

Figure 22.36

12. The AppleTalk connection now appears in the list of printer ports (see Figure 22.37), and you can continue through the installation normally, selecting the proper printer drivers.

Figure 22.37
The newly connected printer appears in the Ports list. You can proceed to install the proper Windows printer drivers.

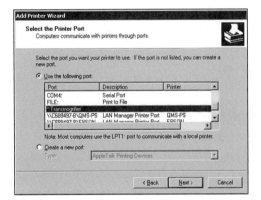

After you've finished installing the printer, you can (and probably should) share the printer connection you've made, for other Windows users who might want to use that printer. I'll describe how to share printers later in this chapter.

USING OTHER NETWORK-CONNECTED PRINTERS

Windows 2000 can use other types of network-connected printers as well. Some printer models come with a built-in network connection, and others have a network adapter option. You can also buy network printer servers, which are small boxes with a network connector and one to three printer connection ports. These devices let you locate printers in a convenient area, which doesn't need to be near a computer.

Printer servers and network computers also take a computational burden away from computers with connected printers. Due to design flaws that started in the original IBM PC and were never addressed, printing on a PC puts a great burden on the computer's processor. It's bad enough when your computer slows down while it prints your documents, but when it slows down because it's printing a document for some other user on the LAN, you'll get annoyed pretty quickly. Network printers solve this problem.

The installation procedures for various printer and server models vary. I'll cover the DLC printing protocol used by some Hewlett-Packard and IBM printers in this chapter; if you have a different brand, you can use this procedure as an example when following your manufacturer's specific instructions.

INSTALLING A DLC PRINTER

Installing a DLC printer is similar to installing an AppleTalk printer, so I'll abbreviate the instructions somewhat.

1. Right-click your LAN connection in Network and Dial-Up Connections and select Properties. Select Install.

2. In the resulting Select Network Component Type dialog, highlight Protocol and click Add.

3. In the Select Network Protocol dialog, highlight DLC Protocol and click OK.

4. Close the Local Area Connection Properties box.

   Connect the printer to your network and set it up before proceeding. Follow the printer's instruction manual to print a test page, which will show the printer's DLC address on the network.

   Then install the printer in Windows by completing these steps.

5. Choose Start, Settings, Printers, and then select Add Printer.

6. Select Local Printer (because the Network option connects only to Windows Network and IPP printers). Uncheck Automatically Detect and Install my Plug and Play Printer, and click Next.

7. Select Create a New Port, and choose Hewlett-Packard Network Peripheral Port.

8. Enter a name for the printer, as in Figure 22.38, and either enter the printer's network card address from the test printout or select Refresh to query the network for available printers. Your new printer's address should appear. Select it by double-clicking, but don't click OK yet.

9. Select Options, and uncheck Information in Logging Level; this prevents the printer from recording messages in your computer's Event log unless a problem occurs. Click OK to close the Options box.

10. Click OK to finish installing the printer connection port. Continue as with a standard printer by selecting the printer manufacturer and model.

Figure 22.38

USING NETWORK RESOURCES EFFECTIVELY

Tips are scattered throughout this chapter, but I want to collect a few of the best ones here for easy reference. The following tips and strategies will help you make the most of your LAN.

USE MY NETWORK PLACES

My Network Places not only serves as a convenient place to collect shortcuts to network resources, but it also appears under My Computer when you open or save files in any application. This feature can save you lots of time when you use the same places over and over.

You can make shortcuts in My Network Places for the handful of the network shared folders that you use most frequently.

You can add the names of subfolders when you make these shortcuts, if you find that you always have to drill your way into the main shared folder to get to the folder you actually want.

MAKE FOLDER SHORTCUTS

You can drag the icon appearing in the address field from any shared folder view to your desktop, to My Network Places, or any other convenient place for reuse later.

I like to organize projects into folders on my desktop and put related network resources in each. For example, I might have three project folders on my desktop, and in each one, three shortcuts to related shared folders.

Because shortcuts aren't the "real thing," you can have several shortcuts to the same place wherever you need them.

USE OFFLINE NETWORK FOLDERS

If you use network resources from a portable computer or a computer with an intermittent network connection (by design or by accident), you can use the Offline Folders feature to keep local copies of important network folders in your own computer for use when the network is unavailable.

→ If you would like to learn more details about Offline Folders, **see** "Offline Folders," **p. 817**.

PUT TOOLS AND DOCUMENTATION ONLINE

Administrators and power users should put management batch files, Registry installation and setup files, special program utilities, and documentation in a shared network folder, for convenient access from any computer on the network. All your network's users don't need to know it's there unless you want them to.

PLAN A WORKGROUP NETWORK CAREFULLY

If you don't have a Windows 2000 domain network, you need to take a little extra care to make your network easy to use.

Each computer in a workgroup network has its own separate user list, and this tends to make the network difficult to manage. The problem is that people tend to do the wrong things to resolve the difficulty. The wrong solutions are to have the users log on to their computers using the Administrator account or to enable the Guest account so that unknown LAN users can have access to shared resources. The problem with using Administrator is that it leaves computers vulnerable to viruses and system attacks virtually all the time. The problem with the Guest account is that, while you are connected to the Internet, even just with a dial-up connection, your LAN is vulnerable to probing by hackers.

The right things to do are as follows:

- Try to put all shared resources on one computer.
- Set up an account on that computer for each user on the network.
- Have all users keep their passwords set to the same thing on the computers they use and on the common computer. Maintaining consistent passwords allows Windows use your username and password to gain access to remote resources through pass-through authentication. In practice, you will never notice anything "passing through"; you'll just be able to access shared files. It just works.

For more suggestions about workgroup management, see Chapter 32, "Managing Users."

ORGANIZE YOUR NETWORK TO FIT YOUR USERS

You should organize shared folders to fit the way users actually work. For example, if your organization frequently passes documents back and forth between users, you could make a shared folder named Inbox, containing a subfolder for each user. Co-workers could deliver documents to each other by dropping them into the appropriate network inbox. Users could each have a shortcut to their inboxes on their desktops for quick access.

SHARING RESOURCES

On a large corporate LAN, most important network resources, shared folders, and printers are set up and tightly controlled by network managers. You might not even be able to share resources from your own computer. This helps control the cost of maintaining and managing the network, but it doesn't help you and your co-workers if you want to share files for a project among yourselves. You might have to plead with your network manager to prepare a common shared folder for you.

On the other hand, you might be able to set up the file sharing yourself. In a workgroup network, it's almost certain you can. Administrators and members of the Administrators and Power Users groups can manage file and printer sharing.

Before deciding to share resources, you should give some thought to just what you want to share, how you want to organize it, and who should have permission to see, use, or change files you've published in the shared folders.

Windows enables you to share your entire hard drive as a single shared resource.

SHARING FOLDERS AND DRIVES

You can easily share a folder with your network cohorts; this capability is built right into Explorer. You just follow these steps:

1. Select a folder in Explorer, or select the name of the hard drive itself at the top of the Explorer view if you want to share the entire disk.

2. Right-click the folder, choose Properties, and then click the Sharing tab.

> **Note**
>
> You might notice that Windows has automatically already shared your entire hard drive with the name c$. Leave this share alone; it lets administrators manage your computer. You can choose a different name if you want to share your entire hard drive—for example, my_c or my_c$.

3. Select Share This Folder. Windows fills in the Share Name field with the name of the folder. If the name contains spaces, it might not be accessible to Windows for Workgroups users, so you might want to shorten or abbreviate the name. You also can enter a comment to describe the contents of the shared folder, as shown in Figure 22.39.

Figure 22.39
When sharing a location, be sure to enter a share name. Comments are optional.

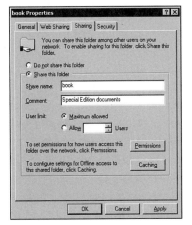

> **Tip #265**
>
> You can prevent other users from seeing your shared folder when they browse the network by adding a dollar sign to the share name—for example, mystuff$. This convention alone does not prevent them from seeing your files if they know the share name.

4. You can restrict the number of outside users who can connect to the shared folder by specifying a user limit, although in practice doing so is probably unnecessary.

Before clicking OK to make the folder accessible, you should consider file security and the ability of other users to keep Offline Folder copies of your files.

If you receive a `File Is in Use By Another` *error when attempting to use one of the files in a folder you have shared, see "File Is in Use by Another" in the "Troubleshooting" section at the end of this chapter.*

CACHING SETTINGS

If you expect network users to use this folder or any of its contents as an Offline Folder, you should check the caching settings. (*Caching* is a computer term for keeping a handy copy of information that resides elsewhere. Caches give you quick access to that information but require care to be sure the copy always matches the original.)

Caching settings influence how the other user's computer will treat the files you're sharing. In the Properties dialog box for the shared folder, select Caching, and instruct Windows how you want it to treat the files you're sharing. Figure 22.40 shows the Caching Settings dialog box.

Figure 22.40
Caching settings control how other computers will manage your files if other users choose to keep them in an Offline Folder.

Your choices are as follows:

No Caching	Uncheck the Allow Caching of Files in This Shared Folder check box to prevent network users from keeping copies of your data in an Offline Folder.
Manual Caching for Documents	This setting, the default, requires remote users to specify which particular documents they want to keep a copy of in an Offline Folder.
Automatic Caching for Programs	Windows automatically copies all files to the Offline Folder, and the remote users execute and view their local copies when possible. You should use this setting when the shared folder contains programs and static data.
Automatic Caching for Documents	Windows automatically copies and synchronizes all files in an Offline Folder. You should use this setting when the files are all required as a set.

Choose the setting that most closely describes your shared files, and click OK.

SHARED FOLDER SECURITY

Sharing security is frequently misunderstood. You can specify the rights of remote users and groups to read, change (that is, read and write), or fully control (read, write, delete, rename, and so on) the files in your shared folder. Figure 22.41 shows the permissions for the book folder.

Figure 22.41
Shared folder permissions apply in *addition* to NTFS file permissions. Only the most restrictive access is granted.

If you are sharing files on a FAT partition, these are the only controls you have at your disposal to manage access to your files. You should probably remove Everyone and add only selected users and groups to grant them rights to the files in your shared folder.

> **Caution**
>
> When you are on a LAN, it is not a good idea to share any folders from a FAT-formatted disk because the network controls are the only controls available. It's too easy for someone to enable a Guest account and give a complete outsider or Internet hacker access to your files. If you do enable sharing of a FAT-partition folder, remove Everyone and grant access only to selected users or groups.

If you have an NTFS formatted hard drive, you need to know that NTFS file permissions work in addition to any permissions you set for the shared folder. The most restrictive access is granted. You can leave the shared folder set to permit Everyone full control, and use NTFS file permissions to completely control access to your shared files, as long as you pay attention to assigning NTFS permissions to your folder.

> **Note**
>
> You must use NTFS permissions anyway because anyone who can access your files over the LAN could log in physically at your computer and get at the files there with only the NTFS permissions protecting them.

Network security is a serious matter, and in a business setting, you should be very sure to understand the risks you're exposing your files to and the ways you can protect them.

You should read Chapter 32, "Managing Users," and Chapter 33, "Managing the Hard Disk," for more information about setting User and Group access to folders using NTFS permissions.

After you set share permissions and cache settings, click OK to make the share available on the network.

 When you have shared a folder, its icon changes to a hand holding the folder like an offering.

SHARING WEB FOLDERS

If you have installed Internet Information Services on your computer then Web folder sharing is available by default. When you view a folder's properties, Web Sharing appears as a tab, as shown in Figure 22.42.

→ To learn more about installing the Web services on your computer, **see** Chapter 18, "Using Internet Information Services to Host a Web Site."

Figure 22.42
Web Sharing appears as a folder property when you install IIS and the FrontPage 2000 Server Extensions.

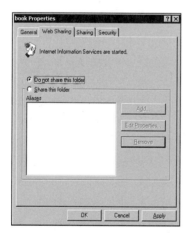

 If Web Sharing does not appear as a tab in a folder's properties, see "Web Sharing Is Not a Choice" in the "Troubleshooting" section at the end of this chapter.

Enabling regular sharing on a folder does not make it available as a Web folder, or vice versa.

To make the folder available to Web visitors using IE5, Office 2000, or FrontPage 2000, select Share This Folder on the Web Sharing tab. A dialog box appears, as shown in Figure 22.43.

Now you can set a URL name for the shared folder; the URL for Web access is http://hostname/foldername, so it's best to enter the name without spaces or punctuation characters.

Figure 22.43
In this dialog, you can set up access to the shared folder. To provide read/write access, check Write and set Application Permissions to None.

By default, the folder is set up for read-only access. Remote Web folder users, regardless of their passwords, see the folder in a standard Explorer view and can copy files from it, but cannot add or modify the files in it.

To enable read/write access to the shared folder, check Write in the Access Permissions section, and set Application Permissions to None.

> **Caution**
>
> If you enable Write access, you must set application permissions to None to prevent outside users from delivering arbitrary programs to your computer that they could then execute on your computer via the Internet.
>
> You must also be sure that local user IUSR_*XXXXX*, where *XXXXX* is your computer's name, is not a member of group Everyone. This could give anonymous Internet visitors (represented by user IUSR_*XXXXX*) read and write permission in your shared folder!

These permission settings work in addition to NTFS permissions, so the same issues pertain to Web sharing as to standard sharing:

- Don't Web-share a folder on a FAT-formatted partition.
- Carefully check NTFS permissions on any folders you share.
- Read Chapters 26, 32, and 33 for important discussions of file and network security.

The most important thing to do after enabling Web sharing is to open a Web browser and attempt to access the shared folder using no username or password, and then with the username and password of a user account that you do not think should have access to the files. If either of these methods works, you do not have effective security in place.

SHARING PRINTERS

You can share any local printer on your computer. It can be a printer directly cabled to your computer or one connected via the network using AppleTalk, LPR, DLC, or other network protocols.

To enable printer sharing, do the following:

1. Choose Start, Settings, Printers, and then select the local printer.

2. Right-click the printer icon and choose Sharing, or select Properties and then select the Sharing tab.

3. Select Shared As, and enter a network-visible name for the printer, as shown in Figure 22.44. Enter up to 14 characters using letters, numbers, and hyphens. Avoid spaces if you have Windows 3.x computers on your network. 8.3 naming is recommended if Windows 3.x computers need to access the share.

Figure 22.44
Enabling sharing for a printer.

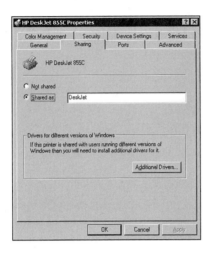

4. If your network has only Windows 2000 computers, click OK, and you're finished. Other network users can now use the shared printer.

Otherwise, continue to the next section to add extra printer drivers for other operating systems.

INSTALLING EXTRA PRINTER DRIVERS

If you have computers running other versions of Windows or other CPU types, you can load the appropriate printer drivers for those operating systems now, and network users will receive them automatically when they connect to your printer. This step is optional, but it's the friendly thing to do.

View the Sharing tab in your printer's Properties dialog box, and select the Additional Drivers button. Windows displays a list of supported operating systems and CPU types.

Check the boxes for the CPUs and operating systems you want to support, and click OK. Windows then goes through any additional operating systems you chose one-by-one and ask for either your Windows 2000 CD-ROM or other operating system installation disks to locate the appropriate drivers, as shown in Figure 22.45.

Figure 22.45
In this dialog, you can locate the appropriate drivers for each operating system as requested.

PART

IV

CH

22

You can find these drivers on the original installation disks for the alternate operating system, or often on disks provided with the printer, which might contain support for many operating systems on the same disk.

SETTING PERMISSIONS

Shared printers have three security attributes that can be assigned to users or groups:

Print	Send output to the printer.
Manage Printers	Change printer configuration settings and share or unshare a printer.
Manage Documents	Cancel or suspend other users' print jobs.

You can use the Security tab in the printer's Properties dialog box to alter the groups and users assigned to each of these permissions. It's actually most useful to modify the Access Control settings, as shown in Figure 22.46.

Figure 22.46
Permissions assigned to a printer apply either to documents pending in the print's queue, the printer itself, or both.

It seems a little confusing at first because the three privileges apply independently to the printer and to documents sent to the printer. The CREATOR OWNER name, for documents, applies to the user who submitted a given print job, so the first two listed permissions shown in Figure 22.46 let Everyone print, and let each person manage (for example, delete) only his or her own documents. The remaining four entries give Administrators and Power Users members full control over the printer and all documents.

You probably don't have to change the default permission settings unless you want to limit use of the printer by outside users in a domain environment only. In this case, delete Everyone, and add specific groups with Print (this printer only) permission.

NOTIFYING USERS WHEN PRINTING IS COMPLETE

You can have Windows send a pop-up message to remote users when print jobs they send to your printer have completed. By default, this feature is turned off when you install Windows 2000.

To enable remote user notification, do the following:

1. Select Start, Settings, Printers.
2. Choose File, Server Properties.
3. Select the Advanced tab.
4. Check Notify When Remote Documents Are Printed.
5. If users on your network tend to use more than one computer at a time, check Notify Computer, Not User, When Remote Documents Are Printed. Checking this option sends the notification to the computer where the print job originated rather than to the user who submitted the print job. If your users tend to move around between computers quite frequently, this feature is probably undesirable.
6. Click OK.

With remote notification enabled, when a print job has completed, a dialog box pops up on the sender's desktop, as in Figure 22.47. No message is sent if the print job is canceled, however.

Figure 22.47
Remote Notification tells a user that a print job submitted over the network has completed.

TRACKING PRINTER USERS

If you want to track usage patterns of your printer, you can instruct Windows to record print job completion and maintenance alerts in the System Event Log, through settings on the Print Server Properties dialog box. Here's how:

1. Select Start, Settings, Printers.
2. Choose File, Server Properties.
3. Select the Advanced tab.

4. Check Log events to record the degree of login required:

Log Spooler Error Events records the most severe printer errors.

Log Spooler Warning Events records less severe errors.

Log Spooler Information Events records successful print job completion.

5. Click OK.

I generally disable Log Spooler Information Events to prevent the system log from recording print activity, which I don't care to keep track of.

If you do care, though, more detailed recording of printer use and management activity is available through Auditing. Auditing provides a way to record printer activity in the Windows Event Security Log.

The Windows Auditing feature records an event when a specified permission has been either granted or denied. The granting or denying of permission implies that someone completed, or tried to complete, the action that the permission controls.

This situation sounds a little more complex than it is. In practical terms, if you audit success and failure of the Print permission, you'll see who submitted print jobs and who tried and was denied. If you audit just failure of the Manage Documents permission, you'll see who tried to delete another user's document and was prohibited.

You can add permissions in the Auditing tab by selecting Add, then choosing a user or group of users to select for auditing, and then choosing permissions and outcomes to audit, as shown in Figure 22.48.

Figure 22.48
Adding an Audit entry to record when Printing permission has been granted or denied to anyone.

Finally, click OK to add the permission to the Audit list, and add more if desired.

PRINTER POOLING

In some offices, the printers are fired up only once a day, but others seem to crank out pages day and night. If your network involves heavy-duty printing, you might find that your printers are the bottleneck in getting your work done. You can get faster printers, and you can also add multiple printers.

If you have two printers shared separately, you'll have to choose one or the other for your printing, and you'll probably encounter bank-line syndrome: The other line always seems to move faster.

The way around this problem is to use printer pooling. You can set up one shared printer queue that sends its output to multiple printers. The documents line up in one list, and multiple printers take jobs from the front of the line, first-come, first served.

To set up pooled printers, follow these steps:

1. Buy identical printers; at least, they must be identical from the software point of view.
2. Set up and test one printer, and configure network sharing for it.
3. Install the extra printer(s) on the same computer as the first. If you use network-connected printers, you need to add the necessary additional network ports.
4. View the printer's properties, and select the Ports tab. Mark Enable Printer Pooling, and mark the ports for the additional printers.

That's all there is to it; Windows passes print jobs to as many printers as you select on the Ports pages.

SEPARATOR PAGES

Windows 2000 has a feature that lets you add a cover page to each print job sent to given printer. The cover page can be configured to show the name of the user who sent the print job, his or her computer name, and so on. On a network with dozens of users sharing a given printer, these cover pages can be very helpful in sorting out whose printouts are whose. On the other hand, using cover pages is wasteful of paper and isn't a good "green" practice unless the confusion around your printers is really significant.

Separator pages have another very important use: They can be used to switch "multiple personality" printers into one language mode or another. For example, some Hewlett-Packard printers accept input in both the PostScript and PCL page description languages. These printers normally detect which format is being used and adjust automatically. They don't always, however, so separator pages can be used to force the issue.

You can set up the pages like this: Create two Windows shared printer icons in the Printers folder, both pointing to the same physical printer on the same LPT port. Configure one with the PostScript driver, and the other with the standard PCL driver. Name the printers appropriately—for example, LaserJet-PS and LaserJet-PCL. Configure each printer with a separator page that forces the printer into the correct mode. This way, you can select the printer driver you want, and the printer will never mistake the language being used. This is really handy if UNIX or Macintosh users are sending output to your printers.

Windows ships with four predefined separator files:

pcl.sep	Forces a LaserJet printer into PCL mode and prints a separator page
sysprint.sep	Forces a LaserJet printer into PostScript mode and prints a separator page
pscript.sep	Forces a LaserJet printer into PostScript mode but doesn't print a separator page
sysprtj.sep	Contains a Japanese font version of sysprint.sep

Separator files are stored in your \winnt\system32 folder. You can use one of the predefined files, or you can create one of your own. To assign a separator page to a given printer, follow these steps:

1. Open the printer's Properties box, and select the Advanced tab.
2. Click the Separator Page button and enter the desired filename, or click Browse to find the file by hand.
3. Click OK.

The first line of a *.sep file contains only one character, which sets the escape character for the rest of the file. Subsequent lines are sent to the printer. Sequences starting with the escape character are interpreted as substitution commands; the sequence is replaced with other text before being sent to the printer. The command substitutions are shown in Table 22.2. In the table, I assume that a backslash (\) is the escape character.

TABLE 22.2   SEPARATOR PAGE SUBSTITUTIONS

Sequence	Is Replaced With
\N	Name of the user who submitted the print job.
\I	Print job number.
\D	Date the job was printed.
\T	Time the job was printed.
\Lxxxxxx	Text *xxxxxx* up to the next escape.
\Ffilename	Contents of file *filename*. This file is copied literally with no substitution. It can be used for a message of the day.
\Hxx	Hexadecimal value *xx*. Particularly useful is \H1B, which emits the ASCII <esc> character used in printer control commands.
\Wnn	Limits the width of the page to *nn* columns.

You can create or modify separator page files using the predefined files as examples. Table 22.2 can help you interpret these files.

Tip #266

> If you have a two-bin printer, you can put colored paper in the second bin and print the separator pages on it so they really stand out. To do so, add the appropriate printer control sequences to the .sep file. At the beginning of the file, reset the printer and switch to bin two. Print the separator page stuff. At the end of the file, switch back to bin one.

SHARING PRINTERS ON THE WEB VIA IPP

If you have installed Internet Information Services on Windows 2000, IPP printing is installed by default. Simply view the Web page `http://hostname/printers`.

The Web pages are generated by a set of nearly two dozen ASP script files that are installed in \winnt\Web\printers. (They make fascinating reading, if you want to learn serious ASP programming!)

Windows 2000 users can access the shared printer across the Internet by viewing the /printers page. Microsoft has made IPP printer drivers available for Windows 9x and Windows NT 4 as well as Windows 2000, so you can print to an IPP printer from computers running any of these operating systems. The add-on software is available at `http://www.windowsupdate.com`.

You can print to the Windows IPP service from any other operating systems that support IPP. You need to know the correct URL for the printer, which is `http://computername/printers/sharename/.printer`. For example, my shared printer \\bali\laserjet is accessible over the Internet as `http://bali.mycompany.com/printers/Laserjet/.printer`.

You don't have to remember this URL, though; you can view the printer's Web page and select Properties. The resulting page lists the IPP network name and the printer's other printing capabilities.

This URL can't be browsed as a Web page; it's meant to be used as the target of IPP software only.

MANAGING NETWORK USE OF YOUR COMPUTER

If you've shared folders on your LAN, you might want to know who's using them. You could need to know this information if, for example, someone were editing a file in your shared folder. If you tried to edit the same file, you'd be told by your word processor that the file was "in use by another." But by whom?

Computer Management can help you out. Right-click My Computer, select Manage, and open the Shared Folders system tool. It displays the shared folders that your computer offers and the number of users attached to them.

You can add new shared folders using the Shares tool with a right-click.

You can also view the current users (sessions) and the files they have in use with the Sessions and Open Files views. This will let you know whom to ask to close a file or, in an emergency, you can disconnect a user or close an open file with the Delete key. (This is a drastic measure and is sure to mess up the remote user, so use it only when absolutely necessary.)

MANAGING NETWORK RESOURCES USING THE COMMAND LINE

If you find yourself repeating certain network and file operations over and over, day after day, it makes sense to try to automate the processes. You might get so used to the graphical interface that you forget the command line, but it's still there, and you can perform drive mappings and printer selections with the command line almost as easily as from the GUI. Batch files, which were so familiar in the old DOS days, are still around and are a great way to perform repetitive tasks.

I use batch files to perform simple computer-to-computer backups of important files. Let's say I want to back up the folder c:\book on my computer to a shared folder of the same name on another computer named abalone. Here's what a batch file to do this might look like:

```
@echo off
net use q: /delete 1>nul 2>nul
net use q: \\abalone\book
xcopy c:/book q: /e /r /c /y
net use q: /delete
exit
```

Of course, I could bring up Explorer, locate my c:\book folder and the abalone book folder, drag the folder from one computer to the other, and repeat this process every time I want to make a copy of my files. But a shortcut to the preceding batch file on my desktop will do the same job with a double-click, and I can add the batch file as a scheduled task to run automatically every night. Now which seems more convenient—that nifty GUI or the humble command-line batch file? Knowing the net utilities gives you an extra set of tools to work with, and their ancient origins shouldn't make them seem less worthy!

The net command comes to us virtually unchanged since the original PC network software developed by Microsoft and IBM back in the early 1980s. There are so many variations of the net command that I think of them as separate commands: net view, net use, net *whatever*. Each net command contains a word that selects a subcommand or operation type.

You can find a complete and detailed description of each command in Appendix A, "Command-Line Reference," which is on the CD-ROM that accompanies this book. You can also get online help by typing net /? or net *command* /?, where *command* is one of the net subcommands.

MAPPING DRIVES WITH net use

The net use command is the most useful of the command-line network functions. net use makes and disconnects drive mappings and establishes printer redirection for command-line programs. The basic command is as follows:

```
net use drive sharename
```

The following example

```
net use q: \\abalone\book
```

maps drive letter q to the shared folder \\abalone\book. You can't replace the shared folder attached to an already mapped drive, so it's best to place commands in the batch file to delete any previous mapping before trying to make a new one:

```
net use q: /delete
net use q: \\abalone\book
```

The /delete command prints an error message if there was no previous message. An elegant solution is to redirect the output of the first net command to NUL, which discards any output. I usually redirect both standard output and standard error output with

```
net use q: /delete 1>nul 2>nul
```

to ensure that this command will do its work silently.

You can add the /persistent:yes option to a net use command to make the drive mapping permanent, matching the function of the Reconnect at Login check box in the graphical drive mapping tool.

You can also map a drive to a subfolder of a shared folder—mimicking the map root function familiar to Novell NetWare veterans. Subfolder mapping lets you run legacy DOS applications that require that certain files or directories be placed in the root directory of a hard disk. You can fool them into running with data on a shared network folder. I like to do this because it lets me store data in a centralized place where it will get backed up regularly.

For example, suppose the hypothetical program runit needs to see its data files in the current root directory, and runs from directory \startdir. I want all the files to reside in a shared network folder, in a subdirectory oldprog of a shared folder named \\server\officedata. This batch file does the trick:

```
@echo off
net use e: /delete 1>nul 2>nul
net use e: \\server\officedata\oldprog
e:
cd \startdir
runit
c:
net use e: /delete
exit
```

Creating a shortcut to this batch file in Windows 2000 lets me run the old program with a double-click.

net use also maps network printers to the legacy DOS printer devices LPT1, LPT2, and LPT3. The capture printer setting found in Windows 9x is not available, and the only way to redirect DOS program output to a network printer is through net use.

The following command directs DOS application LPT1 printer output to the network printer:

```
net use lpt1: \\server\printername
```

The following command cancels it:

```
net use lpt1: /delete
```

THE DISTRIBUTED FILE SYSTEM

One of the new features in Windows 2000 Server is the Distributed File System. Windows 2000 Server lets a domain manager take shared folders from other computers and graft them onto the server's own file system. I think a picture might explain this best. Figure 22.49 shows how a server has had shared folders grafted onto C:\Documents\public. The server now appears to have a folder at C:\Documents\public\brochures even though that directory resides in a shared folder on another computer. The Distributed File System detects that access to anything in folder C:\Documents\public\brochures really refers to \\sales\brochures.

This becomes really interesting if this administrator shares the C:\documents folder, say, as \\server\documents. Now, anyone on the network can access \\server\documents\public\brochures. The server will invisibly have a remote user retrieve the file from the grafted folders without the user even knowing it.

Figure 22.49
The Distributed File System lets a Windows 2000 Server administrator graft shared folders from elsewhere in the network into the Server's own file system, building one virtual file system from several computers.

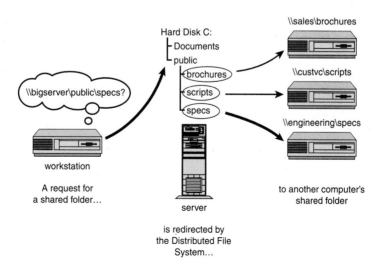

Why is this capability useful? Well, it lets a network administrator build a server that is constructed of interchangeable parts. Bali could be the central server of a huge network, sharing millions of files—with none of them actually stored on Bali! Users would be able to come to one place to find resources, but the workload of serving all these files would be distributed among all the grafted file servers. And if one hard disk failed, it wouldn't take down the whole network. The administrator could simply graft in a replacement file server, instantly restoring service.

Finally, consider this: If every computer on your LAN shared its entire hard drive, and the network administrator grafted every one of these shares into a master folder, you would have a virtual file system containing every single file from every computer in your LAN. Think what the Find Files utility could do with that!

TROUBLESHOOTING

CAN'T FIND ANY PRINTERS IN ACTIVE DIRECTORY

When I use Find Printers, no printers appear in the results list.

You might have selected criteria that no printers match, or you might be specifying the criteria too closely and missing some near but inexact matches. Remove a criterion or two and repeat the search. If your search reveals more printers than you want to look at, try narrowing the search more slowly. Instead of specifying Postscript Level 2 as a Printer Language, for example, try searching for Post. You might be missing a printer that was entered PostScript Lvl 2.

NO CONNECT OPTION FOR WEB PRINTING

I can view a Windows 2000 computer's/printer's Web page and select a printer, but Connect is not shown as an option.

You need to have IPP software installed on the computer that is viewing the Web page, and you must be using Internet Explorer as your Web browser. Windows 95, 98, and NT 4 can get IPP software from http://www.windowsupdate.com. Download the Internet Printing update. Then, when you view the Web page with IE, you can connect and use the printer.

WEB FOLDER APPEARS TO BE EMPTY

When I view a Web folder known to contain files, it appears to be empty. What's wrong?

The Web server that is sharing the folder does not have Directory Listing enabled on the shared folder. The manager of this Web server (who could be you) needs to set this property in the Web Sharing Properties dialog box for the folder.

DIRECTORY LISTING APPEARS INSTEAD OF WEB FOLDER

When I view a Web folder, I see a columnar text listing of filenames, sizes, and dates instead of the expected folder view with icons.

You did not view the folder using the Open dialog box with Open as Web Folder checked, or the Web site you visited does not have WebDAV, FrontPage 2000, or Office 2000 server extensions installed.

WEB SHARING IS NOT A CHOICE

When I view a folder or hard drive's properties, Web Sharing is not available as a choice.

Internet Information Services must be installed, as well as the FrontPage Server Extensions. Check to see that these services are properly installed, as explained in Chapter 18. If the Web Sharing tab is still not available, uninstall the Server Extensions and reinstall them.

FILE IS IN USE BY ANOTHER

When I attempt to edit a file in a folder I've shared on the network, I receive an error message indicating that the file is in use by another user.

You can find out which remote user has the file open by using the Shared Folder tool in Computer Management, as described earlier in this chapter under "Managing Network Use of Your Computer."

You can wait for the remote user to finish using your file, or you can ask that person to quit. Only in a dire emergency should you use the Shared Folder tool to disconnect the remote user or close the file. The only reasons I can think of to do this would be that the remote user's computer has crashed but your computer thinks the connection is still established or that the remote user is an intruder.

TIPS FROM THE WINDOWS PROS: USING COMMAND-LINE UTILITIES

Setting up a new network can be a grueling task. If you've ever set up a dozen computers in a day, you know what I mean. Think how long it took you to set up Windows, install applications, set up printers and network information, and get the desktop just so…then multiply that work by 10 or 20. Then repeat the process any time a new computer is installed or repaired and reformatted.

Network managers do anything they can to minimize the amount of work they need to do to set up and maintain computers. Windows 2000 Server offers a remote installation service that can set up a completely outfitted Windows 2000 workstation in a virgin computer, over the LAN, without laying a finger on it. This is a blessing for them, but what about those of us with workgroup LANs?

The rest of us rely on whatever handy labor-saving tricks we can find to minimize the amount of work needed. Batch files can go a long way to help ease the pain of installing, and they also have two other benefits: They let you make more consistent installations, and they serve as a sort of documentation of whatever configuration they're performing.

My first tip to a workgroup manager is to learn the Windows 2000 command-line utilities; you can set up batch files to make some consistent settings on new computers. Put the batch files in a shared network folder, and you have an installation and configuration toolkit. If a user accidentally disconnects a mapped network drive, that person can visit your folder of handy icons, click MAPDRIVES, and everything can be reset. This can be done with `net use` commands in a batch file.

You can also install printers with the command line. The entire functionality of the Install Printer Wizard is available at the command line; you can pop up graphical utilities like the queue manager, and you even can perform installations and configure printers in a batch file.

Type the following at the command prompt for a full listing of the printer configuration utility's commands:

```
rundll32 printui.dll,PrintUIEntry /?
```

Scroll to the bottom of the list for an eye-popping list of examples. (I warn you, it's ugly. Some experimentation is required to get some of the commands to work, even with the examples given here.)

One really handy use of this command is to install a connection to a network shared printer. This example sets up the local computer to use the shared printer \\bali\laserjet:

```
rundll32 printui.dll,PrintUIEntry /n "\\bali\laserjet" /in
rundll32 printui.dll,PrintUIEntry /n "\\bali\laserjet" /y
```

The first command installs the printer, and the second makes it the default printer.

If you put commands like these in a batch file (using your network's printer names, of course) and put the batch file in a shared network folder, you can add the printers to any computer just by double-clicking the batch file icon. This capability can be a real time-saver when you're configuring many workstations. You could also put these commands in a common login script batch file on your network so that they are executed when your users log in.

Even better, you can push the printers into your network's computers. The /c*name* option lets you install printers on a remote network computer by name. So if I made a batch file named pushpr.bat with these contents:

```
rundll32 printui.dll,PrintUIEntry /n "\\bali\laserjet" /in /c\\%1
rundll32 printui.dll,PrintUIEntry /n "\\bali\laserjet" /y /c\\%1
```

I could install the LaserJet printer on all my network's computers by issuing commands like these:

```
pushpr ambon
pushpr java
pushpr sumatra
```

That *really* can save a bunch of walking around!

CHAPTER 23

WINDOWS UNPLUGGED: REMOTE AND MOBILE NETWORKING

In this chapter

Going Unplugged

Imagine sitting under a tree in the park, sipping an iced tea, reading Web pages, and editing a document from a computer at your office server. You can do this because you've gone "unplugged." You're working with network resources on your own terms, as neatly as if you were at your office, chained to your desk. Working this way is not a farfetched idea anymore!

Local area networks (LANs) were once considered esoteric and difficult to use, but now I hardly stop to think where my files and applications are stored. Who cares whether the file is really in my computer or if it's in another building? To me as a user, they're just in a folder on the desktop. The distinction between my computer and others on the LAN is almost gone.

Windows 2000 extends that same seamlessness to the remote or mobile computer user. Five mechanisms make this seamlessness possible:

- Dial-Up Networking lets you connect by modem to a remote network and use it as if you were directly connected. File sharing, Active Directory, and network printing are available just as if you were wired right to the LAN.

- Roaming profiles let you have access to your "global" My Documents folder and desktop, even from your mobile computer. (Roaming profiles are available only if you're connecting to a Windows 2000 domain network, though.)

- Offline Folders let you view and use shared network folders and files you've designated as important, even when you're not connected or dialed up. Windows gives you this capability by keeping copies of network files stashed away on your own hard drive and invisibly keeping them up-to-date. From your point of view, the network folder is just always there and available.

- Offline Web pages let you mark Web pages and sites for perusal when you're disconnected from the Net.

- Virtual Private Networking lets you exploit any available wide area network connection, including the Internet, to get from your computer to your own LAN, with a high degree of security.

With a little bit of preparation, you'll find that you can take Windows 2000 anywhere and, for the most part, use the applications and data you want without thinking too much about where you are or how you're connected.

Going unplugged is not perfectly seamless, but it's very close, and you'll find you take to it very quickly. You learned about Offline Web pages in Chapter 12, "World Wide Web." Now it's time to tackle the network features. Get that iced tea ready!

Dial-Up Networking

Windows 2000 can connect to a remote Windows network via modem, and after it is connected, the remote computer is a full member of the LAN. All file sharing, printing, and directory services are available just as if you were directly connected, including any Novell,

OS/2, and UNIX file and print services provided on the network. Just dial up, open shared folders, transfer files and email as if you were there, and disconnect when you're finished.

The receiving end of Dial-Up Networking can be handled by the Remote Access Services (RAS) in Windows 2000 Server or by a third-party remote connection hardware device.

Windows 2000 Professional comes with a stripped-down version of RAS, so you can also set up your own Windows 2000 Pro computer to receive a single incoming modem connection. You can do so, for example, to get access to your office computer and LAN from home, provided this access is permitted by your company.

PART
IV
CH
23

I'll discuss incoming calls later in the chapter. First, though, let me tell you how to connect to a remote Windows network.

SETTING UP FOR DIAL-UP NETWORKING

To create a dial-up connection to a remote network or computer, you need an installed modem. You learned how to install modems in Chapter 11, "Internet and TCP/IP Connection Options," so start there to install and configure your modem.

You also must get or confirm the information shown in Table 23.1 with the remote network's or computer's manager.

TABLE 23.1   INFORMATION NEEDED FOR A RAS CONNECTION

Information	Reason
Telephone number	You must know the receiving modem's telephone number, including area code.
Modem compatibility	You must confirm that your modem is compatible with the modems used by the remote network; check which modem protocols are supported (V.90, V.32, and so on).
Protocols in use	The remote network can use TCP/IP, IPX/SPX, NetBEUI, or any combination of these protocols.
TCP/IP configuration	You must know whether the Remote Access Server assigns TCP/IP information automatically (dynamically) via DHCP. Usually, the answer is yes. If not (if your network uses fixed or static IP address information), you must ask what IP address, subnet mask, DNS servers, and domain name to use. Your network might also require you to set WINS server addresses.
Mail servers	You might need to obtain the IP addresses or names of SMTP, POP, Exchange, Lotus Notes, or Microsoft Mail servers if you want to use these applications while connected to the remote network.
User ID and password	You must supply a username and password to the remote dial-up server. If you're using a Windows 2000 or NT RAS server, they are the same as the Windows username and password you use on that remote network. If you're calling a third-party connection server, you might have a separate user ID and password used just for the connection.

Armed with this information, you're ready to create a dial-up connection to the remote network. To do so, just follow these steps:

1. Choose Settings, Network and Dial-Up Connections, and then open the Make New Connection icon.

2. Select Dial-Up to Private Network (see Figure 23.1) and then click Next.

Figure 23.1
Choose Dial-Up to Private Network in New Connection selections.

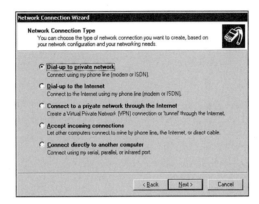

3. Enter the telephone number of the remote dial-in server. You can enter the number directly, including any prefixes or area codes, or you can select Use Dialing Rules and enter the location, regional or area code, and telephone number separately, as shown in Figure 23.2. (This option lets Windows use the correct prefix and area code as it thinks necessary, based on your current location.) Select Next.

Figure 23.2
You can enter the remote access telephone number here. Choose Use Dialing Rules to let Windows determine when to apply prefixes and area codes when it dials.

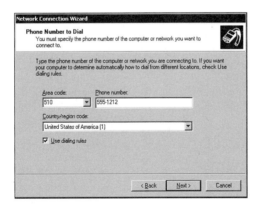

4. Windows then asks whether this connection's name and telephone number should appear in Network and Dial-Up Connections for all users of this computer or just for you.

Select All Users if other users on this computer want to connect to the same remote network or if you want to use this dial-up connection to connect to a remote domain using your roaming profile on that domain.

Note

Don't worry; your password is not shared with other users if you share the connection.

5. Choose a name for the connection (see Figure 23.3). This name will appear as the name of the connection icon in Network and Dial-Up Connections. This dialog contains an additional check box to have Windows put a shortcut to this connection on your desktop.

Note

You can delete a connection shortcut later if you don't want it and can drag the connection icon from Network and Dial-Up Connections to your desktop later if you do.

Figure 23.3
In this dialog, you can make up a name for the connection. Usually, the name of your company or the name of the remote computer is a good choice.

6. Choose Finish. Windows immediately wants to open the connection, but you must set the connection properties first, so select Cancel. Right-click the new connection icon, and select Properties.

The Dial-Up Connection's properties page has five tabs and a heap o' parameters. Most of the time, the default settings will work correctly, but you might need to change some of them. Let me walk you through the most important parameters.

→ For detailed instructions on establishing locations and dialing rules, **see** "Phone and Modem Options," **p. 1055**.

GENERAL

On the General tab of the Properties dialog (see Figure 23.4), you can set your choice of modems if you have more than one installed. You also can set telephone numbers and dialing rules.

Figure 23.4
General Properties include dialing and modem settings.

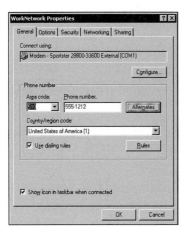

The significant parameters are as follows:

- Connect Using—If you have more than one modem installed, choose which modem to use for this connection. The Configure button lets you set the maximum data rate to use between the computer and the modem, and if your modem permits a choice of protocols (for example, V.90 and K56Flex), you should set the fastest protocol supported by the remote server's modems.

- Area Code, Phone Number, and Region—If the remote server has more than one phone number (or more than one hunt group), you can specify alternative telephone numbers. It's a neat feature if your company has several access points or provides emergency-use-only toll-free numbers.

- Show Icon in Taskbar—This option lets you keep a small connection monitor icon in your task tray when you're connected to the remote network. Opening it lets you quickly disconnect the remote connection, so it's best to leave Show Icon checked.

OPTIONS

The Options tab of the Properties dialog (see Figure 23.5) includes dialing options, choices for being prompted for phone number and passwords, and redialing settings.

The important options are as follows:

- Prompt for Name and Password—If this box is checked, Windows always prompts for your remote connection user ID and password. If it is unchecked, after the first successful connection, Windows will no longer prompt but will use the remembered password. If you are worried that someone might dial the connection by gaining unauthorized access to your computer, leave this box checked; otherwise, you can uncheck it to skip the password step when connecting.

- Include Windows Logon Domain—Check this box if you are calling a Windows 2000 domain network but your computer is not set up as a member of the same domain.

When this box is checked, the dialing dialog box has a space for you to enter the remote domain's name.

Figure 23.5
The Options tab includes dialing and prompting options.

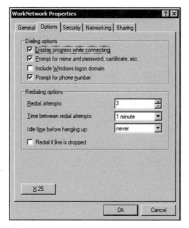

- Prompt for Phone Number—If this box is checked, Windows will display the phone number it's about to dial. Leave it checked if you don't trust Windows to use the correct area code, prefixes, and so on. It's best to leave it checked until you're convinced.

- Redialing Options—If the remote server frequently gives you a busy signal, increase the number of attempts from 3 to, say, 20, and lower the delay from 1 minute to 15 seconds to get quicker redialing action.

- Idle Time Before Hanging Up—If you tend to wander off for hours with your modem still online, you can set this option to a reasonable time, and Windows will automatically disconnect you if no network traffic occurs for the specified time.

- Redial If Line Is Dropped—This option makes Windows redial immediately if your modem connection fails. It's good if you have lousy phone connections but bad if the remote computer disconnects you because its "idle time" runs out before yours does.

SECURITY

On the Security tab, you can select which encryption methods are required or permitted when you're logging on to the remote connection server, as shown in Figure 23.6.

- Security Options—If you are connecting to a Windows 2000 or Windows NT Remote Access Server, select Typical and Require Secured Password. If the Windows domain name, username, and password you'll use for the remote network are the same as those you use to sign in to your own computer, check Automatically Use My Windows Logon.

- Advanced (Custom Settings)—Select Advanced if you are calling a Shiva Remote Access Server. Click the Settings button, and then select Shiva Password Authentication Protocol (SPAP).

Figure 23.6
Dial-up connection
security options.

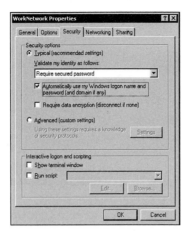

> **Note**
>
> *Shiva* is shorthand for a user account/password verification system manufactured by Shiva Corporation (now owned by Intel). Shiva developed some of the first large-scale dial-up and remote access systems. Large corporations and ISPs must manage huge user account databases, and Shiva's approach of using a single "authentication server" on a network to perform password checks for potentially hundreds of remote access and dial-up devices made account management easy. Shiva's technology became so popular that most remote access systems have an option to defer user validation to a Shiva server. Note that this system only validates a caller's right to connect to the modem; it doesn't grant rights to resources (such as file servers) on the network.

NETWORKING

The Networking tab of the Properties dialog (see Figure 23.7) defines which network protocols and network services are connected through the dial-up connection.

Figure 23.7
On the Networking
tab, you can choose
which network proto-
cols and services are
enabled for the dial-
up connection. Check
everything, and set
the TCP/IP protocol's
properties if neces-
sary.

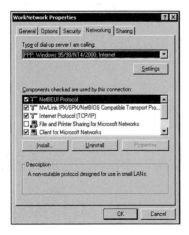

All protocols and services should be checked. By default, Windows does not check File and Printer Sharing, so remote network users cannot use your computer's shared folders and printers. If you want to let the remote network's users see them, check File and Printer Sharing.

Normally, a Remote Access Server automatically assigns your connection the proper IP address, DNS addresses, and other TCP/IP settings through DHCP, so you don't need to alter the Internet Protocol properties.

In the very unlikely event that the network administrator tells you that you must set TCP/IP parameters yourself, select Internet Protocol from the Components list, and click Properties. Enter the supplied IP address and DNS addresses there.

SHARING

Internet connection sharing is used only when using this dial-up connection to provide Internet connectivity to the rest of your LAN, as you'll learn in Chapter 24, "Connecting Your LAN to the Internet." You could use a remote network connection to provide Internet service to your LAN, but generally you won't use connection sharing to join your LAN to another LAN.

After you've finished making any changes to the connection's options on the Sharing tab, select OK. The connection icon is then installed in Network and Dial-Up Connections for use anytime.

MANAGING DIAL-UP CONNECTIONS FROM MULTIPLE LOCATIONS

As you've seen already, Windows lets you enter your current telephone area code and dialing prefix requirements so that it can make modem calls using the customs appropriate for your local phone system. This capability is great if you use a portable computer, as you might wander from office to office and region to region, and these dialing rules might change. For example, at home, you might be in area code 415. At the office, you might be in area code 707 and have to dial 9 to get an outside telephone line. When you're visiting Indianapolis, you're in area code 317 and might need to use a telephone company calling card when making long-distance calls.

Windows offers great support for these variations by letting you define "locations," with a separate local area code and dialing rules. When you use one of your Network and Dial-Up Connections icons, as long as you've told Windows your current location, it can automatically apply the correct set of rules when making a dial-up connection.

→ For detailed instructions on establishing locations and dialing rules, **see** "Phone and Modem Options," **p. 1055**.

However, if you use an ISP with access points in various cities, or your company has different access numbers in various regions, you'll find that this Locations system does not let you associate a different dial-up number with each location. It would be great if it did, but no such luck. (Hey, let's all write to Microsoft and ask for this feature to be added to the next release of Windows 2000.)

If you want to use "local" dial-up numbers for the various locations you visit with your computer, you must set up a separate Network and Dial-Up Connections icon for each access number and use the appropriate icon when making a connection at each location.

Tip #267	Set up and test the first access number you need. Then, when you need to add a new access number, right-click the first one, select Create Copy, rename it, and change its telephone number. I name my icons based on the location of the local number: My ISP-Berkeley, My ISP-Seattle, and so on.
	When you travel and want to make a dial-up connection, select the appropriate dial-up icon, and set your location before you click Dial.

Tip #268	If you travel, you'll find that having your Internet Options set to dial a particular connection automatically is not a great idea. It would dial the chosen connection no matter where you were (and remember, if there's a 50-50 chance of things going wrong, 9 times out of 10 they will). So, if you travel with your computer, you might want to go to the Internet Options Control Panel, select the Connections tab, and choose Never Dial a Connection. This way, you won't be blind-sided by an inadvertent call to Indiana while you're in India.

MAKING A DIAL-UP CONNECTION

Making a remote network dial-up connection is no more difficult than connecting to the Internet. If you're a mobile user who moves between area codes, check your current location first, and then dial.

CHECK YOUR CURRENT LOCATION

Windows can apply automatic dialing rules to select the proper area code, prefix, and dialing codes. If you've changed area codes or phone systems since the last time you made a modem connection, check your location setting by following these steps before dialing into the network:

1. Open the Control Panel, and select Phone and Modem Options.
2. Check your current location in the list of configured dialing locations, as shown in Figure 23.8.
3. Click OK to close the dialog.

Windows should now use the correct area code and dialing prefixes.

CHOOSE A PROFILE OPTION

Before dialing into a remote Windows 2000 Server network that offers roaming user profiles, you must make a quick decision whether to connect using your local profile or use your remote "roaming" profile. Your network manager will tell you if the network provides roaming profiles. You have two options for making the connection:

- If you connect while you're already logged on to your computer, you'll have access to the files, printers, and all other network resources on the remote network, but the My Documents folder and desktop will remain as they were before you made the connection. You'll be "here."

- If you log off from Windows and then log on again using the Log On Using Dial-Up Connection option, you'll be connected with your user profile on the remote network. Your My Documents folder, home directory, desktop layout, and other preferences will be copied to your mobile computer, and you'll be "there."

Figure 23.8
You can select your current location before dialing.

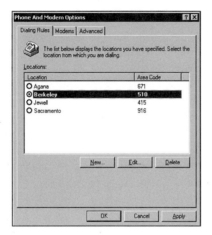

If you don't have a roaming profile, or don't need to use it, use the first method.

If you have an account with a roaming profile on the remote network, and you want to have access to the My Documents folder and settings you use on that network, use the second method.

CONNECT TO A REMOTE NETWORK WITHOUT A ROAMING PROFILE

To connect to a remote network using the profile you're already using in your own computer, make the connection directly, without logging out. Just follow these steps:

1. Open the connection from Network and Dial-Up Connections, or open a shortcut to the connection.

2. Enter your login name, password, and domain, if the remote is different from your computer's, as shown in Figure 23.9. You can also select Properties to adjust the connection's telephone number or dialing properties. (The Dialing From choice appears only if you have defined more than one dialing location and checked Use Dialing Rules.)

Tip #269

Life will be much easier for you if your username and password on your computer are the same as on the remote network. Windows won't have to prompt you for a name and password every time you try to access a remote shared resource.

Figure 23.9
In the Connect dialog, you can enter your username and password for the remote domain. If you're logged in, you can also tell Windows to remember your password and change the dialing properties.

3. Select Dial. Windows shows you the progress of your connection, as you can see in Figure 23.10. The stages are dialing, verifying username and password, and registering your computer on the network.

Figure 23.10
The dialing progress indicator.

If the connection fails, unless you dialed the wrong number, you'll most likely get a reasonable explanation: The password or account name was invalid, the remote system is not accepting calls, and so on. If you entered an incorrect username or password, you are given two more chances to re-enter the information before the other end hangs up on you.

If the connection completes successfully, a new connection icon appears in your taskbar, indicating the established connection speed, as in Figure 23.11.

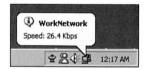

Figure 23.11

You can now use the remote network's resources, as I'll discuss next.

CONNECT TO A REMOTE NETWORK WITH A ROAMING PROFILE

To use the remote network under your user profile on that network, you must log in like this using the remote connection:

1. Log off Windows if you are currently logged on. Choose Start, Shut Down, and select Log off.

Tip #270	If you usually log off rather than shut down your computer, you can skip this two-step process. Just add Log Off directly to the Start menu. Choose Start, Settings, Taskbar & Start Menu, and then select the Advanced tab. Check Display Logoff in the Start Menu Settings list.

2. Press Ctrl+Alt+Del to display the logon dialog. Next, choose the Options button. Then check Log On Using Dial-Up Connection, and select OK.

3. Choose a network connection by selecting the name of the remote connection from the drop-down list, and select Dial.

 If the connection you need to use isn't shown in the list of connection choices, see "Can't Choose Dial-Up Connection at Login" in the "Troubleshooting" section at the end of this chapter.

4. When the Connect dialog appears, enter your username, password, and logon domain for the remote network, as previously shown in Figure 23.9. (You won't have the option to save your password or change the connection properties because you're not logged in.) Select Dial.

Windows then dials the remote network connection and logs in. After your profile settings have been copied, you're online and ready to use the network.

| Note | By default, if the connection fails because the telephone number was wrong, and you can't change it while logging in, you must log in locally, go to the connections Properties page, and either fix the telephone number or check Prompt for Phone Number. You won't have access to change the connection's properties until you're logged in.

The administrator can tell Windows in advance to let anyone add or modify connections without being logged in. In Network and Dial-Up Connections, open the Advanced menu, select Dial-up Preferences, and check Allow Creating and Modifying Connections Before Logon on the Connections tab.

Enabling this option is a security risk, however, and I don't suggest enabling it unless you find yourself frustrated more than twice trying to log on using an incorrect dial-up setting. |
|---|---|

CALLBACKS

For security purposes, some networks don't permit you to just call in; they want to call you, so you not only need the right login name and password, but you also must be in the right spot to gain access to the network. This type of access also generates an audit trail through phone company records.

When this type of security is in force, your network manager will contact you to arrange the predetermined telephone number to use to call you. You cannot access the network from any other location unless you arrange for call forwarding from the original number.

Note	Callbacks to a basic-rate (two-channel) ISDN modem line don't work reliably. If you use an ISDN modem and a remote network requiring callbacks, you should discuss this use with the network manager.

Callbacks can also be used to make the remote host pay for a long phone call. Some businesses use callbacks so that employees can dial in from the field at the company's expense.

When callbacks have been mandated, when you dial, as soon as the remote network has accepted your user information, it hangs up. Windows then informs you that it is waiting for the return call. Within 30 seconds, the remote server will dial the telephone number associated with your login name. If you're there, your modem will be waiting to answer. (If the phone line is also connected to a telephone, you had better tell the people around you not to answer the incoming call!)

If callbacks are optional, you can tell Windows how you want to exercise the option. In Network and Dial-Up Connections, select the Advanced menu, choose Dial-Up Preferences, and select the Callback tab (see Figure 23.12). You can indicate that, after you're connected, you will be given the option of entering a callback number or not. If you choose to be called, the remote server will disconnect and call you back. Windows sets your modem to answer the next incoming call.

Figure 23.12
Callback preferences let you choose whether you want to be called back by the dial-up server, when it's an option.

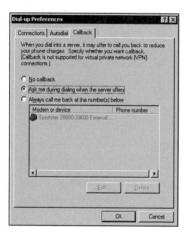

Either way, when your modem picks up the incoming call, the authentication procedure will repeat, and finally you'll be online.

Using Remote Network Resources

When you're connected, you can use network resources exactly as if you were on the network. My Network Places, shared folders, and network printers all function as if you were directly connected.

The following are some tips for effective remote networking by modem:

- Don't try to run application software that is installed on the remote network itself. Starting it could take hours!

■ If you get disconnected while using a remote network, it's a bummer to have to stop what you're doing and reconnect. You can tell Windows to automatically redial Internet and network connections if you're disconnected while you're working. In Network and Dial-Up Connections, from the Advanced menu, choose Dial-up Preferences, and select the Autodial tab (see Figure 23.13). Check any locations you work from where you would like Windows to automatically reconnect you.

Figure 23.13
Autodial properties let you specify that you would like Windows to automatically redial a dropped connection.

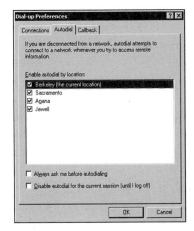

■ You can use My Network Places to record frequently visited remote network folders. You can also place shortcuts to network folders on your desktop or in other folders.

■ If you plan on working with a remote file several times, and you're not concerned that someone else might modify it while you're working, drag a copy to your desktop. Work on it on your computer, and then drag it back when you're finished. That way, you can work with the local copy.

■ Even better than that, mark the files and folders you need as Offline Folders, and let Windows manage the copies for you. I'll describe Offline Folders later in this chapter.

■ If the remote LAN has Internet access, you can browse the Internet while you're connected to the LAN. You don't need to disconnect and switch to your ISP. You might need to make a change in your personal email program, though, as I'll note later.

■ Remember that shortcuts are not the real thing, so you can make and discard them at will. I like the convenience of having shortcuts on my desktop but don't like clutter, so I make and trash shortcuts all the time.

■ I use several different remote networks belonging to my clients. I have a folder for each, and in them I put shortcuts to the appropriate connection and to frequently used folders on those networks. All these folders are in a folder named Client Networks on my desktop. I can choose one and be working within seconds. You can extend this idea to your business: Make folders for specific projects, customers, or clients.

EMAIL AND NETWORK CONNECTIONS

When you're connected to remote LANs as well as an ISP, you might need to be careful with the email programs you use. Most email programs don't make it easy for you to associate different mail servers with different connections.

Although most email servers allow you to retrieve your mail from anywhere on the Internet, most are also very picky about whom they let send email. Generally, to use an SMTP server to send mail out, you must be using a computer whose IP address is known by the server to belong to its network.

For example, if your mail program is set up to send outgoing mail through smtp.myisp.net, you can send mail when you're dialed in to one of My ISP's modem banks. However, if you're connecting through your office, your ISP address will be seen as foreign, and the mail server will not accept email from you. This kind of lockout is done to prevent spam senders from abusing their email servers. You can still pick up email; you just can't send it.

When you configure your chosen email program, see whether you can configure separate "identities" or accounts to use when connected to your ISP and when you're connected to a remote LAN. When you're connected to the LAN, even if you want to pick up mail from an outside POP email server, you must use an outgoing SMTP server that belongs to the LAN you're using.

MONITORING AND ENDING A DIAL-UP CONNECTION

While you're connected, note that the taskbar connection icon flashes to indicate incoming and outgoing data activity. It's a true Windows tool, which means you can have it do pretty much the same thing in about five different ways.

Note

If the connection icon is missing, you should enable it; otherwise, you won't know whether you've been disconnected. To enable it, open Network and Dial-Up Connections. Right-click the connection you're using, select Properties, and check Show Icon in Taskbar When Connected.

- If you hover your mouse cursor over the connection icon, a ToolTip box appears, listing the connection name, speed, and number of bytes transmitted and received.
- If you double-click it, the connection status dialog box appears, as shown in Figure 23.14. From the status dialog, you can get to the connection properties or disconnect.
- If you right-click it, you can select Disconnect, Status, or Open Network and Dial-Up Connections. This is the way to go.

Truthfully, all I ever do with the taskbar icon is make sure it blinks while I'm working and right-click Disconnect when I'm finished.

When you disconnect a remote network connection, the taskbar icon disappears. If you logged in using a remote network profile, you remain logged in using the local copy of this profile until you log out.

Figure 23.14
The connection status dialog displays current connection statistics and lets you disconnect or change connection properties. Right-clicking the connection icon in the taskbar is a quicker way to disconnect.

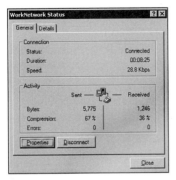

ENABLING DIAL-IN ACCESS TO YOUR COMPUTER

Windows 2000 Professional has a stripped-down Remote Access Server built in, and you can take advantage of it to get access to your work computer from home or from the field, or vice versa. You can also enable remote access temporarily so that a system administrator can maintain your computer.

Caution

RAS is not too difficult to set up, but beware: Permitting remote access opens up security risks. Before you enable dial-in access at work, be sure that your company permits it. In some companies, you could be fired for violating the security policies.

To enable dial-in access, you must be logged on as administrator. Then follow these steps:

1. In Network and Dial-Up Connections, open the Make New Connection icon to start the Network Connection Wizard. Click Next.
2. Choose Accept Incoming Connections, and click Next.
3. Check the modem to be used for incoming connections, as shown in Figure 23.15.

Tip #271

Despite what the wizard dialog box seems to say, you can choose at most one modem. You *can* choose one of each different type of connection: modem and direct parallel port.

4. You then are asked whether you want to additionally permit Virtual Private Network connections to your computer (see Figure 23.16). I'll discuss Virtual Private Networking later in this chapter. You can read ahead to decide whether you want it or check Do Not Allow Virtual Private Connections now. You can always repeat this process to enable it later. It's best to not allow virtual private connections now if you're not sure.

Figure 23.15
In this dialog, you can select the modem to use for incoming dial-up connections.

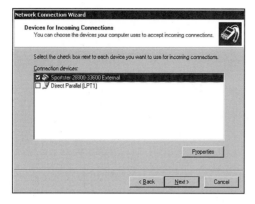

Figure 23.16
Choose Do Not Allow Virtual Private Connections if you're not yet sure whether you want them.

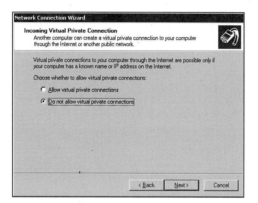

5. Windows then displays a list of your computer's or domain's users. Select the ones who will be permitted to access your computer remotely, as shown in Figure 23.17. This step is very important: Check only the names of those users whom you really want and need to give access. The fewer accounts you enable, the less like that someone might accidentally break into your computer.

Figure 23.17
Here, you can choose users who will be granted the right to remote access of your computer. Check only the names of those users really needing access, and don't check Guest.

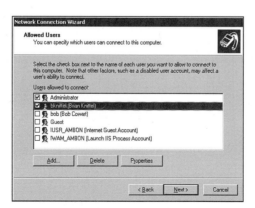

Caution

Under no circumstances should you enable Guest, IUSR_*xxx*, or IWAM_*xxx* (where *xxx* is the name of your computer—for example, IUSR_AMBON) for remote access. The IUSR and IWAM accounts are used exclusively by Internet Information Server for access by Web site visitors, and Guest is used for general network access. There's no way you would ever want to give unprotected access to your network via modem or VPN!

Check only the names of users who need access and who have good (long, complex) passwords.

6. You can enable or enforce callbacks for individual users if you like. Select the username, and click Properties. Then select the Callback tab, as shown in Figure 23.18. You can make callbacks optional or mandatory. You must enter the number for a mandatory callback. If you do, add any dialing prefixes and area code necessary to make the call; Windows doesn't use dialing rules when making callbacks. In the example, I use 9 to get an outside line, a comma to make the modem pause a moment, and then dial the designated number.

Figure 23.18
You can enable callbacks for a user account in this dialog.

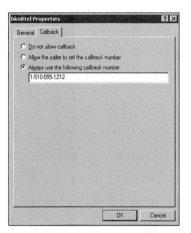

7. Windows displays a list of network protocols and services that will be made available to the dial-up connection, as shown in Figure 23.19. Generally, you can leave all protocols and services checked. Disable one or more only to block access to the remote users.

View the properties page for each checked protocol to specify whether callers have access only to your computer or have access to the LAN via your computer. Unless you have a reason to ban a remote caller (usually you) from reaching the rest of your LAN, you have no reason to disable these services.

Access to legacy Windows servers through the NetBIOS protocol and NetWare servers through IPX/SPX is handled without difficulty.

Figure 23.19
In this dialog, you can choose network services and protocols to be made available to dial-up users. Generally, you can leave all the options checked.

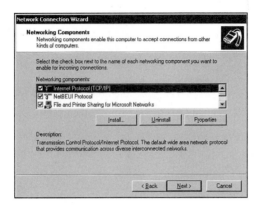

However, the TCP/IP protocol presents a significant problem. Incoming callers must be assigned IP addresses valid on your LAN to be able to communicate with computers other than your own.

If your network has a DHCP server, or if you are using Internet connection sharing, then a caller is automatically allocated a valid IP address, with which it can communicate with your computer and others on the network. No worries.

If your network does not have a true DHCP server on the network, you must manually assign a valid subnet of at least four IP addresses taken from the IP address range of your network. If you don't, incoming callers can access only your computer.

This process is more complex than I can get into here in any detail, unfortunately. You'll have to get a network manager to assign the subnet for you; the first address you enter must have a node number, exclusive of the subnet mask, of one.

Tip #272	If your network has a subnet mask of 255.255.255.0, use the first three numbers of your own IP address, and for the fourth, you must do some experimentation. Find a range of four unused IP addresses, starting with an even multiple of four, which I'll call X. Use the `ping` command to see whether the addresses are in use. For example, if my network address were 192.168.0.1, I might see whether 192.168.0.80 through 192.198.0.83 are free.
	On the properties page, for the starting and ending IP address, use X+1 and X+2, respectively. In my example, I would enter 192.168.0.81 and 192.168.0.82.
	This description makes a DHCP server look really attractive, doesn't it! If you have dedicated DSL Internet access, you might not know that you have a DHCP server already. Most DSL routers can be DHCP servers, too; check with your ISP.

Enabling incoming access is a great way to get access to your own computer from afar, but it is not without risk. The risk is that someone might dial up your computer and find a username with an inadequate or nonexistent password. If a hacker did that, he or she would have access to your computer from wherever he or she was, and you might not even know it was happening. The chances of someone finding your modem's telephone number are less than someone attempting to break in through the Internet. However, you should be sure to follow at least these steps to minimize the risk:

- Disable the Guest account on your computer and all computers on your LAN.
- Don't enable Guest for dial-in access.
- Select as few accounts for access as possible.
- Be sure these accounts have long, complex, secret passwords.

OFFLINE FOLDERS

You might recognize the "Offline" problem: You'll eventually want to have copies of a remote computer's files on your own computer. If you make changes to your copies, the network's copy will be out of date. If someone changes the originals on the remote computer, your copies will be out of date. And trying to remember where the originals came from, where you saved the copies on your computer, and which is the newest copy can get confusing sometimes. Sometimes you copy stuff back and forth and accidentally overwrite a newer file, or miss one that was added since you last looked. The answer to the offline problem is automation. Computers can do anything, right?

Well, I don't know if you ever tried to use My Briefcase in previous versions of Windows, but the answer to that question is "not always." It was a nice idea: You could copy files from an office computer into the special Briefcase folder and take it on a floppy to your portable, or from a remote computer to your "briefcase" via a LAN. The next time you connected, Windows would attempt to reconcile the files in your "briefcase" folder with the originals. The whole process was so confusing I never even tried it on older versions of Windows until I started work on this book. When I did try, it froze, lost files, or crashed my computer every time I used it. Well, as the saying goes, "It's the thought that counts."

In Windows 2000, Microsoft has created Offline Folders to take care of these problems. Here's the skinny: When you mark a folder for offline use, Windows stashes away a copy or *caches* the folder's files somewhere on your hard drive, but all you see is the original shared folder on your screen. When you disconnect, the shared file folder remains on your screen, with its files intact. You do with it as you will—add files, delete files, edit files. Meanwhile, network users can do the same with the original copies. When you reconnect later, Windows will set everything right again.

"Right," I can hear you say, "and if you believe that, I have a bridge to sell you." Okay, I was skeptical too at first, but this time, Microsoft really did it right. You'll find that this feature works, and it's more powerful than it seems at first glance. It has a bewildering array of features, options, and configuration settings, and it took me some time to see why: Offline Folders have several different applications, and each requires a slightly different setup. The following are some of the applications of Offline Folders:

- Maintaining an up-to-date copy of a set of shared files on a server (or desktop computer) and a remote or portable computer. If you keep a project's files in an offline folder, Windows keeps the copies on all your computers up-to-date.

- "Pushing" application software or data from a network to a portable computer. If software or data is kept in an offline folder, your portable can update itself when you connect or dock to the LAN.

- Automatically backing up important files from your computer to an alternative location. Your computer can connect to a dial-up or network computer on a timer and refresh your offline folders automatically.

After I describe all the functions and settings for Offline Folders, I'll give you some scenarios and show how you can set up Offline Folders to help.

Tip #273

> Oh, by the way, for the courageous among you, My Briefcase is still provided with Windows 2000. For what it's worth, I banished the hateful thing from my desktop. You can just drag it to the Recycle Bin. Given the power of Offline Folders, I suggest that you give the ill-fated Briefcase a similar send-off. If you ever want My Briefcase back, you can make another one by using the New context menu. Just right-click the desktop.

Identifying Files and Folders for Offline Use

You can mark specific files, subfolders, or even entire shared folders from a remote server for offline use.

Note

> The server I'm talking about might be in the next room, which isn't very "remote" at all, but that's what I'll call it for simplicity's sake. In this section, a remote server is any one to which you are only sometimes connected. You might connect to it by modem or through a VPN, but it could also be your office server, from which you sometimes unplug and leave.

While you're connected to the remote network, view the desired items in Explorer, either on the left or right pane. You can find a shared folder in Entire Network, Computers Near Me, or, if you've mapped a drive letter to the shared folder, you can select it under My Computer.

Note

> The Offline Folders feature works with folders shared by any network server using Microsoft's standard networking protocols, so you can use shares from Windows, OS/2, Samba, and so on, but not NetWare.
>
> However, you cannot take offline any folder whose full pathname is longer than 64 characters. Windows caches only files whose pathnames are shorter than 64 characters.

When you find the folder or folders you want, select them, and right-click Make Available Offline, or select File, Make Available Offline, as shown in Figure 23.20.

Tip #274

Be cautious about marking entire shared drives or folders available offline unless you're sure how much data they contain, and you're sure you want it all. You could end up with a gigabyte of stuff you don't need! If in doubt, choose just a subfolder or two you're sure you need.

Figure 23.20
Making a network folder available offline. I chose just subfolder ch23 so that I could take the files for this chapter home from the office and work on them over the weekend.

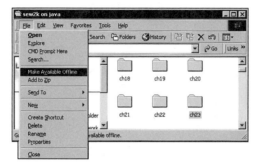

Note

You might run into a bit of a glitch. If you choose a shared folder listed under My Network Places, Make Available Offline isn't a choice. You can select a subfolder, but not the whole shared folder. To make an entire shared folder available offline, select it in one of the other places I mentioned.

If you choose a folder that contains subfolders, Windows asks if you want only the folder and its files, or the folder and also any subfolders it contains, as shown in Figure 23.21. Your call!

Figure 23.21
If you want to make a subfolder available offline, you can choose to keep just the folder or all its subfolders as well.

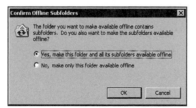

Note

If you select a shortcut to a file and mark it Make Available Offline, Windows does you a favor: It gets the file to which the shortcut points and makes it available offline, too. But Windows doesn't do this with a shortcut to a folder.

 If you get the error "Files of This Type Cannot Be Made Available Offline," see "Can't Make File Available Offline" in the "Troubleshooting" section at the end of the chapter.

The first time you make something available offline, the Offline Files Wizard starts to guide you through some setup. Click Next to get going:

1. If the remote files are available over a LAN, as opposed to a dial-up connection, Windows can update your local copy of the files whenever you log on or off while connected. This is a good choice for a dockable portable computer. If you want this update to occur, check Automatically Synchronize, as shown in Figure 23.22, and select Next.

Figure 23.22
You can choose automatic synchronization if the remote server is directly accessible by LAN, as would be the case with a dockable computer.

2. The wizard offers two options. While you're working offline, Windows can periodically pop up a little reminder on the taskbar. You can also get a desktop shortcut to the folder containing the locally stored files. I don't find either option helpful and prefer to find the files using their original network folder names. I suggest unchecking both options and then selecting Next.

Windows begins copying files from the network server to your hard disk, as shown in Figure 23.23.

Figure 23.23
The Synchronizing dialog indicates that file transfers are underway.

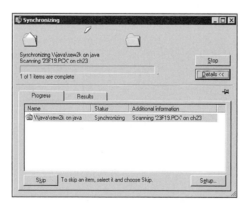

When the synchronization is finished, the network folder or file icon appears with a special "roundtrip" marker to indicate that it is available offline.

When you disconnect from the network by undocking or disconnecting a remote connection, only the offline files and folders remain in the Explorer display, as shown in Figure 23.24.

Figure 23.24
Offline files or folders have a mark added to their icons to show their special status. When you disconnect from the network, only offline folders and files remain.

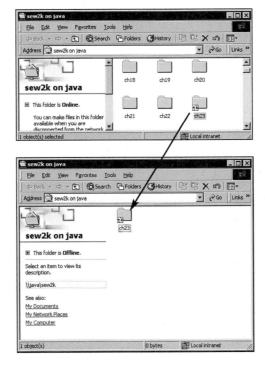

Offline, you can still use the remote folder. You can add, delete, or edit files in it. If you have a drive letter mapped to the offline folder, the drive letter still functions.

> **Note**
>
> This process works so well that it's disconcerting at first because the effect is...well, because there is no effect at all. You can happily copy files to a network folder, and it seems to happen, except they don't show up on the remote server—until you reconnect, that is.

When you reconnect, you should synchronize your offline folders with the network folders so that both sets will be up-to-date.

THE SYNCHRONIZATION MANAGER

You can synchronize files anytime you are connected to the network containing the original shared folder, whether by LAN, modem, or VPN network connection. You can start a synchronization in five ways (of course):

- Manually, from Explorer's Tools menu or by choosing Start, Accessories. This method lets you synchronize any offline folders whose remote server is available.

■ Manually, by right-clicking a specific shared file or folder and choosing Synchronize. This method synchronizes just that file or folder.

■ Automatically, when your computer is connected and idle.

■ Automatically, when you log on, off, or both.

■ Automatically, at specified times and days of the week. For a scheduled synchronization, Windows even automatically makes a dial-up connection if necessary.

As wonderful as the Offline Folder system is, it can't help you if two people modify the same file from two different locations. Windows helps you avoid this problem while you're connected by using the online copy of the file whenever available (see the following tip for one teensy exception). This way, everyone uses the same copy, and Windows can use its standard file and record locking mechanism to control access to the file by multiple users.

Tip #275	Although Windows uses the online copy of the file whenever possible, there is one exception: If the person who shared the files made them available for offline use as "applications," Windows doesn't let you change them, and it uses the local copy when possible. I'll talk about this topic under "Making Your Shared Folders Available for Offline Use" later in this chapter.

During offline use, though, it's possible for both the original and your copy to be changed. When you synchronize, you must pick the "winner," and one set of changes will be lost. If you are keeping copies only of your own files, shared from your own computer, losing one set probably won't be a big problem. You can't work in two places at the same time anyway. If you're dealing with shared files used by many people, though, offline folders are good, but they can't save you from collisions in editing.

Tip #276	If you're collaborating with others on a project and editing files offline, the way to avoid problems is to coordinate with each other before editing and synchronize frequently.

MANUAL SYNCHRONIZATION

You can start synchronization manually after you've reconnected to a network whose files you took offline. You must do so if you connect to the remote server with a dial-up or VPN connection.

In Explorer, choose Tools, Synchronize, or select Start, Programs, Accessories, Synchronize to start the synchronization process. Select the shared folders whose files you want to update, as shown in Figure 23.25, and select Synchronize.

Windows copies update files as necessary and then asks you to resolve any conflicts it encounters. The three types of conflict for any given file are as follows:

■ A file on the server was deleted. Windows asks whether you want to delete your local copy, too, or put your copy back on the server. This situation is illustrated in Figure 23.26.

Figure 23.25
For manual synchro-
nization, check the
network shares whose
folders you want to
update.

Figure 23.26
Synchronization might
require you to recon-
cile missing files.

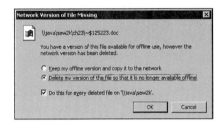

- You deleted your copy of the file. Windows asks whether you want to pick up another
  copy or delete the file from the server.

- Your copy of the file and the server's copy were both edited since you last synchronized.
  Windows asks who wins: Do you want to copy your file to the server, the server's copy
  to your computer (see Figure 23.27), or keep both files under two different names?
  This dialog box is pretty nicely done; you can view either version with the click of a
  button. Note that you can check a box to apply your decision to all file conflicts.

Figure 23.27
When both the origi-
nal and copy have
been modified, you
can view both ver-
sions and can choose
to replace one or
keep both.

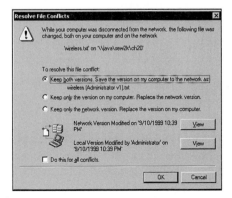

I can't tell you a right or wrong answer for any of these situations. You'll have to determine which is the appropriate answer in each case.

 If you get the error Unable to connect to server, *see "Offline Synchronization Gives* Unable to connect to server *Error" in the "Troubleshooting" section at the end of the chapter.*

After all files have been checked, Windows displays a summary showing you any problems it encountered, as you can see in Figure 23.28.

Figure 23.28
A summary appears when synchronization is complete. The synchronization process might not have updated all files if errors occurred; it stops processing a given folder when it encounters an error.

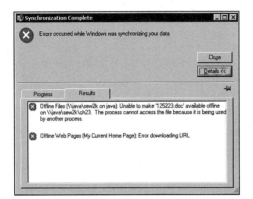

The synchronization summary indicates any significant problems encountered. For example, if someone is editing a document with Word (as I was when I recorded Figure 23.28), the synchronization process stops at that file and continues with the next network share.

Caution

If the process fails because a file is in use, you should repeat the synchronization when no one is editing files in the shared folder; otherwise, you might lose changes to some files.

AUTOMATIC SYNCHRONIZATION

You can tell Windows to perform synchronization automatically on logon, logoff, or when your computer is sitting idle as long as you are connected to the remote network. Although you'll probably never log off while dialed into a remote network, this feature is good for dockable mobile computers that spend a good deal of their time directly connected to a LAN.

If you bring up the Synchronization Manager (in Explorer, by choosing Tools, Synchronize), you can select the Settings button to display the Synchronization Settings dialog, which is shown in Figure 23.29.

You can specify that Windows is to synchronize selected folders each time you log on or log off while connected to a network. You can check which offline files are to be updated (and which offline Web pages too, by the way; I've been ignoring them, but they are updated with the Synchronization Manager, too). You can also select a different set of folders to update, depending on which connection is active: your LAN adapter or any dial-up connection.

Figure 23.29
On the
Synchronization
Settings dialog, you
can specify automatic
synchronization times.

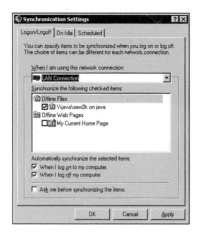

→ For information on updating offline Web pages, **see** "Browsing Offline," **p. 438**.

You might automatically update all folders when connected to your local area connection, except those on servers that you access only via a dial-up connection.

Note

It doesn't make much sense for a dial-up connection to synchronize at logon and logoff unless you use Windows Log on Via Dial Up Connection features.

UPDATE ON IDLE

You can also instruct Windows to synchronize when your computer is sitting idle by using the On Idle tab of the Synchronization Settings dialog. Here, you can also choose which folders to update, depending on which connection is in use. By default, Windows waits for 15 minutes of inactivity before starting an update, and it updates again every 60 minutes. You can change these times by choosing the Advanced button.

Updating when idle is useful if your computer spends a considerable amount of time connected to the LAN, and you have the opportunity to work while you're away from your desk. It seems less useful for a portable computer dialed in by modem.

SCHEDULED SYNCHRONIZATION

Finally, you can instruct Windows to begin synchronizations on a timed schedule. Enabling this feature makes sense only if your computer is *on* at the time of the scheduled update, so it makes more sense for use with desktop computers that stay on most or all of the time. It would be useful to get copies of large files from a LAN server or from a distant server through a VPN connection. The Scheduler can establish a connection before synchronizing.

You can view scheduled synchronizations on the Synchronization Manager's Scheduled tab. The Synchronization Settings dialog lists any currently scheduled updates. To add a new entry, click Add, and use the Scheduled Synchronization Wizard, as follows:

1. Select a network connection that must be active for this update. If it's a dial-up or VPN connection, you can check If My Computer Is Not Connected...Connect For Me, as shown in Figure 23.30. Choose Next to continue.

Figure 23.30
Using the Scheduled Synchronization Wizard, you can select a connection and shared folders to update and enable automatic dialing if necessary.

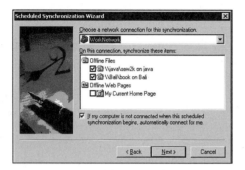

2. Select the time of day and days of the week to perform the update, and select Next.

3. Assign a name to the update job, such as Get Product Specs; select Next; and then select Finish.

4. After the new schedule job is added to the list of scheduled updates, you can add more, delete, or edit scheduled updates.

You manage the scheduling information for scheduled synchronizations just like any other scheduled task. It's a rather complex system with many options (for example, don't synchronize while the computer is running on battery power).

MAKING YOUR SHARED FOLDERS AVAILABLE FOR OFFLINE USE

After you've marked a network file for offline use and then try to use the file, Windows has a tempting choice: You can choose a copy way out there on the network or a copy right on your hard disk. Wouldn't it be nice to use the fast, nearby copy?

Using this copy is reasonable, but there are arguments pro and con: It would be much faster to use the local copy, but if you modify the local copy, then file protection, record locking, and other standard access controls don't work. You might have had the experience of trying to open a Word document that was being edited by someone else on the network. Word doesn't let you because it knows someone else is working on the file. If Word opened a local copy of a document, this protection wouldn't be there.

Windows leaves the choice with the person who shares the network folder. When *you* share folders on your computer, you should specify the way Windows will make this folder available for offline use by others.

On the Folders Sharing properties page, select the Caching button to display the Caching Settings dialog, as shown in Figure 23.31. (You will read about this topic in Chapter 24, "Connecting Your LAN to the Internet.") Make one of the choices explained in Table 23.2.

Figure 23.31
Caching settings tell Windows how to treat the files in your shared folder when other users select them for offline use.

PART

IV

CH

23

TABLE 23.2   CACHING SETTINGS

Option	Description
Allow Caching of Files in This Shared Folder	If this box is unchecked, the files cannot be copied for offline use. Use this setting to protect sensitive or fast-changing data.
Manual Caching for Documents	This setting makes files behave as discussed in this section. Users can select files and folders for offline use and are responsible for synchronizing them. You should use this setting for most cases.
Automatic Caching for Applications	Windows automatically makes any file accessed by the user available offline and uses the cached copy if it can. You should use this setting if your files are programs or are documents that cannot be modified by the remote users.
Automatic Caching for Documents	Windows automatically makes any opened file available offline, but when another user is connected and edits one, Windows edits the network copy for proper file access control. You should use this setting to "push" documents to the other user's computer for offline use.

The amount of disk space allocated to automatically available offline files is limited to an amount set in the Offline Files properties page.

OFFLINE FILES PROPERTIES

You can control your computer's overall treatment of offline files from the Explorer. Select Tools, Folder Options, and then select the Offline Files tab, as shown in Figure 23.32.

Figure 23.32
The Offline Files properties tab makes global settings for the handling of offline files.

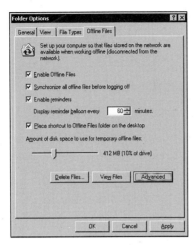

I hope the settings make sense as I've covered all the features they control. I've included them all in Table 23.3.

TABLE 23.3 OFFLINE FILES OPTIONS

Option	Description
Enable Offline Files	Uncheck to disable the entire Offline Files system.
Synchronize All Offline Files Before Logging Off	Check to force the option that might also be made individually for each shared folder.
Enable Reminders	Uncheck to disable the annoying balloon that pops up on the taskbar to remind you that you're offline. If you're under a tree sipping iced tea, you know already.
Place Shortcut to Offline Files on the Desktop	Check to see which files are currently cached.
Amount of Disk Space to Use	Adjust to limit disk space used to cache temporary ("Automatic") offline files. Manually chosen offline files are not counted.
Delete Files	Select to delete temporary and/or manually chosen offline files from the cache. Network copies are *not* deleted. Use this feature to force a refreshed copy of all files.
View Files	Select to display the Offline Files folder, a listing of all cached files. It provides the same view as given by the desktop icon.
Advanced	Select to set how your computer behaves when it goes offline.

You don't need to change any of these options to use Offline folders. However, you can come here if you find the offline warning balloon annoying; or you run short of disk space, and purging Internet Explorer's temporary file cache, your collection of downloaded MP3s, all the .TMP files on the disk, and your games isn't enough, so you must purge the offline files cache.

If you choose the Advanced properties button, you can tell Windows what to do if your network connection is lost unexpectedly (see Figure 23.33).

Figure 23.33
On the Advanced Settings dialog, you can specify which server connections are essential.

You can tell Windows that some network server connections are essential and not to simply go into offline mode if the connection is lost. In the Advanced Settings dialog, you can say that all connections are essential or none are, and then list the names of computers to omit. In Figure 23.33, I've permitted offline operation for all computers except sumatra, which I require.

USING OFFLINE FOLDERS

Earlier, I listed three uses of offline folders. Now that you've read all the details, you should be able to see how the Offline system handles these tasks:

- Maintaining an up-to-date copy of a set of shared files on a server (or desktop computer) and a remote or portable computer. If you manually select a network folder to be available offline, your computer will always have up-to-date files. If you typically connect to the LAN with a docking portable computer, you can synchronize automatically on logon and logoff. If you connect to the network by a dial-up or VPN connection, you must synchronize manually.

- Pushing application software or data from a network to a portable computer. If you put application software or seldom-changed read-only data on a shared network folder and mark it Automatic Caching for Applications, remote users must copy the file across a slow network connection only once. The trick is to have the users always refer to the files by their network shared folder name, even when offline. Windows gives them the cached copy automatically. This capability is a boon for modem users.

- Automatically backing up important files from your computer to an alternative location. You can make a shared folder on a server or computer at your office and create an offline copy of it at home or in your portable. If you do all your work in the offline folder, the synchronization process really is an intelligent backup process. You can even schedule it automatically.

I don't get too enthusiastic about these things usually, but after struggling and suffering with My Briefcase and then working with offline folders, I'd say that they're probably one of the three neatest features I've found in Windows 2000.

Remember, after you've marked folders for offline use, continue to use them in the normal way, referring to them using their full network path filenames or through mapped network drives.

 If you can't find a file that was marked for offline use, see "Offline Files Are Missing" in the "Troubleshooting" section at the end of this chapter.

Finally, you can uncheck Make Available Offline on a file or folder at any time to remove it from the cached file list.

WEB FOLDERS AND WEB PRINTING

If a remote computer with Windows 2000 has Internet Information Services (IIS) installed, has enabled Web Sharing on any folders, and is accessible over the Internet or a corporate intranet, you can access its shared files through Internet Explorer version 5 or higher. This technology lets you copy files to and from a remote computer with a high degree of security, through firewalls that normally block access to file sharing protocols.

When IIS is installed, the computer's shared printers may also be used through the Internet using the Internet Printing Protocol, or IPP. IPP lets remote computers print to shared printers across the Internet, again through firewalls.

You can use these technologies to great advantage if your home base has dedicated Internet access because you can use shared files and printers across the Internet rather than use a modem or VPN network connection.

These applications are all described elsewhere in this book; I just wanted to be sure they were mentioned here as they're great resources for the "unplugged" user.

Installing IIS is covered in detail in Chapter 18, "Using Internet Information Services to Host a Web Site." Using Web Folders and Web Printing is covered in Chapter 24.

VIRTUAL PRIVATE NETWORKING

You know that you can use dial-up networking to connect to your office LAN or desktop computer from afar. But, with the Internet providing network connections and local modem access nearly all over the world, why can't you reach through the Internet to connect to remote networks instead of placing a possibly expensive long-distance call?

Well, in fact, you can. Microsoft networking can use the Internet's TCP protocol to conduct its business, so you can, in fact, use an Internet connection to access shared files and printers, if the computer you want to reach has an Internet connection up and running.

But the Internet is not a friendly place. With tens of millions of people using it every day, you must expect that some percentage of them are up to no good. Network break-ins are everyday news now. It's no wonder that businesses and smart individuals don't want their file sharing services directly exposed to the Internet.

Virtual Private Networking (VPN) provides a way to protect a LAN from direct exposure to the Internet yet let trusted outside users access network resources. Figure 23.34 illustrates a standard Internet connection from a computer through an ISP to a server on the Internet.

Figure 23.34
A standard Internet connection from you to a server. You can connect to the server, but so can 50 million others.

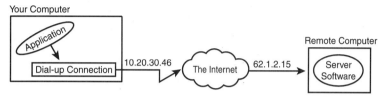

PART

IV

CH

23

The dial-up connection is assigned an IP address, say 10.20.30.46. You can connect to a server across the Internet, which has a public IP address, 62.1.2.15 in this example. The Internet happily routes data back and forth.

This setup is fine if the server is providing only public Web pages, but if the server is providing private pages or shared network folders, it's exposed to perhaps 50 million Internet users, any one of whom might try breaking in. It's just not an acceptable risk. The solution is to install a *firewall* to block network traffic.

→ To learn more details about firewalls and network security, **see** "Set Up Firewalls and NAT Devices," **p. 949**.

In Figure 23.35, the server is protected by a private network and an added firewall. The only problem is the application software can't connect to the server. You can't send data to the new IP address 192.168.1.8, as it's not a visible, connected Internet address. The server is safe from intruders now, but you have no access to it either.

Figure 23.35
A firewall and a private network protect the server from everyone, including the trusted remote user.

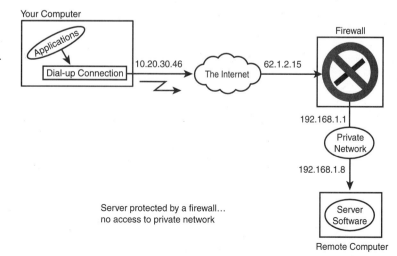

What you really want is to become a direct part of the private network, as if you were there, by safely tunneling through the Internet, as the fanciful Figure 23.36 suggests.

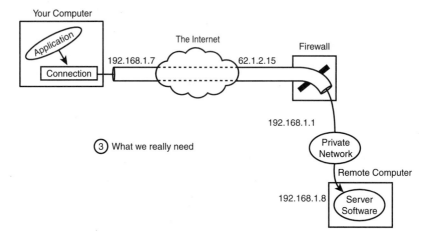

Figure 23.36
What you want is to become part of the private network by somehow creating a tunnel from your computer through the firewall.

Tip #277

An analogy I like to make is that of trying to mail a letter, addressed in Chinese, to a friend in China. The postal service here doesn't know what to make of the address, of course. If you put the letter inside another envelope and address it in English to the main post office in Beijing, the letter will get there. Then the postal service in Beijing can tear open the envelope and forward the contents.

Figure 23.37 shows how a VPN connection does the same thing. When you establish a VPN connection, you are assigned an IP address from the private network. In the figure, I used 192.168.1.7. It's as if you have a new LAN adapter and connection in your computer, in addition to your dial-up connection. But its private IP address is still a nonsense address as far as the Internet is concerned.

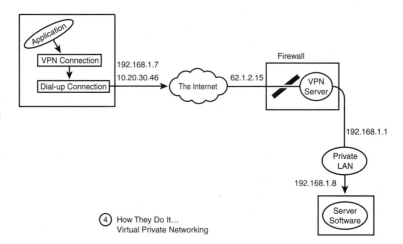

Figure 23.37
A Virtual Private Network connection provides the tunnel. Data destined for the remote network is encrypted and sent to the VPN server, which unencrypts it and passes it in to the private network.

When you send data to a server on your private network, the data is *encapsulated*, that is, put inside another IP packet which is addressed to the VPN server using its public IP address. In Figure 23.37, the encapsulated packet is sent from the dial-up connection at 10.20.30.46 to the VPN server at 62.1.2.15. When the data reaches the VPN server, the original data and addresses are pulled out and are passed into the private network to the server. The return path works the same way.

The system is secure because you can establish the connection with VPN server using your network logon name and password, so it knows it can trust you. And all the encapsulated data can be encrypted, so it is safe from prying eyes.

PART
IV

CH
23

That's a VPN in a nutshell. It actually works, and Windows 2000 comes with all the stuff to make it happen. You can connect to a remote LAN from Windows 2000 Professional using a VPN gateway provided by Windows 2000 Pro, Server, or any of several commercial routers with built-in VPN software.

Windows 2000 supports two encapsulation or repackaging technologies. The *Point-to-Point Tunneling Protocol*, or *PPTP*, was developed by Microsoft and was provided with previous versions of Windows. The *Layer Two Tunneling Protocol*, or *L2TP*, is an industry standard technology, and is faster and better than PPTP. Windows now uses L2TP when it can and PPTP when communicating with older versions of Windows. L2TP requires a certificate for its IPSec-based encryption, though, so if you don't have Windows 2000 Server, your VPN connections will always use PPTP.

ROUTING ISSUES

If the remote network you want to use is a simple, small network with only one subnet or range of IP addresses, you can skip this section. Otherwise, I must address an issue with TCP/IP routing address here, as much as I fear it's a real can of worms.

Take a look at Figure 23.37 again. What happens if you want to communicate with two servers—say a private server through the tunnel and a public Web site on the Internet at the same time?

When you send data to an address that doesn't belong to the private network's range of addresses, Windows has two choices: It can pass the data through the tunnel and let the network on the other end route it on, or it can pass the data directly through the dial-up connection and to the Internet.

It would seem sensible that Windows should always take the second choice because any IP address other than, say, 192.168.1.xxx clearly doesn't belong to the private network and doesn't need protection. That's right as long as the remote network has only one such subnet. Some complex corporate networks have many, with different addresses, so Windows can't just decide from the address of the VPN connection which addresses belong to the private network and which go direct.

If you plan to use a VPN connection and the Internet at the same time, you must find out whether your remote network has more than one subnet. Then follow this advice:

- If the remote network has only one subnet, tell Windows not to use the remote network as its gateway address for all unknown locations. This is the easy case.

- If the remote network has more than one subnet, tell Windows to use the remote network as its gateway, and you can connect to all servers on the remote network. But Internet access goes through the tunnel, too, and from there to the Internet. It slows things down.

- Alternatively, you can tell Windows not to use the remote network gateway; you can manually set routes to other subnets while you're connected. It's tricky and inconvenient. I'll show you how I do it at the end of the chapter, under "Tips from the Windows Pros."

SETTING UP FOR VIRTUAL PRIVATE NETWORKING

VPN connectivity was difficult to install in previous versions of Windows, as it required you to install and configure additional network components. It's now built into Windows 2000 and comes along for free when you install the TCP/IP protocol, so you can just use it "out of the box."

Because VPN is completely built in, it's actually easier to use than a standard dial-up connection. You must know the hostname or IP address of the computer that hosts the VPN connection. It might be a Windows 2000 computer or a special VPN host, just as with dial-up networking.

To establish a VPN connection from your computer to another network, you must know the hostname or IP address of the remote VPN connection. This information corresponds to the telephone number in a dial-up connection; it lets you specify the endpoint of the tunnel. After the connection is made, just as with a dial-up connection, your connection goes into the network beyond the VPN host. You also need a way to connect to the VPN host, whether through a dial-up connection to the Internet or to a Windows 2000 Server network, or a LAN connection. Any way will work, as long as you can send data from your computer to the VPN host. Just follow these steps:

1. Choose Settings, Network and Dial-Up Connections, and open the Make New Connection icon.

2. Select Dial-Up to Private Network through the Internet, and click Next.

3. If you require a dial-up connection to get to the Internet or the network that will carry the VPN connection, you can specify it here, as shown in Figure 23.38. Then select Next. Otherwise, Windows assumes you are connecting through your LAN connection.

4. Enter the hostname or IP address of the remote dial-in server—for example, vpn.mycompany.com—and select Next.

Figure 23.38
You can have Windows automatically dial an Internet connection before making a VPN connection.

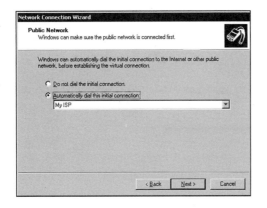

5. Windows asks whether this connection's name and telephone number should appear in Network and Dial-Up Connections for all users of this computer or just for you. Select All Users if other users on this computer want to connect to the same remote network or if you want to use this dial-up connection to connect to a remote domain using your roaming profile on that domain.

Note

Don't worry; your password is not shared with other users if you share the connection.

If you want to log in to the remote network using the VPN connection, make both the VPN connection and the dial-up connection to your ISP available to everyone. This is necessary so Windows can access the connections when you log out and log on again using the VPN connection.

6. Choose a name for the connection, which will appear as the name of the connection icon in Network and Dial-Up Connections. I usually enter VPN *xxxxx*, where *xxxxx* is the name of the remote computer. This dialog contains an additional check box to have Windows put a shortcut to this connection on your desktop.

Note

You can delete a connection shortcut later if you don't want it and can drag the connection icon from Network and Dial-Up Connections to your desktop later if you do.

7. Choose Finish. Windows immediately wants to open the connection, but you must set the connection properties first. To do so, select Cancel. Then right-click the new connection icon, and select Properties.

The Dial-Up Connection's properties page has five tabs. Most of the time, the default settings will work correctly, but you will need to check some of them. Let me walk you through the most important parameters.

GENERAL PROPERTIES

The General tab of the Properties dialog holds the hostname or IP address of your VPN connection server, and if needed, the name of a dial-up connection to use to carry the VPN connection (see Figure 23.39). If you are establishing the VPN connection over a LAN or dedicated Internet connection, you can uncheck Dial Another Connection First.

Figure 23.39
For the Virtual Private Network connection properties, you can specify the hostname and, if necessary, a dial-up connection to use to carry the VPN connection.

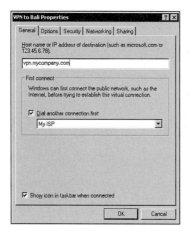

SECURITY

It's unlikely that you will need to change any security settings. The data in a VPN connection is usually carried across the Internet, and a high level of security is required. Your password and data should be encrypted in the strongest fashion possible. Be sure that Require Secured Password and Require Data Encryption are set on the Security tab.

If you are connecting to your own home network and want to use your current login name and password on the remote system, check Automatically Use My Windows Logon Name and Password so that you aren't prompted for it whenever you use the connection.

NETWORKING

It's likely that you want to participate as a full member of the remote network, so leave all Components checked on the Networking tab of the Properties dialog.

As I mentioned, two types of VPN protocols are used by Windows 2000 Server and Professional. Generally, you can leave the Type of VPN server set to Automatic, and Windows will determine to which type it's connected when it makes each call.

You also must deal with the gateway issue I discussed earlier in this chapter under "Routing Issues." Select Internet Protocol, and choose Properties. Leave the IP address and DNS information to Obtain Automatically, and click Advanced.

If the remote network has only one subnet, or if you will set routes to multiple subnets manually, uncheck Use Default Gateway On Remote Network on the resulting dialog (see Figure 23.40).

Figure 23.40
Uncheck Use Default Gateway to let Internet traffic bypass the tunnel while you're connected. If the remote network has more than one subnet, you must manually set routes to them.

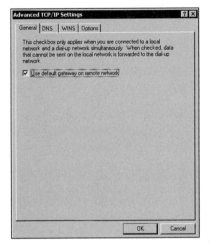

If your remote network uses L2TP, and you have been set up with encryption certificates, select the Options tab, view IPSec properties, and be sure that Use This IP Security Policy is set to Client (Respond Only).

DIALING A VPN CONNECTION

Making a VPN connection follows the same procedure as making a dial-up connection:

1. Select the connection icon from Network and Dial-Up Connections.

2. If this VPN connection requires a dial-up connection, you are prompted with the username and password for your dial-up connection to your ISP. Check for the proper location and dialing rules, and then select Dial. After the connection has been made, Windows proceeds to make the VPN connection.

3. Enter the username and password for access to the remote network. Select Connect.

   Windows then contacts the remote VPN server, verifies your username and password, registers your computer on the network, and creates a connection status on the taskbar, just as for a standard dial-up connection.

You can use the remote network now, access shared files and folders, access printers, synchronize offline folders, and so on.

When you're finished, right-click the connection icon, and select Disconnect.

ENABLING VPN ACCESS TO YOUR COMPUTER

You can enable incoming VPN connections to your computer if it has a dedicated Internet connection. You can then connect to your computer through the Internet from home or in the field; Windows 9x, NT, and 2000 can all connect to a Windows 2000 VPN server. Your Windows Pro computer will accept only one incoming VPN call at a time, however.

Enabling VPN access is exactly the same as enabling dial-in access, so see the section "Enabling Dial-In Access to Your Computer" earlier in this chapter. Follow those instructions, being sure to enable an incoming VPN connection. You don't need to choose any modems to receive incoming modem calls.

When Incoming Calls is configured, your computer can be contacted as the host of a VPN connection. To connect to it, establish a VPN connection as you learned in the preceding section, using your computer's public IP address or hostname as the number to dial.

Note

You must configure the Internet protocol to assign valid IP addresses for incoming connections. This topic, which was discussed in "Enabling Dial-In Access to Your Computer," applies to VPN access, too.

INFRARED NETWORKING

Most portable computers include an infrared data transmission device similar to that used on TV remote controls. Using a data transmission standard called IrDA (after the Infrared Data Association), computers, printers, and handheld organizers can communicate with each other without LAN wiring. Just point them at each other. LAN connections are much faster, so I recommend using them over IrDA any day, but if you don't have a LAN connection, IrDA can give "point and shoot" a whole new meaning.

IrDA comes in two flavors: SIR (Serial Infrared), which tops out at 112Kbps, and FIR (Fast Infrared), which runs up to 4Mbps. Most new portables support either protocol. The advantage of using SIR is that you can attach an expensive adapter to a standard serial port on a desktop computer and get infrared capability.

Note

An FIR adapter connects to an SIR adapter by automatically lowering its transfer rate. The two standards interoperate quite nicely.

Windows 2000 includes support for IrDA file transfers between two capable devices such as laptops, digital cameras, and so on. Because most laptop computers have IrDA software, you can transfer files between two Windows 2000 laptops just by bringing them near each other.

SETTING UP AN INFRARED DEVICE

If your computer has IrDA-compatible hardware installed, Windows detects it and installs support for it during installation. You can tell by checking for a Wireless Link applet in the Control Panel.

If you've added an external serial port IrDA adapter, choose Add/Remove Hardware in the Control Panel, select Add Hardware, choose the device manually, and select Infrared Devices. Finally, choose the proper IrDA device type and serial port information.

 If the Wireless Link icon is not present in the Control Panel, see "Wireless Link Is Not Present in Control Panel" in the "Troubleshooting" section at the end of this chapter.

Open the applet, and confirm that Windows thinks the device is operating properly (see Figure 23.41). If it's not, select Troubleshoot to diagnose and fix the problem.

PART

IV

CH

23

Figure 23.41
Using the Wireless Link Control Panel applet, you can configure file transfer directories and the transfer speed.

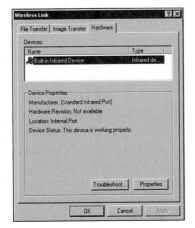

The applet has three tabs. On the first two, you can select the destination folder for files and images received from other computers and digital cameras. The default folder for received files is your desktop. The default folder for received images is the My Pictures folder inside your My Documents folder. You can change these defaults by clicking Properties and selecting a different folder.

On the Hardware tab, you can set the maximum speed for wireless transfers. If you experience a high error rate, try changing the speed from the default 115200bps to 57600 or lower.

INFRARED FILE TRANSFER

When another infrared-capable computer is in range of your computer's beam, your computer makes an interesting sound, a Wireless Link icon appears on the desktop, and a small control icon appears in the task tray (see Figure 23.42). You can instantly send files to the other computer by dragging files to the Wireless icon. Pretty neat!

Figure 23.42
When another infrared file transfer device is in range, the Wireless Link icon (left) appears on the desktop, and the Wireless control icon (right) appears in the task tray.

 If the Wireless Link icon doesn't appear when you think it should, see "Wireless Link Icon Doesn't Appear" in the "Troubleshooting" section at the end of this chapter.

To send files to another computer, you can use any of these three methods:

- Drag and drop the files onto the Wireless Link icon on the desktop.
- Select and right-click a file, choose Send To, and select Infrared Recipient.
- Open the Wireless Link icon, or select Transfer Files from the control icon in the taskbar to bring up the Wireless Link dialog shown in Figure 23.43. Here, you can browse for and select the files to transfer and then click Send to transfer the files.

> **Note**
>
> The Wireless Link dialog is a standard Open File dialog; it's really a little Explorer window. If you drag a file into this dialog, you're moving it to the displayed directory on your own computer. To transfer a file via drag and drop, drag it to the Wireless Link icon.

Figure 23.43
Using the Wireless Link dialog, you can browse for and select files to transfer via the Infrared Link.

After you've selected files to transfer via drag and drop, Send To, or the dialog, progress dialogs appear on both computers, indicating that a file transfer is taking place. Figure 23.44 shows the Sending Files dialog.

On the receiving end, by default, received files are placed on the desktop. You can change the received file directory by opening the Wireless Link properties page from the Control

Panel, from the wireless link task tray icon, or from the Wireless Link dialog. There, you can also disable receipt of infrared transfers.

Figure 23.44
Infrared file transfer progress is shown on dialogs on the sending computer (left) and the receiving computer (right). The sending computer can cancel the transfer with the cancel button; the receiving computer can only close the progress display.

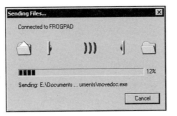

> **Note**
>
> When wireless file transfers are enabled, anyone with a wireless-equipped Windows 2000 computer can zap files onto your computer's desktop. Don't worry, though, because files are never overwritten. If someone sends you a file with the same name as an existing file on your desktop, it's named something like Copy 1 of XXXXXX.

DIGITAL CAMERA IMAGE TRANSFER

When you bring a digital camera with a compatible IrDA interface near your computer, the image transfer utility appears. Follow your camera manufacturer's instructions to copy images from the camera to your computer.

You can specify the directory for image transfers in the Wireless Link properties, from the Control Panel, or from the Wireless Link task tray icon. The default is the My Pictures folder inside your My Documents folder.

INFRARED PRINTING

When your computer has an IrDA interface, you can print to infrared-connected printers. To make a connection to an infrared printer, follow these steps:

1. In Printers, select Add Printer. Choose Local Printer, but do not check Automatically Detect.
2. Under Use the Following Port, choose IR (Local Port), as shown in Figure 23.45.
3. Select the printer's manufacturer and model. If it's not listed, and you have a disk from the manufacturer, select Have Disk and locate the Windows 2000 printer drivers.
4. Supply a name for the printer, choose whether it will be the default printer, and choose whether to share the printer to your LAN.

Now you can use the printer whenever it's in visible range of your computer.

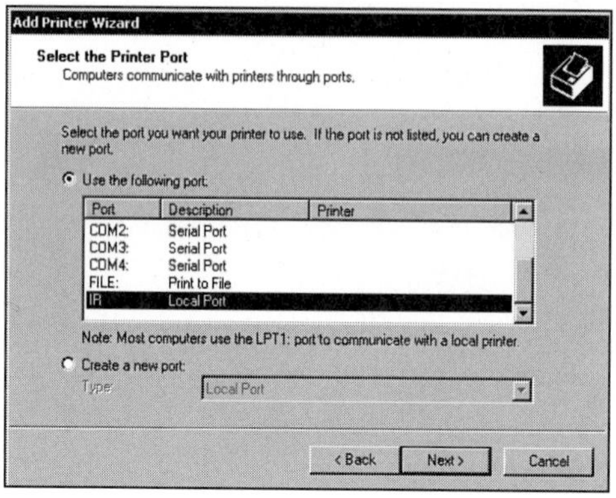

Figure 23.45
Choose IR Port to connect to a wireless printer.

MULTIPLE LAN CONNECTIONS

Microsoft has made it easy for you to manage several different dial-up and VPN connections, but not different LAN connections. Most desktop computers sit where they are installed, gathering dust until they're obsolete, and participate in only one LAN.

But portable computer users often carry their computers from office to office, docking or plugging into several different local LANs. This causes a problem if the network configuration settings are manually set.

Internet Protocol settings are the difficult ones. If your computer is set to use automatic TCP/IP configuration, you won't encounter any problems; your computer will absorb the local information each time you connect.

If your TCP/IP settings are set manually, there is no easy solution. You'll have to manually change the settings each time you connect to a different network. I suggest that you stick a 3-by-5-inch card with the settings for each network in your laptop carrying case for handy reference. At each new location, open Network and Dial-Up Connections, right-click Local Area Connections Properties, select Internet Protocol properties, and make the appropriate changes. (At least you won't have to restart your computer.)

Microsoft said that making multiple local area connections was too difficult to accomplish for Windows 2000 but might address the problem with a future version.

TROUBLESHOOTING

CAN'T CHOOSE DIAL-UP CONNECTION AT LOGIN

When I choose Log On Using Dial-Up Connection, the connection to the remote network is not an available choice.

When you created the connection, you chose For My Use Only rather than For All Users. Because you're now logged out, you don't have access to the connection. You cannot retroactively share the connection. Log on again; then delete and re-create the connection.

VPN CONNECTION FAILS WITHOUT CERTIFICATE

When I attempt to make a VPN connection, I receive the message `Unable to negotiate the encryption you requested without a certificate`.

You are trying to connect to a VPN server with a higher level of encryption than your computer or the other computer is configured to carry out.

If you are attempting to contact a Windows 2000 VPN server, contact your network administrator to get the appropriate certificate installed. If you are calling a Windows NT 4 VPN server, this error probably occurred because you enabled IPSec on the Options tab of the Advanced Internet Protocol properties. In this case, disable IPSec.

CAN'T MAKE FILE AVAILABLE OFFLINE

When I mark files or folders for offline use, I receive the error `Files of this Type Cannot Be Made Available Offline`.

Microsoft has deemed that some file types shouldn't be available offline, for example, Access's .mdb database files. They assume that these files are in use by multiple LAN users, and there's no way to reconcile changes made by offline and online users. This can help a lot of people avoid database damage, but it's annoying if you really do know you want to edit the database file while offline. There is a way to get around this if you are sure you won't take offline any files that might be edited by others while you have them.

If you're on a domain network, ask your domain administrator to modify the Group Policy entry Computer Configuration\Administrative Templates\Network\Offline Files\Files not cached.

If you are on a workgroup network, follow these steps:

1. Log in as Administrator and start the Microsoft Management Console with Start, Run, mmc.

2. Choose Console, Add/Remove Snap-in, Add.

3. Highlight Group Policy and click Add.

4. Leave the Group Policy Object set to Local Computer. Click Finish, Close, and OK.

5. In the left pane, open Local Computer policy and drill down through Computer Configuration, Administrative Templates, and Network to Offline Files.

6. In the right pane, double-click Files Not Cached.

7. Check Enabled, and enter any extensions that should be protected, such as *.dbf. Omit the file types you want to take offline.

8. Click OK and close the MMC console program.

9. Log out, and then log back in.

OFFLINE SYNCHRONIZATION GIVES `Unable to connect to server` ERROR

When I synchronize offline files, I receive the error `Unable to connect to '\\server\file'.` `The specified network name is no longer available.`

The indicated server (actually, any computer sharing a folder you are using offline) might not be might functioning. If you are a mobile user, you also might have checked folders for updating that aren't present in your current LAN or dialed-up network. Windows has no way of knowing which servers should be available and which shouldn't. You must select the servers appropriate to your connection.

OFFLINE FILES ARE MISSING

I can't find files or folders I've clearly marked for offline use.

You can choose from two possible solutions here. First, you might not have synchronized after marking the file, its folder, or a containing folder for offline use. The solution is to go back online and synchronize.

Windows 2000 also has a strange limitation: The full pathname of an offline file can't be more than 64 characters long. Files with longer pathnames are simply ignored and not copied for offline use. Check the name of the file you've found to be missing; if its full path is more than 64 characters long, this is the problem. The solution is to contact the manager of the computer sharing the original folder and ask him or her to make a network share at a deeper level in the folder tree so that the pathname will be shorter. For example, if you need files in the folder \\servername\sharename\folder one\subfolder two\subfolder three\subfolder four\myfolder, ask the manager to make a share called \\servername\subfolder4 so that the path to the desired folder myfolder is shorter.

WIRELESS LINK IS NOT PRESENT IN CONTROL PANEL

I have a wireless adapter in my desktop (or portable computer), but Wireless Link does not appear in the Control Panel.

The IrDA adapter is probably disabled in your computer's BIOS. Shut down and restart your computer. When your BIOS is setting up, press the indicated key to enter its setup utility.

Look at its Built-In Peripherals screen for IrDA options. You must enable IrDA 1.1 support. It might require a DMA and Interrupt port as well, so you might not be able to use infrared and ECP printing at the same time. Save and exit the setup program.

When you restart Windows, it will detect and install support for the infrared connector.

WIRELESS LINK ICON DOESN'T APPEAR

When another computer with an infrared IrDA port is brought near my computer, the Wireless Link icon doesn't appear.

In this case, the problem could be with either computer. If one of the two computers *can* make a wireless link with at least one other computer, then you know the fault lies with the other.

The following are a few points to check:

- Be sure that the wireless optical ports are within a few feet of each other, are pointed relatively directly at each other, and have a clear line of sight between them.
- Check the Device Manager on both computers to be sure that both IrDA ports are working correctly.
- Be sure that both computers have wireless file transfers enabled.
- If all else fails, see whether you can get a handheld video camcorder. These cameras can often "see" the infrared light emitted by IrDA ports. Check to see that the ports on both computers are blinking. If you see one blinking but not the other, you know one computer isn't set up correctly.

TIPS FROM THE WINDOWS PROS: MANUALLY ADDING ROUTING INFORMATION

As I discussed previously (the bit about a can of worms), if you use Virtual Private Networking to connect to a remote network with more than one subnet, you can let Windows set the default gateway to the remote network. This way, you can contact all the hosts on the remote network and its subnets, but all your Internet traffic travels through the tunnel, too, slowing you down. It's irritating.

The alternative is to disable the use of the default gateway and manually add routes to any subnets known to belong to the private network. You can do so at the command line by using the route command, which looks like this:

route add subnet **mask** netmask gateway

The subnet and netmask arguments are the addresses for additional networks that can be reached through the gateway address gateway. To add a route, you must know the remote subnets and your gateway address through the VPN.

You must get the subnet numbers from the network administrator on the remote end. You can find the gateway address from your own computer. Connect to the remote VPN, open a command prompt, and type ipconfig. One of the connections printed will be labeled PPP Adapter or L2TP Adapter. Note the gateway address listed. This address is the internal IP address of the VPN router and the place to send packets destined for other subnets.

Suppose you're connecting to a VPN host through a connection named VPN to Client and find these connection addresses:

```
PPP adapter VPN to Client:
        IP Address. . . . . . . 192.168.005.226
        Subnet Mask . . . . . . 255.255.255.255
        Default Gateway . . . . 192.168.105.225
```

What you need is the gateway 192.168.105.225.

Now, suppose you know that two other subnets are on the remote network: 192.168.10.0 mask 255.255.255.0, and 192.168.15.0 mask 255.255.255.0. You can reach these two networks by adding two route commands:

```
route add 192.168.10.0 mask 255.255.255.0 192.168.105.225
route add 192.168.15.0 mask 255.255.255.0 192.168.105.225
```

Each route command ends with the IP address of the remote end of the VPN connection (it's called the *next hop*).

Check your work by typing route print and looking at its output. You should see only one destination labeled 0.0.0.0; if you see two, you forgot to disable the use of the remote network as the default gateway. See that the two routes you added are shown.

To avoid having to type all this every time, you can use another neat trick. You can put a dialing command and the route commands in a batch file. Use the rasdial command to make the connection and then install the routes, like this:

```
@echo off
rasphone -d "VPN to Client"
route add 192.168.10.0 mask 255.255.255.0 192.168.105.225
route add 192.168.15.0 mask 255.255.255.0 192.168.105.225
```

The rasphone command pops up the connection dialer. When the connection is made, the two routes are added, and you're all set. A shortcut to this batch file lets you connect and set up the routes with a click.

When you disconnect the VPN connection, Windows removes the added routes automatically.

Note that if you have incoming connections enabled at the same time you make the VPN connection, the route add command does not work. Windows suggests using netsh, but danged if I can make it work on Windows 2000 Professional (yet).

For more information about rasdial and route, see Appendix A, "Command-Line Reference," on the CD-ROM that accompanies this book.

CHAPTER 24

CONNECTING YOUR LAN TO THE INTERNET

In this chapter

IT'S A GREAT TIME TO CONNECT YOUR LAN TO THE INTERNET

It's a given now that you will want Internet access on your new network. (How else will you get in those day trades during your coffee break?) In the 1980s, only big corporations and universities had Internet connections, and then, a single 64Kbps connection was probably shared by hundreds of users. Now, accessing the Internet is as much a daily requirement as the morning paper. We expect to have instant access from any keyboard we can get our fingers on, and personally, I get grumpy using anything less than a 400Kbps connection. That's progress, I suppose.

Because you now have your computers all tied together with a nifty local area network (LAN), it seems silly that each user should have to use a modem to gain Internet access individually. No worries: You have a host of options for shared Internet connections. You can use a high-speed connection to serve the entire LAN, or you can share a modem connection made from one designated Windows 2000 computer. Either way, shared access makes online life simpler for everyone on the network.

At the beginning of the Internet boom, independent Internet service providers (ISPs) pioneered inexpensive access. Anyone with a few thousand dollars, a boxful of modems, and a closet to put them in could set up shop as an ISP and make some money. Growth, competition, and consolidation have taken a toll on these "Mom & Pop" operations, and now that the Internet has proven to be more than a passing fad (I hope, or my IRA's sunk!), giant corporations such as AT&T are bullying and buying their way into the market. It's a given that the Internet will evolve into a global, high-speed network, reaching every home and office, and will take over the job of today's telephone, radio, and broadcast television networks. So, these industries are scrambling to be first into your home with fast and cheap Internet connectivity in the hope of retaining your business into the future.

High-speed data connections were once a juicy source of revenue for telephone companies. Now these companies are sensing the threat from other networking media such as cable TV, so prices for high-speed connections are plummeting. Furthermore, new technologies are making their way from the laboratory into the marketplace, making higher- and higher-speed connections less and less expensive. All this progress adds up to very good news for you and me. You won't have to live with that screechy old modem much longer.

In this chapter, I'll show you what your Internet connection options are and give you some of the pros and cons for each. I'll list them in my preferred order, based on what I think are reasonable priorities for a small business. You can adjust them as you see fit. A table at the end of each section summarizes the features and costs of each type of service.

Caution

Combining a LAN with an Internet connection also exposes you to some risks from hackers who have nothing better to do than try to break into your computers. Read Chapter 26, "Network Security," for more details.

THE NUTS AND BOLTS OF THE CONNECTION

You're probably familiar with using a modem to connect your own PC to an Internet service provider and thus to the Internet. When you're connecting an entire network of computers, the process is a little more involved. We'll address five main issues, starting with the physical connection itself. We'll discuss the pros and cons of each of the most common and reasonable alternatives.

THE NEED FOR SPEED

Of the several connection technologies, each has advantages and disadvantages in reliability, speed, and cost.

Speed is everything on the Internet now, and the need for raw speed will become even more important in the future. Remember that everyone on the LAN will be sharing a single connection, so you have to consider the speed requirements for the applications you'll be using over the network and multiply that requirement by the number of *simultaneous* users you'll want to support at that speed. If you have 20 users checking email and occasionally browsing the Web, your speed requirements might be met by a single modem, but if you have just two users who want to use voice and videoconferencing at the same time, you might need a very high-speed connection indeed.

PART

IV

CH

24

You can use these numbers to estimate your need for speed. They are minimum data rates for reasonable performance:

Text email	10Kbps
Web browsing	50Kbps
Voice conferencing	100Kbps
Videoconferencing	500Kbps

Multiply these data rates by the number of simultaneous users you want to give this level of performance. For most offices, you might try the rule of thumb I use: The factor is 1 + (number of computers/8). That is, assume that for every eight computers you'll find one additional user downloading something at any given moment.

For example, for a 12-user network engaging in average Web browsing, you'll want 50Kbps times (1 + 12/8), or at least a 125Kbps connection. For this network, a single shared 56K modem connection would often be annoyingly slow, but a 128Kbps Integrated Services Digital Network (ISDN) connection should be fine. Of course, more speed is *always* better!

HARDWARE TO MAKE THE CONNECTION

When you're using a single computer, you simply use its modem to dial your ISP as needed. On a LAN, you either use a modem in one of the computers or a separate hardware device, called a *router* or *modem/bridge*, connected to your ISP on one end and your LAN on the other. No matter what connection technology you use, you'll want the connection process to be automatic. The connection either needs to be on all the time or must be made auto-matically whenever someone on the network wants to use it. So, you need to use a *dedicated* connection, or you must use *demand-dialing*—that is, a modem that automatically connects whenever a user on the network needs it.

Fortunately, most of the fast, new Internet connection technologies use dedicated, always-on connections. And if you use an analog or ISDN modem to make your connection, Windows 2000 Professional has built-in demand-dialing software called *Internet Connection Sharing*, which does exactly what you need. Third-party hardware and software devices that can tackle this job are also available.

As an overview, Figure 24.1 shows the various ways you can hook up your LAN to an Internet service provider. We'll go into greater detail on each technique later in the chapter.

> **Note**
>
> Microsoft wants to change the name of *Internet Connection Sharing* on Windows 2000 Professional to *Shared Access* to distinguish the service on Windows 2000 Professional from the service on Windows 2000 Server. They really are different under the hood, but the name change is confusing, in my opinion, and came way too late in the Windows develop-ment cycle. If you see references to Shared Access, just know that it's the same as Connection Sharing. I continue to call it *Connection Sharing* because I'm stubborn and slow to change, and besides, any day, the folks at Microsoft might change their minds again.

MANAGING IP ADDRESSES

When you and several other computers are sharing one connection, all your data travels in and out through one wire. Just as every telephone needs its own number, each computer on your LAN needs a unique IP address so that returning Internet data gets sent to the correct computer. With multiple computers, you have a way to manage the job of assigning a dis-tinct IP address to each computer on your LAN.

You will have to make some decisions that depend on the number of computers you have connected to your LAN now and in the foreseeable future. Like telephone numbers, IP addresses are in short supply, and ISPs are reluctant to give you more than a few, at least without charging you for the privilege. The additional costs can add up, so you might want to consider using Windows Internet Connection Sharing or buying a device for carrying out your LAN's Internet connections using a single IP address. They both use the same process, and it's called *Network Address Translation (NAT)*, *circuit proxying*, and also *IP Masquerading*. It works like the telephone receptionist in an office who answers every call from the outside and routes messages to each extension in the office.

Figure 24.1
Note the various ways to connect your LAN to an ISP.

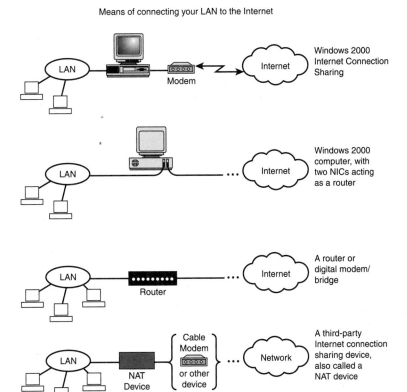

Means of connecting your LAN to the Internet

Windows 2000 Internet Connection Sharing

Windows 2000 computer, with two NICs acting as a router

A router or digital modem/bridge

A third-party Internet connection sharing device, also called a NAT device

You can go about IP addressing in one of two ways:

- Each computer on the network can have its own official, registered IP address, assigned by your ISP. The ISP sends data for all these IP addresses through your connection to your LAN.

- NAT software allows your Internet connection to carry multiple conversations using just one IP address. NAT software carries on the conversations on your behalf, using the one public IP address (see Figure 24.2). NAT has some significant benefits and drawbacks.

The benefits of using NAT are as follows:

- You can use an inexpensive, single-user ISP account to provide Internet access for as many computers as you want.

- NAT conserves IP addresses, which are in short supply due to the worldwide growth of the Internet.

- NAT acts as a basic firewall, preventing hackers from probing your network.

Figure 24.2
A NAT device or program carries on all Internet communications using one IP address. NAT keeps track of outgoing data from your LAN to determine where to send responses from the outside.

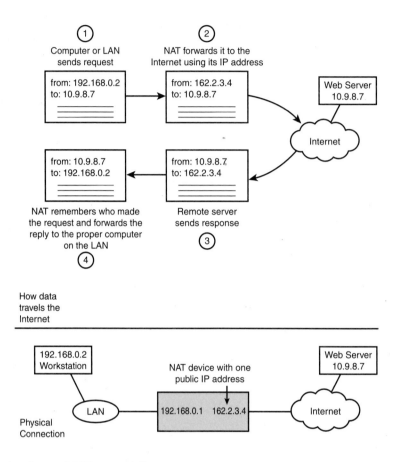

The drawbacks of using NAT are as follows:

- If you want to establish a public Web, FTP, or email server on your LAN, NAT has to be specially configured to direct incoming connections to the server on your network. Configuring NAT this way is not a big problem, but it means you can't have more than one public server of each type.

- NAT doesn't work with all network software. Some vendors' versions of NAT don't support RealAudio, Microsoft VPN software, or other protocols.

The version of NAT that comes with Windows 2000 Server can be enhanced to support new protocols, but the basic Connection Sharing in Windows 2000 Professional cannot.

Another drawback of Windows 2000's Internet Connection Sharing is that the computer with the connection must be powered up anytime anyone on the LAN wants Internet access. If you're sharing a modem connection, the computer has to remain logged in as well. If the computer with the connection is logged out or turned off, so is your connection.

NAT software is built into most DSL *(page 857)* and Frame Relay routers. You can also buy external devices such as the Whistle InterJet, UMAX Technology's UGate for cable and DSL, the Ramp Networks's Webramp system, Farallon's Netopia modem-sharing routers, or other systems for $300 to $1,200. This cost is quickly recovered because you can use a less expensive single-IP address plan from your ISP.

Whether or not you use NAT, each computer needs an IP address of its own for use on your LAN so that the router, modem, or NAT device can direct data to each of your computers. With NAT, you can use *any* IP addresses on your LAN because it's a private network and all communication with the outside world will use the one IP address of your NAT connection. It's best, though, to use addresses from a range that has been set aside just for this purpose. This way, your router always knows which addresses belong to the outside world and which belong inside.

Whatever numbers you use, you have to assign these numbers to the computers on your LAN. Windows 2000 Professional's Connection Sharing service takes care of this task for you automatically. If you don't use Connection Sharing, you can set the addresses manually, or you can use a router that provides Dynamic Host Configuration Protocol (DHCP) service. Many frame relay and DSL routers can do this job as well.

You'll learn a little more about NAT and addressing later on, after we've discussed making the connection itself.

PART
IV

CH
24

Running Your Own Web Servers

If you want to host your own public Web or email servers on your LAN, your network should use an always-on connection so that people around the world can reach your servers at any time. A *demand-dialing connection* is not a good choice for this use because the connection is established only when you try to reach out. Because the connection has to be on all the time, even a permanent dial-up connection is not very attractive because you have to pay per-minute connection charges to the telephone company, and there are 43,200 minutes in a 30-day month. The charges add up fast.

You also need your ISP to assign you a permanent, or *static*, IP address so that your computers' IP addresses don't change from day to day as a dial-up connection's does. Static IP addressing is not available with every connection technology or ISP, so you have to ask when shopping for your service provider.

Finally, you need a domain name service (DNS), which lets users around the world type `http://www.yoursitename.com` into their Web browsers to reach you. This service is provided as part of Windows 2000 Server, but not Professional. In this case, you need to have your ISP provide domain name service. It will probably cost you an extra $5 to $20 a month.

Inverse DNS

If you go for dedicated Internet access, and your ISP assigns you a block of IP addresses, you might want to ask your ISP to enter *Inverse DNS* information for you as well as register your domain name.

The domain name service (DNS) is called into play whenever you use an Internet address such as www.microsoft.com. DNS looks up this name in a directory and returns some computer's IP address—for example, 207.46.131.137. The DNS system can also work in reverse and return the name of a computer given its IP address. For example, the name 4.3.2.1 turns out to be durham2-001.dsl.gtei.net.

When you get routed Internet access, the inverse lookup names for the IP addresses assigned to you either are left undefined or are set to some generic names like cust137.dsl131.someISP.com. If you ask, your ISP can set up names that identify your computers and domain so that anyone on the Internet to whom you connect can find out the name of your computer.

Using inverse DNS has some pros and cons. A pro is that some email servers on the Internet don't accept email from systems without a valid inverse DNS entry. If you run an email server on your network, at least that computer should have an inverse DNS entry. A con is that Web site managers can tell the name of your computer and domain when you visit Web sites, so you give up some privacy.

The choice is up to you. If you want to register your computers, talk to your ISP. You need to email the provider a list of your IP numbers and the names of the computers to which they're assigned.

OTHER SUPPORT SERVICES

In addition to domain name service, you might want to pay your ISP to host email accounts for your users. Many ISPs provide multiple mailboxes for a nominal fee, letting you set up email addresses for each of your users. In addition, you might ask for mail alias service, which lets you assign role-based email addresses like sales@mycompany.com or info@mycompany.com to the appropriate person or persons.

If you choose to run your own public-access Web or email server, you still need your ISP to supply domain name service for you because the DNS system is involved in directing email to servers.

At this point, you've learned the basic service considerations. Now you have to consider what physical type of connection to use. For each of the choices discussed in the following sections, I'll point out how they stack up against the issues just discussed.

Let's look at the choices for getting connected.

CHOOSING A CONNECTIVITY OPTION

You must consider several factors when choosing an Internet connection for your network. Access speed and cost are certainly two of the most important, but you also need to consider the following:

- Reliability of the service and the companies involved.
- Availability of sufficient IP addresses for all the computers you're going to connect if you're not using NAT to hide your network behind a single IP address.

- Availability of static IP addresses if you plan to host public Web sites or an email server. If IP addresses are dynamic—that is, change every time you reconnect—you cannot host a Web or email server.

High-speed Internet connectivity is such a fast-growing business that providers are sometimes overwhelmed with orders, unable to maintain adequate service, and make more promises than they can keep. I know by direct and unhappy experience. The companies in this field range from superb to sincere to incompetent to downright dangerous, so my first recommendation is that you ask for references from current customers of any ISP you consider. Ask if their installation was performed on time, if phone calls are returned in a timely fashion, and if the service has been reliable and has met the advertised specifications. If your business depends on your Internet connection, do your homework and choose an ISP you feel you can trust. This consideration is much more important than cost.

You can choose from several connection types; I've listed them roughly in order of my enthusiasm for them.

A WARNING FOR BUSINESS USERS

My enthusiasm notwithstanding, cable and DSL Internet service are based on new technologies, and the businesses delivering them are new and growing extremely rapidly. I can tell you from direct experience that they can give you a painful, bumpy ride. Some DSL ISPs have already gone bankrupt and stranded their customers.

Customer support ranges from okay to incredibly bad, installation appointments are routinely missed, and even billing can be a terrible mess. Ask a provider for a service level agreement (a guaranteed percentage of uptime and throughput), and the likely reply will be hysterical laughter. If your business depends on your Internet connection to host servers or obtain access, DSL and cable are probably not for you.

It will cost lots more in the short term to set up Frame Relay or dedicated ISDN service, but if you lose business when your connection fails, you probably can't afford the risks that come with DSL and cable Internet access in these early years.

CABLE MODEM

The nation's cable television systems are being outfitted for two-way data connections at an amazing pace. Cable companies have fought for the right to use their existing wiring to carry not only television and radio signals, but also telephone and data communications. The cable company simply adds a small box to your TV cable, providing an Ethernet connection to your computer, router, or hub. Cable-based Internet service typically delivers data from the Internet to you at speeds up to 10Mbps (which is fast!) and from you out to the Internet at up to 128Kbps. See Figure 24.3 for an illustration of how cable modems work.

PART

IV

CH

24

Figure 24.3
Connecting via a cable modem.

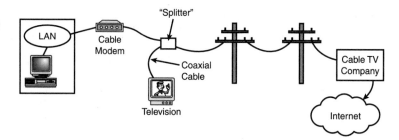

The connection between the cable modem and your LAN can be made in one of several ways. If your cable ISP can supply you with enough IP addresses for all the computers on your LAN, you can just connect the modem directly to your LAN. I *don't recommend* this method, though, because it does not provide any way to prevent outside hackers from attempting to break into your LAN; you don't have a firewall. A better approach would be to connect the modem to a firewall or filtering router, and the router to your LAN, as described in Chapter 26.

Usually, though, cable ISPs provide no more than three IP addresses, and this number won't be enough for you. In this case, or if you want to avoid the security risk of a direct connection, you should use Connection Sharing or NAT. You can connect the cable modem to a separate NAT device and then connect that device to your LAN. Or you can install two network cards in one of your Windows 2000 computers—one to connect to the LAN and one to connect to the cable modem—and use Internet Connection Sharing. Either way, you'll have an unlimited number of IP addresses and a greater measure of security.

Because most Internet activity such as Web browsing involves your sending very short requests to receive relatively large amounts of data back, this imbalance in transfer speeds is not noticeable. If you often use your Internet connection to copy large files to a remote location, however, you would probably find this imbalance irritating, and if you plan to host a Web site on your computer, the speed imbalance really would work against you.

However, some cable Internet services send data through the cable lines *to* you but require a modem to carry data back to your ISP. This kind of service is *not* really cut out for LAN connectivity. If that's all you can get in your area, you'll have to look to another technology to connect your LAN.

If you can get cable service, though, Table 24.1 provides some benchmarks you can use to determine whether connecting to the Internet via your cable company is a good idea.

TABLE 24.1   HOW CABLE STACKS UP

Speed of connection	Downloading is blazingly fast, whereas uploading is slower but still faster than even ISDN. If you've surfed the Net only over a modem connection, cable service will knock your socks off. However, this high bandwidth is shared by all the customers in the neighborhood served by each cable feeder system. So, as more of your friends and neighbors figure out what a great deal cable modems are, your connection will get slower and slower during high-use periods. (With any luck, by then the cable companies will be making enough money that they'll want to invest in speeding up things.)
Type of connection	Cable uses a special external modem with a 10BASE-T Ethernet connection. (Technically, it is called a *modem/bridge*, but don't worry, this term will not be on the final exam.) Cable can be connected directly to one computer or to a 10BASE-T network hub. It requires a dual-speed hub if you use a 100BASE-T network. The connection is always on.
IP addressing	The cable company provides usually no more than three addresses, and the numbers might not even be on the same IP subnetwork. This makes it a bad match for LAN access unless you use a NAT device. A separate NAT device is required to connect more than three computers.
Hosting your own servers	Addresses are usually static, but not always. Check with your ISP. Without static IP addresses, you cannot host a public server. Many cable ISPs expressly prohibit you from running servers over your cable connection.
Cost	The monthly rate is hard to beat; it's typically about $40 a month.

If cable service is available in your area, and you don't spend a lot of time copying data *out* to the Internet, then I say go with cable.

DSL

Digital Subscriber Line (DSL) technology sends a digital data signal over the standard telephone wires between your location and the telephone company's central office. This signal can coexist with a standard telephone connection, so your existing home or office telephone line can be outfitted to carry high-speed Internet traffic, even while you're carrying on a normal telephone conversation on the same line. This technology works by using a *splitter* device at your location and in the telephone company's switching office (see Figure 24.4). At your end is a DSL modem/bridge, and in the central office, the split-off signals of several subscribers are consolidated into fiber-optic connections; from there, your connections are routed to participating ISPs.

Figure 24.4
A DSL modem or router gives you high-speed Internet access over an existing telephone line.

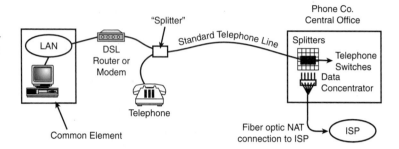

DSL service comes in many flavors; here, you can see the bewildering list of variations:

- ADSL, or Asymmetric Digital Subscriber Line, has different upload and download data rates, just like cable service.

- SDSL, or Symmetric Digital Subscriber Line, uses equal upload and download speeds.

- HDSL, or High Speed Digital Subscriber Line, is just ADSL or SDSL service at speeds of 384Kbps or more.

- IDSL uses a telephone line that formerly was used for ISDN service.

- RADSL, or Rate Adaptive Digital Subscriber Line, might go faster, but the phone company isn't responsible if the line doesn't run faster than the minimum guaranteed speed. In my area, RADSL is offered with the download speed advertised as "between 384K and 1.5Mbps." The closer you are to the phone company's central office and the better the quality of your community's wiring, the faster your service will be. (I had this service installed at home the day I wrote this chapter, in fact, and I lucked out: My line runs at 1.5 Mbps. Your mileage may vary.)

To save my weary fingers, I'll just write DSL and let you imagine the missing letters.

In practice, if DSL service is available to you, you can choose from a list of upload and download speeds and corresponding price schedules. In some cases, DSL data transport (the telephone company part) is bundled with the ISP's fee; in other localities, you pay for the two separately, so you have to be sure to add these figures when comparison shopping.

Tip #278	Prices for DSL can vary, of course, and your needs and budget must be factored in. For home use, I recommend getting service with 128Kbps upload and 384Kbps or higher download speeds. For a shared office connection, or if you plan to run a public Web server on your network, check into 384Kbps or faster symmetric DSL. Of course, if you want to offer streaming video or other bandwidth-intensive applications, you might want to go up to 1.5Mbps or higher.

DSL works just like cable when it comes to connecting the service to your LAN; you might have the additional option of getting a combination DSL modem/router with built-in firewall and NAT capability. This solution is the best, even better than using Windows Internet Connection Sharing, because you don't have to leave one of your Windows 2000 computers turned on all the time. I've used the Flowpoint and Netopia brand DSL routers, and both do a terrific job of providing firewall, NAT, and DHCP services for a small LAN.

Because you can get these feature-packed routers, given a choice, I recommend choosing DSL over cable when you're connecting a LAN to the Internet.

There, I've made my biases known. For the sake of fairness, though, Table 24.2 breaks down the pros and cons of DSL.

TABLE 24.2   HOW DSL STACKS UP

Speed of connection	DSL speeds range from 128Kbps to 6Mbps, depending on how much you're willing to pay and the distance between your location and the phone company's central office.
	As with cable service, DSL's speed is amazing, and you'll be spoiled instantly. You won't be able to stand to use a modem ever again.
Type of connection	DSL service is always on.
	For connections with one to three IP addresses, you are given a DSL modem/bridge with a single 10BASE-T connector. You can cable it to a 10BASE-T hub or directly to a single computer.
	For larger networks, you need to purchase a DSL router such as the Flowpoint 2200 or Farallon Netopia R7100, which are nifty devices with eight-port 10BASE-T hubs built right in.
Managing IP addresses	DSL providers typically assign fixed IP addresses. DSL routers, if used, are up-to-date with NAT and DHCP servers built right in, so they are quite helpful to use if you have a medium- or large-sized LAN. Routers cost more than a modem, but I like the extra NAT, firewall, and DHCP services they provide. If you don't want to use NAT, you can ask your ISP for a block of assigned IP addresses for your network, although you may be charged extra for more than three or four.
Hosting your own servers	No problem here. DSL's fixed IP addresses mean that you can easily set up a public Web site or email server.
Cost	DSL service is aggressively priced to compete with cable service and is a great bargain. DSL plans typically cost $50 to $200 a month, for rates in the 500Kbps ballpark and 1 to 64 IP addresses.
	A DSL router costs about $400, compared with a DSL modem at $100, but is well worth the cost if you want to use the NAT, DHCP, or firewall functions.
	Some ISPs even waive installation, setup, and sometimes equipment costs if you sign up for at least a year's service.

PART

IV

CH

24

You can probably tell that I'm really excited about both DSL and cable service. They provide the fastest connections for the money but are not yet available everywhere. You'll have to check to see whether they're available in your area. The following are a few suggested places to check:

- Your telephone company
- Your cable TV company
- Your current ISP
- http://www.northpoint.com and www.covad.com (DSL)
- http://www.athome.com (cable)
- http://www.rr.com (cable)

If these services are not yet available to you, call these people and complain loudly. Remember, the squeaky wheel gets changed and left by the side of the road. (No, wait, that's not how it goes, is it?)

ISDN

Integrated Services Digital Network (ISDN) is an all-digital telephone service. ISDN was once considered to have great promise as a replacement for ordinary telephone service, but that was before the Internet burst on the scene and made ISDN's maximum 128Kbps data rate seem pitifully slow. ISDN's strong point is that it maintains two simultaneous 64Kbps channels, either of which can carry a telephone or data connection. Or it can use both of its channels together to carry one 128Kbps connection.

Connecting a Windows 2000 LAN via ISDN is a little trickier than with cable or DSL. ISDN Internet connections need an ISDN router (from 3COM, Ascend, Nortel Networks, or other manufacturers) or an ISDN modem, which acts like an ordinary modem but connects to an ISDN telephone line. Routers are more difficult to set up, but in my opinion, they perform better than modems in a LAN setting. In particular, ISDN routers can be set up to demand-dial *and* to automatically switch between 64Kbps and 128Kbps connections, depending on usage. You therefore can save money because telephone companies usually charge for the two data channels as separate telephone calls. If you use an ISDN modem, it functions like a regular modem. You can connect an external ISDN modem to a NAT Internet sharing device, or you can install either an external or internal modem in a Windows 2000 computer and use Internet Connection Sharing.

ISDN is a decent temporary means of connecting your LAN until DSL becomes available in your area. Table 24.3 provides some basic criteria to help you determine whether ISDN is for you.

TABLE 24.3   HOW ISDN STACKS UP

Speed of connection	ISDN connects at speeds of 64Kbps or 128Kbps.
Type of connection	ISDN uses a special digital telephone line.
	ISDN modems have a standard serial adapter, which plugs into a COM port on your computer.
	To get the most out of an ISDN modem, your COM port needs to be able to run at least at 115Kbps and preferably higher.
	ISDN routers have a 10BASE-T network connection to plug into your network.
Managing IP addresses	ISPs can usually set up ISDN accounts with either a single fixed or dynamic IP address, or a block of fixed addresses. You therefore have two options: You can use Connection Sharing and one IP address, or you can use an external ISDN router as long as it has firewall protection.
	ISDN routers typically do not have built-in DHCP servers, so you might have to assign IP addresses on your LAN by hand.
Hosting your own servers	Many ISPs assign static IP addresses to business ISDN customers, especially if you're willing to pay the higher rate for a dedicated 24-hour-a-day connection. For a dedicated connection, ISDN routers can be configured to keep the call permanently established. This configuration gets expensive, though, because ISDN calls are expensive and even local calls are billed.
Cost	Dial-up ISDN service is typically $30 to $50 a month for a single IP address, using demand-dialing for an intermittent connection.
	For direct LAN connections, with multiple IP addresses and an always-on connection, expect to pay the ISP $250 a month, and $200 to $800 a month in telephone connection costs.
	The rates vary considerably from state to state in the U.S.
	You might be able to eliminate per-minute charges if *Centrex* service is available in your area; check with your ISP to see whether you can use it.

The Centrex Sneak

Centrex is a service that phone companies provide to compete with private office phone-switching systems called *key systems*. (You've probably seen that gray box on the wall in the office bathroom; it connects to every phone extension and links to a few outside lines. That's a key system.)

The phone company can set up telephones to act like a key system, except that a line runs from each extension all the way to the phone company's central office. This service is called Centrex (usually—your phone company might have another name for it), and you've encountered it if you've ever had to dial a 9 to get an outside line.

I'll let you in on a little secret: Calls between the extension phones are free because they're internal calls.

This setup is a fairly good deal for businesses, which don't have to buy an expensive switching system and never need to upgrade or repair it. It's a *great* deal for the phone company, which gets to charge a monthly fee

continues

continued

for each extension, instead of just a few outside lines. As a benefit, perhaps in exchange for all that extra revenue, phone companies will install lines in other locations, still as part of the Centrex system, as long as the lines run to the same or nearby central office. Calls to and from these remote extensions are still free. Hmmmm!

If your ISP can have one of its own modem or ISDN telephone lines installed at your location as a remote extension, the call to your ISP is an internal phone call, and it's free…even if it's on 24 hours a day, seven days a week.

Oh, the phone companies *hate* this, but I've found it a neat, if dirty, trick to get a cheap, dedicated Internet connection.

MODEM

A shared connection using a modem? It's not really high tech, but it works, if you enable the Windows Connection Sharing feature. Windows 2000 Professional has built-in support for demand-dialing, so you can set up a modem on just one of the computers on your LAN. With Connection Sharing, when anyone on the LAN attempts to connect to an outside Internet resource, this modem automatically dials your ISP and establishes a connection (see Figure 24.5). After a period of inactivity, it can automatically hang up the modem. Windows 2000 Professional provides built-in NAT for modem connections. Of course, the single 33Kbps to 56Kbps connection is shared by all users trying to transfer information at the same time, so you might find you *really* dislike this approach when the next *Star Wars* movie comes out and everyone tries to download the trailer at the same time.

Figure 24.5
Connection Sharing makes one modem available to an entire network. The host computer acts as a router, a NAT device, and a DHCP server.

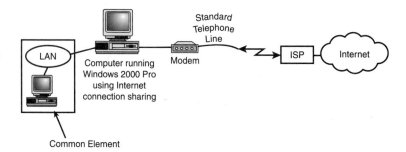

Another downside to Windows Connection Sharing is that it requires the computer with the shared modem to remain turned on and logged in. Keeping the modem turned on poses a security risk, which you'll have to consider. The third-party hardware packages I mentioned don't have this problem.

No matter how you do it, a shared modem connection is a bit cumbersome, at least in an office setting. Still, if DSL or cable service isn't available, it's a workable alternative.

For a dedicated connection, modems share the per-minute-cost drawback of ISDN. In most states, businesses are charged by the minute for even local calls, so month-long phone calls can really add up! Again, Centrex service might be available, which would eliminate the monthly cost. Centrex has worked well for one of my clients. However, few ISPs are interested in establishing dedicated modem connections any more. Table 24.4 gives you the lowdown on shared modem connections.

TABLE 24.4	HOW A MODEM STACKS UP
Speed of connection	A modem provides 33Kbps upload and typically 40 to 50Kbps download.
Type of connection	A modem must be attached to the serial port of a computer or a third-party NAT router. The computer or router then connects to your LAN.
Managing IP addresses	Windows Connection Sharing entails your buying into Microsoft's built-in package, which includes DHCP and NAT. IP address management is automatic, but you are forced into using the numbers Microsoft chose for you.
Hosting your own servers	Sorry, but hosting your own servers isn't likely to be possible because, with modem connections, the IP address assigned to the modem changes every call. It would be like having a phone number that changed every hour.... You could call out okay, but who could ever call you? Few ISPs assign a static, or permanent, IP address for dial-up users. Yours might, but don't get your hopes up.

PART

IV

CH

24

FRAME RELAY

Frame relay is an older technology that was primarily designed for private, dedicated, long-distance connections for the corporate world. It's connected using hardware very similar to DSL, but it requires its own dedicated telephone line from your office to the phone company and some expensive equipment (see Figure 24.6).

Figure 24.6
Frame relay service is reliable but relatively expensive. It requires a router and a line-interface device called a CSU/DSU.

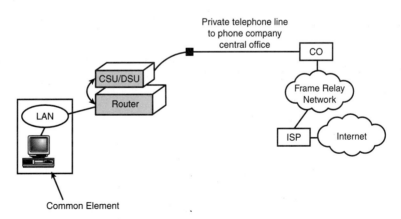

Although installing and setting up frame relay Internet hardware is tough, after the equipment is in, it just plugs into your LAN and virtually no setup is involved with Windows itself.

Frame relay connections are very reliable, and run at data rates similar to DSL, but have a severe disadvantage in price. Consider the typical mid-1999 costs for a 128Kbps (frame relay versus DSL) Internet connection shown in Table 24.5.

TABLE 24.5   128KBPS FRAME RELAY VERSUS 128KBPS DSL

	128Kbps Frame Relay	128Kbps DSL
Installation by telephone company	$1,000	$0–100
Setup by ISP	$400	$0
Required hardware (modem and so on)	$1,200–1,800	$100–600
Monthly data line fee	$325	$40
Monthly Internet service provider fee	$400	$10

On the plus side, a frame relay connection can be used to provide secure, private connections between geographically separate LANs in a company, over a single physical wire, which can also be used for an Internet connection. Frame relay is also more reliable. You might expect service interruptions of no more than three minutes per month versus perhaps three hours per month with DSL service. So you have justifiable business reasons for using frame relay for WAN connectivity, but probably not for Internet service, unless no other options are available. An exception would be for businesses running e-commerce servers or other business applications, for which this high reliability is a business requirement and a reasonable expense.

Table 24.6 provides some basics to help you decide whether frame relay is right for your needs.

TABLE 24.6   HOW FRAME RELAY STACKS UP

Speed of connection	Frame relay connects at 64Kbps to 1.5Mbps.
Type of connection	Frame relay uses a dedicated, leased line managed by the telephone company, a digital modem called a CSU/DSU, and a standard router, usually with a 10BASE-T connector.
Managing IP addresses	Excellent; ISPs provide blocks of IP addresses for frame relay users. Frame relay routers typically have DHCP server software built in.
Hosting your own servers	Excellent; frame relay gives an always-on, high-reliability connection with fixed IP addresses. Most businesses with serious Web sites use frame relay.
Cost	Frame relay is really expensive, next to DSL or cable. A few years ago, it was the only option, so people got used to paying this much. For a small office, it's probably the last resort now.

WIRELESS

Wireless Internet service is now available in limited metropolitan areas. This service is similar to the personal wireless connection offered by companies such as Ricochet, but it's faster—up to 1.5Mbps over a radio connection to an ISP (see Figure 24.7). The disadvantages are limited availability, high cost (roughly the same as frame relay), and the requirement for a line-of-sight path between the ISP and your receiving antenna. The big advantage is that you can be connected immediately because you don't have the weeks' long wait for the telephone company to install a line.

The effort of connecting your Windows 2000 LAN via wireless is about the same as frame relay, though. The hardware is rather hard to set up and configure; but when it's in, you don't have to do any Windows setup at all.

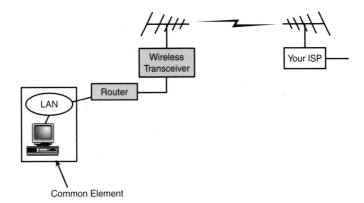

Figure 24.7
Wireless Internet service carries the plug-and-play concept to the LAN.

To see how wireless connections rate, see the "Frame Relay" section earlier in this chapter. Wireless connections are similar to frame relay, with the addition of the pros and cons I just mentioned.

SATELLITE

You might have heard that you can get Internet service via dinner-plate-sized satellite receivers, through several providers such as Hughes's DirecPC. One big plus for satellite service is that it's available anywhere you can see the sky! The download speeds are quite high, comparable to cable modems. But satellite service is not a reasonable choice for connecting your LAN to the Internet. For the types of satellite service available on any reasonable budget, the satellite part of the connection is only one-way: Internet to you. Receiving is simple, but sending data to a satellite takes a lot of very expensive equipment. So, satellite Internet service requires a modem connection to an ISP to carry data from you to the Internet (see Figure 24.8). This technology doesn't mesh with NAT or Connection Sharing because you're actually making two separate outside connections. For this reason, I'm not going to say any more about satellite Internet service: For a LAN, it's not feasible. Its only niche is providing access in places where no other high-speed technology can reach—that is, where no competition exists.

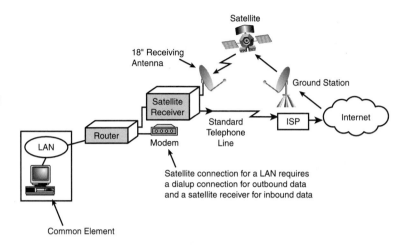

Figure 24.8
Satellite service is a one-direction connection that requires a modem for outbound data. The service is expensive and is not a good choice for LAN connectivity.

COMPARING THE DATA TRANSFER RATES AND SPEED OF EACH CONNECTION TYPE

Table 24.7 shows the data rates and costs of each of the technologies discussed in this chapter.

TABLE 24.7 SUMMARY OF INTERNET CONNECTION TECHNOLOGIES WITH APPROXIMATE COSTS FOR INTERMITTENT SERVICE

Technology	Upload Data Rate	Download Data Rate	Setup Cost	Monthly Cost[2]
DSL	128Kbps	384Kbps	$100	$50
	384Kbps	1.5Mbps	$600	$99
	1.5Mbps	6Mbps	$600	$250
Cable	128Kbps	1–10 Mbps	$100	$40
ISDN	64Kbps	64Kbps	$500	$75[1]
	128Kbps	128Kbps	$500	$100[1]
Modem	33Kbps	50Kbps	$150	$50[1]
Frame Relay	64Kbps 1.5Mbps	64Kbps 1.5Mbps	$3,200 $3,200	$500 $1,500

[1] Add $200 to $800 a month for a dedicated connection if Centrex service is not available.
[2] All prices are average rates, second quarter 1999; prices will vary.

GETTING YOUR SERVICE INSTALLED

You've done your research, you've found out what connection technologies are available to you, and you've checked prices and asked a few selected ISPs for references. Now what? The following sections describe the steps you need to take to get your network connected.

WHEN THE PHONE COMPANY IS INVOLVED

If you choose DSL, ISDN, or frame relay service, you have to get a phone line installed and have to deal with the phone company. If you remember her, conjure up a picture of Lily Tomlin's character "Ernestine" taking your order. Got the picture?

Telephone companies are old, big businesses with their own language. In many countries, they're state-owned monopolies, and in most, they're slow, bureaucratic, and highly regulated. The first lesson you have to learn is that you do it their way or not at all. I'll describe the way things are done in the United States to give you a feel for what needs to happen. If you're dealing with Internet service in another country, you'll probably have to make some adjustments to what follows; check with your local ISPs for expert advice on dealing with your telephone company.

If you're lucky, your Internet service provider will manage all aspects of your order, including provisioning, outside and inside wiring, and equipment setup. If you have to deal with the "telcos" directly, you should be familiar with the terminology they'll throw your way. Table 24.8 should arm you with the verbal weaponry you need.

PART

IV

CH

24

TABLE 24.8	STANDARD TELCO TERMINOLOGY
POTS	We've talked all about high-tech services. Did you know that the name for just plain old telephone service is…exactly that? *POTS* is a real telephone company acronym. It's used this way: "DSL service can run on a standard POTS line."
T1	T1 is a fairly old-fashioned data carrier technology that lets a single pair of wires carry data at 1.5Mbps, which can carry 64 digitized telephone conversations. Telcos use T1 lines to carry phone calls between their offices, and ISDN and frame relay service can also ride on T1 lines.
T3	This technology makes a T1 line look like a drinking straw; it runs at 45Mbps.
CO	The *central office* is a phone company switching center. All the telephone wires in your neighborhood—whether they're carrying POTS, ISDN, DSL, or private data service—funnel into a CO, where they connect to the telephone company's switching equipment. From there, T1 and fiber-optic lines connect the central offices.
Switch	This device in a CO cross-connects the telephone lines of subscribers when they call each other or connects them to *trunk lines*, which connect the switches. Switches were designed to interlink only a certain number of lines at once, so lengthy calls to ISPs tie up the switches' capacity and give fits to the telephone company.
Demarc	In the U.S., the telephone company is responsible for the wiring and proper operation of any service from its office up to the point the wires enter your building. This point is called the *demarcation point*, or just *demarc*. At this point, the telephone company installs a box with screw terminals, where its wires end and yours are attached.

continues

TABLE 24.8   CONTINUED

Outside wiring	The phone company installs *outside wiring* between its street boxes, telephone poles, and so on, and the demarc. The price for this service is included in your installation fee.
Inside wiring	The wiring between the demarc and your networking equipment or telephones is *inside wiring*. This wiring is your responsibility, although the phone company will wire for a fee if you ask. You can also hire a wiring contractor or do it yourself. Some service providers include inside wiring in the setup fee. The DSL services I've installed all included free inside wiring.
Provisioning	The job of determining which wires to use of the thousands installed in the cables running around town, which IP addresses you'll be assigned, and which options to program into the central office's hardware is called *provisioning*. In a company with millions of such resources to track, the process is handled by a separate department. Sometimes you have to speak to a provisioning specialist to select or confirm some options for your service.

ORDERING THE SERVICE

Ordering the service is the most treacherous part of the whole process. I've been involved in dozens of telephone and network service installations, and by far, most of the problems I have encountered are not technical but administrative: Details get lost or left out, orders get lost or set aside, equipment is not shipped, and due dates slip. So, my two most important tips are as follows:

- Hire a consultant. Networking services, especially if they involve the telephone company, have many options and details. If you don't specify them yourself, the odds are that someone in an office cubicle somewhere, someone who has no idea what you're trying to do, will make decisions for you. Don't take that chance. If you're the least bit unsure about this process, hire a consultant to help get set up. Or, at least, have your ISP work with you to order any part of the service that involves the telephone company.

- Don't take anyone's word for granted. Take responsibility for knowing whether the ordering and installation process is progressing. Get the information you need to follow your order through the system. Internet service providers, especially DSL and cable providers, are frenzied right now, and the chances are they'll drop the ball somewhere along the way. Keep on top of them.

I recommend that you keep the following list, which I'll call "talking points" (Thank you, Monica), in front of you when you are ordering your service. Keeping a list may sound fussy, but I have been tripped up at various times by forgetting to ask even just one of these questions.

- Is my location qualified for this service?
- When will you call me to let me know? (This question should be used in response to any "I don't know" answer.)

- Do you assign static IP addresses?
- How many IP addresses can I have, and at what cost?
- For cable only: Will all the IP numbers be on the same subnet? (See "Special Notes for Cable Service" following this list.)
- Can I add on IP addresses later?
- What are the setup, installation, equipment, and monthly service costs?
- Do you offer any discounts for longer-term contracts?
- What equipment is included in the price you quoted?
- Do I need to order service from the telephone company, or do you do that?
- Do other people order or ask for things that I haven't?
- When will the service be installed? At what time of day?
- What sort of inside wiring is needed?
- Do you do inside wiring, and is the cost included in your quote?
- What other equipment will I need?
- Will you waive your setup fee?
- What is my order number?
- Who in your organization is responsible for the next step in getting my order completed? What is that person's phone number? When will I hear from him or her?
- What equipment do I need to have ready when the installer arrives?
- Could you please read back my name, address, phone number, email address, and the details of the order as you've taken them down?
- Do I need to know anything else?

PART

IV

CH

24

> **Note**
>
> Do you have a network connection experience, hint, or horror story you would like to share? Visit our Web site at `http://www.helpwin.com` to share it with us!

Tip #279

> Most of the technologies described in this chapter involve installing a connection of some sort between your location and the ISP or telephone company. So, you're involved with *two* companies. Your best bet is to let your ISP coordinate getting the wiring ordered and installed so that no information falls between the cracks.

SPECIAL NOTES FOR CABLE SERVICE

When you order more than one IP address on cable service, some providers assign IP addresses that have different IP subnet addresses. Giving you different subnet addresses is like giving you telephone extensions with different area codes—yuck!

It makes a big difference if you want to use the TCP/IP protocol for Microsoft Networking (file sharing) on your LAN because your computers would not be able to find each other in Network Neighborhood. Having different subnet addresses makes it impossible to use a router or to use Windows as a direct router. Besides the security risks, if your provider gives you different addresses, use NAT with cable modem service.

Special Notes for ISDN Service

If you are ordering ISDN service, you should know what kind of ISDN modem or router you will be using before you order an ISDN line from the phone company. ISDN provisioning is complex, and most telephone companies can determine the options you need if you tell them the brand of equipment you're using. Also, your ISDN equipment manual may list a special "quick order" code to give your telephone company. You will probably order "2B+D, Data and voice, 64K data" service with no special call functions.

When your ISDN line is installed, be sure to ask the installer for the following information:

- Switch type
- SPID (Service Profile Identifiers) numbers
- Directory numbers

Getting the Equipment Installed

Each of the technologies mentioned in this chapter uses different equipment to make the connection. I'll go through each of them here to tell you what you need to do to make the connection to your LAN. You'll learn how to configure it in the next major section.

Cable

Cable Internet service providers install a cable modem or router, which has a single 10BASE-T Ethernet connector.

If you are connecting your cable modem directly to your LAN and use a 100BASE-Tx network, you might have a problem. If you use a dual-speed hub, you can just plug the cable modem right in. Otherwise, you need to buy a media converter to connect between the cable modem and your hub. A 10BASE-T to 100BASE-Tx media converter costs about $100. I don't recommend making a direct connection in any case because it affords you no firewall protection.

Tip #280

If you want to mix 10- and 100BASE-T equipment, be careful because some so-called "dual-speed" hubs can't mix both speeds at the same time, so the slower connection to your cable modem slows down the entire network. Check with the hub's supplier before you buy!

If you are using a NAT device, plug the cable modem into the NAT device and then the NAT device to your LAN hub. The NAT device manual explains how to configure your computers.

If you're using Windows Internet Connection Sharing, install a second 10BASE-T Ethernet card in the computer that will be the sharing computer. Connect the cable modem to the new network card. This is great because you can use an inexpensive 10BASE-T network card regardless of the network type or speed of your LAN.

Note

Check the documentation on the cable modem to see whether you should use a *straight-through* or *crossover* network cable to make the connection. If the manual says to use a straight-through cable to connect directly to a network card in a computer, use a crossover cable if you connect to your network hub, and vice versa.(Or, do what I do: Ignore the manual, try both, and use whichever one makes the green lights come on.) (The cable service installer will probably make this connection for you anyway.)

DSL

DSL Internet service providers install a DSL modem with a single 10BASE-T Ethernet connector, or a router, which may have a built-in eight-port 10BASE-T hub.

If you are not using NAT, or if you are using built-in NAT software in the DSL router, you can connect the modem or router directly to your 10BASE-T hub. If you can use the hub built into your router, lucky for you.

See the note in the preceding "Cable" section regarding 100BASE-Tx networks, cables, little green lights, and NAT.

MODEM

If you want to use a modem, you can install and configure your modem in the usual Windows way, as described in Chapter 11, "Internet and TCP/IP Connection Options." You'll learn how to set up Internet Connection Sharing in the next major section.

ISDN

If you want to use an ISDN modem and Windows Internet Connection Sharing, you can install the ISDN modem as described in Chapter 11 and proceed to the next section to set up Internet Connection Sharing.

If you are using an ISDN router, you need to follow the instructions provided by its manufacturer. I can't help you much with this installation, but I can tell you the main tasks involved:

■ Install a telephone jack for the ISDN connection near your network hub. Label the jack clearly as "ISDN." ISDN signals don't damage an ordinary telephone, but you might be confused because an ISDN line appears to have no dial tone when you plug in an ordinary phone.

- Connect the ISDN router to the new ISDN line and to your network hub. ISDN devices typically provide a 10BASE-T connection, so you need a media converter if you must connect it to coaxial cable or 100BASE-T network wiring.

- Your ISP should configure the router for you and set it to use demand-dialing or a permanent (in phone terminology, nailed-up) connection, as you like. If you need to set up the router yourself, you need the following:

  From your ISP, the telephone number, username, and password for your dial-up ISDN connection.

  From the telephone company, the switch type, SPIDs, and directory numbers for your new line.

  Your ISP will also assign you a block of network numbers for the router and the computers on your LAN.

FRAME RELAY

Frame relay connections require two hardware devices: a CSU/DSU (which is a type of high-speed digital modem) and a router. I don't have the room to explain how to install and set up this type of connection, nor would you want to read it. (Can you say "Dry"?)

> **Note**
>
> I can, however, recommend an excellent book that covers networking in detail. Pick up a copy of *Upgrading and Repairing Networks, Second Edition*, published by Que.

The main tasks involved are as follows:

- Frame relay service uses leased, dedicated lines provided by the telephone company. If you can, have the telephone company "extend the demarc"—that is, take responsibility for the data line all the way to your computer room (closet, shelf, desk, hut, hovel, or whatever). By doing so, you may save some finger pointing later if you have trouble with the connection.

- Connect the leased line to the CSU/DSU, the CSU/DSU to the router, and the router to your Ethernet network.

- Your ISP will provide all the setup information for the router, or may even configure or install it for you. (For a thousand bucks, it should.)

- Your ISP will assign an IP address for your router and another block of IP addresses for the computers on your LAN. You will have to use whatever numbers the ISP assigns, unless you are using a NAT device between the frame relay router and your LAN. The router may have NAT capability built in, but you probably don't need it. The router can and should be set up to act as a proper firewall to protect your network.

- If you have no Windows 2000 server on your network, the router can probably be configured to act as a DHCP server, which you'll learn about later in this chapter.

WIRELESS

A wireless connection uses equipment installed by your ISP, and it requires the ISP to mount an antenna and test the radio signal. The rest of the setup for wireless connectivity follows the procedure described for frame relay. Your ISP will help you install and set up a router.

CONFIGURING YOUR LAN

You waited weeks for installation day, and the phone installer finally came. The routers and modems arrived, and now all you can think of is all those bits, just waiting to blast their way onto your network. Hang on; we're almost done.

The last step is to set up your network's TCP/IP software to let your computers talk through the Internet connection in a coordinated way. This step depends not so much on the connection type you chose but on the sharing type and IP address system you're using.

You proceed like this:

- If you are using an analog or ISDN modem to dial in to an ISP, follow the instructions in the next section for dial-up Internet Connection Sharing.

- If you are using Internet Connection Sharing to share a DSL or cable connection, see "Configuring Cable/DSL Service for Connection Sharing."

- Otherwise, skip down to "Configuring Direct High-Speed Connections," where I will offer little help.

CONFIGURING A SHARED DIAL-UP CONNECTION

Microsoft has included a demand-dialing NAT service called Internet Connection Sharing as part of Windows 2000 Professional. It works with modem or ISDN connections. The following section describes how to set it up.

SETTING UP THE SHARED CONNECTION

To set up a shared connection, first install and test your modem and ISP information on one computer on the network by configuring a standard dial-up connection. You learned this process in Chapter 11. Be sure that you can access the Internet properly by viewing at least one Web page. Then follow these steps:

1. In Network and Dial-up Connections, right-click the icon for the connection to your ISP, and select Properties.

2. Choose the Internet Connection Sharing tab. Check Enable Internet Connection Sharing for This Connection and Enable On-Demand Dialing (see Figure 24.9).

PART

IV

CH

24

Figure 24.9
Sharing a dial-up connection is a snap.

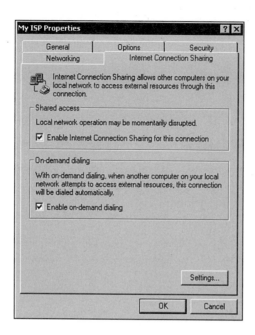

3. If you want an always-on connection, select the Options tab and check Redial if Line Is Dropped. Set the number of Redial Attempts to 99, the Time Between Redial Attempts to 10 seconds, and Idle Time Before Hanging Up to Never.

   Otherwise, if you want a demand-dialing connection, select the Options tab and uncheck Redial if Line Is Dropped. Set the number of Redial Attempts to 10, the Time Between Redial Attempts to 10 seconds, and Idle Time Before Hanging Up to 10 minutes. (I recommend using this time; however, you can change it if you like.)

4. Select the Networking tab. In the list of Components used by the connection, be sure that *only* Internet Protocol (TCP/IP) is checked.

Caution

Selecting only the Internet Protocol (TCP/IP) option is your network's only protection from hackers on the Internet. File and Printer Sharing for Microsoft Networks must be unchecked to disconnect this computer's file sharing from the Internet connection. Other computers on the LAN are protected by NAT.

5. Click OK. Windows then warns you that it is changing the network address of your LAN adapter to 192.168.0.1. It is now the IP address for this computer on your LAN.

6. Open the Computer Management Control Panel, and select Services and Applications. Then open Services.

7. Locate Remote Access Auto Connection Manager. Right-click it and select Start, as shown in Figure 24.10

Figure 24.10
To enable on-demand dialing, you must set the Remote Access Auto Connection Manager Service to start automatically when your computer is booted up.

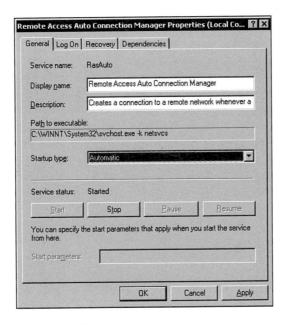

8. Right-click again and select Properties.

9. Change Startup Type to Automatic and click OK.

10. Close the Computer Management Control Panel.

CONFIGURING THE REST OF THE NETWORK

To configure the other computers on the network, each in turn, follow these steps:

1. Bring up Network and Dial-up Connections, and open Local Area Connections Properties.

2. Select Internet Protocol (TCP/IP), and then select Properties.

3. Check Obtain an IP Address Automatically and Obtain DNS Server Address Automatically.

   If you want to provide public access to a Web server running on your LAN but not in the sharing computer, you need to be sure it has a fixed, known IP address. You need to set that computer's IP address manually. You might decide to do so anyway, if you want to know the IP addresses of your computers without having to check them.

   If you want to assign an address manually, you can enter a specific IP address as 192.168.0.*x*, where *x* is a number between 2 and 254. Start with 254 and work downward to avoid conflicts with the automatic numbers Windows passes out. Set the Network mask to 255.255.255.0, the Default Gateway to 192.168.0.1, (the sharing computer), and the DNS Server Information address to 192.168.0.1 as well. Figure 24.11 shows typical settings.

Figure 24.11
If you manually set IP addresses for the other computers on your LAN, you must use addresses 192.168.0.*x* and use the sharing computer as the gateway and DNS server.

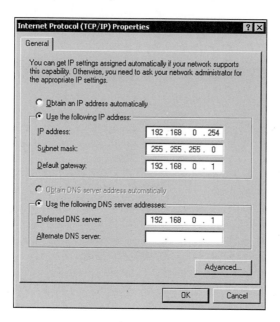

If you enter IP addresses manually, you have to keep track of them yourself, but at least you will always know which number is assigned to each computer. Unless you have a strong preference, I recommend choosing Automatic.

4. Click OK. The computer should reconfigure itself with a new IP address obtained from the computer with the shared dial-up connection.

Now test the shared connection from a computer on your LAN by trying to browse a Web page.

 If the computer can't browse Web pages, see "Can't Access a Shared Modem Connection from the LAN" in the "Troubleshooting" section at the end of this chapter.

MAKING A WEB SERVER AVAILABLE

If you have a Web server running in the sharing computer, it is accessible from the Internet, as are any other TCP/IP services it has installed. If you have a Web server (for example, Internet Information Server) elsewhere on your network, you can make it available to the Internet by telling the Internet Connection Sharing service to redirect incoming Web server requests to the other computer. Remember, the outside world sees only the IP address assigned to your dial-up connection, not the private IP numbers used on your LAN.

> **Note**
> You must redirect server requests only if the service is hosted on a computer other than the one sharing the Internet connection. Any incoming requests that aren't redirected are handled by the sharing computer.

To tell the NAT service in Connection Sharing where to send incoming requests, first go to the computer with the shared Internet connection. Then follow these steps:

1. In Network and Dial-up Connections, right-click the icon for the connection to your ISP and select Properties. Next, choose the Internet Connection Sharing tab.

2. Click the Settings button, and select the Services tab. Then click Add.

3. Fill in the information as shown in Figure 24.12.
   - Name of service —http
   - Service port number—80
   - Check TCP.
   - Name or Address of Server Computer on Private Network—Enter the name or the IP number of the computer that is running IIS. Unless you have manually set the IP addresses on your network, enter the computer's name because IP numbers may change automatically from reboot to reboot.

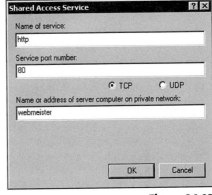

Figure 24.12

4. Click OK.

Now an Internet user who knows your connection's IP address (not the address inside your LAN, but the address of the modem connection) can view Web pages from the server on your LAN by typing the following:

```
http://111.222.333.444
```

The user must substitute your actual IP number, of course.

For this reason, you need a fixed IP number if you want to have a "real" Web site. If your public IP number changes every time your modem disconnects, your site will be very difficult for people to find.

ISDN users with fixed IP addresses and DNS service can ask their ISP to direct requests for www.mycompany.com to your fixed IP address, and *voilà*, you have a Web site.

MAKING OTHER SERVICES AVAILABLE TO THE INTERNET

You can adjust the instructions for making a Web server available to add mappings for other server types as well. If you have any of the following server types running on your LAN, you can use the following service names and TCP port numbers to add entries for any of the servers you have installed:

HTTP (World Wide Web)	80
SMTP (mail receipt)	25

POP3 (mail post office)   110

FTP (needs two entries)   20 and 21

You can add other mappings for RealAudio servers, and so on; you just need to know the server's protocol and port number assignments, which are provided by the software manufacturer. For example, you can redirect incoming connections to Symantec's PCAnywhere remote control software by directing TCP port 5631 and UDP port 5632 to a computer on your LAN that you want to designate as the PCAnywhere host.

However, you cannot tell Connection Sharing to direct Microsoft Virtual Private Networking (VPN) requests to a different computer on the LAN; only the computer with the shared dial-up connection can receive a (single) VPN connection. Unfortunately, the NAT system on Windows 2000 Professional isn't sophisticated enough to redirect incoming VPN connections.

ENABLING NAT FOR NONSTANDARD APPLICATIONS

Connection Sharing's NAT system knows about most of the standard TCP/IP and Microsoft network protocols already, so if a computer in your LAN makes a request to a remote Web server, NAT knows where to send the response.

If you find that you can access a remote TCP/IP service from the sharing computer but not other computers on your LAN, you might have to tell NAT how to recognize an outgoing request so that it can properly route the returning responses. Doing so is especially important when the service uses the UDP protocol, which doesn't carry the connection information that NAT can use to match outgoing and incoming packets.

You must know what port the remote server receives requests on and which protocol it uses, and what ports and protocols its responses are sent through. For example, assume you want to view online video using a fictitious video service. The video service Web site says that its servers listen on TCP port 4321 and send the video stream back to the client on UDP port 4322.

To tell NAT how to redirect responses for this video site, you open the Sharing tab on the Internet Connection, click Settings, and then choose Add on the Applications tab.

CONFIGURING CABLE/DSL SERVICE FOR CONNECTION SHARING

To set up the Shared Connection, follow these steps:

1. Choose the computer that you will use to share the Internet connection. Remember, it needs to be turned on for connection sharing to work. It doesn't have to remain logged in, though.

2. Install a second network card in this computer, using the procedure you learned in Chapter 21, "Instant Networking." Get an inexpensive, plug-and-play 10BASE-T network card; just be sure it's on the Windows hardware compatibility list.

3. Start Windows after adding the card so that Windows can detect and install drivers for the new card.

4. In Network and Dial-Up Connections, you'll now find two Local Network Connection icons. The first is the original LAN connection. The second belongs to your new card, as shown in Figure 24.13. For each, right-click and choose Rename. Rename the two icons LAN Connection and Internet Connection to make their purposes clear.

Figure 24.13
After you add a second network card for the DSL or cable modem, Network and Dial-Up Connections has two Local Connection icons. Rename them LAN Connection and Internet Connection for clarity. Enable Internet Connection Sharing in the Internet Connection icon.

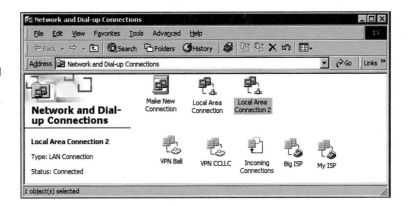

5. Right-click the Internet Connection icon, and select Properties. Configure the Internet Protocol properties as required by your cable or DSL provider, using the provided IP address, network mask, and DNS addresses.

6. Be sure that only Internet Protocol (TCP/IP) is checked to prevent hackers from accessing your network's shared files.

Caution

Step 6 is crucial. Selecting this one option is the only protection your network has from hackers on the Internet. You should uncheck all network components except Internet Protocol (TCP/IP) .

7. Click OK to close the connection's properties page.

8. Test your new high-speed Internet connection by viewing Web pages on the Internet. (If you've never used a high-speed connection before, you will be *really happy* right about here.)

9. Open the Internet Connection properties page again, and select the Sharing tab. Click Enable Internet Connection Sharing for This Connection, as shown in Figure 24.9.

10. Click OK. Windows then warns you that it is changing the network address of your other LAN adapter to 192.168.0.1. It is now the IP address for this computer on your LAN.

The rest of the procedure is the same as for a shared modem connection. See "Configuring the Rest of the Network," earlier in this chapter.

 If, after you set up the other computers on your LAN, the computers can't browse Web pages, see "Can't Access a Shared DSL or Cable Connection from the LAN" in the "Troubleshooting" section at the end of this chapter.

CONFIGURING DIRECT HIGH-SPEED CONNECTIONS

If you are using a router, or a DSL or cable modem without NAT, you have to configure your network using the IP addresses assigned by your ISP. The procedure depends on whether you are using a direct connection to a modem/bridge, a router, a router with NAT, or a third-party NAT device. The following sections describe the process.

MAKING A DIRECT INTERNET CONNECTION

If you are using a cable or DSL modem with no NAT device and no routing capability, you are probably configuring a LAN with only two to five computers. Your ISP should have provided you with a list of IP addresses for your LAN.

Dole these addresses out, one to each computer, using the following procedure on each:

1. Open Network and Dial-Up Connections, and choose Local Area Connection Properties.
2. Select Internet Protocol (TCP/IP) and click Properties.
3. Enter the IP address, Subnet Mask, Default Gateway, and DNS information provided by your ISP.
4. Click OK, and you should be online, simple as that.

Caution

Let me make this point very clear: suggest that you *do not* go this route. It offers you *no* protection from hacking over the Internet. Read Chapter 26, which describes the risks of this approach. I suggest you use a firewall router in between your network and your Internet connection. It can cost under $100 if you do the work yourself.

IP ADDRESSING WITH NAT

If you are using a DSL, cable, frame relay, or other router with built-in NAT capability, or a third-party external NAT device, you have to follow the instructions provided with this hardware to configure the router. Your ISP should help you with this process.

In general, you do the following:

- Receive an IP address for the router or NAT device, which will be your public, or external, IP address.
- Assign private IP numbers to each of the computers on your LAN.

Tip #281

I recommend using numbers 192.168.0.1 through 192.168.0.254, unless the ISP suggests otherwise. These numbers are reserved for private network use and will never conflict with IP addresses assigned on the Internet.

- The LAN side of the router or NAT device will be your gateway. Assign it address 192.168.0.1 and subnet mask 255.255.255.0.

- On each other computer, assign addresses 192.168.0.2 and up, set the subnet mask to 255.255.255.0, set the gateway address to 192.168.0.1 (the address of the NAT device,) and set the DNS information using the addresses supplied by your ISP.

If the router includes a DHCP server, all this IP addressing information can be configured once in the router, and the computers on the network can be set to Obtain an IP Address and Obtain DNS Server Address automatically.

If you have a Web or email server on your LAN that you want to be made public, you must configure NAT to direct incoming connection requests to that server. Write down the private IP address for each server and the type(s) of service it provides.

You must refer to the setup instructions for your particular NAT device or router to enter this information. Your task is to make an entry that says something like this: "When an HTTP connection request appears from the outside world using TCP port 80, send it to address 192.168.100.xxx." The exact commands you use vary from device to device.

IP ADDRESSING WITH A STANDARD ROUTER

Finally, if you're using frame relay, routed ISDN, or another type of connection using a commercial router, your ISP will assign one block of IP numbers for your LAN and another block for the connection between the router and the ISP.

When your LAN is connected to the Internet, the Internet is connected to your LAN. This setup should worry you a *lot!* Hacking, break-ins, and general disruption are definitely on the upswing.

To get a little bit technical: You need to be sure that certain Internet protocols are blocked across your Internet connection. They include Microsoft Networking (file sharing), Remote Administration, Remote Procedure Calls, and Simple Network Management Protocol (SNMP).

Note

Because network security is so important, it gets its own chapter. Refer to Chapter 26 to learn what steps to take to protect your network from assaults—internal, external, and otherwise.

If you need to access your files or administer computers from a remote computer on the Internet, you can do so safely by using Virtual Private Networking, which was described in Chapter 23, "Windows Unplugged: Remote and Mobile Networking."

PART
IV
CH
24

TROUBLESHOOTING

CAN'T ACCESS A SHARED MODEM CONNECTION FROM THE LAN

When I attempt to view an Internet page from a LAN computer, my Web browser doesn't get past "Looking up host www.somewhere.com."

A delay of 30 seconds or so is normal while the dial-up connection is established when you first start using the Internet.

If the connection doesn't progress after 30 seconds, be sure of the following: The sharing computer was turned on when you booted up your computer, the sharing computer is logged in, and your computer is set to obtain its IP address automatically.

Try to make the connection from the sharing computer to be sure the modem is connecting properly. If it's not, see the "Troubleshooting" section at the end of Chapter 11, "Internet and TCP/IP Connection Options," to diagnose the dial-up connection problem.

CAN'T ACCESS A SHARED DSL OR CABLE CONNECTION FROM THE LAN

When I attempt to view an Internet page from a LAN computer, my Web browser doesn't get past "Looking up host www.somewhere.com"

Be sure that the sharing computer was turned on when you booted up your computer, that the connection to the DSL or cable modem is the one marked as "shared," and that your computer is set to obtain its IP address automatically.

Try to view Web pages from the sharing computer to be sure the high-speed connection is functioning. If it's not, see the "Troubleshooting" section at the end of Chapter 16, "Internet Diagnosis Tools," to diagnose the Internet connectivity problem.

TIPS FROM THE WINDOWS PROS: SQUEEZING TOP SPEED FROM YOUR HIGH-SPEED CONNECTION

If you're using a high-speed connection such as DSL or cable, you can make an adjustment to your computer's networking software to get the best speed from your new connection.

Internet TCP/IP software sends data in chunks called *packets*, which are sent in a stream from, say, a Web server to your computer. The receiving computer sends acknowledgments every so often to indicate that the data has been received correctly or to indicate that something was lost or garbled during transmission.

A server sends only a limited amount of data before it expects to receive an acknowledgment. If the limit is reached before an acknowledgment is received, the sender has to stop and wait for one.

Ideally, for the fastest possible transfers, the sender should never have to stop sending because acknowledgments for earlier data arrive before this limit has been reached. Then the sender can go on sending, again hoping that the data will be acknowledged before the limit is reached.

For cable and DSL modems, the data rate is so high and the cross-country travel times so long that a considerable amount of data can be "in flight" before an acknowledgment could possibly be returned. So, to get the maximum use of your DSL or cable connection, you must tell Windows to make the limit larger than normal for a LAN connection.

This limit, called the *receive window*, should be larger than the data rate times the roundtrip time for data traveling back and forth between the two computers. This number is the maximum amount of data in flight. A typical round trip time is .100 seconds for interstate Internet traffic, so for various data rates, the receive window should be at least

At 100Kbps × 0.100 sec / bits per byte	= 1.2KB
500Kbps	6KB
1.5Mbps	19KB
4Mbps	75KB

The default value used by Windows 9x, NT, and 2000 is about 4KB! This means that Windows sends or lets a remote server send only 4KB and then sits and waits while your connection sits idle.

Windows slowly boosts the window size all by itself during a long file transfer, but when you're browsing Web pages with lots of small graphic images, it never gets a chance to boost the window size enough for you to realize the full potential of your fast connection.

For Windows 9x and NT4, you can increase the window size to 64KB. The maximum that you can specify for Windows 2000 is greater than 64KB, but 64KB is a practical maximum for DSL or cable service. To set the receive window, you must use the Registry Editor, which is described in Chapter 35, "The Registry." You must add a Registry value to a key, which contains TCP/IP software parameters.

Caution

Before adding a Registry value, be sure to read Chapter 35, with its dire warnings about the risks of editing the Registry and its urgings for you to back up the Registry before making a change of this sort.

SETTING THE RECEIVE WINDOW IN WINDOWS 2000

To set the receive window in Windows 2000, do the following:

1. Open Registry key HKEY_LOCAL_MACHINE\System \CurrentControlSet\Services\Tcpip\Parameters.

2. Add a new DWORD value, and name it `GlobalMaxTCPWindowSize` to set its value to 20000 (hexadecimal). See Figure 24.14 to see this entry in the Registry Editor.

Figure 24.14
You add value
GlobalMaxTCPWindow
Size in this dialog.
Note that Hexadecimal
must be checked.

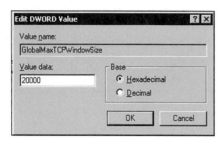

SETTING THE RECEIVE WINDOW IN WINDOWS NT4

To set the receive window in Windows NT4, follow these steps:

1. Open Registry key HKEY_LOCAL_MACHINE\System
   \CurrentControlSet\Services\Tcpip\Parameters.

2. Add a new DWORD value named TcpWindowSize to set its value to ffff (hexadecimal).

SETTING THE RECEIVE WINDOW IN WINDOWS 95/98

To set the receive window in Windows 95/98, do the following:

1. Open Registry key
   HKEY_LOCAL_MACHINE\System\CurrentControlSet\Services\VxD\MSTCP\.

2. Add a new DWORD value named DefaultRcvWindow to set its value to ffff (hexadecimal).

REBOOTING THE COMPUTER

After you make the change, close the Registry Editor and reboot the computer. You should make this change in each computer that uses the high-speed Internet connection.

Tip #282

If you have to make this change for several computers, you can create a Registry file to make your job much easier. Here's how:

1. Use the Registry Editor to make the change in one computer.

2. Highlight the Registry key in which you've added the new value in the left pane.

3. Select Registry, Export Registry File, and save a file named TCPWindow.reg in a shared folder on your network.

4. In Explorer, right-click this file and select Edit. Remove the lines for all the values listed except the one you added. Save the file.

5. On each of the other computers, open the shared folder in Explorer. Right-click the TCPWindow.reg file and select Install to insert the value. Reboot the computer.

CHAPTER 25

NETWORKING MIX AND MATCH

In this chapter

NETWORKING WITH OTHER OPERATING SYSTEMS

In the previous chapters, you learned about basic peer-to-peer and Active Directory networking, but these chapters considered only "vanilla" Windows networks. Real-life networks are seldom so simple. Often these networks have a mix of operating systems, and Windows must get along with them. Also, some optional networking components are not necessary in most environments, but they are used by some network managers for maintenance and monitoring. This chapter covers internetworking and these more obscure parts of the Windows network puzzle.

This point might be shocking, but you must be told: There are people who aren't like us. They use other operating systems. In ancient times, they were thought to be possessed by demons and, more recently, in need of reparative therapy. But times have changed. We now recognize that they can lead perfectly happy, productive lives despite their alternative preferences. The question is, "What happens if you're forced to live or work with them?" Actually, working with them is not only possible, but with enough cross-cultural education, it can be a positive growth experience for all concerned.

Well, okay, your being able to work with them might take more than just sensitivity training; it might require you to install additional protocols and services. But I'm here to help.

On a real-life LAN with multiple operating systems, it's not enough that computers be able to coexist on the same network cable. Interoperation, or *internetworking*, is necessary so that users of these various systems can share files and printers. At best, this sharing can occur without anyone even knowing that alternative platforms are involved. Achieving this kind of seamlessness can range from effortless to excruciating. The ease of internetworking between Windows and another operating systems appears to be directly proportional to Microsoft's interest in capturing the other operating systems' existing customer base. Therefore, you'll find that Novell NetWare access is fully supported, whereas Linux interoperation is entirely absent and left up to you.

INTERNETWORKING WITH NOVELL NETWARE

Novell NetWare was the first PC-based network operating system and for many years was virtually unchallenged as the LAN platform for the business world. It's still arguably the fastest and most efficient file sharing service available for PC networks. NetWare and Windows have been tightly integrated from the start, and Microsoft has made sure that it's virtually effortless to add Windows servers and workstations to a NetWare network.

Behind the scenes, internetworking with NetWare is fairly complex. NetWare uses different protocols and network components, as shown in Table 25.1. Windows networking and NetWare use different protocols to communicate with the file sharing computer and possibly a different network transport protocol.

TABLE 25.1   COMPARISON OF COMPONENTS USED BY WINDOWS NETWORKING AND NETWARE

	Client/Server Protocol	Transport Protocol
Windows Networking	SMB (Server Message Block)	TCP/IP, NetBEUI, and/or IPX/SPX
NetWare 5	NCP (NetWare Core Protocol)	TCP/IP and/or IPX/SPX
NetWare 2 to 4	NCP	IPX/SPX

To simultaneously use files and printers shared by both Windows and NetWare servers, you must reconcile these differences.

To resolve the transport protocol issue, you can use IPX/SPX as the base networking protocol for Windows, or you can use the default TCP/IP and simply install IPX/SPX as an additional protocol choice.

The differences in the fundamental server protocol can be addressed in one of two ways. You can install a separate network client that communicates directly with NetWare servers, or if you have a Windows 2000 Server network, you can install Gateway Service for NetWare (GSNW) on a Windows 2000 Server system. The gateway makes NetWare-based shared resources visible to Microsoft Networking clients. Another Server component, File and Print Services for NetWare (FPNW), works in the opposite direction, making resources from Microsoft Networking servers visible to NetWare users.

This type of translation system has two purposes:

- File and Print Services for NetWare harkens back to the old days of DOS and its strict memory limitations. With only 640KB of memory to work with, it was feasible to load only one type of network access software: NCP or SMB; even just one of them was sometimes a very tight fit. Because NetWare was the dominant networking system, DOS-based computers usually needed to have NetWare drivers installed. So, Microsoft developed FPNW to help sell Windows NT servers; this service made it possible for Novell-based workstations to access Windows NT servers without having to change any client software at all.

- The Gateway service provides a transition path from NetWare-based enterprise networks to Windows 2000-based networks. GSNW makes it possible to swap in new Windows-based servers first, accessible from client workstations expecting to find replaced Novell servers, and then reconfigure the enterprise network later.

However, if your LAN has NetWare servers, your network manager will probably have you install (or will install for you) the Client for Microsoft Networks so you can access NetWare servers without any sort of translation. Nowadays, having two network clients doesn't place any significant burden on memory or your computer.

PART

IV

CH

25

USING A NETWARE CLIENT

The Client for NetWare is a network driver that adds NCP-based networking support to Windows. It's really so well integrated with Windows that after it's installed, you don't have to treat NetWare servers as any different than Windows.

NetWare client software has two functions:

- First, it provides the underlying mechanism Windows uses to recognize that filenames like \\server\volume\file indicate that data is stored on a different computer.

- Second, the client provides support for legacy DOS applications that access network services directly through the NetWare Application Program Interface. These programs include NetWare system configuration utilities such as SYSCON and PCONSOLE, and some application software such as chat, email, database, and client/server programs. When you install a NetWare client in Windows, a driver is added to Windows 2000's MS-DOS subsystem to perform the functions that the IPXODI, NETX, and VLM programs performed in the DOS days of old.

You do have to decide whose client package to install. Both Microsoft and Novell Corporation provide clients. It's a little unclear why they do so, but you can bet that business tactics are the most significant reasons. For you, as an end user, the decision comes down mainly to compatibility and reliability. Historically, Microsoft's client package has been the most reliable and bug free. The Novell client has better compatibility with those old DOS programs, and some NetWare-specific programs absolutely require it.

Note

Microsoft's Client Services for NetWare does *not* operate with NetWare version 5. If you use NetWare 5, you must download and use Novell's client. I'll discuss Novell's client later in the chapter.

If you need to access shared files and printers only from NetWare servers, you're probably better off with the Microsoft standard client. If your company uses NetWare-specific programs, your network manager can tell you whether you must use the Novell client. If you need it, you can download Novell's client from http://www.novell.com. I'll talk more about Novell's client later in the chapter. In the following discussion, I'll refer to the Microsoft client as it's the standard offering supplied with Windows 2000.

Tip #283

One other issue that might affect your decision is security. Microsoft's NetWare client can't encrypt passwords sent to NetWare servers, so if wire-level security is a concern, and you must protect yourself from people using network monitors to sniff out passwords on your LAN, use the Novell client.

CHOOSING NETWORK PROTOCOLS

You also must decide whether to allow Windows networking to use IPX/SPX as a transport protocol. With more than one protocol installed, you can select which ones are used by the File Sharing service and File Services client software in your computer through a process called *binding*. Bindings have the same sort of purpose as the cords and plugs on an old telephone switchboard, letting you select which higher-level services connect to which transport protocols, and which protocols can be used on each network adapter and dial-up connection.

Windows SMB file services can use more than one protocol. It uses any available protocol to a remote machine that has one or more of the same protocols in common. However, this can cause problems if each computer on the network doesn't have the same set of protocols bound to the file services. Windows finds other computers by name using the browser service that runs on just one computer on the LAN. The choice of browser is made by a random process called an *election*, and the browser learns only the names of computers for which it has protocols in common. If the random choice of the browser server happens to pick one that doesn't have a particular protocol bound to Windows file sharing, it doesn't see all the computers on the LAN, and the rest of the network cannot find those computers by name.

Tip #284	This information sounds very complicated, but in practical terms, it comes down to one simple point: If you use more than one network protocol for Windows networking, install the *same* set on *every* computer.

The decision will be made by your network manager if you have a Windows 2000 Server-based network. If you have a peer-to-peer network and must make the decision yourself, here's my advice: Install TCP/IP and IPX/SPX on *every* computer. Windows networking uses both protocols by default.

If you can't install IPX/SPX on some of your Windows computers for some reason, unbind IPX/SPX from Windows file services on *every* computer, using the procedure covered later in the chapter under "Setting Network Bindings."

WORKING WITH NETWARE LOGIN SCRIPTS

Since its early days, NetWare has included a script-processing function that is activated when a user first logs in to a NetWare server. Login scripts let the user and/or network administrator make drive mappings, run email or menu programs, and configure the computer's DOS environment.

NetWare login scripts can still be used with Windows 2000, but using them presents some pros and cons:

- You can make drive mappings just as easily by using the Explorer's Tools menu and set them to be reestablished every time you log in. Windows mappings, deleted in one session, won't be restored when you log in the next time, though, so the NetWare approach is safer in situations in which you want to protect a user from accidentally deleting an essential drive mapping.

- Most NetWare login scripts were designed for the DOS environment and aren't appropriate for Windows. In particular, DOS terminate-and-stay-resident (TSR) programs that were frequently run from login scripts are useless in Windows. Windows can fire up programs at login time with the Startup program group; you don't need the Novell script for this function anymore. On the other hand, the NetWare scripting language is quite powerful and can be used to make very specific configuration settings at startup time, which Windows can't.

If you do use NetWare login scripts with Windows, watch out for the following:

- DOS TSR programs don't work as expected; they are run in separate Command Prompt windows, which immediately terminate.

- External commands run with # inside the login script should use the 32-bit command interpreter cmd, as in #cmd program args, not #command program args.

- DOS environment variables can't be set from the login script.

- Most NetWare scripts assume that drive F: is available for use as a network drive. Be sure that this is the case on your Windows 2000 computer. You might need to reassign your physical drive letters or modify the login script.

You should discuss login scripts with your NetWare system administrator to see whether they are required in your environment. You should also ask for the name of the preferred login server or NetWare Directory Service (NDS) context before installing your NetWare client.

INSTALLING MICROSOFT CLIENT SERVICES FOR NETWARE

After you've done the background research, you can install the Microsoft client, as follows:

1. Open Network and Dial-Up Connections. Right-click Local Area Connection, and select Properties.

2. Select Install, highlight Client, and select Add.

3. Highlight Client Services for NetWare, and click OK to install the client, NWLink NetBIOS, and NWLink IPX/SPX/NetBIOS Compatible Transport.

4. When the Select NetWare Logon dialog appears, as shown in Figure 25.1, ask your NetWare administrator for the proper settings.

5. You must select a primary NetWare logon server if you're going to use a login script:

- On a NetWare 3 network (also called a *bindery security* network), choose a server from the list, or select None.

- On a NetWare NDS network, select the name and context of the NDS tree you've been assigned by your NetWare administrator.

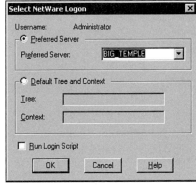

Figure 25.1

6. If your NetWare administrator has configured Windows 2000–compatible login scripts, check Run Login Script. Otherwise, if your NetWare login scripts were designed for a DOS environment, it's best not to run them.

7. After you've installed the client, it's best to proceed directly to the Control Panel to double-check the client's configuration settings.

CONFIGURING MICROSOFT CLIENT SERVICES FOR NETWARE

Both Microsoft's and Novell's NetWare clients have configuration settings that are made from the Control Panel using a new applet that appears after you've installed the client service (see Figure 25.2).

Figure 25.2
The CSNW icon appears in the Control Panel after you install a NetWare client.

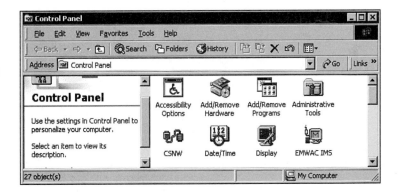

PART

IV

CH

25

You should examine the CNSW (Client Services for NetWare) applet as soon as you install the NetWare client to get familiar with its options. The CNSW applet dialog is shown in Figure 25.3.

Figure 25.3
Client Services for
NetWare Control Panel
applet.

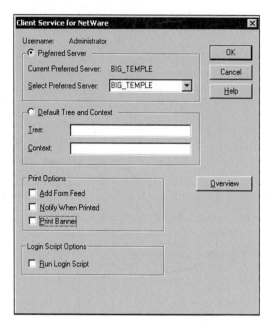

The Preferred Server, Default Tree, and Login Script Options settings are the same as those made when you initially installed the NetWare client, as described previously.

Table 25.2 shows an additional set of printing options that you should set before using the network.

TABLE 25.2 ADDITIONAL PRINTING OPTIONS

Option	Description
Add Form Feed	Adds a form feed (page eject) at the end of each print job sent to any Novell print queue. This option dates back to the days of dot-matrix line printers and is undesirable with laser printers.
Notify When Printed	Displays a pop-up message on your screen whenever a print job sent to a Novell print queue has completed. I find it annoying.
Print Banner	Prints a page with your username before every print job sent to a Novell printer. It wastes paper, so I suggest unchecking it unless your organization really requires it.

Tip #285

By default, Notify When Printed and Print Banner are checked in this applet when you install Client Services for NetWare. I recommend unchecking both of them immediately unless your organization really requires them.

INSTALLING AND USING NOVELL'S CLIENT SOFTWARE

You can also use the Novell client if your needs or network manager so dictate. You can download Novell's client software from the Web site at http://www.novell.com.

Be sure to study the README file or any release notes supplied with the client software. Novell updates the client software from time to time, so you should be sure you're using the most up-to-date instructions.

Before you install Novell's client, be sure you have removed the Microsoft client. Open Network and Dial-Up Connections, view Properties for the Local Area Connection, and be sure that Client Services for NetWare isn't listed. If it is, select it and choose Uninstall. You must restart your computer before proceeding.

To install the Novell client, follow these steps:

1. Download the Novell client software, and unzip it in a folder. It can be a temporary folder or one you'll share on the network for repeated installations.

2. Run setupnw to begin the installation process.

> **Caution**
>
> When you install the Novell client, choose the Typical installation unless you are certain you need to use Custom. If do you use Custom, don't choose the Select All components button. Doing so might inadvertently install conflicting software components and render your network inoperative.

3. The installation reboots your computer after it's finished copying files.

When Windows restarts, the Windows login dialog box is replaced with a Novell login dialog. This dialog contains options to log in to a Novell NDS tree, a legacy Novell server, or just the Windows workstation. The Novell client also installs a sophisticated, full-featured Novell utility icon in the task tray.

> **Note**
>
> If your network uses Microsoft's File and Print Services for NetWare (FPNW) on a Windows 2000 Server, the Novell client can't use the simulated NetWare resources shared by the FPNW server because of software incompatibilities.

SETTING PROVIDER ORDER

Provider order determines which computer name service, Novell's or Microsoft's, is queried first to find a given named file or print server. For example, if you choose a shared printer named \\munich\laserjet, Windows has to identify the machine named munich. It might need to query both the Windows computer name service (Active Directory or the browser service) and the NetWare naming service before it finds the name. When you use a mix of

Microsoft and NetWare servers, you might be able to speed up network operations by setting the provider order so that the most likely name service is examined first. To do so, just follow these steps:

1. Open Network and Dial-Up Connections.

2. From the Advanced menu, select Advanced Settings, and click the Provider Order tab, as shown in Figure 25.4. The dialog lists services used to find access to file servers and print servers, respectively.

Figure 25.4
Provider Order settings let you choose which file or printer service is examined first to find a named remote server.

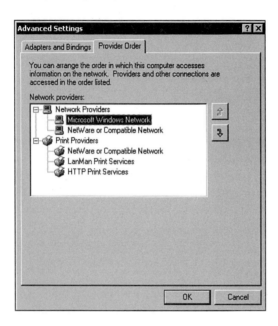

Arrange the services so that the type you use most frequently is listed on top, followed by less often-used services. Highlight a service type, and click the up- or down-arrow button to rearrange the types. In the figure, I've indicated that I most frequently use Windows servers for shared files and Novell servers for printing.

Tip #286	In case you're wondering, comparable network services for data link control (DLC), AppleTalk, and other network printers are never shown here because they are accessed directly as local printers, not network printers. It's strange, but true.

USING NETWARE RESOURCES

After a NetWare client has been installed, you can access NetWare services in the same ways as Windows servers. The only difference, if you're used to the Novell way of naming resources, is that remote folders and files must be specified using standard Windows UNC format.

- NetWare users are familiar with the server\volume:path\file format—for example, MUNICH\SYS:PUBLIC\SYSCON.EXE.
- From Windows, the same file would be \\MUNICH\SYS\PUBLIC\SYSCON.EXE.

This format takes a bit of getting used to, and you must make some changes to existing batch files and programs. But beyond this small difference, you can treat NetWare resources just like Windows resources and therefore can do the following:

- Browse the network from My Network Places.
- Specify remote files or directories using standard UNC names.
- Make drive mappings using the Explorer's Tools menu.
- Make drive mappings from the command line by using the command net use.
- Print to Novell print queues by adding network printers in the usual Windows 2000 way.

The following sections step you through some of these network functions.

 If print job banner pages or extra blank sheets appear in print jobs sent to Novell queues, see "Banner and/or Blank Pages Are Printed on NetWare Printers" in the "Troubleshooting" section at the end of this chapter.

BROWSING THE NETWORK

When locating a file, mapping a network drive, or just exploring the network, you can find a NetWare server in My Network Places or any other network browsing dialog. Expand Entire Network, and you'll notice two network branches: Microsoft Windows Network and NetWare or Compatible Network. Expanding the NetWare branch, you can see any available NDS trees or individual NetWare bindery servers, as shown in Figure 25.5.

 If no Novell servers appear in the browsing list, see "Novell NetWare Servers Can't Be Found" in the "Troubleshooting" section at the end of this chapter.

If some Windows computers are missing from the list, see "Some Computers Are Missing from Entire Network" in the "Troubleshooting" section.

You can drill down into shared volumes (for example, sys), folders, and files if you like.

When you attach to a NetWare server, by default, your Windows login name and password are used to make the connection. You can use an alternative login name and password if you use the Map Network Drive Wizard, which is available from the Explorer's Tools menu. Having different account names and passwords on your Windows and Novell servers can be a bit confusing, however, so your network manager will probably try to make them match. You might need to manually update your passwords to keep them identical on the two server types, however.

Figure 25.5
NetWare trees and servers appear under the NetWare branch of Entire Network.

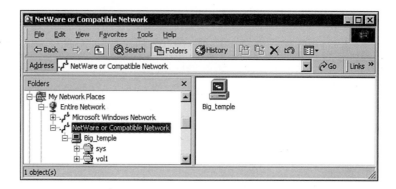

⚠️ *If you get a* `Logon Failed` *error while attempting to attach to a NetWare server, see "Can't Attach to NetWare Servers" in the "Troubleshooting" section at the end of this chapter.*

SYNCHRONIZING NETWARE PASSWORDS

If you use the same account name for both Windows and NetWare, as most people do, you should change your password on both systems to the same thing at the same time. That way, your name and password will work for both networks, and you won't be bothered with entering them by hand every time you attach to a NetWare resource.

Tip #287	Be sure to connect to your Novell server or servers or trees before changing your Windows password so that the password is updated on all servers. You can simply view any NetWare resource on a server in My Network Places to establish a connection.

If your Novell servers use the NDS directory system for security, you're in luck. When you change your Windows password by pressing Ctrl+Alt+Del, your Novell password is set as well for any NDS trees you're currently connected to.

If you use older bindery-based NetWare servers, you must use the old `setpass` DOS utility to update NetWare passwords after changing your Windows password. To do so, follow these steps:

1. Make attachments to any NetWare servers you use by opening My Network Places and browsing into any of their shared volumes.

2. Open a command prompt, and type `pushd \\`*`server`*`\sys\public`, replacing *server* with the name of your primary NetWare server.

3. Change your Windows password by pressing Ctrl+Alt+Del.

4. In the command prompt, type `setpass` and press Enter. Follow the instructions to change your NetWare password.

These steps synchronize all bindery-based NetWare servers.

LISTING YOUR NETWARE CONNECTIONS

On a DOS-based Novell network, you use the whoami command to keep track of your current NetWare connections. This function is available in Windows from any Explorer File menu, or you can access it by right-clicking the desktop and choosing Who Am I, as shown in Figure 25.6.

Figure 25.6
Who Am I appears on the Explorer's File menu to show connections to NetWare servers.

Who Am I displays a list of attached file servers and NDS trees, as shown in Figure 25.7.

Figure 25.7
Who Am I displays currently connected NetWare servers.

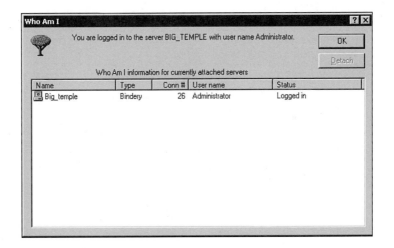

Who Am I lists the servers to which you're connected and the login name used to make the connection. The Type column indicates the NetWare security system in use for the connection to each server: Bindery for NetWare version 3.x servers or NDS for version 4 and higher.

You can disconnect from a server, if desired, by selecting it in the list and choosing Detach.

NETWARE AND THE COMMAND PROMPT

NetWare's DOS origins show most clearly in the set of management and operating utilities it uses to control drive mappings and monitor and configure the network. Its beloved utilities, such as MAP, SYSCON, and PCONSOLE, have very limited usefulness under

Windows because many of them interacted directly with DOS to change its drive listing and printer configuration. These functions simply don't work with Windows 2000 because it's based on Windows NT, not DOS.

If you were a command-line aficionado on your Novell network, you'll have to learn a new way of doing things. You'll probably grumble about it for a while (I sure did!), but eventually the new way will become familiar. Table 25.3 shows some key differences between common NetWare and Windows commands.

TABLE 25.3 COMPARING NETWARE AND WINDOWS COMMANDS

NetWare Command	Windows Command
capture lpt1:=server\queue	net use lpt1: \\server\queue
endcap	net use lpt1: /delete
login	(n/a)
logout	(n/a)
map	net use
map f:=server\vol	net use f: \\server\vol
map root f:=server\vol\folder	net use f: \\server\vol\folder
map del f:	net use f: /delete
pconsole	(Use the Windows Printer controls.)
slist	new view /network:nw

Most of the NetWare utilities listed in this table cannot be used on Windows 2000; they simply don't work or don't work correctly.

You can still use many old DOS NetWare utilities to manage your NetWare servers themselves. Many but not all NetWare management programs run correctly in a Windows Command Prompt window. Some NetWare utilities cannot be used in Windows because the operating system management functions they use were designed for DOS, not Windows 2000.

Note

Windows-based NetWare 4.0 and 5.0 management utilities do *not* work with the Microsoft Client. These utilities run only with the Novell Client.

Tip #288

The easiest way to use a NetWare utility is to open a command prompt and type pushd \\server\sys\public to change the current directory to the NetWare server's utility directory. You can also make shortcuts to any often-used utilities.

The MS-DOS environment is simulated in Windows using two drivers loaded in AUTOEXEC.NT: nw16 and vwipxspx. They provide some but not all the services that the old DOS programs IPX and NETX or VLM shell programs did.

TROUBLESHOOTING A NOVELL NETWORK CONNECTION

If you have problems establishing a connection to a Novell server using the Microsoft client, you can use the built-in Windows Troubleshooter to help diagnose the problem.

To use it, choose Start, Help. On the Search tab, search for NetWare, and select Troubleshooter in the left pane. Then select Client Services for NetWare in the right pane.

INTERNETWORKING WITH OS/2

IBM's OS/2 operating system uses the same fundamental networking functions as Windows. This fact shouldn't be a surprise, as Microsoft developed the networking software used on the original IBM PC, and its relationship with IBM lasted through the release of the first few versions of OS/2. IBM's LAN Server evolved directly from Microsoft's original LAN Manager product, whose name still appears here and there in Windows 2000. You'll see the letters *LM* and the phrase *LanMan* used in some Windows networking components.

Internetworking with OS/2 is quite transparent. Just be sure of two things:

■ Install the NetBEUI protocol on *all* computers on your network. (I discussed the reasoning for installing the same protocols on every computer on your network earlier in this chapter under "Choosing Network Protocols.") If you're using OS/2 Warp, you might not need to do so because OS/2 Warp offers the option of using NetBIOS over TCP/IP. Check with the OS/2 system manager to see whether this option is enabled on your system.

■ Do not apply a Windows 2000 security policy that prohibits the use of the LMHASH password encryption protocol. LMHASH is an old encryption system used to encode passwords stored on servers and transmitted across networks. It was designed for LAN Manager and hence is used by OS/2 LAN Server. Windows NT's and Windows 2000's encryption systems are more secure, so some network managers prevent the network from using LMHASH to gain protection. Doing so, unfortunately, makes it impossible to internetwork between OS/2 and Windows.

To install NetBEUI, do the following on each computer:

1. Open Network and Dial-Up Connections. Right-click Local Area Connection, and select Properties.
2. Select Install, highlight Protocol, and select Add.
3. Highlight NetBEUI Protocol, and click OK. Close Network and Dial-Up Connections.

If some Windows or OS/2 computers are missing from the list of all LAN computers in Computers Near Me or Entire Network in My Network Places, see "Some Computers Are Missing from Entire Network" in the "Troubleshooting" section at the end of this chapter.

INTERNETWORKING WITH UNIX

The UNIX operating system, originally developed in the 1970s at AT&T's Bell Laboratories as a platform for internal software development, is still evolving and growing. UNIX orginally was a commercial operating system distributed at no cost to academic institutions, so a generation of computer scientists learned their art on UNIX systems in college. Most Internet software you're familiar with today was developed on UNIX systems, and it's the most common operating system for high-end graphics and engineering workstations manufactured by Sun Microsystems, Hewlett-Packard, and many other companies. The Open Source phenomenon has also produced the no-cost GNU and Linux UNIX clones, ensuring that a new generation of programmers will continue the tradition of openness, cooperation, and sharing that typify the UNIX community.

This chapter looks at ways to network Windows 2000 with UNIX-type operating systems. Although many of the examples involve Linux (Red Hat Linux 6.0), most of the examples can be translated to almost any UNIX-type operating system.

THE SMB/CIFS PROTOCOL

The Server Message Block (SMB) protocol is the high-level network protocol used for Windows and LAN Manager file and printer sharing. There's no fundamental reason to restrict its use solely by Windows systems, however. To promote interoperation, Microsoft, the Santa Cruz Operation (SCO), Intel, and other companies began the Common Internet File System (CIFS) initiative to extend SMB networking to other operating systems. Networking software used by all versions of Microsoft Windows and OS/2 are fully CIFS-compliant, and CIFS software is available for dozens of other operating platforms. This is the technology of choice for internetworking between Windows and UNIX systems.

CIFS differs from most UNIX file sharing standards in that it is not a stateless protocol. While providing file access for routine access purposes, CIFS also synchronizes the file state between the client and server. It is therefore more efficient than other UNIX file sharing protocols across a reliable network. When CIFS-compatible network software is installed on a UNIX computer, it can participate as a peer in a Windows network.

You can see a list of validated CIFS packages at http://msdn.microsoft.com/workshop/networking/cifs/support.asp. For this chapter, I'll concentrate on just one: the Samba package.

SAMBA

Certainly the most popular UNIX-to-Windows networking package, Samba can be a life-saver for integrated networks. Samba is an open source (read: free) software suite based on the SMB/CIFS protocol. Samba provides transparent access to UNIX resources for Windows clients.

You can get more information about Samba and download a version for your UNIX system from `http://www.samba.org`.

USING SAMBA CLIENT TOOLS

Samba requires a small amount of configuration to make it work within a Windows-based network. For purposes of this chapter, I will describe how Samba works with Linux.

In the following discussion, remember that all the work is done on a Linux computer so that it can participate as a member of a Windows 2000 network.

Most Linux distributions now include Samba and install it by default. The following examples use Samba version 2.0.5a. If you are using an earlier version, I recommend that you upgrade because 2.0.5a includes many enhancements over previous versions.

First, you must decide in what capacity you will be using your Linux system with Samba. At this time, let's look at using Samba in a client scenario within a Windows-based network. Using Samba, you can access file and print services handled by a Windows server.

PART

IV

CH

25

Tip #289

Samba includes command-line tools for accessing Windows resources from Linux. Open source GUI-based tools are also available for easy configuration of Samba tools. Among them, gnomba is a GTK-based GUI config that enables you to browse Windows resources from within Linux or any UNIX-based operating system running Samba. gnomba is similar to the Microsoft Network Neighborhood share browser. You can find gnomba at the following address:

`http://gnomba.darkcorner.net`

To access file services on a Windows server, you must know exactly what resources are available from a given host on the network. Samba includes a program called `smbclient` for just that purpose. This application enables you to find Windows shares and printers from within Linux. `smbclient` is a command-line-based tool. You can see most of the optional switches to `smbclient` simply by executing the following command:

```
smbclient -help
```

The preceding command gives a printout similar to this:

```
Added interface ip=10.0.0.1 bcast=10.255.255.255 nmask=255.0.0.0
Usage: smbclient service <password> [options]
Version 2.0.5a
        -s smb.conf             pathname to smb.conf file
        -B IP addr              broadcast IP address to use
        -O socket_options       socket options to use
        -R name resolve order   use these name resolution services only
        -M host                 send a winpopup message to the host
        -i scope                use this NetBIOS scope
```

```
-N                        don't ask for a password
-n netbios name.          Use this name as my netbios name
-d debuglevel             set the debuglevel
-P                        connect to service as a printer
-p port                   connect to the specified port
-l log basename.          Basename for log/debug files
-h                        Print this help message.
-I dest IP                use this IP to connect to
-E       .                write messages to stderr instead of stdout
-U username               set the network username
-L host                   get a list of shares available on a host
-t terminal code          terminal i/o code {sjis¦euc¦jis7¦jis8¦junet¦hex}
-m max protocol           set the max protocol level
-W workgroup              set the workgroup name
-T<c¦x>IXFqgbNan          command line tar
-D directory              start from directory
-c command string         execute semicolon separated commands
-b xmit/send buffer    changes the transmit/send buffer (default: 65520)
```

Using smbclient, you can look at some of the resources available on a Windows 2000 Professional system on your network. Executing the following command from a Linux terminal shows you the available resources on the computer named SHIVA:

```
smbclient -L \\SHIVA
```

This command provides a listing of the available resources on the system SHIVA:

```
Added interface ip=10.0.0.1 bcast=10.255.255.255 nmask=255.0.0.0
Password:
Domain=[DAYDREAM] OS=[Windows 5.0] Server=[Windows 2000 LAN Manager]

     Sharename      Type        Comment
     ---------      ----        -------
     storage        Disk        User Storage
     IPC$           IPC         IPC Service
     HPLaserJet     Printer
     ken            Disk        Home Directories

     Server                 Comment
     ---------              -------
     SHIVA                  Ken's Laptop
     Workgroup              Master
     ---------              -------
     DAYDREAM               SHIVA
```

This information indicates that two disk shares are available: the ken share as well as the Storage share. Also, notice the printer named HPLaserJet. Now that you've seen what's available, you can mount the Storage share on your system by using another piece of the Samba package, smbmount. smbmount allows you to mount the Windows share on the local Linux file system. The command

```
smbmount //SHIVA/Storage /mnt/winshare -U ken
```

mounts the Storage share on SHIVA, after you are prompted for a password, to the local directory /mnt/winshare. The -U switch tells smbclient what username to use when trying to mount the share.

You also can use a Windows printer from a Linux client. The easiest way to configure a Windows printer is to use the Red Hat GUI-based print tool as root. This way, you can set up an SMB-based printer with a minimal amount of hassle. If you are not using Red Hat Linux, you must edit your /etc/printcap file manually. The number of options involved are beyond the scope of this chapter. A thorough read of the SMB How-To, available from `http://www.linuxdoc.org/HOWTO/SMB-HOWTO.html`, is recommended.

USING SAMBA SERVER TOOLS

Samba also includes tools and servers to make your Linux system look just like a Windows-based network server; this capability lets your Windows computers use files and printers shared by UNIX systems.

The parameters for configuring Samba in a server capacity are contained in the file /etc/smb.conf. The default file included with Samba has comments for every parameter to explain what each one is. Remember, after you have edited the smb.conf file, you must stop and restart the smbd server. To stop smbd, issue this command:

```
/etc/rc.d/init.d/smbd stop
```

Then, to restart it, simply run the following:

```
/etc/rc.d/init.d/smbd start
```

This way, you ensure that your smbd daemon is always running with your current edits.

PART
IV
CH
25

Tip #290	The smb.conf file, with its many options, is rather large. As with many Linux-based administration tasks, you can use an open source GUI-based config tool to work with it. A great GUI-based tool for editing this file is gnosamba. It is highly recommended that you download and use this great application to more easily configure Samba on your Linux system. You can find gnosamba at this address: `http://www.open-systems.com/gnosamba.html`

Now you're ready to look at some quick steps to enable you to share your Linux resources with Windows systems on the network. The following sections cover just the parameters you need to share resources on the network. You can, however, configure many more parameters. As I mentioned earlier in this section, a thorough read of the Samba documentation at `http://www.linuxdoc.org/HOWTO/SMB-HOWTO.html` is recommended.

CONFIGURING GLOBAL SAMBA PARAMETERS

The first section you must configure is the `global` section. Edit /etc/smb.conf, and locate the string "`[global]`":

```
[global]
netbios name = HYDRA
workgroup = DAYDREAM
server string = Daydream Network PDC
```

```
hosts allow = 192.168.1. 192.168.2. 127.
printcap name = /etc/printcap
load printers = yes
security = user
encrypt passwords = yes
smb passwd file = /etc/smbpasswd
username map = /etc/smbusers
```

Now, let's look at each of the global parameters to get a better understanding of the way in which they work:

```
netbios name = HYDRA
```

This parameter defines the name the server shows up as to the Windows clients connecting to it.

```
workgroup = DAYDREAM
```

This parameter defines the workgroup or NT domain you want the server to belong to.

```
server string = Daydream Network PDC
```

The server string shows up in the comment field for your server when browsing the network. It can be anything you like.

```
hosts allow = 192.168.1. 192.168.2. 127.
```

If set, this parameter lists IP addresses of clients allowed to connect to the Samba server. You can specify more than one address and can enter one, two, three, or all four parts of the IP address. Any missing parts are taken as "anything." Setting these addresses is a great way to restrict access to your system to only hosts within your local network.

```
printcap name = /etc/printcap
```

This parameter defines the path and filename for your system's printcap file. This file gives Samba a list of available printers to share.

```
load printers = yes
```

This parameter indicates that you would like to share your printer. To do so, you specify the load printers parameter as yes.

```
security = user
```

This parameter is very important: You can choose from three modes for security purposes:

user—All resources are secured based on the user who is connecting to them.

share—Resources are secured based on the share and any privileges assigned to it.

server—This option tells Samba to use a separate password server to authenticate the client. In this way, a primary domain controller, for instance, could be used to authenticate the user.

For purposes of this chapter, you can use the `user` mode to authenticate your clients.

```
encrypt passwords = yes
```

This parameter is crucial. Because Windows operating systems want to send only encrypted passwords by default, you must enable SMB-encrypted passwords. The only drawback of this approach, however, is that you must maintain a separate password file for Samba. If you choose not to encrypt passwords, you must edit the Registry of every Windows client to have them send plain-text passwords.

```
smb passwd file = /etc/smbpasswd
```

Because you are using encrypted passwords, you now specify the file from which Samba will read the encrypted passwords.

```
username map = /etc/smbusers
```

This parameter is optional. It specifies a path and filename from which you can map UNIX users to Samba client (Windows) users. This way, you can have different logins to each system and have them work transparently when using SMB resources.

Configuring Samba Homes Parameters

Next, let's look at the `homes` section. In this section, you define whether the home directories for the corresponding UNIX users show up after a successful login. This way, you can transparently map a user to his or her home directory. Search /etc/smb.conf for the string `"[homes]"`.

```
[homes]
comment = Home Directories
browseable = no
writable = yes
```

Again, let's examine each of the parameters:

```
comment = Home Directories
```

This parameter indicates the string that shows up in the comment field for the shared resources. It can be anything you like but should be somewhat descriptive.

```
browseable = no
```

This parameter defines whether users' home directories are browseable by clients that do not own them. In most instances, you will probably want to say no here.

```
writable = yes
```

This parameter is really useful only if you have defined the home directories as browseable. A no entry gives guests just read-only access to home directories. You can just leave it set to yes because you don't have the home directories browseable.

CONFIGURING SAMBA PRINTER PARAMETERS

Next, let's look at the `printers` section. Here, you can define parameters specific to your shared printer. Search for "`[printers]`" in /etc/smb.conf.

```
[printers]
comment = All Printers
path = /var/spool/samba
browseable = no
guest ok = no
writable = no
printable = yes
```

Let's look at each specific parameter for the `printers` section:

`comment = All Printers`

Like all the other comment fields, this one is just an arbitrary string of your choosing to define any description of the resource. It is displayed when users browse My Network Places.

`path = /var/spool/samba`

This parameter defines the directory where the server will spool incoming print requests. It is required if you are sharing a printer.

`browseable = no`

The `browseable` parameter, like the `homes` section's `browseable` parameter, defines whether the printer can be seen by any normal domain user without actually trying to connect to it after being authenticated. In this case, you can choose to turn it off.

`guest ok = no`

This parameter gives you the choice of letting guest users print to your printer. In this case, don't allow the guest account by selecting no.

`writable = no`

This parameter enables you to specify whether changes can be made to your printer share. In this case, just use no.

`printable = yes`

If you would like clients to be able to print to your printer and write spool files to your spool directory, you can enter yes for the `printable` parameter.

CONFIGURING SAMBA CUSTOM-DEFINED SERVICE PARAMETERS

Finally, you come to a custom-defined service or section of the smb.conf file. Here, you specify a share for users to store any files or applications that they would like to be available to other connecting clients.

```
[storage]
comment = User Storage
path = /storage
```

```
public = no
writable = yes
write list = @users
```

Now, let's look at the specific parameters for this resource:

```
comment = User Storage
```

Again, the `comment` parameter defines the description for this resource.

```
path = /storage
```

This parameter gives you a chance to specify where the directory you want to share resides on the local system. In this case, you can create a directory at `/storage` for just that purpose.

```
public = no
```

This parameter lets you toggle the option to have the directory available in a browseable list of server resources. In this example, you don't want this to be the case, so you can specify `no`.

```
writable = yes
```

Like the other `writable` parameters in smb.conf, this parameter defines the option to have the directory writable. In this case, you can specify yes because you want clients to use this directory to store files they want publicly available.

```
write list = @users
```

Last is the `write list` parameter. It enables you to define which group clients must belong to in order to write to the directory. In this instance, you want the UNIX group `users` to be the only group able to write to the Storage share.

PART

IV

CH

25

RUNNING testparm

Now that you have finished editing the smb.conf file, you can test to see that the syntax is correct by using the Samba program `testparm`. `testparm` checks smb.conf for internal "correctness" before you actually use it in a production environment. By running

```
/usr/bin/testparm
```

you get a printout like the following if all goes well:

```
Load smb config files from /etc/smb.conf
Processing section "[homes]"
Processing section "[printers]"
Processing section "[storage]"
Loaded services file OK.
Press enter to see a dump of your service definitions
```

Furthermore, you can press Enter to see a dump of all the parameters the server uses to configure itself.

DEFINING SAMBA USERS

Next, you must define the Samba users by adding them to the Samba config files. You can do so by using the command smbadduser. The syntax of the smbadduser command is as follows:

```
/usr/bin/smbadduser unixid:ntid
```

The unixid parameter is the user's name on the UNIX system, and ntid is the client login that will be mapped to the unixid. After running this command, you are prompted to add and confirm a password for the user. At this point, the user you've added can connect and view his or her home directory along with the Storage share defined earlier in the smb.conf. This is the final step in the configuration of Samba.

You can now simply restart smbd, and Windows clients should be able to connect to the resources you have defined. All the resources you've set up will look like normal Windows shares to any client that connects. Because of this transparent presentation of resources, you can merely connect to them in the same manner you would to any other Windows share.

UNIX PRINTING TOOLS

Windows 2000 provides the familiar lpr and lpq programs to print files from Windows to a UNIX printer and check UNIX printer queue status, respectively. The use on Windows 2000 is identical to the use on UNIX; you do have to be careful about the different line ending conventions between Windows and UNIX, however.

The lpr tool simply sends a file or the output of a command-line program to the printer. Windows 2000 also provides tools to let you fully integrate printing services between UNIX and Windows. You can use UNIX-hosted printers directly from the Windows printing system, and you can print to Windows shared printers from UNIX hosts.

PRINTING TO UNIX QUEUES FROM WINDOWS

Windows 2000 has built-in support to send output to UNIX-based printers using the lpr protocol. You can install a standard Windows printer whose output is directed to a UNIX system and can use this printer just as you would any local or networked Windows printer.

→ For instruction on setting up an lpr-based printer, **see** "Using UNIX and LPR Printers," **p. 772**.

PRINTING TO WINDOWS PRINTERS FROM UNIX

You can also install an LPD server on Windows 2000 to let UNIX users print to any local printers shared by your computer. (It can print only to local printers shared by your computer, not to network printers from other machines used by your computer.)

To install this service, follow these steps:

1. Open Network and Dial-Up Connections.
2. Select Advanced, Optional Networking Components.

3. Check Other Network File and Print Services.

4. Click Details, and check Print Services for UNIX.

5. Click OK, and then click Next.

These steps install the service but, because of an installer glitch, don't make the service start when you boot your computer. You might have to finish the job manually, like this:

1. Right-click My Computer, and select Manage.

2. In the left pane, open Services and Applications; then select Services.

3. In the right pane, locate TCP/IP Print Server.

4. If the service's Status is not shown as `Started`, right-click it and select Start.

5. If its Startup Type is not shown as `Automatic`, right-click it and select Properties. Set the Startup Type to `Automatic`, and click OK.

6. Close Computer Management.

Now, UNIX users can send print jobs to your computer by using the command

```
lpr -S computername -P sharename
```

where `computername` is the DNS name or IP address of your computer, and `sharename` is the share name of any of your printers. (You can see the list of printers you're sharing from the command prompt by entering the command `net share`.)

Tip #291	By default, Windows treats incoming print jobs as ASCII text that must be formatted and printed. If the UNIX machine is sending, say, a PostScript file, it prints the PostScript source code rather than the document the file represents. UNIX users must use the appropriate `-o` option to send a binary print job in this case. For example, you can enter the following: `lpr -S ambon -P Laserjet -o l filename.ps`

 If text files are printed with line feeds inserted where just carriage returns were expected, see "Carriage Returns and Line Feeds Are Mangled" in the "Troubleshooting" section at the end of this chapter.

OTHER UNIX NETWORK TOOLS

UNIX operating systems were designed with the network in mind. As such, many different programs and functions are available to the administrator or user. As a nod to the large number of UNIX users and systems, Windows 2000 includes versions of several common UNIX utilities. You can use these tools to monitor, administer, and use UNIX systems from Windows 2000.

Tip #292	You can find third-party Windows versions of many more UNIX commands. The Cygnus Solutions `cygwin` environment is one of the best available. The `cygwin` tools are ports of popular GNU applications and utilities to the Windows environment. The `cygwin` tools are available for free at the following site: `http://sourceware.cygnus.com/cygwin`

finger

The `finger` command is used on UNIX systems to find out about the person behind a computer account name. Windows 2000 doesn't provide a "finger server," but it does provide the standard "finger client" program.

Typing

`C:\>finger username@computername`

tells you the person's full name, whether he or she is logged in on the named computer, and perhaps his or her phone number and other information. For example, typing

`C:\>finger briank@ginger.berkeley.edu`

tells you whether I am logged on to the computer named `ginger.berkeley.edu`.

Typing

`C:\>finger computername`

by itself prints a list of all users currently logged on to the named computer.

Note	Most organizations block finger traffic from passing through their firewalls because it reveals usernames and thus poses a security risk. `finger` is generally used only within an organization.

TELNET

The `telnet` command is perhaps one of the most well-known UNIX network tools. Telnet provides a remote terminal function and on a UNIX system lets you use a shell or command prompt environment on a remote system across a LAN or the Internet. Windows 2000 Professional includes a Telnet client for connecting to other systems running a Telnet server.

Tip #293	On UNIX-based operating systems, Telnet is a relatively insecure protocol. This insecurity can be overcome if you implement any of the widely available security enhancement tools. Of special interest is the TCP wrappers package, which allows you to create host-based access rules for greater network security. This process must be handled by the UNIX system administrator. You can also use the Secure Shell (SSH) package, which I'll describe later in this chapter.

Windows 2000 supplies a Telnet application with Windows 2000, but there's a surprise! This version is a Windows console program, meaning it looks like a Command Prompt window rather than a regular graphical Windows program. It also supports built-in NTLM authentication, so it can securely connect to the Telnet host service provided with Windows 2000 Professional and Server.

To connect to a remote server with Telnet—say `amber.university.edu`—you can issue the command by choosing Start, Run, or in a command prompt, as follows:

```
telnet amber.university.edu
```

Alternatively, you can simply run the Telnet program without naming a remote host to start it in its "prompt" mode. In prompt mode, Telnet prompts for commands like this:

```
Microsoft Telnet>
```

To this prompt, you can issue any of the commands listed in Table 25.4.

TABLE 25.4 TELNET COMMANDS

Command	Description
close	Closes the current host connection.
display	Displays the current program settings.
open hostname	Opens a connection to host hostname.
quit	Exits Telnet.
set	Changes a program setting. Set ? prints a list of available settings.
status	Prints connection status information.
unset	Changes a program setting (see set).
help (or ?)	Prints the list of commands.

When you get to the Telnet prompt, you can issue the open command, as follows, to establish a connection to a Telnet server:

```
open amber.university.edu
```

When a connection is established, the console window becomes a terminal screen. The remote computer's output is displayed in this window, and your keystrokes are sent to the remote server.

In terminal mode, the usual cut and paste shortcut keys are not available. You can cut and paste between the terminal window and the Windows Clipboard by using the window's System menu at the far left. To copy to the Clipboard, click the System icon; then select Edit and Mark. Highlight the desired text, and press Enter. Then, from the System menu, select Edit and Copy. To paste from the Clipboard into the terminal window, open the System menu, and then select Edit and Paste.

Pressing Ctrl+] (the Ctrl key plus the right bracket key) switches from terminal mode back to prompt mode, and when a connection is active, the Enter key switches from prompt mode back to terminal mode.

You can set or unset the following parameters in Telnet:

- NTLM—Enables encrypted authentication if you are connecting to a Windows 2000 Telnet server. (You can leave this setting enabled even if you're connecting to other types of Telnet servers.)

- LOCAL_ECHO—If set, displays what you type as you type it. Normally, this parameter is unset, and the remote terminal echoes your typing to the screen.

- TERM *type*—Lets you specify the control sequences recognized by the Telnet program. Type can be ANSI, VT100, VT100, VT52, or VTNT. The default is ANSI. The program can sometimes autodetect the terminal type and change this setting by itself.

- CRLF—If set, the Enter key sends both a carriage return and line feed character.

To terminate a Telnet session, you can press Ctrl+] and enter the quit command, or simply close the Telnet console window.

If you want to use a graphical user interface Telnet program, you can use Windows' own built-in Hyperterminal program or buy a third-party replacement. These alternatives don't support NTLM authentication needed to connect to a Windows 2000 Telnet server, however.

> **Note**
>
> By default, Telnet connects to the standard Telnet TCP/IP service port #23. You can connect to alternative ports by specifying a port number after the hostname, either on the command line or at the Telnet prompt. For example, `telnet host.company.com 110` connects to the POP3 service on port 110.

Hyperterminal Telnet

The old Hyperterminal program, a relic of the days of character-based dial-up services and bulletin boards, is still around in Windows 2000. You can still use it for direct serial and modem communications, but it has been taught the new trick of communicating through TCP/IP and can serve as a nifty Telnet client.

I don't really have a lot of room to explain it here, but these few pointers might help you along:

- You can create a connection by entering a descriptive name for the service you'll be contacting in the Connection Description dialog.

- In the Connect To dialog, first select TCP/IP (Winsock) in Connect Using. The dialog changes so that you can enter the name of the remote host or its IP address in the Host Address field. The default port is 23 (telnet), but you can enter an alternative port number—for example, 110 for the POP3 service.

■ Notable menu choices are File, Properties, which sets the terminal screen properties; Call, Disconnect, which terminates the connection; and Transfer, for file transfer using XMODEM, and so on. You can also send the output to the printer by using the Transfer menu.

■ You can save the connection (session) information by using the File menu. A shortcut to the saved session file gives you an instant way to make the connection again in the future.

Tip #294	Many network routers use Telnet for configuration and monitoring. If you manage a network, you can make a folder for network management tools and insert shortcuts to Hyperterminal Telnet connections to each of your routers in the folder.

THE TELNET HOST SERVICE

Windows 2000 is the first Microsoft operating system to come equipped with a Telnet server as well as a client. Having both a server and a client sounds like a boon for network managers, as it theoretically lets a remote user connect to and run programs on your Windows 2000 computer. It could conceivably also let a UNIX user connect to and run programs on a Windows 2000 computer.

I don't recommend using the Telnet Host Service for several reasons. First, it's strictly a command-line service, and few Windows applications are terribly useful without a graphical user interface. You could use some command-line management utilities, I grant you. Second, as I've mentioned, Telnet is an insecure protocol. The Windows 2000 Telnet server does use the NTLM password encryption protocol to authenticate users, but this feature can be disabled by hacking into the Registry. The result is that, in the end, using it is more of a risk than a benefit, and you can accomplish the same results by using Windows graphical interface management tools. Third, the Windows 2000 Professional version is limited to two connections from outside users.

Caution	If you're a system administrator, I *really* caution you against using the Telnet service or client to manage your LAN. Administrators will be the prime target of network snoops and Trojan horse authors; you have the passwords they want, and they'll be after you and your computer.

If you *really* want to try it, you must activate it manually:

1. Right-click My Computer and select Manage.
2. Open Services and Applications, and select Services.
3. Select Telnet in the right pane, and right-click Start.

4. Connect to your Telnet server from the command line, and type `telnet localhost`.

5. Type `exit` to disconnect. If you want to stop the service, go back to the Services Manager, right-click Telnet, and select Stop.

Note

If you want Telnet to start every time you boot, right-click Properties, and set the Startup Type to Automatic.

THE BERKELEY r COMMANDS

Most UNIX operating systems also come equipped with a suite of programs collectively referred to as the r commands. This reference is in relation to the fact that all of them are made for running remote commands or shells. You therefore have a great deal of flexibility where the task of remote network management is concerned.

Combined with the scheduling offered by the `cron` command, these tools enable you to write very powerful scripts and therefore maintain your network with a great degree of automation.

Table 25.5 provides a brief list and description of the r commands provided with Windows 2000.

TABLE 25.5   BERKELEY r COMMANDS PROVIDED WITH WINDOWS 2000

Command	Description
rsh	Remote shell, or `rsh`, executes a single command on another network system. `rsh` copies its standard output to the remote system's standard input and redirects the remote system's standard output to the local standard input.
rexec	Remote execute, or `rexec`, executes a single command on a remote system. This command is similar to `rsh`, except that it works with a different host service.
rcp	Remote copy, or `rcp`, is a command for copying files between two systems. `rcp` can even do third-party copies in which neither the source nor the destination reside on the system executing `rcp`.

If you're a UNIX user, you're probably already familiar with these commands.

The r commands are configured on the UNIX end through a file named .rhosts in the UNIX home directory. The syntax of this file is as follows:

```
host.domain.com     username
host2.domain.com      username
host3.domain.com      username
```

Each line lists a remote computer from which you might send a remote command to the UNIX system and the username you use on that remote computer. To use the r commands on a UNIX system from Windows 2000 then, you add a line on your UNIX .rhosts file listing the full domain name of your Windows 2000 computer and your Windows login name.

Tip #295	The Berkeley r commands, although very useful, are also inherently insecure because the commands used by these programs are usually passed in plain text through the network. Additionally, these commands are designed to be run in a trusted network where clients are not always required to reauthenticate themselves. This might not always be the case where today's networks are concerned. Because of these inherent vulnerabilities, it's best not to use these commands across the Internet. You might use the Secure Shell package, which replaces all the r commands as well as adds a greater degree of security via strong encryption. SSH also replaces the very insecure Telnet protocol and offers X11-encrypted forwarding. You can obtain the most current UNIX version of SSH from the following site:
	
	`ftp://ftp.cs.hut.fi/pub/ssh`
	
	You can obtain Windows-based client versions of SSH from this site:
	
	`http://www.datafellows.com`

INTERNETWORKING WITH MACINTOSH

The Apple Macintosh is arguably *the* computer of choice in the graphic arts and publishing worlds. Teetering on the edge of extinction a few years ago, Apple has staged an impressive comeback, and its recent product releases show it's back to stay. Apple's new G4 PowerPC computer outperforms the fastest Pentium machines by a factor of two to four and matches the original Cray 1 supercomputer in calculation power. So, seamless internetworking with the Mac will remain an important part of the Windows 2000 network.

Windows NT 4.0 Server brought AppleTalk file and printer sharing to the Windows world and with it a few headaches because of some significant glitches. The situation has improved in the Windows 2000 version.

The following sections examine some of the problems of having Macs and Windows machines coexist on the same network.

MAC FILES AND NETWORKING

Macintosh files actually consist of two separate parts, or *forks*:

- The data fork, which contains data, document text, program code, and so on
- The resource fork, which contains language-specific strings and dialog box layouts for programs, and the association information to link a document with the application that created it

The two parts can be read and written independently on the Macintosh; it's as if each file is composed of two bundled but separate files. Right away, this is a big problem: Nothing in this structure really corresponds to the structure of Windows. On Windows, like DOS before it, data and resource information are combined in a single file, and program associations and directory information are kept elsewhere in the system. Windows programs aren't aware of a two-part structure, which can lead to conflicts when Windows users and Mac users write to the same file, as you'll soon learn.

Macintoshes use a proprietary file sharing system called AppleTalk File Protocol (AFP), which runs over Ethernet as well as a slower serial-port version called LocalTalk. In contrast, PCs use the Server Message Block, or SMB, protocol for file sharing.

To link Macs and PCs on a network, then, either the Macs must learn to speak SMB or the Windows computers must speak AFP. Both solutions are possible. If you have a Windows 2000 Server computer, it comes with Services for Macintosh (dubbed SFM), which speaks AFP to provide your Windows network's resources to Macs. You can also install SMB software on Macs. I'll go into these solutions in a little bit. First, let's look at some of the differences between the Mac and Windows worlds that have an impact on peaceful coexistence on a LAN.

PLANNING FOR COMPATIBILITY

Before getting to the details of *how* to share files between Macintoshes and Windows computers, let's look at what you must do to be sure that the files—however shared—are going to make sense to both platforms.

FILENAME COMPATIBILITY

Mac filenames cannot exceed 31 characters, including the extension (for example, .doc). Mac filenames can contain any character except the colon (:).

> **Note**
>
> The 31-character limit is the result of the design of the Macintosh Hierarchical File System, or HFS. HFS is Apple's disk formatting standard, and it corresponds to FAT or NFTS on Windows machines.

A second-generation disk formatting system called HFS+ is available as an add-on for users of MacOS 8 or higher. HFS+ solves many of HFS's limitations, just as FAT32 was an advance over FAT16. Table 25.6 shows a comparison of the different formats.

TABLE 25.6   COMPARISON OF MACINTOSH HFS AND HFS+ DISK FORMATS

Feature	HFS	HFS +
User visible name	MacOS Standard	MacOS Extended
Allocation table structure	16 bits	32 bits
Filename length	31 characters	255 characters
Filename encoding	MacRoman	Unicode

Feature	HFS	HFS +
File/folder attributes	Support for fixed-size attributes (FInfo and FXInfo)	Allows for future metadata extensions
OS startup support	System Folder ID	Also supports a dedicated startup file
Catalog node size	512 bytes	4KB
Maximum file size	231 bytes	263 bytes

Windows permits filenames up to 256 characters in length but has a longer list of unacceptable characters: the colon (:), backslash (\), forward slash (/), question mark (?), asterisk (*), quotation mark ("), greater-than symbol (>), less-than symbol (<), and pipe symbol (|).

Therefore, you must be careful when naming files that are to be visible to users in both camps. Mac users cannot see the entire filename if Windows people use more than 33 characters. Likewise, if Mac people use the illegal Windows characters in filenames, Windows users see modified versions of filenames, which might be confusing. Windows automatically replaces illegal characters with legal ones, which might make it difficult to recognize a name. It's best to stick with shorter names using characters legal on *both* operating systems.

A more subtle difference between the MacOS and Windows is the way that document/application associations are made. Windows matches up documents to their application programs with the file extension. For example, Windows associates the .doc extension with Microsoft Word, so you can double-click on a .doc file, and Windows launches Word to display the file.

Macs, on the other hand, store this information in each document file's resource fork. Each file notes its document type (for example, WDBN for a Word document) and its application type through what's called the *Creator code* (MSWD for Microsoft Word). Windows applications don't acknowledge the resource fork and generally remove it when writing a new version of a document file on disk. When it detects that this is about to happen (which isn't always), Windows warns you and gives you the option of preserving the resource data. You should always say Yes. Sometimes, though, the document/application link is lost.

Mac users must get used to this, as double-clicking an edited document doesn't automatically launch the appropriate application. They either must search for the application manually or drag the file and drop it onto the application's icon. (They'll probably exact their revenge by removing the .doc extension from Word document filenames.)

FILE AND VOLUME SIZE LIMITATIONS

Macintosh computers running the Mac operating system (MacOS) versions prior to 7.6.1 can't see further than 2GB into any disk drive, local or networked. If your Windows network shares files from volumes larger than 2GB, your Macs must run OS 7.6.1 or higher.

Furthermore, Macintoshes can't cope with a network server sharing more than 50 volumes if the shared volume names are 27 characters long or fewer, or more than 167 volumes if the share names are 12 characters or fewer. This limitation isn't significant in most environments but might be a problem with one of those humongous CD-ROM servers sharing 50 to 100 CDs.

OS COMPATIBILITY

Before starting to internetwork, you should upgrade your Macs to at least version 7.5.5, or if you'll be sharing volumes larger than 2GB, to version 7.6.1 or higher. If you want to use HFS+ disk formatting, you must upgrade to MacOS 8 or higher.

> **Note**
>
> Apple has made System 7.5.5 available for free download via its FTP site. You must purchase licenses for 7.6 and higher from Apple, however. The site is located at
>
> ```
> ftp://ftp.apple.com/Apple_Support_Area/Apple_Software_Updates/
>    English-North_American/Macintosh/System/Older_System/
> ```
>
> Also, be sure to download the update to System 7.5.5 available in the previous folder.

Also, some Macintosh applications don't properly install themselves when they're installed into a Windows shared folder. An error occurs when more than one user tries to run the application at the same time.

 If Macintosh users get a network error when more than one Mac accesses an application, see "Can't Run Macintosh Application Concurrently" in the "Troubleshooting" section at the end of this chapter.

PRINTING

Windows users can directly print to AppleTalk printers on the network. If you want to get full queueing and spooling for *all* users, you can use Windows 2000 Server's Services for Macintosh to capture and share the printer on the network, where it will be available to both Windows and Mac users. It seems a little strange to make Mac users go through Windows to get their own brand of printers, but it makes access more fair for all.

In general, Windows and Mac users alike can fully utilize any available PostScript printers. Services for Macintosh can also make non-PostScript printers available to Mac users. However, due to Windows printer driver limitations, Mac users can't print at greater than 300dpi resolution on these printers.

INTERNETWORKING OPTIONS

Macintosh and Windows network users can share files in several ways. Windows 2000 Server provides a "gateway" system that lets Macs use files and printers shared by Windows computers as if the shares came from other Macs, and similarly letting Windows users see and use Mac shares. If your network doesn't have Windows 2000 Server, some options are still available, but using the Windows 2000 Server path is the easiest.

SERVICES FOR MACINTOSH ON WINDOWS 2000 SERVER

If you have any familiarity with Windows servers, then you might have at least a passing understanding of file and print services for the Macintosh. In a nutshell, Microsoft provides native AppleTalk services for Macintosh computers connected to the network. When a Macintosh user opens the Chooser—the Mac's equivalent to the Network Neighborhood—and selects AppleTalk, the Windows servers running Macintosh file and print services appear as available. The environment should appear to be seamless to all users.

About the only way that users of either operating system will notice that the other operating system is mucking about on the network is to notice the filename extensions and resource-fork stripping discussed earlier. The effect is that sometimes users must search for the appropriate application to open a file.

 If Macintosh users discover that the Finder can't find the correct application to open a document that has been edited by Windows users, see "Macintosh Files Have Lost Application Associations" in the "Troubleshooting" section at the end of this chapter.

The process of installing and configuring SFM is not complicated, but it has to be done by the administrator of a Windows 2000 Server computer.

> **Note**
>
> When SFM is installed, Windows doesn't let you share any folder that is within an already-shared folder. This side effect is normal. Apparently, Macs run into some sort of trouble if they run into the same material shared two different ways.

As for configuration, you have only two issues to worry about:

- The network administrator needs to make sure that Windows users are defined to match each Macintosh.
- When you're sharing folders on a server with SFM, the Create Shared Folder Properties dialog includes a check box to enable sharing to Macintosh users. You must check this box on any shares you want to make available to Macintosh as well as Windows users.

APPLESHARE IP ON MACINTOSH

Instead of providing the networking gateway on a Windows machine, you can also buy gateway software from Apple to run on one of your Macintoshes.

AppleShare IP (ASIP) is an industry favorite from Apple. ASIP provides file and printer sharing services for both Macintoshes *and* Windows, each in its native file sharing protocol format, using the TCP/IP network transport protocol throughout. ASIP provides an almost complete set of TCP/IP-based services to meet all the basic needs of a workgroup or even large-scale environment with hundreds of users. Services included are Web, email (SMTP, POP, and IMAP), file and printer sharing in both SMB and AFP formats, and FTP.

Its powerful capabilities, easy administration, native SMB support for Windows clients, and relatively low price have made it quite popular. The application is mature, solid, and stable. For small, mixed-platform workgroups, ASIP is an excellent server with a proven track record. It does, however, have one significant limitation: security. Although password and other types of security are built into ASIP, it's not nearly as robust or deep as Windows NT/2000. This point isn't so critical in a workgroup environment where strong security isn't necessary, but when documents and information need to be strongly protected, ASIP, in its raw form, does not have the capabilities.

> **Note**
>
> MacOS version 9 does add some stronger security capabilities to the Macintosh environment. Two enhancements—voiceprint identification and multiple user capability—are wholly new to the MacOS. You can find additional information at
> `www.apple.com/macos/reserve9.html`.

The current version of ASIP is 6.3, which improves the already-powerful administration tools and adds support for MacOS 9. To run ASIP, you need any PowerMac, iMac, or Macintosh Server with a G4, G3, 604e, 604, or 601 CPU, or a 6500 series computer with a 603e microprocessor (got all that?). ASIP 6.3 costs about $450 for a 10-user license and about $1,250 for an unlimited license. This amount seems expensive until you note that it includes a Web server and full email system, as well as integrated Macintosh and Windows file sharing services.

Making ASIP available requires inserting the appropriate information for your network into OpenTransport and setting up Users & Groups, Sharepoints, and other services you want to offer from the server.

Up to 10 ASIP servers can be administered from one machine, even if it's not a server. Also, you can share a common Users & Groups database between servers using ASIP's shared directory service (it's not quite *Active Directory*, but it beats entering users into 10 computers separately).

MacOS X Plus Samba

As you might have guessed, Apple also has a server operating system. This one is called MacOS X Server and is a port of NeXT Software's OpenStep operating system, based on the MACH kernel (one of the many UNIX cores). Although it has the familiar Macintosh interface, the internals hold little in relation to previous MacOS offerings. And for the first time in history, a MacOS command-line interface is available. The point of the matter is this: MacOS X Server is POSIX-compliant and can run a slightly modified version of Samba. Samba can give Windows users on the network access to Macintosh files, whereas Macintosh users can access the shared files via Macintosh networking.

MacOS X's beta and release schedule is uncertain at the time of this writing, but this solution to Macintosh and Windows internetworking will be one to watch carefully. A

Macintosh server could be less expensive than a Windows server because, unlike Microsoft, Apple licenses the server for unlimited users.

VIRTUAL PC

Virtual PC from Connectix (www.connectix.com) allows you to run Windows 9x on your Macintosh. Don't laugh! This emulation software makes a Macintosh look like a PC and runs Windows in a window (ironic). The Windows environment has no idea that it's running on a software emulator, so you can feel free to install all your Windows applications. The connectivity boon here is two-fold. One, you can drag and drop files between the Windows 9x desktop and the Mac desktop. Two, if you plug into the Ethernet network and configure Windows properly, your Windows network will see Virtual PC as a real PC, and networking will be in effect. You can use this virtual Windows computer to share a Mac volume to the network as a Windows share.

Another benefit to VPC is that it enables you to have several different operating systems at hand almost immediately. Because VPC uses files as drive containers, you're limited only to hard drive space on hand (and the 2GB/container limit that VPC imposes). Keep in mind that Connectix supports only DOS 6.22, Windows 95, and Windows 98 with helper files that make working with the guest operating system easier.

DAVE

DAVE, from Thursby Software Systems at www.thursby.com, is a NetBIOS (SMB) client for the Mac. It allows a Macintosh to appear on a Windows network as if it were a Windows client connecting via NetBIOS. The sharing is seamless—if not slightly difficult to configure and slow when it's working. (NetBIOS is not exactly a speed demon, even over Ethernet.) Still, it's a feasible solution for a network with a relatively small number of Macintoshes, with mostly Windows computers.

Thursby Software Systems also sells TSStalk (formerly COPSTalk), an AppleShare client for Windows machines. TSStalk allows Windows users to directly and natively access AppleShare IP 5.x and 6.x networks over AppleTalk as if it were, what else, a Macintosh. Because this is AFP over TCP/IP and not NetBIOS, it's faster. This solution is a decent approach for a network with a relatively small number of Windows computers and mostly Macintoshes.

Both of the preceding solutions can be a great help in an environment that is dominated by one platform or the other. However, there is nothing like a dedicated server that can handle requests from a number of platforms as each new widget on a workstation reduces its overall capabilities by draining its resources. So, despite their excellent capabilities, it's better to avoid them when a server can be put to use, especially when that server already has the capability to do so built in.

SNEAKERNET

If you can't use any of the real internetworking methods to connect Macintosh and Windows computers on your LAN, you can still trade files the old-fashioned way with floppy disks. Macintosh computers can read and write files on floppies formatted by Windows.

A few utilities allow Windows computers to view Macintosh HFS-formatted floppies and files. One of the most revered and well-known is TransMac. This shareware title, available at www.asy.com, is a simple-to-use file viewer that reads HFS-formatted floppies and CD-ROMs. If, however, you plan on doing a lot of Macintosh volume browsing, consider something along the lines of MacOpener from DataViz (www.dataviz.com). This utility so completely integrates itself with your system that its operation is seamless. You can even format floppies in HFS. PC Exchange is yet another option.

ESSENTIAL UTILITIES

Besides internetworking, you need some tools to help both camps read and process each other's files. Prime examples are MacDrive 98 (www.media4.com, $65) and the popular favorite TransMac (www.asy.com, $65), which allows you to mount Mac HFS- and HFS+-formatted media in Windows. Many productivity applications have versions for both Windows and Macintosh, so you can use their documents on both platforms without a hitch. Microsoft's Office 98 for Macintosh is a prime example of cross-platform compatibility. Office 98 Macintosh and Office 2000 share the same file format for all duplicated applications.

You'll also want to be able to convert files for applications that don't have equivalents on both platforms. One solution is MacLink Plus from DataViz (www.dataviz.com, $99.00), which is capable of viewing and converting dozens of file formats, including Office 2000 documents, to Macintosh file formats. Conversions Plus from DataViz ($99.00) does the same thing for Windows. DataViz also has an HFS volume mounting utility for Windows called MacOpener ($59.95), which is also well received.

For text files such as READMEs and other ASCII-based documents, try UltraEdit (www.ultraedit.com, $30), which can handle files to and from Windows, Macintosh, and UNIX with ease. It also makes a great Notepad replacement with its capability to show multiple files in a single window. Another company to watch is Mijenix (www.mijenix.com). This company has a slew of capable utilities that kick the socks off its competitors and are sold for peanuts. PowerDesk 98 ($29.95) is a collection of useful additions to Windows and an impressive replacement for Explorer that comes with a built-in file viewer. Of course, if you buy Fix-It 99, a complete suite of diagnostic and repair utilities for Windows 9x *and* Windows NT, Mijenix throws in PowerDesk ($49.95). ZipMagic turns ZIP archives into folders that seamlessly integrate into the rest of the environment ($39.95).

Last, but by far not the least, is PowerQuest. If you don't have a single PowerQuest utility, you must go out and get at least one—Lost & Found ($65). This miracle utility can recover data from just about any drive that can still spin.

INTERNETWORKING OVER DIAL-UP AND VPN CONNECTIONS

When you use a dial-up or Virtual Private Networking (VPN) connection to reach a remote network with non-Windows servers, you must be sure that the remote servers' protocols are carried over the connection. In this section, I'll refer to dial-up connections, but whatever I say applies to VPN connections as well.

The AppleTalk protocol is not transmitted over a dial-up connection. You can reach Macintosh file servers only if the remote network uses the file and print services for Macintosh gateway service on a Windows 2000 or NT server.

UNIX, OS/2, and NetWare servers can be reached as long as the appropriate protocol (TCP/IP, NetBEUI, and IPX/SPX, respectively) is enabled across the dial-up connection. To confirm whether the protocols are enabled, do the following:

1. Open Network and Dial-Up Connections.
2. Right-click the Connection icon, and select Properties.
3. Select the Networking tab, and verify that the required protocols are checked under Components Checked Are Used by This Connection.

The protocols must also be enabled on the Dial-Up Networking server at the remote end. If you enable incoming connections on your own Windows 2000 Professional computer, verify that the protocols are enabled for your Incoming Connections icon.

> **Note**
>
> For more information about enabling incoming connections to your Windows 2000 Professional computer, see Chapter 23, "Windows Unplugged: Remote and Mobile Networking."

To enable alternative protocols for incoming connections, follow these steps:

1. Open Network and Dial-Up Connections.
2. Right-click the Incoming Connections icon, and select Properties.
3. Select the Networking tab, and verify that the required protocols are checked under Network Components.
4. Select the name of each protocol in turn. Click Properties, and confirm that Allow Callers to Access My Local Area Network is checked.

These steps ensure that all protocols are routed through your computer when you dial in by modem or through a VPN connection.

PART

IV

CH

25

ADVANCED NETWORKING SERVICES

Several Windows networking options and settings are difficult to categorize. These topics must be covered somewhere, so I've collected them here.

SETTING NETWORK BINDINGS

Windows lets you specify how network components are connected. As you learned in Chapter 19, "Overview of Windows 2000 Networking," a network uses many layers of components. Bindings are the connections between these components. Through bindings, you can control whether the file and printer sharing service can be reached by each installed protocol and through which network and/or dial-up adapters.

You'll find step-by-step instructions for setting bindings elsewhere in this book where necessary. Let me give you the general picture here, in case you're arriving at this topic through the index.

To set network bindings, open Network and Dial-Up Connections, and select Advanced, Advanced Settings. Select the Adapters and Bindings tab, as shown in Figure 25.8.

Figure 25.8
On the Adapters and Bindings tab, you can sever the connection between specific network components.

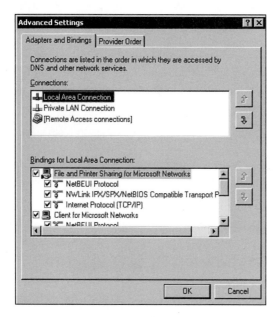

Select a network adapter in the upper part of the dialog. In the bottom, you can check and uncheck services and individual transport protocols to connect or disconnect these services from the selected network adapter.

To set bindings for dial-up connections, you must view the Properties pages of the individual dial-up connections. On the Networking tab, you can check which services and protocols are to be used across the connection.

INSTALLING OPTIONAL NETWORK COMPONENTS

Windows 2000 Professional comes with a few networking components that are not used in most networks but can be essential in others. I won't cover these components in great detail because your network manager will probably install them for you if they're used on your LAN.

The optional components are listed in Table 25.7.

TABLE 25.7   WINDOWS 2000 OPTIONAL NETWORK COMPONENTS

Component	Description
Simple Network Management Protocol	A remote monitoring and measurement tool used by some network management systems. This protocol is discussed next.
RIP Listener	A service to receive network routing information in large networks. Your network manager will indicate whether you need to install it. Don't install unless it's required.
Simple TCP/IP Services	A suite of services that perform simple functions for testing purposes, such as echoing data to a remote computer or generating a stream of data. Don't install these services unless you're instructed to do so by a network manager because they don't do anything useful but can be used by hackers to tie up your network with pointless traffic.
Print Services for UNIX	Printer services for UNIX hosts. These services were covered earlier in this chapter under "Printing to Windows Printers from UNIX."

PART

IV

CH

25

SNMP

The Simple Network Management Protocol, or SNMP, is used by large corporate networks to monitor, measure, and configure network equipment from a central location. It can be used, for example, by monitoring software to detect whether servers or WAN connections have gone offline to alert staff or sound an alarm.

Windows 2000 Professional doesn't come with a tool to *use* the information SNMP can reveal, but it does come with an optional networking component that lets an SNMP monitor measure network activity in your computer.

To install the SNMP service, follow these steps:

1. Open Network and Dial-Up Connections, and select Optional Networking Components.
2. Check Management and Monitoring Tools, and then click Details.
3. Check Simple Network Management Protocol, and click OK.
4. Click Next.

You should immediately configure the SNMP monitor to protect your computer's information with a secret "community name." This name is like a password that remote monitors need to supply before they can extract information from your computer. The default community name is public. Your network manager might supply you with an alternative community name. To set it, do the following:

1. Right-click My Computer, and select Manage.

2. Open Services and Applications, select Services, and locate SNMP Service in the right pane. Double-click it to open its Properties page.

3. Select the Security tab. Select Public, and then click Remove. Next, click Add to enter any community names provided by your network manager. Generally, you assign read-only community rights unless your network manager specifies otherwise.

Note

> SNMP can be a minor security risk because it reveals the names of user accounts on your computer and your computer's network routing information. A community name with write or create permission can alter network routing tables. For this reason, SNMP should be blocked by your network's firewall; therefore, you should *not* install it unless it's necessary.

Tip #296

> If you're a network manager and use SNMP to monitor equipment health, you might find it valuable to know that Windows 2000 Professional and Server come with a utility that can turn specified Windows Event Log entries into SNMP traps (messages) as they happen. This feature is configured by the undocumented program evntwin. This utility can let your network monitor detect and report on full hard drives, security violations, and other significant events.
>
> evntwin can save a list of event-to-trap mappings to a file. Another undocumented utility, evntcmd, can instantly install this file on another computer, even remotely.

TROUBLESHOOTING

NOVELL NETWARE SERVERS CAN'T BE FOUND

I have installed a NetWare client, but version 2.x NetWare servers do not appear under Entire Network in My Network Places.

Windows might not have correctly identified the Ethernet frame type used by these earlier NetWare versions. In Network and Dial-Up Connections, open the Local Area Connection properties. Select NWLink IPX/SPX Compatible Protocol, and open Properties. Under Frame Type, change the setting from Auto to 802.3.

If you have NetWare version 3 or higher servers on the network, you must configure them to use 802.3 framing in addition to the default Ethernet_II.

CAN'T ATTACH TO NETWARE SERVERS

I'm using the Microsoft Client but can't connect to some NetWare servers running version 3 or higher; my password is rejected.

Have the NetWare administrator enable unencrypted passwords on these servers. The Microsoft client can't send encrypted passwords to NetWare servers. (The Novell client does not have this problem.)

BANNER AND/OR BLANK PAGES ARE PRINTED ON NETWARE PRINTERS

When I send printer output to Novell printers, banner pages are printed at the beginning of my print jobs, and/or blank sheets are printed at the end.

Open the CNSW Control Panel applet, and uncheck Print Banner Pages and Add Form Feed.

SOME COMPUTERS ARE MISSING FROM ENTIRE NETWORK

My list of Computers Near Me is incomplete under Entire Network in My Network Places.

The network has elected a browser master that doesn't have all the protocols used by Windows networking computers on your LAN. This is a random selection, so be sure to install and bind the same set of protocols on every workstation in your LAN.

CARRIAGE RETURNS AND LINE FEEDS ARE MANGLED

When plain-text files are sent from UNIX machines to my printers using lpr *and Print Services for UNIX, carriage returns and line feeds are mangled. Line feeds are inserted where just carriage returns were present.*

When it's receiving plain ASCII text for printing, the TCP/IP Print Server replaces both LF (line feed or newline) and CR (carriage return) characters with a carriage return/line feed pair. This messes up print jobs that wanted to overprint lines using just a carriage return.

You can disable the translation of both newlines and carriage returns, or just of carriage returns, by adding a value to the Registry.

→ For instructions and warnings about using the Registry Editor, **see** "Using Regedit," **p. 1344**.

Use the Registry Editor called Regedit to find the key HKEY_LOCAL_MACHINE\System\CurrentControlSet\Control\Print\Printers\ *printername*\PrinterDriverData, where *printername* is the name of the shared printer the UNIX user is using.

To prevent the TCP/IP Print Server from replacing either CR or NL with CR+LF, follow these steps:

1. Select key PrinterDriverData and choose Edit, New, DWORD Value. Enter the name Winprint_TextNoTranslation, and set the value to 1.

2. To prevent the server from replacing CR with CR+LF but still replace LF with CR+LF, add the DWORD value `Winprint_TextNoCRTranslation` with the value 1.

3. After making either of these additions, go to Computer Management, view Services, right-click TCP/IP Print Server, and select Restart.

Some Windows 2000 printer drivers do not correctly implement overprinted lines. You might find that the lines are now correctly stacked on top of each other, but only the text from the topmost line is visible. You might need to use the binary mode flag (`-o l`) in your `lpr` command and add a form feed to the end of your file.

If you later decide to undo the Registry change, you can remove the value item or set its value to 0, and then restart the service.

CAN'T RUN MACINTOSH APPLICATION CONCURRENTLY

When a Macintosh application is installed on a shared folder stored on a Windows 2000 or Windows NT server, an `Unable to Open File` *error occurs on Macintoshes when more than one Macintosh user attempts to run the application concurrently.*

Some Macintosh programs fail to open their application executable files in the proper file sharing mode. You can patch the problem by using a resource editor program on the Macintosh; just follow these steps:

1. Obtain a copy of ResEdit. An excellent resource (pun intended) for all things resource related is ResExcellence (`www.resexcellence.com`). There, you can download a copy of ResEdit as well as gain helpful resource editing skills through the huge collection of step-by-step projects. For novice users, a better program is FileBuddy from SkyTag (`www.skytag.com`).

2. Start ResEdit or FileBuddy. Select Get Info from the File menu. In the dialog that appears, you can select the application.

3. Put a check in the Shared check box.

4. If you're using ResEdit, quit the application and choose Yes to save the changes. In FileBuddy, click OK.

> **Caution**
>
> Resource editing on a Macintosh is as risky as Registry editing in Windows. Always make a copy of whatever file you're going to edit before making changes, and *never* throw out an original, even if it seems that your modified version works like a charm.

MACINTOSH FILES HAVE LOST APPLICATION ASSOCIATIONS

After a shared file has been edited by a Windows user, when Macintosh users open the file, the Macintosh Finder says it can't find the application required to open the document.

The file's resource fork was stripped out when the file was edited in Windows, so the file's Type and Creator codes are missing. The Macintosh user can drag the file and drop it onto the applications' icon or manually locate the application. When the Macintosh user saves the file, the association will be restored for future edits.

The Type and Creator codes can also be set using a Macintosh resource editor, as described previously. However, resource editing is tricky and best not done unless it's an emergency.

Note

> Type and Creator codes are case sensitive. MSWD is not the same as MsWd or mswd. Case can often cause confusion if you must restore the codes if they were stripped on a trip through Windows or DOS.

TIPS FROM THE WINDOWS PROS: THE HOSTS FILE

If you have an office LAN, especially one with mixed and matched computers, you're probably like me and have a chart of computer names and IP addresses posted on your wall—not just computers, but routers, firewalls, monitored devices, and all manner of devices. Who knows? Soon the espresso machine might be wired in, too.

On a corporate or enterprise LAN, the LAN administrators will probably enter each device into the organization's Domain Name Service system, under your own default domain, so that you can type a command like ping firewall instead of having to type ping firewall.mycompany.com or, worse, something like ping 192.168.56.102.

On a workgroup LAN, you probably don't have your own domain name server. Or your network manager hasn't entered names for the devices you use most frequently (for example, ping espresso). On a heterogeneous network, your Macintosh and testbed Linux machines probably aren't in any domain name list anywhere.

The hosts file is the answer to this annoying situation. You can add entries to the file \winnt\system32\drivers\etc\hosts to associate names with IP addresses. The Windows domain-name lookup system looks first in the hosts file before consulting the network, so you can add entries for your own workgroup's computers and devices, regardless of operating system.

The format is simple. Edit the file in Notepad. Add lines to the file, listing IP addresses at the left margin, followed by some whitespace (tabs or spaces), followed by one or more names. You can enter simple names or full domain names. Simple names are assumed to belong to your own domain.

My hosts file looks like this:

```
127.0.0.0 localhost lh
192.168.56.102 firewall fw
192.168.56.45 macone
```

The first entry is the default entry shipped with Windows. localhost stands for "my own computer" and is used for internal testing of the network software. I've added a second name, lh, because I'm lazy and would rather type ping lh than ping localhost.

I added the second entry myself to give a name to my network's firewall. I can now configure the firewall by typing `telnet firewall` or, better yet, `telnet fw` rather than having to look up at that sheet on the wall and type a bunch of numbers.

Finally, there's an entry for my Macintosh computer, `macone`. This way, I can view its Web server's home page from Internet Explorer using `http://macone` rather than having to remember its IP address.

This file also serves as a sort of documentation of my network, as it records important IP addresses. One thing you must watch out for, though, is that Windows checks this file before using the real DNS system to look up names. If you put a name in your LAN's (or the Internet's) DNS system, and the computer's IP address later changes, your hosts file will be incorrect. It's best to use this file only for machines that are in nobody's DNS system.

CHAPTER 26

NETWORK SECURITY

In this chapter

It's a Cold, Cruel World

You might be considering connecting your LAN to the Internet, or you might have done so already. Connecting will probably be more work than you expect (even with, or due to, my advice), but the achievement will be gratifying. After you make just a few keystrokes, a friend in Italy will be able to log on to your network. Millions of potential customers can reach you. You'll be one with the world.

I don't want to spoil your day, but the cruel fact is that, in addition to your customers, friends, mother, and curious, benign strangers, your computer and your LAN will also be exposed to pranksters, hackers, information bandits, thieves, and a variety of other bad guys who, like anyone else, can probe, prod, and test your system. Will your network be up to the task? Even if you have a single computer only occasionally connected to the Internet by modem, you're still at risk.

By this point in the book, you are aware that network design is foremost a task of planning. It's especially true in this case: Before you connect to the Internet, you must plan for security, whether you have a single computer or a large local area network (LAN).

Explaining everything that you can and should do would be impossible. What I want to do in this chapter is give you an idea of what network security entails. I'll talk about the types of risks you'll be exposed to and the means people use to minimize this exposure; then I'll end with some tips and to-do lists. If you want to have a network or security consultant take care of implementation for you, that's great. This chapter will give you the background to understand what the consultant is doing. If you want to go it on your own then consider this chapter to be a survey course, and your assignment is to continue to research, write, and implement a security plan.

Who Would Be Interested in My Computer?

The truth is that as inviting as you think your network or Web site is, hackers are not at all interested in the *public* parts of it. They are trying to find a hole—a security breach—through which they can get into the rest of your computer or into your larger network. After they get inside, the hackers aim to gain access to valuable data and critical system functions. Your credit cards might end up financing someone's excessive and dubious tastes. Your Web site might become a trafficking center for stolen information or pornography. If your Internet server is connected to internal networks, hackers may have a free ride deep inside your company. Even a single computer at home might have something worth using in future exploits.

The Internet is a gateway, but it works both ways, and it's quite simple now for any of the millions of Internet users worldwide to scan hundreds or thousands of computers at a time for potential means of access: the presence of a Web server or file sharing or remote control software. These hackers can then narrow down their search and concentrate their attack on promising candidates. If you're directly connected or just happen to be online at the right time, you could be their next target.

In the corporate and government world, a server is likely to be a conduit to information that you do not want to share with strangers or perhaps even friends and employees. Your servers may be a pathway to proprietary source code, business plans, client lists, credit card numbers, medical records, passwords, classified military information, marketing plans, personnel records, and stock transactions—just to name a few sensitive items. You can't simply ignore the risks that exposing this information brings.

Some organizations do not have any secret, confidential, or proprietary information, and in these settings, they might not have anything to steal; however, the well-being of the server itself can be a target of attack. For example, public service or political organizations want to give away information, but sometimes opposing groups do not want the information disseminated. If hackers can gain entry to cripple the information server, the entire objective is fulfilled. In this case, nothing is stolen—except Freedom of Speech.

Security risks can come from *inside* a network environment as well as from outside. An attack from either direction can be dangerous and costly. Inside, you might be subject to highly sophisticated eavesdropping techniques or even simple theft. I know of a company whose entire customer list and internal pricing database walked out the door one night with the receptionist, whose significant other worked for the competition. The theft was easy; any employee could read and print any file on the company's network.

Everyone—even you, the solitary computer user—should be worried about theft of something even less tangible: your identity. An identity thief, armed with personal information such as your name, birthplace, and Social Security number can often obtain credit cards in your name, forged driver's licenses, and so on.

Think You're Safe? Think Again.

I wanted to give you a practical example, so I did something shady: Last week at 1 a.m., I scanned the Internet for computers with unprotected Windows File Sharing. I picked a block of IP addresses near mine and used common, completely legal programs to find computers that were turned on and connected. Within a few minutes, I had found 20. I went through these 20 to see whether they had shared files or folders. My efforts didn't take long; on the fourth try, I was presented with the contents of someone's entire hard drive. Of course, I immediately closed the display, but not before noticing that one of the folders on the hard drive was named Quicken and probably contained all this person's checking and savings account information.

Within 10 minutes I had hacked into someone's computer, and I wasn't trying very hard or using one of the many sophisticated tools available. I didn't have to attempt to break a password. But even if I'd had to, would that person have noticed his or her computer's hard disk light flickering at 1 a.m.? Would you?

PART

IV

CH

26

TYPES OF ATTACK

Before I talk about how to defend your computer against attack, let's go through the types of attacks you're facing. Hackers can work their way into your servers and network using several methods.

PASSWORD CRACKING

Hackers want two things: user account names and passwords. With both, they have the key to your computer and LAN. With just one, they have half of the key and can start searching for the missing information by simply trying dictionary words and, after that, using random combinations of letters and numbers.

Oddly, in this sophisticated age of bits and bytes, brute force remains an amazingly productive technique. Hacking software is tireless. Armed with a simple program, hackers can scan for promising targets and map out a network in seconds. Password crackers can try thousands of name and password combinations in a short time. If your network is "user friendly" and permits passwords composed of just four letters or numbers, the hackers' programs need only try an average of 800,000 combinations before these programs finds the correct combination. This is a piece of cake.

The attack can be targeted to many services: file sharing, Web servers, mail servers, and FTP servers, just for starters. The hackers might then gain access to shared volumes, mail, Web pages, or anything else stored on your server. With luck, they might be able to download or alter Registry information or names and passwords for other systems linked to yours. A domain administrator password, for example, is quite valuable to crack or obtain, as it is the key to the rest of the network.

SPOOFING

One way of preventing brute force attacks is to instruct network software to accept connections only from trusted IP addresses within a private network. Savvy hackers can send data packets into your network with a "sending address" that appears to belong to one of the trusted internal computers, in a type of attack called *spoofing*. The receiving computer sends its replies to the internal computer being impersonated, not back to the hackers. But the hackers, knowing that they are working blindly, just keep sending in strings of commands, hoping that everything is working. They might be able to mail themselves a password file, alter Registry values, and so on. This technique is actually quite a serious security risk with network services such as rsh, FTP, and telnet.

IMPERSONATION

Hackers can exploit unprotected network routing equipment to direct Web site requests to their servers rather than yours. An identical replacement Web site or network server might be able to collect several usernames and passwords before the complaints of "I can't log on" are recognized as the indication of a serious problem.

EAVESDROPPING

Network monitoring software is commonly available (Windows 2000, in fact, comes with it). Anyone with a physical connection to your network cabling can tap into all the unencrypted information passing by.

Even though some types of network software encrypt login and password information just to avoid this type of monitoring, some older security protocols are static. The encrypted password can be recorded and sent in again later by the hackers to gain access. This is called a *replay* attack. Windows 2000's Kerberos and MSCHAPv2 security protocols are immune from this type of attack because their password encoding mechanism changes from use to use.

> **Caution**
>
> When a Windows 2000 network has to support older versions of Windows and OS/2, it still allows computers to use the old technique, so passwords can still be captured this way.
>
> Many network protocols don't encode passwords at all. For example, the File Transfer Protocol (FTP) and the Post Office Protocol (POP3) send passwords "in the clear." If you pick up your mail using your Windows username and password, Windows 2000's powerful security technology is simply bypassed by the use of these older, insecure technologies. Your password travels through a LAN or even the Internet with no protection whatsoever.

Exploits and Back Doors

Most serious servers and even your Windows 2000 Professional computer have several hundred megabytes of system software installed. You know, and the hackers know, that hundreds or even thousands of bugs are present in all this code, and they will still be there even after years of refinement and service packs. These bugs and undocumented, insecure features can be exploited by hackers to gain access in ways never intended by the system's programmers. If you subscribe to any of the security email lists found on the Internet, you'll receive weekly notifications of such new bugs found in operating systems and software that, when exploited in just the right way, cause a security breach or system failure.

Debugging features built into server programs, called *back doors*, and features that have broader security implications than their programmers anticipated are also quickly discovered and publicized in the hacker community. Several years ago, a legendary bug in many UNIX mail systems allowed any user to mail in a replacement password file for the entire system. Chaos ensued.

Systematic hackers might have as part of their attack a query to find out whether your server is running a specific version of a program that can be exploited. I've seen network diagnostic tools that can determine which version of which operating system a computer is using, via the Internet, simply by analyzing its response to various types of legal and illegal data packets. In a couple of seconds, hackers will know just which bugs and features to attack on your particular computer.

Open Doors

A system program does not have to be flawed with a bug to be a security risk. A program that is perfect from a coding point of view may also be perfect as a jumping-off point for hackers. The experiment I cited earlier is a perfect case. I hacked into a computer simply because it was there, and I could; the door had been left open.

Windows 2000 comes with a built-in Guest user account, which has access to most of the files on the computer and requires no password. Unless this account is disabled, anyone connecting to your computer via a network can see, with no effort, at the very least the names of all your user accounts and maybe more!

Some programs are off-the-shelf security disasters. The Windows NT 3.51 Resource Kit included a remote command server (REMOTE.EXE) that accepted and executed command lines from anyone, with no security of any kind required or allowed. You might think that NT 3.51 is not sold anymore, and this story is old news, but thousands of NT 3.51 installations are still in place.

The lesson here is that major products can contain and even facilitate security breaches. Brand names and the quality of software products are *not guarantees*.

TROJAN HORSES AND VIRUSES

You remember the famous Trojan Horse in the story from ancient Greece. A great wooden horse was built and offered as a gift to the enemy within the fortress. The credulous enemy rolled the great horse into their fort unaware that it was filled with soldiers, who, during the night, disembarked, opened the gates, and wreaked destruction. Blood and ashes were all that was left of the enemy.

The Trojan Horse trick has had a resurgence in popularity, thanks to the Internet and the ease of retrieving software, games, images, and documents. You probably heard about Melissa and Happy99 on the TV news. The infamous Happy99 program was emailed to thousands of people, and those who ran it saw a cute fireworks show with the greeting "Happy 1999!" Meanwhile, the program was perusing the unsuspecting victims' email address books and mailing copies to the victims' friends and co-workers, in the victims' names: "Here's that program I was telling you about!"

This particular Trojan horse was relatively benign, in that once let into the fort, it did nothing more than spawn copies of itself. But what if it had sat silently waiting for passwords to pass by? Or had erased the victims' hard drives, say, a couple of days later after it was sure it had spread itself as far as possible?

Viruses are similar to Trojan horses, except that these programs silently attach themselves to your own programs, spreadsheets, and emails rather than rely on a cute "gift" to induce their spread. Like organic viruses, they simply hope to be carried somewhere by someone doing his or her daily business.

Viruses and Trojan horses are a major concern today. So, let me tell you a few ways to eliminate and avoid them:

- Install antivirus software on your computers.
- Use a virus-checking email server, if possible.

- Configure Word, Excel, and other desktop applications not to automatically enable macros in documents.

- Establish a *firm* policy that email attachments of documents and programs are *not* to be directly opened when received but must be saved to a file and scanned before opening.

- Configure Internet Explorer and other Web browsers to ask before opening Word or Excel documents. Disable ActiveX controls in the "Internet" security zone, or use the "Medium" security setting.

SOCIAL ENGINEERING

A more subtle approach than brute force hacking is to simply call or write someone who has useful information and ask for it. You would be surprised how easy it is to call many organizations' internal "help desks" and ask for a "forgotten" password to be revealed or changed. If hackers learn your user account name and enough information about you to sound credible, they might succeed in getting your password.

This trick is also used in *spam* email, in which ISP or online service customers are mailed official-sounding warnings that, due to some sort of programming glitch, their account information was lost, and their account will be terminated if they don't immediately supply their username and password or credit card number by return email. (P.T. Barnum said there's a sucker born every minute. Sadly, this works out to 1,440 suckers per day, or over half a million per year, and it's not too hard to reach a lot of them with one bulk email.)

These attacks need to be controlled by policy and user education. No one will ever ask you for your own password, for any legitimate reason, anyway. Help desks should never reveal or change a password for an employee or other user without directly calling the user at his or her home or office, or otherwise verifying the caller's identity.

DENIAL OF SERVICE

Many hackers don't have theft in mind. Denial of service attacks are a hacker's way of saying, "If I can't use your computer, you can't either." It could be an act of revenge, a political statement, or simply an exercise in malice and mischief.

Complex systems such as Windows and Internet Information Server (IIS) are vulnerable to malformed data and illegal requests because it's hard enough for programmers to make them work with the correct data, let alone take into account every possible type of incorrect data that can be delivered. Simple, carefully constructed messages can simply stop a server in its tracks. And it's not terribly difficult to tie up an Internet-connected computer with enough meaningless network traffic that no legitimate work can get done or to fill up its hard disk with log entries or junk files.

The result isn't permanent damage or theft of data but the loss of legitimate use of the systems under attack.

YOUR LINES OF DEFENSE

Making your computer and network completely impervious to all these forms of attack is quite impossible, if for no other reason than there is always a human element that you cannot control, and there are always bugs and exploits not yet anticipated.

You *can* do a great deal, however, if you plan ahead. Furthermore, a network is always changing with new features, services, users, and problems. Assessing security is an ongoing task, with issues arising that never could have been foreseen. You must consider updating your security measures as a part of the ongoing maintenance of the system.

In the most general sense, you can approach security of any sort in these two ways:

- Allow anything by default, but block some actions as dictated by safety.
- Block everything by default, and grant access as dictated by need.

Think about these points for a moment. The first strategy requires that you know beforehand everything you need to *prevent*. How will you find out whether you've made a mistake? When someone has done something he or she shouldn't have, that's how.

The second strategy requires that you know in advance everything you'll need to *allow*. And if you make a mistake? Someone won't get the access he or she needs.

Now, which mistake do you think you'll hear about first, and which is going to be easier to fix? Right: the second. When someone can't do what he or she wants to do, you'll hear about it, loudly; so you can then fix the problem. The consequences are that someone may be temporarily inconvenienced, but the impediment can be removed. But if someone does something he or she shouldn't be able to, it's already too late! You won't find out until the damage has already been done. The consequences could be disastrous. So, whenever you can, you should try to choose methods that follow the second strategy: Block by default, permit as needed.

Alas, you usually must make a trade-off between convenience and security. You can more easily think of a few things to prohibit than think of everything you need to allow, so you will be tempted to go the easier route. My suggestion is that you at least give it some thought. You might choose to adopt the simpler, looser strategy if you decide that the risk is small compared to the inconvenience that strict security brings. That's fine: We all take risks every day, just stepping outside the door of our homes. We just need be clear about the nature of those risks.

The following sections delve into the four main lines of computer defense. Each has its own part in a security plan by reducing your risk of attack, protecting you from attack, and preparing you to respond in the event your defenses fail.

You can omit any of these measures, of course, if you weigh what you have at risk against what these efforts will cost you and decide that the benefit isn't worth the effort.

What I'm describing sounds like a lot of work, and it can be. Nevertheless, even if you're a home user, I encourage you to consider each of these steps and to put them into effect with as much diligence as you can muster. Just think of that poor sleeping soul whose hard disk I could have erased the other morning at 1 a.m. (if you missed this poignant example, see the sidebar titled "Think You're Safe? Think Again," earlier in the chapter).

PREPARATION

Preparation involves eliminating unnecessary sources of risk before they can be attacked. Steps you should take include

- Investing time in planning and policies
- Structuring your network to restrict unauthorized access
- Installing only needed services
- Using software known to be secure and (relatively) bug free
- Properly configuring your servers, file systems, software, and user accounts to maintain appropriate access control
- Hiding from the outside world as much information about your systems as possible

ACTIVE DEFENSE

Active defense means actively resisting known methods of attack. Active defenses include

- Firewalls, proxies, and gateways to block dangerous or inappropriate Internet traffic as it passes between your network and the Internet at large
- Encryption and authentication to limit access based on some sort of credentials (such as a password)
- Keeping up-to-date on security and risks, especially with respect to Windows 2000

TESTING, LOGGING, AND MONITORING

Testing, logging, and monitoring involve testing your defense strategies and detecting breaches. These steps should include

- Testing your defenses before you connect to the Internet
- Monitoring Internet traffic on your network and on the connection to your Internet service provider or other networks
- Detecting and recording suspicious activity on the network and in application software

DISASTER PLANNING

Disaster planning is preparation for recovery after an attack, which means

- Making permanent, archived "baseline" backups of exposed servers *before* they're connected to the Internet and anytime system software is changed
- Making frequent backups once online

- Having thorough, written, and tested server restore procedures
- Having written and maintained documentation of your software and network configuration
- Having an incident plan

PREPARATION

The easiest way to defend against attack is to eliminate the object at risk. Taking this point to extreme, you could say that the best-defended computer is one locked in a room with no LAN, no modem, no electricity, and no users.

Don't laugh! Some government agencies, research sites, and major defense corporations go nearly this far. They call it an *airgap defense*. Their offices have a separate, dedicated power supply; closed-circuit air conditioning; no phone lines; no LAN; and so on. (They do still have users, however. One nuclear weapon research facility implemented an airgap defense but then let someone walk out the door with a diskette!)

This system might be very secure, but it's probably more security than you or I want to cope with. Because this is not really an option, you have to decide what kinds of services, connections, permissions, and access to allow.

Tip #297	For each of the defensive measures I'll go through in the following sections, write down how you plan to implement them and what kinds of attacks you expect them to stop. You'll need this list in section on disaster planning when you have to actually think of a way to test each of these measures to be sure they work!

ESTABLISH POLICIES TO MAINTAIN SECURITY

You should decide what security-related features and functions you want to leave in the hands of your users and which you want to restrict. The following are some issues to ponder:

- Do you want to permit access from the Internet directly in to your network, indirectly via a Virtual Private Network (VPN), or not at all?
- Will you allow users to install modems in their computers and configure them to receive calls?
- Do you trust users to create and protect their own shared folders, or should this be done by management only?
- Do you want to run a Web server, FTP server, or other network services, each of which provides benefits but also increases risk?
- Are your users allowed to create passwords without numbers or punctuation?
- Are users allowed to send and receive personal email from the network?

- Are users allowed to install software they obtain themselves?
- Are users allowed to share access to their desktops with NetMeeting, Carbon Copy, PCAnywhere, or other remote-control software?

I want to emphasize the point that security is in part a technical issue and in part a matter of organizational policy. In the old days of centralized computer systems, system administrators too often exercised absolute control over computer usage. Now that computers are on every desktop, you have much more control over what you do with your own computers. But along with this control, security is now in the hands of every individual user. One user with a modem and a lack of responsibility can open a door into the best-protected network.

In a Windows 2000 Server-based network, the Group Policy system is a major technological advance, for it lets a company strike its own balance between absolute central control and complete anarchy. Options that are deemed too dangerous for general use can be blocked. In a Windows 2000 workgroup network or with a single computer, though, no Group Policy lockdown mechanism exists, so *you* are completely responsible for enforcing these decisions.

PUBLISH THE RULES

You should make public your management and personnel policies regarding network security and appropriate use of computer resources. Educate your users in them. The following are some ideas for official policies:

- Require that all accounts be protected by a "good" password with letters and numbers or punctuation.
- Require that all passwords be kept personal and confidential. In particular, they must never be stored in files or sent by email under any circumstances. They should never be given to someone over the phone unless the caller *knows for sure* who's on the other end of the line. Even support staff should follow these rules.
- Do not permit users to run unapproved or unofficial software, especially software obtained from BBSs, over the Internet, or carried in on floppy disk. Virus-scanning software should be available and should be run frequently, and always on files obtained over the Internet.
- Make and communicate a policy on the confidentiality of email, receipt of personal email on corporate computers, personal use of Web browsers, and storage or viewing of potentially offensive material. Whether you decide to be very hard-nosed or permit your users to use their own discretion, you should consider this topic and let your users know in advance.
- Finally, formalize and communicate the disciplinary consequences of failing to comply with security policies.

If your own users don't respect the integrity of your network, you don't stand a chance against the outside world. Making up the rules in advance and ensuring that everyone knows them are crucial to an effective security strategy.

PART

IV

CH

26

STRUCTURE YOUR NETWORK TO RESTRICT OUTSIDE ACCESS

When you use a dial-up connection to the Internet, your computer is directly exposed to the Internet. Any computer anywhere on the Internet can connect to any TCP/IP-based service on your computer. Likewise, a direct connection between the Internet and your LAN means that every computer on your network is completely exposed. This exposure violates the philosophy I began this chapter with: Deny everything; permit what's needed.

Now, when other security measures are followed, the risk of connecting one computer to the Internet may be acceptable. And you can configure the computers themselves to resist attack. When several computers are involved, however, the chances that at least one of them will be configured incorrectly grows proportionately.

Taking this chance is one of the trade-offs I spoke of earlier: You *can* permit a direct connection, but you'll have a lot less to worry about if you restrict what can come in via your Internet connection before troublesome data gets to your computers.

You can get a great deal of control over the traffic permitted by your Internet connection if you choose an appropriate means of making the connection. Figure 26.1 shows how this can be done.

Figure 26.1
The No Connection model, for the greatest security.

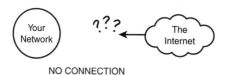

NO CONNECTION

Figure 26.1 shows "No connection." Yes, the best defense is to completely remove the object of attack. If your network contains *very* sensitive information, it should *not* have an Internet connection at all, nor should any user be permitted to connect to the Internet via modem. You can always set up a disconnected workstation or a separate network with Internet access. (Likewise, a computer with very sensitive information might simply not be connected to the LAN at all.) You can bet your booties that Microsoft's corporate financial systems run on a network that isn't within a *mile* of an Internet connection.

In this kind of environment, you should also have strict policies against moving sensitive data from one computer to another. (Depending on your level of paranoia, you also might want to hire security consultants to be sure that no sensitive data leaks out of your office via radio emissions from your monitors, but that's a little beyond what I'm talking about here.)

Figure 26.2 shows the Direct Connection model, the opposite extreme. Here, as I've said, the entire network is exposed to the Internet, and every software service on every computer is vulnerable to attack.

In Figure 26.3, a packet filtering system or device is added between the Internet and your LAN. Packet filtering can occur in any device that connects two separate networks: the LAN and the Internet. Filtering blocks access based on the type of network service requested. The filtering device or software examines each network data packet arriving from or destined for the Internet, and decides whether to let it pass through or to discard it as unwanted. Filtering is usually an option with Internet connection devices, software, or external routers.

Figure 26.2
The Direct Connection model presents no barriers to incoming or outgoing connections.

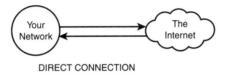

DIRECT CONNECTION

Figure 26.3
The Packet Filtering model permits specified Internet protocols to be passed or blocked, as specified by your security policy.

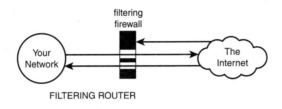

FILTERING ROUTER

Filtering is possible because Internet protocol packets are identified by two parameters: a *protocol type* and a *port number*. Protocol types include UDP and TCP for standard data transfers, ICMP for network condition reporting, RIP for router configuration, and so on. Port numbers are assigned to each network service type and are standardized. By blocking the UDP protocol with port number 161, for example, you can block outside access to the Simple Network Management Protocol (SNMP) service. Microsoft File Sharing can be prevented across the Internet connection by blocking all TCP and UDP protocol packets with port numbers between 137 and 139.

With File Sharing blocked at the point of your Internet connection, it won't matter whether any of your machines are incorrectly configured; no one can get to them.

Filters need to be specified for inbound and outbound connections independently. For example, you might want to prevent outside attempts to connect to your internal Web server but permit access from the inside to outside Web servers.

PART

IV

CH

26

Tip #298

You might have heard that Windows 2000 Professional has a TCP/IP filtering feature. It does, but it is nearly *useless* as a means of protecting your LAN's connection to the Internet. I'll explain why in a bit.

Even if the TCP/IP filtering feature were useful, I would use a separate device for firewall functions anyway. Using the Windows filtering system to protect itself would be like posting a chicken to guard the henhouse. If you want to protect your network with filtering, you need to use a filtering or NAT router or Windows 2000's Internet Connection Sharing.

Figure 26.4 shows another connection scheme, Network Address Translation (NAT), using either Windows 2000's Internet Connection Sharing or a separate router device.

Figure 26.4
NAT (Network Address Translation) adds even greater security, as all incoming connections are blocked unless directed to one specified inside server.

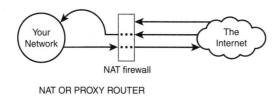

NAT was described in some detail in Chapter 24, "Connecting Your LAN to the Internet." Basically, NAT acts as an intermediary between inside users and the Internet, carrying on all network conversations on their behalf. Only the NAT router (or Windows 2000 shared connection) is visible to the outside world. When someone *outside* your network attempts to connect to a network service at the NAT router's address, NAT simply rejects that request, unless you've explicitly told NAT that certain network protocols are handled by specified internal servers. In that case, it forwards in the incoming data request to the designated server. This setup perfectly meshes with my "block all, permit as needed" philosophy.

A disadvantage to a NAT connection is that, at most, only one server of a given type can be accessible to the outside world. Because packets are directed to a specific internal machine, based on their network protocol and port number, you can have only one visible Web server, mail server, FTP server, or Virtual Private Networking connection point. Because the VPN service built into Windows 2000 Professional permits only one incoming connection, this connection might be too restrictive for you. Windows 2000 Server, though, permits unlimited incoming connections.

NAT and filtering functions are built into many commercial ISDN, DSL, and frame relay routers now, and you can also construct a nifty filtering or NAT router using an old PC and a shareware program such as IPROUTE, WinProxy, or WinGate.

Tip #299	I recommend using an NAT router over using Windows Internet Connection Sharing, again, because I think it's best to separate the protection system from the protected system.

In Figure 26.5, Virtual Private Networking is added to either of the previous two models. If Microsoft Virtual Private Networking packets are permitted through your filter or directed by NAT to a specified computer inside the firewall, then your users can gain unrestricted access to the inside network via the Internet.

Figure 26.5
Virtual Private Networking provides a way for authorized users to bypass the firewall completely. Having this capability might make it more palatable to make the firewall even more restrictive.

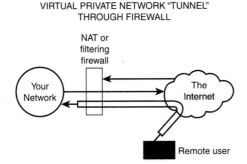

The advantage of this system is that it lets you divide the outside world into two camps: the clean and the unclean, if you will. With a way for authorized users to get into your network without restrictions, you're more likely to be able to shut down many other doors. In fact, Windows 2000's filtering system even has a built-in option to permit *only* VPN connections from the outside, in essence restricting your Internet connection to authorized users only and otherwise eliminating *all* outside access to your network.

You can also provide authorized users an alternative means of accessing the inside network, as shown in Figure 26.6. A modem configured for dial-in access gives authorized users a way to bypass the firewall. Again, this configuration makes it possible for you to make the firewall much more restrictive because it need only allow incoming connections to the one or two services you might want to make available to the outside world.

Figure 26.6
The Dual-Access model gives another way of providing unrestricted, secure access to authorized users.

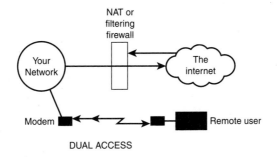

Finally, you can install on one computer the services you want to make available to the world at large, and use two firewalls to isolate that server, as shown in Figure 26.7. This server lies in what is called a *demilitarized zone*, named after the no-man's land between North and South Korea, where limited diplomatic efforts take place, but through which neither side ventures into the land beyond.

Figure 26.7
The demilitarized zone is a more elaborate means of providing limited services to the outside world. A "sacrificial machine" performs public services, and no outside access is allowed into the inside network at all.

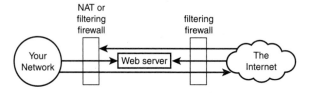

DUAL FIREWALL SYSTEM WITH "DMZ"

The outside firewall lets in only the services offered by the public server. The inside firewall blocks *all* outside access to the internal network, except perhaps incoming Virtual Private Network connections, and only a minimum of access between the inside network and the middle computer.

These seven connection strategies I've listed in increasing complexity give you increasingly more control over the traffic passing between you and the Internet.

Tip #300	I recommend using the firewall and NAT approaches, with the filtering and/or NAT services performed by a separate device such as a DSL router, or a commercial or shareware firewall router. The extra security they afford is well worth the additional cost.

INSTALL ONLY NEEDED SERVICES

Besides limiting access, you should limit the services that are available on the network to just those absolutely required.

The task of configuring, restricting, analyzing, and maintaining network services is hard work, and when you've installed services you don't even need, the task is made even more difficult. You might forget a critical detail, fall behind in applying software updates, or leave yourself open to a security breach. You might even completely forget that the service is installed until the day that you wake up and find something terrible has happened.

Planning and policies make a big difference at this point:

- Don't install any network service, protocol, or feature you don't know you need. Protocols such as RIP and SNMP can pose a great security risk if not managed carefully. If you don't need to share files or printers on a particular computer, don't install File and Printer Sharing for Microsoft Networks.

- Maintain documentation on every computer on your network, showing which protocols and services are installed.

- Maintain a restrictive policy on software installation and modification on your network. Users shouldn't be allowed to install services on their own without consulting someone responsible for maintaining security.

- If you have Windows 2000 Server on your network, the domain administrator can and should prevent users from adding or configuring network services.

- The optional Simple TCP Services network service option provides no useful function, only archaic services that make great denial of service attack targets. Don't install it.

- It's a bad idea to use Windows File Sharing or Virtual Private Networking *and* FTP or POP Mail. Windows File Sharing encrypts its passwords, but FTP and POP don't. FTP and POP invite your users to transmit their passwords across the Internet without encryption, which can reveal your users' passwords to eavesdropping hackers. They could then break in using File Sharing or the VPN connection.

> **Caution**
>
> All of Windows 2000's great security features are for naught if you install services that permit users to expose their passwords.

- Installing Internet Information Server might sound like fun, but don't install it unless you're really sure you need it and are willing to keep up with its frequent bug fixes and maintenance alerts. IIS has been Microsoft's biggest source of strange and dangerous security flaws. All sophisticated services come with a measure of risk, and IIS is very sophisticated.

Tip #301

> If you have a small "workgroup" LAN and can't or don't want to set up a firewall or NAT service, you can still protect your network from Internet attacks: Don't use TCP/IP for File and Printer Sharing. Install the NetBEUI protocol in addition to Internet Protocol (TCP/IP) on all your computers. Also, unbind Internet Protocol from File and Printer Sharing for Microsoft Networks and Client for Microsoft Networks on all your computers. This technique works for small workgroups but isn't acceptable for large LANs or Windows 2000 domain networks.

→ For instructions on setting bindings, **see** "Setting Network Bindings," **p. 924**.

Use Secure and Updated Software

You should be very careful to check out the quality of any software you acquire and install on your computers.

Many useful tools and utilities are available. Shareware and publicly downloadable programs may be great, but you should treat them like ticking bombs until you've checked them out with a virus scanner and tested them on an isolated machine before installing them on a working network server. Even commercial software should be viewed skeptically until it has proven itself in a safe environment. If you want to use a noncommercial program, try to get its source code, and compile it yourself after checking for trap doors or other unexpected features.

PART

IV

CH

26

Tip #302

My philosophy is to use the simplest program possible to accomplish a given job: The smaller the program, the greater the chance that it has been completely tested, and the less the chance that it has undesirable...um, features...which I haven't yet discovered.

Big programs generally have more bugs; this is an inescapable truth. Note that Windows NT version 4 has been around for more than five years, yet its most recent service pack listed fixes to more than 100 bugs. A rule I try to follow is one I call the *Law of Version Numbers*: Avoid versions 1.*x* and *x*.0, where *x* is any number. A corollary is: Wait for Service Pack 2.

When you do decide to install a program, keep up-to-date on security warnings and bug fixes for any program or service you install.

Tip #303

The most important program to keep up-to-date is Windows 2000 itself. I suggest that you keep up-to-date on Windows 2000 bugs and fixes through Microsoft's update program *and* through independent watchdogs. Install Microsoft's Critical Update Notification program from www.windowsupdate.com, and subscribe to the independent bug reporting mailing lists at www.ntbugtraq.com and www.sans.org.

HIDE AS MUCH AS POSSIBLE

Another basic security strategy is to reveal as little information as possible to the outside world. Keep information within your company, on a need-to-know basis. This information includes the following:

- User account names—These names should not be publicized unless you're forced to use them as email account names.

- DNS information—You don't need to publicize the IP addresses or machine names of any but your public servers.

- Modem access numbers—You should share these numbers only with those people who actually need them.

- Shared folder names—You can prevent remote users from seeing shared folders by adding a dollar sign ($) to their names. These shared folders won't appear when the host computer is explored in the Network browser. Users can view or map drives to them, however, provided they know the names.

- IP addresses—A NAT router helps considerably because your internal computers simply cannot be reached from the outside world. Your whole network looks like just one computer to the Internet.

Tip #304

IP numbers, shared folder names, modem access numbers, and so on only assist hackers, so keeping this kind of information hidden can make the hackers' work more difficult. However, a cardinal rule of network security is this: Don't rely on obscurity for security. That is, don't assume that keeping things quiet is adequate protection by itself. Remember my neighbor with the publicly shared hard drive. I found it without any help (see the sidebar titled "Think You're Safe? Think Again" earlier in the chapter).

NAIL DOWN WHAT YOU CAN

To the extent possible, you should restrict things which could be used to reconfigure your network or subvert your security measures.

The following are some tips:

- Don't leave copies of the Policy Editor tool or plug-in on nonadministrative users' computers. You might even be really hard-nosed about it and remove the two Registry Editors.

- Export to a floppy disk, and delete the recovery certificate from the encrypted file system recovery agent's account. Keep the disk locked in a safe place.

- Don't leave computers logged in when unattended.

- Restrict physical access to servers, tape libraries, paper files with passwords, and other sensitive equipment or materials. (I once saw an installation in which a server was kept in a safe.)

- If you have a router (for example, for DSL or frame relay), be sure it's configured with a password.

→ If you want to learn more details about configuring routers with a password, **see** "Secure Your Router," **p. 956**.

- Configure routers with static routing tables, and disable Router Information Protocol (RIP) so that outside forces can't redirect your network traffic.

- Verify that your ISP also uses static routing and has disabled RIP.

PART

IV

CH

26

ACTIVE DEFENSES: BLOCKING KNOWN METHODS OF ATTACK

When your network is in place, your next job is to configure it to restrict access as much as possible. This task involves blocking network traffic known to be dangerous and configuring network protocols to use the most secure communications protocols possible.

SET UP FIREWALLS AND NAT DEVICES

Using a firewall is a most effective technique to secure your network. From the viewpoint of design and maintenance, it is also the most efficient tool because you can focus your efforts on one critical place, the interface between your internal network and the Internet.

NAT devices add an extra measure of security because they permit only outgoing network connections, from your LAN to servers you want to contact on the Internet. Incoming connections are rejected, unless you direct them to specific servers inside your LAN that offer a selected service.

PACKET FILTERING

A *packet filtering firewall* is a router that connects two separate networks, which I'll call the *inside* and *outside* networks. The inside network is your LAN, and the outside network is the link to your ISP. This router connects the two networks by sitting in the middle, with two network cards, or one network card and a modem. It is designated the "gateway" on your LAN so that all traffic between your LAN and the outside world has to pass through the firewall.

This job is usually done by an external router device, such as a DSL or frame relay router, or a purpose-built Internet Connection Sharing device, such as the Whistle or WebRamp products. You can also build your own by using a computer running proxy/firewall software. I've used a shareware program called IPROUTE, available at http://www.mischler.com, for several years and really like its flexibility. It's a small, simple, well-debugged DOS program, and it's off the radar screen of most hackers. It's also somewhat difficult to configure. WinGate and WinProxy offer similar features but are easier to configure.

Filtering works like this: Each Internet data packet contains identifying numbers that indicate the protocol type and the IP address for the source and destination computers. Some protocols also have an additional port number, which identifies the type of service that is to receive the packet. The WWW service, for example, expects TCP protocol packets addressed to port 80. A domain name server listens for UDP packets on port 52.

A packet arriving at the firewall from either side is examined; then it is either passed on or discarded, according to a set of rules that list the protocols and ports permitted or prohibited for each direction. A prohibited packet can be dropped silently, or the router can reject the packet with an error message indicating the requested network service is unavailable. (I prefer the silent treatment. Why tell hackers that a desired service is present but unavailable to them?) Some routers can also make a log entry or send an alert indicating that an unwanted connection was attempted.

Note

For a good introduction to firewalls and Internet security in general, I recommend *Maximum Security, Second Edition*, published by Sams (ISBN: 0-672-31341-3), and *Firewalls and Internet Security: Repelling the Wily Hacker* by William R. Cheswick and Steven M. Bellovin of ATT Bell Labs (Addison & Wesley, ISBN: 0-201-63357-4).

WHICH PROTOCOLS AND PORTS TO BLOCK

Filtering routers usually let you specify the filter in either of two ways: You can specify which protocols and ports to permit and have it block everything else, or you can specify which to block and have it permit everything else. (This information should sound familiar by now!)

You can choose either method. It's safest to block by default, but easier to select just the network services you want to block. Table 26.1 provides some suggestions for network services that should end up being blocked—only in the *incoming* direction—whichever method you use.

TABLE 26.1   BLOCKING NETWORK SERVICES[1]

Protocol	Ports	Description
TCP	20–21	FTP—File Transfer Protocol. (Acceptable if only anonymous logins are permitted.)
TCP	23	TELNET—Clear-text passwords are sent by this remote terminal service, which also is used to configure routers. It's best not to let Internet hackers try to get access to your router.
TCP	54	DNS—Domain Name Service. Block TCP mode "zone" transfers, which reveal machine names.
TCP+UDP	67	BOOTP—Bootstrap Protocol (similar to DHCP). Unnecessary.
TCP+UDP	69	TFTP—Trivial File Transfer Protocol. No security.
TCP	110	POP3—Post Office Protocol.
UDP TCP	137–8 139	NetBIOS—Three ports are used by Microsoft File Sharing.
TCP	135, 1500, 2500	RPC—The Remote Procedure Call protocol is used for COM+, remote Registry editing, and other management functions.
UDP	161–2	SNMP—Simple Network Monitoring Protocol. Reveals too much information.
TCP	515	LPD—UNIX printer sharing protocol supported by Windows 2000.

[1] *You can modify this list to suit your own needs, depending on the network services you have inside your LAN which you do or do not want to have visible to the Internet.*

PART

IV

CH

26

SETTING UP A PACKET FILTER

What you need is a filtering system that permits you to specify which protocols and ports are permitted in and out of the *outside* network port. You may have heard or read that Windows 2000 Professional has an "IP Filtering" security feature built in.

The Windows built-in filtering mechanism is useless, however, because it's applied equally to *all* network interfaces in a given computer. If a Windows 2000 Professional computer is used as a router, it can't discriminate between packets you want to send out to the Internet, hacking attempts coming from the Internet into your LAN, and connections between the computer and its own LAN. If you use Windows 2000 Professional's filtering feature to block, say, Microsoft File Sharing across the Internet, the computer cannot access shared files on your LAN either. If you want to block incoming attempts to use your LAN's Domain Name Service, your LAN cannot use the Internet's Domain Name Service either. This solution is no good at all!

You could use a Windows 2000 Professional computer as a filtering router if it didn't have to do anything else, but it's a terrible way to go. So, if you want to have firewall protection, and you aren't using Windows Connection Sharing or an NAT device, you need to use a separate router for filtering.

> **Note**
>
> The packet filtering system provided in Windows 2000 *Server,* on the other hand, is actually useful. If your network has a Windows 2000 Server computer, your network administrator can implement decent packet filtering on the server.

So, what kind of filtering should you use? You really only need to apply a filter for packets entering the outside, or Internet-side, interface. For an Internet-side-arriving packet filter, follow these basic steps:

1. Block any packet whose sending or source IP address belongs to your LAN. It is called an *anti-spoofing* filter. No legitimate packet would ever arrive from the *outside* with one of your internal IP addresses. If you are using NAT, you should base this on the public IP address of your NAT device. If you aren't using NAT but have a block of IP addresses for your network, block the entire range of IP addresses for your network.

2. Permit any TCP packet without the SYN bit set. This bit indicates a packet that belongs to a connection you've already approved of, so it should just be passed through.

3. Block any packets with protocols and port numbers you don't want to permit across the Internet connection, as listed in Table 26.1.

4. Permit any other packet.

In addition, be sure that your router is set to ignore RIP, which is sometimes used to communicate routing paths from router to router. RIP can be used to redirect your network traffic to an interloper's site.

Now, because I don't know what kind of filtering router you'll use, I can't tell you exactly how to configure it. However, I can give you examples for a few different types of routers.

> **Note**
>
> TCP/IP services are vulnerable to SYN-flooding programs, which inundate the receiving computer with connection establishment requests (called *SYNs*). This deluge of connection requests overflows the receiving computer's queue of pending connection requests. Because the receiving computer cannot discern between forged and real requests, legitimate users are denied access to your TCP-based services.
>
> Having the firewall filter out all packets with the SYN bit set might seem beneficial, but that would block all incoming requests into your network and even make FTP files transfers difficult. You just have to rely on Windows 2000, which is by design "hardened" against SYN flood attacks.

PACKET FILTERING WITH A FLOWPOINT DSL ROUTER

If you want to use DSL service to connect a LAN to the Internet, try to get a full-fledged router rather than a simple modem. Most DSL routers contain good filtering and NAT features, and your ISP will help you configure it.

Note

Unless you have a router, this section won't make a lot of sense to you. Bear in mind that explaining routing in detail would take another book in itself.

If, however, you already have a router, check the manual for your router's configuration commands and some good examples (I hope). Then the information in this section should make more sense, and I hope you'll be able to make the translation. You can use my examples to figure out what information you should have to supply to your router.

Let's use the Flowpoint/2200 DSL router as an example. This router has NAT as a standard feature and IP filtering as an extra cost option. The router is configured via the Telnet program, which lets you enter commands via a simple command-line interface. If your LAN is assigned a subnet of IP addresses from 10.20.30.0 through 10.20.30.15, you can use the following commands:

```
1    remote ipfilter append input drop -sa 10.20.30.0:10.20.30.15 internet
2    remote ipfilter append input accept -tcp noflag internet
3    remote ipfilter append input drop -p tcp -dp 20:21 internet
4    remote ipfilter append input drop -p tcp -dp 23 internet
5    remote ipfilter append input drop -p tcp -dp 54 internet
6    remote ipfilter append input drop -p tcp -dp 67 internet
7    remote ipfilter append input drop -p udp -dp 67 internet
8    remote ipfilter append input drop -p tcp -dp 69 internet
9    remote ipfilter append input drop -p udp -dp 69 internet
10   remote ipfilter append input drop -p tcp -dp 110 internet
11   remote ipfilter append input drop -p udp -dp 137:138 internet
12   remote ipfilter append input drop -p tcp -dp 139 internet
13   remote ipfilter append input drop -p udp -dp 161:162 internet
14   remote ipfilter append input drop -p tcp -dp 515 internet
15   remote setIpOptions rxrip off internet
16   save
17   reboot
```

PART

IV

CH

26

Line 1: This `ipfilter` command blocks any incoming packets with your own LAN's addresses.

Line 2: This `ipfilter` command lets through any TCP packet that is part of an established, already-approved connection. This accounts for about 95 percent of the network traffic, and taking care of it without having to check the remaining rules results in more efficient operation of the router.

Lines 3–14: The remaining `ipfilter` rules drop traffic for protocols you want to block. On any protocol that matches, no packet is accepted.

Line 15: This `ipfilter` command disables the RIP protocol.

It's best to leave configuring to your ISP, if you can, because, as you can see, this task is ugly and difficult stuff, and getting it wrong can mess up your router. Still, when it's done, you can rest a little easier knowing that your full-time connection isn't a worldwide, full-time invitation to mischief.

PACKET FILTERING WITH IPROUTE

I have used a DOS-based shareware router program called IPROUTE from http://www.mischler.com for several network installations. IPROUTE can make a nice filtering router out of an old, discarded 486 computer, two inexpensive network cards, and a floppy drive; no hard disk is needed. You can place it between a DSL or cable modem and your LAN. Setting it up is a bit of work because you have to configure this DOS program with old-fashioned "packet driver" software, but you can't beat the $50 registration price. And it will run for years without rebooting.

The same filter commands for IPROUTE would look something like this:

```
1    filter outside log drop in * 10.20.30.1/28 *
2    filter outside permit in tcp-xsyn * *
3    filter outside log drop in tcp * *:20-21
4    filter outside log drop in tcp * *:23
5    filter outside log drop in tcp * *:54
6    filter outside log drop in tcp * *:67
7    filter outside log drop in udp * *:67
8    filter outside log drop in tcp * *:69
9    filter outside log drop in udp * *:69
10   filter outside log drop in tcp * *:110
11   filter outside log drop in udp * *:137-138
12   filter outside log drop in tcp * *:139
13   filter outside log drop in udp * * 161-162
14   filter outside log drop in tcp * * 515
15   filter dsl permit in * * *
16   rip outside off
```

Line 1: This command sets a rule blocking any incoming packets with your own LAN's addresses.

Line 2: This rule lets through any TCP packet that is part of an established, already approved connection.

Lines 3–14: These rules drop traffic for the protocols you want to block.

Line 15: This rule lets pass any packet not rejected by the earlier rules.

Line 16: This command disables the RIP protocol.

USING NAT OR INTERNET CONNECTION SHARING

By either name, Network Address Translation (NAT) has two big security benefits. First, it hides an entire network behind one IP address. Then, while it transparently passes connections from you out to the Internet, it rejects all incoming connection attempts except those that you explicitly direct to waiting servers inside your LAN. No packet filtering is really necessary when NAT is in use.

You learned how to configure Windows Internet Connection Sharing in Chapter 24, so I won't repeat that information here.

If you have built a network with another type of router or connection sharing device, you must follow the instructions of the NAT device, or your ISP can set up your router. (Your ISP should do the job, as part of its setup fee!)

You can configure NAT in a Flowpoint 2200 DSL router something like this:

```
1    remote setIPTranslate on
2    remote SetSrcIPAddr 155.144.133.130 255.255.255.0 internet
3    eth ip addr 192.168.0.1 255.255.255.0
4    remote AddServer 192.168.0.10 tcp 80    internet
5    remote AddServer 192.168.0.20 tcp 1723 internet
6    remote AddServer 192.168.0.20 47  0     internet
7    save
8    reboot
```

Lines 1–3: These three commands enable NAT and set the external and internal IP addresses.

Lines 4–6: These commands direct incoming HTTP and VPN requests to the servers on the LAN.

On this hypothetical network, the computer at address 192.168.10.10 receives World Wide Web requests, and 192.168.0.20 receives incoming Microsoft Point-to-Point Tunneling Protocol (PPTP) VPN requests. PPTP uses packets of two types: TCP packets using port 1723 and packets using the Generic Routing Encapsulation (GRE) protocol. GRE is so obscure that most routers don't recognize its name, so it's referred to by its protocol number, which is 47. (Why Microsoft chose this technique, I don't know.)

To the outside world, there is only one IP address, 155.144.133.130, which appears to be both a Web server and a Microsoft VPN host.

The same configuration in IPROUTE would look something like this:

```
1    nat outside icmp 155.144.133.130      155.144.133.130
2    nat outside tcp  192.168.0.10:80      155.144.133.130:80
3    nat outside tcp  192.168.0.20:1723    155.144.133.130:1723
4    nat outside 47   192.168.0.20         155.144.133.130
5    nat outside *    *                    155.144.133.130
```

Line 1: This command lets the router respond to PING requests on its translated interface.

Lines 2–4: These three commands direct incoming HTTP and VPN requests to the servers on the LAN.

Line 5: This command lets the router automatically translate any outgoing request.

ADD-ON PRODUCTS FOR WINDOWS

Some new products can be installed right in your own computer to perform firewall features. *Personal firewalls*, which are an emerging technology and for individual computers with dial-up or wired Internet service, might be just the ticket. Products such as BlackICE Defender cost less than $50.

For a review of some of the latest add-on firewall products, check out the page on personal firewalls at Gibson Research's Web site:

```
http://www.grc.com/su-firewalls.htm
```

This Web site also has a nifty Web-based tool called ShieldsUp that will test your computer for Internet hacking vulnerabilities.

SECURE YOUR ROUTER

Securing your router is worth expanding on a bit. If you use a router for your Internet connection and rely on it to provide network protection, you *must* make it require a password. If your router doesn't require a password, *anyone* could connect to it across the Internet and delete the filters you've set up. Most routers as configured by the manufacturers and ISPs *do not* require a password.

To lock down your router, do the following:

- Change the SNMP community name to a secret word.
- Prohibit Write access via SNMP.
- Change all Telnet login passwords, whether administrative or informational.

If you don't want to lock down your router, your ISP can do it for you. If you do it, be sure to give the password to your ISP.

People scan IP addresses on the Internet looking for routers and computers to break in to. As an example, check out these actual log entries from my DSL router, showing that persons unknown attempted to use SNMP and Telnet to access it:

```
06/25/99 23:08:57   Telnet connection up, address 153.37.194.42
06/25/99 23:09:04   Telnet connection down, address 153.37.194.42
08/04/99 18:26:41 * SNMP Authentication Failure (IP address 206.173.138.59)
08/04/99 18:26:48 * SNMP Authentication Failure (IP address 206.173.138.59)
```

Note ·

I used `nslookup` to try to identify the persons using the methods described in Chapter 16, "Internet Diagnosis Tools," to no avail. See "`nslookup`" in Chapter 16 for more details.

USE ENCRYPTION AND AUTHENTICATION

You can use encryption and authentication to limit access based on some sort of credentials (such as a password).

Hackers who have physical access to an Internet data cable or who have hacked their way into computers in an ISP's office can monitor network traffic and read unencrypted passwords.

Microsoft's FTP server and most mail servers use the Windows username and password list to authenticate connections. Because FTP and POP mail protocols do not encrypt their passwords, eavesdropping hackers can use these protocols to obtain valid usernames and passwords for your systems.

This is an elementary security precaution: I strongly recommend that, if you permit TCP/IP file sharing over the Internet, you do not install FTP and Mail services accessible from the outside. If these services are not installed or reachable from the Internet then your users cannot inadvertently expose their usernames and passwords. Permitting these services invites users to expose their passwords.

If you must install a POP or FTP server that uses actual NT usernames and passwords, you should then prohibit file sharing access and VPN connections. Otherwise, you could provide hackers both the key and the door to your network.

SET UP RESTRICTIVE ACCESS CONTROLS

Possibly the most important and difficult step you can take is to limit access to shared files, folders, and printers. You can use the guidelines shown in Table 26.2 to help organize a security review of every machine on your network. I've put some crucial items in boldface.

PART

IV

CH

26

TABLE 26.2   RESTRICTING ACCESS CONTROLS

Access Point	Controls
File Sharing	Unless you have a secure private network (as illustrated in Figures 26.3 through 23.7), do *not* install File and Printer Sharing on any computers that don't need it.
	Block file sharing across your Internet connection. (I'll explain how later in the chapter.)
Passwords	Use Domain or Local Machine policy to specify that passwords are required on all accounts, must be complex, and must be changed frequently. Be sure to set up new accounts with initial passwords of random letters and numbers. **Disable the Guest account**. Limit the number of incorrect password attempts to three.

continues

TABLE 26.2   RESTRICTING ACCESS CONTROLS

Access Point	Controls
Partitions	Use NTFS on all partitions used for shared files and for IIS data. Create separate partitions for FTP files and mail server files. That way, an attempt to stuff your hard drive with junk to disable it will be confined to one volume, while the others continue operating.
Access Control	Don't add users to the Administrators group. Keep the Administrator password a secret. **Don't use the Administrator account for your day-to-day work.** Grant the most restrictive permissions possible on shared folders. Give access only to the users or groups that really need it. Remove Write/Change privileges wherever you can.
Group or Local Policy	Use Windows 2000's Group or Local Security Policy mechanism to enforce good password and security practices on your network's users.
FTP	If you install an FTP server, do not let FTP share a FAT-formatted drive or partition. If you have enabled Anonymous FTP, I *strongly* urge you not to give the Anonymous FTP user (IUSR_XXXXX, where XXXXX is the name of your computer) Write permission in any folder. If your customers or clients need to send you files then create accounts and passwords for them with privileges to write into a specific directory. If you must give the Anonymous FTP account Write permission on a directory, deny it Delete, Change, List Files, and Read access so that remote users can drop off but not pick up files. Isolate the directory in a separate volume. Delete files periodically.
SMTP	Consider storing incoming mail in a separate partition. If your mail server software allows incoming mail to be automatically stored in files, be sure that the Mail server's service login account doesn't have access to any directories but ones you select for mail storage and logging. **Prohibit "relaying"** from outside SMTP servers to outside domains, lest your server be used as a spam relay site.
HTTP (Web)	**Don't enable both Script/Execute permission and Write permission on the same folder.** Enabling both permissions would permit outside users to install and run arbitrary programs on your computer. You should manually install any needed scripts or CGI programs. (The FrontPage extensions can publish scripts to protected directories, but they perform strong user authentication before doing so.)
SNMP	This network monitoring option poses a serious security risk. If installed, it could be used to modify your computer's network settings and, at the very least, will happily reveal the names of all the user accounts on your computer. Don't install SNMP unless you need it, and if you do, **change the "community name"** from `public` to something confidential and difficult to guess.

KEEP UP-TO-DATE

New bugs in major operating systems and applications software are found every week, and patches and updates are issued almost as frequently.

Software manufacturers have become quite forthcoming with information about security risks, bugs, and the like. It wasn't always the case, as they mostly figured if they kept the problems a secret, fewer bad guys would find out about them, and so their customers would be better off. (That, and it saved them the embarrassment of admitting the seriousness of their bugs.) Information is shared so quickly among the bad guys now that it has become essential for companies to inform users of security problems as soon as a defensive strategy can be devised.

In the past few years, Microsoft has itself become quite forthcoming with announcements of security issues with its software, and to stay on top of the game, you have to subscribe and read the periodic announcements. You can subscribe to the Microsoft Security Bulletin service at `http://www.microsoft.com/security`.

The following are some other places to check out:

`http://www.ntbugtraq.com`

`http://www.sans.org`

`http://www.cert.org`

`http://www.first.org`

`http://www.cs.purdue.edu/coast/coast.html`

`http://www.greatcircle.com`

`newsgroups: comp.security.*, comp.risks`

Some of these sites point you toward security-related mailing lists. You should subscribe to Microsoft Security Advisor Bulletins and the SANS and CERT advisories at least, and perhaps other lists in digest form.

TESTING, LOGGING, AND MONITORING

If you've installed a security system, your next step is to make sure it works. You can't second-guess what 100 million potential visitors might do to your computer or network, but you should at least be sure that all your roadblocks stop the traffic you were expecting.

TEST YOUR DEFENSES

Some companies have hired expert hackers to attempt to break into their networks. You can do this too, or you can try to be your own hacker. Before you connect to the Internet, and periodically thereafter, try to break into your own system. Find its weaknesses.

Go through each of your defenses and each of the security policy changes you made, and try each of the things you thought they should prevent. This task can be quite time-consuming but well worth the effort.

PART

IV

CH

26

Try at least the following things from a Windows 2000 computer connected to the Internet outside your network:

- Visit the Internet site www.spinrite.com and view the ShieldsUp page. This Web site attempts to connect to Microsoft Networking and TCP/IP services on your computer to see whether any are accessible from the outside world. Click the Test My Shields! and Probe My Ports! buttons to see whether this testing system exposes any vulnerabilities. This is a great tool! (However, if you're on a corporate network, contact your network manager before trying this. If your company uses intrusion monitoring, this probe might set off alarms and get you in hot water.)

- Attempt file sharing by opening Windows Explorer (*not* Internet Explorer) and entering an address of \\1.2.3.4, where 1.2.3.4 is your computer's IP address or your network's public IP address. You should not be able to see any shared folders, and you shouldn't even be prompted for a username and/or password. If you have more than one public IP address, test *all* of them.

 If you are able to view your computer's shared folders, see "Shared Folders Are Visible to the Internet" in the "Troubleshooting" section at the end of this chapter.

- If you have installed a Web or FTP server, attempt to view any protected pages *without* using the correct username or password. With FTP, try using the login name anonymous and the password guest.

 If you are able to view your computer's shared folders, see "Sensitive Web Pages or FTP Folders Are Visible to the Internet" in the "Troubleshooting" section at the end of this chapter.

If you are not able to view protected Web pages or folders even after providing the correct password, see "Can't View Protected Web Pages" in the "Troubleshooting" section at the end of this chapter.

- Use network testing utilities to attempt to connect to any of the network services you have blocked—for example, SNMP.

 If sensitive network services are found to be accessible, see "Network Services Are Not Being Blocked" in the "Troubleshooting" section at the end of this chapter.

- Attempt to use Telnet to connect to your router, if you have one. If you are prompted for a login, try the name or password admin and the factory default login name indicated in the router's manual.

 If you can access your router, see "Router Is Accessible via Telnet" in the "Troubleshooting" section at the end of this chapter.

Port scanning tools are available to perform many of these tests automatically. For an example, see the ShieldsUp Web page at www.spinrite.com. I caution you to use this sort of tool in addition to, not instead of, the tests I listed here.

MONITOR SUSPICIOUS ACTIVITY

You should monitor the Security Event Log for audit entries indicating suspicious activity. Check FTP, Web, and email server log files frequently. I check them at least once a week on my LAN and look for unauthorized login attempts, spam, or relayed email, and so on. If the log entry lists the IP address of the offending party, I try to contact that party's ISP with evidence of his or her misdoing.

Repeated failed login attempts are a clue that your system may be under attack. I recommend auditing failed login and service requests and monitoring them frequently for signs of probing and attack.

If you have a router set up for packet filtering, you can send alerts when packets have been rejected or at least have the router display information about rejected traffic on its monitor or console display.

Some firewall products, including personal firewall products such as BlackICE Defender (http://www.networkice.com), keep a log of the packets they reject as evidence of possible hacking attempts. Review these logs frequently.

DISASTER PLANNING: PREPARATION FOR RECOVERY AFTER AN ATTACK

If you know a break-in has been successful, you must take immediate action. First, disconnect your network from the Internet. Then find out what happened.

Your server might have merely been browsed, but if the hacker is lucky and skilled, he or she may have gained Administrator privileges. He or she may have planted a virus or a monitoring program to provide him or her with useful information.

Unless you have an exact understanding of what happened and can fix the problem, you should clean out your system entirely. This means that you should reformat your hard drive, install Windows and all applications from CDs or pristine disks, and make a clean start. Then you can look at recent backups to see whether you have any you know aren't compromised, restore them, and then go on.

Having a break-in is a miserable experience and a time of pressure. You not only need to get the server up, but you also have to find out what might have gone wrong with your security measures so that you can fix them as well. Remember that a hacker who has had success is likely to try it again.

A little planning now will go a long way toward helping you through this situation. The key is having a good backup of all critical software.

MAKE A BASELINE BACKUP WHEN YOU CONFIGURE YOUR NETWORK

You should always make a permanent baseline backup of a system before you put it online with the Internet. This backup should be kept permanently. You can use it as a starting point for recovery if your system is compromised.

MAKE FREQUENT BACKUPS WHEN YOU'RE ONLINE

I hate to sound like a broken record on this point, but you should have a backup plan and stick to it. Make backups at some sensible interval and always after a session of extensive or significant changes (for example, after installing new software or adding users). If it helps, use backup software with a built-in scheduler, or use the command scheduler to perform an incremental backup every day or so.

WRITE AND TEST SERVER RESTORE PROCEDURES

I can tell you from personal experience that the only feeling more sickening than losing your system is finding out that the backups you've been diligently making are unreadable. Whatever your backup scheme is, be sure it works!

This step is really difficult to take, but I really urge you to try to completely rebuild a system after an imaginary break-in or disk failure. Use a sacrificial computer, of course, not your main server, and give yourself a whole day. Go through all the steps: Reformat hard disks, reinstall Windows, reinstall tape software, and restore the most recent backups. You might find that your backup system has a hole, a missing piece. Finding the problem with your system before you need the backups is much better than finding it after.

Also, be sure to document the whole process so that you can repeat it later. After a disaster, you'll be under considerable stress, so you might forget a step or make a mistake. Having a clear, written, tested procedure will go a long way toward making the recovery process easier and more likely to succeed.

WRITE AND MAINTAIN DOCUMENTATION

It's in your own best interest to maintain a log of all software installed on your computers, along with software settings, hardware types and settings, configuration choices, network number information, and so on. (Do you vaguely remember that ordeal with a DMA conflict when you installed the tape software last year? How *did* you resolve that problem, anyway?)

This information is often part of a company's "oral tradition," but a written record is an important insurance policy against loss due to memory lapses or personnel changes. Record all installation and configuration details.

Tip #305	Windows has no utilities to print out the configuration settings for software and network systems. I use Print Screen to record the configurations for each program and network component and then paste the images into a WordPad or Microsoft Word document.

The record will serve as a benchmark for your system so that you can immediately recognize any changes that have been introduced by hackers. It will also will help you rebuild the server if a crash occurs.

Then, if you have to reinstall and reconfigure Windows and all applications, could you find all the necessary components?

After you bring up your server, take the time to create a library of all printed and digital archives related to the network. Assign a bookshelf to the operating system and application software manuals. Make a library of CD-ROMs, repair disks, startup disks, utility disks, backup CDs, ZIP disks, tapes, manuals, and notebooks that record your configurations and observations. Keep them all in one place and locked up if possible.

HAVE AN INCIDENT PLAN

A system crash or intrusion is a highly stressful event. A written plan of action made now will help you keep a clear head when things go wrong. The actual event probably won't go as you imagined, but at least you'll have some good first steps to follow while you get your wits about you.

The following are some tips to include in your incident plan:

- Write down exactly what to do to disconnect your systems from the Internet. You don't want a plug-pulling frenzy.
- Write down exactly how to properly shut down computers and servers.
- Make a list of people to notify, including company officials, your computer support staff, your ISP, an incident response team, your therapist, and anyone else who will be involved in dealing with the aftermath.
- Check http://www.first.org to see whether you are eligible for assistance from one of the many FIRST response teams around the world. FIRST (the Forum of Incident Response and Security Teams) can tell you which agencies might best be able to help you in the event of a security incident; call 1-301-975-3359.
- The CERT-CC (the Computer Emergency Response Team Coordination Center) may also be able to help you, or at least get information from your break-in to help protect others. Check http://www.cert.org. In an emergency, call 1-412-268-7090.

  You can find a great deal of general information on effective incident response planning at http://www.cert.org. CERT offers training seminars, libraries, security (bug) advisories, and technical tips as well.

PART

IV

CH

26

SPECIFIC CONFIGURATION STEPS FOR WINDOWS 2000

Many of the points I've mentioned so far in this chapter are general, conceptual ideas that should be helpful in planning a security strategy, but perhaps not terribly helpful in implementing your plans. The following sections provide some specific instructions to tighten security on your Windows 2000 computer or LAN. These instructions are for a single Windows 2000 computer or a workgroup without Windows 2000 Server. Server offers more powerful and integrated security tools than are available with Windows 2000 Professional alone (and happily, it's the domain administrator's job to set it all up).

IF YOU HAVE A STANDALONE WINDOWS 2000 PROFESSIONAL COMPUTER

If you have a standalone system, you need to take only a few steps to be sure you're safe when browsing the Internet:

1. Enable Macro Virus Protection in your Microsoft Office applications.

2. Be very wary of viruses and Trojan horses in email attachments and downloaded software. Install a virus scan program, and discard unsolicited email with attachments without opening it.

3. Keep your system up-to-date with service packs, application software updates, and virus scanner updates.

4. Make the Security Policy changes I suggest below.

5. Use strong passwords. Use letters and numbers; don't use your name or other simple words.

6. Do not install the File Sharing for Microsoft Networks service. Remove it if it's installed now.

IF YOU HAVE A WINDOWS 2000 WORKGROUP ON A LAN

If you have a LAN with an Internet connection, whether it's by modem, with Connection Sharing, NAT, or a direct routed connection, do the following:

1. Follow the first five suggestions from the list in the preceding section. Make the Security Policy changes on *each* computer.

2. Disable the Guest account on each computer.

3. If you connect by modem, you won't have any firewall protection, but the security policy changes will help protect you. You could consider using a different protocol for file sharing purposes and *unbind* TCP/IP from the file sharing service so that Internet hackers can't get at the file sharing system. To do so, perform these steps on each computer on your LAN:

    a. Open Network and Dial-Up Connections. In Local Area Connection, install the SPX/IPX compatible protocol.

    b. Open Network and Dial-Up Connections. On the Advanced menu, under Advanced Settings, select the Adapters and Bindings tab.

    c. Select each LAN connection in turn (Local Area Connection and/or Private LAN Connection), and under File and Printer Sharing for Microsoft Networks, uncheck Internet Protocol.

    d. Restart each computer to make Windows file sharing use the IPX/SPX protocol and not TCP/IP. It also protects your LAN from file sharing access over the Internet.

4. If you connect with Connection Sharing or NAT, these services give you decent firewall protection.

5. If you use a direct, routed connection, configure packet filtering in your router, or add a filtering router between your Internet connection and your LAN. At the very least, block TCP and UDP ports 137–162 to eliminate file sharing, RPC, and SNMP.

TIGHTENING LOCAL SECURITY POLICY

You should set your machine's own (local) security policy whether your have a standalone computer or are on a LAN.

If your computer is part of a Windows 2000 domain, your local security policy setting *may* be superseded by policies set by your domain administrator, but you should set them anyway so that you're protected if your domain administrator doesn't enforce the settings for you.

To configure local security policy, log in as Administrator, and choose Start, Programs, Administrative Tools, Local Security Policy. (If you have not installed the Windows 2000 Administrative Tools option, you can use the Administrator Tools Control Panel applet as well.)

A familiar Explorer view then appears with three main categories in the left pane—Account Policies, Local Policies, and Public Key Policies—as shown in Figure 26.8. Change the following policy entries to these (or more stringent) values to maximize network security. To change the settings, select the policy categories from the left pane, and double-click the policy names in the right pane. Appropriate Properties dialogs appear for each; an example is shown in Figure 26.9. The Effective Policy Setting shows the actual current policy, which takes into account Group Policy from a domain server and the values in effect when you logged on.

Figure 26.8
The Local Policy Editor lets you tighten security by restricting unsafe configuration options.

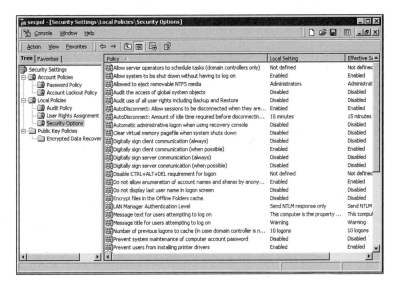

Figure 26.9
Each security policy item has a Properties dialog. You can enter the settings shown in the tables in the following sections.

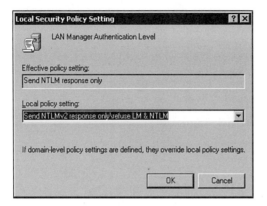

You don't need to change all the policies. I'll list the important ones in the following sections.

ACCOUNT POLICIES

Account policies require long, difficult, frequently changed passwords, and make it hard for users to recycle the same passwords over and over when forced to change. You should lock out accounts that fail several login attempts, locally or over the LAN. Table 26.3 shows the password policies and recommended local settings.

TABLE 26.3 PASSWORD POLICY SETTINGS

Password Policy	Local Setting
Enforce password history	10 passwords remembered
Maximum password age	42 days
Minimum password age	0 days
Minimum password length	8 characters
Passwords must meet complexity requirements of the installed password filter	Enabled
Store password using reversible encryption for all users in the domain	Disabled
User must log on to change the password	Disabled
Account Policy	
Account lockout counter	5 invalid logon attempts
Account lockout duration	30 minutes
Reset account lockout counter after	30 minutes

AUDIT POLICY

You should have an entry in the Event Log whenever someone oversteps his or her bounds. (However, you should not audit Privilege Use because hundreds of spurious entries appear for no apparent reason.) Security options are used to restrict what users can do with system options. Table 26.4 shows the audit policies and recommended settings.

TABLE 26.4   AUDIT POLICY SETTINGS

Audit Policy	Local Setting
Audit account logon events	Failure
Audit account management	Failure
Audit directory service access	Failure
Audit logon events	Failure
Audit object access	Failure
Audit policy change	Success, Failure
Audit privilege use	No auditing
Audit process tracking	Failure
Audit system events	Failure
User Rights Assignment	(no changes necessary)
Disable Ctrl+Alt+Del requirement for logon	Disabled
Do not allow enumeration of account names and shares by anonymous users	Enabled
LAN Manager Authentication Level	Send NTNTLMv2 responses/refuse LM&NTLM. Disable the LM and NTLM password encryption protocols if you don't have older versions of Windows on your LAN and don't want to use dial-up networking or Virtual Private Networking to connect to Windows 2000 with older operating systems. If you have to support Windows 95, use the Send NTLM Response Only setting.
Log-in Message text	The text varies. You can display a sort of "Posted: No Trespassing" warning with this entry. Use something like this: "This computer is property of XYZ Corp. Unauthorized use will be prosecuted."
Message title for users attempting to log on	Warning
Prevent user installation of print drivers	Disabled. If you want to prevent users from installing potentially untested printer and hardware drivers, check out the options for these settings.

PART

IV

CH

26

continues

TABLE 26.4 CONTINUED

Audit Policy	Local Setting
Send unencrypted password to connect to third-party SMB servers	Disabled. Some UNIX and Linux-based systems run Windows-compatible file sharing services (for example, Samba). These packages can't understand Windows password encryption and need passwords to be sent in the clear. If you use one of these servers, you must enable this setting.
Shut down system immediately if unable to log security audits	Disabled. A common hacker trick is to fill up audit logs with junk messages and then break in. If you want to, you can have Windows shut down when the Security Event Log fills. Doing so is probably not necessary and the downside is that it makes your security system a denial of service risk! (Microsoft's public "hack me if you can" Windows 2000 Server was shut down just this way.)
Unsigned driver installation behavior	Not defined. If you want to prevent users from installing potentially untested printer and hardware drivers, check out the options for these settings.
Unsigned nondriver	Not defined. If you want to prevent users from installation behavior installing potentially untested printer and hardware drivers, check out the options for these settings.

When you log out and back in, the new restrictive security policies will take effect.

Tip #306

> If you are working in a Windows 2000 Workgroup environment and have several computers to configure, you can configure one computer and create a template to make the same settings in the others. Select the Security Settings item in the left pane, and choose Action, Export Policy, Local Policy. Save the settings to a template file—for example, secpolicy.inf—on a shared folder on the network. Then, on each computer on your network, you can install the security policy. To do so, log on as Administrator, and run the Local Policy tool. Select Action and Import Policy. Locate the shared template file, and select Open.

You still must export and delete the recovery agent certificate to finish beefing up the security on each computer.

PUBLIC KEY POLICY AND THE ENCRYPTED FILE SYSTEM

Each Windows 2000 computer has a way of recovering encrypted files in the event that the original user account is deleted or if the encrypting certificate is lost or deleted. *Recovery agents* are accounts given the privilege of viewing files encrypted by other users. A domain administrator can designate recovery agents for the whole domain, and individual computer administrators can designate recovery agents for individual computers. Each designated recovery agent needs an encryption certificate, which contains the recovery key.

As I've discussed elsewhere, hackers with physical access to your computer can use a series of tricks to fool Windows into letting them use the recovery agent certificate to access any encrypted file on the system!

You should leave Administrator as the only recovery agent for your local computer, but you should remove the certificate from the computer so that it can't be obtained over the network. To do so, follow the procedure described in Chapter 33, "Managing the Hard Disk."

TROUBLESHOOTING

SHARED FOLDERS ARE VISIBLE TO THE INTERNET

When I use Explorer to view my computer across the Internet, I am prompted for a username and password, and/or shared folders are visible.

If you have this problem, Microsoft file sharing services are being exposed to the Internet. If you have a shared connection to the Internet, you need to install a packet filter to block file sharing services (UDP and TCP ports 137 through 139). If you are using Internet Connection Sharing, you can uninstall File and Printer Sharing for Microsoft Networks on the computer sharing the Internet connection. Otherwise, you should use a filtering router to protect yourself. This problem is serious. Don't leave it unfixed!

SENSITIVE WEB PAGES OR FTP FOLDERS ARE VISIBLE TO THE INTERNET

When I access my Web site from the Internet using a Web browser or anonymous FTP, I can view folders that I thought were private and protected.

First, you must be sure that the shared folders are not on a FAT-formatted disk partition. FAT disks don't support user-level file protection. Share only folders from NTFS-formatted disks.

You must restrict access on the shared folders using NTFS permissions. View the folders in Windows Explorer on the computer running IIS. View the folders' Securities Properties tab. Be sure neither Everyone nor IUSR_XXXX (where XXXX is your computer name) is granted access. On these protected folders, grant Read and Write privileges only to authorized users.

CAN'T VIEW PROTECTED WEB PAGES

When I try to view protected Web pages or change to a protected directory in FTP, I can't view the pages or folders.

View the virtual folder's Properties page in the Internet Information Services management applet. On the Directory Security tab, click Edit under Anonymous Access and Authentication Control. Be sure that Digest Authentication and Integrated Windows Authentication are checked. If they were checked already, view the folder's Security settings in Windows Explorer as described in the previous troubleshooting tip. Make sure that the desired users or groups are granted appropriate NTFS access permissions on the folder and its files and subfolders.

NETWORK SERVICES ARE NOT BEING BLOCKED

I can connect to my computer across the Internet with remote administration tools such as the Registry Editor, with SNMP viewers, or with other tools that use network services. How do I prevent this access?

Look up the protocol type (for example, UDP or TCP) and port numbers of the unblocked services, and configure filters in your router to block these services. Your ISP might be able to help you with this problem. If you don't have a filtering router, you might want to consider uninstalling the services from the computer making the Internet connection.

ROUTER IS ACCESSIBLE VIA TELNET

I can connect to my Internet service router through Telnet across the Internet without providing a secret administrative password. How do I prevent this access?

Configure your router to require a sensible password for access. Choose a password with letters and numbers. Be sure you write it down, and also give it to the technical support department of your ISP. The ISP might even be able to help you change the password.

TIPS FROM THE WINDOWS PROS: BUILDING A FIREWALL/NAT ROUTER

I've mentioned IPROUTE several times in this chapter. It's a nifty $50 shareware router program written by David Mischler, available at `http://www.mischler.com`. Nowadays, old 486 computers can be had for free, if you look around, and network cards can be obtained for about $15, so you can build a neat little filtering router, which can provide NAT service and can even be used to provide a shared modem connection, for under $100. Other programs such as WinGate, WinProxy, and SyGate are easier to use and configure, though. Still, I really like IPROUTE for several reasons:

- It has no per-user licensing fee.
- It can build a full-fledged router. I've used it to build a four-port (four LAN) router.
- It runs on DOS, so it's simpler, cheaper to set up, and more reliable than Windows-based programs.
- It's obscure and less likely to have exploits known to hackers.
- It's very flexible and configurable.
- It's *really* reliable. (Did I say that already?)

You can get information on setting up IPROUTE in many configurations from `www.mischler.com`. Examples include modem dial-on-demand, modem always-on, modem dial-in, and so on. I've used it this way with external ISDN and analog modems.

Here, I'll show you an actually-in-use-today configuration for an IP router using NAT to provide Internet service to a whole LAN, starting with a single-connection DSL or cable modem. This router is set up to share the Internet connection, and it makes visible the Web and email server inside the network.

The computer can be any 486 or faster computer with at least 1MB memory. In this example, I used a 486-66 with 8MB memory. (I didn't bother to remove the unneeded memory.) I disconnected its hard drive and removed the hard drive setup information from the system BIOS, and I also disabled the Error If No Keyboard error in the BIOS setup program. (After getting these routers set up and working, I usually remove the keyboard and monitor.)

The tricky part of setting up one of these routers is locating the Packet Driver software for the particular network cards you use. They are usually on the installation floppy disks, and you have to look up the command-line syntax required for each manufacturer's driver. Packet drivers are software programs that let DOS programs communicate directly with the network cards, and each card has to be assigned an interrupt request (IRQ) number for the software driver itself, as distinct from the network card. The numbers are usually in the range 60 through 69, hexadecimal. The number is usually preceded with 0x. Then you may or may not need to specify the I/O address or IRQ number for the network card. When you use two cards of the same type, you usually do have to, so the software knows which card you're indicating. In any case, the documentation on the card's setup disk will explain how to run the packet driver.

For this example, I found one D-Link brand card and one 3Com card. I used the setup programs provided with each card to configure their IRQ and I/O addresses (no Plug and Play allowed here, folks!). The D-Link card was configured for I/O address 300, interrupt 5, and I assigned the packet driver interrupt number 62. I labeled this card Inside because it is connected to the network hub for the LAN.

I set up the 3Com card for I/O address 330 and interrupt 10, and chose interrupt number 64 for its packet driver. This card I labeled Outside because it's connected to the DSL router with a simple UTP patch cable.

I made a DOS boot disk and installed the files listed in Table 26.5.

TABLE 26.5   CONTENTS OF THE IPROUTE ROUTER BOOT DISK

Filename	Description
COMMAND.COM	File installed when you make any DOS boot disk
AUTOEXEC.BAT	Startup batch file, listed below
DE22XPD.COM	Packet driver provided with D-Link card
3C5X9PD.COM	Packet driver provided with 3Com card
IPR.EXE	IPROUTE program, registered version
CONFIG.IPR	IPROUTE configuration script, listed below

I had to edit two files: AUTOEXEC.BAT, to start up the computer, and CONFIG.IPR, to configure IPROUTE. These two files are shown here.

The AUTOEXEC.BAT file looks like this:

```
@echo off
prompt $p$g

echo.
echo Loading packet drivers...

rem ... inside interface
de22xpd 0x64

rem ... translated outside (dsl) interface
3c5x9pd 0x62

echo.
echo Loading IPROUTE

ipr CONFIG.IPR
```

The CONFIG.IPR file looks like this:

```
; ---------------------------------------------
;    NAT FIREWALL ROUTER CONFIGURATION
; ---------------------------------------------

set log file CON
set log timestamp on
set log brief
set nat send-reset on
set nat send-icmp on
```

The preceding section configures the router to display error messages on the computer's monitor.

```
show version

; ---------------------------------------------
; telnet authentication
; ---------------------------------------------

user admin gloppy23423 *:21
```

This section sets username and password for Telnet administrative access to the router.

```
; ---------------------------------------------
.; interfaces:
;      inside  - internal network
;      outside - OUTSIDE line to internet
; ---------------------------------------------

packet inside  0x64   192.168.0.1/24
packet outside 0x62   203.202.201.200/24
```

The preceding section tells the router the interrupt number of each network card and assigns an IP address to each. The /## number is an alternative way of specifying a subnet mask.

```
; ------------------------------------------------
; set default gateway (address specified by the ISP)
; ------------------------------------------------

route * outside 203.202.201.254
```

This section sets the default gateway and the ISP's router's address.

```
; ------------------------------------------------
; NAT translation rules
;
; handle ping directly
; forward HTTP, SMTP, PPTP, PCAnywhere to machine 192.168.0.4
; ------------------------------------------------
;            proto internal addr     external address
;            ----- -------------     ----------------
nat outside  icmp  203.202.201.200   203.202.201.200
nat outside  tcp   192.168.0.4:80    203.202.201.200:80
nat outside  tcp   192.168.0.4:25    203.202.201.200:25
nat outside  tcp   192.168.0.4:1723  203.202.201.200:1723
nat outside  47    192.168.0.4       203.202.201.200
nat outside  tcp   192.168.0.4:5631  203.202.201.200:5631
nat outside  udp   192.168.0.4:5632  203.202.201.200:5632
nat outside  *     *                 203.202.201.200
```

The preceding section directs incoming Web, mail transfer, VPN, and PCAnywhere connections to a specific internal computer: 192.168.0.4.

```
; ------------------------------------------------
; enable TELNET
; ------------------------------------------------

telnetd do_tel
```

The preceding section enables Telnet access to the router. Do_tel is a subroutine in the script to handle connection requests.

```
; ------------------------------------------------
; Start a command interpreter on the console and exit
; ------------------------------------------------

command
log "ROUTER STARTED"
exit
```

This section ends the startup phase of the router.

```
; ------------------------------------------------
; TELNET handler
; ------------------------------------------------

do_tel:
    log "TELNET ($IPADDR:$PORT)> Connection opened"
    on cdloss drop_tel
    wait .5
    on timeout drop_tel
    send "\r\nlogin: "
    set echo on
```

```
read 20 "\r\n" NAME
send "\r\nPassword:"
set echo off
read 20 "\r\n" PASS
on cdloss bad_pass
authenticate NAME PASS *:21
on cdloss drop_tel
log "TELNET ($IPADDR:$PORT)> $NAME logged in"
send "\r\n\n"
set trace on
command
exit

bad_pass:
log "TELNET ($IPADDR:$PORT)> Authentication failed ($NAME:$PASS)"

drop_tel:
log "TELNET ($IPADDR:$PORT)> connection closed"
exit
```

The preceding subroutine is called when a Telnet connection request is received. It requests a username and password, validates them, and if successful, starts a command interpreter for the caller. Otherwise, it disconnects.

If you use these scripts to build your own router, you need to edit some of the information inside. The following items are specific to my network:

■ The Telnet login name is admin, and the password is gloppy23423. You should change that information!

■ The IP address of my DSL (outside) connection is 203.202.201.200. The network mask given by my ISP was 255.255.255.0. For IPROUTE, you have to convert this number to binary and count the number of 1s (there are 24 in my setup). The outside interface is specified as 203.202.201.200/24 in this case. You have to use the IP address and network mask provided by your ISP.

■ My ISP's gateway address is 203.200.201.254. You can use the gateway provided by your ISP.

■ The IP address of my IPROUTE router is 192.168.0.1. You can use any address you want, but this one is a good as any.

■ The computers on my inside network (my LAN) use IP addresses 192.168.0.2 through 192.168.0.254, with network mask 255.255.255.0 and gateway address 192.168.0.1. They all must be set manually. You can set each computer's DNS Server IP address as specified by your ISP.

■ I have directed incoming Web (HTTP), email transfer (SMTP), Microsoft Virtual Private Networking (PPTP), and Symantec PCAnywhere requests to one particular machine, with address 192.168.0.4. You can delete or alter these entries.

The IPROUTE documentation you get when you download the program provides a complete description of all the scripting commands.

Building routers sounds like a lot of work, but I've been able to set them up in under an hour. Really!

You can try this routine yourself with the free demo version of IPROUTE that runs for 30 minutes and then shuts down. When you register, you can download the unlimited version. What you get for your effort is a very configurable router that will protect your PC or network for less than $100.

CHAPTER 27

TROUBLESHOOTING YOUR NETWORK

In this chapter

WHEN GOOD NETWORKS GO BAD

Today's networks are so easy to install and configure that you can just Plug and Pray, er, I mean Play. But when good networks go bad, it's another story, one with all the makings of a Fox Network special.

Every time I get a call from a client with a network problem, I cringe. I never know whether it's going to take 10 minutes or a week to fix. Sometimes the problem isn't so bad; I've fixed more than one "broken" computer by turning it on. If such an easy fix doesn't present itself immediately, though, a bit of a cold sweat breaks out on my forehead. The problem could be anything. How do you even start to find a nasty problem in the maze of cards, wires, drivers, and hidden, inexplicable system services?

Well, if you work for a corporation with a network support staff, of course, the answer to that question is "Call the Help Desk!" or "Call Bob!" or call whatever or whomever is responsible for network problems in your organization. That's clearly the best way to go! Take a refreshing walk around the block while someone else sweats over your network. (If you're on your own, taking that walk might help anyway, before coming back to the job of discovering what the problem might be.)

I will tell you that, in reading this chapter, you won't find the solution to any network problem you're having. I can't solve your problem here, but I can show you some of the tools available to help you identify the source of a problem you might have.

GETTING STARTED

As a consultant, I've spent many years helping clients with hardware, software, and network problems. The most common—and frustrating—way people report a problem is to say "I can't..." or "The computer won't...." Usually, knowing what *doesn't* happen isn't very helpful at all. To solve a mystery, you have to start with what you *do* know. I always have to ask "What happens when you try...?" The answer to that question usually gets me well on the way to solving the problem. The original report usually leaves out important error messages and symptoms that might immediately identify the problem.

Also, as you work on a problem, pay as much attention to what *does* work as to what doesn't. Knowing what *isn't* broken lets you eliminate whole categories of problems. It also helps you to see whether a problem affects just one computer or all the computers on your local area network (LAN).

The following are some other questions I ask:

- Does the problem occur all the time or just sometimes?
- Can you reproduce the problem consistently? If you can define a procedure to reproduce the problem, try to reduce it to the shortest, most direct procedure possible.
- Has the system ever worked, even once? If so, when did it stop working, and what happened just before that? What changed?

These questions can help you determine whether the problem is fundamental (for example, due to a nonfunctioning network card) or interactive (that is, due to a conflict with other users, with new software, or confined to a particular subsystem of the network). You might be able to spot the problem right off the bat if you look at the scene this way. If you can't, you can use some tools to help narrow down the problem.

Generally, network problems fall into one or more of these categories:

- Application software
- Network clients
- Name-resolving services
- Network protocols
- Addressing and network configuration
- Driver software
- Network cards and hardware configuration
- Wiring/hubs

→ To learn more information about networks and network components, **see** Chapter 19, "Overview of Windows 2000 Networking."

If you can determine which category a problem falls in, you're halfway there. At this point, diagnostic tools and good, old-fashioned deductive reasoning come into play.

You might be able to eliminate one or more categories right away. For example, if your computer can communicate with some other computers but not all, and your network uses a central hub, you can deduce that at least your computer's network card and the wiring from your computer to the hub are working properly.

Windows comes with some diagnostic tools to further help you narrow down the cause of a network problem. In the rest of this chapter, I'll outline the tools and suggest how to use them. (You might also peruse Chapter 16, "Internet Diagnosis Tools," for tips on diagnosing network problems specific to the Internet [TCP/IP] protocol.)

Diagnostic Tools

Each diagnostic tool I'll describe serves to test the operation of one or more of the categories I mentioned in the preceding section. I'll go through this toolkit in roughly the order you should try them.

Some tools can be used to find problems in any of the many networking components. These tools quickly identify many problems.

My Network Places

You might not think of it as a diagnostic tool, but My Network Places can be one. It can quickly tell you whether your computer can communicate with any other computers on your

LAN using the file and printer sharing client services. If at least one other computer is visible and online, then you can be pretty sure that your computer's network card and cabling are okay.

To use it, open My Network Places, and then open Computers Near Me if that icon is present. If Computers Near Me is not present, open Entire Network, select the phrase Entire Contents on the left side of the screen, drill down into Microsoft Windows Network or NetWare or Compatible Network (whichever you're trying to diagnose), and then drill into any workgroups or domains you find.

> **Note**
>
> Computers Near Me appears only if your computer is configured for a Workgroup LAN. It is discussed in more detail in Chapter 24, "Connecting Your LAN to the Internet."

See whether any computers appear here. If at least one other computer appears, your network cabling and network card are probably okay, and you need to check to be sure that each computer on your network has the same set of network protocols installed. If no computers appear, My Network Places doesn't tell why, so you have to begin the process of diagnosing connectivity and/or higher-level problems. The next place to go is the Event Viewer, which might have recorded informative error messages from network components.

EVENT VIEWER

The Event Viewer is another very important diagnostic tool, one of the first to check, as Windows often silently records very useful information about problems with network hardware or software in its Event Log. To display the Event Log, right-click My Computer, select Manage, and select the Event Viewer system tool. (Alternatively, you can choose Start, Programs, Administrative Tools, Event Viewer.)

On the left pane, select the System, Application, and Security logs in turn. The Event Viewer displays Event Log entries, most recent first, on the right (see Figure 27.1).

Figure 27.1
The Event Viewer might display important diagnostic information when you have network problems. View the System, Application, and Security logs in turn.

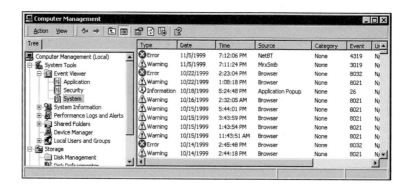

Log entries for serious errors are displayed with a red X circle; warnings appear with a yellow ! triangle. Informational entries (marked with a blue *i*) usually don't relate to problems. Double-click any error or warning entries in the log to view the detailed description and any associated data recorded with the entry.

These messages are usually quite significant and informative to help diagnose network problems; they may indicate that a network card is malfunctioning, that a domain controller for authentication or a DHCP server for configuration can't be found, and so on. The Source column in the error log indicates which Windows component or service recorded the event. These names are usually fairly cryptic. A few of the more common nonobvious ones are listed in Table 27.1.

TABLE 27.1   NETWORK SOURCES OF EVENT LOG ENTRIES

Source	Description
NetBT	Client for Microsoft Networks
MrxSmb	Client for Microsoft Networks
Browser	Name resolution system for Client for Microsoft Networks
Application Popup	(Can come from any system utility; these warning messages are usually significant.)
RemoteAccess	Dial-Up Networking
SMTPSVC	The SMTP mail transport service, part of Internet Information Services (IIS)
W3SVC	The WWW server component of IIS
SNMP	Simple Networking Monitoring Protocol, an optional networking component
IPNATHLP	Internet Connection Sharing
NWCWorkstation	Client for Novell Networks
NwlnkIpx	SPX/IPX Network transport layer
W32Time	Computer clock synchronization service
Dnsapi	DNS client component
Dnscache	DNS client component
atapi	IDE hard disk/CDROM controller

If you're at a loss to solve the problem even with the information given, check the configuration of the indicated component, or remove and reinstall it to see whether you can clear up the problem.

→ To learn more details about the Event Log, **see** "Using the Event Viewer and Log Files," **p. 1179**.

Tip #307

> A problem with one network system usually causes other problems. Therefore, the oldest error message in a sequence of errors is usually the most significant; subsequent errors are just a result of the first failure. Because the Event Log is ordered most-recent-first, you might get the most useful information down a bit from the top of the list.

Tip #308

> The real cause of your problem might reveal itself at system startup time rather than when you observe the problem. Reboot your system, and note the time. Then reproduce the problem. Check the Event Log for messages starting at the reboot time.

DEVICE MANAGER

Hardware problems with your network card will most likely be recorded in the Event Log. If you suspect that your network card is the culprit, and nothing is recorded in the Event Log, check the Device Manager.

To use it, right-click My Computer, select Manage, and choose the Device Manager system tool. Any devices with detectable hardware problems or configuration conflicts appear with a yellow ! icon when you display the Device Manager. If no yellow icons appear, you don't have a *detected* hardware problem. This doesn't mean that you don't have any, but the odds are slim that your network card is the problem.

If devices are shown with ! icons, double-click the device name to see the Windows explanation of the device status and any problems.

→ For more detailed instructions and tips on device troubleshooting, **see** "Driver Signing and the Device Manager," **p. 1090**.

TESTING NETWORK CABLES

If your computer can't communicate with any other on your LAN, and the Device Manager doesn't indicate a faulty network card, you might have a wiring problem. Wiring problems can be the most difficult to solve, as it's quite difficult to prove that data is leaving one computer but not arriving at another. The ping program, which I'll discuss later in this chapter, can help with this problem.

→ To learn how you can use the ping command to diagnose Internet-related network problems, **see** "ping," **p. 560**.

If your computer is not properly wired into the LAN, in many cases, Windows displays an offline icon right on the system tray and indicates that your network card is disconnected. It might not, though, so you shouldn't take a lack of this kind of message to mean that no wiring problems exist.

If you use 10BASE-T wiring, LED indicators should be located at the hub for each computer on the LAN. Check hub-to-hub and computer-to-hub connections for a green Link indicator.

You also can use inexpensive (about $75) cable test devices that check for continuity and correct pin-to-pin wiring order for UTP wiring. They come as a set of two boxes. One gets plugged into each end of a given cable run, and a set of blinking lights tells you whether all four wires are connected and in the correct order. (If you install your own network cabling and/or make your own patch cables, these tools are quite handy to have to check your work.)

With a coaxial (also called ThinNet or 10BASE-2) network, if none of your computers can send data (for example, pings) to any another, a wiring problem is the most likely culprit because a wiring fault usually takes out the whole network. Unfortunately, the network cards don't have any indicator lights to help! You can get a coaxial cable continuity tester, or you might need to manually check each computer's connection.

Note

A *continuity tester* is a small box with two wire probes and a beeper or light. When a sound electrical connection exists between the two probes, the beeper beeps or the light comes on.

To test a coaxial cable with such a tester, you disconnect the cable from the network at both ends. At either end of the cable, you touch one probe to the center pin and the other to the BNC connector's metal outer shell. You should not hear a beep. A beep indicates that the cable is shorted out. Next, have someone at the other end of the cable use a wire to short the other end's center pin to the shell. Now, you should get a beep. No beep indicates that the cable is broken.

Tip #309

I've cured more than one ailing coaxial network by just walking along the chain of computers, from one end to the other, giving each BNC connector a little twist to make sure its little Frankenstein-neck pins are fully locked. Each T-connector has three connections, so be sure to check all three at each computer. This tour has sometimes also revealed missing terminators and improper rearrangements in the network cable made by untrained users.

One helpful technique with coax is to divide the LAN in two, which, with any luck, isolates the fault in one of the halves. You need an extra BNC T-connector and two extra 50-ohm terminators to try this procedure. You disconnect one cable from the computer in the middle of your LAN and attach a terminator to each of the separated ends, as shown in Figure 27.2. When you do so, you make two separate LAN segments, both properly terminated. You can use the ping command to see whether computers in the two segments can communicate with others in the same segment. If one of the segments works, and the other doesn't, you can continue dividing the faulty section in half until you isolate a single network cable or connector.

PART

IV

CH

27

Tip #310

If you have a trusty old volt-ohmmeter, you can check a coaxial Ethernet cable. To do so, unplug the T-connectors from all computers, leaving the cables and terminators attached. Measure the resistance between the center pin and outer shell of one of the connectors. You should read 25 ohms. If a terminator is missing from one end of the cable, or if a break has occurred somewhere in the cable, you'll read 50 ohms. If you read 36 ohms, you've used 72 ohm ARCnet terminators by mistake and need to replace them.

Figure 27.2
Dividing a coaxial network in half to isolate a cabling fault. Disconnect one cable from the computer in the middle of the LAN, and terminate both ends.

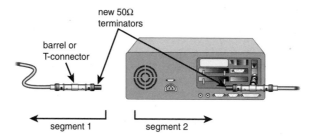

If these quick tricks don't identify the problem, you might have to call in a network wiring professional to test your network cabling. He or she will bring cable testing equipment that is way too expensive for the average business to buy but that can prove or eliminate cabling as a source of problems in mere seconds.

Note

If you really want to get into the guts of your network cabling or are planning a major installation and want to learn more details so that you can oversee a professional installation, I recommend that you read *Practical Network Cabling*, published by Que Corporation.

CHECKING NETWORK CONFIGURATION

If hardware isn't at fault, you may have a fundamental network configuration problem. Often the Event Log or Device Manager gives these problems away, but if they don't, you can use another batch of tools to check the computer's network configuration.

ipconfig

If your computer can't communicate with other computers on your LAN, after you check the Event Log and Device Manager, you can use the `ipconfig` command-line utility to see whether your computer has a valid IP address. Check others on the LAN, too, to ensure that they do as well.

At the command prompt (which you open by choosing Start, Programs, Accessories, Command Prompt), type the following command:

```
>ipconfig /all
```

The results should look something like this:

```
Windows 2000 IP Configuration
        Host Name . . . . . . . . . . . . : AMBON
        Primary DNS Suffix  . . . . . . . : mycompany.com
        Node Type . . . . . . . . . . . . : Broadcast
        IP Routing Enabled. . . . . . . . : Yes
        WINS Proxy Enabled. . . . . . . . : No
        DNS Suffix Search List. . . . . . : mycompany.com

Ethernet adapter Local Area Connection:
        Connection-specific DNS Suffix  . : mycompany.com
        Description . . . . . . . . . . . : Realtek RTL8139(A)
                        PCI Fast Ethernet Adapter
        Physical Address. . . . . . . . . : 00-C0-CA-14-09-7F
        DHCP Enabled. . . . . . . . . . . : No
        IP Address. . . . . . . . . . . . : 202.201.200.166
        Subnet Mask . . . . . . . . . . . : 255.255.255.224
        Default Gateway . . . . . . . . . : 202.201.200.190
        DNS Servers . . . . . . . . . . . : 201.202.203.72
                                            201.202.213.72
```

The most important items to look for are the following:

- Hostname—It should be set to the desired name for each computer. If you just can't correspond with a particular computer, be sure it's turned on and correctly named.

- IP address—It should be set appropriately for your network. If your LAN uses Internet Connection Sharing, the address will be a number in the range 192.168.0.1 through 192.168.0.254. If your LAN uses DHCP for automatic configuration, your network manager can tell you whether the IP address is correct. If you see a number in the range 169.254.0.1 through 192.254.0.254, your computer is set for automatic configuration but no DHCP server was found, so Windows has chosen an IP address by itself. This is fine if your LAN uses this automatic configuration system. However, if there should have been a DHCP server, make sure it's functioning, and restart your computer.

- Network mask—It usually looks like 255.255.255.0, but other settings are possible. At the very least, all computers on the same LAN should have the same network mask.

Each computer on the same LAN should have a valid IP address and network mask. If they don't, check your network configuration.

→ To learn more details about IP addressing, network masks, and configuration, **see** "The IP Route," **p. 661**, and "Configuring Protocols," **p. 726**.

netdiag

netdiag is a comprehensive network connectivity and configuration diagnosis tool included with the Windows 2000 Professional Resource Kit, a set of extra utility programs and diagnostic tools sold by Microsoft.

It's not clear whether Microsoft will provide these tools on the Windows 2000 Professional CD. Browse your Windows 2000 installation CD, and look for a folder named \SUPPORT\TOOLS. If this folder is present, see whether a setup program is inside. If so, good! Run it. It installs a small subset of the Resource Kit, including the netdiag program I'm about to describe.

If it isn't on your CD (or even if it is), get a copy of the Windows 2000 Professional Resource Kit. It costs a few bucks, but every organization with a LAN should have a copy, period. Besides netdiag, it has enough nifty tools and utilities to keep the most tweak-happy computer user satisfied for weeks.

To use this program, issue the command

```
> netdiag ¦ more
```

to run the diagnostics, and page them through the more utility a screenful at a time. Press Enter to see each successive screen.

The output of netdiag is long—over 180 lines on my computer—because it tests quite a number of network subcomponents. Scroll through the output looking for tests marked Failed. They help point you toward fixing a network problem.

If you have a Windows 2000 Server-based domain network, you should refer any failed tests in the Global Results section to your network administrator because they indicate problems with your computer's domain membership.

Note

> I've avoided talking about nonstandard (that is, extra money) Windows 2000 components in this book with this one exception: netdiag is an important tool, and one a network maven shouldn't be without.

MY COMPUTER

You can check your computer's identification and domain membership setup by using My Computer. To do so, right-click My Computer, select Properties, and view the Network Identification tab.

On a Windows 2000 Workgroup network, you should see your computer's name and the name of your workgroup. The workgroup name should be the same on all computers on your workgroup LAN.

On a Windows 2000 domain network, you should see your computer's name displayed as part of a Windows 2000 domain name (for example, my computer AMBON would be called AMBON.mycompany.com on a domain network) and the domain name. Your domain name might not include .com; in any case, though, all computers on the LAN should have the same domain name.

NETWORK AND DIAL-UP CONNECTIONS

You can manually check all installed network protocols and services and their configuration by viewing Network and Dial-Up Connections and viewing the properties for Local Area Connection. Confirm that each required protocol is installed and correctly configured. In general, the settings on each computer on your LAN should match, except that the IP address differs usually only in the last of its four dot-separated numbers. If your LAN uses Automatic IP address configuration, you need to use the `ipconfig` command, which I described earlier, to check the settings.

TESTING NETWORK CONNECTIVITY

A few tools can help you determine whether the network can send data between computers; these tools test the network protocols as well as low-level network hardware layers.

ping

`ping` is a fundamental tool for testing TCP/IP network connectivity. Because most Windows 2000 Professional networks use the Internet (TCP/IP) protocol for file and printer sharing services, as well as for Internet access, most Windows 2000 Professional users can use the `ping` test to confirm that their network cabling, hardware, and the TCP/IP protocol are all functioning correctly. `ping` sends several data packets to a specified computer and waits for the other computer to send the packets back. By default, it sends four packets and prints the results of the four tests.

To see whether the network can carry data between any pair of computers, use the `ipconfig` command (described previously) to find the IP address of the two computers. Then, on one computer, open a Command Prompt window by choosing Start, Programs, Accessories, Command Prompt.

Next, type the following command:

```
> ping 127.0.0.1
```

This command tests the networking software of the computer itself, by sending packets to the special internal IP address 127.0.0.1; this test has the computer send data to itself. It should print the following:

```
Reply from 127.0.0.1: bytes=32 time<10ms TTL=128
Reply from 127.0.0.1: bytes=32 time<10ms TTL=128
Reply from 127.0.0.1: bytes=32 time<10ms TTL=128
Reply from 127.0.0.1: bytes=32 time<10ms TTL=128
```

If it doesn't, the TCP/IP protocol itself is incorrectly installed or configured; check the computer's IP address configuration, or, if that seems correct, remove and reinstall the Internet Protocol from Local Area Connection in Network and Dial-Up Connections. (I have to say, in more than 10 years of working with PC networks, I've never seen this test fail.)

PART

IV

CH

27

If your computer can send data to itself, try another computer on your LAN. Issue the `ping` command again, as in this example:

```
> ping 101.102.103.104
```

Of course, you should use the other computer's real IP address in place of 101.102.103.104. You should get four replies as before:

```
Reply from 101.102.103.104: bytes=32 time<10ms TTL=32
Reply from 101.102.103.104: bytes=32 time<10ms TTL=32
Reply from 101.102.103.104: bytes=32 time<10ms TTL=32
Reply from 101.102.103.104: bytes=32 time<10ms TTL=32
```

These replies indicate that you have successfully sent data to the other machine and received it back.

If, on the other hand, the `ping` command returns `Request timed out`, the packets either didn't make it to the other computer or were not returned. You can run the `netstat` command to see whether the packets were sent and/or received. Here's how: Before you issue another `ping` command, on each computer—both the computer from which you're issuing the command and the computer whose IP address you are testing—issue the following command:

```
> netstat -s -p icmp
```

This command prints statistics for packets using the Internet Control Message Protocol (ICMP), which includes `ping` test packets. In particular, look for these lines:

```
                   Received        Sent
Echos                 0            10
Echo Replies         10             0
```

Note these numbers for each computer, repeat the `ping` test, and then repeat the `netstat` commands. On the sending computer, you should note that the Echos Sent count has gone up by four. On the target computer, see whether the Echos Received and Echo Replies Sent counts have increased. If they haven't, the `ping` tests never reached the test computer. This is the most common case; it may indicate a wiring problem, network card problem, or TCP/IP configuration error.

If the target computer's counts have increased, though, the ping packets were received, but the replies never made it back to the original sending computer. This situation is quite unusual but might indicate that one or the other computer's gateway address or network mask is set incorrectly.

In any case, you can use `ping` to determine which computers can send to which other computers on your LAN or across wide area networks (WANs) or the Internet. `ping` works when given a computer's IP address or its network name.

→ For more information about the `netstat` command, **see** "netstat," **p. 551**.

netmon

Included with Windows 2000 Server *only*, `netmon` is a network monitoring and data capturing program that network administrators can use to perform very meticulous monitoring and analysis of network traffic. If all else fails, a Windows 2000 server computer might be brought in to perform this sort of network monitoring.

→ For more information about netmon, **see** "netmon," **p. 550**.

TESTING NETWORK THROUGHPUT

If your network works but works slowly, you can try to determine the reason by using the Windows Performance monitor tool. The Performance Monitor can display utilization statistics collected from your network card and its drivers. You must first install the Network Monitor Driver to enable the collection of network driver performance statistics. Do so on the most-used computer on your network:

1. In Network and Dial-Up Connections, open Local Area Connections, and select Properties.
2. Select Install, choose Protocol, and select the Network Monitor Driver.
3. Click OK to close the Properties dialog.

Now run the Performance Monitor by choosing Start, Programs, Administrative Tools, Performance. You can use the Performance Monitor to measure network utilization and other network statistics.

MEASURING NETWORK UTILIZATION

In the right pane of the Performance console, you can add an item to the graph of performance statistics like this:

1. Right-click in the graph pane, and select Add Counters.
2. Check Use Local Computer Counters.
3. Select the performance object named Network Segment.
4. Select the counter named Network Segment Utilization.
5. Select All Instances, and click Add.
6. Select Close.

The Performance Monitor then graphs the amount of data traffic on your network connection or connections, expressed as a percentage of the maximum each can carry, and the plot is updated as you watch. Now you can visually monitor the traffic on your network.

→ To learn more details about this nifty system-monitoring application, **see** "Performance Monitor," **p. 1176**.

Ethernet networks generally should not be expected to sustain more than 30 percent average utilization without collisions and conflicts (between computers trying to transmit at the same time), causing the network to slow down significantly. If you see that your network's average utilization is hovering at or more than 30 percent, you might consider breaking your network into several segments and using a switch to route traffic between server (or servers) and the several network segments. This subject is beyond the scope of this book, though, so you should refer to other books or a networking consultant before proceeding.

> **Note**
>
> To learn more information about network design and maintenance, take a look at *Upgrading and Repairing Networks, Second Edition* (ISBN: 0-7897-2034-5), from Que.

To remove counters from the Performance graph, you can select the items in the legend below the graph and click the X icon at the top of the graph. Alternatively, you can right-click the graph and select Properties; next, select the Data tab, select Counters, and then click Remove.

MEASURING BROADCAST ACTIVITY

Broadcast packets are sent when a computer wants or needs every other computer on the LAN to hear its message. These messages can be requests for information or announcements of services the computer makes available. Whatever the reason, a high level of broadcast activity slows network performance because each computer on the LAN must process these messages. An excessive level of broadcast activity may result from misconfigured computers or WAN connections.

To display broadcast activity, repeat the instructions in the preceding section for measuring network utilization, except this time display Broadcast Frames Received/Second:

1. Right-click in the graph pane, and select Add Counters.
2. Check Use Local Computer Counters.
3. Select the performance object named Network Segment.
4. Select the counter named Broadcast Frames Received/Second.
5. Select All Instances, and click Add.
6. Select Close.

You must monitor your network periodically to determine what a normal level of broadcasts is, but if you find more than 10 per second on an average workgroup LAN, a computer on the LAN is probably misconfigured. You can try shutting down computers one at a time to find the culprit.

If you want Windows to keep an eye on these values for you while you do something else, you can set up an alert to notify you any time a specific counter goes above or below a value. To do so, follow these steps:

1. Right-click My Computer, and select Manage.
2. Select Performance Logs and Alerts, and then select Alerts.
3. In the right pane, right-click and select New Alert Settings.
4. Give a name to the alert settings, such as `Watch Network Utilization`.

5. On the General tab, enter a comment such as `Watch for utilization over 40%`.

6. Select Add, and add a set of counters using steps 2 through 6 as I described in the section "Measuring Network Utilization," for example, to add the network segment utilization. You can add any counters you want to monitor.

7. Back on the General tab, select the first listed counter. After Alert When the Value Is:, select Over, and enter an appropriate Limit value—for example, `40` for network segment utilization. Repeat this step for *each counter*.

8. Select the Action tab, and choose Log an Entry in the Application Event Log, and/or Send a Network Message To. If you choose to send a network message, add the login name of the user to receive the pop-up alert message—for example, Administrator.

9. Click OK.

Windows then watches the designated setting or settings and makes an Event Log entry and/or sends a pop-up message to the designated user whenever a listed counter exceeds the specified Limit value.

You can stop and start monitoring of alerts by right-clicking the named alert entry in the right pane and selecting Stop or Start.

Tips from the Windows Pros: Monitoring Your LAN

As businesses increasingly rely on computers by the thousands, flung far and wide around the globe, the job of managing them—that is, monitoring, identifying, and correcting problems—has become an industry of its own. *Enterprise management* is a hot expression in the computer industry now. *Very* pricey software systems have been developed to centrally monitor computers, networks, hubs, routing hardware, UPSs, and even computer room fire alarms. These systems detect problems and can notify staff via pager, email, printouts, or, who knows, probably even carrier pigeon.

The purpose of these systems is to catch problems as they develop, with any luck, before they disrupt people trying to do their work.

Instrumentation is the key here: Equipment has to be designed to be monitored. A TCP/IP-based protocol called Simple Network Management Protocol (SNMP) has been around for years, and "managed" network equipment is capable of being probed and reconfigured via SNMP. Along with this capability comes a hefty price tag, but the net cost of maintaining and dispatching staff to fix problems is much greater.

My small LAN with four users and a handful of development and online servers doesn't need a $20,000 management system, managed hubs, and the like. But, even in my little office, I find myself constantly checking to make sure the servers are up, that they have plenty of disk space, and that the Internet connection is working. What I really want is something to check these things periodically and let me know whether something's amiss.

Part
IV

Ch
27

I guess plenty of other people do, too. Free enterprise is a wonderful thing. I searched the Web and found a handful of packages targeted for small LANs just like mine. If you have a LAN you depend on for your business, you might want to check them out. Hearing about a problem from your pager is a lot nicer than hearing about it from a client or an employee!

Using these products, you can specify a series of computers or devices to be periodically tested. The tests can include `ping`, SNMP, file sharing services, Windows Service activity, disk space availability, server responsiveness, and so on. Failures can be announced to a list of alert recipients via pager, email, or printout. (Different problems may call for different announcement methods, of course. If your LAN is down, an email alert won't get delivered.) Some products can even send announcements to selected employees based on their work schedules.

Using these tools, you can enter a list of your most important network servers and other resources, and rest assured that if something goes wrong with any of them, you'll be notified immediately.

The following are a few products worth investigating. Each of these programs can detect whether a remote server is active, can test various types of network services (for example, file sharing, Web services, and so on), and can send a message to a pager if a failure occurs.

- Enterprise Monitor

    www.mediahouse.com/enterprisemonitor

    (Runs as a Windows Service.)

- Whatsup

    www.ipswitch.com/Products/WhatsUp/whatsup.html

- XperTrak Net

    know-it.com/xtnet.htm

- IPSentry

    www.ipsentry.com

- Servers Alive

    www.woodstone.nu/salive/

- AutoPing

    www.jordan.com/AutoPing/default.asp

Reviewing these products, I found that the product quality is roughly proportional to the price, and it's best, if possible, to use one that runs as a Windows service so that it can do its job even while nobody is logged in to the monitoring computer.

These products are not quite as sophisticated or well designed as their $20,000 cousins, but they might be just the ticket for a small office network.

System Configuration and Customization

CHAPTER 28

TWEAKING THE GUI

In this chapter

GUI: TO TWEAK OR NOT TO TWEAK

I wanted to start this chapter with something cute or meaningful, but all I could think was that, if you know what this title means, you qualify for the Geek-of-the-Year award. For the rest of you, let's get our minds out of the gutter; tweaking the GUI doesn't mean anything lascivious. This chapter describes the graphical user interface and some interesting, useful, and fun stuff you can do with it—changes to help increase your computing efficiency and perhaps even make your computer more fun to use.

As you know, the GUI is the translator that interprets human input into commands the computer can interpret. It's also responsible for displaying output from computer programs and the operating system so that you can understand the results. The Windows 2000 GUI is set up with factory defaults that 90 percent of users will never touch, despite its being highly programmable and easily modifiable through the Control Panel, Folder Options, Properties sheets, and add-on products. If you're a GUI hacker, you know who you are, and if all you want to do is get your work done, well, more power to you because you're the one who's going to get the raise. But playing with the GUI can be fun and can save you time and annoyance.

One of the best GUI hacks I've seen came in an email (yeah, I know I shouldn't run .exe files attached to mail, but I couldn't help myself), which appeared to turn the UI into a Mac booting up System 8. It had the smiley face and everything, and a message—complete with a progress bar—reading

```
Converting your operating system....
```

Scary, but funny.

→ If you want to run Mac apps under Windows 2000, you can. **See** "Macintosh and Windows," **p. 1324**.

Most folks won't modify their GUIs, but it's a shame they don't. Often, not even knowing there is a recourse, users develop headaches from screen flicker, eyestrain from tiny screen fonts, or they live with color schemes they detest. With a little effort, they can rectify these problems. Likewise, means for managing zip archives, altering the right-click Send To options, and handling numerous other functions users have to deal with every day are just a few clicks or Net downloads, Registry hacks, or Properties sheet settings away. Just for fun, you can choose from hundreds of desktop themes, screen savers, wallpaper images, and so on.

Some of this chapter deals with standard display options. Other portions deal with deeper GUI tweaks and tricks. Just skim for the part that interests you.

→ This chapter doesn't cover multimonitor support because it's related more to hardware upgrades than the GUI. **See** "Installing and Using Multiple Monitors," **p. 1104** for coverage of multiple monitors.

DISPLAY PROPERTIES

The most obvious means for altering your GUI settings is via the Display Properties dialog box. From there, you can reach a multitude of GUI settings, mostly affecting display rather than GUI functionality per se:

- Screen saver settings

- Desktop background

- Colors and fonts for GUI elements

- Active Desktop setting

- Color depth and resolution

- Special GUI effects such as menu sliding

- Energy-saving settings

- Device drivers

- Advanced properties such as hardware acceleration

You can most easily reach the display properties by right-clicking the desktop and choosing Properties. The resulting dialog box is shown in Figure 28.1.

Figure 28.1
You can alter a multitude of display attributes from the Display Properties dialog box. Programs such as virus protectors that you have added might introduce additional tabs to this dialog.

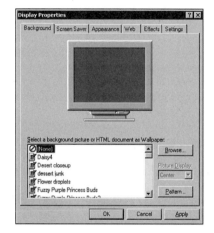

Note

You can also get to the display properties from the Control Panel.

I'll briefly describe this dialog box tab by tab. You've probably used it, so I won't belabor it; however, I will point out the basics and mention any specifics you should be aware of.

BACKGROUND TAB

Normally, you set the background color for your desktop via the Appearance tab. (Check the color setting there for Desktop.) However, many folks like to put up a picture of their pets or favorite nebula as the desktop "wallpaper." To do so, you can just click a picture in the list on the Background tab and click OK to close the box. The None setting defers to the colors in the Appearance tab, whereas any picture you choose will override that color, effectively putting it into the background, showing up only as the color in desktop icon names.

PART

V

CH

28

The picture you want to use probably isn't in the \winnt directory and most likely isn't a .bmp file. On the first score, you're covered. You can just use the Browse button and cruise around to find the picture you want. The second score is trickier. Normally, Windows 2000 doesn't support JPEG images for wallpaper—just BMP and HTML. If you try to load a JPEG or GIF image as wallpaper, you see an error message, like the one shown in Figure 28.2.

Figure 28.2
Active Desktop has to be turned on for JPEG or GIF files to be displayed as wall-paper.

If you do turn on Active Desktop so that you can load such an image, and you want to be able to see the whole image, be sure you don't also have some other Web content (such as your home page) assigned to your Active Desktop. If you do, the wallpaper image will be obscured by the Web page. You *can* effectively mix and match some smaller Active Desktop items and wallpaper. In Figure 28.3, for example, notice that the constantly updated Microsoft stock ticker is running in front of the wallpaper.

Figure 28.3
A JPEG image—taken with a digital cam-era—has been added to the desktop, along with the Microsoft ticker applet.

Active Desktop can be a system resource hog, however, and I generally don't recommend that you use it unless you really insist on having the latest weather, airfares, sports, news, or stock prices scrolling across your desktop at the expense of system performance. A better solution is to turn off Active Desktop and use almost any decent image program (even shareware programs such as ThumbsPlus or PaintShop Pro) to convert your GIF or JPEG images to BMP format.

After you select the image, you can wallpaper by using a single copy of the picture placed in the center of the screen; by tiling, which gives you multiple identical pictures covering the whole screen; or by stretching, which enlarges a picture smaller than your screen resolution so that it fills the screen. Stretching causes the picture to pixilate, so if you want it to look good, make sure to shoot the picture at, or convert it to, a size roughly matching the resolution setting of your display. Then choose the Center option.

 If you've used a photo as a background for your desktop, but it appears blocky, see "Stretched a Bit Thin" in the "Troubleshooting" section at the end of this chapter.

Tip #311	If the image is larger than the screen's resolution, stretching actually shrinks the image to fully fit on the desktop. If stretching is turned off, and the image is larger than the screen, the image is cropped (the edges are cut off).

USING A PATTERN AS A BACKGROUND

Like wallpaper, patterns can be used as a backdrop to the desktop, too, but the advantage is that they consume less memory. Certain patterns, such as Waffle, also make it hard to read your icons. For a pattern to show up, wallpaper has to be set to None in the Background tab because wallpaper always sits on top of the desktop's pattern.

If you don't like the supplied patterns, you can get maniacal and edit one. To do so, set Wallpaper to None, click Pattern, click the pattern you want to use, and click Edit. A new dialog box appears. What you are doing is defining the smallest element of the repeated pattern (a cell). It is blown up in scale to make editing easier. Each click reverses the color of one pixel. The effect when the pattern is applied across a larger area and in normal size is shown in the Sample section to the right. When you like the pattern, click Change to change an existing pattern, or give it a new name and click Add. The pattern is then added to your list of patterns. Finally, click Done.

Patterns always contain only one color plus black. The color is determined by the desktop background color as set on the Appearance tab.

SCREEN SAVER TAB

We all know what screen savers are. On the Screen Saver tab, you can choose from several supplied screen savers and perhaps others that you have installed from other sources. In the old days when phosphors would "burn," screen savers actually did something useful. They prevented a ghost of the image on the screen from being burned into the screen for all time, no matter what is being displayed. Most modern CRTs don't actually need a screen saver to save anything because the phosphors are more durable. And LCDs don't need them either because they don't have any phosphors on the screen at all.

So, what good is a screen saver nowadays, you ask? Well, some older monitor/card combinations go into low-power states when the screen is blanked, so if you choose Blank Screen, there could be some advantage.

The SETI@home Screen Saver

Interested in space exploration? Think life might exist on other planets? If you want to become part of the largest global experiment in massive parallel processing, you can download the SETI@home screen saver to harness your computer's otherwise wasted CPU cycles to sift through signals from outer space, searching for signs of intelligent life out there. (Go to `http://setiathome.ssl.berkeley.edu/` if you're interested in participating.)

SETI@home is a scientific experiment that harnesses the power of hundreds of thousands of Internet-connected computers in the Search for Extraterrestrial Intelligence (SETI). The screen saver downloads and analyzes radio telescope data captured at the world's largest radio telescope in Arecibo, Puerto Rico. It's then shipped to the University of California on 35GB nine-track tape and doled out over the Internet to the participating users. There's a small but captivating possibility that your computer will detect the faint murmur of a civilization beyond Earth.

Your computer, after it is connected to the Internet, gets a "work unit" of interstellar noise downloaded to it from the SETI@home server and starts analyzing it when the screen saver comes up. A work unit requires approximately 20 hours of computing time on a typical Pentium-class computer. If an unnatural noise is detected, you and the people back at the University of California will be alerted. The scientists will attempt to confirm the finding by doing their own analysis and ruling out man-made radio sources such as radar. If it is finally confirmed, you and the team can pack up and head for Sweden to pick up your Nobel Prize. If nothing is found (which is somewhat more likely), the screen saver prompts you to connect to the Internet to download the next work unit.

As of this writing, more than a million computers were participating. This huge, collective-computing model will no doubt set the standard on which massively parallel-processing experiments using small computers will be based in the future. Using what could be called "CPU charities," researchers in many different fields, from medicine to ecology, could have computing power well beyond today's supercomputers at their disposal. This power can be, in essence, donated by computer owners for solving complex mathematical and scientific problems.

Now that beats flying toasters, doesn't it?

Because far too many people leave their computers on all the time (it's not really true that they will last longer that way), efforts have been made by power regulators and electronics manufacturers to devise computer energy-conservation schemes. And, of course, some screen savers are fun to watch. The 3D-Pipes that comes with Windows 2000 Professional is pretty mesmerizing actually.

Some screen savers are mindless; others are more interesting. Some, such as the Marquee, have additional options, such as font, size, and color. You can check out each one as the spirit moves you. Just highlight it on this tab, and click Preview. Don't move the mouse until you're ready to stop the preview.

Screen savers have an .scr extension and are stored in the winnt\system32 folder. Do a search (WIN+F) and look for *.scr. You'll find a bunch of them. On a *dual-boot* machine with Windows 9x, you'll have some in the Windows directory, too. Most files are 100KB or smaller in size.

Double-clicking a screen saver from any window runs it. Just press a key or click the mouse to stop it from running. Many of the .scr files in the Windows directory of a dual-boot machine don't run because of missing DLLs, but some of the simpler ones do. To get a screen saver listed in the dialog box, you have to move it into the winnt\system32 folder, though.

The Web is littered with screen savers. Just do a search. The following are some sources:

- Screen Saver Heaven:
  http://www.galttech.com/ssheaven.shtml
- Screen Savers Bonanza:
  http://www.bonanzas.com/ssavers/

Between those two sources alone, you have access to more than 2,500 screen savers.

The Screen Saver Control Panel supplied with Windows 2000 Professional is pretty lame compared to some other utilities you can download for free. One, called Screen Control by Galt Technology, is pretty useful. Screen Control is a utility that sits in your system tray and lets you run, configure, select, and disable your screen savers. Double-click it, and it launches your current screen saver. Right-click menu choices let you control other goodies, as you can see in Figure 28.4.

Figure 28.4
Utility programs such as this one help you take control of screen savers if you're a collector of such things.

→ The Energy Star settings for monitors are covered under the Power applet discussion. **See** " Power Options," **p. 1063**.

Tip #312	In NT4, you could set a screen saver to work between logins. That is, when the logon box was onscreen, the screen saver could run. Setting the screen saver to work this way required patching the Registry, but it worked. Patching is a terrible idea because it allows a user to install a screen saver that could have a trojan horse virus in it or provide a "back door" into the system. Windows 2000 doesn't allow tampering with this setting, as far as I know, and you should not even attempt to set up a screen saver for the logon screen. Screen savers should be set up only for individual users after they log in.

APPEARANCE TAB

From the Appearance tab (see Figure 28.5), you can seriously alter the look of your entire Windows machine. You can do some serious mischief here, creating some egregious color schemes. Or you can design or choose schemes that improve readability on screens (or eyes) with certain limitations. If, perchance, you're using a monochrome monitor (no color), altering the colors may still have some effect (the amount depends on how you installed Windows), so these settings are not just for systems with color screens.

Figure 28.5
You can click an area of the example to set the color, font, or font size of the Windows screen element.

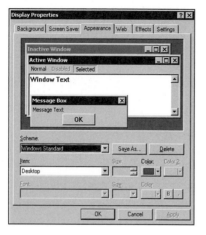

Unless you're upgrading over a preexisting system, your desktop is set to the Windows Standard default color scheme, which is fine for most screens and users. In days past, I made a point of changing the scheme to move out of the "Microsoft blues," which I used to find too cold. But that scheme has grown on me in the past years. I used to soften everything a bit into the beige tones, finding them more relaxing on the eyes.

The color settings options are very flexible and easy to modify. If you're very particular about color choices, you can modify them manually, choosing colors from a palette or even mixing your own with the Custom Colors feature. After they're created, custom colors and color setups can be saved on disk for later use or automatically loaded with each Windows session. For more expedient color reassignments, you can choose from a number of supplied "canned" color schemes.

Note that some elements allow adjusting metrics (size) as well as color. If you have trouble clicking window borders (because they are too small), you can increase the size of that element. Divisions are in screen pixels.

Tip #313

You don't have to choose a scheme and click Apply to see each one. Just click in the Scheme field; then press the up- or down-arrow key to move through the list. The sample elements in the dialog box change to display the color scheme.

Microsoft has incorporated a few color schemes that may make some LCD screens easier to read in challenging lighting or for people who have vision problems. Check out the large and high-contrast schemes.

If you tweak the colors to your liking by altering a scheme, you can save it as a new scheme so that you can go back to the factory-supplied one later if you need to. Just click Save As and name the scheme.

Choosing a color called Other brings up the Color Refiner dialog box. You work with two cursors here. One is the *luminosity bar*, and the other is the *color refiner cursor* (which looks like a crosshair).

You simply drag around these cursors one at a time until the color in the box at the lower left is the shade you want. As you do so, the numbers in the boxes below the color refiner change.

- *Luminosity* is the amount of brightness in the color.
- *Hue* is the actual shade or color. All colors are composed of red, green, and blue.
- *Saturation* is the degree of purity of the color; it is decreased by adding gray to the color and increased by subtracting gray.

You can also type in the numbers or click the arrows next to the numbers if you want, but using the cursors is easier. When you like the color, you can save a color for future use by clicking Add to Custom Colors.

EFFECTS TAB

Introduced in Windows 9x, the Effects tab lets you make some fun changes to the GUI by changing desktop icons and setting some attractive visual effects. If you install some theme manager software, you needn't bother with changing icons most likely, unless you want to change individual icons on-the-fly.

To change an icon, click the icon and then click the Change button. The Change Icon dialog box appears (see Figure 28.6). Explorer.exe is the default .exe file from which potential icons are shown, which is kind of dumb because it contains only about 10 icons. Clear the filename and click OK. You then see a much larger icon collection, stored in shell32.dll from the \system32\ folder. Just click the one you want, and your icon is replaced.

Figure 28.6
You can choose new icons for specific desktop items. Clear the location, and click OK to default to this set.

The applet is looking for .dll, .exe, or .ico files. You might be surprised how many .ico files you have on your computer. Do a search and check it out. If you have a dual-boot machine with another Windows version, you'll have a bunch from it as well. I did a search just now and came up with 211 to choose from. If you set the result display to "large icons," you'll have something like what you see in Figure 28.7. Note the folder and filename of the icon you want because you'll have to browse for it on the Effects tab to load it. (Dragging and dropping doesn't work.)

Figure 28.7
You can conduct a search for icons using *.ico as the search criteria.

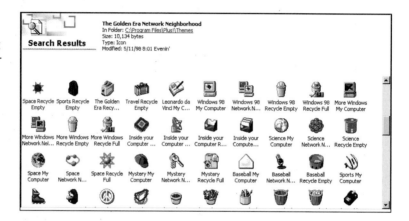

As with screen savers, the Net is littered with icons. Apparently, lots of people have time on their hands and think icons are cute. Do a search for icons, and you'll find literally thousands of them. Typically, they are only about 10KB in size, so you needn't worry about sacrificing too much disk space for them.

Tip #314

If you want to rename a system desktop icon such as My Computer, no fancy Registry hacking is required. Just right-click the item, and choose Rename.

SPECIAL EFFECTS

The special effects settings are just for fun:

Use Transition Effects	Specifies whether to activate animations for menu and file commands. Animations change the appearance of menus and windows when you open and close them.
Smooth Edges of Fonts	Specifies whether to smooth edges of large Screen fonts to make screen fonts more readable. To use this option, you must have a video card and monitor that support a minimum of 256 colors. For best results, your video card and monitor should support high color (16-bit color).

Use Large Icons	Specifies whether to use large icons to represent files, folders, and shortcuts on your desktop. Large icons require more memory than do smaller icons. If you notice a decrease in performance, clear this check box.
Show Icons Using All Possible Colors	Specifies whether to display desktop icons using all the colors supported by your current display and your color palette settings. Again, this option uses more memory, and on a slower video system or computer, it can possibly make icon dragging a bit sluggish.
Show Windows Contents While Dragging	Specifies whether to display window contents as you move or size it. When this check box is cleared, you can see only the outline when you move a window. If you are running in a high color depth (24- or 30-bit) on a slow system, it will be annoying and jerky.
Hide Keyboard Navigation Indicators Until I Use the Alt Key	Specifies whether to suppress the drawing of keyboard shortcuts (the underlined characters in menus and controls) and input focus indicators (the dotted rectangles around objects) until you actually start using the keyboard to navigate in Windows, generally with the Alt, Tab, or arrow keys. I prefer to turn off this option so that I can always see the shortcut key indicator and the active focus object.

WEB TAB

The Web tab of the Display Properties dialog box pertains to Active Desktop, which was introduced with Internet Explorer 4. Like PointCast and Marimba, Active Desktop is based on *push* technology and lets you put live Web content on your desktop, either in small applet windows or covering the bulk of the desktop (for example, a Web page such as MSN.COM). With Active Desktop, you can set up wallpaper that can sport decorative items, ActiveX controls, Dynamic HTML pages, WebCast sites, Java applets, and Microsoft Active Channels. The different components in the wallpaper can be set as separate, resizable windows.

When Microsoft IE4 first appeared a few years ago, the term *push* was bandied about with great enthusiasm. Advertisers hoped that push was to become the technology that would convert your computer to something more like TV, promising advertisers and content providers a semipassive, semicaptive, audience. Microsoft's version of push (Active Desktop) used the otherwise wasted space of the desktop as the canvas for the live Web content. The concept sounded great, but it flopped because the desktop was usually obscured, the applets weren't very useful, and performance of the desktop and stability of the operating system were adversely affected.

Alternative push applets that don't rely on the Active Desktop have appeared, some of which are worth trying. Check out the MSNBC NewsAlert or other ones from popular Web sites such as CNET.com (look for "desktop news") and PointCast, now known as EntryPoint (check pointcast.com). I like the EntryPoint toolbar, incidentally. It's a groovy tool for finding news, checking maps, remembering myriad passwords and credit card numbers for online shopping, and checking portfolio and entertainment goodies such as movie times and theaters.

Figure 28.8 shows an example of Active Desktop Web content. Here, I've added a national weather map and a stock and news ticker (which is actually pretty useful if you micromanage your investments). Clicking a city on the map brings up a Web page with forecasts and such. Clicking a news story in the ticker likewise brings up a Web page about the story. This behavior is typical of Active Desktop applets.

Figure 28.8
Active Desktop objects can be useful, although they make your desktop act a bit sluggish and can cause system slow-down or erratic behavior at times.

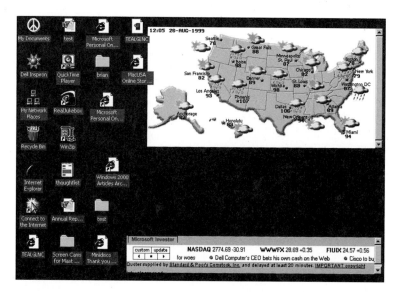

Tip #315

> You can always press WIN+M to clear windows off the desktop and see your Active Desktop and then press Shift+WIN+M to return the windows.

To see how this feature works, click the Web tab, and turn on Show Web Content. Then click New. You then see the Active Desktop Wizard. Click Gallery to go to the Microsoft site that lists some Active Desktop content. Typically, an Active Desktop applet has instructions on the Web page that supplies it.

After you add an item to the Active Desktop, you can position it by hovering your mouse pointer over its upper edge. A frame appears around the object, letting you grab it, and in some cases open menus, close the window, and so on.

After you turn on the Active Desktop feature, Web content is displayed or can be added to your desktop. When you right-click a blank space on the desktop and choose Active Desktop, additional menu options also become available, enabling you to customize and update desktop items.

- Show Web Content turns on the Active Desktop feature.
- Show Desktop Icons displays icons on the desktop or hides them to prevent them from obscuring your Active Desktop windows.
- Lock Desktop Items secures the size and location of Active Desktop items. When this option is selected, Active Desktop items can't be moved or resized.
- Synchronize updates the content of your Active Desktop items.

You can use the Web tab in the Display Properties dialog to turn on or off any content you added, at will. Keeping them in the list but unchecked makes it easy to reactivate push applets later. Uncheck Show Web Content to turn them all off until you're moved again to activate the Active Desktop.

DESKTOP THEMES

Enough for the settings you can make from the Display Properties dialog. How else can you spiff up your user interface? One way is to use *themes*. Themes are collections of icons, sounds, screen savers, and cursors for your Windows 2000 Professional setup. Themes are not much different from what you can achieve by using the related applets in the Control Panel and the icon and desktop settings described previously; using them is just easier when a collection of them is integrated. You can just snap in a theme all at once. Windows 9x provided themes support as part of the Plus! add-on software from Microsoft. By switching a UI theme, you can easily change the whole look and feel of the computer, including error message sounds, desktop background, and so on.

Windows NT didn't have a Plus! program, but you could still incorporate themes using third-party software. However, popular programs for doing so, such as themes.exe from the NT Resource Kit or any other program, do not work until they are updated for Windows 2000. You must resort to changing icons via the Effects tab in the Display Properties dialog because Windows 2000 uses yet another set of new Registry keys that can override HKEY_CLASSES_ROOT entries for special folders.

Windows 2000 setup installs keys at this new location for the Recycle Bin right out of the gate. The complete story is complicated, but the bottom line is that existing utilities cannot update the Recycle Bin icons unless they are updated for Windows 2000. The same applies to My Computer and Network Neighborhood if you ever change them using the Effects tab because Windows 2000 uses the new "super duper" override keys.

So, if you're interested in a program for managing themes on your Windows 2000 Professional machine, make sure it's compatible. Microangelo 2000 is one that works quite well, as does Desktop Architect.

Tip #316	The following are some good places to look for themes:
	Theme Doctor:
	www.themedoctor.com
	Rembrandt:
	http://www.themeworld.com/cgi-bin/redir.pl/rembrndt.zip
	Desktop Architect: Free theme management program, ready for Windows 2000
	http://home1.gte.net/fosterk/da/index.htm
	Microangelo: Extensive theme control, multiuser support, custom desktop folders, and more:
	http://www.impactsoft.com/

SETTINGS TAB

On the Settings tab of the Display Properties dialog box, you can tweak the video driver's most basic settings, such as color depth, refresh rate, and overall desktop size (resolution). These settings are made at a deeper level in the operating system than are the color, font sizes, themes, and so on. Figure 28.9 shows the settings available on the tab.

Figure 28.9
The Settings tab of the Display Properties dialog box controls the video card's device driver. In Windows 2000 Professional, color palette and screen resolution can be adjusted on-the-fly.

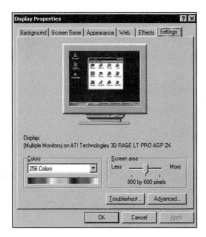

COLOR PALETTE

Assuming your video display card has been properly identified by Windows 2000 Professional, the Colors drop-down list box should include all the legitimate options your card is capable of. Your color depth options are limited by the amount of video RAM on the card and the resolution you choose. The higher the resolution, the more memory is used for pixel addressing, limiting the pixel depth (number of colors that can be displayed per pixel). With many modern cards, this limitation is no biggie, and it's likely that many Windows 2000 Professional users will not have to worry about it except in cases when they have large monitors displaying 1600×1024 and want 32-bit color *and* a high refresh rate. Anyway, the point is that you might have to bow to certain limitations of your card. If you find that setting the color scheme up to high color or true color causes the resolution slider to move left, this is the reason. All modern analog color monitors for PCs are capable of displaying 16 million colors, which is dubbed true color.

You must click the Apply button before the changes are made. When you do, you are warned about the possible effects. The good thing about the new no-reboot video subsystem is that the driver settings should revert within 15 seconds unless you accept them. So, if the screen goes blank or otherwise goes bananas, just wait. It should return to the previous setting.

Tip #317	Unless you have a very fast computer or an intelligent coprocessed AGP video card, you will find that running in true color at a high resolution, such as 1280×1024 or even 1024×768, can be annoying if you have full-window drag turned on (see "Special Effects" earlier in this chapter). When you move a window, it moves jerkily across the screen as your computer tries to redraw the screen image. Drop the color depth to high color or 256 colors (if you don't look at photos much), and you'll be amazed at the improvement in redraw speed.

SCREEN AREA

The Screen Area setting on the Settings tab is something Windows 3.x upgraders will love because, in that operating system, an entirely different driver was required to change the screen resolution. Obviously, we all want to cram as much on the screen as possible without going blind. This setting lets you experiment and even change resolution on-the-fly to best display whatever you're working on. Some jobs, such as working with large spreadsheets, databases, CAD, or typesetting, are much more efficient with more data displayed on the screen. Because higher resolutions require a trade-off in clarity and make onscreen objects smaller, you can minimize eyestrain by going to a lower resolution, such as 640×480 pixels (a pixel is essentially one dot on the screen).

 If you've changed the screen area only to find that you can no longer see some icons or open windows on the desktop, see "Where Did Those Icons Go?" in the "Troubleshooting" section at the end of this chapter.

 If, after toying with the screen resolution, you notice that your once-speedy computer seems to have lost its zip, see "Moving in Slow Motion" in the "Troubleshooting" section at the end of this chapter.

This setting lets you decide as you work. Again, if you find the dialog box doesn't let you choose the resolution you want, drop the color palette setting down a notch and try again.

<table>
<tr><td>Tip #318</td><td>All laptop and notebook computers and LCD monitors have screens that are optimized for one resolution, called the native resolution. Unless a laptop computer is hooked up to an external monitor, don't bother changing the setting from the native, sometimes called suggested, resolution. Choosing a lower one results in blocky display (though still usable in some cases because of intelligent engineering that provides antialiasing). Trying a higher resolution definitely does not work. Check the computer's or monitor's manual if you're in doubt about which external monitor resolutions are supported.</td></tr>
</table>

 If you've connected an external TV monitor to your computer but cannot read the fonts on the screen, see "What Does That Say?" in the "Troubleshooting" section at the end of this chapter.

FONT SIZE

When you switch to a high resolution, such as 1280×1024, some screen elements such as icon names can get quite small and difficult to read. For this reason, you can adjust the font size. Of course, you can do so for some elements such as title bars and dialog boxes via the Fonts settings on the Appearance tab as discussed earlier. Some icon names aren't touched by that change. For a one-stop shop, click the Advanced button on the Settings tab, and look at the Fonts drop-down list on the resulting dialog. Bump the setting up a notch if you want to check out the possible improvement. For any resolution above 640×480, your choices are Small, Large, and Other. Especially for resolutions of 1024×768 or above, you might want to try the Large Fonts.

If you want, you can also choose a custom size font by clicking the Custom button, which lets you declare an amount that you want the fonts scaled up. The range is from 20 percent to 500 percent (of normal). Note that changing screen fonts requires rebooting (and possibly inserting the setup CD).

OTHER ADVANCED SETTINGS

A few other advanced settings are worth examining. On the General tab, notice the reboot options. Unless you have a reason to believe otherwise (that is, your video driver requires it), choose the second or third option. Having to reboot is a nuisance.

On the Adapter tab, the List All Modes button is useful if you're interested in knowing what resolutions, color depths, and refresh rates your adapter card (not your monitor, mind you) is capable of, using the currently installed video driver. (See Figure 28.10.)

Figure 28.10
Here, you can check out the modes your video card and driver combo are capable of producing.

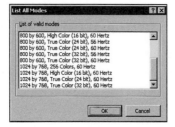

Next, click the Monitor tab, and look at the refresh frequency. For CRTs, you'll want it to be at least 70Hz (cycles per second) to avoid flicker and the resulting eyestrain and headache. Go to 72 or 75Hz if your monitor and card can handle that. Experiment a bit. Sometimes at a higher refresh rate, even if a monitor can handle it, characters begin to blur horizontally because the slew rate of the electronics in the monitor (and possibly the digital-to-analog converters, or DACs, and associated hardware on the card) can't handle the higher line-drawing (raster) speed. In that case, drop it down a notch. But anything less than 70Hz is visible, even if only slightly so.

 If the screen flicker really annoys you, see "Reducing Screen Flicker" in the "Troubleshooting" section at the end of the chapter.

Tip #319	Contrary to some advertising accompanying new flat-panel monitors, LCDs don't give a hoot about high refresh speed. In fact, they don't like high speeds. LCDs use a completely different technology, typically with a transistor for each pixel. The dots don't have to be refreshed as they do in a CRT. I noticed a blurry display on a desktop LCD screen once and tracked down the problem to a 72Hz refresh rate on the video card. I lowered it to 60Hz, and the image cleared up. This advice applies only to LCDs that are attached to analog display cards. Some outboard LCD monitors are driven by their own digital adapter cards, and refresh settings don't affect those cards.

Caution	If you specify a refresh rate that is too high for your monitor, it could damage the monitor. Also, trying to expand the desktop area to a larger size may not work. You just get a mess on the screen. If you have this problem, try using a setting with a lower refresh rate, such as 60Hz or "interlaced." The image may flicker a bit more, but at least it will be visible.

 If, while you're tinkering with the refresh rates for your monitor, the monitor goes blank, don't panic; instead, see "Uh-Oh, My Monitor Died" in the "Troubleshooting" section at the end of this chapter.

 If, after you install a new LCD monitor, you discover that the image is blurry, see "Blurry Images in LCD" in the "Troubleshooting" section at the end of this chapter.

→ If you have a new driver for your display card or monitor and want to install it, **see** " Updating Device Drivers," **p. 1102**.

TWEAK UI

Many Windows experts have become fond of an unsupported Microsoft product called Tweak UI, which is available and freely downloadable from the Microsoft site. Tweak UI is one of the Microsoft "Power Toys" developed by programmers at Camp Bill in Redmond, Washington. Reports are that it works fine in 2000. Versions are available for both Windows 9x and NT. A 2000 version also adds some features. The Windows 98 version requires you to have a Windows 98 CD-ROM, so downloading the NT/Windows 2000 version from the Web would be better. If you happen to be in possession of the Windows 2000 Corporate Preview Program, you'll find a copy of Tweak UI (for 2000) on one of the CDs.

PART

V

CH

28

Tweak UI enables you to make over 100 changes to the Windows 2000 operating system. For example, you can do the following:

- Scroll smoothly in Windows Explorer
- Add special folders to your operating system that have mouse setting refinements
- Add more types of "New" documents when you right-click a folder and choose New
- Add or remove installed programs
- Repair system files, font folders, and icons
- Cover your tracks by erasing temp files, document lists, and history files
- Control whether CDs play automatically when you insert a disk
- Add or remove drives from being displayed in My Computer

The program is easy to use. I downloaded my version from Tucows at

`http://tucows.apollo.lv/shellnt.html`

(You'll also find lots of other system-tweaking programs at this site, by the way.)

If that doesn't work, just use a search engine and look for Tweak UI.

After you download the program, put it in its own folder and run it. A DOS box appears momentarily while an extraction takes place. You end up with several icons (I had six) in the folder, including Help and a readme file. Check the readme file for the latest scoop. Then check the Control Panel. The program should install itself and be reachable from the Control Panel. If it's not, then go back to the Tweak UI folder, look for the file tweakui.inf, right-click it, and choose Install.

Your Control Panel now includes a new icon for the Tweak UI applet. When you run it, you see the dialog box displayed in Figure 28.11.

Figure 28.11
You'll find lots of fun stuff to play with here!

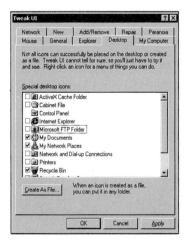

Note

If you want to uninstall Tweak UI, be sure to read its Help file under How to Uninstall.

The following are issues with Tweak UI as it pertains to NT and Windows 2000:

- If you do not have permission to alter the list of drives that appear in My Computer, the My Computer tab is not shown.

- You don't have a Boot tab because Tweak UI doesn't support editing the Windows NT BOOT.INI file. You can use the System Control Panel applet's Startup/Shutdown tab to edit the BOOT.INI file instead.

- You don't have a Repair Associations Now button because Tweak UI doesn't support repairing standard icons and associations under Windows NT. However, Windows 2000 is pretty good at fixing broken shortcuts all on its own.

- Depending on the security permissions granted to the current user, some Tweak UI features may not have any effect. For example, if the current user doesn't have permission to edit the part of the Registry that contains the desktop, then changes to the desktop don't have any result.

POWER TOYS

If you want to go all the way and get wild with your operating system, you can download the entire Power Toys kit (of which Tweak UI is but a part), and get the following applets:

- CabView—Treat .CAB files like ordinary folders.
- CDAutoPlay—Make AutoPlay work on any nonaudio CD.
- Command Prompt—Start a command prompt in the folder of your choice with the click of a button.
- Contents Menu—Get to your files without having to open their folders.
- Desktop Menu—Open items on your desktop from a convenient menu on the taskbar.
- Explore From Here—Open Windows Explorer no matter where you are on the network or on your own computer's file system.
- FindX 1.2—Add drag-and-drop capabilities to your Find menu.
- FlexiCD—Play an audio CD from the taskbar.
- Round Clock—Create a round analog clock without a square window.
- Send To X 1.2—Use this updated version of Send To Any Folder.
- Shortcut Target Menu—Find out the properties for the file to which a shortcut is pointing.
- Telephony Location Selector—Change your dialing location from the taskbar if you're a mobile computer user.
- Xmouse 1.2—Make the focus follow your mouse without clicking in the same way X Window System does for Linux users.

PART

V

CH

28

The entire Power Toys download is available from the Microsoft site or other popular download sites such as www.download.com. Note that the Windows 95 version is compatible with NT. Not all features may work fully with Windows 2000 Professional, and some of the features, such as Desktop Menu, are already integrated into Windows 2000 Professional, so you don't need to use them all. But some of them, such as CabView and Send To X, are priceless.

After you install Send To X, check out the right-click menu choices when clicking a file (see Figure 28.12). Of particular interest are the Send to Desktop, Send to Folder, Send to Clipboard as Name, and Send to Clipboard as Contents options. When you choose Send to Folder, you get a Browse box. Pretty handy.

Figure 28.12
Send To X is a Power Toys add-on that modifies the right-click menu. Note the additional destination choices for the selected item.

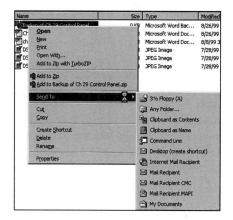

MISCELLANEOUS GUI TIPS

The following sections provide some general tips to help you soup up your Windows 2000 installation.

 If you've become really frustrated because single clicks are interpreted by Windows as double-clicks (and you can't seem to find any mention of the problem in this chapter), never fear; there's an easy solution. See "Single- or Double-Click?" in the "Troubleshooting" section at the end of this chapter.

FONTS PREVIEW TRICK

Chapter 10, "Font Management," explained how you can bring up a Properties sheet for each font and examine the look of the font; however, this technique is a bit cumbersome. Here is a tip for a preview feature you might not have known about.

You must set your interface options to single-click (see the discussion in Chapter 5, "Using the Windows Interface") for this feature to work. After you do that (from the Tools, Folder Options, General tab), when you browse to the Fonts folder, you have a Preview item on the View menu. After you select Preview, when you hover the mouse pointer over a font, a preview of the font is displayed (see Figure 28.13).

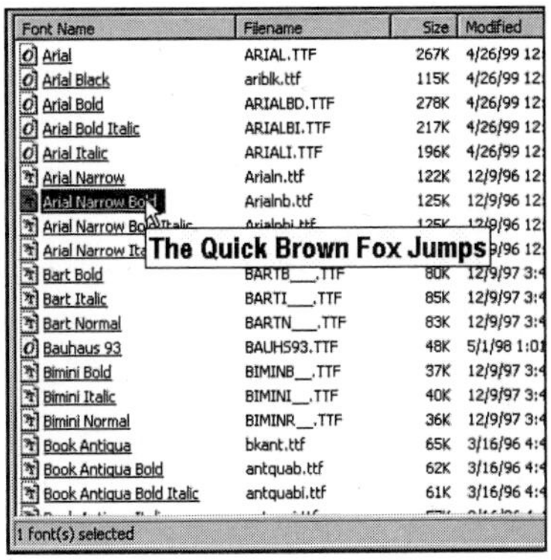

Figure 28.13
You can preview a font just by pointing to it.

Tip #320

Do you hate the personalized menu system and want to turn it off? Just right-click an empty part of the taskbar, choose Properties, click the Start Menu Options tab, and turn off Use Personalized Menus. Now all groups and programs show up. See Chapter 5 for more details about personalized menus.

A BETTER EXPLORER

You don't have to be a pack rat to collect thousands of files on your hard disk—nowadays, that's a cinch. Yet even in the old days with CP/M and DOS, there existed scads of utilities for organizing, archiving, editing, and viewing your files quickly. You might remember XTREE, Eureka, or CP/M Power, just to name a few. So why don't we have cool utilities like this today? Somehow, in Windows, we all got slowed down a bit, even though the GUI lets us drag and drop things in some fairly ingenious ways. But changing drives, opening a file for quick viewing, zipping and unzipping, or quickly formatting a floppy isn't as easy as it should be.

If you're feeling hamstrung by Windows Explorer, check out a fabulous program called DiskJockey, from Clear and Simple Software. If Microsoft wants my advice, I'd say it should buy this product and incorporate it into Windows. It has built-in Zip capability and more than 200 file viewers that let you view documents and images really quickly without leaving the Explorer-like screen. It does this by adding a third pane on the right side of the screen for viewing. Toolbar buttons for printing, file viewing, playing an audio CD, and formatting a disk are all right up front. There's also a pane on the far left for choosing the drive without scrolling the folder pane up and down as is required in Explorer (see Figure 28.14). Top it off with a slew of intelligent preference settings, and you have a valuable time saver on your hands.

I love the ease and speed of viewing seemingly any kind of file—my old Procomm faxes, graphics, even the comments on certain EXE files that identify what they are. This program makes it a snap to pull text out of any file and place it on the clipboard, without having to open Word or some other word processing application.

Check the Web site at www.clear-simple.com to download a demo.

Figure 28.14
DiskJockey is a
replacement Explorer
with more than 200
built-in files viewers,
as well as many other
convenience features.

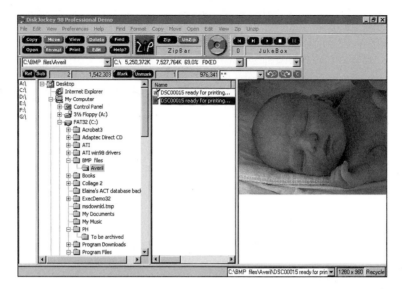

ONE-CLICK INTERNET ACCESS

Here's a software add-in that's a cross between a GUI tweak, a news service (such as
PointCast), and a browser extension. (Then again, who cares about these distinctions anymore?) Like many users, you probably tap the Web more than a few times a day to run a
search, look up a term in Webopedia, check your stock values, or book a flight. An ingenious little add-in to the Windows GUI called EntryPoint might be just the tool to achieve
these ends without the hassle of launching your browser, poring over some portal page
packed with links, or scanning your Favorites folder for a great site you used to figure out a
ZIP code last week.

After installation, a thin EntryPoint toolbar parks itself at your desktop (see Figure 28.15).
It's packed with more information than all your Favorites put together. You get one-click
access to stuff like news, weather, FedEx and UPS package tracking, CD and MP3 player,
research tools such as a thesaurus and dictionary, ZIP and area code lookup, entertainment
listings such as movie and TV listings, stocks, sports, shopping, and so on. There's also a
customizable news marquee with 20 or so actual news categories (not just today's price of
RAM chips). The links on the drop-down menus are essentially no different than those
offered by better portals such as Excite or Yahoo!, but the convenience factor is far greater.
The scrolling marquee for news, stock alerts, and such is a feature I like a lot.

The toolbar logs the user into the EntryPoint network, so this add-in is a live gadget. This
means the menu-based links are updated by the EntryPoint folks, so you don't end up
bumping into "404" errors (page not found), like you so often do with moldy old Favorites
you might have saved last year.

Figure 28.15
The EntryPoint toolbar gives you one-click access to tons of information and sports a scrolling news marquee.

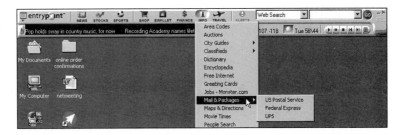

WHICH WINDOWS ARE YOU USING?

If you're dual-booting between Windows 9x and Windows 2000 Professional, you may sometimes wonder which operating system you're running at any given time because the GUIs of these two operating systems are now virtually indistinguishable. Yes, you'll see a few giveaways, such as My Network Places versus Network Neighborhood (assuming your desktop is visible), but in essential look and feel, the similarities easily outweigh the differences. The same goes for NT4.

To determine what's running, you could open the Control Panel, choose System, and read the dialog box. But that's a pain. Instead, you can use these techniques to remind yourself.

- Create a new document on the desktop, such as an empty Notepad file, and call it Windows 98, Windows 95, or Windows 2000. Put it in the lower right of the screen near the system clock. Do so for each operating system that the system boots. Of course, you have to get to the desktop to see this reminder, so the solution isn't perfect.

- For something that's always visible, how about using the position of the taskbar as a clue? You could place the taskbar on the bottom of the screen for Windows 9x and have it on the top of the screen for Windows 2000.

- Although many people like to turn off large icons on the first level of the Start menu (via taskbar Properties, Options), if you leave the large icons turned on, clicking Start displays the operating system name.

- Use the "company name" tip in the following section for putting the operating system name to the right of the system clock on the taskbar.

TWEAKING THE CLOCK TO ADD YOUR COMPANY NAME

You can put your company's name or abbreviation on the taskbar next to the clock, or even an identifier if you have different machines, different operating systems, or different departments. Here's how you do it:

1. Open the Regions applet in the Control Panel.

2. Click the Time tab.

3. Set the time format as hh:mm:ss tttttttt (each t is a placeholder for one character in your message, with eight characters max).

4. Set both AM and PM symbols to your message.

For example, I have mine set to AM - LUCID and PM - LUCID, which is the name of my company (see Figure 28.16). Because what you have effectively done is obliterated the display of AM or PM, you might want to change your time code to 24-hour format. Don't worry about time stamps being messed up in other programs, however. Windows internally uses 24-hour time codes, and even though Outlook Express mail may appear to go out stamped 8:07 LUCID, for example, it really goes out with 24-hour time. The options you are setting on the Time tab of the Regional Options really affect only the display.

Figure 28.16
You can embed a message in the system clock to identify a machine or operating system.

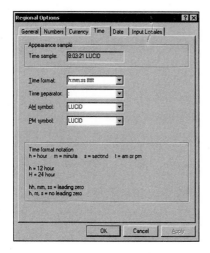

Because this tag also affects programs that have an "insert time stamp" function, you could use it to your benefit, for example, to track not only when a file was opened or edited, but from what department.

 If the items on your taskbar become too small to read when you have a number of applications or documents open at once, see "Taskbar Icons Too Small to Read" in the "Troubleshooting" section at the end of this chapter.

ADMINISTRATOR TOOLS NOT SHOWING UP

A weird quirk of the Windows 2000 Professional GUI is that the Administrative tools don't show up on the Start menu, even if you're signed in as an administrator. You have to dig into the Control Panel and click Administrative Tools.

If you actually poke around in the Start menu with Explorer (right-click the Start button and choose Explorer), you might be surprised to find the Administrative tools are already listed as being on the Administrator Start menu; they just don't show! So how come?

A setting in the taskbar properties controls this feature. Sort of a weird place to have this control, but there it is. To change it, right-click the taskbar, choose Properties, Start Menu Options, and then turn on Display Administrative Tools.

TWEAKING THE SEND TO FOLDER

In Windows 9x, you could add options to the Send To folder at will, simply by dragging shortcuts or programs into the \windows\send to folder. This capability was a great boon, as discussed earlier in the chapter. For example, I have a universal file viewing program called Fview, which creates an ASCII or Hex display of virtually any file. I just put a shortcut to fview.exe in the Send To folder, and I can easily view unknown files, even look into .exe files for hidden clues to what they are, and so on. You get the idea.

Granted, the new Open With command on the right-click menu is helpful because it lets you choose any registered application to open a file with. But then again, it takes a bit of scrolling about in the registered programs window or browsing around the hard disk. Hardly convenient.

Well, Windows 2000 Professional actually has a Send To folder; it's just hidden a bit. You can find it in the Documents and Settings folder of your Win2000 partition. One is available for each user, as you can see in Figure 28.17.

Figure 28.17
Each user has a Send To folder. You can add shortcuts to printers, drives, folders, or programs here, and the operating system adds the item to your Explorer right-click menu.

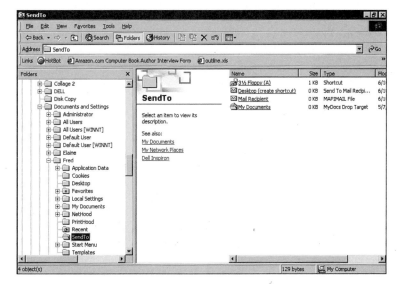

CHANGING THE LOCATION OF THE MY DOCUMENTS FOLDER

This is a very cool tip. As you know, many applications default to saving or opening files in the My Documents folder. What an annoyance! It's enough to make you throw up your hands and surrender to saving your documents where Microsoft wants you to. Well, fret no more. In earlier versions of Windows, you had to hack the Registry to change the location of the My Documents folder, but now changing the location is much simpler.

All you have to do is the following:

1. Right-click My Documents.
2. Choose Properties. The dialog in Figure 28.18 appears.
3. Choose Move, and set the path.

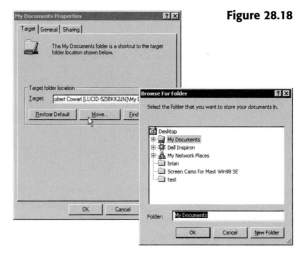

Figure 28.18

CUSTOMIZING TOOLTIPS

You can customize the ToolTip "bubble" that appears when you hover your mouse pointer over any one of your desktop icons. ToolTip bubbles appear, for instance, when you hover your mouse pointer over the My Computer icon; it reads `Displays the files and folders on your computer`.

By default, Windows 2000 Professional desktop or quick-launch icons show a ToolTip that consists of nothing more than the location of the item—for example,

`Location: C:\Program Files\Ulead PhotoImpact`

This information is not very helpful as a tip. In some cases, the name of the program is very obscure at best. You can set up more instructive pop-ups for any items you have added by doing the following:

1. Right-click the icon.
2. Choose Properties.
3. Fill in the Comments field with the text you want for your ToolTip.
4. Click OK, and the next time you hover the mouse pointer over the icon, you will have a customized ToolTip.

These steps do not apply to System icons—such as Network Places, My Computer, Recycle Bin, and so on—only to user-added items.

This feature is new in Windows 2000; it is not available in NT4 or Windows 9x.

CASCADING MY COMPUTER OFF THE START BUTTON

As discussed in Chapter 5, one of the Start menu's options lets you "expand" certain folders such as My Documents and Control Panel from within the Start menu system. The options don't include My Computer, however. Wouldn't it be nice to be able to navigate My Computer without having to clear the desktop? Here's how you can do it:

1. Just drag the My Computer icon onto your Start button and release (see Figure 28.19).
2. Click Start, My Computer, and navigate at will.

Figure 28.19
Dropping My
Computer on the
Start button cascades
it for easy navigating
without clearing the
desktop.

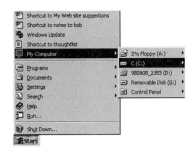

AUTO SCROLLING WITH A THREE-BUTTON MOUSE

Do you have a three-button mouse and wish you had a wheel mouse to make it easier to scroll your Web pages? Don't bother coveting your neighbor's wheel mouse because Internet Explorer and your three-button mouse can do the next best thing. When you're working in an Internet Explorer window, just click the center mouse button. The cursor changes to a two-headed arrow shape. Now move the mouse away or toward you, and the page scrolls. Click again or click another mouse button, and the scrolling function is terminated.

REMAPPING THE KEYBOARD

Do you ever wish certain keys on the keyboard were in different locations? I, for one, have been particularly annoyed about the location of the Ctrl, Caps Lock, and Alt keys ever since IBM moved them back in the eighties with its "improved keyboard." Because IBM was setting the PC standards back then, everyone else had to follow suit. Toshiba was one of the big holdouts, but even its superior keyboard arrangement finally met its fate. For those of us who grew up with standalone terminals, doing word processing with WordStar, programming in dBASE, and using numerous other programs that made heavy use of the Ctrl key, this arrangement was an outrage. The solution for the years before Windows was to use a key remapping program (WordStar even came with one, called Switcher) that reversed the locations of the Ctrl and Shift Lock keys.

Well, with Windows came the Alt key for keyboard shortcuts, and soon we were really in a mess with keyboard placement. Keys floated around for a while, with no fully accepted standard. Oh, and now we have the WIN key, the Windows Menu (right-click menu) key, and many laptops have a special function key for controlling brightness, sound level, and so on. If you're a touch typist, all these rearrangements can be a bit annoying.

Enter the key remapping programs. Many have appeared over the years, and I have been a big fan of them, especially because I insist on programming macros into Microsoft Word so that it behaves like WordStar. Using nothing but Ctrl+key sequences, I can write and edit far more quickly than by using the mouse, the arrow keys, the Home and End keys, and so forth. But all those macros rely on the Ctrl key, most easily reached if it's immediately to the left of the A key.

You can achieve Windows 9x key remapping by using a great little plug-in from Microsoft called Key Remap, which is part of the Power Toys. But alas it doesn't work in Windows 2000. After much combing of the Net, I found another program that works just great under Windows 2000 Professional.

This program, called Remapkey, comes out of Japan, written by a programmer named Hirofumi Yamamoto. Figure 28.20 shows the interface, which is very well designed and easy to use (despite the manual being in Japanese). Virtually all keys of the standard keyboard can be remapped to any other key, including Alt, Ctrl, and Caps Lock. You just drag keys from the upper keyboard to the lower keyboard to remap them.

Figure 28.20
Remapkey for Windows NT works great under Windows 2000 Professional.

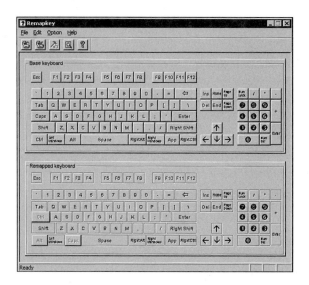

There are potentially many applications for such a program. If you find you are constantly hitting a wrong key, wish your keyboard were arranged a bit differently, or perhaps you are using the computer to acquire data and use only a few keys for special purposes, such a tool might help. For example, you could map the entire keyboard to produce only one character, regardless of which key is struck. Or suppose you want to use the Dvorak keyboard layout to reduce muscular strain and repetitive motion problems.

The Remapkey program has an integrity check that prevents accidentally removing the Ctrl+Alt+Del combination that can be required for system login.

→ In this chapter, we've covered only modifications to the Windows interface. DOS environment configuration is covered in the next chapter.

ADDING MULTIPLE PICTURE FOLDERS

In Chapter 6, "Organizing Your Work," I talked briefly about the My Pictures folder and even badmouthed it a bit. It's true that other programs are better suited to viewing, manipulating, and editing photo images than Explorer is. However, with a little work, you *can* set up a branching folder tree specifically optimized for managing and viewing your images—without using an external program. Here's how:

Folders in Windows 2000 can be customized with HTML code, given background images, and the like. (This is how some of the special folders like Control Panel, Fonts, Printers and so forth display extra information in their left panels, incidentally.)

Microsoft decided to let users customize any folder they like and, for the nonprogrammers among us, provided a wizard and a few templates to make the job easier.

You can actually set up any folder on any disk to include a picture viewer like the one in My Pictures. To do so, just follow these steps:

1. Open the folder in question.
2. Choose View, Customize This Folder.
3. Run the wizard.
4. Turn on the Choose or Edit an HTML Template for This Folder option. If you want a fancy background, turn on that option as well. If you want to add a special comment for the folder, viewable when someone highlights the folder name in an Explorer window, turn on that option. Then click Next.
5. Choose a background and/or caption if prompted, and click Next as many times as necessary to get to the HTML template page.
6. On the template page, choose Image Preview.
7. Click Finish to close the wizard, and your folder is reformatted to include the image preview panel.

→ To learn more details about using the preview panel, **see** "Viewing Thumbnails and Pictures," **p. 222**.

TROUBLESHOOTING

REDUCING SCREEN FLICKER

My CRT is flickering and annoying me. How can I change it?

Increase the refresh rate of the display subsystem to at least 70Hz. Right-click the desktop, choose Properties, and then choose Settings, Advanced, Monitor. Finally, change the refresh rate.

WHERE DID THOSE ICONS GO?

I changed the screen resolution, and now I can't find items off the edge of the screen and I have windows I can't close.

You might have this problem when you switch to a lower resolution from a higher one. Theoretically, Windows is good about relocating desktop icons, but some applications might not do the same. For example, the small AOL Instant Messenger dialog can be off the edge of the screen somewhere, and you can't get to it. Closing and rerunning the program doesn't help. One trick is to switch to the application by pressing Alt+Tab. Then press Alt+spacebar, and press M. This key combination invokes the Move command for the window. Then you can use the arrow keys on the keyboard to move the window (typically to the left and/or up). When you have the title bar of the window in view, press Enter. If this trick doesn't work, switch back to the previous higher resolution, reposition the application window in question closer to the upper-left corner of the screen, and then switch back to the lower resolution. It may help to remember that your screen is always decreased or increased in size starting from the lower-right corner and moving up or down diagonally.

WHAT DOES THAT SAY?

I want to use an external TV monitor, but the output text is illegible.

Some video cards and laptops can be plugged into a TV monitor or regular TV that has video input. But displaying computer output on a TV monitor is problematic for a couple of reasons. For starters, most video display cards don't let you run the TV at anything higher than 640×480 resolution. Don't try anything higher. Also, TV sets (as opposed to professional TV monitors) often *overscan*, pushing the edges of the image off the edge of the screen. The following are a few points to remember when you're using a TV or video projector; whether you're doing presentations, playing games, or giving your eyes a break by moving your focal plane back a bit:

- If your computer and TV have "S" (Super VHS) inputs, use them. They increase the clarity a bit. Don't expect miracles, though.
- Use Display Properties to switch to 640×480 resolution.
- Check to see whether your Display Properties dialog has buttons to center the image on the TV. It's most likely off center or needs resizing when you first try it. Some ATI drivers have advanced properties for fine-tuning TV display.
- Your application may have a "zoom" control for easily increasing the size of text onscreen, without the hassle of reformatting the entire document. MS Office tools such as Excel and Word, for example, have such a feature. Try bumping up the zoom size to increase legibility.

TASKBAR ICONS TOO SMALL TO READ

The taskbar icons are too crowded and small when I have a number of applications or documents open at once.

Increase the size of the taskbar by positioning the pointer on its top boarder and dragging it upward. Make it two or three rows high. I like at least one row for the "quicklauch" section and one or two rows for application and document buttons.

SINGLE- OR DOUBLE-CLICK?

I seem to accidentally run programs and open documents with a slip of the finger.

You probably have Single-Click selection turned on. As a result, one click (or tap, if you're using a touch pad) runs the program or opens the document that is highlighted. Change to Double-Click selection mode by opening a folder window, choosing Tools, Folder Options, and selecting Double Click to Open an Item.

UH-OH, MY MONITOR DIED

I changed my resolution or refresh rate, and now the screen is blank.

Normally, you shouldn't have this problem because Windows 2000 asks you to confirm that a screen resolution works properly and switches back to the previous resolution if you don't confirm. If somehow you changed color depth and resolution, and the system is stuck with a blank screen, you can reboot, press F8 during boot, and choose Safe Mode. Then use Control Panel, System or My Computer, Computer Management to get to the Device Manager. Select the video display, and reset the properties to what the computer was running at before the change. Be sure to reset both the screen resolution *and* the color depth. In the worst case scenario, start with 640×480 and 16 colors. After you've booted successfully, then right-click the desktop, choose Properties, click Settings, and increase the settings one step at a time. Don't change resolution *and* color depth at the same time, though. Increase one first and apply the change. Then adjust the other.

MOVING IN SLOW MOTION

I increased the resolution, but now the screen updates slowly when I drag windows around.

Unless you're doing high-resolution photographic-quality work, you don't need the high-resolution 24-bit or 32-bit color depth settings. These settings just serve to slow down screen redraws when you move windows about. On the Settings tab of the Display Properties dialog, try dropping to 16-bit color or even 256 colors, and enjoy the speed increase.

BLURRY IMAGES IN LCD

I switched to an LCD screen, and the image is blurrier than I expected.

Unlike CRTs, LCDs do not benefit from higher refresh rates. Don't try to use anything above a 60Hz refresh rate for an LCD monitor. Also, check the LCD monitor's internal settings (check its manual) for a "phase adjustment" or focus adjustment to help clear up fuzziness on small text.

STRETCHED A BIT THIN

I set up a picture for my desktop wallpaper, but it looks blocky.

You're stretching a small bitmap. Either use a larger image, or turn off the Stretch setting for the image. See the Display Properties, Background, Picture Display option.

TIPS FROM THE WINDOWS PROS: PIVOTING YOUR DISPLAY

Finally, here's an option you may have been thinking of based on ads you see in computer magazines: pivoting your display. Actually, the Radius monitor for the Macintosh introduced the idea quite a few years ago; now the portrait display is coming around again, this time in the form of a flat panel. A number of LCD monitor makers have introduced pivoting units and the accompanying software that turns the image and negotiates among the mouse driver, the screen driver, and Windows so that the geometry works out right.

Both my co-author and I have been bitten by the LCD bug and have pivoting monitors. Considering that most writing and Web sites are designed to be printed or viewed in the portrait dimension, a portrait monitor makes a tremendous amount of sense. Unlike older CRT models, these modern LCD monitors can be easily pivoted. A click of the software, and the screen image rotates 90 degrees.

All the LCD pivoting drivers come from one company: Portrait Displays, Inc. (www.portrait.com). Its "Pivot" software comes bundled with more and more brands of monitors these days, including those from major makers such as Mag and NEC, Viewsonic, and Compaq.

The new breed of Pivot drivers modifies only your existing driver file, so as long as the chipset on your video controller is recognized, you're in business. Note, however, that the pivoting software can be used only with LCDs and with a very few CRTs that are designed for rotation. I have tried it with my Dell Inspiron 7000 15-inch screen laptop (ATI Rage Pro chipset), and it worked just fine (see Figure 28.21).

Figure 28.21
The pivoting software and monitor combination makes Web page viewing and document writing easier on the mouse hand; you don't have to scroll as much.

CHAPTER 29

CUSTOMIZING VIA CONTROL PANEL APPLETS

In this chapter

SIZING UP THE CONTROL PANEL

As you certainly know, the Control Panel is the central location for making systemwide modifications to everything from accessibility options to user profiles. Microsoft has moved many features around in Windows 2000 Professional, relative to NT, many of which have shown up in the Control Panel. So, before throwing up your hands in frustration, check there (and Table 29.1). The Help system also has a "Where is it now?" feature, which will help you locate seemingly vanished items.

Not all the settings handled by the Control Panel are pivotal to effective or reliable operation of the system. In fact, many of the adjustments you can make from the Control Panel applets are more optional than they are imperative. For example, the Display applet, among other things, can be used to just make Windows a little easier to use or tolerate. Other applets are more imperative, such as applets for setting user rights, installing new hardware, or running system diagnostics.

The preferences settings you make via the Control Panel applets are stored in the Registry. Some are systemwide, whereas others are made on a per-user basis and go into effect when you log in. A few Control Panel settings can be altered from other locations throughout Windows. For example, you can set up printers by choosing Start, Settings, Printers, and you change display settings by right-clicking the desktop. Although the paths may be multifarious, the results are the same; you usually end up running a Control Panel extension (files with .CPL extensions) to do your bidding.

Keep in mind that you must have high-level permissions to modify many of the settings in the Control Panel. User-level settings such as display appearances are not a big deal. However, systemwide settings such as addition and removal of hardware are governed by the security monitor, and you must have the requisite permissions to successfully make modifications.

Tip #321

As you learned in Chapter 5, "Using the Windows 2000 Interface," you can opt to expand the Control Panel, making the applets appear in a fly-out window (by choosing Start, Settings, Control Panel), thus allowing you to avoid opening the whole Control Panel as a window. Using this fly-out window is worthwhile if you use the Control Panel a lot. You can make that setting by choosing Start, Settings, Taskbar and Start Menu. Next, choose the Advanced tab, and check Expand Control Panel in the Start Menu Settings scroll box.

If you use a particular applet a lot, you can drag it to the Start button or the quick launch bar for even faster access.

Not all the Control Panel settings are discussed in detail in this chapter. Because a few of the Control Panel options pertain to other topics, such as networking or printing, or fall under the umbrella of system management, performance tweaking, or system applications, you'll find them in later chapters. Table 29.1 lists each applet and the location of those not discussed here. Also, I won't bore you with covering each and every option in the dialog boxes. Many of the settings are intuitively obvious.

OPENING THE CONTROL PANEL

Choose Start, Settings, Control Panel to open the Control Panel (see Figure 29.1). If you have opted to expand the Control Panel in your Start menu, you can still double-click Control Panel there to open the regular window.

Figure 29.1
A typical Control Panel and applets look like this. Your setup may have more applets, depending on what additional software you have installed.

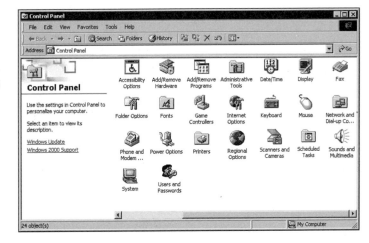

Table 29.1 shows a list of all the standard Control Panel applets and what they accomplish. Following the table, I'll cover each of the included applets (the ones not covered in other chapters) in alphabetical order.

TABLE 29.1   CONTROL PANEL APPLETS

Applet	Description
Accessibility Options	Sets keyboard, mouse, sound, display, and other options for increasing ease of use by those who are visually, aurally, or motor impaired.
Add/Remove Hardware	Installs or removes, disables, or troubleshoots a wide variety of hardware devices such as sound, video, CD-ROM, hard and floppy disk controllers, SCSI controllers, display adapters, keyboard, mouse, and ports.
	Installation of printers is covered in Chapter 9, "Printing and Faxing with Windows 2000."
Add/Remove Programs	Adds, removes, or modifies applications or components of Windows 2000. Also, this applet lets you create a startup disk to start your computer in case the operating system on the hard disk gets trashed accidentally. It supports remote application installation over the LAN.

continues

TABLE 29.1   CONTINUED

Applet	Description
Administrative Tools	Provides shortcuts to administrative tools such as Component Services, Computer Management, ODBC settings, Event Viewer, and Performance Monitor. The Event Viewer is covered in Chapter 31, "System Management and Configuration Tools." Component Services are not covered in this book.
Date/Time	Sets the current date, time, and time zone for the computer.
Display	Sets colors of various parts of Windows display elements, as well as other display-related adjustments, such as desktop background, screen saver, display driver, screen color depth and resolution, refresh rate, energy-saving modes, and active desktop applets.
	The Display applet is covered in detail in Chapter 28, "Tweaking the GUI."
Fax	Installs and sets up faxing service so that you can directly fax from applications. Also, this applet allows you to create and edit fax cover sheets, change properties of all existing fax devices you have installed, and run Fax Service Management from the Microsoft Management Console (MMC).
	Faxing is covered in Chapter 9 as part of printing.
Folder Options	Brings up the same dialog you see from any Explorer window.
	Most of these settings were covered in Chapter 6, "Organizing Your Work." Setting file associations is covered in this one.
Fonts	Adds, deletes, and displays examples of system-installed typefaces for screen display and printer output. Fonts are covered in Chapter 10, "Font Management."
Game Controllers	Adds, removes, and configures game controller hardware, such as joysticks and gamepads.
Internet Options	Brings up the same dialog box you get in Internet Explorer.
	Internet Explorer options are covered in Chapter 12, "World Wide Web."
Keyboard	Sets key repeat rate, cursor blink rate, language of your keyboard, keyboard type, drivers, and troubleshooting.
Mouse	Alters mouse properties such as motion speed, double-click, button orientation, cursor shapes, and other proprietary settings dependent on your mouse driver.
Network and Dial-Up Connections	Same as Properties from My Network Places. Creates new connections, including LAN, dial-up, and VPN. Using this applet, you can add, remove, and modify LAN components (clients, services, and protocols); you also can configure network adapters (NICs).
	These connections are covered throughout Part IV, "Networking."

Applet	Description
Phone and Modem Options	Adds, removes, and sets the properties of the modem(s) connected to your system. Using this applet, you can declare dialing rules (long-distance numbers, call waiting, credit card callings, and so on). You also can add and remove telephony drivers.
Power Options	Provides options for setting the Advanced Power Management (APM) and Advanced Configuration and Power Management (ACMP) functions. Using this applet, you can set timeouts for monitor, hard disk, system standby, and hibernation.
Printers	Adds, modifies, removes, and manages printers you have installed on your system. Using this applet, you can manage the print queue for each printer. The Printers applet is covered in Chapter 9.
Regional Options	Sets how Windows displays times, dates, numbers, and currency.
Scanners and Cameras	Adds, removes, sets properties for, and troubleshoots scanners and digital cameras.
Scheduled Tasks	Sets up automatic execution of applications, utilities, disk cleanup, and so on. Task scheduling is covered in Chapter 30, "Maintaining and Optimizing System Performance."
Sound and Multimedia	Assigns sounds to system events, checks and chooses installed sound drivers, and installs speech engines.
System	Examines and changes your identification (workgroup name, domain name, computer name), installed devices, amount of RAM, type of processor, and so on. Using this applet, you can add, disable, and remove specific devices using the Device Manager; set up hardware profiles; set up user profiles; optimize some parameters of system performance; set environment variables; and set emergency startup options. The use of the System applet is rather complex and thus is covered in Chapters 30 and 31.
Users and Passwords	Adds, deletes, or alters users. Using this applet, you can assign groups, create and change logon passwords, and create certificates. Passwords and security are covered in Chapter 32, "Managing Users."
Wireless Link	Sets aspects of wireless transfer to and from infrared ports (typically for laptops, though some desktops have IR ports).

→ **See** "Infrared Networking," **p. 838**.

Tip #322

Windows NT 4 and 9x included a PCMCIA applet in the Control Panel. It's now gone. It didn't do much anyway, other than let you control whether PC cards beeped when installed and removed. If your system has PC card slot services installed, the system tray contains an icon for PC card control for starting and stopping PC card devices. See Chapter 30 for details.

> **Note**
>
> All the Control Panel setting dialog boxes have a question mark button in their upper-right corners. You can click this button and then click an item in the dialog box that you have a question about. Windows then shows some relevant explanation about the item.

ACCESSIBILITY OPTIONS

Microsoft has made a point of increasing computer accessibility for people who are physically challenged in one way or another. Over the last half decade, Microsoft has increasingly included accessibility options in its operating systems, with features that allow many challenged people to use Windows without major machine or software modifications.

Many people have difficulty seeing characters on the screen, and others have trouble typing on the keyboard or controlling the mouse. People who are partially paralyzed or who have muscle-coordination problems have been at a disadvantage with computers for a long time. Now, with these accessibility options, the playing field is being leveled at least somewhat. Even if you are not disabled, some of the Accessibility options may prove useful for you.

Accessibility options are broken down into several categories, with their respective tabs: Keyboard, Sounds, Display, Mouse, and a few others on the General tab.

ACCESSIBILITY KEYBOARD SETTINGS

The keyboard settings deal with such problems as accidentally repeating keys or pressing combinations of keys. These options fall into three categories: *Sticky keys*, *Filter keys*, and *Toggle keys*.

Sticky keys are settings that, in effect, stay "down" when you press them once. They are good for controlling the function of the Alt, Ctrl, and Shift keys if you have trouble pressing two keys at the same time. To use them, set the Sticky keys option on; then choose the sub-options as you see fit. For some users, the shortcut of pressing the Shift key five times is a good way to activate Sticky keys. If you turn on this option activation method, note that pressing the Shift key five times again turns off Sticky keys. This trick isn't explained clearly in the dialogs. Also, if you choose the Press Modifier Key Twice to Lock option, that means you press, say, Shift twice to lock it. You can then press Shift twice again to unlock it.

Filter keys let you "filter" (remove) accidental repeated keystrokes in case you have trouble pressing a key cleanly once and letting it up. This feature prevents you from typing multiple keystrokes. The shortcut key for turning on this feature works like the one for Sticky keys; it's a toggle.

Tip #323

> Filter keys, when activated, can make it seem that your keyboard has ceased working unless you are very deliberate with keypresses. You have to press a key and keep it down for several seconds for the key to register. If you activate this setting and want to turn it off, the easiest solution is to use the mouse to run or switch to the Control Panel (via the taskbar), run the Accessibility Options applet, turn off Filter Keys, and click Apply or OK.

The Toggle keys option, when turned on, sounds a high-pitched tone when Caps Lock, Scroll Lock, and Num Lock keys are activated and a low-pitched tone when it's turned off again.

Each of these three keyboard features can be used independently or together. Note that a slowdown in performance occurs at the keyboard if sounds are used, as the sound is generated by playing a WAV file. Processing of keypresses doesn't commence until after the keyboard sound finishes, which can result in jerky performance.

When Sticky keys or Filter keys are turned on, a symbol appears in the system tray. The Sticky keys feature is indicated by the three small boxes, representative of the Ctrl, Alt, and Shift keys. The Filter keys feature is represented by the stopwatch, which is representative of the different key timing that goes into effect when the option is working.

ACCESSIBILITY SOUND SETTINGS

The two Accessibility sound settings—Sound Sentry and ShowSounds—are for those with hearing impairments. Instead of playing a sound when an error message or other event that causes a sound occurs, some type of visual display appears onscreen.

With Sound Sentry, a portion of the normal Windows screen blinks, typically the window or application that is generating the error. With ShowSounds turned on, you see some kind of text caption or special icon pop up in a box to report what's going on.

If you choose Sound Sentry, you have a choice of which portion of the screen to blink when an error occurs. Typically, you'll want the window of the application or at least its title bar to flash. Don't make the whole screen flash because it won't indicate which program is producing the warning.

Tip #324	Some programs are finicky about the sound options, especially ShowSounds. If they're not programmed correctly, they don't display a sound. Think of it like closed captioning for TV. Not all shows have it.

ACCESSIBILITY DISPLAY SETTINGS

Special display settings from the Accessibility Options applet increase the screen contrast by altering the display Appearances scheme. Using this applet really is just an easy way to set the display color scheme and font selection for easier reading, just as you could do from the Display applet, as discussed in Chapter 28. The big plus of setting the contrast here is that you can quickly call it up with a shortcut key combination when you need it. Just press Left-Alt, Left-Shift, Prnt Scrn, and the settings go into effect. I have found this feature useful for when my eyes are tired or in imperfect lighting situations. Figure 29.2 shows the effect it had while I was writing this chapter.

Figure 29.2
The effect of turning on the default high-contrast setting.

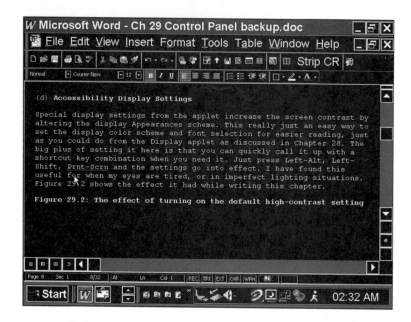

Tip #325

If you choose Custom as the color scheme, you can choose from among the stock color schemes in the Display settings, as described in Chapter 28. It's easier to observe the look of the schemes using the Display applet than in the Accessibility Options applet. Do it there, and then decide which one you like best. Then come back to the Accessibility dialog and make your choice.

ACCESSIBILITY MOUSE SETTINGS

Using the Mouse Settings tab, you can control the mouse with the keypad, in case you have problems controlling your mouse's movements. This feature can bail you out in case your mouse dies for some reason, too, or you simply don't like using the mouse. As is covered in Chapter 5 and Appendix B, "Keyboard Shortcuts and Mouseless Survival Guide" (on the CD-ROM), you can execute many Windows and Windows applications commands using the keyboard shortcut keys. But sometimes an application still responds only to mouse movements and clicks. Graphics programs are a case in point. When you use this Accessibility option, your arrow keys do double duty, acting like pointer control keys.

To use this option, simply turn on the Mouse Keys from the dialog box, and apply the change. Then, to activate the keys, press Left-Alt, Left-Shift, and Num Lock at the same time. The system tray should show a new icon. If the icon has a red line through it, the keys are disabled, so press the Num Lock key to enable them.

Now you can move the pointer around the screen using the arrow keys on the numeric number pad. If you're using a laptop, you'll have to consult the manual for it to determine how to activate the numeric keypad. The normal arrow keys won't cut it.

Click the Settings button if you need to adjust the speed settings for the arrow keys. Turn on the Ctrl and Shift options for speeding up or slowing down the mouse, assuming you can press two keys simultaneously. This setting really speeds things up.

If you adjust the settings, note that you have to click OK and then click Apply before the changes register. Then you can go back and adjust as necessary.

OTHER ACCESSIBILITY SETTINGS (GENERAL TAB)

The final Accessibility tab is General, which is divided into four sections, each of which is described in Table 29.2.

TABLE 29.2   OTHER ACCESSIBILITY SETTINGS

Setting	Description
Automatic Reset	If multiple people are using the same computer, it's a good idea to have the Accessibility features time out if they're not used for a while. If you turn off this option, the settings stay in operation until you manually turn them off, even surviving reboots.
Notification	This setting determines how you're alerted to a feature being turned on or off. By default, a little dialog box appears, but you can change it to a sound.
Serial Key Devices	You can opt to use special input devices designed for the disabled. Just connect such a device to a free serial port, and choose the port (COM1 through COM4) and baud rate.
Administrative Settings	The first option applies your Accessibility settings (such as high contrast, and so on) to the "logon desktop." The logon desktop is what you see when a user is logging on or when you press Ctrl+Alt+Del. It is a different desktop than the user desktop. If you choose this option, all users of the machine have the benefit (or annoyance) of seeing the settings when they are logging on.

The second option, when activated, copies the current Accessibility settings for each new user an administrator adds to the computer. |

ADD/REMOVE HARDWARE

Note that the Add/Remove Hardware applet has been modified in Windows 2000 Professional to include disabling or removing hardware, too. That used to be the province of the System applet.

If you're a hardware maven, you'll be visiting this applet a lot, especially if you're working with non-Plug and Play (PnP) hardware. Plug and Play hardware installation is pretty much a no-brainer because Windows 2000 Professional is good at detecting new hardware and should install it fairly automatically along with the necessary drivers.

Tip #326

Use the System applet, not Add/Remove Hardware, for fine-tuning device settings (such as IRQ and port) and updating devices and drivers. Use the Add New Hardware Wizard only for adding or removing hardware. Also, note that there are other locations throughout Windows for installing some devices, such as printers—which can be installed from the Printers folder—or modems—which can be installed from Phone and Modem Options—even though the effect is the same as using this applet. In other words, the Add New Hardware Wizard can be triggered from a number of disparate locations.

If you've purchased a board or other hardware add-in, first read the supplied manual for details about installation procedures. You might find installation tips and an installation program supplied with the hardware. However, if you can't find any instructions, physically install the hardware and keep reading.

You should close any programs you have running, just in case the installation process hangs the computer. This problem doesn't happen very often in NT-based Windows, but it can. Also, be sure to save your work, and close your applications.

For non-Plug and Play hardware or for Plug and Play stuff that, for some reason, isn't detected or doesn't install automatically, you need to run the applet. The typical scenario is to declare whether you are installing or removing hardware and then let the wizard try searching for Plug and Play hardware. If nothing is found, Windows assumes you're having some trouble with a device. Your currently installed devices are listed with an option to troubleshoot or to add something new. Figure 29.3 shows the dialog. This assumption is sort of weird on the wizard's part, but I guess Microsoft wanted the wizard to perform double duty.

Figure 29.3
When a new Plug and Play device isn't found, you see this box; you can just choose Add a New Device.

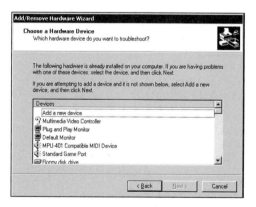

Next, you're asked if you want the wizard to attempt a legacy detection or you want to specify the item yourself. (Legacy hardware interrogation is a science all its own, and I'm always amazed when some old job like a sound card is detected properly.) While the hardware survey is underway, you see a "gas gauge" apprising you of the progress and hear lots of hard disk activity.

If something is found, continue with the wizard, and answer the questions as prompted.

In case the item isn't detected properly, you can simply declare manually what it is you are installing. You're shown a list of hardware types and asked to choose from the category list. Just choose the applicable category, and click Next.

Tip #327

If the category you're looking for isn't one that's listed, choose Other Devices and click Next. Then you can choose from the complete list of all manufacturers and models.

Make sure you choose the precise brand name and model number/name of the item you're installing. You may be prompted to insert your Windows 2000 CD-ROM so that the appropriate driver file or files can be loaded.

Early in the wizard, you have the option of declaring the hardware yourself and skipping the legacy scan. This option can save you time and in some cases is the surer path to installing new hardware. It also lets you physically install the hardware later, should you want to, because the wizard doesn't bother to authenticate the existence of the hardware. It simply installs the new driver.

Tip #328

In some cases, you are given the option of adjusting settings after the hardware is installed and possibly adjusting your hardware to match. (Some legacy cards have switches or software adjustments that can be made to them to control the I/O port, DMA address, and so forth.) You may be told which settings to use in order to avoid conflicts with other hardware in the system.

If, for some reason, you don't want to use the settings suggested by the wizard, you can use your own settings and manually set them. You can do so from the Add/Remove Hardware Wizard or via the Device Manager (from the System applet). See later in this chapter for coverage of the Device Manager.

Caution

In general, be cautious about configuring resource settings manually. When you change settings manually, the settings become fixed, and Windows 2000's built-in device contention resolution is less likely to work. Also, if you install too many devices with manually configured settings, you might not be able to install new Plug and Play devices because none are available. In the worst-case scenario, the system might not even boot if conflicts occur with primary hardware devices such as hard disk controllers or video cards. If you decide to use manual configuration, make sure you know what you're doing, and have in hand the specs for the hardware in question.

In cases in which the wizard detects a conflict, you are alerted upon finishing the wizard. You then have the option of bailing or continuing despite the conflict. You could also back up and choose a different model of hardware, such as one you think is compatible with what you're attempting to install. Figure 29.4 shows a typical message when a conflict is detected.

Figure 29.4
When a hardware conflict is detected, it's reported by the wizard at the end of the installation process.

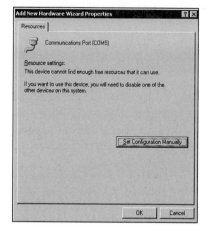

You now have the choice of setting the hardware resources for this device manually. Click Resources to change the settings. You then see something such as the dialog box shown in Figure 29.5.

Figure 29.5
Use caution when manually changing resources for a device. The device at Input/Output Range 03F8-03FF is the conflicting device, as is indicated by the universal "no" symbol over it.

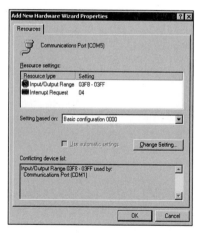

PROVIDING DRIVERS FOR HARDWARE NOT IN THE LIST

When the hardware you're attempting to install isn't on the device list, it's either because the hardware is newer than Windows 2000, or it's really old and Microsoft decided not to include it. What you need to do is obtain the driver from the manufacturer (or Microsoft—check Web sites) and get it ready on disk or on the hard disk, either locally or across the LAN. If the manufacturer supplies a setup disk, forget all this information, and follow those instructions. However, if the manufacturer supplies a driver disk and no instructions, follow along:

1. Run the Add/Remove Hardware applet.

2. Click Next. Then choose the correct class of hardware.

3. Click the Have Disk button.

4. Enter the location of the driver (you can enter any path, such as a directory on the hard disk or network path). Typically, you insert a disk in drive A. Use the Browse button if you need to. You're looking for an .INF file, incidentally.

5. Assuming the wizard finds a suitable driver file, choose the correct hardware item from the resulting dialog box, and follow the onscreen directions.

PART

V

CH

29

Tip #329	If you're not sure which ports and interrupts your other boards are using, you can use the Device Manager to see available and used IRQs, ports, DMAs, and so on.

REMOVING HARDWARE

The Add/Remove Hardware applet obviously also lets you remove hardware. You can use this function of the applet when you plan to remove a card, drive, and so on or if you want to unplug a device. Some devices are hot swappable, and in that case, you needn't worry about taking these steps. Firewire and USB, for example, can be plugged and unplugged with impunity. But COM and LPT ports are not as forgiving of devices suddenly disappearing. Nor are PCMCIA slots. You should alert the operating system before unplugging these items, or the system could get confused.

Tip #330	You can stop PCMCIA cards by clicking the PC card icon in the system tray, which has the same effect as disabling the item from this applet.

To remove a hardware device, follow these steps:

1. Run the Add/Remove Hardware applet.

2. Start the wizard.

3. Choose Uninstall/Unplug a Device.

4. Choose either permanent or temporary removal, depending on your aim.

5. Choose the device to uninstall, and confirm it. You may be prompted to reboot.

ADD/REMOVE PROGRAMS

The issue of adding applications to your system was discussed somewhat in Chapter 5, "Using the Windows Interface," and Chapter 6, "Organizing Your Work," in the context of running your programs and organizing your work. As you know, many programs come with their own installation (Setup) programs that handle all the details of installation, such as file copying, making Registry additions, making file associations, and adding items to the Start menus. You'll rarely add programs through the Add/Remove Programs applet. Most of what you'll use this applet for is to remove applications or portions thereof, and to add and remove Windows components, so let's start there.

As you might expect, not all Windows 9x or NT programs run perfectly under Windows 2000. A major operating system upgrade such as Windows 2000 comes with a few sacrifices, but the stability you gain from it is well worthwhile, I believe. Windows 2000 comes with an internal database of potentially incompatible programs and will warn you about likely difficulty should you insist on running such a program. In some cases, specific information about the program, the upgrade needed, and such is displayed. An example is shown in Figure 29.6.

Figure 29.6
Windows 2000 Professional recognizes a program that has known incompatibilities.

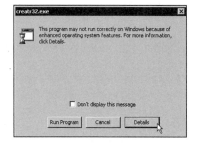

CHANGING OR REMOVING PROGRAMS

You've probably noticed that not all programs show up in the Add/Remove Programs applet in Windows 9x, NT, or Windows 2000 Professional. They don't appear because only programs complying with the 32-bit Windows API standard for installation get their filenames and locations recorded in the system database, allowing them to be reliably erased without adversely affecting the operation of Windows. Many older or less-sophisticated applications simply install in their own way and don't bother registering with the operating system.

Tip #331

In earlier versions of Windows, you could use the Add/Remove Programs applet to create a startup disk as a bailout in case the operating system got trashed beyond bootability. That chore has been moved into the Backup application, which is covered in Chapter 31.

REMOVING EXISTING PROGRAMS

Most modern applications are written in compliance with the Microsoft Windows standards for installation and removal. Thus, you see them in your installed applications list in the Add/Remove Programs applet. This list is mainly the result of the PC software industry's response to complaints from users and critics about tenacious programs that are hard to root out after they're installed. Some ambitious programs spread themselves out all over your hard disk like oil on your garage floor with no easy way of reversing the process. Users complained about the loss of precious disk space, unexplained system slowdowns, and so forth.

If you need help removing a program because it doesn't show up in the Add/Remove Programs list, see "Program Doesn't Show Up" in the "Troubleshooting" section at the end of this chapter.

This problem was the inspiration for such programs as Uninstaller, CleanSweep, and other utilities that monitor and keep a database of the files a program installs; they wipe out these files effectively when you decide to remove the program, also returning any modified Windows settings to their previous state with any luck. This process is better relegated to those writing the operating system, I feel, and Microsoft rightly set up standards for installation and removal of applications, overseen by this applet. Even if an application isn't installed via the Add/Remove Programs applet per se, if well behaved, it should still make itself known to the operating system and register changes it makes, enabling you to make changes and/or uninstall it from there.

What's more, the built-in uninstaller lets you make changes to applications, such as adding or removing suboptions (assuming the application supports that feature).

Use of the uninstall feature of the applet is simple:

1. Run the Add/Remove Programs applet.

2. Check the list of installed applications. A typical list is shown in Figure 29.7. Note that you can sort the applications by some interesting criteria in the sort box, such as frequency of use. (That one helps weed out stuff you almost never use.)

Figure 29.7
Choosing the program to uninstall or change.

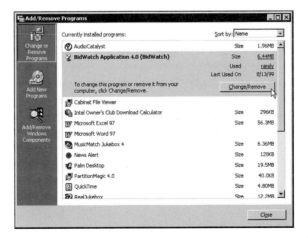

3. Select the program or programs you want to change or uninstall.

4. Click the Change/Remove button.

5. Answer any warnings about removing an application as appropriate.

Tip #332

> Obviously, removing an application can't easily be reversed by, say, restoring files from the Recycle Bin because settings from the Start button and possibly the Registry are deleted.

Some applications (for example, Microsoft Office) prompt you to insert the program CD when you attempt to change or remove the app. These prompts can be annoying, but what can you do? The setup, change, and uninstall programs for some large suites are stored on their CDs, not on your hard disk. So, just insert the disk when prompted.

INSTALLING APPLICATIONS

As you know, installation of new programs is usually as simple as inserting a CD into the drive. The autorun program on most application CDs does the rest. Or, when it doesn't, you can run the Setup on the disk, and the rest is automatic. Ditto for programs you download off the Net. Still, you can install from this applet if you want or if the program's instructions suggest it. This part of the applet provides a front end for running an application's Setup program. Big Whoop. Here's what you do:

1. Click Add New Programs in the left panel.
2. Choose the source:

    - CD or Floppy—Choose this option for CD, floppy, or hard disk folder. You have to browse to get to the hard disk folder.

    - Windows Update—This option runs Internet Explorer, connects to the Microsoft site, and runs Windows Update just as though you had started that process from the Start button. Don't choose this option unless you're trying to update your Windows installation.

3. The wizard is looking for any file named setup.exe incidentally. If it finds this file on the CD or floppy, just choose the desired file, and follow the instructions you see. If the setup program you're looking for isn't called setup.exe then you have a little more work to do. Change the Files of Type drop-down list to Program Files or All Files, and poke around a bit more. But make sure you choose a file that's actually a setup file. If you point to a regular old application, it will just run normally. Nothing weird will happen; you just won't be installing anything.

4. Click Finish to complete the task and make the new software's installation or setup procedure run. Instructions vary depending on the program. If your program's setup routine isn't compatible with the applet, you are advised of this fact. After installation, the new program appears in the list of removable programs only if it's compatible with Windows 2000's install/remove scheme.

INSTALLING PROGRAMS FROM THE NETWORK

As you learned in Chapter 1, "Introducing Windows 2000 Professional," an administrator of a Windows 2000 Server machine can "publish" or "push" applications at workstations.

When an application is published over the LAN, that means users can connect to a remote workstation or server to install the application on their machines.

When you choose Add New Programs, you have another option, showing applications that are available on the network (see Figure 29.8).

Figure 29.8
Installing a program published on a remote LAN server.

Push Technology Meets the LAN

You might have heard the term *push* used in relation to the Web over the past couple of years. Advantages and disadvantages of the push as it applies to the Active Desktop and the Web are covered in Chapter 28. But how does this technology apply to the LAN and to applications? The idea of push is that it's a bit like television or radio. You turn on your TV, and there's the show. You don't have to do anything except choose the channel. Push technology on the Web works the same way. When you're connected, information is sent to your computer on a regular basis—for example, displaying stock prices in a ticker window on your desktop.

The push I'm talking about here with the LAN works much the same way, except that instead of being sent a Web page or stock ticker, you're sent an entire application that gets installed automatically on your computer, according to your system administrator's wishes.

Next, open the box called Category, which you use to narrow down the class of application you want to install. (The system administrator makes up the categories.) When you select such an application for installation, note that the administrator who set it up for publishing may have turned off the possibility for you to make installation choices such as which portions, add-ins, or other options to install.

Note

In the case of pushed (a.k.a. *assigned*) applications, when you log on to the machine or network, the applications assigned to you are added to your machine across the network automatically. In fact, if you accidentally or intentionally delete the application from your computer, it reinstalls itself.

DATE AND TIME

Date/Time is a simple applet you're sure to have used in the past to adjust the system date and time. That is, it adjusts the hardware clock in the computer, which is maintained by a battery on the motherboard. The system date and time are used for a number of purposes, including date- and time-stamping the files you create and modify, stamping email, controlling the scheduler program for automatic application running, and so on.

> **Note**
>
> The Date/Time applet doesn't change the format of the date and time, only the actual date and time. To change formats, see the description of the Regional applet later in this chapter.

To set the date and time, follow these steps:

1. Run the Date/Time applet. The dialog in Figure 28.9 appears.

2. Alter the time and date by typing in the corrections or by clicking the arrows. The trick is to click directly on the hours, minutes, seconds, or AM/PM area before the little arrows to the right of them modify the correct value. So, to adjust the a.m. or p.m., click AM or PM, and then click the little up or down arrow.

Figure 29.9
Changing date and time settings.

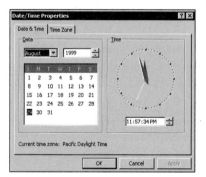

3. Click the Time Zone tab to adjust the zone. Why? It's good practice to have your time zone set correctly for programs such as client managers, faxing programs, time synchronizing programs (see the sidebar titled "Synchronizing to the Ether"), or phone dialing programs. They may need to figure out where you are in relation to others and what the time differential is. Also, if you want your computer's clock to be adjusted automatically when daylight saving time changes, make sure the Automatically Adjust Clock for Daylight Saving Changes check box is selected.

Tip #333

You can also adjust the time and date using the TIME and DATE commands from the DOS prompt. For example, open a DOS box, type C:\>time, and press Enter. This command displays the current time and a prompt to enter the new time, as shown here:

```
The current time is: 21:39:31.78
Enter the new time:
```

Enter the new time or press Enter to leave the time as it is. The same process applies to the date. Type C:\>date and press Enter. The current date is displayed with a prompt to enter the new date, as shown here:

```
The current date is: Thu 11/04/1999
Enter the new date: (mm-dd-yy)
```

For more details about the TIME and DATE commands, see Appendix A, "Command-Line Reference," on the CD-ROM that accompanies this book.

Note

When you're a member of Windows 2000 domain, you should never need to set the clock. It is kept synchronized to the domain controller (Windows 2000 server). This is necessitated by the *Kerberos* security system. If you're part of a workgroup and want to sync your clocks, see the tip about this topic in Chapter 24, "Connecting Your LAN to the Internet."

Synchronizing to the Ether

If you want to ensure that your computer always has the absolute correct time (well, nothing is perfect, but this is pretty close...), download one of the atomic-clock synchronizers you can find on the Web. You can find one called Atom Time at www.atomtime.com. These programs sync your computer's clock to the atomic reference clock in Boulder, Colorado. They are based on the atomic second, the basic unit of International Atomic Time.

To ensure accuracy, this kind of clock even beats the pants off your old Pulsar wristwatch, measuring its ticks on cesium atoms jiggling at 9,192,631,770 vibrations per second. Setting your clock this way is much more accurate than setting a clock according to the less-regular standard solar time, which is based on the earth's rotation. A solar second is 1/60 of a minute, which is 1/60 of an hour, which is 1/24 of a day. Don't have a calculator handy? Use the one in Windows 2000 Professional. You'll find that makes a solar second 1/86400 of a solar day. That's a lot less accurate than a number derived from approximately 9 billion pulsations of a cesium atom.

Programs such as Atom Time are smart in addition to being accurate. They don't need you to specify what time zone you're in. They automatically adjust to the time zone your computer is set to.

DISPLAY PROPERTIES ENERGY USAGE

In Chapter 28, you found out a great deal about changing the display properties. What you didn't learn about was the energy settings, also known as Energy Star options. Energy Star monitors require an Energy Star-compatible video card in the computer to work properly, but most modern ones comply. With complying hardware, you can cut your energy bill and reduce wear on your CRT by having the screen power down after a predetermined period of inactivity.

Powering down is particularly important for LCD monitors because their backlights have a finite lifetime. CRTs are the gas-guzzlers of computers, consuming far more energy than the typical computer box. A typical computer consumes about 50 watts of power, whereas a

CRT at full tilt is more on the order of 120 to 150 watts. In the suspend state, most 17-inch monitors consume only 8 to 10 watts. That's a big difference.

To check and/or set the display energy settings, run the Display applet from the Control Panel. Next, select the Screen Saver tab, and click Power Schemes. You then see the dialog shown in Figure 29.10. This one is for a laptop computer. If you're on a desktop machine, you won't have settings labeled Plugged In and Running on Batteries.

Figure 29.10
Setting the timeouts for the monitor is a good idea. It saves energy and can extend the life of the monitor.

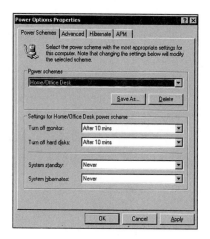

If your adapter/monitor combination isn't Energy Star-compatible, the option is grayed out. Only energy settings that your computer is capable of using are available. Windows 2000 Professional detects APM and ACPI capabilities when first installed.

Earlier Windows versions had timeouts for both lower-power state and power off. Now you have only one. When powered off, a CRT takes a few seconds to come back on, so don't make the setting too short. Something on the order of 30 minutes is pretty reasonable.

FOLDER OPTIONS (REGISTERING APPLICATIONS)

Chapters 5 and 6 described some of the Windows folders options, such as showing hidden and system files, Web view, and so on. But they didn't describe how file types get registered. This aspect of Windows 2000's functioning is important.

Unlike the Macintosh operating system, Windows (due to its DOS legacy) uses file extensions (the last three or four letters after the dot in the filename) to determine what program it will open in. (The Macintosh operating system uses a smarter arrangement, wherein every document file has a "creator" signature in it, telling the operating system what program originated the file.)

In Windows, the relationship between a document file and its application program is called an *association*. Windows 2000 comes with a number of file associations preregistered. For example, clicking a .BMP file opens it in Paint. Likewise, a .TXT file opens in Notepad; a .DOC file, in WordPad; and HTML files, in Internet Explorer. All this is done via the magic of file associations.

When you install a new program that uses a proprietary file type, it creates a new association in the Registry. Files of that type appear in folder windows with a recognizable icon and open automatically in the target program when clicked. All this is very fine, but unfortunately, with so many popular file types around, they are constantly being reassigned to new applications when you install them. Or even unbeknownst to you, this can happen. Install Real Player, for example, and suddenly your WAV, AVI, and MPG files no longer play in the Windows Media Player. Instead, they play in Real Player, and you're inundated with advertisements yanked off the Web and displayed in the Real Player window.

Another popular example is the association with popular graphic image formats, such as JPG and GIF files. Nice image-editing programs ask which image formats you want to associate with the new program. Some applications are not so nice. I'll bet that right now you don't know what program will run when you double-click a JPG file. I'm not sure I know either because it seems to change from week to week.

Occasionally, though, I get ticked off and dig into the Folder Options and reset a specific file association. Here's how to do it.

Let's say you want to associate JPG files with the Kodak Imaging program that comes with Windows 2000 Professional instead of with Internet Explorer.

Just follow these steps to reset a file association:

1. In the Control Panel (or from any folder window's Folder Tools), click Folder Options.

2. Click the third tab, File Types. You then see the dialog box shown in Figure 29.11.

Figure 29.11
Start here to change a file association.

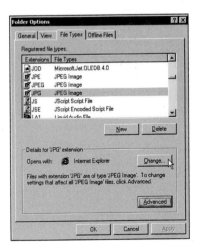

3. Find the file extension type in question, and highlight it.

4. Click Change to open the dialog listing registered applications. In this case, choose Imaging Preview, as shown in Figure 29.12.

5. If the program you want to associate the file type with isn't listed, click Other and browse for it.

6. Check the Always Use This Program box if that's what you want.

7. Click OK to close the dialog box, and the registration is changed.

Figure 29.12

You can add a file type to the Registry and make an association for it by clicking the New button and naming the new extension. Then follow the preceding steps to set up the association for it.

You can click the Advanced button to get into more of the nitty-gritty, but doing so can entail knowledge of DDE and the use of some cryptic coding. If all you want to do is control what program opens a file when clicked, use the preceding steps.

Tip #334	You don't have to officially change an association to easily open a file in a specific program. Right-click the document file in an Explorer window, and choose Open With, Choose Program. Then choose the application from the resulting list, or browse to it. If you want to set the association from that box, check the box labeled Always Use This Program to Open These Files.

GAME CONTROLLERS

If you're serious about playing games on your computer, you need a game controller; that means something more than a mouse. Typical controllers are joystick, gamepad, flight yoke, driving wheel, or other hardware devices designed specifically for the games of your choice. If you're an extreme gamer, normal old joysticks and gamepads won't cut the mustard either. High-tech gaming these days requires high-tech controls. Game controllers have reached the point at which serious flight simulator enthusiasts hook up a yoke and separate rudder foot pedals to more accurately simulate the flying experience.

This book doesn't cover gaming to any extent, but if you are a gamer, and you buy a game controller, it likely comes with an installation program. If not, you can hook up the controller, run the Add/Remove Hardware Wizard, and see whether the controller is installed. If that doesn't do the job for you, run the Game Controllers applet, choose Add, and then choose the type of controller you have (see Figure 29.13).

Figure 29.13
Choosing the type of
game controller to
install.

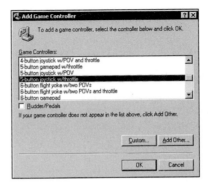

For the last several years, heavy gamers have opted for Windows 95 and 98 as their platforms because of their more extensive support for games. The kinds of hardware direct access and the display driver optimizations that games expect have traditionally been unsupported on the NT platform. The DirectX support on Windows 9x has been superior in this regard.

With Windows 2000, the NT platform begins to change this legacy. As a result, you see options such as game controller settings in the Control Panel. You'll see more people migrating from the Windows 9x platform for gaming as Windows 2000 supports more and more gaming devices and programs simply because it's more stable.

Windows 2000 supports DirectX 7.0, including accelerated video card and sound card drivers that provide better playback for different types of games, for full-color graphics and video, and 3D animation. DirectX automatically determines the hardware capabilities of your computer and then sets your programs' parameters to match. This allows multimedia applications to run on any Windows-based computer and at the same time ensures that the multimedia applications take full advantage of high-performance hardware.

Low-level functions of DirectX 7.0 are supported by the components that make up the DirectX Foundation layer—namely the following:

- DirectDraw
- Direct 3D Immediate mode
- DirectSound
- DirectMusic
- DirectInput
- Direct3D Retained mode
- DirectAnimation
- DirectPlay
- DirectShow
- DirectX Transform

Of particular interest to gamers are DirectDraw (which provides extremely fast, direct access to the accelerated hardware capabilities of a computer's video adapter), DirectInput (for quick processing of game controller input), Direct3D Retained Mode (which supports advanced, real-time, three-dimensional graphics), and DirectPlay (which supports game connections over a modem, the Internet, or a LAN).

Tip #335

When you upgrade from Windows 98, Windows 2000 doesn't automatically set up previously installed game devices. You need to manually add your devices in the Control Panel.

Note

If you want to optimize your computer for gaming or want to build one from the ground up, I suggest you pick up a copy of *Building the Ultimate Game PC*, published by Que. This book will walk you through configuring and optimizing your machine to squeeze every drop of performance from Windows, DirectX, and DirectSound. It also will help you become a seasoned shopper and build your dream machine after you have all the right parts.

After you install a game controller, you can click the Advanced button if you need to alter the controller ID and/or the port to which it's connected. Each game controller should be assigned a different ID. You can share the same game port for a number of controllers by disconnecting one and connecting another. You might be prompted to remove a game controller from the list before a new one can be connected, however, depending on the kind of controller and the port to which it's connected.

- For a custom controller (one not listed in the Add list), click Add, and then click Custom. Fill in the settings for controller type, axes, and number of buttons; then give the controller a name.

- To choose from a list of brand-name controllers, click Add Other, and choose a manufacturer and model. (Some of the devices that show up in this list aren't game controllers, but many are.) If you have a disk of a game port or game controllers, click Have Disk, insert the diskette if necessary, or browse to the appropriate folder location.

KEYBOARD

The Keyboard applet lets you fine-tune the way the keyboard behaves, check the keyboard driver, and perform some keyboard troubleshooting (see Figure 29.14). You can also alter the "input locales" just as in the Regional Settings applet (and is redundant with that feature, so see "Regional Options" later in this chapter for input locales.)

The main attractions here are the repeat rate, the repeat delay, and the cursor blink rate. By altering the key repeat delay (the time after pressing a key before it starts to repeat) and the repeat speed, you can calm down an ill-behaved keyboard or improve usability for someone with a mobility impairment. Altering the delay before the repeat sets in might be helpful if you use applications that require extensive use of, say, the PgUp and PgDn, Enter, or the arrow keys (perhaps in a point-of-sale situation).

Figure 29.14
Adjusting key-repeat speed and delay can be useful for avoiding unwanted characters.

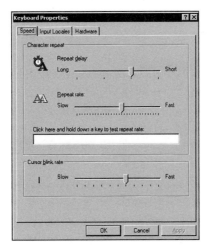

You might also want to change the cursor blink rate if the standard blinking cursor annoys you for some reason. You can't stop it altogether, unfortunately. I prefer a nonblinking one myself.

The defaults for these keyboard settings are adequate for most users and keyboards.

MOUSE

With each passing year, it seems that the mouse, trackpad, roller, graphics tablet, or pointing stick has become more and more the means through which users interact with the computer. I remember when the mouse was an option. Nowadays, you can barely shut down a computer without a mouse, much less use it effectively.

Obviously, then, the mouse being a major means of interface with your computer, it behooves you to optimize its functioning. The Control Panel's Mouse applet lets you do just that, with as many as 10 aspects of your mouse's operation being adjustable (see Figure 29.15):

- Left-right button reversal
- Single or double-click system behavior
- Double-click speed
- Look of the pointers
- Pointer scheme

- Tracking speed
- Acceleration
- "Snap to default" button
- Mouse type and driver
- Troubleshooting

Figure 29.15
Setting mouse properties can help you get your work done more efficiently, though the defaults usually work fine without modification.

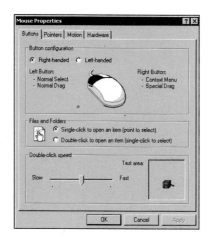

The options vary based on pointing device type, and sometimes you are supplied with even fancier options if your pointing device comes with a custom driver. For example, the Synaptics touch pads let you scroll a window by sliding your finger down the right side of the trackpad. Or you can turn on a little program called *mood pad* that, like a mood ring, changes colors on the screen based on how hard you press on the trackpad.

BUTTONS AND CLICKING

Poor lefties never get a fair shake in life, what with all the right-handed scissors and tools around. Well, they get one here (except for some types of weird, ergonomically shaped mouse devices that don't work well in the left hand). If you're left-handed, you can move the mouse to the left side of the keyboard and then reverse the function of the buttons by using the Mouse applet. Right-clicks then become left-clicks. Of course, DOS programs don't know squat about this mouse setting, but for Windows and Windows programs, the button reverse will work.

The Files and Folders option is the same as the one available via the Control Panel Folders applet or from any Explorer window. It's just an easy place to turn on or off the single-click mode.

On the same tab, you can set the double-click speed. A middle-range setting is appropriate for most folks. Double-click the Jack-in-the-box to try out the new double-click speed. Jack jumps out or back into the box if the double-click registered. If you're not faring well, try adjusting the slider, and then try again. You don't have to click Apply to test the slider settings. Just moving the slider instantly affects the mouse's double-click speed.

POINTER OPTIONS

As you know, the pointer cursor changes based on the task at hand. For example, when you're editing text, it becomes an I-beam. You can customize your cursors for the fun of it or to increase visibility. You can even install animated cursors to amuse yourself while you wait for some process to complete. Just as with icons and screen savers, the Web is littered with Windows cursors, in case you would like to collect a few thousand. Windows 2000 Professional comes with enough to keep me happy, organized into schemes. You can change individual cursors or change a set of them in one fell swoop by using the *cursor schemes*.

Like color schemes and sound schemes, cursor schemes are collections of cursor shapes. When you select a scheme, all the cursors in the scheme go into effect at once. You can choose from about 20 canned schemes.

> **Note**
>
> Use one of the Extra Large cursor schemes if you have trouble seeing the pointer. Also, some of the schemes change the pointer into things that don't resemble pointers and can make selecting or clicking small objects difficult because the pointer's hotspot is difficult to locate. Sometimes the cursor is very distracting and can obscure the very item you want to select or click.

You can change individual cursors in a scheme, if you like. To change a cursor assignment, click a cursor in the list. Then click Browse. The default location is winnt/cursors. Animated cursors move for you in the Browse box (a thoughtful feature). Figure 29.16 shows the Browse dialog box with cursors.

Figure 29.16
You can replace individual cursors in the system. Windows 2000 Professional comes stocked with a sizeable collection of cursor replacements.

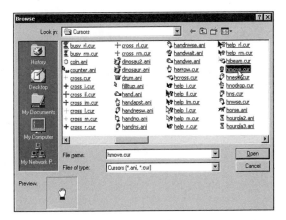

After you custom tailor a set of cursors to your liking, you can save the scheme for later recall. Click Save As, and name it.

Setting the Pointer Motion

As I mentioned earlier, the options you see on the Mouse tabs vary, based on the driver and mouse you have installed. The generic Microsoft mouse driver has three options on the Motion tab, as shown in Table 29.3.

Table 29.3 Motion Tab Settings

Option	Description
Speed	This option sets the speed at which the mouse pointer moves relative to the movement of the mouse. Someone out there in geek land has a sense of humor because mouse motion is actually measured in *Mickeys!* A Mickey equals 1/100 of an inch of mouse movement. The speed setting lets you adjust the relationship of Mickeys to *pixels*. If you want to be very exact in your cursor movement, you can decrease this setting.
Acceleration	This option controls whether the pointer will move more quickly across the screen if you move the mouse fast versus slow. If you are annoyed by slow pointer movement but also want good control when doing close work, increase the acceleration setting, and decrease the speed setting.
Snap to Default	If your mouse driver has this option, you're in luck. It forces the pointer to jump to the selected focus in dialog boxes and windows. It probably saves miles of arm motion over the course of a year's computing.

Tip #336

> In the olden days of Windows, if you used DOS programs that required the mouse, they required DOS mouse drivers. If the DOS mouse driver and the Windows mouse driver's speed settings were different, using the mouse could be annoying because your body's learned hand-eye coordination with one environment didn't match the other. Some DOS mouse drivers let you adjust the speed in that environment, so you could match the two. In Windows 2000 Professional, DOS-environment mouse support is provided by Windows. As my co-author Brian says, DOS support under Windows 2000 Professional is one of the marvels of the modern world because it is so well thought out and extensive.

 If you're frustrated because the mouse pointer still appears on the screen while you're in DOS, see "Using DOS Programs with a Mouse" in the "Troubleshooting" section at the end of the chapter.

Hardware Tab

As with most devices in Windows 2000, the Mouse applet contains a tab that lets you check the driver details (author, version) and whether the device is working properly. By navigating through a few subpages, you can read more about the driver, check the hardware resources such as IRQ used by the mouse, update the driver, and so on. Options vary among mouse devices.

You might also see multiple mouse devices listed as installed and operational on this tab. One of my laptop systems has two mouse devices (an internal trackpad and an external one built into an external ergonomic keyboard). Both are listed on this tab.

→ To learn more details about checking, changing, and updating device drivers, **see** " Updating Device Drivers," **p. 1102**.

Tip #337	If you use an external serial mouse on your laptop, it may not wake up after your laptop goes into a suspended state. For example, if you close the lid to a laptop running Windows 2000 Professional, it will probably go into Standby or Hibernate, depending on your laptop's and Windows settings. When you wake it up, your external mouse might not wake up along with it because the mouse driver may not know to reinitialize the mouse. Here's a way around that problem, short of rebooting: Choose Control Panel, System, Hardware, Device Manager. Next, click Computer. Then choose Action, Scan for Hardware Changes to do a search for new hardware. Because the mouse was not initialized, it fell off the list of current hardware. Doing the scan finds it and reinitializes it. The mouse should now work.

PHONE AND MODEM OPTIONS

The Phone and Modem Options applet lets you add, remove, and set the properties of the modems connected to your system. You can also declare dialing rules (long-distance numbers, call waiting, credit card calls, and so on), and add and remove telephony drivers.

 If you can't get your modem to connect, see "Cannot Connect" in the "Troubleshooting" section at the end of this chapter.

THE WINDOWS TELEPHONY INTERFACE

Windows 2000 (like Windows 9x) has a *telephony* interface, essentially an API that provides the means (hooks) for communications applications to work through the operating system. In fact, this interface is called TAPI. Through TAPI, the operating system provides a standard way for communications applications to access COM ports and devices such as modems and telephone sets when handling data, fax, and voice transmissions.

TAPI empowers applications to make, answer, and hang up calls; put calls on hold; perform call transfer; record voice mail; and make conference calls. Fully TAPI-compliant applications should be able to work with conventional telephone lines, PBX and Centrex systems, and with specialized services such as cellular and ISDN.

Much like the way process contention is handled by TCP/IP for network transmission or by the process scheduler for CPU usage, TAPI allows multiple communications to request the same resources, without a data collision occurring. The advantage to the end user is that you don't have to shut down a program that's waiting for incoming calls before you use a different program to send a fax, for example. Nor do you have to keep entering modem, phone number, dialing options, and COM port settings into each new communications program installed. These settings, just like printer settings, are stored in the system and are available for every communications program, such as Hyperterminal or Dial-Up Networking.

The Phones and Modems applet in the Control Panel offers a central location for altering some TAPI settings, as well as for installing and configuring modems and telephone devices. Installing and configuring a modem were covered in Chapter 11, "Internet and TCP/IP

Connection Options," so I'll dispense with the basics of modem installation here. Refer to that chapter if you're hooking up a new modem.

Tip #338	You can use cell phones for data communications, for example, from a laptop in the field. Remember two points, though. The phone must be set to run in analog mode. Also, in the best of circumstances, you will get only 9600bps throughput because of limitations in the cellular transmission channel.
	To set up cellular communications, you need a modem that is compatible with the cell phone you have and a cable designed specifically for connecting your model of phone to that modem. I use a standard Motorola "flip phone" with a Megahertz cellular-ready modem. With this combo, not much fiddling is required, but I made sure *before* I purchased the modem that it would work with my make and model phone.
	As for settings, I did drop down the transfer rate to 9600 baud, and because my phone is analog/digital, I have to force it into analog mode for each call. This extra step is a bit of an annoyance, but I'll survive. Then I connect the cell phone to the modem, power up the phone, and initiate the dialing sequence. With any luck, I get on the Internet. Don't forget the per-minute cost of cellular connections! The charges can add up. If you do a lot of on-the-road connecting, check out one of the wireless connection options such as Ricochet's or Hughes's service, which are typically offered at a reasonable flat rate for a full 24×7 connection.

Tip #339	Windows 2000 supports *modem aggregation*, which is also called *PPP multilink dialing*. It essentially allows you to group modems together to increase the connection bandwidth. This process is a little tricky and requires multiple phone lines and multiple ISP accounts to work, as well as an ISP that supports synchronization of multiple modems.

In general, your default TAPI and modem properties will probably work fine and won't need to be changed. If you do need to change them, remember that changes affect all applications that use the modem whose properties you modify. To change the modem properties after installation is complete, open the Control Panel, and double-click the Phone and Modem Options icon. The resulting dialog box looks like the one shown in Figure 29.17.

DIALING RULES

On the Dialing Rules tab of the Phone & Modem Options dialog, you can set up your dialog locations and rules pertaining to those locations, such as phone number prefixes for outside lines, calling card access codes, and so on. If you move around (road-warrior style), you can add some new locations to the default one that's already set up for you as the current user.

You can either edit or add a dialing location from this tab. The resulting dialog box is the same in either case, as shown in Figure 29.18. Table 29.4 describes the settings.

Figure 29.17
You can change TAPI and related settings such as modem properties from this applet.

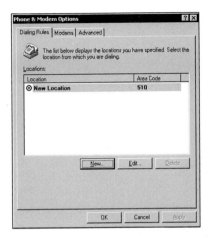

Figure 29.18
This set of properties determines the way communications programs handle phone calls for each location.

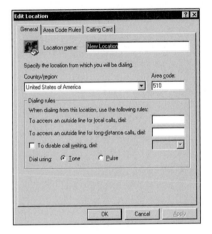

TABLE 29.4   SETTING DIALING RULES FOR EACH LOCATION

Option	Description
Location Name	This field specifies the name of each configuration set. To create a new configuration, use the New button and type a name in the Create New Location dialog box.
Area Code	Type your own area code in this field.
Country/Region	This field contains a drop-down menu that lists the international dialing codes for most countries of the world. Choose the name of the country from which you will be originating calls. The United States, Canada, and many Caribbean countries all use the same Country Code.

continues

TABLE 29.4   CONTINUED

Option	Description
To Access an Outside Line for Local Calls	If your modem line is in an office where you must dial 9 for an outside line or some other code for long distance, type that number here. If you have a direct outside line, leave this field blank.
To Access an Outside Line for Long-Distance Calls	If you have to dial 9 or 8 for long-distance calls, enter that number. Remember that you need to use this field only when your modem is connected to a PBX or other telephone system that uses a special code for toll calls. Do *not* use this field for the 1 prefix that you dial before making long-distance calls. The dialer adds that code automatically.
To Disable Call Waiting, Dial	If your phone service has call waiting, it can be a nuisance and cause your data connection to fail when a phone call comes in while you're online. Most call waiting services let you turn off the service for the duration of the current call by entering *70, 70#, or 1170 before making the call. If you have call waiting, you should turn on this option and enter the code your phone company tells you or choose the correct code. Often your local telephone directory has the necessary code listed. The comma after the code causes a 1- or 2-second pause after dialing the special code, often necessary before dialing the actual phone number.
Tone or Pulse Dialing	Most pushbutton telephones use tone dialing (known in the United States as TouchTone dialing). However, older dial telephones and some cheap pushbutton phones use pulse signaling instead. Chances are good that your telephone circuit will accept tone dialing even if a dial telephone is connected to it. Try it if in doubt. Change to pulse if it doesn't make a connection.

THE OTHER TABS

Two other tabs complete the setup dialog box.

AREA CODE RULES TAB

On the Area Code Rules tab, you can set details about the use of an area code, specifically the use of the 1 prefix for certain exchanges. If you have to dial 1 (but no area code) for certain areas, you can add those prefixes here.

Click New to create a new rule, and fill in the resulting dialog box.

CALLING CARD TAB

You might not need to worry about calling cards at all if you travel using an ISP that has many points of presence. The larger ISPs such as Mindspring, CompuServe, and AOL have local dial-up numbers from most major cities. Some also have 800 numbers that you can use when connecting phones from remote locations. If you need to bill your connection to a telephone company (or long-distance service) calling card, though, you set those options on the Calling Card tab.

Tip #340

If you use more than one calling card, you can create a different location for each one. Telephony programs, such as Phone Dialer or the Send Fax Wizard, normally let you change the location before dialing.

As you probably know from using a calling card for voice calls, to place and charge a call with a calling card, you dial a special string of numbers that includes a carrier access code, your account number, and the number you're calling. In some cases, you have to call a service provider, enter your account number, and wait for a second dial tone before you can actually enter the number you want to call.

To assign a calling card, follow these steps:

1. Click the location you are assigning it to on the Dialing Rules tab of the Phone & Modem Options dialog.

2. Click Edit.

3. Fill in the general information and any area code rules.

4. Click the Calling Card tab.

5. Choose the card type you have. If it's not listed, click New and fill in the resulting dialog box, using the ? (question mark) button for assistance (see Figure 29.19). If your service is one of the presets, all the necessary settings, such as pauses and dialing codes, are made for you.

Figure 29.19
You can use this dialog box to specify how calling card calls are to be placed.

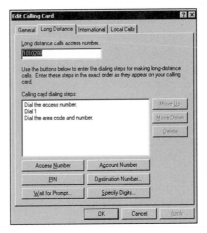

6. Enter your Account Number and Personal ID Number (PIN) if necessary. Not all calling card options require them, so these options may be grayed out.

SETTING OR EDITING CALLING CARD SCRIPTS

If you get into editing the calling card rules for a location, you're in pretty deep. I don't have room here to walk you through a description of every setting and how the dialog box works, but I can give you a few tips.

Basically, you can set up and edit a sequence of events, like a script, in the Edit Calling Card dialog. You can not only change the sequence of events, but you can also enter any specific numbers or other codes. When you make the call, the events progress from the top of the box to the bottom.

You can set up a script for each kind of call: local, long distance, and international. The dialog box looks like the one shown in Figure 29.19.

You can use the Edit Calling Card dialog box when you have to fine-tune a calling card's dialing script. Do so only if the presets for your calling card service don't already work. The six buttons below the steps list insert new steps into the script.

Some services require you to wait for a "bong" tone before continuing with the dialing. If the tone your carrier plays isn't detected by your modem, try experimenting with different pause lengths instead. You typically are allowed a few seconds to enter the remainder of the sequence, so the pause amount may not be critical as long as you have waited for the bong.

If a connection isn't working, and you're fine-tuning these events, it sometimes help to lift the receiver of a phone on the same line and listen (or turn on the modem's speaker), monitoring the sounds. You'll be better able to figure out where a sequence is bombing out.

SETTING MODEM PROPERTIES

So much for dialing rules. The second tab in the Phone & Modem Options dialog—Modems—is for setting modem properties. Typically, you don't need to change your modem properties, so unless you're having difficulty, remember this old adage: If it ain't broke, don't fix it.

To alter a modem's properties, follow these steps:

1. Click the Modems tab.
2. Choose the modem.
3. Click Properties.

Figure 29.20 shows the Properties dialog box for a modem.

Tip #341

> Notice that you can add and remove modems from this Properties dialog box, too, although you can do so just as easily from the Add/Remove Hardware applet.

You can dig pretty deeply into the three tabs in this dialog, especially the Advanced one. As per usual Microsoft strategy on its communications stuff, if you're used to the Windows 9x or NT 4 dialogs, you'll find things have shifted around, and you'll have to do a little hunting. Table 29.5 lists a few notes about some of the more salient settings.

Figure 29.20
You can use this dialog box to tweak the properties for individual modems.

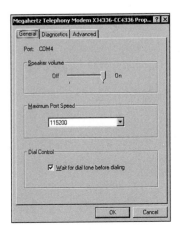

TABLE 29.5   MODEM PROPERTIES SETTINGS

Setting	Description
Port	You can use the drop-down Port menu to specify the COM port to which your modem is connected. If you don't have a drop-down list box, you don't have a choice of ports. This is the case for PCMCIA modems.
Speaker Volume	The Speaker Volume control is a slide setting that sets the loudness of the speaker inside your modem. In some cases, you will have only Off and On as options rather than a variable speaker volume.
Maximum Port Speed	When your modem makes a connection, it tries to use the maximum speed to exchange data with the modem at the other end of the link. As a rule, if you have a 9600bps or faster modem, the maximum speed should be three or four times the rated modem speed (for example, set your modem speed to 38400) to take advantage of the modem's built-in data compression. Note that the Advanced settings' Port Speed setting interacts with this one.
Dial Control	You can choose whether the dialer should wait to detect a dial tone before proceeding.
Extra Initialization Commands	The Extra Settings section is a place to send additional AT commands to your modem. In most cases, you don't need to add any special commands. Because different modem manufacturers use slightly different command sets, you'll have to consult your modem manual for specific commands.

continues

Table 29.5   Continued

Setting	Description
Data Protocol	If you're using a cellular phone with the modem, choose Cellular Protocol in the default settings page's Data Protocol drop-down list. Cell phones use special data error compression and correction protocols to increase connection speed. The modem still works with this setting turned off, but the connection may improve if it's turned on. Don't use Cellular Protocol if your cell phone service doesn't support it.
Advanced Connection Preferences	The Data bits, Parity, and Stop bits settings must be the same at both ends of a data link. The most common settings are 8 data bits, no parity, and one stop bit.
Call Preferences	The two Call Preferences options control the way your modem handles individual calls and whether the line is dropped if the call isn't answered. Place a check mark in the box if you want to use that option. Set the timeouts if you need to. The Idle Time setting could affect your changes if you are making long-distance calls.
Advanced Port Settings	Clicking this button brings up the Advanced Port Settings dialog box. These settings determine how the incoming and outgoing data are buffered by the COM port UARTS. Leave them alone unless you have information from your ISP or modem manufacturer, or you suspect that dropping them will help with connection success. Before you change these settings, drop the maximum port speed, which controls the data transmission speed between the modem and the port. If you do experiment with them, and your throughput drops significantly, return to this screen, and click Defaults to set the sliders and check box back to the original suggested settings.
Distinctive Ring	A tab for this option appears only if your modem supports the feature. "Distinctive ring" is a service from your phone company that provides different ring patterns for different kinds of incoming calls. Depending on the kind of modem you have, you can have between three and six numbers, or addresses, for one telephone line. Each number can have a distinctive ring pattern. You can also assign each ring pattern to a specific type of program. For example, if you have two rings assigned for fax calls, any call received with that ring pattern could be automatically sent to your fax program. Some phone companies have distinctive ring patterns based on the duration of the ring rather than the number of rings. Some modems support this scenario. In general, you should choose the desired number of rings for each kind of incoming call based on settings you get from your phone company. Then check your modem's manual for details on using this feature. You'll have to enable the distinctive ring feature first by clicking the check box before you can alter the ring settings.

DIAGNOSTIC PROPERTIES

You can click the Diagnostics tab in the original Modem Properties dialog box to make it active, as shown in Figure 29.21. The Diagnostics tab asks the modem to identify itself. It can further test the modem's capability to respond to the standard AT command set, display the contents of its internal registers, and display its settings. Click Query Modem to make it so.

Figure 29.21
On this tab, you can query a modem to display its internal name and dump internal settings for viewing.

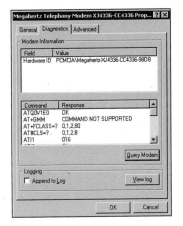

POWER OPTIONS

The Power Options applet provides options for controlling how power is conserved in your computer, whether a desktop machine or portable.

A few years back, Intel and Microsoft began conspiring to devise a plan whereby portable computers could better manage and conserve the battery charge, enabling users to run for longer periods of time without AC power. The result was a standard called Advanced Power Management (APM). Windows 95 shipped with APM. APM took some of the load off applications programmers by letting the operating system and the computer's BIOS handle power management. Under APM, power management was somewhat limited, however, because many of the devices in the computer had no way of communicating with the operating system. For example, waking up the computer when a fax or voice call came into the modem or when a LAN request came into the LAN card was not possible.

The big brother to and outgrowth of APM is the Advanced Configuration and Power Interface (ACPI). Pioneered by Toshiba, Intel, and Microsoft, it aims at controlling all aspects of a computer's power consumption, stem to stern. It can power down CD-ROM drives, displays, hard disks, PC cards, even the fan in a desktop computer's power supply. It also allows the computer to be controlled by "soft" switches. Touch a power key on the keyboard, and the machine goes into a suspend state. Another key wakes it up.

Many recent computers are ACPI-compliant, and Windows 2000 Professional takes advantage of this capability. A machine can benefit from Windows 2000's ACPI support as long as the BIOS, motherboard, Plug and Play devices, and power supply are all in compliance with the ACPI specification.

In a full ACPI implementation, the operating system can keep track of which programs are active and what hardware they require. Hardware not required for an activity can be turned off, including computer subsystems and peripherals. This way, the operating system can direct power to devices as they need it, preventing unnecessary power demands on your system.

A side benefit is that because Windows 2000 controls your computer's resources and configuration, you can install Plug and Play hardware devices without restarting.

ADJUSTING POWER PROPERTIES

The options you see in the Power Options applet vary from computer to computer, based on the hardware installed. For example, the Alarm tab (for battery power) isn't available on desktop machines. But you'll have a few options at the very least.

You can open the applet from the Control Panel or by clicking the battery or AC plug icon in the system tray. Figure 29.22 shows the dialog box and Table 29.6 explains the settings. (The options in yours may be different.)

Figure 29.22
You can adjust the power settings from this dialog box.

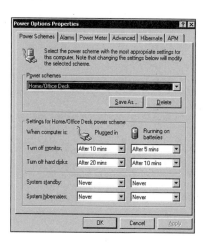

TABLE 29.6 POWER SETTINGS

Setting	Description
Power Schemes	As with sound, cursor, and display schemes, power schemes let you create different arrangements of power settings. You can call them into effect by opening this box and choosing them. Stored in the scheme are only the items on this tab, so a scheme is simply a combination of the settings in the lower portion of the dialog box. Typical schemes are for desktop or laptop computers, which come preset with average timeout values for screen and hard disks. To create your own schemes, simply adjust the timeouts in the bottom section as you like, click the Save As button, and fill in a name.

Setting	Description
Turn Off Monitor	This option sets the time delay before your monitor is told to go into a low power state (roughly 1/10 of the usual energy consumption). The monitor and card must be APM- and preferably ACPI-compliant to do this; most card/monitor combos made in the last four years are. (Monitor energy settings were discussed earlier in this chapter.)
Turn Off Hard Disk	You can tell your hard disks to spin down if not "hit" for the amount of time you enter here. Spinning down can reduce wear and tear on the drive motor and bearings and reduce noise. Of course, it takes as much as 5 seconds for most drives to start up again after resting, so it can slow down your work. If you're serving Web pages, doing lots of real-time transactions of any type, or performing other activities in which the hard disk must be quickly available (such as cutting CDs), set this option to Never.
System Standby	After this period of inactivity, the computer goes into a low power state. From this state, it can quickly restore itself, with all work just as you left it. The process may take 10 seconds or so. If the power source is removed, data is lost.
System Hibernates	After this period of inactivity, the computer stores the system state to the hard disk. Hibernation requires as much hard disk space as you have RAM in the computer. It takes longer to hibernate than to standby, but this process is nonvolatile and uses no battery power from a laptop when in this state. The computer completely shuts down after the system state is saved on the hard disk. When the power switch is turned on again, the state is read into RAM from the hard disk, and you can resume working where you left off. (See the description of the Hibernate tab later in this chapter for Hibernation-related settings.)

Tip #342

If your computer is capable of going into standby or hibernate, you'll have these options on your shutdown menu. Both of these features are great time-savers. If you're like me, you often have 10 or 15 windows open while working and don't want to have to re-create that working environment each time you boot up the computer.

Caution

Saving any work before you manually suspend is always a good idea, just in case your laptop's battery runs down before you resume your work. The Suspend option relies on your computer's battery to the system RAM running in order to store your data and applications. A dead battery will leave you dead in the water. You'll have to reboot when you get to an AC outlet.

ALARMS

If you have a laptop with a recognized battery system, you'll see an Alarms tab in the Power Options Properties dialog box. These settings tell the computer how to handle an impending power outage as the batteries drain down. (See Figure 29.23 for the dialog box in question.)

Figure 29.23
Setting the power alarms ensures you are alerted in time to avoid calamity.

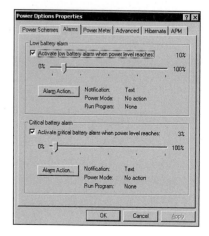

Settings on the tab are described in Table 29.7.

TABLE 29.7 ALARM SETTINGS

Setting	Description
Low Battery Alarm	When should the first alarm ring? Good settings for this option are dependent on your work habits and your battery life. I suggest 15 percent remaining to hear the first alarm. (It's just a little beep, not an air-raid siren, incidentally.)
Critical Battery Alarm	When should the critical alarm (three annoying beeps in repetition) ring? I suggest 10 percent remaining.
Alarm Action	After that, you have the choice of what the computer should do in case you aren't around to power down or plug into AC. Click the Alarm Action button to see this box. Five options face you now. First, choose whether you want to hear an alarm or see a message onscreen, or both, when the respective battery condition is reached. Then you can choose automated evasive actions: standby, hibernate, or shutdown (power off).
	—Remember that maintaining a standby state requires energy. If you choose this option, make sure you can supply power to the computer relatively soon after it goes into standby state.
	—Hibernating takes enough energy to write to the hard disk for about 10 to 20 seconds, which 10 percent power on a healthy laptop battery should be able to do. Then you're home free. It doesn't matter when you get to a power source.
	—Shutdown is dicey because, if you have work open, you may lose it. Notice the option Force Standby Even If a Program Stops Responding. This option applies not only to crashed applications, but also to applications that are prompting you to save or abandon work. If this check box is off, the shutdown process hangs if an application issues such a dialog box and you don't respond. If the check box is checked, Windows gives you the option to save open work as it shuts down applications, but it doesn't wait more than about 10 seconds for you to answer the question. What it does at that point is not predictable, as it depends on the application.

POWER METER

On a laptop running on batteries, you'll have a Power Meter tab displaying the state of your battery charge. You can check the condition of the battery charge using this tab. If you have two batteries, you can display the condition of each. If you want to see an aggregate graph of the combined power of two batteries (instead of a numeric percentage rating), turn off the Show Details of Each Battery check box.

ADVANCED SETTINGS

The remaining tabs of the Power Options Properties dialog may show various additional items based on your machine type. Typically, the settings shown in Table 29.8 are the ones you'll have available for the Advanced tab.

TABLE 29.8 ADVANCED SETTINGS

Setting	Description
Always Show Icon on the Taskbar	With this option on, the battery icon (or AC plug icon when plugged in) appears on the taskbar. Hover the mouse pointer over the little taskbar icon, and wait a second. The remaining battery time is then displayed. On some machines, the setting displays a percentage instead of remaining time.
Prompt for Password When Computer Goes Off Standby	With this option on, you are asked for a password when you restart the computer (such as by lifting the lid of the laptop). If the password is not required, this is an easy entry for an unauthorized user to gain access to your computer.

 If you use a portable computer and don't see a battery icon in the task tray, see "No Battery Icon in System Tray" in the "Troubleshooting" section at the end of this chapter.

HIBERNATE

As mentioned earlier, hibernation is similar to putting your computer in a low-energy standby mode, except that it uses *no* energy once in hibernation. When put into hibernation, the computer stores the system state to the hard disk. Hibernation requires as much hard disk space as you have RAM in the computer. It takes longer to hibernate than to standby, but this process is nonvolatile and uses no battery power from a laptop when in this state. The computer completely shuts down after the system state is saved on the hard disk. When the power switch is turned on again, the state is read into RAM from the hard disk, and you can resume working where you left off.

Let's talk a bit about energy management strategies on laptops for a minute. If your laptop is plugged into AC power, I suggest you use the standby mode rather than hibernate mode for daily use. When you get up to go to lunch or leave overnight, most laptops are wired in such a way that simply closing the lid triggers the low energy standby state. Standby powers off the screen backlight (increasing its life span), drops the telephone line (if you're connected to the Internet), and disconnects the LAN connection (if any). But all your programs and documents are left as is. Just lifting the lid wakes up the computer and prompts you for a password. Enter the password, and you're back where you left off.

More and more desktop machines have standby support nowadays. Compaq machines, for example, have a sleep switch, which triggers standby. If your computer doesn't have a visible switch for standby, it may still work from the Start button's Shut Down dialog box. Just choose Standby instead of Shutdown or Hibernate. Some laptops and desktop machines are triggered to wake up from standby when a LAN request comes in to the machine. Windows 2000 Professional supports this feature on selected machines. Check your computer's specs about this feature. You might need to set a BIOS option typically called Wake on LAN or something like that.

Getting back to the topic of Hibernation, now consider that, in standby mode, your work is in the hands of the computer's RAM primarily. Standby keeps the RAM powered on, and this is dependent on the computer's power source being alive and well. If you want to go home for the day and then come back to work in the morning and be assured that you can pick up where you left off easily, you should use the Hibernate function instead. (Optionally, you can shut down fully, closing all your applications and documents, but I think that approach is a pain. It's virtually as safe to hibernate the machine.) With hibernation, even if the power goes off during the night, or if your laptop's battery croaks, you're still in business. Just apply power as necessary, and start the computer. After power up, Windows 2000 checks to see whether it should resume from the hibernation file stored on disk. It then loads up from that file rather than boots anew.

> **Note**
>
> Your computer has to be APM-compatible and have APM support enabled before hibernate and standby modes will work. See the "APM" section for more details.

The Hibernate tab appears in your Power Options Properties dialog if your computer is capable of hibernating. It has only two sections, as listed in Table 29.9.

TABLE 29.9 HIBERNATE OPTIONS

Enable Hibernate Support	Turn on this option to allow hibernation. Hibernate is then added to the Shut Down dialog box as an option. Also, the necessary Hibernate space on the hard disk is checked for and the file created. This file, called save2disk.bin, is placed in the root of the boot disk.
Disk Space for Hibernation	This setting reports the amount of free space on your system drive (the mandatory location for the hibernation file) and the amount of disk space required to hibernate your machine (equivalent to the amount of RAM in your computer).

APM

The APM tab of the Power Options Properties dialog simply activates the APM driver for the computer and is available as an option only if Windows 2000's autodetection determines that your machine is APM-compatible. You must turn on the Enable Advanced Power Management option if you want Standby and Hibernate modes to work on your computer.

REGIONAL OPTIONS

The Regional settings affect the way Windows displays times, dates, numbers, and currency. When you install Windows, chances are good that the Regional settings are already set for your locale. This will certainly be true if you purchase a computer with Windows 2000 Professional preinstalled on it, from a vender in your country or area.

Running the Regional Options applet from the Control Panel displays the dialog box you see in Figure 29.24.

Figure 29.24
Making changes to the Regional settings affects the display of date, time, and currency in Windows applications that use the internal Windows settings for such functions.

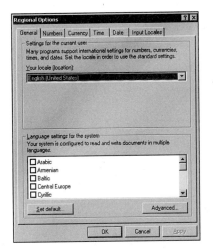

To change the settings, simply click the appropriate tab, and then click the drop-down list box for the setting in question. Examples of the current settings are shown in each section, so you don't need to change them unless they look wrong. Table 29.10 gives the basic breakdown of the Regional settings.

TABLE 29.10   REGIONAL SETTINGS

Setting	Description
Your Locale (Location)	Specifies the country you're in. All other settings change in accordance with the accepted practices in that country, so you probably don't have to bother changing the other options.
Language Settings for the System	Specifies which language groups are currently installed or available on your computer. The selected check boxes indicate which language groups are installed. To install an additional language group, click to select the check box next to the language group. To remove a language group, clear its check box.

continues

TABLE 29.10 CONTINUED

Setting	Description
Numbers	Displays numbers with or without decimals, commas, or leading zeros and with different decimal separators. It also determines whether to display measurements in metric or English units and what your list separator should be. In English, the list separator is a comma (for example, Fred, Jane, and Ted went to the store). In other languages, items listed in a sentence are separated by other punctuation marks.
Currency	Adjusts your currency indicator and the location and number of decimal digits.
Time	Adjusts for 12- or 24-hour time indication, a.m. or p.m. indicators, choice of separators, and leading zeros.
Date	Adjusts date display formats to appear as 3/6/53; 03/06/53; 3/6/1953; 06-03-1953; March 6, 1953; and so on. This setting is useful for time-sensitive programs such as email that need a date stamp that pops the date into text at the touch of a key or translates dates from one format to another.
Input Locales	Lists the input languages and keyboard layouts that are loaded into memory every time you start your computer.
Hot Keys for Input Locales	Specifies which keys (if any) you can use to switch between installed input locales. You can customize the key sequence for each input locale by clicking Change Key Sequence.

SCANNERS AND CAMERAS

Using the Scanners and Cameras applet, you can add, remove, set properties for, and troubleshoot your connection to scanners and digital cameras. As scanners and digital cameras become as omnipresent as the trusty printer, provisions are being made to assist in the transfer of documents and images from them into the computer. Especially with the advent of the digital still camera, many new convenient methods for facilitating the transfer of captured images are being made available. This is a must if the digital camera is to become as prevalent as the standard film camera.

The Scanners and Cameras applet appears in the Control Panel when you install your first scanner or digital camera. You can use this applet to install other scanners, digital still cameras, digital video cameras, and image-capturing devices.

After a device is installed, Scanners and Cameras can link it to a program on your computer. For example, when you press Scan on your scanner, you can have the scanned picture automatically open in the program you want.

With some cameras and scanners, you can create linked events that execute when you do something on the camera or the scanner. Typically, this means pressing a button on the scanner or camera.

Note

You might have noticed that the Wireless Link applet has an option for transferring images from digital cameras. Windows 2000 infrared support simulates a serial port, IrCOMM, and only one image transfer program can use it at a time. As of this writing, few cameras have IR transfer capabilities. This could change, however. If your camera uses infrared to transfer images, open the Wireless Link applet, click the Image Transfer tab, and choose the destination folder for the images.

After you set up the options, orient the IR transmitter/receiver, and begin the transfer. Then follow the camera manufacturer's instructions to select the picture and send it to the computer. Assuming your IR port is functioning properly, the images should transfer. If you turn on the Explore Location After Receiving Pictures option, the Windows Explorer pops up a folder window showing the new files.

In the best of all worlds, detection of your scanner or camera will occur automatically as Windows Plug and Play detection notices the device. But as you know, sometimes running the Add Hardware Wizard is required to force a search. To do that, use this applet to install a scanner device like this:

1. Run the Scanners and Cameras applet, and click Add (see Figure 29.25). (Ideally, you should hook up the device before doing so.) Follow the wizard, and choose the make and model if necessary.

2. Choose the port the device is connected to. You can use the option Automatic Port Select if you don't intend to be consistent with which port you use for this connection, or you don't want to bother guessing which port it's on.

3. When an item is installed, the drivers are added to the boot list at startup, and appropriate features in the operating system are modified for gaining access to the device.

   For example, I installed Nikon CoolPix 900S, which is the camera I have. Once installed, the applet dialog looked like that in Figure 29.25.

Figure 29.25
The Scanners and Cameras dialog after installing a Nikon camera via the Add button.

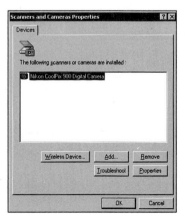

You can check and test a scanner or camera by selecting it and clicking the Properties button. The Properties dialog for the device appears, as you can see in the example in

Figure 29.26. Here, you can alter the port number if you need to and check other settings as applicable. If color profiles are available for the device, you can add or remove them using the Color Management tab.

Figure 29.26
Test your hookup by clicking the Test Scanner or Camera button.

 If your camera or scanner doesn't show up in the installed devices list, see "It's Not Here" in the "Troubleshooting" section at the end of this chapter.

GETTING IMAGES INTO THE COMPUTER

How you acquire images from the device into the computer varies depending on the product. As I mentioned earlier, some cameras use a wireless link (that is, infrared link), and for them, you use the Wireless Link applet in the Control Panel. The Nikon digital camera in this example uses a COM port.

When the physical connection is made, it's a matter of triggering the correct "event" (see the previous explanation). To link a program to a scanner or digital camera event, follow these steps:

1. Open the Scanners and Cameras applet.
2. Click the scanner or camera you want to use, click Properties, and then click the Events tab.
3. In Scanner Events or Camera Events, click the event you want to link to a program.
4. In Send to This Application, click the program you want to receive the image from the scanner or camera. If the Events tab isn't displayed, you're out of luck; the feature isn't available for the selected scanner or digital camera. Also, at this point, most applications don't support linking to scanners and digital cameras using this new technique. It may take some time for software makers to incorporate it, just as it took awhile for *TWAIN* to be supported by the PC industry at large. Also, note that linking is available only with the programs that appear in Send to This Application.

 If you have trouble getting a scanner or camera recognized by your system, see "It's Not Here" in the "Troubleshooting" section at the end of this chapter.

SOUNDS AND MULTIMEDIA

The Sounds and Multimedia applet is your stopping place when it comes to adjustments to your sound system and the sounds the computer makes to alert you of errors, new mail, and so on.

> **Note**
>
> As you might know, you adjust the volume of your computer speakers (and other inputs and outputs) by choosing Start, Programs, Accessories, Entertainment, Volume Controls. Alternatively, you can simply double-click the little speaker next to the clock in the system tray. By single-clicking the same little speaker, you can quickly adjust the master volume control. The Volume Controls are covered in Chapter 7, "Using the Simple Supplied Applications."

When you open the Sounds and Multimedia applet from the Control Panel, you see the dialog box shown in Figure 29.27.

Figure 29.27
You can make adjustments to your audio system from this applet.

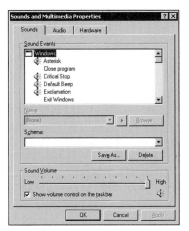

As you can see here, there's a bunch of fun to be had from this box, should you like to twiddle with your sounds. Most of what people do with this applet is change the goofy sounds their computers make in response to specific events.

> **Note**
>
> One way to easily change all the sounds your computer makes is to use sound themes. This topic is covered later in this chapter. If you want to learn more about themes (including sound themes), refer to "Desktop Themes" in Chapter 28. Desktop themes include sound as well as visual settings (for example, screen saver and desktop appearance).

If your computer had a sound card (or motherboard-based sound chip set) when you installed Windows 2000, it's likely Windows established a default set of rather boring sounds for your system, most of which you've probably grown tired of already. Aside from making life more interesting, having different sounds for different types of events is also more informative. You know when you've made an error as opposed to when an application is acknowledging your actions, for example.

The sounds the system uses are stored on disk in the .WAV format. You can create, purchase, or download just about any sound you can think of from the Internet. I downloaded the sound of Homer Simpson saying "Doh!" and the theme from the sixties TV Show "Car 54, Where Are You?" the other day, for example.

→ You can use the Sound Recorder accessory program to create your own WAV files, if you care to. To learn more about it, **see** "Sound Recorder," **p. 268**.

Windows 2000 comes with several sound files now, a big improvement over the measly assemblage of WAV files supplied with some earlier versions of Windows. In fact, just as with the color schemes, you can create and save sound schemes by using the Control Panel's Display applet (covered in Chapter 7); you can set up and save personalized schemes to suit your mood. Microsoft supplies a fairly rich variety of sounds for your auditory pleasure.

Despite the diverse selection, I still use a few of the sounds I've put together using the Sound Recorder. I have one, for example, that says "New Mail" when I receive email. Sometimes I didn't notice the generic "boop" sound when new mail arrived, so I changed it.

If you want to get fancy, you can record from a CD or tape recorder rather than from a microphone. This way, you can sample bits and pieces from your favorite artists by popping the audio CD into the computer and tapping directly into it rather than by sticking a microphone up in front of your boom box and accidentally recording the telephone when it rings. Just check out the Volume Control applet, and figure out which slider on the mixer panel controls the input volume of the CD. Then use the Sound Recorder applet to make the recording. I have a few good ones, such as James Brown's incomparable "Ow!" for an error message sound.

Tip #343	You should make sure that WAV files you intend for system sounds aren't too large. Sound files *can* be super large, especially if they are recorded in 16-bit stereo. As a rule, you should keep the size to a minimum for system sounds because it takes a few seconds for a larger sound to load and play.

You assign sounds to specific Windows events like this:

1. Open the Control Panel, and run the Sounds and Multimedia applet. The dialog box previously shown in Figure 29.28 appears.

2. The top section, Sound Events, lists the events that can have sounds associated with them. Several classes of events are listed on a typical computer, such as Windows, NetMeeting, Windows Explorer, Media Player, Power Configurator, Sound Recorder, or Wireless Link. As you purchase and install new programs in the future, those programs may add their own events to your list. An event with a speaker icon next to it already has a sound associated with it. You can click it and then click the Preview button

to hear the sound. The sound file that's associated with the event is listed in the Name box.

3. Click any event for which you want to assign a sound or change the assigned sound.

4. Open the drop-down Name list, and choose the WAV file you want to use for that event. Some of the event names may not make sense to you, such as Asterisk, Critical Stop, or Exclamation. These names are for the various classes of dialog boxes that Windows 95 displays from time to time. The sounds you're most likely to hear often will be Default Beep, Menu Command, New Mail Notification, Question, Open Program, Close Program, Minimize, Maximize, and Close program. You might want to start by assigning sounds to them and then add others as you feel like it.

5. Repeat these steps for each item you want to assign or reassign a sound to. Then click OK to close the dialog box.

Tip #344	The default folder for sounds is the \winnt\media. If you have a WAV file stored in another folder and want to assign it to an event, use the Browse button to locate it. You don't have to move your sound files into the \winnt\media folder for it to work. However, if you're planning on reassigning sounds regularly, you'll find that the process is easier if you move your WAV files into the media folder first.

At the top of the list of available sounds is an option called <none>, which has the obvious effect: No sound will occur for that event. Assigning all events to <none> effectively silences your laptop for use in a library or other silent setting. You can also silence all sounds easily by choosing the No Sounds sound scheme as explained next.

LOADING AND SAVING SOUND SCHEMES

In the same way that the Display Properties page lets you save color schemes, the Sounds and Multimedia applet lets you save sound schemes. You can set up goofy sounds for your humorous moods and somber ones for those gloomy days. I often tire of a sound scheme, so I have a few setups that I can easily switch to. The ones supplied with Windows 2000 are pretty decent, actually, and considering the amount of work required to set up your own schemes, you'll probably make out best just trying a scheme to see if you like it.

To choose an existing sound scheme, follow these steps:

1. Click the drop-down list button for schemes at the bottom of the dialog box.

2. When a list of existing schemes appears, choose a sound scheme. Now all the events in the upper part of the box will have the new sound scheme's sounds. Check out the sounds as explained previously to see whether you like them.

3. If you like them, click OK.

You can set up your own sound schemes by assigning or reassigning individual sounds, as I've already explained. But unless you *save* the scheme with the Save As button, it'll be lost the next time you change to a new one. So, the moral is, after you get your favorite sounds assigned to system events, save the scheme. Then you can call it up any time you like.

THE AUDIO TAB

Using the Audio tab of the Sounds and Multimedia Properties dialog box, you can simply declare the hardware you want to use for audio playback, recording, and MIDI playback. Most systems offer minimal choices in these departments because typical computers have only a single sound system. You might find something strange in the sound playback and recording settings, such as the option to use your modem for these purposes (if your modem has voice messaging capability). Don't bother trying to use your modem for voice messaging unless you have multiple sound cards in the computer.

The Advanced buttons for the three categories could be useful, however, depending on your sound system's chip set. Some offer options to adjust bass and treble; expanded stereo (sort of a wider sound based on adjustment of the "phase" of the signal going to the amplifier); sample-rate conversion options; equalization optimization based on the kind of speakers you have; and hardware acceleration (use full acceleration if you're a gamer because it affects DirectSound used in some games). Figure 29.28 shows the advanced dialog for an ESS Maestro sound chip-based system.

Figure 29.28

Advanced properties for an ESS Maestro sound system let you choose the types of speakers the computer is attached to.

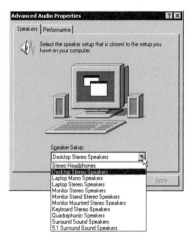

The Use Only Preferred Devices option determines which sound card or cards your programs will use. If you use programs that require a specific type of sound card, and that sound card is selected in Preferred Devices, select this check box. That way, if for some reason your preferred devices aren't available, the program doesn't bomb or freak out by trying to use a sound card that Windows thinks is a reasonable replacement. For any situation I've been in, leaving the check box cleared has never been a problem.

THE HARDWARE TAB

The Hardware tab of the Sounds and Multimedia Properties dialog simply lists all the sound, video, DVD, and other multimedia hardware items currently installed. You can check their properties, current status, and troubleshoot them. You can get to them via the Device Manager just as well, but this tab limits the device list only to multimedia-related hardware.

TROUBLESHOOTING

PROGRAM DOESN'T SHOW UP

A program I'm trying to kill doesn't show up in the Add/Remove Programs applet. How can I remove it?

This is often the case with programs that don't announce themselves thoroughly to Windows as they are being installed. You have to find the program on the hard disk and eliminate it using the Windows Explorer. Finding a program is often as simple as browsing to the Program Files folder, opening it, and looking around for a folder holding the program in question. Often, deleting the folder is all you have to do. Look for an uninstall application there first because it will do a more complete job of removal than just killing the folder, most likely, because some stray DLLs and other support files may be scattered about, not to mention shortcuts in your Start menus that you'll want axed.

As a second (and possibly quicker) means of discovering the location of an unlisted program, you can use its Start menu shortcut to lead you to the application's source. Open the Start menu, and click your way to the application. When you see it, *right-click* it. Now choose Properties from the context menu. Then click Find Target to go directly to the folder where the program resides. Then you can start your dirty work.

If you're trying to kill a program that seems to start up all on its own when you boot up, choose Start, Programs, Startup. Anything in this group autoexecutes upon bootup. Right-click the offending item, and choose Delete. This trick doesn't remove the program from your hard disk, but it prevents the program from starting at boot time.

NO BATTERY ICON IN SYSTEM TRAY

I don't see a battery icon in the system tray. My laptop seems to be brain dead about batteries and power conservation.

Make sure APM is enabled for the computer via the Power Options applet in the Control Panel. Also, make sure the computer complies with APM (check your BIOS settings).

CANNOT CONNECT

My modem isn't connecting for some reason.

More often than not, modem problems are caused by incorrect phone numbers and/or a bad phone line connection. Assuming Windows detected and installed your modem, don't get esoteric in your troubleshooting. Just as you're most likely to find a lost item where you think it should be, it's the silly things that keep modems from working—a bad or incompletely inserted phone wire, bad wall jack, or splitter; or a phone number that's missing an area code (or has an unnecessary area code) being dialed. Another typical goof is to specify an external access number (typically 9), which might be necessary at the office but not on the road. Check the properties for the Dial-Up Networking connection you're trying to use. Also, of course, double-check the user ID and password. You might be dialing in and physically connecting just fine, but the remote server is kicking you off because of incorrect user ID or password.

Finally, recall that a number of troubleshooters are built into Windows 2000. One of them is for modems. Choose Start, Help, and in the right pane, click Troubleshooting.

IT'S NOT HERE

My camera or scanner doesn't show up.

Sometimes starting with the obvious is easiest. Does the device have power? Is your scanner or camera plugged in and turned on? Check the power cables and the data connection. Does the camera have a good power source? Digital cameras eat up batteries at a ravenous rate. Either use fresh batteries or an external power source. (I recommend getting nickel-metal hydride batteries for digital cameras. They work much longer than normal alkalines or Ni-Cad batteries.) If the connection is an infrared one, check the Wireless Link settings, and make sure the camera and computer IR sensor are lined up properly.

Some devices don't connect correctly unless they're turned on. See your device documentation if you need more information.

As per my usual admonition, check your cables! Make sure you have the correct type of cable plugged into the correct ports on both the device and your computer. See your scanner or camera documentation for more information. Your device may be connected to a port that is disabled. A serial port, for example, is often disabled to allow an internal modem to work.

Next, check to see whether the driver for your device is installed. Virtually all cameras and scanners are Plug and Play these days, so Windows 2000 should install the drivers for them automatically. However, you might need to install drivers for some devices manually. See the section in the this chapter covering the Scanners and Cameras applet for details on installing a driver. If that doesn't help, and the device is listed as installed (in Control Panel, Scanners and Cameras), try removing it and reinstalling it via that applet and then reinstalling it (by clicking Remove and then Add).

USING DOS PROGRAMS WITH A MOUSE

Why is the mouse pointer still on the screen while I'm in DOS?

Lots of folks still run DOS programs, even under Windows 9x, NT, and Windows 2000. Most DOS programs are keyboard driven and don't require a mouse. Normally, however, when you run DOS programs in a window, the mouse pointer sits annoyingly on the screen, even though it's useless.

You can hide the mouse pointer when running an MS-DOS program, assuming you don't need it. To hide it, right-click the title bar of the MS-DOS window to display the menu, and then click Hide Mouse Pointer. (If the program switches between character-based and graphics modes, you might need to hide the mouse pointer again.) When the mouse pointer is hidden, you can't see it inside or outside the program's window. To display the mouse pointer, press Alt+Spacebar, and choose Display Mouse Pointer from the resulting menu.

Tips from the Windows Pros: Transferring Images from the Camera to Your PC

What's the best way to get pictures from a camera into a computer?

Efficiently moving photographs from a camera to a computer is something everyone with a digital camera wants to do. Even though most digital cameras come with a digital link of some sort and transfer software that works within Windows, you can waste a lot of time using a slow COM port or infrared link, especially if you have a megapixel camera. The files from these cameras are typically quite large (at least a couple hundred kilobytes each) and, aside from being slow to transfer, can run down your camera's batteries just doing the transfer.

I can think of several better approaches. The approach you use depends somewhat on the computer you have and the type of memory your camera uses, but they all involve removing the media ("digital film") from your camera.

I think the best combination of storage and transfer is a Compact Flash card and PCMCIA adapter. Not all cameras use Compact Flash media, but most do. Here's my technique:

1. Take your pictures.
2. Pop out the Compact Flash card, insert it into the PC card adapter, plug the PC card into the laptop (even when on because PC cards are hot swappable), and Windows 2000 will recognize the card as a disk drive.
3. Switch to Windows Explorer, and check the contents of the new removable drive. All your pictures will be there instantly. No transfer necessary.
4. Now select all the files by pressing Ctrl+A; then press Ctrl+X to cut them.
5. Target the destination folder on your hard disk where you want to move the images, and press Ctrl+V. They are then moved into that folder. Because you used Ctrl+X to cut them from the Compact Flash card, you've effectively cleaned off the card for its next use at the same time. So you don't have to format it in the camera now.

If you're using a desktop machine, go get a Compact Flash card reader, install it, and use the same technique. If your camera relies on Smart Media instead of Compact Flash media, get a gadget that reads that format, such as a Smart Media floppy disk adapter, and then adjust the technique as necessary.

Tip #345

All digital cameras use a numerical naming system for the images they store on the removable media. Some cameras never number two images with the same number. Others always start with some number (Nikon uses DSC0001.jpg). Obviously, a problem arises when collecting images in your computer: New images from each photo session are going to have the same names. If you try to move the images into the same hard disk folder each time, you'll get an error message from Windows asking whether you want to overwrite existing files. Obviously, you don't. You have to create a new folder for each transfer. I do so by creating a parent folder called From Camera. Under that folder, I create folders with simple numeric names, such as 1, 2, 3, and so on. When I get a chance to organize the photos into more traditional categories (I have folders for people, places, parties, travel, flowers, and so on.), I move them and rename them.

MAINTAINING AND OPTIMIZING SYSTEM PERFORMANCE

In this chapter

RUNNING A TIGHT SHIP

If you're reading this chapter, you are probably the kind of user or administrator who is interested in keeping your Windows workstation spinning like a top. Or maybe you have the responsibility of maintaining a myriad of computers on the company LAN, and your charges insist that you do the same for them. You probably like to install and test new video cards, experiment with USB devices, or set up multiple hardware profiles. In short, you must tinker with your hardware. You are also most likely to be interested in improving the performance of your system through system software enhancement and tweaking on a deeper level than figuring out which screen saver will kick in when you're hanging out at the water cooler.

In this chapter, I'll discuss some of the techniques that will best serve you in that process. I'll start with a discussion about specific hardware upgrades you might want to make and how to best take advantage of them should you decide to make such upgrades. Primary among the topics will be the use of the Control Panel's Add/Remove Hardware applet, the Device Manager for configuring hardware add-ins, and troubleshooters.

The remainder of the chapter will deal with configuration of the various program application subsystems—Win32, Win16, DOS, and a bit on OS/2.

UPGRADING YOUR HARDWARE

If you're running Windows 2000 Professional on a full-bore, state-of-the-art system such as a multiprocessor Compaq or a top-notch Pentium III system, and your system has a fast video accelerator, a SCSI drive, and lots of memory, you don't have much more to do in the way of actual hardware optimizing. You might want to consider Windows 2000 Professional's appetite and throw as much RAM as possible at it, adjust the pagefile sizes, or convert as many partitions to NTFS as you can. Some of the settings you can make were discussed in Chapter 29, "Customizing via Control Panel Applets," and the remainder will be discussed in Chapter 31, "System Management and Configuration Tools," and Chapter 33, "Managing the Hard Disk."

By the same token, if you're on a single Windows 2000 Professional workstation doing common, everyday tasks such as word processing, and you're satisfied with the performance of your computer as a whole, you probably don't need to worry about performance boosters anyway. Your system is probably running just fine, and the time you waste trying to fine-tune it could be better spent doing whatever it is you use your computer for (like earning a living).

As discussed in Chapter 3, "Getting Your Hardware and Software Ready for Windows 2000," you might consider several hardware upgrades should you be economy-minded and prefer to fight planned obsolescence rather than comply with the "in with the new, out with the old" mentality. If you want to keep your older computer chassis and slowly change the innards (like I do), or if you're a system administrator who suddenly has the task of upgrading a slew of machines to Windows 2000, you should review the following sections and Chapter 3.

As a brief reminder, you should consider the following areas of hardware upgrades and optimization to increase your throughput.

BIOS SETTINGS

By all means, study the manual supplied with the computer hardware. Often, significant proprietary performance-tuning features go unnoticed until they're discovered buried deep in the manual somewhere. Depending on what's built into the motherboard (for example, what type of bus, CPU, video, and so on), the BIOS options will vary or be more extensive. Some fancy motherboards let you finely tweak the technique the system uses to refresh the RAM chips, let you specify blocks of memory that shouldn't be used by the operating system because a plug-in card needs that memory block, or let you set the internal clock source (tick rate) or CPU type and speed.

Be careful when you're futzing with the BIOS. If your machine is working okay, it probably doesn't have any problems that need addressing. If you're inexperienced in such matters, steer away from making changes to BIOS settings. You can view them, but you should leave the setup program without saving the changes. How you do so varies from machine to machine, but usually a series of Esc keypresses gets you out safely. The following are some points to check:

- Set up your boot order to start with drive C: so that you can skip the floppy stepper motor test. This way, you can speed up booting a tad.

- Check out the BIOS and video shadowing. Most CMOS BIOS setup routines let you turn BIOS and video shadowing on or off. You should ensure that both are turned on, if possible. Sometimes you have the option of choosing the location of the RAM that will be used to hold the relocated code. You might need to do so only if you have an oddball card or another device that is mapped into a portion of system memory normally used for shadowing. I've never had to bother with this setting, and you probably won't either. Just check to see that the setup routine has video and BIOS shadowing enabled.

 If, after tinkering with your BIOS settings, you find that your computer will no longer boot up, see "Altered BIOS Settings Prevent Computer from Booting" in the "Troubleshooting" section at the end of this chapter.

UPGRADING YOUR HARD DISK

One of the most effective improvements you can make to a system is to get a faster and/or larger hard drive, or you can add another drive. SCSI hard disks used to seriously one-up IDE drives, but the new breed of EIDE drives are quite speedy. Don't bother with SCSI unless you need it for fancy RAID setups (see Chapter 33) that rely on proprietary controllers such as mirroring controllers, or you need a chain of drives that exceed the number the EIDE bus will support. An EIDE bus supports four drives (two each on the primary and secondary channels). Adding a CD-ROM drive claims one, leaving you with a maximum of three EIDE hard drives.

The following are some essential considerations for upgrading your hard disk system:

- Delete unnecessary files and applications. Use the Control Panel's Add/Remove Programs applet to remove old applications, and use the Internet Options to clear the Web cache. Open My Computer, right-click a drive icon, choose Properties, and then choose Disk Cleanup to remove files.

- Don't put a hard drive and a CD-ROM drive on the same channel unless necessary. An IDE channel negotiates down to the slowest device on a channel, slowing down the hard disk's effective transfer rate. Make sure the hard drive containing Windows is designated as the Primary Master drive.

- Optimize the hard disk interleave. Carefully check the documentation with the drive and your computer first. Resetting the interleave can take a long time. Optimally, it will be 1:1. Virtually all new drives operate at this speed already, but some older ones don't.

- Defragment the hard disk with the Defragmenter utility (see Chapter 33).

- Upgrade the disk controller. If you're using an ultra-wide SCSI II or later driver, for example, make sure you have a controller that takes maximum advantage of it. If you're using an ISA controller, chuck it. Get on the 100MHz PCI bus, or use a motherboard with a fast internal controller tied right into the 100MHz bus. It should be a direct memory access (DMA) bus-mastering controller if possible.

- Get a faster disk drive. Many new drives can run at high speeds and use wide data paths. Check out the high-rev drives (10KB/sec and above), ultra DMA, Ultra-Wide Fast SCSI II, and so on. Make sure the track-to-track seek time on the drive is quick. Read the fine print on drive specs. Sometimes they quote average access times, which don't represent worst-case scenarios. Check the overall transfer rate of the drive, too, and make sure your controller can accommodate it. Don't buy a super-fast drive if your controller, bus, and CPU can't handle it. If you are doing video editing and playback or anything that requires real-time performance, purchase an A/V-ready drive. These drives are thermally more stable and don't stop midstream to recalibrate the stepper motor that controls the head position.

RAM

Perhaps the most cost-effective upgrade you can make to any Windows-based system is to add RAM. Windows recognizes newly added RAM and adapts internal settings, such as when to swap to disk, to take best advantage of any RAM you throw its way. If your disk is heavily thrashing each time you switch between running applications or documents, you probably need RAM. Power users should be running 128MB minimum for really nice, smooth daily operation with multiple, simultaneously running applications.

ADDING AND REMOVING HARDWARE

One of the tasks that is most common for anyone responsible for configuring and maintaining PCs is adding and removing hardware. The Control Panel contains an applet designed for that purpose; it's called the Add/Remove Hardware applet. You can use it in cases in which the operating system doesn't automatically recognize that you've swiped something or added something new, whether it's a peripheral such as a printer or an internal device such as a DVD-ROM, additional hard disk, or whatever.

If you're a hardware maven, you'll be visiting this applet a lot, especially if you're working with non-Plug and Play hardware. Plug and Play hardware installation is pretty much a no-brainer because Windows 2000 Professional is good at detection and should install items fairly automatically, along with any necessary drivers.

Note that this Control Panel applet has been modified in Windows 2000 Professional to include disabling or removing hardware, too. That task used to be the province of the System applet.

PART

V

CH

30

Tip #346	You use the System applet or the Computer Management Console, not Add/Remove Hardware, for fine-tuning device settings, such as IRQ and port, and updating devices and drivers. You use Add/Remove Hardware only for adding or removing hardware. Also, note that you can find other locations throughout Windows for installing some devices (for example, printers, which can be installed from the Printers folder), even though the effect is the same as using this applet. In other words, the Add New Hardware Wizard can be triggered from a number of disparate locations throughout the operating system.

If you've purchased a board or other hardware add-in, you should first read the supplied manual for details about installation procedures. Installation tips and an install program may be supplied with the hardware. However, if no instructions are included, you can physically install the hardware and keep reading.

Close any programs you have running, just in case the installation process hangs the computer. The computer doesn't hang very often in NT-based Windows, such as Windows 2000 Professional, but it can. Save your work, and close your applications.

For non-Plug and Play hardware, or for Plug and Play stuff that isn't detected or doesn't install automatically for some reason, you must run the Add/Remove Hardware applet. The typical scenario is to declare whether you are installing or removing hardware and then let the wizard, shown in Figure 30.1, try searching for Plug and Play hardware. If nothing is found, Windows assumes you're having some trouble with a device. Your currently installed devices are listed with an option to troubleshoot or to add something new. For veterans, the combination option of adding new hardware or troubleshooting installed hardware seems a bit weird until you get used to it. I guess Microsoft wanted the wizard to perform double-duty.

Next, you're asked whether you want the wizard to attempt a legacy detection or you want to specify the item yourself. (Legacy hardware interrogation is a science all its own, and I'm always amazed when some old job like a sound card is detected properly.) While the hardware survey is underway, you'll see a "gas gauge" apprising you of the progress, and you'll hear lots of hard disk activity.

Figure 30.1
When a new Plug and Play device isn't found, you see this dialog box. Choose Add a New Device.

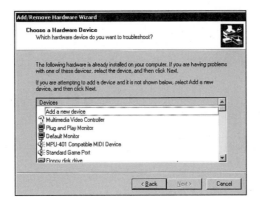

If something is found, continue with the wizard, and answer the questions as prompted.

In case the item isn't detected properly, you can simply declare manually what you are installing. The wizard shows you a list of hardware types and asks you to choose from the category list. Just choose the applicable category, and click Next.

Tip #347

If the category you're looking for isn't listed, choose Other Devices and click Next. Then you can choose from the complete list of all manufacturers and models.

Make sure you choose the precise brand name and model number/name of the item you're installing. You might be prompted to insert your Windows 2000 CD-ROM so that the appropriate driver file(s) can be loaded.

Early in the wizard's steps, you have the option of declaring the hardware yourself and skipping the legacy scan. Choosing this option can save you time and, in some cases, is the surer path to installing new hardware. It also lets you physically install the hardware later, should you want to. The wizard doesn't bother to authenticate the existence of the hardware; it simply installs the new driver.

Tip #348

In some cases, you are given the option of adjusting settings after the hardware is installed and possibly adjusting your hardware to match. (Some legacy cards have switches or software adjustments that can be made to them to control the I/O port, DMA address, and so forth.) You may be told which settings to use to avoid conflicts with other hardware in the system.

If, for some reason, you don't want to use the settings suggested by the wizard, you can use your own settings and manually set them. You can do so from the Add/Remove Hardware Wizard or via the Device Manager (from the System applet). See "Driver Signing and the Device Manager" later in this chapter for coverage of the Device Manager.

> **Caution**
>
> In general, be cautious about configuring resource settings manually. When you change settings manually, the settings become fixed, and Windows 2000's built-in device contention resolution is less likely to work. Also, if you install too many devices with manually configured settings, you might not be able to install new Plug and Play devices because none will be available. In the worst-case scenario, the system might not even boot if conflicts occur with primary hardware devices such as hard disk controllers or video cards. If you decide to use manual configuration, make sure you know what you're doing, and have the specs for the hardware in question at hand.

In cases in which the wizard detects a conflict, you are alerted when you finish walking through the wizard steps. You then have the option of bailing or continuing despite the conflict. You can also back up and choose a different model of hardware, such as one you think is compatible with what you're attempting to install. Figure 30.2 shows a typical message when a conflict is detected.

Figure 30.2
When a hardware conflict is detected, it's reported by the wizard at the end of the installation process.

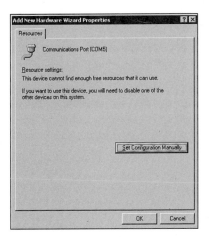

You now have the choice of setting the hardware resources for this device manually. Click Set Configuration Manually to change the settings. You'll see something such as the dialog box in Figure 30.3.

PROVIDING DRIVERS FOR HARDWARE NOT IN THE LIST

When the hardware you're attempting to install isn't on the device list, the problem is either because the hardware is newer than Windows 2000, or it's really old and Microsoft decided not to include it. In this case, you must obtain the driver from the manufacturer (or Microsoft; check Web sites) and get it ready on disk or on the hard disk, either locally or across the LAN. If the manufacturer supplies a setup disk, forget my advice, and follow the manufacturer's instructions. However, if the manufacturer supplies a driver disk and no instructions, follow along with these steps:

Figure 30.3
Use caution when manually changing resources for a device. You may end up choosing a nonavailable resource. In this dialog, the I/O range is not available, though I manually chose it.

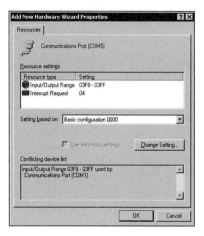

1. Run the Add/Remove Hardware applet.

2. Click Next. Then choose the correct class of hardware.

3. Click the Have Disk button.

4. Enter the location of the driver (you can enter any path, such as a directory on the hard disk or network path). Typically, you insert a disk in drive A:. Use the Browse button if you need to. You're looking for an .INF file, incidentally.

5. Assuming the wizard finds a suitable driver file, choose the correct hardware item from the resulting dialog box, and follow the onscreen directions.

Tip #349

If you're not sure which ports and interrupts your other boards are using, you can use the Device Manager to locate available and used IRQs, ports, DMA, and so on.

 If you've added some hardware and it doesn't work, see "New Hardware Doesn't Work" in the "Troubleshooting" section at the end of this chapter.

REMOVING HARDWARE

The Add/Remove Hardware applet obviously also enables you to remove hardware. You can use this function of the applet when you plan to remove a card, drive, and so on or if you want to unplug a device. Some devices are hot-swappable, and in that case, you needn't worry about taking these steps. Firewire and USB, for example, can be plugged and unplugged with impunity. On the other hand, COM and LPT ports are not as forgiving of devices suddenly disappearing. Nor are PCMCIA slots. You should alert the operating system by running the Add/Remove Hardware applet before unplugging these items, or the system could get confused.

Tip #350	You can stop PCMCIA cards by clicking the PC Card icon in the system tray, which has the same effect as disabling the item from this applet.

To remove hardware, follow these steps:

1. Run the Add/Remove Hardware applet.
2. Start the wizard.
3. Choose Uninstall/Unplug a Device.
4. Choose either permanent or temporary removal, depending on your aim.
5. Choose the device to uninstall, and confirm your selection. You may be prompted to reboot.

USING THE SYSTEM APPLET

One of the tools you're more than likely to rely on frequently for management of the computer's hardware is the Control Panel's System applet. The System applet contains two tabs—Hardware and Advanced—that are most likely to be used when managing hardware.

→ To learn more details about using the tools on the Network Identification tab, **see** "Setting Your Computer Identification," **p. 729**.

→ For more details on the settings on the User Profiles tab, **see** "User Profiles," **p. 1212**.

The General tab isn't good for much. You certainly can't make any settings from it. However, it does tell you what operating system you're running, the registered user's name, the Windows serial number, the type of computer, and the amount of RAM. Checking this tab is a relatively quick way to find out the amount of RAM Windows is detecting—which is particularly useful if you've just added some and you're wondering whether you installed it correctly, or if you're considering adding more RAM and don't recall how well the computer is currently endowed.

The other tabs and settings deal more with user and network-level management, discussed in other chapters. So, let's start with the Hardware tab. Figure 30.4 shows the Hardware tab of the Control Panel's System applet.

The Hardware tab's first option is the Hardware Wizard button. Choosing it has the effect of running the Add/Remove Hardware Wizard, which was covered in the preceding section. There's no sense running the wizard a second time. This button is just a shortcut so that you can direct the operating system to scan for new hardware from this dialog.

PART
V

CH
30

Figure 30.4
The Hardware tab of the System applet is a control center for examining and modifying hardware.

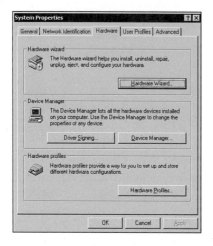

DRIVER SIGNING AND THE DEVICE MANAGER

The second section of the System applet's Hardware tab, Device Manager, lets you dig into the guts of the machine and see what's installed and what's running or problematic; you also can examine or modify hardware drivers from this section.

The first button in this section, Driver Signing, helps prevent bogus files and drivers from invading your operating system and potentially crashing it.

The idea is that all the important code and drivers that are allowed into the critical areas of the operating system should be tested and "signed" by the maker of the files, typically Microsoft. All the Windows 2000 drivers and operating system files supplied on the CD have an embedded *digital signature* from Microsoft. It is supposed to ensure their quality, which it does, short of the bugs that Microsoft decided to let through the production process—typically noncritical ones that will later be fixed. But at least Microsoft's digital signature on a file offers some assurance that the file has been through numerous rigorous testing phases and that the file wasn't overwritten by some other program's installation process. Tacking on a digital signature to a file is not easy, so counterfeit files will not likely become a stock in trade.

You or your administrator can configure three levels of protection on a computer. Clicking the Driver Signing button brings up a dialog for doing just that, as shown in Figure 30.5.

Figure 30.5
Setting the digital signature protection level for a machine can protect against the addition of bogus drivers and system files.

Based on the settings you choose, Windows 2000 either ignores device drivers that have no signature, warns you when it detects device drivers that are not digitally signed (the default), or prevents you from installing device drivers without digital signatures. Table 30.1 lists the options.

TABLE 30.1   CODE SIGNING OPTIONS

Setting	Meaning
Ignore	Any and all device drivers will be installed, without checking for a valid digital signature.
Warn	If you try to install a driver that doesn't have a valid signature, you'll be alerted with a dialog box during the installation process. You can then cancel or continue.
Block	Drivers are always checked for signature. If one valid signature is missing, the installation process stops dead in its tracks.
Apply Setting as System Default	Only if you're logged in as a member of the Administrator group can you alter this setting, because it affects all users. When it is set on, it applies the settings above to all users who log on.

→ An additional tool for verifying the signature of files, including all the system files, is called the File Signature Verification tool. To learn more about it, **see** "Running the File Signature Verification Tool," **p. 1169**.

Leaving the default setting for signature verification is probably the wisest choice for general usage. You should instruct users of the computer to check with you or the administrator if a warning pops up during installation of a program. Then a decision can be made on an ad hoc basis. Using the highest level of protection can be annoying because an installation will simply terminate mysteriously if the signature isn't found. Of course, in certain mission-critical settings, that result may be just what you want.

THE DEVICE MANAGER

The Device Manager is the core tool for managing hardware configuration. In earlier versions of Windows, managing devices meant running around to several different applets, depending on the class of device. Since the Device Manager appeared, checking the existence and status of devices, installing and removing them, and updating drivers for them can be done at this one-stop shop.

You can get to the Device Manager in two main ways:

- Choose Control Panel, System, Hardware, Device Manager.

- Choose Start, Settings, Control Panel, Administrative Tools, and then double-click Computer Management. Open the System Tools branch, and then click Device Manager. You get a different and more powerful view of devices this way, more like the Windows Explorer, because the console tree is in view (see Figure 30.6).

Figure 30.6
The Device Manager through the eyes of the Computer Management Console.

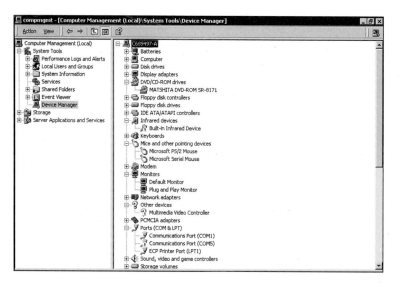

If you open the Device Manager through the Control Panel, you can add the left pane by choosing View, Console Tree, though you'll see only Device Manager on Local Machine in the tree. In either case, it's the same Device Manager. From the Computer Management Console, you can see more information about potential conflicts, such as IRQ, DMA, and so on, but I'll explain more about that soon.

You can click a + (plus) sign to expand a device category to investigate the installed components in the category. I've expanded a couple in the figure. Also note that problematic items are marked with an exclamation mark. You can check on any item's status by right-clicking it and choosing Properties, as you can see in Figure 30.7.

Figure 30.7
You can begin operating on a specific piece of software via Properties.

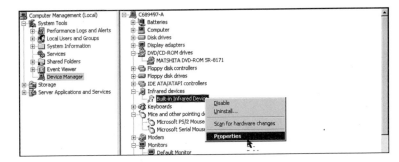

Choosing this option opens a Properties dialog, like the one shown in Figure 30.8. You can do some serious device tweaking from this dialog.

Figure 30.8
A Properties dialog box for a malfunctioning piece of hardware.

Choices on the dialog box vary from device to device. In this case, for the infrared port that's not working, an IrDa tab is available. The most important items are shown in Table 30.2.

TABLE 30.2   PROPERTIES DIALOG TABS

Tab	Options and Notes
General	Status: Check to see whether the device is reported as working properly.
	Troubleshooter: If the device is not working, you can click the troubleshooter to walk through a wizard.
	Device Usage: You can check the hardware configurations that are available on your computer. You also can disable a device in a hardware configuration by clearing the check box next to the hardware configuration.
Settings	The options on this tab vary with the device.

continues

TABLE 30.2 CONTINUED

Tab	Options and Notes
Driver	Driver Details: This tab displays the author of the driver, version, and location on the hard disk. It's worth checking. Most of the drivers will be from Microsoft, unless you installed one from another manufacturer.
	Uninstall: You can use this tab to remove the device drivers for this device. Removing the drivers effectively kills the device. You might have to reboot afterward, but in many cases, it's not required. You can add the device manually later if you change your mind. Sometimes removing and reinstalling a device can clear up problems you were having with it.
	Update Driver: This button runs the Upgrade Device Driver Wizard, which walks you through the process of adding a driver. Refer to the "Adding and Removing Hardware" section earlier in the chapter if you have questions about the process of changing a driver.
Resources	Set Configuration Manually: If you suspect that the device is conflicting with other devices and this is why it's not working, you may be allowed to configure it manually.

If you decide to change the resources for a device, be cautious. Manually setting a device's resource assignment can result in conflicts with other installed devices, and doing so imposes restrictions on the Plug and Play system's capability to dynamically allocate resources in the future. (I mentioned this point in the section on the Add/Remove Hardware applet earlier but repeat it here because it's important.)

To reassign a resource, click the resource in question on the Resources tab, and choose Change Setting. In an attempt to prevent folks from inadvertently doing damage, the manual resource assignment dialog keeps an eye on what you're doing. If you attempt to reassign to a resource that is already in use, you'll be warned about the conflict. Check out Figure 30.9 as an example.

Figure 30.9
If you attempt to reassign a device to a pre-allocated resource, you'll be notified. Here, you can see a COM5 port with an unassigned IRQ and a conflicting I/O range. I'm hoping to assign IRQ 9, but it's taken by the IDE controller.

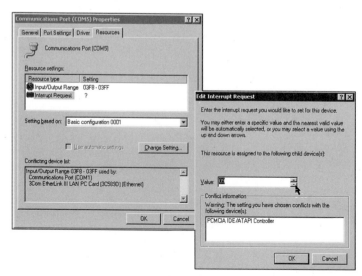

Some drivers don't have resources that can be reassigned. Others have an option button called Reinstall Driver if the system thinks that would solve a nonfunctioning-device problem. In general, devices that are operating properly don't let you reassign the resources.

> **Caution**
>
> Notice the Setting Based On drop-down list on the Resources tab. It lists the hardware configurations in which the currently selected device is enabled. If you choose a hardware configuration other than the default, and you change any resource settings, resource conflicts may occur when you use the default hardware configuration. Resource conflicts can disable your hardware and cause your computer to malfunction or to be inoperable.
>
> If you have multiple hardware configurations (see later in this chapter), the moral of the story is to try to keep the same configurations for hardware between them. It's okay to totally *turn off* specific pieces of hardware for a given saved hardware configuration, but when you start changing the resource allocations for each one, you could end up with a mess.

USING THE COMPUTER MANAGEMENT CONSOLE

Wouldn't it be nice if you could easily see which hardware resources are being used and which are free? This isn't as necessary in these days of Plug and Play as it was when legacy hardware ruled, but it's still required for serious sleuthing. The Computer Management Console lets you do just that. In Windows 9x and NT 4, you could list used and free resources in a variety of sort orders via a trick in the Device Manager (by checking the Computer properties). This trick doesn't work in Windows 2000 Professional. Here's how to see them in Windows 2000:

1. Run Computer Management. (An easy way to run it is to right-click My Computer and choose Manage.)

2. Open System Tools, System Information, Hardware Resources.

3. Click the listing of your heart's desire. Figure 30.10 shows the current assignments on one of my computers. Notice that several items share the same IRQ.

Check the conflicts, DMA, forced hardware, I/O, IRQ, and memory allocations by clicking their respective folders.

→ The Computer Management Console is a powerful tool. This section describes only a small fraction of what it can do. Chapter 31, "System Management and Configuration Tools," covers the program in more detail.

Figure 30.10
Checking hardware resource allocations and conflicts sorted in various orders makes troubleshooting easier.

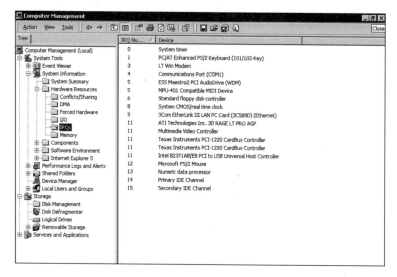

UNDERSTANDING AND RESOLVING HARDWARE CONFLICTS

Windows, together with its Plug and Play technology, has grown far better at detecting and preventing hardware conflicts over the past few years. Still, system conflicts do arise, especially when you're using ISA cards and other legacy hardware. You don't need to throw these items away, however, when they are still perfectly serviceable. For example, I'm still happily using a bunch of ISA network cards I bought probably 10 years ago, and they're effectively operating on my Ethernet backbone.

More often than not, configuration and installation problems are due only to incorrect settings on network, I/O, sound, and other cards. The result is cards that conflict with one another for the same IRQ (interrupt request line), base I/O port address, DMA, or base memory address. Usually, these settings are made by changing jumpers or DIP switches on the board. Legacy items that typically required settings were network cards, bus mouse cards, sound cards, tape backup controllers, SCSI cards, and fax/modem cards.

Note

> Some legacy cards can be configured via software settings rather than DIP switches and jumpers. For example, Novell's popular NE2000 PLUS Ethernet adapter card uses its own utility program to set the IRQ and port address. You might have to run such a configuration program (typically under DOS) to set up the card before it will run correctly under Windows 2000.

As I mentioned earlier, you can force Windows 2000 to use manually declared system resources, such as IRQ, for a given piece of gear. In the Device Manager, choose the item, open its Properties dialog, click the Resources tab, turn off Use Automatic Settings, and enter the resource or resources you want to assign.

> **Caution**
>
> Don't manually assign resources unless you know what you're doing. The result can be an operating system that won't boot or a bunch of other components in your system that no longer work.

In case your understanding of board configuration settings is somewhat foggy, the next few sections provide a quick review.

IRQs

PC architecture includes a means for a piece of hardware to quickly gain the attention of the CPU through a message called an *interrupt request*, or *IRQ*. Interrupts are sent over one of the 15 IRQ wires on the computer's bus. Such a request is a direct line to the CPU, which then services the request accordingly. A common example occurs when data comes in to your system's modem or LAN card. The modem or LAN card triggers the predetermined interrupt line (IRQ), and the CPU then begins to execute the program code that is appropriate for handling that interrupt. In fact, a part of the operating system called the *interrupt handler* is responsible for making it so.

If there were an unlimited supply of IRQs, this scheme would prove acceptable. But there is not. To make matters worse, as a rule, no two items in the computer should share the same IRQ. When two devices attempt to use the same interrupt at the same time, a data collision can happen and the system can hang, or nothing happens at all. If two peripherals are set to use the same IRQ and do so at the same time, a short is produced on the bus.

Under DOS and earlier versions of Windows, some sharing of IRQs is allowed. You might be familiar with this use. For example, under DOS, you can usually share LPT1 (IRQ 7) with other devices as long as you're not printing through the LPT port at the time the second device tries to use it. Windows 2000 (and NT) handles IRQ sharing differently. It does support sharing on PCI machines, but only if no ISA card is sharing the same IRQ as another card. In the case of an ISA card and another ISA card or a PCI card sharing the same IRQ, Windows 2000 switches to a "polling" mode, wherein the CPU regularly checks for and services I/O requests rather than waits for IRQ lines to be activated. Obviously, this process can slow down overall system performance because it creates another software loop that the operating system must service.

The moral of the story is that, because of the throwback state of PC architecture, you might have to leave something out of the system if you have boards that aren't very flexible in their IRQ options. Even if they are, today's computers come from the factory so chock full of hardware that you are often unlikely to find more than one or two IRQs available for additional devices, such as NICs or other expansion boards.

Note

Although some complex add-ons that can provide additional IRQs are available, they are typically available only in high-priced specialty computers.

One solution to the IRQ shortage manufacturers have tried is to incorporate the PCI bus into PCs. PCI is an internal bus that theoretically can support a wide variety of on-board and add-in hardware without consuming IRQs. At least, that's the idea. In reality, PCI often ends up using more IRQs than ISA cards do, for reasons that are shrouded in mystery, but which are most likely in order to maintain compatibility with the variety of operating systems they may be used with. What you will find nowadays in computers incorporating both ISA and PCI buses (meaning virtually all of today's PCs) is that every PCI card requires an IRQ, maybe more!

An emerging standard called the PC99 spec will eventually kill off the ISA bus and implement PCI more fully. When this happens, you'll see an end to IRQ scarcity, but until that time, mind your IRQs and check your BIOS. Why the BIOS? Some computers have a BIOS setting that helps the operating system share PCI IRQs, not surprisingly called PCI IRQ sharing.

If you find yourself short on IRQs or if you have two devices attempting to use the same IRQ and creating a conflict, you can try these possible solutions:

- One solution with PCI cards causing conflicts is to try moving the PCI card to another slot. On some machines, each PCI slot's PCI Interrupt (A through D) is mapped to an ISA-type IRQ. By simply moving a card to a neighboring slot, you may luck out and get your hardware working.

- Another solution for IRQ cram is to set up multiple hardware profiles. You might not get all items to work under one profile, but you can have a couple of profiles and at least not have to throw anything away. You just reboot in another profile when you need access to a specific piece of gear.

- Another workaround is to use USB and SCSI buses (if you have them). As you probably know, USB and SCSI both support multiple devices on the same wire. No IRQs are required other than for the controller (typically 1). Yet USB supports up to 64 devices, and SCSI typically 7. If you're struggling with where to put a scanner, printer, digital camera, or additional external hard drive, consider these buses.

- Finally, a solution I've resorted to is using pass-through connectors on the parallel bus. On one machine, I have a printer, a zip drive, and a scanner. They all work together fine, using the pass-through connectors supplied with the products. The cable from the LPT port leads to the zip drive, out to the scanner, and then off to the printer. Obviously, I can't use them simultaneously, but each device driver seems to know how to trigger its respective child.

Table 30.3 lists the common IRQs in an Intel-based computer using ISA technology. This information, in conjunction with the IRQ and the Conflicts/Sharing nodes of the Computer

Management application, might help you to assign boards effectively. But remember, it's always best to let Windows make hardware assignments unless you are really stuck and something important just won't work. Also, remember that if hardware isn't on the Hardware Compatibility List (HCL), you're better off just going shopping than wasting a day tinkering with settings.

TABLE 30.3   TYPICAL IRQ ASSIGNMENTS IN 80286-BASED OR LATER X86 SYSTEMS

IRQ	Typical Assignment
2	EGA/VGA video (almost never available because it's redirected to IRQ 9)
3	COM2:, COM4: (sometimes available)
4	COM1:, COM3: (usually not available)
5	LPT2: (if a second parallel port is installed, probably available)
6	Floppy disk controller (almost never available)
7	LPT1: (printer port) (almost never available, but if it is, it can be shared only on EISA, MCA, and PCI devices; if an ISA peripheral is detected on the same IRQ, this prevents sharing)
8	System clock (never available)
9	EGA/VGA (seldom available because devices using IRQ 2 are redirected here as well)
10	Often available
11	Often available; note that some 16-bit SCSI cards default to this IRQ
12	PS/2 mouse (available only on systems that don't have a PS/2-style mouse connector
13	Math coprocessor (if installed)
14	IDE hard disk controller (never available)
15	Often available; sometimes used for second channel of IDE hard disk controller

Tip #352	Hardware failures, power failures, and human errors can prevent Windows 2000 from starting successfully. Recovery is easier if you know the configuration of each computer and its history and if you back up critical system files when making changes to your Windows 2000 configuration.
	A good hedge against this problem is to create a technical reference library for all your hardware and software documentation. Your reference library should include the history of software changes and upgrades for each machine, as well as hardware settings such as those described here.

DMA CHANNELS

A typical PC has eight DMA channels, labeled 0 to 7. DMA channels are used for rapidly transferring data between memory and peripherals such as a hard disk, sound cards, and so on, without the help of the CPU. Some cards even use several of these channels at once.

(For example, the Media Vision ProAudio Spectrum 16 uses two DMA channels.) Typical users of DMA channels are

- Memory access controllers
- ECP printer ports
- Floppy disk controllers
- Tape backup controllers
- Network cards
- Scanner cards
- SCSI controllers

Sharing DMA channels is less advised than sharing IRQs. There are exceptions to this rule, but you should never share DMAs that are in use by network cards or hard disk controllers. Important data might be lost. As a rule, try to make sure that no two devices use the same DMA channel at the same time. Table 30.4 shows the typical assignments.

TABLE 30.4   TYPICAL DMA CONTROLLER ASSIGNMENTS

Channel	Typical Assignment
0	Generally used for DMA refresh
1	Available
2	Floppy disk controller
3	Some ECP printer ports
4	DMA controller
5	Available
6	Available
7	Available

Tip #353

Some devices are hidden from view in the Device Manager. Hidden devices include non-Plug and Play devices (devices with earlier Windows 2000 device drivers) and devices that have been physically removed from the computer but have not had their drivers uninstalled. To see hidden devices in the Device Manager list, choose View, Show Hidden Devices. A check mark should appear on the menu, indicating that hidden devices are showing. Click it again to hide them.

I/O PORT ASSIGNMENTS

Using DMA is the fastest way to transfer data between components in the PC. However, an older technology called *memory-mapped I/O* is still in use today. (*I/O* means *input/output*.) In PC architecture, I/O ports are mapped into system memory and therefore are accessed by the CPU using memory addresses. As you might expect, each device that uses an I/O port must have a different port address, or data intended for one device will end up at another.

Check out the I/O folder off the Hardware Resources node in Computer Management, as shown in Figure 30.11, to see a sample list of I/O addresses and assignments. As you can see, this folder contains quite a few assignments. Note that the addresses are in standard memory-mapping parlance—hexadecimal.

Figure 30.11
Typical I/O assignments in a Windows 2000 Professional machine are numerous. Notice the scrollbar. Only about half the assignments are visible in this figure.

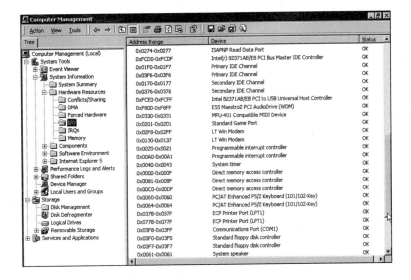

> **Note**
>
> A common source of I/O contention occurs among video cards, SCSI devices, and network cards.

MEMORY ADDRESSES

Similar to the I/O port address, the base memory address is the beginning memory address that some cards or motherboard hardware use to communicate with the CPU. Sometimes this setting is called the *RAM starting address* (or *start address*).

Some older cards (you'll notice this often in network adapters) must have their base memory address set by a jumper or software. Then the device driver for that component needs its software setting to match the jumper. A typical base memory address reads like this: 0xA0000 or just A0000. Sometimes the last digit is dropped, like this: A000.

If you open Computer Management and go to System Information, Hardware Resources, Memory, you'll see memory addresses such as the following:

```
0xA0000-0xBFFFF   PCI bus
```

This address means the memory area between A0000 and BFFFF is fully spoken for use by the PCI bus. (The 0x indicates that it is a hexadecimal address.) So, when setting memory addressing, you must consider not only the base addresses, but also the amount of RAM space the addresses will occupy. Some cards use 16KB of space, and others use 32KB or more. Check the card's manual for options. Using more memory can, in some cases, improve the operation of the card, but it decreases your system's memory availability because that space will be occupied. The end result depends on the type of card.

When you specify a memory address for a card, the operating system reserves that memory area for it. Regular RAM in that area is not used by the CPU, to prevent conflicts that could result from trying to write data or program code into system RAM at that address. Instead, the reserved area is used only by the device driver for your piece of hardware.

Most older ISA cards use an upper memory address that falls somewhere between a000 and FFFF. However, many VL-Bus, PCI, and some ISA cards can use address space above 1MB, or even above 16MB in the case of 32-bit cards. If your card can utilize a high address, it's better to do so because it minimizes the chances of bumping into the operating system.

UPDATING DEVICE DRIVERS

At some point, you'll need to get the latest driver for a device. Perhaps you'll visit the Web site of the company that makes your video card or backup gear, and you'll realize a new download is available. Before you download and install, use this checklist:

1. Do you have permission to upgrade drivers? You need Administrator privileges.
2. Is it really the latest driver? Check the manufacturer's site and the Microsoft site to see what you can find. The following sites are good places to start:
   http://support.microsoft.com/support/downloads
   www.microsoft.com/hcl
   www.windrivers.com

> **Note**
>
> You might want to try running Start, Windows Update, choosing Product Updates, and then choosing Device Drivers. Microsoft may have listed updated device drivers for your system.

3. Does the "new" driver work with Windows 2000 Professional?
4. Did you run Start, Windows Update? It might find and update drivers for you automatically. After the driver passes muster, download it.

After you've downloaded the new driver, install it using these steps:

1. Open the Control Panel or Computer Management Console.
2. In Control Panel, choose System, Hardware, Device Manager. If you're using the Computer Management approach, choose Device Manager in the left pane.
3. Click the device in question, and open its Properties dialog box.

4. In the Properties dialog box, select the Driver tab, and click Details if you want to see what version of the driver you are currently using, or just click Update Driver, as in Figure 30.12, to proceed with updating the driver.

5. When the Update Wizard starts running, click past the first page. On the second page, choose the second option, Display a List.

6. Click Next and then click Have Disk. Browse to the location of the driver. If the driver isn't found on the disk, you're in trouble. The .INF file on the disk and the accompanying driver file(s) must meet the requirements of Windows 2000 to be deemed acceptable for installation. Contact the manufacturer if it looks like a no-go. You might have to download a driver from the manufacturer's Web site.

PART

V

CH

30

Figure 30.12
Updating a driver.

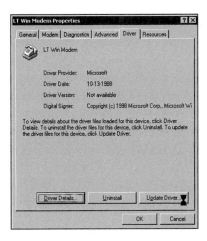

USING THE TROUBLESHOOTERS

The troubleshooters have been mentioned several times in this book, beginning in Chapter 1, "Introducing Windows 2000 Professional." Twelve hardware troubleshooters are supplied with Windows 2000 Professional. Although they won't always solve your problems, they'll at least walk you through a logical train of investigation for your malady, possibly leading you to a conclusion or avenue of thought you hadn't entertained previously.

Buttons for the troubleshooters pop up from time to time while you're using Windows, but if you don't see them, head directly for them from Help:

1. Choose Start, Help.

2. Click Troubleshooting. Notice all the good links!

3. Double-click the Hardware link. You then see a list of troubleshooter wizards, similar to the list in Figure 30.13.

Figure 30.13
The troubleshooters may be of some use helping you solve common problems.

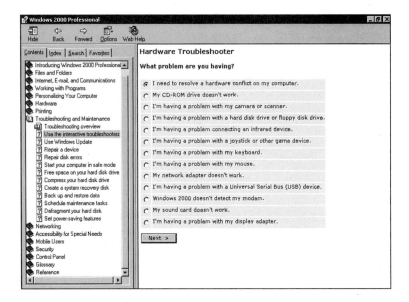

4. Run the troubleshooter that applies. You may be asked some questions that require running the Device Manager to determine the status of your hardware.

Tip #354

If a USB controller doesn't install properly, especially if the controller doesn't show up in the Device Manager, the problem might be in your system BIOS. Some BIOSs have a setting that can enable or disable the USB ports. Shut down and restart. Do whatever your computer requires for you to check the BIOS settings during system startup. Then enter the BIOS setup and enable USB support. When that is done, if the USB controller still doesn't appear in the Device Manager, it's possible that the computer's BIOS might be outdated. Check with the computer's or motherboard's manufacturer for a possible update to support USB under Windows 2000.

Note that you can attempt to troubleshoot a specific installed device by running the Add/Remove Hardware applet from the Control Panel and highlighting the afflicted item.

Installing and Using Multiple Monitors

A terrific feature of Windows 98 that has migrated over to Windows 2000 is the support of multiple monitors on the same machine. Windows 2000 supports up to 10 monitors simultaneously. By using multiple monitors, you can place a large amount of information on your screens at once. Typical applications would be multiple windows for nonlinear video editing with one screen for timeline and the other for preview. Professional graphics or CAD designers who use complex programs with many toolbars will like moving the tools to one monitor, while leaving the work on the faster monitor/card combination. Stock brokering is another typical multiscreen use, allowing multiple tickers, spreadsheets, and such on the screens. Manipulating large spreadsheets is another obvious use.

The following are some rules and tips to know about using multiple monitors:

- Windows 2000 Professional supports up to 10 monitors.

- Because most computers don't have nine or even four (and maybe not even two) PCI slots open, if you want to max out your video system, look into the new breed of multi-monitor video cards. In a single slot, you can drive up to four monitors on some of the cards I've seen. With only two slots, you can drive eight monitors.

- Most multimonitor situations consist of two cards: either two PCIs or a mix of one PCI and one AGP.

- If you mix AGP and PCI, older BIOSs sometimes have a strange habit of forcing one or the other to become the "primary" display. It is the display that Windows first boots on and the one you use for logging on. You might be annoyed if your better monitor or better card isn't the primary display because most programs are initially displayed on the primary monitor when you launch them. Therefore, you might want to flash-upgrade your BIOS if the maker of your computer or motherboard indicates that such an upgrade will advance the multiple-monitor support for your computer by letting you choose which monitor or card you want to make the primary display.

> *If you aren't having luck assigning the primary display, and your secondary card is taking over the role of primary display, see "Setting the Primary Display" in the "Troubleshooting" section at the end of this chapter.*

- The operating system always needs a VGA device, which becomes the primary display. The BIOS detects the VGA device based on slot order, unless the BIOS offers an option for choosing which device is to be treated as the VGA device. Check your BIOS settings to see whether any special settings might affect multimonitor display, such as whether the AGP or PCI card will default to primary display, or the PCI slot order. Slot 1 is typically the slot farthest from the ISA slots.

- The design of the card itself is what makes it capable of operating on multiple monitors with Windows 2000, not the driver. Don't expect any vendors to be able to make that happen. Either the card can support multimonitoring, or it can't. Some cards should technically be able to do so but are not stable enough to handle this capability at this time.

- Very few S3-based cards can support multimonitor operation. One that can is the S3 Trio3D.

- Just because a set of cards supports multimonitoring under Windows 98 doesn't mean it can under Windows 2000. These two operating systems have completely different video architectures.

Follow these steps to install multiple monitors:

1. Boot up your system into Windows 2000, and right-click a blank area of your desktop. From the resulting pop-up menu, select Properties.

2. Go to the Settings tab. Confirm that your display adapter is listed correctly (that is, if you have an ATI Rage Pro, then ATI Rage Pro should be listed under Display). Your display adapter *should not* be listed as VGA, or multimonitoring will not work. If this is the case, you must find and install correct Windows 2000 drivers, or consult your display manufacturer's Web site.

3. Be sure you are in at least 256 colors (16-bit setting, high color is recommended). Then click OK, and when prompted, select Apply Without Restarting.

4. After you've confirmed that you have drivers loaded for your display adapter and that you are in a compatible color depth, shut down and then power off your system.

5. Disconnect the power cable leading to the back of your system, and remove the case cover. Confirm that you have an available PCI slot. Before inserting your secondary display adapter, confirm that it has VGA Disabled selected via either a jumper or a small DIP switch located on the secondary display adapter. (If you cannot locate a jumper or switch, consult the manufacturer's documentation. Another possibility is that you have not selected a compatible secondary display adapter.)

 If you have problems setting jumpers on your video card, see "Setting the Primary Display" in the "Troubleshooting" section at the end of this chapter.

6. Insert your secondary display adapter, secure it properly with a screw, reassemble your system, and reconnect the power. Next, connect a second monitor to the secondary display adapter.

7. Turn on both the monitors, and power up the system. Allow the system to boot into Windows 2000.

8. After you log in, Windows 2000 detects your new display adapter and brings up the Hardware Wizard. Confirm that it detects the correct display adapter and, when prompted, tell Windows 2000 to search for a suitable driver. Then click Next.

9. Windows 2000 then finds information on the display adapter. When you are prompted, insert your Windows 2000 installation CD, and click OK.

10. Windows 2000 then copies files. When the process is completed, click Finish. Windows 2000 then also detects your secondary monitor (if it is a PnP monitor). When you are prompted, click Finish again.

11. Now that all appropriate drivers are installed, right-click a blank portion of your desktop, and select Properties again. Next, go to the Settings tab. You will notice that two Monitor icons now appear in the center window of the display applet representing your two monitors. Left-click the Monitor icon labeled 2, and it is highlighted in blue.

12. Under Display, your secondary adapter should be displayed. In the lower-left corner below the Colors section, check the box labeled Extend My Windows Desktop into This Monitor.

13. When Windows 2000 gives you a warning concerning compatibility, click Yes.

14. While the Monitor icon labeled 2 is highlighted, adjust the color depth and resolution for the new monitor.

15. You might want to change the way your monitors are positioned by left-clicking and holding down the mouse button while you drag the Monitor icons. (Note that the displays must touch along one edge.) When you find a desirable position, just release the mouse button, and the Monitor icon is aligned adjacent to the first Monitor icon. Also note that wherever the two displays meet is the location your mouse will be able to pass from one display to the next, so a horizontal alignment is preferred for a standard desktop monitor arrangement.

16. Click OK. Windows 2000 then asks whether you want to restart or apply your changes. Select Restart to allow Windows 2000 to reboot your system.

17. After the system is rebooted and you log on to your system, multimonitoring should be functional, and you should have an extended desktop displayed on your second monitor. You also should be able to move your mouse into this extended desktop.

Note

You can set up Windows 2000 with more than one secondary display adapter, up to a maximum of nine additional displays. To do so, select another supported secondary display adapter with VGA disabled, and repeat the preceding steps with another monitor attached to the additional secondary adapter.

After you finish these steps, you can drag items across your screen onto alternate monitors. Better yet, you can resize a window to stretch it across more than one monitor. Things get a little weird at the gap, though. You must get used to the idea of the mouse cursor jumping from one screen into the next, too.

 If you're having trouble getting your multimonitor setup to work, see "Setting the Primary Display" in the "Troubleshooting" section at the end of this chapter.

 If you don't have enough open slots for multiple monitors, see "Not Enough Slots" in the "Troubleshooting" section at the end of the chapter.

Using Hardware Profiles

Tucked away within the Control Panel, you'll find the hardware profile settings option that lets you name and save hardware setups just as you can color or sound schemes. The idea of hardware profiles is that they let you start up the computer with different sets of devices to accommodate situations in which different hardware is attached to the machine. Hardware profiles also let you stipulate different settings (such as resource allocations) for each device. In essence, you can have almost a different computer with each hardware profile.

Note

Windows enables or disables devices by simply installing or not installing their drivers at boot time.

Profiles grew out of the need for docking laptops to be able to boot with a new set of driver settings based on whether the laptop was on the road or connected to a docking station with its own external monitor, additional CD-ROM drive, and so on. Profiles have become more capable with Plug and Play, sensing when the computer is "hot-docked" and kicking in the appropriate profile when needed. Also, for complex arrangements such as on a desktop computer stuffed to the gills with devices, it is sometimes necessary to disable some devices so that others can have access to certain limited resources such as interrupt requests (IRQs).

When you first install Windows 2000 on a desktop computer, a hardware profile called Profile 1 is created for it. A laptop should have a Docket Profile or Undocked Profile, depending on whether it senses it is docked or undocked during setup. As you install new devices on the Windows 2000 Professional workstation, they are enabled in the default profile. Table 30.5 shows a typical laptop scenario.

TABLE 30.5   TYPICAL LAPTOP HARDWARE PROFILES

Example	Description
Profile 1: "On the Road"	Use when traveling. Contains enabled modem and printer.
Profile 2: "At the Office"	Use when docked to the docking station or port replicator. Enables LAN card, external monitor, and CD-ROM drive.

You manage the profiles on a system using the System applet. Choose Start, Control Panel, System and then the Hardware tab. Then click Hardware Profiles. You then see the dialog box displayed in Figure 30.14.

Figure 30.14
You can set up and manage new hardware profiles from this dialog.

You must be logged on with Administrator privileges to alter the hardware profiles.

To create a new profile, click Copy to copy the current profile and all the active driver listings into a new profile that you can alter as you like. (Obviously, you can use the Rename button to change the names later, so don't sweat the name.)

After you've copied a profile, you can begin to modify it to meet your needs. Click the profile, and then click Properties. You can declare some aspects of the profile at this stage. You can indicate, for example, whether it's a profile on a laptop computer. Table 30.6 lists some of the options and their meanings.

TABLE 30.6   HARDWARE PROFILE OPTIONS

Option	Description
Delete	Use this option to eliminate a profile. You can't delete the currently active profile.
Wait Until I Select a Hardware Profile	When you boot the computer, you are presented with a list of profiles early in the boot process. If this option is on, the computer will wait forever for you to select the profile to boot into.
Select the First Profile If I Don't Select a Profile in x Seconds	Profiles appear in the list above this setting. The order determines the first profile. You can organize the profiles using the arrow buttons so that the first one is the default profile you want to boot in case you don't intervene.
This Is a Portable Computer	If you're on a desktop, don't check this box. If you're on a laptop that is going to be alternately docked and undocked, check it, and choose the appropriate radio button. The Unknown button is selected by default if Windows can't figure out the docking status at the current time. You can help clear up the confusion by clicking one of the other options.
Include This Profile as an Option When Windows Starts	You can opt to have a profile not appear in the bootup list if you want to keep it on hand for future use but don't want it to show up in the list of profiles to choose from when you boot up.

ALTERING A HARDWARE PROFILE'S DEVICE COMPLEMENT

Windows 2000 is pretty good about detecting and setting up separate hardware profiles for popular docking stations and port replicators. However, if yours isn't detected, you can use the technique presented here to alter what drivers will load with each profile. You can use this technique for personalizing profiles on any kind of computer, be it desktop or portable, for that matter.

The way you differentiate hardware profiles is to first create multiple copies of the same profile, then turn off or on devices in each to suit your needs, and resave them. After settings are made, you reboot. During bootup, you are prompted to choose between them.

Tip #355

You should use different hardware profiles for any computer where you alter the physical setup regularly in a predictable manner, such as switching between two monitors.

The following is the basic game plan for modifying existing profiles:

1. Get your system running with a superset of the hardware you're going to want to use. That is, use as much external stuff—such as hard drives—as possible. This step may require your using the Control Panel's Add/Remove Hardware applet as well (see earlier in this chapter).

2. Choose Control Panel, System. Then click Hardware Profiles.

3. Select the profile you want to use as a basis for your scaled-down (undocked) profile, and click Copy.

4. Name the new profile something meaningful, such as Undocked Laptop.

5. Click the Properties button, and look at the options there. If you're modifying a portable computer, check the appropriate box, and indicate the current state (docked or undocked) and whether you want the new hardware profile to be presented as an option for the user to choose when Windows boots. (Normally, you would want it to show, but you could disable this option if you, for example, were loaning the computer to someone and didn't want to confuse him or her with boot options.) Click OK to close that dialog box.

6. Now comes the tricky part. You must boot up in a specific profile before you can modify the settings therein. Do so, and pick the profile you want to modify.

7. Choose Control Panel, System, and click the Device Manager button.

8. In the Device Manager window, click the + (plus) sign next to any piece of hardware whose inclusion/exclusion in one of your profiles you want to alter. Highlight the specific item, and click Properties.

9. At the bottom of the resulting Properties dialog, use the Device Usage drop-down list to choose whether you want to enable or disable the specific piece of hardware in your current profile.

10. Repeat for each device whose usage will be affected by a given profile.

11. Repeat steps 6 through 10 for each profile you want to adjust.

INSTALLING A UPS

Unless you work in a small office that is a totally laptop-driven shop, it's incumbent upon you to worry about power outages and data loss. The next chapter describes the supplied backup program and data backup strategies, but in this section, I want to talk about UPS systems because using a UPS is a hardware strategy rather than a software-based one.

As you probably know, UPS isn't a competitor to FedEx—well, not in this case anyway. Here I'm talking about power backup. A UPS, or uninterruptible power supply, is a system that provides AC power to your computer in the event of power fluctuations, brownouts, or complete blackouts. A UPS is essentially a box with a battery in it that stays charged all the time. A computer plugs into it like it would a surge protector, except that a UPS is larger, a bit like a car battery.

Electronic circuitry in the UPS continually monitors the AC line voltages, and should the voltage rise above or dip below predefined limits or fail entirely, the UPS takes over, powering the computer and cutting off the computer from the AC wall outlet. An intelligent UPS can also connect to the computer's data inputs (typically through a serial port) to send a data message to the computer's operating system, alerting it of the nature of the power problem. The computer's software can then decide what evasive maneuvers to take. Figure 30.15 shows the relationship between the computer, UPS, and power outlet.

Figure 30.15
Stages of UPS power protection.

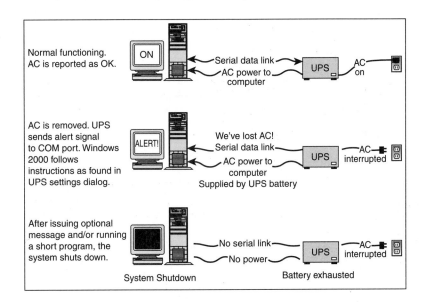

As you might imagine, to prevent data loss, the system's response time must be very fast. As soon as the AC power gets flaky, the UPS must take over within a few milliseconds, at most. Even then, a spike in the voltage could potentially cause data corruption (which is a good reason to use surge protectors).

UPS devices fall into one of the two following categories:

- Standby UPS—This kind of UPS works pretty much as explained in the preceding paragraphs. Normally, power is delivered right from the wall outlet to the computer. When a power outage is detected, the electronics in the UPS (actually *SPS*, for Standby Power System) quickly switch to the battery power. There is necessarily a small lapse in time during the switchover.

- Online UPS—This device is more sophisticated and more expensive as well. It connects *between* the main power and the computer at all times. The main power continually charges the batteries that supply the power to the computer. Small power lapses are avoided because the UPS is constantly providing power from its own inverter, even when the power line is functioning properly. This also has the added advantage of providing power conditioning, which means that it removes spikes, surges, sags, and noise.

UPS CONSIDERATIONS FOR WINDOWS 2000 PROFESSIONAL

Ideally, all your workstations assigned to serious tasks (what work isn't serious?) should have UPS protection of some sort. Although it's true that well-designed programs such as Microsoft Office have auto-backup options that help to restore files in progress if the power goes out, they are not always reliable. Crashes and weird performance of applications and operating systems are enough to worry about, without adding power loss on top. And if the power fails during a disk write, you might have a rude awakening because the hard disk's filesystem could be corrupted, which is far worse than having a lost file or two.

My advice is that you guard against the ravages of power outages at all reasonable costs. With the ever-increasing power and plummeting cost of laptop computers, one of the most economically sensible solutions is to purchase laptops. They take up little space, they are easier to configure because the hardware complement cannot be easily altered, and they have UPSs built in. When the power fails, the battery takes over.

Tip #356	When you're using laptops, make sure your batteries are still working, though. With time, they can lose their capacity to hold a charge. You should cycle them once in a while to check out how long they will run. If necessary, replace them. Also, you should set up the power options on a laptop to save to disk (hibernate) in case of impending power loss. You'll typically want to set hibernation to kick in when 5 to 10 percent of battery power is remaining, just to ensure that the hard disk can start up (if sleeping) and write out the system state onto disk.

In the case of servers, you'll certainly want UPS support, as discussed in the networking section of this book. Windows 2000 Servers can alert any connected workstation users of impending system shutdown as the UPS battery begins to drain. Users are warned to save their work and shut down (assuming they are running on a power source that is also functional, of course).

Before shelling out your hard-earned dough for UPS systems, you should check to see which ones are supported by Windows 2000 Professional. Consult the Hardware Compatibility List on the Microsoft site. Also, consider this checklist of questions:

- What type of UPS do you want: UPS or SPS?
- Do you want to purchase a separate UPS for every workstation or one larger UPS that can power a number of computers from a single location?
- What UPS capacity do you need for each computer? The answer depends on the power draw of the computer box, the size of the monitor, and whether you want peripherals to work on battery, too. To fully protect your network, you should also install a UPS on network devices such as routers, hubs, bridges, modems, telephones, printers, and any other network equipment. Check the real-world specs for the UPS. The capacity is also determined by how long you want the UPS to be able to operate after a complete power outage. If you just want enough time for you or another user to save work, a relatively small UPS will do. If you want to be able to get through a day's work doing stock trades, you'll need a hefty unit.

■ What software support do you want? Do you need to keep a log of UPS activity during the day for later analysis? What about utilities that test the UPS on a regular basis to ensure it's working?

■ As I mentioned previously, Windows 2000 has services built in for responding to a UPS's signal that an outage has occurred. They can be configured to alert users, automatically shut down the system, and/or execute a program of your choice. Automatic and graceful shutdown of the system is important in case a power failure lasts long enough to deplete the UPS batteries. In addition to connected users being warned of an impending shutdown, new users can be prevented from connecting to such a server.

PART

V

CH

30

Tip #357	In some cases, UPS vendors provide software for configuring their devices. You can use them instead of the one provided in Windows 2000.

INSTALLING AND CONFIGURING THE WINDOWS 2000 UPS SERVICE

If you are going to use a UPS that doesn't support signaling to the computer via a data cable, you don't have to worry about installing or configuring the Windows 2000 UPS service. It won't make any difference and isn't needed.

You can install the UPS according the manufacturer's instructions or, if it's a Plug and Play device, follow standard procedures for installing new hardware. Typically, you connect the UPS to the power source, the computer to the UPS, and the serial cable between the UPS and the computer.

Caution	Be aware that normal serial cables do not cut the mustard for connecting a UPS to a Windows 2000 Professional machine. UPS serial cables, even between models from the same manufacturer, use different pin assignments. You're best off using the cable supplied by the maker of the UPS.

Another way to install the driver for a particular UPS model is to go to the Control Panel and run the Power Options applet. You should see the tab displayed in Figure 30.16.

Click Select, and choose the UPS make and model you have and the COM port the UPS data cable is on, if any. The COM port is used to receive signals from the UPS about its charge level and the state of the AC power source.

If your UPS isn't listed, choose Generic Make, select Custom, and make sure to check the signal polarity settings in Table 30.7. For listed UPS devices, the polarities are preset for you.

After you declare the type of UPS, return to the UPS tab of the Power Options Properties dialog, and click Configure to set up what you want Windows 2000 Professional to do in the event of a power interruption. The UPS Configuration dialog is shown in Figure 30.17.

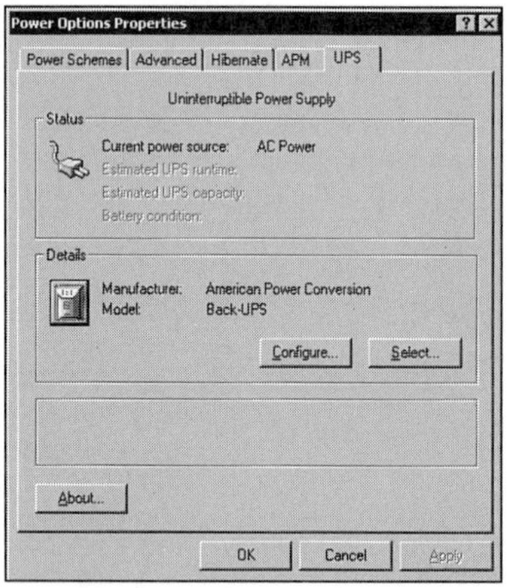

Figure 30.16
You can install a UPS
by clicking Select.

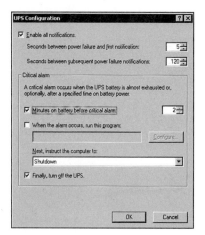

Figure 30.17
Here, you can set the
UPS and system
behavior for cases of
power outage.

Editable items on the tab differ, depending on what UPS you have installed, but they fall
into the following categories:

- The conditions that trigger the UPS device to send a signal, such as regular power supply failure, low battery power, and remote shutdown by the UPS device
- The time intervals for maintaining battery power, recharging the battery, and sending warning messages after power failure
- An optional executable program specified to run when power outage is sensed
- Final behavior of Windows in case of complete discharge of the UPS backup battery (typically a graceful shutdown)

You can use Table 30.7 when you're considering the settings.

TABLE 30.7   THE UPS CONFIGURATION DIALOG BOX

Option	Description
UPS Is Installed On	Check this box if your UPS connects to a COM port. Then choose the COM port from the drop-down list.
Enable All Notifications	Check this box if you want notifications of impending power failure to appear on the users' screens and sent to users currently connected to the computer over the LAN. The message is broadcast over the local node. It doesn't cross a router.
Seconds Between Power Failure and First Notification	Set how much time elapses between the power failure and when the power failure signal is sent to the computer. This figure is subtracted from the total expected battery life to determine when the system should begin shutdown. The range is 0 to 120 seconds.
Time Between Subsequent Power Failure Notifications	If the UPS can keep the system messages going for some time, set this time to determine how often (5 to 300 seconds) the user should be notified of impending doom. Too-frequent messages can be annoying and can unnecessarily alarm users in the case of regularly occurring power fluctuations. Messages sent too seldom can be overlooked.
Minutes on Battery Before Critical Alarm	Set how long after the UPS kicks in a critical notification and/or alarm should sound be issued, warning of imminent system shutdown. Base this setting on the capacity of the UPS and the power load of your system complement. A smart UPS might be able to signal the computer to indicate a critical state. If not, estimate on the conservative side, based on the manufacturer's manual.
When the Alarm Occurs, Run This Program	When the critical alarm goes off, you can optionally choose to run a program of no more than 30 seconds in execution time. (See the next option.)
Next, Instruct the Computer To	Set what should happen after a critical alarm goes off and an optional program runs. You can choose Shutdown or Hibernate. Hibernate allows the machine to return to the previous state after resumption of power.

SETTING POLARITIES FOR A GENERIC UPS

For a smart UPS, serial data lines are used to communicate with the UPS. For a generic UPS, though, the data lines are ignored, and Windows uses the COM port's modem-status signaling lines. AC and battery status are received from the UPS using two of these lines, and a third line, the DTR signal, goes from the computer to the UPS. This signal can tell the UPS to turn itself off when Windows 2000 Professional has finished shutting down. This capability helps extend the life of the UPS batteries by avoiding a full discharge.

If your UPS isn't listed among those supported, Windows 2000 Professional doesn't know what your UPS is capable of and how it sends signals to the computer, if at all. When you choose Generic and then choose Custom, you see a Next button. Clicking it brings up the dialog box shown in Figure 30.18.

Figure 30.18
Here, you can set cus-
tom polarities for a
UPS that Windows
2000 Professional
doesn't know how to
preconfigure.

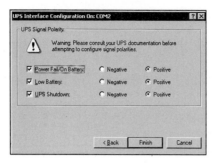

Assuming the UPS has a serial link to the computer, you can set the port and fill in the
blanks as necessary. Turn off all the options if the UPS has no serial link to a COM port. As
the dialog box warns, you should consult the manufacturer or manual to ensure the settings
are correct.

Table 30.8 describes the salient settings in the UPS polarities.

TABLE 30.8 UPS POLARITIES

Setting	Description
Power Fail/On Battery	Can the UPS send a power failure signal on the CTS (clear-to-send) pin of the serial link? If so, check this box, and indicate which voltage polarity (+ or –) signals the failure. These interface voltages indicate the *active* state for the signal. For example, if you select a negative interface voltage for the power failure signal, the normally positive signal becomes negative when a power failure occurs.
Low Battery	Can the UPS send a low-battery signal on the DCD (data-carrier-detect) pin of the serial link? If so, check this box and set the polarity.
UPS Shutdown	Can the UPS receive a signal from the Windows 2000 machine on the DTR (data-terminal-ready) pin of the serial link? (This signal is used to tell the UPS when the battery power is no longer needed either because the AC source was revived or because the computer shuts off.) If so, check the box, and indicate which voltage polarity (+ or –) signals the cessation of battery power need.

RUNNING A COMMAND FILE WHEN THE POWER FAILS

The UPS Configuration dialog box has an option for running an executable file when a
power failure is detected. It is an option only. Warning messages are sent out (assuming
those options are supported and turned on) regardless of whether you choose this option.
However, you might want to run a specific executable before the computer is shut down.

If you use this option, make sure the program or script you choose can execute in 30 seconds or less. Failure to complete execution in 30 seconds jeopardizes the safe shutdown of
your Windows computer.

→ **See** Chapter 36, "Windows Script Host," to learn about how you can write scripts to automate the execution of Windows 2000 Professional internal programs.

Do the following to declare and set up the executable file:

1. In the UPS Configuration dialog box, select the When the Alarm Occurs, Run This Program check box, and then click Configure.

2. In the resulting UPS System Shutdown Program dialog box, select the Task tab.

3. Type the name of the file in the Run field.

4. If you want the scheduled task to run at a specified time, select the Enabled (Scheduled Task Runs at Specified Time) check box, and continue this procedure.

5. Select the Schedule tab, and then select the frequency and start time of the task.

6. You can make additional schedule settings by clicking the Settings tab.

7. Set any additional options you want in the Scheduled Task Completed, Idle Time, and Power Management areas of the Settings tab; then click OK.

8. In the Set Account Information dialog box, type the Run As and password information, and then click OK.

PART

V

CH

30

Tip #358

The command file must reside in your %SystemRoot%\System32 folder and have a file-name extension, such as .EXE, .COM, .BAT, or .CMD.

→ To learn more details about the Run As setting, **see** "Guest and Administrator Accounts," **p. 1195**.

TESTING YOUR UPS CONFIGURATION

Testing your UPS configuration from time to time is wise, just to make sure you aren't let down when a real emergency occurs. Follow these steps to do so:

1. Close any open documents or programs.

2. Simulate a power failure by disconnecting the power to the UPS device. Check to see that, after disconnecting the power to the UPS device, the computer and peripherals connected to the UPS device continue operating and that a warning message appears on the screen.

3. Wait until the UPS battery reaches a low level, at which point a system shutdown should occur.

4. If the UPS service is configured to run a command file, check to see that it executes in under 30 seconds.

5. Restore power to the UPS device.

6. Check the system log in the Event Viewer to ensure that all actions were logged and that no errors occurred.

CONFIGURING THE PROGRAM ENVIRONMENTS

Chapter 28, "Tweaking the GUI," and Chapter 29, "Customizing via Control Panel Applets," covered quite of few of the adjustments that you can make to the Windows 2000 user environment. Those chapters also addressed a variety of settings that affect the operation of Windows on a more rudimentary level, such as Properties sheets for printers and other devices you may have installed on a typical system or network. In addition to all these settings and properties, Windows 2000 allows for fine-tuning of program and system handling under the various operating system environments—32-bit Windows, 16-bit Windows, DOS, OS/2, and POSIX.

As discussed in Chapter 2, "The Design and Architecture of Windows 2000 Professional," and Chapter 3, "Getting Your Hardware and Software Ready for Windows 2000," Windows 2000 Professional runs non–NT-based applications that fall into four classes: MS-DOS, Windows 3.x, OS/2 1.x character-based, and POSIX character-based. You may remember also that this flexibility is achieved via simulated operating environments called environment subsystems. Each subsystem is basically an emulator responsible for providing the API for each operating system and then translating the API calls to the 32-bit Windows subsystem, which passes the commands onto Windows 2000 for processing.

Some optimization and configuration of the various environments are possible, typically to allow for higher compatibility with non-NT and non-Windows 2000 programs. Or, in some cases, the adjustments possible are purely aesthetic or convenience factors. The following sections describe options for configuring applications and subsystems. They also describe some specific programs or classes of programs (such as DOS-based TSRs) and how best to run them under Windows 2000 Professional.

In the following sections, you'll learn about settings for the following:

- Windows 32-bit
- Windows 16-bit
- DOS
- OS/2

→ You also might want to **see** Appendix A on the CD-ROM, "Command-Line Reference," for further details of DOS subsystem tuning and control.

CONFIGURING THE 32-BIT WINDOWS ENVIRONMENT

Aside from the interface tweaking you already learned about in the Control Panel chapter, and the service settings and system administrator applications that you'll learn in the next chapter, there is really precious little in the way of settings to fine-tune the Win32 subsystem. Therefore, user intervention into the internal Win32 performance settings is minimal. The only settings still not covered yet regarding the native 32-bit Windows environment subsystem are as follows:

- Virtual memory settings
- Registry size
- Tasking priority

The following sections discuss these settings.

OPTIMIZING VIRTUAL MEMORY (PAGING) FILE AND REGISTRY SIZES

Windows 2000—like NT, Windows 9x, and Windows 3.1—incorporates a virtual memory scheme. As you are probably aware, virtual memory is a scheme by which an operating system fakes itself into thinking it has more apparent RAM for use by applications than is physically present in the computer. It does so by using a hard disk file called pagefile.sys space to simulate RAM. The Virtual Memory Manager (VMM) constantly tracks the amount of free RAM, and when the available RAM is exhausted, the VMM begins swapping out 4KB chunks of data and instruction code to pagefile.sys. As portions of the data or code are needed, they are swapped back into RAM chips, where they can be operated on by the CPU. The upshot is that more applications and services can run simultaneously than would normally be the case.

The default VMM settings applied when you install Windows 2000 Professional are based on your hard disk space and partition designations. One swap file is created in the root of the partition containing the operating system. Each partition can have its own pagefile.sys, and the size of the file is dynamic, unlike the permanent paging (swap) files that are possible under Windows 3.1. So, if you have several disks or partitions, Windows might decrease the size of a pagefile on one partition and shift paging onto another one as available hard disk space decreases.

Because Windows 2000 Professional is such a huge operating system, it's imperative that paging be intelligent and plentiful. Likewise, RAM is important, as discussed in Chapter 3. If the pagefile needs to be resized, Windows 2000 alerts you and performs the operation, as you see in Figure 30.19.

Figure 30.19
Windows adjusts the pagefile size if it is running low.

If you want to ensure that your hard disk doesn't thrash itself to death and that the system runs efficiently, not making you wait every time you switch between windows or move something around on the screen, you should install at least 128MB of RAM, let Windows manage the pagefile size, and keep lots of free space on your drive.

PART
V

CH
30

The default pagefile size is equal to the amount of RAM in your computer plus 12MB. As disk space dwindles, the file can shrink. The minimum can be no less than about 2MB. Usually, you should leave the pagefile at its recommended size, although you might increase its size if you routinely use programs that require a lot of memory. You can check with the software maker for information about how demanding applications might benefit from increasing the allocation.

If you have multiple partitions or drives, you should economize on the space lost from each drive or partition. This way, you can improve performance on most modern disk systems because multiple disks can process input/output (I/O) requests concurrently in a round-robin fashion.

You can optimize virtual memory use by dividing the space between multiple drives and especially by removing it from slower or heavily accessed drives. To best optimize your virtual memory space, you should divide it across as many physical hard drives as possible. When you're selecting drives, keep the following guidelines in mind:

- Try to avoid having a large pagefile on the same drive as the system files. You should have at least a 2MB pagefile on the boot volume. The system requires this to write events to the system log, send an administrative alert, or automatically restart after a system Stop error occurs in the event of a system failure.

- Avoid putting a pagefile on a fault-tolerant drive, such as a mirrored volume or a RAID-5 volume. Pagefiles don't need fault tolerance, and some fault-tolerant systems suffer from slow data writes because they write data to multiple locations.

- Don't place multiple pagefiles on different partitions on the same physical disk drive.

The following are some other points to consider when you're adjusting the pagefile:

- Setting the pagefile's initial size and maximum size to the same value increases efficiency because the operating system does not need to expand the file during processing. Setting different values for initial and maximum size can contribute to disk fragmentation. Expanding the default size of the pagefile can increase performance if applications are consuming virtual memory and the full capacity of the existing file is being used. To determine how large your pagefile should be based on your system workload, you should monitor the Process (_Total)\Page File Bytes counter in the Performance Monitor. This counter indicates, in bytes, how much of the pagefile is being used.

- Don't put a large pagefile on a disk that is used a lot, such as one used for serving applications and databases. It slows down overall performance.

- The operating system always needs 5MB free on its partition. Make sure you don't use up the whole system boot drive.

- Change the file size a little at a time, and test the performance.

Tip #359

> You should consider compacting your hard disk and upgrading your hard disk, hard disk controller, and/or motherboard for faster disk performance. Before installing a fancy, new IDE hard drive, find out which transfer protocol it uses. If the new drive uses Ultra DMA/66, and your present IDE controller doesn't, you could have booting problems. See whether the drive manufacturer has provided a method of reverting to DMA/33. If not, you might have to turn off DMA support completely in your system BIOS and suffer a large performance hit. Sometimes when you're upgrading a hard drive, upgrading the motherboard at the same time will serve you well, for just this reason.

To change the initial and maximum size of the workstation's pagefile, the file locations, the number of pagefiles, and the size of the Windows 2000 Registry, follow these steps:

1. Open the Control Panel, and run the System applet.

2. Click the Advanced tab; then click Performance Options. In the Virtual Memory area, click Change. You then see the dialog box shown in Figure 30.20.

Figure 30.20
You can set the overall Win32 system performance options in this dialog.

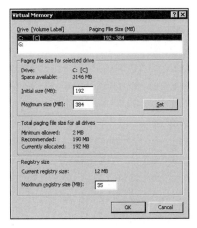

3. Edit the initial size and maximum size if you want to change them, and click Set.

4. Under Registry Size, you can enter a new size (in megabytes) to declare the maximum size of the Registry. Setting a maximum size for the Registry sets an upper limit on the area predesignated (a contiguous block of disk area) for Registry data. You probably will never need to adjust this size, unless you have so many programs installed that the Registry data exceeds the limit you set under Registry Size. Then you would see an error message, and you could increase the size from this dialog box. I've never seen this happen. You can examine this dialog box occasionally to see whether the currently reported Registry size is reaching the maximum file size, but you shouldn't lose any sleep over it. That is, don't mark your calendar to check the Registry size every month.

Tip #360

You must be logged on as an administrator to the local computer to change the Registry size. If you decrease the size of either the minimum or maximum pagefile settings, you must restart your computer to see the effects of those changes. Increasing the size doesn't normally require a restart.

Tip #361

Short on disk space? If you're seriously short on space, you can turn off the VMM and then delete the pagefile. You can't delete it while it's in use, though. So, first, you must turn it off. Next, you can just remove the pagefile using the Control Panel's System applet, reboot, and then delete the inactive file.

You can use the Performance Monitor to get a sense of how much virtual memory is being used. This program is covered in Chapter 31, but I'll mention the technique here. To get started, choose Start, Settings, Control Panel, Administrative Tools, Performance. Next, click the + (plus) button on the toolbar. Choose Pagefile from the Performance Object drop-down list. Then add Usage and Usage peak. View the statistics in whatever way you like. Figure 30.21 shows an example. In this figure, you can see that even with 32 programs running, I'm still only at 79 percent usage, with a peak of 86 percent.

Figure 30.21
You can check virtual memory usage via the Performance Monitor by adding pagefile monitoring for display in the chart.

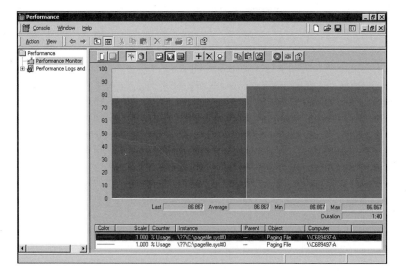

SETTING TASKING PRIORITIES FOR THE 32-BIT ENVIRONMENT

As you know, Windows 2000 is a multithreaded, preemptively multitasking operating system. Left to its own devices, it does an extremely good job of balancing user requests with the need for internal system operations and control. The result from the user's point of view is performance that appears to be highly responsive, even though some internal sleight of hand and task juggling may be going on under the hood.

One setting can slightly improve overall smoothness of Windows 2000's tasking, depending on what you use your computer for. To set it, do the following:

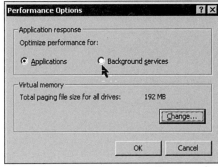

1. Open the Control Panel, run the System applet, and click the Advanced tab.

2. Click Performance Options to open the dialog box shown in Figure 30.22. In this dialog, you can set the tasking priority for all Win32 applications.

Figure 30.22

3. Click either Background Services or Applications.

Normally, Applications is set, ensuring that the foreground application (the window you work with) gets more CPU time slices than programs running in the background. Time slices are also shorter and variably sized, which results in more responsive action from an application as you work in it. Unless you have CPU-intensive applications running in the background, though, you won't notice a difference in foreground performance.

If you're running something important in the background that bogs down too much when you're doing other foreground work on the computer, choose the Background Services option. Examples might be data acquisition programs, communications programs, or a backup utility. The time slices are doled out in longer portions with this setting.

SETTING ENVIRONMENT VARIABLES

Settings that you're not likely to use but that could prove handy are the environment variables. By clicking the Environment Variables button on the System applet's Advanced tab, you can change the environment variables in the resulting dialog (see Figure 30.23).

Figure 30.23
Here, you can examine and alter the system variables.

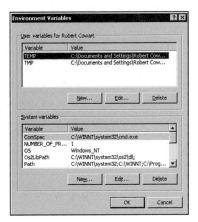

In this dialog, you can create new variables, delete a variable, or edit a variable using the corresponding buttons. Notice that this dialog lists systemwide variables as well as per-user ones. Setting a variable in the System Variables area alters the defaults for all users.

A conflict can occur over system variables as named in different places or commands in the operating system. As a rule, the last value declared for a variable usurps all previous declarations. Windows 2000 Professional sets variables in the following order:

1. System-level variables

2. User-level variables

3. AUTOEXEC.NT-declared variables (but only for MS-DOS or Windows applications when the VDM runs, not within the standard CMD box)

4. Anything subsequent, issued by a user or command-line program, utility, or batch file

Caution

I must make an important distinction here. AUTOEXEC.NT variable settings go into effect only when the execution of an MS-DOS or Windows 3.x program triggers a VDM to be created. AUTOEXEC.NT settings do not affect variables in the standard Command Prompt window. Of course, if you run a Command Prompt window, set environment variables from the prompt, and then run a program, that program inherits the variables from that box. When you close the box, though, those settings are discarded. The next Command Prompt window you open will have only the system-wide and user-level variables as declared by the System dialog box discussed in the preceding paragraphs.

Why modify system variables? Good question. Not many people need to. Probably the most likely reason to modify these variables is to add directories to the system's search path. Or you might have particular applications that require environment variables set. Some command-line utilities also look for environment variables. For example, copy has an env var, which determines whether it prompts before overwriting files.

CONFIGURING THE WINDOWS 3.1 ENVIRONMENT

As you learned in Chapter 3, "Getting Your Hardware and Software Ready for Windows 2000," and Chapter 4, "Installing Windows 2000," in the coverage of installation, if you're upgrading from Windows 3.x, the upgrade is necessarily done via an intermediary upgrade to Windows 9x. At that point, assuming the installation is done into the same Windows directory, DOS and Windows 3.x settings are migrated into Windows 9x, much of it ending up in the Windows 9x Registry, particularly WIN.INI and SYSTEM.INI. Program Manager groups and application settings are imported intact, and your applications should run under Windows 9x.

Subsequently, an upgrade to Windows 2000 results in Windows 2000 inheriting the most important of these settings. So, even after two upgrades, Windows 3.x users should have a fair amount of the look and feel of their familiar Windows 3.1 setup, barring the loss of the Program Manager (that being replaced by the Start button) and the File Manager (replaced by My Computer and/or Windows Explorer).

Like NT, Windows 2000 Professional continues to migrate key Windows 3.1 data at each bootup. When a Windows 3.x program writes its setting into WIN.INI, for example, Windows 2000 Professional sniffs out this setting and registers it. Note that only application-specific information is of interest, not system settings in WIN.INI or SYSTEM.INI. This is because only Windows system settings come to bear when controlling the operating environment.

Even more the case with Windows 3.1 than with the Win32 environment, there is little for you to worry about when it comes to configuration. Windows 3.1 applications generally run quite well and even fail to bring the operating system to a halt in the case of faulty operation. You can say goodbye to General Protection Faults (remember them?).

PART

V

CH

30

Note

> I find it hilarious that the General Protection Fault was replaced by the Kernel-32 Error in Windows 9x, don't you? Is this the trickle-down effect in the rank and file? Or is it a demotion? I guess I just can't get away from my military upbringing.

The most notable exception you're going to find when running Windows 3.x applications, as discussed in Chapter 5, "Using the Windows 2000 Interface," is that you'll see truncated file and folder names in anything that looks at the hard disk directory. You get these shortened names because Windows 3.x applications were hostage to the limitation of DOS's 8.3 file-naming conventions. This limitation can be annoying, especially in a Browse box, but there's absolutely nothing you can do about it. The best thing you can do is upgrade to a Windows 9x, NT 4, or Windows 2000 version of the program.

If you can't upgrade, at least understanding how the truncated names are generated helps a bit. Following are some of the rules governing truncated NTFS and DOS file-naming rules and some hints for using them.

First, consider the rules of Windows 9x, NT 4, and Windows 2000 long filenames:

- Files and directory names can be up to 256 characters in length.
- You can include an extension, separated from the rest of the name by a period, such as *2002 Sales Reports.WKS*. (If associated file extensions are hidden via the Folder Options, the extension is invisible in listings, however.)
- Special characters not allowed are as follows:
  ?, ", \, /, <, >, *, |, and :
- Spaces can be included. No problem.
- Uppercase and lowercase are both allowed, and they appear in listings. However, they aren't interpreted by Windows 2000 Professional or its applications as being different from one another.

Windows 2000 Professional automatically generates shorter DOS-compatible filenames when needed by a Windows 3.x program by doing the following:

- Removing illegal characters and replacing them with _ (an underscore)
- Removing any spaces in the name
- Using only the last period that has three consecutive letters after it as the extension
- Truncating the first name to six letters and adding a tilde (~) and a single-digit number as the last two characters of the first name. Consider these examples:

Windows 2000 Name	DOS Name
Quarterly Sales Reports.WK3	QUARTE~1.WK3
Quarterly Sales Reports. Atlanta.Georgia.WK3	QUARTE~1.WK3
Qrtr[Sales]Reports from Atlanta,Georgia.WK3	QRTR_S~1.WK3

When you use any programs that generate documents you're going to use with DOS and Windows 3.x applications, you might want to adopt a naming convention that makes sense to you when the longer names are converted to shorter DOS names. Try to use only one period, and use the extension that the application expects. Because the first six letters are retained, pack as much description into them as possible. If you use the same first eight letters for several filenames, they'll look almost identical under the Windows 3.x and DOS applications.

ALLOTTING INDEPENDENT MEMORY SPACE FOR WINDOWS 3.1 APPLICATIONS

Chapter 2 described how Windows 2000 creates a virtual DOS machine (VDM) for each DOS program you run, but that all 16-bit Windows 3.x applications are run in the *same* VDM. The result is that, just like in a real Windows 3.x machine, one crashing Windows 3.x application can take down the whole VDM, crashing any other Windows 3.x programs. Well, this isn't necessarily a fact of life. The one adjustment you can make to the Windows 3.x subsystem is to prevent this all-or-nothing situation.

Technically, you're not actually making an adjustment to the subsystem; instead, you're making a setting for individual Windows 3.x applications. Through a simple setting, you can cause an application to request its own VDM. The memory space that it runs in is then totally isolated, protected from other applications that might run amok. The upside is that one errant Windows 3.x application can't take down another. The downside is that any Windows 3.x applications running in their own memory space can't communicate with other Windows 3.1 applications as they would in a true Windows 3.x computer. DLL services, for example, are not running or functional, so data passing between applications is quashed.

You make the setting to the properties for the Windows 3.x program. As an example, I'll use the program that I use to take screen shots for this book; it's a Windows 3.x application called Collage Complete. To change the setting, follow these steps:

1. Create a shortcut for the program in question.
2. Right-click it, and choose Properties. You then see the dialog box shown in Figure 30.24.

Figure 30.24
You can set this option to give a Windows 3.x application its own memory space. You can do so only from a shortcut for the application.

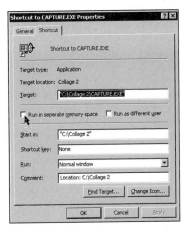

CONFIGURING THE DOS ENVIRONMENT

The DOS environment is highly configurable. You can configure it in several ways:

- By configuring the user variables in the System dialog box, as discussed in the section "Setting Environment Variables"
- By making selections from the DOS window's Control menu
- By making settings in the Properties sheet for the DOS application
- By making settings stored in AUTOEXEC.NT and CONFIG.NT
- By entering environment-altering commands at the command prompt

You can choose from a great number of settings, including the following, all of which can be set for an individual program or as defaults to be used any time a Command Prompt window or DOS program is run. You can make the following settings:

- Set the window font (including TrueType and bitmapped font styles)
- Set the background and foreground colors for normal text
- Set the background and foreground colors for pop-up boxes
- Choose window or full-screen viewing
- Set the default window position on the screen
- Use or turn off the QuickEdit mode
- Use or hide the Windows 2000 mouse pointer in the application

In addition to these settings, you can set environment variables, specify memory requirements (for EMS and XMS), and set other nitty-gritty options using PIF files and the System option in the Control Panel. Unless specified otherwise, Windows 2000 Professional uses the file _DEFAULT.PIF, stored in the \WINNT directory, as the basis for MS-DOS sessions and running applications that don't have a PIF. Practically speaking, PIF files are no longer used, so you just alter the properties for DOS applications by right-clicking the application and making settings. The result of running any DOS application, however, is that Windows 2000 Professional creates a PIF on-the-fly and assigns the default settings to it unless other settings are specified.

SETTING THE COMMAND PROMPT WINDOW PROPERTIES FROM A WINDOW

By far, the simplest means for altering the DOS environment is via the Properties dialog box of a DOS window. If you need to fine-tune the DOS environment, this is most likely the way you will do it.

When you open a Command Prompt window or run a DOS-based program, the window defaults to a standard size, background color, and font. Configuration options on the window's Control menu allow you to alter settings for the specific session. Options in the dialog boxes also let you save the settings to establish new defaults. You can set the properties like this:

1. Choose Start, Run.

2. Enter cmd, and press Enter.

3. On the resulting Command Prompt window, click the upper-left corner to open the Control menu, and choose either Properties or Default.

   • Properties sets the properties for this box and optionally all other boxes with the same title (as seen in the box's title bar) in the future.

   • Default applies the settings to all DOS-based programs and Command Prompt windows from here on out (even with other programs running in them).

The resulting dialog box is the same in either case. You can see it in Figure 30.25.

Figure 30.25
Here, you can set the one-time properties or all-time defaults for DOS boxes.

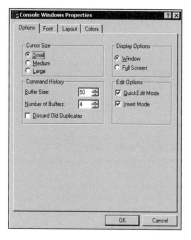

4. Click through the four tabs, and notice the settings. You can click the ? (question mark) button in the dialog box and then click any of the settings to learn more about them.

5. Make changes as necessary, and click OK.

If you're changing the properties for a specific window, you are asked whether you want the settings to apply to future DOS boxes with the same title bar. If you choose Yes, then any time you run the program you're modifying, it defaults to the new settings. What happens internally is that Windows edits the PIF for the DOS application in question (or the _DEFAULT.PIF in the case of a CMD window), storing the settings.

Note	The Control menu's Edit command and its associated cascading menu options are covered in Chapter 8, "Data Sharing Between Applications," which describes the use of the Clipboard and OLE.

PART

V

CH

30

Tip #362	Setting a large buffer size can be a real boon if you run batch files or other programs that normally cause text to scroll off the top of the screen. A large buffer enables you to scroll back the screen and check program flow and error messages.

EDITING ADVANCED SETTINGS FOR A DOS APPLICATION FROM ITS PROPERTIES SHEET

If you're experiencing difficulties while running specific DOS programs, you should read this section to learn about making deeper changes to the properties settings for them. When you manipulate the properties (via the PIF) for a program, Windows 2000 Professional fine-tunes the VDM environment for the particular application, allowing it to run more smoothly, or in some cases simply allowing it to run at all.

MS-DOS applications were designed to run in solitude. They assume that they are the only applications running and usually are memory hogs. Often they want at least 640KB of RAM and perhaps even extended or expanded memory. Running several non-Windows programs simultaneously—especially DOS programs—is like asking for territorial conflict.

To successfully accommodate the many DOS-based applications still in use, Windows 2000 Professional must be ingenious in managing computer resources such as RAM, printers, modems, mouse devices, and display I/O. Significant sleight of hand is required to pull off this task smoothly, but Microsoft has done this fairly well, partly due to the use of PIFs.

PIFs (program information files) are small files stored on disk, usually in the \WINNT directory or in the same directory as the application. They contain settings Windows 2000 Professional uses when it runs a related application. When you modify the properties of a DOS executable or shortcut, Windows 2000, in turn, edits the associated PIF. With the correct settings, the program runs properly, sparing you the aggravation caused by program crashes, sluggish performance, memory shortages, and other annoying anomalies. PIFs have the same initial name as the application but use .PIF as the extension (123.PIF, for example). When you run an MS-DOS application (using any technique), Windows 2000 searches the application's directory and the system search path for a PIF with the same name as the application. If one is found, this file's settings are applied to the DOS environment by the DOS environment subsystem before running the application. If no PIF is found, Windows

2000 uses the default settings stored in a file named _DEFAULT.PIF, stored in the \WINNT directory. These settings work for most DOS applications, but not all.

Tip #363	In earlier versions of Windows, you had to edit a PIF using the PIF Editor. You no longer need to do so. For all intents and purposes, you can forget about the existence of PIFs and focus on a DOS application's properties instead by right-clicking the application and choosing Properties.

DOS property settings can affect many aspects of an application's operation, such as (but not limited to) the following:

- The directory that becomes active when an application starts
- Full-screen or windowed operation upon launch
- Conventional memory usage
- Expanded or extended memory usage
- The application's multitasking priority level
- The application's shortcut keys
- Foreground and background processing

Some DOS programs come with PIFs, knowing you might run them under Windows. PIF settings from a Windows 3.1 computer work under the Windows 2000 Professional environment, so you can copy them to the appropriate directory, or take note of the settings on the Windows 3.x machine and reenter them on the Windows 2000 Professional machine.

Earlier versions of Windows (namely Windows 3.x) sported more settings for DOS programs, but because Windows 2000 Professional is more intelligent than its little brother, many of them are history.

To edit these properties for a DOS program, do the following:

1. Find the program file or a shortcut to it.
2. Right-click and choose Settings. You then see a dialog box like the one shown in Figure 30.26. (In this example, I adjusted the properties for the print spooler supplied with Windows version 1.1, just for kicks.)

Poke through each tab, and use the ? (question mark) button for help on the settings.

Tip #364	You can use the Program tab's Close On Exit setting if you want the program's window to disappear and dump you back into Windows when you exit the program. Otherwise, the remains of the application stay onscreen when you quit, and nothing happens. You then must press any key to return to Windows. In most cases, you'll want this box enabled. You'll want it disabled when you run an application such as `tracert` or a `dir` listing in which you want to read the program's screen output after it completes execution.

Figure 30.26
Setting the advanced property settings for a DOS application.

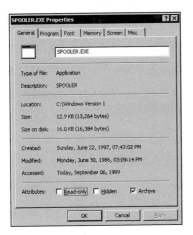

Tip #365

The Screen tab's Usage options determine whether the application initially comes up windowed or full-screen. You still can toggle between views by pressing Alt+Enter. Of course, in full-screen display, the mouse is surrendered to the application. And, unless you stipulate otherwise via the application window's Control menu, when the application is running in a window, Windows takes over the mouse. Then it can be used only for Windows operations.

CUSTOM STARTUP FILES

The Program tab from a DOS program's Properties dialog box has a Windows NT button. You can choose it to further configure the MS-DOS environment with what amounts to the old CONFIG.SYS and AUTOEXEC.BAT commands. In Windows NT and 2000-land, these files are called CONFIG.NT and AUTOEXEC.NT; they are the default files loaded into each DOS VDM. If an application needs a particular environment that would normally be controlled by settings in CONFIG.SYS or AUTOEXEC.BAT, such as a memory-resident program, and you don't want every VDM to use these settings, you can control it. You simply create specialized files that the PIF loads instead of the defaults and then declare the filenames in the PIF.

From the application's Properties dialog box, click the Windows NT button. You then see the dialog box shown in Figure 30.27; here, you can name alternative files to be used. Just enter the names of the files. You should create your own modified files for this use. Start by copying CONFIG.NT and AUTOEXEC.NT and then editing them with a plain text editor such as Notepad. You can find the files in the \SYSTEM32 directory.

When you run a DOS application, Windows 2000 Professional creates a DOS VDM by loading the DOS environment subsystem and sort of "booting up" DOS. In the process, it reads in settings from CONFIG.NT and AUTOEXEC.NT in just the same way real DOS does when it boots. The only difference is the filenames and the file locations. In this case, the files are in the \SYSTEM32 directory (usually \WINNT\SYSTEM32 or \WINDOWS\SYSTEM32) instead of the root directory. Each time you run a DOS application in a new window (each time a VDM is created), Windows 2000 reads the CONFIG.NT and AUTOEXEC.NT files. The great thing about this capability is that you can change the settings and rerun a program, and the new settings get read and go into effect. It's like rebooting DOS after fine-tuning CONFIG.SYS and AUTOEXEC.BAT—except faster.

Figure 30.27
You can further fine-tune the DOS environment by using CONFIG.NT and AUTOEXEC.NT or similar files of your choice.

→ The commands you can place in an AUTOEXEC.NT file are nearly identical to those in DOS. **See** Appendix A, "Command-Line Reference" (on the CD-ROM), for a listing of commands pertinent to an MS-DOS window.

The commands available for CONFIG.NT are shown in Table 30.9.

TABLE 30.9 COMMANDS AVAILABLE FOR CONFIG.NT

Command	Description
country=	Sets the language conventions for the session.
device=	Installs loadable device drivers. Be careful with drivers that attempt to address hardware directly; they don't work. You can load display drivers such as ANSI.SYS and memory managers such as EMM.SYS and HIMEM.SYS.
dos=	Tells Windows 2000 what to do with the Upper Memory Area (where to load DOS, as in dos=high).
dosonly	Allows only DOS programs to be loaded from a COMMAND.COM prompt. POSIX, OS/2, and Windows programs don't run. Note that a COMMAND.COM prompt and a Windows 2000 Command Prompt window's prompt are not the same. If you run COMMAND.COM, you get a DOS box running the DOS command interpreter. Command Prompt windows run Windows 2000 Professional's command interpreter (CMD.EXE), whose command set differs and expands on MS-DOS's.
echoconfig	Activates the display of CONFIG and AUTOEXEC commands as they are executed from the files.
fcbs=	Sets the maximum number of file control blocks (FCBs).
files=	Sets the maximum number of open files.
install=	Loads a memory-resident (TSR) program into memory before the window comes up or an application loads.
loadhigh=	Loads device drivers into the High Memory Area (HMA).
ntcmdprompt	Replaces the COMMAND.COM interpreter with the Windows 2000 interpreter, CMD.EXE. After you load a TSR or when you shell out of an application to DOS, you get CMD.EXE instead, from which you have the added benefits of the Windows 2000 interpreter.
rem	Marks a line as a comment.
stacks=	Indicates the amount of RAM set aside for stacking up hardware interrupts as they come in.

ABOUT THE COMMAND-LINE ENVIRONMENT

Despite the ease of use of the Windows graphical user interface, using the command-line interface remains a useful way to perform many maintenance, configuration, and diagnostic tasks. Many of the most important diagnostic tools such as ping, tracert, and nslookup are only available from the command line, unless you purchase third-party graphical add-ons to perform these functions. Using batch files remains a useful way to encapsulate common management functions; batch files (or shortcuts to batch files) can be placed in shared folders as a way of distributing management functions on a network. Together, command-line utilities and Windows Script Host scripts provide a complete set of building blocks from which you can build very high-level utilities.

→ If you're interested in learning more about using Windows Script Host to automate repetitive system administration tasks, **see** Chapter 36, "Windows Script Host."

The Windows 2000 command-line utilities include many of the same programs found in DOS and earlier versions of Windows. In many cases, the programs have been enhanced considerably. Utilities not found in DOS or Windows 9x are also available.

Command-line programs fall into five categories, as shown in Table 30.10.

TABLE 30.10   CATEGORIES OF COMMAND-LINE PROGRAMS

Types of Commands	Description
Built-in	These commands are built into the command interpreter; for example, dir, copy, and rename.
Native	These commands call .EXE files; for example, sort.exe, net.exe, and more.exe.
Subsystem	These commands are .EXE files from older operating systems that were designed to adjust the environment or interface. They run inside the virtual DOS machine. Examples are DOSKEY, SETVER, himem.sys, and dosx.exe.
Batch file	These commands direct the flow of batch files; for example, for, goto, if, and else.
Configuration	These commands go in AUTOEXEC.NT, CONFIG.NT, and CONFIG.SYS in the root drive. They tune the subsystem during startup.

The command interpreter (the DOS shell) in Windows 2000 Professional is, by default, CMD.EXE. The CMD.EXE command interpreter is similar to the old COMMAND.COM shell but has enhanced batch file functions and also has built-in command-line editing and a command history function similar to that provided by DOSKEY in DOS and Windows 9x. You don't need DOSKEY in Windows 2000, unless you want to use its command aliasing feature. (See the entries for CMD and DOSKEY in Appendix A, on the CD, for more information.)

Tip #366	Many of the built-in commands are significantly enhanced since Windows 9x and NT 4. If you're a batch file programmer, make sure to see Appendix A on the CD, and read about all the enhancements to the batch files and built-in commands.

WHAT'S NEW OR DIFFERENT FROM MS-DOS

Windows 2000 retains and enhances almost all the functionality of MS-DOS. The following sections explain new Windows 2000 commands not found in MS-DOS, changes to MS-DOS commands, and unavailable MS-DOS commands.

WINDOWS 2000 COMMANDS

Table 30.11 explains Windows 2000 system commands not found in MS-DOS.

TABLE 30.11   WINDOWS 2000 COMMANDS

Command	Function
at	Schedules commands and programs to run on a computer at a specified time and date.
cacls	Displays or modifies access control lists (ACLs) of files.
convert	Converts file systems from FAT or FAT32 to NTFS.
dosonly	Prevents starting applications other than MS-DOS–based applications from the COMMAND.COM prompt.
echoconfig	Displays messages when reading the MS-DOS subsystem CONFIG.NT file.
endlocal	Ends localization of environment variables.
findstr	Searches for text in files using regular expressions.
ntcmdprompt	Runs the Windows 2000 command interpreter, CMD.EXE, rather than COMMAND.COM after running a TSR or after starting the command prompt from within an MS-DOS application.
popd	Changes to the directory last set with the pushd command.
pushd	Saves the current directory for use by the popd command and then changes to the specified directory.
setlocal	Begins localization of environmental variables.
start	Runs a specified program or command in a secondary window and in its own memory space.
title	Sets the title of the Command Prompt window.
&&	Command following this symbol runs only if the command preceding the symbol succeeds.
||	Command following this symbol runs only if the command preceding the symbol fails.
&	Separates multiple commands on the command line.
( )	Groups commands.
^	(Escape character.) Allows you to type command symbols as text.
; or ,	Separates parameters.

CHANGES TO MS-DOS COMMANDS

Table 30.12 lists changes and improvements to MS-DOS commands.

TABLE 30.12 CHANGES TO MS-DOS COMMANDS

Command	Changed Features
chcp	This command changes code pages for full-screen mode only.
cmd	CMD.EXE replaces COMMAND.COM.
del	New switches provide many more functions.
dir	New switches provide many more functions.
diskcomp	Switches /1 and /8 are not supported.
diskcopy	Switch /1 is not supported.
doskey	This command is available for all character-based programs that accept buffered input. DOSKEY has been improved by a series of enhancements.
format	A 20.8MB optical drive is supported. Switches /b, /s, and /u are not supported.
label	The symbols ^ and & can be used in a volume label.
mode	This command has had extensive changes.
more	New switches provide many more functions.
path	The %PATH% environment variable appends the current path to a new setting at the command prompt.
print	Switches /b, /c, /m, /p, /q, /s, /t, and /u are not supported.
prompt	New character combinations allow you to add ampersands ($a), parentheses ($c and $f), and spaces ($s) to your prompt.
recover	This command recovers files only.
rmdir	The new /s switch deletes directories containing files and subdirectories.
sort	This command does not require the TEMP environment variable. File size is unlimited.
xcopy	New switches provide many more functions.

UNAVAILABLE MS-DOS COMMANDS

The MS-DOS commands in Table 30.13 are not available at the Windows 2000 command prompt.

TABLE 30.13 MS-DOS COMMANDS NOT AVAILABLE IN WINDOWS 2000

Command	New Procedure or Reason for Obsolescence
assign	Not supported in Windows 2000.
backup	Not currently supported.

continues

TABLE 30.13   CONTINUED

Command	New Procedure or Reason for Obsolescence
choice	Not currently supported.
ctty	Not currently supported.
dblspace	Not supported.
defrag	Windows 2000 automatically optimizes disk use. To optimize a disk manually, right-click it in My Computer, click Properties, and then, on the Tools tab, click Defragment Now.
deltree	The rmdir /s command deletes directories containing files and subdirectories.
diskperf	Not currently supported.
dosshell	Unnecessary with Windows 2000.
drvspace	Not currently supported.
emm386	Unnecessary with Windows 2000. Note: emm386 is not used, but an EMM control does appear in CONFIG.NT for CMD.EXE.
fasthelp	This MS-DOS 6.0 command is the same as the Windows 2000 command help. Windows 2000 also provides an online command reference.
fdisk	Disk Management prepares hard disks for use with Windows 2000.
include	Multiple configurations of the MS-DOS subsystem are not supported.
interlnk	Not supported.
intersrv	Not supported.
join	Increased partition size and an improved file system eliminate the need to join drives.
memmaker	Windows 2000 automatically optimizes the MS-DOS subsystem's memory use.
menucolor	Multiple configurations of the MS-DOS subsystem are not supported.
menudefault	Multiple configurations of the MS-DOS subsystem are not supported.
menuitem	Multiple configurations of the MS-DOS subsystem are not supported.
mirror	Not supported in Windows 2000.
msav	Not supported.
msbackup	Windows 2000 provides the Backup utility (under the Administrative Tools in the Control Panel) for computers with tape drives or the xcopy command for computers without tape drives.
mscdex	You don't need to configure the MS-DOS subsystem to use CD-ROM drives. Windows 2000 provides access to CD-ROM drives for the MS-DOS subsystem. Actually, mscdexnt is the Windows 2000 replacement for mscdex and is run in AUTOEXEC.NT.
msd	You can use the System Information snap-in instead. To start System Information, choose Start, Run, and then type msinfo32.
numlock	Not currently supported.

Command	New Procedure or Reason for Obsolescence
power	Not supported.
restore	Not currently supported.
scandisk	Not supported.
smartdrv	Windows 2000 automatically provides caching for the MS-DOS subsystem.
submenu	Multiple configurations of the MS-DOS subsystem are not supported.
sys	Windows 2000 does not fit on a standard 1.2MB or 1.44MB floppy disk.
undelete	Not supported in Windows 2000.
unformat	Not supported in Windows 2000.
vsafe	Not supported.

PART

V

CH

30

Tip #367

If you are a system administrator or veteran command-line user, you should get a copy of the Windows 2000 Resource kit, which contains many more valuable utilities, both graphical and command-line. In a Windows 2000 LAN of more than two or three computers, at least one computer should have a copy of the Resource Kit.

Monitoring Legacy Programs

Read on if you want to learn how to monitor a 16-bit Windows-based program or an MS-DOS–based program. In Windows 2000, 16-bit Windows-based programs run as separate threads in a multithreaded process called Windows Virtual DOS Machine (NTVDM). As explained in Chapter 2, the NTVDM process simulates a 16-bit Windows environment.

An MS-DOS–based program runs in its own NTVDM process. You can monitor a 16-bit program or an MS-DOS–based program running on your computer with System Monitor by monitoring the NTVDM instance of the Process performance object. Note that 16-bit programs running in an NTVDM appear only if they are started in a separate memory space. If you find that your 16-bit programs are not performing well under Windows 2000, you can access some of the program's properties by right-clicking the name of the program in Windows Explorer and configuring the properties as follows:

- If the program is in a window, and the display performance is slow, on the Screen tab, click Full-Screen.
- If the program is in a window and seems to pause periodically, click the Misc tab, and set the Idle Sensitivity slider to Low.

You can turn off Compatible Timer Hardware Emulation for the program if performance does not improve by changing the previously described settings. To do so, right-click _DEFAULT.PIF or the program name, point to Program, and click Windows NT. In the dialog box that appears, clear the Compatible Timer Hardware Emulation check box. This change typically causes a decrease in performance and should be made only if other efforts fail.

KEEPING A COMMAND PROMPT WINDOW OPEN AFTER EXECUTION OF A PROGRAM

To keep a Command Prompt window open after a program has executed, you can open the window first and then run the program manually. When the program is terminated, the window will stay open. However, if you run the program by entering its name into the Run box or from a shortcut in the Windows GUI, it will close automatically by default. To keep the window open, follow these steps:

1. Create a shortcut to the DOS program or batch file.
2. Right-click the shortcut, and choose Properties.
3. Select the Program tab.
4. Uncheck Close on Exit. The window should now be kept open after the program finishes.

TROUBLESHOOTING

NOT ENOUGH SLOTS

I don't have enough slots for multiple monitors. What should I do?

Some video display cards support more than one monitor; they have a connector for each monitor. Try Appian Technology's 2-port and 4-port Jeronimo cards. With two 4-port and one 2-port card, you could get 10 monitors in three PCI slots. Check the Windows Hardware Compatibility List for details of the latest cards that support multiple monitors all in one card. Also, check www.appiantech.com.

SETTING THE PRIMARY DISPLAY

I can't get my multimonitor system to choose the primary display properly.

As I mentioned in the section about multimonitor arrangements earlier in the chapter, it can be tricky to force Windows 2000 into using a particular video display card as the secondary display. If a display card isn't disabled from running in VGA mode, the computer runs the card's Power-On Self Test (POST). When that happens, Windows 2000 assigns it primary display status. Most users will want to keep their first video card as the primary display, so they must know how to prevent the POST from happening. In Table 30.14, I've compiled some information about display adapters that support multimonitor operation in Windows 2000 and how to disable their VGA modes—and thus their POST.

Many of the adapters that support multimonitors under Windows 2000 have jumpers or switches that allow you to disable VGA mode, allowing the display to operate as a secondary display adapter. The problem is complicated by the fact that most computers with on-board video try to assign primary display status to an add-on card.

As video cards are constantly going through revision, you should consult your owner's manual for exact details of the jumpers and switches being discussed in Table 30.14.

TABLE 30.14 VIDEO CARD JUMPERS AND SWITCHES

Type	Description
Matrox	Of the Matrox series display adapters, only the original Matrox Millennium has a DIP switch located on the lower-right corner of the card allowing the user to disable VGA. Also, be aware that any Matrox display that utilizes the mga64.sys driver can disable VGA and should work as a secondary adapter, but only the original Milleniums have the option to disable VGA with a jumper.
Number Nine	Number Nine has several adapters supporting VGA-disabling: Imagine128, Imagine 128 v2, Revolution 3D, and the Revolution IV. To get any of these displays to function as a VGA-disabled secondary display, the VGA jumper on the adapter must be set to Disable.
3Dlabs Permedia2	3Dlabs Permedia2 chipsets are available on several OEM manufacturer's display adapters. The Permedia2 driver in Windows 2000 is capable of disabling VGA, although many of the available adapters have VGA-disabling jumpers. It is recommended that you set this jumper to VGA-Disable if available.
ATI Technologies	ATI has no card available with a functioning VGA-disable jumper or switch. (There are several models with what appears to be a VGA-disable jumper as well as a VGA INT jumper; the VGA-disable jumper has no function or use in setting up multimonitoring on Windows 2000.) Of the displays ATI offers, only the 3D Rage Pro PCI and 3D Rage Pro AGP 2x support VGA-disabling currently. Of these two chipsets, only those supplied with SGRAM can function as VGA-disabled. You also should be sure you do not have a 3D Rage Pro Turbo chipset. These chipsets function as VGA-disabled displays, but with serious corruption; therefore, they are currently not supported as VGA-disabled displays on Windows 2000.

When you choose an ATI display adapter for use as a VGA-disabled display, look for the off-white SGRAM memory socket (for upgrading display memory, your card may have this socket populated); this socket indicates that the display uses SGRAM. Also, you should double-check that the chipset is one of the two mentioned above, and not a Rage Pro Turbo, IIC, VT2, VT3, VT4, LT, LT Pro, Rage, Rage II, Rage II+, CT, CX, VT, VT2, GT, or GX because none of these chipsets are supported as VGA-disabled displays on Windows 2000. |

ALTERED BIOS SETTINGS PREVENT COMPUTER FROM BOOTING

I've altered my BIOS settings, and now the computer won't start.

This is a bad place to be, and I know the feeling. It's one of those "oops" feelings, just like after you've locked your keys in the car. Today's computer BIOSs have *so* many arcane settings that it's quite possible to alter one that will prevent proper booting. Before you futz with the advanced CMOS settings (not just the simple stuff like time, date, boot order, power settings, ports, and such), read the manual that came with the computer or motherboard. If you decide to change something, write down the old value before doing so. When in doubt, don't alter advanced CMOS settings that affect how the chipset works, whether and where the BIOS and video shadowing is done, and so on. The default settings are designed by the motherboard maker to work under most situations and operating systems. Because Windows is the most popular operating system, you can bet it was already tested and configured for Windows 9x, NT, or 2000 (unless you have an old motherboard).

That said, what do you do if you've changed something in the CMOS and now the computer won't boot? You can try the computer's or motherboard's manual or Web site for information about settings for Windows 2000. If you find nothing, then you should wind back the settings to the factory defaults. Most CMOS setups have a "Set to Default" or similar command you can issue.

If what you've done has changed the hard disk "Type," or if you manually entered the number of sectors, tracks, platters, and so on, and now it won't boot, use the Auto Detect Hard Disk BIOS setting. Virtually all modern BIOSs and hard disks can do a little dance to discover and enter those numbers automatically (this is known as *drive autotyping*).

NEW HARDWARE DOESN'T WORK

I've added some hardware, but it doesn't work.

Try these steps, in this order:

1. Try the troubleshooters included in the Help system, assuming the hardware fits into one of the neatly packaged categories. Open them by choosing Start, Help, Troubleshooting. No good?

2. Try rebooting Windows 2000.

3. Use the Computer Management Console and the Device Manager to check resources assigned to the hardware to be sure that it's not conflicting. Check the hardware's manual to determine whether you should be setting some DIP switches or jumpers on it to avoid conflicts.

4. Remove the item and reboot. Then use the Device Manager to make sure the item is truly removed from the operating system. If it isn't, remove it manually in the Device Manager (by right-clicking and choosing Uninstall), and reboot until it's gone.

5. Power down, add the hardware again (running the Add/Remove Hardware applet if the hardware isn't detected at bootup), and configure as necessary.

6. Contact the manufacturer.

TIPS FROM THE WINDOWS PROS: UPGRADING AND OPTIMIZING YOUR COMPUTER

Following are several tips I've learned over the years that will help save you hours of headaches.

SLEUTHING OUT CONFLICTS

When you're hunting down potential IRQ, memory, and I/O conflicts, try using the Device Manager to help out. Yes, Computer Management, System Information, Hardware Resources, Conflicts Sharing will show you potential conflicts, so that's a good place to look, too. But let me share a trick with the Device Manager that isn't readily apparent.

Normally, a class of devices called Hidden Devices isn't shown. To show them, open the Device Manager (either via Control Panel, System or from Computer Management). Then, on the View menu, click Show Hidden Devices (see Figure 30.28). A check mark next to Show Hidden Devices indicates that hidden devices are showing. Click it again to clear the check mark. Hidden devices include non-Plug and Play devices (devices with earlier Windows 2000 device drivers) and devices that have been physically removed from the computer but have not had their drivers uninstalled.

Figure 30.28
Showing hidden devices can help you track down renegade IRQ conflicts.

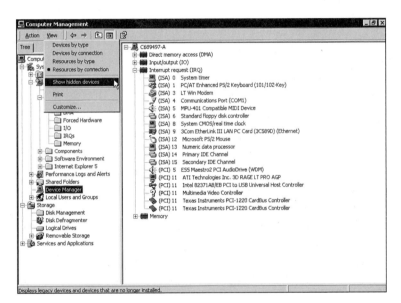

CHANGING YOUR LAPTOP HARD DISK EFFORTLESSLY

So, you want to upgrade or swap out the hard disk on your laptop? Assuming the drive you're replacing actually works okay and is just too small for you, the obvious question is how to do it and not have to lose your data, applications, and the operating system. As you'll learn in Chapter 33, you could use a program such as DriveImage or Ghost to make an image of the hard disk, but doing so can become a problem when you try to copy the data to the new drive; you must boot up with network support or CD-ROM support or use some other tricky scheme for the recovery.

Let me tell you about an approach that works faster, is almost effortless, and is designed specifically for upgrading laptop hard disks. Check out a product called SuperDupe from iGo (www.igo.com). You just plug in a PCMCIA card, attach the new IDE drive to it, and run a program. Everything is copied from drive 1 to drive 2, including the master boot record, boot tracks, partitions (FAT16 and FAT32 only, though), system, applications, and data. If a partition exists on the old drive, it initiates a similar partition on the new drive (though you can override the suggested settings). The remaining room on the new larger drive is simply formatted, making the entire drive usable. And the transfer rate is fast, so it shouldn't take long. You might even consider this approach for a super-fast backup program (assuming you don't mind springing for the additional hard drive).

OPTIMIZING YOUR COMPUTER FOR WINDOWS 2000

Finally, here's my biggest tip....

Optimizing your computer for Windows 2000 is actually pretty easy. I'm very impressed with this operating system's capability to keep on chugging. It doesn't cough or die easily if you mind your manners.

- If you're buying new stuff for an upgrade, consider only hardware that's on the HCL.
- When you're buying a new machine, get it with Windows 2000 Professional preinstalled and from a reputable maker with decent technical support, not just a reputable dealer. The dealer might not be able to solve complex technical problems. Brand-name manufacturers such as Dell, Compaq, Gateway, IBM, and so on have teams of engineers devoted to testing new operating systems and ironing out kinks in their hardware, with help from engineers at Microsoft.

  If you love to upgrade and experiment, more power to you. I used to build PCs from scratch, even soldering them together from parts. Then again, you can also build your own car. (I used to just about do that myself, too.) Or you can buy it preassembled from some company in Detroit. It really isn't worth spending much time fiddling with PC hardware unless you are putting together systems for a specific purpose. With the amazingly low price of computers these days, don't waste your time. And don't cut corners in configuring a new machine. For an extra 50 bucks, you can get goodies such as a modem, network card, and faster video card thrown in. Do it up front, and save the hassle down the road.
- Run Windows Update frequently.
- Keep the hard disks defragmented (see Chapter 34), and make sure you have a decent amount of free space on your drives, especially your WINNT drive.

Note

Chapter 3 contains a lot of discussion about computer upgrades. This is a good starting point whenever you are considering a computer hardware or software upgrade.

SYSTEM ADMINISTRATION AND SYSTEM MAINTENANCE

CHAPTER 31

SYSTEM MANAGEMENT AND CONFIGURATION TOOLS

In this chapter

GETTING UNDER THE HOOD

Windows 2000 Professional is rife with system management and administrative utility programs—so many, in fact, that you can easily become overwhelmed by the number of tools and the multitudinous paths for reaching those tools. As writers who have pounded on Windows systems since the days of version 1.1, my co-author and I can easily report that the mandate of effectively discussing the administrator tools for Windows 2000 Professional was a bit daunting, even to us.

If you're the kind of user who likes to pop the hood, see what's inside, and do a little tinkering, or if you're an administrator who has the job of managing computers in a corporation, this is the chapter for you. You'll want to read through the descriptions of the various tools covered here and learn a bit about how to use them.

Thus far, you've learned about the basic Control Panel utilities and many of the configuration and maintenance tools and applets. Dividing the tools into clearly delineated chapters was somewhat difficult, as many do not fall neatly into a category. The following is how it all shook out in the end:

- Chapter 29, "Customizing via Control Panel Applets," discusses a majority of the Control Panel applets.

- Chapter 30, "Maintaining and Optimizing System Performance," discusses a number of primarily hardware-related tools.

- This chapter discusses the balance of the computer management tools, some of which are very powerful, especially the Microsoft Management Console (MMC), which is a highly customizable toolbox you can build for your own sleuthing purposes. If you did not find a tool you were looking for by skimming the other chapters, it is likely here.

If you're a Windows 9x or NT 4 maven, some tools that you are likely familiar with in those interfaces have changed names and locations in Windows 2000. In some cases, the functionality has been picked up in a completely different tool interface. When this is the case, I'll cite the old and new locations. And, of course, some system management tools, such as the Microsoft Management Console, are completely new in Windows 2000 Professional.

Table 31.1 describes each of the system management tools. With the exception of the Recovery tool (which is described in Chapter 33, "Managing the Hard Disk"), each of these tools is discussed later in this chapter.

TABLE 31.1 SYSTEM MANAGEMENT TOOLS

Tool	Description
Task Manager	A tool for killing crashed applications, listing currently running processes, and checking system performance

Tool	Description
Microsoft Management Console (MMC)	A powerful, expandable interface for major administration of local and remote workstations
Computer Management	A subset of Microsoft Management Console, for extensive control of the local machine
Windows Update (including Rollback)	Online tool via the Internet, for ensuring your system is running the latest software additions and bug fixes
Scheduled Tasks	A utility program for automating execution of programs
File Signature Verification tool	A tool that prevents critical system files from being altered
System File Checker	A command-line executable that verifies system file versions are aligned properly
Performance Monitor	A tool that creates a graphical and/or numeric display of essential system information, such as memory usage, status of the hard disk usage, CPU activity, and network traffic
Event Viewer	A tool for viewing system-generated log files
Recovery Console	A tool that attempts to recover a broken or otherwise nonbooting system

PART

VI

CH

31

TASK MANAGER

The Task Manager is one tool you're bound to frequent, perhaps more than any other. Whenever an application crashes, you believe you're running some suspect process that you want to kill, or you want to check on the state of system resources (for example, RAM usage), you can use the Task Manager. Even as nothing more than an educational tool, the Task Manager is informative.

The Task Manager can display more than 20 parameters of each running process for your edification, such as CPU and memory usage, page faults, and handle count. This information is particularly useful for programmers although everyday users might also find it helpful in troubleshooting the system. For example, you can use it if you want to know how much memory or CPU time a particular program is consuming.

The Task Manager is always available, with a simple press of the "three-finger salute." Press Ctrl+Alt+Del and up pops the Windows Security dialog. This dialog is interesting and useful; Table 31.2 explains some of its features.

TABLE 31.2   BUTTONS ON THE TASK MANAGER

Button	Function
Lock Computer	Use this button to display the Computer Locked dialog box. Your system is then locked, preventing everyone except you or a system administrator from unlocking your system and viewing any open files or programs. To unlock your computer, press Ctrl+Alt+Delete, type your password, and then click OK.
Change Password	Use this button to regularly change your logon password.
Log Off	Use this button to log off the current user and log on a new user.
Shut Down	Use this button to choose logoff (it has a similar effect to the preceding button), power down, standby, or hibernate.
Task Manager	Use this button to list, check status of, or kill any running or crashed tasks and applications. You also can start applications and see a dynamic display of memory and CPU usage.
Cancel	Use this button to go back to what you were doing.

If you choose Task Manager, the dialog in Figure 31.1 appears, with the three tabs described in the following sections.

Figure 31.1
The Task Manager shows you which applications and processes are running and lets you terminate hung programs. It also indicates some important aspects of system performance.

APPLICATIONS TAB

You can click the Applications tab of the Task Manager to see a list of the programs currently running on the computer. Not a lot of information is displayed, only the application name and the status (running or not responding). However, this tab does provide a more complete report than you'll get by glancing at the taskbar buttons or via the dialog box you see if you press Alt+Tab.

You can sort the list by clicking the column heads. If an application has multiple documents open, the application appears only once in the list, probably with the name of the document that is foremost at the time (has the focus). Some applications don't comply with this single-document interface (SDI) approach, listing each new document as a separate application. Some examples are Word, Excel, and PowerPoint.

From this list, you can kill a hung application. If an application has hung, it is probably reported in the list as Not responding. I say probably because sometimes the list reports it as running when it is not. Click the End Task button to terminate the task. If a document is open and unsaved, and if, for some unexpected reason, the program responds gracefully to Windows's attempt to shut it down (which is unlikely), you might see a dialog asking whether you want to save. More likely, Windows 2000 will just ask for confirmation to kill the application, as you can see in Figure 31.2.

PART

VI

CH

31

Figure 31.2
Ending a task that is "not responding," in other words, crashed.

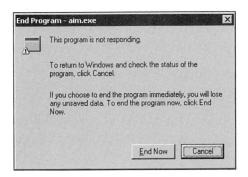

 If you have killed applications and they still appear in the Applications tab listing, see "The Task Manager Is Stalled" in the "Troubleshooting" section at the end of this chapter.

Tip #368

Before you give an application its last rites, pause for a bit. In general, it's not a good idea to kill an application if you can avoid doing so. Terminating an application can cause instability in the operating system (even though it shouldn't in most cases because of the NT kernel design). Or at the least, you can lose data. Try "jiggling" the application in various ways, in hopes of being able to close it gracefully first. Switch to it and back a few times. Give it a little time. Maybe even do some work in another application for a few minutes, or take a trip to the water cooler. Try pressing Esc while the application is open.

When executing some macros in Word, for example, I noticed that one of my macros hangs for no apparent reason. It seems to crash Word. So, I killed it from the Task Manager, losing some work. I later realized the solution was to press Esc, which terminated the macro. Having slow network connections and attempting to link to nonexistent Web pages, printers, or removable media can also cause apparent hangs. Try opening a drive

continues

continued

door, removing a network cable, or performing some other trick to break a loop a program might be in before resorting to killing the program from the Task Manager. This is especially true if you've been working on a document and you might potentially lose data.

Dr. Watson, Come Quick!

You might want to know about a debugging program called Dr. Watson, which is supplied with Windows 2000 Professional. It's primarily designed for programmers or for technical support people who might be helping you resolve a software conflict on the workstation. The program sits in memory, keeping an eagle eye on applications as they run. If one bombs or breaches security, Windows 2000 shuts down the errant program, and Dr. Watson creates an entry in a special log file named Drwtsn32.log. The entry contains key information about what the application did wrong, and some other details of your computer's operation at the time of the error. If you are getting application crashes on a specific program, you can contact the vendor and ask whether the tech support people want to see the log. To start the Dr. Watson program to set up preferences, you can choose Start, Run, and enter drwtsn32. The default settings are fine under most circumstances.

Incidentally, two Dr. Watson programs are actually included with Windows 2000. You'll find both 32-bit and 16-bit versions for the corresponding Windows applications. The programs are named drwtsn32.exe (for 32-bit programs) and drwatson.exe (for 16-bit programs).

By default, drwtsn32.exe creates a Crash Dump file for each error that is generated. It is a binary file that can be opened and examined in a debugger program. These files can be quite large, however. They take up space on your disk and cause a bit of a system slowdown while writing the files to disk. The last time I checked one of these files on one of my machines, it was 45MB. If you don't expect to be debugging a program, you can turn off this feature by running drwtsn32.exe and turning off the Create Crash Dump File option.

Notice that you can also switch to an application in the list or run a new one. Just double-click the application you want to switch to (or click Switch To). Similarly, to run a new application, click New Task, and enter the executable name or use the Browse dialog box to find it. This dialog is no different from the Start, Run dialog box, even though its name is different.

 If you're frustrated because you cannot send the Task Manager to the background, see "Sending the Task Manager to the Background" in the "Troubleshooting" section at the end of this chapter.

PROCESSES TAB

Whereas the Application tab displays only the full-fledged applications you're running, the Processes tab shows *all* running processes, including programs (for example, Photoshop), services (for example, Event Log), or a subsystem (for example, wowexec.exe for running Windows 3.x applications).

By studying the entries in the process list, you can learn some interesting facts about the operating system. For starters, you might be shocked to see just how many separate processes the operating system has to multitask just to keep going (see Figure 31.3). In this example, I've maximized the window and added more columns to the display.

Notice that the highlighted process is ntvdm (NT Virtual DOS Machine); also, notice that wowexec.exe is running in it and is indented a bit. The processes running along with the wowexec (two copies of a screen capture program and Pegasus mail) are also indented. Recall from Chapter 2, "The Design and Architecture of Windows 2000 Professional," that all Windows 3.1 processes run in the same VDM, with wowexec.exe (WOW means "Windows on Windows") being the process that emulates Windows 3.1. Terminating the ntvdm or wowexec process will terminate all three Windows 3.1 applications.

Figure 31.3
Examining running processes. Notice the wowexec.exe process, which is the Windows 3.1 subsystem, and the three Windows 3.1 programs. You can add columns to the display via the View, Select Columns command.

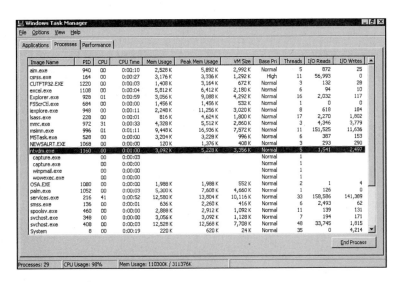

If the true identity of some of the processes is something you're dedicated to uncovering, check the Services snap-in described later in this chapter. Many of the entries in the processes list are system services, the bulk of which load during bootup.

You can observe a bevy of process attributes in the window by adding columns. In Figure 31.3 (shown earlier), 11 columns are displayed. You can choose View, Select Columns to add columns. You then see the options shown in Figure 31.4.

Base Priority (shown as Base Pri as a column head in Figure 31.4) is particularly interesting, as you'll see later because it indicates the base priority of a task.

ALTERING THE PRIORITY OF A TASK

In the beginning, all tasks are created equal. Well, most of them, at least. Looking at Figure 31.4, notice the Base Pri column in the Task Manager. Here, I've set all Normal priority tasks to receive equal CPU time. A few, however, have High Priority, such as winlogon.exe, which is the process that responds to your pressing Ctrl+Alt+Del. You might want to increase or decrease the priority of a process, though changing the priority typically isn't necessary. To do so, right-click the task and choose the new priority.

Figure 31.4
You can add process details to your listing by using this dialog.

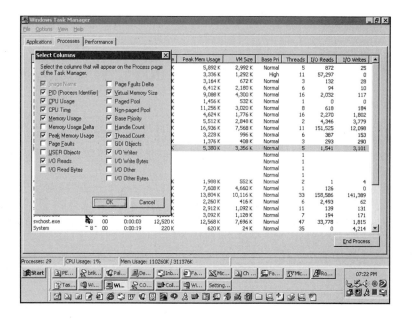

Tip #369

If you have a multiprocessor computer, and you want to assign a task to a given processor, right-click the process and choose the Set Affinity command. Choosing this command guarantees that the process receives CPU time only from the CPU you choose.

PERFORMANCE TAB

The Performance tab of the Task Manager indicates important conditions of your operating system. It shows a dynamic overview of your computer's performance, including CPU usage; memory usage; and totals of handles, threads, and processes (see Figure 31.5).

Although CPU usage is interesting, the most important of these numbers is memory usage. You can easily check in the Physical Memory area to see how much memory is installed in your system, how much is available for use by applications before disk caching begins, and how much the system is using for caching.

Note

System cache is the total current swap and RAM area allocated for system operations.

The Kernel Memory area reports the memory in use strictly by the operating system for running the operating system internals. Nonpaged kernel memory is available only to the operating system. This memory is in physical RAM and can't be paged out to the hard disk because the operating system always needs fast access to it, and it needs to be highly protected. Paged memory can be used by other programs when necessary. Commit memory is memory allocated to programs and the system. Because virtual memory increases the amount of actual memory available, the Commit Peak memory can exceed the maximum physical memory.

Figure 31.5
The Performance tab displays some interesting statistics and a chart of CPU and memory usage over time. By maximizing the window, you can view a greater number of samples.

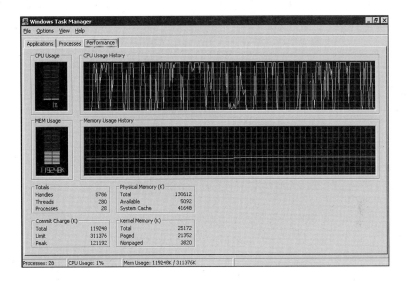

PART

VI

CH

31

In the Totals section, you can see the number of handles, threads, and processes. Threads are discussed in more detail in Chapter 2. Handles are tokens or pointers that let the operating system uniquely identify a resource, such as a file or Registry key, so that a program can access it.

Most of these size reports are of use only to programmers. However, the memory and CPU charts can offer strong, telltale signs of system overstressing. If you see, for example, that your memory usage is consistently nearing the top of its range, you are running too many programs. If the CPU is topped out most of the time, you also could be in trouble. Perhaps you have a background task running that is consuming way too much CPU time. An example could be a background program doing statistical analysis or data gathering.

Tip #370

Turn on the View, Show Kernel Times setting to see the relationship of kernel CPU slices to application CPU slices. (Remember from Chapter 2 that slices are small portions of the CPU's computing time.)

Tip #371

When the Task Manager is running, even if minimized, a green box appears in the system tray, indicating CPU usage. It's a miniature bar graph.

UPDATING THE DISPLAY

The Task Manager updates the display every so often by polling the system for information about running tasks and processes and CPU and memory usage. You can trigger an instant update by choosing View, Refresh Now.

You can also change the frequency at which the data is automatically updated by choosing View, Update Speed, and selecting the desired speed. The speed selections are practically meaningless in terms of an exact time because they vary from system to system as a function of clock speed. The default setting is "normal." You can leave it there for most purposes. Increase the update speed if you are trying to observe the effects of system events that are transitory. Reduce it to display effects over a longer time period in a single window. To analyze data at a specific point in time, choose the Pause option.

COMPUTER MANAGEMENT TOOL

In addition to the Task Manager and Control Panel, another tool named Computer Management is probably the most likely candidate for configuring and administering your PC. To get to it, right-click My Computer (on the desktop), and choose Manage. You then see the window shown in Figure 31.6.

Note

Another means of running the Computer Management tool is through Start, Control Panel, Administrative Tools.

Figure 31.6
You can manage a computer by right-clicking My Computer and choosing Manage.

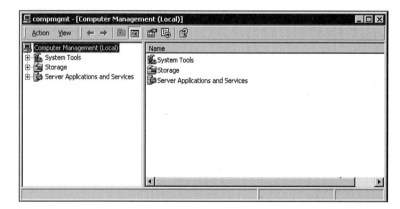

By its size, the command Manage seems humble; however, it is a powerful tool for a Windows 2000 Professional machine. It's actually a subset of the Microsoft Management Console, a topic covered later in this chapter. Computer Management is a serious tool in its own right, however; it includes the components (called *snap-ins*) you most often need for everyday computer management.

Computer Management provides easy access for the following tasks:

- Managing users and groups
- Managing shared devices and drives
- Checking system event logs containing information such as logon times and application errors
- Seeing which remote users are logged in to the system
- Viewing currently running system services, starting and stopping them, and setting automatic startup times for them
- Checking IRQ, DMA, memory, and port assignments for devices; locating device conflicts; and checking installed hardware
- Setting properties for storage devices
- Viewing device configurations and adding new device drivers
- Managing server applications and services such as the domain name service (DNS) or the Dynamic Host Configuration Protocol (DHCP) service

PART

VI

CH

31

THE COMPUTER MANAGEMENT INTERFACE

The Computer Management tool looks similar to the familiar Windows Explorer. It uses a two-pane view, with the *console tree* (for navigation and tool selection) in the left pane and details of the active item shown the right pane.

Items in the tree are called *nodes* (akin to folders in Explorer). The three nodes in Computer Management are as follows:

- System Tools
- Storage
- Server Applications and Services

As you would expect, you can conduct administrative chores by selecting a tool in the console tree and then clicking items in the right pane. When you select an item in the right pane, toolbar and menu options change as appropriate to that item, typically displaying attributes of the item or tool you selected. For example, the System Information branch can show you which IRQs are assigned already, and the Local Users and Groups branch can display the names and properties of all the users on the machine.

In previous versions of Windows NT, you had to hunt around through Control Panel applets to discover properties and settings that are now conveniently grouped together in Computer Management. I'll be honest; things are still a little confusing just because some of the properties available from Computer Management can also be reached via the Control Panel. An example is the Device Manager, which can be reached from the System applet in the Control Panel as well as the System Tools node in Computer Management. It's the same tool, and having multiple paths to the same destination is nothing new in Windows.

Tip #372

You must be assigned Administrator privileges to fully utilize the Computer Management tools. If you're a member of a lesser group, you have limited access to system properties and are locked out of making certain administrative changes to the system.

Experiment with the interface to uncover all that is available from these three little nodes in the left pane. You'll be surprised. Open each node by clicking the + (plus) sign. If you choose View, Details, some helpful information about various items in the right pane is displayed along with the items.

By default, you manage the local computer. To manage a remote computer (assuming you have permission), right-click the topmost item in the tree (Computer Management), and choose Connect to Another Computer.

Also by default, the view is set to Basic. To gain access to more advanced settings in the console, choose View, Advanced.

Note

You can rearrange the columns in the Computer Management window by dragging the column heads left and right.

A few points about each node are listed in the following sections.

SYSTEM TOOLS NODE

Performance Logs and Alerts—Counter logs and trace logs can help you keep track of when system events and errors occur and record them in a log file for later review. You can optionally choose to have a log trigger an alert message, run a program, or add a log entry to another log file when a certain number of errors has occurred or at prespecified times. This flexible service can be used locally or remotely, and it takes some study to effectively master. Unless you are an administrator, you don't have to deal with this tool. You can learn more details about constructing performance logs and alerts via the Computer Management Help system. Learn about viewing other kinds of logs and alerts in the section titled "Using the Event Viewer and Log Files" later in this chapter.

Local Users and Groups—You'll find two folders here: Users and Groups. Click one or the other; then, in the right pane, right-click the name of a person or group, and choose the relevant command, such as Set Password or Properties. Use the Action menu to create a new user.

System Information—This one is a biggie. Opening this folder leads to four subfolders, which in turn lead to a zillion lower folders containing an exact blueprint of your system, hardware, system components, and software environment. (You might have additional nodes in your system because some software you install may add nodes of their own.)

■ System Summary shows you basic information about your computer, operating system revision number, CPU, RAM, virtual memory, pagefile size, BIOS revision, and so on (see Figure 31.7).

Figure 31.7
See a summary of your system properties easily from the System Summary node.

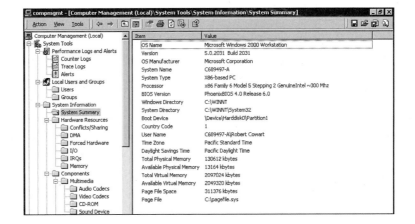

■ Hardware Resources displays hardware-specific settings, such as DMA, IRQs, I/O addresses, and memory addresses. The Conflicts/Sharing node identifies devices that are sharing resources or are in conflict. This information can help you identify problems with a device. Some IRQs can be shared between devices successfully.

■ The Components node provides a truly powerful view of all the major devices in your system. Open any subfolder and click an item. In a few seconds, information pertaining to the item is displayed, such as drive IDs, modem settings, and video display settings. In some cases, you can also see driver details. Check the folder called Problem Devices to see a list of all devices not loading or initializing properly.

■ The Software Environment node is like a super Task Manager. It displays details of 10 categories of software settings. You can see the running tasks, running services, startup files for each user, program groups for each user, environment variables, drivers, OLE registration, network connections, and pending print jobs. Figure 31.8 shows a task listing. Notice that 10 columns of data are available, some of which are offscreen.

Tip #373

Ever wonder why some darned program starts up when you boot, even though it's not in your Startup group? It's probably hiding in the Software Environment, Startup Programs folder. Travel down the path from System Information, Software Environment, Startup Programs, and take a look. I just checked mine and found RealTray and RealJukeboxSystray there. Hey, I don't want these things slowing down my bootup process. Office Startup is there, too. Unfortunately, you can't remove these startup utilities by right-clicking and choosing Delete. You have to use their related Setup programs. For example, to disable RealJukeboxSystray, I had to right-click its icon in the system tray and choose Disable Start Center.

Figure 31.8
Here, you can see a list of running tasks and associated information about the tasks.

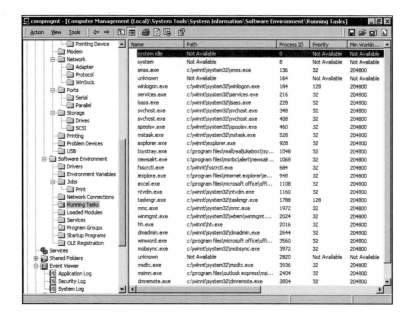

Services—As you learned in Chapters 1 and 2, Windows 2000 is highly modular. Many of the inner housekeeping chores of the operating system are broken down into services that can be added, removed, started, and stopped at any time, without requiring a reboot. A typical Windows 2000 Professional system has between 50 and 60 services running at any one time. You can view which services are running from this node. Use the Services tool (Services node, below) to start and stop services. The Software Environment node (see above) also includes a folder called Services, which is similar to the Services tool but doesn't allow starting and stopping of services. Figure 31.9 shows a typical Services listing. To start, stop, pause, or restart a service, you can use the context menu or the VCR-like buttons on the toolbar. For deeper control of a service, such as to declare what automatic recovery steps should be taken in the case of the service crashing, which hardware profiles it should run in, and more, open its Properties dialog box.

Shared Folders—The functionality of this node amounts to what used to be NetWatcher in previous Windows versions. The three folders under the Shared Folders node are as follows:

- Shares—Allows you to manage the properties of each shared resource. For example, you can alter the access rights for a shared resource so that certain users have read-only access. You can also change share permissions for a resource in the Properties dialog box of any shared resource by right-clicking the resource and clicking Properties.

- Sessions—Allows you to see which users are connected to a share and optionally disconnect them.

- Open Files—Allows you to see which files and resources are open on a share. You also can close files that are open.

Figure 31.9
While you're checking the status of services, you can start, stop, and pause system services from this screen.

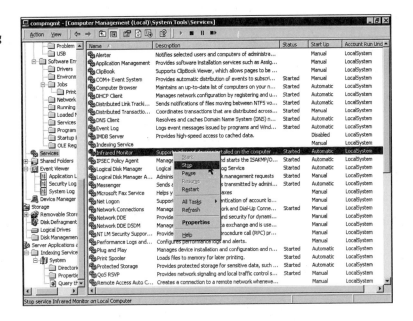

Event Viewer—The Event Viewer allows easy review of hardware and software activities that have been monitored by the operating system and have had entries made in log files (*logs*). Logs are created by the operating system to record system, application, and security events. Logs are very useful because, like a seismograph in earthquake country or a black box in an airplane, they provide a historical record of when events occurred. For example, you can see when services were started, stopped, paused, and resumed; or when hardware failed to start properly; or when removable media or peripherals were removed inappropriately. The logs report the level of danger to the system, as you can see in Figure 31.10. For a shortcut to the Event Viewer, you can choose Start, Control Panel, Administrative Tools, Event Viewer.

Device Manager—This is identical to the Device Manager Control Panel applet and is discussed in further detail in Chapter 29. You can check the status of any device on a computer, see whether it's working properly, update its device driver, check for conflicts with other devices, and so on.

STORAGE NODE

Removable Storage—In this node, you can check the physical location of removable storage devices (such as CD-ROM, DVD-ROM, JAZ, Zip, tapes, and optical disks), check the existence of media pools (typically robot-controlled multidisk gadgets), and check properties of offline media. This node also provides a means for labeling, cataloging, and tracking all your removable media; controls library drives, slots, and doors; and provides drive-cleaning operations.

Figure 31.10
You can easily view system log files from this node.

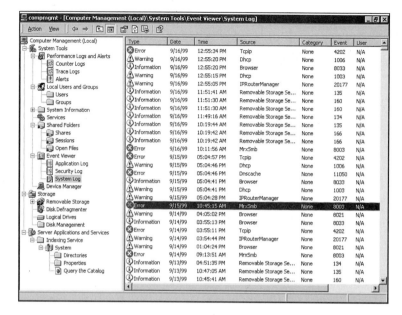

This node can work together with data management or backup programs like the one supplied with Windows 2000 (the Backup program is covered in Chapter 33, "Managing the Hard Disk"), conveying information about storage properties.

Disk Defragmenter—This node runs the disk defragmenter program.

Logical Drives—In this node, you can check basic properties of logical drives and mappings. Logical drive mappings for local drives cannot be changed using tools supplied with Windows 2000, unfortunately. If you want to reassign logical drive letters of your local volumes, you must resort to third-party programs such as PartitionMagic. Use caution when doing so, however. Changing local volume letter assignments can result in problems. For example, an application installed on drive C: expects to find its support files there. If you change the volume letter to D, that application will be unhappy.

Disk Management—This node runs Disk Management (a.k.a. Disk Administrator). For coverage of Disk Administrator, see Chapter 33.

Server Applications and Services Node—Through this node, you can view and manage the properties of any server service or application that is installed on the computer, such as the file indexing service, DNS (domain name service), and DHCP (Domain Host Configuration Protocol). On a Windows 2000 Professional machine, the services are limited somewhat. In a server system, you'll see more options, such as Services for Macintosh, Fax Server, RAS Server, Routing Server, and WINS. Each service has options pertaining to it. For example, the indexing service allows you to choose which directories to include in the indexing service and to query the index for files meeting criteria you specify.

Tip #374	Sometimes you might want to incorporate a list of displayed items into another document. You can export the list as a text file for this purpose. To do so, display the list in question, with the columns arranged as you like. Then choose Action, Export List. You can name the file in the resulting Save As dialog box.

MICROSOFT MANAGEMENT CONSOLE (MMC)

As mentioned previously, the Computer Management tool is actually a subset of something much larger and more extensible—the Microsoft Management Console (MMC). I suppose what happened is that Microsoft finally understood that PC administrators were frustrated by the myriad convoluted means for managing their computers. Managing local or remote machines by hopping around between Control Panel applets, Explorer Properties sheets, and icons such as Network Neighborhood just didn't cut the mustard. Administrators and power users wanted one unified tool, a so-called *single-seat* solution for computer management. They also demanded the ability to construct personalized toolkits to delegate specific administrative tasks to users or groups without jeopardizing the health of the system by giving away the farm.

The Microsoft Management Console does just this. It's a highly extensible tool interface based on modules called snap-ins that perform specialized services. In turn, snap-ins can also be made up of additional extension snap-ins.

When a customized set of snap-ins and extensions is put together, you can save it as an MMC *console* for later use. Consoles are saved as .MSC files that are small in size and easily transportable because, basically, they're just a list of objects and properties. So, you can create an MMC console for, say, co-workers and email it to them, post it on the Web, or make it available in a shared folder on the LAN. Consoles can be exclusively assigned to a specific user or group of users using system policy settings. Because MMC files are editable, you can change them after the fact, adding or removing snap-ins and extensions at will.

Putting together your own MMC consoles is as easy as pie. As when you build a Web page or a brochure, you can start with an existing template of tools and then add or remove snap-ins and extensions. Microsoft supplies a broad selection of tools for futzing with the operating system, and other snap-ins are available from third parties.

The following steps show you how to create a personalized console:

1. To open the base Microsoft Management Console application, choose Start, Run and enter mmc. You then see the window shown in Figure 31.11. The empty console is non-functional until you add some snap-ins. Also, the menu commands apply to the entire console because no individual snap-ins are yet loaded.

PART

VI

CH

31

Figure 31.11
A blank MMC console.

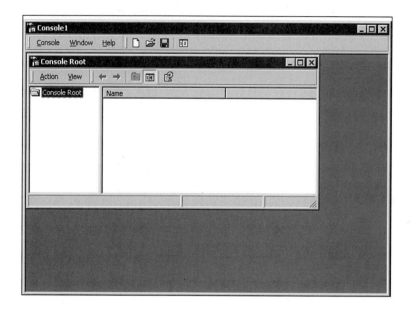

2. Choose Console, Add/Remove Snap-in. On the resulting Add/Remove Snap-in dialog, click the Standalone tab. Choose the insertion point for the snap-in from the drop-down list. (This process is a bit like saving a Favorite in Internet Explorer. You're choosing which branch of the console tree you want the snap-in added to.) Use Console Root because there probably isn't another choice anyway.

3. Click the Add button. Then you see a list of standalone snap-ins, as shown in Figure 31.12.

4. For this example, say you want to add Computer Management to your console. Click it and then click Add. A dialog box comes up asking whether changes you make with this console will apply to the local computer or a remote one. Typically, you choose local. Then click Finish.

5. When you return to the Add/Remove Snap-in dialog (which might require closing the Add Standalone Snap-in dialog box), click the Extensions tab. Now you get to choose the details of

Figure 31.12

the standalone snap-in that you want available in your console (see Figure 31.13). This step is similar to clicking the Details button when you do a custom installation of programs like Office.

Not all snap-ins have extensions.

Figure 31.13
Choosing which extensions of the standalone Computer Management snap-in you want included in your console.

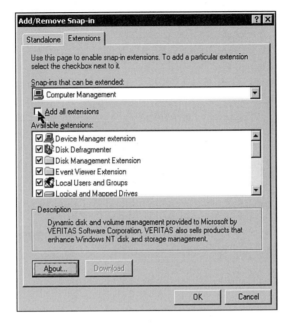

6. Check the extensions you want included in your console. Uncheck the ones you don't want included.

7. Repeat the process to add and set the details for other snap-ins. For example, you might want to add Certificates Management to your console.

Tip #375

You can open a second console window by right-clicking a service in the left pane and then choosing New Window from Here. Then choose Window, Tile Horizontally to arrange the windows.

To save your console, choose Console, Save, and save it in the usual fashion. It is given an .MSC extension. You can later run it by double-clicking it.

 If you're trying to add a snap-in, but it's not listed, see "Cannot Add Snap-In" in the "Troubleshooting" section at the end of this chapter.

CREATING TASKPADS

After you have your console set up, you might want to enable another user to use at least a subset of the snap-ins and extensions in it. You can do so easily by using *taskpads*. A taskpad is a slimmed-down version of your Microsoft Management Console, with limited functionality.

A common usability issue for the first-time user of an MMC snap-in is the inability to discover context menus as the primary way to access snap-in functionality. Taskpads are designed to help novice users discover tasks by providing a way to launch wizards, context menu tasks, and other tasks that would otherwise be difficult to locate.

Taskpads are designed to let the user easily interact with the snap-in. A taskpad may be used as a user interface that can accomplish a variety of functions, including launching executable files, running scripts, accessing Web pages, or even launching another MMC. It does so by displaying the functions as "tasks" in a DHTML page layout. Each task appears as a clickable button.

To create a taskpad, follow these steps:

1. Right-click an item in the console tree. Then choose New Taskpad from the context menu, as you see in Figure 31.14.

2. When the wizard appears, walk through the wizard, and follow the instructions presented to you. This wizard leads you to the Task Creation Wizard. After the two wizards are completed, you'll have a new taskpad. By clicking an item in the resulting window and then on the task icon at the bottom of the window, you or a colleague can perform the task you had intended.

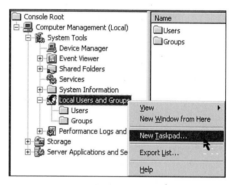

Figure 31.14

You can find an example of the extensibility of the Microsoft Management Console in the Windows 2000 Resource Kit. It includes an MMC snap-in that contains more than 50 special tools for system manipulation, tweaking, and diagnostics. Figure 31.15 shows a some of the tools in the snap-in.

In summary, the Microsoft Management Console is a powerful tool, complex enough to write an entire book about. I hope that this brief introduction is at least enough to get you started in creating your own taskpads. For more information about the Microsoft Management Console, check the following site:

http://www.microsoft.com/management/mmc/download.htm

Figure 31.15
The Windows 2000 Resource Kit contains helpful information and numerous tools for system maintenance.

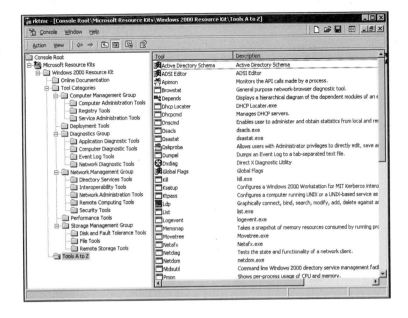

PART

VI

CH

31

Note

You can find a growing gallery of snap-ins for the MMC by clicking Help, Microsoft on the Web, Snap-in Gallery. You can also find a FAQ about the MMC there.

WINDOWS UPDATE AND ROLLBACK

Windows Update, introduced with Windows 9x, is an extension of Windows 2000. It serves to synchronize your operating system files with the newest ones developed at Microsoft. Also, it can download free programs, security updates, bug fixes, drivers, or other extensions to the operating system. Using the Internet and Web technologies for updating your operating system means you don't have to wait for the next release of the operating system or install service packs to get interim updates.

Microsoft is very keen on your visiting the update Web site regularly. To do so, you can simply connect to the Net, choose Start, and then choose Windows Update. A typical page at the Web site looks like the one shown in Figure 31.16.

The ActiveX components that run when you visit the site scan your computer to determine what updates have been made in the past and which ones are outstanding. According to Microsoft, no corporate espionage or personal eavesdropping ensues during the process of system analysis; yet obviously the plug-in has to examine your system to some extent to create a list of potential updates, and something about that list is sent upline so that the Microsoft server can compile the resulting Web page of potential upgrades. However, because Microsoft is probably cautious at this point about being busted for snooping, I don't get weird about this search. Besides, I want the updates.

Figure 31.16
Visit the Windows Update site regularly to keep Windows 2000 Professional up-to-date.

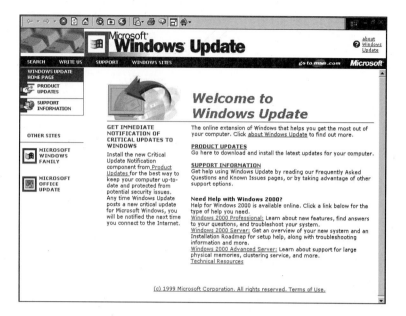

If you don't have the Active Setup component installed already, you see a message offering to install it for you (see Figure 31.17).

Figure 31.17
If the machine you're using hasn't visited the Windows Update site before, you'll likely have to download a plug-in before you can see the list of potential updates.

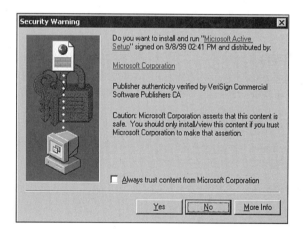

⚠ *If you're seeing Windows Update in the wrong language, see "Wrong Language" in the "Troubleshooting" section at the end of this chapter.*

The look of the pages and the list of updates obviously change from week to week, so I won't waste space here showing you more Web pages. Suffice it to say, you should visit regularly and check especially for the Critical Updates. You also should install the Critical Update Notification component if you want to automatically be warned when important improvements are posted to the Windows Update site. This is essentially a subscription to a

Web page (using push technology). Then, when you are online, your computer will occasionally check with the Microsoft site to determine whether significant updates have been made, typically ones pertaining to system security or serious show-stoppers.

The first time you run it, the update tool creates a database of consummated updates on your computer. This information allows the installer to do the following:

- More quickly determine which updates you haven't installed the next time you visit the site
- Remove items you no longer want
- Roll back the system to its previous state in case an update causes troubles

Look for a History button on the Web page (not the History button on the Internet Explorer toolbar, obviously) to see what you installed and when.

USING ROLLBACK TO UNINSTALL A WINDOWS UPDATE

If you notice unruly system behavior after updating drivers, patches, or system files from Windows Update, you'll probably want to roll back your system to its previous state. Or you may have installed a program and now realize you no longer want it. You can remove such items by using the Update site. Look for instructions about uninstalling items there. You might have to display past updates by clicking the Show Installed Updates button on the Web page. Then you can scroll down to the update and click Uninstall. Figure 31.18 shows an example.

Figure 31.18
You can uninstall unsavory updates by using the Update page, too. Look for uninstall instructions.

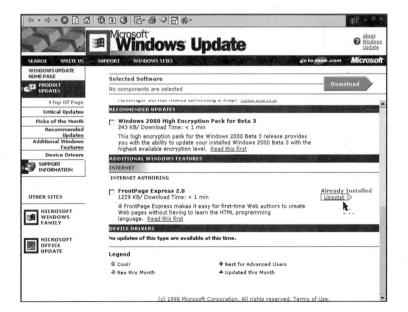

If you don't have Web access, are you sunk? No. Good thing, because you could conceivably make an update only to find it kills your networking or Web access. Some items, such as standalone programs, can be removed via the Control Panel's Add/Remove Programs applet, so check there to remove something such as FrontPage Express or other non-Microsoft applications. Of course, you can't use this approach to roll back system files, patches, or drivers. To do that, you can use Update Wizard Uninstall to accomplish the task instead. The following steps show you how:

1. To start Update Wizard Uninstall, choose Start, Run and then type msinfo32.

2. When the System Information tool comes up, click Support Tools, click Windows, and then click Update Wizard Uninstall (see Figure 31.19).

Figure 31.19
Rolling back an update.

PROTECTING THE WORKSTATION'S SYSTEM FILES

We are all familiar with the problem of an operating system becoming suspiciously unstable after the installation of a new application or a driver or after a system crash. Microsoft has been painfully aware of this problem for some time, and many a technician (whether a Microsoft employee or not) has been forced to instruct a PC user to "reinstall Windows" as the only solution. We all know how much fun that is. If you think Windows operating systems sometimes seem like a house of cards stacked level upon level, waiting for a single *.DLL or other system file to fail, well, you're right. This kind of vulnerability is wholly unacceptable in mission-critical settings, so Microsoft had to come up with preventive measures.

As discussed in Chapter 30, the System applet has a means for setting up options that prevent the often-unintentional destabilization of the operating system from applications or driver installations or, in the worst case, the introduction of viruses that intentionally alter or overwrite system files. Windows 2000's Security Manager and file system work in symphony to help protect critical system files and drivers. Several areas of system functionality help prevent damage from the installation of untested drivers or from modification of system executables such as dynamic link libraries (DLLs). They are as follows:

- System File Protection service—This service is a function of the operating system that continually monitors protected system files, standing guard against attack.
- System File Signature Verification tool—You can use this command-line executable to check the signatures on your essential system components.
- System File Checker tool—You can use this command-line executable to verify that system file versions align properly.

The essential (and automatic) portion of this trio is the first one. Windows 2000's file protection system is enabled by default, and it prevents the replacement of the protected system. System File Protection runs in the background and protects all files installed by the Windows 2000 setup program—.SYS, .DLL, .OCX, .TTF, .FON, and .EXE files. If one is replaced or altered, by default, a dialog box alerts you that a program is attempting to alter a system file.

In Chapter 30, you learned about setting up the three levels of overwrite protection for System File Protection: ignoring, warning, or preventing modification of all system files. Here, I'll talk a bit about a standalone utility supplied with Windows 2000 Professional that you can use to scan for modified files that may have slipped through the detection process.

PART VI
CH 31

RUNNING THE FILE SIGNATURE VERIFICATION TOOL

To verify that system files have a digital signature, follow these steps:

1. Choose Start, Run, and then enter `sigverif` to open the dialog box shown in Figure 31.20.

Figure 31.20
This program checks to see that your system files are signed by a reputable source.

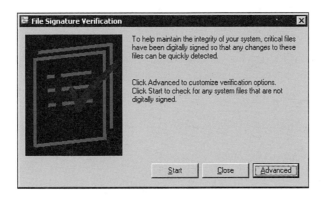

2. Normally, the program searches for any system files not signed, and when you close the program, the results are saved in SIGVERIF.TXT. If you want to search for nonsystem files as well or append to an existing log of found items, click the Advanced button and set up the log file's name, append option, and other related options (see Figure 31.21).

Figure 31.21

3. Back in the File Signature Verification dialog, choose Start. The tool then checks to see which system files are digitally signed and displays its findings. Typically, you see the message displayed in Figure 31.22. If you have logging enabled, the search results are also written to SIGVERIF.TXT in the <system root>\WINNT directory.

Figure 31.22

USING THE SYSTEM FILE CHECKER

Another program, closely related to the File Signature Verification tool, is the System File Checker. This tool looks for protected system files and verifies that their version numbers link up with the operating system and that they haven't been replaced or trashed accidentally. The System File Checker is a command-line program that you set up using a keyboard-entered command. It then runs the next time you boot.

Note

You must be logged in as a system administrator to run this program.

If the System File Checker discovers that a protected file has been overwritten, it retrieves the correct version of the file from the <systemroot>\system32\dllcache folder and then replaces the incorrect file. It uses the following syntax for program execution:

```
sfc [/scanonce] [/scanboot] [/cancel] [/quiet]
Parameters:
/scanonce
```

The preceding syntax scans all protected system files once.

```
/scanboot
```

The preceding command scans all protected system files every time the computer is restarted.

```
/cancel
```

The preceding command cancels all pending scans of protected system files.

```
/quiet
```

This command replaces all incorrect file versions without prompting the user.

> **Note**
>
> What if something or someone has trashed the \system32\dllcache folder? No problem. The `sfc /scanonce` or `sfc /scanboot` commands repair the contents of dllcache if it's unreadable.

System File Protection, if turned on, normally prevents any kind of intrusion that might result in a corrupted file, at least from an outside source such as a third-party program installation. If all is working as planned, you don't have to worry about running this program or the File Signature Verification program with any regularity. If you want to play it super safe, though, protecting also against microscopic bit loss on the hard disk or crafty hacking, you can use the `/scanboot` option to check each time you boot. The verification process doesn't take very long to complete.

TASK SCHEDULER

Using the Task Scheduler, you can set up any program or script (or even open a document) to be run automatically at predetermined times. This utility is very useful for running system maintenance programs or your own scripts and programs when you can't be around to execute them manually.

> **Tip #377**
>
> You could even use the Task Scheduler to run a script that starts or stops a specific system service because services can be started and stopped with this command line:
>
> ```
> net start "service name here"
> ```
>
> or
>
> ```
> net stop "service name here"
> ```
>
> Most folks don't even need to think about this capability, but if you are a software developer and use a special debugging or testing service, this capability might be handy to start it up when you log in. Remember that there is no "when I log off" scheduler entry, so you can't automate shutting off the process when someone logs out.
>
> You can also cause a specific script or program to run when the system boots or when a user (any user) logs on. Why is this different from putting the script or program in the Startup group for All Users? Well, the Task Scheduler lets you specify the logon name to use for this login task. For example, whenever a user logs on, you can have the Task Scheduler run a program with Administrative privileges to record information in a protected file. Using the Task Scheduler this way is similar to using the Run As option. (See Chapter 32, "Managing Users," for more details about Run As.)

> **Note**
>
> When the Task Scheduler runs a task as a different user, the logged-on user cannot see or interact with the program. Be sure that scheduled tasks can operate without user input and exit cleanly when they've done their work.

After you declare tasks to run, the Task Scheduler sits in the background, checking the computer's system clock, and when a predetermined time for a task rolls around, the Task Scheduler runs it as though executed from the specified user.

Note

Obviously, the computer has to be alive to run a task, so if you expect to do a disk cleanup at 4 a.m., make sure you've left the computer on.

Next, I'll explain how to assign tasks to the Task Scheduler and what some of its options are.

Tip #378

If you upgraded from Windows 98 and had tasks assigned in the Task Scheduler there, they should have been converted to the Windows 2000 Professional Task Scheduler.

Follow these steps to get started using the Task Scheduler:

1. Run the Task Scheduler by choosing Start, Settings, Control Panel, Scheduled Tasks. You then see the window shown in Figure 31.23.

   If you have any scheduled tasks, they appear in the list already.

Figure 31.23
You can set up the computer to run tasks automatically at a predetermined time, such as daily, weekly, or monthly.

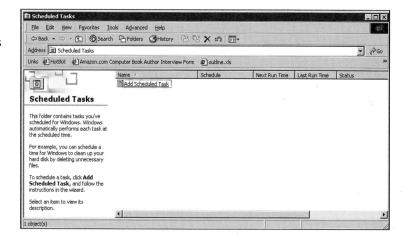

2. Click Add Scheduled Task to invoke a wizard that walks you though adding a new task. If the program isn't listed in the resulting list, click the Browse button to find it. (For system-related applications, the most likely browse locations are in the \winnt or \winnt\system32 folders.)

3. Click Next, and choose how often you want the program to run. Click Next again, and then specify applicable time options, such as time of day, as required (see Figure 31.24).

4. Click Next, and you are prompted to enter the user's name and password so that the task can be executed as though the user (typically, you) were there to run it. (It may already be entered for you, using the current user's name, preceded by the computer name.) After a username and password are set, another user cannot cancel or delete the task unless that user has the correct permissions.

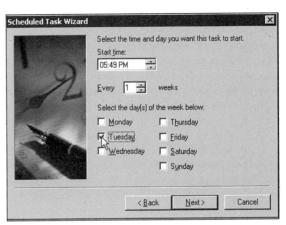

Figure 31.24

Note

The computer name is technically necessary only if you are on a network but want to run the task with local authentication. I cannot think of any reason to do so, unless your domain account doesn't have the correct local rights.

5. Click Next. Then choose Advanced if you want to set advanced options such as idle time, what to do if the computer is running on batteries, and what to do after the task completes and other options, as you see in Figure 31.25. You can set the idle time setting to prevent a task from beginning if you're using the computer to do other work. A computer is idle when no mouse or keyboard activity is occurring.

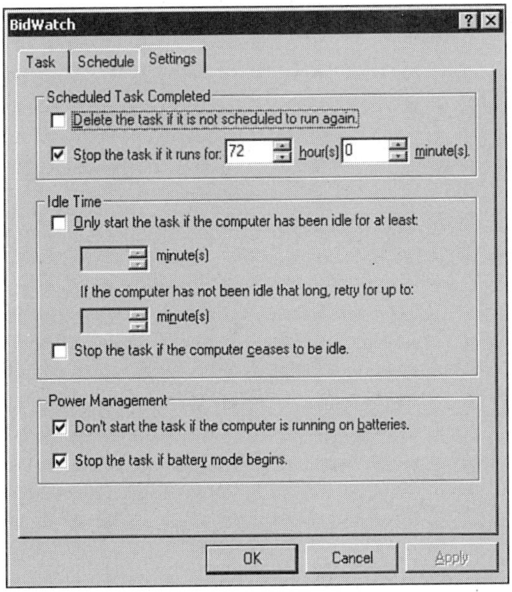

Figure 31.25
You can declare optional program execution options for a scheduled task from this dialog box.

6. Click Finish to close the wizard. The task is then added to the list and will execute at the preassigned time.

At this point, you can do the following:

- Reopen the Task Scheduler from the Control Panel to check the settings (use the Details view).

- Right-click a task, and choose Properties to change the task's timing. You can change the scheduled time as you like, from the second page.

- From the first tab on the Properties dialog, you can disable the task temporarily, without having to delete it.

- Right-click a task, and choose Delete to remove the task from the list. Choosing Delete here doesn't remove it from your hard disk, so don't worry. It just removes the task from the list of tasks to be executed.

- Affect all tasks via commands on the Advanced menu in the Task Scheduler window. You'll see a number of useful items there, as shown in Table 31.3.

TABLE 31.3   ADVANCED SETTINGS FOR THE TASK SCHEDULER

Option	Description
Stop Using Task Scheduler	This option turns off the scheduler, preventing it from running any added tasks. The scheduler won't start automatically the next time you start Windows 2000. To reactivate it, you have to open the Task Scheduler and choose Start Using Task Scheduler.
Pause Task Scheduler	This option temporarily suspends added tasks in the task list. This capability is useful if you are running a program whose operation could be slowed down or otherwise influenced by a scheduled task. To resume the schedules for all tasks, choose Advanced, Continue Task Scheduler. If a task's execution time is now past, it will run at the next scheduled time.
Notify Me of Missed Tasks	If a task can't complete for some reason, a dialog box pops up, letting you know what was missed. For example, if the computer was turned off when a task should have been run, you'll be told of this situation when you boot up next.
AT Service Account	The Task Scheduler runs any commands scheduled using the at command-line utility, which is a carryover from previous versions of Windows NT. By design, commands scheduled by at all run under the same login account. This option lets you specify which account is to be used. You can leave it set to the default LocalSystem setting, or you can turn on This Account to specify a user account.
View Log	This option brings up a text file in Notepad, listing tasks completed, date, and other information about the tasks. Note that some tasks listed in the log might not appear in the Task Scheduler list. This omission can result from system tasks initiated by other services such as synchronization. Check Internet Explorer's Active

Option	Description
	Desktop (Web page subscriptions) or your system settings for offline folders. For coverage of these issues, see Chapter 12, "World Wide Web," and Chapter 23, "Windows Unplugged: Remote and Mobile Networking."

Tip #379

> Remember that some system utilities such as `defrag` are no longer *.EXE files as they are in Windows 9x. You won't find defrag.exe on your disk (unless you're dual-booting with Windows 9x), and in any case, you shouldn't run it. Use dfrg.msc, which is a Microsoft Management Console snap-in. It still runs, but it waits for input from the user to choose the disk and the activity. You would have to create a script to run the defrag program automatically.

Tip #380

> You can run one of your tasks immediately by right-clicking the task in question and hoosing Run.
>
> You also can reach Task Scheduler tasks via the Explorer by going to the \winnt\tasks folder.

 If the Task Scheduler fails to activate properly, see "The Task Scheduler Doesn't Activate Correctly" in the "Troubleshooting" section at the end of this chapter.

You can view scheduled tasks on a remote computer by opening My Network Places, opening the computer in question, and then opening the Scheduled Tasks folder. You need administrative privileges if you want to view the settings on a remote machine. If you want to edit remote settings, the requirements are greater; you can edit tasks on a remote computer running Windows 95 or later, Windows NT 4.0, or Windows 2000 only if that remote computer has remote Registry software installed and shares the *x$* share, where *x* is the hard disk on which the Scheduled Tasks folder resides. That is, it must be shared with an "Administrative Share."

Standard Windows 2000 security permissions apply to tasks you create, so one way to configure tasks is to set NTFS access control lists (ACLs) to set permissions for the task. Settings you make to the ACLs affect which users or groups can view, delete, modify, or use the task. Because ACLs can also apply to the scripts, programs, and documents that make up the tasks, they come into play as well. So, even if you have permission to run a task, you cannot run it unless you have access to the scripts, programs, and documents that the task involves. You set the security for a task by opening its properties and clicking the Security tab. You then see a standard Security dialog.

> **Note**
>
> If you are familiar with the old `at` command-line utility from Windows NT, you'll be happy to know that it still works in Windows 2000. Commands scheduled with `at` appear in the Task Scheduler's list, as well as the list of commands that `at` displays. It's one and the same list. However, if you modify the command within Scheduled Tasks, it will no longer appear in the list displayed by `at`.

Performance Monitor

In previous versions of Windows, a program called the System Monitor was located in the Systems Tools program group. Windows 2000 includes an almost identical tool renamed the Performance Monitor, and you access it through the Control Panel's Administrative Tools folder.

If you're not familiar with it, this tool creates a graphical and/or numeric display of essential system information, such as memory usage, status of hard disk usage, CPU activity, network traffic, and many other quantifiable aspects of your computer's real-time operations. You can display the gathered information in graph, histogram, or numeric format. Displaying this information is useful for trying to get a handle on what's happening with your computer, particularly when you're troubleshooting or tracking down bottlenecks.

Not only does Performance Monitor put up a real-time display, it also interacts with Performance Logs and Alerts (another administrative tool). Using the combination of the two, you can record performance data for later analysis, set up system alerts to send a message, run a program, or start a log specifying whether a counter's value is above, below, or equal to a defined threshold.

> **Note**
>
> Two versions of the Performance Monitor are available: perfmon.exe and perfmon.msc. Running either one brings up the same program.

You can use the Performance Monitor like this:

1. To open the Performance Monitor, choose Start, Run and then type `perfmon.msc`. Its interface is similar to other Microsoft Management Console snap-ins. However, it's not a standalone snap-in, so you can't add it to your MMC.

2. At startup, no parameters are displayed because no counters are running. Click the + (plus) button on the toolbar to add a counter. From the resulting dialog box, choose a computer to measure, the performance object, and then the specific performance counter. Considering all the combinations, you have a seriously flexible tool in your hands. And you can mix and match counters and objects from different computers on the same graph. Therefore, you could, for example, compare some interesting statistics such as disk hits, print jobs, or network requests from different computers on the same graphical display to help you get a sense of bottlenecks in data throughput.

3. Repeat the process of adding counters to your display. As you do, the list at the bottom of the window grows, and each new counter is added to the chart and assigned a color. You can sort the list by clicking the column heads. If you wonder what a given counter is actually measuring, click Explain. You then see a description of the counter, as shown in Figure 31.26.

Tip #381

You can keep the Explain window open and click around on counter names to quickly learn about them, without clicking the Explain button each time.

Figure 31.26
This dialog contains an overwhelming array of possible counters to display. Click Explain to read a description of a selected counter.

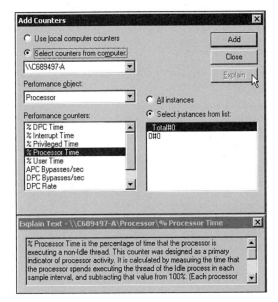

4. To change the format of the display, click the toolbar buttons indicating bar graph (histogram), line graph, or textual display. Figure 31.27 shows a histogram. You also can opt to show a textual display or a chart over time.

Tip #382

To single out one counter in a chart, click the Highlight button in the toolbar; then click the object's name in the list at the bottom of the window.

5. Modify your charts or histograms by using various properties available from the Properties button on the toolbar. Figure 31.28 shows the resulting Properties dialog box.

Figure 31.27
Histogram display.

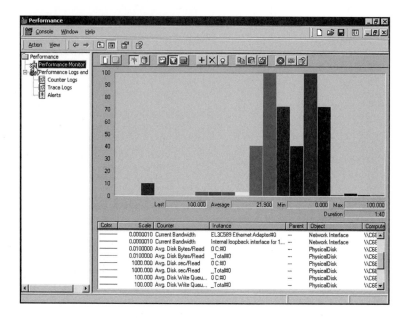

Figure 31.28
The Properties dialog box for the Performance Monitor display offers many options. If you are serious about monitoring system performance, study these options.

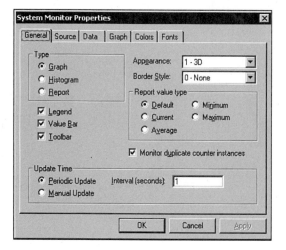

You can add a background grid; add x- and y-axis titles; change the scaling, fonts, colors; and much more. Click the Source tab to locate a log file to display rather than display current events. By changing the display, you can analyze logs you may have stored in the past (see "Using the Event Viewer and Log Files" next). If, at any point, you want to store a snapshot of your display, right-click in the display area, and choose Save As. Give it a name, and it is then stored as an HTML file. Clicking its filename in the Explorer brings it up in Internet Explorer, complete with graphics. This file is basically just a screen shot.

The Physical and Logical Disk counters apparently cost the system a fair bit of extra processing time to compute, so they're disabled by default.

You must issue the command `diskperf -y` and reboot your system to be able to view disk bytes transferred, operations per second, and so on. Disk performance counters always show 0 unless you use this command to enable disk performance monitoring. The counters work until you issue `diskperf -n` and reboot again.

→ **See** the entry for `diskperf` in Appendix A, "Command-Line Reference," on the CD-ROM, for the full command-line syntax.

USING THE EVENT VIEWER AND LOG FILES

The Event Viewer is an administrative application that gives you a window into hardware, software, and system problems and monitors Windows 2000 security events. You can think of an event as any occurrence of significance to the operating system. Many internal system occurrences trigger the display of error message dialog boxes while Windows 2000 is running. For example, if a user attempts to access protected files or remove a printer over which he or she doesn't have control, a message usually appears. The same is true for an impending power-down, in the case of a UPS being triggered. Another example might be a message event generated from an application, such as when it starts a service or runs out of hard disk space.

As you know, Windows 2000 has an intelligent internal security design. So, as you might expect, numerous more subtle events than those described here can generate messages internal to the operating system that are not directly reported to the user. Events such as applications being run, drivers being loaded, or files being copied between directories are common examples. Though kept out of sight, these events are monitored and recorded in log files available for later examination by the system administrator. Many events are stored in the log by default. Others are optional and can be set within dialog boxes pertaining to specific operations. For example, if you open the Printers folder and choose Print Server Properties, Advanced, you'll see options for setting logging of printer errors. You will run across others from time to time as you work with Windows 2000.

TYPES OF LOG FILES

Windows 2000 generates three separate logs (files), though others are possible. These logs are explained in Table 31.4.

TABLE 31.4   WINDOWS 2000 LOG FILES

Type of Log	Description
Application log	The application log contains events logged by applications or programs. For example, a database program might record a file error in the application log. The program developer decides which events to record.
Security log	The security log can record security events such as valid and invalid logon attempts, as well as events related to resource use such as creating, opening, or deleting files. An administrator can specify which events are recorded in the security log. For example, if you have enabled logon auditing, attempts to log on to the system are recorded in the security log.
System log	The system log contains numerous entries pertaining to system events such as booting up, shutting down, loading drivers, and errors with hardware conflicts such as conflicts between ports, CD-ROMs, SCSI cards, or sound cards. For example, the failure of a driver or other system component to load during startup is recorded in the system log. The event types logged by system components are predetermined by Windows 2000 and cannot be altered by the user or administrator.

Now that you have a basic understanding, let's consider the Event Viewer. The Event Viewer is an application that displays each of the log files. Aside from simply displaying a log file, the Event Viewer also lets you do the following:

- Apply sorting, searching, and filtering that make it easier to look for specific events
- Control settings that affect future log entries, such as maximum log size and the time old entries should be deleted
- Clear all log entries to start a log from scratch
- Archive logs on disk for later examination and load those files when needed

Note

Only a user with Administrative privileges can work with the security log. Other users can view the application and system logs, however. By default, security logging is turned off. You can use Group Policy to enable security logging. The administrator can also set auditing policies in the Registry that cause the system to halt when the security log is full.

WORKING WITH EVENT VIEWER LOGS

The following steps explain how you can use the Event Viewer to open the three available logs and more easily view specific events:

1. Open the Event Viewer program in the Administrative Tools group by choosing Start, Programs, Administrative Tools, or access it via the Control Panel. (Remember, if Administrative Tools aren't showing, you turn them on via the Advanced tab of the taskbar's properties.) When you run it, the basic Event Viewer window comes up. Figure 31.29 displays a typical example. (The meaning of each column is explained in the following section.)

Figure 31.29
This typical Event
Viewer screen shows
the system log of the
local computer.

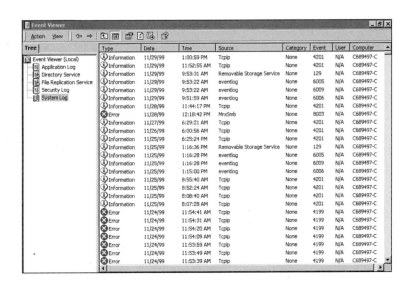

PART

VI

CH

31

2. Choose the log you want to view by clicking it in the left pane. In Figure 31.29, note that two other logs are available as well: Directory Service and File Replication Service. They have red Xs on them because those services have never been run on this machine and therefore are empty.

3. Just as with the File Manager, changes to the log that occur while you're examining it are not always immediately reflected. Press F5 to update the log if you suspect that some system activity has occurred while you've been running the program.

4. Normally, the list is sorted with the most recent events at the top of the list. You can reverse this order if you want by choosing View, Oldest First.

5. You can optionally filter out events that you don't want to wade through. For example, you can show events that occurred only during certain times of the day, events pertaining to a specific user or event ID, or event type (such as only errors or warnings). Just choose View, Filter and fill in the dialog box. (The options are explained in the section titled "Filtering Events.")

6. You might want to search for a specific event. To do so, choose View, Find, and enter the relevant information in the resulting dialog box.

7. If you want to see more information about an event, double-click it. Another dialog box then appears, listing details. An example is shown in Figure 31.30. Details of your security log won't make much sense if you're not a programmer. Even then, the messages are cryptic. The system and application logs offer more in the way of understandable English. Most useful is information about drivers failing to load (often leading you to IRQ and port conflict resolutions).

Figure 31.30
In this dialog, you can double-click an event to display its details. Use the Previous or Next buttons to step through event details quickly.

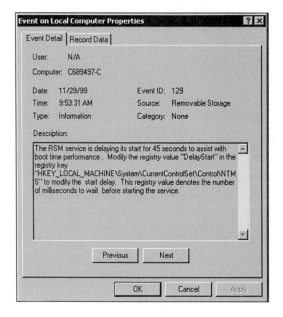

VIEWING A REMOTE COMPUTER'S LOGS

By default, the local computer's log is displayed. If you want to examine a networked computer's log, follow this procedure.

1. Choose Start, Run. Then type mmc, and click OK.
2. On the Console menu, click Add/Remove Snap-in.
3. On the Standalone tab, click Add.
4. Click Event Viewer, and then click Add.
5. Click Another Computer, and then enter the path and name of the computer (for example, \\domainname\computername). Click Finish, click Close, and then click OK.

LOG INTERPRETATION

Careful monitoring of event logs can help you predict and identify the sources of system problems. For example, if log warnings show that a disk driver can read or write to a sector only after several retries, this information could be a foreshadowing that the hard disk sector may die eventually. Logs can also confirm problems with software. If a program crashes, a program event log can provide a record of activity leading up to the event. When a program does crash, you often see a system message informing you that a log entry is being made.

Essentially, each log file consists of a database table with eight columns, which are described in Table 31.5.

TABLE 31.5 DECIPHERING EVENT LOGS

Column Name	Meaning
Type	Indicates the type of event. The five types of events are described in Table 31.6.
Date	Reports the date the event was logged (according to the system clock). Just a reminder: Maintaining accurate event logs is a good reason to ensure that the workstation or server internal clock is set correctly.
Time	Reports the time that the event occurred. Note that if you need to, you can synchronize all workstation clocks by using a command that pulls the time from the server machine for use in the log and other activities. Add the line `net time \\server /set` to the startup file for the machine, replacing the word `server` with the server's name. This line can even be included in the logon script for the user.
Source	Lists the name of the application software or device driver that reported the problem to NT, which then logged it.
Category	Shows the general classification this event falls under. Each of the three logs has different categories of events.
Event	Lists an event number. Event numbers are assigned to events based on a coding system Microsoft has designed. The event ID matches a message file. The message is displayed in the details box for the event.
User	Indicates the specific user for whom the event applies. Many events are related to a specific user. For example, someone might be using the application that logs an error or other event to the application log. That user's name then appears in this field. This information is particularly useful for tracking down attempted security breaches.
Computer	Specifies the computer where the event happened. Of course, this location is almost always the same. It is different only if you export the log data and merge it with exported data from other logs, and then read it back into the Event Viewer. In this case, you might need to see which computer generated which entries. (You can export logs by using the View, Export List command after selecting a log name.)

As mentioned in Table 31.5, five different icons characterize an event, as shown in Table 31.6.

TABLE 31.6 EVENT TYPES

Type of Event	Meaning
Error	Indicates serious trouble of some sort, such as the device driver not loading, IRQ or other hardware conflicts, missing network cards, and so forth.
Warning	Indicates nonserious trouble, but worthy of attention soon, such as being low on hard disk space (which could bring down the system).

continues

TABLE 31.6   CONTINUED

Type of Event	Meaning
Information	Indicates a nonserious situation. Typically, these notices concern successful operations achieved by applications, drivers, or services. For example, when a network driver loads successfully, an Information event is logged.
Success Audit	Indicates success of a procedure. For example, if you opted to audit successful operations from the Print Manager (Printer Folders), a successful attachment to a shared printer by another workstation would be reported as a success audit.
Failure Audit	Similar to a success audit but reversed; indicates that failed attempts are logged. Failures typically occur because the user making the attempt doesn't have the correct privileges. Note that the security log logs only failure events.

Tip #383

Many typical hardware problems—such as conflicting protocols, network card conflicts, and IRQ conflicts—are reported in the system log. The Event Viewer can help you sleuth out possible entries explaining the problem.

FILTERING EVENTS

One way of seeing several similar events you're interested in (for example, to see how many times the same event occurred) is to click the relevant column head in the Event Viewer. Clicking the head sorts the listing according to the column's data. As in Windows Explorer and other Windows programs, the column sorter toggles between ascending and descending order.

A more powerful approach for culling out the items you're interested in is to use filtering. When logs get quite large or if you have a server that supports a high density of workstation activity, this approach might be the most effective technique for ferreting out what you need to examine. The System Log Properties dialog box you use for filtering is shown in Figure 31.31.

After you set up a filter, don't be alarmed if all your entries suddenly seem to have disappeared; they're probably just being filtered. Check the View menu, and you'll see the Filter option selected. Choose it again to eliminate the filter.

SETTING LOGGING OPTIONS

You can stipulate a few settings that affect how log entries are recorded. These settings are most useful in managing the size of your logs so that they don't eat up too much disk space. There are potentially so many loggable events that even a typical day on a busy network server could produce far larger log files than you would want to wade through, or that you would want to devote disk space to.

Figure 31.31
On the Filter tab of the System Log Properties dialog box, you can limit the listing to specific conditions.

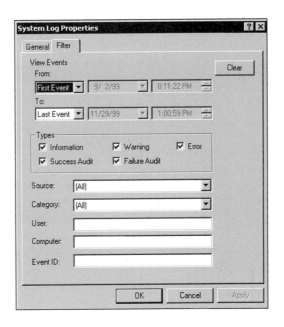

Part

VI

Ch

31

To view or change options for a log file, right-click the log file in question, and choose Properties. Then click the General tab to see the dialog box shown in Figure 31.32.

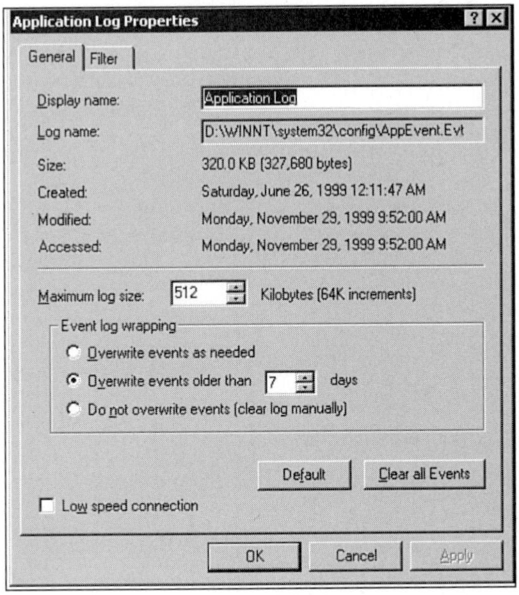

Figure 31.32
Setting a log's options.

The default log settings shown in Figure 31.32 suffice for most systems. If you don't archive the log (see the next section), you should probably have the log "wrap" around after it reaches the maximum log size. The Overwrite Events as Needed option ensures that, when the log fills up, a new event takes the place of the oldest preexisting log entry.

If you really want to ensure that you get to see the log entries, choose the Do Not Overwrite Events option. After the maximum size is reached, subsequent events are not written, and thus lost. If so, you have to use the Action, Clear All Events command to make room for new entries.

USING ARCHIVED LOG FILES

A final option in the Event Viewer lets you create archives of log files and to reload those files for later examination. As a rule, archiving log files isn't of much use unless you're running a very secure operation in which extensive background records of system or network usage are mandated by the government or the corporation where you work. Most likely, in such a secure operation, you'll be doing regular tape or other forms of backup, which might include backups of the log files anyway. In this case, this regimen might meet your security requirements, depending on your tape rotation scheme. If it doesn't, you can archive your event logs. Archiving is a relatively simple process.

Tip #384

One case to be made for archiving is this: Logs can be useful in isolating network or machine failures. By keeping copies of past logs, you have something to compare with current versions that list new failures. By comparing logs, you can perhaps notice how and when the errors began to accumulate. Generally speaking, a network failure starts simple and then increases in frequency until a catastrophic failure occurs. Old logs can help here.

You can store archives as text files, comma-delimited files (text files with a comma between each field for use in database or spreadsheet programs that can import this format), or binary files with the .EVT extension. Only .EVT files retain all the property information for each event. If you want to reload the file for later use, save it as an .EVT file.

Note that the file created by the archiving process isn't affected by any filtering active at the time. That is, all events in the log are written into the archive file.

To archive a log as an .EVT file, follow these steps:

1. View the log you want to archive. That is, run the Event Viewer, and click the log's name. Only that log will be archived.

2. Choose Action, All Tasks, Save Log File As.

3. When you see a standard file save dialog box, choose the drive and directory, give the file a name, and click Save.

To archive a log file as a text file, do the following:

1. View the log you want to archive. That is, run the Event Viewer, and click the log's name. Only that log will be archived.

2. Choose Action, Export List.

3. When you see a standard file save dialog box, choose the drive and directory, give the file a name, choose the type of text file output you want, and click Save.

> **Note**
>
> After you click Save, the log is archived, but the current log isn't cleared. Its contents are unaffected. If your log is full, you have to clear it manually.

To recall an archived log for later examination, do the following:

1. Run the Event Viewer.

2. Choose Action, New, Log View.

3. Choose Saved, and then browse to the log file. You have to choose the type of file (in the Log Type section at the bottom of the dialog box) before actually opening it. This setting determines how the Event Viewer displays event detail data. (Remember this point the next time you save a log file. Name it something that indicates what type of log it is so that, when you reload it, you can do it properly.)

4. When the file is loaded, it's given an arbitrary name. You can then rename it if you want it to say something more than Saved Application Log, Saved Security Log, or Saved System Log.

 If your security log file is empty, see "No Events in Security Log" in the "Troubleshooting" section.

TROUBLESHOOTING

THE TASK MANAGER IS STALLED

My Task Manager seems stuck. It doesn't reflect newly opened or closed applications.

You might have this problem if you've paused the Task Manager. Choose View, Update Speed, and then choose any setting other than Paused. Another approach, if you want to keep it paused, is to choose View, Refresh Now.

SENDING THE TASK MANAGER TO THE BACKGROUND

My Task Manager doesn't drop into the background when I click another program.

Like some Help files, the Task Manager has an Always on Top option. Choose Options, and turn off this setting.

CANNOT ADD SNAP-IN

I'm trying to add a snap-in, but it's not listed, even though I think it's on the system.

If you don't see the snap-in listed, the service and/or snap-in program you want isn't installed. You might have to install it like this:

1. Choose Control Panel, Add/Remove Programs.

2. Find the program or snap-in, and install it.

3. Back at the MMC, try adding the snap-in again.

Remember that two kinds of snap-ins are available: standalone snap-ins and extensions. If you are trying to install an extension, the parent standalone snap-in must have been installed previously. Also, without going through some hassle (namely being on an Active Directory service on a domain), you can't drop snap-ins from another computer into a console you're building. You must have the snap-in on your local machine. Also, remember that snap-ins can't run by themselves. They must be added to an MMC console to work.

WRONG LANGUAGE

I'm seeing Windows Update in the wrong language. Why?

You're probably having this problem because of settings in Windows and Internet Explorer. But let's start at the beginning. The first thing to know is that every copy of Windows has a language tag associated with it. If you're running an English version of Windows 2000 then Windows Update is only going to offer to download English-based add-ins for the operating system.

Now with that said, yes, you can change the language in which you view the Windows Update pages. If you have the wrong Regional settings in Windows and/or in Internet Explorer, you might be dishing up Greek or Italian when you want English. Here's the order in which Windows Update checks for your language preference:

1. Language tag of your copy of Windows and Internet Explorer

2. Your system's Regional Settings

3. Internet Explorer's auxiliary language preferences setting

The catch is that Internet Explorer has a feature called Accept Language, which supersedes the Windows Regional Settings. If you are viewing Windows Update (which is available in multiple languages), Internet Explorer looks to the list of languages in your language preference settings to determine which language to display. This list is prioritized, so if you have Greek as the first language and English as the second, Windows Update is displayed in Greek.

To see the Windows Update site in a different language, you can adjust your Internet Explorer's language preference settings as shown here. Note that changes here affect other multilanguage sites that you view.

1. In Internet Explorer, choose Tools, Internet Options.

2. On the General tab, click the Languages button.

3. Select the language you want, and then use the Move Up button to place your selection at the top of the list of languages. Click OK.

4. Click OK in the Internet Options dialog, and restart your browser.

5. Reload the Windows Update page.

THE TASK SCHEDULER DOESN'T ACTIVATE CORRECTLY

My Task Scheduler doesn't seem to activate correctly. What's the problem?

You can check several things when a Task Scheduler job doesn't activate correctly. Here's the rundown; check these in order:

1. Open the Task Scheduler window, and then open the properties for the task. Make sure the task is actually enabled via the Enabled check box on the Task tab.

2. On the Schedule tab, verify that the schedule is set correctly.

3. Check the permissions for all the items involved in running the task, such as scripts, executables, and so on. Make sure the permissions for those items match those of the user account assigned to the task.

4. If a user whose account a task is set to run in is not logged on at the time the task is scheduled to run, the task runs but is not visible. Check the task log file to see whether the task was running but you didn't know it.

5. Some commands hang, waiting for user input, unless launched with command-line arguments. Research the command or executable you are trying to run. Check Appendix A on the CD-ROM for this book, check the Help file for the program, or issue the command from a Command Prompt window, followed by /? to see a display of options.

6. Check or ask your administrator to check that Task Scheduler service is turned on (by choosing My Computer, Manage).

7. Check the Status column in the Scheduled Tasks window, and look for the task in question. (Use the Details view.) Table 31.7 describes the status types.

TABLE 31.7   SCHEDULED TASK STATUS TYPES

Status	Description
Blank	The task isn't current running, or it already ran and encountered no obstacles.
Running	The task is currently being run.
Missed	One or more attempts to run this task was missed, possibly because the computer was not turned on, or the scheduler was paused at the time.
Could not start	The most recent attempt to start the task failed for some reason. Check the log file if you care to investigate further. The log file, named schedlgu.txt, is stored in the \Winnt folder. This file is used to record the activity of scheduled tasks.

NO EVENTS IN SECURITY LOG

No events are showing in my security log.

By default, security logging is turned off in Windows 2000 Professional. Therefore, no security events are monitored or recorded, and your security log is devoid of entries even if you *do* have the administrative rights required to view them. You can turn security logging on, however, by using the steps outlined here:

1. Choose Start, Run. Then enter mmc /a and click OK.

2. On the Console menu, choose Add/Remove Snap-in, and then click Add.

3. Under Snap-in, choose Group Policy, and then click Add to open a large window.

4. In the Group Policy Object field, Local Computer should be typed in already. If not, enter it. Click Finish, click Close, and then click OK.

5. Back at the Console, open Local Computer Policy, Computer Configuration, Windows Settings, Security Settings, Local Policies, Audit Policy (see Figure 31.33).

6. In the details pane, click the attribute or event you want to audit.

7. Choose Action, Security.

8. In Change Local Policy To, click the options you want, and then click OK.

9. Repeat steps 6, 7, and 8 for other events you want to audit.

Figure 31.33
Turning on security logging takes you on a somewhat circuitous route.

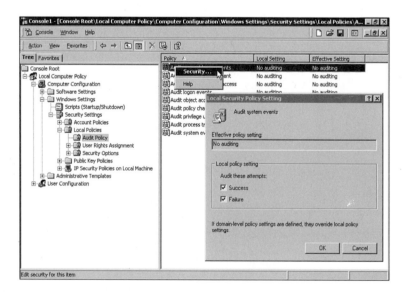

TIPS FROM THE WINDOWS PROS: POWER USER TRICKS

The following tricks are two of my personal favorites. The first is helpful if you frequently work with a laptop computer and want to add a serial mouse without closing all your applications and rebooting.

The second tip is especially helpful if you want to deter workgroup users from using the Windows Update feature without first checking with the system administrator.

ADDING A SERIAL MOUSE TO A LAPTOP WITHOUT REBOOTING

Due to the cramped or otherwise uncomfortable position I have to assume to use my laptop keyboard, I very often plug in an external, ergonomic keyboard with a trackpad on it. Then I can sit back in my chair, keyboard on my lap, or even stand the computer up sideways, as you saw in Chapter 28, "Tweaking the GUI," in the section on rotating the screen image 90 degrees. In any case, I don't always want to power down and then reboot just to plug in the keyboard and mouse.

Now, if the mouse and keyboard were USB devices, this wouldn't be a problem because USB supports hot docking. In the fairly near future, keyboards, mouse devices, graphics tablets, and many other external devices such as cameras, printers, scanners, and PDAs will be USB-enabled. As of the moment, however, they are not.

My keyboard plugs into the PS/2 port, which is no problem. Although making PS/2 connections with a computer turned on is not advisable (it can blow the driver chip for the port), I do it anyway, and on my Dell 7000, it hasn't posed a problem. The keyboard is immediately recognized and works fine. But the rub is that the trackpad, which connects to the serial port (a second PS/2 port is not available for a mouse), isn't recognized. Connecting the mouse doesn't result in anything at all, functionally. For a while, I resorted to rebooting Windows 2000. Hibernating or suspending didn't force a hardware redetection. Another approach was to run Add/Remove Hardware, but that's a pain because it takes too long.

I discovered that the Device Manager can scan hardware and see whether anything new is lying around, without its driver. After I had installed the trackpad software, it was part of the Device Manager's list for the computer. But when the mouse is sensed as unplugged, the operating system marks it as not functioning (with an exclamation mark in the Device Manager). To get it going again, no reboot is necessary. I just had to do the following:

1. Reconnect the mouse.
2. Get to the Device Manager (you can do so from Control Panel, System, or from Computer Management).
3. Click somewhere on the computer's tree, such as the top level, the icon showing the computer name. (This step is imperative, or the next step isn't possible.)
4. Choose Action, Scan for Hardware Changes.
5. Wait about 10 seconds while Windows does its thing. Now the external mouse should work.

REMOVING WINDOWS UPDATE FROM THE START MENU

As good an idea as Windows Update is, unauthorized use of it could be annoying to a system administrator. Corporate system administrators who are responsible for hundreds of PCs need to control what goes on their machines, especially in the way of core operating system updates. It is possible to remove the Windows Update icons that appear in the Start menu, and even prevent the users from accessing the Windows Update site (http://windowsupdate.microsoft.com) from anywhere within Windows.

By using the Windows 2000 Microsoft Management Console's snap-in called Local Computer Policy, you can disable Windows Update on the Start menu. Although you can modify and configure MMC to view policies in many ways, the most generic way to configure a new console root is as follows:

1. Choose Start, Run. Then enter MMC and click OK.

2. From the console, choose Add/Remove Snap-in.

3. Choose Add, Choose Group Policy. Then click Add, Close, and finally OK.

4. Navigate down Local Computer Policy to User Configuration to Administrative Templates to Start Menu & Taskbar.

5. Double-click Disable and Remove Links to Windows Update.

CHAPTER 32

MANAGING USERS

In this chapter

Multiple Users on One Machine

Windows 2000 was designed to be a personalized product, providing security both locally and in a networked environment. One of the ways that Windows 2000 achieves this goal is through user accounts. This chapter explores the ins and outs of creating, managing, and using different user accounts on your Windows 2000 Professional computer.

In many instances, a single computer is used by more than one user, which creates some unique challenges in the computing environment. Suppose, for example, that you share your work computer with a colleague; let's call her Abby. You probably have something on your computer that you don't want Abby to have access to, but how can you deny access to her when she must use the same computer?

Other issues arise with the look and feel of your desktop environment in Windows. Perhaps Abby likes to rearrange the desktop icons to her liking, or maybe she is a big fan of the Windows 3.1 hot dog stand color scheme and has your Windows settings mimicking that. (If you have never seen the hot dog stand color scheme, count yourself lucky!) Worse yet, perhaps Abby has a penchant for sound and has set up a WAV file for every event possible on your computer. To me, nothing is more annoying than hearing a sound every time I touch my keyboard.

User Account Types

User accounts solve these issues by creating what is called a *user profile*. The first time a user logs in to a Windows 2000 system with his or her account, a user profile is created for that user. Understand that the account is what gives the user access to the system, and the user profile is a collection of all user-defined settings and the user's My Documents folder. You can customize your screen saver, wallpaper, folder views, even sounds without affecting other users' environments. The best aspect of user profiles is that they are automatic. The system saves all your changes to your profile when you log out and restores them when you log back in.

> **Note**
>
> If you are in a LAN environment, you should check with your system administrator before trying to customize your profile. Many times corporate LANs include mandatory profiles that prevent users from changing settings.

Before you can get to the promised land of user profiles, you must take a look at user accounts.

Domain and Local Accounts

If your computer is part of a Windows 2000 Server-based network, two different types of user accounts are available: *local accounts* and *domain accounts*. In this type of network, user accounts are usually set up on the server computers by the manager of the network. These accounts are valid on every member computer of the network, so they are called domain accounts.

In addition to domain accounts, accounts that are valid only on one computer can be added to each member computer. These accounts, which can be created by the administrator of the individual computer, are called local accounts.

If your computer isn't part of a Windows 2000 domain network, then you need worry only about local accounts. Each computer on your LAN uses its own separate list of users, and each user is entered into each computer by its own administrator.

For the rest of the discussion of user accounts, I'll talk about local accounts only because a Windows 2000 Professional user generally cannot manage and administer domain accounts, and in no case can he or she modify the profile settings of such a domain account. If you're part of a domain network, you should read the following section on Guest and Administrator accounts. Then you can skip right on down to the discussion of user privileges.

GUEST AND ADMINISTRATOR ACCOUNTS

When you installed Windows 2000, two user accounts were created on your machine. One of them is the Administrator account and the other is the Guest account.

The Guest user account is disabled by default, and I strongly urge you to leave this account disabled. Even though the Guest user account is really on the same level as a normal user account and can't modify system settings or install software, you lose all tracking and accountability. Worse, when a LAN is involved, or when you're connected to the Internet, the Guest account is used for any remote user who doesn't have an account on your computer. Anything Guest has access to, anybody has access to. By default, this is your entire hard drive! The Guest concept might be acceptable on an isolated LAN with no Internet access whatsoever, but in today's world, that's unlikely. It's an idea whose time is past.

The Administrator user account is the exact opposite of the Guest account. In Windows 2000, professional administrators are assumed to be the "benevolent rulers" of the computer. The user who is logged in as Administrator has the power to do just about anything with or to that computer. Because the Administrator account is also a default account, everyone knows about it. As a rule, I always change the name of the Administrator account to something meaningful to me. Changing the name makes it more difficult for someone to break into your system; if users don't have the account name right, they cannot possibly crack the password.

PART

VI

CH

32

Tip #385

I strongly suggest that you do not use the Administrator account—by any name—on a day-to-day basis. Having said that, I know that some people out there want to live on the edge and log in as Administrator daily. If you are one of these "edge-dwellers," you should realize the risk you are assuming.

Being connected to the Internet while logged on as Administrator is the equivalent of painting a big target on your shirt and going jogging at a firing range. Hackers are out there, and they are always watching for an easy target. Running Windows 2000 as Administrator makes you especially susceptible to trojan horse viruses because the trojan horse code then runs with full privileges to your machine. If you are logged on as a normal user, the virus is limited in what it can damage.

If you find that you are logging in and out frequently to do administrative tasks, try using the Run As command. You can do so by opening the Windows Explorer and locating the program that you want to run as a different user. (It could be a Control Panel item, the Microsoft Management Console, or any other executable.) Press the Shift key, right-click the program name, and select Run As, as shown in Figure 32.1. You then can type the username, password, and domain name of the privileged account you want to use.

Figure 32.1
You can choose to run selected applications as a different user than you normally log in as.

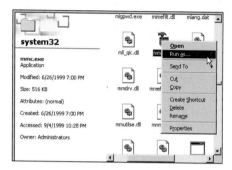

> **Note**
>
> Run As doesn't work with the Windows Explorer, the Printers folder, or desktop icons. Run As also doesn't work with user accounts that are set up with SmartCard authentication systems.

> **Caution**
>
> Change the Administrator password frequently, and ensure that it is kept secure. Remember that the Administrator password is the key to your computer.

CREATING USER ACCOUNTS

Now that I've told you to avoid using either of the default accounts on your machine (at least on a daily basis), you might be wondering how you will get any work done. Of course, you'll need to create personalized user accounts for each user.

When you're creating new accounts, first log in with a privileged account, and then access the administrative tools by choosing Start, Programs, Administrative Tools, Computer Management.

> **Tip #386**
>
> If you don't see Computer Management listed as an administrative tool, don't panic. To show the administrative tools in the Start menu, you must choose Start, Settings, Taskbar. Then choose the Start Menu Options tab, and click Advanced. Finally, check the Show Admin Tools option.

The Computer Management tool is shown in Figure 32.2.

Figure 32.2
You can use the Computer Management tool to configure many options for your Windows 2000 PC.

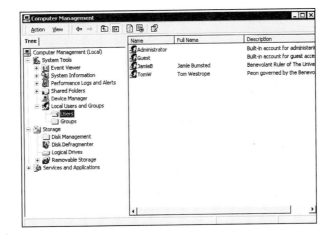

To create a new user account, follow these steps:

1. Navigate to the Users folder in the left pane, click the Action button, and select New User. The New User dialog box then appears, as shown in Figure 32.3.

PART

VI

CH

32

Figure 32.3
You use the New User dialog box in Computer Management to create new user accounts.

2. To add a user, add a username; you also can add the user's full name and a description of the user. You should also enter a preliminary password for this new user. You must enter it twice, of course, to confirm that you didn't make any typographical errors when you entered it. This feature is very helpful because the password you enter is represented by asterisks.

Tip #387

Think of a standard for your usernames. In small organizations, using First Name + Last Initial should work. Be prepared with a contingency plan if you end up with two exact usernames; for example, you could add the middle initial to the username if two are identical.

3. By default, the User Must Change Password at Next Logon option is selected, forcing the user to change the preliminary password when he or she logs on to the computer the next time. This option can be helpful in acting as a check and balance. Even though the administrator can access all resources on the computer, you might not want to know other users' passwords.

4. The User Cannot Change Password option on the New User dialog prevents the user from changing the password. This setting is very helpful if you have a user account that multiple people use. When this option is checked, only the administrator or another privileged account can change the password.

5. The Password Never Expires check box prevents the user's password from expiring. This setting is very convenient for the user, but it really undermines the security of the system. Password security is only as good as the secrecy of the password. Allowing passwords to remain the same indefinitely is like giving would-be hackers a "play till you win" opportunity. I recommend not selecting this option, ever.

6. Last, but definitely not least, the Account Is Disabled setting disables the user account. You should disable user accounts that are no longer active or disable them when users will be away from the office for long periods of time. You should use the disable feature instead of deleting user accounts when at all possible; see the caution on security identifiers for more information.

> **Caution**
>
> Every user account in Windows 2000 has a unique *security identifier*, called an *SID*. This unique identifier ties all security settings to the user account. You can look at the SID as the key ring that contains all your keys to unlock resources on your computer. If you delete a user account, you also delete that SID, and it can never be used again. Even if you create a new user account with the same username and properties, the SID will be different for the new account. You are forced to regenerate all security data, such as group information, file and resources permissions, and so on. As a general rule, you should delete user accounts only when absolutely necessary for organizational purposes.

> **Tip #388**
>
> I suggest that you not deny users access to change their passwords unless you enjoy other users pestering you to do it for them.

7. After you finish checking the boxes you want to implement, click the Create button to create the user account. The New User dialog box is reset to blanks, and you can create another user at this time or click the Close button.

USER ACCOUNT OPTIONS

You will want to look at some more options when dealing with user accounts. If you double-click the user account you just created, you can view the account properties. You go to the user account properties, as shown in Figure 32.4, to manage the user account after creating it. Notice that you have the same check boxes as you did when creating the account. Also, notice the three tabs: General, Member Of, and Profile. Each tab contains configuration information about this user account.

Figure 32.4
The properties interface of a Windows 2000 Professional user account contains three main tabs that you can configure.

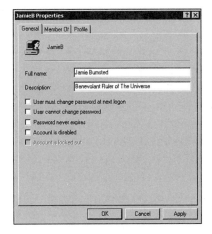

To edit the properties of a user account, do the following:

1. Select the Users folder in the left pane.
2. Double-click the user account that you want to edit in the right pane to bring up the properties of the selected user.

In the Properties dialog box, you have the option of adding users to groups, editing logon scripts and profiles, and specifying password options.

ASSIGNING GROUP MEMBERSHIPS

On the Member Of tab of the Properties dialog, you can add the user to any groups that you feel are necessary. By default, all user accounts are made members of the Users group. This group gives users basic rights to the system. A user account can, and probably will, belong to more than one group. I'll discuss groups and group privileges in more detail later in this chapter.

To add a user to a group, follow these steps:

1. Click the Member Of tab to make it active.
2. Select the Add button.
3. Click the down arrow beside the Look In text box so that you can specify what computer to pull the group options from.
4. Select a group in the upper pane of the window.
5. Click the Add button, and then click OK.

Caution

Do not add any user accounts to the Administrators group unless the account will be used only to perform administrative tasks. Adding a user account to this group and using it for day-to-day activities would expose you to the same risks as using the Administrator account.

STORING USER PROFILES

On the Profile tab of the Properties dialog, you can specify a location in which to store the user's profile. You use this setting only if you want it to be different from the default location, which is C:\Documents and Settings\%USERNAME%. The string %USERNAME% is a placeholder representing the name of the user account.

The following is the procedure to change the default profile path:

1. Click the Profile tab in the Properties dialog.
2. Navigate to the Profile Path text box, and enter the path that you would like to use to store the user's profile. You can use %USERNAME% in this pathname if you want.

SETTING LOGON SCRIPTS

You also can specify a logon script that you want to automatically run when the user logs on. The logon script file is a batch file containing commands to be run each time the user logs in. This file, if specified, should have a .BAT or .CMD extension.

One of the primary uses of logon scripts is to map network drives. The location for logon script files is the local directory %SYSTEMROOT%\System32\Repl\Import\Scripts of the computer that provides validation. If you're working in a domain environment and using a domain account, the primary copy of the logon script resides on one of the domain controllers.

If you want to create logon scripts for your local users, you must save them in the local %SYSTEMROOT%\System32\Repl\Import\Scripts directory. Make sure that all users have at least Read and Execute permissions to this directory, or their logon scripts will not run.

→ If you want to learn more details about setting security options, **see** "Securing Your Files and Folders," **p. 1204**.

To specify a logon script for a user, follow these steps:

1. Move your cursor to the Logon Script text box.
2. Type the name of the logon script file that you want to execute. Do not type the path; it is assumed to be %SYSTEMROOT%\System32\Repl\Import\Scripts.

Tip #389	I have found that the directory %SYSTEMROOT%\System32\Repl\Import\Scripts does not exist by default on Windows 2000 Professional computers. You might have to create the subdirectory Repl\Import\Scripts manually. After you do so, you can create and specify logon scripts to run.

⚠ *If a logon script is specified but does not run, see "Logon Scripts Won't Run" in the "Troubleshooting" section at the end of the chapter.*

SETTING UP HOME DIRECTORIES

On the Profile tab of the Properties dialog, you also can specify the user's home directory. A home directory is the location you want your users to store any and all files that they work on.

Home directories are very useful in a LAN environment because they allow you to access your files from any computer that you log in to during the course of your day. The Home Directory entry on the Profile tab gives you the option either to

- Specify a directory path on the local computer
- Connect a given drive letter to a network pathname for the user's home directory

I recommend mapping the home directory to a network share. This way, when a user logs in, a drive connection mapped in My Computer points to the user's home directory, which is stored in a common place no matter which individual computer the user logs in with. This home directory can be mapped to any drive letter not being used as a local disk. I recommend using the letter *H* for Home or *P* for Personal. Home directories work great for users who don't quite understand the concept of a local area network. They don't have to remember long UNC pathnames, only that the P: drive is the place they should store all their files.

Home directories also help with the protection of data. For example, if your company has one tape backup drive, it can be set up on one computer. All the users' home directories can be placed on that computer and backed up nightly.

When you're creating home directories in a central location, try to keep the naming convention the same for all users. Create a folder on the machine that will store home directories for all users; then you can let Windows 2000 create the home directories themselves inside that folder. If you create a central point to store all home directories, I suggest that you use the pathname to the central store, plus the %USERNAME% environment variable. This way, you create a folder with the same name as the user account, and you can easily keep track of which home directory belongs to which user.

When you specify home directory paths for users, the directories are created automatically. However, in Windows 2000 Professional, I have found that the security is inherited from the parent directory by default. Many times, this means that Everyone has full control. You do not want to allow this control on your home directories. If you remove the inherited security, nobody has access. What this all boils down to is that you must modify the permissions for each user's home directory to allow the user access and to deny everyone else.

To create a home directory container, follow these steps:

1. Working at the computer that you will use to house home directories, navigate to the disk drive that you want to use for home directory storage.

2. Create a folder to house all the users' home directories. (I like to call it Home.) It should be on an NTFS-formatted disk so that user-level access controls can be set up.

3. Right-click the folder you just created, and select Sharing from the drop-down menu.

4. Select Share This Folder, and type a name for the share in the Share Name text box. (The default share name is the name of the folder.) Again, Home is a good choice.

5. Click the Permissions button. You will see that the default share permission is granting Everyone Full Control.

6. Uncheck the Full Control and Change check boxes in the lower pane of the Permissions dialog box. Leave the Read check box selected.

To create each user's home directory, do the following:

1. On the Profile tab of a user's properties, select Connect to a Drive Letter.

2. From the drop-down list provided, choose a drive letter to use when mapping the home directory. I recommend *H* for Home or *P* for Personal.

3. Enter the path to the central store in the text box next to the home directory drive letter. Remember to use the %USERNAME% variable. The entry might look like *computername*\home\%USERNAME%, where *computername* is the name of the computer storing the home directories. This step creates a subfolder for the user in the share folder.

4. Navigate to the home share on the central machine. Right-click the newly created home directory, and select Sharing, Permissions. Remove Everyone by highlighting it and clicking Remove.

5. Click the Add button to add a permission to the user account. Select the username that belongs with the home directory and the Administrator account. Click Add, and then click OK.

6. Highlight Administrator in the upper window, and check all the check boxes, giving the administrator full control.

7. Highlight the user account, and check the Change and Read boxes to give the user Change permission to the folder.

USERS ON A WORKGROUP LAN

So far, you have explored the need for user accounts on your local computer. Now let's delve a little deeper and look at the use of accounts in a workgroup LAN environment. A workgroup-based LAN is generally used in a small business where the number of users and computers is small. My personal recommendation is that a LAN of 10 computers or fewer is manageable in a workgroup setting. Essentially, a workgroup LAN is a group of client computers with no dedicated server. All the resources are distributed throughout all the client computers, and all the user accounts are distributed throughout the client computers. This setup allows users to share files and printers across the network without having to centrally administer the network. One drawback to this setup is that if multiple users use multiple machines, they each need a user account on each computer they will use.

See Figure 32.5 for an example. With a "Bob" account on each computer, Bob can use all three computers and can access shared folders from each. Sharon can use only Computer 2 and can't even access shared resources on the other computers because they don't recognize her login name "Sharon" as valid for access.

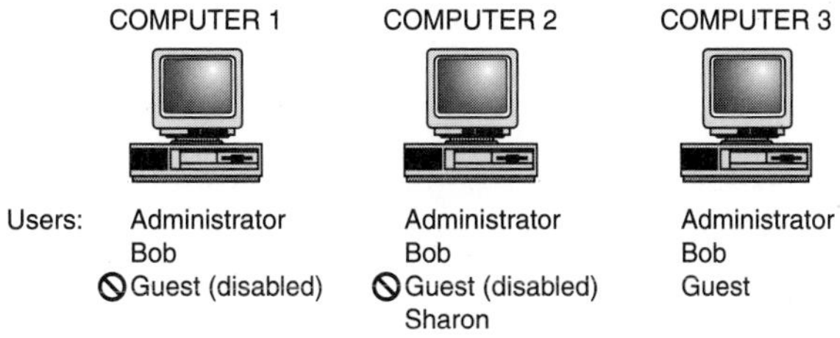

Figure 32.5
In a workgroup LAN, an account must be created on each computer a user wants to use, either directly or through file sharing.

	COMPUTER 1	COMPUTER 2	COMPUTER 3
Users:	Administrator	Administrator	Administrator
	Bob	Bob	Bob
	⊘ Guest (disabled)	⊘ Guest (disabled)	Guest
		Sharon	

PART

VI

CH

32

I should point out that, in this scenario, for network access to be possible, the Bob account must have the same password on all machines. Remember, I said that local accounts are unique to each machine on a workgroup network. For Bob to access resources on a machine he's not directly logged in on, his computer must pass his login name and password to the other computer for it to validate. If no Bob account exists, or the password is different on the networked computer, it rejects his request to access its resources.

SHARING YOUR RESOURCES

To share resources across the network, each user must specify what resources he or she wants to make available for sharing. To be able to share resources, you first must ensure that you have the File and Printer Sharing network component installed. Do so by checking the Local Area Network Connection Properties in Network and Dial-up Connections, as shown in Figure 32.6.

After you have verified that this component is installed in your system, you are ready to do some sharing. To share files on your computer, do the following:

1. Browse to the folder that you want to share, right-click it, and select Sharing to see the Sharing tab shown in Figure 32.7.

Note

If you want to share files, you must share the entire folder that contains the files; you cannot share individual files. However, using Share and NTFS Permissions, you can block access to individual files in a shared directory.

Figure 32.6
The Local Area Network Connection Properties dialog displays network components that are installed and allows you to install new components or configure existing components. Make sure that you have the File and Printer Sharing component installed if you want to share your files or printers.

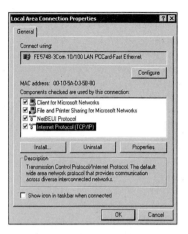

Figure 32.7
The Sharing tab of any folder's Properties dialog box allows you to share the resource.

2. Check the Share This Folder radio button.

3. Enter a share name in the Share Name text box.

4. Enter a descriptive comment in the Comment text box.

5. Specify a user limit using the radio buttons labeled Maximum Allowed or Allow x Number of Users.

6. Set permissions on the share using share permissions and/or NTFS permissions.

 If your users cannot access the resource you have shared, see "Users Cannot Access a Shared Resource" in the "Troubleshooting" section at the end of the chapter.

→ To learn more details about sharing files and folders, **see** "Sharing Folders and Drives," **p. 779**.

SECURING YOUR FILES AND FOLDERS

You can control access to shared resources by using NTFS permissions, share permissions, or both.

NTFS PERMISSIONS

NTFS permissions are used to control access to files and folders for both local and network users. This system gives you total control over other users' access, as long as the folders in question are on an NTFS-formatted disk partition.

→ To learn more details about disk formatting options, **see** "Which File System: FAT, FAT32, or NTFS?" **p. 133**.

Remember, change these settings only when you must control who gets access to a given folder or file. Don't change any of the settings for the Windows folder or the Documents and Settings folders. They are set up correctly when Windows is installed, and removing necessary permissions here can wreak havoc on your computer.

Tip #390	Start with just one folder—perhaps a test folder containing just one file—to test permission settings, and use various user accounts to confirm that the settings do what you want them to before working with "real" folders containing important files.
	Even the most seasoned network administrators sometimes must go around and around with permissions and user accounts before they get them exactly how they want them.

To display or modify NTFS permissions, select a file or folder in the Explorer, right-click Properties, and select the Security tab, as shown in Figure 32.8.

Figure 32.8
You can use the NTFS Permissions dialog box to a folder to restrict access to both network and local users.

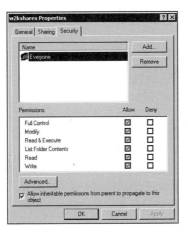

In the top part of the dialog box is the list of users or user groups with access to the file or folder. You can select any of the names in the list to view their associated permissions in the bottom half of the dialog.

The permission properties can each be granted or revoked individually. The permissions are Full Control, Modify, Read & Execute, List Folder Contents, Read, and Write. Their properties are listed in Table 32.1.

TABLE 32.1   NTFS FILE PERMISSION SETTINGS AND THEIR FUNCTIONS

Permission	Properties
Full Control	Gives all the rights listed below, plus lets the user change the file's security and ownership settings.
Modify	Lets a user modify a file's contents or delete a file.
List Folder Contents	Allows the user to see the files in a folder; although other settings might prevent the user from reading or writing those files.
Read & Execute	Allows a user to read a file's contents and/or run an executable file as a program.
Read	Lets a user read a file's contents only.
Write	Lets a user create a new file, write data in an existing file, but not read a file's contents. For a folder, lets users add new files to the folder but not view the folder's contents.

Note that each permission has both an Allow and a Deny check box. To get access to a given resource, a user must be explicitly listed with Allow checked or must belong to a listed group that has Allow checked and must not be listed with Deny access or belong to any group with Deny marked. Deny preempts Allow.

All these permissions are additive. In other words, Read and Write can both be checked to combine the properties of both. Full Control could be marked Allow but Write marked Deny to give all access rights except writing. (This permission would be strange but possible.)

The most productive use of NTFS file permissions is to assign most rights by group membership. One exception is with user home directories or profile directories, to which you usually grant access only to the Administrators group and the individual owner.

INHERITANCE OF PERMISSIONS

One point you should know about NTFS permissions is that, normally, permissions are assigned to a folder (or drive), and all the folders and files within it inherit the permissions of the top-level folder. In Figure 32.8, the folder has a check in Allow Inheritable Permissions from Parent to Propagate to This Object. That's the usual case.

In Figure 32.8, also note that the settings for this folder are visible but grayed out to indicate that you can't change them. If you uncheck the Allow Inheritance box, you uncouple this file or folder from the folder above it and can set its permissions as you like. This is the usual case: If you want to change a file's or folder's permissions, you must "disconnect" it from the folder or drive it's contained in.

When you do uncheck the box, Windows gives you the option of starting with a blank permissions list (Clear) or keeping a copy of the settings it had before (Copy). In either case, the item now has its own independent list of access rights, which you can edit at will.

ADVANCED PERMISSIONS

Besides the basic permissions, advanced properties can be set on NTFS objects as well. As you can see in Figure 32.9, the advanced options for restricting access with NTFS permissions cover just about any situation you could think of. The advanced permissions are explained in Table 32.2. Notice that many of the advanced permissions are two-fold, each part pertaining to a specific function relating to files or folders. The basic permissions listed previously are actually combinations of these more "granular" permissions.

Figure 32.9
You can use the NTFS Advanced Permissions dialog box when general permissions do not provide adequate security.

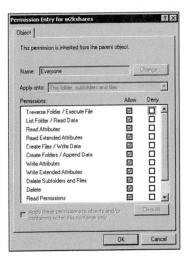

TABLE 32.2   NTFS ADVANCED FILE PERMISSION SETTINGS AND THEIR FUNCTIONS

Permission	Properties
Traverse Folder/Execute File	For folders, this special permission allows a user the right to move through a folder to which he or she doesn't have List access, to reach a file or folder to which he or she does have access. For files, this permission allows the running of applications. (This permission is effective only if the user wasn't granted the Group policy "Bypass Traverse Checking" user right.)
List Folder/Read Data	For folders, allows the user to view the names of files or subfolders inside a folder. For files, allows the user to read the data in a file.
Read Attributes	Allows the user to view the attributes of the file or folder (that is, Hidden, Read-Only, or System).
Read Extended Attributes	Allows the user to view extended attributes of files or folders as defined by another program. (These attributes vary depending on the program.)

continues

TABLE 32.2 CONTINUED

Permission	Properties
Create Files/Write Data	For folders, allows the user to create new files inside the folder. For files, allows the user to add new data or overwrite data inside existing files.
Create Folders/Append Data	For folders, allows the user to create new subfolders. For files, allows the user to append data to the end of an existing file. This permission does not pertain to deleting or overwriting existing data.
Write Attributes	Allows the user to change the attributes of the file or folder.
Write Extended Attributes	Allows the user to change the extended attributes of a file or folder.
Delete Subfolders and Files	For a folder, allows the user to delete subfolders and their contents. This permission applies even if the Delete permission has not been expressly granted on the individual subfolders or their files.
Delete	Allows or denies the user to delete the file. Even if Delete is denied, a user can still delete a file if he or she has Delete Subfolders and Files permission on the parent folder.
Read Permissions	Allows the user to view the file's or folder's permissions assigned to a file or folder.
Change Permissions	Allows the user to change the file's or folder's permissions.
Take Ownership	Allows the user to take ownership of a file or folder.

SHARE PERMISSIONS

Share permissions govern users who are connecting to the resource over the network. These permissions can be set on any shared resource, no matter what disk format you are using (FAT, FAT32, VFAT, or NTFS), and they work in addition to NTFS permissions on the shared files and folders.

You can set three permission levels on a Windows 2000 Professional network share—Full Control, Change, and Read—as shown in Figure 32.10.

- Full Control lets users add or remove other users' permissions to the network share, as well as read and write shared files.

- Change allows network users to create new files in the shared folder, modify existing files, run executable files, and delete files. Change gives the users permission to do anything with the shared directory except govern other users' access.

- Read lets users list folder contents, open files for reading access only, and execute any executables in the share. They cannot create, modify, or delete files.

Figure 32.10
On the Share Permissions tab, you can limit user access to shared resources.

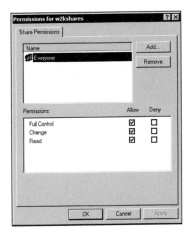

Share permissions do not apply to a local user's access. If a user is logged in locally and directly accesses a folder, share-level permissions are not examined.

It's important to point out that share permissions apply in addition to normal NTFS file access controls and serve to further restrict access. That is, a user who doesn't have read access to a given file by virtue of NTFS file permissions cannot access that file over the network, regardless of the share permissions.

| Tip #391 | If a shared folder is stored on an NTFS-formatted disk partition, and its contents are protected by proper NTFS permissions, you can leave the default share permissions of Full Control for Everyone, with *no* decrease in security. |
| | If the shared folder is stored on a FAT partition, you should use share permissions to control access to the folder through the network. |

ASSIGNING PERMISSIONS TO GROUPS

The best practice for assigning permissions is to assign them to local groups. You can assign the permission for folders and files to a given group, and then add and remove users to or from the group as you need to later on.

But what happens if a user belongs to more than one group with conflicting permissions? Remember that permissions accumulate. Say your colleague Abby is a member of the Users local group and the Accounting local group. She is accessing a shared folder from another computer. The Users group has share permissions of Read to a folder containing the monthly financial statements. The Accounting group has share permissions of Change to the same folder. Because share permissions accumulate, Abby's effective permissions will be Change. The same is true of NTFS permissions. If the Users group has Read NTFS permissions, and Accounting has Change NTFS permissions, Abby's effective permissions will be Change.

When you group NTFS and share permissions together, the most restrictive permissions win out. So, considering the example, if the Users group has share permissions of Read and NTFS permissions of Change, users have effective permissions of Read. Also, if the Accounting group has share permissions of Change and NTFS permissions of Full Control, remote users belonging to the Accounting group have effective permissions of Change. Now let's get really complicated. What if Users has share permissions of Read and NTFS permissions of Change, and Accounting has share permissions of Change and NTFS permissions of Full Control? What are Abby's effective permissions? When in doubt, write it out!

- Share permissions are Read + Change = Change.
- NTFS permissions are Change + Full Control = Change.
- Accumulated permissions are Change + Change = Change.

To calculate effective permissions, follow these steps:

1. Add all share permissions, remembering that share permissions accumulate.
2. Add all NTFS permissions, again remembering that NTFS permissions accumulate.
3. Add the totals from share and NTFS, remembering that the most restrictive of the two wins out.

Note

Remember that share permissions govern only remote users, whereas NTFS permissions govern both local and remote users.

 If you find that a user has access to something he or she shouldn't, see "A User Has Access to a Restricted Object" in the "Troubleshooting" section at the end of the chapter.

SHARING AND SECURING YOUR PRINTERS

The process of sharing and setting security on your shared printers is similar to setting security on your files and folders. If you are installing a new printer and want to set it up for sharing at that time, you can use the Add Printer Wizard, which will walk you through setting up your shared printer, including giving it a location and a brief description about the capabilities of the printer.

→ For detailed instructions on sharing printers on your network, **see** "Sharing Printers," **p. 783**.

Follow these steps to share an existing printer:

1. Navigate to the printers folder and go into the properties of the printer you want to share. Printer Sharing Properties allow you to share your local printer and to provide descriptive information to remote users of the printer.
2. Choose the Sharing tab.
3. Give your printer a share name. It's best to keep the share name to eight or fewer letters.

4. On the Sharing tab, you can specify additional printer drivers for the printer for users of other Windows operating systems.

5. To set permissions on your shared printer, first select the Security tab, as shown in Figure 32.11.

Figure 32.11
On the Security tab, you can manage users and groups that will use your printer.

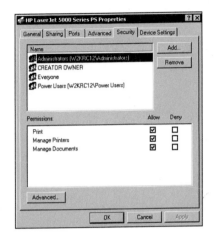

6. Add users or groups to which you want to allow access.

7. Select the appropriate permission for each user or group. See Table 32.3 for an explanation of printer permissions.

TABLE 32.3   NTFS PERMISSIONS FOR PRINTERS

Permission	Explanation
Print	Allows or denies a user permission to connect to the printer and send print jobs.
Manage Printers	Allows or denies the user full control over the printer. The user can pause the printer, restart the printer, manage the queue, and share or unshare the printer.
Manage Documents	Allows or denies the user to manage documents sent to the printer by other users. This permission alone does not allow the user to print to the printer.
Deny	Takes away any or all of the preceding permissions.

USERS ON A DOMAIN LAN

At this point, you have learned about the use of Windows 2000 user and group accounts on a very simple workgroup LAN. Next, you'll explore the possibilities of using Windows 2000 Professional in a Domain LAN environment. Chances are that if you are using Windows

2000 Professional on a domain-based LAN, you will not have to do much administration of user accounts, resources, and permissions (at least not by yourself). You should, however, understand the concepts behind connecting Windows 2000 to a domain-based LAN so that you can efficiently use your computer to its fullest potential.

On a domain-based LAN, the administration of user accounts is generally centralized. Instead of having a user account exist on each computer for each user who may use it, one user account exists on a domain controller. This account is created by the LAN administrator.

Note

A *domain controller* is a network server that maintains the database of domain user accounts.

Resources can be centralized to the server, but many people might still want to share files on their computers as well. If you are a member of a domain-based LAN, you can still share your files and printers in the same manner that you do in a workgroup-based LAN. The only difference is in how you assign permissions. The best practice for assigning permissions in a domain-based environment is to assign all permissions to local groups. Local groups can contain global groups (groups defined across your whole domain network), local users, and global users. This way, you can assign the permission once to a group and then add any users to that group or any group of users to that group who need access.

Another point worth noting is that some global groups are placed into local groups automatically. For example, the global Domain Admins group is automatically placed in the Administrators group on every computer that joins the domain. This placement ensures that the domain administrator has control over decentralized resources, as well as centralized resources.

Note

Local users and local groups exist on the local machine only. Global users and global groups exist in the entire domain.

On a domain network, the network administrators define not only user accounts and groups, but also network security policies, your ability to manage certain aspects of your computer, and the location of user profiles.

USER PROFILES

User profiles contain all the information that the computer needs to personalize your system's look and feel. Your user profile contains your desktop, wallpaper, and shortcut icons. The profile also contains your network settings, network printer definitions, and your personal file folders. Windows 2000 contains four types of user profiles: the default user profile, local user profiles, roaming user profiles, and mandatory profiles.

A default user profile is a profile that is assigned to a user the first time he or she logs in to a computer. When the user logs in for the first time, he or she receives the settings specified in the default user profile. When the user logs off, the default profile is written to a local user profile, including any changes the user made during his or her first session. Because of this process, you can make it a little less painful for users to set up shop on your PC by logging in as a new user and making some general changes.

You can set up custom user profiles like this:

1. Log in to the computer.
2. Make the changes to your computer that you want all users to have, such as power management settings, desktop wallpaper, and so on.
3. Log off the computer.
4. Copy the Administrator user profile to the default user profile on the local computer.
5. Do so by logging back in as Administrator and opening System Properties, as shown in Figure 32.12.
6. Highlight the profile that you want to copy.
7. Click the Copy To button.
8. Enter the path to %SYSTEMROOT%\Documents & Settings\Default User. Then click OK.

Figure 32.12
On the User Profiles tab in System Properties, you can copy a user profile to another location. Just highlight the profile you want to copy, and click the Copy To button.

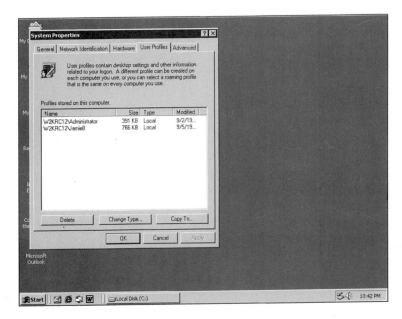

Note

If your computer is located on a Windows 2000 Server-based network, be sure to contact your system administrator before trying to change the default profile. If roaming profiles are enabled, the default profile is located on the Domain Controller, and you cannot change it.

USER PROFILES IN A DOMAIN

Now that you know about local and default user profiles, it's time to bring out the big guns: roaming and mandatory user profiles.

User profiles are used in Windows 2000 Professional no matter what networking model is implemented. However, you can do some pretty nifty things with profiles depending on which network you connect to.

ROAMING PROFILES ON A DOMAIN NETWORK

Remember that a domain network generally consists of global user accounts allowing you to log in to any computer that is a member of the domain. So, how do you get your settings to follow you from one computer to the other? Enter roaming profiles.

When your domain user account is set up, the LAN administrator has the option of specifying a profile path. (This is very similar to the option that you have when creating local users.) If the administrator assigns a network path to your user profile, you are all set to use your roaming profile. When you log in to any computer on the domain network, the domain controller sees that you have a roaming profile path specified. It copies your profile, containing your settings and My Documents folder, to the computer you're currently using. When you log out, it's all copied back. This way, you always see the same settings and files, no matter which computer you use.

If you're worried about the time required to copy all those My Documents files, don't worry. The network manager can specify that they're always to be kept on the central server rather than copied back and forth. In any case, you don't really need to worry about it. You just see the same settings and files, no matter which computer you use anywhere on your company's network.

All this is pretty nifty, but only members of Windows 2000 Server networks get it.

One final point: If you've used a given computer before, the "cached" copy of your profile might still be on the computer. If that computer were unable to copy your profile back to the central server, the next time you log in the local copy might be more up-to-date than the network copy. Windows lets you decide which copy to use in this case.

MANDATORY PROFILES ON A DOMAIN NETWORK

A mandatory user profile is actually a type of roaming user profile. This profile follows a user throughout the domain-based LAN just like a roaming user profile does. The big difference is that any changes made to system settings are not written back to the server copy when the user logs off. This serves as a way to keep a standardized setup on every machine in the LAN.

Using this type of profile can be an excellent way to achieve standardization, which is the key to easier troubleshooting and more comfortable users. Only system administrators can change mandatory user profiles. (Using this can also be a way to create a bunch of frustrated users who find they can't make changes they want, if this kind of enforcement is carried out too harshly.)

USER PROFILES IN A WORKGROUP SETTING

In a workgroup environment, you might think of trying to mimic roaming user profiles by attempting to set a network path as the folder in which to store user profiles. You cannot do so, unfortunately. You can get as far as specifying the remote path to the profile, but it does not follow you from computer to computer because, in a workgroup environment, you do not have a global user account. All accounts are local, and local accounts cannot have a roaming user profile.

Many people (for example, I) have tried to get creative with this and "hack" the Registry to fool Windows 2000 into thinking it does have a roaming profile. It does not work, and even if it did, the process has a couple of major flaws. Because it is not an actual roaming profile, it is not locally cached. If the computer you specified to hold the roaming profiles is down, nobody can log in to his or her own computer. Also, because each user's Registry data is part of the profile, and Windows grabs the Registry file for its exclusive use, a given user could log in only once on the LAN.

USE OF GROUPS

I have talked mostly about user accounts in Windows 2000. Another type of account proves to be very useful, and that is the group account. Group accounts allow you to assign permissions to several users at one time and therefore prevent you from having to assign permissions frequently. After permissions have been assigned to a group, giving users access to resources is as simple as adding them to the group.

PART

VI

CH

32

Just as there are local user accounts and global user accounts, there are local groups and global groups. The same properties apply to group accounts as they do to user accounts. Local groups are local to the machine that they are created on; global groups are valid throughout the domain.

Before I discuss the default groups and what rights they grant to users who are members of the groups, I should discuss how the groups themselves are assigned the rights. When you open the Local Security Policy, you can view the list of rights available for assignment and which groups have been assigned those rights, as you can see in Figure 32.13.

To view and edit local user rights, follow these steps:

1. Open the Microsoft Management Console.
2. Navigate to Local Policies, User Rights Assignment. All your choices are shown on the right side of the screen.
3. To make changes, double-click the right you want to edit.

The available user rights are generally pretty descriptive. Keep in mind, though, you're generally better off leaving them at their default settings.

If you decide you want to make changes to the user rights, you can do so by double-clicking the right you want to change. You then see a listing of what users or groups are currently granted that right, as shown in Figure 32.14.

Figure 32.13
The Local Security Policy snap-in of the Microsoft Management Console allows you to view and edit local user rights assignments.

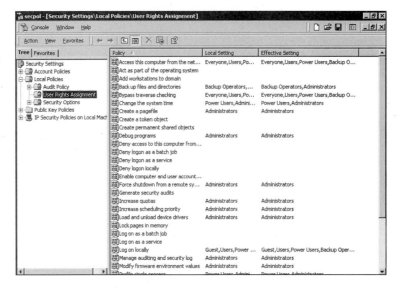

Figure 32.14
You can view groups or users who have been granted specific rights, and you also can add or remove users or groups from this list by unchecking the appropriate check box.

LOCAL GROUPS

The best practice of assigning permissions to resources is to assign them to local groups. You can then place global groups, global users, and local users into those local groups that permissions are assigned to. Your Windows 2000 Professional computer has several default groups available for you to use; they are shown in Figure 32.15.

The default groups included with Windows 2000 Professional are Administrators, Backup Operators, Guests, Power Users, Replicator, and Users. The following sections describe the default groups so that you can see what you have to work with out of the box.

Figure 32.15
Using the Computer Management tool, you can add, remove, or edit local groups. Groups are used to combine similar users and make applying security and permissions a less daunting task.

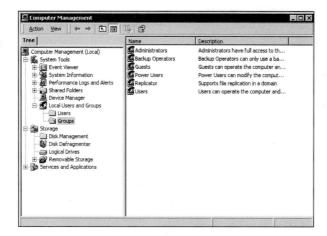

ADMINISTRATORS LOCAL GROUP

The Administrators group is, by default, assigned full permissions to administer the local computer. Remember the discussion earlier that you should not log in to your computer as Administrator? You should also not assign any users to the Administrators group unless that user account will be used only for administrative purposes. Any user account that belongs to the Administrators group is also considered by Windows 2000 to be a "benevolent ruler."

BACKUP OPERATORS LOCAL GROUP

The Backup Operators group gives its members permissions to back up the local computer. This group has interesting permissions, in that even though users belonging to this group might not have access to read or even view certain resources, they still have permission to back them up. There is a caveat, though: These users must do so using a backup program; they can't just copy the files to another location. Windows 2000 Professional includes a backup system utility that you can use to safeguard your data. (Backup is covered in Chapter 33, "Managing the Hard Disk.")

By default, no users are included in the Backup Operators group. I suggest that you create a special user account to perform backups with and add that account to the Backup Operators group. You could get by with adding your personal user account, but in my opinion, you can never be too careful when it comes to computer security. Also, don't forget that you can specify certain programs to be run using a different user account. The addition of this feature makes it even more logical to create a special backup account and to specify that your backup program be run using that account.

GUEST LOCAL GROUP

The Guest group is a local group that has very limited access to the computer. If you remember the discussion of the Guest local user and what you can do with that account, you should realize that the Guest local group is the place where the Guest user account gets it privileges (or lack thereof). Any user account that you add to this group then has the same permissions and rights that the Guest user has. The Guest user can operate the computer and save documents, but cannot make changes to the computer or install software. This is a good group to add users to if they need to do some word processing and would like to use your computer, but if they are normal users of your computer, they would be better suited as members of the Users group.

POWER USERS LOCAL GROUP

Now comes the fun part: the Power Users local group. User accounts in this group basically have permissions to make any changes to the computer, install software, and do all the things that normal users can do as well. The Power Users group does not give members the permission to read or access other users' files or directories. Many people assign their own user accounts as members of the Power Users group so that they can fully administer their computer while they are logged in with their personal account. You should realize that the main difference between a Power User and the Administrator is that the Administrator can view and edit documents that belong to other users, and a Power User cannot. Members of the Power Users group can change system settings and files, so the same security holes apply to them as apply to the Administrator user or members of the Administrators group. Again, I generally assume that there is no such thing as too much security. If you want to be as secure as possible, create a user account that you will use to install software and make system changes with. Then, when you need to run a setup program or make changes with a Control Panel applet, use the Run As feature and specify that privileged account.

REPLICATOR LOCAL GROUP

The Replicator local group is designed for accounts that manage the replication service in a domain. The replication service runs among Windows 2000 Server computers and can include Windows 2000 Professional computers. Traditionally, the replication service is used to keep synchronized copies of logon scripts and security policies on all domain controllers. With replication in place, it does not matter what domain controller validates your login; you get the same script and policy every time. The replication service works by specifying export computers and which directories they export, and specifying import computers and which directories they import to. You should use this local group only when your computer is a member of a domain, and you should always contact your system administrator before trying to set up file replication with your computer. If you do need to use this local group, you should create a specific user account to place in the Replicator group; it should never be an actual user's account.

USERS LOCAL GROUP

The Users local group is the place where most of your actual user accounts should reside. In fact, when you create a new user account, it is automatically assigned as a member of the Users local group. Members of this group can fully use the computer but cannot make system changes (such as adding a local printer or sharing directories).

CUSTOM LOCAL GROUPS

In addition to these built-in local groups, you can create your own custom local groups. Follow these steps to create a local group:

1. Open the Computer Management snap-in of the Microsoft Management Console. To do so, choose Start, Programs, Administrative Tools, Computer Management.

2. Select Local Users and Groups from the right window.

3. Select the Groups folder in either the right or left window.

4. Choose Action, New Group to bring up the New Group dialog box.

5. Type a name for the group in the Group name text box.

6. Type a description in the Description text box.

7. You can add members at this time by clicking the Add button, or you can add them later.

8. When you're finished, click Close.

GROUPS USED IN A WORKGROUP ENVIRONMENT

Now that you have a grasp on groups in general and how they grant permissions and rights to users, let's take a look at how groups can benefit you in a workgroup LAN environment.

Because a workgroup LAN uses the distributed security model, all groups used are local groups. (No central security exists, so you cannot have any central groups.) This means that groups that must cross machines must be replicated on each individual machine. To put it bluntly, this is a lot of work. My suggestion for a small business with a workgroup-based LAN is to find one of your more powerful computers and turn it into a "poor man's server." I don't mean that the computer needs to volunteer time at a soup kitchen; I mean that, even though the computer is used as a workstation for one person, it is also used as a central storage place for shared files. Using the computer this way remedies the problem of having to create multiple groups on multiple machines.

To set up a "poor man's server," follow these steps:

1. Place a shared directory on the selected computer, and give it a meaningful name, such as Share.

2. Evaluate users' needs for accessing the share.point. It is best to divide users into groups by the access they need.

3. Create local groups that correspond to each type of access users need.

Computer number 1 is a prime candidate for the pseudo server. You can begin by placing a shared directory on this computer for central file storage. For simplicity's sake, you can call it Share. Now that you have a shared directory, you must evaluate other users' needs for access to the share. User 1, User 6, and User 11 are all working on a Merit Pay project together. They want to share files related to this project, and because it concerns compensation, other users should not have access to these files. No problem. You can just create a local group on computer number 1, call it Pay, and add the appropriate users to the group. Figure 32.16 illustrates this process.

Figure 32.16
At the top of the dialog box, notice the drop-down menu labeled Look In. In the drop-down box, the default choice is the local machine, but you can select the workgroup that you belong to and choose users from the workgroup.

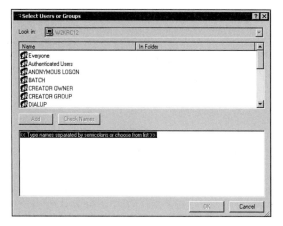

After you assign the appropriate users to the Pay local group, all you must do is assign the appropriate permissions to the shared resources, as discussed earlier in this chapter.

DOMAIN AND GLOBAL GROUPS

If your computer belongs to a domain LAN, you also have global groups to work with. Global groups are created by the LAN administrator and are effective throughout the domain LAN. You probably don't have to worry about assigning permissions to global groups or adding members to them. However, you should realize that if you act as a local administrator of your machine, you might be asked to add a global group to one of your local groups to allow access to your resources.

It is also important to understand that many global groups are automatically assigned as members of your local groups. For example, when you join a domain, the Domain Admins global group is automatically added to the local Administrators group. Also, the Domain users global group is added to the local users group on your machine because, in a domain environment, all global users are allowed access to all domain member computers. This process works from global to local, but not the other way around. Just because you belong to the local administrators group and can administer your computer does not mean you are made a member of the Domain Admins group and allowed to administer the domain. In the same manner, you can have a local user account that does not have access to any other machine on the network because it is not a domain user account.

In a domain environment, you should not use any local user accounts if you can help it. You should be assigned a global domain user account by your system administrator, and that account can be placed in any local group on any member computer. This way, you have user access to all domain members and can also be granted special access to specific member computers. Having this access also eases the administrative load on your LAN administrator.

TROUBLESHOOTING

USERS CANNOT ACCESS SHARED RESOURCE

Share permissions are set up with Everyone to have Full Control. The users get a message telling them they don't have permission to access the folder.

Check to make sure that NTFS permissions are not overriding share permissions on the shared resource. Remember, between the two types of permissions, the most restrictive permission is applied.

LOGON SCRIPTS WON'T RUN

I have set up logon scripts for the all users of my machine, but they run only when I log on.

Make certain that you have specified the logon script properly in the Profile tab of each user account.

Make certain that the logon scripts are stored in the proper directory (%SYSTEMROOT%\System32\Repl\Import\Scripts), and make certain that all users have at least Read and Execute permission to the directory.

A USER HAS ACCESS TO A RESTRICTED OBJECT

A user in the Users local group has access to an object that the Users local group is not assigned permissions for.

Check to see whether the user belongs to any other groups that have been assigned permissions. Remember that permissions accumulate through groups.

TIPS FROM THE WINDOWS PROS: ADDITIONAL SECURITY MEASURES

When speaking of security with your computer, you already know that I am a firm believer in locking things down. For example, when you try to log on to your computer, it automatically displays the username of the last person to log on. To me, because access to the computer is controlled by username and password, it seems silly to give people half of your combination. Also, I generally display a legal notice to all potential users that says "Do not attempt to log on unless you are an authorized user."

You can take care of both of these items in the same spot. To disable the username display, you must navigate to the Local Security Policy and change the Do Not Display Last User Name in Logon Screen option.

You can edit the legal notice text by changing the Message Text for Users Attempting to Logon and the Message Title for Users Attempting to Logon, as shown in Figure 32.17.

Figure 32.17
The Local Security Policy allows you to make your Windows 2000 computer even more secure by not displaying the last user to log on and by displaying a legal notice before logon.

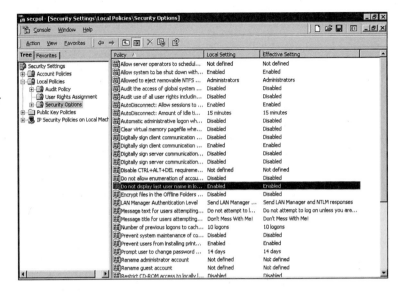

Another way to tighten the security of your workstation is to use the System Policy Editor to make Registry changes. The local system policy works the same in Windows 2000 as it does in Windows NT 4.0. However, with Windows 2000, you'll find an additional policy called Group Policies. If you are on a Windows 2000 Server-based network, contact your system administrator before trying to make changes to your local policy. If group policies are enabled and in use, your local system policy will be overwritten. Also, note that if you are part of a Windows NT 4.0 Server-based network that had a system policy, your local policy settings will be overwritten.

To run the Local Policy Editor, do the following:

1. Choose Start, Run and type poledit to bring up the System Policy Editor.

2. Choose File, New Policy to begin editing a new system policy. Notice that two objects appear in the policy: Default Computer and Default User.

3. Double-click either of these objects to see the options that you can specify.

Note

When you're working in the Policy Editor, it is important to understand what the check boxes mean and how to turn them on and off. An empty (white) check box means that the policy setting will not be applied, and if it is applied already, it will be reversed. A gray check box means that the policy will not be applied, but if it is already there, it will be left alone. A checked check box means that no matter what the setting is, by default, the policy setting will be applied.

When you're working with policies, you should remember that if you make changes to the default user and default computer objects, they will propagate to all the users! Be careful not to lock yourself out of anything. My suggestion is to create a new object in the system policy that corresponds with your username, and then make sure that this system policy is unrestricted. Then you can lock down the default user object without denying yourself access to anything.

To create a personal object in the Policy Editor, follow these steps:

1. Start the Policy Editor.
2. Choose Edit, Add User.
3. Type your username, or click the Browse button to find it.
4. After you create the object, uncheck all the option boxes.

One of my favorite things to lock down on my computer is the Display Control Panel. With it locked down, users cannot make changes to display settings.

Do the following to lock users out of the Display Control Panel:

1. Open the Policy Editor.
2. Double-click the default user object.
3. Click the plus sign next to Control Panel; then click the plus sign next to Display.
4. Check the Restrict Display check box so that a check mark is visible. (See the note on setting policies to make sure you receive the desired results.)
5. Choose from the options dictating how much of the Display Control Panel is locked out.

PART

VI

CH

32

CHAPTER 33

MANAGING THE HARD DISK

In this chapter

HARD DISK MANAGEMENT

For many users and system administrators, intelligent hard disk management forms the core of efficient system management. Until a new technology evolves to replace the hard disk, we're stuck with the problems and limitations created by what is in a sense a crude system of motors, spinning platters, and very delicate parts such as read/write heads floating just microns above a flying surface that can be easily ruined by particles as small as those found in a puff of cigarette smoke. Perhaps some day hard disks will be relics of the past, bookends, like the 5MB drives I have on my bookshelf. (They make good doorstops, too.) Until that time, though, we're stuck with the peculiar vagaries of hard disks. The good news is that high-capacity drives are cheap and plentiful these days.

No doubt, the vast majority of Windows 2000 Professional users will never set up RAID arrays, multiple-booting arrangements, or dynamic disks; use encryption; or need to do any remote disk administration. Perhaps they will perform occasional disk cleanups and defragmenting as well as learn to share folders over the network. These tasks are enough to get by with. Yet, with a bit more knowledge gleaned by reading through this chapter, you will learn how extensive Windows 2000 Professional's hard disk configuration capabilities are.

> **Note**
>
> RAID is short for *redundant array of independent (or inexpensive) disks*. In this hard disk scheme, two or more drives are connected for higher fault tolerance and performance. RAID arrangements are used frequently on servers but aren't generally necessary for personal computers.

This chapter describes the following:

- Using Windows 2000 Professional's disk management tools
- Learning organizational strategies for arranging files and partitions on your hard disk
- Working with the supplied Disk Manager snap-in
- Managing removable storage
- Defragmenting and repairing your drives
- Converting NTFS
- Compressing files
- Encrypting files
- Freeing up space
- Backing up your data
- Using third-party file system tools
- Troubleshooting hard disk problems

WINDOWS 2000 FILE AND STORAGE SYSTEMS

The following sections describe this new dynamic storage model, its benefits, and its drawbacks. You'll also learn about the features and advantages of NTFS5.

Windows 2000 introduces a new concept in storage models, which Microsoft terms *dynamic storage*. Although the old, familiar models of partitions and drives are still supported by Windows 2000, upgrading your hard disk to this new storage type brings with it a new way of thinking about partitions and how they are organized.

> **Caution**
>
> Converting a hard disk to dynamic storage is a one-way process. The only way to change a dynamic disk back to a basic disk is to repartition the drive. Also, note that dynamic disks can be read only by Windows 2000, and they aren't available on portable computers. When you change the disks to dynamic, you can no longer multiboot into another operating system because the familiar boot loader screen disappears for good.

DYNAMIC STORAGE

I can best explain dynamic storage by comparing it to previous methods of structuring a hard disk.

The traditional storage model of disk structure used partition tables. Each hard drive could hold one *primary partition* and one *extended (secondary) partition*. Within this extended partition, you created logical drives. This disk structure is understood and can be accessed by MS-DOS, Windows, and all versions of Windows NT up to release 4.0. The annoyances and limitations of this partition table methodology are artifacts of Microsoft operating systems, incidentally, not something imposed by hard disks themselves or their manufacturers. Some other operating systems don't suffer the same peculiarities.

> **Note**
>
> Storage types are separate from the file systems they contain. Both basic and dynamic disks can contain any combination of FAT16, FAT32, NTFS4, or NTFS5 partitions or volumes.

Dynamic storage is supported only by Windows 2000. With dynamic storage, the restraints of primary and extended partitions are gone. Under this storage model, free space on a hard drive is divided into volumes instead of partitions, and these volumes can be noncontiguous and span one or more disks. In addition, on Windows 2000 Servers, volumes on a dynamic disk can be configured as simple, spanned, mirrored, striped, or RAID-5.

- A *simple* volume uses free space available on a single disk. This space can be a single contiguous region or multiple concatenated regions. Under the basic storage model used by MS-DOS, each partition or logical drive is assigned a separate and distinct drive letter and functions as a distinct region of disk space. Dynamic storage can be configured to see multiple regions of a disk as a single volume, accessed with a single assigned drive letter.

- A *spanned* volume takes the concept of a simple volume and extends it across multiple disks (up to a maximum of 32). All joined regions on these disks are seen as a single volume to programs accessing them.

- A *mirrored* volume is a volume in which data from one disk is mirrored or duplicated on a second disk. This process provides for data redundancy, often called *fault tolerance*. If one disk fails, the data can be accessed from the second disk. A mirrored volume cannot be spanned; each volume must be contained on a single disk. Programs see only one volume, and Windows 2000 ensures that both disks are kept in sync. *Mirroring* is also known in the industry as *RAID-1*.

- A *striped* volume is a volume in which data is stored across two or more physical disks. When data is written to a striped volume space, it is allocated alternately and evenly to each of the physical disks. A striped volume cannot be mirrored or spanned. *Striping* is often termed *RAID-0*. Striping is used to increase storage system throughput.

- A *RAID-5* volume is a combination of a mirrored volume and a striped volume. When data is written to a RAID-5 volume, it is striped across an array of three or more disks, and a parity value is added. If a hard disk belonging to a RAID-5 volume fails, the data can be re-created by the remaining drives using this parity value. Note the difference here between a mirrored volume and a RAID-5 volume.

Note

A mirrored volume contains two disks; if either one fails, the operating system goes to the other for data access.

A RAID-5 volume contains three or more disks, any of which can fail, without the system halting. The operating system then reconstructs the missing data from the information contained on the remaining disks.

What are the advantages of dynamic storage?

- First and foremost, noncontiguous regions of multiple disks can be linked so that they appear as one large region of disk space to any program running under Windows 2000. By linking them, you can increase the size of a disk volume on-the-fly, without reformatting or having to cope with multiple drive letters.

- Second, and perhaps more important from an administrator's point of view, disk and volume management can be performed without restarting the operating system.

Note

Dynamic drive schemes are not available in portable computers.

The catch to all this is that you must be pretty much a "Windows 2000-only" shop; all systems that you want to implement these advanced technologies must be running some incarnation of Windows 2000. The exception to this rule is computers that simply need access servers over a network. Such computers don't care about the nature of the host system. For example, Windows 98 machines could access a Windows 2000 Server sharing a spanned volume or RAID array. The Windows 98 machines don't know that the logical drives or folders being accessed physically span multiple drives or partitions.

ORGANIZATIONAL STRATEGIES

Although the disk systems described in the preceding section are interesting, especially to power users and system administrators who have multiple drives available, most Windows 2000 users will end up setting up their systems with standard partitions and the NTFS file format. But what about other file systems? How should you organize multiple disks? What about preparing your disks, and what kinds of strategies should you consider?

If you're not going to stick with the straight and narrow of running only NTFS on your hard disk, consider these alternative strategies and rules to follow:

- Whenever possible, create a separate partition for your data files. This tip has particular relevance to users who test new software or operating systems. If you store your data on a separate partition, reinstalling an operating system is a simple matter of formatting your system partition and starting from scratch. Although you still must reinstall your programs, using a separate data partition eliminates the need to fuss and ensures you didn't miss a data file somewhere along the line. It also makes backups simple and straightforward. You can do one backup of your system partition; you then need to update this backup only when you add a new device or software program. Data backups can be run on a daily or weekly basis (as determined by how often your data changes) and set to run on your data partition.

Tip #392	When you have a data partition in place, right-click the My Documents icon on your desktop, select Properties, and reset the target folder location to your data partition. Resetting it ensures that all your favorites, application settings, and history files are also kept separate from the system partition. (Windows 2000 domain network users with roaming user profiles have less to worry about on this score, as their My Documents files are copied to the domain server as well as to their local computer.)

PART

VI

CH

33

- Buy a disk image program (such programs are discussed toward the end of this chapter). You can purchase one for less than $50, and it is worth its weight in gold if you like to "tinker" with your system and program configurations. After you have your operating system set up, your principle applications installed, and everything tweaked and configured to perfection, you can create an image of your system on a separate drive or partition. If you need to reinstall your operating system for whatever reason, the complete process—from beginning to end—should take no more than 20 minutes. Couple this program with the separate data partition discussed in the preceding bullet, and you have a system that you can rebuild from scratch with minimal effort or time loss.

When you add, delete, or reconfigure a program, be sure to update your disk image.

Some clients I know have gone so far as to buy and install a separate hard drive just for image storage. At $150 or less for a 6GB drive, a hard drive is probably one of the best investments in crash protection you can buy. As a matter of fact, I'm considering making dedicated image drives a standard system configuration for all computers I sell and maintain.

- If you have more than two IDE hard drives, put both drives on your primary IDE controller and your CD-ROM on the secondary controller. Configuring a system this way puts all the strain on one IDE bus when copying data from drive to drive, but mixing a CD-ROM drive and a hard disk on the same channel is worse. CD-ROM drives transfer data at a much slower rate than hard disks. Mixing fast and slow devices on the same controller forces the controller to run at the slower of the two rates. If you really want good performance with complex drive scenarios (multiple hard disks and CD-R or CD-RW), I suggest that you look into SCSI controllers.

- If you want to install Windows 98 and Windows 2000 in a dual-boot configuration, begin by creating a primary partition for Windows 98 at the head of your drive. Devote the balance of the drive to an extended partition with at least two logical drives: one for Windows 2000 and one for data. Then format the boot drive and the first logical drive (D:) as FAT 32; leave the last logical drive alone for the moment.

Note

To learn more details about setting your computer to dual-boot Windows 2000 and a second operating system, see Chapter 34, "OS Mix and Match." Also, see "Dual Booting Versus Single Booting," in Chapter 4, "Installing Windows 2000."

I suggest this arrangement and format for these reasons:

- FAT32 uses a smaller cluster size than FAT16, so it is a more efficient partition format.

- Windows 98 cannot natively "see" or read an NTFS partition. So, if you want Windows 98 and Windows 2000 to coexist on the same drive, and you want to format your Windows 2000 partition as NTFS (which I recommend), you need to install Windows 98 on the primary boot partition.

- I highly recommend using a separate partition for data. Putting this partition in the middle of your drive reduces the distance your drive heads must move to find a file.

- Windows 2000 can exist anywhere, so given the preceding constraints, this operating system logically gets installed on the third and last partition.

- Set up this way, both operating systems can access the same data files stored on the middle partition. Windows 98 uses the FAT32 format natively, and Windows 2000 can read FAT32 natively.

Note

Remember, however, that although this scheme is convenient in a dual-boot situation, it has its limitations. Neither FAT16 nor FAT32 supports file access security, encryption, or quotas—significant issues for business users. The use of FAT short-circuits most of Windows 2000's security features.

WINDOWS 2000'S DISK MANAGEMENT TOOLS

Windows 2000 comes equipped with a handful of disk management tools, ranging from very powerful ones that can create hard disk stripe sets, create mirror disks, and/or beat it into submission to a couple that are simply convenience items.

The most often-used tools are available right off the Tools tab of a drive's Properties sheet. To reach the Properties sheet, right-click a drive in Explorer. Figure 33.1 shows the Properties tabs for both a FAT drive and an NTFS drive. Notice the difference in the number of tabs. NTFS has more options because of its support for security and quota management.

Figure 33.1
Properties sheets for FAT and NTFS volumes.

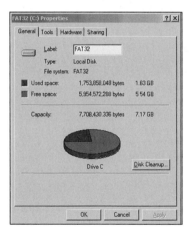
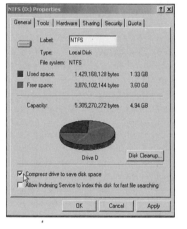

The following sections explain the use of the bulk of hard disk management tools included in Windows 2000 Professional and some of the theory behind the updates that Windows 2000 provides over NT 4.

DISK MANAGER

The familiar standalone Disk Administrator program from NT 4 is gone in Windows 2000, replaced by a Microsoft Management Console (MMC) snap-in contained within the Computer Management program. The Disk Manager in Windows 2000 is responsible for the creation, deletion, alteration, and maintenance of storage volumes in a system. Using the Disk Manager, you also can assign the drive letters used by your CD and hard disk drives.

Figure 33.2 shows the MMC program with the Disk Manager snap-in.

Figure 33.2
The Microsoft
Management Console
has a snap-in for disk
administration that
replaces the NT Disk
Manager program.

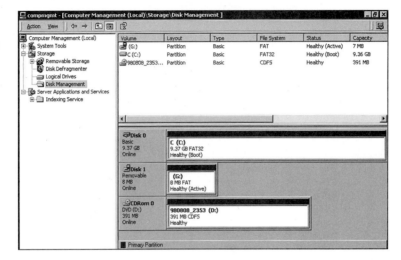

To maintain and configure your storage devices, choose Start, Programs, Administrative Tools, Computer Management. Another means is to right-click My Computer and choose Manage.

→ To learn more details about the Microsoft Management Console and Computer Management, **see** "Microsoft Management Console (MMC)," **p. 1161**.

Tip #393

If the Administrative Tools menu selection is missing from your menu, go to the Start menu and select Settings, Taskbar & Start Menu. On the Advanced tab, go to the Setting window at the bottom of the dialog, and select Display Administrative Tools.

As you know from the discussion in Chapter 31, "System Management and Configuration Tools," this single interface lets you manage both local and remote computers using the various administration utilities shown in the left pane. Using this interface, I will show you how to perform different procedures on your existing and new hard disks. The process is quite simple for most of the operations because you will be presented with a wizard to complete them.

Most operations on disks can be performed by right-clicking the disk or volume you want to affect. As usual, you are presented with a context-sensitive menu from which you can perform any actions relating to the volume or disk you clicked. You can also see, from the graphical layout in the Disk Manager, just what is going on with your disks at any given time. As always, you can select the Help option from within any menu to get an explanation of the operations available to you.

Tip #394

> You can change the way specific types of volumes are displayed in the Disk Manager MMC plug-in by clicking the Settings button at the end of the MMC toolbar. From there, you can select the color you would like to use to represent any of the various disk states that will be shown by the Disk Manager. You can also change the way in which the Disk Manager shows the scaling of each disk. This capability is particularly useful if you would like the scale display to be more representative of the actual physical sizes of your disks. By selecting the Scaling tab from the View Settings dialog, you can change the behavior of the GUI to suit your particular tastes.

ASSIGNING DRIVE LETTERS AND JOINING VOLUMES

Using the Disk Manager, you can easily assign logical drive letters to your hard disks and removable drives such as CD-ROMs. You can't change the drive letter of your boot drive (usually the C: drive), but you can change any of the others.

To change the letter, right-click the disk volume or drive in the bottom-right pane of the Disk Manager, and select Change Drive Letter and Path. A dialog box appears, listing the current drive letter assignment. Click Edit. Under Assign a Drive Letter, choose the desired new letter. Click OK and confirm that you really do want to make the change.

The "Path" part of "Change Drive Letter and Path" is new to Windows 2000. In addition to or instead of assigning a drive letter to a disk drive or partition, you can "graft" the disk volume onto another. Windows lets you specify a folder that will become the mount point for the new drive. For example, I might create a folder named C:\TEMP. Because I want lots of space for it, I can install a new hard drive and, instead of assigning it a drive letter, tell Windows to access it through C:\TEMP. My C:\TEMP files and subfolders are then stored on the alternate drive.

Tip #395

> By using a mount point, you can add space to a hard drive that is available just to the folders under the mount point folder. This is a good way to add space in a controlled fashion for a specific purpose, such as storing scratch files or Web page images.

GRAFTING VERSUS DYNAMIC DISKS

Assigning mount points is different from what happens when you aggregate dynamic disks into one large volume. Although dynamic disks and regular disks (simple disks) both support the use of mount points, dynamic disks can create one large, apparently contiguous disk space. Mount points graft subsequently added drives at a folder, sort of like grafting two trees by tying together a branch from each tree. Figures 33.3 and 33.4 illustrate the differences between the two approaches.

Note

> You can graft new volumes or disks onto a folder only on an NTFS-formatted drive. The new volume can have any format, however.

PART

VI

CH

33

Figure 33.3
You can join drives two different ways. Using mount points is one way, and using dynamic disk aggregation is another.

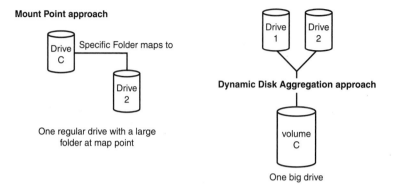

Figure 33.4
Assigning a partition or volume to a folder rather than (or, in addition to) a drive letter joins the volume to an existing volume. The contents of the added volume appear as subdirectories of the mount point folder.

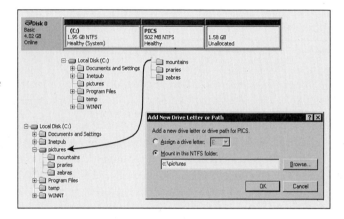

If the folder you specify as the mount point already contains files, they are inaccessible as long as the drive-to-path mapping exists because that folder is now remapped into the new location. The original files reappear if you delete the drive path.

Even if you have several hard drives and CD-ROM drives, you can graft them all together onto your C: drive, making it look like one big file system. It's a great management concept: You can add space to your file system by attaching new disk volumes right into the original folder structure. (UNIX users are probably smirking at this point because the UNIX operating system has worked this way since it was written in the 1970s.)

To graft a disk volume to an existing file system, follow these steps:

1. Create the folder that is to serve as the mount point for the new drive or volume.

2. Highlight the new drive or volume in Disk Management.

3. Right-click Change Drive Letter and Path, and click Add.

4. Select Mount in This NTFS Folder.

5. Enter the folder's pathname, or click Browse to locate it.

6. Click OK to save the path.

Tip #396

When Explorer shows you free disk space on the original drive, it measures only the space on the physical drive, not space on any grafted drives. You'll actually have more space than you think because files on the grafted folders are stored on another volume. If you want, you can also assign a drive letter to the added volume so that you can view and monitor its free space directly.

Alternatively, you can use the command prompt, change to the folder in the grafted volume, and use the DIR command. The DIR command lists free space on the actual current volume.

You can assign a given drive or volume to at most one drive letter, but an arbitrary number of paths. (It's a little bit strange to see the same files appear in several different places, so I recommend that you not go nuts with this feature.)

Tip #397

If you're running out of room on your C: drive, see whether it makes sense in your situation to add lots of space to just one folder (for example, My Documents). If it does, install and format a new hard drive, and assign it a letter. Copy the original folder to the new drive. Then add a path to the new hard drive using the name of the original folder. This way, you can preserve your original data and have lots of room for growth.

By the way, this "grafting" technique works with both basic and dynamic NTFS disks. Only Windows dynamic disks can be "grown" by changing their partition size on-the-fly. If you use a basic-formatted disk, as most users do, the grafting trick is a good one to know.

Tip #398

Another good time to use this feature is when you've backed up application data onto a CD-R or CD-RW. If you want to use the backed-up data in an emergency, you can add a path for your CD-ROM drive to make its files appear in the original data location expected by your application. That way, you can use the data off the CD-R without restoring it to disk or reconfiguring your application. Later, you can delete the path to regain access to the "real" folder.

PART

VI

CH

33

DYNAMIC DISK MANAGEMENT

If you've just installed Windows 2000 Professional, you'll be asked, upon launching the disk administration tool, whether you want to upgrade to dynamic disks. Upgrading is usually the best way to go because of the many advantages of the new dynamic disk storage system. Remember, though, that you can't boot into or read your dynamic disks from any other operating system after you upgrade them. This trade-off is certainly worthwhile for stand-alone Windows 2000 systems but not if you plan on using other systems. For some explanation of the benefits of using dynamic disks, see the section "Windows 2000 File and Storage Systems" earlier in this chapter.

If you're not presented with the option to upgrade to dynamic disks upon launching the Disk Manager from the MMC, don't fret. You can upgrade a disk by running Disk Management, right-clicking the drive's icon in the bottom pane (click the part of the graphical display that reads "Disk 0," "Disk 1," and so on, not on the volume), and choosing Upgrade to Dynamic Disk. Then choose the disk and click OK. Next, just follow the wizard, and you'll be set.

> **Caution**
>
> Don't upgrade to dynamic disks until you read all the material here on the topic and review the Help system's coverage of it in the Disk Manager. As you learned earlier in this chapter, dynamic disks cannot be changed back to basic disks without completely destroying any partitions and reformatting the disk. If you must do that, right-click the volume and select Delete Volume. From there, you can just re-create your simple volume by right-clicking a disk and going through the applicable wizard. Also, remember that other operating systems such as Windows 9x and DOS can't use dynamic disks, so if you intend to multiboot your machine, you should not upgrade the drive.

If you don't seem to have the option of upgrading to dynamic disks, one of two possible reasons might be the cause. First, the disks may have already been upgraded to dynamic disks. Second, if you're using a laptop, you cannot use dynamic disks because they are not supported on portable computers.

> **Note**
>
> You cannot install Windows 2000 onto a dynamic disk partition that you've added to a dynamic disk. This is a limitation of the Windows 2000 Setup program in that it needs to see a partition table in order to install onto the disk. Disk partitions created from a dynamic disk do not contain partition tables and as such cannot be utilized by Setup. The only types of disks that contain partition tables are simple disks and dynamic disks that were upgraded from simple disks.

EXTENDING A DISK

One of the really cool options available in the Disk Manager is the option to extend a disk. Extending is really just another way of "stretching" a simple volume to a specified size when unallocated space is present on the disk. Sometimes you might want to rearrange the way you've set up your disks, so this option can come in very handy.

To perform the actual extend operation on a disk, you need to have an area of the disk that is unallocated. From there, you simply right-click an existing partition and select Extend Volume to bring up the Extend Volume Wizard. The wizard allows you to specify the size that you would like to extend the volume to. Finishing the operation leaves you with a disk that is now larger than before. This operation is not limited to volumes that are mounted as drive letters. You can also perform this task on volumes that are mounted into directories. Figure 33.5 shows the Disk Manager's view of an extended volume.

Figure 33.5
The Disk Manager view of an extended volume. Note that the drive letter is the same on both partitions.

When the Disk Manager extends a disk, it is really just creating a new partition and mapping it to the same drive letter of the partition to be extended. It is, in effect, a spanned volume. Although this approach is a bit different from the traditional method performed by disk utilities such as PartitionMagic, the upside of the Disk Manager approach is that you can extend your disk without having to wait for the volume to be resized and data to be shuffled around. The Disk Manager approach happens very quickly without even rebooting your system.

CREATING A SPANNED VOLUME

A spanned volume is a volume in which the disk space spans multiple partitions and/or disks. Using a spanned volume is a very handy way of taking a couple of small disks and turning them into one large disk, mounted under one drive letter or folder. Simple volumes can also be extended using spanned volumes, as shown in the previous section. Spanned volumes can be created only on dynamic disks.

Creating a spanned volume is a matter of right-clicking an empty partition and selecting Create Volume, which opens the Create Volume Wizard. This wizard enables you to select the spanned volume option. Next, you are given the option to select which disks to include in your spanned volume. At this point, you also can select the amount of space to use for each disk. The total size of your spanned volume is the cumulative total of the space you select on each disk, as shown in Figure 33.6.

Figure 33.6
Selecting the combined disks and partition sizes for a spanned volume in the Create Volume Wizard.

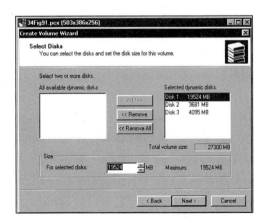

Finally, you are prompted for the mount point and the format for your new spanned volume.

CREATING A STRIPED VOLUME

One of the procedures you can perform with the Disk Manager is creating a striped volume. Creating such a volume is often desirable simply because of the ease of administration as well as the substantial speed gain to be had. Creating a striped volume is really practical only if you're using more than one disk. In fact, you do have to use more than one disk. For the definition of a striped volume, see "Dynamic Storage" earlier in this chapter.

Note

Unfortunately for users, Microsoft decided to leave out the option to create RAID sets from Windows 2000 Professional. This option, as well as mirroring, is included only in the Server, Advanced Server, and Data Center versions of Windows 2000. You are not precluded from using a hardware-based RAID controller with Windows 2000 Professional, however. In devices such as these, the BIOS is used to set up the RAID options, thereby bypassing the operating system.

Note that you can use the Disk Manager in Windows 2000 Professional to manage or create RAID or mirrored sets on a remote system, provided the remote system is a server version of Windows 2000. Thus, I've included the instructions for it here.

When you're creating a striped volume, you are creating partitions of the same size across two or more disks. Bear this point in mind as you plan your implementation because you need to have the same amount of space available on each disk that you want to use for your set.

To create a striped volume, follow these steps:

1. Right-click the first disk, and select Create Volume. The Create Volume Wizard opens.

2. Select Create a Striped Volume. Then select Next.

3. Select the disks you want to include as part of a striped volume, as shown in Figure 33.7. The Create Volume Wizard automatically selects the first free disk as the first in the striped volume. The remaining two disks can be selected from the left column and added to the right column to be selected for the set. When you are done adding disks, click Next.

Figure 33.7
Selecting disks for inclusion into a striped volume.

> **Note**
>
> Notice that the wizard automatically sets the size for all selected disks to the largest amount of free space that is equally available on each disk.

4. You then are prompted for the mount point of your new striped set. The three options here bear further explanation:

   - Assign a Drive Letter—This option assigns your set one drive letter like any normal drive. Selecting this option is the most common method of mounting a striped set, and it will also suffice for most purposes.

   - Mount in an Empty Folder—This option is a bit different from anything previously offered in Windows. By mounting a striped set to a folder, you are effectively creating a mount point within another disk. The mount point isn't actually on another disk in the physical sense. The folder you use just has the amount of storage equal to the size of your striped set. This approach is more closely related to the UNIX approach, where the actual drive letter is not used but the folder is referred to as the mount point. (Mount points were discussed earlier in this chapter.)

   - Do Not Assign a Drive Letter or Drive Path—Selecting this option creates the striped set and leaves it for you to allocate at a later time using either of the two methods mentioned previously.

5. Select the volume format options.

6. When you are presented with a summary of the actions to be performed by the wizard, choose the Finish button so that your new striped volume will be created and mounted under the path you chose in step 4.

> **Note**
>
> In the Explorer, notice that the icon for the folder mount point shows up as a hard disk. This icon appears simply so that you can differentiate between a mounted folder and a plain folder.

PART VI

CH 33

RAID and Dynamic Disk Information Storage

When a basic disk is made a member of a mirror, stripe, or RAID set, it's marked (or "signed") with a tiny hidden partition at the end of the disk drive. This partition tells Windows that the disk is a member of a fault-tolerant disk set. The information about the configuration itself—for example, whether a given disk is the primary or secondary disk in a mirror set—is stored in the Registry. If you think about it, you can see that this is not a great place to store this kind of information: If a disk is damaged, Windows might not be able to read the Registry to find the configuration information. That's why you were always exhorted to update your Emergency Boot Disks when you made changes in the old Windows NT Disk Manager; the disk configuration was stored on the emergency disks, too.

For dynamic disks, Windows creates a 4MB partition at the end of each disk drive in which it stores all the configuration information for all the dynamic drives in your computer. This redundant information helps Windows reconstruct a picture of the whole system if any drives are damaged or replaced, and it's another good reason to use dynamic disks over basic when you're building a Windows 2000 Server.

REMOVABLE STORAGE MANAGER

The Removable Storage Manager is another MMC snap-in. Its job is to track and catalog the data stored on removable storage devices. These devices can take the form of tape backup drives, MO drives, JAZ drives, or the changers that control many removable storage devices. The Removable Storage Manager works by allowing you to create *media pools*—collections of media to which the same management properties (such as security permissions or backup routines) apply.

The Removable Storage Manager is another of those "buried" Windows 2000 features that you're not likely to know about unless you know where to look. The best way to access it is through the Computer Management Console. Just open the Control Panel, click Administrative Tools, and then click Computer Management. In the right pane, expand Storage and click Removable Storage. From here, you can create and manage media pools and also get information about the physical locations for media.

> **Note**
>
> If you're not certain whether a given removable device is compatible with Windows 2000, check the Hardware Compatibility List (HCL) at the Microsoft Web site (www.microsoft.com/hcl).

As implemented, the Removable Storage Manager is limited to the small scope of hardware supported under it. But like many other Windows 2000 features (the Indexing Service, for example), it has tremendous potential when third-party vendors develop hooks to its functions and interface. At the moment, it stands as a useful tool to catalog backup media, such as tapes and optical cartridges, but little else.

See "Backup," later in this chapter, for more details about using removable storage management features as an adjunct to your backup strategies.

DISK DEFRAGMENTER

When an operating system stores data on a hard disk, it places that information in the first available "hole" it can find that isn't already occupied by another file. If the disk already contains several other files, however, that location might not be large enough for the complete file. When this happens, the operating system places as much of the file as it can in the space available and then searches for another open hole for the balance of the file. This process continues until the entire file has been written to disk. Any files not written to a contiguous disk location are considered "fragmented."

The problem with fragmentation is that it slows down the rate at which your hard disk can retrieve information and supply it to the requesting program. Hard disks remain largely mechanical devices and are governed by the laws of physics. To access files stored on a disk, the drive must physically move a small arm to the correct location on a spinning platter. These movements are measured in milliseconds, but milliseconds add up, especially when a file is spread over a hundred unique locations.

Fragmentation is not always a bad thing. If an operating system had to find a contiguous section of disk space for each and every file it stored, as your drive filled, your system would slow. Eventually, your system would reach a point where the disk still had ample free space, but none of this space would be in contiguous blocks big enough to hold a file.

Disk Defragmenter addresses this fragmentation problem by reorganizing all the files on your hard disk so that they are stored as complete units on a single area of the disk. To do so, it identifies any remaining free areas, moves small files there to open up more space, and uses this newly opened space to consolidate larger files. This shuffling process repeats until all the files are shuffled around in this manner and the entire disk is defragmented. It's a bit like moving the furniture around in a room in such a way that you can then remove a wall-to-wall carpet.

The MFT

NTFS contains, at its core, a file called the *master file table (MFT)*. It is similar to the file allocation table in the FAT system. At least one entry exists in the MFT for every file on an NTFS volume, including the MFT itself. The MFT also contains extended information about each file, such as its size, time and date stamps, permissions, data content, and so forth.

As you add more files to an NTFS volume, the number of entries to the MFT grows. When files are deleted from an NTFS volume, their MFT entries are marked as free and may be reused, but the MFT does not shrink. Thus, space used by these entries is not reclaimed from the disk.

NTFS preallocates a specific amount of the volume for storage of the MFT and, in an effort to ensure high performance, tries not to fragment it. NTFS also does its best to allocate free space on the disk intelligently. If you are running low on disk space, it relinquishes reserved and unused MFT areas for your files. If the MFT is running low, it grabs space from the file area for more entries. As you would expect, if you have a large number of files, the MFT becomes larger. If you have a small number of files, the MFT is smaller.

Here's the rub: If you try to pack a zillion files onto an NTFS volume (I can't give you an exact number because it will vary based on volume and file size), and you run out of disk space, you could exhaust the MFT, which can result in a major bummer when the directory table for the volume blows up. You get no warning. If you intend to store a huge number of small files on an NTFS partition, and you think you might unexpectedly run out of room on the volume, you should consider a Registry hack that preallocates more room for the MFT by adding a value to the Registry.

Caution: This procedure modifies the Registry. Do I have to remind you to back up the Registry first? If you aren't a Registry whiz already, be sure to read Chapter 35, "The Registry," before trying this operation.

To add this value, perform the following steps:

1. Run the Registry Editor (Regedt32.exe), and go to the following subkey:

   HKEY_LOCAL_MACHINE\System\CurrentControlSet\Control\FileSystem

2. From the Edit menu, choose Add Value.

3. Type the following information in the resulting dialog box:

   Value Name: NtfsMftZoneReservation

   Data Type: REG_DWORD

   Data: (valid range is 1-4)

continues

continued

NtfsMftZoneReservation is a REG_DWORD value that can take on a value between 1 and 4, where 1 corresponds to the minimum MFT zone size and 4 corresponds to the maximum. The sizes are not absolute. You might have to experiment with the sizing to determine what is best for you. Microsoft supplies no specific details about the number of file entries available under each size.

4. Close the Registry Editor, and restart your computer.

Keep in mind that this is a runtime parameter and it does not affect the format of a volume. Rather, it affects the way NTFS allocates space on all volumes on a given system. Therefore, to be completely effective, the parameter must be in effect from the time a volume is formatted throughout the life of the volume.

For more information, check the following URL:

`http://support.microsoft.com/support/kb/articles/Q174/6/19.ASP`

Tip #399

Defragmenting a large drive with many files on it can take a lot of time. This is the kind of process to use the Task Scheduler to handle, running at night when you're not around and don't need access to your hard disk drive.

When should you defragment your drive? In reality, because today's drives are so fast, you're not likely to notice slowdowns unless you're using very large data files, or you use the same files and/or applications regularly, which can fragment them. But for typical users who are hopping around between programs, creating new files, and deleting files on a regular basis, the average access times they experience with a drive will be acceptable, even when fragmented.

If you start to notice a general hard disk access slowdown, the first thing to suspect is a RAM shortage, or that you have too many files open and your drive's pagefile is being hit too much (that is, swapping is going on). After ruling that out, however, take a trip down defrag lane. Run the program, and it will tell you whether your drive is fragmented enough to make it worth your time to defragment.

Until now, the only way to defragment an NT-based system was to purchase a third-party program such as Diskeeper from Executive Software or Speed Disk from Norton Utilities. With Windows 2000, Microsoft has actually bundled in a limited version of Diskeeper, incorporating defragmentation with the operating system. Keep in mind that for professional defragmenting, you should check out the retail version of Diskeeper. It has some advanced functions not found in Windows 2000, such as the following:

- You can schedule unattended defragmenting.
- You can view LAN-based drives to determine their condition and/or need for defragmenting.
- You can set it to defragment large groups of drives across the LAN.

RUNNING DEFRAG

To run Disk Defragmenter, follow these steps:

1. Choose Start, Programs, Accessories, System Tools, Disk Defragmenter. Alternatively, you can right-click a drive in the Explorer and choose Properties. Then click the Tools tab, and choose Defragment Now.

2. Click the drive you want to defragment, and click Analyze. In a few minutes, the result of the analysis will appear. You'll see a screen like the one shown in Figure 33.8.

Figure 33.8
Running Defrag's analysis on a drive indicates whether you would net any advantage from defragmenting.

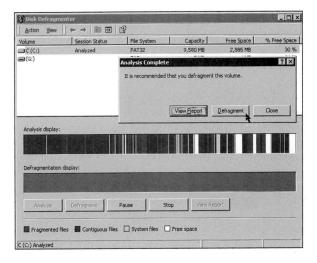

3. Click the View Report button if you're the curious type. You can really get into the numbers here, viewing statistics about the drive, and checking to see where the maximum fragmentation is occurring, the number of fragments, the file sizes, and so on. Figure 33.9 shows an example from my hard disk. You can save the report or print it if you like.

PART
VI
CH
33

Figure 33.9
Details of a defrag analysis can be helpful in determining where most of your fragmentation is occurring. Scroll the top pane, and check to see whether your pagefile is fragmented. Typically, it won't be, but if it is, this is a good reason to defragment.

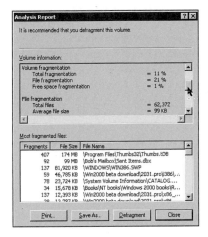

4. If you decide to go ahead and defragment, click the Defragment button and get ready to wait. As the defragmenting progresses, you'll see the progress reported across the bottom graph in the window. The graphic display slowly becomes primarily blue, indicating that most files are now contiguous. You will see some areas of green, indicating system files (possibly a large area if a pagefile is on the drive). You might have some small areas of fragmentation left over as well. Figure 33.10 shows the result of defragmenting an NTFS drive on one of my machines.

Figure 33.10
Results of defragmenting a relatively unpopulated 4GB NTFS partition.

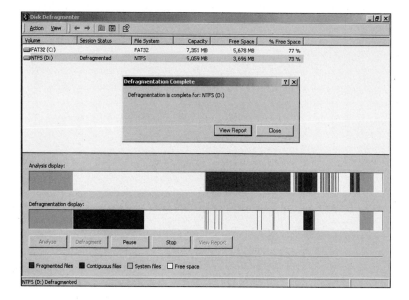

DETECTING AND REPAIRING DISK ERRORS

NTFS was introduced and billed as a "robust and self-healing" file system. All in all, I would have to agree with Microsoft on this one. I have yet to have an NTFS partition go "sour" on me in any way, shape, or form. I've had NTFS partitions that would not boot and key system files that would not run, but for the most part these errors were self-inflicted and usually brought on by playing with fire.

Some other versions of Windows have the ScanDisk program whose job it is to detect and repair the file allocation table (FAT) when you shut down improperly. You also can run it manually from time to time. This program hearkens back to DOS days. From within the Windows 2000 Professional GUI, the replacement program for ScanDisk is called Error Checking.

Tip #400

If you dig a little deeper, you'll find command-line hard disk volume checkers in the %SystemRoot%\System32 directory. They are not called ScanDisk, though, as they were in some previous versions of Windows. Look for chkntfs.exe (for NTFS partitions) and chkdsk.exe (for FAT/FAT32 partitions). For a description of how each works, just add the normal /? switch or see Windows online help. The available commands enable you to turn on or off automatic checking and repair a "dirty" (improperly shut down) drive at bootup.

Error Checking checks the file system for errors and checks the drive for bad sectors (bad spots). To run the program, do the following:

1. In My Computer or the Explorer, right-click the drive you want to check.

2. On the context menu, choose Properties.

3. Click the Tools tab.

4. In the Error-Checking section, click Check Now. A dialog box appears, as shown in Figure 33.11.

Figure 33.11
Checking a disk for errors in the file system and bad spots on the disk.

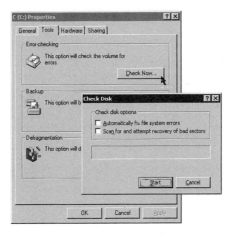

You can run the error check with neither of the option boxes turned on. You are not required to close all open files and programs. However, if you check either of the boxes, you are told that all files must be closed for this process to run. You are given the option of deferring the check until the time you restart your system, however.

The meaning of the options is as follows:

Automatically Fix File System Errors	If file directory errors (for example, lost clusters, files without end-of-file markers, and so on) are found, this option specifies whether the program should fix them.
Scan for and Attempt Recovery of Bad Sectors	This option specifies whether the program should attempt to locate bad sectors, mark them as bad, and recover data from them, writing it in a known good area of the disk. If you select this option, you do not need to select Automatically Fix File System Errors; Windows 2000 fixes any errors on the disk.

Tip #401	If your volume is formatted as NTFS, Windows 2000 automatically logs all file transactions, replaces bad clusters automatically, and stores copies of key information for all files on the NTFS volume.

CONVERT

Convert is a command-line program that converts an existing FAT16 or FAT32 partition to NTFS.

Caution	This conversion process is a one-way street. The only way to revert an NTFS partition back to a FAT partition with the native tools is to reformat the drive. To revert and not lose your data, you must use a program such as PartitionMagic.

The command-line syntax for the Convert program is as follows:

```
CONVERT volume /FS:NTFS [/V]
```

The arguments are as follows:

volume	Specifies the drive letter (followed by a colon), mount point, or volume name
/FS:NTFS	Specifies that the volume is to be converted to NTFS
/V	Specifies that Convert should be run in Verbose mode

Considering the work the Convert program has to do, it's surprisingly fast, even on a well-populated disk.

ENCRYPTION

The Encrypting File System (EFS) provides the core file encryption technology used to store encrypted files on NTFS volumes. When a file is encrypted, the data stored on the hard disk is scrambled in a very secure way. Encryption is transparent to the user who encrypted the file; you do not have to "decrypt" an encrypted file before you can use it. You can work with an encrypted file just as you would any other file; you can open and change the file as necessary. However, any other user or an intruder who tries to access your encrypted files is prevented from doing so. Only the original owner and the computer's designated recovery agent can get into encrypted files. Anyone else receives an Access Denied message when trying to open or copy your encrypted file.

Folders can be marked as encrypted, too. This means that any file created in or copied to an encrypted folder is automatically encrypted. The folder itself isn't encrypted, though. Anyone with the proper file access permissions can see the names of the files in it.

→ To learn more details about recovery agents and how to recover and decrypt files when the username and password of the encryptor have been lost, **see** "Protecting and Recovering Encrypted Files," **p. 1250**.

> **Note**
>
> You can back up an encrypted file without decoding it. If you want to store an encrypted file on a removable disk, use Windows Backup to back up just the desired files to a floppy, zip disk, CD-R, and so on. You must use a Windows-2000 certified backup program to do so.

You encrypt or decrypt a folder or file by setting the encryption property for the folder or file just as you set any other attribute such as read-only, compressed, or hidden (see Figure 33.12).

Figure 33.12
Setting encryption for a specific folder.

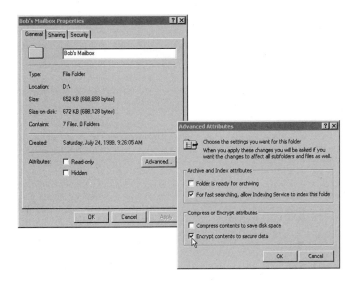

After you set the option to encrypt a folder and click OK on a folder's Properties dialog, you are prompted to confirm the attribute change. From this dialog, you can set the option to encrypt all the subfolders and files within the folder you are encrypting.

It is recommended that you encrypt at the folder level rather than mark individual files so that new files added to the folder will also be encrypted. This point is crucial because most editing programs write a new copy of the file each time you save changes and then delete the original. If the folder containing an encrypted file isn't marked for encryption, too, editing an encrypted file would result in your saving an unencrypted version.

How File Encryption Works

As a kid, you probably played around with simple codes and ciphers in which you exchanged the letters of a message: D for A, E for B, and so on. You might look at this as the process of "adding three" to each letter in your message: Each letter gets bumped to the third next letter in the alphabet. To decode a message, you

continues

continued

subtracted three from every letter to get the original message back. In this code, you could say that the "key" is the number three. Anyone knowing the technique and possessing the key could read and write these secret messages.

Although this example is very simplistic, it illustrates the basic idea of numeric encryption. The cryptographic system used by Windows for the Encrypted File System also uses a numeric technique, but it's extremely complex and uses a key that is 38 digits long for U.S. domestic use or 16 digits for international use. Such a large number means many possible choices, and that means it would take someone a very long time to guess a key and read an encrypted file.

When you mark a file for encryption, Windows randomly generates such a large number, called a unique *file encryption key (FEK)*, which is used to scramble the contents of just that one file. This unique key is itself scrambled with your own personal file encryption key, an even longer number stored in the Windows Certificate database. The encrypted unique key is then stored along with the file.

When you're logged in and try to open an encrypted file, Windows retrieves your personal key, decodes the unique key, and uses that key to decode the contents of the file as it's read off the hard disk.

The reason for the two-step process is to let Windows use a different and unique key for each file. Using different keys provides added security. Even if an attacker managed to guess the key to one file, he or she would have to start afresh to find the key to other files. Yet your personal key can unscramble the unique key to any file you've encrypted. It's a valuable thing, this key, and I'll tell you how to back it up in a certificate file for safekeeping.

As a backup in case your personal key gets lost, Windows lets each computer or domain administrator designate recovery agents, users who are allowed to decode other people's encrypted files. Windows also encrypts the unique FEK for each of the recovery agents. It, too, is stored along with the file, and anyone possessing a recovery key can also read your encrypted files. You'll learn about the benefits and risks of this system in "Protecting and Recovering Encrypted Files" later in this chapter.

You can use EFS to keep your documents safe from intruders who might gain unauthorized physical access to your sensitive stored data (by stealing your laptop or zip disk, for example).

You can also encrypt or decrypt a file or folder using the command line and the following syntax:

```
CIPHER [/E ¦ /D] [/S:dir] [/I] [/F] [/Q] [dirname [...]]
```

The arguments are as follows:

/E	Encrypts the specified directories. Directories are marked so that files added afterward will be encrypted.
/D	Decrypts the folder and halts any further encryption on that folder until reactivated.
/S	Forces the CIPHER command to be recursive; that is, it encrypts all files and folders in the specified folder and all subfolders below it.
/I	By default, the CIPHER command stops when an error is encountered. This parameter forces the encryption process to continue even if errors occur.

/F	Forces the encryption operation on all specified directories, even those already encrypted. Already-encrypted directories are skipped by default.
/Q	Reports only the most essential information about a file or folder's encrypted status.
Dirname	Specifies a pattern or directory.

Used without parameters, CIPHER displays the encryption state of the current directory and any files it contains. You can use multiple directory names and wildcards, but you must place spaces between parameters.

RULES FOR USING ENCRYPTED FILES

When you work with encrypted files and folders, keep in mind the following points:

- Only files and folders on NTFS volumes can be encrypted.

- You cannot encrypt files or folders that are compressed. Compression and encryption are mutually exclusive file attributes. If you want to encrypt a compressed file or folder, you must decompress it first.

- Only the user who encrypted the file and the designated recovery agent(s) can open it. (You'll learn more about recovery agents shortly.)

- If you encrypt a file in a shared directory, it is inaccessible to others. Windows 2000 has no provision to show encrypted files, unlike compressed files, in an alternative color. So, it doesn't take much to lose track of which files are encrypted and which files are not.

- Encrypted files become decrypted if you copy or move the file to a volume or partition that is not formatted with NTFS. You can use Backup to store encrypted files on floppy and other non-NTFS formatted disks.

- You should use Cut and Paste to move files into an encrypted folder. If you use the drag-and-drop method to move files, they are not automatically encrypted in the new folder.

- System files cannot be encrypted.

- Encrypting folders or files does not protect them against being deleted, moved, or renamed. Anyone with the appropriate permission level can manipulate encrypted folders or files. (These users just can't open them.)

- Temporary files, which are created by some programs when documents are edited, are also encrypted as long as all the files are on an NTFS volume and in an encrypted folder. I recommend that you encrypt the Temp folder on your hard disk for this reason. Encrypting your original files keeps them safe from prying eyes, but programs often leave temp files behind—usually in the Temp folder—and these files remain vulnerable.

PART

VI

CH

33

Note

The paging file is also a problem in this regard and unfortunately cannot be protected, as far as I know.

- On a domain network, you can encrypt or decrypt files and folders located on a remote computer that has been enabled for remote encryption. Check with your system administrator to see whether your company's servers support this capability. Keep in mind, however, that opening an encrypted file over a network still exposes the contents of that file while it is being transmitted. A network security protocol such as IPSec must be implemented to safeguard data during transmission.

- You should encrypt folders instead of individual files so that if a program creates temporary files and/or saves new copies during editing, they will be encrypted as well.

- Encrypted files, like compressed folders, perform more slowly than unencrypted ones. If you want maximum performance when folders or files in the folders are being used extensively (for example, by database programs), think twice before encrypting them.

SUGGESTED FOLDERS TO ENCRYPT

I recommend that you encrypt the following folders:

- Encrypt the My Documents folder if you save most of your documents there. Encrypting this folder ensures that any personal documents saved there are automatically encrypted. However, a better alternative would be to create a subfolder under My Document for personal files and encrypt just this folder. This approach relieves you from having to track which files are encrypted and which are not.

Caution

You must not encrypt My Documents if it's stored on a remote network server, as is the case in many installations using Window 2000 Server. Chaos ensues as Windows tries to copy the files over the LAN and back.

- Encrypt your Temp folder so that any temporary files created by programs are automatically encrypted.

Caution

If someone steals your laptop computer or gains physical access to your desktop computer, it's possible that even with all of Windows 2000's file access security and file encryption, that person can gain access to your files. How? There is a trick that allows this to happen, and you should guard against it. Here's how it works: By restarting the computer with an Emergency Repair Disk (ERD) and then reinstalling the operating system from a CD-ROM, a thief can set up himself or herself as the system administrator. If the default file recovery certificate is still on the computer at this point, the intruder can view encrypted files. To guard against this situation, you should export the file recovery certificate to a floppy disk and remove it from the computer. I'll show you how in the next section.

PROTECTING AND RECOVERING ENCRYPTED FILES

Encrypted files are supposed to be very secure; only the user who creates an encrypted file can unscramble it. But this security hangs on your own personal file encryption key, which is stored in the Windows Certificate database (see the sidebar "How File Encryption Works" earlier in this chapter). Where would you be if you accidentally deleted your file encryption certificate, or if your user account was deleted from the system? Could the secret recipe for Aunt Dottie's Zucchini Fritters be lost forever this way? Probably not. The Encrypted File System has a "back door" that lets designated recovery agents open any encrypted file.

The availability of this back door is both good news and bad news. The good news is that encrypted files can be recovered when necessary. The bad news is that this capability opens up a potential security risk, and you need to be sure you take measures to protect yourself against it.

SECURING THE RECOVERY CERTIFICATE

Your ability to recover encrypted files hinges on two factors:

- Being listed by the Windows Local or Group Security Policy as a designated recovery agent
- Possessing the file recovery certificate that holds the recovery key data

With a few dirty tricks, it's possible for someone who steals your computer to get himself or herself in as administrator and pose as the recovery agent. So, if you really want to ensure the privacy of your files with the Encrypted File System, you must save the file recovery certificate on a floppy disk or other removable medium and remove the certificate from your computer.

To back up and remove the recovery certificate, do the following:

1. Be sure that at least one file on your computer has been marked Encrypted by any user.
2. Log in as the local administrator (*XXXX*\Administrator, where *XXXX* is the name of your computer).
3. Start the Microsoft Management Console by choosing Start, Run. Then type mmc and press Enter.
4. Choose Console, Add/Remove Snap-In. Then select Add. Next, highlight the Certificates snap-in and click Add. Select My User Account and click Finish. Finally, click Close and then click OK.
5. In the left pane, open Certificates - Current User, Personal, Certificates.
6. In the right pane, you should see a certificate listed with its Intended Purpose shown as File Recovery, as shown in Figure 33.13. If this certificate is not present, and you're on a domain network, your domain administrator has done this job for you, and you don't need to proceed any further.
7. Right-click the Recovery certificate entry, and select All Tasks, Export to start the Certificate Export Wizard.
8. Select Yes, Export the Private Key, and click Next. Select Personal Information Exchange, uncheck Enable Strong Protection, and uncheck Delete the Private Key if Export Is Successful. Then click Next.

Figure 33.13
Certificate Manager showing the Administrator's file recovery certificate.

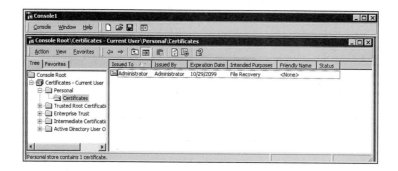

9. Enter a password twice to protect this key. (You must remember this password! I suggest that you make it something fairly simple.) Then click Next.

10. Specify a filename to be used to save the key. Insert a blank, formatted floppy disk, and type A:RECOVERY.PFX. Click Next and then Finish.

11. Right-click the certificate entry again, and select Delete.

12. Label the floppy disk clearly "EFS Recovery Key for *XXX*", where *XXX* is the name of your computer. Store this diskette in a safe place away from your computer.

13. Restart your computer. After it's restarted, log on as Administrator again, and confirm that you can't view the file you encrypted as another user.

> **Caution**
>
> You should back up and delete the Administrator's recovery certificate, but don't delete Administrator as the recovery agent from the Local Security Policy. Leave the Local Security Policy alone. If you delete the entries there, you'll disable EFS.

PROTECTING YOUR OWN FILE ENCRYPTION CERTIFICATE

If your user account is lost, or if you accidentally delete your own file encryption certificate some day, you might lose access to your own files. The recovery agent could still help out, but you can protect yourself by following this procedure:

1. Log on with your own user account. Start the Microsoft Management Console by choosing Start, Run. Then type mmc and press Enter.

2. Choose Console, Add/Remove Snap-In. Then select Add. Next, highlight the Certificates snap-in and click Add. Select My User Account and click Finish. Finally, click Close, and then click OK.

3. In the left pane, open Certificates - Current User, Personal, Certificates.

4. In the right pane, you should see a certificate listed with its Intended Purpose shown as Encrypting File System.

5. Right-click this certificate entry, and select All Tasks, Export to start the Certificate Export Wizard.

6. Select Yes, Export the Private Key, and click Next. Select Personal Information Exchange, uncheck Enable Strong Protection, and uncheck Delete the Private Key if Export Is Successful. Then click Next.

7. Enter a password twice to protect this key. (You must remember this password! I suggest that you make it something fairly simple.) Then click Next.

8. Specify a filename to be used to save the key. Insert a blank, formatted floppy disk, and type A:ENCRYPT.PFX. Click Next and then Finish.

9. Label this disk "EFS for *UUU* on *XXX*," where *UUU* is your user account name and *XXX* is your computer name. Store it in a safe place.

RECOVERING ENCRYPTED FILES ON YOUR OWN COMPUTER

If your user account is deleted or you end up reinstalling Windows from scratch, you'll lose access to your encrypted files because the Encryption database will be lost. You can log on as Administrator and reinstall the encrypted file recovery certificate, or you can log on as yourself and reinstall your file encryption certificate to get the files back with the following procedure:

1. Choose Console, Add/Remove Snap-In. Then select Add. Next, highlight the Certificates snap-in and click Add. Select My User Account and click Finish. Finally, click Close, and then click OK.

2. In the left pane, open Certificates - Current User, Personal, Certificates.

3. In the right pane, right-click and select All Tasks, Import to start the Certificate Import Wizard.

4. Click Next. Enter the name of the certificate file—for example, a:recovery.pfx—and click Next.

5. Enter the password for the certificate, and check Mark the Private Key as Exportable. Click Next twice, and then click Finish.

You should now be able to access the encrypted files. I suggest that you remove the Encrypted check mark from these files. Log on again as the Normal user of these files and reencrypt them if you want.

RECOVERING ENCRYPTED FILES ON A DOMAIN NETWORK

In a Windows 2000 domain network, your network administrator or other designated agents have a master file recovery certificate. If you can't get at your encrypted files, you can send them to the designated agent for recovery. Your network administrator will probably give you a detailed procedure for this task, but here's how it's most often done:

1. Log on as Administrator, and run Windows Backup (by choosing Start, Programs, Accessories, System Tools, Backup).

PART

VI

CH

33

2. Select the Backup tab. Browse to My Computer to find the folders containing the encrypted files, and set the check mark for the folders, or check individual files in the right pane.

3. Under Backup destination, select File. Under Backup Media or File Name, enter a floppy disk or disk filename—for example, `a:recover.bkf` or `c:\temp\recover.bkf`. Click Start Backup.

4. In the Backup Job Information dialog, select Replace the Data on the Media, and click Start Backup.

5. Attach the backup file to a mail message, and send it to your organization's recovery administrator. Alternatively, send the floppy disk.

The administrator will recover the files using the organization's master recovery certificate and return the files to you.

COMPRESSION: HOW IT WORKS, HOW TO USE IT

Windows 2000 ships with built-in provision for file compression that is implemented via NTFS. It's not strictly true that only NTFS files and folders can be compressed because a command-line program called `compress` can compress FAT-based files and folders. However, you must, in turn, use the `expand` command to decompress the resulting files and folders before you can use them. This procedure is awkward. So, for practical purposes, compression is implemented seamlessly into the operating system only on NTFS-formatted volumes.

File compression works by encoding data to take up less storage space. Digital data is compressed by finding repeatable patterns of binary 0s and 1s. The more patterns found, the more the data can be compressed. Text can generally be compressed to about 40 percent of its original size and graphics files from 20 to 90 percent. Some files (namely .EXE files) compress very little because of the lack of repeating data patterns within the program. The amount of compression depends entirely on the type of file and compression algorithm used.

Compressing a file or folder in Windows 2000 is a simple and straightforward process:

1. Open Windows Explorer, and select the file or folder you want.

2. Right-click, and select Properties from the context menu.

3. Select the Advanced button at the bottom of the Properties dialog.

4. In the Advanced Attributes dialog that appears, put a check mark in front of the Compress Contents to Save Disk Space option, as you see in Figure 33.14.

Figure 33.14

5. When you click OK, you are prompted to choose whether you want to compress files and folders, if you're compressing a folder, recursively. Doing so is generally desirable and a safe bet.

To decompress a file or folder, simply repeat the preceding steps and uncheck the Compress Contents to Save Disk Space option.

Two caveats are in order with compression:

- A file or folder can be compressed or encrypted, but not both. These options are mutually exclusive.
- By default, compressed files are shown in the same color as decompressed ones. If you choose Control Panel, Folder Options and select the View tab, you can find an option to display compressed files or folders in an alternate color. Use it. The different color gives you an immediate visual clue as to which files and folders are compressed on your system and which aren't.

Caution

You should keep in mind some disk space requirements when using compression. If you try to compress a volume that's running extremely low on free space, you might see this error message:

```
Compression Error
File Manager/Explorer cannot change compress attributes for:
"path\filename"
```

These error messages indicate that the system needs additional free space to perform compression. The system is not designed to manipulate the data in place on the disk. Additional space is needed to buffer the user data and to possibly hold additional file system metadata. The amount of additional free space required depends on the cluster size, file size, and available space.

PART

VI

CH

33

INDEXING

Windows 2000 Professional comes with a text-search system called the Indexing Service. This system scans files and folders on your hard disk and builds a database of the words it finds in them. This database helps speed up the Search for Files and Directories option when you're looking for words within files or keywords in file descriptions and helps the Internet Information Services Web server perform Web site searches. You can also query the index directly.

Note

Right off the bat, I should reassure you that the Indexing Service pays attention to file privileges when it displays results of searches. It never reports a match for a file the person searching doesn't have permission to view.

Managing the Indexing Service

To view the Indexing Service Manager, right-click My Computer and select Manage. Open Services and Applications, Indexing Service (as shown in Figure 33.15). Under Indexing Service, the manager displays any *catalogs* defined on your system. A catalog is a self-contained index for a folder or group of folders. By default, a System catalog is defined for use by Search for Files and Folders. If you've installed Internet Information Services, you also have a Web index, which can be used by scripts to let visitors to your Web site search its pages.

Figure 33.15
The Indexing Service Manager displays all defined index catalogs.

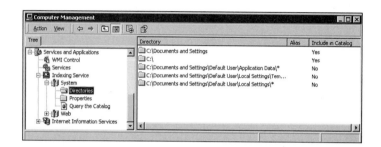

If you want to use the Indexing Service, select Indexing Service in the left pane, and choose Action, Start from the menu. Answer Yes to Do You Want the Indexing Service to Start whenever You Boot Your Computer.

Choosing Yes starts the service, which immediately begins its job of cataloging files on your hard drive. It does its job of scanning files periodically from now on, as long as the computer is turned on.

Indexing Service Properties

You can right-click the Indexing Service entry in Computer Management to adjust the service's global properties. The Generation tab has some useful settings, as shown in Table 33.1.

Table 33.1 Generation Tab Options

Index Files with Unknown Extensions	If this option is checked, the Indexing Service includes all files in the index, regardless of file type. If it is unchecked, only registered file types are indexed. It's probably best to leave the box checked.
Generate Abstracts	If this option is checked, for each indexed file, the Indexing Service extracts and stores the first few sentences of each matching file and displays them on the search results. Check this box with caution because it can consume an enormous amount of disk space. I recommend that you leave it unchecked on the Service's Properties sheet.
Maximum Size	This option sets the maximum length in characters of abstracts. Keep them short. I suggest going no higher than the default 320 characters.

CATALOG PROPERTIES

By default, the Indexing Service Properties settings apply to each catalog managed by the Indexing Service. However, you can select the Properties sheet for each individual catalog by right-clicking the catalog name in the left pane and selecting Properties. Then you can uncheck Inherit Above Settings from Service and customize them on a catalog-by-catalog basis.

A good use of this capability would be to enable abstracts for the Web index if you have installed Internet Information Services and use searching on your Web site.

Note
Under each catalog is an entry named Properties, but it is a display page only. To change the catalog's properties, you must right-click its name in the left pane.

CATALOG DIRECTORIES

You can control which directories (drives and folders) are included in and excluded from a catalog by using the Directories folder. Under any catalog name in the left pane, select the Directories entry, and view the cataloged folders in the right pane.

By default, the System catalog includes the entire C: drive but excludes the Default User folders under \Documents and Settings.

Here, you can add any additional drives to include in your index and add any folders you want to exclude from the index. To add an Include or Exclude entry, right-click in the right pane, and select New, Directory.

In the resulting dialog, enter the full path to the folder to be indexed, or use X:\ to add the entire drive X:. Check Yes or No under Include in Index. If you want to add a directory on a remote computer, enter its full *UNC* network name, for example, \\machine\sharename\folder, and a username and password to be used to access the shared folder.

CONTROLLING INDEXING OF INDIVIDUAL FILES

You can also remove files or folders from all catalogs by using the files' or folders' Properties sheets.

To exclude a file from any catalogs, right-click the file or folder, and select Properties, Advanced. Under Archive and Index attributes on the resulting dialog, you can uncheck For Fast Searching, Allow Indexing Service to Index This File or Folder. Unchecking this box prevents the Indexing Service from ever scanning the file. However, just checking the box is not enough to put the file into an index; the folder must be listed in the catalog's Directories list or in a subfolder of a listed folder.

USING THE INDEXING SERVICE

The System catalog is used automatically by the Start button's Search for Files or Folders item, and it's especially handy when you're searching for a keyword or specific file type. The index is used to hasten the search of any cataloged folder.

The Web folder is used by scripts or FrontPage extensions on the Internet Information Server, which is described in Chapter 18, "Using Internet Information Services to Host a Web Site."

You can also search any catalog directly from the Indexing Service Manager. Select Query the Catalog in the left pane, and a search form appears in the right. Enter any desired keywords, and click Search to begin a query. I was surprised to find that my system's temporary Internet files are included in the catalog, as test queries returned matches based on words in Web pages I had recently visited.

DISK CLEANUP UTILITY

In the course of daily use, Windows 2000 generates thousands of temporary files to aid in system operation. These files are critical to the operation of the programs that use them when the programs are being used. As most people are all too well aware, though, temporary files have a habit of being much more persistent than their name implies. And over the course of time, these files add up in a hurry and consume large amounts of valuable disk space. The Disk Cleanup utility provides you with a safe and reliable way to delete these temporary files from all their various hiding spots and thus free up disk space on your hard drive.

To access this utility, do the following:

1. Choose Start, Programs, Accessories, System Tools, Disk Cleanup. Alternatively, you can right-click a drive in the Explorer, and then choose Properties, General, Disk Cleanup, as you see in Figure 33.16.

Figure 33.16
Running the Disk Cleanup program to find space on your hard disk.

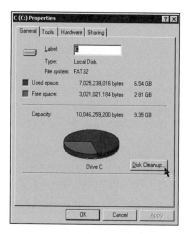

2. In the resulting dialog, choose the drive to analyze. The program then searches this drive for files that can be safely deleted or compressed. The details of this analysis are then displayed in a dialog similar to the one shown in Figure 33.17.

Figure 33.17
Report of a disk cleanup analysis.

Near the top of the dialog is the total amount of disk space you can free on this drive by accepting the selected recommendations listed below. You can exclude or include file groups from the cleanup process by placing a check mark in front of the types listed. When you select an entry, you see a description of which files that group contains and what their purpose is. By selecting a group and then the View Files button, you can see exactly which files are slated for death in the resulting folder window. Use this option if you have any doubts about a group of files, where they reside, or what they do.

The following file groups are available:

- Downloaded Program Files—These files are ActiveX controls and Java applets used by Web pages you have visited. If you delete them, they will simply be reloaded the next time you visit the pages.

- Temporary Internet Files—This one is a biggie. Every time you access a Web page, your browser stores or caches the various elements of that page on the hard disk. When you revisit a page, any elements that have not changed since your last visit are reloaded from the hard disk rather than the site itself to speed the rendering process. Deleting these temporary Internet files frees the largest amount of disk space of any of the group lists. If you use a modem to access the Internet, however, you will notice longer rendering times the next time you return to one of your favorite sites.

Note

Agreeing to delete temporary Internet files does not delete your *cookies* (personalized settings for Web sites), so don't worry about having to reenter user ID information or other such information for sites you visit a lot. Cookies are stored in x:\Documents and

continues

PART

VI

CH

33

Settings*username*\Cookies. Temporary Internet files are stored in x:\Documents and Settings*username*\Local Settings\Temporary Internet Files (where x: is the volume the system is installed on).

- Recycle Bin—Clearing this folder is the same as manually clearing your Recycle Bin. It is a good idea to have a quick look at the files stored there before choosing this option. Select this option, and click the View Files button under the group description; a folder window then opens, listing the contents.

- Temporary Offline Files—Similar to cached Web pages, when you connect to a network location and access a read-only file, a temporary copy is sometimes stored on your hard drive. Clearing these temporary copies does not erase the files you explicitly marked as available for offline use, so this is a safe choice.

- Offline Files—If you use the Synchronization features of Windows 2000 (see Chapter 23, "Windows Unplugged: Remote and Mobile Networking"), selected files and folders from a network connection are stored locally for access while you are disconnected. Do not delete these files unless you're sure you can work without the local copies. You'll lose any changes you made to offline files if you delete them here, so don't make this choice without synchronizing first.

- Compress Old Files—Windows can compress files not accessed within a specified period. To configure this period, select this group and click the More Options button.

- Catalog File for the Content Indexer—The Windows Indexing Service (see the description earlier in this chapter) speeds file searches by building and maintaining indexes on your hard disk. Selecting this option removes any old index files not in use but does not delete any current indexes.

On the Disk Cleanup dialog, also notice the second tab marked More Options. The Windows Components option provides a quick access shortcut to the Windows Components Wizard. From this wizard, you can select major system components (such as IIS and Indexing Services) to add or remove. Also on this tab is a shortcut to Add/Remove Programs under the section labeled Installed Programs.

Tip #402

Running Disk Cleanup weekly does wonders to improve a system's performance. The first time you run it, the program might take quite awhile to run, but with regular exercise, this program speeds up because the disk stays cleaner. Once a month—after you check the contents of the individual folder groups carefully—you should empty all folders of all temporary files. Then follow up by running the built-in defragmentation utility (by choosing Programs, Accessories, System Tools).

USING INTERNET EXPLORER'S CACHE CLEANUP

If you would prefer not to use the Disk Cleanup utility, you can choose a second option for clearing out those disk-hogging cached Internet files.

To access it, open the Control Panel, and select the Internet Options icon. On the Internet Properties dialog, you will find a section titled Temporary Internet Files. The Delete Files button works exactly as advertised. The Settings button allows you to configure options for how often cached files are checked against their original counterparts, how much disk space these cached files are allowed to take up, and which folder they are stored in.

When the disk space setting is exceeded, files are removed on a "First In, First Out" basis; that is, the oldest files are deleted to create space for newer ones.

The Move Folder option lets you specify a location where these temporary files will be stored. I don't see any reason anyone would want to change the location of this folder, unless it's to some network drive dedicated to Web caching. If you have a local drive getting that low on disk space, the operating system must be running like a sloth anyway, and it's a good time to go shopping for a new hard drive.

BACKUP TOOLS AND STRATEGIES

Nobody plans to lose or corrupt an important file. But then again, no one I know gets up in the morning and plans to crash his car either. Things happen, though, and for all the same reasons you buy car insurance, you should also be taking all the necessary steps to safeguard all those bits and bytes that reside on your system's hard drive.

WINDOWS 2000 BACKUP PROGRAM

Windows 2000 is installed with a backup utility that should meet the needs of most individual users. With it, you can back up folders or files—both local and remote—either to a Windows 2000 recognized tape device, to a removable storage device (JAZ drive, MO drive, zip drive, and so on), or to a file on a local or remote drive. If Windows 2000 can read the file (FAT16, FAT32, or NTFS natively), then it can be backed up.

If you have used the Backup tool previously provided with Windows NT 4, the new version included in Windows 2000 will be a welcome change. Long gone are the days of using the AT command in scripts to create your own scheduled and automated backups. The new Backup tool provides a wealth of features that I'm sure many users and system administrators will wonder how they lived so long without.

PART

VI

CH

33

Note

Windows 2000's Backup program is acceptable for an individual user's computer, but it's not really adequate for LAN or server backups because it can't fully back up remote computers. If you're setting up a LAN, you might look into more sophisticated programs such as the server versions of Arcserve or Backup-Exec. If your computer is on a LAN, your system administrator might have a more sophisticated centralized backup system available to you.

REMOVABLE STORAGE SERVICES

Along with a much superior backup application, Windows 2000 brings with it Removable Storage Services. Within the umbrella of Removable Storage Services, you'll find other nifty names and paradigms for handling your zip, tape, or optical storage devices. Microsoft has created Removable Storage Services in the hopes that other applications will make use of this new service, thereby making it easier for developers to concentrate on the actual functionality of the backup program itself. Removable Storage Services handle all the details, and the users only must deal with managing the data that is stored on the media, no matter what program they choose. Additionally, many programs can share the same storage media as opposed to the old way of having different applications write proprietary formats onto media, making the media usable only in the applications that utilized them.

Before beginning a discussion of how to use the backup program, you need a thorough understanding of Removable Storage Services. After you're able to define your media and group them into media pools, you can use them in any program to back up your valuable data with relative ease. This is the foundation on which Windows 2000 builds a clean and powerful set of backup centralization schemes to enable you to have the greatest amount of flexibility and power.

First, open the Computer Management Console from within the Control Panel folder. From there, you can select the Removable Storage tree node to see a list of the various Removable Storage Service components described here (see Figure 33.18).

Figure 33.18
Opening the Removable Storage node from the Computer Management Console.

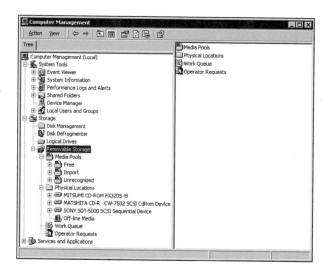

MEDIA POOLS

Windows Backup and other applications that deal with removable media use the Removable Media Services and the Media Pool Manager to catalog used and unused tapes, CD-Rs, zip disks, and so on. This way, Windows knows when a given disk or tape can be erased, when it's time to retire a well-used tape, which tapes are available for reuse, and so on.

Windows 2000 lets you organize your removable media into groups called *media pools*. A media pool is a collection of individual removable storage media (a set of tapes, for example) that share the same management and rotation policies and that are used for a similar purpose. Media pooling supports a wide variety of devices, such as 4mm tape devices, JAZ drives, zip drives, and so on. You therefore have a great deal of flexibility in storage and storage management.

A media pool can span multiple media libraries. This gives you the opportunity to chain multiple CD-R drives to give yourself that extra backup space in a single media pool, for example. (Media pools can also contain other media pools. This capability enriches the situation quite a bit, if you really want to get into setting up hairy removable storage media arrangements.)

Removable Storage Services group media pools into two distinct categories: system media pools and application media pools. System media pools contain media that are in a hold state. That is, the media are not known to have been used by any particular application. For every storage device on your system, the Removable Storage Services automatically create free, unrecognized, and import media pools. The following is a brief description of each type:

- Unrecognized media pool—Media that have so far not been utilized and are unrecognized by Removable Storage Services. Removable Storage Services hold new or unformatted media of any removable type here. By moving unrecognized media to the free media pool, you make them available in your backup application.

- Free media pool—Media that are available to your applications. Media in this pool have not been used by an application but are available for use. You can automatically configure your application media pools to automatically draw media from the System's free media pool as needed. Otherwise, you must manually move free media into your application media pool.

- Import media pool—Media formatted on a different computer system. When you insert a foreign tape or disk into your removable media device, Windows adds an entry for this medium in the import pool. You can then drag this entry to the free pool or another media set.

Recognizing Media Types

You might be wondering how Removable Storage Services recognize all these media types and keep track of them. Simple. Removable Storage Services write an identifier onto each type of medium that allows read-write operations. This identifier is called an *On-Media Identifier*. This way, Removable Storage can identify each type of medium.

By cataloging the On-Media Identifier for each device in a database, Removable Storage Services keep track of what is available to any given media pool and, hence, an application. When you insert a particular medium, Removable Storage Services will look for the On-Media Identifier and make the appropriate decision based on it. If it does not recognize the label, it moves the medium to the unrecognized media pool mentioned previously. If it does recognize the label but not the particular ID of the label, the medium is moved to the import media pool as described previously. Finally, if the label and ID are both recognized, the medium is placed into either the free media pool or any other application media pool it might belong to. This updates the database to inform your backup application the medium is available for use. Note that Removable Storage Services do not write an On-Media Identifier onto read-only or write-once optical media such as CDs or CD-Rs. For these types of discs, the serial number or volume information is used to differentiate them from other media.

The application media pool is created from any backup program that uses Removable Storage Services. You simply create a pool and let Removable Storage Services deal with the details of managing the media.

First, you need to prepare the media as follows:

1. Insert your medium into the drive, and choose Removable Storage, Physical Locations. Then choose the specific drive.

2. Choose the Media node from the Computer Management Console, as shown in Figure 33.19.

Figure 33.19
Preparing the media from the Computer Management Console.

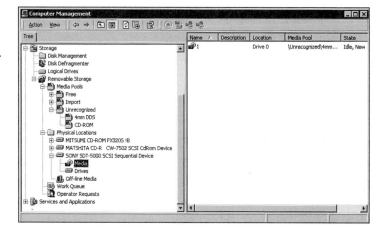

3. In the right pane of the console, right-click the media labeled 1 and select Prepare from the resulting menu. This operation destroys all data on the tape and moves the tape to the system free media pool.

4. Change the default name from 1 to a meaningful name of your choice. Do so by selecting Properties on the drive and changing the name in the Properties tab. A good idea here is to also write this name on the media label itself.

5. Because you want to create a media "pool" (implying more than one piece of media), eject the medium and insert another blank disk, CD, or tape, and then repeat steps 1 through 4. Be sure to give this medium a unique name.

Note

Notice how the right pane of the Computer Management Console still shows the first medium using the name you assigned and that the Library column now reads Off Line Media.

Also note that if the second medium does not appear in the left pane of the console, you can click the device in the MMC and choose Refresh.

6. After you complete the process on the second medium, you can verify that both have been added to the pool by choosing Removable Storage, Media Pools, Free, and then choosing the correct node for your drive, as shown in Figure 33.20.

Figure 33.20
Verifying the free media available in the system media pool from the Computer Management MMC.

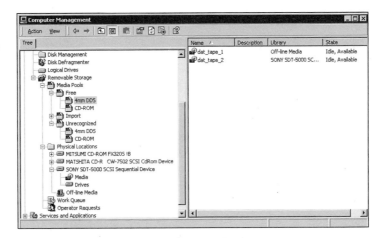

7. Create your own media pool within the application pool of the Backup program. By doing so, you can use your new pool in the Backup program that ships with Windows 2000 Professional.

> **Note**
>
> Applications create their own application media pool upon launching for the first time, provided they support Removable Storage Services. You can create your own media pools only within these applications. You cannot create pools within the system free, import, or unrecognized pools.

If you do not already have an application pool named Backup, you need to now launch the Backup program by selecting Start, Programs, Accessories, System Tools, Backup. After you launch Backup, notice that the tree node titled Backup is automatically created in the Computer Management Console. It is the application media pool for Backup.

CREATING A NEW MEDIA POOL

If you want to create your own media pool, open the Computer Management Console and right-click Removable Storage. Choose Media Pools, Backup, and then select Create Media Pool from the drop-down menu. This action creates a media pool inside the Backup media pool created by Backup. You then are presented with the Create a New Media Pool Properties dialog, as shown in Figure 33.21.

After you've created the pool, you can add a convenient name for this pool. I've chosen Full Backup Pool because I plan to use this pool to perform full system backups on a scheduled basis. Entering a short description next is always a good idea.

Figure 33.21
Creating a new application media pool via the Create a New Media Pool Properties dialog.

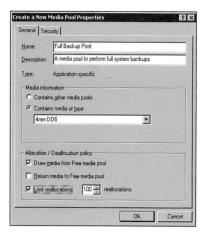

Finally, you need to set the Allocation/Deallocation policies parameters. You can adjust three possible parameters here:

- Draw Media from Free Media Pool—This option makes your media pool automatically take media from the system free media pool. In most cases, this is desirable. If you do not select this option, you must allocate media manually.

- Return Media to Free Media Pool—Selecting this option returns any media used by this pool to the system free media pool. When the media are returned, they are available to any other pool or application. If you plan to use the Backup tool provided with Windows 2000, you shouldn't select this option.

- Limit reallocations—This option is important, especially if you are using magnetic media, such as DAT tapes, because they are susceptible to deterioration and failure after repeated use. This setting allows you to limit the number of times the media gets used in your pool, meaning that you choose the number of times the media can be reused. Tape manufacturers, for example, list the maximum recommended use cycles on the tape's packaging.

Note that security options are available on media pools just as with other objects in Windows 2000. You examine or modify them from the Security tab.

BACKUP

After you have some media prepared, you can perform a data backup using the Backup program that comes supplied with Windows 2000. After you start the Backup program, you are presented with the dialog shown in Figure 33.22.

Figure 33.22
The Welcome tab of
the Backup program.

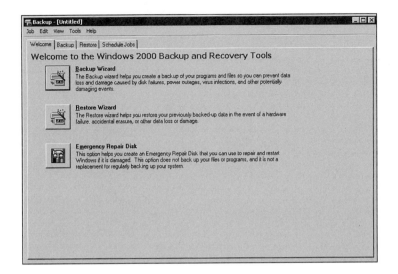

Using the Welcome tab of the Backup program, you can run the Backup Wizard, run the Restore Wizard, or create an Emergency Repair Disk. Yes, the old days of rdisk are gone. You can now create your Emergency Repair Disk (ERD) right here in Backup—with a twist.

Windows 2000 now creates emergency backups in the %SystemRoot%\Repair folder. This folder contains backed-up items such as the Registry, SAM database, and the security and setup log. With this folder, you have a better representation of your system if the need for repairs arises. There is one catch, however. You must actually run the Emergency Repair Disk option from Backup to ever have an up-to-date representation of your system.

To create a backup, select Emergency Repair Disk on the Welcome tab. You then are prompted for a blank floppy disk. Follow the prompts. After you've created the ERD, do the right thing: Label and date it before storing it in a safe place.

PART
VI

CH

33

Note

It's a good idea to go ahead and check the option to back up the Registry because it will give you a better chance of getting your system back to normal in the event of a serious problem.

The Welcome tab also gives you the option of using wizards to back up and restore your data. This approach is easier unless you want more control over the backup process. In that case, click the Backup tab, and you can manually set all the parameters for your backup, as you see in Figure 33.23.

Figure 33.23
Setting up details for a backup.

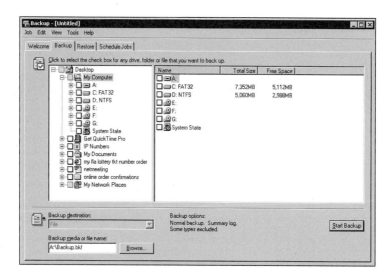

Follow these steps to create a backup:

1. Notice the familiar tree/node view on the left along with the list view on the right. By expanding the C: drive on the left, you get a list of top-level directories on your right. By selecting a check box for any given item, you mark it for backup. By selecting a directory, for instance, you select the directory as well as everything underneath it. This way, you can mark whole directories without the need to manually drill down into each folder on your system.

> **Note**
>
> Note that you can also back up the following:
>
> - System State—This includes boot files, operating system programs, and the Registry. You should always back up System State with any full backup because it's as much a part of the operating system as the Windows directory itself.
> - Network drives—If you've mapped a drive letter for them, you can back them up. (Just as with your local computer, you can back up only networked files for which you have Read permission.)

2. Choose the destination for the backup. On the bottom portion of the Backup tab is a panel with a drop-down list labeled Backup Destination. By opening this list, you can find your media pool, assuming you've created one. If you've not yet created a media pool, File is displayed and this drop-down is grayed out. (See "Creating a Media Pool" earlier in this chapter to learn more details about media pools.)

   You also have the option to back up to a file. This option saves your data to a single file with a .BKF extension. This is very handy for backing up to CD-R, CD-RW, or a zip disk. A backup file can span multiple disks, just has always been the case with Microsoft backup programs.

Tip #403

> Selecting the option to back up to a file is actually a blessing in disguise. Because many people don't have traditional backup devices such as DAT tapes or DLT drives, backing up to a file facilitates backup to other common removable media such as CD-Rs. Backing up your data in this manner is preferable to simply writing files to a CD-R. Normally, if you simply back up files and directories to your CD-R drive, you lose your permissions as well as make all the files read-only by virtue of the fact that they are backed up to read-only media. By backing up to a single file from Backup, you retain these settings and can restore with all of them intact. You can even compress this file before you write it to your CD-R by using your favorite zip program.

3. Before you actually begin backing up, consider the different types of backups available. As you probably know, the operating system provides a means for keeping track of which files have been changed since the last backup—the *archive bit*. Based on whether a file's archive bit is turned on or off, the backup program either backs it up or skips over it. Your job is to set the correct options so the Backup program is relative to this bit. You can find these options by opening the Tools, Options dialog and selecting the Backup Type tab. Here, you can set how your files are backed up to your media, with the following options:

- Normal—The Normal backup does a backup of every file you've selected while also clearing, or turning off, the archive bit on each file. This type of backup sets each file's attribute to signify that it does not need to be backed up again until it has changed.

- Copy—The Copy type of backup simply copies the files to your backup media and leaves the archive bit alone. Using this option, you can have several backups happening on the same files without each of them stepping on each other's toes. In other words, if you use the Copy backup option, using the Normal option still backs up every file because the archive bit is still set on them.

- Differential—This option backs up only the files that have been changed since the last normal or incremental backup, while leaving the archive bit set for each file. With this option, any file backed up looks as though it has not been backed up.

- Incremental—The Incremental option is the same as the Differential option, with the exception that it does, in fact, clear the archive bit on files that it backs up.

- Daily—The Daily option backs up all files that have been modified only on the day that the backup is performed. Be careful with this one because you could end up not backing up everything you want if you do not run nightly backups.

PART

VI

CH

33

Differential Versus Incremental Backups

Let me give you a bit more explanation of the differences between *differential* and *incremental* backups. You can use the differential and incremental options to save time and tapes when backing up frequently. Keep in mind that full backups can take a lot of time and can fill more than one tape or disk.

continues

continued

If you do a full backup and then successive differential backups, each differential backup includes any files changed or added since the full backup. The successive backups do grow in size, but not by much, and you need only two backup sets to fully restore a system: the full backup and the most recent differential.

With incremental backups, only files changed since the last full or incremental backup are saved. With incrementals, the individual backup sets are indeed smaller, but you would need to restore the full and all subsequent incremental backups, in date order, to fully recover all your files. This situation is rather dangerous, in my opinion. I can hardly find my own head some days, let alone a dozen backup tapes.

For a LAN server or business computer, I recommend that you do a full backup weekly and a differential backup daily. For a home computer, you might try a monthly full backup and weekly differential backups.

All the backup options have their places in certain situations. I personally leave the backup type at Normal so that all my files are always backed up, no matter what (see Figure 33.24). You might find that another option suits you better, so feel free to experiment with all these options to find the best one for you.

Figure 33.24
Choose the type of backup from the Backup Type tab of the Tools, Options dialog.

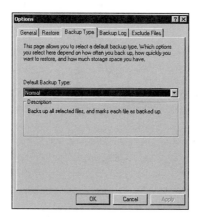

4. Click the Start Backup button to begin the process of backing up your data. The target destination is engaged for the duration of the backup process. You might be prompted to insert media if necessary (for example, if you're backing up to zip disks, and backup data exceeds the amount of space on a disk, you'll have to insert subsequent disks).

RESTORING DATA FROM A BACKUP

"The best laid plans of mice and men oft gang a-glay," as the saying goes. When you've lost data and had enough foresight to have backed it up, you're in luck. Or you hope you are, at least. Backing up is the first half of recovering your data. With any luck, you'll be able to get it back the way it was before whatever bolt of lightning hit your PC. The Restore tab of the Backup dialog comes in at this point. Restoring from a backup is a very simple process, which you can execute in three essential steps:

1. Run the Backup program (by choosing Start, Programs, Accessories, System Tools, Backup).

2. Use the Restore Wizard from the Welcome tab if you want a walkthrough. Alternatively, select the Restore tab, and adjust a few simple parameters.

3. Begin the restore, and insert media if and when prompted.

Of course, you might want to understand a few option and parameter details for better control of your restorations. The following sections discuss them. You should probably read along before doing your first couple of data recoveries. After you have the theories under your belt, then you can proceed.

Notice the left pane of the Restore tab. Here, you can view all the available Backup media pools. You can expand these nodes to display all possible source media and pools. They're displayed in a familiar tree view of the directories and files backed up to each related medium. As with the process of Backup, you simply select the files or folders you want to restore. And, of course, by selecting a top node of the tree, you include everything beneath it.

Next, it's a good idea to look at the settings on the Restore tab of the Options dialog, as shown in Figure 33.25. To open this dialog, choose Tools, Options, and then click the Restore tab.

Figure 33.25
The Restore tab of the Options dialog for the Backup program.

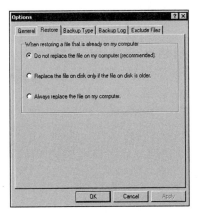

PART

VI

CH

33

Here, you can choose from options that dictate how files will be handled if you are restoring one that already exists in your restore destination. The safest bet here is to not replace any file with a restored version. This is generally the best bet unless you have a specific reason to do so. Reasons for overwriting existing files do crop up, though. For example, if know that you somehow trashed, misedited, or otherwise mangled the file you currently have on disk, you can revert to the last backed-up one. In that case, you need to enable replacement.

Other than the general restore options, the only real option for the restore portion of the Backup program is the option to specify the location in which you want to restore the files. You choose this option from the drop-down list at the bottom of the Restore tab. Three options are available:

- Original Location—This option restores the files to the exact place from which they were backed up. Be careful with this one; it could cause you problems with files that are open. You should make sure you're not trying to restore over a file that may be in use by another application or the system.

- Alternate Location—This option gives you the opportunity to restore the files to a destination of your choosing. If this option is selected, you are prompted for the location to which you want to restore via an entry box beneath the location options. From there, you can use the Browse button to find your restore destination. If you use this option, the directory structure of your backed-up files will be retained in the new destination.

- Single Folder—Selecting this option dumps all the files from your backup to a single folder. Be aware that using this option does not preserve the directory structure of your backed-up data. It simply ignores the structure and restores all the files to the directory you choose.

After you've selected your restore destination, you can click the Start Restore button to begin. Select Advanced on the resulting dialog box. You then can set the options in the Advanced Restore Options dialog (see Figure 33.26).

The options in the Advanced Restore Options dialog are as follows:

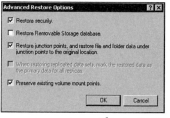

Figure 33.26

- Restore Security—This option enables you to restore the same permissions for the files and folders you're restoring to their original settings. In most cases, choosing this option is best because you don't want to have to set them one-by-one after the restore has finished.

- Restore Removable Storage Database—This one gets a bit tricky. Every time you back up your %SystemRoot% directory, Backup automatically backs up the Removable Storage database. If you select this option, you overwrite the currently active database. In most instances, overwriting is not desirable unless you have a huge database from a previous backup that you want to restore.

- Restore Junction Points, and Restore File and Folder Data Under Junction Points to the Original Location—Turn on this check box if you've created junction points using the linkd command, and you're trying to restore the junction points and the data that the junction points point to. If you don't, only the pointers are restored, not the data. You also should turn on this box if you are restoring a mounted drive's data.

- When Restoring Replicated Data Sets, Mark the Restored Data as the Primary Data for All Replicas—This option is relevant only to Windows 2000 Server and should be grayed out on any machine running Windows 2000 Professional.

- Preserve Existing Volume Mount Points—This option most often applies when you're restoring the data for an entire drive, such as when you're replacing a drive. Typically, you put in a formatted drive, re-create the mount points, and then restore the data. You don't want to overwrite the mount points, so you turn on this option. If you have not re-created the mount points, and you want to restore the entire data and mount points as stored in the backup set, then uncheck this box.

Finally, by selecting the OK button, you can then select OK on the Confirm Restore dialog to start the restore.

SCHEDULING JOBS

Finally, we come to my personal favorite, the Schedule Jobs tab of the Backup dialog. This feature is a great addition to an already very capable backup program. There should really be no reason for most people to not have a reasonably current backup of their system at any given time if they use this tool.

Strategies for scheduling backups vary from person to person or machine to machine. Some people, myself included, are extremely paranoid and go for the "backup every single night" method. As you can guess, backing up this frequently saves a great deal of heartache in the event of a total system meltdown. I can't tell you how many times backing up has saved my neck. On the other hand, say you have a machine at your home or business that rarely gets used or is just acting as a proxy server. This kind of machine really only needs backups at much longer intervals than your personal workstation. In this case, it's usually safe to back up a system like this only every week or so. In the end, it's up to you how you feel you need to schedule your backups. Just remember, your system will probably go down at some point. Being prepared is the best insurance around for this nasty inevitability.

To use the scheduling features of backup, simply double-click any date using the provided calendar. This gives you a chance to use the Backup Wizard. The options for it are very straightforward. In fact, if you read the previous section on backing up, you should have no problem whatsoever using this wizard.

PART

VI

CH

33

Note

> You might be prompted to set the account information for the backup because it may end up running when another logged-in user doesn't have the rights to initiate the backup. When you're prompted, you can specify a "Run As" user and password.

The only other aspect of this program I'd like to mention is the Set Schedule option on the When to Backup section of the wizard. If you choose Later for the time to back up and then click the Set Schedule button (and optionally fill in the Run As box), you see the dialog shown in Figure 33.27.

Figure 33.27
Setting the scheduling options from the Schedule Job dialog.

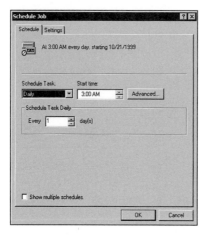

The Schedule Job dialog is actually the same one used when scheduling any common task via Scheduled Tasks, a system tool covered in Chapter 31. You might want to refer to that chapter for some more details on the options.

As you can see from Figure 33.27, I've set my paranoid-style backup to reoccur every day at 3:00 a.m. I set mine this late because I'm usually up to the wee hours writing. So, the backup won't bother me while I'm up, as I should be off my system by 3:00 a.m. By selecting the Advanced button on this dialog, you can confine your backups to a period of days using a start date and end date. And as you change the selection in the Schedule Task drop-down list, the options also change, presenting options relevant to the time period you choose.

The Settings tab on the Schedule Job dialog offers somewhat lower-priority options. You should take a gander at them, though, if you're intending to get serious about automated backups. Among the settings are those that affect idle time and power management. You should consider power settings if you're doing a backup from a laptop running on batteries. The Idle Time options could be useful if there is a possibility that someone will be using the computer when backup begins. .If good responsiveness of the computer is important, you can ensure the backup process stops if someone sits down to the keyboard and begins work. Check the Stop the Task If the Computer Ceases to Be Idle check box.

ALTERNATIVE AND CREATIVE BACKUP STRATEGIES

The following sections provide a few alternative ideas for doing your backups. You can choose from many other possible ideas because of the proliferation of device types and off-site backup services (for example, CD-R, CD-RW, Internet-based services, LAN-based backups, and so on). However, you might find one of these ideas interesting and potentially very helpful in your work setting.

USING OFFLINE FILES AND FOLDERS

Windows 2000 has a little known feature called Offline Files and Folders. The implementation of this tool is aimed at notebook users who connect to the corporate network, update files, and then journey off with their laptops on another adventure.

Here's how it works: The user logs on to the server and marks a network folder as available while offline. This folder and its contents are then replicated to the user's system. While on the road, the user adds new files to the folder and modifies or deletes existing ones. When the user returns and logs back on the network, Windows 2000 automatically synchronizes all changed files—in both directions. For example, if the user deleted a file from the offline folder on his or her notebook, the synchronization process notes the discrepancy and asks whether this file should also be deleted from the server. A similar process takes place for new or modified files.

→ Offline folders are also discussed in the chapter on mobile network users. To learn more about these folders, **see** "Offline Folders," **p. 817**.

"This is all well and good for mobile users," you say. "But why is this topic described under backup strategies?" Because the synchronization process does not give a nit whether you physically disconnect your machine from the network; it can automatically update changed files every time you log off or on. In addition, you can easily force synchronization at any time by using a simple menu command.

Tip #404	Let me describe precisely how I ensure I have a recent backup of my working files throughout the course of a day. Both my main working system and my notebook have network cards, connected by a $10 twisted-pair crossover cable. The notebook has a shortcut to the folders containing all my critical data (book chapters, contact files, business correspondence, and so on), and these folders are enabled for offline access. Whenever I need a break or a distraction arises, I manually force a synchronization between the notebook and my working system. This way, if disaster strikes, I can quickly restore a damaged file by forcing another synchronization. The notebook detects whether something is amiss and offers to right the error.

PART

VI

CH

33

You can follow these steps to set up offline folders. It is assumed that the hardware is already in place to establish a network connection between the two systems. Note that only the system you're configuring for offline folders needs to be running Windows 2000. The other system can be any computer using standard Windows networking services.

1. From the machine for which you want to set up the offline folders, connect to the system where your data files reside.

2. Using Windows Explorer, create a shortcut to these folders (by choosing File, New, Shortcut). It does not matter where this shortcut is created. Two of the most accessible locations are either in My Documents or directly on the desktop.

3. Open this shortcut, and select the file or folder you want to have replicated to your system. If you want to synchronize multiple (top-level) folders, you must do them one at a

time. Go to the File menu, select Make Available Offline, or use the right-click menu's command of the same name.

4. If the selected folder has subfolders, you are given the choice of including subfolders or creating the offline link with just the top-level folder.

5. A synchronization dialog appears, showing a progress bar. When the process is complete, the dialog disappears, and you're in business. Offline folders display a small overlay with two blue arrows to distinguish them from regular folders or shortcuts.

To manually force a synchronization of your offline folders, open Windows Explorer, and from the Tools menu, select the Synchronize command. Then select the Synchronize button at the bottom of the resulting dialog. An alternate path to the same dialog is to choose Start, Programs, Accessories, Synchronize.

To configure automatic synchronization of your offline folders, go to the Items to Synchronize dialog. Choosing the Setup button produces the Synchronization Settings dialog shown in Figure 33.28.

Figure 33.28
The Synchronization Settings dialog box.

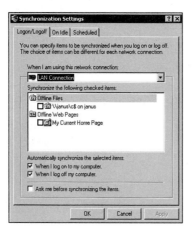

On the Logon/Logoff tab of this dialog, you can specify which network connection to use with which offline configuration. For example, if you use a dial-up connection to synchronize one folder and a LAN connection to synchronize another, each of these configurations can be specified independently of the other.

> **Note**
> When you first set up offline folders, no configurations are selected on the Synchronize the Following Checked Items list. Before your offline folders will automatically update, you need to go to this dialog and select a configuration.

The automatic synchronization options determine when (logging on, logging off, or both) your files will be updated and whether you will be prompted at this time. If you want the synchronization process to be completely transparent, select both Automatically

Synchronize items and leave the Ask Me option off. For complete control over the process, toggle the Ask Me option on. The synchronization process can take several minutes if you have a large number of files or folders set for offline status, and sometimes the changes you've made are not significant. In circumstances like this, rather than wait for your system to trundle through and check the date/time stamps of every file on both the remote and local system, you can cancel the synchronization process.

On the second tab of the Synchronization Settings dialog, On Idle, you can configure a folder or folders for automatic synchronization when your system is idle for X minutes and repeat this process every X minutes if the system remains idle by using the Advanced button.

The Scheduled tab invokes the Scheduled Synchronization Wizard, which lets you select the items to synchronize at a time and interval of your choosing. Using this option is an excellent way to do an unattended backup of your key working files in the wee hours of the morning.

MAKING INACCESSIBLE DEVICES ACCESSIBLE

The backup strategy described here, at first glance, looks a bit convoluted, but if you apply a little thought and creativity, you will be amazed at the range of possibilities that unfold from it.

Every power user has at least one device in his or her computer stable that won't play nice with another. In my case, it happens to be my USB zip drive. The device works flawlessly on my IBM ThinkPad, but the USB port on my main working machine will not work under Windows 2000 until Epox comes out with a BIOS update.

This minor irritation would have remained minor had I not developed such a high regard for my trusty little zip drive. It is fast, convenient, and flexible. It addition, it is a perfect place to copy chapter versions and backups as they evolve. In short, I wanted the same backup flexibility I had on my notebook available to me on my main machine. And being the doggedly persistent person I am, I finally found a way.

Do you remember that crossover cable I talked about earlier? If you have more than one computer in your house, or if you work on computers for a living, go buy one. It has to be the handiest item in my arsenal, and it costs only $10. A crossover cable lets you connect the LAN cards of two computers together into a mini-network without hubs or any other hardware.

As I noted previously, my notebook and my main system "talk" to each other via network cards and my crossover cable. Janus (my working system) can see Penelope (my notebook). Penelope can see and utilize the zip; Janus cannot. But if A can see B, and B can utilize C, then why don't I give A access to C?

Here's how to make it so:

- Computer A can talk to B.
- Computer B has a device (C) attached that A cannot use directly, for whatever reason.

- On computer B, select the device from Windows Explorer and share it (select the device, right-click, and select Share from the pop-up menu displayed). Give it a share name to reflect its function or purpose.

- Now go back to computer A and map a drive to that device (via Windows Explorer, Tools, Map Network Drive). In the folder box, you must specify both the computer name and the device's share name. In my case, it is \\penelope\zip.

I created a shortcut on my desktop for this drive mapping and added it to my Send To menu. Now I can quickly back up a file from Windows Explorer with a single right-click.

GUARDING YOUR PROFILE

Windows 2000 stores your user profile in the folder \Documents and Settings*yourusername*. The subfolders contained here contain all the tweaks, configurations, and data files that make up what you see and access while working under Windows 2000. Guard this folder tree with your life! With a little manipulation, this information can be copied to a safe haven and slipped back into place should the unforeseen occur, and you must reinstall your operating system.

> **Note**
>
> If your computer is a member of a Windows 2000 domain network, and you're set up with a Roaming User Profile, your profile folder is automatically copied from the domain server to your computer when you log in and back again when you log out. It is an automatic backup, of sorts, so you can be a little more relaxed about it.
>
> If you need to restore a profile copy in this environment, you should contact your network administrator because this task is fairly tricky.

The following are some of the invaluable goodies contained on the profile tree:

- Your Favorites folder
- Your History folder
- All the configuration settings and program templates for MS Office
- Your Desktop settings
- The default folder for data files (My Documents)
- Your most recently accessed files list
- The folder your cookies are stored in
- Your SendTo folder
- Your Start menu configuration
- Your section of the Windows Registry
- A bevy of application settings, temp files, and IE history files, in a folder called Local Settings

As you can see, all this stuff is very good, and it's tailored specifically to your computing experience under Windows 2000.

The root folder of your profile (in my case, C:\Documents and Settings\Bob) contains two key files: NTUSER.DAT and a backup of this file, NTUSER. They are your user Registry settings and are locked by the operating system in such a way as to forbid any other program from accessing them directly. Therefore, you cannot copy either of these files while logged on as *yourusername* (even if you have administrative rights under *yourusername)*. An attempted copy operation will fail. The problem is that the rest of the tree structure is useless without these key files because they tell the operating system (and indirectly, the programs that use them) which files can be found where.

Ah, grasshopper, but this problem is not insurmountable. The following steps illustrate how you can wrest a copy of your profile away from the arms of Windows 2000.

Note

The following example uses a network drive as a copy point for simplicity. Realistically, the place you copy your profile is dependent on the resources at hand. The key here is to get it off your system volume and somewhere safe. This location can be a zip drive (if it will fit), a CD-R drive, or at the very least, a separate partition. Personally, I keep my profile backed up to both another partition on my main system and a backup partition on my notebook. I tend to be a bit protective of my data, and for good reason, as you will read shortly.

1. Log off from *yourusername* and log on as Administrator. This is a key step; as noted previously, you cannot properly copy your profile tree while logged on as yourself.

2. In Windows Explorer, create a folder on a network drive you have access to, and name it—for example, Profile Backup.

3. Go to your user profile (in my case, C:\Documents and Settings\Bob), select the highest folder in your profile tree (Bob), and drop it on the network folder you just created (Profile Backup). Go have a cup of coffee; this process could take awhile if you have several data files stored here.

4. Last but not least, make sure you keep this backup profile updated on a routine basis. Most users can generally afford to lose a day or so of work; losing some work is unpleasant, but it is tolerable. But if you're like me, by the end of a busy week, I've probably added 10 or more "gems" to my Favorites list, messed with my NORMAL.DOT template three or four times, and shuffled my Start menu at least once.

The preceding routine is not about protecting your data; that is a separate routine which should be done on a level that reflects the value you place on the data you create every day. What it is about is protecting the configuration settings that represent your daily working environment under Windows 2000.

So, you follow this sage advice and dutifully copy your profile somewhere safe on a routine basis. How is this effort going to reward you? Well, should you need to reinstall your

PART

VI

CH

33

operating system, your efforts are going to reward you by allowing you to re-create your desktop, its shortcuts, and most of your program configurations quickly and painlessly.

Trust Me, It Happens to Everyone

What follows is a personal experience I had right in the midst of writing this very chapter.

Some hard drives run for 10 years; some die an untimely death when they are only a month old—hence the term *Mean* Time Between Failure (MTBF), which is an average estimate of how long the drive manufacturer expects its product to run before it fails. Unfortunately, I ended up on the low end of the bell curve the other day when my three-month old hard drive died a prompt and dramatic death. Luckily, I had made a profile backup the night before onto a partition on my notebook reserved solely for machine-to-machine backups.

I borrowed a spare hard drive from a friend, partitioned it in two (*always, always* make a data partition on your drive), installed the latest build of Windows 2000 on the boot partition, and installed the base productivity programs I use every day (Office 2000 and a smattering of "can't live without" utilities). This last step is an important one. To slide an alternative profile into an existing installation, you must restore your system to a point that closely mirrors when you backed up your earlier profile. In my case, this necessitates installing Office. You do not have to configure or tweak anything; just install it to ensure the Windows 2000 Registry knows it exists.

With all key applications installed, I connected my trusty crossover cable to my notebook, logged off as Bob, and logged back on as Administrator. I connected to the notebook's backup partition and copied my saved profile to my main system. I logged off as Administrator, logged on as Bob, and presto-pocus: My desktop returned, Word found all my tweaked document templates, my Favorites were right where I left them, and Outlook knew exactly where to find my data files. I often find myself cursing as I watch a progress bar tick away at 3 a.m. as I store my day's profile onto my notebook for safekeeping, but when I'm going the other way and fixing a disaster, that progress bar is a lovely sight indeed.

THIRD-PARTY MANAGEMENT TOOLS

Table 33.2 provides a list of tools that you should not be without if you are serious about hard disk tweaking, backup, and recovery. By searching on the Web, you can find any of these programs easily because they are so popular.

TABLE 33.2   THIRD-PARTY TOOLS

Type of Program	Vendor	Product Name
Defragmentation Programs	Executive Software	Diskeeper
Undelete Programs	Executive Software	Undelete
Disk Management Tools	PowerQuest	DriveImage
	PowerQuest	Drive Copy
Compression Programs	Nico Mak Computing	WinZip
	PKWare	PKZip
	Pacific Gold Coast Corp.	TurboZIP
	Info-Zip	Info-Zip

HARD DISK AND SYSTEM TROUBLESHOOTING

Eventually, if you work with computers for long enough, you are going to face some form of hard disk problem. It's not a matter of *if*; it's a matter of *when*. The laws of statistics apply to everyone and everything—and that includes hard drives. In the following sections, when I speak of hard drive problems, I'm not referring to a software program that is acting petulantly or a DLL that has been overwritten by a poorly designed installation routine. I'm talking about the inability to access a critical file, a hard drive that will not boot, or one of those cryptic `Fatal Error - Cannot access hard disk` messages that cause the blood to drain from the face of even the hardiest administrator.

These sections are not meant to be comprehensive. Full books have been written on solving hardware problems, and thousands of individual chapters on hard drives and the multitude of problems they can exhibit. What these sections will do, however, is give you some tried-and-true directions to head in if your hard drive starts to give you grief.

Hard drive problems range from file system structures that have been twisted out of shape to catastrophic, dead-in-the-water hard drive failures. And as any seasoned administrator will tell you, the catastrophic failures are the easy ones to diagnose and fix. More often than not, the inconsistent "what the heck?" problems are the real "head-scratchers."

To keep it simple, let's begin with the most important factor in troubleshooting problems of all shapes and sizes—be it a car that will not start or a computer that will not boot. And that is...

TAKE THE MENTAL APPROACH FIRST

I come from a long line of tradesmen who made a living getting their hands dirty and solving mechanical problems. As a writer and computer consultant, I rarely get my hands dirty anymore, but I have discovered that the principles of problem solving I learned when I was young are the same across all fields. You need to be methodical, and if you are going to make assumptions, they had better be good ones; otherwise, you just might steer yourself down the wrong garden path.

The very first step to take when you have a disk access problem is to stop, sit down, and think. Although this advice might seem obvious, it is seldom realized in practice. People experience what they conclude is a hard drive problem, open their case, and start ripping out components when, in fact, they have a file system problem that could have been easily resolved by running ScanDisk on their drive. Similarly, others start reinstalling operating systems when the problem is not software at all, but a failing CMOS battery that is causing the motherboard to lose sight of the hard drive.

None of this exposition is meant to imply that I'm smarter or better at diagnosing problems than the next guy, and in the end, I might come to the same conclusion as the person who leaped in and started ripping his or her case apart. What separates us, in my humble opinion, is that the steps I use to solve a problem today will apply equally well to a completely different problem I encounter a week from now.

When you have a hard drive problem—or what you think is a hard drive problem—before you pick up a CD-ROM or a screwdriver, get yourself a cup of coffee, and take a few minutes to get a clear picture of the nature of the problem in front of you. The following are some questions you might want to ask yourself:

- When did the problem start?
- What was I doing when I first noticed the problem?
- Is the problem consistent? If so, how? If not, what is missing from the puzzle?

This last point bears some elaboration. Computers, as a whole, are extraordinarily consistent devices. Input goes in here; output comes out over there. In the case of hard drives, you lay out structures on them, and the operating system uses these structures to tell programs where their data is located. When you have inconsistencies at work, one of two forces is at work:

1. You are not seeing or you're overlooking something.
2. You could have more than one problem on your hands.

The key of this forced reflection is to have a "plan" before you react. And the cornerstone of that plan must be to do no further harm and to figure out what the problem is without complicating matters further.

So, the next highly recommended tools to pick up, after you've pondered and had a cup of coffee, are a notepad and a pencil. Begin by jotting down some notes on what happened, what you think the problem is, and what might be a good course of action to solve that problem. Use your notepad to reason out the problem; more often than not, eliminating a piece of flawed logic with an eraser is easier than restoring all the programs to your hard drive.

PROBLEMS AND SOLUTIONS

Hard drive problems fall into two general categories:

- Hardware
- File structure

Hardware-related problems involve the hard drive itself, cabling, power, connections, and the motherboard.

File structure problems involve the tracks and partitions on the hard disk, the boot records, and the files the operating system uses to initialize itself.

If you power up your computer and the BIOS cannot find the attached hard drive, chances are you have a hardware problem. On the other hand, if the BIOS finds and recognizes your hard drive but fails to boot, you likely have a file structure problem. Note the *chances are* and *likely* qualifiers. Bear in mind, as you read through the following scenarios, the complications that can be brought on by compounded problems. In other words, file structure problems and hardware problems can, at times, overlap. For example, a damaged master boot record (MBR) may be the result of a failing hard drive; repairing the MBR might fix a consequence of the problem but not the problem itself.

SCSI Disk Boot Problems

A boot problem can sometimes be caused by SCSI settings that have changed since you installed Windows 2000. The state of the SCSI BIOS at the time you installed Windows 2000 becomes part of the setup of the operating system and is stored in the BOOT.INI file. If you subsequently make a change in the SCSI BIOS after NT is installed, that alone can contradict the stored BOOT.INI file settings and can prevent the operating system from finding the system files and booting up. Don't change the SCSI BIOS settings after you install Windows 2000, or if you do, you should edit BOOT.INI in a text editor (carefully!) to reflect the changes. The BOOT.INI file uses the following syntax:

```
scsi(A)disk(B)rdisk(C)partition(D)\<winnt_dir>
```

Here are the specifics for the parameters in the ARC path when you use the `scsi()` syntax on an X86 computer:

- A is the ordinal number for the adapter linked to the Ntbootdd.sys driver.
- B is the SCSI ID for the target disk.
- C is the SCSI logical unit (LUN). Although it could be a separate disk, most SCSI setups have only one LUN per SCSI ID.
- D is the partition.

SYSTEM STARTS BUT CANNOT FIND THE HARD DRIVE

If the computer fires up (the BIOS information appears and the floppy drive is accessed but nothing more), you have some sleuthing to do. Just follow these steps:

1. Turn off the computer, open it, and check the cables. Are the power and data cables attached to the drive? Is the wide, flat data cable flipped over backward on end? Check to see that pin #1 on the motherboard connects to pin #1 on the drive.

2. Check the settings on the drive to make sure they are correct. If you have a SCSI drive, check the ID number and termination as per the instruction manual for the drive. If you have an IDE drive, check the master/slave settings and channel assignment. If you have two devices on the same IDE channel, both set to master or both set to slave, there will be a conflict. You can have only one master and one slave per IDE channel. You typically change the setting by using a little jumper on the back of the hard drive next to the data and power connectors (ditto for IDE-based CD-ROM drives).

3. Check the BIOS settings by pressing the appropriate key during POST (Power-On Self Test) and having the computer autodetect the drive type. Make sure the drive is listed and/or recognized.

| Tip #405 | Most modern PCs and BIOSs autodetect the hard drive that's connected to the data cable after the drive gets power. You no longer must enter all the explicit information about the drive, such as number of heads, sectors, the landing zone, and so on. Just set the BIOS to Autodetect. |

HARD DRIVE INITIALIZES BUT WILL NOT BOOT

Windows 2000 offers several features that allow you to repair a system that will not start or will not load Windows 2000. These features are useful if some of your system files become corrupted or are accidentally erased, or if you have installed software or device drivers that cause your system to not work properly.

USING SAFE MODE   Using Safe mode, you can start your system with a minimal set of device drivers and services. For example, if newly installed device drivers or software is preventing your computer from starting, you might be able to start your computer in Safe mode and then remove the software or device drivers from your system. Safe mode does not work in all circumstances, especially if your system files are corrupted or missing, or your hard disk is damaged or has failed.

Tip #406	If a symptom does not reappear when you start in Safe mode, you can eliminate the default settings and minimum device drivers as possible causes.

Safe mode starts Windows 2000 using only basic files and drivers (mouse, except serial mouse devices; monitor; keyboard; mass storage; base video; default system services; and no network connections). If your computer does not start successfully using Safe mode, you might need to use the Emergency Repair Disk option discussed in Table 33.3 to repair your system.

TABLE 33.3   SAFE MODE STARTUP OPTIONS

Safe Mode with Networking	Starts Windows 2000 using only basic files and drivers, plus network connections.
Safe Mode with Command Prompt	Starts Windows 2000 using only basic files and drivers. After you log on, the command prompt is displayed instead of the Windows desktop.
Enable Boot Logging	Starts Windows 2000 while logging all the drivers and services that were loaded (or not loaded) by the system to a file. This file, called ntbtlog.txt, is located in the %windir% directory. Safe Mode, Safe Mode with Networking, and Safe Mode with Command Prompt add to the boot log a list of all the drivers and services that are loaded. The boot log is useful in determining the exact cause of system startup problems.
Enable VGA Mode	Starts Windows 2000 using the basic VGA driver. This mode is useful when you have installed a new driver for your video card that is causing Windows 2000 to hang or start and lock up half-way into the initialization process. The basic video driver is always used when you start Windows 2000 in Safe mode (either Safe Mode, Safe Mode with Networking, or Safe Mode with Command Prompt).
Last Known Good Configuration	Starts Windows 2000 using the Registry information that Windows saved at the last shutdown. Use this option only in cases in which you strongly suspect a program has written incorrect or damaging information to the Registry. The last known good configuration does not solve problems caused by corrupted or missing drivers or files. Also, any changes made since the last successful startup are lost.
Debugging Mode	Starts Windows 2000 while sending debug information through a serial cable to another computer.

THE RECOVERY CONSOLE   The Recovery Console feature provides you with a command-line interface that enables you to repair system problems via a limited set of commands. For example, you could use the Recovery Console to enable and disable services, repair a corrupted master boot record, or copy system files from a floppy disk or a CD-ROM. The Recovery Console gives you complete control over the repair process but can be dangerous if not used with caution. If you're not an advanced user, you should stay away from this set of commands.

To run the Recovery Console on a system that will not start, do the following:

1. Insert the Windows 2000 Professional Setup Disk into your floppy drive or, if you have a bootable CD-ROM drive, insert the Windows 2000 Professional CD into your CD-ROM drive.

2. Restart your computer.

3. Follow the directions on the screen. If you're using the Setup disks, you are prompted to insert the other Setup disks into the disk drive. Loading files might take several minutes. Choose the options to repair your Windows 2000 installation and finally to start the Recovery Console.

Note   To see the commands available on the Recovery Console, type `help` at its command prompt.

As an alternative, you can install the Recovery Console on your computer so that it is always available. Note that you must be logged on as Administrator or as a member of the Administrators group to be able to complete this procedure.

1. Log on to Windows as Administrator or as a user with those rights.

2. With Windows running, insert the Windows 2000 Professional CD into your CD-ROM drive.

3. If you're prompted to upgrade to Windows 2000, choose No.

4. At the command prompt, switch to your CD-ROM drive, and then type the following:
   `\i386\winnt32.exe /cmdcons`

5. A dialog box appears, explaining what the Recovery Console is for, telling you it requires about 7MB of hard disk space, and asking whether you want to precede. Click Yes.

6. A wizard starts and copies the files onto your hard disk. That's it.

Now that the Recovery Console is installed, it is listed as one of the operating system options to boot from.

The following are some notes on installing the Recovery Console:

- To run the Recovery Console, you must restart your computer and select the Recovery Console option from the list of available operating systems.

- You must be logged on as Administrator or as a member of the Administrators group to be able to complete this procedure. If your computer is connected to a network, network policy settings may also prevent you from completing this procedure.

- To see the commands available on the Recovery Console, type `help` at the command prompt.

- You can allow a user to run the Recovery Console without logging on by enabling the AutoAdminLogon attribute in the Security Configuration Editor. The AutoAdminLogin attribute is located in the Console tree under Local Computer Policy/Computer Configuration/Windows Settings/Security Settings/Local Policies/ Security Options.

- If your computer does not start, you can run the Recovery Console from the Windows 2000 Professional CD (if you have a bootable CD-ROM drive) or the Setup disks.

Follow these steps to remove the Recovery Console:

1. Restart the computer.
2. Double-click My Computer, and then double-click the hard drive on which you installed the Recovery Console.
3. Choose Tools, Folder Options, View.
4. Click Show Hidden Files and Folders, clear the Hide Protected Operating System Files check box, and then click OK.
5. At the root directory, look for the \Cmdcons folder. If you don't see it, try another partition if your system has multiple partitions. It'll be just off the root.
6. At the root directory, delete the file Cmldr.
7. At the root directory, right-click the BOOT.INI file, and then click Properties.
8. Clear the Read-only check box, and then click OK.
9. Open BOOT.INI in Notepad, and remove the entry for the Recovery Console. It looks similar to this:
   ```
   C:\cmdcons\bootsect.dat="Microsoft Windows 2000 Recovery Console" /cmdcons
   ```
   Delete the entire line of text.
10. Save the BOOT.INI file and close it.
11. Change the attribute for the BOOT.INI file back to Read-only.
12. Hide your system files again by using the Folder options.

Caution

Modifying the BOOT.INI file incorrectly may prevent your computer from restarting. Be sure to delete only the entry for the Recovery Console.

USING AN EMERGENCY REPAIR DISK (ERD)   The Emergency Repair Disk (ERD) utility helps you repair problems with system files, your startup environment (if you have a dual-boot or multiple-boot system), and the partition boot sector on your boot volume. Before you use the Emergency Repair Disk feature to repair your system, you must create an Emergency Repair Disk. You can do so by using the Backup utility. Even if you have not created an Emergency Repair Disk, you can still try to use the Emergency Repair Disk process; however, any changes you have made to your system, such as Service Pack updates, may be lost and may need to be reinstalled.

INSTALL A PARALLEL COPY OF WINDOWS 2000 AND MODIFY THE BROKEN ONE   Before you resort to doing a fresh installation over the top of a dead system, or wiping out the disk and starting over, you might want to try one other approach. This trick can sometimes get you up and running again, assuming you have enough disk space—and some patience. The following procedure creates a back door into a broken installation so that you can remove or change offending drivers, disable some offending services, tweak the Registry, and so on in hopes of getting it back up again. If nothing else, you can do a clean installation and pull in your settings from the old installation.

The basic idea is that you do a clean installation of Windows 2000 into a fresh directory. Then you can use Regedt32 either to alter the Registry of the dead system or pull what you can out of it (such as user settings) into the new one so that you can trash the old installation.

Here are the basic steps:

1. Install Windows 2000 into a fresh directory (a clean installation). For example, if your Windows directory is C:\WINNT, you might use C:\WIN2K for this new installation.
2. Boot up Windows using the newly installed system.
3. Try to repair the old copy by deleting or replacing defective driver files in the original Windows installation directory.

If you suspect that a system service is crashing on bootup and that's what's crashing your computer, you can try editing the old system's Registry to disable the service. Here's how:

1. Run Regedt32.exe from the newly installed version of Windows NT and select the following key:

   HKEY_LOCAL_MACHINE

> **Note**
>
> If you need help running Regedt32, see Chapter 35, "The Registry." Don't tinker with the Registry unless you know what you're doing. Improper editing of the Registry can result in a dead computer.

2. Click Load Hive on the Registry menu, and open the following Registry file on the original Windows NT installation folder

\oldwindowsfolder\System32\Config\System

where *oldwindowsfolder* is the name of the folder of your original Windows installation.

3. Assign this hive a name such as OldSystem. This key contains the old HKEY_LOCAL_MACHINE\System data from your old setup.

4. Browse into the subkey CurrentControlSet if it's displayed. If it's not, look in key Select at Value Current. It will be a number such as 1, 2, or 3. Back in OldSystem, open key ControlSet00*x*, where *x* is the number you found under Current.

5. Browse into the Services key, and look for the likely offending service. Under each service's key is a value named Start, with one of the following values:

   1   Starts in the first phase of bootup (these services are usually used to access file systems)

   2   Starts automatically, just after booting

   3   Starts manually

   4   Disabled

Services with a Start value of 1 are used to boot Windows, and you shouldn't touch them. Services with a Start value of 2 are started just about the same time the Login dialog appears in Windows. If your Windows system boots and then promptly crashes without your help, try setting the Start value of any suspected service(s) to 3 or 4. Be sure to write down the names of the services and their original Start values before you change anything!

6. Select the OldSystem key, and select Registry, Unload Hive.

7. Use Notepad to view file C:\BOOT.INI. You should see two entries for Windows 2000 Professional, one using the original directory and one using the new directory. Note the order in which they're listed.

8. Shut down Windows and reboot. You must select a Windows installation from the two Windows 2000 Professional entries listed. Refer to your notes made in step 7 to determine which entry is which. Select the old (original) installation to boot.

You might need to repeat this process a few times, disabling a different service or two each time. If you can manage to reboot the old system with some system services disabled, uninstall and reinstall those services to recover your installation.

This procedure is a little bit like performing brain surgery with a shovel, but it has resurrected systems for me before.

AS A LAST RESORT... You can reinstall Windows 2000 over a damaged Windows 2000 system. Doing so might be time-consuming, but reinstalling is useful if the emergency repair process does not solve your problem. In most cases, reinstalling your system over an existing installation causes you to lose changes that you have made to system files (such as driver upgrades or system file updates), but you generally retain your program installations and their related configurations.

SLOW FILE ACCESS

If the time it takes Windows 2000 to find and load a file is getting painfully slow, you likely need to defragment your hard drive (see the discussion of defragmenting earlier in this chapter). Run the Disk Defragmenter utility (by choosing Programs, Accessories, System Tools) and see whether defragmenting makes a difference. If your drive is badly fragmented, you might have to run the program more than once.

TIPS FROM THE WINDOWS PROS: QUIETING A NOISY DRIVE

Hard drives vary in the noise output they produce. Sometimes the stepper motors are annoyingly loud. Other drives have loud spindle motors. When a drive is coupled to the body of the computer housing, motor noises can be effectively amplified, increasing the aggravation you experience using a system. If your computer sounds like a garbage disposal from time to time, chances are good that the stepper is not a quiet one, and as the head dances around on the platters, the drive shakes just enough to get the computer chassis rattling a bit, too. It's a bit like the relationship between the strings and the body of a violin.

Spindle motors (the motor that turns the platters at high speed) often start out life quietly, only to get noisy over time as the bearings wear in (or out). This noise is particularly annoying in laptop computers if you happen to use them in a quiet place, such as a library or in a home office. I actually replaced my 8GB IBM 3.5-inch drive once this year (Dell laptop, free of charge thanks to Dell), only to find that within a few months it developed the same annoying whine again, so I gave up and accepted it.

Some environments, such as recording studios, require that a computer be seen and not heard. For desktop systems, there are a couple of solutions. One is to make up some long wires for the keyboard monitor, and so on and relegate the computer to a closet. A more practical approach is to buy an after-market kit that quiets your PC's power supply and hard disk. Check the Web for information about such kits. One kit you might consider is the Hush Kit from Silent Systems (www.silentsystems.com).

The bottom line here is to check out the specs on drive noise if you care about that. Or you can listen for a quiet computer, find out what kind of drive it has, and then order that brand and model the next time you're shopping.

In the case of serious noise (you turn on the computer, and it really does sound like a garbage disposal), well, you're in trouble. This noise is the sign of your hard disk after crashing (the heads are actually rubbing on the surface of the platters) or in the process of crashing. Get out while the getting is good. Back up your data and/or whole drive, and replace it as soon as possible. Then restore the data.

OS MIX AND MATCH

In this chapter

WHY MULTIBOOT?

In today's world of advanced operating systems and low hard disk prices, it certainly is not uncommon for many users to want to experiment with different computing flavors. The world of consumer computing is rife with many different options. With the proliferation of the Internet and its accompanying high-bandwidth needs, whole operating systems are available for free download via many commercial distributors' FTP sites.

Along with just plain curiosity and experimentation, many users use two or more operating systems because of application requirements. Many users create multiboot systems to run specific applications or games in the most optimal environment possible. Windows 98 is far more suited, for example, to games, digital audio, and many other multimedia-type applications. A developer's need changes to Windows NT or Windows 2000 because these operating systems provide the most robust development environment on the Microsoft platform. I need all these operating systems functioning on a single computer to meet my daily application needs. Other than buying multiple computers, multibooting is the most sensible solution.

> **Note**
>
> You should read, or at least skim, this entire chapter before beginning to implement a complex multiboot arrangement. We have not reiterated some considerations under each scenario. Pay particular attention to the issues of file formats, as well as applications and data sharing between operating systems. Then be sure to see "Tips from the Windows Pros: Living with More Than One OS" at the end of the chapter, which covers third-party multiboot solutions.

You can set up dual- or multiboot configurations on your computer so you can choose between operating systems (or between versions of the same operating system) every time you start your computer. Windows 2000 supports dual-booting with the following operating systems:

- Windows NT 3.51 or Windows NT 4.0
- Windows 95 and Windows 98
- Windows 3.1 or Windows for Workgroups 3.11
- MS-DOS
- OS/2

To set up a dual-boot configuration, it's recommended that you use a separate partition for each operating system. Then, during Windows 2000 setup (which typically you do last), you can use the Advanced Setup option to select a folder on an unused partition.

With Windows 2000 Professional, you have all you need to create a multiboot system with a little careful planning and preparation. Along with the lure of running multiple operating systems via a multiboot configuration there are many considerations to be taken into account. A thorough understanding of the pitfalls associated with a multiboot configuration is essential in order for multiple operating systems to coexist peacefully on the same computer. In this chapter, you will find methodologies applicable to some of the possible configurations you can come across when setting up a multiboot system.

For the purposes of this chapter, we will concentrate primarily on Windows 95, Windows 98, Windows NT 4.0, Windows 2000 Professional, and Linux.

Note

Although this chapter provides some solid fundamentals for dual-booting operating systems, an in-depth discussion of the topic could—and in fact does—fill an entire book. For additional details on setting up multiboot scenarios, we recommend that you pick up a copy of *The Multi-Boot Configuration Handbook*, published by Que.

PREPARATION

As discussed in Chapter 3, "Getting Your Hardware and Software Ready for Windows 2000" and Chapter 4, "Installing Windows 2000," it is certainly possible, with a bit of work, to run multiple operating systems on your Windows 2000 Professional computer. So if you just can't part with that trusty old copy of Windows 95 you're running but need to install another operating system, such as Windows 2000 Pro, you're in luck. Or maybe you're running Windows 98, NT 4.0, Linux, or even MS-DOS. Whatever the operating system on your machine at the moment, you've no doubt spent hours and hours fine-tuning it and learning all the little quirks, and you probably have all the settings, applications, and data files arranged to your liking. Well, take heart—you can probably make it live harmoniously with Windows 2000 Professional.

Caution

I strongly recommend that you create an emergency repair disk before you install another operating system on your computer. That way, you can revert to it in case of catastrophe. Installing a new operating system is not always the smoothest path, as you probably know. If an installation doesn't make it all the way through, you'll appreciate being able to gracefully back out.

PART

VI

CH

34

Depending on your current or planned system, running multiple operating systems can be as simple as installing your new copy of Windows 2000 Professional alongside your current operating system. But if you're like me, that will not be the perfect choice. Either way, I'll try to cover all the common methods so you can make the choice that's right for you. After all, if you were the type who settles for things the way they were, you would skip this chapter because a single operating system is all you need.

As the old adage goes, "Fail to plan, plan to fail." This certainly holds true where multibooting operating systems are concerned. After you have decided what operating systems you're going to multiboot, the rest is just a matter of following a few simple procedures. For the purposes of this discussion, we will be using the Windows 2000 Professional boot loader. This gives you enough flexibility and features to boot all the sample operating systems and requires no extra software on your part. Everything you need will reside within each distribution of each operating system you choose to install.

FILE SYSTEM SPECIFICS

Your goal in creating a multiboot system is to have all the operating systems coexist in such a manner that they will be capable of sharing files with each other. Nothing is more frustrating than realizing that you must reboot to retrieve a file, copy it to a floppy, and reboot again to copy into your other operating system. A little bit of knowledge about file systems can save you many headaches down the road.

File systems are the main differentiating factor between the way operating systems access their data. Not all of them use hard disks in the same manner, so you must understand how each deals with itself as well as with each other. Table 34.1 represents the various file system attributes of each operating system discussed in this chapter. Note that in the table, RW stands for read/write and NS stands for not supported.

TABLE 34.1 RELATIONSHIPS BETWEEN FILE SYSTEMS AND OPERATING SYSTEMS

	Fat16	Fat32	NTFS	Extended2
Windows 95	RW	NS	NS[1]	NS[2]
Windows 95b	RW	RW	NS[1]	NS[2]
Windows 98	RW	RW	NS[1]	NS[2]
Windows NT 4.0	RW	NS[3]	RW	NS[4]
Windows 2000	RW	RW	RW	NS[4]
Linux	RW	RW	RW	RW[5]

1. *Windows 9x can read the NTFS file system via a free utility call NTFSDOS. Although NTFSDOS is read-only, it works very well and is highly recommended. You can obtain NTFSDOS from* http://www.sysinternals.com.

2. *Windows 9x can gain read-only access to Linux's extended2 file system by using the free utility FSDEXT2. This utility can be found at* http://www.yipton.demon.co.uk.

3. *You can use the FAT32 utility for Windows NT 4.0 to read and write to FAT32 file systems from Windows NT 4.0. This utility can be obtained from* http://www.sysinternals.com. *This utility is not free.*

4. *Windows NT 4.0 and Windows 2000 can read extended2 file systems by using the free utility EX2FS. This utility can be found at* http://www.chat.ru/~ashedel/ext2fsnt.

5. *Although the 2.2.x Linux kernel does contain a read/write driver for NTFS, you should use the driver only in read-only mode. The write portion of the NTFS driver is still in the very early stages of development and might damage your partition. You can enable read-only support when recompiling your kernel for NTFS support.*

Understanding the interplay between these various file systems is key in creating an efficient multiboot system. Different configurations are available depending on your needs. In the best situations, you want to be able to share files transparently among your various operating systems. By separating the implementation from the presentation, you will give yourself a greater degree of comfort when going through your day-to-day operations.

Where Microsoft operating systems are concerned, you have the choice of sometimes using several different file systems with which to run your system. Each file system has its strengths and weaknesses. Ultimately, you must decide which is best, based on your hardware and the application for which you are creating your multiboot system. The following sections quickly recap file system descriptions, with an eye toward multibooting issues.

FAT16

FAT16 is the oldest file system mentioned in this chapter. It was originally intended for file systems based on the DOS operating system. As such, it is quite antiquated and not often used today. FAT16 might be your only choice in some situations due to its two major advantages:

■ FAT16 is supported by many operating systems, including Windows NT 4.0, Windows 2000, Windows 95/98, OS/2, MS-DOS, and Windows for Workgroups and Linux.

■ The structure of the FAT16 file system is much simpler than the others, giving it much less software overhead. This gives FAT16 increased speed on volumes less than 1GB in size.

One big limitation of FAT16 is the fact that it cannot be installed in partitions greater than 2GB in size. As explained later in the chapter, this limitation has now been overcome by FAT16's newer brother, FAT32.

> **Note**
>
> If you are using the first edition of Windows 95, you can use only the FAT16 file system. Versions of Windows 95 prior to Windows 95 OSR2 will not install on FAT32 partitions. A prompt upgrade to Windows 98 is recommended for this as well as for many other reasons.

FAT32

The FAT32 file system was introduced with Windows 95 OSR2. FAT32 was essentially the answer to most of the shortcomings of FAT16. The following are among FAT32's strengths:

■ FAT32 supports partitions up to 2TB in size (that's 2,048GB to you and me).

■ FAT32 increased the number of clusters (decreasing the cluster size) on the hard disk, making the storage of small files take up less room than it did previously with FAT16.

■ The structure of FAT32 remains very small, providing a notable speed increase over FAT16.

Of course, with all change comes great pain. The introduction of FAT32 caused many more problems than it solved. To this day, Windows NT 4.0 does not natively support FAT32. The addition of FAT32 file support into Windows 2000 is a welcome one, especially for multibooting users. Where standalone servers or workstations are concerned, NTFS is more desirable than FAT32, as explained in the following section.

NTFS

The New Technology File System, or NTFS, brought with it many welcome additions to the world of Microsoft computing, including the following:

- Permissions—NTFS brought with it a concept used in the UNIX world for quite some time. Permissions enable you to configure files and folders to be accessible to specific people, groups of people, or both. This is imperative when you are talking about networked multiuser operating systems.

- Compression—You can now transparently compress folders or files on an NTFS volume.

- Reliability—This was a major improvement over the FAT-type file systems. NTFS is much more reliable, and as such is suited to a server environment. Disk repair applications seldom need to be run on an NTFS file system.

- Large volumes are accessed much quicker with NTFS. Although FAT still rules the 1GB or lower area, NTFS excels at accessing files and folders with great speed over very large disk partitions.

- Encryption came with the version of NTFS supplied with Windows 2000. Now you can lock individual files or folders for high levels of security.

- Dynamic disk arrangements enable you to group drives in one large aggregation (see Chapter 33, "Managing the Hard Disk," for a full discussion). However, beware with dynamic disks—you can't boot anything except Windows 2000 from a dynamic drive, so you can't multiboot with Windows 95/98 on the same drive. You could if it were on another drive, but few people have another drive to spare.

APPLICATION CONSIDERATIONS

Along with all the file system considerations of a multiboot system, application installation problems also can arise unless you install each operating system and compatible applications in a separate partition. This is particularly true of Microsoft operating systems because some of them share the same installed directory names. Because of these potential problems, the following list of precautions is particularly useful:

- It's good practice to isolate operating systems whenever possible to minimize the impact of any catastrophic events such as system crashes, crunched file allocation tables, or applications that run amok. In other words, good disk partitioning is one way to increase protection for all the operating systems you run.

- It is a much cleaner installation if you put Windows 2000 Professional on a separate partition because doing so minimizes the chances that applications running on the different platforms will dump on one another's settings in unexpected ways.

- Sharing the same partition for applications, programs, and the operating system is not ideal. Whenever possible, I prefer to have one partition for the operating system, another for applications, and a third for data. Therefore, following this practice of isolation, along with using yet another partition for each additional operating system, helps keep everything straight.

The last reason is becoming harder to accomplish because so many applications are now integrating themselves more tightly with the operating system. For such applications, you still can easily attain operating system isolation simply by installing the applications twice, once for each operating system. However, the question arises, do you install the application into the same directory for each operating system? This should be decided on a case-by-base basis after you experiment a bit with the application. As a rule, we have found that installing an application for each operating system into the same directory works most of the time and gives you the advantage of not consuming extra hard disk space for each new installation.

If you find that an application acts erratically when shared in this way, install it into a separate directory from each operating system. That is, create a special application folder for each operating system (for example, \Program Files\win98 or \Program Files\linux, and so on) and install problem apps there.

THE WINDOWS 2000 BOOT LOADER

As mentioned earlier in this chapter, one of the great advantages of the approaches we're advocating in this chapter is that we're using the Windows 2000 boot loader. The Windows 2000 boot loader is very functional and reliable. After you've learned some of its basics, you'll have no problem setting up or modifying its default behavior. The following sections explain the functioning of the boot loader.

THE MASTER BOOT RECORD

The *master boot record* (MBR) is the portion of the disk that tells your computer where to find the partition boot sector. All operating systems must be accessed by some type of master boot record, whether it is the system's native code or a multiboot utility. Where they differ, however, is in the code contained in the partition boot sector.

When your system is booted, a resulting chain of events ensues, based on your currently installed operating systems. The following is a simplified version of this chain of events for a single-operating system setup containing only Windows 2000:

1. After POST (power on self test), the system BIOS reads the master boot record (MBR).
2. Control is passed to the master boot record, which then looks for the system partition on the partition table of the startup disk, as defined in your BIOS.
3. After a system partition is found, the master boot record will load sector 0, the partition boot sector, into memory and executes it.
4. The partition boot sector points to NTLDR (NT loader) in the root of the partition and executes that.
5. NTLDR reads the contents of BOOT.INI, located at the root of the partition, and displays the boot menu based on the BOOT.INI operating system entries.

At this point, the user can select the operating system to boot into. Throughout the multi-boot scenarios discussed in this chapter, you'll see this menu change as you add operating systems to your computer.

 If you are having problems with the Windows boot loader, see "Repairing the Windows 2000 Boot Loader" in the "Troubleshooting" section at the end of this chapter.

 If you want to remove the Windows boot loader, see "Removing the Windows 2000 Boot Loader" in the "Troubleshooting" section at the end of this chapter.

THE BOOT.INI SETTINGS FILE

Probably one of the most important files in this process, the BOOT.INI file handles many options for booting your system. For now, you can see your current BOOT.INI by selecting Start, Run and entering `notepad C:\boot.ini`. As you can see, the BOOT.INI file has two sections.

As you read further, you will gain even more knowledge of how the BOOT.INI file works by adding and modifying your own boot selections.

`[boot loader] =`

This section defines two specific settings:

- Timeout—This setting defines how long the system will wait until it boots into the default operating system. This value is in seconds and can be set to –1 to make the system wait until you actually make a manual selection. A setting of 0 makes the system boot immediately into the default operating system.
- Default—This is the default operating system that will boot up, unless there is user intervention.

`[operating systems] =`

This section contains a list of operating systems installed on your computer. You can see the option for Windows 2000 in the BOOT.INI if you've successfully completed an installation.

MULTIBOOT SCENARIOS

The possibilities for multibooting are nearly endless when you consider that a system can have multiple drives, each drive can have multiple partitions, and each partition can have an operating system on it. However, the scenarios discussed next represent the most common and usable configurations. When you understand the scenarios offered here, you should be able to effectively conquer any multiboot setup.

We recommend that you at least read through the first scenario fully, regardless of your own designs. This will give you a better understanding of the overall process. We'll also refer to that scenario so we can reduce repetition. All these configurations assume that you already have a working computer with at least a CD-ROM drive and hard disk.

Note

Always be careful to watch out for the file system interplay between all these operating systems. Always use Table 34.1 as a reference before forging ahead with your installations. This will save you many of the common problems associated with setting up a multiboot system.

Each of the following sections is divided into two types of situations. The first merely adds on to an already running system, and the second is the more ideal method of starting from scratch. We examine both of these methods with each given scenario.

Tip #407

All the following scenarios will work from the assumption that you are able to boot from your CD-ROM drive. Most modern computers have this capability. A little-known fact is that some of the operating systems in these examples are capable of booting from their respective CD-ROM installation disks. Windows NT 4.0 and Windows 2000 Professional can and will boot from your CD-ROM drive, as will OEM versions of Windows 98 and most modern versions of Linux. This method is much quicker and less error prone than the traditional method of booting from a floppy disk. To enable booting from the CD-ROM drive on your computer, consult your computer's operating manual for the proper method to enable this feature from the system BIOS. Because there are many different BIOS manufacturers, there are many different ways to enable this feature.

Booting from the CD-ROM is usually enabled simply by changing the boot sequence from within your system's BIOS so that it checks the CD for an operating system before checking the hard drive. Chapter 4 has more ideas on how to boot from a CD-ROM in case you're having trouble in this department. Look for the troubleshooting tip at the end of the chapter titled "DOS Won't Recognize the CD-ROM Drive."

DUAL-BOOTING WINDOWS 2000 PROFESSIONAL AND WINDOWS 98

Many people want or need to run Windows 98 and Windows 2000 in the same computer. The following sections discuss two ways of doing this:

- In the same partition
- In separate partitions

Note

In a dual-boot scenario, Windows 98 is Windows 2000–aware. You can install Windows 98 after installing Windows 2000 and it will preserve the boot loader. In all other cases (for example, with other operating systems), you must install Windows 2000 last.

PUTTING WINDOWS 2000 PROFESSIONAL AND WINDOWS 98 IN THE SAME PARTITION

If you already have a Windows 95/98 installation, you can simply install Windows 2000 Professional beside it for a dual-boot arrangement from the same partition. As you can see in Table 34.1, Windows 2000 supports all the Windows 9x series file systems. The Windows 2000 installer simply makes an image of the current Windows boot sector and places it on the root of your C: drive in a file called BOOTSECT.DOS. This file then is referenced from C:\BOOT.INI to offer you the choice of booting into your previous Windows install.

Follow these steps to install both Windows 2000 and 9x on the same partition:

1. Assuming you have successfully installed Windows 98 or 95 on your system, begin the Windows 2000 Professional installation wizard by inserting the CD-ROM.

2. If the wizard does not autorun, you can initialize it by choosing Start, Run and then typing D:\i386\winnt, where D: is the letter of your CD-ROM drive.

3. After the wizard has launched, you will be prompted on whether you'd like to upgrade your currently installed Windows 98 system. Select No to install a new copy of Windows 2000 (Clean Install). This way, your existing Windows 98 system will stay intact. This will install Windows 2000, alongside your existing Windows 98 system, into a new system folder called \WINNT. From there, simply install Windows 2000 per the instructions on the installation wizard.

4. When the Windows 2000 installation has concluded, you should be able to successfully boot into either Windows 2000 or Windows 98 via the Windows 2000 boot menu presented at system startup.

Although this configuration is common, it can have its pitfalls. The following are some important things to keep in mind with this configuration:

- Dual-booting Windows 2000 and Windows 98 from the same partition is ill advised, even by Microsoft in its documentation with Windows 2000 Professional. In this configuration, both operating systems will use the same Program Files folder when you install your applications in either one. Be aware, also, that Registry settings for an application on Windows 9x will not follow you into the Registry of Windows 2000, and visa versa. You might have to reinstall some applications in order for them to function correctly in both operating systems. In some instances, you might even have to purchase Windows 9x- or Windows 2000-specific versions of some applications. Finding out which ones you need to do this with is simply a matter of experimenting with each respective operating system.

Tip #408

Don't worry about the Registries stepping on each other. The Registries will not overwrite one another because Windows 9x uses \Windows\user.dat (or if you have your Windows 9x machine set up for multiple users, the user.dat file is not in \windows but in \windows\profiles) and Windows 2000 stores its registries in \documents and settings\<username>.

If there is a problem at all, it will result from the fact that both operating systems will end up sharing a \Program Files folder. This could result in conflicts in software versions or preference settings you make under one operating system not showing up under the other.

Just as a personal anecdote, much of this book was written on a PC sharing Windows 98 and Windows 2000 Professional on the same partition. There were no particularly unsavory events to report other than some annoying inconsistencies in the behavior of Outlook Express under each OS because we wanted to share the same address book and message store regardless of which operating system we were running.

PUTTING WINDOWS 2000 PROFESSIONAL AND WINDOWS 98 IN SEPARATE PARTITIONS

As you have no doubt gathered by now, the preferred approach uses separate partitions. This arrangement is more flexible and foolproof in the long run.

First, you must plan the installation from a file system standpoint. This will give you a better foundation from which to proceed:

- The Windows 98 partition should be a FAT32 file system with C:\windows (the system directory), along with C:\Program Files contained in it.
- Windows 2000 will reside on the second partition with an NTFS file system containing the Windows 2000 %SystemRoot% directory (typically D:\WINNT), along with D:\Program Files.
- A third and final partition will be a FAT32 file system for sharing data between the two operating systems.

This configuration will give you a good amount of flexibility while using either operating system. In Table 34.1, you can see that both operating systems will be capable of reading the FAT32 partition to share files.

Another important advantage of this configuration is that, during a catastrophic failure, no single operating system can destroy the other. This will provide increased data integrity and isolation. As an additional safeguard, you might even want to format the Windows 2000 partition as NTFS so you can create one or two encrypted folders for maximum data security for your most sensitive files.

By studying Table 34.1, you can deduce the only real downside to this configuration: The Windows 9x partition will not be capable of seeing your NTFS-formatted Windows 2000 partition. This really is not too much of an issue if you make good use of the shared-data FAT32 partition. Because of Windows 9x's incapability to read NTFS, you will also not be able to use any applications installed on the Windows 2000 partition. Again, by installing apps on the shared FAT32 partition, this should not pose a problem.

USING FDISK TO DEFINE PARTITIONS

As we've by now hopefully made clear, given the drawbacks associated with installing Windows 2000 and 98 in the same partition, you're probably better off installing each operating system into its own partition.

PART
VI

CH

34

Chapter 4 covered the fact that Setup will enable you to use unpartitioned free space to create a second partition (either NTFS or not) for installing Windows 2000. You also learned about using a third-party program such as PartitionMagic to more flexibly help in that process, especially if you don't have any "free" (meaning unpartitioned) space on your hard disk, which is likely the case.

In lieu of using PartitionMagic (for whatever reason), you can opt to use the trusty old Microsoft-supplied FDISK program to do your partitioning. As you'd expect, you have less flexibility with this program than with PartitionMagic, but it works okay in a pinch (especially on an unpopulated drive or one you're going to wipe), and a knowledge of FDISK can sometimes come in very handy.

The following discussion shows how to start with a blank hard disk, use FDISK to create the partitions, and then install Windows 98 and Windows 2000. The following explains how to define partitions for each operating system:

1. First, boot from the Windows 98 CD-ROM and select the second option, Boot from CD-ROM (see Figure 34.1).

Note

If you are booting from your Windows 9x installation floppy, select the second option, Start Computer with CD-ROM Support.

Figure 34.1
Selecting a CD-ROM boot from the Windows 98 CD-ROM.

```
Microsoft Windows 98 CD-ROM Startup Menu

1. Boot from Hard Disk
2. Boot from CD-ROM

Enter your choice: _
```

2. After selecting Boot from CD-ROM, a second screen will appear. Select Start Computer with CD-ROM Support.

3. After finally booting into DOS, run the FDISK program, which will give you the opportunity to partition your disk so that each operating system can occupy a different partition. This is simply done by typing fdisk at the prompt:

   A:>fdisk

4. When FDISK is loaded, you will be asked whether to enable large disk support if you are using a version of Windows 9x that is newer than Windows 95 OSR2. If you are not prompted with this option, you can simply use the default FAT16 file system because both NT 4.0 and 9x can read FAT16. For the purposes of this configuration, select Yes. This will enable you to later format the disk with the FAT32 file system. If you select No here, you will only be able to create a partition of 2048MB or less using the FAT16 file system.

5. Next, you will be presented with a menu of options for partitioning your hard disk, as shown in Figure 34.2. For the purposes of this installation, select option 1, Create DOS Partition or Logical DOS Drive. This option enables you to create the first partition for installing Windows 9x.

Caution

Using the FDISK editor is a destructive process. If you have any disk partitions currently defined on your system, be sure to have a backup of all your important data because it might be damaged in this process. Unless you are partitioning your disk for the first time, you might find PartitionMagic more suited to the task of configuring your disk partitions. PartitionMagic also has the added advantage of being able to actually resize your existing partitions for a maximum amount of flexibility. More information on PartitionMagic can be found at

http://www.powerquest.com/partitionmagic/index.html

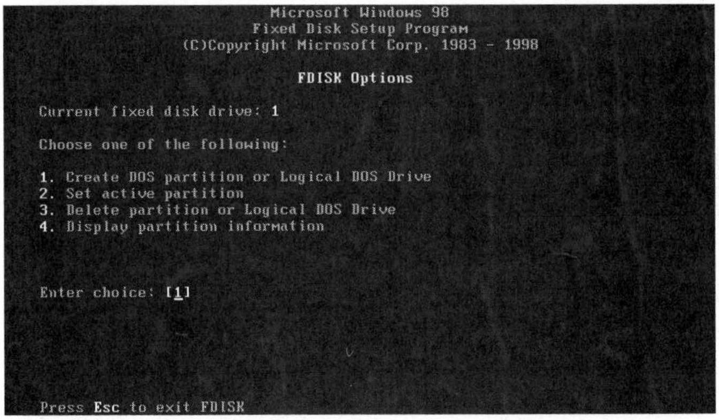

Figure 34.2
The FDISK main
menu screen.

6. Select Create Primary DOS Partition to create a bootable primary partition.

Note

All Microsoft operating systems must be bootable from the first primary partition on the primary IDE bus. The only exclusion to this is a SCSI-based system, which must be bootable from the first primary partition of the SCSI controller-assigned boot disk. This does not mean the system and other files must be installed here; it only means that the Windows boot information must be installed in the MBR (master boot record) of this partition.

7. When asked whether you would like to use the maximum available size for this partition, select No because you will need additional space to be left on the disk for the other two partitions that will house the Windows 2000 system and the shared data partition.

8. Next you are asked for the size of the first partition. This particular setting will vary depending on the operating systems involved and the amount of disk space available.

Table 34.2 (immediately following this set of steps) shows the minimum and recommended sizes for each operating system.

9. Using the information in Table 34.2, enter the desired size for your first primary partition.

PART

VI

Ch

34

> **Note**
>
> Keep in mind that the minimums listed in the table are from Microsoft. You should always make your partitions as large as possible.

10. Next, you must define the first partition as being the *active partition* so that the computer knows from which partition it should try to boot. Press Esc, and you end up with the main FDISK menu. Select the second option, Set Active Partition, to pick the first partition and set it as active.

11. You must now create a logical partition to house your remaining two file systems. This can be done by selecting Create a DOS Partition or Logical DOS Drive from the main FDISK menu, and then selecting Create Extended DOS Partition.

12. Next, FDISK will ask you to define an extended partition, which will house your second operating system. It's advisable that you make that partition roughly the same size as the first partition.

13. The final data partition can be created from either here in FDISK or with the Windows 2000 Professional Disk Administrator.

14. Finally, reboot your system by pressing Esc to exit FDISK. Then press Ctrl+Alt+Delete to restart the computer.

TABLE 34.2   RECOMMENDED HARD DRIVE CAPACITY FOR EACH OPERATING SYSTEM

Operating System	Minimum Size	Recommended Size
Windows 98	205MB to 400MB	2000MB
Windows NT 4.0	124MB	1000MB
Windows 2000 Professional	650MB	2000MB
Linux (Red Hat 6.1)	135MB to 1.2GB	2000MB

INSTALLING WINDOWS 98 INTO THE FIRST PARTITION

After you've defined at least two partitions, you are ready to install Windows 98 into the first one. After that we'll install Windows 2000 in the second one.

1. If you are installing Windows 98 (and you have a bootable version of the installation CD) you can install Windows 98 by booting from the Windows 98 installation CD-ROM. Select Start Windows 98 Setup from CD-ROM to install Windows 98, as shown in Figure 34.3.

> **Note**
>
> If you're having trouble accessing the CD-ROM drive, check the BIOS settings, or as a good little trick, many systems will boot up from a Windows 98 emergency startup disk with CD-ROM support (even one made on another machine). You can boot into DOS this way, with CD-ROM drivers loaded. Then run the Setup program located on the Windows 98 CD. This is discussed more near the end of Chapter 4.

Figure 34.3
Starting the Windows 98 setup from CD-ROM.

2. When you're in the Windows 98 installation program, you will be given the option to format drive C: and continue with the installation. The Windows 98 setup will also require that you format partition D:. Go ahead and do this because you'll have option of converting the partition to the NTFS file system when you run the Windows 2000 setup if you want to go with NTFS.

3. After partitions C: and D: are formatted, continue with the Windows 98 installation, making sure that Windows is placed in the \WINDOWS folder on the C: partition by accepting the default as shown in Figure 34.4.

Caution

If you've been booting from your CD-ROM installation disk, be sure to change the boot sequence in your BIOS so that your hard disk boots before your CD-ROM. This is essential for a successful installation.

Figure 34.4
Make sure the Windows 98 system directory is installed on the C: partition.

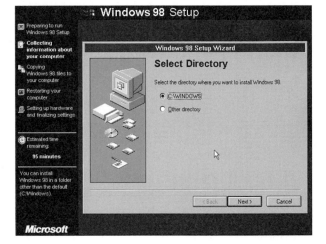

Tip #409

Windows 98 is installed first for a very important reason. Because you will be using the Windows 2000 boot manager to manage your operating system selections, you want to make sure that Windows 98 does not overwrite the Windows 2000 master boot record. Windows 98 will always write its own master boot record to make the system boot into it after an installation. You'll want to make sure that Windows 2000 has the last say in what gets installed at the master boot level so that you can take advantage of its versatile boot loader.

INSTALLING WINDOWS 2000 PROFESSIONAL INTO THE SECOND PARTITION

Continue your multiboot pursuit with the installation of Windows 2000 Professional. Per Microsoft's recommendations, you should run the Windows 2000 installation program from within Windows 98.

1. Insert the Windows 2000 disk. You should be prompted with the dialog box shown in Figure 34.5.

Figure 34.5

2. Because we want to retain the option of booting into Windows 98, we will not select the upgrade method of installation. The Windows NT or 2000 installer will automatically notice that you have an older version of Windows installed and ask you if you'd like to upgrade it. To achieve your goal, click the No button to cancel this action, as shown in Figure 34.5.

3. Select a new installation by clicking the Install Windows 2000 menu selection.

4. The Windows 2000 Setup Wizard will ask you what kind of installation you'd like to perform. Select the Install a New Copy of Windows (Clean Install) as shown in Figure 34.6, and the Windows 98 system will be kept intact and be offered as an additional boot option when the Windows 2000 installation has been successfully completed.

Figure 34.6
Selecting a clean install from the Windows 2000 Professional Setup Wizard.

5. From the Select Special Options page of the Windows 2000 Setup Wizard, you can select the Advanced Options button to specify where you would like the Windows 2000 system folder installed. Most likely, you will want to select the option labeled I Want To Choose the Installation Partition During Setup (see Figure 34.7). This will give you the opportunity to select the D: partition as well as convert it to the NTFS file system further down in the setup.

Tip #410

The other option in this dialog, Windows Installation Folder, enables you to change the name of the folder that will act as the Windows 2000 system root. Because you're installing Windows 2000 into its own separate partition, you can actually use \WINDOWS (rather than the default \WINNT). Actually, you could use your name or anything else that suits you. The folder will be identified to the system via a systemwide variable called %SystemRoot%, no matter what you actually call it on the disk.

Figure 34.7
Enabling the option to choose the Windows 2000 Professional installation directory location from Setup Wizard.

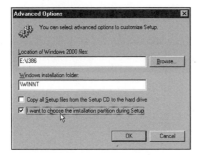

6. After the Windows Setup Wizard copies some files to your hard disk, it will reboot your system and continue the installation from a text-based setup. From this setup, you will have the option to select where you'd like to install your Windows 2000 system. If you've been following along, you would choose the other larger partition you created in the previous section (see Figure 34.8).

Figure 34.8
Selecting the location of the \WINNT install directory from within the text-mode Windows 2000 Setup. Windows NT Setup will offer a similar dialog box.

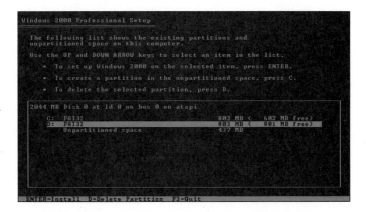

7. Next, you will be given the option to select the type of file system. From here, you can keep your already formatted FAT32 system intact, create a new NTFS or FAT formatted partition, or simply convert your FAT32 partition to NTFS. Because you are installing 2000 into a separate partition, you have the freedom to select the option Convert the Partition to NTFS, which we recommend (see Figure 34.9).

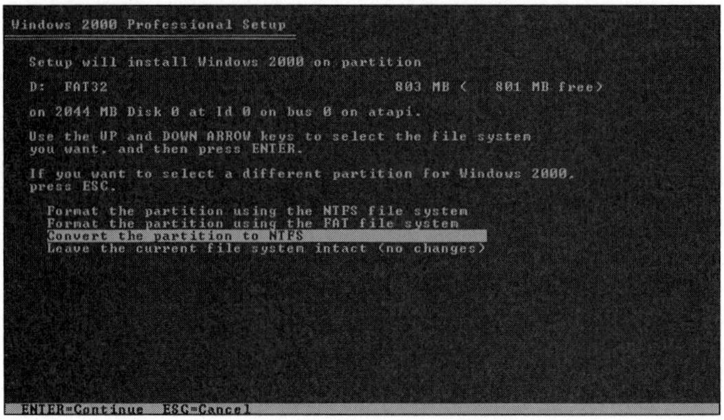

Figure 34.9
Converting the FAT32 file system to NTFS from within the Windows 2000 Professional text-mode setup.

Caution

Be careful! There could be some unsavory repercussions you might not expect if you choose the wrong file system in step 7. If you would like to be able to read the Windows 2000 partition while using Windows 98, you should select the option Leave the Current File System Intact. However, you'll lose the benefits of using NTFS that we discussed earlier in the chapter.

If you choose to convert to NTFS, the installer warns you, too. Sorry if this seems like overkill at this point, but we don't want you to be unhappy, and you can't revert to FAT32 from NTFS without using a third-party program or reformatting the partition.

8. After making your choice, setup will copy files to your hard disk and again reboot your system. The Windows 2000 boot loader will now take control. From here, setup will convert the FAT32 D: partition to NTFS, reboot, and continue with the installation.

9. The Windows 2000 setup will finish its installation and you will be then able to boot into both operating systems using the boot loader at startup.

10. When you restart your computer, you should see the options shown in Figure 34.10.

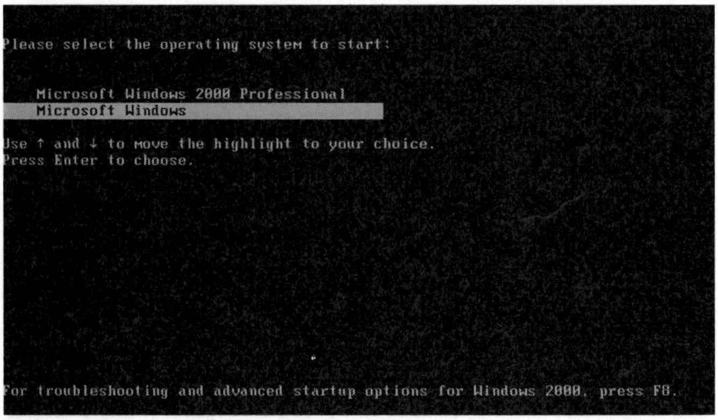

Figure 34.10
The final result! The Windows 2000 boot loader now shows both operating systems at boot time.

Tip #411

Wouldn't it be nice to change the boring name of your Windows 98 boot selection from Microsoft Windows to something a bit more apropos? This can be done as easily as opening the file C:\boot.ini from either operating system and editing the selection's name found in double quotes under the operating systems section.

Note that you must first turn off the read-only attribute by right-clicking the file, selecting Properties, and unchecking the Read-Only check box. After editing this file, be sure to turn the read-only attribute back on. I would be negligent, however, if I didn't warn you that improperly editing this file can leave your system in an unbootable state.

You might want to make a copy of it first, just in case. You can call it BOOT.BACK or something similar. Another approach is to print a hard copy before you edit it.

FORMATTING THE DATA-SHARING PARTITION

Recall that, earlier in this scenario, we discussed the ideal of having a third partition to hold data (and optionally applications) for both operating systems. This way, if one OS crashes or its partition bombs, you just reformat the partition and reinstall the operating system, and your precious data remains intact. Not only that, but backup is expedited. Simply back up the data partition, and rest easy at night knowing that at least your data is secure.

On some of our machines, we're quite content with two partitions only, with data placed either on the Windows 98 partition if it is nonsensitive or on the Windows 2000 NTFS partition (and optionally in an encrypted folder) if it is sensitive. We use a third partition on other machines for neatness and to avoid the possibility of crowding the operating system out of necessary breathing room (swap files, updates, and such).

So, the last step to perform in this scenario is merely to format the remaining shared data partition. This can be done by using PartitionMagic or FDISK, as described earlier in this chapter, or the Windows 2000 Disk Administration program. The idea is to use any remaining disk space for your third partition and format it as FAT32 so that it can be read by both operating systems.

In lieu of a third partition in case you're short on disk space, consider adding a second hard drive and using that for your data and applications.

→ **See** Chapter 33, "Managing the Hard Disk," for more about running and using Disk Management.

After you've created your shared partition, you will be able to see it from both Windows 98 and Windows 2000. From there, simply begin to use it by storing within it files created by your various applications. This will save a great many headaches because you won't have to continuously reboot into Windows 2000 to copy over files that you need to read from Windows 98.

You may optionally store applications there as well. You can create a \Program Files directory on the partition and put your apps there. However, as mentioned much earlier in this chapter, you might have applications that don't like to be shared by two operating systems. In this case, you'll want to install two copies in separate directories or in the \Program Files directories on each operating system's respective partition.

PART

VI

CH

34

One last point (discussed also in Chapter 33) has to do with logical disk names. Always keep logical drive letters in mind when setting up multiboot systems using multiple partitions. When you use file formats that are not compatible among all the operating systems you're using, logical drive letters will likely shift around based on which operating system you're booting.

For example, in the scenario discussed in the preceding section, the third partition's (the data partition) drive letter is likely to get shifted back and forth between D: and E: depending on which operating system is running. Consider Table 34.3 and 34.4 to see what I mean.

TABLE 34.3   LOGIC DRIVE LETTER ASSIGNMENTS IN WINDOWS

Boot Windows 98	Contains	Format	Logical Letter
Partition 1	Windows 98	FAT32	C:
Partition 2	Windows 2000 (invisible)	NTFS	none
Partition 3	Data	FAT32	D:
CD-ROM	N/A	CDFS (CD file system)	E:

TABLE 34.4   LOGIC DRIVE LETTER ASSIGNMENTS IN WINDOWS 2000

Boot Windows 2000	Contains	Format	Logical Letter
Partition 1	Windows 98	FAT32	C:
Partition 2	Windows 2000	NTFS	D:
Partition 3	Data	FAT32	E:
CD-ROM	N/A	CDFS	F:

Notice that under Windows 98 the data partition is D:, whereas under Windows 2000 it is E:. This is not a problem if you store only data on the drive. You simply tell an application to store or retrieve data from the drive in question. You must remember which operating system you're running, though, which can be a petty annoyance, but it's acceptable. If you start to install applications on the data drive, things can become a little more complicated. For example, it becomes more complicated if your applications expect to find support files on a given drive and if Registry entries are pointing to the wrong location. The following is a short discussion of what can be done to remedy the situation in case you want or need static disk volume names, regardless of whether you're booting Windows 98 or Windows 2000.

You might have already thought about using Windows 2000 Disk Management to help. Although it is true that Disk Management can reassign drive letters so that they do not shift around, the new assignments hold true only while in Windows 2000. So, this won't affect how Windows 98 maps drives. In addition, Disk Management won't let you reassign the partition containing the operating system, so reversing D: and E: isn't possible in this case because Windows 2000 is on D: (partition 2). Still, there's hope.

Retail copies of PartitionMagic include a program called DriveMapper that can remap the drive letters under Windows 98. You can run PartitionMagic in Windows 98, use the DriveMapper option, and reassign the data drive to E:, skipping D: altogether when you're running Windows 98. Then make your CD-ROM drive F:. Now, regardless of which operating system you boot into, you'll have the same logical assignments seen in Table 34.5.

TABLE 34.5 LOGICAL DRIVE ASSIGNMENTS AFTER RUNNING DRIVEMAPPER

Boot Windows 98	Contains	Format	Logical Letter
Partition 1	Windows 98	FAT32	C:
Partition 2	Windows 2000 (invisible)	NTFS (invisible)	Nonexistent
Partition 3	Data	FAT32	E:
CD-ROM	N/A	CDFS	F:

Caution

You should be cautious about reassigning drive letters. If possible, reassign letters before you install applications; otherwise, Registry settings, shortcuts, and support files can point to the wrong drive. The best workaround is to reinstall the application under the appropriate operating system after the drive letter is reassigned. Another workaround, though less preferable, is to use the program called MagicMover, which is supplied with retail copies of PartitionMagic. MagicMover has a wizard that can move applications and adjust the Registry as needed. Consult the PartitionMagic user's guide or Help file for more about considerations when reassigning drive letters.

Playing It Safe

Here's the cleanest solution to this whole conundrum of drive letters in Windows 98/Windows 2000 dual-boot situations in which you want a separate data partition whose drive letter doesn't bounce around.

1. Create all three partitions in advance, using PartitionMagic or another utility. Assign them as follows:

    Partition 1: FAT32

    Partition 2: FAT32

    Partition 3: NTFS

2. Install Windows 98 into partition 1. Install Windows 2000 into partition 3. Use partition 2 for data. Without the need or benefit of drive remapping, you'll always see the data drive as D:. Because this required the use of a third-party program, we didn't offer it as the initial solution for sharing a data partition between these two operating systems, even though it is the ideal arrangement.

3. Then, to play it perfectly safe and prevent any programs from dumping on one another from the two operating systems, you can isolate them totally. There are two ways to do this:

    - You can have two program file directories, like this: D:\Program Files 98 and D:\Program Files 2K.

- Alternatively, accept the defaults like this, on each operating system's drive: C:\Program Files and E:\Program Files.

Then simply install applications for each OS in their respective and intended homes. Store only actual data (no applications) on the data partition. This uses a bunch more disk space due to double installation of each application, but all apps are more likely to work in the long run. For example, you won't have to worry about what will happen when you remove an app from one OS and not from the other one.

WINDOWS 2000 PROFESSIONAL AND WINDOWS NT

Installing both Windows NT and Windows 2000 on the same system is also something you might want to do. This configuration is popular for many people already running Windows NT 4.0 who want to try Windows 2000 before completely canning their previous installation. This is a worthwhile pursuit and can be obtained with a little care and planning.

If you already have Windows NT 4.0 installed, you are probably using either the FAT16 file system or NTFS. Looking at Table 34.1, you can see that Windows 2000 supports both of the file systems supported by Windows NT 4.0. When installing Windows 2000 Professional, you simply select a new installation, as opposed to an upgrade, and the installer will handle the rest. As with the previous configuration, Windows 2000 will save your Windows NT 4.0 installation and give you the choice of selecting it at boot time.

This setup also can suffer from the same sort of problems as the Windows 98/Windows 2000 configuration. You must be careful to not overlap your new and old installation directories. This will cause many problems with both the installed and new versions of Windows. Although you can have them coexist on the same partition, it's usually more prudent to just have them occupy separate partitions. This also gives you the added security of not losing everything if one operating system decides to destroy its own partition in a crash.

Caution

Windows 2000 uses an updated version of the NTFS file system: NTFS5. It is strongly recommended that you first update your installed version of Windows NT 4.0 with the latest service pack. This will help ensure that your NT 4.0 installation will be capable of reading your disk after adding Windows 2000 to your system. Service pack 6 is the latest version as of this writing. Failure to do so will probably leave your Windows NT 4.0 system irreparably damaged.

Even with the latest update, however, you won't have all the features of NTFS5. A computer that dual-boots Windows NT and Windows 2000 using NTFS partitions can run into trouble, especially if you use new features of NTFS5 such as compression, encryption, or dynamic disks. After Windows 2000 encrypts a file, for example, that file won't be readable by Windows NT 4.0. The best bet is to load NT4 onto a FAT16 or FAT32 partition. Windows 2000 can be on NTFS then, without difficulty. The other option is to keep Windows NT on NTFS and load Windows 2000 on a FAT16 partition (Windows NT 4.0 can't see FAT32 partitions).

Unlike computers running Windows 9x and Windows NT 4.0 or 2000, we can use the NTFS file system for both operating systems. A close look at Table 34.1 reveals that both Windows NT 4.0 and Windows 2000 support the NTFS file system. You can actually use the same partition configuration in the first scenario and merely substitute Windows NT 4.0 for Windows 98 to achieve your desired results.

Before dual-booting Windows 2000 and Windows NT, consider these points. For folks testing Windows 2000 while keeping the tried-and-true NT 4.0 around, these can be a bit annoying.

- You should upgrade to at least NT 4.0 Service Pack 4 if you want to dual-boot with Windows 2000 Professional sharing NTFS partitions. Upgrade first, and then install Windows 2000 Professional or your NT 4.0 system might not boot.

- If you load both operating systems on the same partition (which we don't suggest), and if that partition is NTFS, you will need to keep it NTFS 4.0 and not upgrade the NTFS partition when installing Windows 2000. This is because Windows NT 4.0 doesn't know how to work with NTFS 5-formatted partitions.

To dual-boot NT and 2000, do the following:

1. Install Windows NT 4.0. Chances are good that you already have it installed, in which case this portion of the job is already complete.

2. You're going to want to have another partition to house Windows 2000. Ideally, use PartitionMagic to create a new partition using the format of your choice, though you can also use the Windows NT Disk Manager to create the partition if you have some free (unpartitioned) space on the disk. Of course, if you have free space, you can install Windows 2000 directly into that because the Setup Wizard gives you that option. (Unlike PartitionMagic, NT Disk Manager cannot resize existing partitions to create a new partition). The new partition can be formatted FAT16, FAT32, or NTFS. If you want to experiment with the more sophisticated features of NTFS 5, you'll be aiming for NTFS, but you can have Setup do the conversion for you.

3. Boot up Windows NT, insert the Windows 2000 setup disk, and choose Install Windows 2000 from the menu. (If the menu doesn't start automatically, look on the CD's root directory for Setup.exe and run it.)

4. Choose Clean Install from the wizard's first page; otherwise, you'll wipe out the Windows NT installation.

5. Accept the agreement, enter the serial number, and follow the wizard.

6. From the Select Special Options page of the Windows 2000 Setup Wizard, select the Advanced Options button to specify where you would like the Windows 2000 system folder installed. You probably will want to select the option labeled I Want To Choose Installation Partition During Setup. This will give you the opportunity to select the D: partition as well as convert it to the NTFS file system later in the setup process.

Tip #412

> The other option in this dialog box, Windows Installation Folder, enables you to change the name of the folder that will act as the Windows 2000 system root. The default is \WINNT. Actually, you could use your name or anything else that suits you. The folder will be identified to the system via a systemwide variable called %SystemRoot%, no matter what you actually call it on the disk.

7. After the Windows Setup Wizard copies some files to your hard disk, it will reboot your system and continue the installation from a text-based setup. From this setup, you will have the option to select where you'd like to install your Windows 2000 system. Choose the partition you created in step 2, or choose any unformatted free space (if you have any).

8. Next, you will be given the option to select how you want the target partition formatted. Because you are installing 2000 into a separate partition from Windows NT, you have the freedom to convert the partition to NTFS, which we recommend though it's not mandatory, by any means. (If you are thinking about adding yet another operating system that might not be capable of reading NTFS, you might want to opt for a version of FAT.)

9. After making your choice, setup will copy files to your hard disk and again reboot your system. The Windows 2000 boot loader will now take control. From here, setup will convert the partition (if applicable), reboot, and continue with the installation.

10. The Windows 2000 setup will finish its installation and you then will be able to boot into both operating systems using the boot loader at startup.

Tip #413

> See the earlier section titled "Formatting the Data-Sharing Partition" for some thoughts about creating a third partition to store data that can be shared between the two operating systems. (There is also some discussion of this topic in Chapter 33.) Because reading NTFS is not an issue in the NT/2000 dual-boot scenario (assuming you have upgraded Windows NT to SP4 before beginning), the file format of the data partition can safely be set to FAT16. You might need to use the Disk Manager in both operating systems to nail down the drive assignments if they don't come up as you'd like. Consistency of drive lettering between the two operating systems is desirable, though not mandatory.

WINDOWS 2000, WINDOWS NT 4.0, AND WINDOWS 9X

This configuration might be one of the less common installations of all. It is, however, very possible to create a setup using all three of these operating systems. Take the following approach:

1. Create three partitions (or four if you want a separate data partition).

2. If you decide you want a data partition, make it FAT16 because NT 4.0 can't see FAT32. FAT16 is the one common denominator. See Table 34.6 for a suggested layout.

As you can see from the table, we're suggesting using FAT16 for all the partitions to ensure maximum compatibility and the least amount of drive letter shifting.

TABLE 34.6   BOOTING WINDOWS 2000, NT 4.0, AND WINDOWS 9X

Partition #	Operating System	Format	Notes
Partition 1	Windows 95 OSR2 or Windows 98	FAT16	Use FAT32 if you don't mind this partition not being seen by NT 4.0.
Partition 2	Windows NT 4.0 SP 4 or later	FAT16	Use NTFS if you are aware of the consequences.
Partition 3	Windows 2000	FAT16	Use NTFS if you want to chance compatibility issues with NT.
Partition 4	Optional Data Partition	FAT16	Use NTFS if you want to hide it from Windows 9x and/or if you want to use features of NTFS.

3. Install Windows 9x in the first partition. If asked whether you want to upgrade to FAT32, say no unless you don't mind having the first partition invisible to Windows NT 4.0. Windows 2000 will still be able to see it, though, even in FAT32.

4. Install Windows NT in the second partition. (Upgrade it to at least Service Pack 4 if you want to try using NTFS for that partition.) Now you should have a dual-boot system. Check it to see that it works acceptably.

5. Install Windows 2000 via a clean install into the third partition. This should add the third operating system to the boot loader.

6. Format the data partition however you like. Remember that for maximum compatibility between all three operating systems, you'll want to use FAT16. However, if you want to experiment with NTFS5 (Windows 2000's file system) for features such as encryption and compression, you can use NTFS. (Use Disk Management in Windows 2000 to upgrade an older formatted NTFS partition to NTFS5.) Be aware, though, that using these newer features on a file or folder might render them unreadable by NT 4.0.

When you're finished, the Windows 2000 boot loader will give you the option of booting into each of the three operating systems. Remember to heed the cautions explained earlier in this chapter regarding sharing data and applications between operating systems.

PART
VI

CH
34

Note

You can't multiboot Windows 95 and Windows 98 with Windows 2000, even if they're on different partitions. The only way to have Windows 95 and Windows 98 on a single machine is with a third-party boot manager such as BootMagic or System Commander. (See the section "Tips from the Windows Pros: Living with More Than One OS," at the end of this chapter.)

WINDOWS 2000 AND LINUX

Using both Windows 2000 and Linux on the same system is a very rewarding multiboot scenario. This gives you two very powerful operating systems that can work in harmony on the same system. Linux can be booted from any type of partition on any installed disk, be it primary or logical. This enables you to create a Linux partition anywhere you have enough space to put it.

If you are installing Linux onto the same disk as any of your Windows 9x/NT/2000 systems, you must have sufficient unused disk space for the installation. If you do not have enough unused space, you can use PartitionMagic. PartitionMagic will actually shrink any partition if you have enough free space in one of your existing Windows file systems.

After you have done this, you can simply follow the rest of the steps to install Linux on your freshly created unused disk space. The best option here is to plan ahead and just install Windows 2000, leaving enough unused space on your disk to accommodate your Linux installation. Alternatively, you could just add a disk to your system for your new Linux installation.

One of the great advantages of this configuration is Linux's capability to read, and sometimes write, nearly every file system under the sun. You'll be able to share files between your two systems with a minimal amount of hassle. Be sure to see Table 34.1 (earlier in this chapter) to properly plan for file sharing between both operating systems.

INSTALLING LINUX

This section deals with the task of installing Linux in a multiboot situation with Windows 2000. Although a complete tutorial on the installation of Linux is out of the scope of this chapter, we will try to cover the essential points needed to make your system multibootable.

This chapter assumes that you are using the current version of Red Hat Linux, which is 6.1 at the time of this writing. For the purposes of this example, you will be installing Linux onto the same disk as your Windows 2000 installation. You must have enough unused disk space (refer to Table 34.2) to see the recommended hard disk requirements for your Linux installation.

Tip #414

If you do not have enough space in your hard drive, consider adding a second disk or using the PartitionMagic program to shrink an existing partition.

Note

As mentioned earlier in this chapter, setting up a multiple booting computer is a broad topic, particularly if Linux is one of the operating systems you want to use. Although the following information provides the basics for dual-booting Windows 2000 with Linux, you'll find much more detailed coverage in *The Multi-Boot Configuration Handbook*, published by Que.

When you have any combination of the previous multiboot scenarios, having Windows 2000 Professional manage booting into Linux is fairly simple. By referring to Table 34.1 (earlier in the chapter), you can see that Linux will be capable of reading and writing all the Windows file systems. At this time it is recommended that you do not use NTFS read/write in Linux because it is still in the very early alpha stages. The read-only version, however, works just fine. This being the case, you might want to reevaluate whether to use NTFS for your Windows 2000 partition. Using FAT32 will give you full read/write capability from Linux without any worries about data corruption from an immature driver.

First, let's cover some of the important aspects of the Red Hat Linux installation procedure.

1. As with Windows 2000, NT, and OEM versions of Windows 98, you can boot from the Red Hat Linux installation CD-ROM. This will bring you to the Red Hat Linux installation program.

2. After some preliminary questions about your keyboard and mouse, you will be prompted for what installation class you want to use. In the examples shown here, I chose the GNOME Workstation class (see Figure 34.11). After you select a Workstation install, the Red Hat installer will automatically set up the unused disk space on your hard disk to run Linux.

Figure 34.11
Selecting the installation class from within the Red Hat installation program.

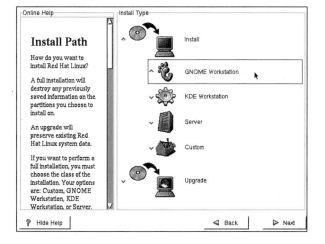

3. The next option offered by the Red Hat installation is whether you'd like automatic partitioning. In this example, you must select the option to manually partition. This step is necessary to create a multiboot system with Windows 2000, using the Windows 2000 boot loader.

4. Click the Next button. You will be able to define the partitions that will make up your Linux system.

5. On the following screen, the Disk Druid tool gives you the option of creating your Linux partitions. Although there are many options for partitioning and mounting Linux

partitions, you can make it much easier on yourself simply by creating a root and swap partition. These are all that is needed to successfully install Linux. On the bottom pane, you can see a representation of your disk, as well as the used and free space available on it (see Figure 34.12).

Figure 34.12
The Red Hat Disk Druid disk partitioning tool.

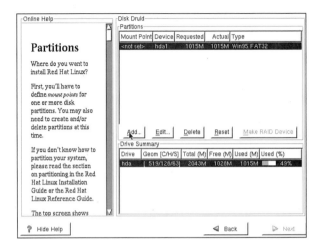

6. Click the Add button, and you can now add a partition for your Linux system. Because you will need to create two partitions, one each for / (or root) and swap, you must plan the sizes of each beforehand.

Tip #415

A good rule of thumb is to create a swap file that is at least the size of your installed memory. This will be enough for most workstation applications. For example, if you are installing Red Hat Linux into a 1024MB partition with 64MB of RAM, you would create a 964MB / (root) partition and a 64MB swap partition.

7. First, click the Add button to define the / (root) partition.

8. Type / into the Mount Point field and make sure the Partition Type is the default Linux Native.

9. In the size field, add the size in megabytes for your root partition.

10. Select OK to create the partition. Notice now that the Free column on the second pane has changed to reflect the remaining space on the partition. This is the space left for your swap partition.

11. Next, click Add and define the swap partition. In the size field, enter the remaining partition space in megabytes.

12. For the partition Type, select Linux Swap, and the Mount Point field will automatically change to reflect that you are creating a swap partition.

13. After you have created these two partitions, you will have the option of continuing with the installation, as shown in Figure 34.13.

Figure 34.13
Root and swap partitions as defined in the Red Hat Disk Druid tool.

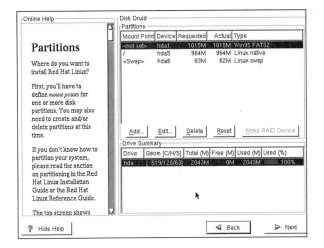

14. Continue with the installation by clicking the Next button. You will be asked whether you'd like to format your root partition. This is perfectly safe and should be performed. You can then continue by again clicking the Next button.

15. Next, you will be asked whether you'd like to create a boot disk for your new Linux system (see Figure 34.14). This step is imperative, so click the Create Boot Disk button. Insert a blank 1.44MB high-density floppy disk when prompted.

16. Next, you are given the option of where to install LILO, the Linux loader. LILO is a boot manager for Linux that can handle other operating systems as well. You can either install LILO on the MBR or the first sector of the Linux boot partition. Most likely, you'll want to use the Windows 2000 boot menu to choose the OS into which you want to boot. If this is the case, select the option to Install LILO on the first sector of the Linux boot partition (see Figure 34.14). This will enable you to retain the Windows 2000 MBR for future use.

Figure 34.14
Boot disk and LILO configuration from the Red Hat Linux installer.

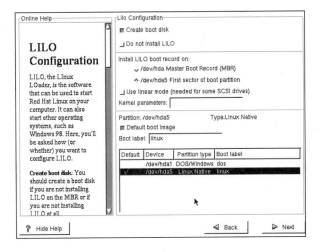

PART

VI

CH

34

Caution

If you were to let LILO install itself on the MBR, you would effectively remove your Windows 2000 MBR and thus replace it with LILO.

Note

Be sure to write down the name of the partition that contains LILO. It will be named something like /dev/hda5. You'll need to know this later when I discuss locating the Linux boot sector.

17. The final section on this screen deals with which partitions show up in LILO, as well as how you want to label the partitions. By default, LILO will add an entry for your Windows 2000 partition and label it dos. This will actually enable you to boot into Windows 2000's boot sector from within LILO by simply typing dos at the LILO prompt. Most likely, you'll want to leave this at its default setting.

18. Next, you'll need to configure your networking and peripherals. Follow the instructions in your Linux distribution manual because this will vary from version to version.

19. The installation will finally create and format your Linux file system and install system packages to complete the installation.

20. When prompted, insert your disk and the installer will create the boot disk for you. This boot disk will enable you to not only boot into Linux in case of an emergency, but also to boot into Linux to take a disk dump of the Linux boot sector. Using this boot sector, you will configure the Windows 2000 boot loader to boot into Linux.

21. After LILO is installed, the Red Hat installation will finish and you may reboot your system.

GETTING THE LINUX BOOT SECTOR

As described earlier, obtaining an image or file dump of the Linux boot sector will enable you to configure the Windows 2000 boot loader to boot into Linux. The following explains how to do so:

1. Format a 1.44MB floppy disk.

2. Shut down and reboot your computer with the Linux boot disk discussed in the previous section.

3. When Linux has finished booting, log in as root using the password you supplied during installation. All the following steps must be performed as root.

4. First, mount a DOS floppy onto your Linux file system to copy the boot sector to it. The floppy also is a safe place to store the boot sector in case it is needed in the future. Remove the boot disk and insert a formatted MS-DOS floppy into your disk drive and type the following command:

```
mount -t msdos /dev/fd0 /mnt/floppy
```

This will make the disk available to you by mounting it in the directory /mnt/floppy.

Tip #416	If you need to format the floppy from within Linux, you may do so by typing the following command from the prompt:

```
fdformat /dev/fd0; /sbin/mkfs -t msdos
```

This command will give you a freshly formatted MS-DOS disk in Linux. From there you can simply mount the disk to get access to it.

5. The next step is to use the program named dd to write the Linux boot sector to the disk. The most important part of this step is to make sure you take the boot sector from the correct partition. This partition is the one that was installed in LILO during the Linux installation. If you're unsure which partition contains the Linux boot sector, issue the following command:

```
more /etc/lilo.conf
```

Which will give you output similar to the following:

```
boot=/dev/hdb1
map=/boot/map
install=/boot/boot.b
prompt
timeout=50
image=/boot/vmlinuz-2.2.5-15
    label=linux
    boot=/dev/hdb5
    read-only
```

6. Note that LILO is installed in /dev/hdb1. Using the dd program, issue the following command:

```
/bin/dd if=/dev/hdb1 of=/mnt/floppy/bootsect.lnx bs=512 count=1
```

This command will copy the Linux boot sector at /dev/hdb1 to a file called bootsect.lnx on your disk.

7. Next, unmount the floppy disk using the following command:

```
umount /dev/fd0 (this is required)
```

8. Finally, reboot the system:

```
/sbin/reboot
```

Be sure to remove the floppy disk from your computer.

Adding Linux to the Windows 2000 Boot Loader

You can add Linux to the Windows 2000 boot loader from either Windows 2000 or Windows 98, if you have it installed. The steps are exactly the same and are not operating system-dependent.

1. First, copy the bootsect.lnx file, which you created in the previous step, from your floppy disk to the root of your C: drive. This can be done from a command prompt or from the Windows 2000 Explorer. This file must be located at the root because it must be referenced from the BOOT.INI file, also found at the root of the C: drive.

Part

VI

Ch

34

2. Modify the BOOT.INI file to add an entry for the newly installed Linux operating system. Before this file can be edited, however, you'll need to disable the read-only attribute. This can be done from a command prompt by typing

   `attrib -r c:\boot.ini`

   Alternatively, you can do this by right-clicking the file from the Windows Explorer, selecting Properties, and deselecting the Read-Only check box as shown in Figure 34.15.

Figure 34.15
Changing the read-only attribute from the file properties dialog, General tab.

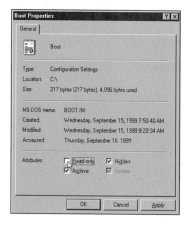

3. Next, add the following line to the next free line of the BOOT.INI file:

   `C:\bootsect.lnx="Red Hat Linux 6"`

4. You can now save BOOT.INI, reboot, and select Red Hat Linux 6 as one of your boot menu options (see Figure 34.16).

Figure 34.16
The Red Hat Linux 6 boot option now appears in the Windows 2000 boot loader.

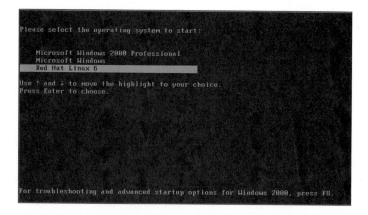

MOUNTING WINDOWS DISKS WITHIN LINUX

Next, you'll want Linux to mount your Windows disks so that you can share files between both operating systems. This will enable you to copy files back and forth without using external media such as floppy disks. All the following steps must be performed as root because they are system-sensitive procedures:

1. First, create the directories within which you will mount the Windows file systems. The normal Linux convention is to create these directories in the /mnt tree.

2. If you are dual-booting Linux with Windows 9x (meaning you are using FAT32), issue the following command to create the directory:

   ```
   mkdir /mnt/windisk1
   ```

   This creates a mount point for the first partition of your first disk.

3. Next, create another directory for the second mount point:

   ```
   mkdir /mnt/windisk2
   ```

> **Note**
>
> These directory names are a matter of taste. You can use whatever name you feel comfortable with at this point. As long as these directories exist, your Windows partitions should mount easily.

4. To test the first mount point, attempt to mount the first FAT32 partition using this command:

   ```
   mnt -t vfat /dev/hda1 /mnt/windisk1
   ```

5. You can examine the contents of this partition by simply executing

   ```
   ls /mnt/windisk1
   ```

6. If the mount was successful, you will see a familiar list of files and directories found on your first Windows 98 partition.

7. Likewise, you can mount the second NTFS partition with the following command:

   ```
   mount -t ntfs /dev/hda2 /mnt/windisk2
   ```

> **Note**
>
> By default, the NTFS file system driver is not enabled in Red Hat Linux. You must consult your documentation to enable this driver. As stated previously, if you use this driver, it is recommended that you use the read-only version. The current read/write version of the NTFS driver is still in the alpha stages as of this writing.

Enabling these file systems to automatically mount in Linux involves a procedure that is out of the scope of this discussion. Although it is possible, only experienced Linux users should attempt to modify the system's boot time mount parameters. Typically, the changes needed to auto-mount foreign file systems are made in /etc/fstab. Red Hat Linux includes a GUI utility, called linuxconf, that makes this task much more simple. Consult the documentation that came with your Linux distribution.

PART

VI

CH

34

MACINTOSH AND WINDOWS

Has a friend ever given you a Macintosh disk and asked if you can read it, or have you wanted to run a particularly cool Mac program and been bummed that you can't? Well, think again.

Reading and writing Mac disks is pretty simple. Actually, the Mac can read and write PC disks, so that is one way around this hassle. Just give the colleague a formatted PC disk and ask him to copy the files you want onto the floppy. Or, you might try a program called Mac-In-DOS. We've tried that and like it. It works in the PC and reads, formats, and writes Mac disks in the PC floppy drive. Search for it on the Web for about $100, or download a free demo.

But if you want to actually run Mac programs on the PC, can you? Well, believe it or not, the answer is yes. Sort of.

Just as there are programs such as SoftPC and SoftWindows that are emulators for the Mac, several Mac emulators can run Mac programs on your PC. One such program we've been experimenting with and are impressed with is called Executor, from ARDI. Executor is a program for reading and writing Macintosh formatted media and running Macintosh programs.

ARDI has implemented the core of the Macintosh operating system independently from Apple Computer, Inc. As such, Executor requires no software (or ROM chip) from Apple, which makes it the only solution for many customers who need to run Macintosh programs who don't already have a Macintosh. (Some of the other emulators require you to have an Apple ROM chip from one of their computers.)

Executor runs as a native Windows application, either in full-screen mode or in a window (see Figure 34.17). You can print from Executor to any printer that your system can talk to (local printers, remote printers, faxes if you have the right software, and so on). You can cut and paste text and graphics between Executor and other applications. You can create shortcuts for a Macintosh application so that Executor will start up and run that application.

Executor implements a virtual 680x0 processor by dynamically translating sections of 680x0 machine instructions into corresponding 80x86 machine instructions. The new 80x86 instructions are then run and saved for later reuse.

Whenever the Macintosh application requests an operating system service, Executor executes the copy of that recompiled service. Each of the 1,200 system services (known to Macintosh developers as operating system calls and toolbox traps) has been implemented as native 80x86 instructions, so they execute without any translation overhead in real-time.

Then ARDI's system services communicate with the world outside its virtual Macintosh by making Win32 system calls, either directly as when Executor addresses the Windows printing subsystem or indirectly through SDL, a library that provides portable access to the display, keyboard, mouse, and sound system.

Note

See http://www.devolution.com/~slouken/SDL for more about SDL.

Figure 34.17
Executor runs many
Mac programs on the
PC under Windows 9x,
Windows NT, and
Windows 2000.

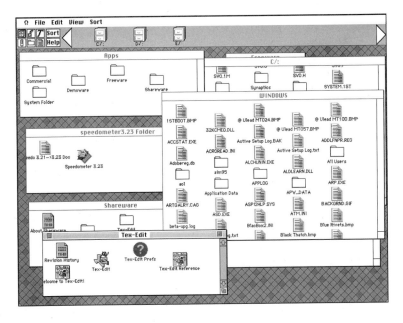

If you refer to Chapter 2, "The Design and Architecture of Windows 2000 Professional," you'll see that this sounds curiously similar to the environment subsystem arrangement that Windows NT-based systems use for running non-NT apps such as DOS, 16-bit Windows, and POSIX.

With Administrative permissions, Macintosh-formatted media can be used directly in a PC. This is useful for transferring information to and from Macintoshes or for loading applications, but for most other uses, it's easier to have Executor store Macintosh formatted files on top of your native file system, whether it's FAT, FAT32, or NTFS. Doing things this way, all file system permissions are obeyed and file sharing is done through Windows 2000's mechanisms, not the Macintosh's.

Unfortunately, Executor will not support applications that are "PowerPC-only," which is an increasing occurrence. Additionally, although ARDI supports a solid core of operating system services, newer services are not supported. Macintosh programs are capable of querying the operating system to determine which services are supported and which aren't, but programmers often make assumptions that are valid for real Macintoshes but that are not valid under Executor. Executor doesn't yet support the system services that were added after Macintosh System 7.0 (Apple is now shipping 9.0), nor does it yet support networking or system software extensions (known as INITs and CDEVs). ARDI has a compatibility database on its Web site at http://www.ardi.com/compat/, which you should check if you're interested in running a particular program.

How fast does it work? I'm sure you're wondering. ARDI claims that CPU-intensive applications run about 8 1/2 times faster on a 500 MHz Pentium III than they did on the fastest 68040-based Macintosh (33 MHz). Graphics applications don't get quite that speedup because they tend to be limited by the speed of accessing video RAM, and Executor doesn't yet use much accelerated video.

As far as stability and security goes, even if you run an application that fails under Executor, all that will happen is that Executor itself will die; unlike a real Macintosh, an application won't take down your entire system.

The makers of the software say they are working to increase compatibility with later versions of the Mac operating system, so keep your eyes peeled on this one, you Mac folks.

Note

For more technical details you can check these two sites:
```
ftp://ftp.ardi.com/pub/SynPaper
http://www.ardi.com/MacHack/machack.html
```

TROUBLESHOOTING

REPAIRING THE WINDOWS 2000 BOOT LOADER

How do I repair the Windows 2000 Boot Loader?

Armed with your recently created emergency disk, you will be able to repair the Windows 2000 boot loader with relative ease. If anything goes wrong, you can simply boot your system from the Windows 2000 Installation CD-ROM. From there, you will be able to select the option to repair a damaged system.

The only repair options you need to select at this point are the options to repair the startup environment and the boot sector. These options will reinstall the boot loader if yours has somehow become corrupt. Your emergency disk will come in handy as the repair mechanism uses it to find your Windows 2000 partition.

REMOVING THE WINDOWS 2000 BOOT LOADER

Why would I want to remove the Windows 2000 Boot Loader?

This might be needed if you have incorrectly installed an operating system and want to remove it to start over. The same process of removing the Windows 2000 boot loader is applicable to the Windows NT 4.0 boot loader. If you choose to perform this step, however, you must be sure that you have an operating system to boot into. For this example, assume you have Windows 98/95 installed and want to return to a state in which it is the only operating system available.

First, while you are booted into Windows 98/95, you must create a bootable system disk. This can be accomplished by selecting the Add/Remove Programs control panel. Then select the Startup Disk tab as shown in Figure 34.18.

After creating a startup disk, reboot your system using the new disk. After you have fully booted into MS-DOS, simply enter the following command from the command prompt:

```
sys C:
```

Figure 34.18
Creating a Windows
98 startup disk.

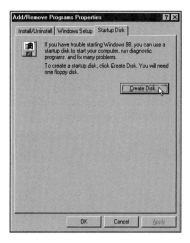

This will install the Windows 98 startup boot sector onto drive C: and remove the Windows 2000 boot loader. Now that you're able to boot back into Windows 9x, simply remove the Windows 2000 %SystemRoot% directory (typically \WINNT).

You can optionally remove the following files to clean up the rest of the Windows 2000 boot loader files:

```
C:\boot.ini
C:\ntldr
C:\ntdetect.com
```

TIPS FROM THE WINDOWS PROS: LIVING WITH MORE THAN ONE OS

If you've never run more than one operating system on the same machine at the same time, you might find that managing those operating systems can be a daunting task. Fortunately, some tricks can save you at your darkest moments.

EASIER HANDLING OF COMPLEX MULTIBOOT SITUATIONS

The Windows 2000 multiboot loader is capable of supporting a large number of multiboot situations—probably more than will fit on the screen in a list. Still, you are somewhat hog-tied when it comes to complex multiboot scenarios. Notwithstanding the issues of file system compatibilities, getting the boot loader to gracefully add or remove operating systems can be problematic. Editing the BOOT.INI file, for example, is a bit of a cryptic process, and you must remember quirky rules about the order of operating system installation.

If you're interested in loading up a killer system with three or more operating systems, we recommend using a program designed specifically for the job. There are a couple that you might consider, as described next.

Once again, the PowerQuest people come to the rescue with their offering, called BootMagic, which is bundled with PartitionMagic. This program uses a graphical interface to help you set up and run multiple operating systems in the same machine, with a minimum of compatibility problems. You can run the setup interface from DOS, Windows 9x, or Windows NT/Windows 2000. The program supports Windows 95/Windows 98, Windows NT 4.0 (server and workstation), Windows NT 3.51 (server and workstation), Windows 3.x (must be installed with DOS 5 or later), MS-DOS 5.0 or later, PC-DOS 6.1 or later, Open DOS, OS/2 3.0 or later, Linux, BeOS, and most other versions of DOS and PC-compatible OSs (check their site at www.powerquest.com for more info).

Another similar program is called System Commander Deluxe, from V Communications. This product has received rave reviews from some magazines. System Commander Deluxe enables you to install and run any combination of PC-compatible operating systems, including Windows 95/98, Windows 3.x, Windows NT, DOS, OS/2, and all of the PC-compatible UNIXes including Linux. Like BootMagic, this program also has a graphical user interface. In addition, it does partition management such as resizing, creation, and deletion. It's not as versatile as PartitionMagic and BootMagic together due to the versatility of PartitionMagic. However, some say it's the better boot manager. It's available from V Communications, Inc. (check their site at www.v-com.com).

RUNNING MULTIPLE OPERATING SYSTEMS AT THE SAME TIME WITH VMWARE

Some people must be able to run multiple operating systems at the same time, not just independently. For example, we needed to do so while writing this book so we could capture certain screen shots of the setup programs running. Program developers must develop and test on different platforms. Why use separate boxes for this when you can do it on the same computer, faster? For a totally flexible multioperating system box, you should definitely check out a program called VMware (www.vmware.com).

VMware is an application that creates a virtual PC in software. You can create as many virtual PCs as you have operating systems. The VMware Virtual Platform is a thin software layer that hosts one OS inside another, letting users run two or more operating systems simultaneously on a PC. Each operating system, when running (not in an emulation mode like the Mac solution explained in this chapter), runs as if it were booted on the PC.

One operating system must act as the host OS to start the computer, obviously. After it boots, the Virtual Platform—which is only 1MB in size—can be started. At that point, the other operating systems can be run.

Currently, Windows NT 4.0 and Linux are the only two host operating systems, although more will be added. MS-DOS, Windows 3.1, Windows 95 and 98, Windows NT, Linux, and FreeBSD UNIX can be run in the Virtual Platform. VMware expects to add more host and supported operating systems in the future.

This program can isolate and protect each operating environment and the applications and data that are running in it. It also supports interoperability among each of these operating systems, including full networking, device and file sharing, and cut-and-paste capabilities.

Each Virtual Platform running on the computer has its own IP address and looks like an individual machine to a network. Each platform is also a secure sandbox, which has two benefits:

- If one operating system crashes, it doesn't take down the whole computer.
- If a virus infects one platform, it can't get out and infect other platforms.

Some hardware processes—such as CPU, memory, and disk access—run at near normal speeds. Performance degradation is not significant, clocking in at only around three percent to five percent compared to running on a PC outside the Virtual Platform.

- Use a hot key to switch between virtual machines.
- Run operating systems already installed on a multiboot computer without reconfiguring.
- Install a virtual machine without repartitioning your disks

CHAPTER **35**

THE REGISTRY

In this chapter

WHAT IS THE REGISTRY?

The *Registry* is Microsoft's answer to the hodgepodge of configuration files, INI files, and mysterious hidden setup files that plagued the early days of DOS and Windows. Programs need a way of saving settings, preferences, file locations, license and registration information, last-viewed file lists, and so on. Before the Registry, you had to take a "create-your-own" approach to storing this information. The result is that you ended up with dozens of setup files scattered all over your hard disk, who knows where, and containing, well, who knows what?

The Registry is the answer to this mess. It provides Windows and 32-bit Windows applications with an organized way to store configuration and preference information. Information is stored in a consistent way, in one place, for all programs. (There are exceptions, of course, which I'll tell you about later.) And it's so easy for programmers to use that nearly every application now uses the Registry.

The Registry itself is a small database system that lets applications and Windows itself efficiently search for, store, and retrieve small bits of information. The Registry was actually introduced in Windows 3.1, in a very inconspicuous way, to hold the "associations" that File Manager made between file extensions and their corresponding applications. The Registry still does this and much more.

Most of the time, you can get by without giving the Registry a second thought. Almost every useful Registry entry is set from a Control Panel applet, an applications preference dialog, or in Windows Setup. From time to time, though, you might have to roll up your sleeves to find the location of an errant device driver, to remove an unwanted startup program, or you might just be curious what kind of information Office 2000 keeps on file about you. This chapter should give you an idea of what the Registry is about and how to go on these kinds of missions.

Two Different Views

One of the advantages of having two authors for this book is that you get two viewpoints. I (Brian) must confess I am a card-carrying Registryphobe; I think Registry tweaking is dangerous and minimally useful. As far as I'm concerned, the Registry is best left alone. I make my living programming with my computer, and the less fancy and more stable it is, the better. "Stock" is the way for me.

For my co-author Bob, who also makes his living with his computer, the Registry is a tweaker's paradise of undocumented adjustments and fascinating Windows trivia. He can change file locations, tune up networking performance, and generally adjust his computer to be "just so." To each his own! We'll both have our say here in telling you how to be careful with the Registry and in showing you how to work with it effectively.

HOW THE REGISTRY IS ORGANIZED

The Registry leaves the plain text files of AUTOEXEC.BAT and WIN.INI far, far behind. It is a specialized database organized a lot like a hard disk: It has several partitions, and its hierarchical structure looks just like a directory structure with folders and files. In fact, the Registry Editor navigates through the Registry using the same expandable list display that Navigator uses to display a disk.

Just as a hard disk contains partitions, the Registry contains separate sections called *hives*. (The reason Microsoft chose the word *hive* is unclear. It had something to do with busy bees, but more than that, the folks there won't say.) In each hive is a list of named *keys* that correspond to the folders on a hard disk. Each key can contain subkeys and *values*, which hold information such as numbers or text strings.

The two top-level keys are as follows:

- HKEY_LOCAL_MACHINE contains all the hardware and machine-specific setup information for your computer. For example, it lists every device driver to load and all your hardware's interrupt settings. It also holds software setup information that is common to all users.
- HKEY_USERS has a key for each user of the computer, in which Windows stores user-specific information, such as color preferences, sounds, and the location of email files.

Through a little bit of software sleight-of-hand, you can find three other top-level keys, which are really subkeys of the other two, as shown in Figure 35.1:

- HKEY_CURRENT_USER is the subsection of HKEY_USERS corresponding to the logged-on user. It holds preferences and software setup information specific to the current user, such the choice of screen saver and Office 2000's default language.
- HKEY_CLASSES_ROOT is the same as HKEY_LOCAL_MACHINE\Software\Classes. It serves the Registry's original purpose of linking filename extensions to application program names, as well as other software-linking information.
- HKEY_CURRENT_CONFIG, which is really HKEY_LOCAL_MACHINE\System\ CurrentControlSet\Hardware Profiles\Current, contains the hardware settings specific to the hardware profile chosen when Windows was started.

The information in these three virtual top-level keys is the same as the parts in the two main keys, several layers down; Windows just gives additional access to it via these top-level pointers. They were not added to make things more confusing for you (really!). They are there to make life easier for programmers, who are spared having to figure out which is the current hardware profile and who is the current user. It's easier to use a key like HKEY_CURRENT_USER\Software\Corel than to figure out that the administrator is logged on, and for administrator, you need to use HKEY_USERS\S-1-5-23-8615631254-1234275354-1349183625-534\Software\Corel.

Figure 35.1
The Registry is composed of two true top-level keys and three virtual top-level keys.

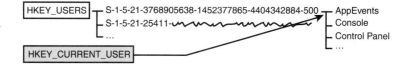

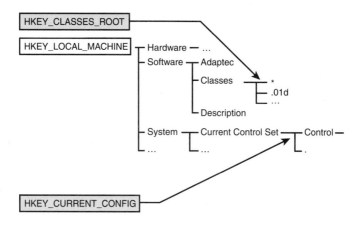

Within each of these top-level keys, subkeys are named just like folders on a hard disk. HKEY_CURRENT_CONFIG, for example, contains four keys: Display, Enum, Software, and System. Display itself contains two keys: Fonts and Settings. With keys, just like folders, you can spell out the full path—HKEY_CURRENT_CONFIG\Display\Settings—or just refer to Settings, if you know you're discussing HKEY_CURRENT_CONFIG\Display.

This information is a little daunting, but remember that, like folders, the purpose of the Registry keys is to organize information sensibly. Instead of having this information in some mysteriously named file, you can pretty much count on finding the settings for your graphics card in the Registry under HKEY_CURRENT_CONFIG\Display\Settings.

> **Caution**
>
> Another similarity between Registry keys and file folders is that both can have access permissions set to prevent unauthorized users from examining or modifying them. I won't go further into this topic, except to recommend that you *don't* attempt to set or modify the default permissions in the Registry. It's too easy to make a mistake that will prevent even Windows itself from having access to the information it needs. If you implement Group Policies, the *Policy Editor* will adjust Registry permissions as necessary.

The Registry database itself is stored in pieces. Although the Registry looks like two hierarchical key structures, various subparts are actually stored in separate files, called *hives*, which I mentioned earlier. HKEY_LOCAL_MACHINE is stored in folder \windows\system32\config, in several files: SAM, SECURITY, SOFTWARE, and SYSTEM.

HKEY_USERS is stored with each user subkey in a separate file. They are kept in each user's profile folder (\Documents and Settings*username*) as a file named NTUSER.DAT, except the Default User key is in \windows\system32\config\DEFAULT.

You generally can't examine or modify these files while Windows is running because Windows maintains exclusive control of them. Backup software uses special Windows program functions to get at them. The exception is that the NTUSER.DAT files for users not currently logged in are not locked in this way, so they can be copied and backed up as normal files.

REGISTRY CONTENTS

So, what's in the Registry, anyway? There's a lot to it; whole books have been written about it. If you want a full-blown guide to the Windows 2000 Registry, check out *Microsoft Windows 2000 Registry Handbook*, published by Que. Short of that, way short, I can still do a quick overview of the Registry to give you some idea of its organization and contents.

You just learned about the five main sections of the Registry. Let's go through them one by one now, and hit on some of each section's highlights.

HKEY_LOCAL_MACHINE

As you might expect, HKEY_LOCAL_MACHINE contains information specific to your computer, settings that aren't user-specific. They include hardware settings and software information that is global for all users.

The main keys in HKEY_LOCAL_MACHINE are shown in Table 35.1.

TABLE 35.1 MAIN KEYS IN HKEY_LOCAL_MACHINE	
HARDWARE	Contains information about the computer's hardware platform and Plug and Play devices, discovered afresh each time the system is booted. No configurable settings are located here.
SAM and SECURITY	Contains the Windows security database. The keys always appear to be empty because only Windows itself is allowed to read or edit the information.
SOFTWARE	Contains systemwide software settings. This key contains many subkeys. The Classes subkey is special and is given its own virtual view as HKEY_CLASSES_ROOT. The other entries are generally named after software manufacturers. I'll describe some of the more interesting keys in a moment.

continues

PART **VI** CH **35**

TABLE 35.1	CONTINUED
SYSTEM	Contains a series of ControlSet### entries, which contain the settings for hardware and system services. One of them is chosen as the CurrentControlSet subkey (which is a virtual view of one of the numbered ControlSets). As you install or remove hardware, Windows rotates through the ControlSet entries, using one as the "current control set." This way, it can keep previous versions to use as a backup.

The fun bits are in the SOFTWARE keys in HKEY_LOCAL_MACHINE. Under SOFTWARE is the special Classes subkey, which I'll describe under HKEY_CLASSES_ROOT. Subkeys named after software manufacturers contain systemwide settings for their various programs.

Under Microsoft, naturally, is a slew of subkeys for the software systems provided with Windows and for any add-ons you've purchased, such as Office. You'll have more than 110 subkeys in HKEY_LOCAL_MACHINE\Software\Microsoft just after installation and more when you start adding your own software.

Most of the juicy settings that control Windows itself are found in HKEY_LOCAL_MACHINE\Software\Microsoft\Windows\CurrentVersion.

I'll discuss just one of these juicy keys. When you log in to your computer, you know that Windows can start up some programs automatically. You can actually set a program to be started up at login in five ways:

1. A shortcut in the Startup folder of your Start menu (in \Documents and Settings\ *yourloginname*\Start Menu\Programs\Startup)

2. A shortcut in \Documents and Settings\All Users\Start Menu\Programs\Startup

3. A key named Run, RunOnce, or RunOnceEx in \HKEY_LOCAL_MACHINE\Software\Microsoft\Windows\CurrentVersion

4. A key named Run, RunOnce, or RunOnceEx in \HKEY_CURRENT_USER\Software\Microsoft\Windows\CurrentVersion

5. A run= or load= entry in WIN.INI in the Windows directory (\windows or \winnt)

The Run keys are often set by software manufacturers who want their software to run whether you want it to or not. Sometimes this is a good thing—as when Windows uses it to start the taskbar program. But this technique is sometimes used to install annoying programs you really don't want.

The RunOnce keys are used mostly by installation programs that need to complete their work after forcing you to reboot your computer. Windows normally deletes these entries after you've logged in once and these programs have run, but they are sometimes not properly removed.

If you're plagued by unwanted or buggy programs when you log in, see "Tracking Down Errant Startup Programs" in the "Troubleshooting" section at the end of this chapter.

HKEY_CURRENT_CONFIG

HKEY_CURRENT_CONFIG is a virtual top-level key containing information Windows uses to initialize during its bootup phase, and very little else. Despite its important-sounding name, you'll find virtually nothing of human interest in here. The information is all set up automatically when you create Hardware Profiles.

By *virtual*, I mean that the keys in HKEY_CURRENT_CONFIG are really contained in other parts of the Registry, and using HKEY_CURRENT_CONFIG is just a convenient way to get at them. A curious feature of this one is that its subkeys come from several different parts of the Registry. Its System\CurrentControlSet subkey comes from one of the HKEY_LOCAL_MACHINE\SYSTEM\ControlSet### keys, and various parts of its Software subkey come from other parts of HKEY_LOCAL_MACHINE.

HKEY_CLASSES_ROOT

HKEY_CLASSES_ROOT is another of these virtual keys, provided to give programmers quick access to HKEY_LOCAL_MACHINE\Software\Classes.

A large part of the Classes section is devoted to the associations the Explorer makes between file types (or filename extensions, like .doc) and the programs that are used to open, display, or edit them. This is the information you're editing when you change associations in the Explorer by choosing Tools, Folder Options, File Types.

These entries contain the nitty-gritty linkage information that Windows uses to track its interchangeable software components called ActiveX Controls, OLE, and other software systems using the COM+ interprocess communication system. These entries are confusing, complex, and best left completely alone. I can say that in the past several years of using Windows I've never needed to touch or look at this stuff or edit it manually.

Table 35.2 gives an overview of the structure of HKEY_CLASSES_ROOT.

TABLE 35.2 THE STRUCTURE OF HKEY_CLASSES_ROOT

Entry	Description
. through .zip	For each listed file extension, the default value assigns a name to the file type. Each of these file type names appears later as a subkey of its own.
	File types that have OLE handlers have a subkey PersistentHandler, which gives a Class ID (a string of numbers like {098f2570-b … -03f3}). They are listed under the CLSID subkey, where the program file for the handler is named.
	Files that have associated programs to edit or display them also have shell or shellx subkeys, which contain the commands Explorer uses when you attempt to open a file using a double-click.

PART

VI

CH

35

continues

	TABLE 35.2 THE STRUCTURE OF HKEY_CLASSES_ROOT
Entry	**Description**
filetype	Each named file type (for example, VBScript) contains the CLSID number of the associated handler for the file type. Windows looks up this information through the CLSID subkey to find the associated program.
CLSID	Contains a subkey for each registered Active-(*something*) handler; the subkeys and values name the handler and point to the file containing its program code.

HKEY_USERS

HKEY_USERS contains a subkey for each authorized user of the computer and an entry named .DEFAULT. The .DEFAULT section contains just that—the basic settings given to each new local user added to the computer. (I say *local* because, on a Windows 2000 domain-based network, when a user logs in for the first time using a domain login name, his or her default Registry entries are obtained from the domain's server, not the local computer.)

The user subkeys of HKEY_USERS have long numeric names. These names are the GUID or Globally Unique User Identification numbers generated by Windows as a computer-friendly representation of the user's name. It's by these numbers that Windows tracks users, whether local or domain-based.

Nothing else is in HKEY_USERS besides these per-user subkeys. They appear as the contents of HKEY_CURRENT_USER when the associated user is logged in, so let's discuss them from this more sensible viewpoint.

HKEY_CURRENT_USER

HKEY_CURRENT_USER contains settings, preferences, and other information specific to the currently logged-in user. This whole section is actually a subkey of HKEY_USERS, as discussed previously, but is provided this way as a username-independent way of getting to the information.

The Software keys in HKEY_CURRENT_USER are similar to the Software subkeys in HKEY_LOCAL_MACHINE. They're grouped by software manufacturer, and Windows entries are stored in HKEY_CURRENT_USER\Software\Microsoft\Windows\CurrentVersion.

BACKING UP AND RESTORING THE REGISTRY

Because the Registry is now the *one* place where all the Windows hardware and software settings are stored, it's also the one thing that Windows absolutely needs to run. You will hear dire warnings from Microsoft, other computer books, installation manuals, and now me: It's very important to back up the Registry before you edit it or before it's changed by installation programs. If a critical entry is lost or changed incorrectly (for example, the name of a driver file for your graphics display adapter), Windows may not be able to start at all.

If you have a Registry problem, before attempting any drastic measures, see "Recovering from a Suspected Registry Problem" in the "Troubleshooting" section at the end of this chapter.

Make it a habit to back up the Registry every time you back up your hard disk and before you install new hardware or software. I can tell you from personal experience that without a Registry backup, something as common as a bad graphics card installation program can cost you a whole day of trying to get your system to boot again! (I don't need to tell you which chapter I was trying to write when this happened, do I?)

BACKING UP THE REGISTRY

You can back up the Registry in Windows 2000 in two main ways: You can back it up as part of a regular disk backup, or you can use the Registry Editor to save a key to a disk file. I suggest that you set your favorite disk backup program to back up the Registry files every time you back up your hard disk. Before you install a piece of new hardware or a significant software package, do a full disk backup, including the Registry. Before you manually edit the Registry for some purpose, use the Registry Editor backup technique.

Tip #417	The Emergency Startup Disk (ESD) contains the most critical, hardware-related information from the Registry. An up-to-date ESD can help you get Windows back on its feet if you have a Registry or driver disaster. You might need it to get Windows running well enough to restore the backups you made earlier. So, the ESD is another Registry backup of a sort. If you *really* want to get a gold star for preparedness, update your ESD after you've added new hardware, when it has proven to be stable and work correctly.

→ To learn how to make an Emergency Startup Disk, **see** "Backup," **p. 1266**.

BACKING UP WITH WINDOWS BACKUP

To run the Backup utility included with Windows 2000, you open the Start menu and choose Programs, Accessories, System Tools, Backup.

Whether you're doing a regular disk backup or just backing up the Registry, check System State either by itself or with other drives or files (see Figure 35.2). Checking this option backs up the Registry along with boot files, Active Directory files, and Certificates, according to Microsoft, and by default includes many other system program files as well—more than 200MB worth on my system. (Such is the state of Windows, I guess!)

Although it's best to perform a full backup to tape or other high-capacity storage media, you can perform a quick System State backup to a disk file in preparation for adding new hardware or software.

→ To learn more about Backup, **see** "Windows 2000 Backup Program," **p. 1261**.

Figure 35.2
Here, you can check System State to add the Registry to your backup set.

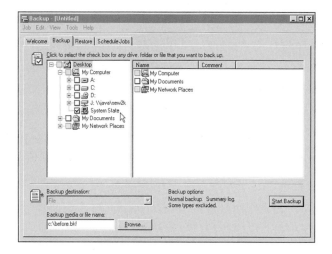

The following are the steps to make a disk-file backup of the Registry:

1. Choose Start, Programs, Accessories, System Tools, Backup.

2. Check System State under My Computer.

3. Choose File from the Backup Destination list.

4. Enter a filename for Backup Media—for example, `c:\before.bkf`.

5. Select Start Backup. The Backup Job Information dialog then appears.

6. Check Replace the Data on the Media with This Backup.

7. You might want to eliminate the system programs from the backup. To do so, click Advanced and uncheck Automatically Backup System Protected Files with the System State (see Figure 35.3). Click OK. (Eliminating these programs reduces the amount of information stored from 210MB to about 10MB.)

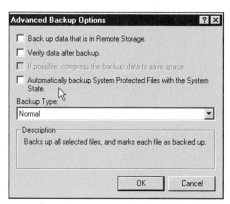

Figure 35.3

Tip #418

If you're backing up prior to installing new software or hardware, I suggest that you back up the system-protected files because the installation might change them as well as Registry entries. If you're backing up prior to manual Registry editing, you are probably safe omitting the system-protected files.

8. Choose Start Backup.

These steps create a file that contains the backed-up Registry. Now, if Registry problems occur after your installation, you can use Backup to restore the Registry to its previous state.

It is a good idea to select System State in *any* backup you make, to disk or tape.

Note

With Backup, you cannot save the System State of a remote computer, only the local computer. For remote or centralized backup services—to back up the Registries of all the computers on your network—you need to buy a third-party backup program. If you're managing a network of computers with or without Windows 2000 Server, you should definitely investigate centralized backup systems.

BACKING UP WITH THIRD-PARTY BACKUP SOFTWARE

Third-party disk backup software made for Windows 2000 includes an option to back up the Registry. Be sure to check this option whenever you are backing up your hard disk. It may have options like the Windows Backup program to back up just the Registry and to back up to a disk file, so you can make a quick backup before attempting Registry edits.

You should check your backup software's manual for instructions on saving Registry and system information when you back up. I suggest that you *always* include the Registry in your backups.

BACKING UP WITH REGEDIT

The Registry Editor, called Regedit, has a mechanism to export a set of Registry keys and values to a text file. By restoring these exported files, you can replace changed or deleted keys and values. But Regedit cannot remove entries you added that were not in the Registry before the backup! So, if an entry you add causes problems, the Registry Editor backup will not help you recover.

If you can't or won't use a more comprehensive backup system before you manually edit the Registry, though, at least use this method: Before you edit the Registry manually, select a key that contains all the subkeys and values you plan to modify. This way, you can back up all the sections you plan to edit in one backup.

To back up a key and its subkeys and values, follow these steps:

1. To run Regedit, choose Start, Run. Type regedit and click OK.
2. Select the key you plan to modify, or a key containing all the keys you plan to modify, in the left pane.
3. Select Registry, Export Registry File (see Figure 35.4).

PART

VI

CH

35

Figure 35.4
Here, you can save a
Registry key with
Regedit.

File type should be set to All Files [*.*]

4. Choose a filename to use to store the Registry keys.

Tip #419

I recommend not using the extension .REG. This extension is associated with Registry entries in the Windows Explorer, and selecting an REG file in the Explorer instantly and silently restores it to the Registry. This operation is far too serious to have happen with just a mouse click or two.

5. Select All Files from the Save As Type list, and enter a name with an extension other than .REG—for example, `c:\before.rg`.

6. Click Save. The chosen key or keys are then saved as a text file.

RESTORING THE REGISTRY

If you've made Registry changes that cause problems, you can try to remember each and every change you made, re-enter the original information, delete any keys you added, and thus undo the changes manually. Good luck! If you were diligent and made a backup before you started, you can simply restore the backup and have confidence that the recovery is complete and accurate.

 If you think you have Registry problems, see "Signs of Registry Problems" in the "Troubleshooting" section at the end of this chapter.

To restore a Registry backup you made, follow the steps described in the following sections.

RESTORING THE REGISTRY FROM WINDOWS BACKUP

The Windows Backup utility's Restore feature lets you replace Registry and other System files saved before a failed installation or change. This step is fairly drastic, so be sure you've exhausted the less invasive procedures before you resort to this method. If you did a full backup, you're fairly safe because all program files will be restored along with the Registry. If you backed up only the Registry itself, there's a chance that the old Registry entries won't solve the problems created by replaced system programs.

Follow these steps to restore the backup:

1. Start Backup, and select the Restore tab.

2. Select Tools, Options. Choose Always Replace the File on My Computer. (You must choose this option because you're replacing files that do exist but that contain the wrong information.) Then click OK.

3. Expand the list of cataloged backups (see Figure 35.5). Then locate the backup you want to restore, and check System State. If you want to restore other files and/or volumes backed up at the same time, check them as well.

Figure 35.5
You can restore a System State Registry backup here.

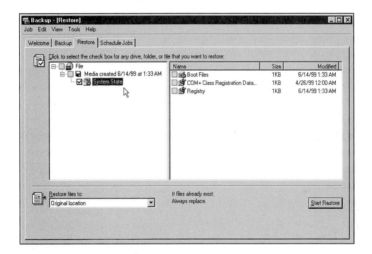

4. Select Start Restore. A dialog box then warns you that you are about to overwrite the current System State. Click OK.

5. When a dialog box offers you Advanced options, you can just click OK to proceed.

6. You then see a dialog box that lets you change the name of the backup set file you're restoring. The name should be the same as when you made the backup—for example, `c:\before.bkf`. Correct it if necessary, and click OK.

7. When the backup is complete, Backup asks you to restart the system. You really must reboot now because the Registry files have not really been restored. The recovered Registry data has been set aside and will only be used the next time Windows starts. If you make any other Registry changes before restarting, they will be lost when the restored files are activated.

RESTORING THE REGISTRY FROM THIRD-PARTY SOFTWARE

Third-party backup software has a Registry restore procedure similar to the one described previously. Follow the instructions for your backup software to restore the Registry (and other files, if applicable), and restart the system.

RESTORING THE REGISTRY FROM REGEDIT

If a Registry editing session has gone awry, and you need to restore the Registry from a Regedit backup, follow these steps:

1. In Regedit, select Registry, Import Registry File.
2. Select All Files from the Files of Type list.
3. Locate the file you used to back up the Registry key or keys—for example, `c:\before.rg`.
4. Select Open.

The saved Registry keys are then imported, replacing any changes or deletions. However, any keys or values you added that were not in the Registry previously are not removed. If they are the cause of the problem, this restore will *not* help.

If the Registry problems persist, you can try a rather drastic measure: You can use Regedit to delete the key or keys that were changed and then import the backup file again. This time, any added keys or values are removed. I suggest you try this approach only with keys related to add-on software, *not* for any of the Microsoft software or hardware keys. (In fact, I don't think you should try it, period.)

Tip #420	My final word on Registry repair: If you encounter problems with the Registry entries for hardware or for Windows itself, and restoring the Registry doesn't help, you are probably better off reinstalling Windows or using the Emergency Repair procedure than trying any further desperate measures to fix the Registry.

Tip #421	If you encounter what you think are Registry problems with add-on software, your best bet is to uninstall the software, if possible, and reinstall it before attempting *any* Registry restores or repairs.

USING REGEDIT

You might never need to edit the Registry manually. Most Registry keys are set by the software that uses them. For example, Office 2000 sets its own preference values, and the Control Panel applets set the appropriate Display, Sound, and Networking Registry entries. In a way, the Control Panel is mostly just a Registry Editor.

You might need to edit the Registry manually if directed by a technical support person who's helping you fix a problem (I hope) or when you're following a published procedure to make an adjustment for which there is no Control Panel setting.

In the latter case, before going any further, I need to say this one last time, to make it absolutely clear: Few circumstances really require you to edit the Registry manually. Be sure you really need to before you do. And, let me add: Back up the Registry, or at least the section you want to change, before making any changes.

Before getting into Registry exploration techniques and some tips and tricks, I'll cover the basics of the Registry Editor.

VIEWING THE REGISTRY

The Registry Editor doesn't have a Start menu item. You must run it from the Start, Run dialog. Just enter `regedit` and click OK.

Regedit displays a two-pane display much like Explorer, as shown in Figure 35.6). The top-level keys, which are listed below My Computer, can be expanded just like drives and folders in the Explorer. In the right pane are the values for each key. The name of the current selected key is shown in the status bar.

Figure 35.6
The Regedit screen shows keys on the left and values on the right.

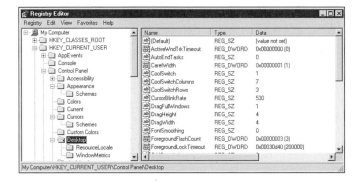

Values have names, just as the files in a folder do, and it's here that configuration information is finally stored. Each key has a (Default) value, which is the value of the key itself, and any number of named values. For example, in Figure 35.6, key HKEY_CURRENT_USER\Desktop is shown. The value of HKEY_CURRENT_USER\Desktop itself is undefined (blank), and the value HKEY_CURRENT_USER\AppEvents\CoolSwitch is 1.

Registry values have a data type, which is usually one of the types shown in Table 35.3.

TABLE 35.3 DATA TYPES

TC here	
REG_SZ	Textual information, a simple string of letters
REG_DWORD	A single number displayed in hexadecimal or decimal
REG_MULTI_SZ	Text in one or more lines
REG_BINARY	Binary data, displayed an arbitrary number of hexadecimal digits

Other data types can be found, but they are obscure, rare, and never require editing by hand.

SEARCHING IN THE REGISTRY

You can search for a Registry entry by key name, value name, or the contents of a value string. First, select a starting point for the search in the left pane. You can select My Computer to select the entire Registry, or you can limit your search to one of the top-level keys or any subordinate key. Next, select Find from the menu, and enter a search string into the Find dialog. The Find feature is not case sensitive, so upper- and lowercase don't matter. You can check any of the Look At boxes, as shown in Figure 35.7, to designate where in the Registry you expect to find the desired text: in the name of a key, in the name of a value, or in the data, the value itself.

Figure 35.7
In this dialog, you can select whether to search key names, value names, or value data.

Check Match Whole String Only to search only for items whose whole name or value is the desired string.

> **Note**
>
> Most of the time I check all the Look At boxes but not Match Whole String Only.

Select Find Next to start the search. The Regedit display indicates the first match to your string, and by pressing F3, you can repeat the search to look for other instances.

> **Tip #1001**
>
> The search function has two limitations:
>
> 1. You can't enter a backslash (\) in the search string when looking for a key or value name; Regedit won't complain, but it won't find anything either.

2. You can't search for the initial HKEY_*xxx* part of a key name. That's not actually part of the name; it's just the section of the Registry in which the key resides.

So, to find a key named, for example, HKEY_CLASSES_ROOT\MIDFile\shell\Play\ Command, you can't type all that in and have Find jump right to the key. When you already know the full pathname of a key, use the left pane of Regedit to browse for the key directly.

EDITING KEYS AND VALUES

Regedit has no Save or Undo menu items. Changes to the Registry happen immediately and permanently. Additions, deletions, and changes are for real. This is the reason for all the warnings to back up before you poke into the Registry.

ADDING A VALUE

To add a value to a key, select the key in the left pane, and choose Edit, New. Select the type of value to add; you can select String Value, Binary Value, or DWORD Value. (The instructions you're following will indicate which type of value to add.) A new value entry then appears in the right pane, as shown in Figure 35.8.

Figure 35.8
New value adds an entry in Rename mode.

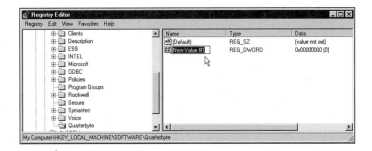

Enter the new value's name, and press Enter to edit the value.

For string values, enter the text of the desired string.

For DWORD values, choose Decimal or Hexadecimal, and enter the desired value in the chosen format (see Figure 35.9).

For binary values, enter pairs of hexadecimal characters as instructed. (You'll never be asked to do this, I promise.)

CHANGING A VALUE

If you want to change a value, double-click a value in the right pane to bring up the Edit Value dialog. Alternatively, you can select it and choose Edit, Modify from the menu, or right-click and select Modify from the context menu. Then make the desired change, and click OK.

PART
VI

CH
35

Figure 35.9
You can choose to enter a DWORD value in either decimal or hexadecimal notation.

That is all you will likely ever need to do with Regedit. It's very unlikely that you will ever be asked to delete a value or add or remove a key. But just for the sake of completeness, I'll describe how in the following sections.

DELETING A VALUE

No big surprises here! To delete a value, select it and choose Edit, Delete from the menu, or right-click and select Delete from the context menu. Confirm by clicking OK.

ADDING A KEY

Keys must be added as subkeys to existing keys; you can't add a top-level key. To add a key, select an existing key in the left pane, and select Edit, New, Key from the menu. Alternatively, right-click the existing key, and select New, Key from the context menu. A new key appears in the left pane, where you can edit its name, as shown in Figure 35.10. Press Enter after you enter the name.

Figure 35.10
A new key appears in Rename mode.

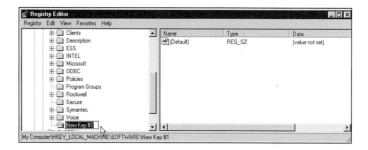

You can delete a key by selecting it in the left pane and choosing Edit, Delete from the menu, or by right-clicking it and selecting Delete from the context menu. Click OK to confirm that you do intend to delete the key. Deleting a key deletes its values and all its subkeys as well, so without the protection of Undo (or a Registry Recycling Bin), this action is serious.

RENAMING A KEY

As you have probably guessed, the pattern for renaming a key follows the Explorer exactly: Choose the key in the left pane and select Edit, Rename, or right-click the key and select Rename. Finally, enter a new name, and press Enter.

Don't attempt to rename keys without a *very good* reason, such as you mistyped the name of the key you were adding.

USING COPY KEY NAME

As you have probably noticed by now, Registry keys can be pretty long, tortuous things to type. The Registry Editor offers a bit of help to finger-fatigued Registry editors (and authors): Choosing Edit, Copy Key Name puts the name of the currently selected key into the Clipboard, so you can paste it elsewhere, should the need arise. For example, when you've found a neat Registry trick, you might want to email your friends about it.

USING REGEDIT ON A REMOTE COMPUTER

The Registry Editor permits administrators to edit the Registry of other computers on a network. Of course, this operation is highly privileged, and you must have administrator privileges on the computer whose Registry you want to edit. To edit a remote computer's Registry, choose Registry, Connect Network Registry. Next, enter the name of the remote computer, or choose Browse to select one graphically; then click OK. (Interestingly, Browse doesn't let you use Active Directory to select a computer to manage, but only the basic Network Neighborhood list.)

If the remote computer grants you access to its Registry, the computer's Registry keys appear in the list along with your own, as shown in Figure 35.11.

Figure 35.11
Viewing and editing a remote computer's Registry.

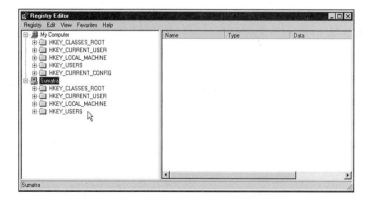

For you to be able to connect to the Registry on a Windows 95 or 98 computer, it must have Remote Management installed. This option must be installed as part of the computer's Network Services through the Network Control Panel. It is not an option with Windows NT and 2000; it is installed automatically.

ADVANCED REGISTRY EDITING WITH REGEDT32

Windows comes with an alternative Registry Editor named Regedt32, which was the version shipped with Windows 95 and NT version 3. The user interface for Regedt32 is more awkward than Regedit's because it doesn't have a left Explorer pane. Instead, each of the top-level keys is opened in a separate window (see Figure 35.12). Other than the display differences and slightly different labeling of the menu choices, the functions in Regedt32 are almost identical to Regedit. However, Regedt32 has three features that Regedit doesn't:

- You can insert REG_MULTI_SZ and REG_EXPAND_SZ values. These two data types are not available in Regedit, and they're needed for certain seldom-seen Registry keys.

- You can attach hives (Registry data files) to the Registry. For example, normally the HKEY_CURRENT_USER hive for a given user is joined to the Registry only while the user is logged in. Regedt32 lets you attach another user's hive to the Registry so that his or her data can be modified while he or she is not logged in.

- You can modify the security attributes of Registry keys and values with Regedt32. Just like files and folders, Registry keys and values have a complete set of Access Control attributes that determine who has rights to read, write, and modify the Registry. Regedt32 lets you examine and modify Registry access rights and auditing.

Figure 35.12
Regedt32 uses an old-style user interface but has some advanced features that Regedit lacks. Each primary key in the Registry is displayed in a separate window.

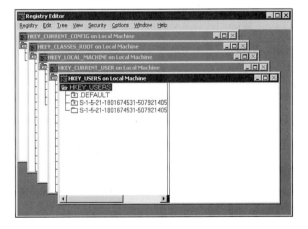

Needless to say, changing Registry key access rights can cause profound problems with Windows, so I encourage you not to make any changes to Registry access settings unless you're explicitly instructed to do so. (I've actually seen this happen. Microsoft sometimes issues security bulletins that tell how to eliminate newly discovered security holes in Windows. Sometimes this process involves controlling access to Registry keys.) The other two special uses of Regedt32 are occasionally valuable, so I'll show you how to take advantage of them next.

ADDING REG_MULTI_SZ AND REG_EXPAND_SZ VALUES

So far, you've learned about three types of Registry values: String, Binary, and DWORD. Actually, the Registry can contain many different data types. Most of them are very odd representations of hardware settings used internally by Windows and never see the light of day, so to speak. For reasons known only to Microsoft planners, however, two fairly important data types were omitted from Regedit: REG_EXPAND_SZ and REG_MULTI_SZ.

These strange-sounding names are the internal names used by Windows programmers, and the three I've described have these geeky names, too:

String is also called REG_SZ.

Binary is called REG_BINARY.

DWORD is called REG_DWORD.

The additional two data types are less often used, but you might be called upon to add or modify one of these values at some time, and Regedt32 is the only way to do so.

REG_MULTI_SZ can contain a list of separate string values and is used, for example, to store the IP address or addresses assigned to a network card. Network cards can be assigned more than one IP address (this technique is used by Web servers to host many different Web sites), so the Registry stores a card's IP addresses in a REG_MULTI_SZ. Regedit can display this data type only as Binary. Now compare the difference between the two displays in Figure 35.13. (I should point out that you no longer need to add extra IP addresses this way as you did in Windows NT 3.5. You can add them directly in Local Area Connection configuration.)

Figure 35.13
Regedt32 (left) can directly display REG_MULTI_SZ data, whereas Regedit must display it as a Binary data value (right).

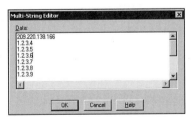
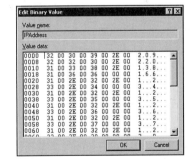

REG_EXPAND_SZ is used when Registry values can contain environment variable strings. For example, the location of each user's profile folder and, within that, folders such as My Documents, are stored with a REG_EXPAND_SZ value. This makes it possible to use the environment variable %USERNAME% as part of the file location. The REG_EXPAND_SZ data type is an indication to Windows that it needs to replace environment variable names in the string rather than interpret any % signs literally. You can't randomly use REG_EXPAND_SZ to get this function, however. The program that uses the Registry value must anticipate it.

PART

VI

CH

35

These Registry data types are not commonly called for, but you might come across references to them in some power-user tips in this book and elsewhere. Now you know the secret to entering them.

EDITING REGISTRY ENTRIES FOR ANOTHER USER

If you open a Registry Editor and look under HKEY_USERS, you will find that the only available subkeys are .DEFAULT and your own, which is also accessible as HKEY_CURRENT_USER. Windows, you remember, stores various parts of the Registry in data files called hives, and usually loads the HKEY_USERS hive only for the currently logged-on user. When you log out on a Windows domain, your Registry data is unloaded from the Registry, and the hive file is copied back to the domain controller where it resides as part of your user profile.

As an administrator, you might find it necessary to edit Registry HKEY_USERS entries for another user. For example, a startup program in HKEY_CURRENT_USER\Software\Windows\CurrentVersion\Run might be causing such trouble that the user can't log in. (Can you tell this is a pet peeve of mine?) If you can't log in as that user, you can edit his or her HKEY_USERS Registry keys in another way:

1. Log on as Administrator.

2. Choose Start, Run. Then type regedt32 and press Enter.

3. Select the HKEY_USERS window.

4. Highlight the top-level key HKEY_USERS (see Figure 37.12).

5. Select Registry, Load Hive.

6. Browse to the profile folder for the desired user. It is in \Documents and Settings\ *username* for a local machine user in a workgroup, or on the domain controller for a Windows Server domain in the folder used for user profiles.

7. Type the filename NTUSER.DAT. (The file does not appear in the browse dialog because it's "super hidden": a hidden system file). Then click Open.

8. A dialog then appears, asking you to enter a name for the hive. While HKEY_USERS normally loads user hives with a long numeric GID name, I suggest that you type the user's logon name. Click OK. The user's Registry data is then loaded and can be edited, as shown in Figure 35.14.

9. When you're finished editing, unload the hive. Select the key you added under HKEY_USERS (for example, the bsmith key in Figure 35.14), and click Registry, Unload Hive. Confirm by clicking Yes on the warning dialog.

Figure 35.14
An offline user's
Registry hive is now
loaded and can be
edited.

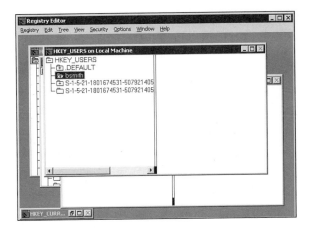

OTHER REGISTRY TOOLS

I've said that, although most Windows adjustments are made via Registry entry changes, most of these settings are made using Control Panel applets, Computer Management tools, and application preferences menus.

There are some nifty changes you can make to Windows's behavior that used to require direct Registry editing. Now, however, you'll find a raft of third-party add-on tools to make these changes more safely via a nice graphical user interface. Let's go through a couple of them.

TWEAKUI

Microsoft produced just such a tool called TweakUI. If you don't geek-speak, its name means "adjust the user interface in cool and arcane ways." You can download TweakUI from Microsoft's Web site at www.microsoft.com. Go to the downloads section, and search for tweakui. Obtain a Windows 2000 version if one is available; otherwise, get the Windows 98 version.

Using TweakUI, you can adjust mouse sensitivity, window movement, and animation effects, the appearance of icons in the Explorer views, the visibility of desktop icons such as Internet Explorer, the visibility of local and network drives in the Explorer, and some security features such as hiding the name of the last-logged-on user.

REGISTRY TOOLKIT

Registry Toolkit is a shareware Registry Editor made by Funduc software with a nifty search-and-replace system. You can scan the Registry, changing all occurrences of one string to another, which is great for some nasty jobs. It also keeps a log of changes made so that edits can be undone. Its user interface isn't very comfortable or slick, but if you need to manage a lot of identical changes in the Registry, this is one tool to check out. It's free to try; $25 to register.

PART

VI

CH

35

REGISTRY PRIVILEGES AND POLICIES

In Windows NT and Windows 2000, like folders and files, Registry keys and values can have permissions set to define who has permission to view and edit them. The Windows Policies system, which allows administrators to restrict users' ability to change their computer configuration, is based on Registry access control.

In a nutshell, Administrative Policies install Registry keys and values that tell Windows administrative programs such as Control Panel to hide certain controls and settings. For example, a policy entry might make the Display Control Panel hide the Power Management settings. These restricting Registry entries are then locked into place with permission settings that prevent the users from seeing or changing them.

You don't manage these entries using Regedit, but by using the Policy Editor and Manager, which is described in Chapter 32, "Managing Users."

Caution

I gave this warning before, but it bears repeating: Trying to manually change Registry privileges is very dangerous. Don't do it! You could easily render your system not only inoperative, but also out of your own reach to repair.

REGISTRY TIPS AND TRICKS

I have said that most important Registry entries are made from Control Panel applets and program preferences. However, a few settings can be made no other way than through manual entries in the Registry. This isn't so different from having to edit CONFIG.SYS or AUTOEXEC.BAT back in the old DOS days, except that you could always get around a bad CONFIG.SYS entry by booting your computer with a floppy disk. No such luck with Windows! As I've warned you, a botched Registry editing job can make Windows unbootable. Nonetheless, some interesting things may make the risk worthwhile (says Bob; maybe, says Brian).

AUTOCOMPLETION OF FILES AND DIRECTORIES ON THE COMMAND LINE

The command prompt can offer autocompletion of filenames and/or directories as you type paths and filenames on the command line. To use this feature, change the value HKEY_CURRENT_USER\Software\Microsoft\Command Processor\CompletionChar to 9 to make the Tab key the completion character. You can type a partial file path and press Tab to view successive matching paths. (Note: When Microsoft releases the Windows 2000 version of TweakUI, this feature will be one of its configuration options.)

STARTING A COMMAND PROMPT IN ANY DIRECTORY

You're familiar with the menu of commands the Explorer presents when you right-click a file: Explore, Open, and so on. You can add a context-menu command for folders to let you instantly start a command prompt window set to that directory like this:

1. Open key HKEY_CLASSES_ROOT\Directory\shell.

2. Add a new key named CmdHere under shell (the name is not important).

3. Edit its (Default) value, and change the value data to CMD &Prompt Here. It becomes the right-click menu prompt.

4. Make a subkey named command under CmdHere.

5. Set its default value data to cmd /k pushd "%1".

Now, in the Explorer, you can right-click CMD Prompt Here and get a command prompt, neatly set to your chosen directory. (This technique can actually be generalized to file types other than Directory, with any appropriate command.)

HIDING CONTROL PANEL APPLETS

Under HKEY_CURRENT_USER\Control Panel\don't load, values named after Control Panel applet files (for example, odbccp32.cpl) prevent them from being visible in the Control Panel. You could use this capability to hide specified Control Panel applets from specific users; this might be best done using a System Policy, however.

CHANGING THE LOCATION OF STANDARD FOLDERS

HKEY_CURRENT_USER\Software\Microsoft\Windows\CurrentVersion\Explorer\Shell Folders contains a list of values that determine which folders Windows associates with standard locations, such as My Pictures, the desktop, and temporary Internet files. These values can be changed to use different directories, although I caution you that the consequences of making a mistake might be really unpleasant.

> **Note**
>
> I have one more tip that's so cool, I put it at the end of the chapter under "Tips from the Windows Pros."

TROUBLESHOOTING

SIGNS OF REGISTRY PROBLEMS

How can I determine whether Windows problems are caused by the Registry?

Registry corruption can take two forms: Either the Registry's database files can be damaged by an errant disk operation, or information can be entered incorrectly, by hand or by a buggy program. No matter what the cause, the result can be a system that won't run. (As I mentioned, I had this problem while writing this chapter. A bad display driver entry caused Windows to reboot over and over.)

Other signs of Registry corruption or errors could be as follows:

- Drivers aren't loaded, or they give errors while Windows is booting.
- Software complains about components that aren't registered or cannot be located.
- Undesirable programs attempt to run when you log in.
- Windows does not boot, or it starts up only in VGA or Safe mode.

RECOVERING FROM A SUSPECTED REGISTRY PROBLEM

How do I recover from a Registry problem?

If any of the signs of a Registry problem occur just after you install new software or hardware, after you've edited the Registry manually, or after an unexpected and unprotected power loss to the computer, then you might have a Registry problem. Try these fixes in turn, checking after each step to see whether the problem is resolved:

1. Use the Repair Wizard to see whether you have any corrupted Windows system files.

2. If the problem occurred right after you installed new software, try uninstalling the software by opening the Control Panel and choosing Add/Remove Software. See whether the software manufacturer has released any updates for the software (especially during the first six months or so after Windows 2000 is released). If an update is available, get it before proceeding. Similarly, if the problem involves previously installed software, not necessarily new, try reinstalling it. I suggest installing it once *without* first uninstalling it. If that fails, uninstall it, and proceed to the next step.

3. Reinstall the software. If problems are indicated by the installer, stop, remove the software, and contact the manufacturer.

4. If you get to this point, get professional technical help if it is available. If your appendix were acting up, would you call a doctor, or would you get out your kitchen knives? Well, if you were stranded on a desert island, you might have to try to take care of the problem yourself.

5. If the problem occurred right after you installed new hardware, try restarting Windows, and press F8 to get the additional startup options. Choose Last Known Good to see whether the problem is solved. Last Known Good uses the previous boot's version of HKEY_LOCAL_CONFIG, so good hardware settings might be preserved there. If the problem persists, try disabling the hardware in the Device Manager. If that solves the problem, you likely have to get an updated driver.

6. If none of these fixes solve the problem, or if you can't get Windows started, try starting Windows in VGA mode. Starting this way circumvents many display driver setup problems. If you suspect the problem is caused by the display driver, set Windows to use the Standard VGA driver and restart. Then reinstall your normal graphics adapter (using the most recent updated driver).

7. If you have a fresh Registry backup, restore it. This fix should return you to a state where you had a working system.

8. Use the Emergency Repair Disk to repair Windows (Repair mode).

9. Reinstall Windows in Upgrade/Replace mode.

10. Reinstall Windows in Clean Install mode.

TRACKING DOWN ERRANT STARTUP PROGRAMS

How do I track down and eliminate startup programs that don't appear in the Start menu but start anyway when I launch Windows?

When I said that all Windows startup information is kept in the Registry, I lied. Actually, to maintain compatibility with older 16-bit Windows software (and even some new software that should know better), the original Windows SYSTEM.INI and WIN.INI files still exist, and Windows 2000 keeps a few of their entries up-to-date with information copied from the Registry. This lets older software that really depends on the old INI file system still function.

Because some older software depended on Windows to start it as Windows started, Windows 2000 still examines SYSTEM.INI for `run` and `load` entries in the `[boot]` section that these older programs might make. It does this when a user logs in.

In addition, Windows examines the Startup folder in the Start Menu Programs folders of both the user logging in and the All Users folder.

Windows also looks in the Registry for values in the following keys:

HKEY_LOCAL_MACHINE\Software\Microsoft\Windows\CurrentVersion\Run

HKEY_LOCAL_MACHINE\Software\Microsoft\Windows\CurrentVersion\RunOnce

HKEY_CURRENT_USER\Software\Microsoft\Windows\CurrentVersion\Run

HKEY_CURRENT_USER\Software\Microsoft\Windows\CurrentVersion\RunOnce

The LOCAL_MACHINE entries are run for all users, and the CURRENT_USER entries are, of course, specific to each individual user.

If you're trying to eliminate a Startup program and can't find it in your own Startup folder, look in the following places:

1. Look for a shortcut or program in the folder \Documents and Settings\Default User\ Start Menu\Programs\Startup.

2. Examine SYSTEM.INI in C:\windows. Look for `load=` or `run=` lines in the `[boot]` section. The program might be run from here.

3. Examine the Startup folders under Programs in both your Start menu and in the All Users Start menu folder. Right-click your Start button, and select Explore to examine these folders. Note: You must have administrator privileges to delete an entry from the All Users Startup folder.

4. Run Regedit, and browse to key HKEY_CURRENT_USER\Software\Microsoft \Windows\CurrentVersion. Look for Run, RunOnce, or RunOnceEx subkeys. Check their values for entries that are starting the undesired program. The RunOnce entries

are often set by installer programs to complete an installation process after rebooting and are sometimes not eliminated properly.

5. Repeat the same process with HKEY_LOCAL_MACHINE\Software\Microsoft\ Windows\CurrentVersion, looking for Run, RunOnce, or RunOnceEx keys.

Note

> If you can't log in as the affected user, and you suspect that the startup program is run from the HKEY_CURRENT_USER Registry entry, see "Editing Registry Entries for Another User" earlier in this chapter.

TIPS FROM THE WINDOWS PROS: POWER MANAGEMENT WHEN LOGGED OUT

In Chapter 31, "System Applets," you learned how to set your system's power management features to turn off your hard drive and monitor when you're away from your computer for a while. These settings are user-specific, and by now, you should be able to guess that they're stored in the Registry under HKEY_CURRENT_USER. But what happens when nobody is logged in? There *is* no current user, right? Well, not really. When nobody is logged in, Windows uses the Registry keys under HKEY_USERS\.DEFAULT as the "current user." This means that desktop and power management settings can be made in .DEFAULT to be applied when you log out.

I use this trick on all my computers to automatically turn off the monitor (and on some, the hard disk) when nobody is logged in. What I've done is set up .DEFAULT to put the monitor in standby when the system's been idle for one minute. When I log out at the end of the workday, the logon screen stays up for a minute; then blink! it's gone. A touch of the mouse brings it back when I want to log in again the next morning. This way, I can strike a balance between saving energy and being kind to the electronics, which hate being completely turned off and on every day.

Naturally, a bit of Registry hacking is involved because you can't get to the Control Panel to make these changes when you're not logged in. You may remember I started this chapter saying I hated Registry hacking in general. In this specific case, it really does some good. Still, you should consider a few caveats before you make these changes on your computer:

1. If your computer is used as a Web server, email server, or file server, it's going to be using its hard disk while you're not logged in. In this case, it's not a good idea to power down the hard disks, just the monitor.

2. Because you're going to edit the .DEFAULT user settings, any new users you create on your computer afterward will inherit this setting. It's best to make this change after adding any users you need. If you later add a new user, wiggle the mouse every so often while logging in the first time, immediately get to the Display properties in Control Panel, and set the power-off times to a reasonable value.

3. As nice as it would be, you can't set up a screen saver to run while you're logged out. It's for security reasons; a nefarious or virus-infected screen saver could mimic the login dialog and capture user passwords. So, power management is your only option.

That said, you can proceed as follows:

1. Log in as Administrator.

2. Open the Power Options Control Panel applet. Note the current settings for Turn off Monitor and Turn Off Hard Disks. Set Turn Off Monitor to After 1 Minute, and Turn Off Hard Disks to either After 5 Minutes or Never, as appropriate. Be sure that System Hibernates, if it appears as a choice, is set to Never.

3. Click OK to save the settings.

4. Start the Registry Editor by choosing Start, Run and typing `regedit`.

5. Back up the Registry using one of the means I described earlier.

6. In the left pane, browse to the key HKEY_CURRENT_USER\Control Panel\ PowerCfg, and highlight it.

7. Select Registry, Export Registry File, and save the file as `loggedout.reg`.

8. Select Registry, Import Registry File. In the file selection dialog, right-click loggedout.reg, and select Edit. When Notepad starts, you should see a file starting with the line `Windows Registry Editor Version 5.00`. This file contains the saved keys and values defining your current power settings.

9. In Notepad, select Edit, Replace. In the Find What box, enter `HKEY_CURRENT_USER`. In the Replace With box, enter `HKEY_USERS\.DEFAULT`. Click Replace All, and then close the Replace dialog.

10. Choose File, Save, and then choose File, Exit.

11. Back in the Import Registry File dialog, select file power.reg again, and click Open to load the power settings into the .DEFAULT user Registry section.

12. Close the Registry Editor.

13. Open the Power Options Control panel, and restore your original settings.

14. Log out, and verify that the monitor goes to standby after a minute. Move your mouse, or press the Shift key to power up the monitor again.

You can use the edited file loggedout.reg to set up other computers. Then copy the file to a floppy disk, or put it into a shared folder. On other computers, just locate the file in the Explorer, and double-click it to load the settings instantly.

PART

VI

CH

35

CHAPTER 36

WINDOWS SCRIPT HOST

In this chapter

BETTER LIVING THROUGH SCRIPTING

Scripting is the process of automating a task on an operating system. Until quite recently, if you wanted to automate something on any of Microsoft's operating systems, your only option was to write a batch file. The batch file language can use almost any command you can run at the command prompt and adds some primitive looping constructs.

You might write a batch file that you run once a week to clean up the temporary folders on your PC, for example. Another common batch file is the logon script that runs when the user logs on to his or her domain. A logon script typically maps various network shares to drive letters or synchronizes the local time on the user's workstation with that of the rest of the network.

Although batch files are useful and easy to write, they just don't have the power to handle complex tasks. Administrators and power users have complained to Microsoft for years about the lack of a decent scripting platform for Windows. Windows Script Host (WSH) is Microsoft's answer. Windows 2000 and Windows 98 support WSH out of the box, and you can download versions of WSH for Windows 95 and NT 4.0.

WSH is a 32-bit language-independent scripting host for ActiveX scripting engines. Because it's a host, it passes on the job of actually interpreting a script file to a language-specific processor or engine. The MS Visual Basic Scripting Edition (VBScript) and MS JavaScript (JScript) development system scripting engines are included along with Windows 2000, so you have everything you need at hand to get started. In addition, you can purchase third-party scripting engines for languages such as Perl, TCL, and Rexx.

This chapter introduces you to scripting on your Windows 2000 Professional workstation. First, I will introduce the VBScript language; then I'll show you how to run and debug scripts in Windows 2000.

You can use other languages with WSH, but VBScript is the best place to start. VBScript has become Microsoft's common scripting language for all sorts of automation, including the automation of Web pages in Internet Explorer and Internet Information Server. It's similar to Visual Basic for Applications (VBA), which is used to program macros in Microsoft Word and Excel. Any experience you gain working with VBScript in one type of application gives you a leg up if you move on to the others.

Note

> Several VBScript examples in this chapter are on the CD-ROM that accompanies this book. You can copy the folder containing the VBScript examples to your desktop so that you can edit as well as run them. The examples on the CD are noted with comments such as "CD Example File WSH001.VBS."
>
> You can run the sample scripts as you read along if you display the folder that contains the WSH folder in Explorer. Double-click a script file to run it with WSH, or right-click it and select Edit to view and/or edit the script with Notepad.

GETTING STARTED WITH VBSCRIPT

VBScript is a subset of Microsoft's Visual Basic programming language. You can think of a programming language as something that allows a programmer to manipulate numbers or strings of letters to produce a useful result. This is a simplified description of a programming language, but adequate to describe VBScript.

VBScript is not like most other programming languages; it doesn't handle user interfaces of any complexity. User interfaces are the "look" of an application—the menus, the toolbars, the dialog boxes, and so on. Sometimes the programming of the user interface can be more complex than the code behind the application's function. VBScript is more than capable of performing calculations and manipulating basic objects behind the scenes, but it cannot generate much of an interactive user interface. It is perfect for scripting, though, because scripts are meant to run with little or no user intervention; therefore, they don't need a user interface.

For the full scoop on VBScript, you can visit the Microsoft Developer's Network Web site at `http://msdn.microsoft.com/scripting`. The MSDN site has the VBScript language reference online, lots of examples, and add-ons you can download. It is *the* definitive VBScript Web site. You can view the VBScript language reference online using Internet Explorer, or you can download it as a Microsoft Help file for use offline.

Although you'll probably need the MSDN reference materials to develop your own scripts, I'll give you an overview of VBScript programming and some examples in this chapter.

> **Note**
>
> You can find a full-scale treatment of VBScript in *Windows Script Host By Example*, published by Que.

The first three VBScript topics I'll cover are variables, operators, and flow control.

VARIABLES

Variables hold the data that you want to process. The data could be either numbers or a series of arbitrary characters (commonly called a *string*). Data is stored in memory as a *variable* and is accessed by a *name*. You refer to it by name to see or change its value. To assign a variable, you use the = sign.

For example, consider the following lines of code:

```
Name = "Sue Smith"
Age = 40
```

In this example, the string value `"Sue Smith"` is stored in variable `Name`, and the integer value 40 is stored in variable `Age`.

Variables can also contain *objects*, which are blocks of data managed by software add-ons to VBScript. Objects are what give VBScript its real power because they let you take advantage of the capabilities of other system programs to perform complex tasks, such as sending email messages, writing files, and installing printers on the computer. I'll cover objects later in this chapter.

In most other programming languages, you have to define the variable type before using it, be it string, integer, object, date, or whatever. But VBScript works the variable type out for itself, making life much simpler for the programmer as a result.

In VBScript, all variables are of one fundamental data type called a *variant*. I'll go into more detail on this topic later, in the section on Advanced VBScript programming.

These restrictions are placed on the names that you can use for variables:

- Names must begin with an alphabetic character.
- They cannot contain an embedded period. For example, House.Big is invalid.
- They must not exceed 255 characters in length.

OPERATORS

VBScript variables can be manipulated with *operators* to perform mathematical or character operations. The + operator adds numeric variables. For example, to compute Sue Smith's age next year, you could use this expression:

```
age = age+1
```

This expression means: Take the variable age, add 1 to it, and store the results in variable age.

With variables containing string values, the & operator concatenates strings. For example,

```
firstname = "Sue"
lastname = "Smith"
fullname = firstname & " " & lastname
```

concatenates "Sue", a blank space, and "Smith" and stores the result in variable fullname. (The + symbol does this as well, but using & is better style.)

Operators are grouped into three classes:

- Arithmetic operators, including +, -, * (multiply), and / (divide)
- Comparison operators—for example, => (is greater than or equal to) and < (is less than)
- Logical operators—for example, AND, OR, and NOT

The comparison and logical operators produce neither a numeric nor string result, but rather a *Boolean* value, either True or False. These operators are used to direct the flow of control in a program, as in this example:

```
if Age >= 40 then
    write "You're not getting older, you're getting wiser"
end if
```

The order of precedence within calculations *does* matter. The expression 1+3*3 produces 10, not 12, because multiplication has higher precedence than addition. (Remember this discussion from high school algebra class?) In this case, 3*3 is computed first, and then it's added to 1. You can use parentheses to force VBScript to evaluate expressions as you desire if necessary. For example, (1+3)*3 produces 12. Remember, expressions in parentheses are computed first.

Sometimes expressions contain operators from more than one category. For example, the following comparison contains both an arithmetic and a comparison operator:

```
if A+B > C then ...
```

In these situations, arithmetic operators are evaluated first, comparison operators are evaluated next, and logical operators are evaluated last. Comparison operators all have equal precedence; that is, they are evaluated in the left-to-right order in which they appear.

Tables 36.1 through 36.3 show all the operators.

TABLE 36.1   ARITHMETIC OPERATORS, IN DESCENDING ORDER OF PRECEDENCE

Operator	Meaning	Example	Result
^	exponentiation	2^5	32
-	unary negation	-5	-5
*	multiplication	2*3	6
/	division	9/2	4.5
\	integer division	9\2	4
mod	modulus (integer remainder)	9 mod 2	1
+	addition	3+5	8
-	subtraction	8-5	3
&	string concatenation	"abc" & "de"	"abcde"

The + operator also concatenates strings, but it's best to get in the habit of using + for numbers and & for strings. Using + makes it clearer to someone reading your program that strings rather than numbers are being manipulated.

TABLE 36.2   COMPARISON OPERATORS

Operator	Meaning	Example	Result
=	equal to	3 = 4	False
<>	not equal to	3 <> 4	True
<	less than	3 < 4	True
>	greater than	3 > 4	False
<=	less than or equal to	3 <= 4	True
>=	greater than or equal to	3 >= 4	False
is	object equivalence	obj1 is obj2	False

TABLE 36.3   LOGICAL OPERATORS, IN DESCENDING ORDER OF PRECEDENCE

Operator	Meaning	Example	Result
not	negation	not (3 = 4)	True
and	conjunction	(3 = 4) and (3 < 4)	False
or	disjunction	(3 = 4) or (3 < 4)	True
xor	exclusion (different)	true xor true	False
eqv	equivalence (same)	false eqv false	True
imp	implication (same, or, second value true)	false imp true	True

> **Note**
>
> Advanced programmers: The logical operators perform bitwise operations on numeric values and logical operations on Boolean values.

Don't worry about all these operators right now. I'll use the more important ones in the examples throughout this chapter. For now, just remember that operators exist for every basic mathematical function, and you can refer back to these tables when you find the need.

FLOW CONTROL

It's all well and good that you can assign values to variables and perform calculations, but the real power of programming is in the ability to perform operations over and over, and to take different actions when conditions require. That's where flow control comes in. Instead of just executing each and every line of a program in order from top to bottom, *conditional statements* make decisions and either execute or skip blocks of commands. With *looping statements*, you can execute certain statements repeatedly.

These statements are important because programs must deal with the vague nature of the real world. Files that were expected to exist might not exist. Folders can contain no files, just a few files, or hundreds of files. A program that interacts with the real world needs to be able to take different actions in response to the reality of the environment in which it's run. Okay, that's enough philosophy. Let's get on with it.

THE If...Then...Else STATEMENT

The If...Then...Else statement examines a condition and, depending on the result, executes one of two sets of statements. Now, consider this example:

```
if Hour(Time()) < 12 then        ' CD Example File WSH001.VBS
    MsgBox "Good morning"        ' see if current hour is in range 0 to 11
else
    MsgBox "Good evening"        ' otherwise, 12 to 23
end if
```

This example executes just one of the message box commands. In plain English, this statement reads: "If the current time is less than 12 noon, then display 'Good Morning.' Otherwise, display 'Good Afternoon.'" Figure 36.1 shows what I saw when I ran the script one morning.

> **Note**
>
> In this chapter and in Microsoft's documentation, you'll see VBScript commands capitalized some times but not others. The case doesn't matter; VBScript is *not case sensitive*. The commands
>
> ```
> IF A = 3 THEN
> if A = 3 Then
> If a = 3 then
> ```
>
> are all the same to VBScript. Microsoft's convention is capitalize the words of VBScript statements, but I think this looks strange and it's too much of a bother, so I'm not going to capitalize most VBScript words in this chapter.
>
> It is helpful to capitalize certain letters in long names such as CreateTextFile, just to make them easier to read, so I do tend to capitalize the names of functions, objects, methods, and properties, as you'll see in this chapter. Remember, the case doesn't matter one bit to VBScript. It just makes the scripts easier for humans to read.

Figure 36.1
The Good morning message was displayed because the hour of the day was less than 12.

The Else statement is not required in all If...Then...Else statements. For example, the following has only the Then part:

```
                        ' CD Example File WSH002.VBS
if Hour(Time()) < 12 then
    MsgBox "It's morning, rise and shine!"
end if
```

If statements can also be nested one inside the other for more complex situations, as shown here:

```
if filetype = ".EXE" then
    if filename = "WSH" then
        MsgBox "This is the WSH program"
    else
        MsgBox "This is some other program"
    end if
else
    MsgBox "This is some other type of file"
end if
```

Here, the "inner" If statement is executed only if the variable filetype is set to ".EXE".

Tip #423

> The indenting of the statements between `If` and `End If` is not essential. VBScript doesn't care as long as each statement is typed on a separate line. This sort of indenting is a convention used by good programmers to help make programs more readable for *humans*. Clear formatting goes a long way toward making a program more understandable and easier to debug.

THE `Select Case` STATEMENT

Nested `If` statements can get messy when you're testing several conditions and the nesting is several layers deep. If you intend to execute a single block of commands based on a condition that can have one of several predetermined values, the `Select Case` statement may be more appropriate.

Suppose you have different commands that you want to run depending on the day of the week. In the following example, I assign to variable `DayNumber` a numeric value (1 to 7) corresponding to the day of the week from Sunday to Saturday:

```
                         ' CD Example File WSH003.VBS
DayNumber = Weekday(Date())
select case DayNumber
    case 2: MsgBox "It's Monday, Football Night on TV"
    case 3: MsgBox "Tuesday, Music lessons"
    case 4: MsgBox "Wednesday, Go see a movie"
    case 5: MsgBox "Thursday, fishing!"
    case 6: MsgBox "Friday, Party Time!"
    case else: MsgBox "Relax, it's the weekend!"
end select
```

When the `Select Case` statement is run, VBScript looks at the value of `DayNumber` and runs just those commands after the one matching `case` entry. You can put more than one command line after each `case` entry if you want, and even sets of complex lines including `If...Then...Else` and other flow-of-control constructions. You can also specify a `Case Else` entry to serve as a catchall case, when the value of the `Select Case` expression doesn't match any of the listed cases. In this example, `Case Else` takes care of the values 1 and 7, for Sunday and Saturday.

Tip #424

> For better readability by humans, VBScript includes predefined *constants* named `vbSunday`, `vbMonday`, `vbTuesday`, and so on, which you can use instead of the numbers 1 through 7. Constants act like variables, except they're predefined by Microsoft and you can't change their values. In the preceding example, I could have typed `case vbMonday:` for the first case, `case vbTuesday:` for the second, and so on. Constants help you make your programs more comprehensible to other readers.

THE `Do...While` LOOP

You can use the `Do While` statement to repeat a block of code over and over until some condition occurs. For example, you might want a script to wait until a file named c:\temp\data.in has been read and deleted by some other process. To keep the script from looking for the file thousands of times per second, you can pause it 5 seconds (5000 milliseconds) between checks, as shown here:

```
' CD Example File WSH004.VBS
set fso = CreateObject("Scripting.FileSystemObject")
do while fso.FileExists("c:\temp\data.in")
    WScript.Sleep 5000
loop
MsgBox "The file c:\temp\data.in has been deleted"
```

There are actually several versions of the Do...While loop, each subtly different:

```
do while expression
    statements
loop
```

```
do until expression
    statements
loop
```

```
do
    statements
while expression
```

```
do
    statements
until expression
```

(Of course, you would use a real logical test in place of *expression* and real VBScript commands in place of *statements*.)

With the first version, VBScript evaluates the logical *expression*. If it's True, VBScript executes the *statement* or *statements* inside the loop and goes back to repeat the test. It executes the set of statements repeatedly, every time it finds that *expression* is True.

In the file-testing example I gave, each time the program finds that the file does not exist, it executes the statements inside the loop, which in this case simply suspends the script for 5 seconds.

The second version loops as long as *expression* is False—that is, until *expression* becomes True. You could also write

```
do while not (expression)
    statements
loop
```

and get the exact same result. It's all the same to the computer! The Until version is provided just so that the program is easier for human readers to understand.

In these first two versions, if the While or Until condition fails before the first go-round, the statements inside will never be executed at all. In the second two versions, notice that the test is at the end of the loop, so the statements inside are always executed at least once.

Look back one more time at the example I gave earlier. If the file c:\temp\data.in exists the first time VBScript encounters the Do statement, it doesn't waste any time. If I had used the version with the test at the end, VBScript would have had to wait 5 seconds before making even the first check. As I said, these are subtle differences, but each version can useful in its own place when you're writing a program.

TERMINATING A LOOP WITH Exit Do

Sometimes it's desirable to get out of a Do...While or other such loop based on results found in the statements inside. In this case, the Exit Do statement can be used to immediately jump out of a loop, to the next command after the "loop" line.

For example, suppose you expect to be able to process five files named FILE1.DAT, FILE2.DAT, and so on. However, if you find that a given file doesn't exist, you might want to stop processing altogether and not continue looking for higher numbered files. The following shows how you might write this up in a script:

```
' CD Example File WSH005.VBS
set fso = CreateObject("Scripting.FileSystemObject")
num = 1
do while num <= 5                          ' process files 1 to 5:
filename = "C:\TEMP\FILE"+ltrim(CStr(num))+".DAT"   ' construct filename
if not FileExists(filename) then           ' see file exists
exit do                                    ' no, terminate early
end if
Process filename                           ' call subroutine process
num = num + 1                              ' go on to next file
loop
```

In this example, the first time through the loop, it sets variable filename to FILE1.DAT and each time through increments variable num by one. It tests to be sure each file whose name is stored in variable filename really exists. If the file does not exist, Exit Do takes the program out of the loop before it attempts to process a missing file.

Generally, the Exit Do statement is used to get out of a loop when something unexpected happens, whereas the While part tests the expected conditions.

You can also use Exit Do when you have to do some work before you can find out whether it's time to exit the loop.

When would you do something like this? You just saw a likely situation in the previous example in which I wanted to process files 1 to 5. The Do While True technique would let me process as many files as are found, from 1 to whatever:

```
                                        ' CD Example File WSH006.VBS
set fso = CreateObject("Scripting.FileSystemObject")
num = 1
do while True                              ' process files 1, 2, 3, etc.
   filename = "C:\TEMP\FILE"+ltrim(Cstr(num))+".DAT"   ' construct filename
   if not FileExists(filename) then        ' see file exists
      exit do                              ' no, terminate early
   end if
   Process filename                        ' call subroutine "process"
   num = num + 1                           ' go on to next file
loop
```

Here, Do While True keeps the loop running indefinitely, until Exit Do ends it.

The Exit Do statement works in any of the four variations of Do...While and Do Until statements.

COUNTING WITH THE For...Next STATEMENT

When a loop needs to run through a set number of iterations, the For...Next statement is usually a better choice than the Do...While statement. The example I used for Exit Do can be rewritten as a For loop like this:

```
                                                 ' CD Example File WSH007.VBS
set fso = CreateObject("Scripting.FileSystemObject")
for num = 1 to 5                                 ' process files 1 to 5:
    filename = "C:\TEMP\FILE"+ltrim(Cstr(num))+".DAT"   ' construct filename
    if not fso.FileExists(filename) then        ' see file exists
        exit for                                ' no, terminate early
    end if
    Process filename                            ' call subroutine "process"
next
```

The For loop sets its variable (num, in this example) to the first value (here, 1) and processes the statements inside. It then increments the variable and repeats the statements until the variable is larger than the number after To (here, 10). This loop thus processes the statements with num = 1, 2, 3, 4 and 5.

In the example, I also used the Exit For statement, which works exactly like the Exit Do does, except that it breaks out of a For loop rather than a Do loop. (Makes sense, doesn't it?!) Exit For ends the For loop immediately, and VBScript continues processing the script with the line after Next.

The For statement itself can be written in either of two ways:

```
for counter = startvalue to endvalue
```

or

```
for counter = startvalue to endvalue step stepvalue
```

Here, counter is the variable to be used; startvalue is the value that the variable is to take the first time through the loop; endvalue is the largest value the variable is to take; and stepvalue, if specified, is the value by which to increment counter each time through. The stepvalue can be negative if you want your loop to count backward, as in this example:

```
                                                 ' CD Example File WSH008.VBS
for number_of_bottles = 100 to 1 step -1
    SingChorus number_of_bottles & " bottles of beer on the wall!"
next
```

> **Note**
>
> This example demonstrates the power of looping commands. Without the `For` loop, you would have to type out each verse
>
> ```
> SingChorus "100 bottles of beer on the wall!"
> SingChorus "99 bottles of beer on the wall!"
> SingChorus "98 bottles of beer on the wall!"
> ```
>
> and on and on. If you use the `For` loop, you can take care of the whole irritating song with just three lines.

If the `Step` clause is left out, the *counter* variable is incremented by one each time.

PROCESSING COLLECTIONS AND ARRAYS WITH `For...Each`

Some special-purpose VBScript functions can return a variable type called a *collection*. A collection is a list of filenames, usernames, or other data contained in a single variable. For example, a directory searching function might return a collection of filenames when you ask for all files named *.TMP. Because you'll probably want to print, view, or manipulate these files, you need a way of accessing the individual items in the collection.

The `For...Each` loop runs through the loop once for each item in a collection. Here's an example:

```
                                        ' CD Example File WSH009.VBS
filelist = ""
set fso = CreateObject("Scripting.FileSystemObject")
set tempfiles = fso.GetFolder("C:\TEMP").Files
for each file in tempfiles
    filelist = filelist & " " & file.name
next
MsgBox "The temp files are:" & filelist
```

In this example, the variable `tempfiles` is set to a collection of all the .TMP files found in folder C:\TEMP. The `For...Each` loop creates a variable named `file`, and each time through the loop it sets `file` to the next object in the collection. The loop runs once for each file. If the collection is empty—that is, if no .TMP files are included in folder C:\TEMP—then the loop doesn't run at all.

You also can use the `For...Each` statement with array variables, executing the contents of the loop once for each element of an array, as shown in this example:

```
dim names[10]
...
for each nm in names
    ...
next
```

I'll explain arrays later in this chapter.

VBSCRIPT FUNCTIONS

Functions are special blocks of VBScript's program code that can be activated (called) by name. A function can be given data to operate on, and it always returns a value to the script that called it. The technical term for a value passed to a function is an *argument*.

For example, the built-in UCase function takes a string variable or value as its argument and returns a string with all the letters set to uppercase. Now, check out this example:

```
str1 = "my file.dat"
str2 = Ucase(str1)
```

In this script, the variable str2 is set to "MY FILE.DAT". The original variable, str1, is left untouched.

CALLING FUNCTIONS AND SUBROUTINES

If you don't care about and don't intend to use the value returned by a function, you omit the parentheses. In that case, you're treating the function as a *subroutine*, which is a fancy name for a function with no value to return. (It does something but doesn't have any information to convey back to the script that called it.)

The following example illustrates two uses of the function MsgBox, first as a function whose value gets saved in a variable, and then as a subroutine:

```
which_button = MsgBox("Is it OK to proceed?", vbYesNo)
MsgBox "Thank you for answering", vbOK
```

In the rest of this chapter, I'll show functions used both ways. Just remember that parentheses are used when you're using the value returned by the function, and they are omitted when you're not.

DOCUMENTATION AND SYNTAX

About 100 predefined functions are available in VBScript, provided for your convenience as a programmer. These functions manipulate strings, perform complex math functions such as square roots, and calculate dates and times.

All these functions are completely explained in the VBScript documentation at Microsoft's Web site http://msdn.microcoft.com/Scripting. To give you an introduction to the type of functions and their applications, I'll go through some of them here. But first, I should explain what you'll see in the online documentation.

The VBScript documentation shows the *syntax*, or required formatting and wording, for each function and statement in the language. For example, the syntax for the MsgBox function looks like this:

```
MsgBox(prompt[, buttons][, title][, helpfile, context])
```

The parentheses tell you that MsgBox is a function. The list inside the parentheses shows that MsgBox can take five arguments. The square brackets ([and]) around some of the arguments aren't meant to be taken literally; that is, you don't type them. Instead, they indicate that the arguments are optional.

The documentation's explanation of each argument tells you what the argument signifies and what value is assumed if you don't supply one—the *default value*.

In the case of MsgBox, you can see that *prompt* is the only required argument. All the other arguments are optional. The simplest use of MsgBox would look like this:

```
x = MsgBox("This is a message to display on the screen")
```

However, you could also use MsgBox with three arguments, like this:

```
x = MsgBox("This is a message to display", vbOK, "This is the title")
```

If you want to specify some of the arguments without specifying the ones in between, you can use commas with nothing between. For example, you could write

```
x = MsgBox("This is a message to display", , "This is the title")
```

to specify the *prompt* and *title* arguments without specifying *buttons*. In this case, the MsgBox program would use the default value for *buttons*.

Finally, notice that the *helpfile* and *context* arguments are surrounded by a single set of brackets, which indicates that you must use both or neither.

Don't worry too much about these details right now. I gave this example just to demonstrate what the documentation will describe.

String Manipulation Functions

Most of the work you'll probably want to do with VBScript will involve manipulating strings such as filenames and usernames, so it's helpful that VBScript has a rich complement of built-in functions to work with strings.

Searching for Strings with InStr() and InStrRev()

I've found that the most common task I perform when working with strings is to determine whether a string contains some other string. For example, if your script is to scan through the contents of a directory looking for .DAT files, it needs a way of finding out whether the string ".DAT" occurs in any given filename.

The InStr function does this job. The statement

```
pos = InStr(filename, ".DAT")
```

sets variable pos to the starting position in variable filename where the string ".DAT" is found. Now, consider this example:

```
filename = "TEST.DAT"
pos = InStr(filename, ".DAT")
```

Here, pos is set to 5. If ".DAT" doesn't occur in filename, pos is set to zero. This way, variable pos lets you know whether the filename is a .DAT file.

When filename might contain both upper- and lowercase characters, the correct test would be as follows:

```
pos = InStr(Ucase(filename), ".DAT")
```

The UCase function returns a string identical to the string it's passed, except that lowercase characters are turned to uppercase. This would detect the .dat in the file named my finances.dat.

Tip #425

Case is a general concern. When you're working with strings, always think through the consequences of having upper- and lowercase characters. To a computer, *a* and *A* are different letters. You usually have to convert user input and filenames to uppercase before performing tests on them.

If the string being sought isn't found in the searched string, InStr returns zero; otherwise, the position is a number greater than zero. This enables you to test whether a string contains another string, regardless of position. For example, this line tests to see whether the variable *the_message* contains the word "warning":

```
if InStr(Ucase(the_message), "WARNING") > 0 Then
```

I used Ucase() to be sure to identify Warning, WARNING, or warning.

If the first argument to InStr is a numeric value, it's interpreted as starting character for the search. In this case, you have to pass three arguments to InStr. The following expression returns the value 4:

```
InStr(2, "ABCABC", "AB")
```

AB occurs at positions 1 and 4 in the string "ABCABC", but you told InStr to start looking at position 2. The first occurrence was skipped.

Function InStrRev() is similar to InStr(), except that it searches starting from the right end of the string. The following line returns 4 because it find the rightmost "AB":

```
InStrRev("ABCABC", "AB")
```

EXTRACTING PARTS OF STRINGS WITH Left(), Right(), AND Mid()

VBScript has several functions to pull pieces out of strings based on the starting position and length of the desired piece.

Function	Returns
Left(*string, length*)	The leftmost *length* characters from *string*
Right(*string, length*)	The rightmost *length* characters from *string*
Mid(*string,start*)	That part of *string* from character position *start* onward
Mid(*string,start,length*)	*length* characters of *string* from position *start*

The following are a few examples:

Expression	Returns
Left("ABCDEF", 3)	"ABC"
Right("ABCDEF", 3)	"DEF"
Mid("ABCDEF", 3)	"CDEF"
Mid("ABCDEF", 3, 2)	"CD"

In real life, you would use these functions with variables. For example, to find the base name of a filename without its filetype or extension, you could use this VBScript code:

```
filename = "My file.DAT"
dot = InStr(filename, ".")
basename = Left(filename, dot-1)
```

This code sets dot to the position of the period in the filename, and basename to that part of the filename up to, but not including, the period. In this case, basename would be set to My file.

If filename doesn't have a period in its name, you have a problem. dot would be set to zero, and VBScript would stop with an error message when you tried to set basename to the left-most –1 characters! Good programming practice requires that you handle this situation as follows:

```
                          ' CD Example File WSH011.VBS
filename = "test.file"
dot = InStr(filename, ".")
if dot = 0 then
    basename = filename
else
    basename = Left(filename, dot-1)
end if
MsgBox filename
```

OTHER STRING OPERATIONS

The following are some more string manipulation functions that you'll find handy:

Function	Returns
Len(*string*)	The length of *string* in characters
Lcase(*string*)	The same *string* but with all alphabetic characters in lowercase
Ucase(*string*)	*string*, with all alphabetic characters in uppercase
Trim(*string*)	*string*, with leading and trailing spaces removed
Ltrim(*string*)	*string*, with leading spaces removed
Rtrim(*string*)	*string*, with trailing spaces removed

The following are a few examples:

Expression	Returns
Len("ABC")	3
Lcase("My Documents")	"my documents"
Ucase("My Documents")	"MY DOCUMENTS"
Trim(" ABC ")	"ABC"
Ltrim(" ABC ")	"ABC "
Rtrim(" ABC ")	" ABC"

DATE AND TIME FUNCTIONS

As you would expect, because computers frequently refer to the date and time, VBScript has a number of built-in functions to make it easy to work with dates and times.

READING THE CLOCK WITH Date(), Time(), AND Now()

Date() and Time() return the current calendar date and local clock time as determined by the operating system. For example, to display the current date and time in a message box, you can use the following code.

```
                                     ' CD Example File WSH012.VBS
MsgBox "The current date is " & Date() & " and the time is " & Time()
```

> **Note**
>
> Using & to join strings with functions that return dates might seem strange, but this is a neat feature of VBScript. Because it knows that the & symbol always operates on strings, it knows to convert the date and time values to their string representations.
>
> The Now() function returns the current time and date combined.
>
> Dates and times are actually stored as numbers. The date is stored as an integer number of days since January 1, 0099, and times are stored as decimal fractions. You don't need to worry about *how* this is done, but it's helpful to know because you can manipulate dates using the arithmetic + operator. For example, the following line assigns today's date plus 1 to the variable *tomorrow*:
>
> tomorrow = date()+1
>
> It's better, though, to use special built-in date and time calculation functions provided in VBScript.

COMPUTING A FUTURE DATE WITH DateAdd

Using the DateAdd function, you can add a specified interval to a given date, time, or combined date/time. The syntax of the function is as follows:

DateAdd(*interval, number, date*)

You use the *date* argument to set the initial date. The *interval* argument is the interval type, such as month, day, or year. And the *number* is the number of intervals to add. Table 36.4 shows a list of interval types. They must be passed to the DateAdd function as a string in quotation marks.

TABLE 36.4   INTERVAL TYPES FOR THE `DateAdd()` FUNCTION

Interval	Description
YYYY	Years
Q	Quarters
M	Months
W	Weeks
D	Days
H	Hours
M	Minutes
S	Seconds

The following are some examples:

Expression	Returns
`DateAdd("M", 2, Date())`	Today's date plus two months
`DateAdd("H", -1, Time())`	The current time minus one hour

THE `DateDiff()` FUNCTION

The `DateDiff()` function calculates the interval between two dates. The syntax is as follows:

`DateDif(interval, date1, date2)`

The `interval` argument describes the format of the result you want returned. Refer to the same Table 36.4 for these values.

For example, `DateDiff("D", "9/9/1999", "1/2/2001")` returns the number of days between September 9, 1999 and January 2, 2001.

This function is especially useful in scripts involving the age of files. For example, you might want to delete a given file if it's older than three hours. If VBScript sets the variable `timestamp` to the last-modified date and time of a file, the following test determines whether the file should be deleted:

`if DateDiff("H", timestamp, time()) > 3 then`

OTHER DATE FUNCTIONS

The following are a few more date and time functions you should be aware of:

Function	Returns
`Day(date)`	Day of the month of the given *date*, from 1 to 31
`Weekday(date)`	Day of the week of the given *date* as a number from 1 to 7, with 1 = Sunday, 2 = Monday, and so on

Month(*date*)	Month of the given *date*, with 1 = January and so on
Weekdayname(*date*)	Day of the week of *date* as a string
MonthName(*date*)	Name of the month in which *date* falls
Hour(*time*)	Hour (0 to 23) of the given *time*
Minute(*time*)	Minute (0 to 59) of the given *time*
Second(*time*)	Second (0 to 59) of the given *time*

VBScript has predefined constants vbSunday, vbMonday, and so on, which you can use to test the values returned by Weekday in If statements and others. vbMonday makes more sense than the number 2 to someone unfamiliar with this function.

The following are some examples of what VBScript returns when the expression is run at 3:10:37 p.m. on Tuesday, January 11, 2000:

Expression	Returns
Day(now())	11
Weekday(now())	3 (for Tuesday)
Month(now())	1 (for January)
WeekdayName(Weekday(now()))	"Tuesday"
MonthName(Month(now()))	"January"
Hour(now())	15
Minute(now())	10
Second(now())	37

INTERACTING WITH THE USER

VBScript is not designed for writing programs with complex user interfaces, but it can display simple messages and receive simple input strings from the user with its MsgBox and InputBox functions.

THE MsgBox() FUNCTION

In its most basic form, MsgBox displays a text message to the user. For example, the following code produces the output shown in Figure 36.2:

```
                              ' CD Example File WSH013.VBS
MsgBox "This message was displayed by VBScript at " & time()
```

You can also use MsgBox to ask simple yes/no questions of the script's user. To do so, you use the advanced form of the MsgBox function, with the following syntax:

```
MsgBox(prompt [, buttons] [, title])
```

The three arguments are as follows: *prompt* specifies the text to display, *buttons* specifies which buttons to offer to the user, and *title* is a text title displayed at the top of the resulting dialog box. You can omit the *buttons* and/or *title* argument; in their absence, VBScript displays just an OK button and the title VBScript. The values for *buttons* needs to be one of those listed in Table 36.5. You can use the constant name or the numeric value.

Figure 36.2
A basic MsgBox displaying a string to the script user.

TABLE 36.5   BUTTONS OPTIONS FOR THE MsgBox() FUNCTION

Constant Name	Value	Displays
VbOKOnly	0	OK button
VbOKCancel	1	OK and Cancel buttons
VbAbortRetryIgnore	2	Abort, Retry, and Ignore buttons
VbYesNoCancel	3	Yes, No, and Cancel buttons
VbYesNo	4	Yes and No buttons
VbRetryCancel	5	Retry and Cancel buttons

For example, you can tell the user that a required file wasn't found and ask how to proceed by using this code:

```
choice = MsgBox("The preferences file is missing, should I proceed?", vbYesNo)
```

VBScript returns either the value vbYes or vbNo, depending on the button clicked. The possible return values for MsgBox are listed in Table 36.6. The value indicates which of the buttons the user selected.

TABLE 36.6   RETURN VALUES FROM THE MsgBox() FUNCTION

Constant Name	Value
VbOK	1
VbCancel	2
VbAbort	3
vbRetry	4
vbIgnore	5
VbYes	6
VbNo	7

You can ask VBScript to display an icon along with the message by adding an additional value to the *buttons* argument, using one of the values listed in Table 36.7.

TABLE 36.7   ICON VALUES TO USE WITH THE MsgBox() FUNCTION

Constant Name	Value	Displays
VBCritical	16	Critical Message icon
VBQuestion	32	Question icon
VbExclamation	48	Exclamation icon
VBInformation	64	Information icon

The following code displays a message with an Information icon:

```
                             ' CD Example File WSH014.VBS
x = 33
MsgBox "The value of variable x is " & x,
➥vbOKOnly + vbInformation, "Debugging Info"
```

The results are shown in Figure 36.3.

Figure 36.3
A MsgBox with a title
and an icon.

You might notice that when I don't care about the return value of the MsgBox function and don't want to assign the value to a variable, I omit the parentheses from the MsgBox call. I discussed this point earlier in the chapter under the section "Calling Functions and Subroutines."

Tip #426

You can use MsgBox to display the contents of variables and values inside your program to help debug it. If you assign a variable

```
debug = True
```

at the top of your program, you can add debugging aids like this throughout the program:

```
if debug then
    MsgBox "The value of variable x is " && x
end if
```

When you get your program working correctly, you can disable all the debugging messages by changing the first line of the program to the following:

```
debug = False
```

Of course, the Windows Script Host debugger is even better at helping you debug your programs. I'll cover debugging later in this chapter.

Tip #427	MsgBox displays a dialog box that stays up until the user clicks on a button. Don't use it in a script that needs to run unattended! Your script will never finish because it will be waiting for a user who isn't watching.
	If you really want to display messages in a script that has to run without user intervention, there's a way to limit the time the message box is displayed. See the Shell.Popup tip in the section "The Popup Method" later in this chapter.

THE InputBox() FUNCTION

VBScript lets you ask your users for a simple text string by using the InputBox function, as in this example:

```
                          ' CD Example File WSH015.VBS
UserName = InputBox("Please enter your first name")
MsgBox "Hello, " & UserName
```

This script displays the input-type dialog box shown in Figure 36.4.

Figure 36.4
The InputBox() function as seen by the user.

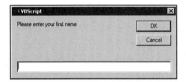

The function returns whatever the user types. In the preceding example, this is stored in variable UserName.

As with MsgBox, you can add additional arguments to the InputBox function to get better control of its appearance. You can use several options, only three of which are really interesting:

```
InputBox(prompt, title, default)
```

Here, *prompt* is the message to display above the input field, *title* is the title to display at the top of the dialog box, and *default* is the character string to put into the editing field when it first appears; the user can then accept or change this value.

A practical use of InputBox is to select a folder for the script to process, as in this example:

```
fldr = InputBox("Enter folder to be cleaned up", "Cleanup Script", "C:\TEMP")
```

VBSCRIPT OBJECTS

The flow control and predefined functions provided with VBScript give you the basic tools to control a script's execution and to manipulate strings, numbers, and dates, but they don't provide any way of interacting with Windows, files, or application software. Those functions are provided by *objects*—add-on components that extend VBScript's internal capabilities.

In the most general sense, objects are little program packages that manipulate and return information. They're the software representation of something tangible, like a file, a folder, a network connection, or an Excel document. Objects have *properties* that describe the attributes of the thing they represent and *methods* that enable you to alter or manipulate the thing.

A file on your hard disk has a size, a creation date, and a name; these are some of the properties you would expect a `File` object to have. You can rename, delete, read, and write a file, so a `File` object should provide methods to perform these tasks.

THE FileSystemObject AND RELATED OBJECTS

Because the properties and methods appropriate for files are different than those for folders or disk drives, Windows Script Host provides a whole set of objects to represent the Windows file system and each of its subcomponents, as shown in Table 36.8.

TABLE 36.8 THE FileSystemObject AND RELATED OBJECTS

Object	Represents
FileSystemObject	The whole file system on your computer
Drive	A single disk drive
Folder	A single folder on a drive
File	An individual file in a folder

> **Note**
>
> You can use objects in any scripting language, not just VBScript. That's part of their power: When a programmer develops a new object, it can be used in VBScript, JavaScript, Word, and Excel macros—in fact, in any language that supports COM, the Common Object Model.

Let's look at the `FileSystemObject` first, as an introduction to objects.

The `FileSystemObject` represents your computer's whole set of disk drives and their contents. (See Table 36.9.) It has only one property, `Drives`, which is actually a collection of `Drive` objects. (I discussed collections earlier in the section on the `For...Each` loop.) The `FileSystemObject` has many methods, though, which can be used not only to manipulate files and folders, but also to test whether a specific file or folder exists.

TABLE 36.9 PROPERTY AND METHODS OF THE FileSystemObject

Property	Methods
Drives	BuildPath
	CopyFile
	CreateFolder

continues

TABLE 36.9   CONTINUED

Property	Methods
	CreateTextFile
	DeleteFile
	DeleteFolder
	DriveExists
	FileExists
	FolderExists
	GetAbsolutePathName
	GetBaseName
	GetDrive
	GetDriveName
	GetExtensionName
	GetFile
	GetFileName
	GetFolder
	GetParentFolderName
	GetSpecialFolder
	GetTempName
	MoveFile
	MoveFolder
	OpenTextFile

To use the FileSystemObject, you use the VBScript function CreateObject, as shown here:

```
set fso = CreateObject("Scripting.FileSystemObject")
```

This example creates a variable named fso. Note the use of the word set; it is a special indicator telling VBScript that I want the variable to refer to an object. You always need to use set when you assign objects to variables.

You need to create only one FileSystemObject in any script you write. From then on, you can use the variable (fso in this example) that refers to this object throughout the script.

As another example, you can use the FileExists method like this to see whether there's a file named C:\temp\secret.doc:

```
                          ' CD Example File WSH016.VBS
set fso = CreateObject("Scripting.FileSystemObject")

if fso.FileExists("c:\temp\secret.doc") then
```

```
    MsgBox "The secret file exists"
end if
```

Now you can see why periods aren't allowed in variable names. Periods are used to string together variable names and property or method names. `fso.FileExists` uses the `FileExists` method with the object `fso`.

> **Note**
>
> As you can see, the method `FileExists` looks and works a lot like a function: It takes an argument and returns a value. But how do you know what the required arguments and possible return values are? You must refer to the object's documentation. In this case, you have to go to Microsoft's Web site at `http://msdn.microsoft.com/scripting`. Look under VBScript, Language Reference, Objects. The methods and properties for each object are shown there with a list of all the arguments they require or allow.

The `Drives` property of `FileSystemObject` returns a collection of `Drive` objects. The `Drive` object has several properties, as shown in Table 36.10.

TABLE 36.10   PROPERTIES AND METHODS OF THE `Drive` OBJECT

Properties	Methods
AvailableSpace	(none)
DriveLetter	
DriveType	
FileSystem	
FreeSpace	
IsReady	
Path	
RootFolder	
SerialNumber	
ShareName	
TotalSize	
VolumeName	

The following script displays the amount of free space on each drive in your computer:

```
                              ' CD Example File WSH017.VBS
set fso = CreateObject("Scripting.FileSystemObject")
set drvs = fso.Drives
for each drv in drvs
    if drv.IsReady then
        ➡MsgBox "Drive " & drv.DriveLetter &
        ➡" has " & drv.FreeSpace & " bytes free"
    end if
next
```

Unfortunately, I don't have the space to discuss each of the objects, methods, and properties in detail. There's enough material here to fill up another book! However, I want you to see how much detail and control you can obtain using the file system objects, so I've listed the Folder and File objects in Tables 36.11 and 36.12, even though I won't discuss them in this chapter.

TABLE 36.11   PROPERTIES AND METHODS OF THE Folder OBJECT

Properties	Methods
Attributes	Copy
DateCreated	Delete
DateLastAccessed	Move
DateLastModified	CreateTextFile
Drive	
Files	
IsRootFolder	
Name	
ParentFolder	
Path	
ShortName	
ShortPath	
Size	
SubFolders	
Type	

TABLE 36.12   PROPERTIES AND METHODS OF THE File OBJECT

Properties	Methods
Attributes	Copy
DateCreated	Delete
DateLastAccessed	Move
DateLastModified	OpenAsTextStream
Drive	
Name	
ParentFolder	
Path	
ShortName	

Properties	Methods
ShortPath	
Size	
Type	

MOVING, COPYING, AND DELETING FILES WITH THE `FileSystemObject`

In your scripts, you'll often want to be able to move, copy, and delete files. VBScript is really useful for these kinds of jobs. The `FileSystemObject` has a number of methods geared exactly for these tasks.

THE `CopyFile` AND `CopyFolder` METHODS

The `CopyFile` method can copy one or more files from one folder to another. The syntax of this method is

```
CopyFile source, destination, overwrite
```

> **Note**
>
> I didn't show parentheses for this method name because the `CopyFile` method returns no value. It can't be used as a function.

source is the path to the file(s) you want to move. It can contain wildcard characters. *destination* is the folder to which you want the files copied, and the *overwrite* argument indicates whether it's acceptable to overwrite existing files. If you use the value `False` for *overwrite*, and a file with the same name of a source file already exists in the destination folder, the `CopyFile` method stops with an error message.

`CopyFile` makes copies and leaves the original *source* files alone. For example, this script copies all files in C:\TEMP into C:\OLDFILES:

```
                              ' CD Example File WSH018.VBS
set fso = CreateObject("Scripting.FileSystemObject")
if not fso.FolderExists("C:\OLDFILES") then
    fso.CreateFolder("C:\OLDFILES")
end if
fso.CopyFile "C:\TEMP\*.*", "C:\OLDFILES", True
```

The `CopyFolder` method can copy whole folders, including subfolders, to another destination. The syntax is similar that of the `CopyFile` method:

```
CopyFolder source, destination, overwrite
```

Here's the example again. This version copies not only C:\TEMP but any subfolders:

```
set fso = CreateObject("Scripting.FileSystemObject")
fso.CopyFolder "C:\TEMP\*.*", "C:\OLDFILES", True
```

THE DeleteFile AND DeleteFolder METHODS

The DeleteFile and DeleteFolder methods, shown here, can delete one or more files and/or folders:

```
DeleteFile source, force
DeleteFolder source, force
```

The *source* argument names the file(s) you want to delete and can contain wildcards. The *force* argument indicates whether you want to force a delete of files if they are found to be read-only. Again, *force* can be either True or False. True tells VBScript to delete read-only files.

The following sample script cleans all .TMP files out of your TEMP directory:

```
                                ' CD Example File WSH019.VBS
set fso = CreateObject("Scripting.FileSystemObject")
fso.DeleteFile "C:\TEMP\*.TMP", True
```

The DeleteFolder method deletes the named folder(s) and any subfolders they contain. Watch out—this is a powerful function!

THE MoveFile AND MoveFolder METHODS

You could move files by copying them and deleting the originals, but VBScript provides the more convenient methods MoveFile and MoveFolder, as shown here:

```
MoveFile source, destination
MoveFolder source, destination
```

Again, the source argument can contain wildcards. If a file already exists in the destination, an error occurs.

THE FileExists AND FolderExists METHODS

Often you might want to check whether a file or folder actually exists before you try to copy, move, or delete it. The FileExists and FolderExists methods can find out for you. Both these methods, shown here, return True if the file or folder already exists:

```
FileExists(fileName)
FolderExists(FolderName)
```

This script tells you whether a C:\TEMP folder is located on your hard disk:

```
                                ' CD Example File WSH020.VBS
set fso = CreateObject("Scripting.FileSystemObject")
if fso.FolderExists("C:\TEMP") then
    msgbox "There is a c:\temp directory!"
end if
```

READING AND WRITING FILES WITH THE TextStream OBJECT

Sometimes you might want a script to create a text file, perhaps to record the results of its processing or just to keep a log of activity. When I write a script that runs on schedule, I usually have it create a text file noting the time it was run and what it did because I'm usually not around to watch when the script runs. Script files might also need to read text files that contain configuration information or data to be processed.

You can create and process text files in a VBScript program by using the `TextStream` object. The `TextStream` object, which represents a named file, gives you properties and methods to write and read strings to and from the file. You can think of the `TextStream` object as a channel between your script program and the file system on your computer. The `TextStream` object's methods and properties are listed in Table 36.13.

TABLE 36.13   PROPERTIES AND METHODS OF THE `TextStream` OBJECT

Properties	Methods
AtEndOfLine	Close
AtEndOfStream	Read
Column	ReadAll
Line	ReadLine
	Skip
	SkipLine
	Write
	WriteLine
	WriteBlankLines

I'll cover only a few of the methods and properties of the `TextStream` object.

THE `OpenTextFile` AND `CreateTextFile` METHODS

`OpenTextFile` enables you, as you might imagine, to open (that is, prepare to read or write) an existing file on your system or to create a new one for output. The `OpenTextFile` method isn't a part of a `TextStream` object, actually. It's part of `FileSystemObject`, and it's used to create a `TextStream`. The syntax for the method is as follows:

```
set variable = FSys.OpenTextFile(filename [, iomode, [, create [, format]]])
```

`Fsys` is a `FileSystemObject` that you've created earlier in your script. `OpenTextFile` returns a `TextStream` object that is stored in a `variable`, which you can then use to work with the file.

The argument `filename` is the name of the file.

`iomode` can be one of three values: 1 indicates that you intend to read strings from the file, 2 indicates that you want to create an empty file to write text into, and 8 indicates that you want to add text to the end of an existing file.

> **Note**
>
> VBScript does not predefine named constants for *iomode*. You can define them yourself, so you can use names rather than numbers, with this command:
>
> `const ForReading = 1, ForWriting = 2, ForAppending = 8`
>
> Someone else reading your script will find `ForWriting` much easier to understand than the number 2.

The *create* argument, if `True`, indicates that if the file doesn't already exist, you want `OpenTextFile` to create an empty one.

format specifies whether to use ASCII or Unicode characters. Omit it to use ASCII.

The following example uses `OpenTextFile` to append a line of text to a file named MYSCRIPT.LOG; it creates the file if the file doesn't exist already:

```
                                  ' CD Example File WSH021.VBS
const ForReading = 1, ForWriting = 2, ForAppending = 8

set Fsys = CreateObject("Scripting.FileSystemObject")
set Tstream = FSys.OpenTextFile("C:\myscript.log", ForAppending, True)
Tstream.WriteLine "This script was run on " & now()
Tstream.Close
```

This script opens file C:\MYSCRIPT.LOG for appending, creating it if necessary. It writes the current time and date to the file and closes the channel. Every time this script is run, it adds one more line to the file. Here's what MYSCRIPT.LOG looks like after running the script three times:

```
This script was run on 12/19/1999 7:08:51 PM
This script was run on 12/19/1999 7:09:03 PM
This script was run on 12/19/1999 7:09:10 PM
```

`CreateTextFile` is similar to `OpenTextFile`, except that it always creates a new, empty file for writing. Its syntax is as follows:

```
set variable = Fsys.CreateObject(filename [, overwrite] [, unicode])
```

The *filename* argument indicates the name of the file to create. By default, VBScript causes an error if the file you specify already exists. If you pass the *overwrite* argument with the value `True`, VBScript simply erases any existing previous file and creates a new, empty one. You should use `CreateTextFile` when you're writing a file that you'll re-create from scratch each time.

THE `Write()` AND `WriteLine()` METHODS

When you're using a `TextStream` object to create a file, the `Write()` and `WriteLine()` methods take text string arguments and write the text into the file. The difference between them is that `WriteLine` adds a carriage return and linefeed character after it writes its text so that subsequent text is written to a new line in the file.

You saw WriteLine used in the example for OpenTextFile in the preceding section. You can use the Write method to write just part of a line so that more can be added before the line is ended with WriteLine. Here's an example:

```
                                    ' CD Example File WSH022.VBS
set Fsys = CreateObject("Scripting.FileSystemObject")
set Tstream = FSys.CreateTextFile("C:\drive summary.txt", True)
Tstream.WriteLine "Drives in this computer:"
for each drive in Fsys.Drives
    Tstream.Write "The " & drive.DriveLetter & " drive has "
    if drive.IsReady then
        Tstream.WriteLine FormatNumber(drive.FreeSpace,0) & " bytes free"
        else
                Tstream.WriteLine "no disk inserted"
        end if
next
Tstream.Close
```

After I run this script, file C:\DRIVE SUMMARY.TXT looks like this on my computer:

```
The A drive has no disk inserted
The C drive has 363,741,184 bytes free
The D drive has 0 bytes free
The J drive has 58,554,368 bytes free
```

> **Note**
>
> In this example, I used the Drive object's IsReady property before trying to check its free space. If you use the FreeSpace property on a floppy or Zip drive with no disk inserted, VBScript stops with an error message. The IsReady test helps you avoid that problem.
>
> Also, when I printed the number of free bytes (drive.FreeSpace), I used the FormatNumber function, which turns the number into a string of characters and adds commas. If I had just printed drive.FreeSpace directly, the numbers wouldn't have been printed with commas, and the output wouldn't have looked as nice.

READING FILES WITH THE ReadLine() METHOD

You can also read text out of a file using a TextFileStream object. In this case, you need to create a TextFileStream with the OpenTextFile method, like this:

```
                                    ' CD Example File WSH023.VBS
const ForReading = 1, ForWriting = 2, ForAppending = 8

set Fsys = CreateObject("Scripting.FileSystemObject")
set Tstream = FSys.OpenTextFile("C:\myscript.log", ForReading)
```

You can then read one line of text at a time using the ReadLine method. Here's an example:

```
txt = Tstream.ReadLine
MsgBox "The first line of myscript.log is: " & txt
```

Readline returns characters from the TextStreamObject file up to, but not including, a carriage return/linefeed character.

> **Note**
>
> You can read a specific number of characters by using the Read method and can read and discard text by using the Skip and SkipLine methods. I won't describe them here, but you can look them up in the online VBScript reference.

THE AtEndOfStream PROPERTY

If you read a file whose length you don't know in advance, you might have to keep reading lines over and over until you reach the end of the file. The AtEndOfStream property tells you that you have reached the end of the file.

This example reads a text file and tells you whether the word error occurs anywhere in the file; it uses the AtEndOfStream property to know when to stop looking:

```
                        ' CD Example File WSH024.VBS
const ForReading = 1, ForWriting = 2, ForAppending = 8

set Fsys = CreateObject("Scripting.FileSystemObject")
set Tstream = FSys.OpenTextFile("C:\myscript.log", ForReading)

do until Tstream.AtEndOfStream
     txt = Tstream.ReadLine
     if InStr("ERROR", UCase(txt)) > 0 then
          MsgBox "The log file contains an error message: " & txt
          exit do
     end if
loop
Tstream.Close
```

THE WshShell OBJECT

Another important object provided with Windows Script Host is the WshShell object. Through this object, you can access environment variables, locate special folders, create shortcuts, run programs, and access your system's Registry.

The properties and methods of the WshShell object are shown in Table 36.14.

TABLE 36.14   PROPERTIES AND METHODS OF THE WshShell OBJECT

Properties	Methods
Environment	AppActivate
SpecialFolders	CreateShortcut
	ExpandEnvironmentStrings
	LogEvent
	Popup
	RegDelete
	RegRead
	RegWrite
	Run
	SendKeys

As with the FileSystemObject, you can create one WshShell object and use it throughout your script. I don't have enough space here to cover all its methods, but I'll go over some important ones.

THE SpecialFolders PROPERTY

The "special folders" on your PC are the folders that contain your Start menu, your Desktop, My Documents, or Windows itself. The SpecialFolders property lets you get the actual pathname of these folders so that you can write files on the desktop or create shortcuts on the Start menu.

The following is an example:

```
                    ' CD Example File WSH025.VBS
Set WShell = CreateObject("Wscript.Shell")
desktop = WShell.SpecialFolders("Desktop")
MsgBox "Your desktop folder is " & desktop
```

The argument to SpecialFolders can be any of the strings listed in Table 36.15.

TABLE 36.15   PERMISSIBLE ARGUMENTS TO THE SpecialFolders PROPERTY

AllUsersDesktop	NetHood
AllUsersStartMenu	PrintHood
AllUsersPrograms	Programs
AllUsersStartup	Recent
Desktop	SendTo
Favorites	StartMenu
Fonts	Startup
MyDocuments	Templates

THE CreateShortcut METHOD

The CreateShortcut method can create a shortcut. The method actually creates an object representing the new shortcut, and you have to fill in the details by setting this new object's properties. This function is quite powerful!

The following example places a shortcut to the calculator accessory (CALC.EXE) on the desktop:

```
                    ' CD Example File WSH026.VBS
Set WShell = CreateObject("Wscript.Shell")
UsrDesktop = Wshell.SpecialFolders("Desktop")
Set SLink = WShell.CreateShortcut(UsrDesktop & "\Calculator.lnk")
SLink.TargetPath = "%systemroot%\System32\calc.exe"
SLink.Save
```

The first three lines of code create the shortcut object in variable slink. You then set the link's TargetPath to point to the actual calculator program and save the object with slink.Save.

Tip #428	Finally! Nearly three-quarters into this chapter it becomes clear how scripting can be very useful to a system administrator. You can set up a script that checks to see whether a set of desired shortcuts exists, and you can create them if they don't. If you run the script inside each user's login script or from the All Users startup folder, you can ensure that the shortcuts are always available to every user.

THE Popup METHOD

The Shell.Popup method displays a message box just as the VBScript MsgBox command does, but you can specify a time limit for it to appear.

Tip #429	If you want to display a message in a script that has to be able to run unattended, you can use the Popup method with a time limit of, say, 20 seconds. That way, if nobody sees the message, the script proceeds anyway. Here's an example:

```
                        ' CD Example File WSH027.VBS
set wss = CreateObject("Wscript.Shell")
wss.Popup "This is a 20 second message", 20
```

THE WScript OBJECT

The WScript object contains information about the running script and can suspend or terminate its execution. Windows Script Host creates a WScript object named Wscript when it runs your script. It's predefined and available for your use.

Table 36.16 shows the methods and properties of the Wscript object.

TABLE 36.16 PROPERTIES AND METHODS OF THE Wscript OBJECT

Properties	Methods
Application	CreateObject
Arguments	ConnectObject
FullName	DisconnectObject
Name	Echo
Path	GetObject
ScriptFullName	Quit
ScriptName	Sleep
StdErr	
StdIn	
StdOut	
Version	

The following sections describe a couple of its properties and methods.

THE Arguments PROPERTY

When you start a script using the command line or a shortcut, you can specify command-line arguments to pass to the script. For example, I can run a script with the following command either from the command line or in a shortcut:

```
wscript c:\wsh\cleanup.vbs "c:\temp" "c:\documents and settings"
```

The two strings `"c:\temp"` and `"c:\documents and settings"` are arguments passed to the script.

The Arguments property returns these arguments as a collection object, which you can run through using a For Each loop. This script cleans out all .TMP files in the folders named in the script's command-line arguments:

```
                              ' CD Example File WSH028.VBS

set FSys = CreateObject("Scripting.FileSystemObject")

set args = Wscript.Arguments
for each arg in args
    if Fsys.FolderExists(arg) then          ' see if any .TMP file exists
      for each file in Fsys.GetFolder(arg).Files
          if InStr(UCase(file.name), ".TMP") > 0 then
            Fsys.DeleteFile arg & "\*.TMP"   ' yes, delete all of them
            exit for              ' no need to keep looking
          end if
      next
    else
      MsgBox "There is no folder named " & arg
    end if
next
```

Tip #430

The Arguments property is one of the most powerful tools for scripting because it lets you write a script in general terms and lets you specify the details when you run the script.

THE Quit METHOD

You can cancel your script at any time by using the Quit method. This method is really helpful inside loops and nested If statements when you find that you can't proceed otherwise. Here's an example:

```
if fsys.FileExists(filename) then
    if MsgBox("The file " & filename & " already exists;
    ➥can I overwrite it?", vbYesNo, "Error") = vbYes then
        Wscript.Quit
    end if
end if
```

Using the `Quit` method is much easier than trying to arrange the `If` and `Else` lines to get past any subsequent parts of the script that would create the file the user didn't want to overwrite.

THE WshNetwork OBJECT

Chances are good that if you're a system administrator, you'll be using Windows Script Host to help with your logon scripting. A good deal of logon scripting involves attaching to network drives and printers, and the `WshNetwork` object provides the methods to help.

Table 36.17 shows the properties and methods of `WshNetwork`.

TABLE 36.17   PROPERTIES AND METHODS OF THE WshNetwork OBJECT

Properties	Methods
ComputerName	AddPrinterConnection
UserDomain	AddWindowsPrinterConnection
UserName	EnumNetworkDrives
	EnumPrinterConnection
	MapNetworkDrive
	RemoveNetworkDrive
	RemovePrinterConnection
	SetDefaultPrinter

To access the network components, you need to create a `WshNetwork` object variable like this:

```
set Wnet = Wscript.CreateObject("Wscript.Network")
```

You can use this one object throughout your entire script.

THE ComputerName, UserDomain, AND UserName PROPERTIES

You can use the `WshNetwork` object to find out details about the currently logged-on user. The following script demonstrates the use of all three properties available:

```
                    ' CD Example File WSH029.VBS
set Wnet = Wscript.CreateObject("Wscript.Network")
UsrName = Wnet.Username
SysName = Wnet.Computername
DomName = Wnet.UserDomain
MsgBox "User: " & UsrName & "@" & DomName & VbCrLf & "Logged on to: " & SysName
```

THE MapNetworkDrive METHODS

Now let's move on to something almost everybody does in a logon script—mapping shared folders to drive letters.

```
Wnet.MapNetworkDrive localName, remoteName
➥[, updateProfile] [, userName] [, password]
```

The *localName* argument should be a drive letter, such as S:, and the *remoteName* argument needs to be a full UNC path such as \\Server1\salesdata. The *updateProfile*, if assigned the value True, reconnects the share each time the user logs on. If you want to use a different username and password to access the shared folder, you can specify them as well, using *username* and *password*. Here's an example:

```
                                ' CD Example File WSH030.VBS
set Wnet = Wscript.CreateObject("Wscript.Network")
Wnet.MapNetworkDrive "S:", "\\Server1\salesdata"
```

OTHER OBJECTS

Windows Script Host provides a few other built-in objects for your use, as shown in Table 36.18. They are of less general use than the ones I showed you in the preceding sections.

TABLE 36.18   OTHER OBJECTS PROVIDED WITH WINDOWS SCRIPT HOST

Object	Purpose
Dictionary	Lets you associate and search for data with key strings; an advanced programming tool
Err	Contains information about errors while processing scripts
Match	Contains the results of pattern matching using the RegExp object
RegExp	Lets you perform sophisticated wildcard-based searching of text strings

You're not limited to the objects provided with WSH and listed in its documentation, however. Other objects provided with Windows aren't as well documented but are available if you know how to use them. Objects are available for advanced applications using the Microsoft Transaction Server and Microsoft Message Queue. There's even an object that can be used to send email messages if your Windows 2000 computer has the Microsoft SMTP server installed; it's shown here:

```
                                ' CD Example File WSH031.VBS
set objSendMail = CreateObject("CDONTS.NewMail")
objSendMail.From    = "brian@coldmail.com"
objSendMail.To      = "bob@warmmail.com"
objSendMail.Subject = "The Book is Nearly Finished!"
objSendMail.Body    = "Bob, the last chapter of the book
is almost complete.  Get that champagne ready!"
objSendMail.Send
set objSendMail = Nothing
```

(The last line "releases" the mail object so that the software that supports it can close up. If your script is this small, you can omit this command, but in a longer script, you might want to release the resources used by complex objects before continuing.)

Even network data transmission can be performed with the right objects to draw on. You can buy an FTP client object, for example, that enables you to send and retrieve files from a script.

You might be surprised to hear that your WSH VBScript code can automate applications such as Word and Excel. Many big applications make their internal functions available as objects to permit automation. Microsoft Excel is one such program. Excel *exposes* its internal objects so that you can create spreadsheets from scripts, and you can even use Excel to perform calculations for your script.

Consider the following example. This script lets the user type an arbitrary mathematical expression, and the script displays its value. Of course, this script works only if you have Excel installed on your computer:

```
                                      ' CD Example File WSH032.VBS
set exl = CreateObject("Excel.Application")
expr = InputBox("Please enter an expression", "Excel Demo")
val =
exl.Evaluate(expr)
msgbox "The value of " & expr & " is " & val
set exl = Nothing
```

ADVANCED VBSCRIPT PROGRAMMING

There's quite a bit more to VBScript than what I've shown you. In fact, there's probably a whole shelf of books devoted to the topic at your local bookstore. I recommend that you check out *Windows Script Host By Example*, also published by Que.

However, I want to cover some important topics here for the more advanced programmers, to help them get going in the right direction. Don't worry if these topics don't make sense now; they're applicable only to the most complex VBScript programs.

PROCEDURES: FUNCTIONS AND SUBROUTINES

Procedures are the building blocks of large VBScript programs. A procedure is a separate section of code in your program that performs a particular task. The two types of procedures are functions and subroutines.

You have already learned about many of the built-in functions in VBScript, but you can create your own, too. You can also create subroutines, which are like functions but don't return a value.

The great power in procedures is that after you have written them once in your code, you can call them as often as you want. You can concentrate on *how* to perform a particular task just once when you write a procedure so that later you can simply *use* the procedure without worrying about the details.

To create a function, you use the Function...End Function statement. The following simple function accepts one argument and returns the value of the argument plus two:

```
function addtwo (value)
    addtwo = value+2
end function
```

You should put all your functions and subroutines *after* the main body of your script. VBScript stops running the script when it encounters the first function or subroutine declaration.

The (value) part tells VBScript that the function expects one argument and is to hold the value in a variable named *value*. The following is an example of how this function might be used elsewhere in the script:

```
a = addtwo(3)
```

When VBScript encounters the expression addtwo(3), it begins to run through the statements of the function, where the variable value is given the value 3. The value to be returned by the function is set when the program assigns a value to variable addtwo; this is the value of the function itself. As you might guess, the end result is that this statement assigns the value 5 to variable a.

In this way, you can extend the built-in functions of VBScript with your own. When you choose names for the argument variables, such as value in the example, you should choose meaningful names that explain what type of information is expected. For example, when a function is to be given a filename, I often name the argument fname, just out of habit.

The following function takes a filename, removes its extension (its filetype), and adds the extension .OLD. You might use this function in a program that is going to update a file if you want to create a backup copy of the file before changing the original. You can use this function to determine the desired name for the backup file, given the original file's name:

```
                                     ' CD Example File WSH033.VBS
function backup_file_name (fname)
idot = instr(fname, ".")
if idot > 0 then
    backup_file_name = left(fname, idot-1)+".OLD"
else
    backup_file_name = fname+".OLD"
end if
end function
```

The Instr function searches its first argument (fname, in this case) for the first occurrence of the second (in this case, just a period character). It returns the value 0 if the second string is not found; otherwise, it returns the position within the first string at which it was found—1, 2, and so on. So, here, idot is set to 0 if no period appears in the filename argument fname, or it is set to a number greater than zero if a period does appear.

The remainder of the function computes the backup filename. If the dot is found, the function constructs the new filename from the first characters of the old name, up to but not including the period, and adds .OLD. If no dot is found in the old name, the function tacks on .OLD anyway. Put into use, the following statements would set variable file1 to MY.OLD, and file2 to SOMEFILE.OLD:

```
file1 = backup_file_name("MY.DATA")
file2 = backup_file_name("SOMEFILE")
```

Subroutines are like functions, except they don't return values. They're used to do some job that can then be taken advantage of by the remainder of your script. For example, the following subroutine takes as its argument the name of a file. It prompts the user whether the file can be deleted, and if the user clicks OK, deletes the file:

```
sub maybe_delete (fname)
    if msgbox("Should I delete file " & fname & "?", vbYesNo) = vbYes then
        fso = CreateObject("Scripting.FileSystemObject")
        fso.DeleteFile(fname)
    end if
end sub
```

This subroutine uses the built-in function MsgBox to ask the script's user whether the file can be deleted. It displays a dialog box with two buttons: Yes and No. If the user clicks Yes, the program uses a FileSystemObject to actually delete the file.

This kind of subroutine would let you use statements like this in your program:

```
maybe_delete filename
maybe_delete "OLD.DATA"
```

You can see how this lets you concentrate on the task at hand (deleting files) as you write the script, knowing that the details of *how* to delete files are taken care of in the subroutine.

> **Note**
>
> In a real script, I would probably create the FileSystemObject at the beginning of the script, so one object could be used throughout. The preceding subroutine would create a new FileSystemObject every time it was called, which is not necessary.

ARRAYS

VBScript supports array variables. Arrays are declared using a dim, or dimension, statement. Array indices start at zero, so the following statement actually creates an eleven-element array, with values var(0), var(1), ... var(9), and var(10):

```
dim var(10)
```

Arrays can be redimensioned with the ReDim statement, like this:

```
ReDim [preserve] varname(subscripts) [, ...]
```

The *preserve* keyword causes VBScript to preserve the existing data in arrays being resized; without *preserve*, the variables are cleared, and all elements are set to Nothing.

VARIABLE SCOPE

By default, when a variable is declared or created in the main body of a script file, it has *global scope*; that is, it's also accessible to every procedure called in the script. Variables defined within procedures, by default, have *private scope*. They're accessible only within the procedure in which they're declared. Another procedure called by this procedure can't access the variable, and when the defining procedure terminates, the variable is destroyed.

You can explicitly create variables with a global scope by using the public statement and private variables by using the private statement. Public variables are accessible to any procedure and are persistent until the script ends. For example, a procedure can use the following statement to declare a variable Fsh and an array MyArray that is available to all procedures in the script:

```
public Fsh, MyArray(10)
```

By default, variables can be used without being declared or dimensioned in advance. Seasoned programmers know that this can lead to hard-to-find bugs, as it's difficult to detect typos; you could simply create a new misspelled variable where you had intended to change the value of a preexisting one. The option explicit statement fixes that by *requiring* you to declare all variables before using them, using a dim, public, or private statement. I recommend this in complex scripts. It takes a little extra work when you first write the program, but it helps eliminate a whole category of bugs.

DATA TYPES

VBScript variables are all stored in one type of variable, called a *variant*. However, the variant knows what kind of data it's representing—string, integer, Boolean, floating point, and so on. You can coerce VBScript into storing variants of a desired subtype by using the built-in conversion functions such as CDbl, CInt, and so on.

CREATING YOUR OWN OBJECTS

The objects provided with VBScript and Windows Script Host can take care of most file operations and network communications. You can use additional components provided by any additional applications you install, such as Word and Excel.

You can also create objects using almost any programming language, such as C, Java, or Visual Basic. This is quite an advanced undertaking, but an experienced programmer can manage it fairly easily. This technology lets you extend VBScript to perform just about any function you could desire, from performing financial calculations to launching rockets. If you're interested, you should read up on the COM and DCOM object models for your programming language of choice.

With your own objects, you can focus on making the program for the object itself work correctly just once. When you use the object in other programs and scripts, you can forget the details of its implementation and focus on using the object to perform a desired job. If this sounds like the rationale for creating subroutines and functions, you're right. Objects have an even greater benefit in that they can have their own variables, functions, and subroutines that are "private"—in other words, for the exclusive use of the program inside the object. This makes it easier to be sure that the object's functions work correctly: No outside program can mess with its data in ways it doesn't expect.

You can even create objects using VBScript as the programming language. It's a strange concept, but the Microsoft Windows Script Components package lets you create objects using VBScript or JScript, complete with properties and methods. These objects can then be used in scripts or other applications. You can find out more details about Windows Script Components online at `http://msdn.microsoft.com/scripting`.

USING WINDOWS SCRIPT HOST

If you're new to programming, you should start at the beginning of the chapter. Otherwise, continue reading for more details about using the Windows Script Host.

CREATING SCRIPT FILES

You can create scripts using any text editor program. Notepad is the easiest to use. You can use a more sophisticated editor such as Microsoft Word or Corel WordPerfect if you want, but you have to be sure to save the script as a plain text file.

Tip #431	When you create a new script using Notepad, be careful when you try to save it with File, Save As. You must set Save as Type to All Files before entering the filename. Then enter a filename ending with .VBS and click Save. If you forget to take this extra step, Notepad will save your file with the name *script*.vbs.txt, which Windows Script Host doesn't recognize as a valid script file.

For your first few scripts, you might start with the examples provided on this book's CD-ROM. Play with them awhile, and use bits and pieces of them to make new scripts for yourself.

RUNNING SCRIPTS ON WINDOWS 2000

WSH identifies a script's base language from the extension of the script filename. For example, a script named LOGON.VBS causes the VBScript engine to be invoked, whereas a script named LOGON.JS invokes the JScript ActiveX engine.

Two versions of the script interpreter are available. Wscript is the windows-based version, and Cscript is the command-line-based version.

As I mentioned before, you can run a script by double-clicking the filename within Windows. Files with the .VBS and .JS extensions are associated with the WSCRIPT.EXE application, which you'll find in the winnt\system32 directory. The following are five other ways to run a script:

- Run the script—Choose Start, Run and enter the script name, using the full pathname to the script file. You can add command-line arguments here, too.

- Run WSCRIPT.EXE directly—Click Start, Run, and enter wscript.exe followed by the script path and name. The advantage of using this method is that you can add switches to modify the behavior of WSCRIPT.EXE at runtime.

- From the command line—Open a command prompt; then type cscript followed by the script name.

■ From the Startup Folder—You can place a script file or a shortcut to a script into your Startup folder under the Start menu, or in the All Users startup folder.

■ From a login script—A script file can be specified to run for a domain user at logon and will be loaded from the netlogon share and executed at logon. Ask your network administrator to set up this file for you if you're unsure how to do it.

Tip #432	WSH has been updated to version 2.0 for Windows 2000. Among other improvements, scripts can be run at logon simply by specifying the script name such as FINANCELOGON.VBS. In the previous version of WSH, the script had to be invoked from a batch or cmd file.

Try running a script now. If, as suggested earlier, you have copied the \wsh folder from the CD accompanying this book onto your desktop, open that folder now, and locate the file called LISTDESK.VBS. Right-click this file, and select Edit from the context menu. Selecting Edit opens the file in Notepad so that you can read and edit it. You should see the following lines of code:

```
' CD Example File ListDesk.vbs
'This file displays all the files on the desktop along with
'the file type.
Set FileSys = CreateObject("Scripting.FileSystemObject")
Set WShell = Wscript.CreateObject("Wscript.Shell")
Desktopfolder = WShell.SpecialFolders("Desktop")
Set Desktop = FileSys.GetFolder(Desktopfolder)
Set DesktopFiles = Desktop.Files
txt = "Your desktop contains: "
For Each file in DesktopFiles
    txt = txt & file.Name & "  (" & file.Type & ")" & vbCrLf
Next
MsgBox txt
```

Close Notepad, and this time, double-click the DESKTOPFILES.VBS file. A message box appears with a list of all the files currently on your desktop. Note that folders are not listed—only files and shortcuts. Running this script on my own desktop gives the list shown in Figure 36.5.

SETTING SCRIPT OPTIONS

The WSCRIPT.EXE and CSCRIPT.EXE executables have a number of switches that modify their behavior at runtime. You can find the full list by typing wscript /? at a command prompt. However, Table 36.19 shows a list of the more important ones.

Figure 36.5
The output of LIST-DESK.VBS.

TABLE 36.19   COMMON VBSCRIPT SWITCHES

Switch	Description
//B	Suppresses error messages while the script is playing.
//I	Interactive mode; the opposite of //B.
//nologo	Prevents logo display.
//T:*nn*	Timeout. Maximum time a script is allowed to run, where *nn* is in seconds.

In addition to command-line switches, a .WSH file can be created for a script. The .WSH file records options for a particular script at runtime. To create a .WSH file, follow these steps:

1. Right-click the script file in Windows Explorer.

2. Select Properties from the context menu, and choose the Script tab on the resulting Properties dialog.

3. Choose the settings you want for the script on the Script tab (see Figure 36.6).

4. Choose OK or Apply. If you click Apply, you need to then choose OK.

Figure 36.6
Setting the script properties for a script file.

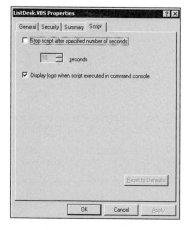

After you click OK or Apply, a .WSH file is created in the same directory as the original script, with the same script name.

Tip #433	If you move the .WSH files and .VBS files to a new location, the Path Setting is not automatically updated. You should create the .WSH file only when you're sure that the original script is staying put.

The .WSH file can be treated as an executable, meaning that you can double-click it to run the script, or you can pass it to the WSCRIPT.EXE or CSCRIPT.EXE applications as the script argument.

DEBUGGING SCRIPTS

VBScript and Windows Script Host are provided for free with Windows as a convenience. But Microsoft doesn't want them to be too terribly convenient, lest they cut into the sales of their profitable Visual Basic and Developer Studio products.

You'll find that you're pretty much left to your own devices when debugging scripts. If you have a problem with a script, WSH displays a message, such as the one shown in Figure 36.7.

Figure 36.7
A WSH Error message indicating a problem with a VBScript statement on the fourth line of the script file. See the "Troubleshooting" section at the end of the chapter for tips for resolving some common error messages.

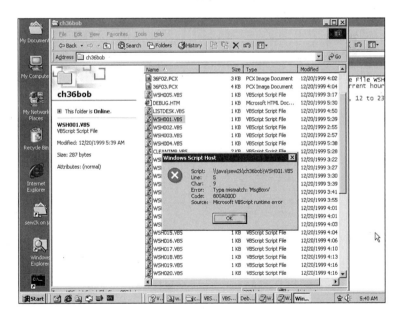

The explanations are usually fairly clear. The line number in the file on which the error occurred is indicated as well as the column number. (Of course, Notepad doesn't display line or column numbers when you're editing a file. You can open the script file from the command-line program Edit, however, which does.)

Some of the error messages returned by Windows Script Host are listed in the "Troubleshooting" section at the end of this chapter, with some discussion.

If your script doesn't do what you expect, you can insert MsgBox statements here and there in your script that display expected values of variables at various points. This ancient program debugging technique is cumbersome but effective.

Microsoft does provide an interactive, graphical script debugging tool, but it's only for VBScript used inside Web pages, not for standalone WSH scripts. You can, however, employ a trick to use the script debugger on your scripts. Put your script into a small Web page, and then use the debugger. When the script has been made to work correctly, you can extract the script contents from the Web page and save it as a .VBS file.

This trick is not convenient, but it works, and it might be the only way to completely debug a complex script. The steps are as follows:

1. Install the Script Debugger. From Control Panel, select Add/Remove Programs. Select Add/Remove Windows Components. Scroll down the list of optional components, and check Script Debugger. Then select Next. When installation is complete, close the installation windows and the Control Panel.

2. You can view the online help for the debugging tool by choosing Start, Programs, Accessories, Microsoft Script Debugger, Microsoft Script Debugger Readme. Ignore the section "Script Debugging in Internet Information Server 4.0" for now.

3. On your desktop, use the right-click menu to select New, Text Document. Name the file DEBUG. Right-click it, and select Rename. Rename the file DEBUG.HTM. Click OK when Windows warns you about renaming the file. (If Windows doesn't warn you, view the Desktop in Windows Explorer. Select Tools, Folder Options, and then select the View tab. Uncheck Hide File Extensions for Known File Types, and click OK. Repeat the renaming process.)

   The DEBUG.HTM icon should appear with an *e* icon.

4. Right-click the DEBUG.HTM icon, and select Open With. Then select Notepad. Enter the following text:

```
<HTML>
<BODY>
<SCRIPT LANGUAGE="VBSCRIPT">
stop

</SCRIPT>
</BODY>
</HTML>
```

5. Paste your script into this file. Here's how: In another Notepad window, edit your script file. Press Ctrl+A and Ctrl+C. In the DEBUG.HTM window, put the cursor on the blank line between stop and the </SCRIPT> tag. Press Ctrl+V. Then save this file by pressing Alt+F, S. Leave this window open.

6. Open Internet Explorer to a blank window. Drag the DEBUG.HTM icon into the IE window, and drop it there. This action should pop up the Microsoft Script Debugger. The word stop will be highlighted in yellow.

You can now use the script debugger to step through and examine the operation of your script. Look at the debugger's View and Debug menus to see the functions available to you.

The following are some basic tips on using the Debugger:

- Press the F8 key to step through the script one statement at a time. You can watch it execute line by line this way.

  If your script uses network or file system objects, Internet Explorer warns you that "Some software (ActiveX controls) on this page might be unsafe." Click Yes to proceed.

- If you suspect trouble at a certain line in the file, put the cursor in this line, and press F9. This action sets a *breakpoint* at this point in the script. Press F5 to let the script run. It stops if and when it encounters the line with the breakpoint. You can clear a breakpoint by pressing F9 again.

- Press F5 to let the script run to completion (or until it encounters a breakpoint or error).

- When you encounter a call to a subroutine or function, you can press Shift+F8 to skip over the contents of the procedure, or you can press F8 to step into the procedure. Inside a procedure, you can press Ctrl+Shift+F8 to let the procedure finish. The debugger stops again immediately after the procedure returns to its caller.

- To view the contents of a variable, select View, Command Window. Type ? *variablename*, where *variablename* is the name of the variable you want to view, and press Enter. Its value is then printed in the Command window.

You can't make any changes to your script with the debugger, however. To make changes, you need to end the debugging session (by selecting Debug, Stop Debugging). Then edit the DEBUG.HTM file using the open Notepad, and save your changes (by pressing Alt+F, S), and refresh (by choosing View, Refresh or pressing F5) in Internet Explorer. Phew! Making changes is a lot of work, but it can be a lifesaver with complex scripts.

> **Note**
>
> Microsoft's Script Debugger help file indicates that Internet Explorer may crash after repeating this process a few times. (What do you expect for free?) If this happens, just kill it with the Task Manager, and start it up again.

When you're finished, select and copy the script contents from the .HTM file, and paste it into your original .VBS script file. Be sure to remove any extra debugging `MsgBox` statements you added during the debugging process.

TROUBLESHOOTING

ERROR MESSAGE `Object doesn't support this property or method`

When I attempt use a property or method with an object, Windows Script Host displays the error `Object doesn't support this property or method`.

There are two possible reasons. One might be that you're using a method or property that isn't valid for the object you're using. You may have mistyped the name; check the Windows Script Host or Visual Basic Scripting documentation to be sure.

This error also occurs if you forget to use `set` when you call `CreateObject` or otherwise obtain the object you're using. Find where the object in trouble was defined, and be sure you used `set` when you assigned the object to a variable.

ERROR MESSAGE `Wrong number of arguments or invalid property assignment`

When I use a method or function, I receive the message `Wrong number of arguments or invalid property assignment`. *What's wrong?*

You might have omitted a required argument or added more arguments than are permitted to a function or object property.

This error can also occur if you omit the `set` keyword when assigning a property that returns an object or collection to a variable. For example, if you omit the `set` keyword in this assignment

```
set args = Wscript.Arguments
```

this error is generated.

ERROR MESSAGE `Type Mismatch`

If I pass the wrong type of value to a function, subroutine, method, or property—for example, I pass `True` *where a string was expected—I receive the* `Type Mismatch` *error. What do I do?*

In this case, find the offending expression, and look up the syntax for each function, subroutine, method, or property.

This error can also occur if you omit the object name with methods—for example, if you type

```
DeleteFile "MyFile.TMP"
```

instead of

```
fso.DeleteFile "MyFile.TMP"
```

or if you misspell the name of a built-in function, procedure, or method. For example, the line

```
MsgBoxx "Hello"
```

generates the `type mismatch` error message.

TIPS FROM THE WINDOWS PROS: CLEANING UP .TMP AND .BAK FILES

I've provided a script to clean up all your .TMP and .BAK files, and all files and folders whose name starts with ~, from every drive and every folder on your computer. This is a handy utility to supplement the Disk Cleanup tool provided with Windows 2000.

> **Caution**
>
> This script also cleans up any mapped network drives, as well as local drives. If you don't want it to clean network drives, you can remove the three lines from `for each drv in drvs` down to its `next` statement, and replace it with a single call `cleanup C:\`.

You can find CLEANTMP.VBS on the CD-ROM accompanying this book.

```
' CD Example File CLEANTMP.VBS

' This script deletes all .TMP and .BAK files from
' every folder on every drive.  It also nukes any folder
' whose name starts with ~

    set fso = CreateObject("Scripting.FileSystemObject")
    set drvs = fso.Drives
    for each drv in drvs
        if drv.IsReady then
            cleanup drv.DriveLetter & ":\"    ' clean each
            ➥drive with a disk
        end if
    next

' Clean out files from one folder, specified by "path". The
' path must end with a \ character.

sub cleanup (path)
    dim sf, fldr

    if AnyFile(path, ".TMP") then             ' clean out
    ➥any files, if at least one exists
        on error resume next                  ' ignore errors
        ➥when deleting files
        fso.DeleteFile path+"*.TMP", False
        on error goto 0                       ' stop on errors
        ➥in the program itself
    end if

    if AnyFile(path, ".BAK") then
        on error resume next
        fso.DeleteFile path+"*.BAK", False
        on error goto 0
    end if

    set sf = fso.GetFolder(path).Subfolders
    ➥' examine each subfolder
    for each fldr in sf
```

```
            if Left(fldr.name,1) = "~" then
                on error resume next
                fso.DeleteFolder(fldr.name), True
                ➥' it's a ~ folder: delete it
                on error goto 0
            else
              cleanup path & fldr.name & "\"  ' any other
              ➥folder: call cleanup recursively to clean
            end if
        next
end sub

' Determine if any file with the specified extension "extn"
' exists in the folder 'path'.  The path must end with a \ character,
' and the file extn must start with a period.

function AnyFile(path, extn)
    AnyFile = False                       ' assume we find none

    for each file in fso.GetFolder(path).Files
    ➥' look at each file in the folder
      if InStr(UCase(file.name), extn) > 0 then
      ➥' does its name contain the extension?
          AnyFile = True
          ➥' yes, we can stop looking
          exit for
      end if
    next
end function
```

To use the script, just double-click it from the WSH folder on the CD-ROM, or from a copy on your own hard disk.

INDEX